International Law

International Law: Text, Cases and Materials provides not only an essential introduction to the core concepts and foundational principles of international law, but also a detailed overview of each established area in which international law operates.

Featuring cases, materials, and illustrative figures throughout to enhance the level of context and detail provided, the book covers everything a student of international law requires. Topics include the law of treaties, international organisations, the international protection of human rights, responsibility in international law, jurisdiction, diplomatic and consular law, territory in international law, the law of the sea, international air and space law, international economic law, international environmental law, and international humanitarian law.

This comprehensive textbook will be essential reading not only for any course on international law, but also as a starting point for those wishing to grasp the context of a particular area of international law before exploring further.

David Pataraia is a professor at Tbilisi Ivane Javakhishvili State University, Georgia. Professor Pataraia has been a practising lawyer and held certain high-ranking positions in Georgia, inter alia, he served as a commissioner in the Georgian National Communication Commission, the parliamentary secretary of the President of Georgia and the head of the administration of the President of Georgia.

International Law
Text, Cases and Materials

David Pataraia

Routledge
Taylor & Francis Group

LONDON AND NEW YORK

First published 2022
by Routledge
2 Park Square, Milton Park, Abingdon, Oxon OX14 4RN

and by Routledge
605 Third Avenue, New York, NY 10158

Routledge is an imprint of the Taylor & Francis Group, an informa business

© 2022 David Pataraia

British Library Cataloguing-in-Publication Data
A catalogue record for this book is available from the British Library

Library of Congress Cataloging-in-Publication Data
Names: Pataraia, David, author.
Title: International law : text, cases, and materials / David Pataraia.
Description: Abingdon, Oxon [UK]; New York, NY : Routledge, 2021. |
    Includes bibliographical references and index.
Identifiers: LCCN 2021025341 (print) | LCCN 2021025342 (ebook) |
    ISBN 9781032101248 (hardback) | ISBN 9781032101231 (paperback) |
    ISBN 9781003213772 (ebook)
Subjects: LCSH: International law.
Classification: LCC KZ3410 .P375 2021 (print) | LCC KZ3410 (ebook) |
    DDC 341—dc23
LC record available at https://lccn.loc.gov/2021025341
LC ebook record available at https://lccn.loc.gov/2021025342

ISBN: 978-1-032-10124-8 (hbk)
ISBN: 978-1-032-10123-1 (pbk)
ISBN: 978-1-003-21377-2 (ebk)

DOI: 10.4324/9781003213772

Typeset in Berling
by Apex CoVantage, LLC

Contents

Table of cases and materials

3. PRINCIPLES OF INTERNATIONAL LAW CONCERNING FRIENDLY RELATIONS AND CO-OPERATION AMONG STATES IN ACCORDANCE WITH THE CHARTER OF THE UNITED NATIONS

4. THE NOTION OF THE SUBJECTS OF INTERNATIONAL LAW AND THE STATE AS THE MAIN SUBJECT

5. OTHER SUBJECTS OF INTERNATIONAL LAW

6. THE LAW OF TREATIES

7. INTERNATIONAL ORGANISATIONS

8. THE INTERNATIONAL PROTECTION OF HUMAN RIGHTS

9. RESPONSIBILITY IN INTERNATIONAL LAW

10. JURISDICTION

11. DIPLOMATIC AND CONSULAR LAW

12. TERRITORY

13. THE LAW OF THE SEA

14. INTERNATIONAL AIR AND SPACE LAW

15. INTERNATIONAL ECONOMIC LAW

16. INTERNATIONAL ENVIRONMENTAL LAW

17. INTERNATIONAL HUMANITARIAN LAW

Figures

Preface

This book is the product of decades dedicated to academic activity at the Ivane Javakh-ishvili Tbilisi State University. Time, personal experience, and empirical evidence all serve as a proof that innovative types of textbooks, which attempt to present the subject to a reader in a wide variety of perspectives and ways, make the study of the general course in international law a much simpler and more enlightening a journey.

Therefore, to make the book even friendlier to the students and would-be readers, the following format has been selected:

- The book's architecture is based on the proven approach according to which general issues are discussed at first and then the separate areas of international law;
- Subtitles are assigned to the parts of the sections and subsections of the book in order to highlight each topic of particular interest in the book;
- At the beginning of each chapter, the reader will discover not only the headings of the sections and subsections, but also the subtitles of the topics discussed in the chapter, with reference to the pages;
- On the first page of each section and subsection, a list of essential terms and respective sources of international law can be found, which are further discussed in the text that follows and are also linked to the Index at the end of the book;
- Footnotes are designed in accordance with the generally accepted rules of academic writing. In addition, non-conventional but essential approaches to particular subjects, which provide a broad perspective to a reader as well as a wide array of alternative viewpoints on topics discussed, are also presented in the footnotes. Therefore, the reader should pay particular attention to the footnotes to acquire a broader and a more complete understanding of the topics discussed. Finally, certain articles and paragraphs that are sources of international law and to which the text refers, are clearly indicated to help readers identify the real content of the specific norms.
- Figures in the book are inserted with the intention of facilitating a better understanding of the subject and simplifying the process of comprehension of the materials that might sometimes be confusing;
- At the end of each chapter are annexed the minimal necessary excerpts from cases and materials that were discussed in the chapter. The selected parts of the cases and the materials are displayed without footnotes, which, in certain cases, could have been

an integral part of the original text but are omitted with a specific intent of making these parts of the book more convenient for a reader to follow.

Generally, this book is a guide, with the focal points being the central issues, leading through the labyrinth of the complex world of international law. It will be a faithful assistant for persons interested in comprehending the basic concepts and approaches of the field of international law.

NOTE TO READERS

This publication is designed to provide accurate and authoritative information in regard to the subject matter covered. It is based upon sources believed to be accurate and reliable and is intended to be current as of the time it was written. To confirm that the information has not been affected or changed by recent developments, traditional legal research techniques should be used, including checking primary sources where appropriate.

David Pataraia
Professor of International Law at Ivane
Javakhishvili Tbilisi State University
2021

Acknowledgments

I would like to express special gratitude to my teacher, Academician Levan Alexidze, an outstanding professor of international law and the founder of the Georgian School of International Law, who has been a teacher and an educator to many generations of international lawyers in Georgia.

I would like to thank my alma mater, the Ivane Javakhishvili Tbilisi State University, which assisted significantly with the large task of preparing this book.

I am grateful to Giorgi Murghvashvili, who supported me in editing and proofreading this book.

Finally, I would like to extend my gratitude to the team at Routledge – Russell George, Emily Kindleysides, Chloe James, Evie Lonsdale, Philip Stirups, as well as Kate Fornadel and the Apex CoVantage team – for being very patient and helpful along the way.

David Pataraia

CHAPTER 1

The essence of law and the nature of international law

DOI: 10.4324/9781003213772-1

INTRODUCTORY REMARKS

general notion of law
sources of law
formal characteristics of law
legal systems
national law
international law
public international law
common characteristics of law
normative phenomena

Law as a generalised notion

In this chapter, the term 'law' shall be understood as a general notion encompassing all legally binding norms (the **general notion of law**) that are reproduced through the **sources of law**. In turn, the sources of law are such predefined forms as particular laws, secondary legislation, and precedents as well as other sources of law, which are precisely predetermined and arranged in each legal system.

The particular angle of the general notion of law presented in this book

This book defines the general notion of law primarily with an emphasis on the **formal characteristics of law** and mainly with the purpose of highlighting the specifics of international law.

Introspecting into the specifics of international law

There are many theoretical models which aim to define the system of rules known as international law. Some of these explanations are outlined in this book, with the intention of making the essence of international law easy to grasp for a would-be reader.

To introspect into the peculiarities of international law, it is necessary to have a clear picture of the following starting points in mind:

1   The law is composed of two **legal systems** – **national law** (also referred to as the municipal law, domestic law, or internal law) and **international law** (also referred to as **public international law**).
2   As regards national law, it has different appearance in different countries.
3   Although there can be no simple answer to the question 'What is law?' nevertheless, there are some **common characteristics of law** that unite the law in all its forms, distinguishing it from other **normative phenomena**.

LEGAL SYSTEMS

legal systems
legal families
civil law family
common law family
customary law family
religious law family
mixed national legal systems family
precedents

Diversity of the legal systems

As noted earlier, **legal systems** exist in the form of either national law (encompassing independent national legal systems of the states) or international law. The national law, in its turn, according to the widely recognised generalisation, is made up today of five **legal families.**[1]

---

1 For instance, it is named by Rene David as the family of laws or legal families: '[T]he Romano-Germanic family, the Common law family and the family of Socialist law. These three groups, whatever their merits

Legal families

- Civil law family
- Common law family
- Customary law family
- Religious law family
- Mixed national legal systems family

Civil law family

The civil law family stems mainly from Roman law heritage. Its examples vary considerably from country to country. Nevertheless, they also display some shared characteristics. In the civil law family states, the ethos of the positive general rules prevails, manifested primarily in the form of the comprehensive legal codes. In these countries, the law is substantially constituted by the legislature (though other state organs which are empowered to introduce the secondary legislation also participate in the law-making process). At the same time, case law is of secondary importance in these jurisdictions. Germany, France, Italy, and Georgia are examples of countries with a civil law system.

Common law family

The nations of the common law family rather tend to abandon the ethos of generalisation and major codification; in parallel with the statutes, they rely on **precedents** (which are certain judicial decisions that have already been made).[2] Hence, the law in such countries is to a considerable degree developed by judges moderating between the adversarial parties. The United Kingdom (except Scots law, which on the whole has a mix of the characteristics of the civil law and common law families), Ireland, and the United States (except Louisiana, which also combines elements of both the civil and common law families) represent the common law family.

---

and whatever their extension throughout the world, do not however take into account all contemporary legal phenomena.' Rene David and John E. C. Brierley, *Major Legal Systems in the World Today* (3rd edn, Stevens & Sons 1985) 22.

2 'In English law, judgments and decisions can represent authoritative precedent (which is generally binding and must be followed) or persuasive precedent (which need not be followed). It is that part of the judgment that represents the legal reasoning (or **ratio decidendi*) of a case that is binding, but only if the legal reasoning is from a superior court and, in general, from the same court in an earlier case. Accordingly, *ratio decidendis* of the *House of Lords are binding upon the *Court of Appeal and all lower courts and are normally followed by the House of Lords itself. The *ratio decidendis* of the Court of Appeal are binding on all lower courts and, subject to some exceptions, on the Court of Appeal itself. *Ratio decidendis* of the High Court are binding on inferior courts, but not on itself. The *ratio decidendis* of inferior courts do not create any binding precedent.' *A Dictionary of Law*, Elizabeth A. Martin (ed) (5th edn, Oxford University Press 2002, reissued with new covers 2003) 374.

Customary law family

In the customary law family countries, certain patterns of behaviour (or customs) are accepted as legal rules of conduct. These are, as a rule, unwritten and are frequently distributed by elders, passed down from generation to generation. Customary law practices can be observed in the mixed national legal systems family countries, where they have combined with the elements of the civil law or common law families. The influence of the customary law family may be seen in some Asian and African nations.

Religious law family

In the religious legal family countries, the law originates from the religious texts and traditions (for instance, nowadays, the Islamic law tradition countries).

Mixed national legal systems family

In the mixed national legal systems family states, two or more of the previously mentioned legal families operate together.

The interplay between the legal families

These different families of national law crosscut each other's boundaries and operate under permanent interaction, sharing each other's experience and, at times, departing from the original trademark characteristics.

THEORIES OF LAW

philosophy of law
natural law legal theory
legal positivism
law of nature
positive law
rule of the reason
The Unanimous Declaration of the Thirteen United States of America
ordinance of reason
just law
legal validity problem
legal realism
critical legal theory
normative theory
law as integrity
divine law

Primary schools of thought

There are two prominent schools of thought in the **philosophy of law** of the Western legacy – **natural law legal theory** and **legal positivism**.

Natural law school of thought

The origination of the natural law legal theory is usually associated with the philosophy of ancient Greece[3] and Rome. It was the most influential legal theory in Europe until the rise of legal positivism. Over the long history of its development, numerous authors (in this context, usually labelled as the naturalists) developed a great variety of different approaches and conclusions. Nevertheless, some general characteristics of the natural law approach can still be identified.

In brief, the natural law school of thought distinguishes the **law of nature** (also referred to as the natural law)[4] from **positive law**. The first is pre-existent to the positive law (the natural law is also regarded as the higher law) and is the universal **rule of the reason** (or a body of the universal and general rules of the reason), which is independent of the will of human authority. In the case of positive law, on the other hand, legal norms are established by the rulers.

The naturalists find the source of the natural law in God, in nature of human (a universalised conception of human nature), or in the idea of justice and, in all cases, refer to reason.

The vital function of the natural law is to establish a valid order as opposed to the arbitrariness of the rulers. At the same time, the naturalists claim that all the legal norms establish a rational standard for conduct, and, by definition, they must be reasonable.[5]

The substantive and procedural natural law

The rule of reason may be discovered either in terms of the substantial meanings (answering the question 'What shall be the content of the law?') or procedural understandings (answering the question 'How is a law made?').

As prominently articulated by a well-known scholar, Lon L. Fuller (1902–1978), who contributed to the rethinking of the naturalist approach in the twentieth century, 'we may

---

3 'The philosophers of ancient Greece, where the idea of natural law originated, considered that there was a kind of perfect justice given to man by nature and that man's laws should conform to this as closely as possible.' ibid 326.

4 In this context, the terms 'law of nature' and 'natural law' do not refer to the physical laws of nature – the laws that science aims to describe (such as Newton's so-called laws of motion).

5 As James Leslie Brierly wrote, 'it has to be admitted that natural law implied a belief in the rationality of the universe which seems to us to be exaggerated. It is true that when medieval writers spoke of natural law as being discoverable by reason, they meant that the best human reasoning could discover it, and not, of course, that the results to which any and every individual's reasoning led him was natural law.' James Leslie Brierly, *The Law of Nations: An Introduction to the International Law of Peace*, Humphrey Waldock (ed) (6th edn, Oxford University Press 1972) 20.

speak of a procedural, as distinguished from a substantive natural law. What I have called the internal morality of law is in this sense a procedural version of natural law.'[6]

The substantive or traditional natural law theory

According to Thomas Hobbes (1588–1679), the first and fundamental law of nature (he finally enunciates 20 laws of nature which are the precepts or the general rules of reason) stipulates that 'every man ought to endeavour peace, as far as he has hope for obtaining it; and when he cannot obtain it, that he may seek, and use, all helps, and advantages of war'.[7] The first branch of the rule contains the first and fundamental law of nature, which is 'to seek peace and follow it', and the second branch is 'the sum of the right of nature, which is: by all means we can to defend ourselves'.[8]

For John Locke (1632–1704), the law of nature is reason in itself ('reason, which is that law'), 'stands as an eternal rule to all men, *legislators* as well as others', and thus represents the will of God ('of which that is a declaration').[9] According to John Locke, the substantial content of the law of nature is to 'preserve oneself and the rest of mankind'.

The outstanding reflection of natural law theory can be discovered in **The Unanimous Declaration of the Thirteen United States of America** (July 4, 1776):

When in the Course of human events, it becomes necessary for one people to dissolve the political bands which have connected them with another, and to assume among the powers of the earth, the separate and equal station to which the Laws of Nature and of Nature's God entitle them, a decent respect to the opinions of mankind requires that they should declare the causes which impel them to the separation.

We hold these truths to be self-evident, that all men are created equal, that they are endowed by their Creator with certain unalienable Rights, that among these are Life, Liberty and the Pursuit of Happiness.

The procedural naturalism

Lon L. Fuller developed eight 'principles of legality', which constitute the 'inner morality of law' and, therefore, are placed into the very concept of the law so that no law that fails to meet these standards can be considered valid. Hence, to count as genuine, the rules have to meet the eight minimal requirements cumulatively; namely, they should be:

6 'The term "procedural" is, however, broadly appropriate as indicating that we are concerned, not with the substantive aims of legal rules, but with the ways in which a system of rules for governing human conduct must be constructed and administered if it is to be efficacious and at the same time remain what it purports to be.' Lon L. Fuller, *The Morality of Law* (Revised edn, Yale University Press 1969) 96–97.

7 Thomas Hobbes, *Leviathan or the Matter, Form and Power of a Commonwealth, Ecclesiastical and Civil*, Henry Morley (intro), LL.D., Professor of English Literature at University College, London (2nd edn, George Routledge and Sons 1886) XIV, 66.

8 David Pataraia, *Traditional Theoretical Approaches in International Relations* (Jus Press 2017) 55.

9 *Two Treatises of Government by John Locke* (A new edition corrected. published 1821 (MDCCCXXI) by Printed for Whitmore and Fenn and C. Brown) Book II, 191, 305.

1   General – reflecting the 'economic prudence' to spread the talents of the lawmakers by putting them to work on drafting general rules and not overloading them case by case.

2   Promulgated – as the law is established for the application and it is reasonable 'at least to make available to the affected party the rules he is expected to observe'.

3   Prospective – as the law shall be applicable only to future behaviour, not the past, since it is reasonable to assume that a person must, first of all, know the rule to obey it.

4   At least minimally clear and intelligible – as the 'desideratum of clarity represents one of the most essential ingredients of legality' since it is reasonable that a person must understand the rule to follow it.

5   Free of contradictions – since it is reasonable that a person must realise which rule to obey.

6   Possible to obey – as 'a law commanding the impossible seems such an absurdity that one is tempted to suppose no sane lawmaker, not even the most evil dictator, would have any reason to enact such a law.'

7   Relatively constant – as the law shall not be subjected to being altered and hanged continuously on an everyday basis, since instability is a challenge which greatly affects obedience to laws.

8   Administered in a way that there must be 'congruence between official action and declared rule'. 'This congruence may be destroyed or impaired in a great variety of ways: mistaken interpretation, inaccessibility of the law, lack of insight into what is required to maintain the integrity of a legal system, bribery, prejudice, indifference, stupidity, and the drive toward personal power.'[10]

Two mainstream lines of argumentation

Thus, among the naturalists discussed earlier, two mainstream lines of argumentation/thinking on the law of nature can be observed:

- The first line of argumentation views the law of nature in terms of its substantial meaning – as in the case of the classical authors mentioned earlier. Such considerations are mostly focused on the preservation of an individual human or a group of humans or the protection of human dignity or the common good. Accordingly, the morality of law is primarily related to the protection of human life and dignity or the common good. The logical assumptions of the naturalists are sometimes applied to the so-called 'state of nature', which is a condition in which society exists 'without a fear for the common power' (e.g. has not yet constituted a state).[11]

10 Fuller (n 6) 49–81.
11 For example, 'Thomas Hobbes does not argue that the mankind has experienced as a common developmental stage a historically universal existence in the state of nature described by him, however, he is certain that some societies existed in the same state of nature in his age. To give more weight to his arguments, he brings the example of the savage tribes in America, whose manner of existence, in his opinion, was brutish. In addition, he argues that the state of the human existence in the state of

- The second line of argumentation views the law of nature in terms of its 'procedural' meaning – as in order to become a law, the norms should cumulate/possess the valid (procedural) characteristics of law.[12]

The law as the ordinance of reason

Thomas Aquinas (1225–1274) was convinced that the law 'is nothing else than an **ordinance of reason** for the common good, made by him who has care of the community, and promulgated.'[13]

Many naturalists share the conclusion that the law is an ordinance of reason, the fundamental pattern of which is composed by the law of nature.[14] Accordingly, for naturalists all positive legal norms shall be practically reasonable and be in synchrony with the law of nature. Otherwise, they are not law. At the same time, it is practically reasonable in itself to establish a 'rational' standard constraining human behaviour in relation to other human beings and vice versa.

In general, the comprehension of the law as the ordinance of reason opens the door for morality by recognising the maxim that what is reasonable (for all humans) is, at the same time, synchronised with morality.

In substantial terms, the morality of law was often disclosed by the so-called classical naturalists in the protection of human life and dignity or the common good. Hence, in such a version, the natural law legal theory overlapped with the so-named natural law moral theory. Sometimes, the classical naturalists also referred to the concept of '**just law**' deduced from natural law and proclaimed the well-known formula 'an unjust law is no law at all'.[15]

---

nature can easily be observed during a civil war; by observing the human existence without a fear for the common power and the degeneration of the lives of people accustomed to live under the peaceful government.' Pataraia (n 8) 52.

12 However, a dilemma arises as to why the society should maintain the order established even by the ideally arranged law-making process, when the material norms of law do not comply with the substantial natural law. Therefore, the cogitation on the idea of law developing some procedural characteristics of the valid law – for instance, the 'principles of legality' presented in this chapter, accordingly, such conditions as the promulgation and clarity of law, the possibility of obeying the law, and so forth – from the viewpoint of the substantive naturalists, might be significant but certainly are not sufficient prerequisites to establish the legal order which is harmonised with the natural law.

13 J. Budziszewski, *Commentary on Thomas Aquinas's Treatise on Law* (Cambridge University Press 2014) 53.

14 Some of them demonstrated a more complex interplay of the appearances of law; for example, by distinguishing, in addition to the law of nature and positive law, divine law. 'Aquinas identified four different kinds of law: the eternal law, the natural law, the divine law, and human (positive) law. . . . According to Aquinas, (genuine or just) positive law is derived from natural law.' Brian Bix, 'Natural Law Theory' in Dennis Patterson (ed), *A Companion to Philosophy of Law and Legal Theory* (2nd edn, Blackwell Publishing Ltd 2010) 213.

15 'A more reasonable interpretation of statements like "an unjust law is no law at all" is that unjust laws are not laws "in the fullest sense." . . . This only indicates that we do not think that the title in this case carries with it all the implications it usually does. Similarly, to say that an unjust law is "not really law"

The morality of law was prominently expressed by John Finnis (born 1940), a famous contemporary naturalist: '[N]o theorist can give a theoretical description and analysis of social facts without also participating in the work of evaluation, of understanding what is really good for human persons, and what is really required by practical reasonableness.'[16]

As it is mentioned earlier, natural law itself is considered by naturalists as the domain of reason. Hence, introspection into the essence of the law of nature is the process of rational thinking ('the best human reasoning') and the making of a logical chain of conclusions (in the case of many classical naturalists, the drawing up of a logical chain of deductions from the assumption acknowledged as a fundamental rule of reason). Besides, in order to identify a material norm as a rule of natural law, writers often pay attention as to whether the precept is combined with the value-laden adjectives like 'inherent', 'inalienable', 'essential', 'fundamental', or 'natural'.

The field in which authors commonly detect substantial natural norms is human rights. As James Leslie Brierly (1881–1955), an outstanding international lawyer, noted, by referring to certain fundamental, inherent, or natural rights, the '[w]riters differ in enumerating what these rights are, but generally five rights are claimed, namely self-preservation, independence, equality, respect, and intercourse.'[17]

Finally, it is noteworthy that the perpetuity of the law of nature was traditionally considered a crucial characteristic. However, over time, some authors theorised on the possibility of developing the law/laws of nature together with the corresponding evolution of the source, which the authors regarded as the originator of such law/laws. Nevertheless, in classical and pure terms, natural law must be discovered as an eternal rule, and only such material or 'procedural' rule (or rules) of reason which may be comprehended as being perpetual shall be referred to as the rule (or rules) of the law of nature.

Legal positivism school of thought

The legal positivism school of thought saw its rise to prominence sometime later. Since the early nineteenth century, natural law assumptions and deductions have been strongly challenged by the new approach, primarily stemming from the writings of such prominent thinkers like Jeremy Bentham (1748–1832) and John Austin (1790–1859). According to Jeremy Bentham:

> Right . . . is the child of law: from real laws come real rights; but from imaginary laws, from laws of nature, fancied and invented by poets, rhetoricians, and dealers in moral and intellectual poisons, come imaginary rights, a bastard brood of monsters.[18]

---

may only be to point out that it does not carry the same moral force or offer the same reasons for action as laws consistent with "higher law."' ibid 214.

16 John Finnis, *Natural Law and Natural Rights* (2nd edn, Oxford University Press 2011) 3.

17 Brierly (n 5) 49.

18 *The Oxford Dictionary of Quotations*, Elizabeth Knowles (ed) (5th edn, Oxford University Press 2001) 2.91.

'The term "positivism" derives from the Latin positum, which refers to the law as it is laid down or posited. Broadly speaking, the core of legal positivism is the view that the validity of any law can be traced to an objectively verifiable source.'[19]

For the classical positivist thinkers, a rule may be considered a law when it comes from a recognised authority and can be enforced by the very authority that issued it (for example, according to Austin, laws are the commands of the sovereigns backed up with the threat of a sanction), such as a king, a parliament, or any ruler who has legislative power within a particular defined territory.

Positivists generally claim that the law is 'a matter of social facts' (which can be explained 'that the laws of a society exist and have meaning if and only if human beings create them and give them meaning') and does not necessarily have a moral character.[20]

Consequently, the positivist thinkers distinguish law from morality. They argue that as long as it was passed validly, even an 'immoral' law is a law, albeit a 'bad' law. This premise does not mean that the positivist writers are not critical of the merits of the laws. Jeremy Bentham, for instance, was a positivist who criticised 'bad' laws. However, his criticism was not about the validity of such laws.[21]

Modern legal positivism

As was articulated by Herbert Lionel Adolphus Hart (1907–1992), a remarkable positivist writer of the twentieth century, 'we shall take Legal Positivism to mean the simple contention that it is in no sense a necessary truth that laws reproduce or satisfy certain demands of morality, though in fact they have often done so.'[22]

He criticised the standpoint of naturalists and 'the claim that laws of proper conduct may be discovered by human reason' and argued that the norms of law which 'require men to behave in certain ways' are prescriptive in nature, in contrast to the laws which

---

19 Raymond Wacks, *Philosophy of Law: A Very Short Introduction* (2nd edn, Oxford University Press 2014) 25.

20 'The first is the *social fact thesis*: what constitutes the law in a certain society is ultimately a matter of social facts – facts about the mental states and behavior of certain individuals. Put more simply, the social fact thesis states that the laws of a society exist and have meaning if and only if human beings create them and give them meaning. The second thesis . . . is the *separability thesis*: there is no necessary connection between law and morality. . . . For many years, the social fact and separability theses jointly defined the position known as *legal positivism*, but in the late twentieth century, positivists began to abandon separability, leaving the social fact thesis as their sole defining thesis.' Jeffrey Brand, *Philosophy of Law Introducing Jurisprudence* (Bloomsbury 2013) 5.

21 'The arch-positivist of the modern era, Jeremy Bentham, was a dedicated social reformer who forcefully attacked the laws of England throughout his life. In doing so, however, he attacked them as bad laws, and did not claim that they were non-laws because they were bad.' Stephen Guest, Adam Gearey, James Penner, and Wayne Morrison, *Jurisprudence and Legal Theory* (University of London Press 2004) 64.

22 HLA Hart, *The Concept of Law* (2nd edn, Clarendon Press 1994) 185–186.

'formulate the course or regularities of nature' and which can be detected by observation and reasoning.[23]

As a positivist author, Hart paid particular attention to the structure of (positive) law and the legal rules. He enumerated the three so-called 'defects' of the regulations in the 'simple form of social life'; namely, uncertainty, static character, and inefficiency. 'The remedy for each of these three main defects in this simplest form of social structure consists in supplementing the primary rules of obligation with secondary rules'.[24] The primary rules, he said, govern conduct; the secondary rules, in turn, prescribe the procedural methods by which the primary rules 'may be conclusively ascertained, introduced, eliminated, varied, and the fact of their violation conclusively determined.'[25] Such secondary rules consist of the rules of recognition, the rules of change and the rules of adjudication.[26]

With the identification of these types of rules, Hart aimed to reflect the comprehensive system of law and to elaborate a more accurate approach to the validity of law. In the end, he found the source of the validity of the primary rules in the rules of recognition.[27]

The different perspectives on the question of the validity of the naturalist and positivist approaches

Thus, one of the critical issues which gives impetus to a confrontation between these two schools of thought concerns the **legal validity problem**: namely,

---

23 '[P]rescriptive laws may be broken and yet remain laws, because that merely means that human beings do not do what they are told to do; but it is meaningless to say of the laws of nature, discovered by science, either that they can or cannot be broken. If the stars behave in ways contrary to the scientific laws which purport to describe their regular movements, these are not broken but they lose their title to be called "laws" and must be reformulated.' ibid 187.

24 ibid 94.

25 ibid.

26 The rule of recognition 'is accepted and used for the identification of primary rules of obligation.' 'In the day-to-day life of a legal system its rule of recognition is very seldom expressly formulated as a rule; though occasionally, courts in England may announce in general terms the relative place of one criterion of law in relation to another, as when they assert the supremacy of Acts of Parliament over other sources or suggested sources of law.' The rule of change 'empowers an individual or body of persons to introduce new primary rules for the conduct of the life of the group, or of some class within it, and to eliminate old rules.' Finally, the rules of adjudication are provided 'to make authoritative determinations of the question whether, on a particular occasion, a primary rule has been broken. . . . Besides identifying the individuals who are to adjudicate, such rules will also define the procedure to be followed.' ibid 95–97, 100–101. The secondary rules are identified in the Constitutions or other legislation (for example, the rules of adjudication, in addition, are reflected in the so-called processual codes) of certain countries.

27 'There are therefore two minimum conditions necessary and sufficient for the existence of a legal system. On the one hand, those rules of behaviour which are valid according to the system's ultimate criteria of validity must be generally obeyed, and, on the other hand, its rules of recognition specifying the criteria of legal validity and its rules of change and adjudication must be effectively accepted as common public standards of official behaviour by its officials.' ibid 116.

- Is it just a matter of the source of the norm ('an objectively verifiable source'), as is assumed by the positivist thinkers? or
- Is it about the content of the norm (to be in synchrony with the substantive natural law) or the valid law-making process (to be in synchrony with the procedural natural law), as is assumed by the representatives of the natural law school of thought?[28]

Other theories and approaches

In the philosophy of law, in parallel with the mainstream schools of thought, other more or less influential theories of law were developed, such as **legal realism**,[29] **critical legal theory**,[30] and so forth.

Normative theory

One of the most outstanding other approaches is the so-called '**normative theory**' developed by Hans Kelsen (1881–1973), the famous Austrian jurist and philosopher, who elaborated the 'pure theory of law', which shares some essential aspects with legal positivism (for example, with an emphasis on positive forms of law, the separability thesis which assumes that there is no necessary connection between law and morality). However, at the same time, the pure theory of law is a unique approach since it is based on the ethos of a pure normative model, which founds the validity of every norm of a legal system on the higher norm and ultimately arrives at the realm of presupposition (the basic norm, which 'is a hypothesis and a wholly formal construct').[31]

Kelsen recognised that

> [a]ll laws are created by human actions, but human actions are facts and they belong to the realm of the 'is,' whereas laws are norms and belong to the realm of the 'ought.' It is another of Kelsen's unquestioned beliefs that there is an unbridgeable gap between the 'is' and the 'ought'; that norms cannot derive their existence from facts.[32]

---

28 It must be made clear that the naturalists also did not exclude the power of the rulers to make positive laws; however, the source of validity for positive laws were found in natural law.

29 'There are two "schools" of realism: the American and the Scandinavian. While they share certain similarities, they also differ fundamentally in their approach and methodology. . . . In particular, although the American movement was largely pragmatist and behaviourist, emphasizing "law in action" (as opposed to legal conceptualism), the Scandinavians were preoccupied with mounting a philosophical attack on the metaphysical foundations of law.' Wacks (n 19) 108.

30 'The most general statement of critical legal theory was the slogan, "Law is politics".' *The Blackwell Guide to the Philosophy of Law and Legal Theory*, Martin P. Golding and William A. Edmundson (eds) (Blackwell Publishing 2005) 80.

31 Wacks (n 19) 41.

32 Joseph Raz, 'Kelsen's Theory of the Basic Norm' (1974) 19(1) *The American Journal of Jurisprudence* 96.

Therefore, he concluded that 'the objective validity of a norm . . . does not follow from the factual act, that is to say, from an *is*, but again from a norm authorizing this act, that is to say, from an *ought*.'[33]

Hence, according to the pure theory of law, norms possess a validity when they are derived from higher norms existing at hierarchically higher levels. These latter norms, again, obtain their validity in a similar way, and so forth until touching the basic norm (in German – *Grundnorm*), whose validity can no longer be obtained from the normative delegation but has to be presupposed. In other words, '[s]ince the actual, legal, chain of validity comes to an end, we inevitably reach a point where the "ought" has to be presupposed, and this is the presupposition of the basic norm.'[34]

On the other hand, there is a need to find the right connection between the national legal system of a given state and international law, since Kelsen was convinced that 'there can be just one normative system and just one basic norm'[35] of a given country. ('No one can serve two masters,' pointed out Kelsen.)

However, there can be 'two monistic constructions' – (1) 'international law which from the viewpoint of the primacy of national law is regarded as merely a part of national law' and (2) 'international law which from the viewpoint of the primacy of the international legal order is regarded as a legal order superior to all national legal orders delegating these legal orders.'

> For the first, starting from the validity of a national legal order, the reason for the validity of international law [as well as any particular national legal order] is the presupposed basic norm, according to which the establishment of the historically first constitution of the state is a law-creating fact. For the second, starting from international law, the reason for its validity is the presupposed basic norm, according to which the custom of the states is a law-creating fact.[36]

At the same time, in Kelsen's concept, the 'historically first constitution of the state' has a complex meaning. He wrote that

> the basic norm . . . refers directly to a specific constitution, actually established by custom or statutory creation, by and large effective, and indirectly to the coercive order created according to this constitution and by and large effective; the basic norm thereby furnishes the reason for the validity of this constitution and of the coercive order created in accordance with it.[37]

---

33 Hans Kelsen, *Pure Theory of Law*, Max Knight (tr) (University of California Press 1967) 9.

34 'At some stage, in every legal system, we get to an authorizing norm that has not been authorized by any other legal norm, and thus it has to be presupposed to be legally valid. The normative content of this presupposition is what Kelsen has called the basic norm.' 'The Pure Theory of Law' (2016) *Stanford Encyclopedia of Philosophy* <https://plato.stanford.edu/entries/lawphil-theory/> accessed 16 March 2021.

35 Raz (n 32) 110.

36 Kelsen (n 33) 339.

37 ibid 201.

In sum, Kelsen preferred a monistic picture for every national legal order in which each state had its own unified legal order based on the primacy of international law. Moreover, in addition, he claimed that ultimately, the basic norm's 'validity depends on efficacy'.[38] As it was summarised by Kelsen, the '[b]eginning and end of the validity of a national legal order are determined by the legal principle of effectiveness', which is 'a norm of positive international law'.[39]

Law as integrity

The other authoritative theory originated in the common law world and was developed by a renowned American jurist and philosopher, Ronald Dworkin (1931–2013), who promoted the meaning of '**law as integrity**'.[40] He elaborated the theory based on the analysis of the cases and the existing discretion of the judges in the decision-making process (mostly in the common law family countries).[41]

> [P]ositivism generally claims that law consists of rules determined by social facts. Where . . . rules run out [Hard cases], the problem can be resolved only by the exercise of a subjective, and hence potentially arbitrary, discretion. . . . If, however, there is more to law than rules, as Dworkin claims, then an answer may be found in the law itself. Hard cases . . . may, in other words, be decided by reference to the legal materials; there is no need to reach outside the law and so to allow subjective judgements to enter.

Hence,

> Dworkin's account of the judicial function requires the judge to treat the law as if it were a seamless web. There is no law beyond the law. Nor, contrary to the positivist thesis, are there any gaps in the law. Law and morals are inextricably intertwined.[42]

---

38 Wacks (n 19) 41. 'If the validity of a legal order requires the effectiveness of its basic norm, it follows that when that basic norm of the system no longer attracts general support, there is no law. This is what happens after a successful revolution. The existing basic norm no longer exists, and, Kelsen says, once the new laws of the revolutionary government are effectively enforced, lawyers may presuppose a new basic norm. This is because the basic norm is not the constitution, but the presumption that the altered state of affairs ought to be accepted in fact.' ibid 43.

39 Kelsen (n 33) 338, 336.

40 Ronald Dworkin, *Law's Empire* (The Belknap Press of Harvard University Press 1986) 94.

41 'Law as integrity asks a judge deciding a common-law case . . . to think of himself as an author in the chain of common law. He knows that other judges have decided cases that, although not exactly like his case, deal with related problems; he must think of their decisions as part of a long story he must interpret and then continue, according to his own judgment of how to make the developing story as good as it can be.' ibid 238–239.

42 Wacks (n 19) 51, 55.

To demonstrate the 'law as integrity', Dworkin distinguished the rules, principles ('a standard that is to be observed, not because it will advance or secure an economic, political, or social situation deemed desirable, but because it is a requirement of justice or fairness or some other dimension of morality'), and policies ('that kind of standard that sets out a goal to be reached, generally an improvement in some economic, political, or social feature of the community (though some goals are negative, in that they stipulate that some present feature is to be protected from adverse change)'),[43] which are in the hands of the judges to interpret the law and to apply the appropriate legal sources of law.[44]

As Dworkin argued, '[l]egal systems characteristically generate controversial or hard cases such as these in which a judge may need to consider whether to look beyond the strict letter of what the law is to determine what it ought to be.' Hence, it is critical for the law to be properly applied to implement 'an interpretive process under which individual rights are paramount.'[45]

To answer the question 'Do judges have to have discretion?' Dworkin 'revisited' the naturalist approach and concluded that

> judges should decide hard cases by interpreting the political structure of their community in the following, perhaps special way: by trying to find the best *justification* they can find, in principles of political morality, for the structure as a whole, from the most profound constitutional rules and arrangements to the details of, for example, the private law of tort or contract.[46]

43 Ronald Dworkin, *Taking Rights Seriously* (Harvard University Press 1978) 22. According to Dworkin, some court decisions reveal that, in addition to rules, the law includes principles. For example, he wrote: 'In 1889 a New York court, in the famous case of *Riggs* v. *Palmer*, had to decide whether an heir named in the will of his grandfather could inherit under that will, even though he had murdered his grandfather to do so. The court began its reasoning with this admission: "It is quite true that statutes regulating the making, proof and effect of wills, and the devolution of property, if literally construed, and if their force and effect can in no way and under no circumstances be controlled or modified, give this property to the murderer." But the court continued to note that "all laws as well as all contracts may be controlled in their operation and effect by general, fundamental maxims of the common law. No one shall be permitted to profit by his own fraud, or to take advantage of his own wrong, or to found any claim upon his own iniquity, or to acquire property by his own crime." The murderer did not receive his inheritance.' ibid 23.

44 'Dworkin claims that, while rules "are applicable in an all-or-nothing fashion", principles and policies have "the dimension of weight or importance". In other words, if a rule applies, and it is a valid rule, a case must be decided in a way dictated by the rule. A principle, on the other hand, provides a reason for deciding the case in a particular way, but it is not a conclusive reason: it will have to be weighed against other principles in the system. Principles differ from policies in that the former is "a standard to be observed, not because it will advance or secure an economic, political, or social situation, but because it is a requirement of justice or fairness or some other dimension of morality". A "policy", however, is "that kind of standard that sets out a goal to be reached, generally an improvement in some economic, political, or social feature of the community". Principles describe rights; policies describe goals.' Wacks (n 19) 55.

45 ibid 52, 50.

46 Ronald Dworkin, '"Natural" Law Revisited' (1982) 34(2) *University of Florida Law Review* 165–188.

The complex interaction between the legal approaches

In numerous countries, the positive law approach, which posits that the law comes from an objectively verifiable source, represents the main pattern. This approach is sometimes nourished by the viewpoint from the natural law schools of thought (and in some instances, other theories as well; for example, the normative theory influenced the development of the strong normative hierarchy system in many countries); however, in general, a particular rule of natural law or at least recognition of the law of nature as a source of the law shall be made through the lenses of positive law.

The same applies to international law. The most frequently used sources of international law – treaty and custom – are the expression of positive law. The third source – the general principles of law, which as a source of international law was affirmed in the twentieth century – also should primarily be considered as a form of positive law. However, at the same time, sometimes it may be regarded as an acknowledged open window into the world of natural law. The chapter ahead in this book contains a more detailed examination of this matter.

An example of the implementation of the naturalist approach in international law is the Nuremberg trials of Nazi war criminals, which used the principle that certain acts constitute 'crimes against humanity', even if, at the moment they are committed, they do not fall under the specific regulations of the positive law. Nevertheless, this provision was applied to particular persons only after its recognition in the Nuremberg Charter (positive law).[47]

The reflection of the natural law legal theory can be found in many international documents on human rights (for example, the Universal Declaration of Human Rights, the European Convention on Human Rights, and so forth), in which, however, the '[n]atural law is conceived of not as a "higher law" in the constitutional sense of invalidating ordinary law but as a benchmark against which to measure positive law.'[48]

Nonetheless, in certain states, other legal approaches prevail. For instance, in the Islamic law tradition (religious law) countries, albeit with some modifications stipulated by the modern era (which are implemented in various proportions in these countries), the concept of **divine law** remains a foundational pattern, which itself is expressed in positive forms, but the rulers have limited power in the law-making process.[49]

---

47 The Charter of the International Military Tribunal, commonly known as the Nuremberg Charter, which was annexed to and formed an integral part of the London Agreement. The jurisdiction of the Tribunal was defined under Article 6 of the Charter, and Paragraph (c) of this Article recognised the 'Crimes against humanity'.

48 Wacks (n 19) 14.

49 'Two terms are used to refer to law in Islam: Shariah and fiqh. Shariah refers to God's divine law as contained in the Quran and the sayings and doings of Muhammad (hadith). Fiqh refers to the scholarly efforts of jurists (fuqaha) to elaborate the details of shariah through investigation and debate. Muslims understand shariah to be an unchanging revelation, while fiqh, as a human endeavor, is open to debate, reinterpretation, and change.' *The Oxford Dictionary of Islam*, John L. Esposito (ed in chief) (Oxford University Press 2003) 148.

In addition, sometimes the legal systems acknowledge the interpretive power of certain authorities: basically, the courts and arbitral tribunals – for example, the competence to dispense a case based on the principles of fairness and justice. The interpretive power of such authorities varies from country to country and from the legal system to the legal system. However, in any case, it is limited and is usually used if the positive norm applicable to a case is unclear or might fail to resolve the issue adequately for other reasons. In international law, for such competence, the obligatory agreement (consent) of the parties concerned is foreseen, which in itself represents a positive form. This matter will be discussed in detail later in this book.

THE ESSENCE OF LAW

There are many sayings and interpretations concerning the meaning of law, which, due to their inherent sharpness in addressing the essence of law, have been widely popular. To cite the few, the following sayings/interpretations are the sharpest in shedding light on its principal mission:

- 'An unjust law is no law at all.' – Thomas Aquinas (1225–1274)
- 'Laws are the sovereigns of sovereigns.' – Louis XIV (1638–1715)
- 'A state is better governed which has but few laws, and those laws strictly observed.' – René Descartes (1596–1650)
- 'Where law ends, tyranny begins.' – William Pitt (1708–1778)
- 'The law is the last result of human wisdom acting upon human experience for the benefit of the public.' – Samuel Johnson (1709–1784)[50]

a) The law as a normative system

descriptive
prescriptive
mores
moral
source of origin
duty generation
sanction

---

50 *Civilization's Quotations: Life's Ideal,* [compiled] by Richard Alan Krieger (Algora Publishing 2002) 236, 233, 238.

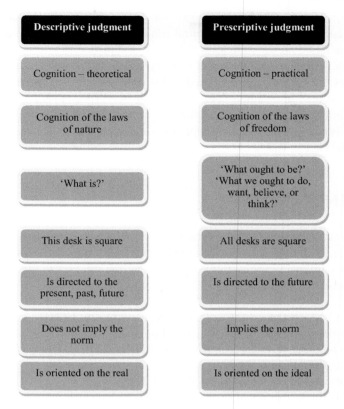

FIGURE 1.1 Descriptive and prescriptive judgments

Normative dimension

For example, 'prudence, justice, strength, self-control is a virtue.' – This sentence is normative in nature because it implies that you have to be reasonable, just, firm and restrained. So the question or judgment is formed normatively, if:

1 it explicitly or implicitly includes a prescriptive 'what ought to be?';
2 it determines some norms or standards;
3 it is future based, carried out in prescriptive (not in descriptive) format/manner;
4 it has an obligatory nature and remains obligatory ('ought to be', 'must') even in cases when the prescriptive rules are not followed. If prescriptive suggestions are not fulfilled, that will not imply the same scientific results which entail non-confirmed experiments in the natural sciences;
5 it is evaluative.[51]

---

51 Pataraia (n 8) 35.

Normative systems

The normative systems manifest the social rules of conduct established with the aim of prescribing norms regulating coexistence between humans.

Multiple varieties of the normative systems exist – for example, such particular arrangements as the rules of a game or a language or such systematised bodies of norms as **moral**, **mores**, and law, which establish the general rules of conduct in a society.

Each normative system can be comprehended and distinguished by answering questions about:

1   the **source of origin** (authors usually refer to a god, a human, a society, and so forth);
2   **duty generation** (from the outside or internally);
3   the category of **sanction**.

Consequently, significant differences can be detected between the normative systems. For instance, if regarding the moral, essentially, duty generation (which stipulates the fulfilment of norms) proceeds internally in an individual; concerning the law, as well as the mores, a duty is predominantly generated from the outside.[52]

Hans J. Morgenthau, a prominent thinker of 'political realism' (which is one of the most influential theories on international relations), for example, first, enumerated only three types of normative systems regulating the conduct 'in all higher societies' and secondly, identified sanctions as the distinguishing characteristic between them. He outlined:

> Three types of norms or rules of conduct operate in all higher societies: ethics, mores, and law. Their distinctive characteristics have been much debated in the literature of philosophy and jurisprudence. For the purpose of this study it is sufficient to point out that every rule of conduct has two elements: the command and the sanction. No particular command is peculiar to any particular type of norm – 'thou shalt not kill' can be a command of ethics, mores, or law. It is the sanction that differentiates these three different types of rules of conduct. . . . If A kills B and afterward feels pangs of conscience or of remorse, we are in the presence of a sanction peculiar to ethics and, hence, of an ethical norm. If A kills B and unorganized society reacts with spontaneous demonstrations of disapproval, such as business boycott, social ostracism, and the like, we have to do with a sanction peculiar to the mores, and, hence, to a norm of the mores. If, finally, A kills B and organized society reacts in the form of a rational procedure with predetermined police action, indictment, trial, verdict, and punishment, the sanction is of a legal nature and the norm, therefore, belongs in the category of law.[53]

---

52 See a wide variety of possible theoretical models and alternative explanations on this matter in Pataraia (n 8) 32–33.

53 Hans J. Morgenthau, *Politics among Nations: The Struggle for Power and Peace* (7th edn, revised by Kenneth W. Thompson and W. David Clinton, McGraw-Hill 2006) 236.

b) The law as a systematised body of norms

> norm
> rules and principles
> legal right
> sources of law
> hierarchy of sources
> complex arrangement of international law
> key imperative of the legal dimension

Prescription

Every **norm** prescribes a rule of conduct (action). Therefore, the norm is a founder of the standards accordingly either of right and wrong (e.g. rules of the game), good and evil (moral) or lawful and unlawful (law).

Ordinary rules or principles

Legal norms appear in the form of either ordinary rules or principles.[54] Both legal rules and legal principles are legal norms because they both suggest what ought to be in legal terms. Nevertheless, there is a difference between legal rules and principles:

- In the case of legal principle, a norm has a general nature and represents a generalised standard (perspective) for an undetermined number of cases that imply the application of the general norm. In addition, a legal principle also provides guidance for the interpretation or application of a legal rule.
- On the other hand, in respect of legal rule, the norm of conduct is applicable only in well-predetermined circumstances and refers to only particular legal relationships (case).

Legal right

There is no **legal right** without the law. The legal norms determine rights and obligations. Every right includes the obligation (of another person/persons) in itself.

---

54 In international law, this distinction has become conventional. The formulation 'rules and principles of international law' is emphasised in many international documents and in the approaches of the International Court of Justice as well. See the Court's Advisory Opinion on *Legal Consequences of the Construction of a Wall in the Occupied Palestinian Territory* of 9 July 2004 (ICJ Reports 2004, 136), for example, Paragraph 114. All ICJ cases are available at <www.icj-cij.org/en/list-of-all-cases>.

Addressees of legal norms

Mostly, legal norms represent the rule of conduct (1) for an unlimited number of persons and (2) for multiple applications. However, legal norms do not always appear to have such a nature – for example, the norms established by an 'individual legal act', which are intended for one-time application[55] and the norms defined by the bilateral international treaty, which are valid only for the parties to the treaty concerned.

Sources of law

Legal norms are presented in pre-defined formats (forms), which are named the '**sources of law**'.

In formal terms, the sources of law are the forms which can be perceived by the human senses and which take shape either as a binding custom (e.g. international custom) or in any other legal format – such as laws, edicts, decrees, rescripts, orders, ordinances, statutes, resolutions, rules, judicial decisions, and the list can be continued further.

Systematised body of norms

Sources and norms of law are ordered in the system of:

- **Hierarchy** (in national law)
- **Complex arrangement** (in international law)

First, the complex arrangement of international law concerns the sources of law and reflects the framework where all of them are placed at the same level without normative hierarchy. However, there are other ordering models in relation to the legal norms of international law regardless of the forms (sources of law) in which they are allocated. These models manage the priority and validity matters in the non-hierarchical system of sources of law. The peremptory and dispositive norms in international law represent one such model. A more detailed description of the complex arrangement system will be provided later in this book.

A key imperative of the legal dimension

Meanwhile, for the legal approach, the principal objective is the implementation of the norms holding legal validity. '**Legal norms are to be kept**' – this is the **key imperative of the legal dimension**: that is to say, a self-sufficient imperative.

At the same time, as suggested earlier, determination of the legal validity *per se* depends on the legal approach one supports. Accordingly, the positivists find validity to be located in an objectively verifiable source; the followers of the law of nature approach in the compliance of a norm with requirements of the (substantive or procedural) law of nature; the

---

55 For instance, Article 2 (Concept and types of legal acts) of the Law of Georgia on Normative Acts.

advocates of the normative theory in the higher norms existing at hierarchically higher levels; the divine law countries in the will of the God, and so forth. However, if a legal norm possesses legal validity, it shall be respected. Hence, in the legal dimension, the effectiveness of a legal norm is preferred over chaos.

c) The law as instituted by the state or the interstate system

> vertical arrangement principle
> interstate system
> horizontal arrangement model
> anarchy
> theories of International Relations
> principle of hierarchy
> principle of anarchy
> law-making
> law-applying

The law as established by the state or interstate system

The law is the body of norms which is developed by the social constructs (structures) named as the 'state' or the 'interstate system'.

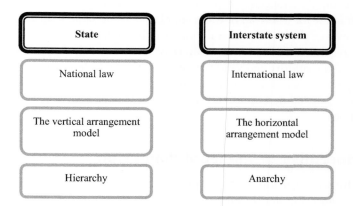

FIGURE 1.2 The state and the interstate system

Law as a mirror of the state or interstate system

Law reflects the structure in which it is established and mirrors the arrangement model of a state or the interstate system.

A state is a complexly interlinked structure which basically is erected on a **vertical arrangement principle** with an implied presence of hierarchy and subordination.

Unlike a state, the **interstate system** is grounded on the model of independent states with no central authority above them (**horizontal arrangement model**). Hence, this model in the International Relations[56] theory is called **anarchy**. In the state of anarchy, there is no hierarchy (supreme authority). Moreover, the state of anarchy is a crucial theoretical tenet for the mainstream **theories of International Relations**.

Ordering principles of national and international law

Therefore, the sources of national law are built on the **principle of hierarchy**, while the sources of international law are arranged on the **principle of anarchy**.

It means that:

- The sources of national law are arranged according to the position in the system of the authority that has adopted them.
- The sources of international law are ordered in the complex arrangement system, but there exists no hierarchy between them.

Key functions

An arrangement model of a system in which and through which the law is instituted corresponds to the disposition of the functions [concerning the law] in this system. The key functions are commonly understood to include:

A   **Law-making** dimension/function

   1   Standards-developing function – the so-called legislative function, which, along with the establishment of the ordinary rules of interaction, allocates governmental power in society.

B   **Law-applying** dimension/function

   2   Order-maintaining function – 'to control . . . [subjects] by coercion and threats of coercion so as to maintain peace and order.'[57]

   3   Order-restoring function – 'to adjust actual conflicts once they have broken out. Here the goal is to restore the peace and order of the ordering framework rather than to maintain it.'[58]

In states, these principal functions are distributed between state authorities.

1   The legislative function is performed by the state authorities recognised by the legal system of a given country to introduce and modify the legislation.
2   The order-maintaining function usually is exercised by the executive branch of government.

---

56 International Relations – the academic discipline of international relations.
57 David A. Funk, 'Major Functions of Law in Modern Society Featured' (1972) 23(2) *Case Western Reserve Law Review* 282.
58 ibid 283–284.

3   The order-restoring function is primarily fulfilled by the judiciary system, which aims to dispense justice. The exercise of the order-restoring function also includes adjusting disputes between private parties (the natural and legal persons), private parties and public officials or state authorities, as well as when only officials and/or state authorities are involved in the conflict (for instance, the conflicts regarding the allocations of governmental power). There are many types of conflicts which can and should be resolved through the fulfilment of the adjudicative function, including conflicts related to the interpretation of legal norms. However, in addition to the courts, the arbitral tribunals are also usually involved in the exercise of the adjudicative function, as well as empowered administrative agencies (for example, in certain states, the so-called independent regulatory bodies).

Thus, the implementation of law-making and law-applying functions within the states is primarily accommodated on hierarchical (inherently centralised) arrangement model, in the sense that in every state, there is the hierarchy between the state organs performing each of the aforementioned powers. Namely, in numerous countries, the parliament is the supreme legislative body and, hence, the supreme authority concerning the law-making function; the government, on the other hand, possesses the supreme responsibility for maintaining order and so forth.

In contrast, in the interstate system, the exercise of law-making and law-applying functions by the subjects of interstate interaction is realised in a decentralised manner (each subject is both a lawmaker and 'an arm of the law'), reflecting the horizontal arrangement model of organisation in the interstate system.

d) The law as applied through the structure which has instituted it

legal order
legal responsibility
legal sanctions
nullity
criminal sanctions
remedies
legal capacity

Law-applying

The structure (state or interstate system) not only institutes but also directs the application of the law.

As outlined earlier, law-applying refers to all the mechanisms which contribute to the maintenance and restoration of legal order.

In states, law-applying usually refers to the activity of state bodies or officials through which they establish, change, and abolish the legal rights and duties of natural or legal persons, as well as the state bodies and officials themselves, or resolve questions about applying the legal responsibility for violation of the legal norms.

However, law-applying is a rather complicated undertaking since, in everyday life, natural or legal persons also voluntarily obey the legal norms regardless of any command from the executive or judiciary bodies. As remarkably outlined by Herbert Lionel Adolphus Hart: 'The power thus conferred on individuals to mould their legal relations with others by contracts, wills, marriages, &c., is one of the great contributions of law to social life.'[59]

Hence, in this chapter, law-applying includes all the forms of the implementation of legal rights and obligations.

Legal order

Without application, the law is the mere combination of words fully distanced from its core objective of establishing the **legal order**.

As famously emphasised by Thomas Hobbes: '[T]he laws are of no power to protect them without a sword in the hands of a man, or men, to cause those laws to be put in execution.'[60] The same idea in the words of Thomas Fuller finds the following expression: 'Law cannot persuade where it cannot punish.'[61]

Therefore, a formula can be introduced which says that the establishment of a legal order by the legal norms can only happen after their application: Law + Law-applying = Legal norms in action = Legal order

FIGURE 1.3 Legal order

Legal responsibility

There are differences between law-applying and the application model of other normative systems, which to a significant degree determine the specifics of law. One important difference is the system of **legal responsibility**, which grants the law its specific obligatory and effective nature.

Thus, the addressees of law have to adhere to and comply with the norms of law. Otherwise, they will be subjected to the **legal sanctions**, such as the (legal) **nullity** of a legal relationship

59 Hart (n 22) 28.
60 Hobbes (n 7) XXI, 101.
61 *Civilization's Quotations: Life's Ideal* (n 50) 236.

(for instance, the nullity of marriage) or a legal norm;[62] the **criminal sanctions** (also called the penal sanctions), **remedies**[63] (for example, the civil or administrative remedies), and so on, which are the guarantying mechanisms of the legal responsibility system. As prominently articulated by Herbert Lionel Adolphus Hart, 'centrally organized effective system of sanctions . . . are therefore required not as the normal motive for obedience, but as a guarantee that those who would voluntarily obey shall not be sacrificed to those who would not.'[64]

Legal capacity

Meanwhile, legal responsibility may be introduced only against persons who possess **legal capacity** ('power to create or enter into a legal relation under the same circumstances in which a normal person would have the power to create or enter into such a relation')[65] and are liable to legal sanctions since not every person can be regarded as a person bearing legal responsibility (for example, a child).

e) The mission of law – to avoid conflicts and to establish civil peace

> conflicts
> reasons for the conflicts
> absence of equal opportunities
> conflicts of interest
> civil peace

62 'NULLITY. . . . In a figurative sense, and in law, it means that which has no more effect than if it did not exist, . . . nullities have been divided into absolute and relative. Absolute nullities are those which may be insisted upon by any one having an interest in rendering the act, deed or writing null, even by the public authorities, . . . Relative nullities can be invoked only by those in whose favor the law has been established'. Nam H Nguyen, *Essential 25000 English Law Dictionary*, 15791 <https://bit.ly/3h5euKQ> accessed 16 March 2021. 'absolute nullity. Civil law. 1. An act that is void because it is against public policy, law, or order. – The nullity is noncurable. It may be invoked by any party or by the court. . . . relative nullity. Civil law. 1. A legal nullity that can be cured by confirmation because the object of the nullity is valid. The nullity may be invoked only by those parties for whose interest it was established. . . . 2. The state of such a nullity.' *Black's Law Dictionary*, Bryan A. Garner (ed in chief) (9th edn, Thomson Reuters 2009) 1173.

63 'remedy (redress. relief) n. Any of the methods available at law for the enforcement, protection, or recovery of rights or for obtaining redress for their infringement. A civil remedy may be granted by a court to a party to a civil action.' *A Dictionary of Law* (n 2) 423.

64 Hart (n 22) 198.

65 'specif., the satisfaction of a legal qualification, such as legal age or soundness of mind, that determines one's ability to sue or be sued, to enter into a binding contract, and the like', *Black's Law Dictionary* (n 62) 235.

Conflicts

Conflicts accompany the coexistence of human beings. The **reasons for the conflicts** are many, but the primary source lies within the human being itself, including the inherent **absence of equal opportunities** and **conflicts of interest** stemming from the limited resources to satisfy human aspirations and desires.

Normative systems as the instruments for the avoidance of conflicts

The normative systems help avoid and check conflicts.

The normative systems are established universally in every social setting where humans interact. Starting with the family, which is the first unit of social order, continuing with the educational or working communities, and finishing with a state, which itself is a sizeable social structure made up of small and large substructures, humans tend to establish and develop norms and place them in a distinctive system to ensure rules are followed.

Civil peace

Consequently, every normative system has a particular significance and influence over the lives of human beings. Nevertheless, because of the apparent effectiveness of its application model, the law is the most effective way to establish **civil peace**.

Primary addressees of national and international law

National law regulates the interaction of the state, other legal (juridical) persons, and natural (physical) persons. However, natural persons (human beings) are the primary addressees of national law.

International law refers to many structures (entities) of the interstate system, including states; however, its primary concern is the legal regulation of the international interaction between states.

Hence, national law exists for humans, international law for states.

THE NOTION OF INTERNATIONAL LAW

Among the many famous definitions of international law widely accepted in academia, some of them are presented below to the attention of the reader:

- [T]he law of nations is originally no other than the law of nature applied to nations.' – Emer de Vattel (1714–1767)[66]

---

66 'This is the law which Grotius, and those who follow him, call the internal law of nations, on account of its being obligatory on nations in point of conscience. Several writers term it the natural law of nations.' Emer de Vattel, *The Law of Nations, or, Principles of the Law of Nature, Applied to the Conduct and Affairs of Nations and Sovereigns, with Three Early Essays on the Origin and Nature of Natural Law and on Luxury,* Béla Kapossy and Richard Whatmore (ed and intro), Thomas Nugent (tr) (Liberty Fund, Inc. 2008) 68

- 'Law of Nations or International Law (*Droit des gens, Völkerrecht*) is the name for the body of customary and conventional rules which are considered legally binding by civilised States in their intercourse with each other.' – Lassa Francis Lawrence Oppenheim (1858–1919)[67]
- '[T]he norms designated as "international law" are really "law" in the same sense as national law.' – Hans Kelsen[68]
- 'Public international law covers relations between states in all their myriad forms, from war to satellites and from trade to human rights, and regulates the operations of the many international and regional institutions.' – Malcolm N. Shaw (born 1947)[69]

DEVELOPMENT OF INTERNATIONAL LAW

Renaissance
multi-centric state system
Peace of Westphalia
universalism
law of nations
Francisco de Vitoria
Francisco Suárez
Alberico Gentili
Hugo Grotius
De Jure Belli ac Pacis
Samuel von Pufendorf
Richard Zouche
Emer de Vattel
Reformation
first wave of international law
Hague Peace Conferences
First World War
second wave of international law
League of Nations
Kellogg-Briand Pact
Second World War
third wave of international law
United Nations Organisation
non-state actors

67 L. Oppenheim, *International Law: A Treatise, Vol. I: Peace* (1st edn, Longmans, Green and Co 1905) 3.
68 Hans Kelsen, *General Theory of Law & State*, A. Javier Trevino (intro) (Transaction Publishers 2006) 328.
69 Malcolm N. Shaw, *International Law* (8th edn, Cambridge University Press 2017) 2.

> Cold War
> Decolonisation
> web of international governmental organisations
> human rights
> United Nations Conference on the Human Environment
> globalisation
> information revolution
> cybersecurity
> COVID-19
> global problems

To the basics

The basics of the law prescribing the relations among nations were designed during the European **Renaissance**.[70] However, many scholars travel further back in history to trace the roots of this law. For example, scholars concentrate on the co-operative agreements between peoples of the ancient Middle East; the profound cultural traditions of ancient Israel, the Indian subcontinent, and China; the prominent political philosophy of ancient Greece and the relations between the Greek city-states; and the rich political and legal legacy of the Roman Empire.

The modern sense of international law

However, in the modern understanding, international law cannot arise in a space without a **multi-centric state system** and the interaction of more or less equal actors.

Consequently, for example, the Roman Empire's *jus gentium*[71] and modern international law cannot in a proper sense be viewed as being analogous because the Roman era in the broad European space in this context was largely monocentric (i.e. Rome-centric – 'All roads lead to Rome').

---

70 'In 15th-century Italy, a revival of interest in classical learning and secular studies, along with a flowering of artistic production, gave rise to the Renaissance (meaning "rebirth"). The movement soon spread to northern Europe, reshaping the continent's cultural landscape.' *History of the World Map by Map*, Rob Houston (Lead Senior ed) (DK Publishing 2018) 160.

71 '*Ius gentium*. yūs gān´tē-ūm. jus jen´tē-um. n. "Law of peoples." (1) In Roman law, *ius gentium* was originally the law applicable to persons lacking Roman citizenship, but, in Imperial Rome, its scope expanded to denote natural law rules supposedly applicable to all persons of any nationality, including Roman citizens. *Ius gentium* thus engulfed the *ius civile* applicable to Roman citizens in Justinian's Code. (2) In more modern usage, a body of law that is universally accepted by the international community as a whole (usually, though not always, based on a theory of natural law). The term is not synonymous with "international law."' Aaron X. Fellmeth and Maurice Horwitz, *Guide to Latin in International Law* (Oxford University Press 2009) 155.

The same can be said about the period before the **Peace of Westphalia** of 1648 concerning most of Europe and the large parts of the world under the rule of Europeans, when the Roman Catholic Church's authority, the Holy Roman Empire's unique position, and, therefore, the prevalence of so-called **universalism** (which was embodied in the papacy and the Holy Roman Empire and, to some degree, stipulated the hierarchical political arrangement between certain European countries) as a core systemic principle prevented the creation of the essentially multi-centric interrelationships. Hence, in that era, Europe was not divided into sovereign states in the modern sense.[72] Meanwhile, according to a contemporary understanding, states are considered organisational entities ruled by an effective government, entitled with centralised political power over their own territory and permanent population, being independent of external political control.

The issue of terminology

Starting from the eighteenth and nineteenth centuries in the English-speaking world, the term 'international law', which first was coined by Jeremy Bentham in 1780, was applied.[73] Before and after, for a certain period of time, the English term for this particular legal system was '**law of nations**'.

New European approach to international law

In general, the road to the new European approach to international law can be more directly traced back to:

- the prominent theoretical thinkers of the sixteenth through eighteenth centuries; and
- the Peace of Westphalia and the political processes which took place during that era.[74]

In this respect, as a theoretical legacy, we shall pay dues to the works of:

- **Francisco de Vitoria** (1486–1546), the Spanish philosopher, theologian, and jurist who is best known for his scientific attempt to safeguard the rights of the indigenous peoples of South America against Spanish colonists and for his ideas on putting limits on the right of justifiable warfare. Like the other thinkers of that era listed here, he

---

72 'Medieval kings were not in this position; internally, they shared power with their barons, each of whom had a private army; externally, they acknowledged some sort of allegiance to the Pope and to the Holy Roman Emperor.' Peter Malanczuk, *Akehurst's Modern Introduction to International Law* (7th revised edn, Routledge 1997) 10.

73 'The word international, it must be acknowledged, is a new one; though, it is hoped, sufficiently analogous and intelligible. It is calculated to express, in a more significant way, the branch of law which goes commonly under the name of the *law of nations*.' Jeremy Bentham, *An Introduction to the Principles of Morals and Legislation* (Clarendon Press 1907) 326.

74 'Modern international law has its origins in the Europe of the sixteenth and seventeenth centuries.' David Harris and Sandesh Sivakumaran, *Cases and Materials on International Law* (8th edn, Sweet & Maxwell 2015) 10.

recognised the importance of the law of nature for the development of the foundations of the law of nations, stressing that this legal system must be based on the universal law of nature and, therefore, non-Europeans should also be subjected to its reign.

- **Francisco Suárez** (1548–1617), the Spanish philosopher, theologian, and jurist, one of the greatest medieval scholastic philosophers, whose writings include treatises on law, the relationship between church and state, metaphysics, and theology. Francisco Suárez is often regarded as a 'philosopher'[75] of international law. At the same time, he was convinced that the '[s]upranational unity is the source of the law of nations which . . . is not that part of natural law which governs the association of peoples, but a positive law, primarily of a customary and consensual nature, accepted by all peoples as the basis for their mutual relations.'[76]
- **Alberico Gentili** (1552–1608), Italian jurist who concluded that the law of nations should reflect the actual practices of civilised nations, limited by moral but not necessarily by religious considerations. He argued in favour of transforming the law of nature from a theological concept into a concept of secular philosophy and, due to his works, is often called 'the originator of the secular school of thought in international law'.[77]
- **Hugo Grotius** (1583–1645), the Dutch jurist who is widely considered to be a founding father of international law in its modern understanding since he was the most consistent in organising the knowledge of his predecessors and his unique scientific approach into a comprehensive system. The cornerstone of his system was the secularist and rationalist rethinking of the law of nature[78] and its role in the law of nations. His well-known work ***De Jure Belli ac Pacis*** (*On the Law of War and Peace*) was first published in 1625 and became one of the leading works on international law.
- Other prominent scientists made essential contributions to the development of international law, such as:

  - The German naturalist writer and jurist **Samuel von Pufendorf** (1632–1694).
  - The English positivist writer and legal scholar **Richard Zouche** (1590–1661).
  - The Swiss jurist **Emer de Vattel**, who combined the arguments of naturalists and positivists, and so forth.

As regards the second significant basis which contributed to the foundation of the new international order under the law of nations, the Peace of Westphalia was a series of peace treaties. These treaties largely resulted in the ending of the so-called European wars

75 'The American internationalist James Brown Scott, in an endearing analogy, considered Francisco de Vitória to be the founder, Francisco Suárez the philosopher and Hugo Grotius the organizer of International Law.' Paulo Emílio Vauthier Borges de Macedo, 'The Law of War in Francisco Suárez: The Civilizing Project of Spanish Scholasticism' (2012) 2(22), jul./dez. Revista da Faculdade de Direito da UERJ 1, 2.

76 Sergio Moratiel Villa, 'The Philosophy of International Law: Suarez, Grotius and Epigones' (1997) (320), September–October *International Review of the Red Cross*, 543–544.

77 Shaw (n 69) 17.

78 'In his influential work, *De Jure Belli ac Pacis*, he asserts that, even if God did not exist, natural law would have the same content.' Wacks (n 19) 6.

of religion, as well as the protracted Dutch War of Independence (the Eighty-Years War) against the Spanish Monarchy and the Thirty Years' War (1618–1648) in the Holy Roman Empire.[79]

The first wave of modern international law

Certainly, the formation of modern international law was facilitated by many political, religious, and cultural processes which developed in Europe over the centuries (for example, in 1517, Martin Luther published 95 theses, initiating to a considerable degree the so-called **Reformation**, which ultimately led to the decline of the political power of the Roman Catholic Church and the idea of universalism).

At the same time, undoubtedly, the international relations based on the Peace of Westphalia did not receive their contemporary form from the beginning, nor was the way ahead on the developmental trajectory without significant setbacks and hurdles to overcome. However, the foundation has been laid by the system-forming principles, which were strengthened by the Peace of Westphalia, and has led to the development of the new interstate model in Europe and, hence, the respective legal system (international law).[80] The two core principles underpinning the new system were as follows:

- *Rex est imperator in regno suo*, which meant that the ruler was sovereign within his or her own domain.
- *Cuius regio, eius religio*, which meant that the religion of the ruler was to dictate the religion of those ruled, a principle that prohibited interference in the internal affairs of other states on religious grounds.[81]

---

79 '[T]he treaty between Spain and Holland entered into Jan. 30, 1648, at Münster, which forms no diplomatic part of what is called the treaty of Westphalia, although it is an important prelude to it; the treaty between Sweden, the emperor, and the states of the empire, Oct. 24, 1648, at Osnabrück, being the first part of the treaty of Westphalia; finally, a treaty between France, the emperor and the states of the empire, Oct. 24, 1648, at Münster, being the second part of the treaty of Westphalia. This peace was not even general. France and Spain continued in a state of war until the peace of the Pyrenees, (Nov 1659), which was thus a complement to the treaties of Westphalia. The former brought peace to Germany and the north, the latter to the south.' *Cyclopaedia of Political Science, Political Economy, and the Political History of the United States by the Best American and European Writers*, John J. Lalor (ed), Volume 1 (Maynard, Merrill, and Co. 1899) 189.

80 'Consequently the treaty of Westphalia has been justly considered as the foundation of positive international law in Europe, and this treaty has been taken as the point of departure of this law.' ibid 189.

81 'Not all scholars agree on this. Some see the modern state emerging much earlier, others much later. But there is no doubt that the Peace of Westphalia is an important turning point in European politics and in world history. The Treaty established two core principles. The first was *rex est imperator in regno suo*. Literally, it means that the king is sovereign within his own domain and not subject to the political will of anyone else. . . . The second principle was *cuius regio, eius religio*. This principle confers upon the king the power to determine which religion is practised in his realm.' Martin Griffiths, Terry O'Callaghan and Steven C. Roach, *International Relations the Key Concepts* (2nd edn, Routledge 2008) 246–247.

Therefore, the Peace of Westphalia was without a doubt a significant political-legal foundation for the **first wave of modern international law** (the classical system of international law [1648–1918]), which was based on the recognition of sovereign states as the subjects of international law and on the essentially unlimited right to wage wars for the protection of national interests. Nevertheless, the system-maintaining principles mentioned here were initially limited to only certain European superpowers. Hence, the new world order was established for these superpowers in the predominantly Eurocentric world.

The last decades of this wave indicated the inclusion of certain non-European nations (for example, the United States and Japan) in the international power relations and the promulgation of a new humanitarian approach to interstate relations when, by the humanisation of warfare, the beginning of a new era of international law was announced. In this respect, the highly impressive new rules were approved during the **Hague Peace Conferences** of 1899 and 1907.

The second wave of modern international law

The **second wave of international law** (1919–1945) was formally inaugurated after the **First World War** when significant steps were taken in the direction of:

- spreading the system-maintaining principles beyond superpowers;
- attempting to institutionalise the international community against war; and
- limiting the use of force.

Consequently, the major developments during the second wave include granting independence to an extensive list of nations, the creation of the **League of Nations**, and the equipping of the international legal system with the general restriction of the use of force under the **Kellogg-Briand Pact** of 1928.

The third wave of modern international law

After the **Second World War**, the main challenge for the interstate system became the avoidance of a third world war. At this stage, the notable developments in science and technology led to the unparalleled improvements in the means of warfare, which had the potential to lead the humankind to the perpetual peace attained 'in the great graveyard of the human race'.[82] To avoid such deplorable events, the states began to reform the existing system of international relations.

- They formed the new collective security system under the auspices of the **United Nations Organisation (UN)** and placed the ultimate restriction on the threat or use of force at the heart of that very system.
- The other focus during the development of the **third wave of international law** was the process of **Decolonisation**, which resulted in the establishment of dozens of newly

---

82 The words of Immanuel Kant in his noble work *Perpetual Peace: A Philosophical Essay*.

independent states. The different political and economic interests of these newly independent states, along with their diverse cultural backgrounds, enriched international law with new perspectives.

- The recognition of the main challenge (avoidance of a third world war) also led to the need for more complex institutionalisation of interstate interaction. More interlinked co-operation was considered the crucial precondition for maintaining international peace, which stipulated the creation of the **web of international governmental organisations**.
- The processes mentioned here also led to an increase in the importance of the **non-state actors** in international relations, with some of them even being entitled to become the subjects of international law.
- Meanwhile, the development of humankind fuelled the progress in thinking with respect to **human rights**, which were identified as the significant focus of international law.[83]
- The process of Decolonisation 'was followed in the 1960s by a focus on economic development to provide the basic necessities for the poorest two thirds of the world and higher standards of living for all. In the 1970s, global values for nature and the environment emerged, as illustrated by the **United Nations Conference on the Human Environment** held in Stockholm in 1972.'[84]

On the whole, the third wave of development of international law was influenced and given its shape by the bipolar configuration of the interstate system and the power relations of the **Cold War**.

New challenges

The collapse of the Soviet Union and the end of the Cold War in the early 1990s led to systemic turbulences in interstate affairs, which has yet to transform into a new and protracted equilibrium.

At the same time, since the 1970s and 1980s, **globalisation** as a process of interaction and integration of individuals and legal entities, as well as governments around the world, has dramatically accelerated due to advances in transportation and communication technology. Many authors designated 'the rapid technological advances in computers, communications, and software that have led to dramatic decreases in the cost of processing and

---

83 'A State-sovereignty-oriented approach has been gradually supplanted by a human-being-oriented approach.' *Prosecutor v Dusko Tadić* a/k/a 'DULE', Decision on the Defence Motion for Interlocutory Appeal on Jurisdiction of 2 October 1995, Tadić (IT-94–1). All cases of the International Criminal Tribunal for the Former Yugoslavia are available at the official website of the Tribunal <www.icty.org/en/cases>. In this book, materials from the website are used, taking into account the disclaimer and applicable legal rules.

84 United Nations, *Prototype Global Sustainable Development Report* (New York: United Nations Department of Economic and Social Affairs, Division for Sustainable Development 2014) <http://sustainabledevelopment.un.org/globalsdreport/> accessed 16 March 2021.

transmitting information' as the '**information revolution**'.[85] However, the process of the globalisation in itself has autonomously become a new challenge for the interstate system and international law as well. For example, during the so-called information revolution, the problem of **cybersecurity** and its regulation by legal norms emerged.

The latest developments have also brought up at the core of the agenda such large-scale challenges as, for example, the terrorism, migration, and so on, which significantly alter the boundaries that existed during the Cold War.

Finally, the **COVID-19** pandemic clearly demonstrated to humanity how vulnerable it is, even with all the latest technological advancement, and the rethinking of international law along the lines of the new crisis is once again back on the agenda for the interstate system. Many commentators argue that international law must solve all the problems which threaten the very existence of life; therefore, all **global problems** (which 'possess a large-scale risk potential, and present a high level of threat in the event that they are not resolved')[86] should be the focus of attention for the interstate legal system, i.e. international law. The problems of that type usually include the threat of unleashing of a third world war; environmental degradation; pandemic; demographic problems (uncontrolled population growth in the poorest countries and birth-rate decrease in developed countries); food crises and famine; resource and energy crises; international terrorist threats; national, socio-cultural, and religious conflicts; conflicts of civilisations; and so on.[87]

Consequently, like the interstate system, international law is now in the process of being rethought in order to find a model that will be consistent with and will fundamentally reflect new realities.

Nonetheless, until now, contemporary international law has essentially retained the core framework it inherited from the early post–World War II period (targeting the avoidance of war and institution of peace in the interstate system), on which, in order to address the new challenges and objectives in the contemporary world, new principles and norms are gradually grafted. Furthermore, the new global threats are still perceived through the lenses of a more complex understanding of the concept of peace, which includes all aspects confronting the establishment of international peace. For example, in his remarks to the Security Council on the COVID-19 pandemic, UN Secretary-General António Guterres articulated that 'the pandemic also poses a significant threat to the maintenance of international peace and security – potentially leading to an increase in social unrest and

---

85 Robert O. Keohane and Joseph S. Nye, *Power & Interdependence* (4th edn, Pearson 2012) 213. At the same time, Robert O. Keohane and Joseph S. Nye, the prominent thinkers of the 'neoliberal institutionalism' (the theory on international relations, also referred to as the theory of 'complex interdependence'), outlined: 'Traditionally, political activity has focused first at the local level, only extending to national and international spheres as the activity being regulated escaped jurisdictional boundaries. The contemporary information revolution, however, is inherently global, since "cyberplace" is divided on a nongeographical basis. The suffixes "edu," "org," and "com" are not geographical; and even where a country suffix appears in an address, there is no guarantee that the person being reached actually resides in that jurisdiction.' ibid 212.

86 See 'Global Problems' <http://planetaryproject.com/global_problems/> accessed 16 March 2021.

87 ibid.

violence that would greatly undermine our ability to fight the disease.'[88] The complex understanding of peace will be examined later in this book.

SPECIFICS OF INTERNATIONAL LAW

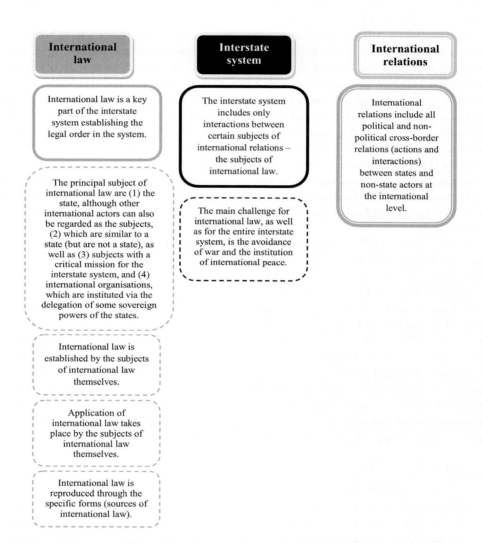

International law

International law is a key part of the interstate system establishing the legal order in the system.

The principal subject of international law are (1) the state, although other international actors can also be regarded as the subjects, (2) which are similar to a state (but are not a state), as well as (3) subjects with a critical mission for the interstate system, and (4) international organisations, which are instituted via the delegation of some sovereign powers of the states.

International law is established by the subjects of international law themselves.

Application of international law takes place by the subjects of international law themselves.

International law is reproduced through the specific forms (sources of international law).

Interstate system

The interstate system includes only interactions between certain subjects of international relations – the subjects of international law.

The main challenge for international law, as well as for the entire interstate system, is the avoidance of war and the institution of international peace.

International relations

International relations include all political and non-political cross-border relations (actions and interactions) between states and non-state actors at the international level.

FIGURE 1.4 International law – interstate system – international relations

88 'Secretary-General's Remarks to the Security Council on the COVID-19 Pandemic [as Delivered]' (9 April 2020) <www.un.org/sg/en/content/sg/statement/2020-04-09/secretary-generals-remarks-the-security-council-the-covid-19-pandemic-delivered> accessed 16 March 2021.

a) Interstate system

complex network of relations
third wave of international law development
interstate legal system
interstate system
horizontal (anarchic) arrangement model
sovereign equality
superpowers
privileged legal position
consent

A complex web

There is a very **complex network of relations** at the international level, in which states, as well as other entities and persons, engage. During the period described in this book as the **third wave of international law development**, the international network shifted to an even more complicated web of relations, in which numerous entities and persons participate.

Nevertheless, only a few of them have acquired the status of a genuine member (actor) of the **interstate legal system**, elevating them to the status of a subject of international law. Hence, in this book, the **interstate system** refers to the systemic and arranged relationships between those subjects, i.e. the states and other subjects of international law.

Horizontal model

The interstate system, as emphasised earlier, is essentially built on the **horizontal (anarchic) arrangement model**, based mainly on the principle of **sovereign equality** of states.

A unique legal position of the superpowers

However, preliminarily, the substantial areas are defined in which maintenance of international peace and security are to a significant degree reserved for the **superpowers** by virtue of their holding a **privileged legal position** (especially in the UN Security Council, which has five permanent members – China, France, the Russian Federation, the United Kingdom of Great Britain and Northern Ireland, and the United States of America). On the other hand, other domains follow the logic of the horizontal arrangement of states.

At the same time, the possession in certain areas of a privileged legal position by superpowers also means that these states have a great responsibility to the entire interstate system. Certainly, with great power comes great responsibility.

Establishment of law by consent (approval)

Finally, for the establishment of law in the interstate system, there is no alternative to **consent** (approval) as the sole mechanism since, in the international order, there exists no legal superiority (subordination) in relations between the subjects.

b) State as the main subject of international law

notion of the subject
law-making process
right to apply the legal norms
other subjects of international law
people
sui generis territorial entities
sui generis non-territorial entities
international organisations
universal subjectivity
limited subjectivity
subjectivity of individuals

A complex notion of the subject of international law

In international law, the **notion of the subject** of international law is defined in rather complex terms, which primarily state that a subject is a person who participates in the **law-making process** and affords itself the **right to apply the legal norms**.[89]

A state as the main subject of international law

On the whole, international law indeed is an interstate law. Hence, a state is a principal subject.

Other subjects

However, the international legal order is also maintained by the **other subjects** (international law actors), namely:

- The **people** in the process of self-determination (usually, the people on the road to independence), based on the principle of equal rights and self-determination of peoples;

89 The notion of the subject of international law will be addressed more precisely later in this book.

- The *sui generis*[90] territorial entities;
- The *sui generis* non-territorial entities; and
- International organisations (intergovernmental organisations).

Scope of subjectivity

The scope of subjectivity depends on the type of subjectivity to which a given entity belongs (a state, a *sui generis* territorial entity, and so on). Only states obtain unlimited and **universal subjectivity**.

The limited subjectivity of the other subjects of international law

The subjectivity of the other actors of international law is limited and corresponds to the degree of their accommodation at the interstate level (**limited subjectivity**).

This limitation is determined by the role (mission, functions) of a given entity. Namely, the scope of subjectivity:

- for the people is defined by the process of self-determination, which means that they are entitled to participate in international legal activities only concerning the issues related to their self-determination process;
- for the *sui generis* territorial entities is ensured in areas where their international status is recognised by other subjects of international law;
- for the *sui generis* non-territorial entities is stipulated by their mission; and
- for the international organisations is determined by the assigned functions and competencies stemming from their foundational treaties (or other instruments).

Subjectivity of individuals

At the same time, in the scholarship dedicated to international law, the problem of **subjectivity of individuals** persists. However, individuals *per se* are not actors at the interstate level, and respectively, of international law, since they, as individuals, are not entitled to participate in the law-making process and the execution of international norms.

For example, regardless of the existence of international law norms with direct reference to the humans, establishment and application of these norms through the power mechanisms is indeed reserved for the interstate level. Hence, in this regard as well, the states (and other subjects of international law) hold the responsibility to the other states (and other subjects of international law) on the interstate level.

---

90 'SUI GENERIS [L. *sui* + *genus*, *generis* / class, kind] Of its own kind. Unique; in a class by itself. Different from others.' Lazar Emanuel, *Latin for Lawyers* (1st edn, Emanuel Publishing Corp 1999) 402.

c) Sources and norms of international law

consensual nature
no hierarchy
international treaties
international custom
general principles of law
unilateral acts
subsidiary sources
soft law
jus cogens norms
dispositive norms

The consensual nature of the sources of law

The sources of international law maintain a **consensual nature**. The subjects constitute them. Under the original concept of international law, applying the norms to a subject that has not given its consent is not permitted.

The sources of law

There is **no hierarchy** between the sources of international law.

There are three sources of international law:

- **international treaties**;
- **international custom**; and
- **general principles of law.**

In international law, a special place is occupied by the **unilateral acts** of states, the **subsidiary sources** of international law – the judicial decisions and the teachings of the most highly qualified publicists – and the **soft law**.

Complex arrangement of international law

In international law, there exists a complex arrangement model between norms (rules and principles). The principal framework for their validity is provided by the concept of *jus cogens* **norms**, which envisages that all the rules of international law are either *jus cogens* or other norms (**peremptory and dispositive norms** of international law). The peremptory norms of general international law are developed from the sources of international law, and they can be changed in the same way through a new norm with the same legal force. They are a set of rules which are peremptory in nature and from which no derogation is allowed under any circumstances.

d) International law as applied by subjects

> enforcement system
> pacific settlement of disputes
> international legal responsibility
> reciprocity
> collective action
> public opinion
> only opportunity

Application of international law

The subjects of international law not only constitute the international norms but also act individually or collectively to apply these norms, including through enforcement and dispute resolution mechanisms.

Enforcement system

Generally, the **enforcement system** of international law is supported by the integrated model of **pacific settlement of disputes**; **international legal responsibility**; and such mechanisms as **reciprocity**, **collective action**, and **public opinion**.

- Reciprocity is a type of enforcement which stipulates that if a particular subject offends against another subject, the other will respond by returning the same behaviour.
- Through collective action, several subjects act together to persuade a subject to comply with its legal obligations.
- Usually, the states and other subjects of international law avoid negative publicity, so the threat of negative public opinion regarding their behaviour may often be an effective enforcement mechanism.

Dispute resolution

In the interstate system, a comprehensive dispute resolution system is introduced, which includes several international institutions on the global, regional, or bilateral levels, such as the international courts and arbitral tribunals (tribunals established on a parity basis or permanent arbitral tribunals), as well as other bodies with competence in the conclusion of a controversy.

However, (1) the power of international adjudicative institutions is limited to the extent established by their constituent sources, and (2) their jurisdiction covers only the subjects of international law that recognise their competence to make binding decisions.

The application system described here as the only opportunity

It is of utmost importance to clearly comprehend that the contemporary law-applying system of international law is the only opportunity to implement the rules of law in the horizontal framework of the interstate system.

e) Avoidance of war and institution of peace

> war and peace
> Eurocentric
> third world war
> co-operation in various fields
> negative peace
> positive peace
> Declaration on the Right of Peoples to Peace
> sacred right to peace

The mission of international law

The main concerns for international law are **war and peace**, whereas the primary aim of national law is to avoid the conflicts between humans and establish civil peace.

The great thinkers who contributed to the establishment and development of modern international law intended precisely such a mission (the avoidance of war and institution of peace) for international law. Moreover, across the centuries, when the world appeared to be principally **Eurocentric**, the law of nations emerged mostly in the form of peace treaties. Meanwhile, Europe is the birthplace of the 'law of nations'. Accordingly, the legacy of that period and its European roots are easily recognisable in contemporary international law.

Avoidance of a third world war

The mission of avoidance of war and institution of peace fuelled the development of the entirety international law, as well as its particular areas.

Meanwhile, after the Second World War, the main concern was the avoidance of a **third world war** and the survival of humanity. Consequently, a collective security system was developed, in which the superpowers hold the qualitatively different and privileged responsibility of maintaining international peace and are equipped with respective legal instruments in the UN Security Council.

Co-operation in various fields

At the same time, the idea that **co-operation in various fields** is necessary for the maintenance of international peace and security is embodied in international law. Thus, the accomplishment of this idea flourished with the creation of a web of multilinked international institutions with corresponding developments of the interstate system.

The meaning of peace

Traditionally, peace and war were interlinked notions. Peace was defined in terms of the absence of war or military hostilities. Such understanding was usually referred to as '**negative peace**' (*absentia belli*).

However, in parallel with this understanding of peace, a more all-encompassing notion was developed, which included the elimination of all or at least the major preconditions/causes of war. Such introspection was expressed in a well-known work, *Perpetual Peace: A Philosophical Essay*, by one of the most famous thinkers of all times – Immanuel Kant (1724–1804).

> In the Kant's opinion, ceasing of the military activities represents only a temporary truce while the reservations and underlying causes for war, including latent causes for the future conflict have not been eradicated. Only when all the underlying causes for war are eliminated, including those on which parties are silent but which have the potential to materialize into a war at the later stage, can the perpetual peace be realized . . . . Consequently, Immanuel Kant diverts into offering a positive definition of peace, whereby in his analysis peace is presented as the condition where all the reservations and potential points for inflaming a conflict are settled and the incentives for starting a war between the parties concerned becomes obsolete.[91]

Over time, the meaning of **positive peace** was developed. It 'aimed at the creation of conditions of equity and social justice preventing recourse to violence. Positive peace requests measures to prevent and put an end to deprivation of rights and liberties, domination of peoples by other peoples.'[92]

Such an understanding of peace gradually covered both the direct underlying causes for war as well as numerous indirect motivations, i.e. the factors which potentially could stipulate instability in the interstate system and, therefore, challenge international peace, as was stressed concerning the COVID-19 pandemic by the UN Secretary-General António Guterres in his statement mentioned earlier.

The right to peace

The Charter of the United Nations proclaimed the basic principles necessary for an enduring international peace. However, in 1984, the UN General Assembly adopted the Resolution and its annex, the **Declaration on the Right of Peoples to Peace**.[93] According

---

91 Pataraia (n 8) 108.

92 Djacoba Liva Tehindrazanarivelo and Robert Kolb, 'Peace, Right to, International Protection' (2006) *Max Planck Encyclopedia of Public International Law* <https://opil.ouplaw.com/view/10.1093/law:epil/9780199231690/law-9780199231690-e858> accessed 16 March 2021.

93 A/RES/39/11 of 12 November 1984. All UN General Assembly resolutions are available at the official website of the UN <www.un.org/en/sections/documents/general-assembly-resolutions/>. In this book, materials from the website are used according to applicable legal rules.

to the Declaration, the General Assembly 'solemnly' proclaimed 'that the peoples of our planet have a **sacred right to peace**' and 'that the preservation of the right of peoples to peace and the promotion of its implementation constitute a fundamental obligation of each State'. Hence, the UN General Assembly announced the start of a new era in which peace should be envisioned as a right. 'Consequently, the step has been taken from an abstract philosophical ideal to a more concrete political-legal principle.'[94]

CASES AND MATERIALS (*SELECTED PARTS*)

Legal families

Rene David and John E. C. Brierley, *Major Legal Systems in the World Today* (3rd edn, Stevens & Sons 1985) 22–36.

'18. Romano-Germanic family

A first family may be called the Romano-Germanic family. This group includes those countries in which legal science has developed on the basis of Roman *jus civile*. Here the rules of law are conceived as rules of conduct intimately linked to ideas of justice and morality. To ascertain and formulate these rules falls principally to legal scholars who, absorbed by this task of enunciating the "doctrine" on an aspect of the law, are somewhat less interested in its actual administration and practical application. These matters are the responsibility of the administration and legal practitioners. Another feature of this family is that the law has evolved, primarily for historical reasons, as an essentially private law, as a means of regulating the private relationships between individual citizens; other branches of law were developed later, but less perfectly, according to the principles of the "civil law" which today still remains the main branch of legal science, Since the nineteenth century, a distinctive feature of the family has been the fact that its various member countries have attached special importance to enacted legislation in the form of "codes".'

'19. Common law family

A second family is that of the Common law, including the law of England and those laws modelled on English law. The Common Law, altogether different in its characteristics from the Romano-Germanic family, was formed primarily by judges who had to resolve specific disputes. Today it still bears striking traces of its origins. The Common law legal rule is one which seeks to provide the solution to a trial rather than to formulate a general rule of conduct for the future. It is then much less abstract than the characteristic legal rule of the Romano-Germanic family. Matters relating to the administration of justice, procedure, evidence and execution of judgments have, for Common law lawyers, an importance equal, or even superior, to substantive legal rules because, historically, their immediate pre-occupation has been to re-establish peace rather than articulate a moral basis for the social order. Finally, the origins of the Common law are linked to royal power. It was developed as a system in those cases where the peace of the English kingdom was threatened, or when some other important consideration required, or

94 Tehindrazanarivelo and Kolb (n 92).

justified, the intervention of royal power. It seems, essentially, to be a *public* law, for contestations between private individuals did not fall within the purview of the Common law courts save to the extent that they involved the interest of the crown or kingdom. In the formation and development of the Common law- a public law issuing from procedure-the learning of the Romanists founded on the *jus civile* played only a very minor role. The divisions of the Common law, its concepts and vocabulary, and the methods of the Common law lawyer, are entirely different from those of the Romano-Germanic family.'

'23. Muslim, Hindu, and Jewish laws

But law may also be seen as a model of ideal behaviour, one not to be confused with the actual rules by which individuals act which courts apply. European universities, in their pre-nineteenth-century tradition, paid very little attention to national or customary laws of the time and taught, almost exclusively, an ideal law constructed on the basis of Roman law. In Muslim countries, in the same way, more attention is given to the model law linked to the Islamic religion than to local custom (treated as a phenomenon of fact) or the laws and decrees of the sovereign (treated as merely administrative measures) and neither of these is thought to possess the full dignity of law. The same can be said of Jewish law and, in a very different context, Hindu law.'

'24. Far East

The situation in the Far East, especially China is completely different. Here there is no question of studying an ideal law distant from rules laid down by legislators or simply followed in practice: here the very value of law itself has traditionally been put into question.'

'25. Black Africa and Malagasy Republic

. . . There too, in milieux in which the community' cohesion prevails over any developed sense of individualism; the principal objective is the maintenance or restoration of harmony rather than respect for law. The Western laws adopted in Africa are often hardly more than a veneer, the vast majority of the population still lives according to traditional ways which do not comprise what we in the West call law and without heed to what is very often nothing more than an artificially implanted body of rules.'

Natural law

Thomas Hobbes, *Leviathan or the Matter, Form and Power of a Commonwealth, Ecclesiastical and Civil*
(2nd edn, George Routledge and Sons 1886) 65–67, 71–72.

'Chapter XIV. Of the First and Second Natural Laws, and of Contracts

"The right of nature", which writers commonly call *jus naturale,* is the liberty each man hath, to use his own power, as he will himself, for the preservation of his own nature; that is to say, of his own life; and consequently, of doing anything, which in his own judgement and reason he shall conceive to be the aptest means thereunto.

By "liberty," is understood, according to the proper signification of the word, the absence of external impediments: which impediments may oft take away part of a man's power to do what he would; but cannot hinder him from using the power left him, according as his judgement and reason shall dictate to him.

A "law of nature," *lex naturalis*, is a precept or general rule, found out by reason, by which a man is forbidden to do that which is destructive of his life, or taketh away the means of preserving the same; and to omit that, by which he thinketh it may be best preserved. For though they that speak of this subject, use to confound *jus* and *lex*, "right" and "law:" yet they ought to be distinguished; because "right," consisteth in liberty to do, or to forbear; whereas "law," determineth and bindeth to one of them; so that law and right differ as much as obligation and liberty; which in one and the same matter are inconsistent.

And because the condition of man, as hath been declared in the precedent chapter, is a condition of war of every one against every one; in which case every one is governed by his own reason; and there is nothing he can make use of, that may not be a help unto him, in preserving his life against his enemies; it followeth, that in such a condition, every man has a right to everything; even to one another's body. And therefore, as long as this natural right of every man to everything endureth, there can be no security to any man, how strong or wise soever he be, of living out the time, which Nature ordinarily alloweth men to live. And consequently it is a precept, or general rule of reason, "that every man ought to endeavour peace, as far as he has hope of obtaining it; and when he cannot obtain it, that he may seek, and use, all helps, and advantages of war." The first branch of which rule, containeth the first, and fundamental law of Nature; which is, "to seek peace, and follow it." The second, the sum of the right of Nature, which is, "by all means we can, to defend ourselves."

From this fundamental law of Nature, by which men are commanded to endeavour peace, is derived this second law; "that a man be willing, when others are so too, as far forth, as for peace, and defence of himself he shall think it necessary, to lay down this right to all things; and be contented with so much liberty against other men, as he would allow other men against himself." For as long as every man holdeth this right, of doing anything he liketh; so long are all men in the condition of war. But if other men will not lay down their right, as well as he; then there is no reason for anyone to divest himself of his: for that were to expose himself to prey, which no man is bound to, rather than to dispose himself to peace. This is that law of the Gospel; "whatsoever you require that others should do to you, that do ye to them." And that law of all men, *quod tibi fieri non vis, alteri ne feceris*.

To "lay down" a man's "right" to anything, is to "divest" himself of the "liberty," of hindering another of the benefit of his own right to the same. For he that renounceth, or passeth away his right, giveth not to any other man a right which he had not before; because there is nothing to which every man had not right by Nature: but only standeth out of his way, that he may enjoy his own original right, without hindrance from him; not without hindrance from another. So that the effect which redoundeth to one man, by another man's defect of right, is but so much diminution of impediments to the use of his own right original.

Right is laid aside, either by simply renouncing it; or by transferring it to another. By "simply renouncing;" when he cares not to whom the benefit thereof redoundeth. By "transferring;" when he intendeth the benefit thereof to some certain person or persons. And when a man hath in either manner abandoned, or granted away his right; then is he said to be "obliged," or "bound," not to hinder those, to whom such right is granted, or abandoned, from the benefit of it: and that he "ought," and it is his "duty," not to make void that voluntary act of his own'.

'Chapter XV. Of Other Laws of Nature

From that law of Nature, by which we are obliged to transfer to another, such rights, as being retained, hinder the peace of mankind, there followeth a third; which is this, "that men perform their covenants made;" without which, covenants are in vain, and but empty words; and the right of all men to all things remaining, we are still in the condition of war.

And in this law of Nature consisteth the fountain and original of "justice." For where no covenant hath preceded, there hath no right been transferred, and every man has right to everything; and consequently, no action can be unjust. But when a covenant is made, then to break it is "unjust:" and the definition of "injustice," is no other than "the not performance of covenant." And whatsoever is not unjust, is "just."'

Natural law

John Locke, *Two Treatises of Government*
(A new edition corrected. published 1821 (MDCCCXXI) by Printed for Whitmore and Fenn and C. Brown) Book II, 189–190, 191–192, 200, 204.

'Chapter II.

Of the State of Nature

§ 4. To understand political power right, and derive it from its original, we must consider, what state all men are naturally in, and that is, *a state of perfect freedom* to order their actions, and dispose of their possessions and persons, as they think fit, within the bounds of the law of nature, without asking leave, or depending upon the will of any other man.

A *state* also *of equality*, wherein all the power and jurisdiction is reciprocal, no one having more than another; there being nothing more evident, than that creatures of the same species and rank, promiscuously born to all the same advantages of nature, and the use of the same faculties should also be equal one amongst another without subordination or subjection, unless the lord and master of them all should, by any manifest declaration of his will, set one above another, and confer on him, by an evident and clear appointment, an undoubted right to dominion and sovereignty.'

'§ 6. But though this be a *state of liberty*, yet *it is not a state of license*: though man in that state have an uncontroulable liberty to dispose of his person or possessions, yet he has not liberty to destroy himself, or so much as any creature in his possession, but where some nobler use than its bare preservation calls for it. The *state of nature* has a law of nature to govern it, which obliges every one: and reason, which is that law, teaches all mankind, who will but consult it, that being all *equal* and *independent*, no one ought to harm another in his life, health, liberty, or possessions: for men being all the workmanship of one omnipotent, and infinitely wise maker; all the servants of one sovereign master, sent into the world by his order, and about his business; they are his property, whose workmanship they are, made to last during his, not one another's pleasure: and being furnished with like faculties, sharing all in one community of nature, there cannot be supposed any such *subordination* among us, that may authorize us to destroy one another, as if we were made for one another's uses, as the inferior ranks of creatures are for ours. Every one, as he is *bound to preserve himself,* and not to quit his station wilfully, so by the like reason, when his own preservation comes not in competition, ought he, as much as he can, to *preserve the rest of mankind* and may not, unless it be to do justice on an offender, take away, or impair the life, or what tends to the preservation of the life, the liberty, health, limb, or goods of another.

§ 7. And that all men may be restrained from invading others rights, and from doing hurt to one another, and the law of nature be observed, which willeth the peace and *preservation of all mankind,* the *execution* of the law of nature is, in that state, put into every man's hands, whereby every one has a right to punish the transgressors of that law to such a degree, as may hinder its violation: for the *law of nature* would, as all other laws that concern men in this world, be in vain, if there were nobody that in the state of nature had a *power to execute* that law, and thereby preserve the innocent and restrain offenders. And if any one in the state of nature may punish another for any evil he has done, every one may do so: for in that *state of perfect equality* where naturally there is no superiority or jurisdiction of one over another, what any may do in prosecution of that law, every one must needs have a right to do.'

'Chapter III.

Of the State of War

§ 16. The *state of war* is a state of *enmity* and *destruction*: and therefore declaring by word or action, not a passionate and hasty, but a sedate settled design upon another man's life *puts him in a state of war* with him against whom he has declared such an intention, and so has exposed his life to the other's power to be taken away by him, or any one that joins with him in his defence, and espouses his quarrel; it being reasonable and just, I should have a right to destroy that which threatens me with destruction: for, *by the fundamental law of nature, man being to be preserved* as much as possible, when all cannot be preserved, the safety of the innocent is to be preferred: and one may destroy a man who makes war upon him, or has discovered an enmity to his being, for the same reason that he may kill a *wolf* or a *lion*; because such men are not under the ties of the common-law of reason, have no other rule, but that of force and violence, and so may be treated as beasts of prey, those dangerous and noxious creatures, that will be sure to destroy him whenever he falls into their power.'

'§ 21. To avoid this *state of war* (wherein there is no appeal but to heaven, and wherein every the least difference is apt to end, where there is no authority to decide between the contenders) is one great reason of men's putting themselves into society, and quitting the state of nature: for where there is an authority, a power on earth, from which relief can be had by *appeal*, there the continuance of the *state of war* is excluded, and the controversy is decided by that power.'

Natural law

Lon L. Fuller, *The Morality of Law*
(Revised edn, Yale University Press 1969) 96–98.

'III. The Concept of Law

What I have tried to do is to discern and articulate the natural laws of a particular kind of human undertaking, which I have described as "the enterprise of subjecting human conduct to the governance of rules." These natural laws have nothing to do with any "brooding omni-presence in the skies." Nor have they the slightest affinity with any such proposition as that the practice of contraception is a violation of God's law. They remain entirely terrestrial in origin and application. They are not "higher" laws; if any metaphor of elevation is appropriate they should be called "lower" laws. They are like the natural laws of carpentry, or at least those laws respected by a carpenter who wants the house he builds to remain standing and serve the purpose of those who live in it.'

'With the positivists certainly no clear pattern emerges. Austin defined law as the command of a political superior. Yet he insisted that "laws properly so-called" were general rules and that "occasional or particular commands" were not law. Bentham, who exploited his colorful vocab-ulary in castigating the law of nature, was at all times concerned with certain aspects of what I have called the internal morality of law. Indeed, he seemed almost obsessed with the need to make the laws accessible to those subject to them. On the other hand, in more recent times Gray has treated the question whether law ought to take the form of general rules as a matter of "little importance practically," though admitting that specific and isolated exercises of legal power do not make a fit subject for jurisprudence. For Somlo retroactive laws might be condemned as unfair, but in no sense are to be regarded as violating any general premise underlying the concept of law itself.

With respect to thinkers associated with the natural law tradition it is safe to say that none of them would display the casualness of a Gray or Somlo toward the demands of legal morality. On the other hand, their chief concern is with what I have called substantive natural law, with the proper ends to be sought through legal rules.'

Legal positivism

Jeremy Bentham, *An Introduction to the Principles of Morals and Legislation* (Oxford: Clarendon Press, MCMVII) 18, 324, 326–327, 329

'[1] 6. A great multitude of people are continually talking of the Law of Nature; and then they go on giving you their sentiments about what is right and what is wrong: and these sentiments, you are to understand, are so many chapters and sections of the Law of Nature.

7. Instead of the phrase, Law of Nature, you have sometimes, Law of Reason, Right Reason, Natural Justice, Natural Equity, Good Order. Any of them will do equally well. This latter is most used in politics. The three last are much more tolerable than the others, because they do not very explicitly claim to be any thing more than phrases: they insist but feebly upon the being looked upon as so many positive standards of themselves, and seem content to be taken, upon occasion, for phrases expressive of the conformity of the thing in question to the proper standard, whatever that may be. On most occasions, however, it will be better to say *utility: utility* is clearer, as refer-ring more explicitly to pain and pleasure.'

'XXIII. Now *law*, or *the law*, taken indefinitely, is an abstract and collective term; which, when it means any thing, can mean neither more nor less than the sum total of a number of individual laws taken together. It follows, that of whatever other modifications the subject of a book of jurisprudence is susceptible, they must all of them be taken from some circumstance or other of which such individual laws, or the assemblages into which they may be sorted, are susceptible.'

'2 In most of the European languages there are two different words for distinguishing the abstract and the concrete senses of the word *law*: which words are so wide asunder as not even to have any etymological affinity. In Latin, for example, there is *lex* for the concrete sense, *jus* for the abstract; in Italian, *legge* and *diritto*; in French, *loi* and *droit*; in Spanish, *ley* and *derecho*; in German, *gesetz* and *recht*. The English is at present destitute of this advantage.

In the Anglo-Saxon, besides *lage*, and several other words, for the concrete sense, there was the word *right*, answering to the German *recht*, for the abstract as may be seen in the compound *folc-right*, and in other instances. But the word *right* having long ago lost this sense, the modern English no longer possesses this advantage.'

'XXV. In the second place, with regard to the *political quality* of the persons whose conduct is the object of the law. These may, on any given occasion, be considered either as members of the same state, or as members of different states: in the first case, the law may be referred to the head of *internal*, in the second case, to that of *international* jurisprudence.

Now as to any transactions which may take place between individuals who are subjects of different states, these are regulated by the internal laws, and decided upon by the internal tribunals, of the one or the other of those states: the case is the same where the sovereign of the one has any immediate transactions with a private member of the other: the sovereign reducing himself, *pro re natâ*, to the condition of a private person, as often as he submits his cause to either tribunal; whether by claiming a benefit, or defending himself against a burthen. There remain then the mutual transactions between sovereigns, as such, for the subject of that branch of jurisprudence which may be properly and exclusively termed *international*.

With what degree of propriety rules for the conduct of persons of this description can come under the appellation of *laws*, is a question that must rest till the nature of the thing called a *law* shall have been more particularly unfolded.

It is evident enough, that international jurisprudence may, as well as internal, be censorial as well as expository, unauthoritative as well as authoritative.'

'XXVIII. Fourthly, in point of *expression*, the laws in question may subsist either in the form of *statute* or in that of *customary* law.

As to the difference between these two branches (which respects only the article of form or expression) it cannot properly be made appear till some progress has been made in the definition of a law.

XXIX. Lastly, The most intricate distinction of all, and that which comes most frequently on the carpet, is that which is made between the *civil* branch of jurisprudence and the *penal*, which latter is wont, in certain circumstances, to receive the name of *criminal*.'

Legal positivism

John Austin, *The Province of Jurisprudence Determined*
(London: John Murray, Albemarle Street 1832) 5, 6–7, 11–13, 18, 29.

'Having stated the essentials of a law or rule, I shall distinguish laws established by political superiors, from laws set by men to men (but *not* by political superiors), and from that Divine law which is the ultimate test of human.

Having distinguished laws established by political superiors, from the laws (properly so called) to which they are related by resemblance, and from the laws (improperly so called) to which they are nearly related by a strong analogy, I shall advert to the improper applications of the term *law* which are merely metaphorical or figurative.

Every *law* or *rule* (taken with the largest signification which can be given to the term *properly*) is a *command*. Or, rather, laws or rules, properly so called, are a *species* of commands.

Now since the term *command* comprises the term *law*, the first is the simpler as well as the larger of the two. But simple as it is, it admits of explanation. And, since it is the *key* to the sciences of jurisprudence and morals, its meaning should be analyzed with precision.'

'If you express or intimate a wish that I shall do or forbear from some act, and if you will visit me with an evil in case I comply not with your wish, the *expression* or *intimation* of your wish is a *command*. A command is distinguished from other significations of desire, not by the style in which the desire is signified, but by the power and the purpose of the party commanding to inflict an evil or pain in case the desire be disregarded. If you cannot or will not harm me in case I comply not with your wish, the expression of your wish is not a command, although you utter your wish in imperative phrase. If you are able and willing to harm me in case I comply not with your wish, the expression of your wish amounts to a command, although you are prompted by a spirit of courtesy to utter it in the shape of a request. . . .

A command, then, is a signification of desire. But a command is distinguished from other significations of desire by this peculiarity: that the party to whom it is directed is liable to evil from the other, in case he comply not with the desire.

Being liable to evil from you if I comply not with a wish which you signify, I am *bound* or *obliged* by your command, or I lie under a *duty* to obey it. If, in spite of that evil in prospect, I comply not with the wish which you signify, I am said to disobey your command, or to violate the duty which it imposes.

Command and duty, are, therefore, correlative terms: the meaning denoted by each being implied or supposed by the other. Or (changing the expression) wherever a duty lies, a command has been signified; and whenever a command is signified, a duty is imposed.'

'It appears, then, from what has been premised, that the ideas or notions comprehended by the term *command* are the following. 1. A wish or desire conceived by a rational being, that another rational being shall do or forbear. 2. An evil to proceed from the former, and to be incurred by the latter, in case the latter comply not with the wish. 3. An expression or intimation of the wish by words or other signs.

It also appears from what has been premised, that *command*, *duty* and *sanction* are inseparably connected terms: that each embraces the same ideas as the others, though each denotes those ideas in a peculiar order or series.

"A wish conceived by one, and expressed or intimated to another, with an evil to be inflicted and incurred in case the wish be disregarded," are signified directly and indirectly by each of the three expressions. Each is the name of the same complex notion.

But when I am talking *directly* of the expression or intimation of the wish, I employ the term *command*: The expression or intimation of the wish being presented *prominently* to my hearer; whilst the evil to be incurred, with the chance of incurring it, are kept (if I may so express myself) in the background of my picture.

When I am talking directly of the chance of incurring the evil, or (changing the expression) of the liability or obnoxiousness to the evil, I employ the term *duty*, or the term *obligation*: The liability or obnoxiousness to the evil being put foremost, and the rest of the complex notion being signified implicitly.

When I am talking *immediately* of the evil itself, I employ the term *sanction*, or a term of the like import: The evil to be incurred being signified directly; whilst the obnoxiousness to that evil, with the expression or intimation of the wish, are indicated indirectly or obliquely.

To those who are familiar with the language of logicians (language unrivalled for brevity, distinctness and precision), I can express my meaning accurately, in a breath. Each of the three terms *signifies* the same notion; but each *denotes* a different part of that notion, and *connotes* the residue.

Commands are of two species. Some are *laws* or *rules*. The others have not acquired an appropriate name, nor does language afford an expression which will mark them briefly and precisely. I must, therefore, note them, as well as I can, by the ambiguous and inexpressive name of "*occasional* or *particular* commands."

The term *laws* or *rules* being not unfrequently applied to occasional or particular commands, it is hardly possible to describe a line of separation which shall consist in every respect with established forms of speech. But the distinction between laws and particular commands, may, I think, be stated in the following manner.

By every command, the party to whom it is directed is obliged to do or to forbear.

Now where, it obliges *generally* to acts or forbearances of a *class*, a command is a law or rule. But where it obliges to a *specific* act or forbearance, or to acts or forbearances which it determines *specifically* or *individually* a command is occasional or particular. In other words, a class or description of acts is determined by a law or rule, and acts of that class or description are enjoined or forbidden generally. But where a command is occasional or particular, the act or acts, which the command enjoins or forbids, are assigned or determined by their specific or individual natures, as well as by the class or description to which they belong.

The statement which I have now given in abstract expressions, I will endeavour to illustrate by apt examples.

If you command your servant to go on a given errand, or *not* to leave your house on a given evening, or to rise at such an hour on such a morning, or to rise at that hour during the next week or month, the command is occasional or particular. For the act or acts enjoined or forbidden, are specifically determined or assigned.

But if you command him *simply* to rise at that hour, or to rise at that hour always, or to rise at that Pour *till further orders*, it may be said, with propriety, that you lay down a *rule* for the guidance of your servant's conduct.'

'A law is a command which obliges a person or persons.

But, as contradistinguished or opposed to an occasional or particular command, a law is a command which obliges a person or persons, and obliges *generally* to acts or forbearances of a class.

In language more popular but less distinct and precise, a law is a command which obliges a person or persons to a *course* of conduct.

Laws and other commands are said to proceed from *superiors*, and to bind or oblige *inferiors*.'

'Like other signification of desire, a command is express or tacit. If the desire be signified by words (written or spoken), the command is express. If the desire be signified by conduct (or by any signs of desire which are *not* words), the command is tacit.

Now when customs are turned into legal rules by decisions of subject judges, the legal rules which emerge from the customs are tacit commands of the sovereign legislature. The state, which is able to abolish, permits its ministers to enforce them: and it, therefore, signifies its pleasure, by that its voluntary acquiescence, "that they shall serve as a law to the governed."

My present purpose is merely this: to prove that the positive law styled *customary* (and all positive law made judicially) is established by the state directly or circuitously, and, therefore, is *imperative*. I am far from disputing, that law made judicially (or in the way of improper legislation) and law made by statute (or in the properly legislative manner) are distinguished by weighty differences.'

Legal positivism

Herbert Lionel Adolphus Hart, *The Concept of Law*
(2nd edn, Clarendon Press 1994) 214, 236–237

'International law presents us with the converse case. For, though it is consistent with the usage of the last I so years to use the expression 'law' here, the absence of an international legislature, courts with compulsory jurisdiction, and centrally organized sanctions have inspired misgivings, at any rate in the breasts of legal theorists. The absence of these institutions means that the rules for states resemble that simple form of social structure, consisting only of primary rules of obligation, which, when we find it among societies of individuals, we are accustomed to contrast with a developed legal system. It is indeed arguable, as we shall show, that international law not only lacks the secondary rules of change and adjudication which provide for legislature and courts, but also a unifying rule of recognition specifying "sources" of law and providing general criteria for the identification of its rules. These differences are indeed striking and the question "Is international law really law?" can hardly be put aside. But in this case also, we shall neither dismiss the doubts, which many feel, with a simple reminder of the existing usage; nor shall we simply confirm them on the footing that the existence of a union of primary and secondary rules is a necessary as well as a sufficient condition for the proper use of the expression "legal system".'

'Bentham, the inventor of the expression "international law", defended it simply by saying that it was "sufficiently analogous" to municipal law. To this, two comments are perhaps worth adding. First, that the analogy is one of content not of form: secondly, that, in this analogy of content, no other social rules are so close to municipal law as those of international law.'

Pure theory of law

Hans Kelsen, *Pure Theory of Law*
Max Knight (tr) (University of California Press 1967) 320, 323, 214–217.

'42. The Essence of International Law

a) The Legal Nature of International Law

According to the traditional definition, international law is a complex of norms regulating the mutual behavior of states, the specific subjects of international law.

In accordance with the concept of law here accepted, so-called international law is "law," if it is a coercive order, that is to say, a set of norms regulating human behavior by attaching certain coercive acts (sanctions) as consequences to certain facts, as delicts, determined by this order as conditions, and if, therefore, it can be described in sentences which – in contradistinction to legal norms – may be called "rules of law".'

'b) International Law as a Primitive Legal Order

International law, as a coercive order, shows the same character as national law, i.e. the law of a state, but differs from it and shows a certain similarity with the law of primitive, i.e. state-less society in that international law (as a general law that binds all states) does not establish special organs for the creation and application of its norms. It is still in a state of far-reaching decentralization. It is only at the beginning of a development which national law has already completed. General norms are created by custom or treaty, which means: by the members of the legal community themselves, not by a special legislative organ. And the same is true for the application of the general norms in a concrete case. It is the state itself, believing its rights have been violated, which has to decide whether the fact of a delict exists for which another state is responsible. And if this other state denies the asserted delict, and if no agreement can be reached between the two parties concerned, no objective authority exists competent to decide the conflict in a legally regulated procedure. And it is the state whose rights have been violated which is authorized to react against the violator by reprisals or war as the coercive acts provided for by international law. The technique of self-help, characteristic of primitive law, prevails.'

The legal character of international law

Andrew Clapham, *Brierly's Law of Nations: An Introduction to the Role of International Law in International Relations*
(7th edn, Oxford University Press 2012) 77–78, 79, 80.

'It has often been said that international law ought to be classified as a branch of ethics rather than of law. The question will clearly depend on the definition of law which we choose to adopt; in any case it does not affect the value of the subject one way or the other, though those who deny the legal character of international law often speak as though "ethical" were a depreciatory epithet. In fact it is both practically inconvenient, and contrary to sensible legal thinking to deny the legal character of international law.

It is inconvenient because, if international law is nothing but international morality, it is certainly not the whole of international morality, and it is difficult to see how we are to distinguish it from those other, admittedly moral, standards which we apply in forming our judgments on the conduct of states. Ordinary usage certainly uses two tests in judging the "rightness" of a state's act, a moral test and another one which is somehow felt to be independent of morality. Every state habitually commits acts of selfishness which are often gravely injurious to other states, and yet are not contrary to international law; but we do not on that account necessarily judge them to have been "right". It is confusing and pedantic to say that both these tests are moral. Moreover, it is the pedantry of the theorist and not of the practical person; for questions of international law are invariably treated as legal questions by the foreign ministries which conduct our international business, and in the courts, national or international, before which they are brought. Legal forms and methods are used in diplomatic controversies and in judicial and arbitral proceedings, and authorities and precedents are cited every day in argument.'

'It is only in quite modern times, when we have come to regard it as natural that the state should be constantly making new laws and enforcing existing ones, that to identify law with the will of the state has become even a plausible theory. We can agree that today the only essential conditions for the existence of law are: the existence of a political community, and the recognition by its members of settled rules binding upon them in that capacity. International law seems generally to satisfy these conditions.'

'The best view is that international law is in fact just a system of customary law, upon which has been erected, almost entirely within the last century, a superstructure of 'conventional' or treaty-made law, and some of its chief defects are precisely those that the history of law teaches us to expect in a customary system.

It is a common mistake to suppose that the most conspicuous defect of international law is the frequency of violations. Actually international law is normally observed because, as we shall see, the vast majority of demands that it makes on states are not exacting; and states generally find it convenient to observe the law. This fact receives little notice however, because the interest of most people in international law is not with the ordinary routine of international legal business, but in the rare and often sensational occasions on which it is flagrantly broken. Such breaches generally occur either when some great political issue has arisen between states, or in that part of the system which professes to regulate the conduct of war. So our diagnosis of what is wrong with the system will be mistaken if we fail to realize that most customary rules and the great majority of treaties are, on the whole, regularly observed in international relations. And this is no small service to international life, however far it may fall short of the ideal by which we judge the achievements of the system. If we fail to understand this, we are likely to assume, as many people do, that all would be well with international law if we could devise a better system for enforcing it.'

The legal character of international law

David Harris and Sandesh Sivakumaran, *Cases and Materials on International Law* (8th edn, Sweet & Maxwell 2015) 5, 10–11.

'1   INTRODUCTION

Notes

2   *The Austinian Handicap.* "Is international law 'law'?" is a standard question asked of international lawyers. Its sometimes irritating persistence is very largely the responsibility of John Austin, an English jurist of the first part of the nineteenth century and a familiar friend of any student who has taken a course in jurisprudence He defines laws "properly so-called" as commands and "positive law", which he regarded as the "appropriate matter of jurisprudence", as the commands of a sovereign. A sovereign he defined as a person who received the habitual obedience of the members of an independent political society and who, in turn, did not owe such obedience to any other person. Rules of international law did not qualify as rules of "positive law" by this test and, not being commands of any sort, were placed

by Austin in the category of "laws improperly so-called". This uncompromising and unhappily phrased rejection of international law's claim to be law of the same order as municipal law has, to this day, upset international lawyers and placed them on the defensive. Although international law is still not "law" according to Austin's test, most international lawyers would at least dispute that that test is more helpful than certain others (e.g. that of Pollock, quoted by Brierly) by which international law could be said to be "law".'

Sources of international law

DOI:10.4324/9781003213772-2

ARTICLE 38 OF THE STATUTE OF THE INTERNATIONAL COURT OF JUSTICE

International Court of Justice
ICJ
Charter of the United Nations Organisation
Statute of the International Court of Justice
international conventions
international custom
general principles of law
judicial decisions
teachings of the most highly qualified publicists
ex aequo et bono
two primary regular law-creating sources

International Court of Justice

The **International Court of Justice** (commonly referred to as the **ICJ**) is the 'principal judicial organ of the United Nations'. It was established in 1945 by the **Charter of the United Nations Organisation** and **Statute of the International Court of Justice** and began to operate in April 1946.

Article 38 of the Statute of the International Court of Justice

1 The Court, whose function is to decide in accordance with international law such disputes as are submitted to it, shall apply:

   a   **international conventions**, whether general or particular, establishing rules expressly recognized by the contesting states;
   b   **international custom**, as evidence of a general practice accepted as law;
   c   the **general principles of law** recognized by civilized nations;
   d   subject to the provisions of Article 59,[95] **judicial decisions** and the **teachings of the most highly qualified publicists** of the various nations, as subsidiary means for the determination of rules of law.

2 This provision shall not prejudice the power of the Court to decide a case *ex aequo et bono*, if the parties agree thereto.

---

95 'The decision of the Court has no binding force except between the parties and in respect of that particular case.'

Ex aequo et bono

Ex aequo et bono is a Latin phrase that means 'from equity and goodness' and, in this context, refers to the power of International Court of Justice to dispense certain cases based on the principles of fairness and justice[96] if the parties agree to it.

Day-to-day founders of international legal rights and obligations

The first two sources of international law pointed out in Article 38 – international treaty and international custom – constitute the international legal rights and obligations on a daily basis, i.e. they are **two primary regular law-creating sources**. Therefore, the majority of international rules exist in those forms.

General principles of law

The third source – the general principles of law – are the maxims which are recognised by civilised nations. Usually, these principles are discovered and manifested primarily in judicial decisions and the teachings of the most highly qualified publicists, which in turn serve as the subsidiary means.

INTERNATIONAL TREATY

pacta sunt servanda
apparently (*ex facte*) expressed consent
bilateral
multilateral
local treaties
regional treaties
global treaties
Vienna Convention on the Law of Treaties
general multilateral treaties
Vienna Convention on Succession of States in respect of Treaties
universal treaties
general international law
political agreements
political (no legal) obligations

---

96 'A decision *ex aequo et bono* may be sought especially when the law governing a dispute is unclear (*non liquet*) or might fail to resolve the dispute adequately for other reasons.' *Guide to Latin in International Law* (n 71) 91.

Introductory remark

The general principles of the contract law of national law apply to the treaties in international law as well.

Pacta sunt servanda

The *pacta sunt servanda* ('agreements are to be kept')[97] principle is the legal basis of treaty law. Without such an acceptance, treaties would become futile. Thus, this is a structural principle of international law.

Form of the international treaty

International treaties are made through an **apparently (*ex facte*) expressed consent**. Usually, they are concluded in the written form. However, at the same time, an unwritten form is also not forbidden.

Foundational formula

The foundational formula to enter into an international treaty may be presented as follows:

Consent on the content + consent on the obligatory nature = the conclusion of the treaty

Types of international treaties

All international treaties are either **bilateral** (between two subjects of international law) or **multilateral** (between three or more subjects of international law).

The multilateral treaties might be concluded at either the local, the regional or the global levels. The **local treaties** are international agreements which bind a very limited number of participants. The **regional treaties** usually cover a certain geographical area. Finally, **global treaties** involve the subjects of international law across the world.

All global treaties aim to regulate the issues corresponding to the certain area of global interest. Some of them address specific issues on the international agenda (for instance, numerous environmental treaties examined later in this book). However, at the same time, certain global treaties are more general in nature and are the result of the codification and progressive development of a specific area of international law (for example, the **Vienna Convention on the Law of Treaties** of 1969).

---

97 *A Dictionary of Law* (n 2) 350. 'This Latin phrase, which may be roughly translated as "treaties shall be complied with," describes a significant *general principle of international law* – one that underlies the entire system of treaty-based relations between sovereign states.' American Society of International Law and the International Judicial Academy, '*Pacta Sunt Servanda*' (2008) <http://bit.ly/2KWAwCb> accessed 16 March 2021.

The right to choose whether or not to become a party to a treaty

The subjects of international law have the right to choose whether or not to become a party to a treaty. An international treaty is an agreement between the states or the other subjects of international law, and thus it has an obvious consensual basis. Therefore, according to the general principle of law, a treaty usually does not create either obligations or rights for a third party without its consent. (The exceptions to this rule will be discussed later.)

Besides, in principle, the parties to the agreement determine who will become a party to the treaty, i.e. for whom the treaty will establish the legal obligations.

However, in certain cases, some international documents and international law scholars refer to the right to participate in an international treaty, if (1) the treaty directly concerns the subject of international law or (2) in the case of the so-called **general multilateral treaties**,[98] which according to the **Vienna Convention on Succession of States in respect of Treaties** of 1978 are defined as 'treaties which deal with the codification and progressive development of international law and those the object and purpose of which are of interest to the international community as a whole'. Some authors designate such international treaties which 'are of general interest, and which have a global sphere of action, or . . . are intended for the creation of generally accepted norms of international law' as **universal treaties**[99] and argue that as long as such treaties affect the rights of all states, '[t]his inevitably means that all States have the right to participate in the drafting and adoption of such treaties.'[100] However, some other authors only regard the treaties whose binding force is in fact recognised by all or almost all the states as universal.

Moreover, certain scholars also attempted to link the concept of general multilateral treaties with the meaning of **general international law**. As a result, they argued that such treaties are able to generate general international law, which is binding on all states without exception. However, according to a more acknowledged approach, general customary international law, general principles of law, and particular norms of international law of universal application (such as the peremptory norms) which may also be enshrined in the treaties are considered to be the general international law.

Therefore, in principle, the 'general multilateral treaties containing rules of general (conventional) law are a source of international law for the contracting parties – and for no one else. Any justification for an extra-contractual effect of such treaties requires recourse to some other validating ground'.[101]

---

98 In the Draft Articles on the Law of Treaties (the 1962 version), the International Law Commission the 'general multilateral treaties' considered agreements in which, as a rule, every state has the right of participation. Article 8 (Participation in a treaty) '1. In the case of a general multilateral treaty, every State may become a party to the treaty unless it is otherwise provided by the terms of the treaty itself or by the established rules of an international organization.' Report of the International Law Commission covering the work of its Fourteenth Session, 24 April–29 June 1962, Official Records of the General Assembly, Seventeenth Session, Supplement No. 9 (A/5209) <https://legal.un.org/ilc/guide/1_1.shtml> accessed 16 March 2021.

99 I. I. Lukashuk, 'Parties to Treaties: The Right of Participation' in *Recueil Des Cours, Collected Courses*, 1972-I (reprinted by H Charlesworth & Co Ltd. Huddersfield 1993) 293.

100 ibid.

101 G. M. Danilenko, *Law-Making in the International Community* (Martinus Nijhoff Publishers 1993) 53.

Political agreements

Sometimes the subjects of international law conclude agreements which do not possess the status of an international treaty, i.e. the status of a legal document. They are called **political agreements**.

The first principal difference between political agreements and international treaties lies in the essence of political agreements since, under the framework of those agreements, only **political (no legal) obligations** can be taken by the parties. However, in practice, it is not easy to find the clear-cut differences between these documents because of the similarities in appearance, name, and so forth.

Distinctive marks

Nevertheless, some specific guiding characteristics can be identified which may help in locating the distinctions between these two types of documents:

1   As a rule, in the political agreements, the parties clearly emphasise that this agreement does not create legally binding obligations.
2   Generally, international treaties consist of three parts. The final part of the treaty defines the procedural norms (notably, the rules of entry into force, termination, and so on). This part is not included in political agreements.
3   If the marks mentioned here do not determine the exact status of the document, it is necessary to conduct a careful study of the preceding documents (protocols of negotiations, parties' intentions, and so on).

INTERNATIONAL CUSTOM

general practice
opinio juris
Continental Shelf case
normative power of the factual
International Law Commission
ILC
Draft Conclusions on Identification of Customary International Law
rationality
material essence/context
obviousness
representativeness
constant and uniform usage
North Sea Continental Shelf cases
general customary international law
special customary international law

> regional custom
> local custom
> *Right of Passage over Indian Territory case*
> *Asylum case*

Foundational formula

The international custom represents evidence of the **general practice** (the *usus*[102] or objective component) accepted as law (the ***opinio juris*** or subjective component).

General practice + *opinio juris* = international custom

The normative power of the factual

As the International Court of Justice in the **Continental Shelf** case (*Libyan Arab Jamahiriya/Malta*) said: 'It is of course axiomatic that the material of customary international law is to be looked for primarily in the actual practice and *opinio juris* of States'.[103]

Therefore, the concept of the '**normative power of the factual**' shall be considered as the source from which the legal force of the international custom originates.

General practice

The general practice is the outcome of the physical and verbal acts and, under particular circumstances, the inaction of the subjects in the local, regional, and global frameworks.

So far, under the subjects which have the capacity to establish customary international law among themselves, the states are primarily considered. However, there can also be a rethinking of the matter which allows the other international law subjects to participate in the international custom's generation process. Recently, the **International Law Commission** (commonly referred to as the **ILC**), a subsidiary organ of the United Nations General Assembly, which is instituted to promote the progressive development of international law and its codification process,[104] recognised such a capacity concerning the international organisations in its Text of the Draft Conclusions on Identification of Customary International Law (here referred to as the **Draft Conclusions on Identification of Customary International Law**). However, in the commentaries, the ILC articulated the limited scope of the application of the Conclusion regarding the ability of the international organisations to develop customary international law:

> The practice of international organizations in international relations (when accompanied by *opinio juris*) may count as practice that gives rise or attests to rules of

---

102 The *usus* refers to the actual practice, or how subjects behave and what they say and do. There is also the following maxim concerning custom: *Usus fit ex iteratis actibus*; this means 'Usage is made by repeated acts.' *Guide to Latin in International Law* (n 71) 285.

103 *Continental Shelf* case (*Libyan Arab Jamahiriya/Malta*), Judgment of 3 June 1985, ICJ Reports 1985, 13.

104 The role and functions of the International Law Commission will be discussed later.

customary international law, but only those rules (a) whose subject matter falls within the mandate of the organizations, and/or (b) that are addressed specifically to them (such as those on their international responsibility or relating to treaties to which international organizations may be parties).[105]

For general practice, a specific, undefined time interval and a distribution of practice among the subjects is needed. The modes of practice leading to the creation of the international customary norm are:

1   For the origination – either an action or a statement of a subject; and
2   For the reaction – either an action or a statement or an abstention from acting (also referred to as omission or inaction) of another subject (or subjects).

Preconditions of the general practice

1   The prerequisites for the originating modes of practice mentioned here are:

   a)   The **rationality** of action for the general practice, which means that only rational action (not any action) of the subject may be considered a starting point for the generation of a norm to elevate it to the status of an international custom.
   b)   The **material essence/context** of an action or a statement. For instance, while it may be observed that in normal circumstances the heads of states virtually always shake hands when they meet, it doesn't necessarily mean that they do so because they are legally obliged by international law;
   c)   The **obviousness** of an action or a statement leading to the general practice, which means that only actions or statements which are clear and to a certain degree devoid of ambiguity may be regarded as a starting point for the generation of an international custom.
   d)   The **representativeness** of an action or a statement leading to the general practice, which means that only actions and statements by the authorised persons (in case of states, for instance, the president or the prime minister) may be considered as a source for developing the general practice.

2   As regards the reaction of another subject (or subjects) leading to the establishment of the general practice, in order to carry out the necessary reaction, the **constant and uniform usage** of a rule by initialising subject and another subject (or subjects) is essential.
3   The international custom may also be generated through the realisation of the ability to develop the general (common) practice from a legal norm (treaties, international customs of other subjects), as well as from political or other rules (if the necessary *opinio juris* arises).

---

105 (5) Commentary to the Conclusion 4 of the ILC Draft Conclusions on Identification of Customary International Law of 2018, adopted by the International Law Commission at its seventieth session, in 2018, and submitted to the General Assembly as a part of the Commission's report covering the work of that session (A/73/10). <http://bit.ly/2Qdkfud> accessed 16 March 2021.

Opinio juris

The second component of the international custom – the *opinio juris sive necessitatis* (an opinion of law or necessity) or simply *opinio juris* – is the belief that an action (or an omission) was carried out as a legal obligation. This principle is a subjective element used to specify whether the practice of a party is grounded in a belief that it has a legal obligation to take a particular action. Consequently, the *opinio juris* is reflected in the particular acts of subjects or in omissions as far as those acts or omissions are done with the belief that the given party is obligated by law to act or refrain from doing something in a particular way.

In the **North Sea Continental Shelf** cases (*Federal Republic of Germany v Denmark, Federal Republic of Germany v Netherlands*), the International Court of Justice determined the difference between mere customs (i.e. habits) and customary (international) law:

> Not only must the acts concerned amount to a settled practice, but they must also be such, or be carried out in such a way, as to be evidence of a belief that this practice is rendered obligatory by the existence of a rule of law requiring it. The need for such a belief, i.e., the existence of a subjective element, is implicit in the very notion of the *opinio juris sive necessitatis*. The States concerned must therefore feel that they are conforming to what amounts to a legal obligation. The frequency, or even habitual character of the acts is not in itself enough. There are many international acts, e.g., in the field of ceremonial and protocol, which are performed almost invariably, but which are motivated only by considerations of courtesy, convenience or tradition, and not by any sense of legal duty.[106]

In practice, a wide variety of sources may be used to demonstrate the existence of *opinio juris*, such as domestic legislation, national and international judicial decisions, press releases and other governmental statements, diplomatic correspondence, official manuals on legal questions, and the list can be continued further.

Persistent objector

If during the process of the formation of a rule of customary international law, a subject of international law objected to it, such a rule is not opposable to the subject concerned for as long as the subject maintains its objection. However, the objection should be clearly expressed, made known to other subjects, and maintained persistently. At the same time, as the ILC concluded in its Draft Conclusions mentioned earlier, '[f]ailure to react over

---

106 *North Sea Continental Shelf* cases (*Federal Republic of Germany v Denmark, Federal Republic of Germany v Netherlands*), Judgment of 20 February 1969, ICJ Reports 1969, 3. According to the Commentary (6) to the Conclusion 9 of the ILC Draft Conclusions on Identification of Customary International Law of 2018, 'without acceptance as law (*opinio juris*), a general practice may not be considered as creative, or expressive, of customary international law; it is mere usage or habit. In other words, practice that States consider themselves legally free either to follow or to disregard does not contribute to or reflect customary international law (unless the rule to be identified itself provides for such a choice).'

time to a practice may serve as evidence of acceptance as law (*opinio juris*), provided that States were in a position to react and the circumstances called for some reaction.'[107]

General or special customary international law

There may exist either **general customary international law** or **special customary international law**,[108] which is also referred to as the **regional custom** in case of regional proliferation of a rule or **local custom** if a customary norm is established between the particular countries and even between two countries, as the International Court of Justice suggested in the **Right of Passage over Indian Territory** case *(Portugal v India)*.[109]

The general customary international law applies to all states while special custom prescribes the relations between a smaller set of countries. General customary international law contains norms relating to diplomatic immunity, to the high seas, to the methods and means of warfare, and so forth.

Thus, the special customary international law operates within the regions or particular countries as, for instance, the law of asylum in Latin America, which was examined by the International Court of Justice in the **Asylum** case *(Colombia v Peru)*. Finally, the Court concluded that: 'The Party which relies on a custom of this kind must prove that this custom is established in such a manner that it has become binding on the other Party.'

This means that the special international customary law should be justified either via the aforementioned positive forms (for example, the domestic legislation, national and international judicial decisions) or the party which relies on such a custom as a legally binding norm expressed in a constant and uniform usage shall otherwise prove that this custom is established in such a manner that it has become binding on the other party.[110]

Final remark

To sum up, the international custom is a form of unwritten consent and represents a dynamic source which fills international law with air extracted from practice.

---

107 Paragraph 3 of the Conclusion 10 of the ILC Draft Conclusions on Identification of Customary International Law of 2018.

108 The ILC uses the term 'particular customary international law' in its Conclusion 16 of the Draft Conclusions on Identification of Customary International Law of 2018: '1. A rule of particular customary international law, whether regional, local or other, is a rule of customary international law that applies only among a limited number of States.'

109 'It is difficult to see why the number of States between which a local custom may be established on the basis of long practice must necessarily be larger than two. The Court sees no reason why long continued practice between two States accepted by them as regulating their relations should not form the basis of mutual rights and obligations between the two States.' *Right of Passage over Indian Territory* case *(Portugal v India)*, Judgment of 12 April 1960, ICJ Reports 1960, 6.

110 'The Colombian Government must prove that the rule invoked by it is in accordance with a constant and uniform usage practised by the States in question, and that this usage is the expression of a right appertaining to the State granting asylum and a duty incumbent on the territorial State.' *Asylum* case *(Colombia v Peru)*, Judgment of 20 November 1950, ICJ Reports 1950, 266.

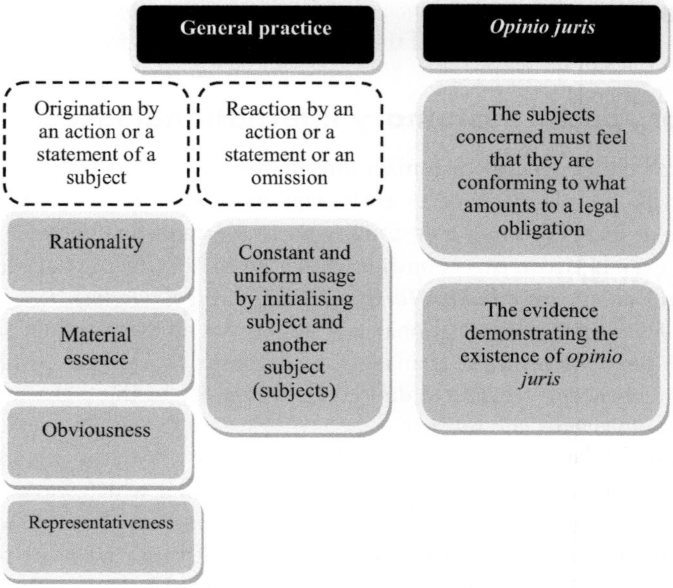

FIGURE 2.1 The establishment of international custom

GENERAL PRINCIPLES OF LAW

Permanent Court of International Justice
PCIJ
Case of the S.S. 'Lotus'
general principles of international law
Dissenting Opinion of Judge Tanaka
South West Africa cases
principle *pacta sunt servanda*
principle of good faith
principle of effectiveness
opinio juris
principle *lex posterior derogat legi priori*
principle *lex specialis derogat legi generali*
principle of estoppel
principle of *res judicata*
principle of judicial impartiality
principle of humanity

General meaning

The general principles of law have been embodied in the statutes of the **Permanent Court of International Justice** (PCIJ was established after World War I)[111] and the International Court of Justice (as mentioned earlier, the ICJ was constituted after World War II), with the following formulation: 'The general principles of law recognised by civilised nations'.[112]

The problem of identification and application of the general principles of law

Certainly, the general principles of law are an undervalued and misjudged source of international law. In practice, the states, as well as the other subjects of international law and both the Permanent Court of International Justice and the International Court of Justice were 'cautious' about resorting to the general principles of law.[113] Therefore, the use of this source among the subjects of international law, as well as in the decisions of the international courts and tribunals has been somewhat limited. Such caution primarily stemmed from the following reasons:

- 'Civilised nations' – The reference in the statutes of the PCIJ and ICJ to this notion was the source of contradiction and disagreement from the very beginning. Perhaps, for the supporters of this formulation, the notion initially covered mostly the countries with a Western legacy of jurisprudence (the common law and civil law legal families). Nevertheless, over time and currently, in the era of non-discrimination and sovereign equality of the states, the formulation came under logical fire for certain discriminatory allusion attributed to it. That's why in modern times, several persons, as well as the legislations of particular countries, refer to the general principles of law being recognised (1) by the 'community of nations', (2) in 'municipal systems', or (3) 'by the parties'. Even the PCIJ in the *Case of the S.S. 'Lotus' (France v Turkey)* (usually referred to as the *Lotus* case), which will be examined in more detail later in this book, in relation to the principles only stated: 'The rules of law binding upon States therefore emanate from their own free will as expressed in conventions or by usages generally accepted as

---

111 'Between 1922 and 1940 the PCIJ dealt with 29 contentious cases between States, and delivered 27 advisory opinions.' International Court of Justice, 'Permanent Court of International Justice' <www.icj-cij.org/en/pcij> accessed 16 March 2021.

112 In Article 38 (I)(3) of the Statute of the Permanent Court of International Justice, and in Article 38 (1)(c) of the Statute of the International Court of Justice.

113 'In practice, both the PCIJ and ICJ have been cautious and have often restricted "General Principles" to a limited role that some would see as a subsidiary function'. 'In general, the two courts have adhered to an apparently more positivistic approach by according conventional and customary law a presumptive priority in application, except where these conflict with a *jus cogens* "principle"'. M. Cherif Bassiouni, 'A Functional Approach to "General Principles of International Law"' (1990) 11(3) *Michigan Journal of International Law* 800, 801.

expressing principles of law and established in order to regulate the relations between these co-existing independent communities or with a view to the achievement of common aims.'[114]

However, in the proper understanding of the phrase 'recognised by civilised nations', it essentially covers all the existing states because, without the legal system, there cannot be a state. A state may be a part of a particular 'major' legal family[115] or combine the approaches and principles of the legal families, or it even may be assumed that a country may itself establish a legal system with new and unique characteristics. Therefore, every such state which fits the aforementioned description shall be regarded as civilised in terms of legal dimension. However, in practice, the majority of scholars, as well as the judges of the international courts, generally consider the Western legal families in order to disclose such general principles of law, though theoretically, the majority of them recognise that the Islamic law tradition and other non-Western bodies of law should also be covered by the very formulation in the Statute.[116] Some writers who did special research into this matter inferred that only in sporadic cases did the ICJ and its judges even mention Islamic law and, generally, without having substantial training in the sources and interpretations of the Islamic legal tradition.[117] Thus, for the Eurocentric international lawyers, the other 'legal worlds' remain so far mainly unexplored, whereas the examination of all major legal families and traditions seems determinative to involve legitimation, particularly in relation to the general principles of law.

- Uncertainty – as a mainstream legal approach of the twentieth century and up until the present, positivism stipulated the elimination of those sources of law which have no positive forms. Hence, in international law, the conventional and customary law received a presumptive privilege as the sources based on the positive data. On the other hand, the general principles of law may be of either positive or non-positive origin. For this reason, the positivists tend to acknowledge this source of law as being the product of the comparative research of positive data, which leaves no possibility for ambiguity. In turn, the naturalists claim that the insertion of the general principles of

---

114 *Case of the S.S. 'Lotus' (France v Turkey)*, Judgment No. 9 of 7 September 1927, PCIJ Ser A (1927) – No.10. All PCIJ cases are available at <www.icj-cij.org/en/pcij>.

115 Often also referred to as major legal system. However, in this book, we specifically identify only two systems of law – national law and international law – with the term 'legal system' .

116 'Since its inception, a majority of judges on the ICJ has always resisted reading Article 38(1)(c) to require the ICJ to consider Islamic law and other non-Western bodies of law as norms that should be taken into account as the ICJ develops its interpretation of international law.' Clark B. Lombardi, 'Islamic Law in the Jurisprudence of the International Court of Justice: An Analysis' (6 January 2007) 8(1) *Chicago Journal of International Law* (note 31), 92.

117 'In two of the cases, the official judgment itself mentioned Islamic law – although, as we shall see, neither of these two judgments discussed Islamic law in any meaningful way. In seven other cases, judges filed separate opinions concurring with or dissenting from the judgment and mentioning Islamic law.' 'References are always brief, never supported by substantial explanation or citation, and show little reflection on the thorny question of how modern judges with little or no formal training in Islamic law can speak convincingly about the meaning of the Shari'ah.' ibid 94, 115.

law into the statutes of the courts is a recognition which provides for the opportunity to incorporate the principles of the natural law into international law.

Nonetheless, in both cases, the uncertainty is not limited to the aforementioned clash between the approaches. Even positivists are not able argue with certainty which positive data should be included for the examination and whether the data from all legal families and every 'civilised nation' needs to be given a proper consideration or not. On the other hand, how may the natural law assumptions which stem from the Western philosophy be traced to the non-Western legal families or the holistic rule of the reason which covers the entire world be discovered?

The general principles of law as a coequal source of international law

The problems discussed earlier have led some people to the underestimation of the general principles of law, allocating to them only a subsidiary function in cases when a rule established by treaty or custom is obscure or unclear (the interpretative function of the general principles of law).

Some others argued that the general principles of law could be used only when a norm was not established via the treaties and customs (the 'gap filler' function of the general principles of law). The 'gap filler' function was articulated by Judge Shigeru Oda in his Dissenting Opinion: 'In the case of international law, the Statute of the Permanent Court of International Justice introduced the clause "the general principles of law recognized by civilized nations" mainly to avoid a *non liquet*[118] resulting from the lack of any positive rules.'[119]

Although in particular cases the general principles of law may additionally undertake the functions mentioned earlier, they are the coequal sources of international law.

Different paths to the origination of the general principles of international law

Various ways for generating general principles of law can be identified:

1   Principles of national law that are recognised by civilised nations – obtained from the domain of national law, which is the most common way to assume the existence of general principles of law. For the identification of the principles, the inductive method of comparative research must be employed, aiming to specify a legal principle of all

---

118 '*Non liquet* . . . "It is unclear." A judgment denoting that the tribunal refuses to render an award or judgment in the belief that the law supplies no rule applicable to the case before it. This term was widely used by Roman jurisprudes such as Cicero and Quintilian, but has become less common in modern times when tribunals are commonly expected to fill gaps in the law by the application of legal reasoning.' *Guide to Latin in International Law* (n 71) 198.

119 *Military and Paramilitary Activities in and against Nicaragua (Nicaragua v United States of America)*, Judgment of 27 June 1986, ICJ Reports 1986, 14, Dissenting Opinion of Judge Oda.

major legal families in the world and particular countries in or outside the major legal families.

   a) Challenge. At this level, the main challenge is the determination of the pattern of the positive data or the identification of the legal families and the number of nations which should be included in this pattern. The conventional approach to this matter may be summarised as follows: (1) All major legal families shall be embraced by the research (including non-Western legal traditions); and (2) a vast majority of countries shall be covered in a sample, which will lead to a final conclusion that a particular principle is the universal one.

2   Principles of law that are derived from the unique character of international interaction and which are recognised by civilised nations, obtained from the domain of international relations. Several principles emanate from the foreign policies of states, international declarations, international treaties and customs, scholarly works and writings, and international case law. This path is used either for the determination of a particular principle or for interpretative purposes.[120] Within this understanding, the term the '**general principles of international law**' is usually utilised, which is sometimes considered a synonymous notion with the general principles of law. However, some scholars discovered a difference between the two terms. For the distinction, they emphasise that '[w]hile the expression general principles of law refers to legal principles derived from national legal systems, the term general principles of international law encompasses legal principles entirely derived from international conventional and customary rules, and they typically possess customary status.'[121]

    When considering principles directly enshrined in the valid international treaties and customs, the principles, of course, can be applied as located in the sources of international law which are determined in Paragraphs 1(a) and 1(b) of Article 38 of the ICJ Statute (international treaty and international custom). However, if the principles are not located in the established norms of the treaty or custom but are discovered merely from the international interaction, in such cases, it is possible to refer to the general principles of international law within the meaning of Paragraph 1(c) of Article 38 of the Statute, so long as 'the word "law" in that paragraph is not qualified and, hence, the general principles of law referred therein may be general principles of national or international law.'[122]

   a) Challenge. At this level, the main challenge consists in determining the demarcation line between the general principles of law and customary international

---

120 'For example, in the *South West Africa Cases* (1962), Judge Jessup employed one of these principles – that of "separateness" of treaty provisions – which may be resorted to when a treaty provision has become inoperative. In that case, the question arose by reason of the fact that the League of Nations was no longer in existence. By using the principle of "separateness," Jessup determined that the life of the League was not necessary to the operation of a treaty provision.' Bassiouni (n 113) 799.

121 Fabián O. Raimondo, *General Principles of Law in the Decisions of International Criminal Courts and Tribunals* (Martinus Nijhoff Publishers 2008) 41.

122 ibid.

law norms (principles). Since the research of the international practice is the acknowledged method for the justification of both elements (general practice and *opinio juris*) of the custom's establishment, it is usually hard to find a correct measure for the distinction. That's why international lawyers refer to the same principle in some instances as a principle (rule) of customary law and, on the other occasions, as a general principle of law. However, these two forms are substantially the separate sources of international law. Therefore, in order to eliminate the previously discussed uncertainty, the following solutions may be suggested:

(i) The establishment of the particular method(s) for the exploration of the general principles of law at the international level, which would be distinct from the technique of affirming the existence of the customary norms.

(ii) One of the methods which may be offered is to concentrate on the substantial meaning of a given principle (even if it is found in the established norms of the treaty or custom), and if the principle expresses the general characteristics of the legal dimension (such as the corollaries of the principle of legality) or has a structural nature, it should be evaluated as a general principle of law. For example, the principle of *opinio juris*, which by itself is a structural principle establishing international custom, should be regarded as a general principle of law derived in this context, predominately from the unique character of international interaction.

3   Principles of law which reflect the ideas of natural law. Such principles may be derived from the domain of the reason. However, the application of the natural law approach in international law is a difficult issue. After examining international case law, only minimal direct or indirect references to the natural law concept can be discovered. The most cited opinion in this context is the **Dissenting Opinion of Judge Tanaka** in the ***South West Africa*** cases *(Ethiopia v South Africa, Liberia v South Africa)*.[123] Firstly, Judge Kotaro Tanaka introduced a remarkable definition of the natural law: 'If a law exists independently of the will of the State and, accordingly, cannot be abolished or modified even by its constitution, because it is deeply rooted in the conscience of mankind and of any reasonable man, it may be called "natural law" in contrast to "positive law".' Then, based on the interpretation of the ICJ Statute, he thought that the concept of human rights was included in the general principles of law. Moreover, he argued that the fact that the provision of the Statute on the general principles of law 'does not require the consent of States as a condition of the recognition of the general principles', it challenges the existing concept of international law, according to which 'international law is nothing but the law of the consent and auto-limitation of the State.' Finally, Judge Tanaka concluded: 'From this kind of source international law could have the foundation of its validity extended beyond the will of States, that is to say, into the sphere of natural law and assume an aspect of its supra-national and

---

123 *South West Africa (Ethiopia v South Africa, Liberia v South Africa)*, Judgment of 18 July 1966, ICJ Reports 1966, 6, Dissenting Opinion of Judge Tanaka.

supra-positive character.'[124] However, this opinion did not receive sufficient support among the other members of the Court.

a) Challenge. The naturalist understanding of the general principles of law faces the following challenges:

(i) There exists substantial ambiguity in relation to either the objective method as to how such a rule (or rules) can be discovered or what the pattern or data should be for the examination and enumeration of such rules.

(ii) As concluded earlier in this book, the incorporation of the naturalist path into the law needs initial general recognition through the positive law, which, in this case, can be considered granted only if we assume that the aforementioned formulation of the statutes stipulates such interpretation allowing the inclusion of the natural law principles into international law. However, there is continuing disagreement on this matter. On the other hand, even if we suggest that such an interpretation is valid and the ICJ Statute should be regarded as granting the general recognition for the naturalist path, then the Paragraph 1(c) of Article 38 by itself creates the limits for the application of the naturalist approach by formulation – 'recognised by civilised nations'. So, if one discovers a rule in the reason or the 'conscience of humankind' (ordinary path for the exploration of natural laws), additionally, this rule must be recognised by civilised nations. The question is whether or not such recognition is justifiable without examining all major legal families. Even Judge Tanaka, who suggested in his Dissenting Opinion that this 'recognition is of a very elastic nature', analysed some legal families, municipal systems of the states, and 'the attitude of delegations of member States in cases of participation in resolutions, declarations, etc.'

(iii) At the same time, another challenge consists of finding the material general principles, regardless of the researcher's choice, either in the non-positive data ('conscience of humankind') or in the legal families or other positive data. Even the most referred field of natural laws – human rights – manifests vital differences in this regard. It seems that even the list of the natural laws noted earlier – self-preservation, independence, equality, respect, and interaction – should be subjected to comparative analysis. For example, the European understanding of equality is not consistent with the comprehension of this issue in the Islamic law tradition. Although the Muslim countries generally adhere to contemporary international law sources and international institutions, the 'human rights issue related to Islam can be summarized as (in)equality based on religion, (in)equality based on gender, and use of certain penalties.'[125] It is noteworthy that many Muslim countries which ratified the human rights treaties made exceptions based on the Islamic law tradi-

---

124 ibid.
125 Maurits Berger, 'Islamic Views on International Law' in P. Meerts (ed), *Culture and International Law* (Cambridge University Press 2008) 112.

tion. Hence, by applying the naturalist approach to the general principles of law, there is a need for the unified rules of reason encompassing at least all 'civilised nations' to be discovered.

Structural principles

Some general principles of law are the building blocks for international law and for the other sources of international law and judicial decisions as well. These principles are:

- The **principle *pacta sunt servanda*** – the agreements are to be kept;
- The **principle of good faith** – a general presumption that the parties to a legal relationship will deal with each other honestly and fairly, i.e. in good faith;
- The **principle of effectiveness** – is based on the idea of a normative power of practice, which stipulates the legal outcomes;[126]
- ***Opinio juris*** – the belief that an action (or an omission) was carried out as a legal obligation;
- The **principle *lex posterior derogat legi priori*** – a later norm [law] prevails over an earlier norm [law]; and
- The **principle *lex specialis derogat legi generali*** – a norm [law] governing a specific subject matter prevails over a norm [law] which governs general matters.

The general principles of all of international law or the different areas of international law

The distinction between general principles of law can be made either on the principles of the whole of international law (such as the structural principles) or on principles which exist in different branches of international law.

The examples of the general principles of whole of international law are:

- The **principle of estoppel** – that prevents a party from denying or alleging a particular fact based on previous conduct, allegation, or denial made by a party;
- The **principle of *res judicata*** – that precludes continued litigation of a case on the same issues between the same parties, when the final judgment was already made; and
- The **principle of judicial impartiality** – the decisions of a judge may not be based on bias, prejudice, or preference.

As regards the general principles of law recognised in a particular branch of international law, one such principle is the **principle of humanity** in international humanitarian law (also referred to as a fundamental general principle of the law of armed conflict). The principle of humanity provides that civilians must not be attacked and must be treated

---

126 David Pataraia, *Rechtsnachfolge im Völkerrecht, Dismembration der Sowjetunion und Georgien* (Jus Press 2019) 5, 6.

humanely and that even concerning the combatants, superfluous injury or unnecessary suffering is prohibited.

UNILATERAL ACTS OF STATES

promise
waiver
recognition
protest
International Law Commission
Guiding Principles

Forms of unilateral acts

The unilateral acts of states are among the essential sources of the obligations of the states under international law. They may comprise various substantive legal acts – **promise**, **waiver**, **recognition**, **protest**.

The principles of effectiveness and good faith are the core legal guides for the unilateral acts. The first principle contributes to the establishment, modification, or revocation of such acts, and both of them constitute the fundament for the binding character of the unilateral acts.

Guiding Principles

The **International Law Commission** adopted a set of ten 'Guiding Principles', together with commentaries applicable to unilateral declarations of states.[127] In this document, the ILC notes some examples of unilateral acts of states:

> Besides the declarations made by France in 1974 on the cessation of nuclear tests in the atmosphere, the public nature of the declaration made by Egypt on 24 April 1957 on the Suez Canal and Jordan's waiver of claims to the West Bank territories represent an important indication of their authors' intention to commit themselves.

The Guiding Principles as determined by ILC are:

1 Declarations publicly made and manifesting the will to be bound may have the effect of creating legal obligations. The binding character of such declarations is based on good faith.

127 Guiding Principles applicable to unilateral declarations of States capable of creating legal obligations with commentaries thereto, International Law Commission, 58th session, 2006 <http://bit.ly/363f5HK> accessed 16 March 2021.

2 Any state possesses the capacity to undertake legal obligations through unilateral declarations.

3 To determine the legal effects of such declarations, it is necessary to take account of their content, of all the factual circumstances in which they were made, and of the reactions to which they gave rise.

4 A unilateral declaration binds the state internationally only if it is made by an authority vested with the power to do so.

5 Unilateral declarations may be formulated orally or in writing.

6 Unilateral declarations may be addressed to the international community as a whole, to one or several states, or other subjects of international law.

7 Unilateral declarations entail obligations for the formulating state only if it is stated in clear and specific terms.

8 A unilateral declaration which conflicts with a peremptory norm of general international law is void and does not create a legal obligation.[128]

9 No obligation may result for other states from the unilateral declaration of a state. However, the other state or states concerned may incur obligations in relation to such a unilateral declaration to the extent that they clearly accepted such a declaration.

10 A unilateral declaration that has created legal obligations for the state making the declaration generally cannot be revoked arbitrarily. In assessing whether revocation would be arbitrary, consideration should be given to:

a) any specific terms of the declaration relating to revocation;

b) the extent to which those to whom the obligations are owed have relied on such obligations; and

c) the extent to which there has been a fundamental change in the circumstances.

A fundamental change in the circumstances

The term 'fundamental change in the circumstances' refers to Article 62 of the 1969 Vienna Convention on the Law of Treaties. Converting this rule in respect to the unilateral acts, it shall be concluded that a subject may appeal on this ground if the existence of those circumstances has constituted an essential basis for the party's unilateral act or

---

128 Currently, the International Law Commission is working on the matter of peremptory norms of general international law (*jus cogens*). According to the Text of the Draft Conclusions and Draft Annex on the Peremptory Norms of General International Law (*jus cogens*) provisionally adopted by the Drafting Committee on first reading in 2019 (A/CN.4/L.936), the Drafting Committee does not refer to '*invalidity* of a unilateral act which is contrary to a peremptory norm of international law', as in the case of the Guiding Principles applicable to unilateral declarations of states capable of creating legal obligations. Under the draft conclusion 15 [16] '1. A unilateral act of a State manifesting the intention to be bound by an obligation under international law that would be in conflict with a peremptory norm of general international law (*jus cogens*) *does not create such an obligation*. 2. An obligation under international law created by a unilateral act of a State *ceases to exist* if and to the extent that it conflicts with a new peremptory norm of general international law (*jus cogens*).' <https://legal.un.org/ilc/guide/1_14.shtml> accessed 16 March 2021.

the effect of the change is radically to transform the extent of the obligations still to be performed under the unilateral act.

Finally, the ILC itself regards the criteria defined in the tenth principle (determining whether or not a withdrawal is arbitrary) to be an open-ended list which is not complete and may be further developed.

SUBSIDIARY MEANS

> actual source of law
> law-applying
> law-making
> development of law

The essence of the subsidiary means

According to the ICJ Statute, the judicial decisions and the teachings of the most highly qualified publicists obtain the value of subsidiary means (subsidiary sources of law).

The true essence of the subsidiary means is that:

- They are not the **actual source of law**.
- They assist in the **law-applying** process (including the verification of the existence of rules and principles of law and the verification of the proper interpretation of the existing rules and principles of law).
- They assist in the **law-making** process (the **development of law**).

Judicial decisions

In international law, the judicial decision has no binding force except between the parties and only with respect to that particular case (as, for example, it is defined with respect to the ICJ according to the Article 59 of the ICJ Statute), i.e. the doctrine of precedent as known in the common law legal family does not exist in international law. In aggregate, the legal nature of a judicial decision in international law is more similar to that usually attributed to a judicial decision in civil law countries (despite differences in this respect between such countries).

Nevertheless, in practice, we can explore the fact that the subjects of international law, as well as qualified publicists, frequently quote judicial decisions as a reliable measure for the applicable legal position. Besides, the courts and tribunals themselves, in the parts of the decisions that state the reasons on which they are based (which is the obligation of each international court and tribunal), often refer to the previous judicial decisions of international courts and tribunals, as well as other bodies of international adjudication, and sometimes also to the decisions of the national courts to articulate and solidify international legal norms.

Teachings of the most highly qualified publicists

Regarding the teachings of the most highly qualified publicists of the various nations, initially, of course, the influence of distinguished writers on the foundation and development of modern international law should be outlined. With legal positivism ascending on the throne as a mainstream legal approach, logically, the importance of writings began to decline. However, until now, as in the case of judicial decisions, the prominent writers are also considered to be authoritative sources for taking appropriate legal positions.

SOFT LAW

> quasi-legal instruments
> hard law
> political agreements
> policy declarations
> final acts
> decisions of the organs of the international organisations
> International Law Commission

The meaning of soft law

Nowadays, in the scholarship dedicated to international law as well as in practical matters, the term 'soft law' has been widely employed to emphasise (legally) non-binding **quasi-legal instruments**.

The subjects of international law sometimes wish to adopt and test through soft law instruments certain rules and principles before they become laws in the near or distant future.

In sum, soft law means that:

- It is not a **(hard) law**.
- It has a limited normative force.
- It shall be understood in the sense of programs rather than prescriptions, guidelines rather than strict obligations.

Consequently, soft law covers the quasi-legal instruments which are neither strictly binding in nature nor entirely lacking in legal significance.

Forms of soft law

Although, there is an almost infinite number of various forms of soft law, it is possible to generalise its most widely used and recognised forms:

1   In international relations, many **political agreements**, **policy declarations**, and '**final acts**' published at the conclusion of international conferences neither exist in the

form of law nor have legal force; for instance, the Helsinki Final Act of 1975 is a major example of soft law. Hence, the political agreements, declarations, and other documents of that kind are widely considered to be soft law.

2   Other examples of soft law, which come from the web of international organisations, are the **decisions of the organs of the international organisations**.

However, occasionally, these decisions may have a mandatory character deriving its force from the foundational treaties of the respective organisations. Consequently, such a binding decision may be regarded as a secondary source of legal obligations (derived source of law). Most such decisions address administrative matters like budgets, internal staff, and so forth. More rarely, from the web of international organisations, there emerge the organs of internal structure with the power to make mandatory decisions on substantial statutory issues, which are determined in the founding treaties of the organisations. The Security Council of the United Nations, for instance, is one of the few international bodies with the power to bind states on substantial statutory matters, for example, under Article 25 of Charter: 'The Members of the United Nations agree to accept and carry out the decisions of the Security Council in accordance with the present Charter.'

Nevertheless, decisions of the internal organs of international organisations generally appear as recommendations. For example, the UN General Assembly is only granted the authority to initiate studies, discuss different issues, and make recommendations which are devoid of legally binding force. Decisions of this type are considered to be soft law.

Soft law as an instrument for the determination and development of law

At the same time, the political agreements, declarations, 'final acts', and so on, as well as the non-obligatory decisions of the internal organs of international organisations, may be regarded as significant instruments for the interpretation and development of law as with the aforementioned original subsidiary means.

In this respect, the considerable role belongs to, for instance, the **International Law Commission**, which was established by the UN General Assembly in 1947 to undertake the mandate of the Assembly, under article 13 (1) (a) of the Charter, to initiate studies and make recommendations for the purpose of 'encouraging the progressive development of international law and its codification.' Consequently, the similar provision was passed in the Statute of the International Law Commission: 'The International Law Commission shall have for its object the promotion of the progressive development of international law and its codification.'[129]

As regards the formation of the Commission, the Statute of the International Law Commission provides that: 'The Commission shall consist of thirty-four members who shall be persons of recognized competence in international law.' The members of ILC are elected by the UN General Assembly from a list of candidates nominated by the governments of member states of the UN. At the same time, '[n]o two members of the Commission shall be nationals of the same State'.[130]

---

129 Paragraph 1 of Article 1 of the Statute of the International Law Commission.
130 Paragraph 1 of Article 2, Article 3, and Paragraph 2 of Article 2 of the Statute of the International Law Commission.

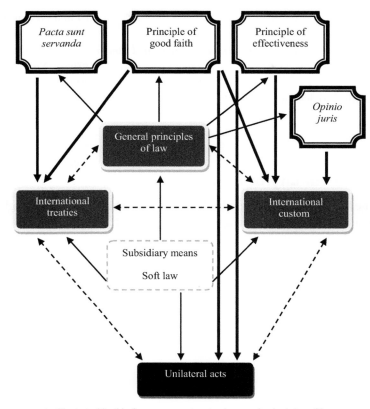

As illustrated in this figure, some structural general principles of law
may be treated as the basics (guides) of the binding character
of sources of international law

FIGURE 2.2 A distinctive look at the basics of the binding force of sources of international law

THE COMPLEX ARRANGEMENT OF INTERNATIONAL LAW – IS THERE A HIERARCHY?

priority
validity
Vienna Convention on the Law of Treaties
lex posterior derogat legi priori
lex specialis derogat legi generali
Military and Paramilitary Activities in and against Nicaragua case
principle of harmonisation
Article 103 of the UN Charter
law of nature theory
international value system

> *erga omnes*
> *jus cogens*
> *Barcelona Traction, Light and Power Company, Limited* case
> *East Timor* case
> *jus dispositivum*
> Draft Articles on Responsibility of States for Internationally Wrongful Acts
> universal jurisdiction

Priority and validity of norms

Generally, the hierarchy in the law establishes the relationships of inferiority and superiority between the norms. These relationships can have several connotations. However, they are mostly considered as a matter of:

- **Priority** between the norms without addressing their validity dimension directly. The principles and rules instituting such priority govern mere precedence between the norms for a specific moment and which rule shall the subject apply to conform with its legal obligations.
- **Validity** of norms, when every norm has to derive its validity from a higher norm, and if it contradicts the higher norm, then it becomes null and void.[131]

National law

National legal systems are hierarchical. The hierarchical structure varies from state to state and depends on the form of government. Nevertheless, as a rule, there is a hierarchy between the sources of law and the corresponding norms, commensurate with the place occupied by the governmental body (in the law-making process) that creates them. Hence, the national law is guided by the principle – *lex superior derogat inferiori*[132] (a norm [law] higher in the hierarchy supersedes the lower one).

In general, by examining this principle, the *lex superior* can be understood as:

1 A norm derived from the source which has a higher standing in the hierarchy, and such a comprehension suggests the existence of a hierarchy between the sources of law; and
2 A norm which has higher status based on the other structural rule (approach), as, for example, in case of the introduction of the system of peremptory norms in international law.

---

131 The conventional phrase 'null and void' is a legal doublet and actually redundant, as *null* means *void*: that is, having no legal force.
132 *Lex superior* – '"Higher law." (1) A body of law of greater legitimacy than another body of law. (2) A body of law that supersedes another, conflicting body of law. Contrast with *Lex inferior.*' *Guide to Latin in International Law* (n 71) 177.

The first understanding applies to national law, while the second applies to international law. The latter subject will be discussed in more detail later in this section.

International law as a non-hierarchical system of the sources of law

Unlike national law, international law is traditionally regarded as a non-hierarchical system of the sources of law. The three primary sources of international law, therefore, are equal in rank and status.[133]

Thus, since there is no hierarchy between the sources of law in international law, the rules of the priority and validity described next should apply regardless of the source through which the norms are established. Hence, for example, the norms created by international custom may prevail over the norms enshrined in a treaty and vice versa.

Besides, while there is no hierarchy between the sources of international law and system-forming subjects (which possess sovereign equality) create rules for themselves through various techniques and processes, there is a need to find the building blocks to interlink these norms.

The complex arrangement system in relation to the norms

Consequently, in international law, there exists a complex arrangement system between the norms, which correlate with each other by particular principles and rules determining either mere precedence between the conflicting norms or validity of norms.

The principle of integrated interpretation of norms

At the same time, in international law, there exists the principle of integrated interpretation of norms, emphasising both the unity of international law and the assertion that the rules must not be interpreted in isolation. For instance, the **Vienna Convention on the Law of Treaties** of 1969 provides a general rule for the interpretation of a treaty, which states that together with the context, there shall be taken into account any subsequent

---

133 Although there is no hierarchy between the sources of international law, some writers have emphasised that the treaty norms are easier to locate, ascertain, and apply than, for example, the customary norms, the precise content of which can be onerous to discover; some scholars have disclosed other arguments for the treaty primacy thesis. Thus, these writers have assumed that there may be a kind of *informal hierarchy* between them. 'This informal hierarchy follows from no legislative enactment but, emerges as a "forensic" or a "natural" aspect of legal reasoning. Any court or lawyer will first look at treaties, then custom and then the general principles of law for an answer to a normative problem.' Fragmentation of International Law: Difficulties Arising from the Diversification and Expansion of International Law, Report of the Study Group of the International Law Commission Finalized by Martti Koskenniemi, A/CN.4/L.682, 13 April 2006, page 47, paragraph 85. On the other hand, the informal treaty primacy thesis has always coexisted with other approaches which proved that general custom should rank higher (informally), as there can be no treaty law without a pre-existing framework of general customary law governing its formation.

agreements regarding interpretation, any subsequent practice in the application of the treaty, and 'any relevant rules of international law applicable in the relations between the parties'.[134] This wording is broad enough to cover all the sources of international law.[135]

General principles of law

As a starting point for the priority dimension between the international law norms, the following general principles of law may be considered:

1   *Lex posterior derogat legi priori* (a later norm [law] prevails over an earlier norm [law]). 'A maxim meaning that a legal rule arising after a conflicting legal rule prevails over the earlier rule to the extent of the conflict';[136] and
2   *Lex specialis derogat legi generali* (a norm [law] governing a specific subject matter [*lex specialis*] prevails[137] over a norm [law] which governs general matters [*lex generalis*]). 'The priority given to *lex specialis* is considered justified by the fact that the *lex specialis* is intended to apply in specific circumstances regardless of the rules applicable more generally where those circumstances may be absent.'[138]

These general principles of law may govern the precedency only if the conflicting norms are in force:

*   between the same parties; and
*   on the identical subject matter.

Meanwhile, the first maxim is sometimes hard to apply to international law since customary law and general principles of law come into being gradually, so no precise date can generally be assigned to their creation.

As regards the second principle, a rule may be general or special only in relation to some other rule:

*   concerning its subject matter; or
*   concerning its parties.

Therefore, for instance, on identical subject matter, the bilateral norm prevails over the multilateral rule between the same parties.

134 Paragraph 3 of Article 31 of the Vienna Convention on the Law of Treaties.
135 '[I]n future dear and authoritative guidance might be given indicating the relationship between treaty and later custom. Article 31(3)(c) provides the basic tool.' Philippe Sands, 'Treaty, Custom and the Cross-Fertilization of International Law' (27 January 2014) 1(1) *Yale Human Rights and Development Journal* Article 4, p. 105.
136 *Guide to Latin in International Law* (n 71) 174.
137 During the application of these maxims within the national law, the word 'repeal' is usually used. So, for instance, the first maxim in English reads: 'A later law repeals an earlier'. However, with regard to international law, in both cases, the word 'prevail' seems more accurate.
138 *Guide to Latin in International Law* (n 71) 177.

In sum, the approach that the special norm has a priority over a general norm has a long history of application with respect to international law norms.[139]

At the same time, the *lex specialis* maxim acquires greater importance in international law because there is no hierarchy between the sources. For example, based on this principle, the following approach concerning the relationship between international treaty norms and general customary law rules is recognised: as the International Court of Justice concludes in the **Military and Paramilitary Activities in and against Nicaragua case** *(Nicaragua v United States of America)*, in the event of divergence between treaty norms and the rules of general customary international law, for the parties to a treaty, amongst themselves, the treaty provisions apply as *lex specialis*.[140]

However, this finding concerns only the relationship which the Court has examined, i.e. the treaty – the general customary international law. Nonetheless, in some instances, the customary norms also may be considered as *lex specialis*: for example, the special customary law norms against the norms of general customary law or global treaties.

Sometimes, the parties to a more general treaty may explicitly agree that no derogation from the certain provisions of the treaty is permissible by means of a special agreement between some of the parties of that treaty. In such cases, the *lex specialis* maxim cannot stipulate prevalence of a norm (a bilateral, local, regional, or another multilateral norm) established between the more limited parties. A well-known example of such a regulation is, for instance, Article 6 of the Geneva Convention for the Amelioration of the Condition of the Wounded and Sick in Armed Forces in the Field of 12 August 1949, which reads: 'No special agreement shall adversely affect the situation of the wounded and sick, of members of the medical personnel or of chaplains, as defined by the present Convention, nor restrict the rights which it confers upon them.'[141]

Compatible norms

If two norms are in force on the same subject matter concerning two subjects of international law, but the subjects have said nothing of their mutual relationship, at first, they shall implement these norms under the **principle of harmonisation**, i.e. as compatible norms.

However, if such harmonisation is not assumed from the text of the norms – i.e. they are not compatible – the aforementioned general principles of law start the operation

---

139 'Its rationale is well expressed already by Grotius: What rules ought to be observed in such cases [i.e. where parts of a document are in conflict]. Among agreements which are equal . . . that should be given preference which is most specific and approaches most nearly to the subject in hand, for special provisions are ordinarily more effective than those that are general.' Fragmentation of International Law: Difficulties Arising from the Diversification and Expansion of International Law (n 133) page 36, paragraph 59.

140 *Military and Paramilitary Activities in and against Nicaragua (Nicaragua v USA)*, Judgment of 27 June 1986, ICJ Reports 1986, 14.

141 Also see the identical provisions of the Articles 6 of the second Geneva Convention for the Amelioration of the Condition of Wounded, Sick and Shipwrecked Members of Armed Forces at Sea and the third Geneva Convention relative to the Treatment of Prisoners of War of 12 August 1949.

maintaining a presumption of intent to derogate from the earlier or general norm. 'This may be the case for example when the treaties deal with wholly different topics and were negotiated by officials from different administrations.'[142]

Incompatibility between the norms

In case of incompatibility between the norms (when a later or special norm is so far incompatible with an earlier or general one that the two norms are not capable of being applied at the same time), the conflict between the norms leads:

1 to the termination of the earlier or general norm; or
2 only to the suspension in operation 'if it appears from the later [or special norm] . . . or is otherwise established that such was the intention of the parties.'[143]

Special cases regarding the continuation of the existence of the identical norms reflected in the different sources of international law

Addressing the jurisdiction and admissibility matter, in the case concerning *Military and Paramilitary Activities in and against Nicaragua (Nicaragua v United States of America)*, the International Court of Justice initially deduced that the general customary international law norms (principles) exist independently of treaty law norms (principles). In other words,

> Principles such as those of the non-use of force, nonintervention, respect for the independence and territorial integrity of States, and the freedom of navigation, continue to be binding as part of customary international law, despite the operation of provisions of conventional law in which they have been incorporated.[144]

Therefore, such norms of general customary international law continue their existence in the background, are binding, and prevail when, for some reason, the treaty providing the identical rule no longer is in force, or, for example, as in the case concerning *Military and Paramilitary Activities in and against Nicaragua*, the jurisdiction of the Court fails to

---

142 Fragmentation of International Law: Difficulties Arising from the Diversification and Expansion of International Law (n 133) page 119, paragraph 230.

143 As regards the earlier-later treaty norms, under Article 59 of the Vienna Convention on the Law of Treaties:

    1 A treaty shall be considered as terminated if all the parties to it conclude a later treaty relating to the same subject matter and:

        (a) it appears from the later treaty or is otherwise established that the parties intended that the matter should be governed by that treaty; or

        (b) the provisions of the later treaty are so far incompatible with those of the earlier one that the two treaties are not capable of being applied at the same time.

    2 The earlier treaty shall be considered as only suspended in operation if it appears from the later treaty or is otherwise established that such was the intention of the parties.'

144 *Military and Paramilitary Activities in and against Nicaragua (Nicaragua v United States of America)*, Judgment of 27 June 1986.

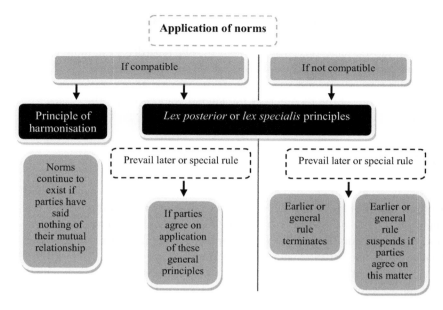

FIGURE 2.3 Application of norms under the *lex posterior* or *lex specialis* principle

apply with respect to the treaty. Hence, if at first two states incorporated a customary international law rule in a new treaty and later, they terminate this treaty, these states cannot claim that, between them, the customary norm was overridden by the treaty rule, so there is no legal regulation on that matter at all. On the contrary, a rule of customary international law is not erased and persists as a binding rule between these states as well.

This finding of the Court can be extended to certain norms of international law possessing the ability of universal application, such as the peremptory norms and the general principles of law. For example, if a rule of the general principles of law is incorporated into a treaty, it continues to be binding as the part of the general principles of law.

Article 103 of the UN Charter

Considering the hierarchy model between the norms in international law, sometimes there is a reference to **Article 103 of the UN Charter**, which reads:

> In the event of a conflict between the obligations of the Members of the United Nations under the present Charter and their obligations under any other international agreement, their obligations under the present Charter shall prevail.

In the meantime, this Article technically emphasises a conflict only between the obligations under UN Charter (the international treaty) and any other international agreement and does not formally concern customary law or the general principles of law. In addition, this Article covers only divergence 'between the obligations' and does not directly relate to the hierarchy between the norms.

Essentially, the question therein is not of the validity of norms but the priority of obligations.

However, substantially, this Article at least may be regarded as an indirect contribution to clarifying the issue of priority between the norms since the state has the duty not to fulfil an obligation arising under that other 'international agreement' which is in conflict with the obligations of the members of the United Nations under the Charter.

Law of nature theory and the concept of the international value system

Until now, international law has remained a system in which the states (also other subjects of international law in limited scale) have an ability to institute international norms through the sources of international law and, correspondingly, have the right to replace or modify these norms in either a bilateral or a multilateral format. Actually, this is a true understanding of the basics of contemporary international law.

However, this understanding was challenged by the supporters of the **law of nature theory** and the concept of the **international value system**. Both aim to restrict the unlimited freedom of states (and other subjects of international law) in law-making and, therefore, target to find a centre of gravity in international law.

The approach of the law of nature is deeply integrated into international law through the sources of law: for example, concerning the human rights field. Hence, in any case, the law of nature can provide a legal obligation if it is duly incorporated into the international law sources by consent or acknowledgement undertaken by the relevant parties. Consequently, as such, the approach of the law of nature does not make much of a contribution (with the independent model) to the question of hierarchy.

Furthermore, the substantive law of nature is usually rooted in the foundational conception of self-survival (preservation of life). By adjusting this concept to the interstate level, it might be considered a preservation of a state, correspondingly, of the sovereignty of the main subject of international law since, without sovereignty, the entity will not be treated as a state. Thus, the law of nature itself maintains the sovereignty of a state and, accordingly, the basics of modern international law that it is not permitted to apply a norm to a certain state without its own consent.

As regards the concept of the international value system, the UN Charter embraced the idea of an international community with shared values and common interests. Subsequently, this idea was further developed by the concepts of ***erga omnes*** obligations and ***jus cogens*** norms.

Concept of *erga omnes*

The significant challenge to the unrestricted freedom of states (and other subjects) to institute, replace, and modify all norms of international law emerged with the birth of the concept of *erga omnes*, which has been used as a legal term to describe the obligations owed by individual states to the community of states as a whole.

In a well-known judgment of the International Court of Justice – *Barcelona Traction, Light and Power Company, Limited* case (*Belgium v Spain*) – the obligations *erga omnes* are determined as follows:

> In particular, an essential distinction should be drawn between the obligations of a State towards the international community as a whole, and those arising vis-à-vis another State in the field of diplomatic protection. By their very nature the former are the concern of all States. In view of the importance of the rights involved, all States can be held to have a legal interest in their protection; they are obligations *erga omnes*.

Afterward, the Court identifies these obligations as derived, for instance, 'from the outlawing of acts of aggression, and of genocide, as also from the principles and rules concerning the basic rights of the human person, including protection from slavery and racial discrimination.'[145]

Moreover, in the number of other decisions, the Court has reaffirmed the notion of obligations towards the international community as a whole. For example, in the *East Timor* case *(Portugal v Australia)*, the Court said that 'Portugal's assertion that the right of peoples to self-determination, as it evolved from the Charter and from United Nations practice, has an *erga omnes* character, is irreproachable.'[146]

In the meantime, the obligations *erga omnes* do not represent all the obligations derived from the norms that have universal coverage. They are an expression of a value-loaded concept; consequently, many (though not all) *erga omnes* obligations have emerged in the fields of human rights and humanitarian law.

Thus, this concept reflects the significance of the international value system, existing at the level of the international community of states. At the same time, this concept in some part overlaps with the obligations under the UN Charter.

However, the concept of the *erga omnes* obligations does not indicate the presence of a normative hierarchy in international law in terms of either priority or validity.[147]

Peremptory norms of general international law

Only regarding the next concept – *jus cogens* norms of general international law – does there exist in international law model of hierarchy between the norms which governs the

---

145 *Barcelona Traction, Light and Power Company, Limited (Belgium v Spain)*, Judgment of 5 February 1970, ICJ Reports 1970, 3.

146 *East Timor (Portugal v Australia)*, Judgment of 30 June 1995, ICJ Reports 1995, 90.

147 'A norm which is creative of obligations *erga omnes* is owed to the "international community as a whole' and all States – irrespective of their particular interest in the matter – are entitled to invoke State responsibility in case of breach. The *erga omnes* nature of an obligation, however, indicates no clear superiority of that obligation over other obligations. Although in practice norms recognised as having an *erga omnes* validity set up undoubtedly important obligations, this importance does not translate into a hierarchical superiority.' Fragmentation of International Law: Difficulties Arising from the Diversification and Expansion of International Law (n 133) page 193, paragraph 380.

validity of the norms. Among the norms of international law, the peremptory (imperative) norms of general international law (*jus cogens* norms) occupy the highest hierarchic position over all the other rules and principles.[148] Accordingly, all norms of international law are either *jus cogens* or **jus dispositivum** (norms which can be replaced by subjects in their bilateral or multilateral dealings).

According to Article 53 (Treaties conflicting with a peremptory norm of general international law ['*jus cogens*']) of the Vienna Convention on the Law of Treaties of 1969:

> A treaty is void if, at the time of its conclusion, it conflicts with a peremptory norm of general international law. For the purposes of the present Convention, a peremptory norm of general international law is a norm accepted and recognized by the international community of states as a whole as a norm from which no derogation is permitted and which can be modified only by a subsequent norm of general international law having the same character.

Hence, there must be four cumulative criteria for a norm to be specified as the *jus cogens*, namely:

1 the character as a norm of the general international law;
2 the acceptance and recognition by the international community of the states as a whole,
3 the prohibition of the derogation, and
4 the permission of its modification only by a subsequent norm of general international law having the same character.

The peremptory norms of general international law are universally applicable, and they serve to protect fundamental and paramount values of the international community. As stated in the Text of the Draft Conclusions and Draft Annex on the Peremptory Norms of General International Law (*jus cogens*) provisionally adopted by the ILC Drafting Committee on first reading:[149] 'Peremptory norms of general international law (*jus cogens*) reflect and protect fundamental values of the international community, are hierarchically superior to other rules of international law and are universally applicable.'[150] The International Law Commission is currently continuing to work on the matter of the peremptory norms of general international law (*jus cogens*).

---

148 'Indeed, the Commission has already concluded that *jus cogens* norms are hierarchically superior to other rules, and that conclusion ought to be a sufficient basis to include hierarchical superiority as a characteristic element of *jus cogens*.' Paragraph 23 of the Second report on *jus cogens* by Dire Tladi, Special Rapporteur, International Law Commission, Sixty-ninth session, Geneva, 1 May–2 June and 3 July–4 August 2017.

149 Peremptory Norms of General International Law (*jus cogens*), Text of the Draft Conclusions and Draft Annex on the Peremptory Norms of General International Law (*jus cogens*) provisionally adopted by the Drafting Committee on first reading in 2019, International Law Commission.

150 Draft Conclusion 3 [3(2)], General nature of peremptory norms of general international law (*jus cogens*).

Formation of the peremptory norms of general international law

The peremptory norms of general international law are created through the sources of international law.

Although customary international law is the most common basis for *jus cogens* norms, international treaties, as well as the general principles of law, may also serve as the foundation for the peremptory norms of general international law. For example, the general principles of law are considered the source of the principle of elementary considerations of humanity.[151]

At the same time, a peremptory norm of general international law undergoes a rather complicated process of development. In order to achieve acceptance and recognition from the international community of states as a whole, the consent by 'a very large majority of states' is required. This, of course, does not mean the requirement of unanimous recognition by all members of the community of states; however, among the very large majority, all significant elements of the community of states shall be included; specifically, the recognising states should represent all geopolitical axes of the world and all principal legal systems.

Such an acceptance and recognition, therefore, mostly requires a combination of the sources of international law since, for example, for certain states, the norm may be established by the international treaty while for others, it might be based on international custom.

Finally, the evidence of acceptance and recognition that a norm of general international law has obtained a peremptory character may take a wide range of forms. Among other ways, such evidence can be expressed in the following forms: '[P]ublic statements made on behalf of States; official publications; government legal opinions; diplomatic

---

151 In the ICJ Judgment on merits delivered on 9 April 1949, the Court stated: 'Such obligations are based . . . on certain general and well-recognized principles, namely: elementary considerations of humanity, even more exacting in peace than in war', *Corfu Channel (United Kingdom of Great Britain and Northern Ireland v Albania)*, ICJ Reports 1949, 4. 'The ICJ was in fact faced with a paradoxical situation, where the laws of war were in fact more protective of persons than the laws of peace. While the former included a treaty that imposed obligations on States laying minefields, the latter did not contain any such provision or any other provision aiming at the protection of persons from harm. . . . The Court avoided the illogical conclusion that people are more protected during wartime than during peacetime through reference to "considerations of humanity" as a principle that should guide the determination and application of more specific obligations pending on States.' Irini Papanicolopulu, 'Considerations of Humanity in the Enrica Lexie Case' (30 November 2015) <www.qil-qdi.org/considerations-of-humanity-in-the-enrica-lexie-case/> accessed 16 March 2021. 'Auch die allgemeinen Rechtsgrundsätze können zwingende Normen enthalten oder auch erzeugen. So wäre eine Mindestrespektierung der Menschenwürde, auch wenn diese bisher nur in einigen Verträgen zum Schutz der Menschenrechte und in Verfassungsordnungen aller anerkannten Rechtsysteme niedergelegt ist, von der Völkerrechtsordnung auch dann zwingend zu beachten, dieser Grundsatz im völkerrechtlichem Gewohnheitsrecht, d.h. in der Staatenpraxis, noch keinen Ausdruck gefunden haben sollte', Karl Doehring, *Völkerrecht: ein Lehrbuch* (2., neubearbeitete Auflage, C. F. Müller Verlag 2004) 124–125.

correspondence; legislative and administrative acts; decisions of national courts; treaty provisions; and resolutions adopted by an international organization or at an intergovernmental conference.'[152]

Additionally, for the determination of the peremptory character of the norms of general international law, the essential role is occupied by such subsidiary means as the decisions of international courts and tribunals, the works of expert bodies established by states or international organisations, and the teachings of the most highly qualified publicists.

A non-exhaustive list of peremptory norms of general international law

The identification of the particular *jus cogens* norms, in reality, is a rather complicated undertaking. This is clearly evidenced by the dissensions regarding the nature of the prohibition on the threat or use of force. Article 2(4) of the UN Charter prohibits the threat or use of force. Therefore, the prohibition includes both the use and the threat of force. The prohibition of the use of force is often claimed to be a rule of a peremptory character. The prohibition of the threat of the use of force, on the other hand, is generally not regarded as possessing the same status.

The International Court of Justice, in the judgment on the ***Military and Paramilitary Activities in and against Nicaragua*** case (*Nicaragua v United States of America*), stated that

> A further confirmation of the validity as customary international law of the principle of the prohibition of the use of force expressed in Article 2, paragraph 4, of the Charter of the United Nations may be found in the fact that it is frequently referred to in statements by State representatives as being not only a principle of customary international law but also a fundamental or cardinal principle of such law. The International Law Commission, in the course of its work on the codification of the law of treaties, expressed the view that 'the law of the Charter concerning the prohibition of the use of force in itself constitutes a conspicuous example of a rule in international law having the character of *jus cogens*.[153]

In recent years, the International Law Commission, in this context, referred to the prohibition of aggression[154] as being the peremptory norm of general international law.

As argued in the **Draft Articles on Responsibility of States for Internationally Wrongful Acts**, with commentaries (or simply Draft Articles on Responsibility of States for Internationally Wrongful Acts) of 2001 of the International Law Commission: 'Those peremptory norms that are clearly accepted and recognized include the prohibitions of aggression,

---

152 Draft Conclusion 8 [9(1)(2)] (Evidence of acceptance and recognition) of the Text of the Draft Conclusions and Draft Annex on the Peremptory Norms of General International Law (*jus cogens*) provisionally adopted by the Drafting Committee of the International Law Commission on first reading.

153 *Military and Paramilitary Activities in and against Nicaragua (Nicaragua v United States of America)*, Judgment of 27 June 1986.

154 The interrelationship between the terms 'use of force', 'aggression', and 'armed attack' will be discussed in a section of this book 'Peaceful co-existence – Refraining from the threat or use of force.'

genocide, slavery, racial discrimination, crimes against humanity and torture, and the right to self-determination.'[155]

In 2019, the Drafting Committee of the International Law Commission provided the following interim non-exhaustive list of norms *jus cogens*:

> (a) The prohibition of aggression; (b) The prohibition of genocide; (c) The prohibition of crimes against humanity; (d) The basic rules of international humanitarian law; (e) The prohibition of racial discrimination and apartheid; (f) The prohibition of slavery; (g) The prohibition of torture; (h) The right of self-determination.[156]

Hence, a more or less complete illustrative list of *jus cogens* norms does not exist in international law. The main concern of the states in introducing such a list is that it would, by definition, not be exhaustive and would entail a risk that other equally important rules of international law would, in effect, be given an inferior status.[157]

Legal consequences of the derogation from the *jus cogens* norms and the breach of obligation arising under a peremptory norm of general international law

Ordinarily, as it was officially endorsed by the Vienna Convention on the Law of Treaties of 1969, the concept of the peremptory norms of general international law was focused on the invalidity of treaty norms derogating from the *jus cogens* norms. As regards the pre-existing treaties, they are annulled when inconsistent peremptory norms of general international law come into existence. Hence, under the concept of the peremptory norms of general international law, the invalidity appears as a true legal sanction. On the other hand, as regards the separability of treaty provisions, save in exceptional cases, a treaty which conflicts with a peremptory norm of general international law is void in whole.[158]

---

155 Paragraph 5 of the commentary to the Article 26 (Compliance with peremptory norms) of the Draft Articles on Responsibility of States for Internationally Wrongful Acts, available at <http://bit.ly/35UsXEa> accessed 16 March 2021. The text of the Draft Articles appeared in the annex to General Assembly Resolution A/RES/56/83 of 12 December 2001 (Annex – Responsibility of States for internationally wrongful acts).

156 Annex of the Text of the Draft Conclusions and Draft Annex on the Peremptory Norms of General International Law (*jus cogens*) provisionally adopted by the Drafting Committee of the International Law Commission on first reading.

157 See the position of the Nordic States during the debate in the Sixth Committee on first report on *jus cogens* by Dire Tladi, Special Rapporteur of ILC, sixty-eighth session of International Law Commission, Geneva, 2 May–10 June and 4 July–12 August 2016, <https://legal.un.org/ilc/guide/1_14.shtml> accessed 16 March 2021.

158 The exceptions to the general rule are provided for in Draft Conclusion 11 of the Text of the Draft Conclusions and Draft Annex on the Peremptory Norms of General International Law (*jus cogens*) provisionally adopted by the Drafting Committee of the International Law Commission on first

At the same time, although Article 53 formally refers to treaty law, it is widely accepted that (1) all existing norms establishing an international legal obligation – including customary norms, obligations instituted by the unilateral acts of states, and norms of the binding resolutions of international organisations – which are in conflict with a peremptory norm (while derogating from this norm), (2) as well as the legal relationships developed based on such norms or obligations, by the direct application of the established concept concerning the treaties, become null and void.[159]

Meanwhile, the extensive dissemination of the notion of *jus cogens* raised questions relating to the legal effects of noncompliance with the *jus cogens* other than the nullity of the norms. Indeed, a subject of international law may derogate from the peremptory norm of general international law by instituting a norm, but it can breach an international obligation derived from the peremptory norm by an act or omission without establishing any conflicting norm. At the same time, even if the noncompliance is provided by a newly developed norm, these shall be considered as:

1   derogation from a peremptory norm of general international law that from a legal point of view makes such a norm invalid; and
2   breach of the international obligation derived from the peremptory norm of general international law by a respective act (since the creation of a norm is simultaneously considered to be an act), leading to the supplemented execution of the ordinary international responsibility model since the 'derogation model' as such does not exclude such an execution.

For example, if a state commits an act of aggression against another state; in the aftermath, the aggressor annexes the territory of the state which fell victim to the act of aggression; and a third state recognises the act of annexation, this recognition (as a unilateral act of states) shall be regarded as:

---

reading: 'A treaty which becomes void because of the emergence of a new peremptory norm of general international law *(jus cogens)* terminates in whole, unless: (a) the provisions that are in conflict with a peremptory norm of general international law *(jus cogens)* are separable from the remainder of the treaty with regard to their application; (b) it appears from the treaty or is otherwise established that acceptance of the said provisions was not an essential basis of the consent of any party to be bound by the treaty as a whole; and (c) continued performance of the remainder of the treaty would not be unjust.'

159 According to the Text of the Draft Conclusions and Draft Annex on the Peremptory Norms of General International Law *(jus cogens)* provisionally adopted by the Drafting Committee on first reading in 2019, the Drafting Committee does not refer to 'invalidity' in cases of customary international law, unilateral acts of states and the obligations created by resolutions, or decisions or other acts of international organisations which are contrary to a peremptory norm of international law. It uses the following formulations: Concerning the customary international law – 'does not come into existence' and 'ceases to exist'; regarding the unilateral acts of states – 'does not create such an obligation' and 'ceases to exist'; and with respect to the resolutions of international organisations – 'does not create obligations'. Hence, at the moment, the propositions of the Drafting Committee do not mirror precisely the terms and scenario of Article 53 of the 1969 Vienna Convention on the Law of Treaties.

1 being in conflict with a peremptory norm of general international law stipulating the invalidity of the recognition and, as such, not creating valid legal relationships because the prohibition of aggression is widely accepted to be the peremptory norm of general international law, and the 'annexation by the use of force' in itself is regarded as the manifestation of an act of aggression; and

2 the act violating the international obligation derived from the peremptory norm, triggering the appropriate international responsibility (ordinary international responsibility model) against the third state.

The determination of the subsequent consequences of the serious breaches of *jus cogens* has been much debated in the works that led to the adoption by the International Law Commission of the Draft Articles on Responsibility of States for Internationally Wrongful Acts mentioned earlier. This document introduces the articles that prescribe the legal consequences of a serious breach by a state of an obligation arising under a peremptory norm of general international law. 'A breach of such an obligation is serious if it involves a gross or systematic failure by the responsible State to fulfil the obligation.'[160]

Among other things, firstly, the Draft Articles on Responsibility of States for Internationally Wrongful Acts defines the obligation of the states to bring to an end through lawful means any serious breaches of international law; secondly, it proclaims the duty of the states not to recognise as lawful a situation created by a serious breach of *jus cogens* norms; and finally, it applies the ordinary international responsibility model to this case, too, such as, if appropriate, to give guarantees and assurances of non-repetition; a duty to make reparation in conformity with international law; and the list can be further continued.[161] Hence, such breaches shall be treated through the lenses of the ordinary model of international responsibility. At the same time, no circumstance precluding wrongfulness under the rules on the responsibility of states for internationally wrongful acts may be invoked concerning any act of a state which is not in conformity with an obligation arising under a norm of *jus cogens*.

In addition, there may be enumerated other legal consequences of the breach of obligation arising from a peremptory norm of general international law. For example, various domestic courts have concluded that the violation of *jus cogens* norms by an individual may permit states' courts to exercise **universal jurisdiction** upon a particular individual.

The distinction between *jus cogens* and *erga omnes*

As noted on the distinction between *jus cogens* and *erga omnes* in the Report of the Study Group of the International Law Commission on Fragmentation of International Law:

> [A]ll *jus cogens* norms constitute *erga omnes* obligations. But the equation does not work the other way around. From the fact that all States have an interest in the fulfilment of

---

160 Paragraph 2 of Article 40 of the Draft Articles on Responsibility of States for Internationally Wrongful Acts.

161 Articles 40 and 41 of the Draft Articles on Responsibility of States for Internationally Wrongful Acts.

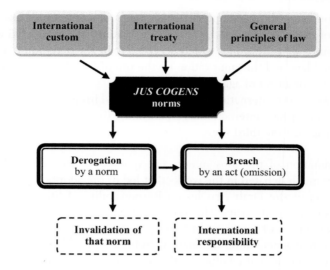

FIGURE 2.4 Peremptory norms of general international law

an obligation it does not necessarily follow that those norms are peremptory – that is to say, they do not necessarily render conflicting obligations null and void.[162]

Thus, the two concepts have different foci. Whereas at the very heart of the peremptory norms approach is the superiority which is to be given to a certain number of fundamental obligations and the validity of norms (and respective obligations), the focus of *erga omnes* obligations is essentially on the legal interest of all states in being entitled to invoke the international responsibility of every state which violates those obligations.

INTERNATIONAL LAW AND NATIONAL LAW

monism
doctrine of incorporation
dualism
doctrine of transformation
Exchange of Greek and Turkish Populations case
implementation
incorporation
transformation
reference

162 Fragmentation of International Law: Difficulties Arising from the Diversification and Expansion of International Law (n 133) page 204, paragraph 404.

> general reference
> individual reference
> self-executing norms
> non-self-executing norms

Preliminary remarks

In the international law scholarship as well as in the practice of the states, three theories about the relationship between international law and national law have emerged. Two of them are monistic, and one is dualistic.

Monism

Monism considers international law and national law to be parts of the one unitary coherent system. They, in sum, are concerned with the same subject matter and thus can come into conflict. If there is a conflict, either the international law prevails (the first version), or international law is one part of the entire body of national law of a state (the second version).[163] Monism contributed to a significant degree to the development of the **doctrine of incorporation**[164] (concerning the implementation of the international law), which is convinced that the norms of international law automatically form part of national law.

Dualism

Dualism considers international law and national law to be two separate legal systems operating and existing independently of one another because of differences in subjects, sources, and content. Consequently, the transformation of international law into national law is required to make international law binding on a domestic level. Therefore, international and national laws as independent systems can never come into conflict. The dualist theory largely stipulated the establishment of the **doctrine of transformation**,[165] otherwise

---

163 For example, the German approach in the second half of the nineteenth century under which the international law was regarded as a mere 'external state law' – in German '*Außenstaatsrecht*'.

164 '[D]octrine of incorporation. The doctrine that rules of international law automatically form part of municipal law. It is opposed to the doctrine of transformation, which states that international law only forms a part of municipal law if accepted as such by statute or judicial decisions.' *A Dictionary of Law* (n 2) 160. The same distinction (between two terms – transformation and incorporation) is expressed in many other articles and monographs.

165 '[T]his theory holds that the rules of international law are not part of municipal law without specific legislation – and is based on the concept of a dualism between international law and municipal law. "To be binding, [international] law must have received the assent of the nations who are to be bound by it. This assent may be express, as by treaty or the acknowledged concurrence of governments, or may be implied from established usage. . . . Nor, in my opinion, would the clearest proof of unanimous assent on the part of other nations be sufficient to authorize the tribunals of this country to apply,

known as the doctrine of adoption,[166] which argues that international law forms only a part of national law if accepted as such by the use of the appropriate constitutional machinery (for example, by the device of ratification), internal legislation (through the creation of parallel [transformed] material internal norms), or judicial decisions.

Different approaches of states

By studying the practice of states, it may be concluded that in the national laws of the countries, different approaches concerning this very issue has been maintained. Therefore, it is difficult to find the right model regarding the relationship between international law and national law. However, some common general legal attitudes still may be discovered.

Two autonomous systems

Indeed, international law and national law are the two systems of law. These two systems interact with each other, while both retain autonomy because each system regulates separate subject fields, and each refers to its particular sphere:

- The international law orders the conduct of states (and other subjects of international law) with respect to the interstate level.
- The national law prescribes the interaction of the state, other legal persons, and natural persons within the state.

So the first creates and modifies the rights and obligations among subjects of international law, the second between the subjects of national law.

Each law is supreme at its level

Accordingly, if we attempt to find a recognised theoretical view tied to reality, we will come to the conclusion that each law is supreme on its own level (sphere).

---

without an Act of Parliament, what would practically amount to a new law. In so doing we should be unjustifiably usurping the province of the legislature": *The Franconia (R. v. Keyn) (1876) 2 Ex. D. 63* at 203 *per* Cockburn C.J.' *Parry & Grant Encyclopaedic Dictionary of International Law*, John P. Grant and J. Craig Barker (3rd edn, Oxford University Press 2009) 611.

166 '[A]doption, doctrine of [–]The doctrine, otherwise called the doctrine of transformation . . . to the effect that "rules of international law are not to be considered as part of English law except in so far as they have already been adopted and made part of our law by the decisions of the judges, or by Act of Parliament, or long established custom", in contrast to "the doctrine of incorporation which says that the rules of international law are incorporated into English law automatically and considered to be part of English law unless they conflict with an Act of Parliament": *Trendtex Trading Corporation v. Central Bank of Nigeria [1977] Q.B. 529* at 533 *per* Lord Denning M.R., who, having accepted the doctrine of adoption without question in *R. v. Secretary of State for the Home Department, ex parte Thakrar [1974]*.' ibid 12.

Prohibition of invoking national law for the justification of non-performance of international law

Undoubtedly, it is not applicable to refer to national law to justify non-compliance with international norms (and corresponding obligations).[167] This approach is prescribed in the Vienna Convention on the Law of Treaties (1969): 'A party may not invoke the provisions of its internal law as justification for its failure to perform a treaty.'[168]

Duty to bring national law in conformity with international law

Meanwhile, despite the existence of the autonomous subject matters, international law and national law are intertwined in some instances. Therefore, there could be a conflict of obligations of a state at the international and domestic levels resulting in the failure of a state on the national plane to act in conformity with international law. In response to such a situation, there exists under international law the general duty to bring national law in compliance with international law. In this respect, the Opinion of the Permanent Court of International Justice of 1925 on the *Exchange of Greek and Turkish Populations* case *(Greece v Turkey)* should be recalled:

> [A] principle which is self-evident, according to which a State which has contracted valid international obligations is bound to make in its legislation such modifications as may be necessary to ensure the fulfilment of the obligations undertaken.[169]

Mutual interdependence between these two legal systems

Thus, in the international sphere, international law has supremacy over national law. However, this does not mean that national law is irrelevant at the interstate level. 'International law does not entirely ignore municipal law. For instance, . . . municipal law may be used as evidence of international custom or of general principles of law, which are both sources of international law.'[170] Some parts of international law originate with the vital assistance of national law.

Besides, both the national and international courts have recognised the need to resort to the other's sphere of operation in order to interpret certain norms.

---

167 'The general rule with regard to the position of municipal law within the international sphere is that a state which has broken a stipulation of international law cannot justify itself by referring to its domestic legal situation.' Shaw (n 69) 100.

168 Article 27 (Internal law and observance of treaties).

169 *Exchange of Greek and Turkish Populations* (*Greece v Turkey*), Advisory Opinion No. 10 of 21 February 1925, PCIJ Ser B (1925) – No. 10.

170 Malanczuk (n 72) 64.

Implementation of international norms into the national law

On the other hand, the attitude of national law towards international law is not easy to summarise since the internal legal systems of different states vary significantly in this respect. However, the existence of the general duty to bring the national law in conformity with the obligations under international law stipulates the duty of **implementation** of international norms into the domestic legislation of the states.

Meanwhile, international law generally does not dictate how international obligations are to be implemented within the domestic sphere. Therefore, it is commonly up to each state to determine how to give effect to its international obligations (freedom of choosing the form of implementation).

Conventional means for the implementation of international law

Nevertheless, there exist some traditional means for the implementation of international law into national law, namely:

- **Incorporation** – recognising the international law norms automatically as part of a national legal system and permitting their direct application.
- **Transformation** – considering that, for the domestic application of international law, it is necessary to adopt domestic constitutional machinery, legislation, or judicial decisions.

At the same time, in the practice of states, there is a mere technical tool of implementation introduced – the **reference** method as an acceptance of international law rules as part and parcel of national law, which consists of the adoption of internal nonmaterial rules concerning the international law-national law relationship:

- **General reference** – for example, the general reference in the constitutions of states about the acceptance of international law rules as an integral part of the national law (i.e. international law direct application rule) or concerning the precedence of international law over the domestic normative acts. Such a way serves as a technical tool for the general incorporation mode.[171]

---

171 Under Article 25 [Primacy of international law] of Basic Law of the Federal Republic of Germany: 'The general rules of international law shall be an integral part of federal law. They shall take precedence over the laws and directly create rights and duties for the inhabitants of the federal territory.' According to Article 4 (paragraph 5) of the Constitution of Georgia: 'The legislation of Georgia shall comply with the universally recognised principles and norms of international law. An international treaty of Georgia shall take precedence over domestic normative acts unless it comes into conflict with the Constitution or the Constitutional Agreement of Georgia.' Under the Supremacy Clause (VI.2) of the United States Constitution, 'all Treaties made, or which shall be made, under the Authority of the United States, shall be the supreme Law of the Land; and the Judges in every State shall be

- **Individual reference** – a reference to a particular international norm (usually, either a treaty, a certain rule of a treaty, or a customary norm). Such a method is a technical tool for the special incorporation mode.

The self-executing and non-self-executing international norms

However, in practice, the ways of international law implementation may vary from one model to another, combining the doctrines and means mentioned earlier.

Sometimes the distinct approach is stipulated by the existence of **self-executing** and **non-self-executing** international norms. The self-executing norms can be directly applied in national law. The non-self-executing norms require supplementary implementing legislation before their application in national law.

A comprehensive practice of implementation of different sources of international law

Actual state practice is more complex and differs even concerning the particular sources of international law. Some countries implement international treaties by practising primarily one doctrine – for example, the doctrine of transformation – whereas, regarding the implementation of the obligations based on international custom, they can in principle refer to another – the doctrine of incorporation.[172]

---

bound thereby, any Thing in the Constitution or Laws of any State to the Contrary notwithstanding.' Furthermore, the US legal system appears amenable to customary international law as well as to international treaties. As the US Supreme Court in the *Paquete Habana* case stated: 'International law is part of our law, and must be ascertained and administered by the courts of justice of appropriate jurisdiction, as often as questions of right depending upon it are duly presented for their determination.'

172 For instance, the doctrine of incorporation generally has become the leading approach of English law regarding customary international law. 'As far as the rules of customary international law are concerned the English courts have generally adopted the doctrine of incorporation. Provided that they are not inconsistent with Acts of Parliament or prior authoritative judicial decisions, then rules of customary international law automatically form part of English law: customary international law is incorporated into English law.' Tim Hillier, *Sourcebook on Public International Law* (Cavendish Publishing Limited 1998) 40. However, international treaties, in principle, do not automatically become part of English law. As Lord Oliver noted in relation to the *International Tin Council* case (*J. H. Rayner (Mincing Lane) Ltd v Department of Trade and Industry*): 'Treaties, as it is sometimes expressed, are not self-executing. Quite simply, a treaty is not part of English law unless and until it has been incorporated into the law by legislation.' At the same time, the model of the United Kingdom concerning the implementation of international treaties is more complicated. For example, sometimes the individual reference (special incorporation mode) is introduced. 'Treaties may be incorporated indirectly into United Kingdom law, including by reference to treaty provisions in primary legislation. For example, section 2 of the Asylum and Immigration Appeals Act 1993 provides "Nothing in the immigration rules . . . shall lay down any practice which would be contrary to the [Refugee] Convention"'. Martin Dixon, Robert McCorquodale, and Sarah Williams, *Cases & Materials on International Law* (6th edn, Oxford University Press 2016) 111, 113.

There may be an inverse combination of the application of these two doctrines, as well as the individual configuration of the approaches visible in the actual practice of different states.

CASES AND MATERIALS (*SELECTED PARTS*)

International custom

Draft Conclusions on Identification of Customary International Law of 2018, International Law Commission
Adopted by the International Law Commission at its seventieth session, *Yearbook of the International Law Commission*, 2018, vol. II, Part Two.

Part One Introduction

Conclusion 1 Scope

The present draft conclusions concern the way in which the existence and content of rules of customary international law are to be determined.

Part Two Basic approach

Conclusion 2 Two constituent elements

To determine the existence and content of a rule of customary international law, it is necessary to ascertain whether there is a general practice that is accepted as law (*opinio juris*).

Conclusion 3 Assessment of evidence for the two constituent elements

1   In assessing evidence for the purpose of ascertaining whether there is a general practice and whether that practice is accepted as law (*opinio juris*), regard must be had to the overall context, the nature of the rule, and the particular circumstances in which the evidence in question is to be found.
2   Each of the two constituent elements is to be separately ascertained. This requires an assessment of evidence for each element.

Part Three A general practice

Conclusion 4 Requirement of practice

1   The requirement of a general practice, as a constituent element of customary international law, refers primarily to the practice of States that contributes to the formation, or expression, of rules of customary international law.
2   In certain cases, the practice of international organizations also contributes to the formation, or expression, of rules of customary international law.
3   Conduct of other actors is not practice that contributes to the formation, or expression, of rules of customary international law, but may be relevant when assessing the practice referred to in paragraphs 1 and 2.

Conclusion 5 Conduct of the State as State practice

State practice consists of conduct of the State, whether in the exercise of its executive, legislative, judicial or other functions.

Conclusion 6 Forms of practice

1   Practice may take a wide range of forms. It includes both physical and verbal acts. It may, under certain circumstances, include inaction.
2   Forms of State practice include, but are not limited to: diplomatic acts and correspondence; conduct in connection with resolutions adopted by an international organization or at an intergovernmental conference; conduct in connection with treaties; executive conduct, including operational conduct "on the ground"; legislative and administrative acts; and decisions of national courts.
3   There is no predetermined hierarchy among the various forms of practice.

Conclusion 7 Assessing a State's practice

1   Account is to be taken of all available practice of a particular State, which is to be assessed as a whole.
2   Where the practice of a particular State varies, the weight to be given to that practice may, depending on the circumstances, be reduced.

Conclusion 8 The practice must be general

1   The relevant practice must be general, meaning that it must be sufficiently widespread and representative, as well as consistent.
2   Provided that the practice is general, no particular duration is required.

Part Four Accepted as law (*opinio juris*)

Conclusion 9 Requirement of acceptance as law (opinio juris)

1   The requirement, as a constituent element of customary international law, that the general practice be accepted as law (*opinio juris*) means that the practice in question must be undertaken with a sense of legal right or obligation.
2   A general practice that is accepted as law (*opinio juris*) is to be distinguished from mere usage or habit.

Conclusion 10 Forms of evidence of acceptance as law (opinio juris)

1   Evidence of acceptance as law (*opinio juris*) may take a wide range of forms.
2   Forms of evidence of acceptance as law (*opinio juris*) include, but are not limited to: public statements made on behalf of States; official publications; government legal opinions; diplomatic correspondence; decisions of national courts; treaty provisions; and conduct in connection with resolutions adopted by an international organization or at an intergovernmental conference.

3   Failure to react over time to a practice may serve as evidence of acceptance as law (*opinio juris*), provided that States were in a position to react and the circumstances called for some reaction.

Part Five Significance of certain materials for the identification of customary international law

Conclusion 11 Treaties

1   A rule set forth in a treaty may reflect a rule of customary international law if it is established that the treaty rule:

   (a) codified a rule of customary international law existing at the time when the treaty was concluded;
   (b) has led to the crystallization of a rule of customary international law that had started to emerge prior to the conclusion of the treaty; or
   (c) has given rise to a general practice that is accepted as law (*opinio juris*), thus generating a new rule of customary international law.

2   The fact that a rule is set forth in a number of treaties may, but does not necessarily, indicate that the treaty rule reflects a rule of customary international law.

Conclusion 12 Resolutions of international organizations and intergovernmental conferences

1   A resolution adopted by an international organization or at an intergovernmental conference cannot, of itself, create a rule of customary international law.
2   A resolution adopted by an international organization or at an intergovernmental conference may provide evidence for determining the existence and content of a rule of customary international law, or contribute to its development.
3   A provision in a resolution adopted by an international organization or at an intergovernmental conference may reflect a rule of customary international law if it is established that the provision corresponds to a general practice that is accepted as law (*opinio juris*).

Conclusion 13 Decisions of courts and tribunals

1   Decisions of international courts and tribunals, in particular of the International Court of Justice, concerning the existence and content of rules of customary international law are a subsidiary means for the determination of such rules.
2   Regard may be had, as appropriate, to decisions of national courts concerning the existence and content of rules of customary international law, as a subsidiary means for the determination of such rules.

Conclusion 14 Teachings

Teachings of the most highly qualified publicists of the various nations may serve as a subsidiary means for the determination of rules of customary international law.

Part Six Persistent objector

Conclusion 15 Persistent objector

1   Where a State has objected to a rule of customary international law while that rule was in the process of formation, the rule is not opposable to the State concerned for so long as it maintains its objection.
2   The objection must be clearly expressed, made known to other States, and maintained persistently.
3   The present draft conclusion is without prejudice to any question concerning peremptory norms of general international law (*jus cogens*).

Part Seven Particular customary international law

Conclusion 16 Particular customary international law

1   A rule of particular customary international law, whether regional, local or other, is a rule of customary international law that applies only among a limited number of States.
2   To determine the existence and content of a rule of particular customary international law, it is necessary to ascertain whether there is a general practice among the States concerned that is accepted by them as law (*opinio juris*) among themselves.

General practice + *Opinio juris*

Continental Shelf case (Libyan Arab Jamahiriya/Malta), Judgment of 3 June 1985,
    International Court of Justice
ICJ Reports 1985, 13.

26. The Parties are broadly in agreement as to the sources of the law applicable in this case. Malta is a party to the 1958 Geneva Convention on the Continental Shelf, while Libya is not; the Parties agree that the Convention, and in particular the provisions for delimitation in Article 6, is thus not as such applicable in the relations between them. Both Parties have signed the 1982 United Nations Convention on the Law of the Sea, but that Convention has not yet entered into force, and is therefore not operative as treaty-law; the Special Agreement contains no provisions as to the substantive law applicable. Nor are there any other bilateral or multilateral treaties claimed to be binding on the Parties. The Parties thus agree that the dispute is to be governed by customary international law. This is not at all to Say, however, that the 1982 Convention was regarded by the Parties as irrelevant: the Parties are again in accord in considering that some of its provisions constitute, to a certain extent, the expression of customary international law in the matter. The Parties do not however agree in identifying the provisions which have this status, or the extent to which they are so treated.

27. It is of course axiomatic that the material of customary international law is to be looked for primarily in the actual practice and *opinio juris* of States, even though multilateral conventions may have an important role to play in recording and defining rules deriving from custom, or indeed in developing them. There has in fact been much debate between the Parties in the present case as to the significance, for the delimitation of – and indeed entitlement to – the continental shelf, of State practice in the matter, and this will be examined further at a later stage in the present judgment. Nevertheless, it cannot be denied that the 1982 Convention is of major importance, having been adopted by an overwhelming majority of States; hence it is clearly the duty of the Court, even

independently of the references made to the Convention by the Parties, to consider in what degree any of its relevant provisions are binding upon the Parties as a rule of customary international law.

Opinio juris

North Sea Continental Shelf cases (Federal Republic of Germany v Denmark, Federal Republic of Germany v Netherlands), Judgment of 20 February 1969, International Court of Justice
ICJ Reports 1969, 3.

77. The essential point in this connection – and it seems necessary to stress it – is that even if these instances of action by non-parties to the Convention were much more numerous than they in fact are, they would not, even in the aggregate, suffice in themselves to constitute the *opinio juris*; – for, in order to achieve this result, two conditions must be fulfilled. Not only must the acts concerned amount to a settled practice, but they must also be such, or be carried out in such a way, as to be evidence of a belief that this practice is rendered obligatory by the existence of a rule of law requiring it. The need for such a belief, i.e. the existence of a subjective element, is implicit in the very notion of the *opinio juris sive necessitatis*. The States concerned must therefore feel that they are conforming to what amounts to a legal obligation. The frequency, or even habitual character of the acts is not in itself enough. There are many international acts, e.g. in the field of ceremonial and protocol, which are performed almost invariably, but which are motivated only by considerations of courtesy, convenience or tradition, and not by any sense of legal duty.

78. In this respect the Court follows the view adopted by the Permanent Court of International Justice in the Lotus case, as stated in the following passage, the principle of which is, by analogy, applicable almost word for word, *mutatis mutandis*, to the present case (PCIJ, Series A, No. 10, 1927, at p. 28):

> Even if the rarity of the judicial decisions to be found . . . were sufficient to prove . . . the circumstance alleged . . ., it would merely show that States had often, in practice, abstained from instituting criminal proceedings, and not that they recognized themselves as being obliged to do so; for only if such abstention were based on their being conscious of having a duty to abstain would it be possible to speak of an international custom. The alleged fact does not allow one to infer that States have been conscious of having such a duty; on the other hand, . . . there are other circumstances calculated to show that the contrary is true.

The special customary international law

Asylum case (Colombia v Peru), Judgment of 20 November 1950, International Court of Justice
ICJ Reports 1950, 266.

The Party which relies on a custom of this kind must prove that this custom is established in such a manner that it has become binding on the other Party. The Colombian Government must prove that the rule invoked by it is in accordance with a constant and uniform usage practised by the States in question, and that this usage is the expression of a right appertaining to the State granting asylum and a duty incumbent on the territorial State. This follows from Article 38 of the Statute of the Court, which refers to international custom "as evidence of a general practice accepted as law".

In support of its contention concerning the existence of such a custom, the Colombian Government has referred to a large number of extradition treaties which, as already explained, can have no bearing on the question now under consideration. It has cited conventions and agreements which do not contain any provision concerning the alleged rule of unilateral and definitive qualification such as the Montevideo Convention of 1889 on international penal law, the Bolivarian Agreement of 1911 and the Havana Convention of 1928. It has invoked conventions which have not been ratified by Peru, such as the Montevideo Conventions of 1933 and 1939. The Convention of 1933 has, in fact, been ratified by not more than eleven States and the Convention of 1939 by two States only.

It is particularly the Montevideo Convention of 1933 which Counsel for the Colombian Government has also relied on in this connexion. It is contended that this Convention has merely codified principles which were already recognized by Latin-American custom, and that it is valid against Peru as a proof of customary law. The limited number of States which have ratified this Convention reveals the weakness of this argument, and furthermore, it is invalidated by the preamble which states that this Convention modifies the Havana Convention.

Finally, the Colombian Government has referred to a large number of particular cases in which diplomatic asylum was in fact granted and respected. But it has not shown that the alleged rule of unilateral and definitive qualification was invoked or – if in some cases it was in fact invoked-that it was, apart from conventional stipulations, exercised by the States granting asylum as a right appertaining to them and respected by the territorial States as a duty incumbent on them and not merely for reasons of political expediency. The facts brought to the knowledge of the Court disclose so much uncertainty and contradiction, so much fluctuation and discrepancy in the exercise of diplomatic asylum and in the official views expressed on various occasions, there has been so much inconsistency in the rapid succession of conventions on asylum, ratified by some States and rejected by others, and the practice has been so much influenced by considerations of political expediency in the various cases, that it is not possible to discern in all this any constant and uniform usage, accepted as law, with regard to the alleged rule of unilateral and definitive qualification of the offence.

The Court cannot therefore find that the Colombian Government has proved the existence of such a custom. But even if it could be supposed that such a custom existed between certain Latin-American States only, it could not be invoked against Peru which, far from having by its attitude adhered to it, has, on the contrary, repudiated it by refraining from ratifying the Montevideo Conventions of 1933 and 1939, which were the first to include a rule concerning the qualification of the offence in matters of diplomatic asylum.

General principles of law

Military and Paramilitary Activities in and against Nicaragua (Nicaragua v United States of America), Judgment of 27 June 1986, International Court of Justice, Dissenting Opinion of Judge Oda

51. I do not deny that once a judicial institution is duly seised of a dispute which is not primarily legal, that dispute may be held justiciable, as a matter of principle. In many systems of domestic law, *non liquet* is generally rejected, even if a directly applicable rule of law is lacking, and a judicial court, in relying on the exclusion of *non liquet*, is in theory able to pass judgment. . . .

Speaking of English law, Sir Frederick Pollock in his note on Maine's Ancient Law stated:

> [English judges] are bound to find a decision for every case, however novel it may be; and that decision, so far as it goes beyond drawing inferences of fact, will be authority for other like cases in future; therefore it is part of their duty to lay down new rules if required. Perhaps this is really the first and greatest rule of our customary law.
>
> (Maine, *Ancient Law*, with introduction and notes by Sir Frederick Pollock, 1906, p. 48.)

52. In the case of international law, the Statute of the Permanent Court of International Justice introduced the clause "the general principles of law recognized by civilized nations" mainly to avoid a *non liquet* resulting from the lack of any positive rules. The Model Rules on Arbitral Procedure prepared by the International Law Commission in 1958 state that "the tribunal may not bring in a finding of *non liquet* on the ground of the silence or obscurity of the law to be applied" (Art. 11) (*Yearbook of the International Law Commission*, 1958, Vol. II, p. 84). Here it is important to note that the exclusion of *non liquet* is connected with the absence of an alternative forum.

53. It is definitely not my intention to have the Court declare, as a matter of principle, that disputes relating to use of force or intervention are non-justiciable, nor to contend that the Court is incapable of dealing with the present dispute once it is properly entertained. Yet my opinion is that the fact that the Court *can* entertain a case *once* it is properly seised is a different matter from the suggestion that the Court *must* exercise jurisdiction.

Let me quote a well-known passage from the 1963 Judgment in the case concerning the *Northern Cameroons*:

> In its Judgment of 18 November 1953 on the Preliminary Objection in the Nottebohm case . . . the Court had occasion to deal at some length with the nature of seisin and the consequences of seising the Court. As this Court said in that Judgment: 'the seising of the Court is one thing, the administration of justice is another'. It is the act of the Applicant which seises the Court but even if the Court, when seised, finds that it has jurisdiction, the Court is not compelled in every case to exercise that jurisdiction. There are inherent limitations on the exercise of the judicial function which the Court, as a court of justice, can never ignore. There may thus be an incompatibility between the desires of an applicant, or, indeed, of both parties to a case, on the one hand, and on the other hand the duty of the Court to maintain its judicial character. The Court itself, and not the parties, must be the guardian of the Court's judicial integrity.
>
> (I.C.J *Reports* 1963, p. 29.)

Principles of law which reflect the ideas of natural law

South West Africa (Ethiopia v South Africa, Liberia v South Africa), Judgment of 18 July 1966, International Court of Justice, Dissenting Opinion of Judge Tanaka

Human rights have always existed with the human being. They existed independently of, and before, the State. Alien and even stateless persons must not be deprived of them. Belonging to diverse kinds of communities and societies – ranging from family, club, corporation, to State and international community, the human rights of man must be protected everywhere in this social hierarchy, just as copyright is protected domestically and internationally. There must be no legal vacuum in the protection of human rights. Who can believe, as a reasonable man, that the existence of human rights depends upon the internal or international legislative measures, etc., of the State and that accordingly they can be validly abolished or modified by the will of the State?

If a law exists independently of the will of the State and, accordingly, cannot be abolished or modified even by its constitution, because it is deeply rooted in the conscience of mankind and of any reasonable man, it may be called "natural law" in contrast to "positive law".

Provisions of the constitutions of some countries characterize fundamental human rights and freedoms as "inalienable", "sacred", "eternal", "inviolate", etc. Therefore, the guarantee of fundamental human rights and freedoms possesses a super-constitutional significance.

If we can introduce in the international field a category of law, namely *jus cogens*, recently examined by the International Law Commission, a kind of imperative law which constitutes the contrast to the *jus dispositivum*, capable of being changed by way of agreement between States, surely the law concerning the protection of human rights may be considered to belong to the *jus cogens*.

As an interpretation of Article 38, paragraph 1 (c), we consider that the concept of human rights and of their protection is included in the general principles mentioned in that Article.

Such an interpretation would necessarily be open to the criticism of falling into the error of natural law dogma. But it is undeniable that in Article 38, paragraph 1 (c), some natural law elements are inherent. It extends the concept of the source of international law beyond the limit of legal positivism according to which, the States being bound only by their own will, international law is nothing but the law of the consent and auto-limitation of the State. But this viewpoint, we believe, was clearly overruled by Article 38, paragraph 1 (c), by the fact that this provision does not require the consent of States as a condition of the recognition of the general principles. States which do not recognize this principle or even deny its validity are nevertheless subject to its rule. From this kind of source international law could have the foundation of its validity extended beyond the will of States, that is to say, into the sphere of natural law and assume an aspect of its supra-national and supra-positive character.

The above-mentioned character of Article 38, paragraph 1 (c), of the Statute is proved by the process of the drafting of this article by the Committee of Jurists. The original proposal made by Baron Descamps referred to "*la conscience juridique des peuples civilisés*", a concept which clearly indicated an idea originating in natural law. This proposal met with the opposition of the positivist members of the Committee, represented by Mr. Root. The final draft, namely Article 38, paragraph 1 (c), is the product of a compromise between two schools, naturalist and positivist, and therefore the fact that the natural law idea became incorporated therein is not difficult to discover (see particularly Jean Spiropoulos, *Die Allgemeine Rechtsgrundsätze im Völkerrecht*, 1928, pp. 60 ff.; Bin Cheng, *op. cit.*, pp. 24–26).

Furthermore, an important role which can be played by Article 38, paragraph 1 (c), in filling in gaps in the positive sources in order to avoid *non liquet* decisions, can only be derived from the natural law character of this provision. Professor Brierly puts it, "its inclusion is important as a rejection of the positivistic doctrine, according to which international law consists solely of rules to which States have given their consent" (J. L. Brierly, *The Law of Nations*, 6th ed., p. 63). Mr. Rosenne comments on the general principles of law as follows:

> "Having independent existence, their validity as legal norms does not derive from the consent of the parties as such. . . . The Statute places this element on a footing of formal

equality with two positivist elements of custom and treaty, and thus is positivist recognitions of the Grotian concept of the co-existence implying no subjugation of positive law and so-called natural law of nations in the Grotian sense."

(Shabtai Rosenne, *The International Court of Justice*,
1965, Vol. II, p. 610.) *Barcelona Traction,
Light and Power Company, Limited (Belgium v Spain)*,
Judgment of 5 February 1970.

33. When a State admits into its territory foreign investments or foreign nationals, whether natural or juristic persons, it is bound to extend to them the protection of the law and assumes obligations concerning the treatment to be afforded them. These obligations, however, are neither absolute nor unqualified. In particular, an essential distinction should be drawn between the obligations of a State towards the international community as a whole, and those arising vis-à-vis another State in the field of diplomatic protection. By their very nature the former are the concern of all States. In view of the importance of the rights involved, all States can be held to have a legal interest in their protection; they are obligations *erga omnes*.

34. Such obligations derive, for example, in contemporary international law, from the outlawing of acts of aggression, and of genocide, as also from the principles and rules concerning the basic rights of the human person, including protection from slavery and racial discrimination. Some of the corresponding rights of protection have entered into the body of general international law (*Reservations to the Convention on the Prevention and Punishment of the Crime of Genocide, Advisory Opinion, I.C.J. Reports 1951*, p. 23); others are conferred by international instruments of a universal or quasi-universal character.

35. Obligations the performance of which is the subject of diplomatic protection are not of the same category. It cannot be held, when one such obligation in particular is in question, in a specific case, that all States have a legal interest in its observance. In order to bring a claim in respect of the breach of such an obligation, a State must first establish its right to do so, for the rules on the subject rest on two suppositions:

"The first is that the defendant State has broken an obligation towards the national State in respect of its nationals. The second is that only the party to whom an international obligation is due can bring a claim in respect of its breach."

(*Reparation for Injuries Suffered in the Service of the
United Nations, Advisory Opinion, I.C.J. Reports
1949*, pp. 181–182.)

Erga omnes

East Timor (Portugal v Australia), Judgment of 30 June 1995, International Court of Justice
ICJ Reports 1995, 90.

29. However, Portugal puts forward an additional argument aiming to show that the principle formulated by the Court in the case concerning *Monetary Gold Removed from Rome in 1943* is not applicable in the present case. It maintains, in effect, that the rights which Australia allegedly breached were rights *erga omnes* and that accordingly Portugal could require it, individually, to respect them regardless of whether or not another State had conducted itself in a similarly unlawful manner.

In the Court's view, Portugal's assertion that the right of peoples to self-determination, as it evolved from the Charter and from United Nations practice, has an *erga omnes* character, is irreproachable. The principle of self-determination of peoples has been recognized by the United Nations Charter and in the jurisprudence of the Court (see *Legal Consequences for States of the Continued Presence of South Africa in Namibia (South West Africa) notwithstanding Security Council Resolution 276 (1970), Advisory Opinion, I. C. J. Reports 1971*, pp. 31–32, paras. 52–53; *Western Sahara, Advisory Opinion, I. C. J. Reports 1975*, pp. 31–33, paras. 54–59); it is one of the essential principles of contemporary international law. However, the Court considers that the *erga omnes* character of a norm and the rule of consent to jurisdiction are two different things. Whatever the nature of the obligations invoked, the Court could not rule on the lawfulness of the conduct of a State when its judgment would imply an evaluation of the lawfulness of the conduct of another State which is not a party to the case. Where this is so, the Court cannot act, even if the right in question is a right *erga omnes*.

Jus cogens

Peremptory Norms of General International Law (*jus cogens*), Text of the Draft Conclusions and Draft Annex provisionally adopted by the Drafting Committee on first reading in 2019, International Law Commission
(A/CN.4/L.936)

Part One Introduction

Draft conclusion 1
Scope

The present draft conclusions concern the identification and legal consequences of peremptory norms of general international law (*jus cogens*).

Draft conclusion 2 [3(1)]
Definition of a peremptory norm of general international law (jus cogens)

A peremptory norm of general international law (*jus cogens*) is a norm accepted and recognized by the international community of States as a whole as a norm from which no derogation is permitted and which can be modified only by a subsequent norm of general international law having the same character.

Draft conclusion 3 [3(2)]
General nature of peremptory norms of general international law (jus cogens)

Peremptory norms of general international law (*jus cogens*) reflect and protect fundamental values of the international community, are hierarchically superior to other rules of international law and are universally applicable.

Part Two
Identification of peremptory norm of general international law (*jus cogens*)

Draft conclusion 4
Criteria for the identification of a peremptory norm of general international law (jus cogens)

To identify a peremptory norm of general international law (*jus cogens*), it is necessary to establish that the norm in question meets the following criteria:

(a) it is a norm of general international law; and
(b) it is accepted and recognised by the international community of States as a whole as a norm from which no derogation is permitted and which can be modified only by a subsequent norm of general international law having the same character.

Draft conclusion 5
Bases for peremptory norms of general international law (jus cogens)

1 Customary international law is the most common basis for peremptory norms of general international law (*jus cogens*).
2 Treaty provisions and general principles of law may also serve as bases for peremptory norms of general international law (*jus cogens*).

Draft conclusion 6 [6, 8]
Acceptance and recognition

1 The requirement of "acceptance and recognition" as a criterion for identifying a peremptory norm of general international law (*jus cogens*) is distinct from acceptance and recognition as a norm of general international law.
2 To identify a norm as a peremptory norm of general international law (*jus cogens*), there must be evidence that such a norm is accepted and recognized as one from which no derogation is permitted and which can only be modified by a subsequent norm of general international law having the same character.

Draft conclusion 7
International community of States as a whole

1 It is the acceptance and recognition by the international community of States as a whole that is relevant for the identification of peremptory norms of general international law (*jus cogens*).
2 Acceptance and recognition by a very large majority of States is required for the identification of a norm as a peremptory norm of general international law (*jus cogens*); acceptance and recognition by all States is not required.

3   While the positions of other actors may be relevant in providing context and for assessing acceptance and recognition by the international community of States as a whole, these positions cannot, in and of themselves, form part of such acceptance and recognition.

Draft conclusion 8 [9(1)(2)]
Evidence of acceptance and recognition

1   Evidence of acceptance and recognition that a norm of general international law is a peremptory norm (*jus cogens*) may take a wide range of forms.
2   Such forms of evidence include, but are not limited to: public statements made on behalf of States; official publications; government legal opinions; diplomatic correspondence; legislative and administrative acts; decisions of national courts; treaty provisions; and resolutions adopted by an international organization or at an intergovernmental conference.

Draft conclusion 9 [9(3)(4)]
Subsidiary means for the determination of the peremptory character of norms of general international law (jus cogens)

1   Decisions of international courts and tribunals, in particular of the International Court of Justice, are a subsidiary means for determining the peremptory character of norms of general international law (*jus cogens*).
2   The works of expert bodies established by States or international organizations and the teachings of the most highly qualified publicists of the various nations may also serve as subsidiary means for determining the peremptory character of norms of general international law (*jus cogens*).

Part Three
Legal consequences of peremptory norms of general international law (*jus cogens*)

Draft conclusion 10 [10(1)(2)]
Treaties conflicting with a peremptory norm of general international law (jus cogens)

1   A treaty is void if, at the time of its conclusion, it conflicts with a peremptory norm of general international law (*jus cogens*). The provisions of such a treaty have no legal force.
2   If a new peremptory norm of general international law (*jus cogens*) emerges, any existing treaty which is in conflict with that norm becomes void and terminates. The parties to such a treaty are released from any obligation further to perform the treaty.

Draft conclusion 11
Separability of treaty provisions conflicting
with a peremptory norm of general international
law (jus cogens)

1   A treaty which, at the time of its conclusion, conflicts with a peremptory norm of general international law (*jus cogens*) is void in whole, and no separation of the provisions of the treaty is permitted.

2   A treaty which becomes void because of the emergence of a new peremptory norm of general international law (*jus cogens*) terminates in whole, unless:

    (a)   the provisions that are in conflict with a peremptory norm of general international law (*jus cogens*) are separable from the remainder of the treaty with regard to their application;

    (b)   it appears from the treaty or is otherwise established that acceptance of the said provisions was not an essential basis of the consent of any party to be bound by the treaty as a whole; and

    (c)   continued performance of the remainder of the treaty would not be unjust.

Draft conclusion 12
Consequences of the invalidity
and termination of treaties conflicting with
a peremptory norm of general international law (jus cogens)

1   Parties to a treaty which is void as a result of being in conflict with a peremptory norm of general international law (*jus cogens*) at the time of the treaty's conclusion have a legal obligation to:

    (a)   eliminate as far as possible the consequences of any act performed in reliance on any provision of the treaty which conflicts with a peremptory norm of general international law (*jus cogens*); and

    (b)   bring their mutual relations into conformity with the peremptory norm of general international law (*jus cogens*).

2   The termination of a treaty on account of the emergence of a new peremptory norm of general international law (*jus cogens*) does not affect any right, obligation or legal situation created through the execution of the treaty prior to the termination of the treaty, provided that those rights, obligations or situations may thereafter be maintained only to the extent that their maintenance is not in itself in conflict with the new peremptory norm of general international law (*jus cogens*).

Draft conclusion 13
Absence of effect of reservations
to treaties on peremptory norms of general international
law (jus cogens)

1   A reservation to a treaty provision that reflects a peremptory norm of general international law (*jus cogens*) does not affect the binding nature of that norm, which shall continue to apply as such.

2   A reservation cannot exclude or modify the legal effect of a treaty in a manner contrary to a peremptory norm of general international law (*jus cogens*).

Draft conclusion 14 [15]
Rules of customary international law conflicting with a peremptory norm of general international law (jus cogens)

1   A rule of customary international law does not come into existence if it conflicts with a peremptory norm of general international law (*jus cogens*). This is without prejudice to the possible modification of a peremptory norm of general international law (*jus cogens*) by a subsequent norm of general international law having the same character.
2   A rule of customary international law not of a peremptory character ceases to exist if and to the extent that it conflicts with a new peremptory norm of general international law (*jus cogens*).
3   The persistent objector rule does not apply to peremptory norms of general international law (*jus cogens*).

Draft conclusion 15 [16]
Obligations created by unilateral acts of States conflicting with a peremptory norm of general international law (jus cogens)

1   A unilateral act of a State manifesting the intention to be bound by an obligation under international law that would be in conflict with a peremptory norm of general international law (*jus cogens*) does not create such an obligation.
2   An obligation under international law created by a unilateral act of a State ceases to exist if and to the extent that it conflicts with a new peremptory norm of general international law (*jus cogens*).

Draft conclusion 16 [17(1)]
Obligations created by resolutions, decisions or other acts of international organizations conflicting with a peremptory norm of general international law (jus cogens)

A resolution, decision or other act of an international organization that would otherwise have binding effect does not create obligations under international law if and to the extent that they conflict with a peremptory norm of general international law (*jus cogens*).

Draft conclusion 17 [18]
Peremptory norms of general international law (jus cogens) as obligations owed to the international community as a whole (obligations erga omnes)

1   Peremptory norms of general international law (*jus cogens*) give rise to obligations owed to the international community as a whole (obligations *erga omnes*), in which all States have a legal interest.

2   Any State is entitled to invoke the responsibility of another State for a breach of a peremptory norm of general international law (*jus cogens*), in accordance with the rules on the responsibility of States for internationally wrongful acts.

Draft conclusion 18 [19(1)]
Peremptory norms of general international law (jus cogens) and circumstances precluding wrongfulness

No circumstance precluding wrongfulness under the rules on the responsibility of States for internationally wrongful acts may be invoked with regard to any act of a State which is not in conformity with an obligation arising under a peremptory norm of general international law (*jus cogens*).

Draft conclusion 19 [20(1)(2), 21]
Particular consequences of serious breaches of peremptory norms of general international law (jus cogens)

1   States shall cooperate to bring to an end through lawful means any serious breach by a State of an obligation arising under a peremptory norm of general international law (*jus cogens*).
2   No State shall recognize as lawful a situation created by a serious breach by a State of an obligation arising from a peremptory norm of general international law (*jus cogens*), nor render aid or assistance in maintaining that situation.
3   A breach of an obligation arising under a peremptory norm of general international law (*jus cogens*) is serious if it involves a gross or systematic failure by the responsible State to fulfil that obligation.
4   This draft conclusion is without prejudice to the other consequences that a serious breach by a State of an obligation arising from a peremptory norm of general international law (*jus cogens*) may entail under international law.

Draft conclusion 20 [10(3), 17(2)]
Interpretation and application consistent with peremptory norms of general international law (jus cogens)

Where it appears that there may be a conflict between a peremptory norm of general international law (*jus cogens*) and another rule of international law, the latter is, as far as possible, to be interpreted and applied so as to be consistent with the former.

Draft conclusion 21 [14]
Procedural requirements

1   A State which invokes a peremptory norm of general international law (*jus cogens*) as a ground for the invalidity or termination of a rule of international law is to notify other States concerned

of its claim. The notification is to be in writing and is to indicate the measure proposed to be taken with respect to the rule of international law in question.

2   If none of the other States concerned raises an objection within a period which, except in cases of special urgency, shall not be less than three months, the invoking State may carry out the measure which it has proposed.

3   If any State concerned raises an objection, then the States concerned are to seek a solution through the means indicated in Article 33 of the Charter of the United Nations.

4   If no solution is reached within a period of twelve months, and the objecting State or States concerned offer to submit the matter to the International Court of Justice, the invoking State may not carry out the measure which it has proposed until the dispute is resolved.

5   This draft conclusion is without prejudice to the procedural requirements set forth in the Vienna Convention on the Law of Treaties, the relevant rules concerning the jurisdiction of the International Court of Justice, or other applicable dispute settlement provisions agreed by the States concerned.

Part Four
General provisions

Draft conclusion 22 [22, 23]

The present draft conclusions are without prejudice to consequences that specific peremptory norms of general international law (*jus cogens*) may otherwise entail under international law.

Draft conclusion 23 [24]
Non-exhaustive list

Without prejudice to the existence or subsequent emergence of other peremptory norms of general international law (*jus cogens*), a non-exhaustive list of norms that the International Law Commission has previously referred to as having that status is to be found in the annex to the present draft conclusions.

Annex

(a)   The prohibition of aggression;
(b)   The prohibition of genocide;
(c)   The prohibition of crimes against humanity;
(d)   The basic rules of international humanitarian law;
(e)   The prohibition of racial discrimination and apartheid;
(f)   The prohibition of slavery;
(g)   The prohibition of torture;
(h)   The right of self-determination.

International law and National law

Exchange of Greek and Turkish Populations (Greece v Turkey), Advisory Opinion No. 10 of 21 February 1925, Permanent Court of International Justice
PCIJ Ser B (1925) – No.10.

The Turkish Delegation however maintains that the Convention contains a reference to national legislation and in support of this contention invokes amongst other things Article 18, according to which:

"The High Contracting Parties undertake to introduce in their respective laws such modifications as may be necessary with a view to ensuring the execution of the present Convention."

This clause, however, merely lays stress on a principle which is self-evident, according to which a State which has contracted valid international obligations is bound to make in its legislation such modifications as may be necessary to ensure the fulfilment of the obligations undertaken. The special nature of the Convention for the Exchange of Greek and Turkish Populations, which closely affects matters regulated by national legislation and lays down principles which conflict with certain rights generally recognized as belonging to individuals, sufficiently explains the express inclusion of a clause such as that contained in Article 18. But it does not in the least follow because the contracting Parties are obliged to bring their legislation into harmony with the Convention, that that instrument must be construed as implicitly referring to national legislation in so far as that is not contrary to the Convention.

International Law Commission

Statute of the International Law Commission
Adopted by the General Assembly in Resolution 174 (II) of 21 November 1947, as amended by Resolutions 485 (V) of 12 December 1950, 984 (X) of 3 December 1955, 985 (X) of 3 December 1955 and 36/39 of 18 November 1981.

STATUTE OF THE INTERNATIONAL LAW COMMISSION

Article 1

1   The International Law Commission shall have for its object the promotion of the progressive development of international law and its codification.
2   The Commission shall concern itself primarily with public international law, but is not precluded from entering the field of private international law.

CHAPTER I
ORGANIZATION OF THE INTERNATIONAL LAW COMMISSION

Article 2

1   The Commission shall consist of thirty-four members who shall be persons of recognized competence in international law.
2   No two members of the Commission shall be nationals of the same State.

3　In case of dual nationality a candidate shall be deemed to be a national of the State in which he ordinarily exercises civil and political rights.

Article 3

The members of the Commission shall be elected by the General Assembly from a list of candidates nominated by the Governments of States Members of the United Nations.

Article 4

Each Member may nominate for election not more than four candidates, of whom two may be nationals of the nominating State and two nationals of other States.

Article 5

The names of the candidates shall be submitted in writing by the Governments to the Secretary-General by 1 June of the year in which an election is held, provided that a Government may in exceptional circumstances substitute for a candidate whom it has nominated before 1 June another candidate whom it shall name not later than thirty days before the opening of the General Assembly.

Article 6

The Secretary-General shall as soon as possible communicate to the Governments of States Members the names submitted, as well as any curricula vitae of candidates that may have been submitted by the nominating Governments.

Article 7

The Secretary-General shall prepare the list referred to in article 3 above, comprising in alphabetical order the names of all the candidates duly nominated, and shall submit this list to the General Assembly for the purposes of the election.

Article 8

At the election the electors shall bear in mind that the persons to be elected to the Commission should individually possess the qualifications required and that in the Commission as a whole representation of the main forms of civilization and of the principal legal systems of the world should be assured.

Article 9

1　Those candidates, up to the maximum number prescribed for each regional group, who obtain the greatest number of votes and not less than a majority of the votes of the Members present and voting shall be elected.
2　In the event of more than one national of the same State obtaining a sufficient number of votes for election, the one who obtains the greatest number of votes shall be elected, and, if the votes are equally divided, the elder or eldest candidate shall be elected.

Article 10

The members of the Commission shall be elected for five years. They shall be eligible for re-election.

Article 11

In the case of a vacancy, the Commission itself shall fill the vacancy having due regard to the provisions contained in articles 2 and 8 above.

Article 12

The Commission shall sit at the European Office of the United Nations at Geneva. The Commission shall, however, have the right to hold meetings at other places after consultation with the Secretary-General.

Article 13

Members of the Commission shall be paid travel expenses, and shall also receive a special allowance, the amount of which shall be determined by the General Assembly.

Article 14

The Secretary-General shall, so far as he is able, make available staff and facilities required by the Commission to fulfil its task.

CHAPTER II
FUNCTIONS OF THE INTERNATIONAL LAW COMMISSION

Article 15

In the following articles the expression "progressive development of international law" is used for convenience as meaning the preparation of draft conventions on subjects which have not yet been regulated by international law or in regard to which the law has not yet been sufficiently developed in the practice of States. Similarly, the expression "codification of international law" is used for convenience as meaning the more precise formulation and systematization of rules of international law in fields where there already has been extensive State practice, precedent and doctrine.

A. PROGRESSIVE DEVELOPMENT OF INTERNATIONAL LAW

Article 16

When the General Assembly refers to the Commission a proposal for the progressive development of international law, the Commission shall follow in general a procedure on the following lines:

(a) It shall appoint one of its members to be Rapporteur;

(b) It shall formulate a plan of work;

(c) It shall circulate a questionnaire to the Governments, and shall invite them to supply, within a fixed period of time, data and information relevant to items included in the plan of work;

(d) It may appoint some of its members to work with the Rapporteur on the preparation of drafts pending receipt of replies to this questionnaire;

(e) It may consult with scientific institutions and individual experts; these experts need not necessarily be nationals of Members of the United Nations. The Secretary-General will provide, when necessary and within the limits of the budget, for the expenses of these consultations of experts;

(f) It shall consider the drafts proposed by the Rapporteur;

(g) When the Commission considers a draft to be satisfactory, it shall request the Secretary-General to issue it as a Commission document. The Secretariat shall give all necessary publicity to this document which shall be accompanied by such explanations and supporting material as the Commission considers appropriate. The publication shall include any information supplied to the Commission in reply to the questionnaire referred to in subparagraph (c) above;

(h) The Commission shall invite the Governments to submit their comments on this document within a reasonable time;

(i) The Rapporteur and the members appointed for that purpose shall reconsider the draft, taking into consideration these comments, and shall prepare a final draft and explanatory report which they shall submit for consideration and adoption by the Commission;

(j) The Commission shall submit the draft so adopted with its recommendations through the Secretary-General to the General Assembly.

Article 17

1 The Commission shall also consider proposals and draft multilateral conventions submitted by Members of the United Nations, the principal organs of the United Nations other than the General Assembly, specialized agencies, or official bodies established by intergovernmental agreement to encourage the progressive development of international law and its codification, and transmitted to it for that purpose by the Secretary-General.

2 If in such cases the Commission deems it appropriate to proceed with the study of such proposals or drafts, it shall follow in general a procedure on the following lines:

(a) The Commission shall formulate a plan of work, and study such proposals or drafts, and compare them with any other proposals and drafts on the same subjects;

(b) The Commission shall circulate a questionnaire to all Members of the United Nations and to the organs, specialized agencies and official bodies mentioned above which are concerned with the question, and shall invite them to transmit their comments within a reasonable time;

(c) The Commission shall submit a report and its recommendations to the General Assembly. Before doing so, it may also, if it deems it desirable, make an interim report to the organ or agency which has submitted the proposal or draft;

(*d*) If the General Assembly should invite the Commission to proceed with its work in accordance with a suggested plan, the procedure outlined in article 16 above shall apply. The questionnaire referred to in paragraph (c) of that article may not, however, be necessary.

B. CODIFICATION OF INTERNATIONAL LAW

Article 18

1 The Commission shall survey the whole field of international law with a view to selecting topics for codification, having in mind existing drafts, whether governmental or not.
2 When the Commission considers that the codification of a particular topic is necessary and desirable, it shall submit its recommendations to the General Assembly.
3 The Commission shall give priority to requests of the General Assembly to deal with any question.

Article 19

1 The Commission shall adopt a plan of work appropriate to each case.
2 The Commission shall, through the Secretary-General, address to Governments a detailed request to furnish the texts of laws, decrees, judicial decisions, treaties, diplomatic correspondence and other documents relevant to the topic being studied and which the Commission deems necessary.

Article 20

The Commission shall prepare its drafts in the form of articles and shall submit them to the General Assembly together with a commentary containing:

(*a*) Adequate presentation of precedents and other relevant data, including treaties, judicial decisions and doctrine;
(*b*) Conclusions defining:

   (i) The extent of agreement on each point in the practice of States and in doctrine;
   (ii) Divergencies and disagreements which exist, as well as arguments invoked in favour of one or another solution.

Article 21

1 When the Commission considers a draft to be satisfactory, it shall request the Secretary-General to issue it as a Commission document. The Secretariat shall give all necessary publicity to the document, including such explanations and supporting material as the Commission may consider appropriate. The publication shall include any information supplied to the Commission by Governments in accordance with article 19. The Commission shall decide whether the opinions of any scientific institution or individual experts consulted by the Commission shall be included in the publication.
2 The Commission shall request Governments to submit comments on this document within a reasonable time.

Article 22

Taking such comments into consideration, the Commission shall prepare a final draft and explanatory report, which it shall submit with its recommendations through the Secretary-General to the General Assembly.

Article 23

1   The Commission may recommend to the General Assembly:

   (a)   To take no action, the report having already been published;
   (b)   To take note of or adopt the report by resolution;
   (c)   To recommend the draft to Members with a view to the conclusion of a convention;
   (d)   To convoke a conference to conclude a convention.

2   Whenever it deems it desirable, the General Assembly may refer drafts back to the Commission for reconsideration or redrafting.

Article 24

The Commission shall consider ways and means for making the evidence of customary international law more readily available, such as the collection and publication of documents concerning State practice and of the decisions of national and international courts on questions of international law, and shall make a report to the General Assembly on this matter.

CHAPTER III
COOPERATION WITH OTHER BODIES

Article 25

1   The Commission may consult, if it considers it necessary, with any of the organs of the United Nations on any subject which is within the competence of that organ.
2   All documents of the Commission which are circulated to Governments by the Secretary-General shall also be circulated to such organs of the United Nations as are concerned. Such organs may furnish any information or make any suggestions to the Commission.

Article 26

1   The Commission may consult with any international or national organizations, official or non-official, on any subject entrusted to it if it believes that such a procedure might aid it in the performance of its functions.
2   For the purpose of distribution of documents of the Commission, the Secretary-General, after consultation with the Commission, shall draw up a list of national and international

organizations concerned with questions of international law. The Secretary-General shall endeavour to include on this list at least one national organization of each Member of the United Nations.

3   In the application of the provisions of this article, the Commission and the Secretary-General shall comply with the resolutions of the General Assembly and the other principal organs of the United Nations concerning relations with Franco Spain and shall exclude both from consultations and from the list, organizations which have collaborated with the nazis and fascists.

4   The advisability of consultation by the Commission with intergovernmental organizations whose task is the codification of international law, such as those of the Pan American Union, is recognized.

Principles of international law concerning friendly relations and co-operation among states in accordance with the Charter of the United Nations

DOI: 10.4324/9781003213772-3

THE NOTION OF THE PRINCIPLES OF INTERNATIONAL LAW CONCERNING FRIENDLY RELATIONS AND CO-OPERATION AMONG STATES IN ACCORDANCE WITH THE CHARTER OF THE UNITED NATIONS

ten principles of international law
basic principles of international law
Declaration on Principles of International Law concerning Friendly Relations and
Co-operation among States in accordance with the Charter of the United Nations
normative carcass
in the context of the other principles
policy-making role
constant motion

The ten principles

There are **ten principles of international law** relating to friendly relations and co-operation among states which are established through the sources of international law.

Meaning of the principles of international law relating to friendly relations and co-operation among states

In general, these ten principles:

1   are the **basic principles of international law** as noted in the **Declaration on Principles of International Law concerning Friendly Relations and Co-operation among States in accordance with the Charter of the United Nations** of 1970 adopted by the General Assembly of the United Nations. Consequently, all states shall be guided by these principles in international affairs and shall aim to develop their mutual relations based on the strict observance of the principles mentioned earlier.[173] At the same time, it is of crucial importance to distinguish these principles from the general principles of law, since

173 A/RES/2625(XXV) of 24 October 1970.

a) they are not independent sources of international law;
b) they were developed through the sources of international law; and
c) their main focus is the friendly relations and co-operation among states;

2 form the **normative carcass** for the friendly relations and co-operation among states, due to each principle having the normative essence representing a complex of certain widely recognised norms of international law;

3 shall be explained interdependently, because under the Declaration on Principles of International Law concerning Friendly Relations and Co-operation among States in accordance with the Charter of the United Nations: 'In their interpretation and application the above principles are interrelated and each principle should be construed **in the context of the other principles**'. Therefore, there exists a complicated interdependence between these principles;

4 have a **policy-making role**, since they indicate the direction for the development of the interstate system. Consequently, these principles have the future-oriented character;

5 reflect the essence of the interstate system and develop alongside the changes in the system. Therefore, they happen to be in **constant motion**, and their normative content modifies accordingly.

Besides, some norms of these principles have the binding force of *jus cogens*.

THE FORMATION OF THE PRINCIPLES OF INTERNATIONAL LAW RELATING TO FRIENDLY RELATIONS AND CO-OPERATION AMONG STATES

seven principles
Charter of the United Nations Organisation
Woodrow Wilson's Fourteen Points
Paris Peace Conference
Treaty of Versailles
Covenant of the League of Nations
Helsinki Declaration on Principles Guiding Relations between Participating States
Helsinki Final Act

The principles enshrined in the UN Charter

Seven principles have been generated based on the **Charter of the United Nations Organisation** signed on 26 June 1945 in San Francisco at the conclusion of the United Nations Conference on International Organisation and came into force on 24 October 1945.

Historical development of these principles

However, some of them trace their roots to the past few centuries. For instance, there is a consensus that the principle of sovereign equality of states arose from the Peace of

Westphalia (1648). From that time on, the nation-states were regarded as principally equal actors in international relations.

Woodrow Wilson's Fourteen Points (of 1918), the **Paris Peace Conference** of 1919–1920, and the **Treaty of Versailles** of 1919 and its Part I, the crown jewel of Versailles – the **Covenant of the League of Nations** – are the significant landmarks in the process of forming the principles of international law concerning friendly relations and co-operation among states.

1970 Declaration on Principles of International Law

At the turn of the sixties, an item on principles of international law concerning friendly relations and co-operation among states was inscribed on the agenda of the General Assembly of the United Nations. In 1970, the Declaration on Principles of International Law concerning Friendly Relations and Co-operation among States in accordance with the Charter of the United Nations was unanimously adopted by the General Assembly.

Helsinki Declaration

The next landmark was the **Helsinki Declaration on Principles Guiding Relations between Participating States** of the Final Act of the Conference on Security and Co-operation in Europe held in Finland during the summer of 1975 (or simply the **Helsinki Final Act**).[174] Thirty-five states, including the USA, Canada, and all European states except Albania and Andorra signed the declaration in an attempt to improve relations between the Communist bloc and the West.

The Final Act added three new principles to the already-existing seven principles of international law concerning friendly relations and co-operation among states.

THE LIST OF THE PRINCIPLES OF INTERNATIONAL LAW RELATING TO FRIENDLY RELATIONS AND CO-OPERATION AMONG STATES

Principles Guiding Relations between Participating States
fundamental rights of states
equality
independence
peaceful co-existence

---

174 The Helsinki Final Act is available on the official website of the OSCE <www.osce.org/helsinki-final-act>.

Seven principles

According to the Declaration on Principles of International Law concerning Friendly Relations and Co-operation among States in accordance with the Charter of the United Nations of 1970, the principles of international law relating to friendly relations and co-operation among states are:

1   The principle that states shall refrain in their international relations from the threat or use of force against the territorial integrity or political independence of any state or in any other manner inconsistent with the purposes of the United Nations.
2   The principle that states shall settle their international disputes by peaceful means in such a manner that international peace and security and justice are not endangered.
3   The duty not to intervene in matters within the domestic jurisdiction of any state, in accordance with the Charter.
4   The duty of states to co-operate with one another in accordance with the Charter.
5   The principle of equal rights and self-determination of peoples.
6   The principle of sovereign equality of states.
7   The principle that states shall fulfil in good faith the obligations assumed by them in accordance with the Charter.

Ten principles

According to the Helsinki Final Act of 1975, the principles of international law relating to friendly relations and co-operation among states are called the **Principles Guiding Relations between Participating States**, which are:

1   sovereign equality, respect for the rights inherent in sovereignty;
2   refraining from the threat or use of force;
3   inviolability of frontiers;
4   territorial integrity of states;
5   peaceful settlement of disputes;
6   non-intervention in internal affairs;
7   respect for human rights and fundamental freedoms, including the freedom of thought, conscience, religion, or belief;
8   equal rights and self-determination of peoples;
9   co-operation among states; and
10 fulfilment in good faith of obligations under international law.

The fundamental rights of states

The principles of international law relating to friendly relations and co-operation among states are the basis for contemporary understanding of the notion of the **fundamental rights of states**, which are closely interlinked with the three ideas (legal concepts) concerning the architecture of the modern interstate world: namely, the ideas of **equality**, **independence**, and **peaceful co-existence**.

EQUALITY – SOVEREIGN EQUALITY, RESPECT FOR THE RIGHTS INHERENT IN SOVEREIGNTY

legal equality of states
artificially equal
exclusive competences within their territory and in their internal affairs
same capacity to make international law
compulsory international process, jurisdiction, or settlement
duty to respect the personality of other states
sovereign equality, respect for the rights inherent in sovereignty

Legal equality of states

The **legal equality of states** is one of the building blocks on which the current world order was founded.

However, the legal equality of states shall not trick us into believing that this principle makes all states **artificially equal** since state capabilities and power-projecting abilities do sometimes differ rather significantly. Nor does it suggest that the states shall be equal in relation to each field of interaction since there are specific areas in which the responsibility of certain states exceeds the capabilities of a state or the group of states (e.g. the system of the UN Security Council).

The contemporary understanding of the legal equality of states

The modern understanding of the idea of legal equality of states suggests that irrespective of their size or power:

- all states have the same functions, such as maintaining order in their respective societies, making the internal rules of universal application, conducting wars, and maintaining peace;
- in principle, states have **exclusive competences within their territory and in their internal affairs**;
- every state in the interstate system has the **same capacity to make international law**, which first of all means that, without its consent, no international legal rule can be made which constitutes legal obligations or rights of a state, especially in the forms of ordinary sources of international law – international treaties or customs;
- the states cannot be subjected to **compulsory international process, jurisdiction, or settlement** without their consent; and
- every state has the **duty to respect the personality of other states**.

In sum, the equality of states is a legal concept which is rooted in the post-Westphalian world order and is mainly linked with the principle of '**sovereign equality, respect for the rights inherent in sovereignty**'.

Sovereign equality according to the Declaration on Principles of International Law

As is emphasised in the Declaration on Principles of International Law concerning Friendly Relations and Co-operation among States in accordance with the Charter of the United Nations,

> [A]ll States enjoy sovereign equality. They have equal rights and duties (obligations) and are equal members of the international community, notwithstanding differences of an economic, social, political or other nature.
>
> In particular, sovereign equality includes the following elements:

- States are juridically equal;
- Each State enjoys the rights inherent in full sovereignty;
- Each State has the duty to respect the personality of other States;
- The territorial integrity and political independence of the State are inviolable;
- Each State has the right freely to choose and develop its political, social, economic and cultural systems;
- Each State has the duty to comply fully and in good faith with its international obligations and to live in peace with other States.

INDEPENDENCE – NON-INTERVENTION IN INTERNAL AFFAIRS

Draft Declaration on the Rights and Duties of States
true nature of international law
Military and Paramilitary Activities in and against Nicaragua case
prohibited intervention
element of coercion
armed intervention
aggression
attempted threats

The notion of independence of states

The independence of states as an idea is also rooted in the post-Westphalian world order and is linked with the principles of 'sovereign equality, respect for the rights inherent in sovereignty', 'non-intervention in internal affairs', and 'refraining from the threat or use of force'.

The legal idea of independence

The legal concept of independence was defined in the **Draft Declaration on the Rights and Duties of States** prepared in 1949 by the International Law Commission. According to the Draft Declaration:

> Every State has the right to independence and hence to exercise freely, without dictation by another State, all its legal powers, including the choice of its own form of government. . . . Every State has the right to exercise jurisdiction over its territory and over all persons and things therein, subject to the immunities recognized by international law.[175]

The legal idea of independence is maintained by the **true nature of international law** as it was originally developed since, as defined by the International Court of Justice under the landmark judgment on the *Military and Paramilitary Activities in and against Nicaragua* **case** *(Nicaragua v United States of America)*: In international law 'there are no rules, other than such rules as may be accepted by the state concerned, by treaty or otherwise, whereby the level of armaments of a sovereign state can be limited, and this principle is valid for all states without exception.'[176]

At the same time, the existence of the *jus cogens* norms cannot serve as proof to argue the opposite because peremptory norms are also (1) founded on the concept, which itself is shared and accepted by the states and (2) any specific *jus cogens* rule shall also be accepted and recognised by the international community of states as a whole to become a norm from which no derogation is permitted.

Non-intervention in internal affairs

The principle of non-intervention in the internal affairs of the states stands as a safeguard of the independence of the states.

The general notion of the prohibited intervention

The **prohibited intervention** comprises economic, political, military, or any other type of measures to coerce another state 'in order to obtain from it the subordination of the exercise of its sovereign rights and to secure from it advantages of any kind.'[177]

As defined by the International Court of Justice in the *Military and Paramilitary Activities in and against Nicaragua* case (*Nicaragua v United States of America*):

> A prohibited intervention must accordingly be one bearing on matters in which each State is permitted, by the principle of State sovereignty, to decide freely. One of these

---

175 Articles 1 and 2 of the Draft Declaration on the Rights and Duties of States.
176 *Military and Paramilitary Activities in and against Nicaragua (Nicaragua v United States of America)*, Judgment of 27 June 1986.
177 Declaration on Principles of International Law concerning Friendly Relations and Co-operation among States.

is the choice of a political, economic, social and cultural system, and the formulation of foreign policy. Intervention is wrongful when it uses methods of coercion in regard to such choices, which must remain free ones. The element of coercion . . . forms the very essence of prohibited intervention.[178]

The element of coercion

Therefore, particular attention should be paid to determining the **element of coercion** when defining an act as an illegal intervention. Some scholars who have tackled this question accentuate certain features from the nature of a coercive act. For example, they argue that the interference in principle should be violent or 'dictatorial' and must have a real impact on the state in question for an act to be regarded as an illegal intervention. All this suggests that in its minor forms or a simple intervention shall not be considered to be an act of prohibited intervention.

The relationship between the two terms – intervention and aggression

Consequently, the principle of non-intervention includes, but is not limited to, the prohibition of the threat or use of force against the territorial integrity or political independence of any state. The prohibited intervention, therefore, contains the **armed intervention** and so is a general notion which includes the acts of **aggression**.

The direct or indirect intervention

The prohibited intervention may be exercised directly or indirectly. Both forms of intervention are regarded as violations of international law. No state shall organise, assist, foment, finance, incite, or tolerate subversive, terrorist, or armed activities directed towards the violent overthrow of the government of another state or interfere in civil strife in another state.

The attempted threats against the personality of the state

Finally, the principle of non-intervention prohibits **attempted threats** against the personality of the state or its political, economic, and cultural elements. As it is prescribed under the Charter of the Organisation of American States:

> No state or group of states has the right to intervene, directly or indirectly, for any reason whatever, in the internal or external affairs of any other state. The foregoing principle prohibits not only armed force but also any other form of interference or

178 *Military and Paramilitary Activities in and against Nicaragua (Nicaragua v United States of America),* Judgment of 27 June 1986.

attempted threat against the personality of the state or against its political, economic and cultural elements.[179]

PEACEFUL CO-EXISTENCE – REFRAINING FROM THE THREAT OR USE OF FORCE

The following sayings/interpretations about war demonstrate how multifaceted war is as a social phenomenon and how important it was to impose restrictions on the use of force:

- 'War is hell.' – Napoleon I (1769–1821);
- 'War is the continuation of politics by other means.' – Karl von Clausewitz (1780–1831);
- 'The ability to get to the verge without getting into the war is the necessary art. . . . We walked to the brink and we looked it in the face.' – John Foster Dulles (1888–1959);
- 'Civilization is nothing more than the effort to reduce the use of force to the last resort.' – Josè Ortega y Gasset (1883–1955).[180]

The historical origins

right to war
just war
Covenant of the League of Nations
direct treatment to the war
Kellogg-Briand Pact
general renunciation of war
Stimson Doctrine
non-recognition of international territorial changes
ex injuria jus non oritur
United Nations Charter
principle of refraining from the threat or use of force
individual or collective self-defence
collective security system

Right to war

Historically, the **right to war** was regarded as an inherent and unlimited right of a state.[181] Efforts to restrain this unlimited right periodically appeared and reappeared on the agenda

179 Article 19 of the OAS Charter.
180 *The Yale Book of Quotations*, Fred R. Shapiro (ed) (Yale University Press 2006) 546, 157, 219; *The Oxford Dictionary of Quotations* (n 18) 3.26.
181 'The term "State" appeared rather late in human history. Only at the turn of the fifteenth century, the term began to be used in a sense that may be compared to its contemporary use.' David Raič, *Statehood and the Law of Self-Determination* (Kluwer Law International 2002) 20.

through the centuries, mostly in connection with the concept of the **just war**, which argued that some wars could be morally justifiable if they did not violate specific predefined criteria on the just causes of war.[182]

Covenant of the League of Nations

The tangible legal limitation (at the global level) on the right to conduct a war was included after the First World War in the **Covenant of the League of Nations**, which declared any war against any of its members as a war against the whole League and therefore, against every member of the League separately:

> Any war or threat of war, whether immediately affecting any of the Members of the League or not, is hereby declared a matter of concern to the whole League, and the League shall take any action that may be deemed wise and effectual to safeguard the peace of nations. In case any such emergency should arise, the Secretary General shall on the request of any Member of the League forthwith summon a meeting of the Council.

At the same time, the Covenant assigned peaceful conflict resolution mechanisms and restricted the **direct treatment to the war**. According to the Covenant:

> The Members of the League agree that if there should arise between them any dispute likely to lead to a rupture, they will submit the matter either to arbitration or to inquiry by the Council, and they agree in no case to resort to war until three months after the award by the arbitrators or the report by the Council. In any case under this Article the award of the arbitrators shall be made within a reasonable time, and the report of the Council shall be made within six months after the submission of the dispute.[183]

However, even with regard to the prohibition of the direct resort to war, some authors argue that the provisions of the Covenant, as well as some subsequent international documents of that era, covered only certain types of war.[184]

Kellogg-Briand Pact

The next significant accomplishment in placing restrictions on the right to war was the **Kellogg-Briand Pact** (General Treaty for Renunciation of War as an Instrument of National Policy) of 1928, sometimes called the Pact of Paris after the city in which it was signed. The

---

182 Starting with the Indian Hindu epic the Mahabharata, continuing with the ancient Roman approaches, the Christian thinkers, and so on.

183 Articles 11 and 12 of Covenant of the League of Nations.

184 'In short, the Covenant does not limit the use of armed force for sanctioning purposes, but only the war as declared war; furthermore the limit does not encounter war itself, as a measure considered under a substantial point of view, but only places a temporal condition . . . to make use of it.' Giuliana Scotto, 'The Use of Force in International Law: On the Historical Evolution and Actual Content of the Prohibition' (2019) *Munich, GRIN Verlag* <www.grin.com/document/489008> accessed 4 April 2021.

Pact was a short agreement (only three articles) emphasising the **general renunciation of war** as an instrument for the solution of international controversies. According to the Pact:

> The High Contracting Parties solemnly declare in the names of their respective peoples that they condemn recourse to war for the solution of international controversies, and renounce it, as an instrument of national policy in their relations with one another. . . . The High Contracting Parties agree that the settlement or solution of all disputes or conflicts of whatever nature or of whatever origin they may be, which may arise among them, shall never be sought except by pacific means.[185]

Stimson Doctrine

In the shadow of this Pact, the **Stimson Doctrine**, as the official policy of the United States, was announced in 1932 via a note addressed to Japan and China on the **non-recognition of international territorial changes** executed by force. The doctrine was an application of the principle of *ex injuria jus non oritur*, which stipulates that unjust acts cannot be translated into law.

United Nations Charter

After World War II, advances on the prohibition of war were successfully completed in Article 2 (4) of the **United Nations Charter**, which established the normative essence of the **principle of refraining from the threat or use of force**:

> All Members shall refrain in their international relations from the threat or use of force against the territorial integrity or political independence of any state, or in any other manner inconsistent with the Purposes of the United Nations.

Thus, in this context, the Charter replaced the traditional notion of war with the term 'force' and prescribed to refrain either from (1) the threat or (2) the use of [armed] force.[186] The replacement was accomplished to avoid the legal uncertainties stemming from the

---

185 Articles I and II of the Kellogg-Briand Pact. 'But even in this case we have a twofold weakness. On the one hand, only the resort to war, and not to every kind of use of armed force, is prohibited (therefore armed reprisals remain lawful, as indeed attested by the practice of those years; as well as all those methods of resorting to armed force not falling within the notion of war); on the other hand, no sanctioning mechanism alternative to the war is established, particularly no restriction in the use of armed force is provided for in the case of violation of the prohibition to refrain from resorting to war. Despite the fact that, within 1939, 63 States had adhered to the Pact of Paris, the convulsive thirties of the twentieth century testify the fragility of this system and quickly ruined towards the second great world conflict.' Scotto (n 184).

186 The general tendency in state practice, embodied in the Declaration on Principles of International Law concerning Friendly Relations and Co-operation among States in accordance with the Charter of the United Nations of 1970, is to limit its meaning to military force.

term 'war' in the aftermath of the First World War by focusing on the relatively neutral and technical notion of 'force'.

However, unlike the Kellogg-Briand Pact, the Charter did not choose as the only option the general renunciation of war as an instrument of national policy in foreign affairs. The general prescription is filled with practical rules and systems. Firstly, the principle of peaceful settlement of international disputes has been advanced. Secondly, the legal mechanisms to respond against the aggression were developed, namely:

- the **individual or collective self-defence**; and
- the **collective security system** (UN Security Council or General Assembly mechanisms, including Chapter VI [Pacific settlement of disputes] and Chapter VII [Action with respect to threats to the peace, breaches of the peace, and acts of aggression).

Aggression

aggression is the most severe form of violation of the principle
crime of aggression
UN General Assembly Resolution, Definition of Aggression
acts of aggression
annexation by the use of force
lawful use of force
first use of armed force
sufficient gravity
collective security system
use of force
armed attack

Aggression and the principle of refraining from the threat or use of force

Firstly, **aggression is the most severe form of violation of the principle** which stipulates refraining from the threat or use of force. No consideration is given to the cause of aggression; whether it is political, economic, military, or otherwise, it may not serve as justification for an act of aggression against a state.

Besides, the aggression:

- is a derogation from and violation of the imperative norm of general international law;
- is a crime against international peace (referred to as the **crime of aggression**); and
- triggers appropriate international responsibility.

UN General Assembly Resolution

In 1974, the UN General Assembly adopted by consensus Resolution 3314 (XXIX), annexing the Definition of Aggression to the Resolution (UN **General Assembly Resolution,**

Definition of Aggression). The Definition begins with a very broad identification of what shall be considered an aggression:

> Aggression is the use of armed force by a State against the sovereignty, territorial integrity or political independence of another State, or in any other manner inconsistent with the Charter of the United Nations, as set out in this Definition. Explanatory note: In this Definition the term 'State': (a) Is used without prejudice to questions of recognition or to whether a State is a member of the United Nations; (b) Includes the concept of a 'group of States' where appropriate.[187]

Subsequently, the Definition enumerates specific examples of the **acts of aggression**:

> Any of the following acts, regardless of a declaration of war, shall . . . qualify as an act of aggression:

(a) The invasion or attack by the armed forces of a State of the territory of another State, or any military occupation, however temporary, resulting from such invasion or attack, or any **annexation by the use of force** of the territory of another State or part thereof;

(b) Bombardment by the armed forces of a State against the territory of another State or the use of any weapons by a State against the territory of another State;

(c) The blockade of the ports or coasts of a State by the armed forces of another State;

(d) An attack by the armed forces of a State on the land, sea or air forces, or marine and air fleets of another State;

(e) The use of armed forces of one State which are within the territory of another State with the agreement of the receiving State, in contravention of the conditions provided for in the agreement or any extension of their presence in such territory beyond the termination of the agreement;

(f) The action of a State in allowing its territory, which it has placed at the disposal of another State, to be used by that other State for perpetrating an act of aggression against a third State;

(g) The sending by or on behalf of a State of armed bands, groups, irregulars or mercenaries, which carry out acts of armed force against another State of such gravity as to amount to the acts listed above, or its substantial involvement therein.[188]

Criteria for the identification of an aggression

However, under this document, even in a case of the formal presence of the aforementioned manifestations of aggression, it is not sufficient to determine an act to be an aggression.

---

187 Article 1 of the Annex to the UN General Assembly Resolution A/RES/3314(XXIX) of 14 December 1974 (Definition of Aggression).

188 Article 3 of the Annex to the UN General Assembly Resolution A/RES/3314(XXIX) (Definition of Aggression).

There are specific criteria for the identification of aggression and the application of this Definition to a given case:

- The scope of the UN Charter determines the application of the Definition, including its provisions concerning the **lawful use of force**, namely, in cases of (1) the individual or collective self-defence; (2) the reaction of the UN collective security system; and (3) the application of the right to self-determination, freedom, and independence of peoples 'under colonial and racist regimes or other forms of alien domination' and specifically 'the right of these peoples to struggle to that end and to seek and receive support, in accordance with the principles of the Charter'.[189]
- The **first use of armed force** by a state in contravention of the Charter may constitute *prima facie*[190] evidence of an act of aggression if the UN Security Council does not evaluate the act differently.
- The UN Security Council may, in conformity with the UN Charter, 'conclude that a determination that an act of aggression has been committed would not be justified in the light of other relevant circumstances, including the fact that the acts concerned or their consequences are not of **sufficient gravity**.'[191]
- The acts manifesting an aggression listed here are not exhaustive, and the UN Security Council may determine that other acts constitute aggression under the provisions of the UN Charter. Nonetheless, the term 'force' as provided in the Definition of Aggression does not cover all its possible manifestations, such as economic or other types of coercion or the threat of force, which were omitted on purpose.[192] The discretion of the Security Council with respect to the determination of aggression, therefore, is not unlimited and is framed by the UN Charter and the Definition of Aggression provided here.

---

189 Article 7 of the Annex to the UN General Assembly Resolution A/RES/3314(XXIX) (Definition of Aggression): 'Nothing in this Definition, and in particular article 3, could in any way prejudice the right to self-determination, freedom and independence, as derived from the Charter, of peoples forcibly deprived of that right and referred to in the Declaration on Principles of International Law concerning Friendly Relations and Co-operation among States in accordance with the Charter of the United Nations, particularly peoples under colonial and racist regimes or other forms of alien domination: nor the right of these peoples to struggle to that end and to seek and receive support, in accordance with the principles of the Charter and in conformity with the above-mentioned Declaration.'

190 'PRIMA FACIE [L. *primus* / first + *facies* / face, form, figure; at first view, on its face] On first appearance.' Emanuel (n 90) 297.

191 Article 2 of the Annex to the UN General Assembly Resolution A/RES/3314(XXIX) (Definition of Aggression).

192 Same approach is maintained by the General Assembly Resolution A/RES/2625(XXV) of 1970 (Declaration on Principles of International Law concerning Friendly Relations and Co-operation among States in accordance with the Charter of the United Nations), which the principle that states shall refrain in their international relations from the threat or use of force links solely with the military force. Economic and other types of coercion, on the other hand, are covered under the principle of non-intervention.

The comprehensive content of aggression

On the whole, the term 'aggression' obtains a rather complex content which means that the provisions mentioned earlier shall be understood and applied as a set of interrelated claims crosscutting and, at times, constraining each other.

Thus, aggression is (1) the use of armed force by a state (the act of aggression shall be imputable to the subject responsible) (2) against another state or in any other manner inconsistent with the Charter of the United Nations (e.g. very rarely also against the people who obtained the status of a subject of international law)[193] (3) against the sovereignty, territorial integrity, or political independence of another subject (the goal) (4) stipulating the existence of sufficient gravity (the real outcome should be large scale and, in fact, threatening to the sovereignty, territorial integrity, or independence of another subject). At the same time, (5) although the UN Security Council has a prevailing role in defining the act of aggression, (6) the first use of armed force by a state in contravention of the UN Charter may constitute *prima facie* evidence of an act of aggression, and (7) the subject of international law which sustained aggression has the immediate right to individual or collective self-defence. However, (8) there are certain limits even in cases in which the use of force is lawful, while violating the scope of rights to self-defence, self-determination, or even the mandate granted by the UN **collective security system** may be considered as the origin of a new (another) aggression.

The interrelationship between the terms 'use of force', 'aggression', and 'armed attack'

The UN Charter refers to the terms '**use of force**', 'aggression', and '**armed attack**' on different occasions. However, in the Charter, these terms are not defined, and thus, there is a need to identify the correlation between these terms.

Some authors use these terms interchangeably; however, many others refer to the so-called 'cascading relationship' between the terms 'use of force', 'aggression', and 'armed attack', where the first term denotes a broader concept, the second a narrower understanding, and the third an even more limited meaning.[194]

---

193 As stressed in the UN General Assembly Resolution A/RES/37/43 of 3 December 1982: 'Considering that the denial of the inalienable rights of the Palestinian people to self-determination, sovereignty, independence and return to Palestine and the repeated acts of aggression by Israel against the peoples of the region constitute a serious threat to international peace and security.'

194 'If some States occasionally insisted that the concepts were one and the same, most agreed that there existed a cascading relationship between the terms "use of force", "aggression" and "armed attack". As one delegate noted: "Article 2, paragraph 4, prohibited also the threat of force and was therefore concerned with a broader concept than the use of armed force. A more limited concept was invoked in Article 1 and 39 of the Charter, and a still more limited one of "armed attack" in Article 51. "' Tom Ruys, *"Armed attack" and Article 51 of the UN Charter: Customary Law and Practice* (Cambridge University Press 2010) 134.

A more plausible version of the interrelationship is provided by the contextual explanation of these terms. For example, taking into account the meanings introduced in the UN Charter, the following conclusions can be generalised:

1   The right to self-defence. The term 'armed attack' is referred to in Article 51 of the UN Charter as a precondition for the exercise of the inherent right of individual or collective self-defence. Since an armed attack triggers the right to self-defence, there should be the least of requirements to protect the country concerned, so long as there may be no time to examine whether the act of aggression takes place or not. Thus, not every armed attack is tantamount to aggression. At the same time, not every illegal use of force justifies self-defence, such as the minor violations of the prohibition of the use of force not fulfilling the requirements for the use of armed force in self-defence which are discussed next.

2   The principle of refraining from the threat or use of force. The term 'use of force' is formulated in Article 2(4) of the UN Charter denoting the principle of refraining from the threat or use of force. In practice, the term has two connotations – either it includes both the threat or use of armed force against the territorial integrity or political independence of any state or in any other manner inconsistent with the purposes of the United Nations or only designates a narrower meaning not covering the threat of armed force.

At the same time, the prohibition prescribed in Article 2(4) of the UN Charter only relates to friendly relations and co-operation among states, and hence, it is adopted to limit the interstate use of force. On the other hand, although initially under the UN Charter, the terms 'aggression' and 'armed attack' were focused on the states as well; over time, particular non-state entities also were gradually considered as addressees to be protected against an aggression and armed with the right to exercise self-defence. Moreover, post-9/11, further discussions took place concerning the armed attacks by the non-state groups which should be regarded as triggering the right to self-defence.[195]

3   The collective response. The term 'aggression', finally, is introduced in the UN Charter in Article 1(1), which defines one of the primary purposes of the UN: namely, to take effective collective measures for the prevention and removal of threats to the peace, and for the suppression of acts of aggression or other breaches of the peace; in Article 39, which relates to the authority of the UN Security Council regarding threats to peace, breaches of the peace, and acts of aggression; and in Article 53(1), concerning the regional arrangements or agencies for enforcement action.

Besides, describing the aggression, the General Assembly Resolution on the Definition of Aggression reviewed earlier refers to 'use of armed force'. This definition, embracing both direct and indirect use of force against the territorial integrity or political independence of any state or in any other manner inconsistent with the purposes of the United Nations, in its turn displays a significant similarity to Article 2(4) of the UN Charter, which prohibits the threat or use of force. However, it does not include a threat, since for an act to be qualified as aggression, the real use of armed force has to take place.

---

195 As in the case of the NATO approach against the Taliban and al Qaida. See the subsection Right to self-defence.

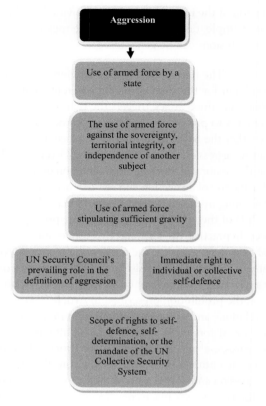

FIGURE 3.1 The complex content of aggression

Right to self-defence

armed attack
individual self-defence
collective self-defence
response to the armed attack
necessity
proportionality
Caroline case
Military and Paramilitary Activities in and against Nicaragua case
right of armed reprisal
necessary minimum required to repulse an attack
right to anticipatory or pre-emptive self-defence
principle of immediacy
Institut de Droit International
doctrine of protection of nationals abroad
Washington Treaty

Article 51 of the UN Charter

As defined under Article 51 of the UN Charter:

> Nothing in the present Charter shall impair the inherent right of individual or collective self-defence if an **armed attack** occurs against a Member of the United Nations, until the Security Council has taken measures necessary to maintain international peace and security. Measures taken by Members in the exercise of this right of self-defence shall be immediately reported to the Security Council and shall not in any way affect the authority and responsibility of the Security Council under the present Charter to take at any time such action as it deems necessary in order to maintain or restore international peace and security.

The meaning of the right to self-defence

Generally, the right to self-defence is considered a natural or inherent right of a state (and, in exceptional cases, of non-state actors). Summarising the formulation of Article 51 of the UN Charter, the right to self-defence:

- includes the rights of **individual self-defence** and self-defence together with allies (**collective self-defence**). However, where collective self-defence is invoked, it is expected that the state for whose benefit this right is exercised would have declared itself to be a victim of an armed attack;
- comes into existence if an armed attack occurs against a member of the United Nations. Nevertheless, this formulation doesn't mean that only the UN member states have the right to self-defence; other states and certain subjects of international law (namely, the units of self-determination in some instances) can be considered persons possessing the right to self-defence on the basis of general customary international law and a broader interpretation of the aforementioned Article; and
- lasts until the UN Security Council has taken the measures necessary to maintain international peace and security.

However, in international law, there are additional scopes of application of the right to self-defence:

1 The self-defence shall be a **response to the armed attack**. The concept of armed attack includes not only direct attacks carried out by the armed forces of a state but also, for instance, 'sending by a State of armed bands to the territory of another State'.[196]

---

196 *Military and Paramilitary Activities in and against Nicaragua (Nicaragua v United States of America)*, Judgment of 27 June 1986. In addition, according to some authors and certain statements by states, within the meaning of an armed attack triggering the right to self-defence, situations can be considered when non-state actors, including terrorist groups, launch attacks against a victim state from external bases and if the territorial state is 'unwilling or unable' to suppress the threat itself (provided that 'unwilling or unable' test will be applied). Supporters of this position have often referred to the situation in Syria. However, this approach is not yet generally recognised in international law.

2   The self-defence shall be exercised by taking into account the criteria of **necessity** and **proportionality**, which are essential components of the normative framework of the right to self-defence. The core idea of necessity was defined in the nineteenth century with respect to the case of the ship *Caroline* (also known as the **Caroline case**)[197] by US Secretary of State Daniel Webster, who emphasised that the state had to demonstrate that the 'necessity of that self-defense is instant, overwhelming, and leaving no choice of means, and no moment of deliberation'. In the same case, the second criterion of self-defence – proportionality – was also articulated. Thus, the response should be proportional in the sense that a certain equilibrium should be maintained between an attack and a response. If there is no equilibrium reached and the self-defence overreaches to turn into an act of aggression, the responding party which initially was attacked may, in the end, attain the status of an aggressor. With the passage of time, these criteria gradually attained the status of general customary international law. As the International Court of Justice concludes in the **Military and Paramilitary Activities in and against Nicaragua case** *(Nicaragua v United States of America)*: There is a 'specific rule whereby self-defence would warrant only measures which are proportional to the armed attack and necessary, a rule well established in customary international law'.[198] Generally, the necessity and proportionality constitute a limit both to the power of states to resort to force *(jus ad bellum)* and to the power to choose the means and methods of warfare *(jus in bello)*.

3   The necessity criterium stipulates the conclusion that minor violations of the prohibition of the use of force should not be considered as empowering a corresponding minor use of force in self-defence. As is stressed by the Eritrea-Ethiopia Claims Commission: '[T]he predicate for a valid claim of self-defence under the Charter is that the party resorting to force has been subjected to an armed attack. Localized border encounters between small infantry units, even those involving the loss of life, do not constitute an armed attack for purposes of the Charter.'[199] Hence, the use of force in self-defence is employed only as a last resort.

---

197 In 1837, a group of Canadian insurrectionists motivated to inflame the Canadian people to break away from the Great Britain and establish an independent Canada executed their plans on the Canadian side of the Niagara River. American advocates of the Canadian insurrectionists shipped arms across the Niagara River using the US steamer *Caroline*. A British Royal Navy force captured the steamer with a number of its crew aboard, pushed it into the current, fired at the steamer, and set it adrift over Niagara Falls. The *Caroline* grounded above the falls to later break up and be swept over by the falls. Following this incident, an intensive diplomatic row broke out, mainly expressed in the exchange of notes and letters between US Secretary of State Daniel Webster and British Special Minister Lord Ashburton. Even though the parties (the US and British governments) never gave their official position as to whether the British attack on the *Caroline* was justified or not, the dispute was resolved through negotiations, resulting in the Webster-Ashburton Treaty of 1842 (dedicated primarily to the resolution of various border disputes existing at that time between the United States and Canada).

198 *Military and Paramilitary Activities in and against Nicaragua (Nicaragua v United States of America)*, Judgment of 27 June 1986.

199 Eritrea-Ethiopia Claims Commission, PCA, Case No 2001–02, Arbitral award of 19 December 2005, *Jus Ad Bellum* Ethiopia's Claims 1–8 between the Federal Democratic Republic of Ethiopia and the State of Eritrea <https://pca-cpa.org/en/cases/71/> accessed 16 March 2021.

4   In self-defence, the use of force is restricted to the **necessary minimum required to repulse an attack**. Mere punitive measures are forbidden.

5   A target state is under obligation to immediately report to the Security Council concerning the actions taken in self-defence.

Right to anticipatory or pre-emptive self-defence

Before the onset of the UN Charter, customary international law generated the **right to anticipatory or pre-emptive self-defence**, if it was consistent with the conditions as laid down in the *Caroline* case. After the UN Charter system was established, a unilateral pre-emptive response was commonly regarded as unlawful since the Charter links the right to self-defence with the occurrence of an armed attack. Therefore, under a narrow interpretation of Article 51, the response shall be immediate as a direct reply to an actual armed attack in conformity with the **principle of immediacy**.

Nevertheless, in the post–Cold War period, the issue of whether a state is entitled to anticipatory or pre-emptive self-defence has been raised frequently. Some scholars have argued for a long time that it was not the intention of the UN Charter to override the pre-existing customary right of anticipatory attacks in self-defence. Several states insist that this right persists, and, in some instances, a state should have the right to use pre-emptive force.[200] Moreover, they often emphasise the developments in modern weaponry, which allow for the possibility of launching an attack with tremendous speed, thus reducing the states' ability to effective self-defence.

A more adaptive model is provided by the Resolution adopted by the **Institut de Droit International** in 2007, which proclaims that the right to self-defence arises 'in the case of an actual or manifestly imminent armed attack'. In addition, it may be exercised 'only when there is no lawful alternative in practice in order to forestall, stop or repel the armed attack'.[201]

In sum, the doctrine supporting the right to anticipatory or pre-emptive self-defence, even in relation to an imminent armed attack, is not conventional, and neither the International Court of Justice nor the UN Security Council has given its authoritative and clear opinion on this matter.

The doctrine of protection of nationals abroad

A further issue within this subject is whether the right to self-defence may be invoked in case of an attack on the state nationals in a foreign country. The states who affirm the adequacy and applicability of the **doctrine of protection of nationals abroad** in this context appeal to the inherent right to self-defence, which has a customary nature and, therefore, should not be limited by a narrow interpretation of Article 51.

200   The notable example is the so-called Bush Doctrine, which was manifested by the President of the United States George W. Bush and his administration following the 11 September 2001 terrorist attacks against the United States.

201   Institut de Droit International. Tenth Commission, Present Problems of the Use of Armed Force in International Law, Resolution of 27 October 2007, Paragraph 3.

According to this approach, the customary right to self-defence has an autonomous nature and may be stretched to cover the protection of nationals in other countries, because the nationals (permanent population) form a part of the essential elements of a statehood, so such an attack should be regarded as an attack against the state itself.

On the other hand, a vast majority of scholars and states argue that attacks on the nationals of a state abroad do not entitle the home state to invoke the right to self-defence since the language of Article 51 and even the customary principles of self-defence cannot be stretched to include the doctrine of protection of nationals abroad, and therefore, actions undertaken under the logic of the aforementioned doctrine cannot be regarded as acts of self-defence. Moreover, justification of the self-defence based on such a broad interpretation of its content threatens the key tenets of the contemporary world order, where the prohibition on the threat or use of force is the system-making principle. At the same time, in fact, the practice of states in support of this approach is minimal, noncoherent and rather limited. Consequently, on the whole, with respect to self-defence, this doctrine also may not be considered the internationally acknowledged approach of international law.

Additional new developments

In the post-9/11 era, discussions were developed regarding armed attacks by non-state groups which may be regarded as establishing the right to self-defence. The most well-known example in this context is the NATO approach against the Taliban and al Qaida, who, over time, were identified as targets of the counterterrorist actions. It is noteworthy that, in the statement by the North Atlantic Council of NATO, initially, there was no state specified as being responsible for the armed attack.[202]

NATO invoked Article 5 of the **Washington Treaty** (NATO's founding treaty) for the first time in its history on 12 September 2001, 24 hours after the terrorist attacks ('acts of barbarism') against the United States, when the terrorists used aircraft as missiles. 'If it is determined that this attack was directed from abroad against the United States, it shall be regarded as an action covered by Article 5 of the Washington Treaty', the North Atlantic Council of NATO stated conditionally in its widely known statement of 12 September 2001. Article 5 of the Washington Treaty stipulates that an armed attack against one or several members shall be considered as an attack against all. The member states finally agreed that an armed attack triggering the right of individual or collective self-defence had taken place. Additionally, the member countries recognised the need for a unique approach to counter-terrorism, as well as the necessity of responding to changing circumstances in the world and the corresponding adjustment of the preconditions triggering the right to collective self-defence.[203]

---

202 Subsequently, on 20 September 2002, 'terrorists and their infrastructure in Afghanistan' were named the targets of the first retaliatory strike. Over time, the US and NATO response and operations were directed 'against the Taliban regime in Afghanistan and the Al Qaida network'.

203 'The commitment to collective self-defence embodied in the Washington Treaty was first entered into in circumstances very different from those that exist now, but it remains no less valid and no less

Collective security system

collective security
system for the maintenance of international peace and security
regional arrangements
Chapter VII of the UN Charter
Chapter VI of the UN Charter
Uniting for Peace Resolution
conflict prevention
peacemaking
peacekeeping
peace enforcement
peacebuilding
sanctions
use of armed force
Military Staff Committee
UN blue helmet or beret

Collective security – the general definition

Collective security can be understood as a regional or global security order in which each state in the system accepts that the security of a single member is the concern to all, and therefore, every state commits to respond to threats and breaches of peace collectively.

UN system for the maintenance of international peace and security

Although the exact expression 'collective security' is not formulated in the UN Charter, it is often used to refer to the **system for the maintenance of international peace and security** under the UN Charter and the corresponding provisions of the **regional arrangements**.

The UN system for the maintenance of international peace and security is based on four core elements:

1   The prohibition of the threat or use of force (legal basis);
2   The identification of the principal organ of the UN for the maintenance of international peace, which is the Security Council (responsible organ);
3   The establishment of the legal obligation of the member states to carry out the Security Council's decisions (authorised organ); and

essential today, in a world subject to the scourge of international terrorism.' Statement by the North Atlantic Council of 12 September 2001, <www.nato.int/docu/pr/2001/p01-124e.htm> accessed 16 March 2021.

4   The equipment of the Security Council with essential instruments for the maintenance of international peace and security (equipped organ).

The principal provisions of the UN Charter on collective security, among others, are:

- Firstly, '[i]n order to ensure prompt and effective action by the United Nations, its Members confer on the Security Council primary responsibility for the maintenance of international peace and security, and agree that in carrying out its duties under this responsibility
  the Security Council acts on their behalf' (Article 24 of the UN Charter).
- Secondly, '[a]ll Members of the United Nations, in order to contribute to the maintenance of international peace and security, undertake to make available to the Security
  Council, on its call and in accordance with a special agreement or agreements, armed
  forces, assistance, and facilities, including rights of passage, necessary for the purpose
  of maintaining international peace and security' (Article 43 of the UN Charter) if
  another arrangement is not assumed between the UN, the UN members. and a particular member state (for example, in case of the neutrality).
- Thirdly, Article 103 of the UN Charter reviewed earlier, which prescribes priority of
  the states' obligations under the Charter in the event of a conflict between the obligations of the UN members under the Charter and their obligations under any other
  (including regional) international agreement.

In general, the UN system for the maintenance of international peace and security is a
significant scaled response to any:

- threat to peace,
- breach of peace, or
- act of aggression.

The terms 'threat to the peace', 'breach of peace', and 'act of aggression' are not defined
anywhere in the UN Charter. However, there are established the other norms of international
law which clarify the scope of the application of these terms. A significant contribution to this
process is provided by the mandatory decisions of the UN Security Council.

Threat to peace

To constitute a threat to peace, a situation must have the potential of provoking an armed
conflict between the states in the short or medium term. After the end of the Cold War,
the UN Security Council developed a broader definition of this term through several
resolutions covering, among other things, civil wars, massive violations of human rights or
international humanitarian law, the incidence of humanitarian crises, and terrorism. For
example, the Resolution on Iraq recognised that the results of human rights repression
constituted a threat to peace and security.[204] Simultaneously, the Resolution on Tribu-

---

204 'Gravely concerned by the repression of the Iraqi civilian population in many parts of Iraq, including
most recently in Kurdish-populated areas, which led to a massive flow of refugees towards and across

nal concerning the former Yugoslavia determined the 'widespread and flagrant violations of international humanitarian law',[205] the Haiti Resolution considered the incidence of humanitarian crises,[206] and the Resolution on the situation in Afghanistan acknowledged continuing violations of international humanitarian law and human rights and the sheltering and training of terrorists and planning of terrorist acts[207] as preconditions constituting a threat to peace and security.

Breach of peace

Breach of peace means a serious outbreak of armed hostilities (1) which is not so severe as to amount to an act of aggression (if there is an offender state) or (2) if there is no possibility to identify the offender party. The Security Council has determined a breach of peace in those situations which involved the use of armed force. Until now, it has referred to the breach of peace on only several occasions. These cases include, for example, the invasion of South Korea by North Korea, the Argentinean invasion of the Falklands/Malvinas, the war between Iran and Iraq, and the Iraqi invasion and military occupation of Kuwait.[208]

Act of aggression

During its three-quarters-of-a-century existence, the Security Council has consistently refrained from assessing different situations which flared into armed hostilities as acts of aggression directly. In cases with a consistent set of events unfolding to apply this term, the Security Council pronounced either breach of peace (as, for instance, in case of the Iraqi invasion of Kuwait) or threat to peace (as in the case of the Turkish military intervention in Cyprus).[209] There are specific reasons the Security Council is cautious in designating a situation as an act of aggression. Nevertheless, the most significant is that by the direct application of the term 'act of aggression', the Council would clearly

---

international frontiers and to cross-border incursions which threaten international peace and security in the region.' S/RES/688(1991) of 5 April 1991. All UN Security Council resolutions are available at the official website of the UN <http://unscr.com/en/resolutions>.

205 'Expressing once again its grave alarm at continuing reports of widespread and flagrant violations of international humanitarian law occurring within the territory of the former Yugoslavia, and especially in the Republic of Bosnia and Herzegovina, including reports of mass killings, massive, organized and systematic detention and rape of women, and the continuance of the practice of "ethnic cleansing", including for the acquisition and the holding of territory, determining that this situation continues to constitute a threat to international peace and security', S/RES/827(1991) of 5 April 1991.

206 '[I]ncidence of humanitarian crises, including mass displacements of population, becoming or aggravating threats to international peace and security.' S/RES/841(1993) of 16 June 1993.

207 S/RES/1267(1999) of 15 October 1999.

208 S/RES/82(1950) of 25 June 1950, S/RES/502(1982) of 3 April 1982, S/RES/598(1987) of 20 July 1987, S/RES/660(1990) of 2 August 1990.

209 'Gravely concerned about the situation which has led to a serious threat to international peace and security.' S/RES/353(1974) of 20 July 1974.

denote the aggressor state, i.e. the guilty side, which bears full responsibility for committing the act of aggression. Additionally, now this would appear as a precondition to prosecute the responsible persons for the crime of aggression. To make such a decision, all permanent member states should have similar assessments of the situation. However, in fact, this is too hard to achieve in the complicated political framework of the Security Council of the UN.

Chapters VI and VII of the UN Charter

Once the UN Security Council has determined the existence of one of the aforementioned preconditions, it may take a decision which is binding upon the member states of the UN under **Chapter VII of the UN Charter** (Action with respect to threats to the peace, breaches of the peace, and acts of aggression), but until that moment, it can issue recommendations under **Chapter VI of the UN Charter** (Pacific settlement of disputes).

Although the primary responsibility for the maintenance of international peace and security lies with the Security Council, other principal organs of the UN also may have power in this respect, but only within the specific confines set by the Charter. For example, the General Assembly may make recommendations to the members of the UN or to the Security Council itself. It has the capacity to advocate the means of finding consensus on difficult issues and represents a forum to sound out grievances and exchange opinions; the International Court of Justice may resolve disputes between the states, provide a view on discrepant legal matters, and so forth.

Uniting for Peace Resolution

However, at the time of the outbreak of hostilities in Korea in 1950, the UN General Assembly interpreted the UN Charter in such a way that, in the extremal circumstances, to facilitate adequate action in case of a deadlock in the Security Council, the General Assembly was empowered to perform the functions of the Security Council without replacing the primary responsibility of the latter to maintain international peace and security.

General Assembly Resolution 377(V)A, adopted in 1950, is commonly known as the **Uniting for Peace Resolution**. The Resolution resolves that

> if the Security Council, because of lack of unanimity of the permanent members, fails to exercise its primary responsibility for the maintenance of international peace and security in any case where there appears to be a threat to the peace, breach of the peace, or act of aggression, the General Assembly shall consider the matter immediately with a view to making appropriate recommendations to Members for collective measures, including in the case of a breach of the peace or act of aggression the use of armed force when necessary, to maintain or restore international peace and security.

In addition, the General Assembly decided that in such cases, it may meet using the mechanism of the emergency special session if it is not in session at the time.[210]

However, this Resolution was the source of a serious friction between the superpowers since the UN system was originally designed in such a way that, when addressing the threat to peace, breach of peace, or act of aggression, these superpowers were necessary participants in the decision-making process on behalf of the UN, and in the UN Security Council format, they possess the right of veto regarding the nonprocedural decisions. Furthermore, the UN security system decisions should not have been made when the countries on the UN Security Council were directly opposed to them and, of course, if the peace enforcement measures under Chapter VII were to be targeted against these superpowers.

This approach initially was agreed on in order not to further aggravate already fragile inter-state relations of the post–Second World War era so that the struggle for peace did not lead into a third world war.[211] Hence, the initial idea for setting up the UN Security Council was explicitly directed at, among other things, avoiding a repetition of the World War.

Sometimes, when the UN Security Council is ineffective, representatives of several countries try to resort to actions through the UN General Assembly, referring to this Resolution. However, despite their efforts to define this approach as an established rule of customary law, it cannot be considered as such, since it contradicts the origins of the UN system and has continuously been opposed by certain superpowers, as well as other countries.

UN mechanisms for the maintenance of international peace and security

There are several mechanisms for the maintenance of the international peace and security which may be triggered by the UN under the Charter; however, the mechanisms triggered shall be adequate and proportional as a response to the situation at hand. Over the years, these mechanisms have evolved to take a systemic shape.

These mechanisms include:

1   conflict prevention;
2   peacemaking;
3   peacekeeping;
4   peace enforcement; and
5   peacebuilding.

---

210 Over the years, the General Assembly has held several special sessions or emergency special sessions on such issues as disarmament, the question of Palestine, the situation in Afghanistan, and so on.

211 The rationality of this approach has been proved over the course of time, as with regard to the Korean peninsula, when there was a severe clash between the superpowers, and the UN member states, disregarding the primary power of the Security Council, made this decision, they might have addressed the situation at that moment, but, nevertheless, the negative consequences of those long-standing decisions remain to this day and from time to time threaten international peace and security.

Over time, the boundaries between these UN mechanisms for the maintenance of international peace and security have become increasingly blurred since, in fact, peace operations are rarely limited to one type of activity.

Conflict prevention

Conflict prevention is a fundamental UN mission, which consists of focused diplomatic measures to contain tensions and disputes among or within the states from escalating into violent conflict.

An early warning represents the essential component of prevention. Consequently, numerous UN officials consistently monitor developments worldwide to explore the threats to international peace and security, thereby helping the UN Security Council and the Secretary-General engage in preventive action. The Secretary-General, in turn, organises the works of their envoys and special representatives who are involved in preventive diplomacy around the world.

Peacemaking

Peacemaking implies actions targeted at bringing hostile parties to an agreement, essentially through such peaceful means as foreseen in Chapter VI of the UN Charter: namely, negotiation, enquiry, mediation, conciliation, arbitration, judicial settlement, and regional agencies or arrangements. The UN members may bring any dispute or any situation which might lead to international friction or trigger a dispute between the countries to the attention of the Security Council or the General Assembly. Addressing an issue brought before the Security Council, it may recommend appropriate procedures or methods for the adjustment of the situation at hand.

Peacekeeping

In literal understanding, peacekeeping means the preservation of peace that already exists. Thus, it could be undertaken at either (1) the pre–military conflict stage or (2) the post–military conflict stage. Peacekeeping is a mechanism not explicitly identified in the UN Charter, which might be authorised by the UN Security Council. However, in fact, it interlinks the activities of the UN General Assembly, the Security Council, the Secretariat, troops and police contributors, the host governments, and the main parties to the conflict. The first such mission was the UN Truce Supervision Organisation, established in 1948 for peacekeeping purposes in the Middle East.

Initially, peacekeeping was devised as a military mechanism to observe ceasefires and separate forces of the conflicting sides after a military conflict had already broken out. Over time, however, this mechanism obtained a more complex form by engaging numerous militaries, police officers, and civilians united with the sole aim of assisting in the establishment of a sustainable peace. Therefore, to date, UN peacekeeping operations have often played an active role in peacemaking efforts, as well as engaging in early peacebuilding activities.

Peacekeeping operations are guided by such principles as:

- consent of the parties, which ensures that the UN will have the co-operation of the warring parties;
- impartiality, which means that peacekeeping must be exercised without favour or prejudice to any party; and
- non-use of force, except in self-defence and defence of the mandate, which emphasises the duty of the peacekeepers not to resort to force to carry out their functions.

Peace enforcement

Peace enforcement involves the injection of coercive measures into a situation where peace does not exist and where usually at least one of the parties does not want international involvement. From the legal point of view, it means the application by the explicit authorisation of the Security Council of certain coercive measures under the Chapter VII of the UN Charter.

Among these measures, **sanctions**, adopted according to the Article 41 of the Charter, are 'complete or partial interruption of economic relations and of rail, sea, air, postal, telegraphic, radio, and other means of communication, and the severance of diplomatic relations'.[212]

If the Security Council decides that these measures would be inadequate, it may authorise the **use of armed force** under Article 42 by air, sea, or land forces through such measures as demonstrations; blockades; and other operations by air, sea, or land forces of members of the UN.

The peace enforcement shall be used specifically to maintain or restore international peace and security in those situations where the Security Council has concluded to take action to counter the threat to peace, breach of peace, or act of aggression.

Peacebuilding

Peacebuilding is a long-term process aimed at attaining the necessary conditions for sustainable peace. By encouraging the peacebuilding process, the UN is focused on the development of the capabilities of a country to overcome the challenges that may lead to a violent conflict. The peacebuilding efforts commonly include supporting dialogue and reconciliation between the parties at conflict, assisting in the restoration of the economy, strengthening governmental structures so that they manage to perform their basic functions better, and so forth. In the UN peacebuilding process, not only are the principal bodies of the UN usually involved, but also a wide variety of the UN system organisations and offices, including the field operations.

---

212 'The Security Council may decide what measures not involving the use of armed force are to be employed to give effect to its decisions, and it may call upon the Members of the United Nations to apply such measures. These may include complete or partial interruption of economic relations and of rail, sea, air, postal, telegraphic, radio, and other means of communication, and the severance of diplomatic relations.' Article 41 of the UN Charter.

Military personnel of peacekeeping operations and armed forces to maintain the peace enforcement

At the beginning, there was envisioned the establishment of a standing military force under the UN Security Council and its subsidiary body, the **Military Staff Committee**, whose main functions under the UN Charter were

> to advise and assist the Security Council on all questions relating to the Security Council's military requirements for the maintenance of international peace and security, the employment and command of forces placed at its disposal, the regulation of armaments, and possible disarmament.[213]

Nevertheless, very quickly, the original mission of the Military Staff Committee was subdued by the power games of the Cold War, and the early rejection of an autonomous, permanent UN military force has greatly narrowed the operational capabilities of the Committee itself. At the same time, the UN peacekeeping activities predominately developed under the auspices of the UN Secretariat, which addressed all the member states to provide troop contingents to implement the Security Council's mandates. Hence, to date, the UN Secretariat, rather than the Military Staff Committee, occupies a central position in the military management activities of the UN.

Thus, the United Nations has no military force of its own. The military and police personnel of the peacekeeping operations are provided voluntarily by the member states. A force commander is responsible for the military aspects of the operation; however, military contingents are accountable to their own national defence entities. The peacekeepers wear their countries' uniforms but are identified as the UN Peacekeepers by the **UN blue helmet or beret**.

As regards the peace enforcement operations, all members of the UN shall make available on the call of the Security Council their armed forces, a required type of assistance, as well as the facilities in accordance with the special agreement or agreements with the Security Council determining, among other things, the numbers and types of troops, their general location, the nature of the facilities and assistance to be provided, and so forth.

In fact, there may be a state or group of states which express readiness to be involved in an operation, and the Security Council may authorise their participation. Moreover, peace enforcement operations, as a rule, are beyond the ability of the UN to engage in command, control, and planning operations of the armed forces. Consequently, those functions may be carried out under a mandate authorised by the Security Council by a coalition of states or by a regional organisation such as NATO.

Regional arrangements

The significant parts of the world collective security system are the so-called regional arrangements or institutions, which aim to provide peace and security at the regional level, such as NATO, OSCE, and others. Moreover, the UN Security Council shall

213 Article 47(1) of the UN Charter.

encourage the development of the pacific settlement of local disputes through such regional arrangements and utilise such regional arrangements or agencies for the peace-keeping or peace enforcement actions undertaken under its authority.

Humanitarian intervention

doctrine of humanitarian intervention
Article 2(4) of the UN Charter
doctrine of responsibility to protect
doctrine of protection of nationals abroad
just cause
right intention
necessity and proportionality
last resort
unlawfulness of humanitarian intervention
legitimacy of humanitarian intervention

Doctrine of humanitarian intervention

The **doctrine of humanitarian intervention** stipulates that under international law, the states are permitted in exceptional cases to use armed forces abroad in order to alleviate overwhelming humanitarian suffering.

The origin of the doctrine dates back to such prominent authors as Hugo Grotius and Emer de Vattel, who, in this context, were driven by the purpose of defending the peoples from the suffering and tyranny imposed on them by their rulers. During the nineteenth and early twentieth centuries, the doctrine had widespread acceptance under general customary international law.

However, in the UN Charter era, its lawfulness is questionable since the prohibition of the use of force has become a cardinal principle of international law. Indeed, contemporary international law (including **Article 2(4) of the UN Charter**) prohibits entirely any threat or use of force between the states except in cases of individual or collective self-defence under Article 51 or when applying collective measures to maintain or restore international peace and security under the authorisation of the UN Security Council.[214]

---

214 The third case, which allows the use of force under international law in exceptional circumstances as a result of the application of the right to self-determination, is the right of the people under colonial and racist regimes or other forms of alien domination and does not directly concern the relations of a state to another state. Hence, the states can use force lawfully only in the aforementioned two scenarios.

Features of humanitarian intervention

According to the conventional approach, humanitarian intervention:

1 involves the threat or use of military force as a central feature;[215]
2 is undertaken without the authorisation of the UN Security Council system;[216]
3 entails the intervention in the internal affairs of a state without its consent;
4 should be motivated by mere humanitarian objectives and as such, it should not ultimately threaten the territorial integrity, political independence, or the very existence of a particular state; and
5 should be conducted only in cases of a humanitarian disaster of sufficient gravity.

Doctrine of responsibility to protect

The doctrine of humanitarian intervention is sometimes interlinked with the **doctrine of responsibility to protect** (R2P), which asserts that where a state fails in its responsibility to protect its own population, it loses some of its sovereign rights in favour of external collective interference in its internal affairs. The 2005 World Summit Outcome Document (endorsed by the UN General Assembly) accepted this doctrine, however, only with reference to genocide, war crimes, ethnic cleansing, and crimes against humanity and, even in such cases, explicitly reaffirmed the authority of the UN Security Council in accordance with the Charter to initiate the collective action.[217] Hence, the doctrine of responsibility to protect is principally aimed at ensuring that the UN Security Council does take an action and, according to an accurate interpretation, should not cover cases of unilateral use of force.

New challenges

In the aftermath of the large-scale humanitarian disasters in the former Yugoslavia (specifically, in Bosnia) and the genocide in Rwanda causing terrible consequences, the responses to those challenges were (1) the demonstration of the problems of the UN system and (2) in the case of former Yugoslavia, the military measures undertaken by the North Atlantic Treaty Organisation (NATO) either by arbitrary expansion of the UN mandate or, in certain cases, without Security Council mandate at all.

More recently, the attention of the international community has shifted to Syria, especially as concerns grow that intervention is necessary to put a stop to the continuous

---

215 However, some authors also include in the definition non-military forms of intervention.
216 Sometimes, under the humanitarian intervention, coercive measures authorised by the UN Security Council are considered. However, from a legal standpoint, those actions should be treated as measures according to Chapters VI and VII of the UN Charter for maintaining or restoring international peace and security, even they are stipulated by an undoubtedly humanitarian context.
217 'In this context, we are prepared to take collective action, in a timely and decisive manner, through the Security Council, in accordance with the Charter, including Chapter VII'. UN General Assembly Resolution A/RES/60/1 16 September 2005, Paragraph 139.

killings and the human rights violations as a result of the actions undertaken by Syria's governing Assad regime and the Islamic State, also known as the Islamic State of Iraq and Syria (ISIS). However, the inability of the UN to effectively respond to the Syrian crisis through the unified approach and the clash of interests between the United States, Russia, China, and the neighbouring states of Syria have led to large-scale disasters and massive migration affecting many neighbouring states, as well as some European ones.

These events gave a new impetus to discussions on the question of the lawfulness of humanitarian interventions.

Arguments maintaining the lawfulness of humanitarian intervention

Some scholars supporting the doctrine of humanitarian intervention argue that, so long as in the genuine cases of humanitarian intervention, an acting state or coalition of states neither seeks a territorial change nor challenges the political independence of the state which is subjected to intervention, such humanitarian intervention is not covered or precluded by Article 2(4) of the UN Charter. Nevertheless, this approach is unacceptable since an armed intervention undertaken in ideal cases with the sole purpose of protecting the human rights is still, in fact, a violation of the very essence of the territorial integrity or political independence of a state.

The other arguments are rooted in the **doctrine of protection of nationals abroad**. This doctrine is unavailing with respect to the self-defence principle, as analysed earlier, but many jurists, by referring to the doctrine of humanitarian intervention, continue to affirm the right of a state to use armed forces for the protection of its citizens suffering injuries on the territory of another state if the state in question fails to address those concerns. In addition, this approach finds significant support in the practice of such states as the USA, the United Kingdom, Israel, and so forth. However, because in those cases, the armed forces are mandated primarily with the protection of several foreigners, it becomes questionable whether such an operation is at all related to the right of humanitarian intervention.

Certainly, if under the terms of humanitarian intervention, we count all interventions determined by the humanitarian objectives in spite of how many persons are affected, the protection of the nationals also may be included. However, usually when applying this term, the states and scholars are considering the 'disasters of sufficient gravity', which by definition should involve numerous persons in a territory and cannot be narrowed down to the human rights violations sustained by only a few foreigners in the territory of the country under focus.

A special case of the doctrine of protection of nationals abroad has often been used during recent decades in situations where one country deliberately grants citizenship wholesale to the population of neighbouring countries (the so-called 'process of passportisation') to implement its political interests and when needed to motivate its interventionism with the humanitarian goal of protection of citizens. An example of such an application of the doctrine of humanitarian intervention is clearly recognisable in Russia's behaviour towards some of its neighbouring countries.

Finally, some authors vindicate the lawfulness of humanitarian intervention only in cases of such international crimes as genocide or crimes against humanity, stating that the protection of the lives of individuals is the minimal essential quality that any legal system should be able to deliver. These crimes destroy the basis of human existence, and therefore, humanitarian intervention is in the interests of humanity and should be legally permissible. Nonetheless, in fact, it is always difficult to assert whether there is a real case of genocide or crime against humanity. It is the business of judges to ascertain this, not political leaders, who, as a rule, are governed by national interests and pronounce political, partial, and subjective assessments. Moreover, the horrors of human suffering are sometimes used to manipulate the conscience of the international community not to betray the political and power interests that lie behind those objectives.

What would a genuine humanitarian intervention involve?

The supporters of the lawfulness of humanitarian intervention argue that the following preconditions for the use of force with regard to the humanitarian intervention are in conformity with international law:

- **Just cause** – there is convincing, impartial evidence, accepted by the international community in whole, of extreme humanitarian distress of sufficient gravity to require immediate and urgent relief;
- **Right intention** – humanitarian intervention shall only aim to offer relief to humans in disaster to rescue their lives and health;
- **Necessity and proportionality** – the proposed use of force should be necessary and proportionate with the aim of relief of humanitarian suffering and must be strictly limited in time and scope to this aim;
- **Last resort** – it must be clear that there is no practicable alternative to the use of force if lives are to be saved.

Regional arrangements as the mechanisms for humanitarian intervention

This new interventionism, or willingness to use force in the name of protection of humanitarian values, played a major role in shaping international relations after the Cold War, when the world order entered a phase of readjustment and political turbulence. Amid the emerging dominance of the USA of the post–Cold War era, it caused a range of unilateral actions, including under the format of the NATO.

The action undertaken by NATO in response to the Kosovo crisis stands as the clearest example of such unilateralism and attempts to modify the exclusive competence of the UN Security Council in the event of humanitarian intervention. Although in 1998, the UN Security Council at first reacted to the dramatic situation existing in Kosovo by imposing an arms embargo[218] and later 'endorsed and supported' the

---

218 '8. Decides that all States shall, for the purposes of fostering peace and stability in Kosovo, prevent the sale or supply to the Federal Republic of Yugoslavia, including Kosovo, by their nationals or from their territories or using their flag vessels and aircraft, of arms and related matériel of all types, such as weapons and ammunition, military vehicles and equipment and spare parts for the aforementioned,

Organisation for Security and Co-operation in Europe (OSCE) Kosovo Verification Mission and the North Atlantic Treaty Organisation (NATO) Air Verification Mission over Kosovo,[219] nevertheless, in 1999, NATO initiated 'a broad range of air operations' against the Federal Republic of Yugoslavia without the authorisation of the Security Council with the formal intention of preventing a potential Serb slaughter of the ethnic Albanians. So the initial mandate was unilaterally replaced by the decisions adopted under the NATO format. However, the proponents of those NATO decisions endeavoured to discover the legal basis for the intervention in the Security Council Resolutions mentioned earlier.

The other significant challenge to the longstanding UN collective security system was pronounced by the African Union (AU), which formally claimed for itself the right to intervene in the affairs of its member states in instances of gross human rights violations.[220] The supporters of such regulation argue that since the member states of the Union have given their express consent to military intervention under the Constitutive Act of African Union, the use of force would fall outside the scope of the prohibition of Article 2(4) of the UN Charter and not be in violation of its principles.

Unilateral use of force

The notable example of the unilateral use of force, referring to the humanitarian intervention doctrine, was exercised in Syria by US military forces.[221] In addition, other countries have also undertaken unilateral military actions in Syria, indicating several strategic and humanitarian objectives. For example, Turkish operations in Northern Syria[222] and Israeli strikes in Syria mostly targeted locations and convoys near the Lebanese border.

---

and shall prevent arming and training for terrorist activities there;' S/RES/1160(1998) of 31 March 1998.

219 'Welcoming the agreement signed in Belgrade on 16 October 1998 by the Minister of Foreign Affairs of the Federal Republic of Yugoslavia and the Chairman-in-Office of the Organization for Security and Cooperation in Europe (OSCE) providing for the OSCE to establish a verification mission in Kosovo (S/1998/978), including the undertaking of the Federal Republic of Yugoslavia to comply with resolutions 1160 (1998) and 1199 (1998), Welcoming also the agreement signed in Belgrade on 15 October 1998 by the Chief of General Staff of the Federal Republic of Yugoslavia and the Supreme Allied Commander, Europe, of the North Atlantic Treaty Organization (NATO) providing for the establishment of an air verification mission over Kosovo (S/1998/991, annex), complementing the OSCE Verification Mission'. S/RES/1203(1998) of 24 October 1998.

220 '[T]he right of the Union to intervene in a Member State pursuant to a decision of the Assembly in respect of grave circumstances, namely: war crimes, genocide and crimes against humanity;' Article 4(h) of the Constitutive Act of the African Union.

221 Officially, US policy towards Syria since 2014 has prioritised counterterrorism operations against the Islamic State, but it has also included nonlethal assistance to Syrian opposition groups, diplomatic efforts to reach a political settlement to the civil war, and humanitarian aid to Syria and regional countries affected by refugee outflows.

222 However, Turkish leaders claimed that the Adana agreement of 1998 gives Ankara the right to enter Syrian territory.

As discussed earlier, international law permits the use of force on the territory of another state without the consent of the state concerned only in self-defence (on a very limited scale) or with the authorisation from the UN Security Council. Neither of the conditions was satisfied in the case of these military operations in Syria. The advocates of new interventionism, particularly in the US, argued that the principles of responsibility to protect and humanitarian intervention provide a legal justification for intervention without the UN mandate. In addition, they have advanced a few similar cases – for example, the so-called Bangladesh crisis, an armed intervention into East Pakistan conducted by India in 1971 to remedy the massive human rights violations inflicted on the people of East Bengal by the Pakistani army, when the Security Council failed to pass any resolution condemning the Indian intervention, and especially the NATO air campaign of 1999 in Kosovo – as precedents that would justify intervention in Syria under those principles.

Is a humanitarian intervention legally justifiable?

It is clear that humanitarian intervention is an emerging norm of customary international law, which might serve as an additional exception to the prohibition against the use of force at some point in the future, if the relevant conditions for the modification of the existing legal model for the use of force are satisfied.

Nevertheless, so far, in order to legally justify coercive military measures in those cases, the authorisation given by the UN Security Council is of crucial importance. As regards the regional organisations, the legal basis of the measures they spearhead is Article 53 of the UN Charter, which clearly restricts regional organisations from undertaking enforcement measures without the authorisation of the Security Council.[223]

Moreover, the prohibition on the use of force is widely accepted as the *jus cogens* norm. To modify its content and to limit the exclusive competence of the Security Council, it is necessary either to acquire the appropriate consent from the states representing the relevant general practice and *opinio juris* leading to the emergence of the general customary international law norm or the conclusion of the global treaty accepted by a very large majority of states.

Meanwhile, the substantiality and recurrence of use of force without Security Council authorisation in terms of uniform practice and *opinio juris* are rather limited.

Besides, a self-repeating feature uniting all these cases was the firm protest by the majority of states, including the permanent members of the UN Security Council and, at times, the NATO members too. Furthermore, in the case of Kosovo, some of the states that took part in the operations insisted that this intervention did not set a precedent.

Finally, if the question of the **unlawfulness of humanitarian intervention** at the current moment is more or less clear, several writers, as well as officials, still tend to consider the matter of the **legitimacy of humanitarian intervention** separately. As concluded by the

---

223 'The Security Council shall, where appropriate, utilize such regional arrangements or agencies for enforcement action under its authority. But no enforcement action shall be taken under regional arrangements or by regional agencies without the authorization of the Security Council', Article 53(1) of the UN Charter.

Independent International Commission on Kosovo[224] in 2000, the NATO military intervention was 'illegal but legitimate'. It emphasised that this 'intervention was illegal because it did not receive prior approval from the United Nations Security Council.' On the other hand, the Commission regarded this intervention as legitimate 'because all diplomatic avenues had been exhausted and because the intervention had the effect of liberating the majority population of Kosovo from a long period of oppression under Serbian rule.'[225]

Neutrality

abstention
impartiality
neutrality in a particular war
neutralist policy
traditional neutrality
permanent neutrality
Non-Aligned Movement
South countries
Western or Eastern Blocs
Hague Conventions of 1899 and 1907
Advisory Opinion on *Legality of the Threat or Use of Nuclear Weapons*

The general notion of neutrality

Neutrality in the interstate system by definition means (1) no interference in the conflict of others and (2) the equal treatment of the parties to the conflict. Hence, the two classical duties of the subjects of international law claiming neutrality are to remain uninvolved (**abstention**) and to treat the conflicting parties equally (**impartiality**).

Those who possess neutral status basically are the states; however, it can occasionally be granted to the other subjects of international law as well. For example, according to the Lateran Pacts of 1929, the Holy See is proclaimed as a subject which 'desires to take, and shall take, no part in any temporal rivalries between other States'.[226]

For centuries, the concept of neutrality has contributed to international peace on the one hand and, on the other hand, to the protection of the interests of those states which had no intention of engaging in a conflict. Besides, neutrality was beneficial for the parties

---

224 The Independent International Commission on Kosovo was created in August 1999 on the initiative of Swedish Prime Minister Göran Persson. Richard Goldstone (South Africa) and Carl Tham (Sweden) chaired and co-chaired the Commission, respectively.

225 Independent International Commission on Kosovo, *The Kosovo Report: Conflict, International Response, Lessons Learned* (Oxford University Press 2000) 4.

226 Article 24 of the Treaty of Conciliation between the Italian Republic and the Holy See.

to the conflict since the existence of such neutral territories that did not constitute a threat to them opened up the pacified neutral fields for the implementation of political and even economic goals. Therefore, neutrality was seen as an essential approach to satisfy multiple diverging interests while security measures in the world were minimal.

Models of neutrality

Over the centuries, neutrality took various forms that can be generalised under three different models:

- **Neutrality in a particular war** – which commonly is constituted by an official declaration of a subject of international law towards the belligerents.
- **Neutralist policy** (also called **traditional neutrality**) – which is a foreign policy standpoint wherein a subject of international law intends to remain neutral in future armed conflicts.
- **Permanent neutrality** – which is commonly established by an international treaty pronouncing that a particular subject of international law will be neutral towards the belligerents of all future armed conflicts and also, during peacetime, will not enter into any legal commitments which, in the event of a conflict, would prevent the neutral from honouring its obligations stemming from its status as a neutral subject.

Permanent neutral states

As is well known, Switzerland's neutrality has deeper roots than any of Europe's other major neutral states. Finally, after an interruption in the policy of neutrality during the Napoleonic Wars, Switzerland received recognition of its international status as a permanently neutral state at the Congress of Vienna in 1815.[227] In addition, this status was guaranteed under the protocol of four powers (Austria, Russia, Great Britain, and Prussia).[228]

The neutrality of Austria was pronounced in the Soviet-Austrian Memorandum of 1955, when Austria gave its approval to make a declaration in a form which obligated Austria to practice neutrality internationally in perpetuity, which was modelled on Switzerland's case,[229] and to take all proper steps to obtain international recognition of the declaration

227 ART. XCII. 'The provinces . . . shall form a part of the neutrality of Switzerland, as it is recognised and guaranteed by the Powers.' The General Treaty of the Final Act of the Congress of Vienna, 9 June 1815 <http://bit.ly/2F9l4io> accessed 16 March 2021.

228 Art. IV. 'The Neutrality of Switzerland shall be extended to that territory, which is placed north of a line to be drawn from Ugina (including that Town) to the south of the Lake of Annecy, and from thence to the Lake of Bourget, as far as the Rhone, in the same manner as it has been extended to the Provinces of Chablais and Faucigny by Article XCII of the Final Act of the Congress of Vienna.' Protocol of the Conference of Paris, 3 November 1815.

229 '1.) In the sense of the declaration already given by Austria at the conference in Berlin in 1954 to join no military alliances and to permit no military bases on its territory, the Austrian Federal Government

confirmed by the Austrian Parliament. Following the Memorandum, Austria received a guarantee from the great powers of the inviolability and integrity of its territory.

Neutralist policy

The neutral status of Sweden and Finland was developed on a different legal and political foundation.

Sweden has maintained its neutrality ever since the end of the Napoleonic Wars. However, Sweden is pursuing a neutralist policy as a primary line in the country's foreign policy, which is to be distinguished from permanent neutrality. In the twentieth century, Sweden's policy of neutrality, for the most part, successfully kept it out of two World Wars. Besides, neutrality has grown to be part of Swedish foreign policy identity.[230]

Meanwhile, the roots of the neutral status of Finland are only a few decades old, partly being the result of the Winter War of 1939–1940 between the USSR and Finland. The starting point of its neutrality is considered to be the recognition granted by the Soviet Union during the Cold War.

Establishment of a neutral status

To obtain a neutral status in the sense of either traditional neutrality or permanent neutrality, the subject of international law first shall agree to become a neutral subject. This choice should usually be validated by domestic procedures and respective documents. Secondly, without the engagement of all neighbouring countries and superpowers, there cannot be sufficient acknowledgement of the status. In addition, this process sometimes involves a formal guarantor. For instance, Switzerland has its neutrality guaranteed by four powers, Austria by four former occupying powers, and Finland by the Soviet Union.

At the same time, the forms of initial recognition and guarantee of neutral status vary significantly. Sometimes they are provided by a bilateral treaty (as in the case of Finland) or the multilateral treaty (as concerning Switzerland).

More recently, the UN format has been used for the recognition of neutral status. In 1995, the UN General Assembly adopted the Resolution on Permanent Neutrality of Turkmenistan. Under this Resolution, the UN recognises and supports the status of permanent neutrality declared by Turkmenistan and calls upon members of the UN to respect and support this status.[231]

---

will make a declaration in a form which will obligate Austria internationally to practice in perpetuity a neutrality of the type maintained by Switzerland.' Memorandum on the outcome of the negotiations between the government delegations from Austria and the Soviet Union (Moscow, 15 April 1955).

230 There are five members of the European Union that still describe themselves as neutral countries in some form: Austria, Ireland, Finland, Malta, and Sweden. With the development of the EU's Common Security and Defence Policy, the extent to which they are, or should be, neutral is widely debated.

231 A/RES/50/80 of 12 December 1995.

Non-Aligned Movement

The power dynamics of the Cold War stimulated the creation of the **Non-Aligned Movement** (NAM).[232] The concept of non-alignment rests on the attitude of abstention and, therefore, overlaps with the institute of neutrality. However, it should be considered separately since the non-alignment movement unites a group of developing countries (also called the **South countries**) which simply do not want to be officially aligned with or against any major power bloc – originally, the **Western or Eastern Blocs**.

In addition, the contemporary mission of this movement is formulated as the contribution to the acceleration and enhancement of national development by strengthening and expanding South-South technical co-operation in the context of international development.

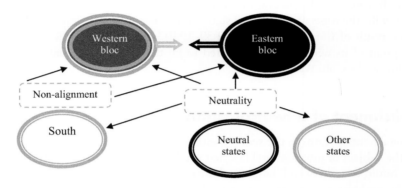

FIGURE 3.2 The bipolar system among states during the Cold War

1899 and 1907 Hague Conventions

Neutrality became part of the excellent codification exercise that started in the nineteenth century; however, the culmination of the codification process was reached with the **Hague Conventions of 1899 and 1907**.[233] At least five out of more than ten Hague Conventions of 1907 addressed the question of neutrality, one was devoted to neutrality in relation to the war on land (Convention (V) respecting the Rights and Duties of Neutral Powers and Persons in Case of War on Land), and the others to neutrality during the naval war.[234] Although

---

232 The Non-Aligned Movement was established in Belgrade in 1961. To date, its members are the majority of UN member states.

233 The Hague Conventions of 1899 and 1907 are a number of international treaties and declarations reached at two international peace conferences at the Hague. The First Hague Conference was held in 1899 and the Second Hague Conference in 1907. Along with the Geneva Conventions, the Hague Conventions were among the first legal documents codifying the law of war and the law of neutrality. A third conference was planned for 1914 and later rescheduled for 1915, but it did not take place due to the start of World War I.

234 Convention (VIII) relative to the Laying of Automatic Submarine Contact Mines, Convention (XI) relative to certain Restrictions with regard to the Exercise of the Right of Capture in Naval War,

many of those provisions are outdated by now, certain rules from those conventions are still binding on the parties to an armed conflict, at least to the extent that the principles of the Hague Conventions are declaratory of customary international law. Under the **Advisory Opinion on *Legality of the Threat or Use of Nuclear Weapons*** of 1996, the International Court of Justice reaffirmed the continued survival of neutrality as an established part of customary international law.[235]

As regards the principles of neutrality formulated in the 1907 Hague Conventions, they may be generalised as follows:

1   A neutral should not fight.
2   The territory of a neutral should be inviolable.[236]
3   The belligerents should respect the inviolability of the territory of a neutral subject.
4   A neutral should defend its territory by force if necessary. If a neutral takes action to defend its territory in response to violations of its neutrality, these actions are not to be regarded as hostile acts.
5   A neutral is under an obligation to make sure that activities contradicting its neutral status do not take place within its territory.[237]
6   A neutral should maintain impartiality, including with respect to trade with belligerent parties.[238]
7   A neutral may render services as an intermediary, recipient of refugees, and supporter of the victims, including the escaped prisoners of war and the sick and wounded belonging to the belligerent armies.

Convention (XII) relative to the Creation of an International Prize Court (which never entered into force) and Convention (XIII) concerning the Rights and Duties of Neutral Powers in Naval War.

235 'The Court finds that as in the case of the principles of humanitarian law applicable in armed conflict, international law leaves no doubt that the principle of neutrality, whatever its content, which is of a fundamental character similar to that of the humanitarian principles and rules, is applicable (subject to the relevant provisions of the United Nations Charter), to all international armed conflict, whatever type of weapons might be used.' *Legality of the Threat or Use of Nuclear Weapons*, Advisory Opinion of 8 July 1996, ICJ Reports 1996, 226.

236 'The territory of neutral Powers is inviolable.' Article 1 of the Convention (V) respecting the Rights and Duties of Neutral Powers and Persons in Case of War on Land.

237 Such activities included the transit of a belligerent's troops or convoys of either munitions of war or supplies across the territory of a neutral power; the erection on the territory of a neutral power a wireless telegraphy station or other apparatus for the purpose of communicating with belligerent forces on land or sea; and the formation or recruiting of a corps of combatants by agencies opened in the territory of a neutral power to assist the belligerents. Articles 2, 3, 4 of the Convention (V) respecting the Rights and Duties of Neutral Powers and Persons in Case of War on Land.

238 Some writers stressed that, in fact, the neutrals went on trading with the enemy during both World Wars. For example, Sweden supplied Nazi Germany with iron ore crucial for the war industry, Switzerland permitted transports between Italy and Germany, and so on. However, trading with belligerents was not generally restricted by the Hague Conventions. On the other hand, these Conventions apparently entail certain limits of trade: for instance, restricting the selling of munitions to belligerents by a neutral power or obliging a neutral to maintain the principle of impartiality.

Neutrality in the UN Charter era

Thus, the concept of neutrality emerged at the time when conflicts between states were still considered to be matters confined to regional affairs. After the gradual formation of the collective security system, which reached its most developed form within the UN Charter, these conflicts were gradually given a global spotlight. Besides, there is a question as to whether the traditional concept of neutrality is compatible with the new world order: namely, with the UN Charter.

This issue became especially relevant when the General Assembly of the UN elected the permanently neutral state of Austria as a non-permanent member of the Security Council in 1972. This was the first time that a permanently neutral state had obtained a seat on the Council. The second significant case was Switzerland, whose leaders and people were in a protracted debate for a long time concerning the possibility of membership in the UN since they feared that their neutrality would be violated if they decided to join the UN. To ensure that it would not be, the UN declared the permanent neutrality of a member state to be compatible with its obligations under the system of the collective security. This approach was reaffirmed several times earlier and after, specifically with regard to Turkmenistan in 1995, when the UN General Assembly stated that 'the adoption by Turkmenistan of the status of permanent neutrality does not affect the fulfilment of its obligations under the Charter and will contribute to the achievement of the purposes of the United Nations'[239] and, more recently in 2017, with the UN General Assembly declaring 12 December to be the International Day of Neutrality.[240] This resolution was nourished by the point of view that neutrality contributes to the strengthening of peace and security in different regions around the globe and plays an essential role in implementing the principles of preventive diplomacy.

Finally, in 2002, after the referendum in which the Swiss voters approved entry into the UN, Switzerland applied to the UN and became its 190th member state.

However, the debates about the interoperability of the institute of neutrality with the UN collective security system persist.

Some authors consider the obligations under the UN Charter to be incompatible with permanent neutrality status. Namely, under Article 2(5) of the UN Charter, the member states are required to assist the Organisation at all times and refrain from giving assistance to any state against which the UN is taking preventive or enforcement actions.

Nevertheless, the opponents to this standpoint stress that:

- Generally, permanently neutral states, as well as all other members of the UN, are free to pronounce themselves to be neutral regarding the conflicts in situations in which it is hard to establish which state has to bear responsibility for the breakout of the armed hostilities.
- There are two types of enforcement measures under Chapter VII of the UN Charter: Measures not involving the use of armed force (according to Article 41) and military

---

239 A/RES/50/80 of 12 December 1995.

240 The UN General Assembly Resolution A/RES/71/275 of 13 February 2017 was introduced by Turkmenistan.

measures (in accordance with Article 42). However, neither comes into effect without the authorisation of the Security Council, imposing a duty on the member states to apply such measures. Additionally, participation in those actions depends on the Security Council's call. Moreover, according to Article 43, to make available to the Security Council the armed forces, assistance, and facilities, including rights of passage, the conclusion of a special agreement or agreements is required. In sum, it can be argued that when accepting permanently neutral states into the UN (due to the knowledge of their neutrality), a duty arises not to force these countries to abandon their neutrality. Therefore, the Security Council shall take into account such a state of affairs.

The permanent neutral states, on the other hand, may argue that the law of neutrality can only be applied exclusively to armed conflicts between two or more states (consequently, it does not apply to internal conflicts). By such a definition, the law of neutrality does not relate to the measures authorised by the UN Security Council as the Security Council works on behalf of the international community to restore international peace and security and is not a belligerent party to any conflict.

PEACEFUL CO-EXISTENCE – PACIFIC SETTLEMENT OF DISPUTES

> negotiation
> enquiry
> mediation
> conciliation
> arbitration
> judicial settlement
> resort to regional agencies or arrangements

Article 33 of the UN Charter

Under Article 33 of the UN Charter:

1   The parties to any dispute, the continuance of which is likely to endanger the maintenance of international peace and security, shall, first of all, seek a solution by **negotiation, enquiry, mediation, conciliation, arbitration, judicial settlement, resort to regional agencies or arrangements**, or other peaceful means of their own choice.
2   The Security Council shall, when it deems necessary, call upon the parties to settle their dispute by such means.

Direct negotiation, good offices, and mediation

procedure of the pacific settlement of disputes
formats
direct negotiation at the highest level
third party
substantive suggestions towards achieving a settlement
draft ideas on the pacific settlement of a dispute
consultative character
Hague Convention for the Pacific Settlement of International Disputes of 1899
Hague Convention for the Pacific Settlement of International Disputes of 1907

Forms of negotiation

Direct negotiation is the initial and principal **procedure of the pacific settlement of disputes**.

It might be conducted in several **formats**. The most efficient of them is a **direct negotiation at the highest level**. However, in general, this form is implemented if the necessary preconditions are fulfilled, such as the adjustment of detailed organisational tasks, agenda, and so on, and appropriate draft suggestions are prepared. Consequently, the subjects of international law also use the format of direct negotiations through special missions, which are a significant tool to prepare the aforementioned direct negotiations at the highest level.

Main targets of direct negotiation are either (1) the settlement of a dispute by this form or (2) the agreement on some other peaceful mechanism for the dispute resolution.

Good offices and mediation

Good offices and mediation are the other procedures for the pacific settlement of disputes where the **third party** is already engaged – either individuals, states, international organisations, or other subjects of international law – in order to aid the contending parties to come to a settlement. The parties can apply these forms of the pacific settlement of disputes only with explicit consent.

By becoming involved in the dispute resolution, the third party contributes to the establishment of contacts between the parties, delivers one party's claim and proposals to the other party and vice versa, and participates in the negotiating process.

The difference between good offices and mediation

It is generally agreed that there are some differences between the procedures of good offices and mediation:

- Good offices maintain the settlement without necessarily offering the disputing parties **substantive suggestions towards achieving a settlement**.
- There is a mediation ongoing when the third party is entitled to actively engage in the conduct of the negotiations between the parties and has the right to submit before the parties the **draft ideas on the pacific settlement of a dispute**.

However, in reality, the dividing line between the two procedures is often difficult to draw as they often tend to merge into one another.

The consultative character of good offices and mediation

The approaches which have been developed through the procedures of good offices and mediation have a **consultative character** and so are not obligatory for the parties. As is stressed in the **Hague Convention for the Pacific Settlement of International Disputes of 1899**:

> Good offices and mediation, either at the request of the parties at variance, or on the initiative of Powers strangers to the dispute, have exclusively the character of advice and never have binding force.[241]

At the same time, there is the similar provision in the **Hague Convention for the Pacific Settlement of International Disputes of 1907**,[242] which replaced the Hague Convention for the Pacific Settlement of International Disputes of 1899 between contracting parties to the later Convention. Hence, for particular states which did not ratify the later Convention, the previous Convention remains in force.

Inquiry and conciliation

detailed study of facts
differences of opinion on factual matters
neutral persons
basics of the dispute
General Act for the Pacific Settlement of International Disputes
Revised General Act for the Pacific Settlement of International Disputes
parity basis

---

241 Article 6 of the Hague Convention for the Pacific Settlement of International Disputes of 1899.

242 The Hague Conventions for the Pacific Settlement of International Disputes are available on the official website of the Permanent Court of Arbitration <https://pca-cpa.org/en/documents/pca-conventions-and-rules/> accessed 16 March 2021. In this book, materials from the website are used taking into account the disclaimer and applicable legal rules.

Inquiry

The inquiry procedure is committed to helping the parties in the **detailed study of facts** when **differences of opinion on factual matters** interfere with a pacific settlement of a dispute between the parties. This procedure implies the involvement of **neutral persons** (for instance, in the form of an international commission of inquiry) to conduct an inquiry. The commission of inquiry checks only the facts – the actual side of the case – and reports the results of this examination to the parties involved. International commissions of inquiry are constituted by special agreement between the parties in conflict. The settled procedure defines their scope of operation. In the inquiry, both sides must be heard.[243]

Conciliation

In the process of conciliation, the engagement of the neutral persons is higher. In such a case, the third party or commission investigates the **basics of the dispute** and prepares a report (the terms of a settlement). Therefore, conciliation unites elements of both inquiry and mediation.

Under the **General Act for the Pacific Settlement of International Disputes** of 1928 and the **Revised General Act for the Pacific Settlement of International Disputes** (the amendments were made by the UN General Assembly in 1949):[244]

> The disputes referred to in the preceding article shall be submitted to a permanent or special conciliation commission constituted by the parties to the dispute. . . .[245] The task of the Conciliation Commission shall be to elucidate the questions in dispute, to collect with that object all necessary information by means of enquiry or otherwise, and to endeavour to bring the parties to an agreement. It may, after the case has been examined, inform the parties of the terms of settlement which seem suitable to it, and lay down the period within which they are to make their decision.[246]

Establishment and decisions of the commissions of inquiry and conciliation

Commissions of inquiry and conciliation are established (1) on a **parity basis**, (2) based on an agreement between the parties via a third person (the state or another subject of international law), or (3) under any other rule.

---

243 Article 10 of the Hague Convention for the Pacific Settlement of International Disputes of 1899.
244 A/RES/268(III) A of 28 April 1949 (Restoration to the General Act of 26 September 1928 of its original efficacy).
245 Article 2 of the General Act for the Pacific Settlement of International Disputes and the identical Article 2 of the Revised General Act for the Pacific Settlement of International Disputes.
246 Article 15 of the General Act for the Pacific Settlement of International Disputes and the identical Article 15 of the Revised General Act for the Pacific Settlement of International Disputes.

The decisions of both types of commissions have consultative character and are not mandatory for the parties.

Inquiry and conciliation within specified institutional frameworks

In practice, high importance is afforded to the inquiry and conciliation procedures within the United Nations (for example, the United Nations investigations and fact-finding missions), the UN Specialised Agencies, and regional international organisations.

International arbitration

special tribunal
permanent body
arbitration clause
compromise
Permanent Court of Arbitration
PCA
panel of independent potential arbitrators
Arbitration Rules 2012
conciliation

Establishment of international arbitral tribunals

International arbitral tribunals are created by the will of the parties. The parties institute an arbitral tribunal on a parity basis (a **special tribunal**) or by application to a **permanent body**.

Under the Hague Convention for the Pacific Settlement of International Disputes of 1899, '[i]nternational arbitration has for its object the settlement of differences between States by judges of their own choice, and on the basis of respect for law.'[247]

The arbitration clause or compromise

The reference to arbitration can be formulated either in the form of the **arbitration clause** or in the document, which is called a **compromise**. An arbitration clause is a specific provision in a contract which is devoted to arbitration.[248] A compromise is an agreement to submit a dispute to arbitration, which parties commonly enter into after a dispute has arisen.

---

247 Article 15 of the Hague Convention for the Pacific Settlement of International Disputes of 1899.

248 See the muster of the 'model arbitration clause for treaties and other agreements' in the Arbitration Rules 2012 of Permanent Court of Arbitration: 'Any dispute, controversy or claim arising out of or in relation to this [agreement] [treaty], or the existence, interpretation, application, breach, termination,

Generally, in the arbitration clause or the compromise, the following issues are being determined:

- rules of formation of the arbitral tribunal;
- object of dispute;
- reference to the sources of law;
- rule of procedure for the arbitration; and
- obligation of the parties to fulfil the decision of the arbitral tribunal.

The decision of the international arbitral tribunal

The decision of the arbitral tribunal is legally binding. The decision is final and cannot be appealed. The decision can be revised only when new circumstances are detected or the arbitration clause or compromise provisions (i.e. procedural rules) are violated.

Permanent Court of Arbitration

In order to facilitate 'an immediate recourse to arbitration for international differences, which it has not been possible to settle by diplomacy', the **Permanent Court of Arbitration (PCA)** was established under the Hague Conventions for the Pacific Settlement of International Disputes of 1899 and 1907 (accordingly, Articles 20 and 41 of the Conventions).

The PCA has a three-part organisational structure consisting of an Administrative Council, a **panel of independent potential arbitrators**, and a Secretariat – the International Bureau, headed by the Secretary-General.

The Administrative Council is composed of the diplomatic representatives of the signatory powers accredited to the Hague and the Minister for Foreign Affairs of the Netherlands, who acts as the President of the Council. The Administrative Council is a body which exercises general guidance on the work of the arbitration and oversees its policies and budgets and whose duty is 'the establishment and organization of the International Bureau, which . . . [is] under its direction and control.'[249]

The International Bureau, established in the Hague, provides administrative support to tribunals and other establishments under the framework of the PCA (for example, the Fact-finding Commissions of Inquiry), serves as the official channel for communication, and ensures safe custody of documents. It has custody of the archives and conducts all the administrative duties.

An official list of potential arbitrators is maintained. Each member state may appoint up to four persons 'of known competency in questions of international law, of the highest moral reputation and disposed to accept the duties of arbitrators'[250] for a renewable six-year term. The arbitrators included on the list are known as the Members of the Court. The

---

or invalidity thereof, shall be settled by arbitration in accordance with the PCA Arbitration Rules 2012.'

249 Article 28 of the Hague Convention for the Pacific Settlement of International Disputes of 1899.

250 Accordingly, Articles 23 and 44 of the Hague Conventions for the Pacific Settlement of International Disputes of 1899 and 1907.

Members from each member state together form a 'national group', which, in turn, has the right to nominate candidates for election to the International Court of Justice.

However, as described on the official website of the Permanent Court of Arbitration,

> [w]hen the PCA appoints an arbitrator, it is not restricted to appointing individuals on any particular list. The PCA will appoint the individual it considers most appropriate, subject to the parties' agreement and the rules governing the arbitration. Nor are parties to PCA arbitrations required to appoint arbitrators from any given list.[251]

The lawsuit is usually divided into two phases – written pleadings and oral discussion. During the first part of the procedure, the parties submit and exchange all relevant documents in support of their case.

Several years ago, the Permanent Court of Arbitration published the **Arbitration Rules 2012** (without replacing the previously adopted PCA Rules), which are the PCA's newest set of procedural rules. The Rules are for use in arbitrating disputes involving at least one state, state-controlled entity, or intergovernmental organisation. According to Paragraph 1 of Article 1 of the Arbitration Rules 2012:

> Where a State, State-controlled entity, or intergovernmental organization has agreed with one or more States, State-controlled entities, intergovernmental organizations, or private parties that disputes between them in respect of a defined legal relationship, whether contractual, treaty-based, or otherwise, shall be referred to arbitration under the Permanent Court of Arbitration Arbitration Rules 2012 . . . then such disputes shall be settled in accordance with these Rules subject to such modification as the parties may agree.

Hence, the parties have a choice to use the previously adopted PCA Rules; the Arbitration Rules 2012; or, under the respective agreement, apply modified arbitration rules.

At the same time, under the Arbitration Rules 2012:

> Agreement by a State, State-controlled entity, or intergovernmental organization to arbitrate under these Rules with a party that is not a State, State-controlled entity, or intergovernmental organization constitutes a waiver of any right of immunity from jurisdiction in respect of the proceedings relating to the dispute in question to which such party might otherwise be entitled. . . . The Rules allow parties to choose an arbitral tribunal of one, three, or five persons; and . . . The choice of arbitrators is not limited to persons who are listed as Members of the PCA. . . . If the parties have not previously agreed on the number of arbitrators, and if within 30 days after the receipt by the respondent of the notice of arbitration the parties have not agreed on the number of arbitrators, three arbitrators shall be appointed.[252]

---

251 <https://pca-cpa.org/en/faq/> accessed 16 March 2021.
252 Paragraph 2 of Article 1, Introduction and Paragraph 1 of Article 7 of the Arbitration Rules 2012.

Hence, the parties determine the number and appointment method of the arbitrators. If three arbitrators are to be appointed, each party usually appoints one arbitrator, and the two arbitrators thus appointed choose the third arbitrator, who acts as the presiding arbitrator of the tribunal. In cases when the parties or the appointed arbitrators do not appoint or agree on the arbitrators, the appointing authority shall, at the request of any party, constitute the arbitral tribunal. The Secretary-General of the Permanent Court of Arbitration serves as appointing authority or may designate another appointing authority.

Conciliation under the PCA framework

There is an established, integrated PCA dispute resolution system that links the procedures for **conciliation** with possible arbitration under the various 'PCA Optional Arbitration Rules'. Under the PCA dispute resolution system, conciliation is very similar to mediation. At the same time, it is a method for resolving differences without the need to resort to arbitration.

The party initiating conciliation sends the other party a written invitation to conciliate, briefly identifying the subject of the dispute. The conciliation proceedings commence when the other party accepts the invitation. According to the PCA Optional Conciliation Rules, '[t]here shall be one conciliator unless the parties agree that there shall be two or three conciliators. . . . In conciliation proceedings with two conciliators, each party appoints one conciliator'. In conciliation proceedings with one or three conciliators, the parties shall endeavour to reach an agreement, accordingly, on the name of a single conciliator or a third conciliator. At the same time, the parties may agree to apply any other procedure with regard to the appointment of conciliators.

The ultimate goal of conciliation is for the parties to agree to resolve the dispute. If the conciliation ends in a positive outcome, the parties draw up and sign a written settlement agreement, or, upon request, the conciliator can also participate in the drafting of such an agreement.

Advantages of arbitration

The main advantages of arbitration, as opposed to the courts (either national or international), are that:

1   It affords the parties involved the most influence on the process since, at first, by mutual agreement, they must decide whether or not to refer the issue to the arbitration; if they proceed to arbitration, they participate in the selection of arbitrators, determine the procedures, and so on.
2   The issue may be settled in a shorter period of time.
3   The arbitration may be less formal and more confidential (less public).
4   While only states have to stand in certain international courts to settle the legal disputes (for example, in the International Court of Justice), the other subjects of international law may prefer to resolve their disputes in arbitration.

Advantages of court adjudication

On the other hand, court adjudication (either national or international) also has its benefits:

1   As opposed to the non-permanent arbitral tribunals, the courts are readily available since they are the permanent entities staffed with experienced, committed full-time judges.

2   Arbitration can be more expensive than going to court.

3   The rule that the decision of arbitration is final and cannot ordinarily be appealed on the substantive issues may be regarded as an advantage of going to arbitration since it is a time-consuming mechanism. However, on the other hand, it may be riskier for the parties to have no chance to appeal on substantial matters, which is allowed in the case of national courts, as well as, in certain cases, in international courts.

International courts

ad hoc
Permanent Court of International Justice
PCIJ
Covenant of the League of Nations
International Court of Justice
ICJ
Statute of the International Court of Justice
contentious cases
advisory opinions
special agreement
articles in the treaty
unilateral statement
Food and Agriculture Organisation
World Health Organisation
United Nations Educational, Scientific and Cultural Organisation
ex aequo et bono
equity and goodness

Variety of international courts

There are several courts at the international level.

The jurisdiction of certain courts is general, without limitation as to areas (for example, the Permanent Court of International Justice and International Court of Justice, which will be discussed in detail later in this chapter); the others cover only specific fields and are commonly referred to as the 'specialist' international courts or tribunals (for example, the International Criminal Court).

Certain courts operate at the global level (for example, the courts listed earlier); some others have jurisdiction at the regional level (as, for instance, the European Court of Justice, the European Court of Human Rights, and the Inter-American Court of Human Rights).

International courts are usually permanent institutions. However, sometimes temporary or so-called ***ad hoc***[253] tribunals are also created (such as the Nuremberg International Military Tribunal and the Tokyo International Military Tribunal).

---

253 'AD HOC [L. *ad* + *hic, haec, hoc* / this] For this; for this particular purpose only. Someone or something selected or designated for a special purpose, as an *ad hoc* committee; also used to describe an act done at the spur of the moment, as an *ad hoc* solution or an *ad hoc* demonstration.' Emanuel (n 90) 12.

Finally, at the interstate level, certain permanent judicial bodies have been instituted (for instance, the International Tribunal for the Law of the Sea), which are not formally designated as 'courts' but should be considered international courts since they share the basic characteristics of such courts: namely, (1) they are constituted by international treaties delegating judicial powers to these institutions; (2) they are judicial bodies made up of certain judges or 'members', and the parties to a particular dispute do not participate in the selection of judges; (3) the parties to a particular dispute shall comply with mandatory procedural rules without the ordinary right to change them by mutual agreement; and so on.

The decisions of certain international courts are final. For example, the judgments of the International Court of Justice are final and without appeal. However, some international judicial bodies provide for the possibility of appeal. For instance, in the International Criminal Court, the prosecutor and the defence have the right to appeal a Trial Chamber's decision on the verdict. An appeal is decided by the Appeals Chamber.

Permanent Court of International Justice

The **Permanent Court of International Justice (PCIJ)** began operation after World War I. The Court's establishment was provided for in the **Covenant of the League of Nations**. It was an international court attached to the League of Nations. 'Between 1922 and 1940 the PCIJ dealt with 29 contentious cases between States, and delivered 27 advisory opinions.'[254] By the Resolution for the Dissolution of the League of Nations, adopted by the Assembly on 18 April 1946, the Court and the League both ceased to exist.

International Court of Justice

The **International Court of Justice** (also referred to as the **ICJ**) was established based on the UN Charter and **Statute of the International Court of Justice** of 1945. The ICJ is located in the Peace Palace in the Hague, which also houses the Permanent Court of Arbitration.

The ICJ is one of the six principal organs of the United Nations.

The composition of the ICJ

As defined by Statute:

> The Court shall be composed of a body of independent judges, elected regardless of their nationality from among persons of high moral character, who possess the qualifications required in their respective countries for appointment to the highest judicial offices, or are jurisconsults of recognized competence in international law.[255]

254 See on the official site of the International Court of Justice, <www.icj-cij.org/en/pcij> accessed 16 March 2021.

255 Article 2 of the Statute of the International Court of Justice.

The Court shall consist of fifteen members, no two of whom may be nationals of the same state.[256]

The members of the Court shall be elected by the General Assembly and by the Security Council from a list of persons nominated by the national groups in the Permanent Court of Arbitration. . . . In the case of Members of the United Nations not represented in the Permanent Court of Arbitration, candidates shall be nominated by national groups appointed for this purpose by their governments under the same conditions as those prescribed for members of the Permanent Court of Arbitration by Article 44 of the Convention of The Hague of 1907 for the pacific settlement of international disputes.[257]

The General Assembly and the Security Council shall proceed independently of one another to elect the members of the Court.[258]

The judges are elected to nine-year terms and may be re-elected.

The parties to the Statute of the ICJ

As stated in Article 93 of the UN Charter, all UN members are *ipso facto* parties to the Court's Statute. Non-UN member states may also become parties to the Court's Statute under Article 93. For example, before becoming a UN member state, Switzerland applied this procedure in 1948 to become a party.[259]

The main functions of the ICJ

International Court of Justice:

* Settles legal disputes submitted to it by the states. Only states may be parties in contentious cases presented before the Court.
* Provides advisory opinions on legal questions submitted to it by duly authorised international bodies, the UN General Assembly, or the Security Council.

Consequently, there are the two types of ICJ cases – **contentious cases** and **advisory opinions**.

The contentious cases

Concerning the contentious cases, the framework of the jurisdiction of the ICJ is based on:

256 Article 3 of the Statute of the International Court of Justice.
257 Article 4 of the Statute of the International Court of Justice.
258 Article 8 of the Statute of the International Court of Justice.
259 Liechtenstein (as from 29 March 1950), San Marino (as from 18 February 1954), Japan (as from 2 April 1954), and Nauru (as from 29 January 1988) also fell into this category before joining the United Nations.

- **Special agreement** concluded by the parties of the dispute.
- **Articles in the treaty.** Some treaties contain jurisdictional articles in which the state agrees to accept the jurisdiction of the Court concerning the interpretation or application of the treaty in the future.
- **Unilateral statement.** A declaration by a state on the recognition of the jurisdiction of the Court as compulsory on any other state that has undertaken the same obligation. The states which are the parties to the Statute of the Court may 'at any time declare that they recognize as compulsory *ipso facto* and without special agreement, in relation to any other State accepting the same obligation, the jurisdiction of the Court.'[260]

The condition for transferring the case to the Court is contained in the Charters of such specialised organisations as the **Food and Agriculture Organisation** (FAO),[261] the **World Health Organisation** (WHO),[262] and the **United Nations Educational, Scientific and Cultural Organisation** (UNESCO),[263] as well as in conventions on international crimes, conventions in the field of international environmental law, and some other international treaties.

As of 2021, more than seventy states have deposited the declarations recognising the jurisdiction of the Court as compulsory with the Secretary-General of the United Nations.[264] Most of these unilateral statements contain reservations that exclude from the reach of the ICJ certain categories of disputes.[265] In some cases, the states exclude in their declarations potential disputes with particular states,[266] or those disputes which emerged in a certain period of time, or when an agreement has been reached between the parties to the

260 Article 36 of the Statute of the International Court of Justice.
261 The Food and Agriculture Organisation is a specialised agency of the United Nations that guides the international efforts to defeat hunger.
262 The World Health Organisation is a specialised agency of the United Nations that is a directing and coordinating authority on international health work.
263 The United Nations Educational, Scientific and Cultural Organisation is a specialised agency of the United Nations, whose principal objective is to contribute to peace and security in the world by promoting collaboration among nations through education, science, culture and communication.
264 An example of such a declaration is the declaration from Georgia: 'I have the honour on behalf of the Republic of Georgia to declare that, in accordance with paragraph 2 of Article 36 of the Statute of the International Court of Justice, the Republic of Georgia recognizes as compulsory *ipso facto* and without special agreement, in relation to any other State accepting the same obligation, the jurisdiction of the Court in all legal disputes referred to in paragraph 2 of Article 36 of the Statute of the International Court of Justice. Tbilisi, 16 June 1995. (Signed) Alexander Chikvaidze, Minister of Foreign Affairs of the Republic of Georgia.'
265 For example, the declaration from Japan: 'This declaration does not apply to . . . (3) any dispute arising out of, concerning, or relating to research on, or conservation, management or exploitation of, living resources of the sea.'
266 Commonly, such a limitation is based on the condition of reciprocity; however, in some instances, the declarations refer to the particular group of states, as in the case of the United Kingdom of Great Britain and Northern Ireland, which accepted as compulsory *ipso facto* and without special convention the jurisdiction of the ICJ over *all disputes arising after 1 January 1987*, with regard to situations or facts subsequent to the same date, other than '(ii) any dispute with the government of any other country which is or has been a Member of the Commonwealth.'

dispute on some other method of peaceful settlement, and so forth. Of the five permanent members of the Security Council, only one – the United Kingdom of Great Britain and Northern Ireland – made a statement that continues to operate up to the present time. Previously, it was done by France and the US, but they withdrew their statements, while China and Russia never made such statements. Meanwhile, even in the declaration of the United Kingdom, there are several categories of disputes which are left out of the reach of the ICJ.

The Court shall decide the disputes in accordance with international law. That is why the Statute reflects the exhaustive list of the ordinary sources and subsidiary means of international law in Article 38. Nevertheless, this provision does not prejudice the power of the Court to decide a case **ex aequo et bono**,[267] if the parties agree to it. As noted earlier, a decision *ex aequo et bono*, i.e. in accordance with **equity and goodness**, may be performed primarily when the rule of international law governing a dispute is unclear or might fail to resolve the dispute adequately for some other reason.

The advisory opinions

Under Article 96 of the UN Charter:

> 1. The General Assembly or the Security Council may request the International Court of Justice to give an advisory opinion on any legal question. 2. Other organs of the United Nations and specialized agencies, which may at any time be so authorized by the General Assembly, may also request advisory opinions of the Court on legal questions arising within the scope of their activities.

As noted earlier, only the states are eligible to appear before the court to settle their disputes, while other subjects of international law are devoid of such a right, including the international governmental organisations, which cannot be parties to a contentious case before the ICJ. However, there is assigned a special procedure – the advisory procedure, which is only available to five United Nations organs (General Assembly, Security Council, Economic and Social Council, Trusteeship Council, Interim Committee of the General Assembly – the permanent intersessional Committee), authorised UN Specialised Agencies, and one Related Organisation (International Atomic Energy Agency).[268] To open up an advisory proceeding, a written request for an advisory opinion should be sent to the Registrar by the United Nations Secretary-General or the director or secretary-general of the entity requesting the opinion.

Advisory opinions are not generally binding, except in rare cases where its binding force is directly articulated (for instance, as in the Convention on the Privileges and Immunities of the United Nations, the Convention on the Privileges and Immunities of the Specialised Agencies of the United Nations, and the Headquarters Agreement between the United

---

267 As mentioned earlier, *Ex aequo et bono* is a Latin phrase meaning '[f]rom equity and goodness. A manner of deciding a case pending before a tribunal with reference to the principles of fairness and justice in preference to any principle of positive law.' *Guide to Latin in International Law* (n 71) 91.

268 See on the official site of the International Court of Justice, <www.icj-cij.org/en/organs-agencies-authorized> accessed 16 March 2021.

Nations and the United States of America). Consequently, from a legal point of view, the effect an advisory opinion will ordinarily have is entirely dependent on the decision of the requesting organ, agency, organisation and on the whole, on the subjects of international law.

CASES AND MATERIALS (*SELECTED PARTS*)

Principles of international law concerning friendly relations and co-operation among states

Declaration on Principles of International Law concerning Friendly Relations and Co-operation among States in accordance with the Charter of the United Nations
Annex to the UN General Assembly Resolution – A/RES/2625(XXV) of 24 October 1970.

The General Assembly . . .

1   *Solemnly proclaims* the following principles:

The principle that States shall refrain in their international relations from the threat or use of force against the territorial integrity or political independence of any State or in any other manner inconsistent with the purposes of the United Nations

Every State has the duty to refrain in its international relations from the threat or use of force against the territorial integrity or political independence of any State, or in any other manner inconsistent with the purposes of the United Nations. Such a threat or use of force constitutes a violation of international law and the Charter of the United Nations and shall never be employed as a means of settling international issues.

A war of aggression constitutes a crime against the peace, for which there is responsibility under international law.

In accordance with the purposes and principles of the United Nations, States have the duty to refrain from propaganda for wars of aggression.

Every State has the duty to refrain from the threat or use of force to violate the existing international boundaries of another State or as a means of solving international disputes, including territorial disputes and problems concerning frontiers of States.

Every State likewise has the duty to refrain from the threat or use of force to violate international lines of demarcation, such as armistice lines, established by or pursuant to an international agreement to which it is a party or which it is otherwise bound to respect. Nothing in the foregoing shall be construed as prejudicing the positions of the parties concerned with regard to the status and effects of such lines under their special regimes or as affecting their temporary character.

States have a duty to refrain from acts of reprisal involving the use of force.

Every State has the duty to refrain from any forcible action which deprives peoples referred to in the elaboration of the principle of equal rights and self-determination of their right to self-determination and freedom and independence.

Every State has the duty to refrain from organizing or encouraging the organization of irregular forces or armed bands including mercenaries, for incursion into the territory of another State.

Every State has the duty to refrain from organizing, instigating, assisting or participating in acts of civil strife or terrorist acts in another State or acquiescing in organized activities within its territory directed towards the commission of such acts, when the acts referred to in the present paragraph involve a threat or use of force.

The territory of a State shall not be the object of military occupation resulting from the use of force in contravention of the provisions of the Charter. The territory of a State shall not be the object of acquisition by another State resulting from the threat or use of force. No territorial acquisition resulting from the threat or use of force shall be recognized as legal. Nothing in the foregoing shall be construed as affecting:

(a)   Provisions of the Charter or any international agreement prior to the Charter regime and valid under international law; or
(b)   The powers of the Security Council under the Charter.

All States shall pursue in good faith negotiations for the early conclusion of a universal treaty on general and complete disarmament under effective international control and strive to adopt appropriate measures to reduce international tensions and strengthen confidence among States.

All States shall comply in good faith with their obligations under the generally recognized principles and rules of international law with respect to the maintenance of international peace and security, and shall endeavour to make the United Nations security system based on the Charter more effective.

Nothing in the foregoing paragraphs shall be construed as enlarging or diminishing in any way the scope of the provisions of the Charter concerning cases in which the use of force is lawful.

The principle that States shall settle their international disputes by peaceful means in such a manner that international peace and security and justice are not endangered

Every State shall settle its international disputes with other States by peaceful means in such a manner that international peace and security and justice are not endangered.

States shall accordingly seek early and just settlement of their international disputes by negotiation, inquiry, mediation, conciliation, arbitration, judicial settlement, resort to regional agencies or arrangements or other peaceful means of their choice. In seeking such a settlement the parties shall agree upon such peaceful means as may be appropriate to the circumstances and nature of the dispute.

The parties to a dispute have the duty, in the event of failure to reach a solution by any one of the above peaceful means, to continue to seek a settlement of the dispute by other peaceful means agreed upon by them.

States parties to an international dispute, as well as other States shall refrain from any action which may aggravate the Situation so as to endanger the maintenance of international peace and security, and shall act in accordance with the purposes and principles of the United Nations.

International disputes shall be settled on the basis of the Sovereign equality of States and in accordance with the Principle of free choice of means. Recourse to, or acceptance of, a settlement procedure freely agreed to by States with regard to existing or future disputes to which they are parties shall not be regarded as incompatible with sovereign equality.

Nothing in the foregoing paragraphs prejudices or derogates from the applicable provisions of the Charter, in particular those relating to the pacific settlement of international disputes.

The principle concerning the duty not to intervene in matters within the domestic jurisdiction of any State, in accordance with the Charter

No State or group of States has the right to intervene, directly or indirectly, for any reason whatever, in the internal or external affairs of any other State. Consequently, armed intervention and all other forms of interference or attempted threats against the personality of the State or against its political, economic and cultural elements, are in violation of international law.

No State may use or encourage the use of economic political or any other type of measures to coerce another State in order to obtain from it the subordination of the exercise of its sovereign rights and to secure from it advantages of any kind. Also, no State shall organize, assist, foment, finance, incite or tolerate subversive, terrorist or armed activities directed towards the violent overthrow of the regime of another State, or interfere in civil strife in another State.

The use of force to deprive peoples of their national identity constitutes a violation of their inalienable rights and of the principle of non-intervention.

Every State has an inalienable right to choose its political, economic, social and cultural systems, without interference in any form by another State.

Nothing in the foregoing paragraphs shall be construed as reflecting the relevant provisions of the Charter relating to the maintenance of international peace and security.

The duty of States to co-operate with one another in accordance with the Charter

States have the duty to co-operate with one another, irrespective of the differences in their political, economic and social systems, in the various spheres of international relations, in order to maintain international peace and security and to promote international economic stability and progress, the general welfare of nations and international co-operation free from discrimination based on such differences.

To this end:

(a) States shall co-operate with other States in the maintenance of international peace and security;
(b) States shall co-operate in the promotion of universal respect for, and observance of, human rights and fundamental freedoms for all, and in the elimination of all forms of racial discrimination and all forms of religious intolerance;
(c) States shall conduct their international relations in the economic, social, cultural, technical and trade fields in accordance with the principles of sovereign equality and non-intervention;
(d) States Members of the United Nations have the duty to take joint and separate action in co-operation with the United Nations in accordance with the relevant provisions of the Charter. States should co-operate in the economic, social and cultural fields as well as in the field of science and technology and for the promotion of international cultural and educational progress.

States should co-operate in the promotion of economic growth throughout the world, especially that of the developing countries.

The principle of equal rights and self-determination of peoples

By virtue of the principle of equal rights and self-determination of peoples enshrined in the Charter of the United Nations, all peoples have the right freely to determine, without external interference, their political status and to pursue their economic, social and cultural development, and every State has the duty to respect this right in accordance with the provisions of the Charter.

Every State has the duty to promote, through joint and separate action, realization of the principle of equal rights and self-determination of peoples, in accordance with the provisions of the Charter, and to render assistance to the United Nations in carrying out the responsibilities entrusted to it by the Charter regarding the implementation of the principle, in order:

(a) To promote friendly relations and co-operation among States; and
(b) To bring a speedy end to colonialism, having due regard to the freely expressed will of the peoples concerned;

and bearing in mind that subjection of peoples to alien subjugation, domination and exploitation constitutes a violation of the principle, as well as a denial of fundamental human rights, and is contrary to the Charter.

Every State has the duty to promote through joint and separate action universal respect for and observance of human rights and fundamental freedoms in accordance with the Charter.

The establishment of a sovereign and independent State, the free association or integration with an independent State or the emergence into any other political status freely determined by a people constitute modes of implementing the right of self-determination by that people.

Every State has the duty to refrain from any forcible action which deprives peoples referred to above in the elaboration of the present principle of their right to self-determination and freedom and independence. In their actions against, and resistance to, such forcible action in pursuit of the exercise of their right to self-determination, such peoples are entitled to seek and to receive support in accordance with the purposes and principles of the Charter.

The territory of a colony or other Non-Self-Governing Territory has, under the Charter, a status separate and distinct from the territory of the State administering it; and such separate and distinct status under the Charter shall exist until the people of the colony or Non-Self-Governing Territory have exercised their right of self-determination in accordance with the Charter, and particularly its purposes and principles.

Nothing in the foregoing paragraphs shall be construed as authorizing or encouraging any action which would dismember or impair, totally or in part, the territorial integrity or political unity of sovereign and independent States conducting themselves in compliance with the principle of equal rights and self-determination of peoples as described above and thus possessed of a government representing the whole people belonging to the territory without distinction as to race, creed or colour.

Every State shall refrain from any action aimed at the partial or total disruption of the national unity and territorial integrity of any other State or country.

The principle of sovereign equality of States

All States enjoy sovereign equality. They have equal rights and duties and are equal members of the international community, notwithstanding differences of an economic, social, political or other nature.

In particular, sovereign equality includes the following elements:

(a) States are juridically equal;
(b) Each State enjoys the rights inherent in full sovereignty;
(c) Each State has the duty to respect the personality of other States;

(d) The territorial integrity and political independence of the State are inviolable;

(e) Each State has the right freely to choose and develop its political, social, economic and cultural systems;

(f) Each State has the duty to comply fully and in good faith with its international obligations and to live in peace with other States.

The principle that States shall fulfil in good faith the obligations assumed by them in accordance with the Charter

Every State has the duty to fulfil in good faith the obligations assumed by it in accordance with the Charter of the United Nations.

Every State has the duty to fulfil in good faith its obligations under the generally recognized principles and rules of international law.

Every State has the duty to fulfil in good faith its obligations under international agreements valid under the generally recognized principles and rules of international law.

Where obligations arising under international agreements are in conflict with the obligations of Members of the United Nations under the Charter of the United Nations, the obligations under the Charter shall prevail.

Helsinki principles

Helsinki Declaration on Principles Guiding Relations between Participating States, the Final Act of the Conference on Security and Co-operation in Europe of 1975

III. Inviolability of frontiers

The participating States regard as inviolable all one another's frontiers as well as the frontiers of all States in Europe and therefore they will refrain now and in the future from assaulting these frontiers.

Accordingly, they will also refrain from any demand for, or act of, seizure and usurpation of part or all of the territory of any participating State.

IV. Territorial integrity of States

The participating States will respect the territorial integrity of each of the participating States.

Accordingly, they will refrain from any action inconsistent with the purposes and principles of the Charter of the United Nations against the territorial integrity, political independence or the unity of any participating State, and in particular from any such action constituting a threat or use of force.

The participating States will likewise refrain from making each other's territory the object of military occupation or other direct or indirect measures of force in contravention of international law, or the object of acquisition by means of such measures or the threat of them. No such occupation or acquisition will be recognized as legal.

VII. Respect for human rights and fundamental freedoms, including the freedom of thought, conscience, religion or belief

The participating States will respect human rights and fundamental freedoms, including the freedom of thought, conscience, religion or belief, for all without distinction as to race, sex, language or religion.

They will promote and encourage the effective exercise of civil, political, economic, social, cultural and other rights and freedoms all of which derive from the inherent dignity of the human person and are essential for his free and full development.

Within this framework the participating States will recognize and respect the freedom of the individual to profess and practice, alone or in community with others, religion or belief acting in accordance with the dictates of his own conscience.

The participating States on whose territory national minorities exist will respect the right of persons belonging to such minorities to equality before the law, will afford them the full opportunity for the actual enjoyment of human rights and fundamental freedoms and will, in this manner, protect their legitimate interests in this sphere.

The participating States recognize the universal significance of human rights and fundamental freedoms, respect for which is an essential factor for the peace, justice and well-being necessary to ensure the development of friendly relations and co-operation among themselves as among all States.

They will constantly respect these rights and freedoms in their mutual relations and will endeavour jointly and separately, including in co-operation with the United Nations, to promote universal and effective respect for them.

They confirm the right of the individual to know and act upon his rights and duties in this field.

In the field of human rights and fundamental freedoms, the participating States will act in conformity with the purposes and principles of the Charter of the United Nations and with the Universal Declaration of Human Rights. They will also fulfil their obligations as set forth in the international declarations and agreements in this field, including inter alia the International Covenants on Human Rights, by which they may be bound.

Aggression

Definition of Aggression. Annex to the UN General Assembly Resolution – A/RES/3314(XXIX) of 14 December 1974

Article 1

Aggression is the use of armed force by a State against the sovereignty, territorial integrity or political independence of another State, or in any other manner inconsistent with the Charter of the United Nations, as set out in this Definition.

Explanatory note: In this Definition the term "State":

(a) Is used without prejudice to questions of recognition or to whether a State is a member of the United Nations;
(b) Includes the concept of a "group of States" where appropriate.

Article 2

The first use of armed force by a State in contravention of the Charter shall constitute prima facie evidence of an act of aggression although the Security Council may, in conformity with the Charter, conclude that a determination that an act of aggression has been committed would not be justified in the light of other relevant circumstances, including the fact that the acts concerned or their consequences are not of sufficient gravity.

Article 3

Any of the following acts, regardless of a declaration of war, shall, subject to and in accordance with the provisions of article 2, qualify as an act of aggression:

(a) The invasion or attack by the armed forces of a State of the territory of another State, or any military occupation, however temporary, resulting from such invasion or attack, or any annexation by the use of force of the territory of another State or part thereof;

(b) Bombardment by the armed forces of a State against the territory of another State or the use of any weapons by a State against the territory of another State;

(c) The blockade of the ports or coasts of a State by the armed forces of another State;

(d) An attack by the armed forces of a State on the land, sea or air forces, or marine and air fleets of another State;

(e) The use of armed forces of one State which are within the territory of another State with the agreement of the receiving State, in contravention of the conditions provided for in the agreement or any extension of their presence in such territory beyond the termination of the agreement;

(f) The action of a State in allowing its territory, which it has placed at the disposal of another State, to be used by that other State for perpetrating an act of aggression against a third State;

(g) The sending by or on behalf of a State of armed bands, groups, irregulars or mercenaries, which carry out acts of armed force against another State of such gravity as to amount to the acts listed above, or its substantial involvement therein.

Article 4

The acts enumerated above are not exhaustive and the Security Council may determine that other acts constitute aggression under the provisions of the Charter.

Article 5

1 No consideration of whatever nature, whether political, economic, military or otherwise, may serve as a justification for aggression.

2 A war of aggression is a crime against international peace. Aggression gives rise to international responsibility.

3 No territorial acquisition or special advantage resulting from aggression is or shall be recognized as lawful.

Article 6

Nothing in this Definition shall be construed as in any way enlarging or diminishing the scope of the Charter, including its provisions concerning cases in which the use of force is lawful.

Article 7

Nothing in this Definition, and in particular article 3, could in any way prejudice the right to self-determination, freedom and independence, as derived from the Charter, of peoples forcibly deprived of that right and referred to in the Declaration on Principles of International Law concerning Friendly Relations and Co-operation among States in accordance with the Charter of the United Nations, particularly peoples under colonial and racist regimes or other forms of alien domination: nor the right of these peoples to struggle to that end and to seek and receive support, in accordance with the principles of the Charter and in conformity with the above-mentioned Declaration.

Article 8

In their interpretation and application the above provisions are interrelated and each provision should be construed in the context of the other provisions.

Complex arrangement of international law
Individual or collective self-defence

Military and Paramilitary Activities in and against Nicaragua (Nicaragua v United States of America), Judgment of 27 June 1986, International Court of Justice
ICJ Reports 1986, 14.

175. The Court does not consider that, in the areas of law relevant to the present dispute, it can be claimed that all the customary rules which may be invoked have a content exactly identical to that of the rules contained in the treaties which cannot be applied by virtue of the United States reservation. On a number of points, the areas governed by the two sources of law do not exactly overlap, and the substantive rules in which they are framed are not identical in content. But in addition, even if a treaty norm and a customary norm relevant to the present dispute were to have exactly the same content, this would not be a reason for the Court to take the view that the operation of the treaty process must necessarily deprive the customary norm of its separate applicability. Nor can the multilateral treaty reservation be interpreted as meaning that, once applicable to a given dispute, it would exclude the application of any rule of customary international law the content of which was the same as, or analogous to, that of the treaty-law rule which had caused the reservation to become effective.

176. As regards the suggestion that the areas covered by the two sources of law are identical, the Court observes that the United Nations Charter, the convention to which most of the United States argument is directed, by no means covers the whole area of the regulation of the use of force in international relations. On one essential point, this treaty itself refers to pre-existing customary international law; this reference to customary law is contained in the actual text of Article 51, which mentions the "inherent right" (in the French text the "droit naturel") of individual or collective self-defence, which "nothing in the present Charter shall impair" and which applies in the event of an armed attack. The Court therefore finds that Article 51 of the Charter is only meaningful on the basis that there is a "natural" or "inherent" right of self-defence, and it is hard to see how this can be other than of a customary nature, even if its present content has been confirmed and influenced by the Charter. Moreover the Charter, having itself recognized the existence of this right, does not go on to regulate directly all aspects of its content. For example, it does not contain any specific rule whereby self-defence would warrant only measures which are proportional to the armed attack and necessary to respond to it, a rule well established in customary international law. Moreover, a definition of the "armed attack" which, if found to exist, authorizes the exercise of the "inherent right" of self-defence, is not provided in the Charter, and is not part of treaty law. It cannot therefore be held that Article 51 is a provision which "subsumes and supervenes" customary international law. It rather demonstrates that in the field in question, the

importance of which for the present dispute need hardly be stressed, customary international law continues to exist alongside treaty law. The areas governed by the two sources of law thus do not overlap exactly, and the rules do not have the same content. This could also be demonstrated for other subjects, in particular for the principle of non-intervention.

Pacific settlement of disputes
Action with respect to threats to the peace,
breaches of the peace, and acts of aggression

Charter of the United Nations
Entry into force: 24 October 1945

CHAPTER VI: PACIFIC SETTLEMENT OF DISPUTES

Article 33

1   The parties to any dispute, the continuance of which is likely to endanger the maintenance of international peace and security, shall, first of all, seek a solution by negotiation, enquiry, mediation, conciliation, arbitration, judicial settlement, resort to regional agencies or arrangements, or other peaceful means of their own choice.
2   The Security Council shall, when it deems necessary, call upon the parties to settle their dispute by such means.

Article 34

The Security Council may investigate any dispute, or any situation which might lead to international friction or give rise to a dispute, in order to determine whether the continuance of the dispute or situation is likely to endanger the maintenance of international peace and security.

Article 35

1   Any Member of the United Nations may bring any dispute, or any situation of the nature referred to in Article 34, to the attention of the Security Council or of the General Assembly.
2   A state which is not a Member of the United Nations may bring to the attention of the Security Council or of the General Assembly any dispute to which it is a party if it accepts in advance, for the purposes of the dispute, the obligations of pacific settlement provided in the present Charter.
3   The proceedings of the General Assembly in respect of matters brought to its attention under this Article will be subject to the provisions of Articles 11 and 12.

Article 36

1   The Security Council may, at any stage of a dispute of the nature referred to in Article 33 or of a situation of like nature, recommend appropriate procedures or methods of adjustment.

2   The Security Council should take into consideration any procedures for the settlement of the dispute which have already been adopted by the parties.
3   In making recommendations under this Article the Security Council should also take into consideration that legal disputes should as a general rule be referred by the parties to the International Court of Justice in accordance with the provisions of the Statute of the Court.

Article 37

1   Should the parties to a dispute of the nature referred to in Article 33 fail to settle it by the means indicated in that Article, they shall refer it to the Security Council.
2   If the Security Council deems that the continuance of the dispute is in fact likely to endanger the maintenance of international peace and security, it shall decide whether to take action under Article 36 or to recommend such terms of settlement as it may consider appropriate.

Article 38

Without prejudice to the provisions of Articles 33 to 37, the Security Council may, if all the parties to any dispute so request, make recommendations to the parties with a view to a pacific settlement of the dispute.

CHAPTER VII: ACTION WITH RESPECT TO THREATS TO THE PEACE, BREACHES OF THE PEACE, AND ACTS OF AGGRESSION

Article 39

The Security Council shall determine the existence of any threat to the peace, breach of the peace, or act of aggression and shall make recommendations, or decide what measures shall be taken in accordance with Articles 41 and 42, to maintain or restore international peace and security.

Article 40

In order to prevent an aggravation of the situation, the Security Council may, before making the recommendations or deciding upon the measures provided for in Article 39, call upon the parties concerned to comply with such provisional measures as it deems necessary or desirable. Such provisional measures shall be without prejudice to the rights, claims, or position of the parties concerned. The Security Council shall duly take account of failure to comply with such provisional measures.

Article 41

The Security Council may decide what measures not involving the use of armed force are to be employed to give effect to its decisions, and it may call upon the Members of the United Nations to apply such measures. These may include complete or partial interruption of economic relations and of rail, sea, air, postal, telegraphic, radio, and other means of communication, and the severance of diplomatic relations.

Article 42

Should the Security Council consider that measures provided for in Article 41 would be inadequate or have proved to be inadequate, it may take such action by air, sea, or land forces as may be necessary to maintain or restore international peace and security. Such action may include demonstrations, blockade, and other operations by air, sea, or land forces of Members of the United Nations.

Article 43

1   All Members of the United Nations, in order to contribute to the maintenance of international peace and security, undertake to make available to the Security Council, on its call and in accordance with a special agreement or agreements, armed forces, assistance, and facilities, including rights of passage, necessary for the purpose of maintaining international peace and security.
2   Such agreement or agreements shall govern the numbers and types of forces, their degree of readiness and general location, and the nature of the facilities and assistance to be provided.
3   The agreement or agreements shall be negotiated as soon as possible on the initiative of the Security Council. They shall be concluded between the Security Council and Members or between the Security Council and groups of Members and shall be subject to ratification by the signatory states in accordance with their respective constitutional processes.

Article 44

When the Security Council has decided to use force it shall, before calling upon a Member not represented on it to provide armed forces in fulfilment of the obligations assumed under Article 43, invite that Member, if the Member so desires, to participate in the decisions of the Security Council concerning the employment of contingents of that Member's armed forces.

Article 45

In order to enable the United Nations to take urgent military measures, Members shall hold immediately available national air-force contingents for combined international enforcement action. The strength and degree of readiness of these contingents and plans for their combined action shall be determined within the limits laid down in the special agreement or agreements referred to in Article 43, by the Security Council with the assistance of the Military Staff Committee.

Article 46

Plans for the application of armed force shall be made by the Security Council with the assistance of the Military Staff Committee.

Article 47

1   There shall be established a Military Staff Committee to advise and assist the Security Council on all questions relating to the Security Council's military requirements for the maintenance of international peace and security, the employment and command of forces placed at its disposal, the regulation of armaments, and possible disarmament.
2   The Military Staff Committee shall consist of the Chiefs of Staff of the permanent members of the Security Council or their representatives. Any Member of the United Nations not permanently represented on the Committee shall be invited by the Committee to be associated with it when the efficient discharge of the Committee's responsibilities requires the participation of that Member in its work.
3   The Military Staff Committee shall be responsible under the Security Council for the strategic direction of any armed forces placed at the disposal of the Security Council. Questions relating to the command of such forces shall be worked out subsequently.
4   The Military Staff Committee, with the authorization of the Security Council and after consultation with appropriate regional agencies, may establish regional sub-committees.

Article 48

1   The action required to carry out the decisions of the Security Council for the maintenance of international peace and security shall be taken by all the Members of the United Nations or by some of them, as the Security Council may determine.
2   Such decisions shall be carried out by the Members of the United Nations directly and through their action in the appropriate international agencies of which they are members.

Article 49

The Members of the United Nations shall join in affording mutual assistance in carrying out the measures decided upon by the Security Council.

Article 50

If preventive or enforcement measures against any state are taken by the Security Council, any other state, whether a Member of the United Nations or not, which finds itself confronted with special economic problems arising from the carrying out of those measures shall have the right to consult the Security Council with regard to a solution of those problems.

Article 51

Nothing in the present Charter shall impair the inherent right of individual or collective self-defence if an armed attack occurs against a Member of the United Nations, until the Security Council has taken measures necessary to maintain international peace and security. Measures taken by Members in the exercise of this right of self-defence shall be immediately reported to the Security Council and shall not in any way affect the authority and responsibility of the Security Council under the present Charter to take at any time such action as it deems necessary in order to maintain or restore international peace and security.

CHAPTER VIII: REGIONAL ARRANGEMENTS

Article 52

1   Nothing in the present Charter precludes the existence of regional arrangements or agencies for dealing with such matters relating to the maintenance of international peace and security as are appropriate for regional action provided that such arrangements or agencies and their activities are consistent with the Purposes and Principles of the United Nations.
2   The Members of the United Nations entering into such arrangements or constituting such agencies shall make every effort to achieve pacific settlement of local disputes through such regional arrangements or by such regional agencies before referring them to the Security Council.
3   The Security Council shall encourage the development of pacific settlement of local disputes through such regional arrangements or by such regional agencies either on the initiative of the states concerned or by reference from the Security Council.
4   This Article in no way impairs the application of Articles 34 and 35.

Article 53

1   The Security Council shall, where appropriate, utilize such regional arrangements or agencies for enforcement action under its authority. But no enforcement action shall be taken under regional arrangements or by regional agencies without the authorization of the Security Council, with the exception of measures against any enemy state, as defined in paragraph 2 of this Article, provided for pursuant to Article 107 or in regional arrangements directed against renewal of aggressive policy on the part of any such state, until such time as the Organization may, on request of the Governments concerned, be charged with the responsibility for preventing further aggression by such a state.
2   The term enemy state as used in paragraph 1 of this Article applies to any state which during the Second World War has been an enemy of any signatory of the present Charter.

Article 54

The Security Council shall at all times be kept fully informed of activities undertaken or in contemplation under regional arrangements or by regional agencies for the maintenance of international peace and security.

Neutrality

Legality of the Threat or Use of Nuclear Weapons, Advisory Opinion, 8 July 1996, International Court of Justice
ICJ Reports 1996, 226.

88. The Court will now turn to the principle of neutrality which was raised by several States. In the context of the advisory proceedings brought before the Court by the WHO concerning the *Legality of the Use by a State of Nuclear Weapons in Armed Conflict*, the position was put as follows by one State:

The principle of neutrality, in its classic sense, was aimed at preventing the incursion of belligerent forces into neutral territory, or attacks on the persons or ships of neutrals. Thus: 'the territory of neutral powers is inviolable' (Article 1 of the Hague Convention (V) Respecting the Rights and Duties of Neutral Powers and Persons in Case of War on Land, concluded on 18 October 1907); 'belligerents are bound to respect the sovereign rights of neutral powers . . .' (Article 1 to the Hague Convention (XIII) Respecting the Rights and Duties of Neutral Powers in Naval War. concluded on 18 October 1907), 'neutral states have equal inter& in having their rights respected by belligerents . . .' (Preamble to Convention on Maritime Neutrality, concluded on 20 February 1928). It is clear, however, that the principle of neutrality applies with equal force to transborder incursions of armed forces and to the transborder damage caused to a neutral State by the use of a weapon in a belligerent State.

(Nauru, Written Statement (1), p. 35, IV E.)

The principle so circumscribed is presented as an established part of the customary international law.

89. The Court finds that as in the case of the principles of humanitarian law applicable in armed conflict, international law leaves no doubt that the principle of neutrality, whatever its content, which is of a fundamental character similar to that of the humanitarian principles and rules, is applicable (subject to the relevant provisions of the United Nations Charter), to all international armed conflict, whatever type of weapons might be used.

International Court of Justice

Statute of the International Court of Justice

Entry into force: 24 October 1945
Chapter I: Organization of the Court (Articles 2–33)
Chapter II: Competence of the Court (Articles 34–38)
Chapter III: Procedure (Articles 39–64)
Chapter IV: Advisory Opinions (Articles 65–68)
Chapter V: Amendment (Articles 69 and 70)

Article 2

The Court shall be composed of a body of independent judges, elected regardless of their nationality from among persons of high moral character, who possess the qualifications required in their respective countries for appointment to the highest judicial offices, or are jurisconsults of recognized competence in international law.

Article 3

1   The Court shall consist of fifteen members, no two of whom may be nationals of the same state.
2   A person who for the purposes of membership in the Court could be regarded as a national of more than one state shall be deemed to be a national of the one in which he ordinarily exercises civil and political rights.

Article 4

1   The members of the Court shall be elected by the General Assembly and by the Security Council from a list of persons nominated by the national groups in the Permanent Court of Arbitration, in accordance with the following provisions.

2   In the case of Members of the United Nations not represented in the Permanent Court of Arbitration, candidates shall be nominated by national groups appointed for this purpose by their governments under the same conditions as those prescribed for members of the Permanent Court of Arbitration by Article 44 of the Convention of The Hague of 1907 for the pacific settlement of international disputes.

3   The conditions under which a state which is a party to the present Statute but is not a Member of the United Nations may participate in electing the members of the Court shall, in the absence of a special agreement, be laid down by the General Assembly upon recommendation of the Security Council.

Article 10

1   Those candidates who obtain an absolute majority of votes in the General Assembly and in the Security Council shall be considered as elected.

2   Any vote of the Security Council, whether for the election of judges or for the appointment of members of the conference envisaged in Article 12, shall be taken without any distinction between permanent and non-permanent members of the Security Council.

3   In the event of more than one national of the same state obtaining an absolute majority of the votes both of the General Assembly and of the Security Council, the eldest of these only shall be considered as elected.

Article 13

1   The members of the Court shall be elected for nine years and may be re-elected; provided, however, that of the judges elected at the first election, the terms of five judges shall expire at the end of three years and the terms of five more judges shall expire at the end of six years.

2   The judges whose terms are to expire at the end of the above-mentioned initial periods of three and six years shall be chosen by lot to be drawn by the Secretary-General immediately after the first election has been completed.

3   The members of the Court shall continue to discharge their duties until their places have been filled. Though replaced, they shall finish any cases which they may have begun.

4   In the case of the resignation of a member of the Court, the resignation shall be addressed to the President of the Court for transmission to the Secretary-General. This last notification makes the place vacant.

Article 16

1   No member of the Court may exercise any political or administrative function, or engage in any other occupation of a professional nature.

2   Any doubt on this point shall be settled by the decision of the Court.

Article 17

1 No member of the Court may act as agent, counsel, or advocate in any case.
2 No member may participate in the decision of any case in which he has previously taken part as agent, counsel, or advocate for one of the parties, or as a member of a national or international court, or of a commission of enquiry, or in any other capacity.
3 Any doubt on this point shall be settled by the decision of the Court.

Article 18

1 No member of the Court can be dismissed unless, in the unanimous opinion of the other members, he has ceased to fulfill the required conditions.
2 Formal notification thereof shall be made to the Secretary-General by the Registrar.
3 This notification makes the place vacant.

Article 21

1 The Court shall elect its President and Vice-President for three years; they may be re-elected.
2 The Court shall appoint its Registrar and may provide for the appointment of such other officers as may be necessary.

Article 22

1 The seat of the Court shall be established at The Hague. This, however, shall not prevent the Court from sitting and exercising its functions elsewhere whenever the Court considers it desirable.
2 The President and the Registrar shall reside at the seat of the Court.

Article 25

1 The full Court shall sit except when it is expressly provided otherwise in the present Statute.
2 Subject to the condition that the number of judges available to constitute the Court is not thereby reduced below eleven, the Rules of the Court may provide for allowing one or more judges, according to circumstances and in rotation, to be dispensed from sitting.
3 A quorum of nine judges shall suffice to constitute the Court.

Article 26

1 The Court may from time to time form one or more chambers, composed of three or more judges as the Court may determine, for dealing with particular categories of cases; for example, labour cases and cases relating to transit and communications.
2 The Court may at any time form a chamber for dealing with a particular case. The number of judges to constitute such a chamber shall be determined by the Court with the approval of the parties.
3 Cases shall be heard and determined by the chambers provided for in this article if the parties so request.

Article 34

1   Only states may be parties in cases before the Court.
2   The Court, subject to and in conformity with its Rules, may request of public international organizations information relevant to cases before it, and shall receive such information presented by such organizations on their own initiative.
3   Whenever the construction of the constituent instrument of a public international organization or of an international convention adopted thereunder is in question in a case before the Court, the Registrar shall so notify the public international organization concerned and shall communicate to it copies of all the written proceedings.

Article 35

1   The Court shall be open to the states parties to the present Statute.
2   The conditions under which the Court shall be open to other states shall, subject to the special provisions contained in treaties in force, be laid down by the Security Council, but in no case shall such conditions place the parties in a position of inequality before the Court.
3   When a state which is not a Member of the United Nations is a party to a case, the Court shall fix the amount which that party is to contribute towards the expenses of the Court. This provision shall not apply if such state is bearing a share of the expenses of the Court

Article 36

1   The jurisdiction of the Court comprises all cases which the parties refer to it and all matters specially provided for in the Charter of the United Nations or in treaties and conventions in force.
2   The states parties to the present Statute may at any time declare that they recognize as compulsory *ipso facto* and without special agreement, in relation to any other state accepting the same obligation, the jurisdiction of the Court in all legal disputes concerning:

a   the interpretation of a treaty;
b   any question of international law;
c   the existence of any fact which, if established, would constitute a breach of an international obligation;
d   the nature or extent of the reparation to be made for the breach of an international obligation.

3   The declarations referred to above may be made unconditionally or on condition of reciprocity on the part of several or certain states, or for a certain time.
4   Such declarations shall be deposited with the Secretary-General of the United Nations, who shall transmit copies thereof to the parties to the Statute and to the Registrar of the Court.
5   Declarations made under Article 36 of the Statute of the Permanent Court of International Justice and which are still in force shall be deemed, as between the parties to the present Statute, to be acceptances of the compulsory jurisdiction of the International Court of Justice for the period which they still have to run and in accordance with their terms.

6   In the event of a dispute as to whether the Court has jurisdiction, the matter shall be settled by the decision of the Court.

Article 38

1   The Court, whose function is to decide in accordance with international law such disputes as are submitted to it, shall apply:

a   international conventions, whether general or particular, establishing rules expressly recognized by the contesting states;
b   international custom, as evidence of a general practice accepted as law;
c   the general principles of law recognized by civilized nations;
d   subject to the provisions of Article 59, judicial decisions and the teachings of the most highly qualified publicists of the various nations, as subsidiary means for the determination of rules of law.

2   This provision shall not prejudice the power of the Court to decide a case *ex aequo et bono*, if the parties agree thereto.

Article 40

1   Cases are brought before the Court, as the case may be, either by the notification of the special agreement or by a written application addressed to the Registrar. In either case the subject of the dispute and the parties shall be indicated.
2   The Registrar shall forthwith communicate the application to all concerned.
3   He shall also notify the Members of the United Nations through the Secretary-General, and also any other states entitled to appear before the Court.

Article 42

1   The parties shall be represented by agents.
2   They may have the assistance of counsel or advocates before the Court.
3   The agents, counsel, and advocates of parties before the Court shall enjoy the privileges and immunities necessary to the independent exercise of their duties.

Article 43

1   The procedure shall consist of two parts: written and oral.
2   The written proceedings shall consist of the communication to the Court and to the parties of memorials, counter-memorials and, if necessary, replies; also all papers and documents in support.
3   These communications shall be made through the Registrar, in the order and within the time fixed by the Court.
4   A certified copy of every document produced by one party shall be communicated to the other party.
5   The oral proceedings shall consist of the hearing by the Court of witnesses, experts, agents, counsel, and advocates.

Article 45

The hearing shall be under the control of the President or, if he is unable to preside, of the Vice-President; if neither is able to preside, the senior judge present shall preside.

Article 46

The hearing in Court shall be public, unless the Court shall decide otherwise, or unless the parties demand that the public be not admitted.

Article 55

1   All questions shall be decided by a majority of the judges present.
2   In the event of an equality of votes, the President or the judge who acts in his place shall have a casting vote.

Article 56

1   The judgment shall state the reasons on which it is based.
2   It shall contain the names of the judges who have taken part in the decision.

Article 57

If the judgment does not represent in whole or in part the unanimous opinion of the judges, any judge shall be entitled to deliver a separate opinion.

Article 58

The judgment shall be signed by the President and by the Registrar. It shall be read in open court, due notice having been given to the agents.

Article 59

The decision of the Court has no binding force except between the parties and in respect of that particular case.

Article 60

The judgment is final and without appeal. In the event of dispute as to the meaning or scope of the judgment, the Court shall construe it upon the request of any party.

Article 65

1   The Court may give an advisory opinion on any legal question at the request of whatever body may be authorized by or in accordance with the Charter of the United Nations to make such a request.

2 Questions upon which the advisory opinion of the Court is asked shall be laid before the Court by means of a written request containing an exact statement of the question upon which an opinion is required, and accompanied by all documents likely to throw light upon the question.

Article 67

The Court shall deliver its advisory opinions in open court, notice having been given to the Secretary-General and to the representatives of Members of the United Nations, of other states and of international organizations immediately concerned.

The notion of the subjects of international law and the state as the main subject

DOI: 10.4324/9781003213772-4

THE NOTION OF THE SUBJECT OF INTERNATIONAL LAW

legal rights and duties
legal personality
legal capacity
natural persons
physical persons
legal entities
fictitious persons
juridical person

> legal person
> international (legal) personality
> international claim
> Advisory Opinion on *Reparation for Injuries Suffered in the Service of the United Nations*
> active participant at the interstate level
> universal subjectivity
> limited subjectivity

The general meaning of the subject of law

Generally, the subject of a law is the person (individuals and entities) who possesses the **legal rights and duties** (obligations) or to whom the legal norms refer.

Legal personality and legal capacity

Alongside the concept of the subject of law, national legal systems also recognise the notions of '**legal personality**' and '**legal capacity**'. Legal personality is the ability to enjoy rights and be bound by obligations and as such, it is a prerequisite to legal capacity.

There are two kinds of persons who possess the legal personality – **natural persons (physical persons)** and **legal entities**. Legal entities, which are commonly referred to as artificial or **fictitious persons** (Lat. – *persona ficta*), include states and other subjects of international or national law (such organisational entities as associations, cooperatives, corporations, companies, partnerships, and so on). To denote legal entities, the term '**juridical person**' or '**legal person**' is also applied. Although, in general, the terms 'juridical person' and 'legal person' cover all fictitious persons (including states), in certain cases in this book, depending on the context, these terms may only refer to the legal entities incorporated under the national legislation of the state (for example, associations, cooperatives, corporations, companies, partnerships, and so forth).

Legal capacity is the ability of any person to amend, enter into, transfer, implement, and so on rights and duties.

International personality

With respect of international law, the term '**international (legal) personality**' denotes an entity possessing international rights and duties, which has, additionally, the capacity to maintain its rights by bringing **international claims**. According to the ICJ **Advisory Opinion on *Reparation for injuries suffered in the service of the United Nations***:

> Competence to bring an international claim is, for those possessing it, the capacity to resort to the customary methods recognized by international law for the establishment, the presentation and the settlement of claims. Among these methods may be mentioned protest, request for an enquiry, negotiation, and request for submission

to an arbitral tribunal or to the Court in so far as this may be authorized by the Statute.[269]

The essence of the subject of international law

Nevertheless, the meaning of the subject of international law is more complicated, and to fully recognise the complex characteristics of this notion, we have to:

- Choose between the subject as being a beneficiary of rights and a bearer of duties or the subject as being an **active participant at the interstate level**. In the first case, numerous actors can be identified to whom the norms of international law refer directly. On the other hand, if we are to follow the second version, the list of the subjects of international law will be significantly reduced in number.
- Find the exact characteristics of the notion of a subject of international law.

It is clear that in international law scholarship, the notions mentioned here (subject, legal personality, legal capacity, international personality) are mainly intertwined. Hence, the subject is the entity which possesses the international personality expressed in the capacity (1) to establish norms of international law for itself, (2) to obtain and generate the rights and duties directly under these norms, and (3) to amend, transfer, and implement these rights and duties. Only such a person may be considered the active participant at the interstate level since the key to the generation of international law is only afforded to a limited number of subjects, and after entering this building, their responsibility lies only before each other to apply (enforce and determine) these obligatory rules and principles.

In sum, the subject of international law is the person who:

- could be the author of the norms of international law (direct participant of the law-making process); and
- has the ability to implement the norms of international law (in the making of which it participates) by, among other things, bringing an international claim.

Who are the subjects of international law?

The subjects of international law are:

- states; and
- the other subjects of international law which obtain not a **universal subjectivity** as the states do, but possess only a **limited subjectivity**.

---

269 *Reparation for Injuries Suffered in the Service of the United Nations*, Advisory Opinion of 11 April 1949, ICJ Reports 1949, 174. 'Personality in international law necessitates the consideration of the interrelationship between rights and duties afforded under the international system and capacity to enforce claims.' Shaw (n 69) 156.

The following are regarded as being among the other subjects of international law:

1   Peoples (based on the principle of equal rights and self-determination of peoples);
2   *Sui generis* territorial entities (e.g. Taiwan, Hong Kong), *sui generis* non-territorial entities (e.g. the Holy See, the Sovereign Order of Malta); and
3   International organisations (as a rule, only international governmental organisations).

STATE

state is an institution
state is a compulsory association which organises domination
Badinter Arbitration Commission

The state as an institution (related to the territory and people)

As James Leslie Brierly explained: 'A **STATE** is an *institution* , that is to say, it is a system of relations which men establish among themselves as a means of securing certain objects, of which the most fundamental is a system of order within which their activities can be carried on.'[270]

The state as a compulsory association organising domination

International law scholars most commonly refer to the Max Weber's (1864–1920) definition, according to which 'the modern **state is a compulsory association which organizes domination**. It has been successful in seeking to monopolize the legitimate use of physical force as a means of domination within a territory.'

The definition of the Badinter Arbitration Commission

When defining a state, the Arbitration Commission of the Conference on Yugoslavia, commonly known as the **Badinter Arbitration Commission**[271] (which was established on 27 August 1991 by the European Economic Community and its member states to provide the Conference on Yugoslavia with legal advice),[272] articulated 'that the state is commonly

---

270 Brierly (n 5) 126.
271 Sometimes also referred to as the Badinter Arbitration Committee.
272 'On 27 August 1991 the European Community (EC) resolved to establish a peace conference on Yugoslavia (the Brussels Declaration). Within the framework of the peace conference an Arbitration

defined as a community which consists of a territory and a population subject to an organized political authority; that such a state is characterized by sovereignty'.[273]

The general legal characteristics of states

The exclusive and general legal characteristics of states were explained by James Crawford (1948–2021) as follows:

(1) In principle, States have plenary competence to perform acts, make treaties and so on in the international sphere. . . .

(2) In principle States are exclusively competent with respect to their internal affairs, . . .

(3) In principle States are not subject to compulsory international process, jurisdiction, or settlement without their consent, given either generally or in the specific case.

(4) In international law States are regarded as 'equal.'[274]

Traditional criteria of statehood

criteria of statehood
Montevideo Convention on the Rights and Duties of States
elements of statehood
permanent population
defined territory
government
capacity to enter into relations with other states
North Sea Continental Shelf cases
movable territory
effective control

Commission was established for the purpose of resolving differences between "the relevant authorities" (not specifically identified). The Arbitration Commission consisted of five members, all being presidents of constitutional courts of EC members states and was headed by the French lawyer, Robert Badinter. The Arbitration Commission was subsequently endorsed by the United States (US) and the then Union of Soviet Socialist Republics (USSR).' Peter Radan, 'The Badinter Arbitration Commission and the Partition of Yugoslavia' (1997) 25(3) *Nationalities Papers* 537.

273 Badinter Arbitration Commission, Opinion No. 1 of 29 November 1991, Paragraph 1 (b). See in Alain Pellet, 'The Opinions of the Badinter Arbitration Committee: A Second Breath for the Self-Determination of Peoples' (1992) 3 *EJIL* 178 <ejil.org/pdfs/3/1/1175.pdf> accessed 16 March 2021.

274 James Crawford, *The Creation of States in International Law* (2nd edn, Clarendon Press in Oxford, Oxford University Press 2007) 40–41 (footnotes omitted).

The Montevideo Convention on the Rights and Duties of States

The most authoritative description of the constitutive **criteria of statehood** is provided in Article 1 of the 1933 **Montevideo Convention on the Rights and Duties of States**.

The Montevideo Convention on the Rights and Duties of States is a treaty signed at Montevideo, Uruguay, on 26 December 1933, during the Seventh International Conference of the American States. The Convention entered into force on 26 December 1934.

Traditional criteria of statehood

Article 1 of the Montevideo Convention lays down the so-called traditional criteria of statehood. These criteria (sometimes also called the **elements of statehood**) are:

- **permanent population**;
- **defined territory**;
- **government**; and
- **capacity to enter into relations with other states**.

On the whole, the Montevideo Convention has identified the most significant provisions on the rights and duties of states: for example, that:

> States are juridically equal, enjoy the same rights, and have equal capacity in their exercise. The rights of each one do not depend upon the power which it possesses to assure its exercise, but upon the simple fact of its existence as a person under international law.[275]

The meaning of the criteria of statehood

The criteria of statehood should be applied to the establishment of states, as well as the continuation of the existence of states.

On the whole, in order to regard an entity as a state, the criteria of statehood should be cumulatively met. Hence, only in such cases an entity may have the right to claim the rights and duties of a state under international law.

At the same time, international law defines the principal meaning of each of the criteria of statehood separately.

No lower limit on the size

International law imposes no lower limits on the size of the population and territory a state shall mandatorily possess to be considered a state. For instance, there is no defined minimum of a territory which would serve as a prerequisite for statehood; however, a

---

275 Article 4 of the Montevideo Convention.

piece of land in the possession of a state traditionally was regarded to be essential for the recognition of the establishment or continuation of the existence of the state.

As was articulated by the prominent scholar Lassa Oppenheim:

> State territory is that defined portion of the surface of the globe which is subjected to the sovereignty of a state. A state without a territory is not possible, although the necessary territory may be very small. . . . The importance of state territory lies in the fact that it is the space within which the state exercises its supreme authority.[276]

Permanent population

On the other hand, the traditional approach concerning criterion of the population stipulates that a population shall be permanent and demonstrate a strong link with an entity claiming statehood.

Usually, such a connection is due to the fact that individuals consider themselves (1) members of a state (as in the case of the established states providing the concepts of nationality and citizenship) and (2) having firm legal and political ties with the entity in question.

The population of a state may be mono-ethnic or multi-ethnic, there might be only one dominant religion or multiple religions, and so forth. However, international law does not prescribe any rule in relation to the necessary composition of a population.

Defined territory

As regards the state territory, it must be defined with certain boundaries. Meanwhile, in practice, the frontiers of the state may be disputable. However, a dispute regarding the boundaries of a state is not an insurmountable obstacle which cancels the existence of a state, if the boundaries are specified between certain subjects but are only disputed by certain other subjects (i.e. the territory has 'a sufficient consistency' as was concluded by the German-Polish Mixed Arbitral Tribunal in the *Deutsche Continental Gas-Gesellschaft v Polish State* case [1929]).[277]

The International Court of Justice also favoured this position in the **North Sea Continental Shelf** cases (*Federal Republic of Germany v Denmark; Federal Republic of Germany v Netherlands*):

> The appurtenance of a given area, considered as an entity, in no way governs the precise delimitation of its boundaries, any more than uncertainty as to boundaries

---

276 L. Oppenheim, *International Law: A Treatise*, Ronald F. Roxburgh (ed) Volume 1: *Peace* (3rd edn, Longmans, Green and CO 1920) 305, 307.

277 'In order to say that a State exists . . . it is enough that this territory has a sufficient consistency, even though its boundaries have not yet been accurately delaminated, and that the State actually exercises independent public authority over that territory.' *Deutsche Continental Gas-Gesellschaft v Polish State* (1929), Annual Digest, 5 (1929–30) No. 5.

can affect territorial rights. There is for instance no rule that the land frontiers of a State must be fully delimited and defined, and often in various places and for long periods they are not, as is shown by the case of the entry of Albania into the League of Nations.[278]

The composition of the state territory

The state territory consists of the land territory (embracing inland waters), the sea territories (including the internal waters and territorial sea), the subsoil beneath its land and sea territory, and the airspace above the land and sea territory to the edge of the earth's atmosphere.

However, traditionally, only the earth's solid surface was considered a crucial characteristic of the state territory, since all other types of state territories either relate to or derive from the possession of the land.

The state territory is delineated by state borders. Nevertheless, there are other places outside the state borders where the states have the jurisdictional powers, such as military bases abroad, the premises of diplomatic and consular missions, the sea zones under mixed legal regime, and the leased territories and the territories under certain servitudes.

Besides, in the actual practice, ships, aircraft, and space objects are also to some degree interlinked with the principle of territoriality since the military or the other governmental ships and aircraft operated for non-commercial purposes everywhere and the ships and aircraft operated for commercial purposes in some instances (for example, the ships on the high seas) are usually assimilated into a state territory as a **'movable territory'** under the jurisdiction of a respective owner state (of the military or other governmental ships, aircraft, and space objects) or the flag state (for example, merchant ships on the high seas).

The Permanent Court of International Justice considered the issue of movable territories in its well-known *Case of the S.S. 'Lotus' (France v Turkey)* and stated that '[a] corollary of the principle of the freedom of the seas is that a ship on the high seas is assimilated to the territory of the State the flag of which it flies, for, just as in its own territory, that State exercises its authority upon it, and no other State may do so.'[279]

Nonetheless, strictly speaking, no territory outside the state borders may be regarded as a state territory. In such cases, the sovereign rights of a state with regard to a foreign, mixed, or international territory may be outlined, which, in turn, can be only accorded by international law.

Government

The criterion of a government does not demand the implementation of any particular type of governance. It does not require that a government be either democratic or legitimate. The traditional approach was based on a single prescription that a government should exercise

---

278 *North Sea Continental Shelf* cases *(Federal Republic of Germany v Denmark, Federal Republic of Germany v Netherlands)*, Judgment of 20 February 1969.
279 *Case of the S.S. 'Lotus' (France v Turkey)*, Judgment No. 9 of 7 September 1927.

effective control over the population and the territory. Hence, the ability of efficient control over the people in a certain territory is the primary precondition set for a government.

On the other hand, a government must be sovereign, which means that it shall be capable of acting independently of internal forces, as well as foreign governments. The independence of a government allows it to limit the authority through its will in relations with other subjects of international law, i.e. by creating the norms of international law, as well as other rules, and, based on such rules, restrict its unlimited independence.

Capacity to enter into relations with other states

Although the fourth criterion of statehood is sometimes regarded as a necessary element, it finds no universal recognition. This state of affairs was partly stipulated by the fact that only the first three criteria of the Montevideo Convention derived from the so-called doctrine of the three elements (in German *Drei-Elemente-Lehre*) popularised by the German writer Georg Jellinek, which became the approach acknowledged worldwide. These criteria in Jellinek's wording were the state territory (*Staatsgebiet*), the state population (*Staatsvolk*) and the state government (*Staatsgewalt*).[280]

At the same time, criticism of the fourth criterion of statehood also stemmed from the uncertainties conditioned by the terms 'enter into relations' and 'capacity'. Many scholars argued that the first term ('enter into relations') corresponded with the recognition of an entity by other states, the scope of which itself is debatable. Secondly, the meaning of 'capacity' in this context was essentially interlinked with independence and sovereignty.[281] Hence, some authors saw no necessity to introduce the additional criterion, which might already be covered by such elements of statehood as the population and the government, since independence and sovereignty were undoubtfully regarded as essential features of those terms.

However, despite the criticism, the capacity to enter into relations with other states is still regarded as one of the traditional criteria of statehood.

The concept of sovereignty

internal sovereignty
external sovereignty
totality of state competences under international law
highest authorities on the earth
Corfu Channel case
territorial sovereignty
sovereign rights
territories under a mixed legal regime
Lateran Pacts

---

280 Georg Jellinek, *Allgemeine Staatslehre* (Dritte Auflage, Verlag von O. Haring 1914) 394–434.
281 *Parry & Grant Encyclopaedic Dictionary of International Law* (n 165) 574.

Internal and external sovereignty

The modern notion of sovereignty is rooted in the ideas of Jean Bodin (1530–1596), whose political philosophy was significantly affected by the doctrine of sovereignty. Jean Bodin defined sovereignty in his work *Republic* as 'the absolute and perpetual power of a Republic, that is to say the active form and personification of the great body of a modern State'.[282]

Generally, sovereignty is the ability to hold so-called **internal sovereignty** and **external sovereignty**, or pursue domestic and foreign policy independently.

The internal aspect of sovereignty is the exclusive competence of a state to conduct its domestic policy freely without any interference from other internal forces.

The external aspect of sovereignty is the right of the state to determine its relations independently with other subjects of international law without any restraint or control exercised by other subject(s) of international law.

Other characteristics of the state's sovereignty

At the same time, sovereignty is also used as a concept which denotes the **totality of state competences under international law**. In addition, sovereignty also has another meaning: namely, that the states are the **highest authorities on the earth** (*suprema potestas*).

In the *Corfu Channel* case (*UK v Albania*), which was the first public international law case heard before the International Court of Justice between 1947 and 1949, Judge Alejandro Alvarez pointed out the following: 'By sovereignty, we understand the whole body of rights and attributes which a State possesses in its territory, to the exclusion of all other States, and also in its relations with other States. Sovereignty confers rights upon States and imposes obligations on them.'[283]

The sovereignty of the state may be restricted only by international law.

The interrelationship between the sovereignty and the traditional criteria of statehood

Sovereignty is related to all traditional criteria of statehood.

1   It is an integral feature of elements such as the population and the government since every government and in those countries where the people are the source of political legitimacy and government, a population shall also have the ability to hold the so-called internal sovereignty and external sovereignty independently.
2   It overlaps with the capacity to enter into relations with other states since such a capacity should be exercised through concomitant external sovereignty.
3   It relates to a state territory since, in the strict sense, the full-fledged sovereignty of a state can only be exercised on a state territory.

282 Pierre Mesnard, 'Bodin, Jean' in Donald M. Borchert (ed in chief), *Encyclopedia of Philosophy*, 1 Volume (2nd edn, Thomson Gale 2006) 621.
283 *Corfu Channel (UK v Albania)*, Judgment of 9 April 1949, ICJ Reports 1949, 4, Separate Opinion by Judge Alvarez.

Hence, the concept of sovereignty unites all the criteria of statehood by arranging all of them under the specific focus, which is the pursuit of domestic and foreign policy objectives independently. In other words, it is a concept which is related to all elements of statehood but belongs to the state as a whole.

Territorial sovereignty

Sovereignty – an essential attribute of a state – with regard to a state territory is known as the **territorial sovereignty** (of the state). Therefore, the term 'territorial sovereignty' should be understood as referring only to the state territory.

Over time, areas outside a state territory emerged to which states also to some extent claimed 'sovereignty'. As long as the full sovereignty of the state can be exercised only on a state territory, in those situations, a more precise term would be **sovereign rights**.

Therefore, sovereign rights refer to the limited or functional authority of a state (within the limits established by international law) in relation to the territories and properties located outside its borders. For instance, the **territories under a mixed legal regime** such as the respective maritime zones – the contiguous zone, the exclusive economic zone, the continental shelf – in the law of the sea. The territories under a mixed legal regime primarily hold international status, but at the same time, the particular functional sovereign rights of the respective state are preserved: for example, sovereign right to the establishment and use of artificial islands, installations, and structures in the exclusive economic zone.

Sovereignty and other subjects of international law

Strictly speaking, the term 'sovereignty' predominantly refers to states. However, sometimes in international law, the term also concerns some other subjects of international law.

For example, the term is applied in several provisions of the Conciliation Treaty (a part of the **Lateran Pacts**) of 1929, such as: 'Italy recognizes the sovereignty of the Holy See in international matters' or the 'sovereignty and exclusive jurisdiction over the Vatican City, which Italy recognizes as appertaining to the Holy See'.[284]

Hence, in rare cases, 'sovereignty' may also be applied in relation to other subjects of international law.

Recognition

	establishment of the relationship
	development of the relationship
	recognition of some status
	acceptance of the international status
	targets of recognition

---

284 Articles 2 and 4 of the Conciliation Treaty.

Constitutive theory
Declaratory theory
political existence of the state
legal existence of the state
individual recognition
collective recognition
unconditionality of recognition
irrevocability of recognition
de jure recognition
de facto recognition
ad hoc recognition

Recognition as a unilateral act

Recognition is a unilateral act, and all general rules mentioned in this book with respect to unilateral acts apply to it similarly.

The functions of recognition

Basically, the functions of recognition are:

1   **establishment of the relationship** between the persons;
2   **development of the relationship** between the persons; and
3   **acceptance of the international status** of the particular target of recognition.

Recognition usually establishes or serves as the legal basis for the development of relations between two subjects. This is the conventional meaning of this unilateral act in every case of its application.

When there is a conflict between different legal positions concerning the legal status of a certain target of recognition, only then recognition may obtain the third meaning as a tool for the acceptance of international status. In international law, the **recognition of some status** is a formal acknowledgement of it as being legal and may involve the acceptance or the granting of rights.

The targets of recognition

The **targets of recognition** under international law may be:

- a subject: a state (statehood), a government, an international personality of the certain person (e.g. belligerents, *sui generis* territorial entities, and so on);
- legal status of the territory (e.g. acquisition of the title to the territory); or
- international legal status of the particular issue or situation (e.g. neutrality and so on).

Recognition of states

There are two classic theories on the recognition of statehood:

- **Constitutive theory** – 'A State is, and becomes, an International Person through recognition only and exclusively.'[285] – Lassa Oppenheim
- **Declaratory theory** – The existence of the state as 'an international person', is independent on recognition by the other states. An act of recognition refers to an already-existing factual situation.[286] Hence, a subject owns international rights and duties based on that factual situation.

Under the Montevideo Convention on Rights and Duties of States:

> The **political existence of the state** is independent of recognition by the other states. Even before recognition the state has the right to defend its integrity and independence, to provide for its conservation and prosperity, and consequently to organize itself as it sees fit, to legislate upon its interests, administer its services, and to define the jurisdiction and competence of its courts.
>
> The exercise of these rights has no other limitation than the exercise of the rights of other states according to international law.[287]

Nevertheless, the question of the **legal existence of the state** is not explicitly provided for in this formulation of the Convention.

The actual meaning of recognition during the different standpoints concerning the status of a subject

Although it is clear that recognition as such does not create a new state and 'the existence or disappearance of the state is a question of fact', in practice, when there is a conflict between different standpoints concerning status, recognition has a constitutive power in the context of two subjects (recognising subject and recognised subject). In this case, the state, as an international person, indeed exists for those who recognise it under such a status.

On the other hand, when there is no conflict between the viewpoints, recognition may be considered an automatic act.

In both cases, recognition contributes to the establishment or development of relations between two subjects.

---

285 Oppenheim (n 276) 134.
286 For example, the Badinter Arbitration Commission articulated in its Opinion No. 1 'that the answer to the question should be based on the principles of public international law which serve to define the conditions on which an entity constitutes a state; that in this respect, the existence or disappearance of the state is a question of fact; that the effects of recognition by other states are purely declaratory.'
287 Article 3 of the Montevideo Convention.

Individual and collective recognition

Recognition can be either individual or collective. **Individual recognition** represents a basic form. **Collective recognition** signifies a special form (for instance, recognition through the international conferences). According to a more acknowledged approach, membership in the international intergovernmental organisation (of which only states are members) is evidence of collective recognition as a state, which also includes the states that will not cast votes but, based on the founding international treaty (or other instrument), have the obligation to maintain friendly relations and co-operation with other member states.

The unconditionality and irrevocability of recognition

Recognition shall be **unconditional**.

A subject may simply refuse to deal with some other subject. However, a lawful *de jure* **recognition** is generally **irrevocable**. ˙

Express or tacit recognition

The recognition of a subject may be express or tacit. 'The latter results from any act which implies the intention of recognizing the new state' (Article 7 of the Montevideo Convention on the Rights and Duties of States).

Recognition is express when a special document on recognition is sent to the subject which is being recognised, when an official statement is published, or when any legal document (for example, an international treaty) is concluded with this subject.

De facto and *de jure* recognition

The official recognition of a state (as well as of a government or other entity) can be carried out either *de facto* or *de jure* (the *de jure* recognition is sometimes also called the full recognition). At the same time, due to the fact that the legal approach and interstate practice are not quite clear on this issue, it is difficult to discover the conventional distinction between these two forms.

Moreover, confusion is also exacerbated by the fact that sometimes the target of recognition is a government (recognition of governments), while in other cases, that target is a state. On most occasions, *de facto* declarations of recognition refer to governments, and only in specific cases do they directly relate to new states.[288]

For instance, the United Kingdom recognised the Soviet government *de facto* in 1921, but *de jure* recognition of the Soviet Union as a state was made in 1924 (after the end of the civil war). Replying to the question on the trade agreement signed between the United

---

288 'Probably the last clear example for *de facto* recognition of a State was the recognition of Israel in 1948 by Great Britain.' Jochen Abr. Frowein, 'Recognition' in R. Bernhardt (ed), *Encyclopedia of Public International Law*, 10 States· Responsibility of States· International Law and Municipal Law, (Elsevier Science Publishers B.V. 1987) 342.

Kingdom and the Russian Soviet Federative Socialist Republic, the British Prime Minister formulated his response in the following words: 'This is purely a trading agreement recognising the soviet government as *de facto* government of Russia, which undoubtedly it is' (22 March 1921).[289]

Meanwhile, some scholars suggest that there is no huge difference between *de facto* and *de jure* recognition.[290] Some others see the significance in establishing clear boundaries between these concepts.

If we suggest that there is a difference between these two forms of recognition, the most appropriate version of the differences may be formulated as follows:

1   When recognition is granted in an explicit form (and not in a tacit form), it should always be treated as *de jure* recognition, unless the recognising subject underlines that its recognition is only *de facto* recognition.

2   *De jure* recognition is durable, and the formal explicit acceptance of the existence of a subject is usually embodied by the exchange of permanent missions.

3   *De facto* recognition is more preliminary and done with a dose of hesitancy: 'Recognition *de facto* implies that there is some doubt as to the long-term viability of the government in question.'[291]

4   Both forms produce legal effects; however, the effect of *de facto* recognition is limited within the particular legal consequences and mostly aims to safeguard the affairs of its citizens and institutions or maintain the specific political or economic interests.

5   *De facto* recognition can be followed by recognition *de jure*, or it may be withdrawn.

6   *De facto* recognition of a state may be revoked in case of non-fulfilment of the prerequisite conditions of statehood or based on some political considerations which have defined the prior recognition.

7   A lawful *de jure* recognition may be revoked only in certain circumstances, which are defined for the unilateral acts of international law. For instance, a fundamental change in the circumstances can lead to the right of revocation of any unilateral act, i.e. including *de jure* recognition, within the meaning and the strict limits of the rule determined in the 1969 Vienna Convention on the Law of Treaties.[292] At the same time, the practice of recent years with regard to *de jure* recognition has proved that if such recognition is considered to be a consequence of an unlawful act or acts and, therefore, is illegal in itself, it can be revoked. On the other hand, if *de jure* recognition is a consequence of the derogation from peremptory norms, it has no legal force (is invalid), and, therefore, from the legal point of view, there is no need to withdraw such recognition.

---

289 George Grafton Wilson, 'British Recognition de Facto and de Jure of the U.S.S.R.' (January 1934) 28(1) *The American Journal of International Law* 100.

290 'If one thinks of recognition as having an evidential value, then presumably *de jure* recognition would have greater evidential force than *de facto* recognition; but the difference is probably not very great.' Malanczuk (n 72) 88.

291 Shaw (n 69) 341.

292 Article 62 of the Vienna Convention on the Law of Treaties.

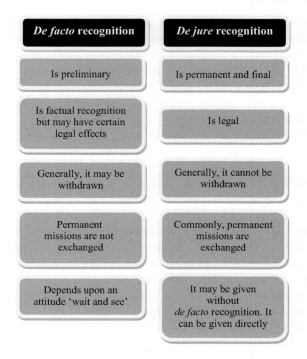

FIGURE 4.1 The mainstream version of the distinction between *de facto* and *de jure* recognition

Ad hoc recognition

Still, the primary forms of recognition are *de facto* and *de jure*. However, some authors additionally highlight ***ad hoc* recognition** as a separately standing form of recognition. By distinguishing recognition of such a type, these authors suggest that *ad hoc* recognition is not official and only signifies entry into relations with the subject concerning a particular issue or cause (for example, the protection of the citizenry or the exchange of prisoners of war) while *de facto* and *de jure* recognitions are official.

State succession

Succession = Substitution + Continuation
preconditions of succession
succession of international organisations
succession of other subjects of international law
unification of states
one or more state's incorporation in another state
dissolution of a state
separation of part or parts of the territory of a state

transfer of part of the territory of a state
cession
adjudication
annexation
identity
continuity
Vienna Convention on Succession of States in respect of Treaties
Vienna Convention on Succession of States in respect of State Property, Archives and Debts
discontinuity and continuity of rights and obligations
clean slate theory
universal succession theory
continuity theory
tabula rasa
uti possidetis
Frontier Dispute case
moving treaty boundaries
preservation and safety of state archives

The formula of succession

Succession = Substitution + Continuation: this is the prominent formula by Max Huber (1874–1960).[293]

Substitution means the **preconditions of succession**. Continuation means the succession in itself.

Succession as a realised continuation in the rights and duties

There emerges a category of succession when one subject of law becomes extinct in whole or in part and is substituted by another subject of law. Consequently, the rights and duties of the predecessor are transferred to the successor. Therefore, succession is a realised continuation in rights and duties.

Various targets of the institute of succession

In international law, the general principle of law – the succession – is not limited to the succession of states. There exists the **succession of international organisations**, as well as the **succession of other subjects of international law** may be considered.

---

293 M. Huber, *Die Staatensuccession, Völkerrechtliche und Staatsrechtliche Praxis im 19. Jahrhundert* (Verlag von Duncker & Humblot 1898) 18.

State succession

The preconditions of state succession are
When the predecessor subject becomes extinct:

- **Unification of states;**
- **One or more state's incorporation in another state** (in accordance with international law);
- **Dissolution of a state.**

When the predecessor subject becomes replaced on the part of its territory:

- **Separation of part or parts of the territory of a state;**
- **Transfer of part of the territory of a state (cession.** Sometimes, in this context, **adjudication** is also mentioned; however, the adjudication is only a confirming mechanism of the acquisition of territory).[294]

The notion of state succession is not applicable to revolution, a coup, or the change of government and constitutional changes because, in all these cases, the state, as a defined individuality and a subject of international law, does not cease to exist in whole or in part.

Another issue is the problem of **annexation**, which is prohibited in modern international law. Generally, annexation is one of the preconditions of state succession; however, today it is obviously an illegal form. Meanwhile, regarding the historical cases (before the prohibition of the annexation), it may be assumed as a precondition of state succession.

Identity and continuity

Succession is closely related to the concepts of **identity** and **continuity** (of subjects).

Continuity, in this case, means an incessancy, and when there is a continuous existence of a given subject (state), the question of succession does not arise. On the other hand, if the subject exists continuously, it is, at the same time, identical to itself. In other words, in this case, these two categories coincide.

However, there are situations when there is no continuity in the state existence, but the question of identity is still on the agenda. For example, if state A is voluntarily incorporated into state B, and over time, it separates and re-establishes the independent country A, the legal model of identity without continuity arises (regarding the previously existing A), and additionally, the rules of succession may also be applied (concerning state B). Therefore, in this context, both legal models – state succession and identity – can create a legal framework if their rules are compatible, or if that is not the case, the concerned parties can choose between one of the aforementioned legal models. The succession model links state A with state B and its certain international rights and obligations, while identity refers to the rights and obligations of state A before the incorporation if the rights and obligations are not outdated and inconsistent with the modern state of affairs.

---

294 See the subsection of this book dealing with adjudication.

To define the issue of identity, an observer needs to examine both the objective and subjective criteria.

The objective criteria in this case are:

- the official name of the state;
- state symbols;
- constitution and legal system;
- size of the territory and the population;
- economic and military power; and so on.

The subjective criteria are:

- self-perception of a given state (on the issue of identity); and
- counter-perception of other states and subjects of international law regarding this state.

The fields of state succession

The traditional fields of state succession in international law are:

- succession of states in respect of treaties;
- succession of states in respect of state property, archives, and debts;
- nationality of natural persons in relation to the succession of states;
- national law and state succession;
- private property of foreigners and state succession; and
- membership in international organisations and state succession.

The treaties on succession at the global level

Although the state succession is one of those issues which the states have long been trying to arrange, it still remains the field of international law where, in fact, the conclusion of the universally recognised or even almost universally recognised treaties has failed. Indeed, even those international documents that have been elaborated over time could not obtain the support needed, which is necessary to establish the widely recognised treaty norms. Namely:

- **Vienna Convention on Succession of States in respect of Treaties**, which was done at Vienna in 1978 and after almost two decades (in 1996) entered into force but has been supported by only a small number of states.
- **Vienna Convention on Succession of States in respect of State Property, Archives and Debts**, which was signed in Vienna in 1983 but failed to enter into force.
- The UN General Assembly Resolution 'Nationality of natural persons in relation to the succession of States' of 2000,[295] whose follow-up actions have not been implemented by the states up until now since there is no global treaty on this matter concluded.

---

295 A/RES/55/153 of 12 Dec. 2000 – Nationality of natural persons in relation to the succession of States and its Annex: Nationality of natural persons in relation to the succession of States.

The theories on state succession

Over time, several theories concerning state succession were developed. All the theories developed in this respect were allocated between two poles – the **discontinuity and continuity of rights and obligations**. Some of them tended to argue that the successor state is completely free from the obligations of the predecessor state since the successor state does not exercise its sovereignty over the territory in virtue of a transfer of authority from its predecessor (the so-called negative theory, **clean slate theory**, or option theory). The others primarily represent a variation of the oldest theory on state succession called the **universal succession theory**, which was propounded by Hugo Grotius using the Roman analogy of succession on the death of a natural person (the **continuity theory**, popular continuity theory, or organic substitution theory).

For example, the clean slate theory shares the *tabula rasa* rule concerning state succession, denying the transfer of rights and obligations. It appears to have emerged as a consequence of linking the understanding of international law as deriving from the sovereign will and the deduced assumption that international legal relations are intensely personal. Hence, when the sovereignty of one state on a certain territory comes to an end and is substituted by another subject, no transfer (succession) of rights or obligations between the old and the new subject shall take place.

The discontinuity approach has been doubtfully applied to the new states, primarily in the process of Decolonisation (the 'newly independent States') by the Vienna Conventions on Succession of States.[296] Such a position resulted in the strong opposition to these conventions by a large group of states.

At the same time, the thesis of the clean slate (or *tabula rasa*) was sometimes referred to by the practice concerning international claims. When international claims are regarded as truly 'personal', the discontinuity was revoked in relation to the international claims during the succession, since the extinction of either the claimant state or the defendant state was considered as leading to the extinction of the claim itself.[297]

The universal succession theory and other theories which were convinced in the continuation during the state succession argued that rights and obligations may pass to states as long as they are considered to have essentially inherited the legal identity of the former subject. Thus, these approaches award the rights and obligations of the predecessor to a successor sovereign.

---

296 For example, Article 16 of the Vienna Convention on Succession of States in respect of Treaties: 'A newly independent State is not bound to maintain in force, or to become a party to, any treaty by reason only of the fact that at the date of the succession of States the treaty was in force in respect of the territory to which the succession of States relates.'

297 For instance, the Robert B. Brown Claim case, which arose out of the annexation of the South African Republic by the United Kingdom. Robert B. Brown was a US citizen and suffered a denial of justice in the South African Republic in 1895. The British-American Tribunal [*Robert E. Brown (United States v Great Britain)*] of 1923 rejected the claim. According to the decision of the Tribunal: 'The contention of the American Agent amounts to an assertion that a succeeding State acquiring a territory by conquest without any undertaking to assume such liabilities is bound to take affirmative steps to right the wrongs done by the former State. We cannot endorse this doctrine.'

However, the existing rules of international law have found a middle way between the discontinuity and continuity models, as long as in particular fields (for example, political treaties) there exists no obligation to transfer the rights and obligations under the state succession model, while in certain areas, the continuation thesis prevails (for example, multilateral agreements, which are open to all countries for participation).

Generally applicable rules on state succession

Although, as noted earlier, the conclusion of the widely recognised global treaties concerning state succession has failed, rules can still be identified which may be considered the general customary international law norms for the majority of states and also as the international treaty norms, only for a smaller number of states (the parties to the Vienna Convention on Succession of States in respect of Treaties).

The dispositive character of the general rules on state succession

At the same time, almost all general rules on succession of states possess a dispositive nature. Therefore, the predecessor and successor states can change these rules by agreements among themselves. There was a case, for example, after the dissolution of the Soviet Union,[298] when the successor states initially concluded international agreements in several fields in accordance with the Vienna Conventions mentioned earlier, but subsequently, for example, with respect to state assets and debts based on the bilateral agreements, the Russian Federation implemented the so-called 'zero option' and took on a vital part of the rights and obligations.[299]

The fields where the parties cannot change the norms

Nevertheless, there are certain norms which cannot be modified by the concerned parties in the process of succession.

Firstly, the peremptory norms of general international law cannot be affected by state succession. The successor country shall fulfil the obligations established by the peremptory norms, even if it did not exist at the time of the development of a particular norm.

Secondly, the norms regarding boundaries and other territorial regimes also cannot be affected by the process of succession. In sum, international law provides a clear prescription that a succession of states does not as such affect a boundary established by the bilateral or multilateral norms of international law or obligations and rights established by them and relating to the regime of a boundary. Besides, examples of such arrangements also include demilitarised zones, rights of transit, and other servitudes.

---

298 In 1991, after the dissolution of the Soviet Union, the 12 successor states of USSR and the three Baltic states obtained independence.

299 See Pataraia (n 126) 91–118.

Uti possidetis

However, when a certain precondition for state succession emerges – for example, the dissolution of a state (as a precondition) – the problem of the borders of the new states appears since only some of them are the defined state frontiers of the predecessor state.

In this case, the principle of the ***uti possidetis***[300] has been considered as a solution, which initially was applied to the Decolonisation issues in America and Africa but is today recognised as a general principle of law. As it was concluded by the International Court of Justice in the ***Frontier Dispute*** case *(Burkina Faso/Republic of Mali)*, whereas

> the two Parties have . . . expressly requested the Chamber to resolve their dispute on the basis, in particular, of the 'principle of the intangibility of frontiers inherited from colonization', the Chamber cannot disregard the principle of *uti possidetis juris*, the application of which gives rise to this respect for intangibility of frontiers.[301]

Hence, in this context, the primary aim of the principle of *uti possidetis* is to secure respect for the territorial (including administrative) boundaries which exist at the time independence is achieved.

Succession of states in respect of the treaties

During the succession of states in respect of the treaties, there are some general rules which are widely recognised.

For example, according to the rule of the **moving treaty boundaries**, where an existing state acquires territory, usually, the treaties of the predecessor state cease to be applicable with regard to that territory, while the treaties of the successor state extend to the area, unless the application of the treaty to that territory would be incompatible with the object and purpose of the treaty or would radically change the conditions of its operation.

As for the other approach, usually, political or military treaties are considered as individual (personal) treaties and cannot be transferred to a new person on the sole basis of the succession. In turn, the rights and obligations obtained on the legal basis of the treaties, which are open to all countries for participation, in principle are transferrable.

With respect to other types of treaties, the rules vary according to the nature of the territorial change (preconditions of succession).

Succession of states in respect of state (public) property, state archives, and state debts

The differentiated approach is applied to the succession of states in respect of state (public) property, state archives, and state debts.

For instance, during the dissolution of a state, the successor states inherit more rights and duties with regard to the state property than in the case of the separation of a part or

---

300 *Uti possidetis* is a Latin phrase meaning '"As you possess, so may you possess." An archaic maxim meaning that a state that has acquired possession of territory with intent to annex it has thereby established sovereignty over that territory.' *Guide to Latin in International Law* (n 71) 286.

301 *Frontier Dispute (Burkina Faso/Republic of Mali)*, Judgment of 22 December 1986, ICJ Reports 1986, 554.

parts of the territory. In the latter case, under the state property which shall pass to the successor state is regarded:

- the immovable state property of the predecessor situated in the territory to which the succession of states relates;
- the movable state property of the predecessor state connected with the activity of the predecessor state in respect of the territory to which the succession of states relates; and
- the movable state property of the predecessor state, other than that mentioned earlier, which shall pass to the successor in an equitable proportion.

However, in the case of the dissolution of a state, the immovable state property situated outside the predecessor's territory is added to the aforementioned list of properties which shall be passed to the successor in equitable proportions.

With regard to the state debts, which means any financial obligation of a predecessor state arising in conformity with international law towards a third state, an international organisation, or any other subject of international law, unless the concerned states agree on another arrangement, the state debt of the predecessor state shall pass to the successor state in an equitable proportion, considering, in particular, the property, rights, and interests which are passed to the successor state in relation to that state debt.

In respect of state archives, which means all documents of whatever date and kind produced or received by the predecessor state, the fundamental virtues are the **preservation and safety of state archives**, as well as the protection of the rights of the peoples of the concerned states 'to development, to information about their history and to their cultural heritage'.[302]

Accordingly, by taking into consideration these virtues, the state archives shall pass to the successor if they exclusively or principally concern ('relate directly') the territory of the successor state or 'should be in the territory of a successor State for normal administration of its territory'.[303] At the same time, if they are merely 'connected with the interests of the territory' of the successor state, there is the rule of the availability of state archives to the successor state, which stipulates the delivery of appropriate reproductions of the state archives to a successor state. In all other cases, the successor states should allocate the state archives 'in an equitable manner, taking into account all relevant circumstances' and the fundamental virtues mentioned earlier.

Extinction of statehood

> presumption of the state's existence
> prerequisite conditions of statehood
> Failed State

---

302 For example, Article 31 (4) of the Vienna Convention on Succession of States in respect of State Property, Archives and Debts.

303 For example, Article 31(1) of the Vienna Convention on Succession of States in respect of State Property, Archives and Debts.

> moment of extinction of the statehood
> principle of effectiveness
> voluntary extinction of a state
> involuntary extinction of a state
> Badinter Arbitration Commission

The interdependence of the topics

The extinction of statehood is intertwined with many of the previously discussed topics:

- statehood;
- state succession;
- identity and continuity;
- date of the succession of states, which is determined in the Vienna Conventions on Succession of States as 'the date upon which the successor State replaced the predecessor State in the responsibility for the international relations of the territory to which the succession of States relates';
- annexation;
- the principle of effectiveness; and so forth.

Presumption of the state's existence

It is noteworthy that the state is not inevitably extinguished even by substantial changes in the territory under its sovereign possession, its population, or the government. At the same time, under international law, the scale of changes which is necessary for extinction to take place is not defined. Instead, under international law, there exists a **presumption of the state's existence**, which means that until the moment a new international status comes into existence, the existing status of that subject is preserved.

The non-fulfilment of the **prerequisite conditions of statehood** (criteria of statehood) is a permanent challenge for the states. As outlined earlier, the criteria of statehood are essential both at the stage of the creation of a state and throughout its existence. However, due to the presence of the presumption, during the dispute, the prevailing approach is that the state continues to exist.

Meanwhile, another problem concerning the extinction of statehood is the concept of a '**Failed State**' and the strength of the presumption of state existence in this regard. In international relations, there are many states which are regarded as states; however, as concerns their operation, the fulfilment of the prerequisite conditions of statehood is disputable.

The moment of extinction

Another problem is the determination of the **moment** (date) **of extinction of the statehood** since it is sometimes a process and not a single moment in time (date).

Annexation and extinction of statehood

The extinction of statehood is closely related to the problem of annexation. As has been noted before, today, annexation which is accomplished by the threat or the use of force is an illegal act, and furthermore, the annexation by the use of force being the manifestation of aggression represents derogation from the peremptory norm of general international law.

History after the Second World War has proved that prohibition on annexation is generally effective. Moreover, this postulate was demonstrated in various cases when the attempted annexations were not finalised.

However, in this relation, there appears another significant building block of international law: namely, the **principle of effectiveness**.

In practice, there is no strict deadline. Basically, it takes a 'long' time to increase the power of effectiveness. Nevertheless, at the present moment, this principle has a complicated linkage with the peremptory norms of general international law. Effectiveness cannot change the legal sanction of the derogation from the *jus cogens* norms, which means that every international norm or obligation justifying or recognising the annexation undertaken by the use of force, as well as its legal consequences, shall be void.

Voluntary or involuntary extinction of statehood

The extinction of statehood may be either voluntary or involuntary.

Examples of **voluntary extinction of a state** include the incorporation of the German Democratic Republic into the Federal Republic of Germany (1990), the unification of North Yemen (Yemen Arab Republic) and South Yemen (People's Democratic Republic of Yemen) and creation of the Republic of Yemen (1990), the dissolution of the Soviet Union and creation of the new states (1991), and so forth.

A modern example of the **involuntary extinction of a state** is the case of Yugoslavia. This case has confirmed that involuntary extinction stipulates various legal problems, including the problems of continuity and identity. For a long time (1992–2000), the Federal Republic of Yugoslavia (Serbia-Montenegro) argued that it continued the legal and political personality of the Socialist Federal Republic of Yugoslavia. However, in the international community, there was no unified position – not even in the United Nations, where the Security Council was more categorical that the Socialist Federal Republic of Yugoslavia had ceased its existence. The position of the official Belgrade was that other republics had separated from the Socialist Federal Republic of Yugoslavia while the core of the state continued its existence.

However, the UN Security Council maintained the opposite position:

> Noting that the claim by the Federal Republic of Yugoslavia (Serbia and Montenegro) to continue automatically the membership of the former Socialist Federal Republic of Yugoslavia in the United Nations has not been generally accepted.[304]

304 S/RES/757(1992) of 30 May 1992.

The same position was declared in 1992 by the **Badinter Arbitration Commission** in its Opinion No. 9: '[T]he SFRY's membership of international organizations must be terminated according to their statutes and that none of the successor states may thereupon claim for itself alone the membership rights previously enjoyed by the former SFRY'. As regards the new entity, the 'Federal Republic of Yugoslavia' (FRY), which was constituted on 27 April 1992 by Montenegro and Serbia, in its Opinion No. 10, the Badinter Arbitration Commission stated that 'the FRY (Serbia and Montenegro) is a new state which cannot be considered the sole successor to the SFRY'.[305]

In 2000, the Federal Republic of Yugoslavia accepted this position of the UN (and other subjects), and FRY was admitted as a new member state of the United Nations.

Consequently, the case of Yugoslavia confirms the importance of the subjective criteria for defining the issues of identity and continuity – i.e. the self-perception of the subject (on the issue of identity) and the counter-perception of other subjects of international law.

CASES AND MATERIALS (*SELECTED PARTS*)

The notion of the subject of international law

Reparation for Injuries Suffered in the Service of the United Nations, Advisory Opinion, 11 April 1949, International Court of Justice
ICJ Reports 1949, 174.

The questions asked of the Court relate to the "capacity to bring an international claim"; accordingly, we must begin by defining what is meant by that capacity, and consider the characteristics of the Organization, so as to determine whether, in general, these characteristics do, or do not, include for the Organization a right to present an international claim.

Competence to bring an international claim is, for those possessing it, the capacity to resort to the customary methods recognized by international law for the establishment, the presentation and the settlement of claims. Among these methods may be mentioned protest, request for an enquiry, negotiation, and request for submission to an arbitral tribunal or to the Court in so far as this may be authorized by the Statute.

This capacity certainly belongs to the State; a State can bring an international claim against another State. Such a claim takes the form of a claim between two political entities, equal in law, similar in form, and both the direct subjects of international law. It is dealt with by means of negotiation, and cannot, in the present state of the law as to international jurisdiction, be submitted to a tribunal, except with the consent of the States concerned.

When the Organization brings a claim against one of its Members, this claim will be presented in the same manner, and regulated by the same procedure. It may, when necessary, be supported by the political means at the disposal of the Organization. In these ways the Organization would find a method for securing the observance of its rights by the Member against which it has a claim.

---

305 Opinions No. 4–10 of the Badinter Arbitration Commission are included in Annex 3 to the following article – Danilo Türk, 'Recognition of States: A Comment' (1993) 4 *European Journal of International Law* 74–91.

But, in the international sphere, has the Organization such a nature as involves the capacity to bring an international claim? In order to answer this question, the Court must first enquire whether the Charter has given the Organization such a position that it possesses, in regard to its Members, rights which it is entitled to ask them to respect. In other words, does the Organization possess international personality? This is no doubt a doctrinal expression, which has sometimes given rise to controversy. But it will be used here to mean that if the Organization is recognized as having that personality, it is an entity capable of availing itself of obligations incumbent upon its Members.

To answer this question, which is not settled by the actual terms of the Charter, we must consider what characteristics it was intended thereby to give to the Organization.

The subjects of law in any legal system are not necessarily identical in their nature or in the extent of their rights, and their nature depends upon the needs of the community. Throughout its history, the development of international law has been influenced by the requirements of international life, and the progressive increase in the collective activities of States has already given rise to instances of action upon the international plane by certain entities which are not States. This development culminated in the establishment in June 1945 of an international organization whose purposes and principles are specified in the Charter of the United Nations. But to achieve these ends the attribution of international personality is indispensable.

The Charter has not been content to make the Organization created by it merely a centre "for harmonizing the actions of nations in the attainment of these common ends" (Article 1, para. 3). It has equipped that centre with organs, and has given it special tasks. It has defined the position of the Members in relation to the Organization by requiring them to give it every assistance in any action undertaken by it (Article 2, para. 5), and to accept and carry out the decisions of the Security Council; by authorizing the General Assembly to make recommendations to the Members; by giving the Organization legal capacity and privileges and immunities in the territory of each of its Members; and by providing for the conclusion of agreements between the Organization and its Members. Practice – in particular the conclusion of conventions to which the Organization is a party – has confirmed this character of the Organization, which occupies a position in certain respects in detachment from its Members, and which is under a duty to remind them, if need be, of certain obligations. It must be added that the Organization is a political body, charged with political tasks of an important character, and covering a wide field namely, the maintenance of international peace and security, the development of friendly relations among nations, and the achievement of international co-operation in the solution of problems of an economic, social, cultural or humanitarian character (Article 1); and in dealing with its Members it employs political means. The "Convention on the Privileges and Immunities of the United Nations" of 1946 creates rights and duties between each of the signatories and the Organization. . . . It is difficult to see how such a convention could operate except upon the international plane and as between parties possessing international personality.

In the opinion of the Court, the Organization was intended to exercise and enjoy, and is in fact exercising and enjoying, functions and rights which can only be explained on the basis of the possession of a large measure of international personality and the capacity to operate upon an international plane. It is at present the supreme type of international organization, and it could not carry out the intentions of its founders if it was devoid of international personality. It must be acknowledged that its Members, by entrusting certain functions to it, with the attendant duties and responsibilities, have clothed it with the competence required to enable those functions to be effectively discharged.

Accordingly, the Court has come to the conclusion that the Organization is an international person. That is not the same thing as saying that it is a State, which it certainly is not, or that its legal personality and rights and duties are the same as those of a State. Still less is it the same thing as saying that it is "a super-State", whatever that expression may mean. It does not even imply that all its rights and duties must be upon the international plane, any more than all the rights and duties of a State must be upon that plane. What it does mean is that it is a subject of international law and capable of possessing international rights and duties, and that it has capacity to maintain its rights by bringing international claims.

State

State succession

Respect for the fundamental rights of the individual

and the rights of peoples and minorities

Badinter Arbitration Commission on Yugoslavia, Opinion No. 1 of 29 November 1991
In Alain Pellet, 'The Opinions of the Badinter Arbitration Committee: A Second Breath for the Self-Determination of Peoples', 3 EJIL (1992) 178.

Opinion No. 1

'The President of the Arbitration Committee received the following letter from Lord Carrington, President of the Conference on Yugoslavia, on 20 November 1991:

We find ourselves with a major legal question.

Serbia considers that those Republics which have declared or would declare themselves independent or sovereign have seceded or would secede from the SFRY which would otherwise continue to exist.

Other Republics on the contrary consider that there is no question of secession, but the question is one of a disintegration or breaking-up of the SDRY as the result of the concurring will of a number of Republics. They consider that the six Republics are to be considered equal successors to the SFRY, without any of them or group of them being able to claim to be the continuation thereof.'

'1)   The Committee considers:

   a)   that the answer to the question should be based on the principles of public international law which serve to define the conditions on which an entity constitutes a state; that in this respect, the existence or disappearance of the state is a question of fact; that the effects of recognition by other states are purely declaratory;

   b)   that the state is commonly defined as a community which consists of a territory and a population subject to an organized political authority; that such a state is characterized by sovereignty;

   c)   that, for the purpose of applying these criteria, the form of internal political organization and the constitutional provisions are mere facts, . . . '

   'd)   that in the case of a federal-type state, which embraces communities that possess a degree of autonomy and, moreover, participate in the exercise of political power within the framework of institutions common to the Federation, the existence of the state implies that the federal organs represent the components of the Federation and wield effective power;

   e)   that, in compliance with the accepted definition in international law, the expression "state succession" means the replacement of one state by another in the responsibility for the international relations of territory. This occurs whenever there is a change in the territory of the state. The phenomenon of state succession is governed by the principles of international law, from which the Vienna Conventions of 23 August 1978 and 8 April 1983 have drawn inspiration. In compliance with these principles, the outcome of succession should be equitable, the states concerned being free of terms of settlement and conditions by agreement.'

'2) The Arbitration Committee notes that:

a) although the SFRY has until now retained its international personality, notably inside international organizations, the Republics have expressed their desire for independence; . . .

b) The composition and workings of the essential organs of the Federation, be they the Federal Presidency, the Federal Council, the Council of the Republics and the Provinces, the Federal Executive Council, the Constitutional Court or the Federal Army, no longer meet the criteria of participation and representatives inherent in a federal state;

c) The recourse to force has led to armed conflict between the different elements of the Federation which has caused the death of thousands of people and wrought considerable destruction within a few months. The authorities of the Federation and the Republics have shown themselves to be powerless to enforce respect for the succeeding ceasefire agreements concluded under the auspices of the European Communities or the United Nations Organization.

3) Consequently, the Arbitration Committee is of the opinion:

- that the Socialist Federal Republic of Yugoslavia is in the process of dissolution;
- that it is incumbent upon the Republics to settle such problems of state succession as may arise from this process in keeping with the principles and rules of international law, with particular regard for human rights and the rights of peoples and minorities;
- that it is up to those Republics that so wish, to work together to form a new association endowed with the democratic institutions of their choice.'

Criteria of statehood
Rights and Duties of States

The Montevideo Convention on the Rights and Duties of States
of 1933
Entry into force: 26 December 1934.

Article 1

The state as a person of international law should possess the following qualifications:

(a) a permanent population;
(b) a defined territory;
(c) government; and
(d) capacity to enter into relations with the other states.

Article 2

The federal state shall constitute a sole person in the eyes of international law.

Article 3

The political existence of the state is independent of recognition by the other states. Even before recognition the state has the right to defend its integrity and independence, to provide for its conservation and prosperity, and consequently to organize itself as it sees fit, to legislate upon its interests, administer its services, and to define the jurisdiction and competence of its courts.

The exercise of these rights has no other limitation than the exercise of the rights of other states according to international law.

Article 4

States are juridically equal, enjoy the same rights, and have equal capacity in their exercise. The rights of each one do not depend upon the power which it possesses to assure its exercise, but upon the simple fact of its existence as a person under international law.

Article 5

The fundamental rights of states are not susceptible of being affected in any manner whatsoever.

Article 6

The recognition of a state merely signifies that the state which recognizes it accepts the personality of the other with all the rights and duties determined by international law. Recognition is unconditional and irrevocable.

Article 7

The recognition of a state may be express or tacit. The latter results from any act which implies the intention of recognizing the new state.

Article 8

No state has the right to intervene in the internal or external affairs of another.

Article 9

The jurisdiction of states within the limits of national territory applies to all the inhabitants.

Nationals and foreigners are under the same protection of the law and the national authorities and the foreigners may not claim rights other or more extensive than those of the nationals.

Article 10

The primary interest of states is the conservation of peace. Differences of any nature which arise between them should be settled by recognized pacific methods.

Article 11

The contracting states definitely establish as the rule of their conduct the precise obligation not to recognize territorial acquisitions or special advantages which have been obtained by force whether this consists in the employment of arms, in threatening diplomatic representations, or in any other effective coercive measure. The territory of a state is inviolable and may not be the object of military occupation nor of other measures of force imposed by another state directly or indirectly or for any motive whatever even temporarily.

Article 12

The present Convention shall not affect obligations previously entered into by the High Contracting Parties by virtue of international agreements.

Article 13

The present Convention shall be ratified by the High Contracting Parties in conformity with their respective constitutional procedures. The Minister of Foreign Affairs of the Republic of Uruguay shall transmit authentic certified copies to the governments for the aforementioned purpose of ratification. The instrument of ratification shall be deposited in the archives of the Pan American Union in Washington, which shall notify the signatory governments of said deposit. Such notification shall be considered as an exchange of ratifications.

Recognition

Lassa Oppenheim, *International law: a treatise*
Vol. I. – Peace (1st edition, Longmans, Green and Co 1905) 108–110

'§ 71. As the basis of the Law of Nations is the common consent of the civilised States, statehood alone does not include membership of the Family of Nations. There are States in existence, although their number decreases gradually, which are not, or not fully, members of that family because their civilisation, if any, does not enable them and their subjects to act in conformity with the principles of International Law. Those States which are members are either original members because the Law of Nations grew up gradually between them through custom and treaties, or they are members which have been recognised by the body of members already in existence when they were born. For every State that is not already, but wants to be, a member, recognition is therefore necessary. A State is and becomes an International Person through recognition only and exclusively.

Many writers do not agree with this opinion. They maintain that, if a new civilised State comes into existence either by breaking off from an existing recognised State, as Belgium did in 1831, or otherwise, such new State enters of right into the Family of Nations and becomes of right an International Person. They do not deny that practically such recognition is necessary to enable every new State to enter into official intercourse with other States. Yet they assert that theoretically every new State becomes a member of the Family of Nations *ipso facto* by its rising into existence, and that recognition supplies only the necessary evidence for this fact.

If the real facts of international life are taken into consideration, this opinion cannot stand. It is a rule of International Law that no new State has a right towards other States to be recognised by them, and that no State has the duty to recognise a new State. It is generally agreed that a new State before its recognition cannot claim any right which a member of the Family of Nations has towards other members. It can, therefore, not be seen what the function of recognition could be if a State entered with its birth really of right into the membership of the Family of Nations. There is no doubt that statehood itself is independent of recognition. International Law does not say that a State is not in existence as long as it is not recognised, but it takes no notice of it before its recognition. Through recognition only and exclusively a State becomes an International Person and a subject of International Law.'

Formation and existence of states

Constitutive theory
Declaratory theory

James Crawford, *The Creation of States in International Law*
(2nd edn, Clarendon Press in Oxford, Oxford University Press 2007) 4, 5, 6.

'[I]t has long been asserted that "The formation of a new State is . . . a matter of fact, and not of law." This position was supported by a wide spectrum of legal opinion. For example, one of the most common arguments of the declaratory theory . . . is that, where a State actually exists, the legality of its creation or existence must be an abstract issue: the law must take account of the new situation, despite its illegality.'

'Neither theory of recognition satisfactorily explains modern practice. The declaratory theory assumes that territorial entities can readily, by virtue of their mere existence, be classified as having one particular legal status: it thus, in a way, confuses "fact" with "law". For, even if effectiveness is the dominant principle, it must nonetheless be a legal principle. A State is not a fact in the sense that a chair is a fact; it is a fact in the sense in which it may be said a treaty is a fact: that is, a legal status attaching to a certain state of affairs by virtue of certain rules or practices.'

'Fundamentally the question is whether international law is itself, in one of its most important aspects, a coherent or complete system of law. According to predominant nineteenth-century doctrine there were no rules determining what were "States" for the purposes of international law; the matter was within the discretion of existing recognized States. The international law of that period exhibited a formal incoherence that was an expression of its radical decentralization.

But if international law is still, more or less, decentralized in terms of its basic structures, it is generally assumed that it is a formally complete system of law. For example this is taken to be the case with respect to the use of force and nationality, fields closely related to the existence and legitimacy of States. This work investigates the question whether, and to what extent, the formation and existence of States is regulated by international law, and is not simply a "matter of fact".'

Sovereignty

Corfu Channel (United Kingdom of Great Britain and Northern Ireland v Albania), Judgment of 9 April 1949, International Court of Justice, Separate Opinion by Judge Alvarez

Questions which concern the sovereignty of States deserve special consideration, for the main issues in the present dispute have their primary origin in that notion or will affect it.

By sovereignty, we understand the whole body of rights and attributes which a State possesses in its territory, to the exclusion of all other States, and also in its relations with other States.

Sovereignty confers rights upon States and imposes obligations on them.

These rights are not the same and are not exercised in the same way in every sphere of international law. 1 have in mind the four traditional spheres-terrestrial, maritime, fluvial and lacustrine to which must be added three new ones – aerial, polar and floating (floating islands). The violation of these rights is not of equal gravity in all these different spheres.

Some jurists have proposed to abolish the notion of the sovereignty of States, considering it obsolete. That is an error. This notion has its foundation in national sentiment and in the psychology of the peoples, in fact it is very deeply rooted. The constituent instrument of the International Organization has especially recognized the sovereignty of States and has endeavoured to bring it into harmony with the objects of that Organization. . . .

This notion has evolved, and we must now adopt a conception of it which will be in harmony with the new conditions of social life. We can no longer regard sovereignty as an absolute and individual right of every State, as used to be done under the old law founded on the individualist regime, according to which States were only bound by the rules which they had accepted. To-day, owing to social interdependence and to the predominance of the general interest, the States are bound by many rules which have not been ordered by their will. The sovereignty of States has now become an *institution*, an *international social function* of a psychological character, which has to be exercised in accordance with the new international law.

Uti possidetis

Frontier Dispute (Burkina Faso/Republic of Mali), Judgment of 22 December 1986,
    International Court of Justice
    ICJ Reports 1986, 554.

19. The characteristic feature of the legal context of the frontier determination to be undertaken by the Chamber is that both States involved derive their existence from the process of decolonization which has been unfolding in Africa during the past 30 years. Their territories, and that of Niger, were formerly part of the French colonies which were grouped together under the name of French West Africa (AOF). Considering only the situation which prevailed immediately before the accession to independence of the two States, and disregarding previous administrative changes, it can be said that Burkina Faso corresponds to the colony of Upper Volta, and the Republic of Mali to the colony of Sudan (formerly French Sudan). It is to be supposed that the Parties drew inspiration from the principle expressly stated in the well-known resolution (AGH/Res.16 (1)), adopted at the first session of the Conference of African Heads of State and Government, meeting in Cairo in 1964, whereby the Conference solemnly declared that all member States of the Organization of African Unity "solemnly . . . pledge themselves to respect the frontiers existing on their achievement of national independence", inasmuch as, in the preamble to their Special Agreement, they stated that the settlement of the dispute by the Chamber must be "based in particular on respect for the principle of the intangibility of frontiers inherited from colonization". It is clear from this text, and from the pleadings and oral arguments of the Parties, that they are in agreement as regards both the applicable law and the starting-point for the legal reasoning which is to lead to the determination of the frontier between their territories in the disputed area.

20. Since the two Parties have, as noted above, expressly requested the Chamber to resolve their dispute on the basis, in particular, of the "principle of the intangibility of frontiers inherited

from colonization", the Chamber cannot disregard the principle of *uti possidetis juris*, the application of which gives rise to this respect for intangibility of frontiers. Although there is no need, for the purposes of the present case, to show that this is a firmly established principle of international law where decolonization is concerned, the Chamber nonetheless wishes to emphasize its general scope, in view of its exceptional importance for the African continent and for the two Parties. In this connection it should be noted that the principle of *uti possidetis* seems to have been first invoked and applied in Spanish America, inasmuch as this was the continent which first witnessed the phenomenon of decolonization involving the formation of a number of sovereign States on territory formerly belonging to a single metropolitan State. Nevertheless the principle is not a special rule which pertains solely to one specific system of international law. It is a general principle, which is logically connected with the phenomenon of the obtaining of independence, wherever it occurs. Its obvious purpose is to prevent the independence and stability of new States being endangered by fratricidal struggles provoked by the challenging of frontiers following the withdrawal of the administering power.

21. It was for this reason that, as soon as the phenomenon of decolonization characteristic of the situation in Spanish America in the 19th century subsequently appeared in Africa in the 20th century, the principle of *uti possidetis*, in the sense described above, fell to be applied. The fact that the new African States have respected the administrative boundaries and frontiers established by the colonial powers must be seen not as a mere practice contributing to the gradual emergence of a principle of customary international law, limited in its impact to the African continent as it had previously been to Spanish America, but as the application in Africa of a rule of general scope.

22. The elements of *uti possidetis* were latent in the many declarations made by African leaders in the dawn of independence. These declarations confirmed the maintenance of the territorial status quo at the time of independence, and stated the principle of respect both for the frontiers deriving from international agreements, and for those resulting from mere internal administrative divisions. The Charter of the Organization of African Unity did not ignore the principle of *uti possidetis*, but made only indirect reference to it in Article 3, according to which member States solemnly affirm the principle of respect for the sovereignty and territorial integrity of every State. However, at their first summit conference after the creation of the Organization of African Unity, the African Heads of State, in their Resolution mentioned above (AGH/Res. 16 (1)), adopted in Cairo in July 1964, deliberately defined and stressed the principle of *uti possidetis juris* contained only in an implicit sense in the Charter of their organization.

23. There are several different aspects to this principle, in its well-known application in Spanish America. The first aspect, emphasized by the Latin genitive *juris*, is found in the pre-eminence accorded to legal title over effective possession as a basis of sovereignty. Its purpose, at the time of the achievement of independence by the former Spanish colonies of America, was to scotch any designs which non-American colonizing powers might have on regions which had been assigned by the former metropolitan State to one division or another, but which were still uninhabited or unexplored. However, there is more to the principle of *uti possidetis* than this particular aspect. The essence of the principle lies in its primary aim of securing respect for the territorial boundaries at the moment when independence is achieved. Such territorial boundaries might be no more than delimitations between different administrative divisions or colonies all subject to the same sovereign. In that case, the application of the principle of *uti possidetis* resulted in administrative boundaries being transformed into international frontiers in the full sense of the term. This is true both of the States which took shape in the regions of South America which were dependent on the Spanish Crown, and of the States Parties to the present case, which took shape within the vast territories of French West Africa. *Uti possidetis*, as a principle

which upgraded former administrative delimitations, established during the colonial period, to international frontiers, is therefore a principle of a general kind which is logically connected with this form of decolonization wherever it occurs.

State succession

Vienna Convention on Succession of States in respect of Treaties of 1978
Entry into force: 6 November 1996.

PART I.
GENERAL PROVISIONS

Article 1 Scope of the present Convention

The present Convention applies to the effects of a succession of States in respect of treaties between States.

Article 2 Use of terms

1   For the purposes of the present Convention:

  (**a**) "treaty" means an international agreement concluded between States in written form and governed by international law, whether embodied in a single instrument or in two or more related instruments, and whatever its particular designation;

  (**b**) "succession of States" means the replacement of one State by another in the responsibility for the international relations of territory;

  (**c**) "predecessor State" means the State which has been replaced by another State on the occurrence of a succession of States;

  (**d**) "successor State" means the State which has replaced another State on the occurrence of a succession of States;

  (**e**) "date of the succession of States" means the date upon which the successor State replaced the predecessor State in the responsibility for the international relations of the territory to which the succession of States relates;

  (**f**) "newly independent State" means a successor State the territory of which immediately before the date of the succession of States was a dependent territory for the international relations of which the predecessor State was responsible;

  (**g**) "notification of succession" means in relation to a multilateral treaty any notification, however phrased or named, made by a successor State expressing its consent to be considered as bound by the treaty;

  (**h**) "full powers" means in relation to a notification of succession or any other notification under the present Convention a document emanating from the competent authority of a State designating a person or persons to represent the State for communicating the notification of succession or, as the case may be, the notification;

  (**i**) "ratification", "acceptance" and "approval" mean in each case the international act so named whereby a State establishes on the international plane its consent to be bound by a treaty;

  (**j**) "reservation" means a unilateral statement, however phrased or named, made by a

State when signing, ratifying, accepting, approving or acceding to a treaty or when making a notification of succession to a treaty, whereby it purports to exclude or to modify the legal effect of certain provisions of the treaty in their application to that State;

(**k**) "contracting State" means a State which has consented to be bound by the treaty, whether or not the treaty has entered into force;

(**1**) "party" means a State which has consented to be bound by the treaty and for which the treaty is in force;

(**m**) "other State party" means in relation to a successor State any party, other than the predecessor State, to a treaty in force at the date of a succession of States in respect of the territory to which that succession of States relates;

(**n**) "international organization" means an intergovernmental organization.

2 The provisions of paragraph 1 regarding the use of terms in the present Convention are without prejudice to the use of those terms or to the meanings which may be given to them in the internal law of any State.

Article 3 Cases not within the scope of the present Convention

The fact that the present Convention does not apply to the effects of a succession of States in respect of international agreements concluded between States and other subjects of international law or in respect of international agreements not in written form shall not affect:

(**a**) the application to such cases of any of the rules set forth in the present Convention to which they are subject under international law independently of the Convention;

(**b**) the application as between States of the present Convention to the effects of a succession of States in respect of international agreements to which other subjects of international law are also parties.

Article 4 Treaties constituting international organizations and treaties adopted within an international organization

The present Convention applies to the effects of a succession of States in respect of:

(**a**) any treaty which is the constituent instrument of an international organization without prejudice to the rules concerning acquisition of membership and without prejudice to any other relevant rules of the organization;

(**b**) any treaty adopted within an international organization without prejudice to any relevant rules of the organization.

Article 5 Obligations imposed by international law independently of a treaty

The fact that a treaty is not considered to be in force in respect of a State by virtue of the application of the present Convention shall not in any way impair the duty of that State to fulfil any obligation embodied in the treaty to which it is subject under international law independently of the treaty.

Article 6 Cases of succession of States covered by the present Convention

The present Convention applies only to the effects of a succession of States occurring in conformity with international law and, in particular, the principles of international law embodied in the Charter of the United Nations.

Article 8 Agreements for the devolution of treaty obligations or rights from a predecessor State to a successor State

1   The obligations or rights of a predecessor State under treaties in force in respect of a territory at the date of a succession of States do not become the obligations or rights of the successor State towards other States Parties to those treaties by reason only of the fact that the predecessor State and the successor State have concluded an agreement providing that such obligations or rights shall devolve upon the successor State.
2   Notwithstanding the conclusion of such an agreement, the effects of a succession of States on treaties which, at the date of that succession of States, were in force in respect of the territory in question are governed by the present Convention.

Article 9 Unilateral declaration by a successor State regarding treaties of the predecessor State

1   Obligations or rights under treaties in force in respect of a territory at the date of a succession of States do not become the obligations or rights of the successor State or of other States Parties to those treaties by reason only of the fact that the successor State has made a unilateral declaration providing for the continuance in force of the treaties in respect of its territory.
2   In such a case, the effects of the succession of States on treaties which, at the date of that succession of States, were in force in respect of the territory in question are governed by the present Convention.

Article 10 Treaties providing for the participation of a successor State

1   When a treaty provides that, on the occurrence of a succession of States, a successor State shall have the option to consider itself a party to the treaty, it may notify its succession in respect of the treaty in conformity with the provisions of the treaty or, failing any such provisions, in conformity with the provisions of the present Convention.
2   If a treaty provides that, on the occurrence of a succession of States, a successor State shall be considered as a party to the treaty, that provision takes effect as such only if the successor State expressly accepts in writing to be so considered.
3   In cases falling under paragraph 1 or 2, a successor State which establishes its consent to be a party to the treaty is considered as a party from the date of the succession of States unless the treaty otherwise provides or it is otherwise agreed.

Article 11 Boundary regimes

A succession of States does not as such affect:

(a) a boundary established by a treaty; or
(b) obligations and rights established by a treaty and relating to the regime of a boundary.

Article 12 Other territorial regimes

1 A succession of States does not as such affect:

(a) obligations relating to the use of any territory, or to restrictions upon its use, established by a treaty for the benefit of any territory of a foreign State and considered as attaching to the territories in question;
(b) rights established by a treaty for the benefit of any territory and relating to the use, or to restrictions upon the use, of any territory of a foreign State and considered as attaching to the territories in question.

2 A succession of States does not as such affect:

(a) obligations relating to the use of any territory, or to restrictions upon its use, established by a treaty for the benefit of a group of States or of all States and considered as attaching to that territory;
(b) rights established by a treaty for the benefit of a group of States or of all States and relating to the use of any territory, or to restrictions upon its use, and considered as attaching to that territory.

3 The provisions of the present article do not apply to treaty obligations of the predecessor State providing for the establishment of foreign military bases on the territory to which the succession of States relates.

Article 13 The present Convention and permanent sovereignty over natural wealth and resources

Nothing in the present Convention shall affect the principles of international law affirming the permanent sovereignty of every people and every State over its natural wealth and resources.

Article 14 Questions relating to the validity of a treaty

Nothing in the present Convention shall be considered as prejudging in any respect any question relating to the validity of a treaty.

PART II.
SUCCESSION IN RESPECT OF PART OF TERRITORY

Article 15 Succession in respect of part of territory

When part of the territory of a State, or when any territory for the international relations of which a State is responsible, not being part of the territory of that State, becomes part of the territory of another State:

(**a**) treaties of the predecessor State cease to be in force in respect of the territory to which the succession of States relates from the date of the succession of States; and

(**b**) treaties of the successor State are in force in respect of the territory to which the succession of States relates from the date of the succession of States, unless it appears from the treaty or is otherwise established that the application of the treaty to that territory would be incompatible with the object and purpose of the treaty or would radically change the conditions for its operation.

PART IV.
UNITING AND SEPARATION OF STATES

Article 31 Effects of a uniting of States in respect of treaties in force at the date of the succession of States

1   When two or more States unite and so form one successor State, any treaty in force at the date of the succession of States in respect of any of them continues in force in respect of the successor State unless:

   (a)   the successor State and the other State party or States Parties otherwise agree; or
   (b)   it appears from the treaty or is otherwise established that the application of the treaty in respect of the successor State would be incompatible with the object and purpose of the treaty or would radically change the conditions for its operation.

2   Any treaty continuing in force in conformity with paragraph 1 shall apply only in respect of the part of the territory of the successor State in respect of which the treaty was in force at the date of the succession of States unless:

   (a)   in the case of a multilateral treaty not falling within the category mentioned in article 17, paragraph 3, the successor State makes a notification that the treaty shall apply in respect of its entire territory;
   (b)   in the case of a multilateral treaty falling within the category mentioned in article 17, paragraph 3, the successor State and the other States Parties otherwise agree; or
   (c)   in the case of a bilateral treaty, the successor State and the other State party otherwise agree.

3   Paragraph 2 (a) does not apply if it appears from the treaty or is otherwise established that the application of the treaty in respect of the entire territory of the successor State would be incompatible with the object and purpose of the treaty or would radically change the conditions for its operation.

Article 32 Effects of a uniting of States in respect of treaties not in force at the date of the succession of States

1   Subject to paragraphs 3 and 4, a successor State falling under article 31 may, by making a notification, establish its status as a contracting State to a multilateral treaty which is not in force if, at the date of the succession of States, any of the predecessor States was a contracting State to the treaty.

2   Subject to paragraphs 3 and 4, a successor State falling under article 31 may, by making a notification, establish its status as a party to a multilateral treaty which enters into force after the date of the succession of States if, at that date, any of the predecessor States was a contracting State to the treaty.

3   Paragraphs 1 and 2 do not apply if it appears from the treaty or is otherwise established that the application of the treaty in respect of the successor State would be incompatible with the object and purpose of the treaty or would radically change the conditions for its operation.

4   If the treaty is one falling within the category mentioned in article 17, paragraph 3, the successor State may establish its status as a party or as a contracting State to the treaty only with the consent of all the parties or of all the contracting States.

5   Any treaty to which the successor State becomes a contracting State or a party in conformity with paragraph 1 or 2 shall apply only in respect of the part of the territory of the successor State in respect of which consent to be bound by the treaty had been given prior to the date of the succession of States unless:

    (**a**)   in the case of a multilateral treaty not falling within the category mentioned in article 17, paragraph 3, the successor State indicates in its notification made under paragraph 1 or 2 that the treaty shall apply in respect of its entire territory; or

    (**b**)   in the case of a multilateral treaty falling within the category mentioned in article 17, paragraph 3, the successor State and all the parties or, as the case may be, all the contracting States otherwise agree.

6   Paragraph 5 (*a*) does not apply if it appears from the treaty or is otherwise established that the application of the treaty in respect of the entire territory of the successor State would be incompatible with the object and purpose of the treaty or would radically change the conditions for its operation.

Article 33 Effects of a uniting of States in respect of treaties signed by a predecessor State subject to ratification, acceptance or approval

1   Subject to paragraphs 2 and 3, if before the date of the succession of States one of the predecessor States had signed a multilateral treaty subject to ratification, acceptance or approval, a successor State falling under article 31 may ratify, accept or approve the treaty as if it had signed that treaty and may thereby become a party or a contracting State to it.

2   Paragraph 1 does not apply if it appears from the treaty or is otherwise established that the application of the treaty in respect of the successor State would be incompatible with the object and purpose of the treaty or would radically change the conditions for its operation.

3   If the treaty is one falling within the category mentioned in article 17, paragraph 3, the successor State may become a party or a contracting State to the treaty only with the consent of all the parties or of all the contracting States.

4   Any treaty to which the successor State becomes a party or a contracting State in conformity with paragraph 1 shall apply only in respect of the part of the territory of the successor State in respect of which the treaty was signed by one of the predecessor States unless:

    (**a**)   in the case of a multilateral treaty not falling within the category mentioned in article 17, paragraph 3, the successor State when ratifying, accepting or approving the treaty gives notice that the treaty shall apply in respect of its entire territory; or

    (**b**)   in the case of a multilateral treaty falling within the category mentioned in article 17, paragraph 3, the successor State and all the parties or, as the case may be, all the contracting States otherwise agree.

5   Paragraph 4 (*a*) does not apply if it appears from the treaty or is otherwise established that the application of the treaty in respect of the entire territory of the successor State would be incompatible with the object and purpose of the treaty or would radically change the conditions for its operation.

Article 34 Succession of States in cases of separation of parts of a State

1   When a part or parts of the territory of a State separate to form one or more States, whether or not the predecessor State continues to exist:

(*a*)   any treaty in force at the date of the succession of States in respect of the entire territory of the predecessor State continues in force in respect of each successor State so formed;

(*b*)   any treaty in force at the date of the succession of States in respect only of that part of the territory of the predecessor State which has become a successor State continues in force in respect of that successor State alone.

2   Paragraph 1 does not apply if:

(*a*)   the States concerned otherwise agree; or

(*b*)   it appears from the treaty or is otherwise established that the application of the treaty in respect of the successor State would be incompatible with the object and purpose of the treaty or would radically change the conditions for its operation.

Article 35 Position if a State continues after separation of part of its territory

When, after separation of any part of the territory of a State, the predecessor State continues to exist, any treaty which at the date of the succession of States was in force in respect of the predecessor State continues in force in respect of its remaining territory unless:

(*a*)   the States concerned otherwise agree;

(*b*)   it is established that the treaty related only to the territory which has separated from the predecessor State; or

(*c*)   it appears from the treaty or is otherwise established that the application of the treaty in respect of the predecessor State would be incompatible with the object and purpose of the treaty or would radically change the conditions for its operation.

Article 36 Participation in treaties not in force at the date of the succession of States in cases of separation of parts of a State

1   Subject to paragraphs 3 and 4, a successor State falling under article 34, paragraph 1, may, by making a notification, establish its status as a contracting State to a multilateral treaty which is not in force if, at the date of the succession of States, the predecessor State was a contracting State to the treaty in respect of the territory to which the succession of States relates.

2   Subject to paragraphs 3 and 4, a successor State falling under article 34, paragraph 1, may, by making a notification, establish its status as a party to a multilateral treaty which enters into force after the date of the succession of States if at that date the predecessor State was a contracting State to the treaty in respect of the territory to which the succession of States relates.

3   Paragraphs 1 and 2 do not apply if it appears from the treaty or is otherwise established that the application of the treaty in respect of the successor State would be incompatible with the object and purpose of the treaty or would radically change the conditions for its operation.

4   If the treaty is one falling within the category mentioned in article 17, paragraph 3, the successor State may establish its status as a party or as a contracting State to the treaty only with the consent of all the parties or of all the contracting States.

Article 37 Participation in cases of separation of parts of a State in treaties signed by the predecessor State subject to ratification, acceptance or approval

1   Subject to paragraphs 2 and 3, if before the date of the succession of States the predecessor State had signed a multilateral treaty subject to ratification, acceptance or approval and the treaty, if it had been in force at that date, would have applied in respect of the territory to which the succession of States relates, a successor State falling under article 34, paragraph 1, may ratify, accept or approve the treaty as if it had signed that treaty and may thereby become a party or a contracting State to it.

2   Paragraph 1 does not apply if it appears from the treaty or is otherwise established that the application of the treaty in respect of the successor State would be incompatible with the object and purpose of the treaty or would radically change the conditions for its operation.

3   If the treaty is one falling within the category mentioned in article 17, paragraph 3, the successor State may become a party or a contracting State to the treaty only with the consent of all the parties or of all the contracting States.

Other subjects of international law

DOI: 10.4324/9781003213772-5

THE PEOPLE AS A SUBJECT OF INTERNATIONAL LAW

The preconditions of international subjectivity of the peoples

The 'peoples' acquire independent subjectivity in international law basically as a result of the struggle for independence or, in particular cases, upon the international credentials granted by the decisions of states and other subjects of international law (for example, concerning the inclusion of a people in the process of Decolonisation). The status of people can be generalised as a subject which is not the state but which is considered an international person in specific cases and areas.

The genesis of the principle of equal rights and self-determination of peoples

peoples as the possessors of the inherent right to decide their own destiny
representative government
popular sovereignty
American Declaration of Independence
Declaration of Human and Civic Rights
right to autonomous development
right to independent statehood
principle of self-determination

> legal principle
> right of secession
> Era of Decolonisation
> peoples
> Declaration on the granting of independence to colonial countries and peoples
> International Covenant on Civil and Political Rights
> International Covenant on Economic, Social and Cultural Rights
> universally recognised human right
> Declaration on Principles of International Law concerning Friendly Relations and
> Co-operation among States in accordance with the Charter of the United Nations
> Helsinki Final Act
> Vienna Declaration and Programme of Action
> modes implementing the right to self-determination

Preliminary remark

It is especially notable that the meaning of the self-determination of peoples is one of the most controversial issues in international law.

Enlightenment

The original idea that peoples are the **possessors of the inherent right to decide their own destiny** is rooted in the philosophy of the enlightenment era.

In fact, the concepts of **representative government** and **popular sovereignty** that John Locke and Jean-Jacques Rousseau (1712–1778) advocated together with the other famous scholars of that era lie at the heart of self-determination as it was first developed in Europe and some other parts of the world. At that point in history, these concepts facilitated the belief that the authority of a state should be created and sustained by the consent of its people.

Different contexts of self-determination

Then, in the course of time, references to the self-determination of peoples were made in different contexts, such as:

* Decolonisation – for example, the **American Declaration of Independence** of 4 July 1776, where the initial ideas of enlightenment regarding the system of government were combined with the context set by the Decolonisation.[306]

---

306 'That, whenever any form of Government becomes destructive of these ends, it is the Right of the People to alter or to abolish it. . . . Prudence, indeed, will dictate that Governments long established should not be changed for light and transient causes. . . . Such has been the patient sufferance of these Colonies; and such is now the necessity which constrains them to alter their former Systems of Government.' American Declaration of Independence.

- Revolution and coup – for instance, the **Declaration of Human and Civic Rights** passed by the National Assembly of France on 26 August 1789, where the aforementioned concepts of enlightenment contributed to the justification of the revolution.
- Consolidation – for example, the process of unification of Italy and Germany, when self-determination provided the consolidating ground;
- Autonomism – when many peoples living on the parts of the territories of the states claimed their **right to autonomous development**.
- Secessionism – for instance, the division of the Ottoman and Austro-Hungarian empires, when as a result of growing nationalism, the originating idea (of self-determination) shifted to the concept of self-determination as a **right to independent statehood** of particular peoples.

The principle of self-determination

The **principle of self-determination** materialised politically after World War I. The President of the United States of America, Woodrow Wilson, declared self-determination 'an imperative principle of action'. However, Wilson's purpose for incorporating self-determination into the Covenant of the League of Nations failed. That is why this principle could not obtain the status of a **legal principle** at that stage. Moreover, it was not clear to whom self-determination would apply. Indeed, without a clearly identifiable unit, the practical application of this principle was regarded as a danger to peace and stability.

Only after World War II was self-determination reshaped from a political into a legal principle, when it was included in the Charter of the United Nations as one of the principles of friendly relations among states. This principle appeared in precise wording in the Charter in two places: namely, in Article 1(2), Chapter I, containing the purposes of the Organisation, and Article 55, Chapter IX, dedicated to international economic and social co-operation.

According to Article 1: 'The Purposes of the United Nations are: . . . 2. To develop friendly relations among nations based on respect for the principle of equal rights and self-determination of peoples, and to take other appropriate measures to strengthen universal peace'.

A similar formulation can be found in Article 55 of the Charter: 'With a view to the creation of conditions of stability and well-being which are necessary for peaceful and friendly relations among nations based on respect for the principle of equal rights and self-determination of peoples, the United Nations shall promote . . .'

Era of Decolonisation

Although these provisions were not intended to incentivise the **right of secession**, the appearance of the legal principle in the Charter has proved to be a significant facilitator of the **Era of Decolonisation**, when, with regard to particular territories and peoples, self-determination was applied as a legal obligation in maintaining the process of Decolonisation and establishing the numerous newly independent states. Therefore, the content of self-determination is one of the most ambivalent provisions of the Charter. In addition, the meaning of the term '**peoples**' also remains uncertain, since no definition of it was included in the Charter.

Declaration on the granting of independence to colonial countries and peoples

The remarkable expression of the trend prevailing in the era of Decolonisation was the **Declaration on the granting of independence to colonial countries and peoples** of 1960, which was adopted by the UN General Assembly.[307]

According to the Declaration: 'All peoples have the right to self-determination; by virtue of that right they freely determine their political status and freely pursue their economic, social and cultural development.' At the same time, the 'subjection of peoples to alien subjugation, domination and exploitation constitutes a denial of fundamental human rights.' With this formulation, the Declaration opened the window for a rethinking of the principle of self-determination as being linked with fundamental human rights.

Two International Human Right Covenants

As the next notable milestone in the development of the principle of self-determination, the two International Human Rights Covenants of 1966 should be considered – the **International Covenant on Civil and Political Rights** and the **International Covenant on Economic, Social and Cultural Rights**. Indeed, there is a reference to the principle of self-determination in Article 1, which is identical in both these covenants: '1. All peoples have the right of self-determination. By virtue of that right they freely determine their political status and freely pursue their economic, social and cultural development.'

With its inclusion in the International Human Rights Covenants, the self-determination of peoples – a legal principle that primarily concerned the area of Decolonisation – received a new hypostasis as a **universally recognised human right**.

The contemporary developments of the principle of equal rights and self-determination of peoples

Finally, the actors of the interstate system have reaffirmed their commitment to the self-determination principle by another three significant documents – the UN General Assembly's **Declaration on Principles of International Law concerning Friendly Relations and Co-operation among States in accordance with the Charter of the United Nations** of 1970, the **Helsinki Final Act** of 1975, and the **Vienna Declaration and Programme of Action** of 1993. Nowadays, these are regarded as the documents from which numerous general customary norms originate, which, among other things, define the legal nature of the self-determination principle.

According to the Declaration on Principles of International Law Concerning Friendly Relations:

---

307 A/RES/1514(XV) of 14 December 1960 – Declaration on the granting of independence to colonial countries and peoples.

Every state has the duty to promote, through joint and separate action, realization of the principle of equal rights and self-determination of peoples . . . in order:

(a) to promote friendly relations and co-operation among states; and
(b) to bring a speedy end to colonialism, having due regard to the freely expressed will of the peoples concerned; and bearing in mind that subjection of peoples to alien subjugation, domination and exploitation constitutes a violation of the principle, as well as a denial of fundamental human rights, and is contrary to the Charter.

This formulation emphasises the colonial context of the principles of equal rights and self-determination of peoples, 'bearing in mind that subjection of peoples to alien subjugation, domination and exploitation' violates both the principle of self-determination and fundamental human rights.

Furthermore, the Declaration defines the **modes implementing the right to self-determination** by the peoples, which are (1) the establishment of a sovereign and independent state, (2) the free association or integration with an independent state, and (3) the acquisition of any other political status freely determined by the will of the people.

With respect to this principle, the Helsinki Final Act prescribes the requirement to understand and interpret the right to self-determination in the context of all relevant rules of international law:

> The participating States will respect the equal rights of peoples and their right to self-determination, acting at all times in conformity with the purposes and principles of the Charter of the United Nations and with the relevant norms of international law, including those relating to territorial integrity of States.

Lastly, the Vienna Declaration and Programme of Action, which is the most recent document, underlines the importance of finding the balance between the self-determination of peoples and the territorial integrity of states:

> [T]he World Conference on Human Rights recognizes the right of peoples to take any legitimate action, in accordance with the Charter of the United Nations, to realize their inalienable right of self-determination. . . . [T]his shall not be construed as authorizing or encouraging any action which would dismember or impair, totally or in part, the territorial integrity or political unity of sovereign and independent States conducting themselves in compliance with the principle of equal rights and self-determination of peoples and thus possessed of a Government representing the whole people belonging to the territory without distinction of any kind.

Defining self-determination

to maintain people's existence
sufficient protection and development
external self-determination

internal self-determination
cultural autonomy
economic autonomy
political autonomy
Advisory Opinion on *Namibia*
Advisory Opinion on *Western Sahara*
freely expressed will of peoples
Frontier Dispute case
uti possidetis
East Timor case
erga omnes
Advisory Opinion on *Accordance with International Law of the Unilateral Declaration of Independence in respect of Kosovo*
Quebec case
separatism
secessionism
principles of inviolability of frontiers and territorial integrity of states

The general meaning of self-determination

Generally, the self-determination of a person essentially implies the process which allows a person to be in control of his/her own life and decisions. Therefore, by applying this meaning to the peoples in the interstate system, in the broader sense, it is possible to proceed from the original idea that every people possess the inherent right to decide their own destiny – **to maintain people's existence** and ensure **sufficient protection and development**.

People may maintain their existence without challenging the territorial integrity of a state. However, sometimes, when determining their political status, the peoples claim independence referring to the aforementioned legal provisions and, notably, to the Articles of the International Covenants considering self-determination as a universally recognised right of 'all peoples'.

Nevertheless, for reasons arising from the requirements of international peace and security, the right to self-determination needs to be balanced with the necessity to uphold the inviolability of frontiers and the territorial integrity of states. However, is it possible to find a middle ground or a point of equilibrium between these seemingly conflicting ideas?

During the practical application of the principle of self-determination, a distinction has been made between the two concepts – **external self-determination** and **internal self-determination**.

External self-determination

External self-determination is a mode of self-determination which aims at the formation of an independent state, the integration into or association with a third state, or free determination of any other political status.

In general, the concept of external self-determination has been developed with regard to the colonial context.

Internal self-determination

Internal self-determination, in turn, refers to the right of all peoples to participate in the decision-making processes within the state.

Meanwhile, in practice, outside the colonial context, the right to self-determination is mostly fulfilled through internal self-determination. This includes the ability of a people to determine their political destiny within a state by such mechanisms as **cultural autonomy** (the extraordinary model of the protection of language, culture, and autonomous educational systems), **economic autonomy** (autonomy in the economic fields, e.g. taxes, distribution of wealth), and **political autonomy** (autonomous government).

The case law

Over time, the International Court of Justice has made an essential contribution to the affirmation of particular approaches and rules regarding the self-determination principle.

The Court considered this principle in the **Advisory Opinion on *Namibia*** (*Legal Consequences for States of the Continued Presence of South Africa in Namibia (South-West Africa) notwithstanding Security Council Resolution 276 (1970)*) of 1971 (addressing the question of the UN Security Council), according to which it validated the practice of the UN concerning the non-self-governing and trust territories and confirmed that the development of international law made the principle of self-determination applicable to all such territories.[308]

The next case in which the Court discussed the principle of self-determination was the **Advisory Opinion on *Western Sahara*** of 1975 (addressing the question of the UN General Assembly). In this Opinion, the Court emphasised the need to pay regard to the **freely expressed will of peoples** in the colonial context. On the other hand, it identified that when colonial peoples were exercising their right of self-determination, there was a legal obligation to hold a referendum or to conduct a vote for the free expression of the will of a people in any other form, except if a population was not the people in terms of self-determination or in some other cases in which 'special circumstances' were at hand.[309]

---

308 '[T]he subsequent development of international law in regard to non-self-governing territories, as enshrined in the Charter of the United Nations, made the principle of self-determination applicable to all of them. The concept of the sacred trust was confirmed and expanded to all "territories whose peoples have not yet attained a full measure of self-government" (Art. 73). Thus it clearly embraced territories under a colonial regime.' *Legal Consequences for States of the Continued Presence of South Africa in Namibia (South-West Africa) notwithstanding Security Council Resolution 276 (1970)*, Advisory Opinion of 21 June 1971, ICJ Reports 1971, 16.

309 'The validity of the principle of self-determination, defined as the need to pay regard to the freely expressed will of peoples, is not affected by the fact that in certain cases the General Assembly has dispensed with the requirement of consulting the inhabitants of a given territory. Those instances were based either on the consideration that a certain population did not constitute a "people" entitled to

Under the ***Frontier Dispute*** case (*Burkina Faso/Republic of Mali*), the ICJ examined the relationship between self-determination and ***uti possidetis***, which is understood to be 'the intangibility of frontiers inherited from colonisation' or a principle of international law that 'freezes the territorial title' at the moment a colony achieves independence; 'it stops the clock, but does not put back the hands.'[310]

The next relevant case in this context is the ***East Timor*** case (*Portugal v Australia*), under which the Court asserted that 'the right of peoples to self-determination, as it evolved from the Charter and from United Nations practice, has an ***erga omnes*** character.'[311]

More recently, the ICJ issued the **Advisory Opinion on** *Accordance with International Law of the Unilateral Declaration of Independence in respect of Kosovo* of 2010 (addressing the question of the UN General Assembly). However, the ICJ Advisory Opinion did not fulfil the expectations that it would clarify the issues connected to the extent of the right to self-determination. It limited the 'scope and meaning of the question' to 'whether or not the declaration of independence [of Kosovo] is in accordance with international law'.[312] Finally, the ICJ outlined its following findings:

1   The general international law contains no universal prohibition of the declarations of independence, and
2   '[T]he adoption of declaration of independence [of Kosovo] of 17 February 2008 did not violate general international law' (after considering the particular materials concerning the Kosovo case, including, the UN Security Council Resolution 1244[313] and the 'Constitutional Framework for Provisional Self-Government').[314]

Furthermore, the ICJ reaffirmed the existence of the right to external self-determination with regard to (1) the non-self-governing territories and (2) 'peoples subject to alien subjugation, domination and exploitation' but, outside this context, only enumerated the

---

self-determination or on the conviction that a consultation was totally unnecessary, in view of special circumstances.' *Western Sahara*, Advisory Opinion of 16 October 1975, ICJ Reports 1975, 12.

310   *Frontier Dispute (Burkina Faso/Republic of Mali)*, Judgment of 22 December 1986.

311   *East Timor (Portugal v Australia)*, Judgment of 30 June 1995.

312   'A number of participants in the present proceedings have claimed, although in almost every instance only as a secondary argument, that the population of Kosovo has the right to create an independent State either as a manifestation of a right to self-determination or pursuant to what they described as a right of "remedial secession" in the face of the situation in Kosovo. . . . The General Assembly has requested the Court's opinion only on whether or not the declaration of independence is in accordance with international law. Debates regarding the extent of the right of self-determination and the existence of any right of "remedial secession", however, concern the right to separate from a State.' *Accordance with International Law of the Unilateral Declaration of Independence in Respect of Kosovo*, Advisory Opinion of 22 July 2010, ICJ Reports 2010, 403.

313   S/RES/1244 (1999) of 10 June 1999 – The situation relating to Kosovo.

314   '[W]hich defined the responsibilities relating to the administration of Kosovo between the Special Representative of the Secretary-General and the Provisional Institutions of Self-Government of Kosovo.' *Accordance with International Law of the Unilateral Declaration of Independence in Respect of Kosovo*, Advisory Opinion of 22 July 2010.

primary debatable approaches without interpreting the state of affairs in this regard.[315] At the same time, even concerning the 'peoples subject to alien subjugation, domination and exploitation', the Court did not specify whether it referred only to the peoples in the Decolonisation process or the peoples outside the colonial context should also be covered.[316]

Although the Advisory Opinion's scope was very limited, even the finding of the ICJ that the adoption of the declaration of independence of Kosovo did not violate general international law stipulated the firm disagreements between the members of the Court. For example, Judge Abdul G. Koroma, in his Dissenting Opinion, articulated that

> the International law does not confer a right on ethnic, linguistic or religious groups to break away from the territory of a State of which they form part, without that State's consent, merely by expressing their wish to do so. To accept otherwise, to allow any ethnic, linguistic or religious group to declare independence and break away from the territory of the State of which it forms part, outside the context of decolonization, creates a very dangerous precedent.[317]

In contrast to the cautious position of the ICJ, the Supreme Court of Canada, under its landmark judgment of 1998 in *Reference by the Governor in Council concerning Certain Questions relating to the Secession of Quebec from Canada* case (so-called the **Quebec case**) with regard to the secession of Quebec from Canada,[318] elaborated the general legal approach which led to the following clarification:

> In summary, the international law right to self-determination only generates, at best, a right to external self-determination in situations of former colonies; where a people

315 'Whether, outside the context of non-self-governing territories and peoples subject to alien subjugation, domination and exploitation, the international law of self-determination confers upon part of the population of an existing State a right to separate from that State is, however, a subject on which radically different views were expressed by those taking part in the proceedings and expressing a position on the question. Similar differences existed regarding whether international law provides for a right of "remedial secession" and, if so, in what circumstances.' ibid.

316 Although the ICJ did not consider the problem deeper, it utilised the wording of the 'Declaration on the granting of independence to colonial countries and peoples'. Besides, it noted that '[a] great many new States have come into existence as a result of the exercise of this right.' Additionally, the Court stated that '[t]here were, however, also instances of declarations of independence outside this context.' Hence, based on the contextual analysis, the formulation 'peoples subject to alien subjugation, domination, and exploitation' may be interpreted as relating only to the Decolonisation process.

317 *Accordance with International Law of the Unilateral Declaration of Independence in Respect of Kosovo*, Advisory Opinion of 22 July 2010, ICJ Reports 2010, 403, Dissenting Opinion of Judge Koroma.

318 *Reference by the Governor in Council concerning Certain Questions relating to the Secession of Quebec from Canada*, Judgment of 20 August 1998, Supreme Court of Canada, Case number 25506, Report [1998] 2 SCR 217. available at <https://scc-csc.lexum.com/scc-csc/scc-csc/en/item/1643/index.do> accessed 16 March 2021. The Court examined Quebec's right to independence under Canadian and international law. While acknowledging the right to self-determination, the Court ultimately determined that Quebec does not have the right to secede unilaterally.

is oppressed, as for example under foreign military occupation; or where a definable group is denied meaningful access to government to pursue their political, economic, social and cultural development. . . . In other circumstances, peoples are expected to achieve self-determination within the framework of their existing state.[319]

The necessity of finding the balancing point between the self-determination of peoples and inviolability of frontiers and territorial integrity of states

Although the meaning of the self-determination of peoples remains one of the most controversial issues of international law, it is still possible to discover the point at which the self-determination of peoples on one side and inviolability of frontiers and territorial integrity of states on the other side might be balanced. Combining international law norms and the contemporary practice of the subjects of international law, we may arrive at the following conclusions:

1   The external self-determination is suitable if the actors of the interstate system generally apply it to certain processes, cases, or situations, as in the case of Decolonisation, including trust and mandated territories and non-self-governing territories (the ordinary mode).

2   A particular form of the (ordinary) external self-determination is a situation when a people enjoy the right to external self-determination based on the internal legislation of a state or according to the particular norms of international law as, for example, if this right is specified in the Constitution or in the founding international treaty of the state concerned.

3   Outside the ordinary modes, which are widely recognised to be the triggering mechanisms of the right to external self-determination, the extraordinary preconditions for the application of the right to external self-determination may be the following cases:

    a)   Where a people 'is oppressed, as, for example, under foreign military occupation', or where 'a definable group is denied meaningful access to government to pursue their political, economic, social and cultural development' and if all this has led to the gross or systematic violations of human rights. In all situations mentioned earlier, the peoples in question are entitled to a right to external self-determination because they have been denied the opportunity to exercise the right to self-determination internally.

    b)   Where a people do not have the chance to survive within a particular state and appeal for the right to sufficient protection, such as in case of 'widespread or systematic' violation of universally recognised human rights (including crimes against humanity and acts of genocide). This approach is often referred to as the 'remedial theory' ('remedial right of secession' or 'qualified secession doctrine'),[320]

---

319 ibid.

320 'In the doctrine of modern international law there is a certain view that the right to external self-determination can be exercised if certain groups are subject to a repressive regime ("Remedial Theory").

which, however, according to the assessment of some scholars, is not well developed or widely recognised.

4   By including the principle of self-determination in the International Human Rights Covenants, the interstate system acknowledges that the first and foremost aim is the protection of a human as a member of a people[321] since '[b]y virtue of that right every individual may choose to belong to whatever ethnic, religious or language community he or she wishes.'[322] Consequently, implementation of the right to 'free determination of the political status' shall be understood as being interlinked with the other human rights, and, therefore, it should not lead to a massive violation of human rights.

5   Furthermore, nowadays, the international community is well aware of the challenges posed by **separatism**. According to the general definition: 'Separatism is the ideas or activities advocating separation of a group or a territorial unit from a state (country), state institutions, or a larger group, usually in the form of autonomy or independence.'[323] Several forms of separatism can be identified. Based on the intensity criterion, the researchers specify the so-called 'latent separatism', which is stipulated by such preconditions as the beliefs, attitudes, narratives, ideologies, or 'active separatism', which is expressed in various active actions. Usually, separatism arises from the combination of such factors as ethnic, religious, and racial distinctiveness; the collective memories of the past autonomous or independent existence; and so forth. The most radical form of separatism represents **secessionism**, which may broadly be defined as the belief that a part of a state should become separate and independent from the rest. 'The majority of secessionist movements are based on presumed ethnic differences between the seceding region and the larger state entity.'[324]

There are some thousand large groups of individuals in the world that can theoretically claim their singularity and the right to pursue their own economic, social, and cultural development paths freely. If every such group applies the broader

---

According to some commentators, the right to self-determination can be transformed into the right of secession if certain minority groups are oppressed and eliminated from participation in state political life, and if all this have led to gross violations of human rights, including acts of genocide.' Farhad Mirzayev, 'Abkhazia' in Christian Walter, Antje Von Ungern-Sternberg, and Kavus Abushov (eds), *Self-Determination and Secession in International Law* (Oxford University Press 2014) 197. '[T]here is a strong presumption in favour of the existence of a qualified or remedial right of secession for minority-peoples within existing States. As has been seen there is a considerable weight of opinion in favour of the existence of such a qualified right and this position is not contradicted by state practice; to the contrary, this position was confirmed in the cases of Bangladesh and Croatia.' Raič (n 181) 365.

321 As the Badinter Arbitration Commission noted: 'Article 1 of the two 1986 International Covenants on human rights establishes that the principle of the right to self-determination serves to safeguard human rights.' Opinion No. 2, Paragraph 3.

322 Badinter Arbitration Commission, Opinion No. 2, Paragraph 3.

323 Mikhail A. Alexseev, 'Separatism' in William A. Darity Jr. (ed in chief), *International Encyclopedia of the Social Sciences*, Volume 7 (2nd edn, Macmillan 2008) 450.

324 Erin K. Jenne, 'Secession' in George Thomas Kurian (ed in chief), *The Encyclopedia of Political Science* (CQ Press, a division of SAGE 2011) 1524.

understanding of the right to free determination of the political status and demands external self-determination, it will have serious repercussions for international peace and security. That is why the contemporary international law considers the **principles of inviolability of frontiers and territorial integrity of states** to be the mainstream model for the organisation of the modern interstate system, while external self-determination as a solution is considered to be a special case.

6   Therefore, internal self-determination is, at this stage, the primary mode for the realisation of the principle of equal rights and self-determination of peoples. At the same time, with regard to particular cases, there is a need to find an appropriate mechanism for internal self-determination which is sufficient to maintain people's existence and assure the minimum necessary standards of protection and development. Hence, this mechanism may be a self-government model or may amount to a certain form of autonomy within a particular state.

The self-determination unit

> people
> nation
> common historical tradition
> racial or ethnic identity
> cultural homogeneity
> linguistic unity
> religion or ideological affinity
> territorial connection
> common economic life
> objective criteria
> minorities
> subjective criteria
> self-consciousness
> recognition from others

Introductory remark

According to contemporary international law, the unit of both internal and external self-determination is a **people** and not a **nation** or any other ethnic, linguistic, or religious group.

What does the term 'people' mean?

1   'People' means the entire population of a state.
2   'People' means a group of individuals forming a distinctive group on a particular territory.

In the context of self-determination, under the format of UNESCO, there are seven characteristics outlined that define 'people' ('a group of individual human beings who enjoy some or all of the following common features'): A **common historical tradition, racial or ethnic identity, cultural homogeneity, linguistic unity, religion or ideological affinity, territorial connection,** and **common economic life.**[325]

In addition, several authors also contributed to the definition of the term 'people' in the context of self-determination by adding other particular qualities.[326]

After summing up all these opinions, the following **objective criteria** can be outlined for determining whether a group of individuals forms a 'people' under the '2' meaning listed earlier:

1   Such a group should live on a territory forming a distinct politico-geographical area, with a definable territory and the territorial integrity of that area.
2   Such a group should be homogeneous, i.e. must be united based on at least some of the characteristics enumerated earlier.
3   Such a group should make up the majority of the population of that territory.
4   Such a group should have/display a realised capacity to form a viable political entity with some kind of an organisational formation which guides the desire for self-determination of the people.

Hence, according to this meaning, mere '**minorities**', which do not constitute the majority of the population even within a particular definable territory or do not meet other qualities outlined earlier, do not have the right to self-determination. However, this does not mean that minorities are not under the protection of international law. Furthermore, as stressed by the Badinter Arbitration Commission on Yugoslavia,

> the – now peremptory – norms of international law require states to ensure respect for the rights of minorities. . . . Where there are one or more groups within a state constituting one or more ethnic, religious or language communities, they have the right to recognition of their identity under international law.[327]

In addition, the essential characteristics of a people possessing the right to self-determination are not only the objective characteristics described here but also **subjective criteria,**

---

325 See the Final Report and Recommendations, International Meeting of Experts on further study of the concept of the rights of peoples, 27–30 November 1989, United Nations Educational, Scientific and Cultural Organisation, Division of Human Rights and Peace, Paragraph 22.

326 Christopher Waters summarised the so-called two-part test 'in determining when a group is designated as a "people"': 'The first prong considers whether the group shares "a common racial background, ethnicity, language, religion, history, and cultural heritage" including the "territorial integrity of the area the group is claiming". The second prong considers "the extent to which individuals within the group self-consciously perceive themselves collectively as a distinct "people" and the degree to which the group can form a viable political entity'. Christopher Waters, 'South Ossetia' in Christian Walter, Antje von Ungern-Sternberg, and Kavus Abushov (eds), *Self-Determination and Secession in International Law* (n 320) 185.

327 Badinter Arbitration Commission, Opinion No. 2, Paragraph 2, Opinion No. 1, Paragraph 1 (e).

such as **self-consciousness** and **recognition from others** (for example, from the neighbouring peoples). Indeed, for the purpose of self-determination:

1   A people, as a unit of self-determination, begins to exist only when it becomes aware
    of its own identity and distinctiveness.
2   It is crucial how the other actors regard the self-consciousness of the people.

What does the term 'nation' mean?

The definition of a nation is an utterly difficult undertaking. Its perception differs from
one country to another and from one cultural framework to another.[328] In English, the
term 'nation' is usually used either (1) in close connection with a territory and sovereign people living there, or (2) it designates a coherent ethnic community bound by
common ancestry and culture, which may not necessarily be associated with a specific
geographical area (for example, Jews before the establishment of Israel). The first
meaning prevails in such concepts as 'international relations' and 'international law';
the second perception encompasses national groups living in parts of the territories of
one or more states. The first understanding refers to the bond of a social group by the
civic criterion (such as citizenship); the second is based primarily on such characteristics as ethnicity and origin. Hence, according to the understandings described here:

1   Nation means the entire population of a state or even a state itself.
2   Nation means the group of individuals comprising a distinctive unity based on ethnic-
    ity, common history, and so on, i.e. a national group.

Application of the self-determination principle to these meanings of 'people' and 'nation'

The '1' meanings of a people and a nation provided in this chapter do not match the
requirements of the self-determination principle.

---

328 For example, in the Soviet state, from the beginning, the Bolsheviks propagandised the principle of
     self-determination of nations, and in relation to nationalities, the '[p]olicies aimed at satisfying their
     "national aspirations" were central to the communist reconstruction of society.' Generally, in the Rus-
     sian Empire and the Soviet Union, several words were utilised to designate the meaning of ethnic and
     other distinct groups, among them, in the Soviet period, such terms included 'nation' (in Russian,
     natsiya) and 'nationality' (in Russian, *natsionalnost*, 'meaning not citizenship but ethnic origin inher-
     ited from parents'), which were predominantly linked with ethnicity, and *narodnost*, a 'denationalised'
     community of smaller groups which were united 'by customs, religious practices, and physical type'.
     Jeremy Smith, 'Nationalities Policies, Soviet' in James R. Millar (ed in chief), *Encyclopedia of Russian
     History* (Macmillan Reference USA 2004) 1010–1011, 1026.

As regards the '2' understandings of a people and a nation, people's '2' meaning is the right addressee of the self-determination principle while nation's '2' sense can be relevant for self-determination only in combination with the '2' meaning of people, i.e. only when people at the same time are substantially mono-ethnic. These conclusions apply to both internal and external self-determination. However, to claim external self-determination, a unit shall also meet additional preconditions outlined next.

The external self-determination units

The external self-determination units are:

The ordinary cases

1 Peoples in the Decolonisation process, including the peoples of the Trust and mandated territories and the peoples on the territories treated as non-self-governing under Chapter XI of the UN Charter.
2 Peoples possessing the right to external self-determination as defined by national or international law.

The extraordinary cases

3 Peoples under oppression or those denied meaningful access to government to pursue their political, economic, social, and cultural development.
4 Peoples who are unable to maintain their own existence and ensure sufficient protection within the existing state.

The *sui generis* cases

5 Peoples on any other territories to which the parties apply external self-determination as a suitable solution.

The first case shall be linked with the Decolonisation process. The second case refers to a situation in which external self-determination is foreseen in the internal constitutional norms of a state or when there are the particular norms of international law (e.g. the founding international treaty)[329] authorising such a status of the people. The third case may be regarded as granting the right to external self-determination if the oppression or denial of meaningful access to the government fed violations of human rights of sufficient gravity. The fourth case is limited to the previously defined situations when gross or systematic violations of universally recognised human rights are committed against a given people. The fifth case refers to a situation in which external self-determination is applied

---

329 For example, Clause 26 of the Treaty on the Creation of the USSR of 1922 formally included the provision that each Republic had the right to leave the Union.

with the consent of all concerned parties, provided that such an application is not in conflict with the peremptory norms of general international law.

Mandated and trust territories and non-self-governing territories

> Central Powers
> Allied Powers
> Associated Powers
> mandate system
> trusteeship system
> Question of Palestine
> Palestine Liberation Organisation
> non-member observer State status in the United Nations
> Axis Powers
> trusteeship agreements
> UN Trusteeship Council
> non-self-governing territories
> non-self-governing territories system
> Special Committee on Decolonisation
> Committee of 24
> Special Political and Decolonisation Committee
> administering authorities
> international personality of a particular form
> sovereignty
> Advisory Opinion on *International Status of South West Africa*
> popular sovereignty over natural resources

From mandate system to trusteeship system

After the end of the First World War and the collapse of the **Central Powers**,[330] the **Allied Powers** and **Associated Powers**[331] established a **mandate system** under the League of Nations for the former colonies and certain parts of the defeated powers.

---

330 Germany, Austria-Hungary, Ottoman Empire (Turkey), and the Kingdom of Bulgaria.

331 The chief Allied Powers in the First World War were the British Empire, France, and the Russian Empire, which were legally linked by the Treaty of London of 5 September 1914. Other states that had been, or came to be, allied by treaty to one or more of those powers were also called Allies, such as Portugal, Japan, and Italy. Other countries that were arrayed against the Central Powers (for instance, the United States after its entry in World War I in 1917) were called the Associated Powers, not Allied Powers.

Under Article 22 of the Covenant of the League of Nations, the mandate system was divided into three classes – A ('Certain communities formerly belonging to the Turkish Empire'), B ('Other peoples, especially those of Central Africa'), and C Mandates ('South-West Africa and certain of the South Pacific Islands') 'according to the stage of the development of the people, the geographical situation of the territory, its economic conditions and other similar circumstances'. To all these Mandates was 'applied the principle that the well-being and development of such peoples form a sacred trust of civilisation and that securities for the performance of this trust should be embodied in this Covenant.'

Hence, the different Mandates were established by a series of international agreements with the distinct 'degree of authority, control, or administration to be exercised by the Mandatory', which was determined by international treaties between the Allied and Associated Powers[332] and the states of the former Central Powers, with the substantial engagement (approval) of the Council of the League of Nations.

In the aftermath of the World War II and the demise of the League of Nations, the mandate system was, generally, transformed into the United Nations **trusteeship system** with the supervisory role of the UN under Chapters XII (International Trusteeship System) and XIII (The Trusteeship Council) of the UN Charter and by individual agreements with the states administering them. However, 'two Mandates survived the dissolution of the League without being transferred to the Trusteeship system – Palestine and South West Africa.'[333]

The question of Palestine

The **question of Palestine** was the source of longstanding uncertainty in relation to the Mandate and the status of Palestine and, up until now, of the continuing clash of legal approaches concerning that region. Hence, the State of Palestine has not yet reached UN membership, even though a vast majority of states have recognised it as a state.

However, in 1974, the UN General Assembly had already recognised the 'inalienable rights of the Palestinian people to self-determination' and the **Palestine Liberation Organisation** (PLO) to be the representative of the Palestinian people. At the same time, the Palestine Liberation Organisation was granted non-state observer status and the right to participate in the sessions of the Assembly, as well as in the other UN platforms. (This was later reaffirmed several times.) In 1988, the UN General Assembly replaced the designation 'Palestine Liberation Organisation' with the designation 'Palestine' in the United Nations system.[334]

---

332 Under Treaty of Versailles, the United States, the British Empire, France, Italy, and Japan were referred to as the 'Principal Allied and Associated Powers' and. together with other parties to the Treaty (for their part), were designated the 'Allied and Associated Powers'. The opposite party to the treaty was Germany.

333 Crawford (n 274) 580.

334 A/RES/3210 of 14 October 1974 (Invitation to the Palestine Liberation Organization), A/RES/3236(XXIX) of 22 November 1974 (Question of Palestine), A/RES/3237(XXIX) of 22

In 2012, the UN General Assembly decided 'to accord to Palestine **non-member observer State status in the United Nations**'.[335] Thus, to date, Palestine participates at the international level in the status of a state for the subjects which have recognised as such, and the subjects of international law which did not recognise Palestine as a state regard it as a self-determination unit.[336]

The question of South West Africa (Namibia)

The last mandated territory was South West Africa. The General Assembly revoked the mandate for South West Africa (present day Namibia) in 1966 and placed that territory under the 'direct responsibility of the United Nations' when South Africa failed to fulfil its obligations under the Mandate.[337] However, Namibia did not achieve full independence until 1990.

The trusteeship system and the categories of trust territories

Under Article 77 of the UN Charter, the trusteeship system was applied by means of **trusteeship agreements** between an administering power and the UN[338] to the following territories:

1   Territories held under Mandates established by the League of Nations after World War I.
2   Territories detached from 'enemy States' or **Axis Powers**[339] as a result of World War II.
3   Territories voluntarily placed under this system by states responsible for their administration.

November 1974 (Observer status for the Palestine Liberation Organization), A/RES/43/177 of 5 December 1988 (Question of Palestine).

335 A/RES/67/19 of 9 November 2012 (Status of Palestine in the United Nations).

336 The UN General Assembly by its Resolution A/RES/67/19 of 9 November 2012 expressed 'the hope that the Security Council will consider favourably the application submitted on 23 September 2011 by the State of Palestine for admission to full membership in the United Nations'. Nevertheless, as of the time this book was written, Palestine did not enjoy 'full membership' in the UN; however, at the same time, by its Resolution S/RES/2334 (2016), the Security Council supported 'the two-State solution'.

337 A/RES/2145(XXI) of 27 October 1966 (Question of South West Africa).

338 For example, the 'Trusteeship Agreement for the Territory of Nauru, approved by the General Assembly of the United Nations on 1 November 1947' between the governments of Australia, New Zealand, and the United Kingdom (the joint Administering Authority) and the UN, which was terminated by the UN General Assembly (A/RES/2347 (XXII) of 19 December 1967) based on the submission of the Administering Authority 'following the resumed talks between representatives of the Nauruan people and of the Administering Authority'. So the trust territory of Nauru became the state of Nauru.

339 In World War II, the Axis Powers were Germany, Italy, and Japan, and the major Allied Powers were the United Kingdom, France, the Soviet Union, the United States, and China.

In the early years of the UN, 11 territories were accommodated under the trusteeship system. Ten were former mandates under the League of Nations, and just one (Somaliland) belonged to the category of those detached from 'enemy States'. The third option of Article 77, noted earlier, was never used.

The functions of the United Nations concerning trusteeship agreements for all areas not designated as 'strategic', which were under the direct supervision of the UN Security Council, were exercised by the General Assembly. At the same time, the **UN Trusteeship Council** was empowered as the key organ for day-to-day supervision under the trusteeship system.

The targets of the trusteeship system

The principal purpose of the trusteeship system was the maintenance of the political, economic, and social advancement of territories concerned, as well as their development towards self-government and self-determination.

The current situation

Currently, all territories under the trusteeship system have either attained the status of an independent state or have voluntarily associated themselves with the existing state. The UN Security Council in 1994 terminated the Trusteeship Agreement (the Trusteeship Agreement for the former Japanese Mandated Islands, which was designated as strategic) for the last territory – Palau, administered by the United States so long as the objectives of the trusteeship agreement have been fully attained.[340] Palau became independent and joined the United Nations in 1994.

Finally, with no territories left under its supervision, the trusteeship system completed its essential task.

Non-self-governing territories

When the UN was founded, almost a third of the world's population lived in territories that were under some form of control exercised by other countries. The mandate and trusteeship systems were established for the self-government or independence of particular colonial territories; however, they were limited in scope.

To address in a more extensive form the need for the protection of the 'inhabitants' of the 'other dependent territories', the UN Charter introduced the concept of **non-self-governing territories** as a broader notion covering the territories whose people were yet to attain the full measure of self-government and established the corresponding **non-self-governing territories system** (Chapter XI: Declaration Regarding Non-Self-Governing Territories).

---

340 'Determines, in the light of the entry into force on 1 October 1994 of the new status agreement for Palau, that the objectives of the Trusteeship Agreement have been fully attained, and that the applicability of the Trusteeship Agreement has terminated with respect to Palau.' S/RES/956 of 10 November 1994.

The system binds administering powers (1) to recognise that the interests of the inhabitants of the dependent territories are paramount, (2) to agree to promote social, economic, political, and educational progress in those territories, and (3) to assist in developing appropriate forms of self-government (Article 73). On the other hand, the United Nations monitors progress towards self-government in these territories. It maintains a list of places that the United Nations General Assembly deems to be 'non-self-governing', and member states have the obligation to regularly transmit the information to the UN Secretary-General 'relating to economic, social, and educational conditions in the territories for which they are respectively responsible other than those territories to which Chapters XII and XIII apply' (Article 73 e).

Initially, several states identified a number of territories under their administration that were not self-governing and placed them on the UN list. Over time, as a result of the Decolonisation process, most of the enumerated territories were removed from this list. There are only 17 non-self-governing territories remaining today. For example, in the Pacific region, such territories as American Samoa, Guam (administered by the United States), French Polynesia, New Caledonia (administered by France), Pitcairn (administered by the United Kingdom), and Tokelau (administered by New Zealand).

The ambiguity related to the definition of non-self-governing territories

However, the uncertain definition of non-self-governing territories in the UN Charter fed substantial disagreements. Thus, in 1960, the UN General Assembly adopted the Principles which should guide members in determining whether or not an obligation exists to transmit the information called for under Article 73 e of the Charter.[341] According to the Principles, Chapter XI should apply to the territories which:

1 'were then known to be of the colonial type';
2 did not attain 'a full measure of self-government', which may be fulfilled either by attaining the status of a sovereign independent state, by free association with an independent state, or through integration with an independent state; or
3 '[are] geographically separate and . . . distinct ethnically and/or culturally from the country administering [them]'.

Prima facie, there is an obligation to transmit the information on such territories. However, to sum up whether a territory is non-self-governing or not, other elements should be also be taken into account.

> These additional elements may be, inter alia, of an administrative, political, juridical, economic or historical nature. If they affect the relationship between the metropolitan State and the territory concerned in a manner which arbitrarily places the latter in a position or status of subordination, they support the presumption that there is an obligation to transmit information under Article 73 e of the Charter.

341 A/RES/1541(XV) of 15 December 1960.

The non-self-governing territories and the principle of self-determination

Hence, the principles noted here affirmed that the main focus of the non-self-governing territories system was the process of Decolonisation. And, logically, the principle of self-determination was applied to non-self-governing territories.

In 1961, the General Assembly instituted the Special Committee on the Situation with regard to the Implementation of the Declaration on the Granting of Independence of Colonial Countries and Peoples (also referred to as the **Special Committee on Decolonisation**)[342] as a subsidiary organ, in order to monitor the implementation of the 1960 Declaration on the Granting of Independence of Colonial Countries and Peoples and to provide the appropriate recommendations on this matter. The Special Committee on Decolonisation was made up of 24 members (after its expansion in 1962); therefore, it is usually called the **Committee of 24** or simply C-24.[343] The Special Committee submits its recommendations to the **Special Political and Decolonisation Committee** (Fourth Committee), which is one of the Main Committees of the General Assembly.

Administering authorities

In the trusteeship and non-self-governing territories system, the UN and the following states were engaged as the **administering authorities**: Australia, Belgium, Denmark, France, Italy, the Netherlands, New Zealand, Portugal, South Africa (which was replaced by the United Nations), Spain, the United Kingdom, and the United States.[344]

International status of the mandated, trust, and non-self-governing territories

All systems discussed in this chapter accepted the principle of the international responsibility of the administering authority to carry out aims as determined under an assignment. Therefore, these subjects hold exclusive responsibility towards other actors in the inter-state system concerning the mandated tasks.

However, the question which came up on the agenda concerned the territories themselves and whether the population of those territories possessed at least the **international personality of a particular form** or not. The second topic for debates was the issue of the existence and location of '**sovereignty**' over the mandated, trust, and non-self-governing territories and whether these territories and the peoples in them did have sovereignty of a particular type. The debate, among other things, also was stipulated by the multiplicity

---

342 A/RES/1654(XVI) of 27 November 1961 (The situation with regard to the implementation of the Declaration on the granting of independence to colonial countries and peoples).

343 'Currently, the C-24 consists of 29 members. . . . The officers of the C-24 are called the bureau which consists of the Chair, Vice-Chairs and Rapporteur.' <www.un.org/dppa/decolonization/en/c24/about> accessed 16 March 2021.

344 See the 'List of former Trust and Non-Self-Governing Territories' on the official site of the UN <www.un.org/dppa/decolonization/en/history/former-trust-and-nsgts> accessed 16 March 2021.

of legal arrangements concerning such territories and the different modifications of the mandated, trust, and non-self-governing territories, which varied greatly.

Even within a particular type of mandate system, there are substantial differences between the forms which are implemented in reality. For example, whereas some of the 'A' Mandates of the League of Nations period had their own governments (notably, Iraq under the British Mandate), others were subjected to the 'full powers of legislation and administration' of the administering states (as in the case of the Palestine under the British Mandate). As James Crawford stated,

> [I]n fact France exercised direct rule throughout the period of the Mandates. Syria and Lebanon, under Mandate governments, made Treaties of Alliance with the Mandatory Powers, carried on international litigation in their own name and had their own nationality. But their status approximated to that of international protectorates[345] rather than protected States.[346]

As regards other mandated, trust, and non-self-governing territories, in the vast majority of cases, they had no local governments.

For example, according to the Trusteeship Agreement for the Former Japanese Mandated Islands (also known as the Trusteeship Agreement for the Territory of the Pacific Islands) of 1947 between the US and the UN, administering authority (the US) had 'full powers of administration, legislation, and jurisdiction over the territory' and ensured that the trust territory played 'its part, in accordance with the Charter of the United Nations, in the maintenance of international peace and security'. On the other hand, the administering authority held the responsibility towards the people of the territory to

> foster the development of such political institutions as are suited to the trust territory and shall promote the development of the inhabitants of the trust territory toward self-government or independence, as may be appropriate to the particular circumstances of the trust territory and its peoples and the freely expressed wishes of the peoples concerned.[347]

Sovereignty

The term 'sovereignty' in relation to the mandated, trust, and non-self-governing territories is usually regarded as inappropriate. As Sir Arnold McNair notably formulated in his

---

345 Although there existed different types of the protectorates, generally, the term 'protectorate' referred to a dependent territory possessing local autonomy and some independence but without separate statehood. The protectorates were under the suzerainty of a greater sovereign state, which offered protection and exercised only limited jurisdiction. Hence, a protectorate remained an autonomous part of a sovereign state with local rulers. Therefore, they were different from colonies. At the same time, a state which was under the protection of another state but still maintained independence was known as a protected state and was distinct from protectorates. Examples of protectorates were German New Guinea (1884–1919), British Cyprus (1878–1914), Saar Protectorate (1947–1956) (French protectorate), and so forth.

346 Crawford (n 274) 570.

347 Articles 3, 5, 6 of the Trusteeship Agreement for the Former Japanese Mandated Islands.

Separate Opinion to the ICJ **Advisory Opinion on *International Status of South West Africa*** of 1950 (which was given at the request of the UN General Assembly):

> The Mandates System (and the 'corresponding principles' of the International Trusteeship System) is a new institution – a new relationship between territory and its inhabitants on the one hand and the government which represents them internationally on the other – a new species of international government, which does not fit into the old conception of sovereignty and which is alien to it.[348]

Indeed, the term 'sovereignty' as the capacity to pursue domestic and foreign policy independently principally refers to states. Under international law, it is also transferred to certain *sui generis* subjects of international law and, in terms of popular sovereignty, is applied to peoples as well.

The mandated, trust, and non-self-governing units generally were not considered as independent entities like the states or even, for example, as having the same status as the Holy See. So the meaning of the state sovereignty, as well as its modified version which was developed in relation to the status of the Holy See, may be not suitable in this regard.

Regarding the meaning of 'popular sovereignty', the original understanding that the authority of a state should be created and sustained by the consent of its people may be relevant in this context, provided that such an understanding on a theoretical level concerns all peoples, including the peoples in the mandated, trust, and non-self-governing territories. However, in relation to the mandated, trust, and non-self-governing territories, this concept had minimal usage. On the other hand, in practice, more often a developed model of popular sovereignty was applied in terms of **popular sovereignty over natural resources** (right of peoples and nations to permanent sovereignty over their natural wealth and resources), which was reaffirmed by UN General Assembly Resolution in 1962.[349]

International personality

Firstly, as noted earlier, only the administering authorities hold responsibility towards the other actors of the interstate system. There were different legal instruments developed with an intention to establish such a responsibility – on the one hand, the norms of general international law or the obligations incorporated within the League of Nations and the United Nations systems, and on the other hand, the multilateral agreements in relation to the mandate system, the bilateral trusteeship agreements concerning the trusteeship system, and particular legal instruments regarding the non-self-governing territories. In individual cases, the different legal regimes commanded distinct levels of the international

---

348 *International Status of South West Africa*, Advisory Opinion of 11 July 1950, ICJ Reports 1950, 128, Separate Opinion by Sir Arnold McNair.

349 '7. Violation of the rights of peoples and nations to sovereignty over their natural wealth and resources is contrary to the spirit and principles of the Charter of the United Nations and hinders the development of international co-operation and the maintenance of peace.' A/RES/1803(XVII) of 14 December 1962 (Permanent sovereignty over natural resources).

responsibility of an administering authority, even within the one type of the system (either the mandate, trusteeship, or non-self-governing territories system).

However, international personality was also accorded to the self-determination units in various proportions. Peoples living on the mandated, trust, and non-self-governing territories, first of all, were considered to perform in such a status. Therefore, although at different scales, they all exercised an international personality on the basis of the self-determination principle. Among them, the peoples of the non-self-governing territories had the smallest number of international rights, and the peoples in certain territories (for example, Iraq under the British Mandate) had the largest.

Besides, concerning the international status of the peoples on the mandated and trust territories, the ICJ, in its Advisory Opinion on *International Status of South West Africa*, proclaimed the 'right of the population to have the Territory administered in accordance with' the mandate.

In addition, engagement of the mandated and trust territories in the process of the termination of the international mandates by such mechanisms as the plebiscites conducted by the peoples of the territories also contributed to their international status. Moreover, sometimes the termination was implemented by the treaties with the participation of the self-determination unit, as in the case of the British Mandate for Iraq, which was factually terminated through the agreement between the new state, the Mandate holder, and the Council of the League of Nations.

International administration of territories

international regime
international personality
international mandate
administrative functions
United Nations Transitional Authority in Cambodia
United Nations Transitional Administration for Eastern Slavonia, Baranja, and Western Sirmium
United Nations Interim Administration Mission in Kosovo
United Nations Transitional Administration in East Timor

The general meaning

The international administration of territories refers to situations in which territory and people on that territory are placed under a form of **international regime**.

Such international regimes vary greatly. Sometimes the governmental functions in a particular territory and the **international personality** of the concerned territory and people are carried out almost completely by a person who is empowered to act in such a status under international law, i.e. an international organisation, a state, or a group of states under an **international mandate**: for example, as in the vast majority of cases of mandated and trust territories examined earlier in this chapter. At the same time, the international subjectivity of such a people is undertaken by the administering authority only within the limits of the mandate.

However, at times, the administering authority has very limited rights concerning the territory and people since it performs only particular **administrative functions**. Hence, the people in this territory and their local government structures exercise a significant portion of international personality (which is partly shared with the proxy authority within the framework of the international mandate), for example, as in the case of Kosovo after 2008, when Kosovo declared its independence.

The international administration of territories for the maintenance of international peace and security

Sometimes the UN has considered the international administration of territories an appropriate model for the fulfilment of its primary purpose – the maintenance of international peace and security, which is enshrined in Article 1(1) of the Charter.

In these cases, the UN has assumed direct control over the territories. By the way, the UN, as a proxy subject, has adopted decisions which have had an immediate effect on the ground in relation to the local population. Notably, international territorial administrations are empowered to guarantee much more than the mere absence of armed conflict.

Decisions made by such missions are limited by the mandate, however, may relate to all spheres of public life and all fields of public power; in other words, these missions may exercise legislative, executive, and judicial authority within a territory and over a people.

The cases of international administration of territories

The UN has become engaged in important administrative functions in several cases, including the following:

- **United Nations Transitional Authority in Cambodia** during 1992–1993 under the 1991 Paris Peace Agreements, which assigned the United Nations to establish civil administrative functions in that country: namely, to control and supervise the activities of the administrative structures, including the police; ensure respect for the human rights; and organise and conduct free and fair elections. In 1992, the UN Security Council authorised the establishment of this mission.[350]
- **United Nations Transitional Administration for Eastern Slavonia, Baranja, and Western Sirmium**, in the eastern parts of Croatia between 1996 and 1998. Instituted by the UN Security Council Resolution of 1996, this mission was armed with military and civilian components to, among other things, supervise the demilitarisation, establish a temporary police force, undertake tasks relating to civil administration and public services, and organise the elections.[351]

350 S/RES/745 of 28 February 1992.
351 S/RES/1037 of 15 January 1996, Paragraphs 1, 10.

- **United Nations Interim Administration Mission in Kosovo**, which was established by the UN Security Council Resolution of 1999. The Resolution prescribed the deployment in Kosovo, under the United Nations auspices, of international civil and security presences in order to provide an interim administration for Kosovo and exercise the function of transitional administration while establishing and overseeing the development of provisional democratic self-governing institutions.[352] Initially, the task of the United Nations Interim Administration Mission in Kosovo was comprehensive, with authority over the territory and people of Kosovo, including all legislative and executive powers and administration of the judiciary. Despite Kosovo declaring independence in 2008, the United Nations Interim Administration Mission in Kosovo still continues, but its day-to-day functions have been minimised.
- The **United Nations Transitional Administration in East Timor**, which was established by the UN Security Council Resolution in 1999 to institute an effective administration on the territory; exercise all legislative and executive authority, including the administration of justice during the transitional period; and support capacity building for self-government.[353] East Timor became an independent country in 2002.

Insurgents, belligerents, and national liberation movements

Additional Protocol I to the four 1949 Geneva Conventions
international conflict
international humanitarian law
insurrection against government
interim organised government by the armed conflict
Palestine Liberation Organisation
South West Africa People's Organisation

Limited international personality

The insurgents, belligerents, and national liberation movements have a limited international personality. For the accretion of their international status, a significant role belongs to, for example, the 1977 **Additional Protocol I to the four 1949 Geneva Conventions**, according to which, in the instances of colonial domination, alien occupation, or racist regimes, a struggle of the people to exercise the right to self-determination is regarded as an **international conflict**.[354] In this context, the principal aim is to ensure the compliance

---

352 S/RES/1244 of 10 June 1999, Paragraphs 5, 10.

353 S/RES/1272 of 25 October 1999, Paragraphs 1, 2.

354 Paragraph 4 of Article 1 (On General Principles and Scope of Application) of the Protocol I Additional to the Geneva Conventions of 12 August 1949 provides: The situations referred to in the preceding paragraph [Conventions of 12 August 1949 for the Protection of war victims, shall apply in the

of the parties involved in an armed conflict with **international humanitarian law**. At the same time, in many other cases as well, the appearance of insurgents, belligerents, and national liberation movements at the international level is stipulated by the principle of self-determination.

The distinction between insurgents, belligerents, and national liberation movements

From time to time, in praxis, there is no evidential difference between the insurgents, belligerents, and national liberation movements. In addition, over time, a particular actor who could be characterised as belonging to any of these groups might easily transform into another. Nevertheless, from a legal point of view, these notions display significant differences:

- Insurgents are a group of human beings who participate in an **insurrection against their government**. Insurgency is the halfway point between substantially irregular or unorganised civil disorders and the conduct of organised war.
- Belligerents signify something like a state of war and not merely a civil conflict. They are a group of insurgents who possess an **interim organised government by the armed conflict**, occupy a substantial part of the territory, and have an internal organisation capable of and willing to enforce the laws of war.
- In the course of the international anti-colonialist trend, the status of the national liberation movement regarding certain actors appeared in international politics and law. National liberation movements represent not only themselves and the territory they control, but also the whole of the people, who are in the process of implementing the right to self-determination.

Recognition of status

In international relations, persons may be regarded as insurgents, belligerents, or national liberation movements if they are recognised as having such a status. In this case, recognition definitely possesses a constitutive power.

For a long time, the subjects of international law have recognised the actors engaged in the activities mentioned here as insurgents, belligerents, and national liberation movements. Hence, in certain circumstances, they may be entitled to international personality and, therefore, considered subjects having certain rights and duties under international law. Accordingly, they can enter into relationships with states, international organisations, and other subjects of international law; conclude international treaties and configure the

---

situations referred to in Article 2 Common to those Conventions] 'include armed conflicts in which peoples are fighting against colonial domination and alien occupation and against racist régimes in the exercise of their right of self-determination, as enshrined in the Charter of the United Nations and the Declaration on Principles of International Law concerning Friendly Relations and Co-operation among States in accordance with the Charter of the United Nations.'

customary rules; and acquire rights and obligations under the norms of international humanitarian law.

Besides, international law has accorded to national liberation movements the capacity to participate in the proceedings of the United Nations, as well as other international organisations and international conferences.

For instance, under the Resolution of 1974,[355] the General Assembly of the UN decided to invite the national liberation movements recognised by the Organisation of African Unity and/or the League of Arab States in their respective regions to participate in the United Nations Conference on the Representation of States in Their Relations with International Organisations as observers. The Conference,[356] in its own capacity, adopted the resolution on the status of the national liberation movements.

Moreover, in 1988, the General Assembly reaffirmed[357] that the **Palestine Liberation Organisation** and the **South West Africa People's Organisation** were entitled to have their communications relating to the sessions and work of the General Assembly issued and circulated directly, and without an intermediary, as official documents of the Assembly. Besides, it stated that these two organisations were entitled to have their communications relating to the sessions and work of all international conferences convened under the auspices of the General Assembly of the UN issued and circulated directly, and without an intermediary, as official documents of these conferences.

Summary

Meanwhile, the international subjectivity (personality) of insurgents, belligerents, and national liberation movements is not of a general nature. They hold a functionalised subjectivity which is mainly associated with the struggle of a people to exercise the right to self-determination and with the standards on the conduct of hostilities.

SUI GENERIS ENTITIES

> territorial entities
> traditional entities
> recognised missions

The *sui generis* territorial entities

The *sui generis* **territorial entities**, or the territorial entities other than states, are the subjects of international law in specific cases. Their status can be generalised as territorial

---

355 A/RES/3247 (XXIX) of 29 November 1974.

356 United Nations Conference on the Representation of States in Their Relations with International Organisations, Vienna, Austria, 4 February–14 March 1975.

357 A/RES/43/160 of 9 December 1988.

entities which are not recognised as states but are considered as international units in specific cases and areas.

The main reason for this status lies in the history of these entities and in the fact that they essentially exercise governmental functions in their respective territories.

The *sui generis* non-territorial entities

The *sui generis* non-territorial **traditional entities** are subjects of international law based on the historical developments and the highly significant role of these entities in the inter-state system. Their status can be generalised as entities which are not states but are considered international persons in specific cases and areas.

The principal reason for such a status lies in the history of these entities and in the fact that they exercise the specific **recognised missions** in the body of world politics.

Taiwan

Republic of China
People's Republic of China
self-determination unit
recognition of governments
presumption of the recognised government
subjective criteria

Historical background

The **Republic of China** (ROC) is one of the founders of the UN and was a permanent member of the UN Security Council until the relevant decisions in the UN were adopted in 1971.

The Chinese Civil War led to the Republic of China's loss of the mainland to the Communists, and in 1949, the ROC government retreated to Taiwan (followed by over a million people from mainland China). Although the government of the Republic of China continued to claim for a long time to be the sole legitimate government of China, its effective jurisdiction since 1949 has been limited to Taiwan and its surrounding islands.

In 1971, at its 26th session, the General Assembly adopted Resolution 2758 (Restoration of the lawful rights of the **People's Republic of China** in the United Nations), in which the General Assembly declared that 'the representatives of the Government of the People's Republic of China are the only lawful representatives of China to the United Nations and that the People's Republic of China is one of the five permanent members of the Security Council' and decided

> to restore all its rights to the People's Republic of China and to recognize the representatives of its Government as the only legitimate representatives of China to the United Nations, and to expel forthwith the representatives of Chiang Kai-shek

from the place which they unlawfully occupy at the United Nations and in all the organizations related to it.

After 1971, mostly indicating that it was the Republic of China,[358] Taiwan has been trying to obtain status and re-establish its participation in the United Nations, but without any success.

Under its One-China Policy, the People's Republic of China (PRC) refused to conduct diplomatic relations with any country that recognised the Republic of China. Today, more than ten United Nations member states (as well as some other subjects) recognise the ROC, but many other states maintain unofficial ties through representative offices and institutions that function as *de facto* embassies and consulates. Although Taiwan is fully self-governing, most international organisations in which the People's Republic of China holds membership either refuse to grant membership to Taiwan or allow it to participate only as a non-state actor (as a specific unit).

Taiwan's international status

- Taiwan is not a state for the vast majority of the subjects of international law. On the one hand, it has almost all the objective characteristics of a state because for more than half a century, factually, there has been formed the particular territory (Taiwan and its surrounding islands) and the independently governed people with (1) the capacity to enter into relations with other states, (2) valid international treaties, (3) limited *de jure* recognition, and so on. However, on the other hand, both the People's Republic of China's One-China Policy and Taiwan's policy itself remained as obstacles to independent statehood since, for a long time, its government and people did not assert and follow the clear path to become independent. Moreover, their vision was that the Republic of China was representing the whole of China.[359]

358 In the more recent 'Requests' for the inclusion of a supplementary item in the agenda of the UN General Assembly session, this subject was named: Republic of China in Taiwan (1993, 1994), Republic of China on Taiwan (1995, 1999, 2000), Taiwan, Republic of China (1996), Republic of China (Taiwan) (2002, 2003), and Taiwan (2004–2007). For example, see the 'Request for the inclusion of a supplementary item in the agenda of the fifty-sixth session [of the UN General Assembly]: Need to examine the exceptional international situation pertaining to the Republic of China on Taiwan, to ensure that the fundamental right of its twenty-three million people to participate in the work and activities of the United Nations is fully respected.' Letter dated 8 August 2001 from the representatives of Belize, Burkina Faso, Chad, Dominica, El Salvador, the Gambia, Nicaragua, Palau, Senegal, and Tuvalu to the United Nations, addressed to the Secretary-General <https://digitallibrary.un.org/record/446790#record-files-collapse-header> accessed 14 April 2021.

359 In most cases, diplomatic relations with the Republic of China did not constitute an international acceptance of the Republic of China (Taiwan) as an independent state, but rather represented a recognition of the ROC as the representative of all of China. Moreover, for a long time, the government of the ROC required its diplomatic allies to recognise the Republic of China as the sole legitimate representative of China. Only since the 1990s has its policy changed to seeking dual recognition with

- In most cases, Taiwan is a particular (specific) unit (entity) for international law. In several norms of international treaties and customary norms of international law, it can be seen as a separate customs territory of Taiwan, Penghu, Kinmen, and Matsu (Chinese Taipei), a fishing entity,[360] a meteorological entity, an aviation entity, an investment entity (e.g. under the bilateral investment treaties).[361]

The significance of the Taiwan example for international law

The Taiwan example:

- emphasises the importance of the international model of the **recognition of governments** and the power of the **presumption of the recognised government** at the interstate level. Although China is one of the central pillars of the international security system and a permanent member of the UN Security Council, even with regard to this superpower, replacing the Republic of China's government with the effective government of China controlling the main territory of the country took a rather long time.
- confirms the significance of the principle of effectiveness, since in the course of time, this principle acquires more power, and at some point, the normative power of practice at the interstate level prevails over the presumption of the recognised government.
- identifies for the establishment of international status the importance of obviousness and consistency of the subjective self-perception of the entity and the perception of the others (the **subjective criteria**), since, for a long time, there was uncertainty on both

---

the People's Republic of China. As outlined in the *2020–2021 Taiwan at a Glance* 'since 1991, the government has acknowledged that its jurisdiction extends only to the areas it controls.' (1st edn, Ministry of Foreign Affairs, Republic of China (Taiwan) 2020) 24. However, the People's Republic of China consistently contradicts the 'model of parallel representation of divided countries' (a model that exists, for example, in the case of the two Koreas). As is emphasised in the Report of Jaushieh Joseph Wu, Minister of Foreign Affairs of the Republic of China (Taiwan) (at the Foreign and National Defense Committee of the Legislative Yuan on 28 September 2020): 'China has never ceased attempts to suppress Taiwan in the international arena. . . . As such, it is pressing forward with attempts to impose the "one country, two systems" model on Taiwan and has continued to intensify its rhetorical assault and military intimidation. Following on Hong Kong, Taiwan has become China's next target. China's egregious acts have been a unilateral attempt to undermine the status quo of stability across the Taiwan Strait.' Available at <https://bit.ly/3g9xeM1> accessed 14 April 2021.

360 'Pursuant to paragraph 1 of the Protocol, the Separate Customs Territory of Taiwan, Penghu, Kinmen and Matsu shall become a Member of the World Trade Organization on 1 January 2002.' Protocol of Accession of the Separate Customs Territory of Taiwan, Penghu, Kinmen and Matsu to the Marrakesh Agreement Establishing the World Trade Organisation, done at Doha on 11 November 2001, available at <https://docs.wto.org>. Taiwan is identified as the 'Fishing Entity of Taiwan', for example, in relation to the Convention for the Conservation of Southern Bluefin Tuna of 1993. See <www.fao.org/fishery/rfb/ccsbt/en#Org-OrgsInvolved> accessed 14 April 2021.

361 Since the 1990s, Taiwan may also be regarded as a self-determination unit striving for independent statehood.

sides about the legal status of the Republic of China (Taiwan), a consequence of which, to a significant extent, is the fact that the current status of this entity is so multifaceted.

Hong Kong

> lease of the New Territories
> One Country, Two Systems
> Sino-British Joint Declaration
> broad autonomous status
> specific unit
> Hong Kong, China

Historical background

After the First Opium War (1839–1842), the occupation of the Hong Kong Island by the British forces was formalised according to the Treaty of Nanking of 1842. Under the Treaty, it was stated that: 'His Majesty the Emperor of China cedes to Her Majesty the Queen of Great Britain, etc., the Island of Hongkong, to be possessed in perpetuity by Her Britannic Majesty, Her Heirs and Successors'.[362] A Royal Charter was issued the same year proclaiming Hong Kong to be a Crown Colony. Under the Convention of Friendship of 1860, the areas of the Kowloon Peninsula and Stonecutters Island were added to the Colony's original territory.[363] Finally, to protect the Colony and, generally, the interests of the Crown in the region, which were potentially threatened by the rapid expansion of other countries' interests in and around the China, the vast territory (so-called 'New Territories')[364] was leased to the Great Britain rent-free for 99 years by the Convention between the United Kingdom and China Respecting an Extension of Hong Kong Territory of 1898 (**lease of the New Territories**). Under the Convention, it was determined that 'the limits of British territory shall be enlarged under lease to the extent indicated generally on the annexed map.'

In 1997, Hong Kong became a Special Administrative Region (SAR) of the Peoples Republic of China with a high degree of autonomy.

Based on the principle of '**One Country, Two Systems**', formulated in the **Sino-British Joint Declaration** of 1984, Hong Kong has a different political and economic system from China. Except for the military defence and foreign diplomatic and political affairs, Hong Kong maintains its autonomous legislative, executive, and judiciary powers. Meanwhile, Hong Kong develops relations directly with subjects of international law in a broad range of fields.

---

362 Article III of the Treaty of Nanking.

363 Article VI of the Convention of Friendship. 'Approximately 3.5 square miles of territory were added to the Colony's original 32 square miles by this convention in the form of Stonecutters Island and the Kowloon Peninsula south of present-day Boundary Street.' The United States of America, Department of State, International Boundary Study, No. 13, April 13 1962, China Hong Kong Boundary (Country Codes: CH-HK), The Geographer Office of the Geographer Bureau of Intelligence and Research <https://docplayer. net/12052355-International-boundary-study-china-hong-kong-boundary.html> accessed 16 March 2021.

364 'The New Territories include approximately 355 square miles' ibid.

Hong Kong's international status

- Hong Kong is not a state.
- It is the sovereign territory of the People's Republic of China with **broad autonomous status**, which is guaranteed for 50 years after the transfer of rights (in relation to Hong Kong) formerly held by the United Kingdom to the People's Republic of China in 1997 (i.e. until the middle of the 21st century).
- It is a self-governing territory without the claim to independence.
- On the other hand, it is a particular, **specific unit** (entity) under international law. In different norms of international law, it can be seen as a free zone, a separate customs territory, a separate immigration territory, and so forth. According to the Hong Kong's Basic Law, '[r]epresentatives of the Government of the Hong Kong Special Administrative Region may, as members of delegations of the Government of the People's Republic of China, participate in negotiations at the diplomatic level directly affecting the Region conducted by the Central People's Government.' At the same time, 'Hong Kong Special Administrative Region may on its own, using the name **"Hong Kong, China"**, maintain and develop relations and conclude and implement agreements with foreign states and regions and relevant international organizations in the appropriate fields, including the economic, trade, financial and monetary, shipping, communications, tourism, cultural and sports fields.' 'The Hong Kong Special Administrative Region may, using the name "Hong Kong, China", participate in international organizations and conferences not limited to states.' Finally, the Hong Kong may establish 'official or semi-official economic and trade missions in foreign countries and shall report the establishment of such missions to the Central People's Government for the record.'[365]
- In a broad range of fields, Hong Kong has concluded a large number of treaties since 1997. Regarding these international treaties, Hong Kong may be considered as an international person, a particular (specific) unit (entity) with international obligations.

The significance of the Hong Kong example for international law

The Hong Kong example:

- confirms the importance of history and historical developments for the establishment of international status since, for more than one and a half centuries of existence under

---

365 Articles 150, 151, 152 and 156 of the Basic Law of the Hong Kong (adopted at the Third Session of the Seventh National People's Congress on 4 April 1990, promulgated by Order No. 26 of the President of the People's Republic of China on 4 April 1990, effective as of 1 July 1997). These Articles are cited from *The Basic Law of the Hong Kong Special Administrative Region of the People's Republic of China* (Constitutional and Mainland Affairs Bureau 2015). As it is outlined in the Welcome Message of the Erick Tsang Kwok-wai – the Secretary for Constitutional and Mainland Affairs: 'The Constitutional and Mainland Affairs Bureau (CMAB) is responsible for overseeing the full and faithful implementation of the Basic Law. We develop and maintain a constructive working relationship between the HKSAR Government and the Central People's Government as well as other Mainland authorities in accordance with the principles of "one country, two systems", "Hong Kong people administering Hong Kong" and a high degree of autonomy.' <https://www.cmab.gov.hk/en/about/welcome.htm> accessed 6 May 2021.

British rule, it has developed into a political and economic system which is distinct from China and is characterised by a strong self-governing tradition.

- clearly denotes the influence of the subjective factors on the formation of the state – which means either the subjective self-perception of the entity (in this case – ' One Country, Two Systems') or the counter-perception of the others towards an entity since Hong Kong has no substantial claim to be an independent state and, as noted earlier, without the official declaration of its international status (i.e. independent statehood), there can be no recognition of that status by the other actors.
- acknowledges the true variety and diversity of *sui generis* territorial entities, which can have different colours, i.e. distinct legal positions under international law.

The Holy See and the Vatican City

> Vatican City
> sovereignty of the Holy See in the international realm
> neutrality of Holy See and Vatican City
> neutral and inviolable territory
> in conformity with its traditions and the requirements of its mission to the world
> concordats
> Permanent Observer State at the United Nations
> derived subject of international law

Historical background

The so-called Papal States were territories on the Italian Peninsula under the sovereign rule of the Pope from the eighth century until 1870. Italian unification was completed with the annexation of the Papal States. In 1871, Rome became the capital of the Kingdom of Italy.[366]

---

366 'The popes fostered a special relationship with the Franks by playing upon the Carolingians' veneration of St Peter, and finally in response to papal pleas Charles led an expedition to Italy which resulted in the take-over of the Lombard kingdom in 774. The momentous repercussions of this step included the creation of a papal state which remained a major factor on the Italian scene until 1870.' *The Oxford Illustrated History of Medieval Europe*, George Holmes (ed) (Oxford University Press 1988) 20. 'The Italians entered the Papal States in September 1870 and, through the backing of a plebiscite held in early October, annexed the Papal States and Rome to the Kingdom of Italy.' 'Issues Relevant to U.S. Foreign Diplomacy: Unification of Italian States' Office of the Historian, Foreign Service Institute, United States Department of State <https://history.state.gov/countries/issues/italian-unification> accessed 8 May 2021. 'Shortly after the events of Porta Pia, with a law of February 3, 1871, the capital of the Kingdom of Italy was moved to Rome . . . and the king made his official entrance in the city on July 2, 1871.' Cristina Mazzoni, 'Capital City: Rome 1870-2010.' (2010) Annali D'Italianistica, vol. 28, 14, JSTOR, <www.jstor.org/stable/24016385> accessed 8 May 2021.

Lateran Pacts

After that, the Holy See had no formal sovereign territory until 1929, when the Lateran Pacts (which consisted of the Treaty of Conciliation, the Financial Convention, and the Concordat) were signed,[367] which legalised the international status of the Holy See and its sovereignty over the **Vatican City**.

In 1984, Italy and the Holy See signed the Agreement amending the Lateran Concordat. At the same time, the parties declared new understandings concerning some initial principles and rules of the Lateran Pacts in order 'to assure, by means of appropriate specifications, the best application of the Lateran Pacts and the agreed upon amendments, and willing to avoid any difficulties of interpretation thereof.'[368]

The Holy See

The Holy See[369] signifies the following meanings:

1   On the one hand, it designates the episcopal jurisdiction of the Catholic Church in Rome directed by the Bishop of Rome – the Pope, who, at the same time, is 'the head of the College of Bishops,[370] the Vicar of Christ, and the Pastor of the universal Church here on earth'.[371]

367 'The Lateran Pacts of 1929 contained three sections – the Treaty of Conciliation (27 articles) which established Vatican City as an independent state, restoring the civil sovereignty of the Pope as a monarch, the Financial Convention annexed to the treaty (3 articles) which compensated the Holy See for loss of the papal states, and the Concordat (45 articles), which dealt with the Roman Catholic Church's ecclesiastical relations with the Italian State.' <www.uniset.ca/nold/lateran.htm> accessed 16 March 2021.

368 For example, it was pronounced that 'the principle of the Catholic religion as the sole religion of the Italian State, originally referred to by the Lateran Pacts, shall be considered to be no longer in force.' Available at <http://bit.ly/37kyYux> accessed 16 March 2021.

369 Holy See – from Latin: *Sancta Sedes* – 'holy chair'. For example, see <www.usccb.org/offices/general-secretariat/holy-see> accessed 16 March 2021.

370 'Can. 336 The head of the College of Bishops is the Supreme Pontiff, and its members are the Bishops by virtue of their sacramental consecration and hierarchical communion with the head of the College and its members. This College of Bishops, in which the apostolic body abides in an unbroken manner, is, in union with its head and never without this head, also the subject of supreme and full power over the universal Church. Can. 337 §1 The College of Bishops exercises its power over the universal Church in solemn form in an Ecumenical Council.' Code of Canon Law, Part II: The Hierarchical Constitution of the Church. This book uses the English version of the Code of Canon Law, which is available at <www.intratext.com/IXT/ENG0017/_INDEX.HTM> accessed 16 March 2021.

371 'Can. 331 The office uniquely committed by the Lord to Peter, the first of the Apostles, and to be transmitted to his successors, abides in the Bishop of the Church of Rome. He is the head of the College of Bishops, the Vicar of Christ, and the Pastor of the universal Church here on earth. Consequently, by virtue of his office, he has supreme, full, immediate and universal ordinary power in the Church, and he can always freely exercise this power.' Code of Canon Law, ibid.

2   One the other hand, the Holy See denotes the central authority of the Catholic Church, composed of the Roman Pontiff, the Secretariat of State, the Council for the public affairs of the Church, and the other Institutes of the Roman Curia.[372]

3   In terms of international law, the Holy See:

   a)   is an independent sovereign entity. According to the Treaty of Conciliation, 'Italy recognizes the **sovereignty of the Holy See in the international realm** as an attribute inherent in its nature in conformity with its tradition and with the requirements of its mission to the world.'[373]

   b)   holds the Vatican City in Rome as its sovereign territory. Some international scholars also regard it as the 'government' of the Vatican City.[374] According to the Treaty of Conciliation, 'Italy recognizes the full ownership and the exclusive and absolute power and jurisdiction of the Holy See over the Vatican as it is presently constituted, together with all its appurtenances and endowments, creating in this manner Vatican City for the special purposes and under the conditions given in this Treaty.'[375]

   c)   concludes the international treaties.[376]

   d)   maintains diplomatic relations with other subjects of international law.

The Holy See is administered in the name of the Pope by the Roman Curia (*Curia Romana*),[377] which is similar to a centralised government.[378] The Roman Curia consists of a complex of offices, including the Secretariat of State under the Cardinal Secretary of State, which directs and coordinates the Curia, the Council for the public affairs of the Church, the Congregations, the Tribunals and other Institutes.

372   'Can. 361 In this Code the terms Apostolic See or Holy See mean not only the Roman Pontiff, but also, unless the contrary is clear from the nature of things or from the context, the Secretariat of State, the Council for the public affairs of the Church, and the other Institutes of the Roman Curia.' Code of Canon Law, ibid.

373   Article 2, the Treaty of Conciliation is available on the official website of the Vatican <www.vatican-state.va/phocadownload/laws-decrees/LateranTreaty.pdf> accessed 16 March 2021.

374   '[I]n the case of the Vatican City the strength and influence of the government – the Holy See – have compensated for a tiny territory and the lack of a permanent population.' Crawford (n 274) 223.

375   Article 3 of the Treaty of Conciliation.

376   For example, Concordat between the Holy See and the German Reich (1933), Concordat between the Holy See and Spain (1953), Concordat between the Holy See and the Republic of Poland (1993), and so forth. See <www.vatican.va/roman_curia/secretariat_state/index_concordati-accordi_en.htm> accessed 16 March 2021.

377   'Can. 360 The Supreme Pontiff usually conducts the business of the universal Church through the Roman Curia, which acts in his name and with his authority for the good and for the service of the Churches. The Curia is composed of the Secretariat of State or Papal Secretariat, the Council for the public affairs of the Church, the Congregations, the Tribunals and other Institutes. The constitution and competence of all these is defined by special law.' Code of Canon Law, Part II: The Hierarchical Constitution of the Church, (n 370).

378   'In exercising supreme, full, and immediate power in the universal Church, the Roman pontiff makes use of the departments of the Roman Curia which, therefore, perform their duties in his name and with his authority for the good of the churches and in the service of the sacred pastors.' <www.vatican.va/roman_curia/index.htm> accessed 16 March 2021.

The Treaty of Conciliation prescribed the **neutrality of Holy See and Vatican City**:

> In regard to the sovereignty appertaining to it also in the international realm, the Holy See declares that it desires to remain and will remain outside of any temporal rivalries between other States and the international congresses called to settle such matters, unless the contending parties make a mutual appeal to its mission of peace; it reserves to itself in any case the right to exercise its moral and spiritual power. Consequently, Vatican City will always and in every case be considered **neutral and inviolable territory**.[379]

Statehood and the Vatican City

- Vatican City essentially has no permanent population in the meaning of a state population. Its population is transient and exists only to support the work of the Holy See.
- The 'government' of the Vatican is the Supreme Pontiff and the institutions, which exercise their authority in the name of the Pope.[380] The pope himself is the head of the Catholic Church, its highest hierarchy, and his authority extends further beyond the rule of the Vatican City.
- There is no sufficient and uniform recognition of the Vatican City as a state by the subjects of international law.
- Therefore, Vatican City cannot be regarded as a state in the traditional sense of statehood.[381]

379 Article 24.
380 As described on the official website of the Vatican, the form of government in the 'Vatican City State' is absolute monarchy. Its head is the Supreme Pontiff, who has the fullness of legislative, executive, and judicial powers. In addition to the Supreme Pontiff, legislative power is exercised in his name by the Pontifical Commission for the Vatican City State (*Pontificia Commissione per lo Stato della Città del Vaticano*), which is made up of a Cardinal President and other Cardinals, appointed for a five-year term. Executive power is delegated to the President of the Pontifical Commission, who, in this capacity, assumes the name of President of the Governorate (*Governatorato*). Judicial power is exercised, on behalf of the Supreme Pontiff, by certain organs of the judicial system. <https://bit.ly/2XyneCg> accessed 16 March 2021.
381 However, some scholars regard the Vatican City as the state. For example, James Crawford first refers to the words of Duursma: 'As Duursma notes: The criterion of independence aims to distinguish one State from another so that one territorial entity is not just the continuation of another territorial entity. The Holy See however is neither a State nor a territorial entity. Moreover, it is an authority which partly coincides with certain Vatican temporal governmental institutions and which operates from inside the Vatican City. Thus the presence of the Holy See cannot preclude the Vatican City's statehood, because the Vatican City is not subject to any external influence.' Finally, Crawford concludes: 'For all these reasons, it is clear that the Vatican City is a State in international law, despite its size and special circumstances.' Crawford (n 274) 225.

Statehood and the Holy See

- The Holy See is a central authority for Catholics worldwide; it cannot be asserted to have a 'permanent population' in the meaning of a state population.
- The Holy See holds sovereignty over the Vatican City; however, its international status is independent of the ownership of any territory. Moreover, the Holy See does not participate in the interstate system as a government of any territory. Its international mission extends further beyond the rule of the Vatican City.
- Therefore, the Holy See cannot be regarded as a state in the traditional sense of statehood, and particular references to it as a state should be interpreted as indicating only its international legal personality.

The Holy See's and Vatican's international status

- Based on Lateran Pacts, the sovereignty of the Holy See has been restored as an inherent attribute **in conformity with its traditions and the requirements of its mission to the world**. Accordingly, as mentioned earlier, its sovereignty is independent of the territory.
- The primary subject of international law is the Holy See as *sui generis* entity. The personality of the Holy See is distinct from the personality of Vatican City, although the supreme authority of both is exercised by the Pope. The Holy See can act in its name in the interstate system. It can enter into legally binding international treaties, including the specific treaties known as **concordats**. It has diplomatic relations with an impressive majority of the UN members, is a 'member-state' of various intergovernmental international organisations, and became a **Permanent Observer State at the United Nations**[382] on 6 April 1964.[383] The Holy See owns certain 'edifices', which enjoy immunity in the same manner as granted by international law to the headquarters of the diplomatic agents of foreign states.[384]

---

382 As of the time this book was written, there were two permanent 'Non-member States' in the UN – the Holy See and Palestine. Both were identified as 'Non-member States' with a standing invitation to participate as observers in the sessions and the work of the General Assembly, 'the international conferences convened under the auspices of the Assembly or other organs of the United Nations, as well as in United Nations conferences', and with the permanent observer missions at the UN Headquarters. The General Assembly redefined the scope of the participation of the Holy See in the work of the United Nations by its Resolution A/RES/58/314 of 1 July 2004.

383 Generally, there are five types of permanent observers at the UN: (1) Non-Member States, (2) Specialised Agencies of the UN system, (3) Intergovernmental organisations not part of the UN system, (4) National liberation movements recognised by the UN General Assembly, and (5) Non-governmental organisations.

384 According to Article 15 of the Treaty of Conciliation, '[t]he property indicated in Article 13 hereof and in paragraphs (1) and (2) of Article 14, . . . and all other edifices in which the Holy See shall subsequently desire to establish other offices and departments although such edifices form part of the territory belonging to the Italian State, shall enjoy the immunity granted by International Law to the headquarters of the diplomatic agents of foreign States. Similar immunity shall also apply

- However, in international relations, the Vatican City also participates as a **derived subject of international law**. This participation is primarily stipulated by the fact that the Vatican is a unit related to the territory, and its international personality should, therefore, be limited to the issues directly related to that territory. (However, as is summarised by James Crawford, such a practice is not always consistent.)[385] Thus, the Vatican is a member of the International Telecommunication Union and the Universal Postal Union.[386] Besides, the Vatican has some international treaties concluded (e.g. the Monetary Agreement between the European Union and the Vatican City State [2009], in which the Vatican is represented by the Holy See).

Hence, the Vatican City, from the legal point of view, shall be considered as a *sui generis* territorial entity with a limited international personality.[387]

---

with regard to any other churches (even if situated outside Rome) during such time as, without such churches being open to the public, the Supreme Pontiff shall take part in religious ceremonies celebrated therein.'

385 'It would be significant if accessions to multilateral treaties by the Vatican City had been restricted to cases where the primary application of the treaty was to the territory of the Vatican itself, whilst accession by the Holy See had taken place in cases of humanitarian treaties or treaties that were relevant to the more general religious or cultural purposes of the Holy See. To some extent (for example, with the functional international organizations) this may be the case, but practice with respect to multilateral treaties has not been entirely consistent. Thus the Vatican City signed the International Wheat Agreement of 1956 and the Convention on the Recovery Abroad of Maintenance, but the Holy See signed the 1958 Convention on the Recognition and Enforcement of Foreign Arbitral Awards, and the 1965 Convention on Transit Trade of Land-Locked States. On the other hand, the Holy See has ratified the two Vienna Conventions on Diplomatic and Consular Relations, various international humanitarian law conventions, and various conventions relating to cultural property and copyright.' Crawford (n 274) 227–228.

386 See at <www.itu.int/online/mm/scripts/gensel8> ([in Italian] referred to as Città Del Vaticano – Vatican City) <www.upu.int/en/Universal-Postal-Union/About-UPU/Member-Countries?csid=-1&cid=324#mb-1> (named as the Vatican, ISO Code 3166/Alpha-2: VA and listed as a 'member country') accessed 16 March 2021. In addition to ITU and the UPU, the official website of the Vatican lists the following other international organisations in which the Vatican participates as a member: International Grains Council, International Telecommunications Satellite Organisation, European Telecommunication Satellite Organisation, European Conference of Postal and Telecommunications, International Institute of Administrative Sciences <https://bit.ly/2XBQh7W> accessed 16 March 2021.

387 At the same time, since 'the full ownership, exclusive dominion, and sovereign authority and jurisdiction of the Holy See over the Vatican' is recognised (Article 3 of the Treaty of Conciliation) and, on the whole, there is 'the presence of the Holy See' in the governance of the Vatican City, the existence of the Vatican's autonomous will is questionable. Consequently, one can dispute whether such an entity can be considered a separate subject of international law at all. However, whereas, in fact, the Vatican City directly enters into particular international relations on its behalf, concludes agreements with other subjects of international law, and is regarded as holding international responsibility on some matters, it should also be identified as the subject of international law, at least within the scopes of such international treaties. Besides, as noted earlier, the 'presence' of the Holy See in the governance of the Vatican City must be regarded as a process of forming the internal will of the Vatican City and 'cannot preclude' the Vatican City's separate existence because the Vatican City is not subject to 'any external influence.' See n 381.

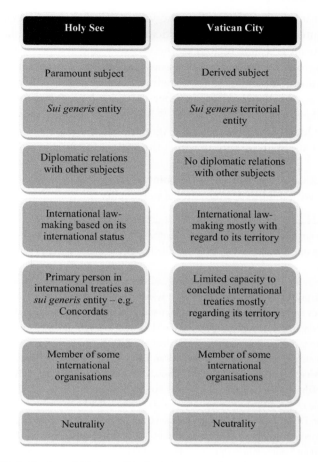

FIGURE 5.1 The Holy See's and Vatican City's international status

The Sovereign Order of Malta

> lay religious order
> Hospitallers
> hospitaller mission
> Grand Master
> Defence of the (Catholic) faith and assistance to the poor

Historical background

The birth of the Sovereign Order of Malta can be traced back to the eleventh century. 'Some merchants from the maritime republic of Amalfi obtained an authorization from the

Caliph of Egypt to build in Jerusalem a church, convent and hospital named after St. John Baptist to assist pilgrims.'[388] Pope Paschal II officially recognised the religious community of the Hospitallers of St. John of Jerusalem with the Bull of 1113. He placed the community under papal protection and conferred on it the privilege of electing its superiors without interference from other lay or religious authorities. Hence, the religious community developed into the '**lay religious order**' dedicated to serving the sick, poor, and pilgrims.[389]

The Order (also known as the Knights of Malta or simply **Hospitallers**) continued its international activity for almost 1,000 years, even when it was expelled from its former territorial bases in the Holy Land, Cyprus, Rhodes, and Malta. In 1834, the Order finally settled down in Rome, where it owns the Magistral Palace and the Magistral Villa on the Aventine Hill. The long history of the Order is reflected in its full name: Sovereign Military Hospitaller Order of St John of Jerusalem of Rhodes and of Malta.

Starting from the second part of the 19th century, the original **hospitaller mission** became the main focus of the Order.

As articulated on the official website of the Order:

> Its 13,500 members, 80,000 permanent volunteers and qualified staff of 42,000 professionals – most of whom are medical personnel and paramedics – form an efficient network that includes everything from emergency relief for refugees and the displaced living through war and conflict, to intervention in areas hit by natural disasters, hospital work, medical care and social services.[390]

Basic legal documents

The primary legal documents of the Order are the Constitutional Charter and the Code. Under the Constitutional Charter:

> The Order is a subject of international law and exercises sovereign functions. . . . Legislative, executive and judicial functions are reserved to the competent bodies of the Order according to the provisions of the Constitution and Code.[391]

388 <www.orderofmalta.int/history/1048-to-the-present/> accessed 16 March 2021.

389 'It was under the leadership of Blessed Fra' Gerard, founder and first Master, that the religious community became a lay religious order. Thanks to the bull of 15 February 1113, Pope Paschal II recognised the Order of St. John, placing it under the protection of the Church and granting it the right to freely elect its superiors, without interference from other lay or religious authorities.' In addition, it is remarkable that '[t]he Constitution of the Kingdom of Jerusalem obliged the Order to assume the military defence of the sick and pilgrims and to protect its medical centres and main roads. Defence of the faith was then added to the hospitaller mission and the Order adopted the eight-pointed cross, still today its symbol.' ibid, accessed 16 March 2021. 'February 15, 2013, marked the 900th anniversary of the papal bull "Pie postulatio voluntatis" which is one of the foundation documents of the Order of Malta. . . . Under papal protection, Gerard's hospital in Jerusalem developed into the international Order of the Hospital, which then evolved into a military religious order that ruled over Rhodes (1310–1522) and Malta (1530–1798).' 'Malta Study Center Curates National Exhibit' (2013) <http://bit.ly/3heGehH> accessed 16 March 2021.

390 <www.orderofmalta.int/humanitarian-medical-works/> accessed 16 March 2021.

391 Article 3 (Sovereignty), Par. 1 and 2.

The Order is a legal entity recognized by the Holy See. . . . The Order has diplomatic representation to the Holy See, according to the norms of international law.[392]

Current period

The Order is divided internationally into six territorial Grand Priories, six Sub-Priories and 48 national associations. The head of the Sovereign Order of Malta is the **Grand Master**.

The bilateral diplomatic relations which the Sovereign Order of Malta maintains with more than 100 states, the European Union, and some other subjects of international law (for example, the Holy See); its permanent observer status at the United Nations; and the international Cooperation Agreements concluded with over 50 states assist its humanitarian activities and allow safe access in crisis-stricken regions.

The Sovereign Order of Malta's international status

- The international personality of the Sovereign Order of Malta is provided in conformity with its traditions and the requirements of its mission to the world.
- The present mission of the Order in the interstate system is summed up in its motto: *Tuitio fidei et obsequium pauperum* (**Defence of the [Catholic] faith and assistance to the poor.**)
- The Sovereign Order of Malta is recognised by a number of states as a subject of international law possessing an international personality. However, its international personality is framed within the mission discussed earlier and in relation only to those subjects of international law which have recognised its international personality. In this context, recognition gains a constitutive nature.[393]
- The Sovereign Order of Malta has permanent observer missions to the United Nations and its Specialised Agencies. It has relations at an ambassadorial level with the European Union.
- The Sovereign Order of Malta has diplomatic relations with more than 100 states and other subjects of international law. It has the capacity to enter into international treaties with the subjects of international law.
- Its two headquarters in Rome, as well as the land and buildings forming part of Fort Saint Angelo in Malta (the Order signed an Agreement with the Maltese Government in 1999, which granted the Order the exclusive right of use of the Fort for a term of 99 years),[394] enjoy extraterritoriality.

---

392 Article 4 (Relations with the Apostolic See), Par. 1 and 5.

393 'In *Scarfo v Sovereign Order of Malta* 24 ILR 1 (1957), Tribunal of Rome, Italy, the Tribunal seemed to indicate that the sovereignty of the Order is opposable to Italy because of the latter's recognition of the fact. This may mean that other States would not be bound to accept or give effect to that sovereignty without such recognition.' Dixon, McCorquodale, and Williams (n 172) 162.

394 'The Government grants to the Order for the period of duration of this Agreement provided in Article 15. [99 years] the right of use of the land and buildings forming part of Fort Saint Angelo, as shown delineated in green on the plan contained in the Annex . . . to be used by the Order for its international

- The Sovereign Order of Malta cannot be regarded as a state according to international law as it does not possess the essential criteria for statehood.
- The Sovereign Order of Malta shall be considered a *sui generis* entity.

International Committee of the Red Cross and International Red Cross and Red Crescent Movement

> International Committee of the Red Cross
> private association
> functional international legal personality
> four Geneva Conventions of 1949
> Additional Protocols
> International Red Cross and Red Crescent Movement
> International Federation of Red Cross and Red Crescent Societies
> National Red Cross and Red Crescent Societies
> partial, functional international legal personality

Historical background

International Committee of the Red Cross (ICRC) was created in 1863 in Geneva. Among its five founding members was Henry Dunant (1828–1910), who, the year before, had published a crusading book, *A Memory of Solferino*, calling for improved care for wounded soldiers during wartime.[395]

The current state of affairs

Operating as a **private association** in accordance with the Swiss Civil Code,[396] ICRC implements several functions at the international level (the ICRC's **functional international**

---

humanitarian and cultural activities as well as the other activities mentioned in the following provisions of this Agreement.' Paragraph 1 of Article 2 of the Agreement. The Agreement is available on the official website of the Ministry for Foreign and European Affairs of Malta <https://bit.ly/3aAR8uD> accessed 16 March 2021.

395 In the book, Henry Dunant described his experiences and what he witnessed in the battle of Solferino, and at the same time, he made two suggestions. Firstly, 'each state should establish in time of peace a relief society to aid the army medical services in time of war', and secondly, 'state should conclude a treaty that would facilitate the activities of these relief societies and guarantee a better treatment of the wounded'.

396 Article 2 of the Statutes of ICRC.

legal personality) and 'is generally accepted that the ICRC, although a private organization under Swiss law, has an international legal personality.'[397]

States parties (signatories) to the **four Geneva Conventions of 1949** and their **Additional Protocols** of 1977 (Protocol I, Protocol II) and 2005 (Protocol III), as well as other subjects of international law based on the general customary international law (in certain cases), allowed the ICRC the mandate to protect victims of international and non-international armed conflicts. Such victims include prisoners of war, civilian internees, the population of occupied territories, refugees, and other groups.

In 1993, the Agreement between the International Committee of the Red Cross and the Swiss Federal Council to determine the legal status of the Committee in Switzerland (Status Agreement) was concluded. According to the Agreement: 'The Federal Council recognizes the international juridical personality and the legal capacity in Switzerland of the International Committee of the Red Cross.'[398]

ICRC's international personality

- ICRC's international status is constituted through crucial international treaties and customary norms of international humanitarian law.
- ICRC has concluded many international treaties with the states (e.g. headquarters agreements), international organisations, and other subjects of international law.
- ICRC's international personality is maintained with the aforementioned Status Agreement.
- In international law, there are many rules of customary international law concerning ICRC.[399]
- In certain cases, the ICRC enjoys immunity from state jurisdiction.
- ICRC has observer status at the United Nations. In 1990, the United Nations General Assembly decided 'to invite the International Committee of the Red Cross to participate in the sessions and the work of the General Assembly in the capacity of observer.'[400]
- ICRC has the capacity to maintain its rights by bringing international claims.

Consequently, the ICRC is neither a classical non-governmental organisation nor an international governmental organisation. It is rather recognised as a traditional *sui generis*

---

397 *Prosecutor v Blagoje Simic, Milan Simic, Miroslav Tadic, Stevan Todorovic, Simo Zaric*, Decision of 27 July 1999 on the prosecution motion under rule 73 for a ruling concerning the testimony of a witness, International Criminal Tribunal for the former Yugoslavia, Footnote 9.

398 Article 1 of the Status Agreement, available at <https://casebook.icrc.org/case-study/agreement-between-icrc-and-switzerland> accessed 16 March 2021.

399 'The ratification of the Geneva Conventions by 188 States can be considered as reflecting the *opinio juris* of these State Parties, which, in addition to the general practice of States in relation to the ICRC as described above, leads the Trial Chamber to conclude that the ICRC has a right under customary international law to non-disclosure of the Information.' *Prosecutor v Blagoje Simic, Milan Simic, Miroslav Tadic, Stevan Todorovic, Simo Zaric*, Decision of 27 July 1999 on the prosecution motion under rule 73 for a ruling concerning the testimony of a witness, Paragraph 74.

400 A/RES/45/6 of 16 October 1990.

entity – a non-governmental organisation operating at the international level with a partial functional international legal personality (subjectivity).

The International Red Cross and Red Crescent Movement

ICRC is the most significant traditional 'component' of the **International Red Cross and Red Crescent Movement**.

> The International Red Cross and Red Crescent Movement is a global human-itarian network of 80 million people that helps those facing disaster, conflict and health and social problems. It consists of the International Committee of the Red Cross, the **International Federation of Red Cross and Red Crescent Societies** and the 191 **National Red Cross and Red Crescent Societies.**[401]

The Movement has the Statutes of the International Red Cross and Red Crescent Movement, adopted by the 25th International Conference of the Red Cross at Geneva in 1986. According to the Statutes:

> The components of the Movement, while maintaining their independence within the limits of the present Statutes, act at all times in accordance with the Fundamen-tal Principles and cooperate with each other in carrying out their respective tasks in pursuance of their common mission.[402]

The International Federation of Red Cross and Red Crescent Societies

The International Federation of Red Cross and Red Crescent Societies (IFRC) was con-stituted in 1919.[403] 'The war had shown a need for close cooperation between Red Cross Societies, which, through their humanitarian activities on behalf of prisoners of war and combatants, had attracted millions of volunteers and built a large body of expertise.'[404]

IFRC 'is a membership organization established by and comprised of the National Societies.'[405]

> The Federation is an independent humanitarian organization which is not gov-ernmental, political, racial or sectarian in character . . . The general object of the Federation is to inspire, encourage, facilitate and promote at all times all forms of

---

401 <www.icrc.org/en/who-we-are/movement> accessed 16 March 2021.
402 Article 1 of the Statutes of the International Red Cross and Red Crescent Movement.
403 In 1919, the name was 'League of Red Cross Societies', which was changed in 1983 to 'League of Red Cross and Red Crescent Societies' and then in 1991 to 'International Federation of Red Cross and Red Crescent Societies.'
404 <www.ifrc.org/en/who-we-are/history/?print=true> accessed 16 March 2021.
405 Article 1 of the Constitution of IFRC.

humanitarian activities by the National Societies, with a view to preventing and alleviating human suffering and thereby contributing to the maintenance and the promotion of peace in the world.[406]

In 1996, the status agreement with Switzerland was concluded. IFRC enjoys the status of observer at the United Nations. In 1994, the United Nations General Assembly decided 'to invite the International Federation of Red Cross and Red Crescent Societies to participate in the sessions and the work of the General Assembly in the capacity of observer'.[407]

However, generally, IFRC does not enjoy the functional international legal personality to the same degree as the International Committee of the Red Cross.[408] On the whole, IFRC is neither a national non-governmental organisation nor an international governmental organisation. It is rather recognised as an international non-governmental organisation operating at the international level with a small **partial, functional international legal personality**.

INTERNATIONAL ORGANISATIONS

> international governmental organisations
> international non-governmental organisations
> international organisation
> association of states
> *sui generis* treaty
> functions transcend national boundaries
> complex internal organisational structure
> independent will
> Advisory Opinion on *Reparation for Injuries Suffered in the Service of the United Nations*

The wide variety of international organisations

There is a great deal of difference between the international organisations concerning their scope (material scopes – functions, goals, and so on; geographical scopes – global organisations and regional organisations), membership, and other important criteria.

---

406 Article 6 of the Statutes of the International Red Cross and Red Crescent Movement.

407 A/RES/49/2 of 19 October 1994.

408 For example, if the ICRC's mandate is based on the four Geneva Conventions of 1949, their Additional Protocols, and many other international law norms, we can find very limited direct reference to the IFRC in global international documents and norms: e.g. Article 4 (International Committee of the Red Cross and International Federation of Red Cross and Red Crescent Societies) of the Protocol Additional to the Geneva Conventions of 12 August 1949, and relating to the Adoption of an Additional Distinctive Emblem (Protocol III), of 8 December 2005.

International governmental and non-governmental organisations

For international law, the essential measure of distinction between international organisations is the membership criterion. Accordingly, concentrating on this criterion, two different types of organisations can be identified:

- Intergovernmental organisations or **international governmental organisations** (IGOs) (often referred to as international organisations, sometimes as international public organisations) are the organisations composed primarily of sovereign states or also of intergovernmental organisations and other subjects of international law. The international governmental organisations are the subjects of international law.
- **International non-governmental organisations** (INGOs) (sometimes referred to as international private organisations) have the same mission as the non-governmental organisations (NGOs); however, their field of operation is not national but international. As a rule, the members of the INGOs are private juridical persons or natural persons. These include worldwide organisations such as Amnesty International, Greenpeace International, the International Olympic Committee, and so forth. They generally are not considered to be subjects of international law. In principle, they have no right to create norms of international law, no right to apply (enforce and determine) international law norms in the same manner as full-fledged subjects of international law do, and so on. Accordingly, unlike intergovernmental organisations, they do not possess significant elements of international legal personality. However, there may be exceptions to the general rule, as in the case of the International Federation of Red Cross and Red Crescent Societies, which, as an international non-governmental organisation, has at its disposal minimal partial functional international legal personality.

The principal characteristics of an international governmental organisation

An international governmental organisation (in this book also referred to as an **international organisation**) is:

- essentially an **association of states**;
- commonly established by a *sui generis* **treaty** (which means that such treaties not only create international rights and obligations between the parties, as ordinary treaties, but also constitute an institutional framework with complex relationships between organs of the internal structure) between states (and sometimes, in addition, by some other subjects of international law) or in rare cases, by other instrument governed by international law;
- an entity whose **functions transcend national boundaries**;
- an entity with a **complex internal organisational structure**; and
- an entity which possesses **independent will** and, consequently, is a separate subject of law.

On the one hand, the international organisation is a secondary creation which is instituted and operated by the states and other subjects of international law. However, on the other hand, to generate the decisions by the internal organs, the concerted decision-making system is required. Consequently, the decisions agreed on in such a multilateral manner become independent from those actors who cast a vote in their favour.

Status of international governmental organisations

The appearance of international governmental organisations since the nineteenth century, raises a critical question about their status in international law, to which the International Court of Justice responded with its **Advisory Opinion on** *Reparation for Injuries Suffered in the Service of the United Nations* in 1949:

> In the opinion of the Court, the Organization was intended to exercise and enjoy, and is in fact exercising and enjoying, functions and rights which can only be explained on the basis of the possession of a large measure of international personality and the capacity to operate upon an international plane.[409] Every international governmental organisation can perform legal acts such as entering into agreements with states and other subjects of international law, bringing claims before certain adjudicating bodies, and so on.

Meanwhile, the international legal personality of an international governmental organisation is limited in scope as laid down in the foundational instrument, and, thus, this international legal personality is granted to it by the states (and sometimes, in addition, by some other subjects) which instituted it.

INDIVIDUALS

> individuals
> directly possesses rights and duties
> directly participates in the law-making
> applies the international law norms

The increasing role of individuals

In modern international law, the importance of **individuals** has been significantly increased. The human progress, scientific and technological development, the process of globalisation, and the democratisation of world processes have led to the elevation and inclusion of certain natural persons (as private persons) in interstate affairs. Nevertheless, the question which still remains is as follows: Can individuals be considered subjects of international law?

---

409 *Reparation for Injuries Suffered in the Service of the United Nations*, Advisory Opinion of 11 April 1949.

Two versions of the notion of a subject of law

If we conclude that a subject of international law is a person who is an addressee of the international legal norms, endowed by these norms with rights and obligations, then individuals are undoubtedly subjects of international law since there are many international legal norms that directly address individuals, mainly in the fields of international human rights law, international criminal law, and international humanitarian law.

However, the concept of a subject of international law, as already noted, is not identical to the corresponding concept in national law. And if we consider that a subject of international law is a person who (1) **directly possesses rights and duties** based on international law, (2) **directly participates in the law-making** process, and (3) **applies the international law norms**, including by bringing international claims, then the individual cannot be considered to possess an international legal personality.

Individuals are not the subjects of international law

Although individuals have rights and duties based on international law, can sometimes bring international claims against subjects of international law (e.g. against the member states of the European Convention on Human Rights, when in particular cases, individuals may apply to the European Court of Human Rights) and moreover, certain individuals have a significant impact on foreign policy and international decision making, they still do not have a general and worldwide right to implement their international rights and duties. Moreover, as individuals, they do not participate in the international law-making process.

CASES AND MATERIALS (*SELECTED PARTS*)

The Purposes of the United Nations
Non-self-governing territories
International trusteeship system

Charter of the United Nations

CHAPTER I: PURPOSES AND PRINCIPLES

Article 1

The Purposes of the United Nations are:

1   To maintain international peace and security, and to that end: to take effective collective measures for the prevention and removal of threats to the peace, and for the suppression of acts of aggression or other breaches of the peace, and to bring about by peaceful means, and in conformity with the principles of justice and international law, adjustment or settlement of international disputes or situations which might lead to a breach of the peace;

2   To develop friendly relations among nations based on respect for the principle of equal rights and self-determination of peoples, and to take other appropriate measures to strengthen universal peace;

3   To achieve international co-operation in solving international problems of an economic, social, cultural, or humanitarian character, and in promoting and encouraging respect for human rights and for fundamental freedoms for all without distinction as to race, sex, language, or religion; and

4   To be a centre for harmonizing the actions of nations in the attainment of these common ends.

CHAPTER IX: INTERNATIONAL ECONOMIC AND SOCIAL CO-OPERATION

Article 55

With a view to the creation of conditions of stability and well-being which are necessary for peaceful and friendly relations among nations based on respect for the principle of equal rights and self-determination of peoples, the United Nations shall promote:

a   higher standards of living, full employment, and conditions of economic and social progress and development;

b   solutions of international economic, social, health, and related problems; and international cultural and educational cooperation; and

c   universal respect for, and observance of, human rights and fundamental freedoms for all without distinction as to race, sex, language, or religion.

CHAPTER XI: DECLARATION REGARDING NON-SELF-GOVERNING TERRITORIES

Article 73

Members of the United Nations which have or assume responsibilities for the administration of territories whose peoples have not yet attained a full measure of self-government recognize the principle that the interests of the inhabitants of these territories are paramount, and accept as a sacred trust the obligation to promote to the utmost, within the system of international peace and security established by the present Charter, the well-being of the inhabitants of these territories, and, to this end:

a   to ensure, with due respect for the culture of the peoples concerned, their political, economic, social, and educational advancement, their just treatment, and their protection against abuses;

b   to develop self-government, to take due account of the political aspirations of the peoples, and to assist them in the progressive development of their free political institutions, according to the particular circumstances of each territory and its peoples and their varying stages of advancement;

c   to further international peace and security;

d   to promote constructive measures of development, to encourage research, and to co-operate with one another and, when and where appropriate, with specialized international bodies with a view to the practical achievement of the social, economic, and scientific purposes set forth in this Article; and

e   to transmit regularly to the Secretary-General for information purposes, subject to such limitation as security and constitutional considerations may require, statistical and other information of a technical nature relating to economic, social, and educational conditions in the territories for which they are respectively responsible other than those territories to which Chapters XII and XIII apply.

Article 74

Members of the United Nations also agree that their policy in respect of the territories to which this Chapter applies, no less than in respect of their metropolitan areas, must be based on the general principle of good-neighbourliness, due account being taken of the interests and well-being of the rest of the world, in social, economic, and commercial matters.

Chapter XII: International trusteeship system

Article 75

The United Nations shall establish under its authority an international trusteeship system for the administration and supervision of such territories as may be placed thereunder by subsequent individual agreements. These territories are hereinafter referred to as trust territories.

Article 76

The basic objectives of the trusteeship system, in accordance with the Purposes of the United Nations laid down in Article 1 of the present Charter, shall be:

a   to further international peace and security;

b   to promote the political, economic, social, and educational advancement of the inhabitants of the trust territories, and their progressive development towards self-government or independence as may be appropriate to the particular circumstances of each territory and its peoples and the freely expressed wishes of the peoples concerned, and as may be provided by the terms of each trusteeship agreement;

c   to encourage respect for human rights and for fundamental freedoms for all without distinction as to race, sex, language, or religion, and to encourage recognition of the interdependence of the peoples of the world; and

d   to ensure equal treatment in social, economic, and commercial matters for all Members of the United Nations and their nationals, and also equal treatment for the latter in the administration of justice, without prejudice to the attainment of the foregoing objectives and subject to the provisions of Article 80.

Article 77

1   The trusteeship system shall apply to such territories in the following categories as may be placed thereunder by means of trusteeship agreements:

   a   territories now held under mandate;
   b   territories which may be detached from enemy states as a result of the Second World War; and
   c   territories voluntarily placed under the system by states responsible for their administration.

2   It will be a matter for subsequent agreement as to which territories in the foregoing categories will be brought under the trusteeship system and upon what terms.

Article 78

The trusteeship system shall not apply to territories which have become Members of the United Nations, relationship among which shall be based on respect for the principle of sovereign equality.

Article 79

The terms of trusteeship for each territory to be placed under the trusteeship system, including any alteration or amendment, shall be agreed upon by the states directly concerned, including the mandatory power in the case of territories held under mandate by a Member of the United Nations, and shall be approved as provided for in Articles 83 and 85.

Article 80

1   Except as may be agreed upon in individual trusteeship agreements, made under Articles 77, 79, and 81, placing each territory under the trusteeship system, and until such agreements have been concluded, nothing in this Chapter shall be construed in or of itself to alter in any manner the rights whatsoever of any states or any peoples or the terms of existing international instruments to which Members of the United Nations may respectively be parties.

2   Paragraph 1 of this Article shall not be interpreted as giving grounds for delay or postponement of the negotiation and conclusion of agreements for placing mandated and other territories under the trusteeship system as provided for in Article 77.

Article 81

The trusteeship agreement shall in each case include the terms under which the trust territory will be administered and designate the authority which will exercise the administration of the trust territory. Such authority, hereinafter called the administering authority, may be one or more states or the Organization itself.

Article 82

There may be designated, in any trusteeship agreement, a strategic area or areas which may include part or all of the trust territory to which the agreement applies, without prejudice to any special agreement or agreements made under Article 43.

Article 83

1 All functions of the United Nations relating to strategic areas, including the approval of the terms of the trusteeship agreements and of their alteration or amendment shall be exercised by the Security Council.
2 The basic objectives set forth in Article 76 shall be applicable to the people of each strategic area.
3 The Security Council shall, subject to the provisions of the trusteeship agreements and without prejudice to security considerations, avail itself of the assistance of the Trusteeship Council to perform those functions of the United Nations under the trusteeship system relating to political, economic, social, and educational matters in the strategic areas.

Article 84

It shall be the duty of the administering authority to ensure that the trust territory shall play its part in the maintenance of international peace and security. To this end the administering authority may make use of volunteer forces, facilities, and assistance from the trust territory in carrying out the obligations towards the Security Council undertaken in this regard by the administering authority, as well as for local defence and the maintenance of law and order within the trust territory.

Article 85

1 The functions of the United Nations with regard to trusteeship agreements for all areas not designated as strategic, including the approval of the terms of the trusteeship agreements and of their alteration or amendment, shall be exercised by the General Assembly.
2 The Trusteeship Council, operating under the authority of the General Assembly shall assist the General Assembly in carrying out these functions.

CHAPTER XIII: THE TRUSTEESHIP COUNCIL

COMPOSITION

Article 86

1 The Trusteeship Council shall consist of the following Members of the United Nations:

a those Members administering trust territories;
b such of those Members mentioned by name in Article 23 as are not administering trust territories; and
c as many other Members elected for three-year terms by the General Assembly as may be necessary to ensure that the total number of members of the Trusteeship Council is equally divided between those Members of the United Nations which administer trust territories and those which do not.

2 Each member of the Trusteeship Council shall designate one specially qualified person to represent it therein.

FUNCTIONS AND POWERS

Article 87

The General Assembly and, under its authority, the Trusteeship Council, in carrying out their functions, may:

a   consider reports submitted by the administering authority;
b   accept petitions and examine them in consultation with the administering authority;
c   provide for periodic visits to the respective trust territories at times agreed upon with the administering authority; and
d   take these and other actions in conformity with the terms of the trusteeship agreements.

Article 88

The Trusteeship Council shall formulate a questionnaire on the political, economic, social, and educational advancement of the inhabitants of each trust territory, and the administering authority for each trust territory within the competence of the General Assembly shall make an annual report to the General Assembly upon the basis of such questionnaire.

VOTING

Article 89

1   Each member of the Trusteeship Council shall have one vote.
2   Decisions of the Trusteeship Council shall be made by a majority of the members present and voting.

PROCEDURE

Article 90

1   The Trusteeship Council shall adopt its own rules of procedure, including the method of selecting its President.
2   The Trusteeship Council shall meet as required in accordance with its rules, which shall include provision for the convening of meetings on the request of a majority of its members.

Article 91

The Trusteeship Council shall, when appropriate, avail itself of the assistance of the Economic and Social Council and of the specialized agencies in regard to matters with which they are respectively concerned.

Self-determination

Declaration on the granting of independence to colonial countries and peoples
The UN General Assembly Resolution – A/RES/1514(XV) of 14 December 1960

The General Assembly . . .
Declares that:

1 The subjection of peoples to alien subjugation, domination and exploitation constitutes a denial of fundamental human rights, is contrary to the Charter of the United Nations and is an impediment to the promotion of world peace and co-operation.

2 All peoples have the right to self-determination; by virtue of that right they freely determine their political status and freely pursue their economic, social and cultural development.

3 Inadequacy of political, economic, social or educational preparedness should never serve as a pretext for delaying independence.

4 All armed action or repressive measures of all kinds directed against dependent peoples shall cease in order to enable them to exercise peacefully and freely their right to complete independence, and the integrity of their national territory shall be respected.

5 Immediate steps shall be taken, in Trust and Non-Self-Governing Territories or all other territories which have not yet attained independence, to transfer all powers to the peoples of those territories, without any conditions or reservations, in accordance with their freely expressed will and desire, without any distinction as to race, creed or colour, in order to enable them to enjoy complete independence and freedom.

6 Any attempt aimed at the partial or total disruption of the national unity and the territorial integrity of a country is incompatible with the purposes and principles of the Charter of the United Nations.

7 All States shall observe faithfully and strictly the provisions of the Charter of the United Nations, the Universal Declaration of Human Rights and the present Declaration on the basis of equality, non-interference in the internal affairs of all States, and respect for the sovereign rights of all peoples and their territorial integrity.

Self-determination

Legal Consequences for States of the Continued Presence of South Africa in Namibia (South-West Africa) notwithstanding Security Council Resolution 276 (1970), Advisory Opinion, 21 June 1971, International Court of Justice
    ICJ Reports 1971, 16.
    52. Furthermore, the subsequent development of international law in regard to non-self-governing territories, as enshrined in the Charter of the United Nations, made the principle of self-determination applicable to all of them. The concept of the sacred trust was confirmed and expanded to all "territories whose peoples have not yet attained a full measure of self-government" (Art. 73). Thus it clearly embraced territories under a colonial regime. Obviously the sacred trust continued to apply to League of Nations mandated territories on which an international status had been conferred earlier. A further important stage in this development was the Declaration on the Granting of Independence to Colonial Countries and Peoples (General Assembly resolution 1514 (XV) of 14 December 1960), which embraces all peoples and territories which "have not yet attained independence". Nor is it possible to leave out of account the political history of mandated territories in general. All those which did not acquire independence, excluding Namibia, were placed under trusteeship. Today, only two out of fifteen, excluding Namibia, remain under United Nations tutelage. This is but a manifestation of the general development which has led to the birth of so many new States.

Western Sahara, Advisory Opinion, 16 October 1975, International Court of Justice
ICJ Reports 1975, 12.

58. General Assembly resolution 2625 (XXV), "Declaration on Principles of International Law concerning Friendly Relations and Co-operation among States in accordance with the Charter of the United Nations" – to which reference was also made in the proceedings – mentions other possibilities besides independence, association or integration. But in doing so it reiterates the basic need to take account of the wishes of the people concerned:

> "The establishment of a sovereign and independent State, the free association or integration with an independent State or the emergence into any other political status freely determined by a people constitute modes of implementing the right of self-determination by that people." . . .

Resolution 2625 (XXV) further provides that:

> "Every State has the duty to promote, through joint and separate action, realization of the principle of equal rights and self-determination of peoples in accordance with the provisions of the Charter, and to render assistance to the United Nations in carrying out the responsibilities entrusted to it by the Charter regarding the implementation of the principle, in order: . . .
>
> (b) To bring a speedy end to colonialism, having due regard to the freely expressed will of the peoples concerned."

59. The validity of the principle of self-determination, defined as the need to pay regard to the freely expressed will of peoples, is not affected by the fact that in certain cases the General Assembly has dispensed with the requirement of consulting the inhabitants of a given territory. Those instances were based either on the consideration that a certain population did not constitute a "people" entitled to self-determination or on the conviction that a consultation was totally unnecessary, in view of special circumstances.

Accordance with International Law of the Unilateral Declaration of Independence in respect of Kosovo, Advisory Opinion, 22 July 2010, International Court of Justice
ICJ Reports 2010, 403.

55. While many of those participating in the present proceedings made reference to the opinion of the Supreme Court of Canada in *Reference by the Governor in Council concerning Certain Questions relating to the Secession of Quebec from Canada* ([1998] 2 *Supreme Court Reporter (SCR)* 217; 161 *Dominion Law Reports (DLR)* (4th) 385; 115 *International Law Reports (ILR)* 536), the Court observes that the question in the present case is markedly different from that posed to the Supreme Court of Canada.

The relevant question in that case was:

> "Does international law give the National Assembly, legislature or government of Quebec the right to effect the secession of Quebec from Canada unilaterally? In this regard, is there a right to self-determination under international law that would give the National Assembly,

legislature or government of Quebec the right to effect the secession of Quebec from Canada unilaterally?"

56. The question put to the Supreme Court of Canada inquired whether there was a right to "effect secession", and whether there was a rule of international law which conferred a positive entitlement on any of the organs named. By contrast, the General Assembly has asked whether the declaration of independence was "in accordance with" international law. The answer to that question turns on whether or not the applicable international law prohibited the declaration of independence. If the Court concludes that it did, then it must answer the question put by saying that the declaration of independence was not in accordance with international law. It follows that the task which the Court is called upon to perform is to determine whether or not the declaration of independence was adopted in violation of international law. The Court is not required by the question it has been asked to take a position on whether international law conferred a positive entitlement on Kosovo unilaterally to declare its independence or, *a fortiori*, on whether international law generally confers an entitlement on entities situated within a State unilaterally to break away from it. Indeed, it is entirely possible for a particular act – such as a unilateral declaration of independence – not to be in violation of international law without necessarily constituting the exercise of a right conferred by it. The Court has been asked for an opinion on the first point, not the second . . .

122. The Court has concluded above that the adoption of the declaration of independence of 17 February 2008 did not violate general international law, Security Council resolution 1244 (1999) or the Constitutional Framework. Consequently the adoption of that declaration did not violate any applicable rule of international law.

Self-determination

Reference by the Governor in Council concerning Certain Questions relating to the Secession of Quebec from Canada, Judgment of 20 August 1998, Supreme Court of Canada
Case number 25506, Report [1998] 2 SCR 217.

136 The population of Quebec cannot plausibly be said to be denied access to government. Quebecers occupy prominent positions within the government of Canada. Residents of the province freely make political choices and pursue economic, social and cultural development within Quebec, across Canada, and throughout the world. The population of Quebec is equitably represented in legislative, executive and judicial institutions. In short, to reflect the phraseology of the international documents that address the right to self-determination of peoples, Canada is a "sovereign and independent state conducting itself in compliance with the principle of equal rights and self-determination of peoples and thus possessed of a government representing the whole people belonging to the territory without distinction".

137 The continuing failure to reach agreement on amendments to the Constitution, while a matter of concern, does not amount to a denial of self-determination. In the absence of amendments to the Canadian Constitution, we must look at the constitutional arrangements presently in effect, and we cannot conclude under current circumstances that those arrangements place Quebecers in a disadvantaged position within the scope of the international law rule.

138 In summary, the international law right to self-determination only generates, at best, a right to external self-determination in situations of former colonies; where a people is oppressed, as for example under foreign military occupation; or where a definable group is denied meaningful access to government to pursue their political, economic, social and cultural development. In all

three situations, the people in question are entitled to a right to external self-determination because they have been denied the ability to exert internally their right to self-determination. Such exceptional circumstances are manifestly inapplicable to Quebec under existing conditions. Accordingly, neither the population of the province of Quebec, even if characterized in terms of "people" or "peoples", nor its representative institutions, the National Assembly, the legislature or government of Quebec, possess a right, under international law, to secede unilaterally from Canada.

139 We would not wish to leave this aspect of our answer to Question 2 without acknowledging the importance of the submissions made to us respecting the rights and concerns of aboriginal peoples in the event of a unilateral secession, as well as the appropriate means of defining the boundaries of a seceding Quebec with particular regard to the northern lands occupied largely by aboriginal peoples. However, the concern of aboriginal peoples is precipitated by the asserted right of Quebec to unilateral secession. In light of our finding that there is no such right applicable to the population of Quebec, either under the Constitution of Canada or at international law, but that on the contrary a clear democratic expression of support for secession would lead under the Constitution to negotiations in which aboriginal interests would be taken into account, it becomes unnecessary to explore further the concerns of the aboriginal peoples in this Reference.

(2) Recognition of a Factual/Political Reality: the "Effectivity" Principle

140 As stated, an argument advanced by the *amicus curiae* on this branch of the Reference was that, while international law may not ground a positive right to unilateral secession in the context of Quebec, international law equally does not prohibit secession and, in fact, international recognition would be conferred on such a political reality if it emerged, for example, via effective control of the territory of what is now the province of Quebec.

141 It is true that international law may well, depending on the circumstances, adapt to recognize a political and/or factual reality, regardless of the legality of the steps leading to its creation. However, as mentioned at the outset, effectivity, as such, does not have any real applicability to Question 2, which asks whether a right to unilateral secession exists.

142 No one doubts that legal consequences may flow from political facts, and that "sovereignty is a political fact for which no purely legal authority can be constituted . . .," H. W. R. Wade, "The Basis of Legal Sovereignty", [1955] *Camb. L.J.* 172, at p. 196. Secession of a province from Canada, if successful in the streets, might well lead to the creation of a new state. Although recognition by other states is not, at least as a matter of theory, necessary to achieve statehood, the viability of a would-be state in the international community depends, as a practical matter, upon recognition by other states. That process of recognition is guided by legal norms. However, international recognition is not alone constitutive of statehood and, critically, does not relate back to the date of secession to serve retroactively as a source of a "legal" right to secede in the first place. Recognition occurs only after a territorial unit has been successful, as a political fact, in achieving secession.

143 As indicated in responding to Question 1, one of the legal norms which may be recognized by states in granting or withholding recognition of emergent states is the legitimacy of the process by which the *de facto* secession is, or was, being pursued. The process of recognition, once considered to be an exercise of pure sovereign discretion, has come to be associated with legal norms. See, e.g., *European Community Declaration on the Guidelines on the Recognition of New States in Eastern Europe and in the Soviet Union*, 31 I.L.M. 1486 (1992), at p. 1487. While national interest and perceived political advantage to the recognizing state obviously play an important role, foreign states may also take into account their view as to the existence of a right to self-determination on the part of the population of the putative state, and a counterpart domestic evaluation, namely, an examination of the legality of the secession according to the law of the state from which the territorial unit purports to have seceded. As we indicated in our answer to Question

1, an emergent state that has disregarded legitimate obligations arising out of its previous situation can potentially expect to be hindered by that disregard in achieving international recognition, at least with respect to the timing of that recognition. On the other hand, compliance by the seceding province with such legitimate obligations would weigh in favour of international recognition. The notion that what is not explicitly prohibited is implicitly permitted has little relevance where (as here) international law refers the legality of secession to the domestic law of the seceding state and the law of that state holds unilateral secession to be unconstitutional.

144 As a court of law, we are ultimately concerned only with legal claims. If the principle of "effectivity" is no more than that "successful revolution begets its own legality" (S. A. de Smith, "Constitutional Lawyers in Revolutionary Situations" (1968), *7 West. Ont. L. Rev.* 93, at p. 96), it necessarily means that legality follows and does not precede the successful revolution. *Ex hypothesi*, the successful revolution took place outside the constitutional framework of the predecessor state, otherwise it would not be characterized as "a revolution". It may be that a unilateral secession by Quebec would eventually be accorded legal status by Canada and other states, and thus give rise to legal consequences; but this does not support the more radical contention that subsequent recognition of a state of affairs brought about by a unilateral declaration of independence could be taken to mean that secession was achieved under colour of a legal right.

145 An argument was made to analogize the principle of effectivity with the second aspect of the rule of law identified by this Court in *the Manitoba Language Rights Reference, supra*, at p. 753, namely, avoidance of a legal vacuum. In that Reference, it will be recalled, this Court declined to strike down all of Manitoba's legislation for its failure to comply with constitutional dictates, out of concern that this would leave the province in a state of chaos. In so doing, we recognized that the rule of law is a constitutional principle which permits the courts to address the practical consequences of their actions, particularly in constitutional cases. The similarity between that principle and the principle of effectivity, it was argued, is that both attempt to refashion the law to meet social reality. However, nothing of our concern in the *Manitoba Language Rights Reference* about the severe practical consequences of unconstitutionality affected our conclusion that, as a matter of law, all Manitoba legislation at issue in that case was unconstitutional. The Court's declaration of unconstitutionality was clear and unambiguous. The Court's concern with maintenance of the rule of law was directed in its relevant aspect to the appropriate remedy, which in that case was to suspend the declaration of invalidity to permit appropriate rectification to take place.

146 The principle of effectivity operates very differently. It proclaims that an illegal act may eventually acquire legal status if, as a matter of empirical fact, it is recognized on the international plane. Our law has long recognized that through a combination of acquiescence and prescription, an illegal act may at some later point be accorded some form of legal status. In the law of property, for example, it is well known that a squatter on land may ultimately become the owner if the true owner sleeps on his or her right to repossess the land. In this way, a change in the factual circumstances may subsequently be reflected in a change in legal status. It is, however, quite another matter to suggest that a subsequent condonation of an initially illegal act retroactively creates a legal right to engage in the act in the first place. The broader contention is not supported by the international principle of effectivity or otherwise and must be rejected.

Palestinian question

The situation in the Middle East, including the Palestinian question. The UN Security Council Resolution – S/RES/2334 (2016)
of 23 December 2016
The Security Council . . .

Condemning all acts of violence against civilians, including acts of terror, as well as all acts of provocation, incitement and destruction,

Reiterating its vision of a region where two democratic States, Israel and Palestine, live side by side in peace within secure and recognized borders,

Stressing that the *status quo* is not sustainable and that significant steps, consistent with the transition contemplated by prior agreements, are urgently needed in order to

(i) stabilize the situation and to reverse negative trends on the ground, which are steadily eroding the two-State solution and entrenching a one-State reality, and

(ii) to create the conditions for successful final status negotiations and for advancing the two-State solution through those negotiations and on the ground,

1 Reaffirms that the establishment by Israel of settlements in the Palestinian territory occupied since 1967, including East Jerusalem, has no legal validity and constitutes a flagrant violation under international law and a major obstacle to the achievement of the two-State solution and a just, lasting and comprehensive peace;

2 Reiterates its demand that Israel immediately and completely cease all settlement activities in the occupied Palestinian territory, including East Jerusalem, and that it fully respect all of its legal obligations in this regard;

3 Underlines that it will not recognize any changes to the 4 June 1967 lines, including with regard to Jerusalem, other than those agreed by the parties through negotiations;

4 Stresses that the cessation of all Israeli settlement activities is essential for salvaging the two-State solution, and calls for affirmative steps to be taken immediately to reverse the negative trends on the ground that are imperilling the two-State solution;

5 Calls upon all States, bearing in mind paragraph 1 of this resolution, to distinguish, in their relevant dealings, between the territory of the State of Israel and the territories occupied since 1967;

6 Calls for immediate steps to prevent all acts of violence against civilians, including acts of terror, as well as all acts of provocation and destruction, calls for accountability in this regard, and calls for compliance with obligations under international law for the strengthening of ongoing efforts to combat terrorism, including through existing security coordination, and to clearly condemn all acts of terrorism;

7 Calls upon both parties to act on the basis of international law, including international humanitarian law, and their previous agreements and obligations, to observe calm and restraint, and to refrain from provocative actions, incitement and inflammatory rhetoric, with the aim, inter alia, of de-escalating the situation on the ground, rebuilding trust and confidence, demonstrating through policies and actions a genuine commitment to the two-State solution, and creating the conditions necessary for promoting peace;

8 Calls upon all parties to continue, in the interest of the promotion of peace and security, to exert collective efforts to launch credible negotiations on all final status issues in the Middle East peace process and within the time frame specified by the Quartet in its statement of 21 September 2010;

9 Urges in this regard the intensification and acceleration of international and regional diplomatic efforts and support aimed at achieving, without delay a comprehensive, just and lasting peace in the Middle East on the basis of the relevant United Nations resolutions, the Madrid terms of reference, including the principle of land for peace, the Arab Peace Initiative and the Quartet Roadmap and an end

to the Israeli occupation that began in 1967; and underscores in this regard the importance of the ongoing efforts to advance the Arab Peace Initiative, the initiative of France for the convening of an international peace conference, the recent efforts of the Quartet, as well as the efforts of Egypt and the Russian Federation;

10 Confirms its determination to support the parties throughout the negotiations and in the implementation of an agreement;
11 Reaffirms its determination to examine practical ways and means to secure the full implementation of its relevant resolutions;
12 Requests the Secretary-General to report to the Council every three months on the implementation of the provisions of the present resolution;
13 Decides to remain seized of the matter.

Kosovo question

The situation relating Kosovo. The UN Security Council Resolution – S/RES/1244 (1999) of 10 June 1999
The Security Council . . .

1 Decides that a political solution to the Kosovo crisis shall be based on the general principles in annex 1 and as further elaborated in the principles and other required elements in annex 2;
2 Welcomes the acceptance by the Federal Republic of Yugoslavia of the principles and other required elements referred to in paragraph 1 above, and demands the full cooperation of the Federal Republic of Yugoslavia in their rapid implementation;
3 Demands in particular that the Federal Republic of Yugoslavia put an immediate and verifiable end to violence and repression in Kosovo, and begin and complete verifiable phased withdrawal from Kosovo of all military, police and paramilitary forces according to a rapid timetable, with which the deployment of the international security presence in Kosovo will be synchronized;
4 Confirms that after the withdrawal an agreed number of Yugoslav and Serb military and police personnel will be permitted to return to Kosovo to perform the functions in accordance with annex 2;
5 Decides on the deployment in Kosovo, under United Nations auspices, of international civil and security presences, with appropriate equipment and personnel as required, and welcomes the agreement of the Federal Republic of Yugoslavia to such presences;
6 Requests the Secretary-General to appoint, in consultation with the Security Council, a Special Representative to control the implementation of the international civil presence, and further requests the Secretary-General to instruct his Special Representative to coordinate closely with the international security presence to ensure that both presences operate towards the same goals and in a mutually supportive manner;
7 Authorizes Member States and relevant international organizations to establish the international security presence in Kosovo as set out in point 4 of annex 2 with all necessary means to fulfil its responsibilities under paragraph 9 below;
8 Affirms the need for the rapid early deployment of effective international civil and security presences to Kosovo, and demands that the parties cooperate fully in their deployment;
9 Decides that the responsibilities of the international security presence to be deployed and acting in Kosovo will include:

(a) Deterring renewed hostilities, maintaining and where necessary enforcing a ceasefire, and ensuring the withdrawal and preventing the return into Kosovo of Federal and Republic military, police and paramilitary forces, except as provided in point 6 of annex 2;

(b) Demilitarizing the Kosovo Liberation Army (KLA) and other armed Kosovo Albanian groups as required in paragraph 15 below;

(c) Establishing a secure environment in which refugees and displaced persons can return home in safety, the international civil presence can operate, a transitional administration can be established, and humanitarian aid can be delivered;

(d) Ensuring public safety and order until the international civil presence can take responsibility for this task;

(e) Supervising demining until the international civil presence can, as appropriate, take over responsibility for this task;

(f) Supporting, as appropriate, and coordinating closely with the work of the international civil presence;

(g) Conducting border monitoring duties as required;

(h) Ensuring the protection and freedom of movement of itself, the international civil presence, and other international organizations;

10 Authorizes the Secretary-General, with the assistance of relevant international organizations, to establish an international civil presence in Kosovo in order to provide an interim administration for Kosovo under which the people of Kosovo can enjoy substantial autonomy within the Federal Republic of Yugoslavia, and which will provide transitional administration while establishing and overseeing the development of provisional democratic self-governing institutions to ensure conditions for a peaceful and normal life for all inhabitants of Kosovo;

11 Decides that the main responsibilities of the international civil presence will include:

(a) Promoting the establishment, pending a final settlement, of substantial autonomy and self-government in Kosovo, taking full account of annex 2 and of the Rambouillet accords (S/1999/648);

(b) Performing basic civilian administrative functions where and as long as required;

(c) Organizing and overseeing the development of provisional institutions for democratic and autonomous self-government pending a political settlement, including the holding of elections;

(d) Transferring, as these institutions are established, its administrative responsibilities while overseeing and supporting the consolidation of Kosovo's local provisional institutions and other peacebuilding activities;

(e) Facilitating a political process designed to determine Kosovo's future status, taking into account the Rambouillet accords (S/1999/648);

(f) In a final stage, overseeing the transfer of authority from Kosovo's provisional institutions to institutions established under a political settlement;

(g) Supporting the reconstruction of key infrastructure and other economic reconstruction;

(h) Supporting, in coordination with international humanitarian organizations, humanitarian and disaster relief aid;

(i) Maintaining civil law and order, including establishing local police forces and meanwhile through the deployment of international police personnel to serve in Kosovo;

(j) Protecting and promoting human rights;

(k) Assuring the safe and unimpeded return of all refugees and displaced persons to their homes in Kosovo;

12 Emphasizes the need for coordinated humanitarian relief operations, and for the Federal Republic of Yugoslavia to allow unimpeded access to Kosovo by humanitarian aid

organizations and to cooperate with such organizations so as to ensure the fast and effective delivery of international aid;

13 Encourages all Member States and international organizations to contribute to economic and social reconstruction as well as to the safe return of refugees and displaced persons, and emphasizes in this context the importance of convening an international donors' conference, particularly for the purposes set out in paragraph 11 (g) above, at the earliest possible date;

14 Demands full cooperation by all concerned, including the international security presence, with the International Tribunal for the Former Yugoslavia;

15 Demands that the KLA and other armed Kosovo Albanian groups end immediately all offensive actions and comply with the requirements for demilitarization as laid down by the head of the international security presence in consultation with the Special Representative of the Secretary-General;

16 Decides that the prohibitions imposed by paragraph 8 of resolution 1160 (1998) shall not apply to arms and related matériel for the use of the international civil and security presences;

17 Welcomes the work in hand in the European Union and other international organizations to develop a comprehensive approach to the economic development and stabilization of the region affected by the Kosovo crisis, including the implementation of a Stability Pact for South Eastern Europe with broad international participation in order to further the promotion of democracy, economic prosperity, stability and regional cooperation;

18 Demands that all States in the region cooperate fully in the implementation of all aspects of this resolution;

19 Decides that the international civil and security presences are established for an initial period of 12 months, to continue thereafter unless the Security Council decides otherwise;

20 Requests the Secretary-General to report to the Council at regular intervals on the implementation of this resolution, including reports from the leaderships of the international civil and security presences, the first reports to be submitted within 30 days of the adoption of this resolution;

21 Decides to remain actively seized of the matter.

Sui generis entities

Lateran Pacts of 1929 between the Holy See and Italy, the Treaty of Conciliation

Article 1

Italy recognizes and reaffirms the principle established in the first Article of the Statute of the Kingdom of 4 March 1848, according to which the Catholic, Apostolic and Roman Religion is the only religion of the State.

Article 2

Italy recognizes the sovereignty of the Holy See in the international realm as an attribute inherent in its nature in conformity with its tradition and with the requirements of its mission to the world.

Article 3

Italy recognizes the full ownership and the exclusive and absolute power and jurisdiction of the Holy See over the Vatican as it is presently constituted, together with all its appurtenances and endowments, creating in this manner Vatican City for the special purposes and under the conditions given in this Treaty.

The boundaries of the said City are set forth in the map which constitutes Attachment I of the present Treaty, of which it is forms an integral part.

It remains understood that St. Peter's Square, although forming part of Vatican City, will continue to be normally open to the public and to be subject to the police power of the Italian authorities, who will stop at the foot of the steps leading to the Basilica, although the latter will continue to be used for public worship, and they will, therefore, abstain from mounting the steps and entering the said Basilica, unless they are asked to intervene by the competent authority.

Whenever the Holy See consider it necessary, for the purpose of particular functions, to close St. Peter's Square temporarily to the free passage of the public, the Italian authorities will withdraw beyond the outer lines of Bernini's Colonnade and their extension, unless they have been asked to remain by the competent authority.

Article 4

The sovereignty and exclusive jurisdiction over Vatican City which Italy recognizes as pertaining to the Holy See means that within the same City there cannot be any interference on the part of the Italian Government and that there is no other authority there than that of the Holy See.

Article 5

In order to put the provisions of the preceding Article into effect, before the present Treaty comes into force the Italian Government will see to it that the territory forming Vatican City is freed from every lien and from possible occupants. The Holy See will arrange to close the means of access to the City, enclosing the open parts, except St. Peter's Square.

It is furthermore agreed that, in respect of the buildings existing there and belonging to religious institutes or entities, the Holy See will make provisions directly to regulate its relations with them, with the Italian State abstaining from any involvement.

Article 6

Italy will see to it, by means of agreements made with the entities concerned, that an adequate supply of the water in its possession is fully assured to Vatican City.

Italy will furthermore provide for connection with the State railways by constructing a railway station within Vatican City, in the location indicated on the attached map (Attachment I), and by permitting the movement of railway vehicles belonging to the Vatican on the Italian railways.

It will further provide for the connection, even directly with other States, of the telegraph, telephone, radiotelegraph, radiotelephone, broadcasting, and postal services in Vatican City.

Finally, it will also provide for the coordination of other public services.

All the provisions just mentioned will be made at the expense of the Italian State and within the period of one year from the entry into force of the present Treaty.

The Holy See, at its own expense, will see to the arrangement of the existing means of access to the Vatican, and those others which it may consider necessary to open in the future.

Agreements will be subsequently concluded between the Holy See and Italy concerning the circulation, on and over Italian territory, of land vehicles and aircraft belonging to Vatican City.

Article 7

The Italian Government undertakes not to permit the construction within the territory surrounding Vatican City of any new buildings which have a view into the Vatican, and for the same purpose undertakes to provide for the partial demolition of such buildings already standing, from the Porta Cavalleggeri and along the Via Aurelia and the Viale Vaticano.

In accordance with the provisions of International Law, it is forbidden for aircraft of any kind whatsoever to fly over the territory of the Vatican.

In Piazza Rusticucci and in the areas adjoining the Colonnade, wherever the extra-territoriality referred to in Art. 15 does not extend, any alterations of buildings or streets that could affect Vatican City will be effected by mutual agreement.

Article 8

Italy, considering the person of the Supreme Pontiff to be sacred and inviolable, declares that any attempt against his person or any incitement to commit such an attempt is punishable by the same penalties as all similar attempts and incitements to commit the same against the person of the King.

Offences and public insults committed within Italian territory against the person of the Supreme Pontiff, whether by means of speech, deeds or writing, are punished in the same manner as offences and insults against the person of the King.

Article 9

In accordance with the provisions of International Law, all persons having permanent residence within Vatican City are subject to the sovereignty of the Holy See. Such residence is not lost by reason of the mere fact of temporary residence elsewhere, unless accompanied by the loss of a dwelling place in the City itself or by other circumstances proving that such residence has been abandoned.

On ceasing to be subject to the sovereignty of the Holy See, the persons referred to in the preceding paragraph who, according to the provisions of Italian law, independently of the factual circumstances considered above, are not to be considered as possessing another citizenship, will be regarded in Italy as certainly being Italian citizens.

While such persons are subject to the sovereignty of the Holy See, the provisions of Italian legislation will be applicable to them within the territory of the Kingdom of Italy, even in those matters wherein personal law must be observed (when such matters are not regulated by rules issued by the Holy See) and, in the case of persons considered to possess another citizenship, the legislative provisions of the State to which they belong.

Article 10

The dignitaries of the Church and the persons belonging to the Papal Court, who will be indicated in a list to be agreed upon by the Contracting Parties, will always and in every case, even when not citizens of the Vatican, be exempt, as far as Italy is concerned, from military service, jury duty, and any other obligation of a personal nature.

This provision also applies to regular officials whose services are declared to be indispensable by the Holy See, who are permanently employed with fixed salary by the offices of the Holy See as well as the Dicasteries and Offices to be indicated in Articles 13, 14, 15, and 16, existing outside of Vatican City. The names of such officials will be set forth in another list to be agreed upon as above mentioned, and which will be brought up to date each year by the Holy See.

Ecclesiastics who, for reasons of office, participate outside Vatican City in the issuance of enactments of the Holy See are not subject, on that account, to any hindrance, investigation, or disturbance on the part of the Italian authorities.

Every foreign person holding an ecclesiastical office in Rome enjoys the personal guarantees belonging to Italian citizens in virtue of the laws of the Kingdom.

Article 11

The central entities of the Catholic Church are exempt from any interference on the part of the Italian State (except as provided by Italian law in regard to acquisitions made by corporate persons) and from conversion with regard to real estate.

Article 12

Italy recognizes the right of the Holy See to active and passive Legation, according to the general rules of International Law.

Envoys of foreign Governments to the Holy See continue to enjoy, within the Kingdom, all the prerogatives and immunities enjoyed by diplomatic agents under International Law, and their headquarters may continue to remain within Italian territory enjoying the immunities due them under International Law, even if their States do not have diplomatic relations with Italy.

It is understood that Italy commits itself to leave free always and in every case the correspondence from all States, including belligerents, to the Holy See and vice versa, as well as to allow free access to the Apostolic See by Bishops from all over the world.

The Contracting Parties commit themselves to establish normal diplomatic relations between them, by means the accreditation of an Italian Ambassador to the Holy See and of a Papal Nuncio to Italy, who will be the Dean of the Diplomatic Corps, in accordance with the customary right recognized by the Congress of Vienna by the Act of 9 June 1815.

In consequence of the sovereignty hereby recognized and without prejudice to the provisions established by Article 19 hereafter, the diplomats of the Holy See and the diplomatic couriers dispatched in the name of the Supreme Pontiff enjoy within Italian territory, even in time of war, the same treatment as that enjoyed by diplomatic personages and official couriers of other foreign Governments, according to the provisions of International Law.

Article 13

Italy recognizes the full ownership of the Holy See over the patriarchal Basilicas of St. John Lateran, Saint Mary Major and St. Paul, with their annexed buildings (Attachment II, 1, 2 and 3).

The State transfers to the Holy See the free management and administration of said Basilica of St. Paul and its attached Monastery, also paying over to the Holy See the sum of capital corresponding to the sums set aside annually for that Basilica in the budget of the Ministry of Education.

It is likewise understood that the Holy See is the free owner of its dependent building of San Callisto, adjoining Santa Maria in Trastevere (Attachment II, 9).

Article 14

Italy recognizes the full ownership by the Holy See of the Papal Palace of Castel Gandolfo, together with all endowments, appurtenances, and dependencies thereof (Attachment II, 4), which are now already in the possession of the Holy See, and Italy also obliges itself to hand over to the Holy See, within six months after the coming into force of the present Treaty, Villa Barberini in Castel Gandolfo, together with all endowments, appurtenances, and dependencies thereof (Attachment II, 5).

In order to consolidate the ownership of the real estate situated on the northern side of the Janiculum Hill belonging to the Sacred Congregation of Propaganda Fide and other ecclesiastical institutions, and facing the Vatican Palaces, the State commits itself to transfer to the Holy See or other bodies indicated by it, all real estate belonging to the State or to third parties existing in said area. The properties belonging to said Congregation and other institutions and those to be transferred are marked on the attached map (Attachment II, 12).

Finally, Italy transfers to the Holy See, in full and free ownership, the former conventual buildings in Rome attached to the Basilica of the Twelve Holy Apostles and to the churches of San Andrea della Valle and San Carlo ai Catinari, with all annexes and dependencies thereof (Attachment III, 3, 4 and 5), and will hand them over, free of all occupants, within one year after the entry into force of the present Treaty.

Article 15

The properties indicated in Article 13 hereof and the first and second paragraphs of Article 14, as well as the Palaces of the Dataria, of the Cancelleria, and of Propaganda Fide in Piazza di Spagna, the Palace of the Holy Office with its annexes, that of the Convertendi (now the Congregation for the Eastern Church) in Piazza Scossacavalli, the Palace of the Vicariate, and the other edifices in which the Holy See will in the future desire to locate others of its Dicasteries, even if such edifices form part of the territory of the Italian State, will enjoy the immunities granted by International Law to the headquarters of the diplomatic agents of foreign States.

The same immunities apply also with regard to other churches (even if situated outside Rome) during such time in which, without such churches being open to the public, religious ceremonies are celebrated in them with the participation of the Supreme Pontiff.

Article 16

The buildings mentioned in the three preceding Articles, as well as those used as headquarters of the following Pontifical institutions: the Gregorian University, the Biblical, Oriental, and Archaeological Institutes, the Russian Seminary, the Lombard College, the two Palaces of St. Apollinaris, and the Clergy Retreat House of Sts. John and Paul (Attachment III, 1, 1bis, 2, 6, 7, 8), will never be subject to liens or to expropriation for reasons of public utility, save by previous agreement with the Holy See, and will be exempt from taxes, whether ordinary or extraordinary, whether payable to the State or to any other body whatsoever.

It is possible for the Holy See to give all the buildings above mentioned or referred to in the three preceding Articles the arrangement it deems fit, without need of the authorization or consent of the Italian governmental, provincial, or communal authorities, which authorities can in this regard rely safely on the noble artistic traditions which the Catholic Church possesses.

Article 17

As from 1 January 1929, compensation of whatsoever nature payable by the Holy See, by other central bodies of the Catholic Church and by bodies administered directly by the Holy See even outside of Rome, to dignitaries, employees and paid workers, even temporary ones, will be exempt within Italian territory from any tax whether payable to the State or to any other body.

Article 18

The treasures of art and science existing within Vatican City and the Lateran Palace will remain open to scholars and visitors, reserving to the Holy See full liberty to regulate the access of the public.

Article 19

Diplomats and envoys of the Holy See, diplomats and envoys of foreign Governments accredited to the Holy See, and dignitaries of the Church arriving from abroad and travelling to Vatican City, holding passports of their States of origin, furnished with the visa of the Papal representative abroad, will be able to have access to Vatican City through Italian territory without any other formality. The same applies for the above-mentioned persons who, holding a regular pontifical passport, will travel to Vatican City from abroad.

Article 20

Goods arriving from abroad and destined for Vatican City or destined for institutions or offices of the Holy See outside its boundaries, will always be admitted from any point of the Italian frontier and in any seaport of the Kingdom for transit through Italian territory, with full exemption from customs fees and duty.

Article 21

All Cardinals enjoy in Italy the honours due to Princes of the Blood. Those Cardinals who reside in Rome outside Vatican City are, for all effects, citizens thereof.

During the vacancy of the Holy See, Italy shall make special arrangements to see that nothing impedes the free transit and access of Cardinals through Italian territory to the Vatican, and shall provide that no impediment or limitation is placed on their personal liberty.

Italy shall also see that within its territory surrounding Vatican City no acts are committed which could possibly disturb the meetings of the Conclave.

The same provisions also apply for Conclaves held outside of Vatican City and for Councils presided over by the Supreme Pontiff or his Legates, also with regard to all Bishops summoned to attend them.

Article 22

At the request of the Holy See, or by its delegation which may be given in individuals cases or permanently, Italy will provide within its territory for the punishment of crimes committed within

Vatican City, except when the author of the crime will have taken refuge in Italian territory, in which event he will be certainly prosecuted according to the provisions of Italian laws.

The Holy See will hand over to the Italian State persons who may have taken refuge within Vatican City and who have been accused of acts, committed within Italian territory, which are considered to be criminal by the laws of both States.

The same provisions will apply in regard to persons accused of crimes who may have taken refuge within the buildings declared to be immune in Art. 15 hereof, unless the persons in charge of such buildings prefer to invite the Italian police agents to enter them in order to arrest such persons.

Article 23

The regulations of International Law will apply for the execution, within the Kingdom, of sentences pronounced by the Courts of Vatican City.

On the other hand, all sentences and measures emanating from ecclesiastical authorities and officially communicated to the civil authorities, concerning ecclesiastical or religious persons and concerning spiritual or disciplinary matters, will without exception have full legal force in Italy, also with all civil effects.

Article 24

In regard to the sovereignty appertaining to it also in the international realm, the Holy See declares that it desires to remain and will remain outside of any temporal rivalries between other States and the international congresses called to settle such matters, unless the contending parties make a mutual appeal to its mission of peace; it reserves to itself in any case the right to exercise its moral and spiritual power.

Consequently, Vatican City will always and in every case be considered neutral and inviolable territory.

Article 25

By a special Convention written below and joined to the present Treaty, which constitutes Attachment IV to the same and forms an integral part thereof, provision is made for the liquidation of the credits of the Holy See with respect to Italy.

Article 26

The Holy See holds that with the agreements signed today it is guaranteed sufficiently what it requires in order to provide with due liberty and independence for the pastoral governance of the Diocese of Rome and of the Catholic Church in Italy and in the world; it declares that the "Roman Question" has been definitely and irrevocably settled and therefore eliminated and it recognizes the Kingdom of Italy under the Dynasty of the House of Savoy with Rome as the capital of the Italian State.

Italy, on its part, recognizes Vatican City State under the sovereignty of the Supreme Pontiff.

The law of May 13, 1871, no. 214 is hereby abrogated together with any other disposition contrary to the present Treaty.

Article 27

Within four months after the signature thereof, the present Treaty will be submitted to the Supreme Pontiff and the King of Italy for ratification, and will enter into force from the very act of the exchange of ratifications.

Given in Rome this eleventh day of February, One Thousand Nine Hundred and Twenty-Nine.

The law of treaties

DOI: 10.4324/9781003213772-6

BASIC DOCUMENTS ON THE LAW OF TREATIES

Vienna Convention on the Law of Treaties
Vienna Convention on Succession of States in respect of Treaties
Vienna Convention on the Law of Treaties between States and International
Organisations or between International Organisations

Foundational treaties

At the current stage, the basic general multilateral conventions on the law of treaties are:

- **Vienna Convention on the Law of Treaties** (1969);
- **Vienna Convention on Succession of States in respect of Treaties** (1978); and
- **Vienna Convention on the Law of Treaties between States and International Organisations or between International Organisations** (1986 – is not yet in force)[410] [hereinafter referred in this chapter as Vienna Convention (1986)].

Vienna Convention (1969)

Nowadays, the Vienna Convention on the Law of Treaties (1969) [hereinafter referred to in this chapter as Vienna Convention (1969)] is the most foundational international treaty regarding the law of treaties between the states. Although under the Convention, it does not directly affect the legal force of the treaties not covered by the Convention, it can also apply to the agreements concluded by the other subjects of international law or in accordance with any other rules of international law. As stated in the Vienna Convention (1969):

> The fact that the present Convention does not apply to international agreements concluded between States and other subjects of international law or between such other subjects of international law, or to international agreements not in written form, shall not affect:
>
> (a) The legal force of such agreements;
> (b) The application to them of any of the rules set forth in the present Convention to which they would be subject under international law independently of the Convention;
> (c) The application of the Convention to the relations of States as between themselves under international agreements to which other subjects of international law are also parties.[411]

---

410 Article 85(1) of the Vienna Convention (1986): 'The present Convention shall enter into force on the thirtieth day following the date of deposit of the thirty-fifth instrument of ratification or accession by States or by Namibia, represented by the United Nations Council for Namibia.'
411 Article 3 of the Vienna Convention (1969).

PRINCIPLES OF THE LAW OF TREATIES

> *pacta sunt servanda*
> *pacta tertiis nec nocent nec prosunt*
> non-invocation of internal law for justifying non-performance of a treaty
> non-retroactivity of treaties
> application of successive treaties relating to the same subject matter

An illustrative list of principles of the law of treaties

The law of treaties is founded on the following principles:

- *Pacta sunt servanda* (agreements are to be kept) – According to the Vienna Convention (1969)[412] and the identical provision of Vienna Convention (1986),[413] this is defined as follows: 'Every treaty in force is binding upon the parties to it and must be performed by them in good faith.'
- *Pacta tertiis nec nocent nec prosunt* – 'A treaty does not create either obligations or rights for a third State without its consent'.[414] But there are also exceptions to this general rule: (1) peremptory norms of international law; (2) agreements against aggressor;[415] and (3) If the third party uses the right, then '[a] State exercising a right . . . shall comply with the conditions for its exercise provided for in the treaty or established in conformity with the treaty.'[416]
- **Non-invocation of internal law for justifying non-performance of a treaty** – 'A party may not invoke the provisions of its internal law as justification for its failure to perform a treaty.'[417]
- **Non-retroactivity of treaties**

  Unless a different intention appears from the treaty or is otherwise established, its provisions do not bind a party in relation to any act or fact which took place or any situation which ceased to exist before the date of the entry into force of the treaty with respect to that party.[418]

---

412 Article 26 of the Vienna Convention (1969).
413 Article 26 of the Vienna Convention (1986).
414 Article 34 of the Vienna Convention (1969) and similar Article 34 of the Vienna Convention (1986).
415 Article 75 of the Vienna Convention (1969).
416 Article 36 (2) of the Vienna Convention (1969) and the similar Article 36 (3) of the Vienna Convention (1986).
417 Article 27 of the Vienna Convention (1969) and the Vienna Convention (1986).
418 Article 28 of the Vienna Convention (1969) and the Vienna Convention (1986).

- Application of successive treaties relating to the same subject-matter

When all the parties to the earlier treaty are parties also to the later treaty but the earlier treaty is not terminated or suspended in operation under article 59, the earlier treaty applies only to the extent that its provisions are compatible with those of the later treaty.[419]

A treaty shall be considered as terminated if all the parties to it conclude a later treaty relating to the same subject matter and: (a) it appears from the later treaty or is otherwise established that the parties intended that the matter should be governed by that treaty; or (b) the provisions of the later treaty are so far incompatible with those of the earlier one that the two treaties are not capable of being applied at the same time. . . . The earlier treaty shall be considered as only suspended in operation if it appears from the later treaty or is otherwise established that such was the intention of the parties.[420]

DEFINITION AND STRUCTURE OF AN INTERNATIONAL TREATY

written form
nonwritten form
registration
diplomatic languages
official languages
preamble
text part
final part
depositary
agreement
protocol
covenant
convention
pact
exchange of letters

General definition

An international treaty is an agreement concluded between the subjects of international law and governed by international law.

---

419 Article 30 (3) of the Vienna Convention (1969) and the Vienna Convention (1986).
420 Article 59 (1) of the Vienna Convention (1969) and the Vienna Convention (1986).

Definition provided by the Vienna Conventions

According to the relevant Article of the Vienna Convention (1969), which determines the treaty for the purposes of this Convention:

> 'Treaty' means an international agreement concluded between States in written form and governed by international law, whether embodied in a single instrument or in two or more related instruments and whatever its particular designation.[421]

The similar accents are articulated in the corresponding provision of the Vienna Convention (1986) that treaty means international agreement, concluded in written form and which is governed by international law:

> (a) "treaty" means an international agreement governed by international law and concluded in written form:
>
>   (i) between one or more States and one or more international organizations; or
>   (ii) between international organizations, whether that agreement is embodied in a single instrument or in two or more related instruments and whatever its particular designation.[422]

Written or nonwritten forms

Consequently, an international treaty is usually concluded in **written form**, but, at the same time, under international law, the **nonwritten form** is not prohibited.

Registration

To encourage the written form, the institute of **registration** was established. 'Treaties shall, after their entry into force, be transmitted to the Secretariat of the United Nations for registration or filing and recording, as the case may be, and for publication.'[423]

Moreover, Article 102 of the Charter of United Nations prescribes that every treaty 'entered into by any Member of the United Nations after the present Charter comes into force shall as soon as possible be registered with the Secretariat and published by it', and no party to any such treaty or international agreement which has not been registered 'may invoke that treaty or agreement before any organ of the United Nations.'

Languages

Multilateral international treaties are usually made in **diplomatic languages** (English, French, Russian). In the United Nations, there are six **official languages** – English, French, Russian, Chinese, Spanish, and Arabic.

---

421 Article 2 (1) (a) of the Vienna Convention (1969).
422 Article 2 (1) (a) of the Vienna Convention (1986).
423 Article 80 (1) of the Vienna Convention (1969) and Article 81 (1) of the Vienna Convention (1986).

Structure of an international treaty

Generally, an international treaty is made up of the following components:

- **Preamble** – determines the objectives, tasks, principles of the treaty;
- **Text part** – defines the content of the agreement; and
- **Final part** – formulates procedural norms.

The depositary of a treaty

The designation of the **depositary** of a treaty may be made by the negotiating subjects, either in the treaty itself or in some other manner. The functions of the depositary are keeping custody of the original text and any full powers; preparing certified copies of the original text; receiving and keeping custody of any instruments, notifications, and communications relating to the treaty; registering the treaty with the Secretariat of the United Nations; and so on.

Designation of international treaties

An international treaty also may be titled as an (international) **agreement, protocol, covenant, convention, pact,** and so forth or be concluded in the form of an **exchange of letters.** Regardless of designation, all these agreements are equally considered international treaties under international law, and the rules which apply to them are the same.

CONCLUSION OF AN INTERNATIONAL TREATY BETWEEN STATES

negotiations
authentication of text
signature *ad referendum*
initialling of a text
consent to be bound by a treaty
signature
exchange of instruments constituting a treaty
ratification
acceptance, approval
accession
entry into force
reservations

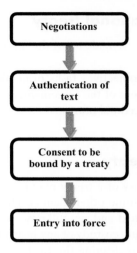

FIGURE 6.1 Stages (phases) of the conclusion of an international treaty

Negotiations

Negotiations can be made in the form of direct diplomatic negotiations or international conference. The adoption of the text of a treaty takes place by the consent of all the subjects participating in its elaboration, with the exception of international conferences, where the text is adopted by the vote of two-thirds of the subjects 'present and voting', unless the same majority decides to apply a different rule.

Persons representing a state

Every subject of international law shall be presented in due and proper form. In the case of states, the following persons may hold full powers:

1 Heads of state, heads of government, and ministers for foreign affairs, for the purpose of performing all acts relating to the conclusion of a treaty;
2 Heads of diplomatic missions, for the purpose of adopting the text of a treaty between the accrediting state and the state to which they are accredited;
3 Representatives accredited by states to an international conference or an international organisation or one of its organs, for the purpose of adopting the text of a treaty in that conference, organisation, or organ;
4 A person who produces appropriate full powers; and
5 A person for whom it appears from the practice of the states concerned or other circumstances that they intended to consider that person as representing the state for such purposes and to dispense with full powers (persons who, without holding any of conventional posts such as the president, head of government, and so forth, are known as officials representing that country).[424]

---

424 Article 6 of the Vienna Convention (1969).

Authentication of text

The goal of the stage of the **authentication of text** is to get an authentic and definitive text. Once a treaty has been authenticated, subjects of international law cannot unilaterally change its provisions. If the subjects which negotiated a given treaty do not agree on specific procedures for authentication, a treaty will usually be authenticated by signature, signature *ad referendum*, or the initialling by the representatives of those subjects.[425]

Signature *ad referendum*

The term **signature *ad referendum*** is used in the international law of treaties to indicate that the signature needs the final confirmation of the responsible authority. The signature *ad referendum* of a treaty by a representative, if confirmed by his authority, constitutes a full signature of the treaty.

Initialling of a text

The **initialling of a text** represents a signature of the treaty when it is established that the negotiating subjects have already so agreed.

Initialling is to mark or sign (a document) with one's initials in order to authorise an authentic and definitive text or validate that the text is ready for signature or – although unusual – prepared for a provisional application.

Consent to be bound by a treaty

Consent to be bound by a treaty represents the next step in the conclusion of an international treaty. As noted earlier, every subject of international law is engaged in the law-making process, and without its consent, no international obligation may arise. Therefore, the consent to be bound by a treaty is a significant step in the creation of rights and obligations under treaties.

The means of expressing consent

There are various means of expressing consent, according to the Vienna Convention (1969):

- **Signature**;
- **Exchange of instruments constituting a treaty**;
- **Ratification**;
- **Acceptance, approval**;
- **Accession**; and
- Any other means if so agreed.

425 Article 10 of the Vienna Convention (1969).

Generally, similar provisions are provided in practice regarding the other subjects of international law with particular differences. Nevertheless, we will next focus on the Vienna Convention (1969) and the mechanisms of consent by the states.

Signature

The signature of its representative expresses the consent of a state to be bound by a treaty if the treaty provides that signature shall have that effect, or it is otherwise established that the negotiating parties agreed that signature should have such an effect. Moreover, according to the Vienna Convention (1969), initialling and signature *ad referendum* are also considered for the purposes of signature. The initialling of a text constitutes a full signature only when the negotiating parties specifically so agree. Without this agreement, it cannot be regarded as the final signature. On the other hand, the signature *ad referendum* automatically constitutes a full signature of the treaty if a state in focus later confirms it.[426]

However, in some instances, the mere signing of a treaty does not make a state a party to the treaty: namely, when the treaty is subject to acceptance, approval, or ratification. In such cases, the signature will essentially mean that the state representatives have agreed upon a text and will additionally express the willingness of the signatory party to continue the treaty-making process. It also stipulates an obligation on a signing state to refrain, in good faith, from acts that would endanger the purpose and existence of the object of the treaty.

Exchange of instruments constituting a treaty

The consent of states to be bound by a treaty is expressed by instruments exchanged between them when:

(a) The instruments provide that their exchange shall have that effect; or
(b) It is otherwise established that those States were agreed that the exchange of instruments shall have that effect.[427]

Ratification

As regards the ratification, numerous multilateral treaties provide for states to express their consent to be bound by signature subject to ratification. The determination of an authority who is entitled to ratify international treaties is an internal affair of a particular state. Usually, the states assign such a function to such organs as a supreme legislative body (parliament), a head of a state, or both of them.[428] Under international law, the ratification is considered a means of the consent of a state to be bound by a treaty only when:

426 Article 12 of the Vienna Convention (1969).
427 Article 13 of the Vienna Convention (1969).
428 As in the case of the United States, where the Senate does not ratify treaties. Instead, the Senate formally gives its advice and consent by a two-thirds vote, empowering the President to proceed with

(a) The treaty provides for such consent to be expressed by means of ratification;

(b) It is otherwise established that the negotiating States were agreed that ratification should be required;

(c) The representative of the State has signed the treaty subject to ratification; or

(d) The intention of the State to sign the treaty subject to ratification appears from the full powers of its representative or was expressed during the negotiation.[429]

Acceptance and approval

Concerning the means of acceptance or approval, consent of a state to be bound by a treaty is expressed under conditions similar to those which apply to ratification. Hence, these means imply the prior signature provided by the representative of the state. In practice, the acceptance and approval are usually used instead of ratification when the treaty itself refers specifically to these procedures, or it is otherwise established that the negotiating states were agreed on that and, at a domestic level, under the respective legislation, this treaty is not subject to ratification. Usually, acceptance and approval procedures are exercised by the executive branch of the government of a country. At the same time, the states independently define the internal organs that are empowered to conduct acceptance or approval.

The suitable organs and persons

In sum, the choice of the means of the state's consent is internationally determined since it is defined under the treaty's final part or through negotiations resulting in the conclusion of the treaty. However, implementation of the means mentioned earlier and the state organs entitled to exercise a particular mechanism are internal issues of a given state. Consequently, a state determines according to its national legislation the appropriate organs and persons for this type of a task.

Accession

And finally, the instrument of accession is provided for subjects who join a treaty after it is already in force and when accession is allowed (it is established that the negotiating parties were agreed that the consent of a subject to be bound by a treaty may be expressed by means of accession). The accession shall be implemented by the means determined under the treaty for consent. Therefore, if, for example, ratification is considered a mechanism of consent, then accession to the treaty shall be fulfilled through the authority which is responsible for ratification according to national law.

---

ratification. This procedure means that under the US Constitution, a power to conclude a binding treaty is a coordinated effort between the executive and legislative branches.

429 Article 14 of the Vienna Convention (1969).

The application of the means of consent

There are procedural rules concerning the starting moment of the application of the means of consent.

> Unless the treaty otherwise provides, instruments of ratification, acceptance, approval or accession establish the consent of a State to be bound by a treaty upon:
>
> (a) Their exchange between the contracting States;
> (b) Their deposit with the depositary; or
> (c) Their notification to the contracting States or to the depositary, if so agreed.[430]

Entry into force

Entry into force is the final stage of the conclusion of an international treaty. It means that a treaty acquires legal force; however, until that moment, obligations determined by a treaty may be legally binding for the subjects who admitted their proper consent and developed the appropriate general practice harmonised with these rules as the norms of customary law.

Meanwhile, there is another mechanism for applying a treaty before its entry into force – the so-called 'provisional application' of a treaty:

> A treaty or a part of a treaty is applied provisionally pending its entry into force if:
> (a) The treaty itself so provides; or (b) The negotiating States have in some other manner so agreed.[431]

The procedure of entry of a treaty into force is described as a rule in the final procedural part of a treaty. Negotiating subjects may define specific means (signature, exchange of instruments constituting a treaty, ratification, acceptance, approval), quantity (of subjects who shall admit their consent to be bound by a treaty), and dates (or other conditions) for entry of a treaty into force.

1. A treaty enters into force in such manner and upon such date as it may provide or as the negotiating States may agree.
2. Failing any such provision or agreement, a treaty enters into force as soon as consent to be bound by the treaty has been established for all the negotiating States.[432]

In the process of the entry into force, if the consent of a subject to be bound by a treaty is established on a date after the treaty has come into force, the treaty enters into force for that subject on that date, unless the treaty provides otherwise.

---

430 Article 16 of the Vienna Convention (1969).
431 Article 25 of the Vienna Convention (1969).
432 Article 24 of the Vienna Convention (1969).

Reservations

Reservations mean a unilateral statement made by a party when signing, ratifying, accepting, approving, or acceding to a treaty, whereby it aims to exclude or modify the legal effect of certain provisions of the treaty in their application to that subject.

A reservation, an express acceptance of a reservation, and an objection to a reservation, as well as withdrawal of a reservation or an objection to a reservation, must be formulated in writing and communicated to the contracting parties.

Generally, if a treaty expressly authorises a reservation, it does not require any subsequent acceptance by the other contracting parties.

As a rule, concerning the multilateral treaties without a limited number of parties reservations are allowed. In such cases, the following conventional rule applies:

> A State may, when signing, ratifying, accepting, approving or acceding to a treaty, formulate a reservation unless:
>
> **(a)** The reservation is prohibited by the treaty;
> **(b)** The treaty provides that only specified reservations, which do not include the reservation in question, may be made; or
> **(c)** In cases not falling under sub-paragraphs (a) and (b), the reservation is incompatible with the object and purpose of the treaty.[433]

Reservations are not permitted in relation to bilateral international treaties as long as this kind of treaty needs both parties to agree to all terms before it can become binding for them.[434] Hence, if such a reservation before the entry into force of a treaty is submitted, it results in the reopening of negotiations to modify the terms of the agreement.

As regards multilateral treaties with limited parties, reservations are rarely allowed. When it appears from the limited number of the negotiating parties and the object and purpose of a treaty that the application of the treaty in its entirety between all the parties is an essential condition of the consent of each one to be bound by the treaty, a reservation requires acceptance by all the parties.

Finally, in general,

> a reservation is considered to have been accepted by a State if it shall have raised no objection to the reservation by the end of a period of twelve months after it was notified of the reservation or by the date on which it expressed its consent to be bound by the treaty, whichever is later.[435]

---

433 Article 19 of the Vienna Convention (1969).

434 According to the approach of the International Law Commission, such a unilateral statement made by a party cannot be called reservation. See Paragraph 1.6.1 – 'Reservations to bilateral treaties', the Guide to Practice on Reservations to Treaties of 2011.

435 Paragraph 5 of Article 20 of the Vienna Convention (1969).

A complex picture of international rights and obligations provided by reservations

On the whole, reservations make a very complex picture of international rights and obligations, where acceptance of a reservation by another contracting party (if it is needed) or the reservation itself (when there is no necessity for acceptance) moves the engaged subjects into diverse legal relationships. Namely, the reservation modifies for the reserving state in its relations with that other party the provisions of the treaty to which the reservation relates to the extent of the reservation, and vice versa. At the same time, the reservation does not modify the provisions of the treaty for the other parties to the treaty. Therefore, multiple legal conditions might appear based on different rights and obligations for different subjects of the same treaty.

Impermissible reservations

However, over time, numerous disagreements have arisen between the parties to several treaties, regarding the limits of reservations, especially with regard to the provision on the impermissibility of a reservation if 'the reservation is incompatible with the object and purpose of the treaty.'

Some international bodies outlined the specific fields in which the general approach of the Vienna Convention (1969) on reservations 'is inappropriate' to address the problem of reservations in such fields. For example, the UN Human Rights Committee in 1994 adopted General Comment No. 24, which states that

> it is the Vienna Convention on the Law of Treaties that provides the definition of reservations and also the application of the object and purpose test in the absence of other specific provisions. But the Committee believes that its provisions on the role of State objections in relation to reservations are inappropriate to address the problem of reservations to human rights treaties. Such treaties, and the Covenant specifically, are not a web of inter-State exchanges of mutual obligations. They concern the endowment of individuals with rights.[436]

On the whole, the Committee targeted to interpret the rules of international law in such a way as to limit the right of the states' parties concerning reservations in the human rights field. Some states, by contrast, declared that monitoring bodies (such as the UN Human Rights Committee) cannot decide whether a reservation is permissible or not since their functions should be restricted to making recommendations to the parties to the respective treaty which the monitoring body has established.

At the same time, there are the particular rules which are shared between the subjects of international law in general; for instance, reservations that offend against the

---

436 UN Human Rights Committee, CCPR General Comment No. 24, 'Issues Relating to Reservations Made upon Ratification or Accession to the Covenant or the Optional Protocols thereto, or in Relation to Declarations under Article 41 of the Covenant' (4 November 1994) <www.refworld.org/docid/453883fc11.html> accessed 16 March 2021.

peremptory norms of general international law would not be compatible with the object and purpose of a treaty.

To overcome the disagreements and misunderstandings, the International Law Commission developed a comprehensive document, the 'Guide to Practice on Reservations to Treaties', which was annexed to the UN General Assembly Resolution in 2013.[437] The document resolved many disputable issues, including the matter discussed earlier. According to the ILC approach, the

> following may assess, within their respective competences, the permissibility of reservations to a treaty formulated by a State or an international organization:
>
> - contracting States or contracting organizations;
> - dispute settlement bodies;
> - treaty monitoring bodies.[438]

CONCLUSION OF INTERNATIONAL TREATIES AND OTHER SUBJECTS OF INTERNATIONAL LAW

limited international personality
particular nature of a certain subject
Vienna Convention on the Law of Treaties between States and International
Organisations or between International Organisations
act of formal confirmation

Similar terms, principles, structure, and means

The conclusion of international treaties by other subjects of international law represents part of international treaty law. Therefore, in this case, the same terms, principles, structure, and means as regarding the treaties of states are generally applicable.

Differences

However, there are significant distinctions, first of all, rooted in the modern concept of international law, where other subjects possess **limited international personality** unlike that of the states which possess full and unconditional international personality. Consequently, the capacity of the other subjects of international law to conclude international treaties is determined via their international status. For instance, the capacity of international organisations to conclude international treaties is governed and restricted by the

---

437 A/RES/68/111 of 19 December 2013.
438 Article 3.2 (Assessment of the permissibility of reservations) of the Text of the guidelines constituting the Guide to Practice on Reservations to Treaties.

founding rules of the organisations, i.e. constituent instruments, and decisions and resolutions adopted in accordance with them.[439]

On the other hand, differences in the conclusion of international treaties are maintained through the **particular nature of a certain subject**. For example, the composition of international organisations stipulates such distinctions concerning the means of expressing consent as they are not the states, and specific methods available to states are not applicable to them.

International organisations

Concerning international organisations, main terms and specifics have been defined under the **Vienna Convention on the Law of Treaties between States and International Organisations or between International Organisations**, in which the 'international organisation' means an intergovernmental organisation. Although this convention has not entered into force until now, many norms formulated there are considered rules and principles of customary international law and general principles of law. For instance, the Vienna Convention (1986) determines who can represent the international organisation, which can be regarded as an established rule of general customary international law:

> A person is considered as representing an international organization for the purpose of adopting or authenticating the text of a treaty, or expressing the consent of that organization to be bound by a treaty, if:
>
> (a) that person produces appropriate full powers; or
> (b) it appears from the circumstances that it was the intention of the States and international organizations concerned to consider that person as representing the organization for such purposes, in accordance with the rules of the organization, without having to produce full powers.[440]

Regarding the stages of negotiation, authentication of text, consent to be bound by a treaty, entry into force, reservations, and so on, we can emphasise the similarities with the law of treaties between states in terms, approaches, and so forth. For example, as it is prescribed according to the relevant Article of the Vienna Convention (1986):

> The text of a treaty between international organizations is established as authentic and definitive: (a) by such procedure as may be provided for in the text or agreed upon by the organizations participating in its drawing up; or (b) failing such procedure, by the signature, signature *ad referendum* or initialling by the representatives of those States and those organizations of the text of the treaty or of the Final Act of a conference incorporating the text.[441]

However, as noted earlier, there are also significant differences basically caused by the specific nature of the international organisations themselves. For example, the specific

439 Article 6 (3) of the Vienna Convention (1986).
440 Article 7 of the Vienna Convention (1986).
441 Article 10 (2) of the Vienna Convention (1986).

Article of the Vienna Convention (1986) which does not consider ratification as an appropriate means for an international organisation and instead articulates the **act of formal confirmation**: 'The consent of an international organization to be bound by a treaty may be expressed by signature, exchange of instruments constituting a treaty, act of formal confirmation, acceptance, approval or accession, or by any other means if so agreed.'[442] Thus, the act of formal confirmation means an international act corresponding to that of an act of ratification by a state whereby an international organisation constitutes its consent to be bound by a treaty.[443]

INTERPRETATION OF INTERNATIONAL TREATIES

> good faith
> ordinary meaning
> context
> object and purpose of the treaty
> special meaning
> supplementary means of interpretation

The principle of good faith

The general principle of law '**good faith**' is considered to be a foundational principle for the interpretation of international treaties. According to the aforementioned principle, every treaty shall be interpreted in good faith (1) in accordance with the **ordinary meaning** to be given to the terms of the treaty, (2) by introspecting into its **context** and (3) with a view to the **object and purpose of the treaty**.

Ordinary and special meaning

An ordinary meaning is a general basis for an interpretation. However, a **special meaning** shall be given to a term if it is defined that the parties so intended.

Context

The context for the interpretation shall comprise the text, its preamble, and its annexes, as well as any agreement or instrument relating to the treaty which was made between all the parties in connection with the conclusion of the treaty.

> There shall be taken into account, together with the context: (a) Any subsequent agreement between the parties regarding the interpretation of the treaty or the application of its provisions; (b) Any subsequent practice in the application of the

---

442 Article 11 (2) of the Vienna Convention (1986).
443 Article 2, paragraph 1.b bis of the Vienna Convention (1986).

treaty which establishes the agreement of the parties regarding its interpretation; (c) Any relevant rules of international law applicable in the relations between the parties.[444]

There are also the **supplementary means of interpretation**, which include the preparatory work done on the treaty and the circumstances of its conclusion.

Authentic texts

When a treaty has been authenticated in two or more languages, the text is equally authoritative in each language, unless the treaty provides otherwise or the parties agree that in case of divergence between the translations, a particular text shall prevail. On the other hand, when a comparison of the authentic texts discloses a difference of meaning which the application of means of interpretation does not remove, the meaning which best reconciles the texts, having regard to the object and purpose of the treaty, shall be adopted.[445]

AMENDMENT AND MODIFICATION OF INTERNATIONAL TREATIES

> amendment
> modification
> rights or obligations of the other parties
> object and purpose of the treaty

The general meanings

According to the Vienna Conventions (1969 and 1986), the term **amendment** denotes an agreement between the parties to change the provisions of a treaty with respect to all parties. In contrast, the term **modification** refers to an agreement concluded between particular subjects intended to alter provisions of a multilateral treaty among themselves. However, the modification can shift from its original form and become an amendment if all the parties accept the intended modification of a treaty.

Amendment of treaties

In international treaty law, there is the general rule regarding amendments that they shall undergo the same formalities as was the case during the initial elaboration of the treaty. Commonly, in order to adopt amendments, the international treaties lay down specific

444 Article 31 of the Vienna Convention (1969).
445 Article 33 of the Vienna Convention (1969).

requirements which should be satisfied. In the absence of such provisions, there is an obligation that notifications be sent to all the contracting parties, and an agreement must be reached between the parties so that the amendments may be adopted. Every subject entitled to become a party to the treaty shall also be entitled to become a party to the treaty as amended.

The amending agreement does not bind any subject already a party to the treaty which does not become a party to the amending agreement. A subject which becomes a party to the treaty after the entry into force of the amending agreement shall, failing an expression of a different intention by that subject, '(a) be considered as a party to the treaty as amended; and (b) be considered as a party to the unamended treaty in relation to any party to the treaty not bound by the amending agreement.'[446]

Modification of treaties

Due to the diverging interests of the subjects of international law at an international level, amendment of treaties with a large number of parties proves to be a complicated process. Meanwhile, some of the parties may wish to modify the treaty as between them alone. Therefore, in the international treaty law, an institute of the modification of multilateral treaties between particular parties (modifying agreement *inter se*)[447] is introduced, which is allowed if:

1   the treaty provides the possibility of such modification;
2   although the treaty does not directly permit the modification, it is at least not prohibited by its provisions, and additionally

    a   does not affect the **rights or obligations of the other parties** to the treaty; or
    b   does not contravene with the **object and purpose of the treaty**.[448]

At the same time, the parties intending a modification have the general obligation to notify the other parties of their intention to conclude such an agreement as well as to communicate the text of the modification to the treaty.

INVALIDITY, TERMINATION, AND SUSPENSION OF THE OPERATION OF AN INTERNATIONAL TREATY

non-separability of treaty provisions
absolute invalidity
relative invalidity

---

446 Article 40 of the Vienna Conventions (1969 and 1986).
447 *Inter se* is a Latin phrase and means: '[b]etween themselves'. *Guide to Latin in International Law* (n 71) 142.
448 Article 41 of the Vienna Conventions (1969 and 1986).

vitiation of consent
coercion of a representative
coercion of a party
incompetence of an agent
error
fraud
corruption
manifest violation of a provision of the fundamental importance of internal rule
lack of the appropriate full powers
violation of notified specific restrictions on authority
termination
withdrawal
suspension
denunciation
material breach of a treaty
supervening impossibility of performance
fundamental change of circumstances

Preliminary remark

Under international law, there are some general rules established regarding the invalidity, termination, and suspension of operation of international treaties.

Application of the provisions of the treaty or other international law norms

Firstly, the validity of a treaty, the termination of or withdrawal from a treaty, or the suspension of the operation of a treaty may take place only as a result of the application of the provisions of the treaty or based on the other norms of international law.[449]

Obligations imposed by international law independently of a treaty

Secondly, the invalidity, termination of or withdrawal from a treaty or the suspension of the operation of a treaty as a result of the application of the law of treaties shall not in any way impair the obligations of a party imposed by international law independently of a treaty.[450]

449 Article 42 of the Vienna Conventions (1969 and 1986).
450 Article 43 of the Vienna Conventions (1969 and 1986).

The non-separability and separability of treaty provisions

Thirdly, in the law of treaties, the **non-separability of treaty provisions** is the general rule, including concerning the invalidity, termination, or suspension of operation of an international treaty, unless the treaty provides another rule or the parties agree otherwise. However,

> If the ground relates solely to particular clauses, it may be invoked only with respect to those clauses where: (a) the said clauses are separable from the remainder of the treaty with regard to their application; (b) it appears from the treaty or is otherwise established that acceptance of those clauses was not an essential basis of the consent of the other party or parties to be bound by the treaty as a whole; and (c) continued performance of the remainder of the treaty would not be unjust.[451]

Loss of a right to invoke a ground for invalidating, terminating, withdrawing from, or suspending the operation of a treaty

Fourthly, there exists a condition which may lead to a loss of the right to invoke a ground for invalidating, terminating, withdrawing from, or suspending the operation of a treaty, if the subject shall have expressly or implicitly agreed that the treaty is valid, remains in force, or continues to operate, as the case may be.[452]

The consequences of invalidity

The invalidity of a treaty means nullity of the treaty or of its particular provisions, and such a treaty or its provisions have no legal force. As a result, each contracting party may require any other party to establish whenever possible in their mutual relations the position which would have existed if the acts had not been performed.

However, a ground for invalidating a treaty may be invoked only with respect to the whole treaty, except where it relates solely to a particular clause which is separable, acceptance of this clause was not an essential basis of the consent from the other party or parties, and if performance of the remainder of the treaty would not be unjust.

Grounds for invalidity

Concerning their legal outcomes, the grounds for invalidity may be either grounds for **absolute invalidity** or **relative invalidity**. In the case of absolute invalidity, the treaty is null and void from the moment it was concluded, whether a ground was invoked by a party or not. As regards the grounds for relative invalidity, in such circumstances, the treaty is valid until a party makes a claim about the invalidity of a treaty: i.e. such a treaty is probably voidable rather than void.

451 Article 44 (3) of the Vienna Conventions (1969 and 1986).
452 Article 45 of the Vienna Conventions (1969 and 1986).

Illegality of the object

A treaty is absolutely void if, at the time of its conclusion, it derogates from a peremptory norm of general international law (*jus cogens*). According to the Vienna Conventions (1969 and 1986), if a treaty is in conflict with a peremptory norm of general international law, the parties shall 'eliminate as far as possible the consequences of any act performed in reliance on any provision which conflicts with the peremptory norm of general international law.'

Vitiation of consent

The **vitiation of consent** or defective intention is one of the conventional grounds for invalidity. It can be either grounds for absolute or relative invalidity. These grounds include (1) **coercion of a representative and** (2) **coercion of a party** (absolute invalidity) and (3) **incompetence of an agent**, (4) **error**, (5) **fraud**, and (6) **corruption** (relative invalidity).

Coercion of a representative of a subject

The expression by a subject of a consent to be bound by a treaty which has been attained by coercing the representative of that party through acts or threats directed against him or her has no legal effect.[453]

Coercion of a subject by the threat or use of force

'A treaty is void if its conclusion has been procured by the threat or use of force in violation of the principles of international law embodied in the Chatter of the United Nations.'[454]

Incompetence of an agent

The following preconditions are included in this ground of invalidity:

- **Manifest violation of a provision of the fundamental importance of internal rule** regarding the competence to conclude treaties. The general rule prescribes that the non-compliance with internal law or internal rules (as in the case of international organisations), requirements regarding the competence to conclude treaties may not be invoked as a reason for invalidating the consent of a party. Nevertheless, the general approach has legal force unless the violation of an internal provision is manifest and concerns a rule of fundamental importance. A violation is manifest if it would be objectively evident to any party conducting itself in the matter in accordance with normal practice and in good faith.[455]

453 Article 51 of the Vienna Conventions (1969 and 1986).
454 Article 52 of the Vienna Convention (1986), similar Article 52 of the 1969 Vienna Convention.
455 Article 46 of the Vienna Conventions (1969 and 1986).

- **Lack of the appropriate full powers** if the representative is not the person who, according to international law, is *ex officio* assignee of a subject (the heads of state or government, ministers for foreign affairs, and so forth).
- **Violation of notified specific restrictions on authority** to express consent to be bound if the restriction was notified to the negotiating parties prior to the expressing of consent.[456]

Error

An error relating only to the wording of the text of a treaty does not affect its validity. The subject may invoke an error in a treaty as invalidating its consent if the error (1) relates to a fact or situation which was assumed by that party to exist at the time when the treaty was concluded and (2) formed an essential basis of its consent to be bound by that treaty. However, this rule shall not apply if the subject in question contributed to the error due to its own conduct or if the circumstances were such as to put that subject on notice of a possible error.[457]

Fraud

A subject may invoke fraud as invalidating its consent to be bound by the treaty if it has been induced to conclude the treaty due to the fraudulent conduct of another negotiating party.[458]

Corruption of a representative of a subject

Expression of consent by the representative of one subject which was attained through the corruption of its representative via direct or indirect means by another negotiating subject may be invoked by the first subject as a reason for invalidating its consent to be bound by the treaty.[459]

Difference between the termination of a treaty, withdrawal from a treaty, and suspension of the operation of a treaty

(1) **Termination** of a treaty, (2) **withdrawal** from a treaty, and (3) **suspension** of the operation of a treaty differ from each other in the legal outcomes which they produce. In the first case, the treaty is terminated entirely for all parties, and in the second case, it is terminated for a withdrawing party while, in the third case, it is only temporarily suspended.

---

456 Article 47 of the Vienna Conventions (1969 and 1986).
457 Article 48 of the Vienna Conventions (1969 and 1986).
458 Article 49 of the Vienna Conventions (1969 and 1986).
459 Article 50 of the Vienna Conventions (1969 and 1986).

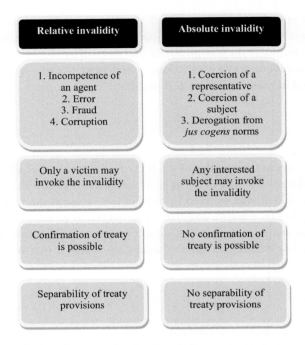

FIGURE 6.2 The grounds for relative or absolute invalidity

The withdrawal of a party from a bilateral treaty simultaneously means the complete termination of a treaty, whereas withdrawal from a multilateral treaty will not typically result in its termination.

Grounds for the termination of or withdrawal from a treaty

The grounds for the termination of or withdrawal from a treaty can be squared down to the following options:

1　Termination of or withdrawal from a treaty

   a)　under its provisions (e.g. expiration of term of the treaty), or

   b)　by consent of the parties;[460]

2　Termination by unilateral will – **denunciation**;[461]

3　Termination of a treaty implied by the conclusion of a later treaty;

4　**Material breach of a treaty;**[462]

460　Article 54 of the Vienna Conventions (1969 and 1986).
461　Article 56 of the Vienna Conventions (1969 and 1986).
462　Article 60 of the Vienna Conventions (1969 and 1986).

5   Supervening impossibility of performance;[463]
6   Fundamental change of circumstances (*clausula rebus sic stantibus*);[464] and
7   Emergence of a new peremptory norm of general international law (*jus cogens*).[465]

Grounds for the suspension of the operation of treaties

The grounds for the suspension of the operation of treaties:

1   Suspension of the operation of a treaty

    a)   based on its provisions, or
    b)   by the consent of the parties;[466]

2   Suspension of the operation of a multilateral treaty due to the agreement between particular parties only;[467]
3   Material breach of a treaty;[468]
4   Supervening impossibility of performance;[469] and
5   Fundamental change of circumstances.[470]

Denunciation of or withdrawal from a treaty containing no direct provision regarding denunciation or withdrawal

Denunciation of or withdrawal from a treaty is a special form of termination of (a full termination) or withdrawal from (termination of a treaty regarding withdrawing party) an international treaty by the unilateral will of a party. Generally, a treaty which includes no provision on denunciation or withdrawal is not subject to them. The denunciation of or withdrawal from a treaty is allowed only when such a provision and corresponding procedures are determined in the treaty or '(a) it is established that the parties intended to admit the possibility of denunciation or withdrawal; or (b) a right of denunciation or withdrawal may be implied by the nature of the treaty.'[471] At the same time, in case of referring to the (a) or (b) preconditions, a party shall deliver a notice on its intention to denounce or withdraw from a treaty no less than twelve months prior.

The terms 'denunciation' and 'withdrawal', in practice, are usually used with regard to bilateral as well as multilateral treaties. However, more proper utilisation of these notions

---

463   Article 61 of the Vienna Conventions (1969 and 1986).
464   Article 62 of the Vienna Conventions (1969 and 1986). The *clausula rebus sic stantibus* is a Latin phrase and means 'By the clause the situation thus remaining'. *Guide to Latin in International Law* (n 71) 55.
465   Article 64 of the Vienna Conventions (1969 and 1986).
466   Article 57 of the Vienna Conventions (1969 and 1986).
467   Article 58 of the Vienna Conventions (1969 and 1986).
468   Article 60 of the Vienna Conventions (1969 and 1986).
469   Article 61 of the Vienna Conventions (1969 and 1986).
470   Article 62 of the Vienna Conventions (1969 and 1986).
471   Article 56 of the Vienna Conventions (1969 and 1986).

stipulates the following possible distinction between them: Denunciation should be mostly practised concerning the bilateral treaties. At the same time, even though denunciation is also applied in relation to multilateral agreements, withdrawal is the term which best corresponds to such a case.

Material breach of a treaty

A material breach of a treaty consists of a repudiation of the treaty not sanctioned by international law or the violation of a provision which is essential for the accomplishment of the object or the purpose of the treaty.

A material breach of a multilateral treaty by one of the parties entitles:

- the other parties due to the unanimous agreement to suspend the operation of the treaty in whole or in part or to terminate it either (a) between themselves and the defaulting subject or (b) between all the parties;
- a party particularly affected by such a breach to invoke it as a precondition for suspending the operation of the treaty in whole or in part between itself and the defaulting subject;
- any party other than the defaulting subject if the treaty is of such a character that a material breach of its provisions by one party radically changes the position of every party concerning the further performance of its obligations under the treaty.

Nevertheless, these rights do not apply to provisions relating to the protection of the humans contained in treaties of a humanitarian character.[472]

Supervening impossibility of performance

Supervening impossibility of performance is considered as grounds for termination or withdrawal: 'if the impossibility results from the permanent disappearance or destruction of an object indispensable for the execution of the treaty. If the impossibility is temporary, it may be invoked only as a ground for suspending the operation of the treaty.'[473]

Fundamental change of circumstances

A fundamental change of circumstances is considered ground for terminating or withdrawing from a treaty, or suspending the operation of a treaty if '(a) the existence of those circumstances constituted an essential basis of the consent of the parties to be bound by the treaty; and (b) the effect of the change is radically to transform the extent of obligations still to be performed under the treaty.'[474]

---

472 Article 60 of the Vienna Conventions (1969 and 1986).
473 Article 61 of the Vienna Conventions (1969 and 1986).
474 Article 62 of the Vienna Conventions (1969 and 1986).

However, this is not applicable in the case of boundaries or 'if the fundamental change is the result of a breach by the party invoking it either of an obligation under the treaty or of any other international obligation owed to any other party to the treaty.'[475]

Severance of diplomatic or consular relations

And finally, a special case is the severance of diplomatic or consular relations between parties to a treaty. In this respect, there is a rule that the severance of diplomatic or consular relations does not affect the legal relations established between the subjects of the treaty 'except insofar as the existence of diplomatic or consular relations is indispensable for the application of the treaty.'[476]

ARMED CONFLICTS AND INTERNATIONAL TREATIES

> UN General Assembly Resolution, Effects of armed conflicts on treaties
> armed conflict does not *ipso facto* terminate or suspend the operation of treaties
> armed conflict does not terminate international treaties with third parties
> prohibition of benefit to an aggressor state
> norms of peaceful coexistence

The general approach

The Vienna Conventions on the Law of Treaties of 1969 and 1986 do not deal with the effects of armed conflict on treaties, apart from stating that the provisions of the conventions shall not prejudice any question that may arise regarding a treaty from the outbreak of hostilities between states.[477] Afterward, the International Law Commission prepared a separate project on this matter.

The UN General Assembly Resolution 'Effects of armed conflicts on treaties'

Under the UN General Assembly Resolution, Effects of armed conflicts on treaties (Resolution 66/99 of 2011), the General Assembly takes note of the articles on the effects of armed conflicts on treaties presented by the International Law Commission.[478] Up until now, the Annex of Resolution, enshrining the articles concerning the effects of armed conflicts on treaties, remains an example of soft law; however, it partly is composed of certain rules which make up the general international law norms on this matter.

---

475 Article 62 (2) of the Vienna Conventions (1969 and 1986).
476 Article 63 of the Vienna Conventions (1969 and 1986).
477 Article 73 of the Vienna Convention (1969) and Article 74 of the Vienna Convention (1986).
478 A/RES/66/99 of 9 December 2011.

Established rules

On the whole, this field of international treaty law has been very controversial until now. However, we can discover some shared rules which are reflected in practice and may have mandatory power founded either on international treaties or international customs.

1   Armed conflict does not *ipso facto* [479] terminate or suspend the operation of treaties between states which are parties to the conflict.[480]
2   The outbreak of an **armed conflict does not terminate international treaties with third parties.**
3   When a treaty itself prescribes the provisions regulating its operation in situations of an armed conflict, those provisions shall apply.[481]
4   During an armed conflict, a subject which is a party to that conflict has the full capacity to conclude treaties in accordance with international law.[482]
5   A subject exercising the right to individual or collective self-defence is entitled to suspend in whole or in part the operation of a treaty to which it is a party insofar as that operation is incompatible with the exercise of that right.[483]
6   Against the aggressor state, the victim of aggression can rely on the rules of international law concerning the material breach of a treaty since the aggressor state is in violation of a vast complex of norms. On the other hand, the aggressor has no right to terminate or suspend the international treaty if the termination or suspension gives it the advantage since a **prohibition of benefit to an aggressor state** exists in international law.
7   Commonly, the international **norms of peaceful coexistence** between the belligerent parties are considered as stagnant. (In particular cases, the rules of the supervening impossibility of performance or fundamental change of circumstances are applicable.) However, in the Annex of UN General Assembly Resolution 66/99 is formulated an indicative list of treaties the subject matter of which involves an implication that they continue to operate in whole or in part during the armed conflicts. The following treaties have such subject matter:

- Treaties on the law of armed conflict, including treaties on international humanitarian law;
- Treaties declaring, creating, or regulating a permanent regime or status or related permanent rights, including treaties establishing or modifying land and maritime boundaries;

479 *Ipso facto* is a Latin phrase and means "'[b]y the fact itself." By virtue of the fact alone and without other, intervening facts; by the very nature of the facts.' *Guide to Latin in International Law* (n 71) 144.
480 Article 3 of the Annex to the Resolution 66/99 'Effects of armed conflicts on treaties'.
481 Article 4 of the Annex to the Resolution 66/99 'Effects of armed conflicts on treaties'.
482 Article 8 of the Annex to the Resolution 66/99 'Effects of armed conflicts on treaties'.
483 Article 14 of the Annex to the Resolution A/RES/66/99 of 9 December 2011 'Effects of armed conflicts on treaties'.

- Multilateral law-making treaties;
- Treaties on international criminal justice;
- Treaties of friendship, commerce, and navigation and agreements concerning private rights;
- Treaties for the international protection of human rights;
- Treaties relating to the international protection of the environment;
- Treaties relating to international watercourses and related installations and facilities;
- Treaties relating to aquifers and related installations and facilities;
- Treaties which are constituent instruments of international organisations;
- Treaties relating to the international settlement of disputes by peaceful means, including resort to conciliation, mediation, arbitration, and judicial settlement; and
- Treaties relating to diplomatic and consular relations.[484]

CASES AND MATERIALS (*SELECTED PARTS*)

The law of Treaties

Vienna Convention on the Law of Treaties
of 1969
Entry into force: 27 January 1980

PART I.
INTRODUCTION

Article 1 Scope of the present Convention

The present Convention applies to treaties between States.

---

484 lso included in the indicative list are treaties relating to diplomatic relations. While the experience is not well documented, it is not unusual for embassies to remain open in time of armed conflict. In any event the provisions of the Vienna Convention on Diplomatic Relations suggest its application in time of armed conflict. Indeed, Article 24 of that Convention provides that the archives and documents of the mission shall be inviolable "at any time"; this phrase was added during the Vienna Conference in order to make clear that inviolability continued in the event of armed conflict.' 'As in the case of treaties relating to diplomatic relations, so also in the case of treaties relating to consular relations, there is a strong case for placing such treaties within the class of agreements which are not necessarily terminated or suspended in case of an armed conflict. *It is well recognized that consular relations may continue even in the event of severance of diplomatic relations or of armed conflict.*' International Law Commission's Commentaries 71, 73 on the Indicative list of treaties, Draft Articles on the effects of armed conflicts on treaties, with commentaries, 2011.

Article 2 Use of terms

1   For the purposes of the present Convention:

(a) "treaty" means an international agreement concluded between States in written form and governed by international law, whether embodied in a single instrument or in two or more related instruments and whatever its particular designation;

(b) "ratification", "acceptance", "approval" and "accession" mean in each case the international act so named whereby a State establishes on the international plane its consent to be bound by a treaty;

(c) "full powers" means a document emanating from the competent authority of a State designating a person or persons to represent the State for negotiating, adopting or authenticating the text of a treaty, for expressing the consent of the State to be bound by a treaty, or for accomplishing any other act with respect to a treaty;

(d) "reservation" means a unilateral statement, however phrased or named, made by a State, when signing, ratifying, accepting, approving or acceding to a treaty, whereby it purports to exclude or to modify the legal effect of certain provisions of the treaty in their application to that State;

(e) "negotiating State" means a State which took part in the drawing up and adoption of the text of the treaty;

(f) "contracting State" means a State which has consented to be bound by the treaty, whether or not the treaty has entered into force;

(g) "party" means a State which has consented to be bound by the treaty and for which the treaty is in force;

(h) "third State" means a State not a party to the treaty;

(i) "international organization" means an intergovernmental organization.

2   The provisions of paragraph 1 regarding the use of terms in the present Convention are without prejudice to the use of those terms or to the meanings which may be given to them in the internal law of any State.

Article 3 International agreements not within the scope of the present Convention

The fact that the present Convention does not apply to international agreements concluded between States and other subjects of international law or between such other subjects of international law, or to international agreements not in written form, shall not affect:

(a) the legal force of such agreements;

(b) the application to them of any of the rules set forth in the present Convention to which they would be subject under international law independently of the Convention;

(c) the application of the Convention to the relations of States as between themselves under international agreements to which other subjects of international law are also parties.

Article 4 Non-retroactivity of the present Convention

Without prejudice to the application of any rules set forth in the present Convention to which treaties would be subject under international law independently of the Convention, the Convention applies only to treaties which are concluded by States after the entry into force of the present Convention with regard to such States.

Article 5 Treaties constituting international organizations and treaties adopted within an international organization

The present Convention applies to any treaty which is the constituent instrument of an international organization and to any treaty adopted within an international organization without prejudice to any relevant rules of the organization.

PART II.
CONCLUSION AND ENTRY INTO FORCE OF TREATIES

Section 1. Conclusion of treaties

Article 6 Capacity of States to conclude treaties

Every State possesses capacity to conclude treaties.

Article 7 Full powers

1   A person is considered as representing a State for the purpose of adopting or authenticating the text of a treaty or for the purpose of expressing the consent of the State to be bound by a treaty if:

(a)   he produces appropriate full powers; or
(b)   it appears from the practice of the States concerned or from other circumstances that their intention was to consider that person as representing the State for such purposes and to dispense with full powers.

2   In virtue of their functions and without having to produce full powers, the following are considered as representing their State:

(a)   Heads of State, Heads of Government and Ministers for Foreign Affairs, for the purpose of performing all acts relating to the conclusion of a treaty;
(b)   heads of diplomatic missions, for the purpose of adopting the text of a treaty between the accrediting State and the State to which they are accredited;
(c)   representatives accredited by States to an international conference or to an international organization or one of its organs, for the purpose of adopting the text of a treaty in that conference, organization or organ.

Article 8 Subsequent confirmation of an act performed without authorization

An act relating to the conclusion of a treaty performed by a person who cannot be considered under article 7 as authorized to represent a State for that purpose is without legal effect unless afterwards confirmed by that State.

Article 9 Adoption of the text

1   The adoption of the text of a treaty takes place by the consent of all the States participating in its drawing up except as provided in paragraph 2.
2   The adoption of the text of a treaty at an international conference takes place by the vote of two thirds of the States present and voting, unless by the same majority they shall decide to apply a different rule.

Article 10 Authentication of the text

The text of a treaty is established as authentic and definitive:

(a)   by such procedure as may be provided for in the text or agreed upon by the States participating in its drawing up; or
(b)   failing such procedure, by the signature, signature ad referendum or initialling by the representatives of those States of the text of the treaty or of the Final Act of a conference incorporating the text.

Article 11 Means of expressing consent to be bound by a treaty

The consent of a State to be bound by a treaty may be expressed by signature, exchange of instruments constituting a treaty, ratification, acceptance, approval or accession, or by any other means if so agreed.

Article 12 Consent to be bound by a treaty expressed by signature

1   The consent of a State to be bound by a treaty is expressed by the signature of its representative when:

(a)   the treaty provides that signature shall have that effect;
(b)   it is otherwise established that the negotiating States were agreed that signature should have that effect; or
(c)   the intention of the State to give that effect to the signature appears from the full powers of its representative or was expressed during the negotiation.

2   For the purposes of paragraph 1:

(a)   the initialling of a text constitutes a signature of the treaty when it is established that the negotiating States so agreed;
(b)   the signature ad referendum of a treaty by a representative, if confirmed by his State, constitutes a full signature of the treaty.

Article 13 Consent to be bound by a treaty expressed by an exchange of instruments constituting a treaty

The consent of States to be bound by a treaty constituted by instruments exchanged between them is expressed by that exchange when:

(a)   the instruments provide that their exchange shall have that effect; or

(b) it is otherwise established that those States were agreed that the exchange of instruments should have that effect.

Article 14 Consent to be bound by a treaty expressed by ratification, acceptance or approval

1 The consent of a State to be bound by a treaty is expressed by ratification when:

    (a) the treaty provides for such consent to be expressed by means of ratification;

    (b) it is otherwise established that the negotiating States were agreed that ratification should be required;

    (c) the representative of the State has signed the treaty subject to ratification; or

    (d) the intention of the State to sign the treaty subject to ratification appears from the full powers of its representative or was expressed during the negotiation.

2 The consent of a State to be bound by a treaty is expressed by acceptance or approval under conditions similar to those which apply to ratification.

Article 15 Consent to be bound by a treaty expressed by accession

The consent of a State to be bound by a treaty is expressed by accession when:

(a) the treaty provides that such consent may be expressed by that State by means of accession;

(b) it is otherwise established that the negotiating States were agreed that such consent may be expressed by that State by means of accession; or

(c) all the parties have subsequently agreed that such consent may be expressed by that State by means of accession.

Article 16 Exchange or deposit of instruments of ratification, acceptance, approval or accession

Unless the treaty otherwise provides, instruments of ratification, acceptance, approval or accession establish the consent of a State to be bound by a treaty upon:

(a) their exchange between the contracting States;

(b) their deposit with the depositary; or

(c) their notification to the contracting States or to the depositary, if so agreed.

Article 17 Consent to be bound by part of a treaty and choice of differing provisions

1 Without prejudice to articles 19 to 23, the consent of a State to be bound by part of a treaty is effective only if the treaty so permits or the other contracting States so agree.

2 The consent of a State to be bound by a treaty which permits a choice between differing provisions is effective only if it is made clear to which of the provisions the consent relates.

Article 18 Obligation not to defeat the object and purpose of a treaty prior to its entry into force

A State is obliged to refrain from acts which would defeat the object and purpose of a treaty when:

(a) it has signed the treaty or has exchanged instruments constituting the treaty subject to ratification, acceptance or approval, until it shall have made its intention clear not to become a party to the treaty; or

(b) it has expressed its consent to be bound by the treaty, pending the entry into force of the treaty and provided that such entry into force is not unduly delayed.

SECTION 2. RESERVATIONS

Article 19 Formulation of reservations

A State may, when signing, ratifying, accepting, approving or acceding to a treaty, formulate a reservation unless:

(a) the reservation is prohibited by the treaty;

(b) the treaty provides that only specified reservations, which do not include the reservation in question, may be made; or

(c) in cases not failing under subparagraphs (a) and (b), the reservation is incompatible with the object and purpose of the treaty.

Article 20 Acceptance of and objection to reservations

1 A reservation expressly authorized by a treaty does not require any subsequent acceptance by the other contracting States unless the treaty so provides.

2 When it appears from the limited number of the negotiating States and the object and purpose of a treaty that the application of the treaty in its entirety between all the parties is an essential condition of the consent of each one to be bound by the treaty, a reservation requires acceptance by all the parties.

3 When a treaty is a constituent instrument of an international organization and unless it otherwise provides, a reservation requires the acceptance of the competent organ of that organization.

4 In cases not falling under the preceding paragraphs and unless the treaty otherwise provides:

(a) acceptance by another contracting State of a reservation constitutes the reserving State a party to the treaty in relation to that other State if or when the treaty is in force for those States;

(b) an objection by another contracting State to a reservation does not preclude the entry into force of the treaty as between the objecting and reserving States unless a contrary intention is definitely expressed by the objecting State;

(c) an act expressing a State's consent to be bound by the treaty and containing a reservation is effective as soon as at least one other contracting State has accepted the reservation.

5   For the purposes of paragraphs 2 and 4 and unless the treaty otherwise provides, a reservation is considered to have been accepted by a State if it shall have raised no objection to the reservation by the end of a period of twelve months after it was notified of the reservation or by the date on which it expressed its consent to be bound by the treaty, whichever is later.

Article 21 Legal elects of reservations and of objections to reservations

1   A reservation established with regard to another party in accordance with articles 19, 20 and 23:

(a) modifies for the reserving State in its relations with that other party the provisions of the treaty to which the reservation relates to the extent of the reservation; and

(b) modifies those provisions to the same extent for that other party in its relations with the reserving State.

2   The reservation does not modify the provisions of the treaty for the other parties to the treaty inter se.

3   When a State objecting to a reservation has not opposed the entry into force of the treaty between itself and the reserving State, the provisions to which the reservation relates do not apply as between the two States to the extent of the reservation.

Article 22 Withdrawal of reservations and of objections to reservations

1   Unless the treaty otherwise provides, a reservation may be withdrawn at any time and the consent of a State which has accepted the reservation is not required for its withdrawal.

2   Unless the treaty otherwise provides, an objection to a reservation may be withdrawn at any time.

3   Unless the treaty otherwise provides, or it is otherwise agreed:

(a) the withdrawal of a reservation becomes operative in relation to another contracting State only when notice of it has been received by that State;

(b) the withdrawal of an objection to a reservation becomes operative only when notice of it has been received by the State which formulated the reservation.

Article 23 Procedure regarding reservations

1   A reservation, an express acceptance of a reservation and an objection to a reservation must be formulated in writing and communicated to the contracting States and other States entitled to become parties to the treaty.

2   If formulated when signing the treaty subject to ratification, acceptance or approval, a reservation must be formally confirmed by the reserving State when expressing its consent to be bound by the treaty. In such a case the reservation shall be considered as having been made on the date of its confirmation.

3   An express acceptance of, or an objection to, a reservation made previously to confirmation of the reservation does not itself require confirmation.
4   The withdrawal of a reservation or of an objection to a reservation must be formulated in writing.

SECTION 3. ENTRY INTO FORCE AND PROVISIONAL APPLICATION OF TREATIES

Article 24 Entry into force

1   A treaty enters into force in such manner and upon such date as it may provide or as the negotiating States may agree.
2   Failing any such provision or agreement, a treaty enters into force as soon as consent to be bound by the treaty has been established for all the negotiating States.
3   When the consent of a State to be bound by a treaty is established on a date after the treaty has come into force, the treaty enters into force for that State on that date, unless the treaty otherwise provides.
4   The provisions of a treaty regulating the authentication of its text, the establishment of the consent of States to be bound by the treaty, the manner or date of its entry into force, reservations, the functions of the depositary and other matters arising necessarily before the entry into force of the treaty apply from the time of the adoption of its text.

Article 25 Provisional application

1   A treaty or a part of a treaty is applied provisionally pending its entry into force if:

   (a) the treaty itself so provides; or
   (b) the negotiating States have in some other manner so agreed.

2   Unless the treaty otherwise provides or the negotiating States have otherwise agreed, the provisional application of a treaty or a part of a treaty with respect to a State shall be terminated if that State notifies the other States between which the treaty is being applied provisionally of its intention not to become a party to the treaty.

PART III. OBSERVANCE, APPLICATION AND INTERPRETATION OF TREATIES

Section 1. Observance of treaties

Article 26 "Pacta sunt servanda"

Every treaty in force is binding upon the parties to it and must be performed by them in good faith.

Article 27 Internal law and observance of treaties

A party may not invoke the provisions of its internal law as justification for its failure to perform a treaty. This rule is without prejudice to article 46.

SECTION 2. APPLICATION OF TREATIES

Article 28 Non-retroactivity of treaties

Unless a different intention appears from the treaty or is otherwise established, its provisions do not bind a party in relation to any act or fact which took place or any situation which ceased to exist before the date of the entry into force of the treaty with respect to that party.

Article 29 Territorial scope of treaties

Unless a different intention appears from the treaty or is otherwise established, a treaty is binding upon each party in respect of its entire territory.

Article 30 Application of successive treaties relating to the same subject matter

1   Subject to Article 103 of the Charter of the United Nations, the rights and obligations of States Parties to successive treaties relating to the same subject matter shall be determined in accordance with the following paragraphs.
2   When a treaty specifies that it is subject to, or that it is not to be considered as incompatible with, an earlier or later treaty, the provisions of that other treaty prevail.
3   When all the parties to the earlier treaty are parties also to the later treaty but the earlier treaty is not terminated or suspended in operation under article 59, the earlier treaty applies only to the extent that its provisions are compatible with those of the later treaty.
4   When the parties to the later treaty do not include all the parties to the earlier one:

   (a)   as between States Parties to both treaties the same rule applies as in paragraph 3;
   (b)   as between a State party to both treaties and a State party to only one of the treaties, the treaty to which both States are parties governs their mutual rights and obligations.

5   Paragraph 4 is without prejudice to article 41, or to any question of the termination or suspension of the operation of a treaty under article 60 or to any question of responsibility which may arise for a State from the conclusion or application of a treaty the provisions of which are incompatible with its obligations towards another State under another treaty.

SECTION 3. INTERPRETATION OF TREATIES

Article 31 General rule of interpretation

1   A treaty shall be interpreted in good faith in accordance with the ordinary meaning to be given to the terms of the treaty in their context and in the light of its object and purpose.
2   The context for the purpose of the interpretation of a treaty shall comprise, in addition to the text, including its preamble and annexes:

   (a)   any agreement relating to the treaty which was made between all the parties in connection with the conclusion of the treaty;

(b) any instrument which was made by one or more parties in connection with the conclusion of the treaty and accepted by the other parties as an instrument related to the treaty.

3 There shall be taken into account, together with the context:

(a) any subsequent agreement between the parties regarding the interpretation of the treaty or the application of its provisions;

(b) any subsequent practice in the application of the treaty which establishes the agreement of the parties regarding its interpretation;

(c) any relevant rules of international law applicable in the relations between the parties.

4 A special meaning shall be given to a term if it is established that the parties so intended.

Article 32 Supplementary means of interpretation

Recourse may be had to supplementary means of interpretation, including the preparatory work of the treaty and the circumstances of its conclusion, in order to confirm the meaning resulting from the application of article 31, or to determine the meaning when the interpretation according to article 31:

(a) leaves the meaning ambiguous or obscure; or
(b) leads to a result which is manifestly absurd or unreasonable.

Article 33 Interpretation of treaties authenticated in two or more languages

1 When a treaty has been authenticated in two or more languages, the text is equally authoritative in each language, unless the treaty provides or the parties agree that, in case of divergence, a particular text shall prevail.

2 A version of the treaty in a language other than one of those in which the text was authenticated shall be considered an authentic text only if the treaty so provides or the parties so agree.

3 The terms of the treaty are presumed to have the same meaning in each authentic text.

4 Except where a particular text prevails in accordance with paragraph 1, when a comparison of the authentic texts discloses a difference of meaning which the application of articles 31 and 32 does not remove, the meaning which best reconciles the texts, having regard to the object and purpose of the treaty, shall be adopted.

SECTION 4. TREATIES AND THIRD STATES

Article 34 General rule regarding third States

A treaty does not create either obligations or rights for a third State without its consent.

Article 35 Treaties providing for obligations for third States

An obligation arises for a third State from a provision of a treaty if the parties to the treaty intend the provision to be the means of establishing the obligation and the third State expressly accepts that obligation in writing.

Article 36 Treaties providing for rights for third States

1   A right arises for a third State from a provision of a treaty if the parties to the treaty intend the provision to accord that right either to the third State, or to a group of States to which it belongs, or to all States, and the third State assents thereto. Its assent shall be presumed so long as the contrary is not indicated, unless the treaty otherwise provides.
2   A State exercising a right in accordance with paragraph 1 shall comply with the conditions for its exercise provided for in the treaty or established in conformity with the treaty.

Article 37 Revocation or modification of obligations or rights of third States

1   When an obligation has arisen for a third State in conformity with article 35, the obligation may be revoked or modified only with the consent of the parties to the treaty and of the third State, unless it is established that they had otherwise agreed.
2   When a right has arisen for a third State in conformity with article 36, the right may not be revoked or modified by the parties if it is established that the right was intended not to be revocable or subject to modification without the consent of the third State.

Article 38 Rules in a treaty becoming binding on third States through international custom

Nothing in articles 34 to 37 precludes a rule set forth in a treaty from becoming binding upon a third State as a customary rule of international law, recognized as such.

PART IV.
AMENDMENT AND MODIFICATION OF TREATIES

Article 39 General rule regarding the amendment of treaties

A treaty may be amended by agreement between the parties. The rules laid down in Part II apply to such an agreement except insofar as the treaty may otherwise provide.

Article 40 Amendment of multilateral treaties

1   Unless the treaty otherwise provides, the amendment of multilateral treaties shall be governed by the following paragraphs.
2   Any proposal to amend a multilateral treaty as between all the parties must be notified to all the contracting States, each one of which shall have the right to take part in:

(a)   the decision as to the action to be taken in regard to such proposal;
(b)   the negotiation and conclusion of any agreement for the amendment of the treaty.

3   Every State entitled to become a party to the treaty shall also be entitled to become a party to the treaty as amended.
4   The amending agreement does not bind any State already a party to the treaty which does not become a party to the amending agreement; article 30, paragraph 4 (b), applies in relation to such State.

5 Any State which becomes a party to the treaty after the entry into force of the amending agreement shall, failing an expression of a different intention by that State:

(a) be considered as a party to the treaty as amended; and

(b) be considered as a party to the unamended treaty in relation to any party to the treaty not bound by the amending agreement.

Article 41 Agreements to modify multilateral treaties between certain of the parties only

1 Two or more of the parties to a multilateral treaty may conclude an agreement to modify the treaty as between themselves alone if:

(a) the possibility of such a modification is provided for by the treaty; or

(b) the modification in question is not prohibited by the treaty and:

(i) does not affect the enjoyment by the other parties of their rights under the treaty or the performance of their obligations;

(ii) does not relate to a provision, derogation from which is incompatible with the effective execution of the object and purpose of the treaty as a whole.

2 Unless in a case falling under paragraph 1 (a) the treaty otherwise provides, the parties in question shall notify the other parties of their intention to conclude the agreement and of the modification to the treaty for which it provides.

PART V. INVALIDITY, TERMINATION AND SUSPENSION OF THE OPERATION OF TREATIES

Section 1. General provisions

Article 42 Validity and continuance in force of treaties

1 The validity of a treaty or of the consent of a State to be bound by a treaty may be impeached only through the application of the present Convention.

2 The termination of a treaty, its denunciation or the withdrawal of a party, may take place only as a result of the application of the provisions of the treaty or of the present Convention. The same rule applies to suspension of the operation of a treaty.

Article 43 Obligations imposed by international law independently of a treaty

The invalidity, termination or denunciation of a treaty, the withdrawal of a party from it, or the suspension of its operation, as a result of the application of the present Convention or of the provisions of the treaty, shall not in any way impair the duty of any State to fulfil any obligation embodied in the treaty to which it would be subject under international law independently of the treaty.

Article 44 Separability of treaty provisions

1   A right of a party, provided for in a treaty or arising under article 56, to denounce, withdraw from or suspend the operation of the treaty may be exercised only with respect to the whole treaty unless the treaty otherwise provides or the parties otherwise agree.

2   A ground for invalidating, terminating, withdrawing from or suspending the operation of a treaty recognized in the present Convention may be invoked only with respect to the whole treaty except as provided in the following paragraphs or in article 60.

3   If the ground relates solely to particular clauses, it may be invoked only with respect to those clauses where:

(a)   the said clauses are separable from the remainder of the treaty with regard to their application;

(b)   it appears from the treaty or is otherwise established that acceptance of those clauses was not an essential basis of the consent of the other party or parties to be bound by the treaty as a whole; and

(c)   continued performance of the remainder of the treaty would not be unjust.

4   In cases falling under articles 49 and 50, the State entitled to invoke the fraud or corruption may do so with respect either to the whole treaty or, subject to paragraph 3, to the particular clauses alone.

5   In cases falling under articles 51, 52 and 53, no separation of the provisions of the treaty is permitted.

Article 45 Loss of a right to invoke a ground for invalidating, terminating, withdrawing from or suspending the operation of a treaty

A State may no longer invoke a ground for invalidating, terminating, withdrawing from or suspending the operation of a treaty under articles 46 to 50 or articles 60 and 62 if, after becoming aware of the facts:

(a)   it shall have expressly agreed that the treaty is valid or remains in force or continues in operation, as the case may be; or

(b)   it must by reason of its conduct be considered as having acquiesced in the validity of the treaty or in its maintenance in force or in operation, as the case may be.

Section 2. Invalidity of treaties

Article 46 Provisions of internal law regarding competence to conclude treaties

1   A State may not invoke the fact that its consent to be bound by a treaty has been expressed in violation of a provision of its internal law regarding competence to conclude treaties as invalidating its consent unless that violation was manifest and concerned a rule of its internal law of fundamental importance.

2   A violation is manifest if it would be objectively evident to any State conducting itself in the matter in accordance with normal practice and in good faith.

Article 47 Specific restrictions on authority to express the consent of a State

If the authority of a representative to express the consent of a State to be bound by a particular treaty has been made subject to a specific restriction, his omission to observe that restriction may not be invoked as invalidating the consent expressed by him unless the restriction was notified to the other negotiating States prior to his expressing such consent.

Article 48 Error

1   A State may invoke an error in a treaty as invalidating its consent to be bound by the treaty if the error relates to a fact or situation which was assumed by that State to exist at the time when the treaty was concluded and formed an essential basis of its consent to be bound by the treaty.
2   Paragraph 1 shall not apply if the State in question contributed by its own conduct to the error or if the circumstances were such as to put that State on notice of a possible error.
3   An error relating only to the wording of the text of a treaty does not affect its validity; article 79 then applies.

Article 49 Fraud

If a State has been induced to conclude a treaty by the fraudulent conduct of another negotiating State, the State may invoke the fraud as invalidating its consent to be bound by the treaty.

Article 50 Corruption of a representative of a State

If the expression of a State's consent to be bound by a treaty has been procured through the corruption of its representative directly or indirectly by another negotiating State, the State may invoke such corruption as invalidating its consent to be bound by the treaty.

Article 51 Coercion of a representative of a State

The expression of a State's consent to be bound by a treaty which has been procured by the coercion of its representative through acts or threats directed against him shall be without any legal effect.

Article 52 Coercion of a State by the threat or use of force

A treaty is void if its conclusion has been procured by the threat or use of force in violation of the principles of international law embodied in the Charter of the United Nations.

Article 53 Treaties conflicting with a peremptory norm of general international law ("jus cogens")

A treaty is void if, at the time of its conclusion, it conflicts with a peremptory norm of general international law. For the purposes of the present Convention, a peremptory norm of general international law is a norm accepted and recognized by the international community of States as a whole as a norm from which no derogation is permitted and which can be modified only by a subsequent norm of general international law having the same character.

SECTION 3.
TERMINATION AND SUSPENSION OF THE
OPERATION OF TREATIES

Article 54 Termination of or withdrawal from a treaty under its provisions or by consent of the parties

The termination of a treaty or the withdrawal of a party may take place:

(a) in conformity with the provisions of the treaty; or
(b) at any time by consent of all the parties after consultation with the other contracting States.

Article 55 Reduction of the parties to a multilateral treaty below the number necessary for its entry into force

Unless the treaty otherwise provides, a multilateral treaty does not terminate by reason only of the fact that the number of the parties falls below the number necessary for its entry into force.

Article 56 Denunciation of or withdrawal from a treaty containing no provision regarding termination, denunciation or withdrawal

1   A treaty which contains no provision regarding its termination and which does not provide for denunciation or withdrawal is not subject to denunciation or withdrawal unless:

(a) it is established that the parties intended to admit the possibility of denunciation or withdrawal; or
(b) a right of denunciation or withdrawal may be implied by the nature of the treaty.

2   A party shall give not less than twelve months' notice of its intention to denounce or withdraw from a treaty under paragraph 1.

Article 57 Suspension of the operation of a treaty under its provisions or by consent of the parties

The operation of a treaty in regard to all the parties or to a particular party may be suspended:

(a) in conformity with the provisions of the treaty; or
(b) at any time by consent of all the parties after consultation with the other contracting States.

Article 58 Suspension of the operation of a multilateral treaty by agreement between certain of the parties only

1   Two or more parties to a multilateral treaty may conclude an agreement to suspend the operation of provisions of the treaty, temporarily and as between themselves alone, if:

(a) the possibility of such a suspension is provided for by the treaty; or

(b) the suspension in question is not prohibited by the treaty and:

(i) does not affect the enjoyment by the other parties of their rights under the treaty or the performance of their obligations;

(ii) is not incompatible with the object and purpose of the treaty.

2 Unless in a case falling under paragraph 1 (a) the treaty otherwise provides, the parties in question shall notify the other parties of their intention to conclude the agreement and of those provisions of the treaty the operation of which they intend to suspend.

Article 59 Termination or suspension of the operation of a treaty implied by conclusion of a later treaty

1 A treaty shall be considered as terminated if all the parties to it conclude a later treaty relating to the same subject matter and:

(a) it appears from the later treaty or is otherwise established that the parties intended that the matter should be governed by that treaty; or

(b) the provisions of the later treaty are so far incompatible with those of the earlier one that the two treaties are not capable of being applied at the same time.

2 The earlier treaty shall be considered as only suspended in operation if it appears from the later treaty or is otherwise established that such was the intention of the parties.

Article 60 Termination or suspension of the operation of a treaty as a consequence of its breach

1 A material breach of a bilateral treaty by one of the parties entitles the other to invoke the breach as a ground for terminating the treaty or suspending its operation in whole or in part.

2 A material breach of a multilateral treaty by one of the parties entitles:

(a) the other parties by unanimous agreement to suspend the operation of the treaty in whole or in part or to terminate it either:

(i) in the relations between themselves and the defaulting State; or

(ii) as between all the parties;

(b) a party specially affected by the breach to invoke it as a ground for suspending the operation of the treaty in whole or in part in the relations between itself and the defaulting State;

(c) any party other than the defaulting State to invoke the breach as a ground for suspending the operation of the treaty in whole or in part with respect to itself if the treaty is of such a character that a material breach of its provisions by one party radically changes the position of every party with respect to the further performance of its obligations under the treaty.

3 A material breach of a treaty, for the purposes of this article, consists in:

(a) a repudiation of the treaty not sanctioned by the present Convention; or

(b) the violation of a provision essential to the accomplishment of the object or purpose of the treaty.

4 The foregoing paragraphs are without prejudice to any provision in the treaty applicable in the event of a breach.

5 Paragraphs 1 to 3 do not apply to provisions relating to the protection of the human person contained in treaties of a humanitarian character, in particular to provisions prohibiting any form of reprisals against persons protected by such treaties.

Article 61 *Supervening impossibility of performance*

1 A party may invoke the impossibility of performing a treaty as a ground for terminating or withdrawing from it if the impossibility results from the permanent disappearance or destruction of an object indispensable for the execution of the treaty. If the impossibility is temporary, it may be invoked only as a ground for suspending the operation of the treaty.
2 Impossibility of performance may not be invoked by a party as a ground for terminating, withdrawing from or suspending the operation of a treaty if the impossibility is the result of a breach by that party either of an obligation under the treaty or of any other international obligation owed to any other party to the treaty.

Article 62 *Fundamental change of circumstances*

1 A fundamental change of circumstances which has occurred with regard to those existing at the time of the conclusion of a treaty, and which was not foreseen by the parties, may not be invoked as a ground for terminating or withdrawing from the treaty unless:

   (a) the existence of those circumstances constituted an essential basis of the consent of the parties to be bound by the treaty; and
   (b) the effect of the change is radically to transform the extent of obligations still to be performed under the treaty.

2 A fundamental change of circumstances may not be invoked as a ground for terminating or withdrawing from a treaty:

   (a) if the treaty establishes a boundary; or
   (b) if the fundamental change is the result of a breach by the party invoking it either of an obligation under the treaty or of any other international obligation owed to any other party to the treaty.

3 If, under the foregoing paragraphs, a party may invoke a fundamental change of circumstances as a ground for terminating or withdrawing from a treaty it may also invoke the change as a ground for suspending the operation of the treaty.

Article 63 *Severance of diplomatic or consular relations*

The severance of diplomatic or consular relations between parties to a treaty does not affect the legal relations established between them by the treaty except insofar as the existence of diplomatic or consular relations is indispensable for the application of the treaty.

Article 64 *Emergence of a new peremptory norm of general international law ("jus cogens")*

If a new peremptory norm of general international law emerges, any existing treaty which is in conflict with that norm becomes void and terminates.

Reservations to treaties. Annex to the UN General Assembly Resolution – A/RES/ 68/111 of 19 December 2013

Text of the guidelines constituting the Guide to Practice on Reservations to Treaties

3. PERMISSIBILITY OF RESERVATIONS AND INTERPRETATIVE DECLARATIONS

3.1 Permissible reservations

A State or an international organization may, when signing, ratifying, formally confirming, accepting, approving or acceding to a treaty, formulate a reservation unless:

(a) the reservation is prohibited by the treaty;
(b) the treaty provides that only specified reservations, which do not include the reservation in question, may be made; or
(c) in cases not falling under subparagraphs (a) and (b), the reservation is incompatible with the object and purpose of the treaty.

3.1.1 Reservations prohibited by the treaty

A reservation is prohibited by the treaty if it contains a provision:

(a) prohibiting all reservations;
(b) prohibiting reservations to specified provisions to which the reservation in question relates; or
(c) prohibiting certain categories of reservations including the reservation in question.

3.1.2 Definition of specified reservations

For the purposes of guideline 3.1, the expression "specified reservations" means reservations that are expressly envisaged in the treaty to certain provisions of the treaty or to the treaty as a whole with respect to certain specific aspects.

3.1.3 Permissibility of reservations not prohibited by the treaty

Where the treaty prohibits the formulation of certain reservations, a reservation which is not prohibited by the treaty may be formulated by a State or an international organization only if it is not incompatible with the object and purpose of the treaty.

3.1.4 Permissibility of specified reservations

Where the treaty envisages the formulation of specified reservations without defining their content, a reservation may be formulated by a State or an international organization only if it is not incompatible with the object and purpose of the treaty.

3.2 Assessment of the permissibility of reservations

The following may assess, within their respective competences, the permissibility of reservations to a treaty formulated by a State or an international organization:

- contracting States or contracting organizations;
- dispute settlement bodies;
- treaty monitoring bodies.

3.2.1 Competence of the treaty monitoring bodies to assess the permissibility of reservations

1   A treaty monitoring body may, for the purpose of discharging the functions entrusted to it, assess the permissibility of reservations formulated by a State or an international organization.
2   The assessment made by such a body in the exercise of this competence has no greater legal effect than that of the act which contains it.

4.5.1 Nullity of an invalid reservation

A reservation that does not meet the conditions of formal validity and permissibility set out in Parts 2 and 3 of the Guide to Practice is null and void, and therefore devoid of any legal effect.

4.5.2 Reactions to a reservation considered invalid

1   The nullity of an invalid reservation does not depend on the objection or the acceptance by a contracting State or a contracting organization.
2   Nevertheless, a State or an international organization which considers that a reservation is invalid should formulate a reasoned objection as soon as possible.

4.5.3 Status of the author of an invalid reservation in relation to the treaty

1   The status of the author of an invalid reservation in relation to a treaty depends on the intention expressed by the reserving State or international organization on whether it intends to be bound by the treaty without the benefit of the reservation or whether it considers that it is not bound by the treaty.
2   Unless the author of the invalid reservation has expressed a contrary intention or such an intention is otherwise established, it is considered a contracting State or a contracting organization without the benefit of the reservation.
3   Notwithstanding paragraphs 1 and 2, the author of the invalid reservation may express at any time its intention not to be bound by the treaty without the benefit of the reservation.
4   If a treaty monitoring body expresses the view that a reservation is invalid and the reserving State or international organization intends not to be bound by the treaty without the benefit of the reservation, it should express its intention to that effect within a period of twelve months from the date at which the treaty monitoring body made its assessment.

CCPR General Comment No. 24, Issues Relating to Reservations Made upon Ratification or Accession to the Covenant or the Optional Protocols thereto, or in Relation to Declarations under Article 41 of the Covenant of 4 November 1994, UN Human Rights Committee

Adopted at the Fifty-second Session of the Human Rights Committee, CCPR/C/21/Rev.1/Add.6, General Comment No. 24. (General Comments).

4. The possibility of entering reservations may encourage States which consider that they have difficulties in guaranteeing all the rights in the Covenant nonetheless to accept the generality of obligations in that instrument. Reservations may serve a useful function to enable States to adapt specific elements in their laws to the inherent rights of each person as articulated in the Covenant. However, it is desirable in principle that States accept the full range of obligations, because the human rights norms are the legal expression of the essential rights that every person is entitled to as a human being . . .

8. Reservations that offend peremptory norms would not be compatible with the object and purpose of the Covenant. Although treaties that are mere exchanges of obligations between States allow them to reserve inter se application of rules of general international law, it is otherwise in human rights treaties, which are for the benefit of persons within their jurisdiction. Accordingly, provisions in the Covenant that represent customary international law (and a fortiori when they have the character of peremptory norms) may not be the subject of reservations. Accordingly, a State may not reserve the right to engage in slavery, to torture, to subject persons to cruel, inhuman or degrading treatment or punishment, to arbitrarily deprive persons of their lives, to arbitrarily arrest and detain persons, to deny freedom of thought, conscience and religion, to presume a person guilty unless he proves his innocence, to execute pregnant women or children, to permit the advocacy of national, racial or religious hatred, to deny to persons of marriageable age the right to marry, or to deny to minorities the right to enjoy their own culture, profess their own religion, or use their own language. . . .

11. The Covenant consists not just of the specified rights, but of important supportive guarantees. These guarantees provide the necessary framework for securing the rights in the Covenant and are thus essential to its object and purpose. Some operate at the national level and some at the international level. Reservations designed to remove these guarantees are thus not acceptable . . .

13. The issue arises as to whether reservations are permissible under the first Optional Protocol and, if so, whether any such reservation might be contrary to the object and purpose of the Covenant or of the first Optional Protocol itself. It is clear that the first Optional Protocol is itself an international treaty, distinct from the Covenant but closely related to it. Its object and purpose is to recognize the competence of the Committee to receive and consider communications from individuals who claim to be victims of a violation by a State party of any of the rights in the Covenant. States accept the substantive rights of individuals by reference to the Covenant, and not the first Optional Protocol. The function of the first Optional Protocol is to allow claims in respect of those rights to be tested before the Committee. Accordingly, a reservation to an obligation of a State to respect and ensure a right contained in the Covenant, made under the first Optional Protocol when it has not previously been made in respect of the same rights under the Covenant, does not affect the State's duty to comply with its substantive obligation. A reservation cannot be made to the Covenant through the vehicle of the Optional Protocol but such a reservation would operate to ensure that the State's compliance with that obligation may not be tested by the Committee under

the first Optional Protocol. And because the object and purpose of the first Optional Protocol is to allow the rights obligatory for a State under the Covenant to be tested before the Committee, a reservation that seeks to preclude this would be contrary to the object and purpose of the first Optional Protocol, even if not of the Covenant. A reservation to a substantive obligation made for the first time under the first Optional Protocol would seem to reflect an intention by the State concerned to prevent the Committee from expressing its views relating to a particular article of the Covenant in an individual case. . . .

17. As indicated above, it is the Vienna Convention on the Law of Treaties that provides the definition of reservations and also the application of the object and purpose test in the absence of other specific provisions. But the Committee believes that its provisions on the role of State objections in relation to reservations are inappropriate to address the problem of reservations to human rights treaties. Such treaties, and the Covenant specifically, are not a web of inter-State exchanges of mutual obligations. They concern the endowment of individuals with rights. The principle of inter-State reciprocity has no place, save perhaps in the limited context of reservations to declarations on the Committee's competence under article 41. And because the operation of the classic rules on reservations is so inadequate for the Covenant, States have often not seen any legal interest in or need to object to reservations. The absence of protest by States cannot imply that a reservation is either compatible or incompatible with the object and purpose of the Covenant. Objections have been occasional, made by some States but not others, and on grounds not always specified; when an objection is made, it often does not specify a legal consequence, or sometimes even indicates that the objecting party nonetheless does not regard the Covenant as not in effect as between the parties concerned. In short, the pattern is so unclear that it is not safe to assume that a non-objecting State thinks that a particular reservation is acceptable. In the view of the Committee, because of the special characteristics of the Covenant as a human rights treaty, it is open to question what effect objections have between States inter se. However, an objection to a reservation made by States may provide some guidance to the Committee in its interpretation as to its compatibility with the object and purpose of the Covenant.

18. It necessarily falls to the Committee to determine whether a specific reservation is compatible with the object and purpose of the Covenant. This is in part because, as indicated above, it is an inappropriate task for States parties in relation to human rights treaties, and in part because it is a task that the Committee cannot avoid in the performance of its functions. In order to know the scope of its duty to examine a State's compliance under article 40 or a communication under the first Optional Protocol, the Committee has necessarily to take a view on the compatibility of a reservation with the object and purpose of the Covenant and with general international law. Because of the special character of a human rights treaty, the compatibility of a reservation with the object and purpose of the Covenant must be established objectively, by reference to legal principles, and the Committee is particularly well placed to perform this task. The normal consequence of an unacceptable reservation is not that the Covenant will not be in effect at all for a reserving party. Rather, such a reservation will generally be severable, in the sense that the Covenant will be operative for the reserving party without benefit of the reservation.

Armed conflicts and international treaties

Effects of armed conflicts on treaties, Annex to the UN General Assembly Resolution –
   A/RES/66/99
   of 9 December 2011

Part One
Scope and definitions

Article 1 Scope

The present articles apply to the effects of armed conflict on the relations of States under a treaty.

Article 2 Definitions

For the purposes of the present articles:

(a) "Treaty" means an international agreement concluded between States in written form and governed by international law, whether embodied in a single instrument or in two or more related instruments and whatever its particular designation, and includes treaties between States to which international organizations are also parties;

(b) "Armed conflict" means a situation in which there is resort to armed force between States or protracted resort to armed force between governmental authorities and organized armed groups.

Part Two
Principles

Chapter I Operation of treaties in the event of armed conflicts

Article 3 General principle

The existence of an armed conflict does not ipso facto terminate or suspend the operation of treaties:

(a) As between States parties to the conflict;
(b) As between a State party to the conflict and a State that is not.

Article 4 Provisions on the operation of treaties

Where a treaty itself contains provisions on its operation in situations of armed conflict, those provisions shall apply.

Article 5 Application of rules on treaty interpretation

The rules of international law on treaty interpretation shall be applied to establish whether a treaty is susceptible to termination, withdrawal or suspension in the event of an armed conflict.

*Article 6 Factors indicating whether a treaty is susceptible to termination,
withdrawal or suspension*

In order to ascertain whether a treaty is susceptible to termination, withdrawal or suspension in the event of an armed conflict, regard shall be had to all relevant factors, including:

(a) The nature of the treaty, in particular its subject matter, its object and purpose, its content and the number of parties to the treaty; and
(b) The characteristics of the armed conflict, such as its territorial extent, its scale and intensity, its duration and, in the case of non-international armed conflict, also the degree of outside involvement.

Article 7 Continued operation of treaties resulting from their subject matter

An indicative list of treaties, the subject matter of which involves an implication that they continue in operation, in whole or in part, during armed conflict, is to be found in the annex to the present articles.

Chapter II Other provisions relevant to the operation of treaties

Article 8 Conclusion of treaties during armed conflict

1   The existence of an armed conflict does not affect the capacity of a State party to that conflict to conclude treaties in accordance with international law.
2   States may conclude agreements involving termination or suspension of a treaty or part of a treaty that is operative between them during situations of armed conflict, or may agree to amend or modify the treaty.

*Article 9 Notification of intention to terminate or withdraw from
a treaty or to suspend its operation*

1   A State intending to terminate or withdraw from a treaty to which it is a Party, or to suspend the operation of that treaty, as a consequence of an armed conflict shall notify the other State Party or States Parties to the treaty, or its depositary, of such intention.
2   The notification takes effect upon receipt by the other State Party or States Parties, unless it provides for a subsequent date.
3   Nothing in the preceding paragraphs shall affect the right of a Party to object within a reasonable time, in accordance with the terms of the treaty or other applicable rules of international law, to the termination of or withdrawal from the treaty, or suspension of its operation.
4   If an objection has been raised in accordance with paragraph 3, the States concerned shall seek a solution through the means indicated in Article 33 of the Charter of the United Nations.

5   Nothing in the preceding paragraphs shall affect the rights or obligations of States with regard to the settlement of disputes insofar as they have remained applicable.

Article 10 Obligations imposed by international law independently of a treaty

The termination of or the withdrawal from a treaty, or the suspension of its operation, as a consequence of an armed conflict, shall not impair in any way the duty of any State to fulfil any obligation embodied in the treaty to which it would be subject under international law independently of that treaty.

Article 11 Separability of treaty provisions

Termination, withdrawal from or suspension of the operation of a treaty as a consequence of an armed conflict shall, unless the treaty otherwise provides or the Parties otherwise agree, take effect with respect to the whole treaty except where:

(a)   The treaty contains clauses that are separable from the remainder of the treaty with regard to their application;
(b)   It appears from the treaty or is otherwise established that acceptance of those clauses was not an essential basis of the consent of the other Party or Parties to be bound by the treaty as a whole; and
(c)   Continued performance of the remainder of the treaty would not be unjust.

Article 12 Loss of the right to terminate or withdraw from a treaty or to suspend its operation

A State may no longer terminate or withdraw from a treaty or suspend its operation as a consequence of an armed conflict if, after becoming aware of the facts:

(a)   It shall have expressly agreed that the treaty remains in force or continues in operation; or
(b)   It must by reason of its conduct be considered as having acquiesced in the continued operation of the treaty or in its maintenance in force.

Article 13 Revival or resumption of treaty relations subsequent t o an armed conflict

1   Subsequent to an armed conflict, the States Parties may regulate, on the basis of agreement, the revival of treaties terminated or suspended as a consequence of the armed conflict.
2   The resumption of the operation of a treaty suspended as a consequence of an armed conflict shall be determined in accordance with the factors referred to in article 6.

Part Three
Miscellaneous

Article 14 Effect of the exercise of the right to self-defence on a treaty

A State exercising its inherent right of individual or collective self-defence in accordance with the Charter of the United Nations is entitled to suspend in whole or in part the operation of a treaty to which it is a Party insofar as that operation is incompatible with the exercise of that right.

Article 15 Prohibition of benefit to an aggressor State

A State committing aggression within the meaning of the Charter of the United Nations and resolution 3314 (XXIX) of the General Assembly of the United Nations shall not terminate or withdraw from a treaty or suspend its operation as a consequence of an armed conflict that results from the act of aggression if the effect would be to the benefit of that State.

Article 16 Decisions of the Security Council

The present articles are without prejudice to relevant decisions taken by the Security Council in accordance with the Charter of the United Nations.

Article 17 Rights and duties arising from the laws of neutrality

The present articles are without prejudice to the rights and duties of States arising from the laws of neutrality.

Article 18 Other cases of termination, withdrawal or suspension

The present articles are without prejudice to the termination, withdrawal or suspension of treaties as a consequence of, inter alia: (a) a material breach; (b) supervening impossibility of performance; or (c) a fundamental change of circumstances.

Annex

Indicative list of treaties referred to in article 7

(a) Treaties on the law of armed conflict, including treaties on international humanitarian law;
(b) Treaties declaring, creating or regulating a permanent regime or status or related permanent rights, including treaties establishing or modifying land and maritime boundaries;
(c) Multilateral law-making treaties;
(d) Treaties on international criminal justice;
(e) Treaties of friendship, commerce and navigation and agreements concerning private rights;
(f) Treaties for the international protection of human rights;
(g) Treaties relating to the international protection of the environment;

(h)   Treaties relating to international watercourses and related installations and facilities;
(i)   Treaties relating to aquifers and related installations and facilities;
(j)   Treaties which are constituent instruments of international organizations;
(k)   Treaties relating to the international settlement of disputes by peaceful means, including resort to conciliation, mediation, arbitration and judicial settlement;
(l)   Treaties relating to diplomatic and consular relations.

CHAPTER 7

International organisations

DOI: 10.4324/9781003213772-7

INTERNATIONAL INSTITUTIONS

international conferences
international organisations
peace conferences
political or economic conferences
diplomatic conferences
decision-making
unanimously
consensus
consensus minus one or two

> majority
> International Telecommunication Union
> Universal Postal Union
> Permanent Court of Arbitration
> League of Nations
> Treaty of Versailles
> International Labour Organisation

Introductory remarks

There are many institutional frameworks of international co-operation between the subjects of international law from which here are reviewed the **international conferences** and **international organisations**. Each of them has a unique niche in the inter-state system.

International conference

The international conference is a meeting of the representatives of two or more states (and sometimes other subjects of international law also) for consideration of any political, economic, legal, or other issues.

The international conference is an institution which (1) embodies a temporary framework (2) on a particular issue (3) with minimal internal organisational structure (4) finalising its work, as a rule, with the international treaty or the final document.

Different names

The international conference may also be called a 'congress' (for example, Congress of Vienna of 1815) or a 'gathering' (for instance, Berlin gathering of 1871) or can have another designation, but the term 'conference' has been widely used and is an established title for this type of international meetings.

The forms of international conferences

The primary forms of international conferences are **peace conferences, political or economic conferences**, and **diplomatic conferences**. (The latter are dedicated to the codification of international law.)

Convening an international conference

International conferences are convened either by states or by international organisations. As a rule, the representative of the inviting side or a host subject opens the conference. The first session of a conference is mainly dedicated to the election of the internal bodies (like the mandate organs, the editorial bodies, and so on). However, these issues or some of them may be solved preliminarily through diplomatic channels. The work of the conference will be held in plenary sessions and committees (commissions). The plenary sessions are usually public while the committees' sessions are generally closed.

International organisation

The international organisation is an institution:

- embodying a temporary as well as a non-temporary institutional framework;
- founded by an international treaty or in rare cases, by other instrument governed by international law (for example, the resolutions adopted by an international organisation or international conference);
- whose competence is predefined and limited by the foundational instrument;
- which is established to deal with a particular issue. Consequently, international organisations are commonly regarded as holding a functional authority;
- made up predominantly of multiple and complex internal organisational structure; in rare cases, it may also possess a simple internal organisational structure as in the case of the Danube Commission, which is an international intergovernmental organisation constituted by the Convention Regarding the Regime of Navigation on the Danube signed in Belgrade in 1948;
- with a structure which primarily consists of highest (general assembly [conference] of all members), executive (executive council, executive committee or presidium, and so on) bodies and a standing secretariat, headed by a secretary-general or a director. Besides, within the framework of international organisations, there are usually auxiliary consultative bodies (commissions, committees, working groups, and so forth) also set up; and
- which is an independent subject of international law possessing an independent will.

Decision-making process

There are several procedural mechanisms for **decision-making** in international institutions (and their internal bodies). The decisions can be made either **unanimously** (every participant shall provide the consent), by **consensus** (the absence of any objection expressed by a participant**), consensus minus one or two** (if accordingly, only one or two participants object to a decision, the decision will still stand), or by a **majority** of votes, which may be simple or qualified (three-quarters of the vote, two-thirds, and so on).

International organisations – historical background

The organisational co-operation between the states on specific matters in the meaning of modern international organisations is a child of the nineteenth century. The first fully fledged international organisations of a worldwide nature with functions in particular fields were the **International Telecommunication Union** (founded in 1865 as the International Telegraph Union) and the **Universal Postal Union** (established in 1874 as the General Postal Union). Both of these institutions later became Specialised Agencies of the United Nations.

In the aftermath of the Hague Peace Conference (1899) and the Convention for the Pacific Settlement of International Disputes, the **Permanent Court of Arbitration** was established – the first permanent intergovernmental organisation to provide a forum for the resolution of international disputes, which set to work in 1902.

The forerunner of the United Nations was the **League of Nations**, which was the first worldwide international organisation with general functions in the broad areas established in 1919 under the **Treaty of Versailles**: 'to promote international cooperation and to achieve peace and security'. On 18 April 1946, the Assembly of the League of Nations adopted the Resolution for the Dissolution of the League of Nations (at the closing meeting of its twenty-first and last session held in Geneva). According to the Resolution:

> With effect from the day following the close of the present session of the Assembly, the League of Nations shall cease to exist except for the sole purpose of the liquidation of its affairs as provided in the present resolution.

Meanwhile, the **International Labour Organisation** was also created under the Treaty of Versailles (as an affiliated agency of the League) and was one of the first ice breakers in the promotion of social justice internationally, with a primary focus on developing labour standards.

UNITED NATIONS

Among the many popular interpretations of the role of the United Nations Organisation, the following statements seem to be the most accurate to disclose the crucial aspects of the principal mission it intends to realise:

- 'Mankind must put an end to war or war will put an end to mankind.' – John F. Kennedy (1917–1963);[485]
- 'More than ever before in human history, we share a common destiny. We can master it only if we face it together.' – Kofi Annan (1938–2018).[486]

---

485 Speech to United Nations General Assembly, 25 September 1961. *The Oxford Dictionary of Quotations* (n 18) 11.21.

486 'Secretary-General Emphasizes Important Role of United Nations for New Millennium', Press Release SG/SM/7262 (15 December 1999), available on the official website of the UN <www.un.org/press/en/1999/19991215.sgsm7262.doc.html> accessed 16 March 2021.

Foundation of the United Nations

original member states of the UN
United Nations Day
international legal order
collective measures
effectiveness
rationality
co-operation
protection of rights
diversification
principal organs of the UN

To the origins of the organisation

The name 'United Nations' is usually associated with United States President Franklin D. Roosevelt, who was its primary advocate as the designation of the Allied Powers of World War II. The name was first used in the 'Declaration by United Nations' of 1942, according to which each party pledged itself 'to employ its full resources, military or economic, against those members of the Tripartite Pact and its adherents with which such government [was] at war'. Later the name 'United Nations' was applied to the new post-war global peacekeeping organisation.

The United Nations Charter was signed on 26 June 1945 by the representatives of 50 countries. Poland signed it later and became one of the 51 **original member states of the UN**.

The United Nations officially came into existence on 24 October 1945, when the Charter was ratified by the permanent members of the Security Council and by a majority of other original member states. Therefore, **United Nations Day** is celebrated on 24 October.

The purposes of the founders

The primary foundational mission of the United Nations' member states was to avoid a third world war. In the meantime, the founders had in this regard a very negative experience to dwell on, mainly due to the example of the League of Nations, which had been set up with similar hopes. However, the results fell way short of expectations. Therefore, the new concept for the universal international organisation (United Nations Organisation) certainly reflects the negative experience and the unique challenges of that period in history. In sum, the crucial novelty was the sophisticated approach to eliminating the threat of World War III.

The principal purpose of the UN, as defined in the Charter, is to maintain international peace and security. To enforce this mission, a multifaceted approach was developed (as the only way). This approach comprises the following:

- **International legal order** – which should have been established by the explicitly formulated mandatory legal norms (the mandatory legal pattern) to conduct interstate relations. This pattern should have been embodied in international law with well-defined sources specified in the Statute of the International Court of Justice.
- **Collective measures** for the prevention and elimination of the threats to international peace – which included the concept of collective security and diverse measures for maintenance of international peace.
- **Effectiveness** – which aims 'to take effective collective measures for the prevention and removal of threats to the peace, and for the suppression of acts of aggression or other breaches of the peace.'[487]
- **Rationality** – however, for the sake of the effectiveness of the system, the model should have been based on realist logic for it to work. At that moment, in the interstate system, there were the states considered to be superpowers holding a higher degree of responsibility for maintaining international peace. Therefore, a unique role in the collective security system was assigned to those superpowers. Additionally, the model of collective security should have been very cautious against these states since the collective actions addressing the threats to the peace, breaches of the peace and acts of aggression, when the superpowers directly opposed them, and of course, the use of force against these superpowers, could have led not to international peace, but rather to a possible new world war being unleashed. Consequently, in these cases, these superpowers had to enjoy the veto power, which was implemented under the format of the UN Security Council.
- **Co-operation** – which was understood as a significant building block of the multifaceted approach to maintaining international peace and consisted of the development of friendly relations among nations in all essential matters: namely, achieving international co-operation for solving international problems of a political, economic, social, cultural, or humanitarian character. So tying the nations to the web of interconnected relationships in various fields of co-operation was considered in itself to be a principal instrument for maintaining international peace.
- **Protection of rights** – which is an essential prerequisite for maintaining peace and preventing large-scale warfare. It includes (1) the protection of the rights of states, (2) the preservation of peoples based on the respect for the principle of equal rights and self-determination,[488] and (3) the protection of humans on the basis of the respect for human rights and fundamental freedoms for all without discrimination based on race, sex, language, or religion.[489]
- **Diversification** – identification of multiple targets with one primary goal – 'the maintenance of international peace and security' – which is the embodiment of differentiated and, at the same time, holistic approach in the Charter. On the other hand, the United Nations structure is also diversified, where generally, there is no obvious formal hierarchy between the **principal organs of the UN**, and each of them represents a pillar for implementing its primary mission. The overarching framework of

---

487 Article 1 of the Charter.
488 ibid.
489 ibid.

the United Nations incorporates six principal organs, numerous other internal bodies of the UN, as well as a vast array of Specialised Agencies, programs, funds, and Related Organisations, which keep ties with the UN while operating under differing levels of independence.

The UN Membership

Membership in the United Nations, according to Article 4 (1) of the Charter, is open to all 'peace-loving states which accept the obligations contained in the . . . Charter and, in the judgment of the Organization, are able and willing to carry out these obligations.'

States are admitted to become the UN members via the decision of the General Assembly and upon the recommendation of the Security Council. To become the UN member state, firstly, the affirmative votes of the nine members of the Security Council are required, provided that none of its five permanent members has voted against the application; a two-thirds majority vote affirming the admission of a new member in the General Assembly is also necessary.

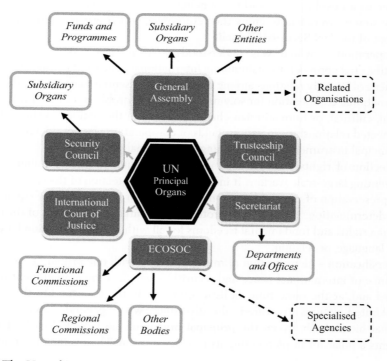

FIGURE 7.1 The United Nations system

General Assembly

> resolutions
> decisions
> no legally binding force
> soft law
> regular annual sessions
> special sessions
> emergency special sessions
> Main Committees of the General Assembly
> preamble
> operative part
> important questions
> voice of the United Nations

The General Assembly as a deliberative organ

The General Assembly, the principal deliberative organ of the UN, meets annually in New York. At the sessions of the General Assembly, the member states address issues related to existing international challenges, debate **resolutions,** and make **decisions** on the issues discussed under the agenda, most of which already passed the examination of several subsidiary bodies of the General Assembly.

These documents hold **no legally binding force** (except certain documents, for example, concerning the payments to the regular and peacekeeping budgets of the UN). However, since their adoption needs a majority vote of the members, they embody the beliefs of the international community and are generally considered to be a form of **soft law**.

Terms of reference

The General Assembly may discuss any questions or any matter within the scope of its competence or in relation to the powers and functions of any internal organ set up under the Charter, and within the scope of its competence, may make recommendations to the members of the United Nations or the principal organs of the UN, including, the Security Council, on any of such questions or matters except 'while the Security Council is exercising in respect of any dispute or situation the functions assigned to it'.[490]

The General Assembly meets in **regular annual sessions, special sessions,** and **emergency special sessions**. The sessions consist of formal and informal meetings.

490 Article 10 and Article 12 of the Charter.

The regular annual sessions

The regular annual session begins on Tuesday of the third week of September and runs for one year. Starting from its 44th session (1989–1990), the General Assembly has been formally regarded as being 'in session' for the whole year.

The first part of the session is usually called the 'main part of the session', which includes the general debate and the majority of the work of the **Main Committees of the General Assembly**. The period from January to September is called the 'resumed part of the session'.

Special sessions

Under the UN Charter, special sessions can be held 'as occasion may require' and 'shall be convoked by the Secretary-General at the request of the Security Council or of a majority of the Members of the United Nations.'[491]

In general, a special session deals with one subject, has a very short agenda, and lasts from one to several days. Eventually, a special session usually adopts one or two outcome documents.

Emergency special sessions

In 1950, the General Assembly initiated a controversial process by its well-known 'Uniting for Peace' Resolution examined earlier, which led to a rethinking of the recognised prerogative of the Security Council concerning the threats to international peace and security. According to the Resolution, the General Assembly decided that if the Security Council failed to exercise its primary responsibility for the maintenance of international peace and security 'because of lack of unanimity of the permanent members', the General Assembly could hold an emergency special session within 24 hours to consider the same matter.

An emergency special session is generally convened in the same manner as a special session. As of now, ten emergency special sessions have been held.[492]

The President and Committees of the General Assembly

491 Article 20 of the Charter.
492 There is no strict time limit for an emergency special session. For example, 'The tenth Emergency Special Session on "Illegal Israeli actions in occupied East Jerusalem and the rest of the Occupied Palestinian Territory" opened in 1997 and has never been formally closed. Member States decided to "temporarily adjourn" and to authorize the PGA to resume the session upon request from a Member State. As of September 2017 the tenth Emergency Special Session has been resumed fourteen times.' *The GA Handbook: A Practical Guide to the United Nations General Assembly*, Johann Aeschlimann and Mary Regan (eds) (Permanent Mission of Switzerland to the United Nations 2017) 1.2.

A full list of the emergency special sessions is available on the UN website <www.un.org/en/ga/sessions/emergency.shtml> accessed 16 March 2021.

For each regular annual session, the General Assembly elects its President and Vice-Presidents for a one-year non-renewable term of office by a simple majority vote 'at least three months before the opening of the session over which they are to preside'.[493] The main functions of the President are to ensure strict protection of the General Assembly Rules of Procedure, declare the opening and closing of each plenary meeting of the session, direct the discussions in plenary meetings, and, in general, facilitate the work of the General Assembly. A special session also assigns its President – normally, the President of the continuing regular session.

In addition, there are various subsidiary organs of the General Assembly, which are divided into the following categories: Boards, Commissions, Committees, Councils and Panels, Working Groups, and so forth.

The General Assembly has six Main Committees, which are commonly referred to as the 'committees of the whole' since all UN member states participate in them. These Main Committees are:

1   Disarmament and International Security Committee (First Committee);
2   Economic and Financial Committee (Second Committee);
3   Social, Humanitarian and Cultural Committee (Third Committee);
4   Special Political and Decolonization Committee (Fourth Committee);
5   Administrative and Budgetary Committee (Fifth Committee);
6   Legal Committee (Sixth Committee).

There are also established the General Committee, which is composed of the President and 21 Vice-Presidents of the General Assembly and the Chairmen of the six Main Committees, in order to prepare and oversee the organisational issues for the sessions of the General Assembly, and the Credentials Committee, which is appointed at the beginning of each regular session and consists of nine members, who are appointed by the General Assembly on the proposal of the President.

The resolutions and decisions

There is no distinction in legal force between the 'resolutions' and 'decisions' of the internal organs of the United Nations.

Typically, the resolutions are adopted on material matters (for example, the General Assembly resolutions express the approaches of the member states, develop policy recommendations, specify mandates to the UN Secretariat and the subsidiary bodies of the General Assembly, and decide on all questions regarding the UN budget); the decisions, on the other hand, regard the procedural issues and are usually divided into 'elections' and 'other decisions' (for example, the General Assembly elects the non-permanent members of the UN Security Council, the members of the Economic and Social Council, the members of its own subsidiary bodies, and the members of the International Court of Justice

493 Rule 30 of the General Assembly Rules of Procedure.

[jointly with the Security Council], and appoints, on the recommendation of the Security Council, the Secretary-General and elects its President and the Vice-Presidents).[494]

Besides, unlike votes on the adoption of the General Assembly resolutions, elections are held by secret paper ballot. The 'other decisions' are commonly made in relation to the procedural matters and are generally very short. Moreover, on simple procedural matters, oral decisions can be taken, which are, as a rule, made by consensus.

The General Assembly resolutions, as well as the resolutions of the other internal organs of the UN, generally consist of two parts – **preamble** and **operative part**. The preamble reflects the background and motives for the resolution. The operative or material part presents the opinion of the organ or the action to be taken. Its paragraphs are numbered. Sometimes the resolutions have annexes with additional texts, such as the text of a convention.

Symbol patterns of the resolutions and decisions of the General Assembly

'From 1946–1975, the first 3,541 resolutions were consecutively numbered, with the session indicated in roman numerals.'[495] At the same time, the special sessions were assigned the designations 'S' and 'ES.' For instance, the well-known Resolution 3314 (XXIX) (Definition of Aggression) refers to the 3314th Resolution, adopted in twenty-ninth regular annual session; A/RES/2252 (ES-V) (Humanitarian assistance) indicates the 2252nd Resolution, adopted at the fifth emergency special session. 'Beginning in 1976, 31st session, the symbol includes the session information and order of adoption of the resolution'.[496]

Hence, the UN General Assembly regular annual sessions are commonly designated in the following pattern – A/RES/[number of the session]/[number of the resolution (starting with 1 for each session)]; the special sessions are symbolised as A/RES/S and the emergency special sessions as A/RES/ES. For example, A/RES/ES-8/2 (Question of Namibia) refers to the 2nd Resolution of the eighth emergency special session.

---

494 For instance, according to the Rules of procedure, Rule 141 – 'When the Security Council has submitted its recommendation on the appointment of the Secretary-General, the General Assembly shall consider the recommendation and vote upon it by secret ballot in private meeting.' Rule 142 – 'The General Assembly shall each year, in the course of its regular session, elect five non-permanent members of the Security Council for a term of two years.' Rule 145 – 'The General Assembly shall each year, in the course of its regular session, elect eighteen members of the Economic and Social Council for a term of three years'. Rule 30 – 'Unless the General Assembly decides otherwise, the General Assembly shall elect a President and twenty-one Vice-Presidents at 9 least three months before the opening of the session over which they are to preside. The President and the Vice-Presidents so elected will assume their functions only at the beginning of the session for which they are elected and shall hold office until the close of that session.'

495 <https://research.un.org/en/docs/ga/resolutions> accessed 16 March 2021.

496 ibid.

As regards the decisions of the General Assembly, the following pattern is used – decision [number of the session]/[sequential number of the decision].[497]

Adoption of the resolutions and decisions

Each member of the United Nations has no more than five representatives in the General Assembly. Today, the United Nations member states are the 193 sovereign states that have equal representation in the General Assembly. At the same time, each member of the General Assembly has only one vote.

The resolutions/decisions of the General Assembly are adopted either by consensus (without taking a vote. If there is just one member state that requests a vote, then consensus is not reached) or by a vote. In the case of a vote, the decisions are made by simple majority or by a two-thirds majority of the members present and voting (i.e. casting an affirmative or negative vote).

The resolutions/decisions on **important questions** (such as the recommendations concerning the maintenance of international peace and security, the election of the non-permanent members of the Security Council, the election of the members of the Economic and Social Council, the election of members of the Trusteeship Council, the admission of new Members to the United Nations, the suspension of the rights and privileges of membership, the expulsion of Members, questions relating to the operation of the trusteeship system, and budgetary questions) shall be made by a two-thirds majority of the votes. At the same time, the General Assembly may decide by a simple majority to include additional issues among the 'important questions'.

Additionally, sometimes the General Assembly also utilises an absolute majority rule (the majority of all member states, which currently amounts to 97): for instance, for the election of members of the International Court of Justice and the Human Rights Council.

The principal mission of the General Assembly

On the whole, we might metaphorically call the General Assembly the **voice of the United Nations** in all matters.

---

497 'Decisions of the General Assembly are published in the sessional cumulation of resolutions and decisions. They are not issued as individual documents and have no document series symbol assigned to them. From 1945–1975, decisions were unnumbered. At the 31st session (1976), a numbering system similar to that for resolutions was established: pattern: General Assembly decision session/sequential number . . . examples: decision 50/411 decision ES-7/11. For decisions adopted at regular sessions: the first set of numbers is reserved for decisions related to elections and appointments, the second set for decisions related to matters other than elections and appointments.' ibid.

Security Council

permanent members of the Security Council
primary responsibility for the maintenance of international peace and security
mandatory resolutions
decisions
presidential statements
procedural matters
abstention from voting
action of the United Nations

Composition of the Security Council

The Security Council consists of 15 members of the United Nations. China, France, Russia, the United Kingdom of Great Britain and Northern Ireland, and the United States of America are **permanent members of the Security Council**. The General Assembly elects for a term of two years

> ten other Members of the United Nations to be non-permanent members of the Security Council, due regard being specially paid, in the first instance to the contribution of Members of the United Nations to the maintenance of international peace and security and to the other purposes of the Organization, and also to equitable geographical distribution.[498]

The principal powers of the Security Council

The United Nations Members 'confer on the Security Council **primary responsibility for the maintenance of international peace and security**'.[499] The specific powers granted to the Security Council for the discharge of this responsibility are laid down in Chapters VI (Pacific Settlement of Disputes), VII (Action with Respect to Threats to the Peace, Breaches of the Peace and Acts of Aggression), VIII (Regional Arrangements), and XII (International Trusteeship System) of the Charter.

Mandatory power of the Security Council's decisions

On the other hand, the UN members agree to accept and carry out the 'decisions of the Security Council' in accordance with the Charter,[500] which means that the Security Council is the UN body that can pass **mandatory resolutions** that the UN member states are

---

498 Article 23 of the Charter.
499 Article 24 of the Charter.
500 Article 25 of the Charter.

legally obliged to obey. The Security Council is also the only organ of the United Nations that can authorise the use of force and thereby physically carry out the enforcement of its resolutions. In addition to the resolutions, the Security Council also issue its **decisions** and **presidential statements**.

Security Council resolutions, decisions, and presidential statements

As in the case of the General Assembly, the decisions of the Security Council are usually on procedural matters, but they are unnumbered and have no document series symbol assigned to them.

Presidential statements are issued following consultations without a vote and currently are indicated with a symbol pattern: S/PRST/[year]/[number of the statement].

Resolutions of the Security Council are the individual documents which have been consecutively numbered since 1946. Their symbol pattern is S/RES/[number of the resolution](year). For instance, S/RES/757(1992) (Bosnia and Herzegovina), mentioned earlier, refers to the 757th Resolution, which was adopted in 1992.

The decision-making process

Each member of the Security Council has one vote. The Security Council decides on **procedural matters** by an affirmative vote of nine members. Resolutions and decisions on all other matters are made by an affirmative vote of nine members, including the concurring votes of the permanent members (the meaning of 'concurring votes' in practice has been reinterpreted, and abstentions are included within this definition).

If a permanent member is a party to a dispute, according to the Article 27(3) of the Charter, this state has the obligation of **abstention from voting** in cases of Chapter VI and under Article 52(3) of the Chapter VIII (Regional Arrangements). Therefore, this rule does not apply to Chapter VII when the Security Council authorises the measures concerning, respectively, threat to the peace, breach of the peace, or an act of aggression.

In sum, abstentions under Article 27(3) are mandatory only if all of the following conditions apply:

- The decision falls under Chapter VI or Article 52(3);
- The issue is considered a dispute;
- A Security Council member is considered a party to the dispute; and
- The decision is not procedural in nature.[501]

---

501 There have been more than ten cases of Article 27(3) abstentions, as well as several cases in which the question of abstentions was either raised or considered without success. For instance, discussing the Czechoslovak Question in 1948, the Draft Resolution failed adoption due to the veto by the USSR. Chile called the veto an 'abuse' and, referring to Article 27(3), stated that this Article seeks 'to prevent a member of the Council from acting as judge in its own case and participating in the decision that may be taken against it.' Nevertheless, the attempt was not successful.

Meanwhile, any state not a member of the UN Security Council or the United Nations, if it is a party to a dispute under consideration by the Security Council, shall be invited to participate, without a vote, in the discussions relating to the dispute.

The principal mission

Consequently, we can think of the Security Council as the **action of the United Nations** in the matters of war and peace.

The primary functions

The Security Council:

- determines threats to the peace, breaches of the peace or acts of aggression;
- calls upon the parties to a dispute to settle it by peaceful means;
- recommends methods of adjustment or terms of settlement of a dispute;
- in some instances, can resort to the imposition of sanctions or even authorise the use of force to maintain or restore international peace and security; and
- submits annual and, when necessary, special reports to the General Assembly for its consideration.

Economic and Social Council

international economic, social, cultural, educational, health, and related matters
recommendations
human rights and fundamental freedoms
Specialised Agencies
regular reports
United Nations coordinator in matters of the co-operation, development and protection of rights

Composition of the Economic and Social Council

The Economic and Social Council (ECOSOC) consists of 54 members of the United Nations elected by the General Assembly. Eighteen members of the Economic and Social Council shall be elected each year for a term of three years. Each member of the Economic and Social Council has one representative.

Functions

1   The Economic and Social Council may make or initiate studies and reports with respect to **international economic, social, cultural, educational, health,**

and related matters and may make **recommendations** with respect to any such matters to the General Assembly to the Members of the United Nations, and to the specialized agencies concerned.

2 It may make recommendations for the purpose of promoting respect for, and observance of, **human rights and fundamental freedoms** for all.[502]

Within its competence, the Economic and Social Council may prepare draft conventions for submission to the General Assembly, convene international conferences, make suitable arrangements for consultation with non-governmental organisations, and set up commissions in economic and social fields and for the promotion of the human rights.

The role of the Economic and Social Council regarding the UN Specialised Agencies

The Economic and Social Council oversees the work of the UN **Specialised Agencies** (international organisations). It enters into agreements with these agencies defining the terms under which the agency concerned shall be brought into relationship with the United Nations and obtains **regular reports** from them. Through its relationship with these outside agencies, ECOSOC often reviews their work and suggests areas of development.

The principal mission

Therefore, we can treat the Economic and Social Council as the **United Nations coordinator in matters of the co-operation, development, and protection of** (human) **rights**.

Decision-making

Decision-making in the Economic and Social Council is carried out by a majority of the members present and voting.

Trusteeship Council

> eleven trust territories
> self-government
> self-determination
> administering authority
> Decolonisation process
> significant contributor to the process of Decolonisation

502 Article 62 of the Charter.

Establishment of the Trusteeship Council

The Trusteeship Council was established in 1945.

According to Chapter XIII of the UN Charter, the Trusteeship Council was composed of the UN members administering the trust territories, the five permanent members of the Security Council, and

> as many other Members elected for three-year terms by the General Assembly as may be necessary to ensure that the total number of members of the Trusteeship Council is equally divided between those Members of the United Nations which administer trust territories and those which do not (Article 86).

In addition, a member of the Trusteeship Council authorised one specially qualified person to represent that member on the Council.

At the same time, each member of the Council had one vote. The Council adopted its decisions by a majority of the members present and voting.

The purposes of the Trusteeship Council

In the early years of the UN, the Trusteeship Council was assigned the international supervision of **eleven trust territories** (seven in Africa and four in Oceania) that had been placed under the administration of seven members of the UN. The Trusteeship Council exercised its competence to ensure that adequate steps were taken to prepare the peoples of these territories for **self-government** and **self-determination**.

It considered the reports submitted by the **administering authority**, accepted petitions and examined them in consultation with the administering authority, provided for periodic visits to the respective trust territories at times agreed upon with the administering authority, and took these and other actions in conformity with the terms of the trusteeship agreements.[503]

The principal mission

Over time, the Trusteeship Council played a historical role in the **Decolonisation process** as all the territories placed under the trusteeship system have by now attained self-government or independence, either as independent states or by joining other countries.[504] Hence, the size of the Trusteeship Council was gradually reduced, since the Council was intended to have a composition of an equal number of the administering and non-administering states and the permanent members of the UN Security Council. Consequently, without administrating states, ultimately it came to include only five permanent members of the Security Council.

In sum, the principal mission of the Trusteeship Council may be disclosed as being a **significant contributor to the process of Decolonisation**.

503 Article 87 of the Charter.
504 As noted earlier, the last was Palau, which became a member state of the United Nations in 1994.

The current state of affairs

The Trusteeship Council suspended operation on 1 November 1994. According to the Resolution of 1994, the Council amended its rules of procedure to drop the obligation to meet annually and agreed to meet upon the occasion on its own decision or the decision of its President or at the request of a majority of its members, the UN General Assembly, or the Security Council.

Nowadays, the United Nations and member states are in the process of finding the right position and functions for the Trusteeship Council in the UN system. Otherwise, the urgency of the elimination of the Council would be more actively placed on the agenda.

Secretariat

administrative and substantive support
Secretary-General
chief administrative officer of the United Nations
international character of the responsibilities
international civil servants
neural system of the United Nations

Functions of the Secretariat

As one of the principal organs of the UN, the Secretariat offers **administrative and substantive support** to all the activities of the UN, beginning from translation services to preparing studies on any topic of interest to the Organisation.

Staff members

It unites the Secretary-General and tens of thousands of international UN staff members who carry out the day-to-day work of the UN under the Charter and mandate assigned by the General Assembly and the Organisation's other principal organs.

Secretary-General

The Secretariat is headed by the **Secretary-General**, who is appointed by the General Assembly upon the recommendation of the Security Council. Secretary-General is the **chief administrative officer of the United Nations** and, as such, represents the Organisation before third persons, including all meetings of the General Assembly, the Security Council, the Economic and Social Council, and so forth.

The Secretary-General makes an annual report to the General Assembly on the work of the Organisation. Meanwhile, Secretary-General may bring to the attention of the

Security Council any matter which, based on the opinion of the Secretary-General, might be threatening international peace and security.[505]

The international character of the responsibilities of the staff and the Secretary-General of the UN

The staff of the Secretariat

> shall not seek or receive instructions from any government or from any other authority external to the Organization. They shall refrain from any action which might reflect on their position as international officials responsible only to the Organization. . . . Each Member of the United Nations undertakes to respect the exclusively **international character of the responsibilities** of the Secretary-General and the staff and not to seek to influence them in the discharge of their responsibilities.[506]

So individuals working within the Secretariat are the **international civil servants**, meaning that in the Secretariat, they do not represent their home states; instead, their work should be dedicated to the realisation of the goals and the mission of the Organisation.

The principal mission

Therefore, we can consider the Secretariat the **neural system of the United Nations**, which is responsible for the movement of the whole body of the Organisation.

International Court of Justice

> judicial organ of the United Nations
> Peace Palace in The Hague
> legal disputes
> advisory opinions

The principal mission

The International Court of Justice is the **judicial organ of the United Nations**.

505 Articles 98, 99 of the Charter.
506 Article 100 of the Charter.

The location of the International Court of Justice

The International Court of Justice is the only one of the six principal organs of the United Nations not located in New York (United States of America). Its seat is at the **Peace Palace in The Hague** (Netherlands).

The Court's role

The Court's role is to settle, in accordance with international law, **legal disputes** submitted to it by the states (contentious cases) and to give out **advisory opinions** on legal questions referred to it by the UN General Assembly; the Security Council; or the other organs of the United Nations, the Specialised Agencies, and the (UN) Related Organisations authorised by the UN General Assembly.

Other issues

A more detailed description of the composition, functions, and activities of the Court is found earlier in this book.[507]

UNITED NATIONS SPECIALISED AGENCIES AND RELATED ORGANISATIONS

decentralised UN system
diversification
Specialised Agencies as independent organisations
ILO
FAO
UNESCO
ICAO
WHO
IBRD
IFC
IDA
WBG
MIGA
ICSID
IMF
UPU
ITU
WMO
IMO

507 The chapter 'International courts'.

WIPO
IFAD
UNIDO
UNWTO
Related Organisations
IAEA
WTO
IOM
Chief Executives Board for Coordination

Diversification

The existence of the **decentralised UN system** is mainly rooted in the founding concept of the United Nations, where **diversification** represents the vital precondition for international peacebuilding. Thus, diversification prevails in the internal structure of the United Nation, as well as in the whole UN System.

The Specialised Agencies as independent organisations

For instance, although the Specialised Agencies are an important part of the whole of the UN system, they, at the same time, enjoy the status of independent international organisations: autonomous subjects of international law (the **Specialised Agencies as independent organisations**).

Activities of the Specialised Agencies

The Specialised Agencies carry out their activities 'in economic, social, cultural, educational, health, and related fields' as defined by the Article 57 (1) of the UN Charter and possess their own highest and executive bodies, secretariats, and budgets.

Linkage/relations with the UN

However, on the other hand, according to the Article 63 of the UN Charter, such agencies agree to adjust their work and policies through agreements with the UN. The Economic and Social Council 'may enter into agreements with any of the agencies referred to in Article 57' and 'may co-ordinate the activities of the specialized agencies through consultation with and recommendations to such agencies and through recommendations to the General Assembly and to the Members of the United Nations'.

Such agreements are subject to approval by the UN General Assembly. Additionally, according to Article 17 (3) of the Charter, the General Assembly considers and approves 'any financial and budgetary arrangements' concerning the Specialised Agencies and examines the administrative budgets of such agencies 'with a view to making recommendations to the agencies concerned.'

Each specialised agency negotiates its agreement with ECOSOC, which leads to a very complex system in which different organisations maintain different types of relationships with the UN. Hence, only such agencies which were brought into relationship with the United Nations under Articles 57 and 63 of the Charter may be referred to as Specialised Agencies.

For example, the UN concluded the agreement mentioned earlier with the World Tourism Organisation under the Resolution of the General Assembly of 2003 by

> [h]aving considered Economic and Social Council resolution 2003/2 of 10 July 2003, the annex to which contains the text of the draft agreement negotiated by the Committee on Negotiations with Intergovernmental Agencies of the Economic and Social Council and the World Tourism Organization Committee on the Negotiations for the Conversion of the Organization into a Specialized Agency.[508]

At the same time, the General Assembly approved the Agreement between the United Nations and the World Tourism Organisation, which was annexed to the Resolution. The Agreement included the following provision on the new status of the World Tourism Organisation:

> The United Nations recognizes the World Tourism Organization as a specialized agency of the United Nations responsible for taking such action as may be appropriate under its Statutes for the accomplishment of the objectives set forth therein. . . . The United Nations recognizes the decisive and central role of the World Tourism Organization, as an intergovernmental organization, in world tourism, as enshrined in its Statutes.[509]

An illustrative list of the Specialised Agencies

The following are the United Nations Specialised Agencies:

- **ILO** – The International Labour Organisation's primary goals are: promotion of rights in the workplace, encouragement of decent employment opportunities, and enhancement of social protection and strengthening of the dialogue on work-related issues. It is a tripartite UN agency, which brings together governments, employers, and workers' representatives from the member states.
- **FAO** – The United Nations Food and Agriculture Organisation's three main goals are: eradication of hunger, food insecurity and malnutrition; elimination of poverty and the driving forward of economic and social progress for all; and the sustainable management and utilisation of natural resources.
- **UNESCO** – The United Nations Educational, Scientific and Cultural Organisation's responsibility is the coordination of international co-operation in education, science, culture, and communication.

---

508 A/RES/58/232 of 23 December 2003.
509 Article 1 of the Agreement between the United Nations and the World Tourism Organisation <https://digitallibrary.un.org/record/509663?ln=en#record-files-collapse-header > accessed 16 March 2021.

- **ICAO** – The International Civil Aviation Organisation is established by the states to manage the administration and governance of the Convention on International Civil Aviation (Chicago Convention).
- **WHO** – The World Health Organisation's primary role is to give direction to and coordinate international health-related issues at the international level. The objective of the Organisation, as defined in the WHO Constitution, is 'the attainment by all peoples of the highest possible level of health'. At the same time, according to the Constitution, health 'is a state of complete physical, mental and social well-being and not merely the absence of disease or infirmity'.
- **IBRD, IFC, and IDA** – Nowadays, the World Bank Group (**WBG**) comprises a group of five legally separate but, at the same time, affiliated organisations, such as the International Bank for Reconstruction and Development (IBRD), the International Finance Corporation (IFC), the International Development Association (IDA), the Multilateral Investment Guarantee Agency (**MIGA**), and the International Centre for Settlement of Investment Disputes (**ICSID**). On the whole, the institutions of the World Bank Group are established to provide loans, technical assistance, and policy advice in order to encourage the sustainable economic development of the subjects of international law around the world. Three of the World Bank Group organisations – namely, the IBRD, the IFC, and the IDA – are Specialised Agencies of the UN.
- **IMF** – The International Monetary Fund is working to foster global monetary co-operation, secure financial stability, facilitate international trade, promote high employment and sustainable economic growth, and reduce poverty around the world.
- **UPU** – The Universal Postal Union is the primary forum for co-operation between postal sector players and helps ensure a truly universal network of up-to-date products and services.
- **ITU** – The International Telecommunication Union's principal purpose is to coordinate telecommunication operations and services throughout the world.
- **WMO** – The World Meteorological Organisation's main goal is to promote international co-operation on a global scale for the development of meteorology, climatology, and operational hydrology as well as to reap the benefits of their application.
- **IMO** – The International Maritime Organisation's central role is to create a regulatory framework for the shipping industry that is fair and effective, universally adopted, and universally implemented.
- **WIPO** – The World Intellectual Property Organisation's mission is to lead the development of a balanced and effective international intellectual property system that enables innovation and creativity for the benefit of all.
- **IFAD** – The International Fund for Agricultural Development is mainly dedicated to eradicating rural poverty in developing countries.
- **UNIDO** – United Nations Industrial Development Organisation's mission is to promote and accelerate inclusive and sustainable industrial development in the member states.
- **UNWTO** – The World Tourism Organisation promotes tourism as a driver of economic growth, inclusive development, and environmental sustainability and offers leadership and support to the sector in advancing knowledge and tourism policies worldwide.

Related Organisations

In addition, the important actors in the global interstate co-operation are other international intergovernmental organisations (the so-called **Related Organisations**), which have concluded special agreements (the Agreement concerning the Relationship) with the UN but do not possess the status of Specialised Agencies, such as the International Atomic Energy Agency (**IAEA**), the World Trade Organisation (**WTO**), and the International Organisation for Migration (**IOM**).[510]

These organisations are designated as the UN 'Related Organisations', which 'has to be understood as a default expression, describing organizations whose cooperation agreement with the United Nations has many points in common with that of Specialized Agencies, but does not refer to Article 57 and 63 of the United Nations Charter, relevant to Specialized Agencies.'[511]

Chief Executives Board for Coordination

The UN System **Chief Executives Board for Coordination** (CEB) is the highest coordination forum of the United Nations, which aims to adjust the activities of more than 30 members. The membership of the CEB includes the United Nations itself, the Specialized Agencies, the Related Organisations, and the funds and programmes established by the UN General Assembly.

The UN System Chief Executives Board for Coordination meets twice a year under the chairmanship of the UN Secretary-General and reports to the Economic and Social Council and the General Assembly of the UN.

EUROPEAN COMMUNITIES AND THE EUROPEAN UNION

For many centuries, Europe was the theatre of the most brutal and bloody wars. However, to the credit of the Europeans, they are also responsible for taking the most radical steps in order to establish peace between the European nations:

---

510 According to the Agreement concerning the Relationship between the United Nations and the International Organisation for Migration: 'The United Nations recognizes the International Organization for Migration as an essential contributor in the field of human mobility, in the protection of migrants, in operational activities related to migrants, displaced people and migration-affected communities, including in the areas of resettlement and returns, and in mainstreaming migration in development plans.' As regards the status, the Agreement determines that the IOM 'by virtue of its Constitution, shall function as an independent, autonomous and non-normative international organization in the working relationship with the United Nations established by this Agreement', A/RES/70/296 of 25 July 2016.

511 Was published on the official website of the UN <www.unsystem.org/members/related-organizations> accessed 19 December 2020. Available at <www.scoop.it/topic/united-nations-undesa-undspd-ecosoc-unsdn-unngls-by-dr-lendy-spires?page=6> accessed 16 March 2021.

- 'World peace cannot be safeguarded without the making of creative efforts proportionate to the dangers which threaten it.' – Robert Schuman (1886–1963).[512]
- 'Living up to Europe's rallying cry – never again war – is our eternal duty, our perpetual responsibility. We must all remain vigilant.' – Jean-Claude Juncker (born 1954).[513]

From economic to political union

European Coal and Steel Community
European Atomic Energy Community
European Economic Community
Merger Treaty
Amsterdam Treaty
single institutional structure
European Communities
European Parliament
Schengen Agreement
Single European Act
Treaty of Maastricht
European Union
European Community
Treaties of Amsterdam and Nice
Treaty of Lisbon

The idea of a united Europe

The idea of a united Europe is rooted in the scientific legacy of Western thinking. The most prominent philosopher in this regard is Immanuel Kant, who in his *Perpetual Peace: A Philosophical Essay* depicted the concept of a federation of free states (based on the rethinking model of international law) as a crucial precondition for perpetual peace.[514]

512 'Luxembourgian-born French prime minister . . . Declaration, 9 May 1950. This declaration on behalf of the French government, which laid the foundation for the European Union, was drafted by Jean Monnet.' *The Yale Book of Quotations* (n 180) 673.

513 'State of the Union 2018, Annual State of the EU address by President Juncker at the European Parliament', available on the official website of the EU <https://ec.europa.eu/commission/priorities/state-union-speeches/state-union-2018_en> accessed 16 March 2021. In this book, materials from the website are used according to applicable legal rules.

514 '[H]e promotes the model of the bond (community) of peoples (Völkerbund) which he equates with the bond (community) of peace (Friedensbund – *foedus pacificum*), free federalism (freie Föderalism) and federative community (föderative Vereinigung). He suggests that the reason, from her throne of the supreme lawgiving moral power, absolutely condemns war as a morally lawful proceeding (als Rechtsgang) and makes a state of peace an immediate duty.' Pataraia (n 8) 131.

In the twentieth century, the first concrete proposals for the integration of Europe were made by Richard von Coudenhove-Kalergi (1894–1972) in 1923,[515] and this object was pursued by the private Pan European Union, which he founded.

After World War II

Since World War II, the new European interstate architecture has been determined by a combination of the following developments:

1   the complex economic and political co-operation between the Western European countries;
2   the process of the harmonisation of approaches regarding democracy, the rule of law, and so on; and
3   the need for Euro-Atlantic consolidation against the common threat of the Soviet Union.

The first development was institutionalised through European Communities and finalised by the European Union, the second with the establishment of the Council of Europe, and the third through NATO (also, in part, by the Western European Union [WEU]).[516]

Timeline of the crucial events and treaties of the European Communities and the European Union

*   1951 – The Treaty of Paris establishing the **European Coal and Steel Community** (ECSC) was signed; the founding members were Belgium, West Germany, France, Luxembourg, Italy, and the Netherlands. The Treaty came into force in 1952 and expired in 2002.
*   1957 – The Treaties of Rome were signed, one establishing the **European Atomic Energy Community** (EURATOM) and the second establishing the **European Economic Community** (EEC). The Treaties came into force in 1958.
*   1967 – The **Merger Treaty** (signed in 1965 and abrogated by the **Amsterdam Treaty** signed in 1997) combined the executive bodies of the European Communities into a **single institutional structure** (a single Council and a single Commission). Although each Community remained legally independent, they shared common institutions (before this Treaty, they already shared the Parliamentary Assembly and Court of Justice) and were together known as the **European Communities**.
*   1973 – The first expansion (UK, Ireland, and Denmark) took place.

515 His book, *Pan-Europa*, was published in 1923.
516 'In 1954, the Western European Union (WEU) was created to strengthen security policy cooperation between the countries of Europe. . . . The WEU marked the beginnings of a security and defence policy in Europe in 1954. However, its role has not developed further, since the majority of its powers have been transferred to other international institutions, notably NATO, the Council of Europe and the EU.' Klaus-Dieter Borchardt, *The ABC of European Union Law* (Luxembourg: Publications Office of the European Union 2010) 10.

- 1979 – The European Monetary System (EMS), including the Exchange Rate Mechanism was established.
- 1979 – A directly elected **European Parliament** was instituted.
- 1981 – The second expansion (Greece) took place.
- 1985 – The **Schengen Agreement** was signed, leading to the creation of the Schengen Area. The Schengen treaties and the rules adopted under them operated independently from the European Union. But in 1999, they were incorporated into the legal framework of the European Union by the Amsterdam Treaty while providing opt-outs for the only two EU member states that had remained outside the Area: Ireland and the United Kingdom.
- 1986 – The third expansion (Spain, Portugal) took place.
- 1986 – The **Single European Act** was signed, which set the European Communities an objective of establishing a single market by 31 December 1992 and codified European political co-operation. The Act came into force in 1987.
- 1990 – East Germany incorporated into united Germany, leading to the integration of East Germany into the European institutional system.
- 1992 – The **Treaty of Maastricht** (the Treaty on **European Union**) was signed and came into force in 1993. According to the Treaty, 'the High Contracting Parties establish among themselves a European Union'. In addition, there was the formulation that 'The Union shall be founded on the European Communities, supplemented by the policies and forms of cooperation established by this Treaty.'[517] At the same time, through the Treaty of Maastricht, the word 'Economic' was removed from the EEC, so it became simply the **European Community** (EC) (Title II. Provisions Amending the Treaty Establishing the European Economic Community with a View to Establishing the European Community.) However, the Treaty of Maastricht was the first step on the path leading ultimately to a modern European institutional system. Further developments came in the form of the **Treaties of Amsterdam and Nice**, which entered into force in 1999 and 2003, respectively.
- 1995 – Fourth expansion (Austria, Finland, Sweden) took place.
- 1999 – The single currency was introduced (since 2002, the euro has replaced the currencies of most of the member states).
- 2002 – The European Coal and Steel Community was finally integrated into the European Community.
- 2004 – Fifth expansion (Czech Republic, Hungary, Poland, Slovakia, Slovenia, Estonia, Latvia, Lithuania, Cyprus, Malta) took place.
- 2007 – The **Treaty of Lisbon**, initially known as the Reform Treaty, was signed. The European Union was given a single consolidated legal personality under this Treaty. Previously, the European Community and the European Union had different statuses. The Lisbon Treaty ended this dual system. The word 'Community' is replaced throughout by the word 'Union'. 'The Union shall be founded on the present Treaty and on the Treaty on the Functioning of the European Union.[518] Those two Treaties

---

517 Article A of the Title I (Common Provisions) of the Treaty of Maastricht.

518 Treaty on the Functioning of the European Union (TFEU) originated as the treaty establishing the European Economic Community (the EEC treaty).

shall have the same legal value. The Union shall replace and succeed the European Community.'[519] Unlike the European Economic Community Treaty, no extreme changes have ever been made to the European Atomic Energy Community Treaty, which remains in force. Notably, Euratom has not merged with the European Union and therefore preserves a separate international legal personality, although it has the same membership.

- 2007 – Second wave of the fifth expansion (Bulgaria, Romania) took place.
- 2013 – Sixth expansion (Croatia) took place.
- 2016 – The UK held a Membership Referendum and voted to leave the European Union.
- 2020 – The UK left the European Union on 31 January 2020.[520]

From the European Union's three pillars concept to the system of the distribution of competences

> Treaty on European Union
> Single Market and the European Communities Policies pillar
> Common Foreign and Security Policy pillar
> Police and Judicial Cooperation in Criminal Matters pillar
> supranationalism
> Treaty of Lisbon
> merged legal personality

519 Article 1 of the Treaty on European Union (TEU) (as amended by the Treaty of Lisbon in its EU Official Journal version dated 17 December 2007).

520 'When the United Kingdom leaves the European Union on 31 January 2020, after full ratification of the Withdrawal Agreement, we will enter into the transition period. This time-limited period was agreed as part of the Withdrawal Agreement and will last until at least 31 December 2020. . . . The transition period is a time-limited period, starting on 1 February 2020. The exact terms of the transition period are set out in Part Four of the Withdrawal Agreement. It is currently foreseen that the transition period ends on 31 December 2020. It can be extended once by up to one to two years. Such a decision must be taken jointly by the EU and United Kingdom before 1 July 2020. . . . The United Kingdom will no longer be a Member State of the European Union and of the European Atomic Energy Community as of 1 February 2020. As a third country, it will no longer participate in the EU's decision-making processes. . . . However, all institutions, bodies, offices and agencies of the European Union continue to hold the powers conferred upon them by EU law in relation to the United Kingdom and to natural and legal persons residing or established in the United Kingdom throughout the transition period. The Court of Justice of the European Union continues to have jurisdiction over the United Kingdom during the transition period. This also applies to the interpretation and implementation of the Withdrawal Agreement.' See the official website of the EU <https://ec.europa.eu/commission/presscorner/detail/en/QANDA_20_104> accessed 16 March 2021.

> EU exclusive competences
> shared competences
> supportive competences
> special competences

The original three pillars

Initially, with the Treaty of Maastricht (the **Treaty on European Union**), the construction of the European Union was founded on the following three pillars:

1　The **Single Market and the European Communities Policies pillar** maintained economic, social, and environmental policies. It comprised the European Community (EC), the European Coal and Steel Community (ECSC) until its expiry in 2002, and the European Atomic Energy Community (EURATOM).
2　The **Common Foreign and Security Policy pillar** took under its arms the foreign policy and military matters of the EU.
3　The **Police and Judicial Cooperation in Criminal Matters pillar** brought together co-operation in the fight against crime.

Meanwhile, **supranationalism** was mostly associated with the first pillar and generally corresponded to the three European Communities whose organisational structure was unified in 1967. In the second and third pillars, the powers of the European bodies were significantly limited.

Treaty of Lisbon

However, after the **Treaty of Lisbon** came into force, the European Union's 'three pillars' concept was abandoned. The new architecture of the EU was established, which simplified EU construction. In sum, the Treaty of Lisbon replaced the 'three pillars' concept with a **merged legal personality** for the Union and incorporated the institutional framework in which the competences in various policy areas were distributed between member states and the Union.

The distribution of competences

The following areas of the **EU exclusive competences** have been established: Customs union, competition rules for the single market, monetary policy for the eurozone countries, conservation of marine biological resources under the common fisheries policy, and international agreements in specific circumstances.[521]

---

521 'The Union shall also have exclusive competence for the conclusion of an international agreement when its conclusion is provided for in a legislative act of the Union or is necessary to enable the Union to exercise its internal competence, or in so far as its conclusion may affect common rules or alter their

The spheres of the **shared competences** (with member states) are single market, employment and social affairs; economic, social and territorial cohesion; agriculture and fisheries (excluding the conservation of marine biological resources); environment; consumer protection; transport; trans-European networks; energy; area of freedom; security and justice; common safety concerns in public health matters; and so forth.

At the same time, there are also the so-called **supportive competences** of the EU in the areas, where the EU can only coordinate or complement the activities of the member states. Notably, such areas include industry, culture, tourism, and so forth.

In addition, the EU may have **special competences** in particular fields: for example, based on the 'flexibility clause', which, under strict conditions, enables the EU to take action outside its typical areas of competences.

The European Union's structure

Treaty on European Union
TEU
Treaty on the Functioning of the European Union
TFEU
European Parliament
European Council
Council
European Commission
Court of Justice of the European Union
European Central Bank
Court of Auditors
voice of the EU's citizens
common general political approach of the EU member states
maintenance and consolidation of the national interests of the member states
voice of the EU
CJEU
right of legislative initiative
European Investment Bank
legislator
ordinary legislative procedure
conciliation committee
special legislative procedure

scope.' Article 3 (2) of the Treaty on the Functioning of the European Union (the consolidated version of 01/03/2020).

The principal decision-making bodies of the European Union

The contemporary structure of the EU was instituted by two founding treaties – the **Treaty on European Union (TEU)** and the **Treaty on the Functioning of the European Union (TFEU)**.[522] The 'institutions' of the EU are the following seven principal decision-making bodies:

- **European Parliament**,
- **European Council**,
- **Council** (of Ministers),
- **European Commission**,
- **Court of Justice of the European Union**,
- **European Central Bank**, and
- **Court of Auditors**.

The EU's unique institutional structure

- The European Council sets the EU's broad priorities, which bring together national and EU-level leaders.
- Members of the European Parliament, who are directly elected, represent the European (EU) citizens. All citizens of an EU country are automatically citizens of the EU, which gives them certain important extra rights and responsibilities (such as the right to move and reside freely within the territory of the member states without discrimination; the right to vote and stand as a candidate in both European and certain municipal [local] elections [as defined in the Council Directive 94/80/EC of 19 December 1994 concerning the municipal elections and the Annex thereto] in the EU country in which he or she resides under the same conditions as nationals of that state; the right to have his or her affairs handled impartially, fairly and within a reasonable time by the institutions, bodies, offices and agencies of the Union [right to good administration]; and so forth).
- The European Commission, whose members are appointed by the national governments, promotes the interests of the EU as a whole.
- The governments defend their national interests in the Council of the EU.

European Parliament

The European Parliament exercises, jointly with the Council, legislative and budgetary functions. It also carries out functions of political control and consultation and is responsible for electing the President of the Commission.

---

522 The consolidated versions of the founding treaties of the EU are available at <https://eur-lex.europa. eu>. In this and subsequent subsections, the consolidated versions from 1 March 2020 are referred to. At the same time, in this book, some other materials (international treaties as well as other documents) concerning the EU are also 'reused' from this website. The website <https://eur-lex.europa. eu> itself is a significant contribution to the development of the publicity of EU legal documents as well as of international law.

The European Parliament is composed of representatives of the Union's citizens, who are elected for a term of five years by direct universal suffrage in a free and secret ballot. They shall not exceed 705 (704 plus the President) as modified following the UK's departure from the EU.

Representation of the citizens shall be degressively proportional, with a minimum threshold of 6 members per member state. No member state shall be allocated more than 96 seats. Meanwhile, the European Council adopts by unanimity, upon the initiative of the European Parliament and with its consent, a decision establishing the composition of the European Parliament (the composition is determined by the European Council Decision (EU) 2018/937 of 28 June 2018).

Therefore, the European Parliament is the **voice of the EU's citizens**.

European Council

The European Council defines the 'general political directions' and priorities. It does not exercise legislative functions.

The European Council consists of the heads of state or government of the member states, together with its President and the President of the Commission. As a rule, it meets twice every six months.

The decisions of the European Council are taken by consensus, except where the founding treaties of the EU provide otherwise. If a vote is taken, neither the European Council President nor the President of the Commission take part.

Consequently, the European Council directs a **common general political approach of the EU member states**.

Council

The Council (also referred to as the Council of Ministers or the Council of the European Union) exercises, jointly with the European Parliament, legislative and budgetary functions. It also carries out policy-making and coordinating functions.

The Council consists of a representative from each member state at the ministerial level. It meets in different configurations: The General Affairs Council, the Foreign Affairs Council, and so forth. The Council meets in public when it deliberates and votes on a draft legislative act.

The Council shall act by a qualified majority except where the founding treaties of the EU provide otherwise. Currently, a qualified majority is defined as 'at least 55% of the members of the Council, comprising at least fifteen of them and representing Member States comprising at least 65% of the population of the Union.'[523] At the same time, a blocking minority must include at least four Council members representing more than 35% of the EU population.

In sum, the Council represents a platform for the **maintenance and consolidation of the national interests of the member states**.

---

523 Article 16 (4) of the Treaty on European Union.

Commission

The Commission 'promotes the general interests of the Union'. It oversees the application of the Union law under the control of the Court of Justice of the European Union; executes the budget; manages programs; and exercises coordinating, executive, and management functions. 'With the exception of the common foreign and security policy, and other cases provided for in the Treaties, it shall ensure the Union's external representation.'[524]

The Commission, as a body, is responsible before the European Parliament. However, it should be completely independent in carrying out its responsibilities. Besides, the members of the Commission do not represent the views of their country of origin but rather the common interest of the EU. Therefore, the members of the Commission shall be chosen based on their general competence and European commitment from the persons whose independence is beyond doubt.

After a rather lengthy process of appointing the President and selecting the Commissioners, finally,

> [t]he President, the High Representative of the Union for Foreign Affairs and Security Policy and the other members of the Commission shall be subject as a body to a vote of consent by the European Parliament. On the basis of this consent the Commission shall be appointed by the European Council, acting by a qualified majority.[525]

The Commission's term of office is five years.

According to the European Council Decision of 28 November 2019, the current Commission (College of Commissioners) is a team of 27 Commissioners (each responsible for a portfolio). 'A new Commission, consisting of one national of each Member State, including its President and the High Representative of the Union for Foreign Affairs and Security Policy, ... [is] appointed until 31 October 2024 .'[526]

The Commission meets, as a general rule, at least once per week. Decisions of the Commission are taken based on collective responsibility. Decisions are usually taken by consensus, but voting can also take place. In the latter case, decisions are taken by a simple majority, in which each commissioner has one vote.

On the whole, metaphorically, we can treat the Commission as the **voice of the EU**.

European Court of Justice

The Court of Justice of the European Union (usually referred to as European Court of Justice or simply **CJEU** or ECJ) includes 'the Court of Justice, the General Court and specialised courts'[527] and is based in Luxembourg.

Hence, the CJEU is divided into two permanent courts with separate registries and individual rules of procedure. Moreover, the cases handled by the General Court are identified using a 'T' (Tribunal) (T – / –), whilst those referred to the Court of Justice are designated with a 'C' (Court) (C – / –).

---

524 Article 17 (1) of the Treaty on European Union.
525 Article 17 (7) of the Treaty on European Union.
526 European Council Decision (EU) 2019/1989 of 28 November 2019 appointing the European Commission.
527 Article 19 of the Treaty on European Union.

The Court of Justice consists of one judge from each of the 27 member states. Eleven Advocates-General assist it. The Court deals mostly with requests for preliminary rulings from national courts to clarify a point concerning the interpretation of EU law, the particular actions for annulment of the EU legal acts, actions for failure to fulfil obligations by a member state and appeals on points of law against judgments and orders of the General Court.

The General Court is made up of two judges from each member country. It primarily deals with actions brought by natural or legal persons against acts of the EU bodies, competition law, state aid, trade, agriculture, trademarks, environment and consumers protection.

The judges and the Advocates-General of the Court of Justice and the judges of the General Court are chosen from persons whose independence is beyond doubt and who meet the conditions specified in the Treaty on the Functioning of the European Union (TFEU). They are appointed by common accord of the governments of the member states for a six-year term.

On the whole, the CJEU:

a) interprets the EU law;
b) settles legal disputes between national governments and EU institutions;
c) rules on actions brought before it by natural or legal persons against an EU institution, if they feel it has somehow infringed their rights; and
d) rules in other cases as provided for in founding treaties.

The most typical types of cases brought before the CJEU are:

- interpreting the EU law – which is undertaken for the harmonised interpretation of EU legal obligations;
- enforcing the EU law – which is practised against the government of a member state for failing to comply with EU law;
- annulling EU legal acts – when legal acts violate EU treaties or fundamental rights;
- ensuring the EU takes action – when the EU Parliament, Council, and Commission should make particular decisions but fail to meet the obligation; and
- sanctioning EU institutions (actions for damages) – which result from the actions or inactions of the EU or its staff.[528]

European Central Bank

The European Central Bank (ECB) manages the euro and conducts, together with the national central banks of the member states whose currency is the euro, the monetary policy of the EU. Its main aim is to keep prices stable, thereby supporting and stimulating economic growth and job creation. In the areas falling within its responsibilities, the ECB shall be consulted on all proposed Union acts, and all proposals for regulation at national level, and may give an opinion.

ECB has the following decision-making bodies: (1) Governing Council – the main decision-making body which consists of the Executive Board plus the governors of the national central banks from the 19 euro area countries. (2) Executive Board – handles the day-to-day running of the ECB and consists of the ECB President and Vice President and

---

528 See the 'most common types' of cases at <https://europa.eu/european-union/about-eu/institutions-bodies/court-justice_en> accessed 16 March 2021.

four other members appointed to eight-year terms by the European Council, acting by a qualified majority. Under the ECB's rules, board members do not represent a particular country, nor are they responsible for keeping track of economic conditions in one state. Instead, all board members are jointly responsible for monetary policy for the entire euro area. (3) General Council – has more of an advisory and coordinating role. It is made up of the ECB President and Vice President and the governors of the central banks from all the EU countries. (4) Supervisory Board – meets every three weeks to carry out the ECB's supervisory tasks.

European Court of Auditors

The European Court of Auditors (ECA) looks after the interests of the EU taxpayers. It works to improve the European Commission's management of the EU budget and reports on the EU finances.

The European Court of Auditors is a collegiate body of 27 members, one from each member state. The members of the ECA are appointed by the Council, after consulting the Parliament, for renewable six-year terms. They choose one of their members as the President for a renewable term of three years.

The EU legislative procedure

EU legal acts consist of legislative and non-legislative acts adopted by the EU institutions. The legal acts of the EU may generally be introduced in the areas in which the EU has either exclusive competences or shared competences; however, based on the principle of subsidiarity, the EU may intervene only if it can act more effectively.

A comprehensive procedure is envisaged for the adoption of legislative acts in which particular principal institutions and advisory bodies of the EU, as well as the citizens and the member states, are involved. Non-legislative acts, on the other hand, are not subject to these procedures and can be introduced by the EU institutions according to the specific rules.

- The **right of legislative initiative** – Generally, legislative acts may be adopted only based on the Commission's proposal where an EU legislative act is adopted by an ordinary or special legislative procedure (which will be examined later), except where the founding treaties of the EU provide otherwise. On the other hand, the Commission is also engaged in the adoption process of the other acts through a proposal mechanism – however, only when the founding treaties explicitly so provide.

  At the same time, the Commission does not have the exclusive right of legislative initiative to propose a legal act in every area in which the European Union has the competence: for instance, in the field of the Common Foreign and Security Policy, to which the 'intergovernmental method' (intergovernmental decision-making procedures) still applies.[529]

---

529 'The Union shall conduct the common foreign and security policy by: (a) defining the general guidelines; (b) adopting decisions defining: (i) actions to be undertaken by the Union; (ii) positions to be taken by the Union; (iii) arrangements for the implementation of the decisions referred to in points

The EU citizens also enjoy the right to 'initiative of inviting the European Commission' if at least one million citizens of the Union from at least one-quarter of the member states 'approach the Commission directly with a request inviting it to submit a proposal for a legal act for the purpose of implementing the Treaties'.[530] In addition, the European Parliament and the Council may also request the Commission to submit the proposals for legislative acts. However, as in the cases of the citizens' initiatives, also in relation to the request of the European Parliament and Council, the Commission can decide not to submit a proposal.

- The **legislator** – For any type of legislative act to become legally binding, it must be adopted by the legislator. In most cases, the legislator is the European Parliament and the Council (Council of Ministers) jointly. This procedure is called an **ordinary legislative procedure**.[531] The ordinary legislative procedure applies in more than 80 defined policy areas comprising the majority of the 'areas of competence' of the EU.

Thus, at most times, there are three central institutions involved in the ordinary legislative procedure: (1) European Parliament, (2) Council (Council of Ministers) and (3) the European Commission. The Commission proposes new legislative acts, and the Parliament and Council adopt them. Therefore, in order to adopt a legislative act, the co-legislators must, during the procedure, agree on a shared text acceptable to both the European Parliament and the Council. Thus, to this end, the responsible institutions should communicate with each other. Such communications commonly take place in the form of the so-called 'trilogues', which are the informal tripartite meetings on legislative proposals between representatives of the European Parliament, Council, and Commission.

If the European Parliament and the Council cannot agree on a common text, at a stage of the second reading, a **conciliation committee** (which is composed of an equal number of representatives from the two co-legislators) seeks to find a solution. If the Conciliation Committee does not agree on the joint text within six weeks, it is assumed that the proposed act was not adopted.[532] At the same time, the Commission

---

(i) and (ii); and by (c) strengthening systematic cooperation between Member States in the conduct of policy.' Article 25 of the Treaty on European Union.

530 According to Article 3 of the Regulation (EU) 2019/788 of the European Parliament and of the Council of 17 April 2019 on the European citizens' initiative: '1. An initiative is valid if: (a) it has received the support of at least one million citizens of the Union in accordance with Article 2(1) ("signatories") from at least one quarter of the Member States; and (b) in at least one quarter of the Member States, the number of signatories is at least equal to the minimum number set out in Annex I, corresponding to the number of the Members of the European Parliament elected in each Member State, multiplied by the total number of Members of the European Parliament, at the time of registration of the initiative.' All legislative or non-legislative acts of the EU are available at <https://eur-lex.europa.eu>.

531 'The ordinary legislative procedure shall consist in the joint adoption by the European Parliament and the Council of a regulation, directive or decision on a proposal from the Commission.' Article 289 (1) of the Treaty on the Functioning of the European Union.

532 'The Conciliation Committee, which shall be composed of the members of the Council or their representatives and an equal number of members representing the European Parliament, shall have the task of reaching agreement on a joint text, by a qualified majority of the members of the Council or their representatives and by a majority of the members representing the European Parliament within six

also takes part in the conciliation committee's proceedings by providing all necessary initiatives to facilitate the reconciliation process.

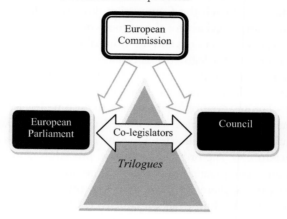

FIGURE 7.2 The EU ordinary legislative procedure

Sometimes, the legislator might be only one of the co-legislators – however, with the participation of the second institution (either the Parliament or Council). Hence, 'in certain more sensitive policy areas'[533] provided for by the Treaties, the adoption of a regulation, directive, or decision by the Council with the participation of the European Parliament, or by the latter with the participation of the Council, constitutes a **special legislative procedure**.[534] Hence, a special legislative procedure:

1   is a derogation from the ordinary legislative procedure;
2   is followed only in exceptional cases, when the founding treaties of the EU explicitly refer to such a procedure; and
3   is implemented by either the Council or Parliament (in the status of a sole legislator) after consulting or obtaining the consent of the second co-legislator.

According to the founding treaties of the EU, in the majority of cases, as a legislator of the special legislative procedure is designated the Council.[535] On

weeks of its being convened, on the basis of the positions of the European Parliament and the Council at second reading.' Article 294 (10) of the Treaty on the Functioning of the European Union.

533 <https://eur-lex.europa.eu/legal-content/EN/TXT/?uri=LEGISSUM%3Aai0016> accessed 16 March 2021.

534 'In the specific cases provided for by the Treaties, the adoption of a regulation, directive or decision by the European Parliament with the participation of the Council, or by the latter with the participation of the European Parliament, shall constitute a special legislative procedure.' Article 289 (2) of the Treaty on the Functioning of the European Union.

535 Moreover, as noted on the official website of the EU: 'The Council is, in practice, the sole legislator.' <www.consilium.europa.eu/en/council-eu/decision-making/special-legislative-procedures/> accessed 16 March 2021.

such occasions, the Council mostly acts unanimously. The European Parliament is required to give its consent to a legislative proposal or be consulted on it. Thus, in practice, there are two types of procedures established – (1) consultation and (2) consent. In case of consultation, the Parliament may approve, reject or propose amendments to a legislative proposal. Council is not legally obliged to take account of Parliament's opinion, but it can only take a decision after it has received that opinion. As regards the consent, the Parliament has the power to accept or reject a legislative proposal, but cannot amend it. The Council has no power to overrule the Parliament's opinion.[536]

The Commission generally retains the right of legislative initiative concerning the special legislative procedure as well,[537] and it is rarely required to seek 'opinion from the Commission'.[538] At times, under the founding treaties, mandatory consultation of other EU institutions or bodies in a special legislative procedure is prescribed.[539]

- Specific cases – In addition, '[i]n the specific cases provided for by the Treaties, legislative acts may be adopted on the initiative of a group of Member States or of the European Parliament, on a recommendation from the European Central Bank or at the request of the Court of Justice or the **European Investment Bank**.'[540] The European Investment Bank is the lending institution of the EU, which offers a wide range of financial products to the 'public and private sectors'.

- The Union's advisory bodies – The European Parliament, the Council, and the Commission are assisted by an Economic and Social Committee and a Committee of the Regions, which exercise the advisory functions.[541] Where the foundational treaties of

536 'Handbook on the Ordinary Legislative Procedure' (2019) <http://bit.ly/2Qsw2Fb> accessed 16 March 2021.

537 See the official website of the EU <www.consilium.europa.eu/en/council-eu/decision-making/special-legislative-procedures/> accessed 16 March 2021.

538 'The European Parliament ►C3, acting by means of regulations on its own initiative in accordance with a special legislative procedure ◄ after seeking an opinion from the Commission and with the ►C3 consent ◄ of the Council, shall lay down the regulations and general conditions governing the performance of the duties of its Members. All rules or conditions relating to the taxation of Members or former Members shall require unanimity within the Council.' Article 223 (2) of the Treaty on the Functioning of the European Union.

539 'The Council shall, acting unanimously in accordance with a special legislative procedure and after consulting the European Parliament and the European Central Bank, adopt the appropriate provisions which shall then replace the said Protocol.' Article 126 (14) of the Treaty on the Functioning of the European Union.

540 Article 289 (4) of the Treaty on the Functioning of the European Union.

541 '2. The Economic and Social Committee shall consist of representatives of organisations of employers, of the employed, and of other parties representative of civil society, notably in socio-economic, civic, professional and cultural areas.

3. The Committee of the Regions shall consist of representatives of regional and local bodies who either hold a regional or local authority electoral mandate or are politically accountable to an elected assembly. . . .

5. The rules referred to in paragraphs 2 and 3 governing the nature of the composition of the Committees shall be reviewed at regular intervals by the Council to take account of economic,

the EU so provide (as a rule, for policies concerning the respective spheres of interests of the Committees), these advisory bodies should be consulted by the EU institutions involved in the legislative procedure. The Committees, in turn, shall submit their opinions within 'a time limit which may not be less than one month'.[542]

The legal nature of the European Union

> European Union Law
> **supranational organisation**
> ***sui generis* organisation**
> **unique international status**

Three versions

The reasoning on the legal nature of the European Union leads to three possible conclusions:

1   The EU is an international organisation.
2   The EU represents a federal-type structure.
3   The EU possesses a unique international status.

The EU as an international organisation

The first conclusion may be made based on certain features which the EU has in common with international organisations:

*   The EU was founded through the international treaties.
*   A membership system exists. Any European state which respects the values referred to in the Treaty on European Union[543] and is committed to promoting them may apply to become a member state of the Union.

---

social and demographic developments within the Union. The Council, on a proposal from the Commission, shall adopt decisions to that end.' Article 300 of the Treaty on the Functioning of the European Union.

542 'The European Parliament, the Council or the Commission shall, if it considers it necessary, set the Committee, for the submission of its opinion, a time limit which may not be less than one month from the date on which the chairman receives notification to this effect. Upon expiry of the time limit, the absence of an opinion shall not prevent further action.' Articles 304 and 307 of the Treaty on the Functioning of the European Union.

543 'The Union is founded on the values of respect for human dignity, freedom, democracy, equality, the rule of law and respect for human rights, including the rights of persons belonging to minorities. These values are common to the Member States in a society in which pluralism, non-discrimination,

- It has a complex internal organisational makeup, partly similar to the international organisations, with comprehensive relationships between them, but also with a unique engagement of the member states' constitutional bodies and citizens in the structure.
- It possesses a functional authority limited by international treaties.

The EU as a federal-type structure

The second conclusion can be made based on certain features which constitute essential attributes of the federal type of governance structure:

- International treaties led to the institution of the Union with its own 'sovereign' rights and responsibilities.
- The member states have ceded some of their sovereign powers to the Union, and the tasks which have been assigned to the European Union are very different from those of other international organisations.
- It has a very comprehensive internal organisational setup where essentially the member states' constitutional bodies and citizens are involved.
- The European Union possesses the so-called *sui generis* legal framework. The EU is a creation which came into existence through the international treaties (international law). However, these treaties also provide the mechanisms for autonomous EU law-making, which itself results in the complex norms named together with the EU foundational and other particular treaties noted later, as well as customary norms and the general principles of Union law as the **European Union Law**.
- There is the direct applicability of Union law to both the member states and their citizens, and the Union law takes precedence over the national law in case of a conflict between them.
- The Union has a united citizenship model, a single market, a single currency, common foreign and security policy and justice system, and so forth.

The EU as a creation with a unique international status

However, despite the similarities to the federal-type structures, the EU and its internal organs:

- differ from the substantially centralised organisation of the federal-type structures;
- do not have the sovereign power to choose their objectives as the authorities of the federal-type structures are able to do; and
- only have powers in certain areas specified in the foundational international treaties.

Therefore, the third deduction may be developed if we consider together all the separate features mentioned here and notice the specifics of the EU and distinctions from the traditional international organisations and the federal-type structures.

---

tolerance, justice, solidarity and equality between women and men prevail.' Article 2 of the Treaty on European Union.

Consequently, when assessing the nature of the EU in legal scholarship, the following descriptions are most prevalent: '**supranational organisation**' or '*sui generis* **organisation**'. Thus, these terms, in this context, mean that the European Union possesses a **unique international status** which comprises the features of the international organisations as well as the federal-type structures.

However, this conclusion may be valid only at the present moment. The EU is in constant motion, and its institutions continue to evolve. Until now, it has developed in the direction of supranationalism. But there is no evidence to suggest this trend will maintain its current trajectory.

European Union law

primary legislation
secondary legislation
general principles of Union law
regulations
directives
decisions
recommendations
opinions
rule of law
principle of legality
principle of certainty
principle of protection of legitimate expectations
NV Algemene Transport- en Expeditie Onderneming van Gend en Loos v Netherlands Inland Revenue Administration case
Flaminio Costa v ENEL case

The main question

The European Union possesses its own legal framework, named the European Union law. However, continued disagreement arose about the essence of this framework. There may be only three possible answers to the aforementioned debate regarding the nature of the European Union law:

1 It is a part of international law.
2 It is a model of national law.
3 It is a separate legal system.

As examined earlier, according to the mainstream approach, only two systems of law exist – international law and national law. So, according to this approach, all legal norms should be located within either international law or the national law system. The recognition of European Union law as a separate legal framework leads to the conclusion that it is a specific model of law, which, therefore, cannot be included in the scope of any of the existing systems of law.

The composition of the European Union law

The EU law consists of **primary legislation** and **secondary legislation**. The sources of the primary legislation are at the top of the hierarchy between the norms of the EU law. It is followed by the other international law norms forming the EU legislation and secondary sources of the EU law, which stem from the primary sources of law and include all the various types of legal acts which the institutions of the EU can undertake.

First of all, the primary sources of the European Union law are the founding international treaties of the EU (the Treaty on European Union, the Treaty on the Functioning of the European Union), the sectoral EURATOM Treaty and the Charter of Fundamental Rights of the European Union.

The other principal sources of the EU law are:

1   the international agreements of the EU – for instance, the Association agreements with non-member states;
2   the agreements and legal customs – concluded or established between the member states – which add to or modify EU primary or secondary legislation;
3   the **general principles of Union law** – which may be derived from shared legal principles in the EU member states or general principles found in international law or European Union law.

As regards EU secondary legislation, in sum, EU institutions may take five types of legal acts:[544]

1   The legally binding acts:

a)   **Regulations** – are directed to all member states. They are binding in their entirety; are directly applicable, provided that they automatically become law in each member state; do not need to be transformed ('transposed') into national law; and may create rights and obligations directly enforceable in the national court.[545]

b)   **Directives** – are directed to all or specific member states. They are used primarily to ensure that member states adjust their own laws for the application of

---

544   'To exercise the Union's competences, the institutions shall adopt regulations, directives, decisions, recommendations and opinions. A regulation shall have general application. It shall be binding in its entirety and directly applicable in all Member States. A directive shall be binding, as to the result to be achieved, upon each Member State to which it is addressed, but shall leave to the national authorities the choice of form and methods. A decision shall be binding in its entirety. A decision which specifies those to whom it is addressed shall be binding only on them. Recommendations and opinions shall have no binding force.' Article 288 of the Treaty on the Functioning of the European Union.

545   For example, Regulation (EU) 2019/1148 of the European Parliament and of the Council of 20 June 2019 on the marketing and use of explosives precursors, amending Regulation (EC) No 1907/2006 and repealing Regulation (EU) No 98/2013 (Text with EEA relevance).

common standards and are binding upon any of the member states to whom they are addressed concerning the intended results to be achieved; however, the national authorities are free to the choose the implementation methods.[546]

c) **Decisions** – are binding on those to whom they are addressed (member states, natural or legal persons) and cover situations specific to those member states or persons.[547]

2   The non-binding acts, which may provide guidance as to the interpretation and content of the European Union law:

a) **Recommendations** – are directed to all or specific member states, other EU bodies, and individuals. They allow the EU institutions an opportunity to promote shared approaches and incentivise a line of action without imposing any legal obligation.[548]

b   **Opinions** – allow the EU institutions to manifest a statement without imposing a legal obligation. They may be issued either by the principal EU decision-making bodies or the Committee of the Regions and the European Economic and Social Committee.[549]

At the same time, the EU institutions also may issue the non-legislative acts, such as the simple legal instruments, delegated acts, or implementing acts.

The general principles of Union law

The general principles of law are mentioned several times in the founding treaties of the Union. The term 'general principles of the Union's law' is used in the Treaty on European Union: 'Fundamental rights, as guaranteed by the European Convention for the Protection of Human Rights and Fundamental Freedoms and as they result from the constitutional traditions common to the Member States, shall constitute general principles of the Union's law.'[550] The formulation 'general principles common to the laws of the Member States' is utilised in the Treaty on the Functioning of the European Union when determining that

---

546 For example, Directive 2014/65/EU of the European Parliament and of the Council of 15 May 2014 on markets in financial instruments and amending Directive 2002/92/EC and Directive 2011/61/EU Text with EEA relevance.

547 For example, Decision No 1080/2011/EU of the European Parliament and of the Council of 25 October 2011 granting an EU guarantee to the European Investment Bank against losses under loans and loan guarantees for projects outside the Union and repealing Decision No 633/2009/EC.

548 For example, Council Recommendations 'Promoting the use of and sharing of best practices on cross-border videoconferencing in the area of justice in the Member States and at EU level', 2015/C 250/01.

549 For example, Opinion of the Economic and Social Committee on the Proposal for a Council Regulation (EEC) on the Statistical Classification of Economic Activities in the European Communities, 90/C 182/01.

550 Article 6 (3) of the Treaty on European Union.

the Union can be held responsible for damages 'caused by its institutions or by its servants in the performance of their duties'.[551] The identical wording is reflected in the Charter of Fundamental Rights of the European Union concerning the same context. On another occasion, in the Charter, the formulation 'general principles recognised by the community of nations' is articulated with respect to the principles of legality and proportionality of criminal offences and penalties.[552]

The Protocol (No. 24) on Asylum for Nationals of Member States of the European Union (1997) corresponds to the Treaty on European Union and states that 'fundamental rights, as guaranteed by the European Convention for the Protection of Human Rights and Fundamental Freedoms, constitute part of the Union's law as general principles'.

Hence, in the treaties, there is no exact definition of the aforementioned terms, which have fed the discussions as to (1) whether all these formulations are interchangeable and refer to the same concept and (2) whether these formulations and a source of international law – the general principles of law – are essentially identical in meaning.

It is obvious that the wording 'general principles recognised by the community of nations' should be explained as a modified version of the formulation of the ICJ statute on the general principles of law. As concerns the other terms, the 'general principles of the Union's law' (or the general principles of the Union law) and 'general principles common to the laws of the member states', formally, some differences between them might be discovered since the first term articulates the principles of the Union law but the second refers to the shared principles of the national laws of the member states.

Although European lawyers tend to acknowledge the substantial peculiarities inherent in the concept 'general principles of the Union's law',[553] in general, it, as well as other terms mentioned here are all interlinked with the meaning of the general principles of law (the source of international law). They share formal characters, provided that they are (1) general, (2) not precisely and exhaustively enumerated, (3) discovered by the inductive method of comparative research, and (4) explored from the selected data of the legal norms.

However, in international law, among the general principles of law are primarily understood the universal legal principles of the entire world. Notwithstanding, as in the case of the other sources of international law, there is also a possibility of introducing the regional patterns of the general principles of law, which may be covered under the definition of Article 38(1)(c) of the Statute of the ICJ. So we cannot eliminate such an interpretation allowing the existence of the general principles of regional international law, which might be extracted from the regional patterns of data. Hence, the discovery of such principles

---

551 Article 340 of the Treaty on the Functioning of the European Union.

552 Article 41 (3) (Right to good administration) and Article 49 (2) of the Charter of Fundamental Rights of the European Union.

553 'A comparison between general principles of EU law and general principles of law of article 38(1)(c) of the Statute of the ICJ is often sketched, especially to underline the specificity of general principles of EU law.' Emanuel Castellarin, 'General Principles of EU Law and General International Law' in Mads Andenas, Malgosia Fitzmaurice, Attila Tanzi, and Jan Wouters (eds), *General Principles and the Coherence of International Law, Queen Mary Studies in International Law*, Volume 37 (Brill Nijhoff 2019) 133.

can only be undertaken through comparative research of the regional legal families and the corresponding countries. Following such a logical chain, for instance, the general principles of the European Union law may be considered to belong to regional general principles of law.

The general principles of Union law, such as the fundamental rights and the **rule of law**, are applied by the European Court of Justice and the national courts of the member states. The latter is part of the European value system (the Anglo-Saxon tradition of the 'rule of law' and its continental counterpart 'legal state'), whose conceptual basics could be discovered in ancient political philosophy – consider, e.g., the formula by Aristotle: Law should govern. However, the rule of law should not be considered a mere and formalistic 'supremacy of statute law'[554] because it unites the substantive normative contents (principles). Notably, as its corollaries are considered (1) the **principle of legality**, providing that the actions undertaken by public bodies shall occur under and within the law; and (2) the **principle of certainty**, requiring the legal rules to be clear and precise and that no retroactive measures be taken, except in legally justified circumstances. Furthermore, according to the principle of certainty, public authorities shall act and perform their duties within a reasonable time. Another principle is the **principle of protection of legitimate expectations**, which is recognised as a sub-principle of the rule of law and means that every person who, as a result of administrative action, has particular reasonable expectations concerning prospective administrative activities may require that these expectations are met unless there arises an overwhelming public interest for not allowing this.

On the other hand, a different category of general principles of Union law may be identified, including the so-called structural principles, which establish the normative support for the overall fabric of the European Union law.

European Union law as international law

The prevailing view concerning the essence of the European Union law is that it is *sui generis* in nature, sharing with both the international and the national legal system some common characteristics. In this context, the most cited decisions of the Court of Justice of the European Union are the ***NV Algemene Transport- en Expeditie Onderneming van Gend en Loos v Netherlands Inland Revenue Administration*** case (case 26–62) and the ***Flaminio Costa v ENEL*** case (case 6–64).

In the first case, the Court concluded that the 'European Economic Community constitutes a new legal order of international law'. Hence, it emphasised that the EEC was a creation with a new legal order; however, at the same time, the wording 'of international law' lexically means that this new legal order is a part of international law.[555]

---

554 See the detailed examination of this matter in Pataraia (n 8) 117–123.

555 'The European Economic Community constitutes a new legal order of international law for the benefit of which the states have limited their sovereign rights, albeit within limited fields, and the subjects of which comprise not only the Member States but also their nationals.' Judgment of 5 February 1963 – Case 26–62 *NV Algemene Transport – en Expeditie Onderneming van Gend & Loos v Netherlands Inland Revenue Administration* [1963] EU:C:1963:1 <http://bit.ly/363NPIS> accessed 16 March 2021.

In the second case, the Court stated that '[b]y contrast with ordinary international treaties, the EEC Treaty has created its own legal system which, on the entry into force of the Treaty, became an integral part of the legal systems of the Member States and which their courts are bound to apply.'[556] Thus, this formulation articulated a special (non-ordinal) character of the Treaty and the establishment of 'its own legal system'.

The interpretations of the CJEU have been logically applied to the EU and European Union law. However, while some summarised these interpretations as providing a justification of the separate standing of the European Union law from international law, others referred only to the *sui generis* status of the EU legal framework. In certain cases, the EU institutions themselves tend to recognise the first understanding. As noted on the official website of the European Parliament: 'The European Union has legal personality and as such its own legal order which is separate from international law.'[557]

In sum, the principal argument in favour of the independent status of the EU law mainly stems from (1) the unique supranational architecture of the EU, (2) the direct application of the legal norms to domestic legal systems, and (3) the effective enforcement mechanism as a significant advancement on the ability of international law to take legal effect at the national level. Nevertheless, are these arguments enough to suggest that the EU law might be considered a separate legal system? Analysing everything comprehensively, we must conclude that none of the aforementioned arguments preclude the possibility of placement of the EU law within the scope of international law.

For example, concerning the EU law, we should remember that it is a complex creation, the primary sources of which are international treaties and other sources of international law. So there may be no dispute on the status of this part of the EU law. Undoubtedly, they are components of international law.

As regards the secondary legislation of the EU, indeed, it possesses a special nature since some types of legal acts are directly applicable laws automatically incorporated into the legal systems of the member countries. Besides, the regulations, directives and decisions differ from the ordinary soft law instruments of the international organisations with their mandatory nature.

However, some particular decisions of the internal organs of certain international organisations may be considered to be a system which is closer to the EU secondary legislation – for example, the mandatory resolutions of the UN Security Council – except the fact that such resolutions usually constitute obligations for the states and other subjects of international law without a self-acting incorporation into the body of national legislations of the member countries.

Furthermore, in certain cases the ordinary international treaties and customary norms of international law may also be automatically incorporated into national law – notably, in countries which recognise the incorporation method for the implementation of international law norms. Therefore, as is rightly stressed by Timothy Moorhead, '[i]t is counter-intuitive to suppose that the resulting obligations arising as a matter of Union legislation,

556 The Judgment of 15 July 1964 – Case 6–64 *Flaminio Costa v ENEL* [1964] EU:C:1964:66 <http://bit.ly/350P8bu> accessed 16 March 2021.

557 <www.europarl.europa.eu/factsheets/en/sheet/6/sources-and-scope-of-european-union-law> accessed 16 March 2021.

and equivalent in status to the Treaty articles as far as domestic orders are concerned, are not themselves norms of international law.'[558]

On the whole, it seems preferable to conclude that the European Union is a *sui generis* institution with 'a new legal order of international law', i.e. possessing its particular *sui generis* legal framework of international law.

THE COUNCIL OF EUROPE

> Statute of the Council of Europe
> specialised internal institutions
> Venice Commission
> Revised Statute of the European Commission for Democracy through Law

The leading human rights organisation

The Council of Europe is the continent's leading human rights organisation. It can be considered the conscience of Europe.

At the same time, the Council of Europe is the continent's one of the oldest regional organisations, founded in 1949 to promote human rights, democracy, and the rule of law in Europe.

Foundation and development

The Council of Europe was founded by the Treaty of London. The Treaty of London or the **Statute of the Council of Europe** was signed by ten states: Belgium, Denmark, France, Ireland, Italy, Luxembourg, the Netherlands, Norway, Sweden, and the United Kingdom.

Nowadays the Council of Europe has 47 members and six observer subjects: Canada, Israel (observer to the Parliamentary Assembly), Japan, Mexico, the United States, and the Holy See.

The Council of Europe has its headquarters in Strasbourg, France.

Internal bodies of the Council of Europe

The primary internal organs of the Council of Europe are:

- Committee of Ministers – composed of the 47 foreign ministers or their permanent diplomatic representatives located in Strasbourg (Permanent Representatives to the Council of Europe). It is the main decision-making body of the organisation. 'The

---

558 Timothy Moorhead, 'European Union Law as International Law' (2012) 5(1) *European Journal of Legal Studies* 126.

Committee of Ministers is the organ which acts on behalf of the Council of Europe.'[559] The Committee meets at ministerial level once a year and at Deputies' level (Permanent Representatives) weekly. There is a very diverse voting system in the Committee of Ministers. Taking into consideration the importance of a question, its resolutions are made either (1) by simple majority vote of the representatives entitled to sit on the Committee, (2) by unanimous vote of the representatives casting a vote and a majority of the representatives entitled to sit on the Committee, or (3) a two-thirds majority of all the representatives entitled to sit on the Committee.

- Parliamentary Assembly – the 'deliberative organ of the Council of Europe',[560] composed of 324 representatives (and the same number of substitutes) appointed by the 47-member states' national parliaments. (Member states have the different number of representatives described in the Statute.) The Assembly elects the Secretary General, the Human Rights Commissioner, and the judges to the European Court of Human Rights. It 'may discuss and make recommendations upon any matter within the aim and scope of the Council of Europe'.[561]
- Congress of Local and Regional Authorities – composed of the Chamber of Local Authorities, the Chamber of Regions, and three committees, 'it brings together 648 elected officials representing more than 150 000 local and regional authorities.'[562] It is a pan-European political assembly for advancing local and regional democracy, developing local and regional governance, and strengthening authorities' self-government.
- Secretariat – headed by the Secretary General, who is appointed by the Parliamentary Assembly on the recommendation of the Committee of Ministers[563] for a five-year term. The Secretary General is responsible before the Committee of Ministers for the work of the Secretariat. The Secretary General represents the organisation.
- European Court of Human Rights – the permanent judicial body which serves as the guarantor for all Europeans for the rights safeguarded by the European Convention on Human Rights.[564]

Other important bodies of the Council of Europe are the Commissioner for Human Rights and the Conference of International Non-Governmental Organisations (INGOs) of the Council of Europe (which is the representative body of the INGOs enjoying participatory status with the Council of Europe).

The Council of Europe promotes human rights in many fields: the abolition of the death penalty, non-discrimination and the fight against racism, upholding freedom of expression, gender equality, protection of children's rights, defence of cultural diversity, and so forth.

As regards the abolition of the death penalty, it is particularly remarkable that the Council of Europe member states no longer apply the death penalty.

---

559 Article 13 of Statute of the Council of Europe.
560 Article 22 of Statute of the Council of Europe.
561 Article 23 of Statute of the Council of Europe.
562 <www.coe.int/en/web/about-us/structure> accessed 16 March 2021.
563 Article 36 of Statute of the Council of Europe.
564 The presentation of the mechanism of the European Court of Human Rights is discussed in the chapter on the international protection of human rights.

Supplementary institutions

Integrated into the structure of the Council of Europe are **specialised internal institutions**, which command different levels of autonomy but are, indeed, inalienable parts of the Council.

One of the most prominent of these specialised institutions is the European Commission for Democracy through Law (better known as the **Venice Commission**), which was established in May 1990 by 18 member states of the Council of Europe. Nowadays, the Commission has 62 member states – the 47 Council of Europe member states, plus 15 other countries – and is the Council of Europe's 'independent consultative body' on constitutional matters. Its plenary sessions are held in Venice, Italy. The Venice Commission is composed of one member and one substitute with respect to each member appointed by a member state for a four-year term who may be reappointed.

Under Article 1 of the **Revised Statute of the European Commission for Democracy through Law** (adopted by the Committee of Ministers in 2002) the Venice Commission's objectives are:

- strengthening the understanding of the legal systems of the participating states, notably with a view to bringing these systems closer;
- promoting the rule of law and democracy;
- examining the problems raised by the working of democratic institutions and their reinforcement and development.

THE NORTH ATLANTIC TREATY ORGANISATION

> **North Atlantic Treaty**
> **one-for-all and all-for-one**
> **NATO political and military structures and International Staff**

The principal mission

The mission of the North Atlantic Treaty Organisation is to ensure the freedom and security of all the member states in both political and military terms.

NATO has standing forces on active duty to contribute to the collective self-defence efforts of the alliance on a permanent basis.

Foundational treaty

The **North Atlantic Treaty** (also referred to as the Washington Treaty) is the foundational agreement of the North Atlantic Treaty Organisation (NATO). The Treaty was signed in Washington, DC, in 1949. At first, there were 12-member states of NATO. In 1952, Greece and Turkey joined; in 1955 the Federal Republic of Germany; and so forth. As of today, the list of the NATO members is expanded to 30 states. It is especially noteworthy that in 1954, the USSR also made a statement on membership, which was rejected.

One-for-all and all-for-one

Collective defence is at the heart of the North Atlantic Treaty and is determined in Article 5, which is known as the '**one-for-all and all-for-one**' article:

> The Parties agree that an armed attack against one or more of them in Europe or North America shall be considered an attack against them all and consequently they agree that, if such an armed attack occurs, each of them, in exercise of the right of individual or collective self-defence recognised by Article 51 of the Charter of the United Nations, will assist the Party or Parties so attacked by taking forthwith, individually and in concert with the other Parties, such action as it deems necessary, including the use of armed force, to restore and maintain the security of the North Atlantic area. Any such armed attack and all measures taken as a result thereof shall immediately be reported to the Security Council. Such measures shall be terminated when the Security Council has taken the measures necessary to restore and maintain international peace and security.

Articles 4 and 5 of the North Atlantic Treaty

Article 4 (which prescribes the joint consulting duty in the event that the territorial integrity, political independence, or security of any of the parties is threatened) and Article 5 can only be invoked at the request of a NATO member. Nevertheless, Article 5 has only been invoked once, immediately following the 11 September 2001, terrorist attacks against the United States.

The provision of this Article 'in Europe or North America' and Article 6 of the North Atlantic Treaty[565] stipulate the different perceptions in practice. However, in fact, these Articles could not have been invoked for the 1964 Gulf of Tonkin incident, the 1968 Pueblo incident, or the 1982 Falklands War, because those incidents did not take place in Europe or North America.

---

565 Article 6 of the treaty was revised by Article 2 of the Protocol to the North Atlantic Treaty on the accession of Greece and Turkey and also on 16 January 1963, when the North Atlantic Council noted that insofar as the former Algerian Departments of France were concerned, the relevant clauses of this Treaty had become inapplicable as from 3 July 1962. Finally, the revised Article prescribes: 'For the purpose of Article 5, an armed attack on one or more of the Parties is deemed to include an armed attack:

1 on the territory of any of the Parties in Europe or North America, on the territory of Turkey or on the islands under the jurisdiction of any of the Parties in the North Atlantic area north of the Tropic of Cancer;

2 on the forces, vessels, or aircraft of any of the Parties, when in or over these territories or any other area in Europe in which occupation forces of any of the Parties were stationed on the date when the Treaty entered into force or the Mediterranean Sea or the North Atlantic area north of the Tropic of Cancer.'

An Alliance of 30 equals

The Alliance takes all its decisions by common accord, so all 30 members have to agree before any decisions are made. On 27 March 2020, North Macedonia became NATO's 30th member, upon depositing its instrument of accession to the Washington Treaty with the US State Department in Washington, DC.[566]

Structure

The structure of NATO is multi-faceted and can be divided conditionally into the **NATO political and military structures and International Staff**.

Political bodies

- North Atlantic Council (NAC) – the principal decision-making body, which oversees political and military processes relating to security issues which affect the interests of the Alliance as a whole. Each member country has a seat at the NAC. It meets at different levels (at the level of heads of state and government, at the level of foreign and defence ministers, and at least once a week and sometimes more frequently at the level of the permanent representatives or 'ambassadors'). Decisions made by the NAC have the same status and validity at whatever level it meets. The meetings of the NAC are chaired by the Secretary General, and the decisions are only made based on unanimity and common accord.
- Nuclear Planning Group (NPG) – whereas the North Atlantic Council is the ultimate authority within NATO, the NPG operates as the senior decision-making body of the Alliance on nuclear matters. NPG meets when necessary at the level of Ambassadors and once a year at the level of Ministers of Defence (except France, which has decided not to participate).
- Subordinate Committees – the framework within which the member countries can exchange information on a variety of subjects on their agendas, from political issues to issues of a more technical nature. In addition to the NAC, the NPG and the Military Committee (MC), there are also a number of committees which report directly to the Council: for example, the Political Committee (which exchanges information and discusses assessments on political and regional developments of interest to allies), the Partnerships and Cooperative Security Committee (which is responsible for all NATO's outreach programmes with non-member countries), and so forth.
- NATO delegations – each member country has a permanent delegation at NATO's political headquarters in Brussels. Each delegation is headed by an 'ambassador' (also called 'permanent representative'), who represents a government in the Alliance's consultation and decision-making process.

566 NATO Secretary General Jens Stoltenberg made the following comment: 'North Macedonia is now part of the NATO family, a family of thirty nations and almost one billion people. A family based on the certainty that, no matter what challenges we face, we are all stronger and safer together.' <www.nato.int/cps/en/natolive/news_174589.htm> accessed 16 March 2021.

Military bodies

- Military Committee (MC) – NATO's senior military authority and the primary source of military advice to the NAC and the NPG, it is composed of the Chiefs of Defence of NATO member countries; the International Military Staff, the Military Committee's executive body; and the military command structure, composed of Allied Command Operations and Allied Command Transformation. The MC meets frequently at the level of countries' permanent Military Representatives (MILREP) to NATO, representing their Chief of Defence (CHOD) (a civilian official represents Iceland, which has no military forces) after meetings of the NAC to follow up on the Council decisions and at its highest level, at the level of Chiefs of Defence three times a year.
- International Military Staff (IMS) – the executive body of the Military Committee, which consists of a staff of approximately 500 and is composed of military and civilian personnel from the NATO member countries.[567]
- Military representatives – each member country is represented in NATO's military structure.

International Staff

- Secretary General and the International Staff – the Secretary General is the Alliance's top international civil servant and chief spokesperson, chairs major political bodies (such as NAC, NPG), and is responsible for managing the process of consultation and decision-making within the Alliance, ensuring that decisions are implemented. The Secretary General heads the Organisation's International Staff, which provides advice, guidance, and administrative support. The Secretary General is nominated and, on the basis of consensus, appointed by the member governments for an initial period of four years, which can be extended by mutual consent.

ORGANISATION FOR SECURITY AND CO-OPERATION IN EUROPE

> Helsinki Final Act
> Conference on Security and Co-operation in Europe
> Charter of Paris for a New Europe

From the Conference to the Organisation

The Organisation for Security and Co-operation in Europe (OSCE) has no founding charter determining membership criteria, purpose, structure, and so on. In contrast to previously described organisations, it started as a gathering, bringing together

---

567 'International Military Staff' <www.nato.int/cps/en/natohq/topics_64557.htm?> accessed 16 March 2021.

representatives of 35 Eastern, Western and non-aligned countries, mainly to discuss the challenges posed by the Cold War, with the opposing blocks having direct clash lines and Europe being at the centre of the Cold War power gravity. A positive development from the preparatory work was the signing in 1975 of the **Helsinki Final Act**.

Consequently, the structure of co-operation was initially established and maintained in the format of the **Conference on Security and Co-operation in Europe** (CSCE). Then, the follow-up meetings took place during the 1970s and 1980s in Belgrade, Madrid, and Vienna.

With the collapse of Communist system in Europe in the late 1980s and early 1990s, the establishment of single Germany in 1990, the break-up of the Warsaw Pact (the military structure of East Axis) in 1991, and the dissolution of the Soviet Union at the end of 1991, the bipolar international order came to an end.

The large-scale transformation of the political landscape in the world and, most dramatically, in Europe put at the very front of the CSCE agenda the challenge of and the need for reformulation of the mission and form of the Conference. As a result, the participating subjects convened a special Summit in Paris in 1990 (which resulted in the **Charter of Paris for a New Europe**, a comprehensive document of shared values that went beyond the Helsinki Final Act) followed by other Summits, which determined the institutional development of the Conference into a full-scale international organisation. At the Budapest Summit in 1994, the participants adopted the US proposal to name it the Organisation for Security and Co-operation in Europe. This decision took effect on 1 January 1995.

The principal mission of the OSCE

The focus of the OSCE is co-operation between the states by promoting the collective security system in the region. In sum, OSCE maintains a comprehensive approach to security that encompasses politico-military, economic, environmental, and human aspects. Therefore, it addresses a wide range of security-related issues, such as arms control, security-building measures, human rights, national minorities, economic and environmental activities, and so on.

Equality of members

All 57 participants (including the Holy See) enjoy equal status, and decisions are taken by consensus on a politically, but not legally, binding basis.

The primary bodies of OSCE

- Summit – periodic meeting of OSCE heads of state or government, which is the highest decision-making body. The decisions of the Summit are adopted by consensus.
- Ministerial Council – the annual meeting of foreign ministers of participants (except in years with a Summit). Between Summits, it is the central decision-making and governing body of the OSCE.

- Permanent Council – the regular body for political consultation and decision-making (meets on a weekly basis in Vienna). It consists of permanent representatives of the participating states and the Holy See.
- Forum for Security Co-operation – the regular body for arms control (meets weekly in Vienna).
- Chairman-in-Office – Chairmanship is held for one calendar year by a participant of the Organisation designated as such in a decision taken at a Summit. Its functions are chairing Summits, Ministerial Councils, the Permanent Council and subsidiary bodies; coordinating and consulting on current OSCE activities; and so forth. The Chairman-in-Office is assisted by the outgoing and the incoming Chairmen-in-Office, and together, they form the OSCE Troika.
- Secretary General and Secretariat – located in Vienna with a documentation office in Prague.
- Specialised bodies – the Office for Democratic Institutions and Human Rights, the High Commissioner on National Minorities, the OSCE Representative on Freedom of the Media, and so on.
- OSCE Parliamentary Assembly – with an international secretariat located in Copenhagen, the Assembly is made up of 323 parliamentarians from the 56 OSCE participants (the Holy See may send two representatives to the Assembly's meetings as guests of honour). It aims to promote parliamentary engagement in the activities of the OSCE and facilitate inter-parliamentary dialogue and co-operation on OSCE-related issues.

The current challenges

However, it is especially noteworthy that in the post–Cold War era, OSCE is still searching for its mission, as well as efficient political and security mechanisms in the turbulent region, which is still under the pressure of the regional military and geopolitical rivalry.

ORGANISATION OF AMERICAN STATES

> Pan American Union
> Inter-American system
> Inter-American Treaty of Reciprocal Assistance
> Protocol of Managua
> Inter-American System of Human Rights

From the Pan American Union to the Organisation of American States

The idea of an international organisation promoting peace and co-operation among the countries of a particular region was perhaps first implemented on the American continent with the establishment of the **Pan American Union** (International Union of American Republics) in 1890. The Union is assumed to have been the initial promoter of the **Inter-American system**.[568] In 1948, it became the Organisation of American States (OAS) after the Charter of the OAS (entered into force in 1951) was signed in Bogota, Columbia.

Under the OAS Charter:

> The American States establish by this Charter the international organization that they have developed to achieve an order of peace and justice, to promote their solidarity, to strengthen their collaboration, and to defend their sovereignty, their territorial integrity, and their independence. Within the United Nations, the Organization of American States is a regional agency.[569]

The current situation

Nowadays, the OAS framework brings together all 35 states of the Americas and institutes the principal governmental forum to engage in discussions regarding political, juridical, and social challenges on the agenda in the hemisphere. At the same time, it granted the status of permanent observer to 69 states, as well as the European Union (EU). The OAS headquarters is located in Washington, DC.

The principles of the Organisation

The fundamental principles envisaged in the Charter,[570] which are mandatory for the members of the Organisation, have to be paid special interest. The charter contains 14 principles.

Among them are enumerated the following universal principles:

- 'International law is the standard of conduct of states in their reciprocal relations'.
- 'International order consists essentially of respect for the personality, sovereignty, and independence of States, and the faithful fulfillment of obligations derived from treaties and other sources of international law'.
- 'Good faith shall govern the relations between States'.
- 'Every State has the right to choose, without external interference, its political, economic, and social system'.
- and so forth.

---

568 At that time, various institutions were created which should be considered the building blocks of the inter-American system, such as the Pan American Health Organization (1902), the Inter-American Juridical Committee (1906), the Inter-American Children's Institute (1927), the Inter-American Commission of Women (1928), the Pan American Institute of Geography and History (1928), and so forth.

569 Article 1 of the OAS Charter.

570 Article 3 of the OAS Charter.

At the same time, the OAS is a regional organisation oriented to uphold the particular interests of the regional states. In this respect, the Charter emphasises the principles of:

- the solidarity of the American countries based on the effective exercise of representative democracy;
- hemispheric defence, which means that an act of aggression against one American state is an act of aggression against all the other American states;
- the economic co-operation which is essential to the common welfare and prosperity of the peoples of the continent; and
- the elimination of extreme poverty;
- and so on.

The Charter's contribution to the development of international law

Generally, the OAS Charter represents a treaty reflecting or, in some instances, even developing very significant norms of international law concerning the fundamental rights and duties of states, pacific settlement of disputes, collective security, and so forth. Some of them are derived from the UN Charter (e.g. principles of international law concerning friendly relations and co-operation among states mentioned earlier); some others from regional international law, for example, the following provision of OAS Charter:

> The political existence of the State is independent of recognition by other States. Even before being recognized, the State has the right to defend its integrity and independence, to provide for its preservation and prosperity, and consequently to organize itself as it sees fit, to legislate concerning its interests, to administer its services, and to determine the jurisdiction and competence of its courts. The exercise of these rights is limited only by the exercise of the rights of other States in accordance with international law.[571]

This provision is nearly identical (with very slight stylistic changes) to Article 3 of the Montevideo Convention on the Rights and Duties of States of 1933.

The component parts of the OAS

- The General Assembly – the supreme organ of the Organisation. It comprises the delegations of all the member states; and determines the mechanisms, policies, actions, and mandates of the Organisation.
- The Meeting of Consultation of Ministers of Foreign Affairs – is held in order to consider problems of an urgent nature and of common interest to the member states and conducts consultations on such matters. When one or more of the member states

---

571 Article 13 of OAS Charter.

that have ratified the **Inter-American Treaty of Reciprocal Assistance** (Rio Treaty)[572] requests that the Meeting of Consultation be called under that Treaty,[573] the Permanent Council decides by vote of an absolute majority of the states that have ratified the Treaty whether such a meeting should be held.

- The Councils – comprise the Permanent Council and the Inter-American Council for Integral Development; both report directly to the General Assembly.

  - According to the Charter: 'The Permanent Council shall keep vigilance over the maintenance of friendly relations among the Member States, and for that purpose shall effectively assist them in the peaceful settlement of their disputes'.[574] The Council fulfils the mandates of the General Assembly and the Meeting of Consultation of Ministers of Foreign Affairs, whose implementation has not been assigned to any other body. The Council also serves as the Preparatory Committee for the General Assembly.

  - The Inter-American Council for Integral Development reports directly to the General Assembly. It was established when the **Protocol of Managua** (Amendment to the Charter of OAS) entered into force in 1996, and it aims at promoting co-operation among the American states for the purpose of achieving integral development and, in particular, helping to eliminate extreme poverty.

- The Inter-American Juridical Committee – serves as an advisory body to the organisation on juridical matters and promotes the progressive development and codification of international law.

- The Inter-American Commission on Human Rights (IACHR) – was established in 1960. The **Inter-American System of Human Rights** is composed of two entities – the Commission and the Inter-American Court of Human Rights.

- The General Secretariat is 'the central and permanent organ of the Organization'[575] pursuing certain administrative functions and serving as a depository of inter-American treaties and agreements. The Secretary General of the Organisation is elected by the General Assembly for a five-year term and may not be re-elected more than once or succeeded by a person of the same nationality.

- The Specialised Conferences – are intergovernmental meetings to deal with specific technical matters or to develop particular aspects of inter-American co-operation when either the General Assembly or the Meeting of Consultation of Ministers of Foreign Affairs so decides.

- The Specialised Organisations – are intergovernmental organisations founded by multilateral agreements. They carry out specific functions concerning technical matters of common interest to the American states, such as the Pan American Health Organisation, the Inter-American Children's Institute, the Inter-American Institute for Cooperation on Agriculture, and so on.

---

572 The Rio Treaty is an agreement signed in 1947 in Rio de Janeiro among countries of the Americas. The central principle defined in its articles is that an attack against one is to be considered an attack against them all (known as the 'hemispheric defence' doctrine).

573 Article 13 of the Inter-American Treaty of Reciprocal Assistance.

574 Article 84 of the OAS Charter.

575 Article 107 of the OAS Charter.

THE AFRICAN UNION

> Organisation of African Unity
> Treaty Establishing the African Economic Community
> African Charter on Human and Peoples' Rights
> Constitutive Act of the African Union
> African Charter on Human and Peoples' Rights

Foundation of the Organisation of African Unity

The **Organisation of African Unity** (OAU) was founded in 1963, with 32 signatory governments from the African continent. African countries took part in the conference in the Ethiopian capital setting up the OAU, which marked the appearance of the first pan-African organisation.

The principal objectives

Initially, the primary purpose of the Organisation was the eradication of colonialism and the overcoming of racial discrimination. Consequently, its first resolutions were against apartheid and concerned the liberation movements. On the whole, the OAU was the manifestation of the pan-African vision for an Africa that should be united, free and able to rule its own destiny.

The African Union

In 2002, the OAU was replaced by the African Union (AU). Under the **Constitutive Act of the African Union**, it was determined that 'This Act shall replace the Charter of the Organisation of African Unity.'[576] Nowadays, the Union is a 55-member organisation consisting of all the recognised states on the African continent. The AU's headquarters are located in Addis Ababa, Ethiopia.

The new vision – to achieve greater unity

The creation of a new Union was conditioned on what was at that time the new vision to 'achieve greater unity and solidarity between the African countries and the peoples of Africa',[577] which was about moving ahead with more determination on the path of unity. It was also about a change of perspective due to the definition of common policies in priority areas such as peace and continental security; integration of African economies;

---

576 Article 33 of the Constitutive Act of the African Union.
577 Article 3 (a) of the Constitutive Act of the African Union.

the free movement of people, goods, and capital; food security; the fight against poverty; protection of the environment; health; and so on.

The internal organs of the African Union

* The Assembly of the Union – is the supreme organ and comprises heads of state and government from all member states, determines the policies of the Union, establishes its priorities, adopts its annual programs, and monitors the implementation of its decisions.
* The Executive Council – is composed of the Ministers of Foreign Affairs or such other ministers or authorities as are designated by the governments of the member states. It meets at least twice a year in regular sessions. It may also meet in an extraordinary sessions. The Executive Council is entitled to coordinate and take certain decisions on policies in areas of common interest to the member states, give consideration on the issues which are brought before it, and monitor the implementation of the policies of the Assembly.
* The Pan-African Parliament – is one of the nine organs which were introduced in 1991 by the **Treaty Establishing the African Economic Community** (Abuja Treaty). Its current authority is to exercise advisory, consultative and budgetary oversight powers. The Parliament is composed of members from the states that have ratified the Protocol establishing it (five members per member state).
* Judicial and Human Rights Institutions

    * The African Commission on Human and Peoples' Rights (ACHPR) was established in 1987 to oversee and interpret the **African Charter on Human and Peoples' Rights** (also known as the Banjul Charter).
    * Initially, in 1998, it was decided to establish the African Court on Human and Peoples' Rights to complement and reinforce the functions of the African Commission on Human and Peoples' Rights by its binding decisions, but the Court officially started to operate in 2006, when the first judges were elected and sworn in. The Court consists of 11 judges elected by the Assembly of the Union from African jurists nominated by the states which are parties to the Protocol establishing the Court. Under the Protocol: 'The Court may entitle relevant Non-Governmental Organisations with observer status before the Commission, and individuals to institute cases directly before it';[578] however, only in cases in which there is a declaration made by a state on accepting this competence of the Court.

        In 2008, the AU Assembly decided to merge the African Court of Justice (which never came onto existence) with the African Court on Human and Peoples' Rights into a single court. (The new combined court is yet not operational.)[579]

---

578 Paragraph 3 of Article 5 of the Protocol to the African Charter on Human and Peoples' Rights on the Establishment of an African Court on Human and Peoples' Rights.

579 See the status of the Protocol on the Statute of the African Court of Justice and Human Rights of 2008 at <https://au.int/en/treaties>.

- The Commission – serves as the African Union's secretariat. The Commission is composed of the Chairman, his or her deputy or deputies, and the Commissioners.
- The Permanent Representatives Committee – exercises the day-to-day business of the AU on behalf of the Assembly and Executive Council.
- The Specialised Technical Committees – are the set of internal organs whose purpose is to work in close collaboration with Commission departments to ensure the harmonisation of AU projects and programs.
- The Peace and Security Council – is 'a standing decision-making organ for the prevention, management and resolution of conflicts'.[580] It has 15 members. All are elected by the AU Executive Council and confirmed by the Assembly at its next session. Members are elected according to the principle of equitable regional representation and national rotation. The principle of consensus guides its decisions. Where consensus is not possible, decisions on procedural matters are taken by a simple majority and, on substantive issues, by a two-thirds majority. Under Protocol: 'The Member States agree to accept and implement the decisions of the Peace and Security Council, in accordance with the Constitutive Act.'[581]
- The Financial Institutions – The AU Constitutive Act provides for three specific financial organs to be created: the African Central Bank, the African Investment Bank, and the African Monetary Fund.[582] The mission of these institutions is to implement economic integration projects as stressed in the Treaty Establishing the African Economic Community (Abuja Treaty).
- The Economic, Social, and Cultural Council – was established in 2004 as an advisory organ to the AU composed of civil society organisations.
- Legal Organs – The AU Commission on International Law was created in 2009 as an independent advisory organ; the AU Advisory Board on Corruption was established as part of the African Union Convention on Preventing and Combating Corruption, which entered into force in August 2006.

The current state of affairs

Finally, it is notable that the institutional architecture of the African Union is still in the process of development. Even though the African nations have fruitful experience with respect to institutional co-operation in the format of the Organisation of African Unity, the new vision of a unified Africa requires gradual implementation by approximating it with best practices the world can offer, which ultimately will result in the creation of a modern institutional framework.

---

580 Paragraph 1 of Article 2 of the 2002 Protocol Relating to the Establishment of the Peace and Security Council of the African Union.
581 Paragraph 3 of Article 7 of the Protocol Relating to the Establishment of the Peace and Security Council of the African Union.
582 Article 19 of the Constitutive Act of the African Union.

THE LEAGUE OF ARAB STATES

> Pact of the League of Arab States
> Arab World
> Joint Defence and Economic Co-operation Treaty

Foundation

The League of Arab states (also referred to as the Arab League) is an organisation that consists of the states in and around North Africa, the Horn of Africa, and the Arabian Peninsula. The representatives of the seven founding member states – Egypt, Iraq, Lebanon, Saudi Arabia, Syria, Transjordan (now Jordan) and Yemen – concluded the **Pact of the League of Arab States** (also is referred to as the Charter of the League of Arab States) in 1945. Gradually, the other 15 countries joined the organisation. The headquarters of the Arab League is located in Cairo, Egypt.

The principal objectives of the League

Since its establishment, the principal objective of the League was to create the institutional framework to ensure the countries in the **Arab World** could maintain their common cultural and spiritual heritage, as well as uphold security and political and economic interests. Accordingly, in international affairs, the League has been used as a forum for the Arab states to coordinate their policy attitudes, deliberate on matters of common concern, settle certain disputes between the member states, and reduce the possibility of conflicts in the region.

To address the security challenges, Joint Defence Council was established under the Joint Defence and Economic Co-operation Treaty of 1950 to coordinate the joint defence of the Arab League member states. The Treaty defined that it 'shall consist of the Foreign Ministers and the Defence Ministers of the Contracting States or their representatives. Decisions taken by a two-thirds majority shall be binding on all the Contracting States.'[583] Over time, the League's security architecture faced global geopolitical and regional challenges. Since the old mechanisms were not so effective, from time to time, proposals for the development of the system appeared on the agenda. And this process is still ongoing.

Overall, the League maintains a vital symbolic significance as a voice of a common aspiration for more Arab unity and coordination.

---

583 Article 6 of the Treaty. This book uses the translation of the original Pact of the League of Arab States, as well as the Joint Defence and Economic Co-operation Treaty provided on the website of the Avalon Project at the Yale Law School: Documents in Law, History and Diplomacy, Lillian Goldman Law Library <https://avalon.law.yale.edu/20th_century/arableag.asp> accessed 19 July 2021.

The main components of the League of Arab States

- The Council – is composed of the representatives of the member states. Each state has one vote. According to the original Pact: 'The Council shall be entrusted with the function of realising the purpose of the League and of supervising the execution of the agreements concluded between the member States . . .'[584] It meets in regular sessions at different levels – at the Summit level, the ministerial level (the Ministers of Foreign Affairs level), and the level of permanent representatives. Besides, it meets in extraordinary sessions whenever the need arises. The original Pact provided that the 'decisions of the Council taken by a unanimous vote shall be binding on all the member States of the League; those that are reached by a majority vote shall bind only those that accept them.'

> This was changed in 2005 to provide that if unanimity cannot be reached, the following procedure is to be followed: • the decision is delayed until the next session; • if the matter is urgent, a special session is held within one month; • if it is not possible to achieve unanimity in the next session, a two-thirds majority of the attending states is required for the vote to pass on substantive matters, and a simple majority is adequate for voting on other matters. The amendment removed the provision that decisions are binding only on those who voted for them.[585]

The council has different powers in different configurations. For example, whereas the Summit is the highest decision-making body in the League of Arab States, the Council of Foreign Ministers is the second-highest decision-making level. The latter discusses issues and prepares them for decision-making by the Summit and is also responsible for making decisions on certain significant issues.

- Specialised Ministerial Councils – are formed 'in all sectors to support joint Arab action such as Arab Interior Ministers Council, Arab Health Ministers Council, Arab Information Ministers Council and others.'[586]
- Special Committees – are established to study and draft proposals on areas of common interest and co-operation. Such committees include the Arab Permanent Committee on Human Rights, committees on financial, administrative, information, and legal affairs.
- Economic and Social Council (also is referred to as the Arab ECOSOC) – was established by the Joint Defence and Economic Cooperation Treaty and is composed of

---

584 Article 3 of the Pact.

585 Mervat Rishmawi, *The League of Arab States Human Rights Standards and Mechanisms, Open Society Foundations and Cairo Institute for Human Rights Studies*, 61. Available at <https://www.opensocietyfoundations.org/newsroom/engaging-arab-league-promoting-human-rights> accessed 7 June 2021.

586 See at the official website of the Ministry of Foreign Affairs of the Kingdom of Bahrain 'League of Arab States' <https://www.mofa.gov.bh/Default.aspx?tabid=119&language=en-US> accessed 7 June 2021.

the ministers of economic and financial matters of all the contracting states or their representatives. It is involved in the implementation of the economic and social provisions of the Charter of the League of Arab States, as well as policy development in this regard. The Council participates in preparatory meetings for Arab economic and social development summits. In addition, it approves the creation of any Arab League's specialised organisation/institution.

• The Arab Parliament – was established in 2005 and is composed of four members of each member state of the Arab League, which are selected from their national parliaments or national assemblies. 'The League Summit in 2014 affirmed the "consultative nature of the Arab Parliament for the time being".'[587]

• The General Secretariat – runs day-to-day affairs and is composed of a Secretary-General and other officials. The General Secretariat of the Arab League serves as the administrative organ of the organisation and the executive body of the Council and Specialised Ministerial Councils as well. The Council (at the ministerial level) appoints the Secretary-General for a period of five years.

The specialised institutions

The League has become an umbrella organisation responsible for numerous specialised organisations created to promote the interests of the Arab countries. Such specialised institutions include the Arab League Educational, Cultural and Scientific Organisation; the Arab Labour Organisation; the Arab Organisation for Agricultural Development; the Arab Administrative Development Organisation; the Arab States Broadcasting Union, the Arab Industrial Development and Mining Organisation, and so forth.

THE ASSOCIATION OF SOUTHEAST ASIAN NATIONS

> ASEAN Declaration
> Treaty of Amity and Co-operation
> Declaration of ASEAN Concord
> Agreement of Establishment of the Permanent Secretariat
> New Vision 2020
> ASEAN Community
> ASEAN Charter
> Entities Associated with ASEAN

Foundation

The Association of Southeast Asian Nations (ASEAN) was established in 1967 as a platform for the integration and deepening of the co-operation between the countries in Southeast Asia (and, in general, for the promotion of Pan-Asianism) with the signing of the **ASEAN Declaration** (Bangkok Declaration) by the founding states of ASEAN:

587 Rishmawi (n 585) 49.

Indonesia, Malaysia, the Philippines, Singapore, and Thailand. Later, five other states in the region joined the organisation, forming the current roster of ten member states.

The additional agreements

In 1976, three agreements were signed: The **Treaty of Amity and Co-operation**, which stressed the fundamental principles of co-operation in the region, reaffirming the principles of the UN Charter and adding the regional principle of effective co-operation among the member states; the **Declaration of ASEAN Concord**, which aimed at increasing political and economic coordination and co-operation; and the **Agreement of Establishment of the Permanent Secretariat** to harmonise the national secretariats established under the 1967 ASEAN Declaration.

ASEAN Community

The ASEAN framework supports the integrative processes among its member states. Thus, recent events and developments have brought the Southeast Asian Nations to the establishment of the community.

On the 30th Anniversary of ASEAN, a **New Vision 2020** was adopted – ASEAN as 'a concert of Southeast Asian nations'. In 2003, at the 9th ASEAN Summit, the ASEAN Leaders resolved that an ASEAN Community shall be established. In 2007 the leaders affirmed their strong commitment to accelerate the establishment of an **ASEAN Community** by 2015 and signed the Cebu Declaration on the Acceleration of the Establishment of an ASEAN Community.

Components of the ASEAN Community

The structure of the ASEAN Community comprises three pillars:

- the ASEAN Political-Security Community;
- the ASEAN Economic Community; and
- the ASEAN Socio-Cultural Community.[588]

ASEAN Charter

The legal basis for the Community was created by the **ASEAN Charter**, which entered into force in 2008. The implementation of this Charter was a step forward in the transition

---

588 Together with the Initiative for ASEAN Integration (IAI) Strategic Framework and IAI Work Plan Phase II, they form the Roadmap for the ASEAN Community. 'The ASEAN Political-Security Community Blueprint, the ASEAN Economic Community Blueprint, the ASEAN Socio-Cultural Community Blueprint and the IAI Work Plan 2 (2009–2015), as annexed, shall constitute the Roadmap for an ASEAN Community (2009–2015), and each ASEAN Member State shall ensure its timely implementation'. Association of Southeast Asian Nations, *Roadmap for an ASEAN Community 2009–2015* (ASEAN Secretariat 2009) 2.

to the operation of the Association under a new legal order and the establishment of a number of new organs for the development of its structure.

Hence, as in cases of other regional international organisations with similar missions mentioned earlier, the ASEAN is also another expression of the trend towards regional integration.

The principles of the ASEAN Charter

The ASEAN Charter stipulates the principles upon which the members shall act. There are the principles which emphasise the specifics of the ASEAN way: namely,

(l) respect for the different cultures, languages and religions of the peoples of ASEAN, while emphasising their common values in the spirit of unity in diversity;

(m) the centrality of ASEAN in external political, economic, social and cultural relations while remaining actively engaged, outward-looking, inclusive and non-discriminatory; and

(n) adherence to multilateral trade rules and ASEAN's rules-based regimes for effective implementation of economic commitments and progressive reduction towards elimination of all barriers to regional economic integration, in a market-driven economy.[589]

Internal organs

- The ASEAN Summit – comprises the heads of state or government of the member states. It is the supreme policy-making body of the Association, appoints the Secretary-General of ASEAN, and takes 'decisions on key issues pertaining to the realisation of the objectives of ASEAN, important matters of interest to Member States and all issues referred to it by the ASEAN Coordinating Council, the ASEAN Community Councils and ASEAN Sectoral Ministerial Bodies'.[590]

- The ASEAN Coordinating Council – is composed of ASEAN foreign ministers and meets at least twice a year. It coordinates the implementation of agreements and decisions of the ASEAN Summit and approves the appointment and termination of the Deputy Secretaries-General upon the recommendation of the Secretary-General.

- The ASEAN Community Councils – comprise the ASEAN Political-Security Community Council, the ASEAN Economic Community Council, and the ASEAN Socio-Cultural Community Council. Each ASEAN Community Council has 'under its purview' the respective ASEAN Sectoral Ministerial Bodies. 'Each ASEAN Community Council shall meet at least twice a year and shall be chaired by the appropriate Minister from the Member State holding the ASEAN Chairmanship'.[591]

- The ASEAN Sectoral Ministerial Bodies – were created to strengthen co-operation in different sectors in support of the ASEAN integration and community building.

- The ASEAN Secretariat and Secretary-General of ASEAN – The Secretary-General of ASEAN serves as Chief Administrative Officer of the Association and is appointed by the ASEAN Summit for a non-renewable term of office of five years and selected from among the nationals of the ASEAN member states based on an alphabetical rotation.

589 Article 2 of the Charter.
590 Paragraph 2 of Article 7 of the Charter.
591 Paragraph 5 of Article 9 of the Charter.

- The Committee of Permanent Representatives to ASEAN – Each ASEAN member state appoints a Permanent Representative to ASEAN with the rank of Ambassador based in Jakarta, Indonesia (where the ASEAN headquarters is located). They collectively constitute a Committee of Permanent Representatives.
- The ASEAN National Secretariats – are established in every member state and represent 'the national focal point' of Association.
- The ASEAN Human Rights Body – serves as a framework of promotion and protection of human rights and fundamental freedoms.
- The ASEAN Foundation – supports 'the Secretary-General of ASEAN and collaborates with the relevant ASEAN bodies to support ASEAN community building by promoting greater awareness of the ASEAN identity, people-to-people interaction, and close collaboration among the business sector, civil society, academia and other stakeholders in ASEAN.'[592]

The other institutions

Additionally, the Charter includes a provision on the engagement of international regional institutions in the process of integration; these institutions are called the **Entities Associated with ASEAN**. There are currently many entities registered in such a status. For instance: the ASEAN Inter-Parliamentary Assembly, the ASEAN Alliance of Health Supplement Associations, the ASEAN Chemical Industries Council, the ASEAN Institute for Peace and Reconciliation, the ASEAN Chess Confederation, and so on.

CASES AND MATERIALS (*SELECTED PARTS*)

The principal organs of the United Nations

Charter of the United Nations

CHAPTER III: ORGANS[593]

Article 7

1 There are established as principal organs of the United Nations: a General Assembly, a Security Council, an Economic and Social Council, a Trusteeship Council, an International Court of Justice and a Secretariat.

592 Paragraph 1 of Article 15 of the Charter.
593 'The Charter has been amended five times. . . . In 1965, Articles 23 was amended to enlarge the Security Council from 11 to 15 members. . . . In 1965, Article 27 was amended to increase the required number of Security Council votes from 7 to 9. . . . In 1965, Article 61 was amended to enlarge the Economic and Social Council from 18 to 27 members. . . . In 1968, Article 109 was amended to change the requirements for a General Conference of Member States for reviewing the Charter. . . . In 1973, Article 61 was amended again to further enlarge the Economic and Social Council from 27 to 54 members'. See 'Can the UN Charter be amended, and how many times has this occurred?' on the official website of the UN <https://ask.un.org/faq/140440> accessed 16 March 2021.

2   Such subsidiary organs as may be found necessary may be established in accordance with the present Charter.

Article 8

The United Nations shall place no restrictions on the eligibility of men and women to participate in any capacity and under conditions of equality in its principal and subsidiary organs.

CHAPTER IV: THE GENERAL ASSEMBLY

COMPOSITION

Article 9

1   The General Assembly shall consist of all the Members of the United Nations.
2   Each Member shall have not more than five representatives in the General Assembly.

FUNCTIONS AND POWERS

Article 10

The General Assembly may discuss any questions or any matters within the scope of the present Charter or relating to the powers and functions of any organs provided for in the present Charter, and, except as provided in Article 12, may make recommendations to the Members of the United Nations or to the Security Council or to both on any such questions or matters.

Article 11

1   The General Assembly may consider the general principles of co-operation in the maintenance of international peace and security, including the principles governing disarmament and the regulation of armaments, and may make recommendations with regard to such principles to the Members or to the Security Council or to both.
2   The General Assembly may discuss any questions relating to the maintenance of international peace and security brought before it by any Member of the United Nations, or by the Security Council, or by a state which is not a Member of the United Nations in accordance with Article 35, paragraph 2, and, except as provided in Article 12, may make recommendations with regard to any such questions to the state or states concerned or to the Security Council or to both. Any such question on which action is necessary shall be referred to the Security Council by the General Assembly either before or after discussion.
3   The General Assembly may call the attention of the Security Council to situations which are likely to endanger international peace and security.
4   The powers of the General Assembly set forth in this Article shall not limit the general scope of Article 10.

Article 12

1 While the Security Council is exercising in respect of any dispute or situation the functions assigned to it in the present Charter, the General Assembly shall not make any recommendation with regard to that dispute or situation unless the Security Council so requests.

2 The Secretary-General, with the consent of the Security Council, shall notify the General Assembly at each session of any matters relative to the maintenance of international peace and security which are being dealt with by the Security Council and shall similarly notify the General Assembly, or the Members of the United Nations if the General Assembly is not in session, immediately the Security Council ceases to deal with such matters.

Article 13

1 The General Assembly shall initiate studies and make recommendations for the purpose of:

a promoting international co-operation in the political field and encouraging the progressive development of international law and its codification;

b promoting international co-operation in the economic, social, cultural, educational, and health fields, and assisting in the realization of human rights and fundamental freedoms for all without distinction as to race, sex, language, or religion.

2 The further responsibilities, functions and powers of the General Assembly with respect to matters mentioned in paragraph 1 (b) above are set forth in Chapters IX and X.

Article 14

Subject to the provisions of Article 12, the General Assembly may recommend measures for the peaceful adjustment of any situation, regardless of origin, which it deems likely to impair the general welfare or friendly relations among nations, including situations resulting from a violation of the provisions of the present Charter setting forth the Purposes and Principles of the United Nations.

Article 15

1 The General Assembly shall receive and consider annual and special reports from the Security Council; these reports shall include an account of the measures that the Security Council has decided upon or taken to maintain international peace and security.

2 The General Assembly shall receive and consider reports from the other organs of the United Nations.

Article 16

The General Assembly shall perform such functions with respect to the international trusteeship system as are assigned to it under Chapters XII and XIII, including the approval of the trusteeship agreements for areas not designated as strategic.

Article 17

1   The General Assembly shall consider and approve the budget of the Organization.
2   The expenses of the Organization shall be borne by the Members as apportioned by the General Assembly.
3   The General Assembly shall consider and approve any financial and budgetary arrangements with specialized agencies referred to in Article 57 and shall examine the administrative budgets of such specialized agencies with a view to making recommendations to the agencies concerned.

VOTING

Article 18

1   Each member of the General Assembly shall have one vote.
2   Decisions of the General Assembly on important questions shall be made by a two-thirds majority of the members present and voting. These questions shall include: recommendations with respect to the maintenance of international peace and security, the election of the non-permanent members of the Security Council, the election of the members of the Economic and Social Council, the election of members of the Trusteeship Council in accordance with paragraph 1 (c) of Article 86, the admission of new Members to the United Nations, the suspension of the rights and privileges of membership, the expulsion of Members, questions relating to the operation of the trusteeship system, and budgetary questions.
3   Decisions on other questions, including the determination of additional categories of questions to be decided by a two-thirds majority, shall be made by a majority of the members present and voting.

Article 19

A Member of the United Nations which is in arrears in the payment of its financial contributions to the Organization shall have no vote in the General Assembly if the amount of its arrears equals or exceeds the amount of the contributions due from it for the preceding two full years. The General Assembly may, nevertheless, permit such a Member to vote if it is satisfied that the failure to pay is due to conditions beyond the control of the Member.

PROCEDURE

Article 20

The General Assembly shall meet in regular annual sessions and in such special sessions as occasion may require. Special sessions shall be convoked by the Secretary-General at the request of the Security Council or of a majority of the Members of the United Nations.

Article 21

The General Assembly shall adopt its own rules of procedure. It shall elect its President for each session.

Article 22

The General Assembly may establish such subsidiary organs as it deems necessary for the performance of its functions.

CHAPTER V: THE SECURITY COUNCIL

COMPOSITION

Article 23

1   The Security Council shall consist of fifteen Members of the United Nations. The Republic of China, France, the Union of Soviet Socialist Republics, the United Kingdom of Great Britain and Northern Ireland, and the United States of America shall be permanent members of the Security Council. The General Assembly shall elect ten other Members of the United Nations to be non-permanent members of the Security Council, due regard being specially paid, in the first instance to the contribution of Members of the United Nations to the maintenance of international peace and security and to the other purposes of the Organization, and also to equitable geographical distribution.
2   The non-permanent members of the Security Council shall be elected for a term of two years. In the first election of the non-permanent members after the increase of the membership of the Security Council from eleven to fifteen, two of the four additional members shall be chosen for a term of one year. A retiring member shall not be eligible for immediate re-election.
3   Each member of the Security Council shall have one representative.

FUNCTIONS AND POWERS

Article 24

1   In order to ensure prompt and effective action by the United Nations, its Members confer on the Security Council primary responsibility for the maintenance of international peace and security, and agree that in carrying out its duties under this responsibility the Security Council acts on their behalf.
2   In discharging these duties the Security Council shall act in accordance with the Purposes and Principles of the United Nations. The specific powers granted to the Security Council for the discharge of these duties are laid down in Chapters VI, VII, VIII, and XII.
3   The Security Council shall submit annual and, when necessary, special reports to the General Assembly for its consideration.

Article 25

The Members of the United Nations agree to accept and carry out the decisions of the Security Council in accordance with the present Charter.

Article 26

In order to promote the establishment and maintenance of international peace and security with the least diversion for armaments of the world's human and economic resources, the Security Council shall be responsible for formulating, with the assistance of the Military Staff Committee referred to in Article 47, plans to be submitted to the Members of the United Nations for the establishment of a system for the regulation of armaments.

VOTING

Article 27

1   Each member of the Security Council shall have one vote.
2   Decisions of the Security Council on procedural matters shall be made by an affirmative vote of nine members.
3   Decisions of the Security Council on all other matters shall be made by an affirmative vote of nine members including the concurring votes of the permanent members; provided that, in decisions under Chapter VI, and under paragraph 3 of Article 52, a party to a dispute shall abstain from voting.

PROCEDURE

Article 28

1   The Security Council shall be so organized as to be able to function continuously. Each member of the Security Council shall for this purpose be represented at all times at the seat of the Organization.
2   The Security Council shall hold periodic meetings at which each of its members may, if it so desires, be represented by a member of the government or by some other specially designated representative.
3   The Security Council may hold meetings at such places other than the seat of the Organization as in its judgment will best facilitate its work.

Article 29

The Security Council may establish such subsidiary organs as it deems necessary for the performance of its functions.

Article 30

The Security Council shall adopt its own rules of procedure, including the method of selecting its President.

Article 31

Any Member of the United Nations which is not a member of the Security Council may participate, without vote, in the discussion of any question brought before the Security Council whenever the latter considers that the interests of that Member are specially affected.

Article 32

Any Member of the United Nations which is not a member of the Security Council or any state which is not a Member of the United Nations, if it is a party to a dispute under consideration by the Security Council, shall be invited to participate, without vote, in the discussion relating to the dispute. The Security Council shall lay down such conditions as it deems just for the participation of a state which is not a Member of the United Nations.

CHAPTER X: THE ECONOMIC AND SOCIAL COUNCIL

COMPOSITION

Article 61

1   The Economic and Social Council shall consist of fifty-four Members of the United Nations elected by the General Assembly.
2   Subject to the provisions of paragraph 3, eighteen members of the Economic and Social Council shall be elected each year for a term of three years. A retiring member shall be eligible for immediate re-election.
3   At the first election after the increase in the membership of the Economic and Social Council from twenty-seven to fifty-four members, in addition to the members elected in place of the nine members whose term of office expires at the end of that year, twenty-seven additional members shall be elected. Of these twenty-seven additional members, the term of office of nine members so elected shall expire at the end of one year, and of nine other members at the end of two years, in accordance with arrangements made by the General Assembly.
4   Each member of the Economic and Social Council shall have one representative.

FUNCTIONS AND POWERS

Article 62

1   The Economic and Social Council may make or initiate studies and reports with respect to international economic, social, cultural, educational, health, and related matters and may make recommendations with respect to any such matters to the General Assembly to the Members of the United Nations, and to the specialized agencies concerned.
2   It may make recommendations for the purpose of promoting respect for, and observance of, human rights and fundamental freedoms for all.
3   It may prepare draft conventions for submission to the General Assembly, with respect to matters falling within its competence.
4   It may call, in accordance with the rules prescribed by the United Nations, international conferences on matters falling within its competence.

Article 63

1 The Economic and Social Council may enter into agreements with any of the agencies referred to in Article 57, defining the terms on which the agency concerned shall be brought into relationship with the United Nations. Such agreements shall be subject to approval by the General Assembly.
2 It may co-ordinate the activities of the specialized agencies through consultation with and recommendations to such agencies and through recommendations to the General Assembly and to the Members of the United Nations.

Article 64

1 The Economic and Social Council may take appropriate steps to obtain regular reports from the specialized agencies. It may make arrangements with the Members of the United Nations and with the specialized agencies to obtain reports on the steps taken to give effect to its own recommendations and to recommendations on matters falling within its competence made by the General Assembly.
2 It may communicate its observations on these reports to the General Assembly.

Article 65

The Economic and Social Council may furnish information to the Security Council and shall assist the Security Council upon its request.

Article 66

1 The Economic and Social Council shall perform such functions as fall within its competence in connection with the carrying out of the recommendations of the General Assembly.
2 It may, with the approval of the General Assembly, perform services at the request of Members of the United Nations and at the request of specialized agencies.
3 It shall perform such other functions as are specified elsewhere in the present Charter or as may be assigned to it by the General Assembly.

VOTING

Article 67

1 Each member of the Economic and Social Council shall have one vote.
2 Decisions of the Economic and Social Council shall be made by a majority of the members present and voting.
3.

PROCEDURE

Article 68

The Economic and Social Council shall set up commissions in economic and social fields and for the promotion of human rights, and such other commissions as may be required for the performance of its functions.

Article 69

The Economic and Social Council shall invite any Member of the United Nations to participate, without vote, in its deliberations on any matter of particular concern to that Member.

Article 70

The Economic and Social Council may make arrangements for representatives of the specialized agencies to participate, without vote, in its deliberations and in those of the commissions established by it, and for its representatives to participate in the deliberations of the specialized agencies.

Article 71

The Economic and Social Council may make suitable arrangements for consultation with non-governmental organizations which are concerned with matters within its competence. Such arrangements may be made with international organizations and, where appropriate, with national organizations after consultation with the Member of the United Nations concerned.

Article 72

1   The Economic and Social Council shall adopt its own rules of procedure, including the method of selecting its President.
2   The Economic and Social Council shall meet as required in accordance with its rules, which shall include provision for the convening of meetings on the request of a majority of its members.

The European Union's institutions

Consolidated version of the Treaty on European Union
of 01.03.2020

TITLE I
COMMON PROVISIONS

Article 1

(Ex Article 1 TEU)

By this Treaty, the HIGH CONTRACTING PARTIES establish among themselves a EUROPEAN UNION, hereinafter called 'the Union', on which the Member States confer competences to attain objectives they have in common.

This Treaty marks a new stage in the process of creating an ever closer union among the peoples of Europe, in which decisions are taken as openly as possible and as closely as possible to the citizen.

The Union shall be founded on the present Treaty and on the Treaty on the Functioning of the European Union (hereinafter referred to as 'the Treaties'). Those two Treaties shall have the same legal value. The Union shall replace and succeed the European Community.

Article 2

The Union is founded on the values of respect for human dignity, freedom, democracy, equality, the rule of law and respect for human rights, including the rights of persons belonging to minorities. These values are common to the Member States in a society in which pluralism, non-discrimination, tolerance, justice, solidarity and equality between women and men prevail.

Article 5

(Ex Article 5 TEC)

1   The limits of Union competences are governed by the principle of conferral. The use of Union competences is governed by the principles of subsidiarity and proportionality.
2   Under the principle of conferral, the Union shall act only within the limits of the competences conferred upon it by the Member States in the Treaties to attain the objectives set out therein. Competences not conferred upon the Union in the Treaties remain with the Member States.
3   Under the principle of subsidiarity, in areas which do not fall within its exclusive competence, the Union shall act only if and in so far as the objectives of the proposed action cannot be sufficiently achieved by the Member States, either at central level or at regional and local level, but can rather, by reason of the scale or effects of the proposed action, be better achieved at Union level.

   The institutions of the Union shall apply the principle of subsidiarity as laid down in the Protocol on the application of the principles of subsidiarity and proportionality. National Parliaments ensure compliance with the principle of subsidiarity in accordance with the procedure set out in that Protocol.
4   Under the principle of proportionality, the content and form of Union action shall not exceed what is necessary to achieve the objectives of the Treaties.

   The institutions of the Union shall apply the principle of proportionality as laid down in the Protocol on the application of the principles of subsidiarity and proportionality.

TITLE III
PROVISIONS ON THE INSTITUTIONS

Article 13

1   The Union shall have an institutional framework which shall aim to promote its values, advance its objectives, serve its interests, those of its citizens and those of the Member States, and ensure the consistency, effectiveness and continuity of its policies and actions.
   The Union's institutions shall be:

   * the European Parliament,
   * the European Council,
   * the Council,
   * the European Commission (hereinafter referred to as 'the Commission'),
   * the Court of Justice of the European Union,

- the European Central Bank,
- the Court of Auditors.

2   Each institution shall act within the limits of the powers conferred on it in the Treaties, and in conformity with the procedures, conditions and objectives set out in them. The institutions shall practice mutual sincere cooperation.

3   The provisions relating to the European Central Bank and the Court of Auditors and detailed provisions on the other institutions are set out in the Treaty on the Functioning of the European Union.

4   The European Parliament, the Council and the Commission shall be assisted by an Economic and Social Committee and a Committee of the Regions acting in an advisory capacity.

Article 14

1   The European Parliament shall, jointly with the Council, exercise legislative and budgetary functions. It shall exercise functions of political control and consultation as laid down in the Treaties. It shall elect the President of the Commission.

2   The European Parliament shall be composed of representatives of the Union's citizens. They shall not exceed seven hundred and fifty in number, plus the President. Representation of citizens shall be degressively proportional, with a minimum threshold of six members per Member State. No Member State shall be allocated more than ninety-six seats.

   The European Council shall adopt by unanimity, on the initiative of the European Parliament and with its consent, a decision establishing the composition of the European Parliament, respecting the principles referred to in the first subparagraph.

3   The members of the European Parliament shall be elected for a term of five years by direct universal suffrage in a free and secret ballot.

4   The European Parliament shall elect its President and its officers from among its members.

Article 15

1   The European Council shall provide the Union with the necessary impetus for its development and shall define the general political directions and priorities thereof. It shall not exercise legislative functions.

2   The European Council shall consist of the Heads of State or Government of the Member States, together with its President and the President of the Commission. The High Representative of the Union for Foreign Affairs and Security Policy shall take part in its work.

3   The European Council shall meet twice every six months, convened by its President. When the agenda so requires, the members of the European Council may decide each to be assisted by a minister and, in the case of the President of the Commission, by a member of the Commission. When the situation so requires, the President shall convene a special meeting of the European Council.

4   Except where the Treaties provide otherwise, decisions of the European Council shall be taken by consensus.

5   The European Council shall elect its President, by a qualified majority, for a term of two and a half years, renewable once. In the event of an impediment or serious misconduct, the European Council can end the President's term of office in accordance with the same procedure.

6   The President of the European Council:

a)   shall chair it and drive forward its work;
b)   shall ensure the preparation and continuity of the work of the European Council in coop-
      eration with the President of the Commission, and on the basis of the work of the General
      Affairs Council;
c)   shall endeavour to facilitate cohesion and consensus within the European Council;
d)   shall present a report to the European Parliament after each of the meetings of the Euro-
      pean Council.

The President of the European Council shall, at his level and in that capacity, ensure the external
representation of the Union on issues concerning its common foreign and security policy, without
prejudice to the powers of the High Representative of the Union for Foreign Affairs and Security
Policy.
The President of the European Council shall not hold a national office.

Article 16

1   The Council shall, jointly with the European Parliament, exercise legislative and budgetary
     functions. It shall carry out policy-making and coordinating functions as laid down in the
     Treaties.
2   The Council shall consist of a representative of each Member State at ministerial level, who
     may commit the government of the Member State in question and cast its vote.
3   The Council shall act by a qualified majority except where the Treaties provide otherwise.
4   As from 1 November 2014, a qualified majority shall be defined as at least 55 % of the
     members of the Council, comprising at least fifteen of them and representing Member
     States comprising at least 65% of the population of the Union.
        A blocking minority must include at least four Council members, failing which the qual-
     ified majority shall be deemed attained.
        The other arrangements governing the qualified majority are laid down in Article
     238(2) of the Treaty on the Functioning of the European Union.
5   The transitional provisions relating to the definition of the qualified majority which
     shall be applicable until 31 October 2014 and those which shall be applicable from
     1 November 2014 to 31 March 2017 are laid down in the Protocol on transitional
     provisions.
6   The Council shall meet in different configurations, the list of which shall be adopted in
     accordance with Article 236 of the Treaty on the Functioning of the European Union.
        The General Affairs Council shall ensure consistency in the work of the different
     Council configurations. It shall prepare and ensure the follow-up to meetings of the
     European Council, in liaison with the President of the European Council and the
     Commission.
        The Foreign Affairs Council shall elaborate the Union's external action on the basis of
     strategic guidelines laid down by the European Council and ensure that the Union's action
     is consistent.

7   A Committee of Permanent Representatives of the Governments of the Member States shall be responsible for preparing the work of the Council.

8   The Council shall meet in public when it deliberates and votes on a draft legislative act. To this end, each Council meeting shall be divided into two parts, dealing respectively with deliberations on Union legislative acts and non-legislative activities.

9   The Presidency of Council configurations, other than that of Foreign Affairs, shall be held by Member State representatives in the Council on the basis of equal rotation, in accordance with the conditions established in accordance with Article 236 of the Treaty on the Functioning of the European Union.

Article 17

1   The Commission shall promote the general interest of the Union and take appropriate initiatives to that end. It shall ensure the application of the Treaties, and of measures adopted by the institutions pursuant to them. It shall oversee the application of Union law under the control of the Court of Justice of the European Union. It shall execute the budget and manage programmes. It shall exercise coordinating, executive and management functions, as laid down in the Treaties. With the exception of the common foreign and security policy, and other cases provided for in the Treaties, it shall ensure the Union's external representation. It shall initiate the Union's annual and multiannual programming with a view to achieving interinstitutional agreements.

2   Union legislative acts may only be adopted on the basis of a Commission proposal, except where the Treaties provide otherwise. Other acts shall be adopted on the basis of a Commission proposal where the Treaties so provide.

3   The Commission's term of office shall be five years.

   The members of the Commission shall be chosen on the ground of their general competence and European commitment from persons whose independence is beyond doubt.

   In carrying out its responsibilities, the Commission shall be completely independent. Without prejudice to Article 18(2), the members of the Commission shall neither seek nor take instructions from any Government or other institution, body, office or entity. They shall refrain from any action incompatible with their duties or the performance of their tasks.

4   The Commission appointed between the date of entry into force of the Treaty of Lisbon and 31 October 2014, shall consist of one national of each Member State, including its President and the High Representative of the Union for Foreign Affairs and Security Policy who shall be one of its Vice-Presidents.

5   As from 1 November 2014, the Commission shall consist of a number of members, including its President and the High Representative of the Union for Foreign Affairs and Security Policy, corresponding to two thirds of the number of Member States, unless the European Council, acting unanimously, decides to alter this number.

   The members of the Commission shall be chosen from among the nationals of the Member States on the basis of a system of strictly equal rotation between the Member States, reflecting the demographic and geographical range of all the Member States. This system shall be established unanimously by the European Council in accordance with Article 244 of the Treaty on the Functioning of the European Union.

6   The President of the Commission shall:

   a)   lay down guidelines within which the Commission is to work;

   b)   decide on the internal organisation of the Commission, ensuring that it acts consistently, efficiently and as a collegiate body;

   c)   appoint Vice-Presidents, other than the High Representative of the Union for Foreign Affairs and Security Policy, from among the members of the Commission.

   A member of the Commission shall resign if the President so requests. The High Representative of the Union for Foreign Affairs and Security Policy shall resign, in accordance with the procedure set out in Article 18(1), if the President so requests.

7   Taking into account the elections to the European Parliament and after having held the appropriate consultations, the European Council, acting by a qualified majority, shall propose to the European Parliament a candidate for President of the Commission. This candidate shall be elected by the European Parliament by a majority of its component members. If he does not obtain the required majority, the European Council, acting by a qualified majority, shall within one month propose a new candidate who shall be elected by the European Parliament following the same procedure.

   The Council, by common accord with the President-elect, shall adopt the list of the other persons whom it proposes for appointment as members of the Commission. They shall be selected, on the basis of the suggestions made by Member States, in accordance with the criteria set out in paragraph 3, second subparagraph, and paragraph 5, second subparagraph.

   The President, the High Representative of the Union for Foreign Affairs and Security Policy and the other members of the Commission shall be subject as a body to a vote of consent by the European Parliament. On the basis of this consent the Commission shall be appointed by the European Council, acting by a qualified majority.

8   The Commission, as a body, shall be responsible to the European Parliament. In accordance with Article 234 of the Treaty on the Functioning of the European Union, the European Parliament may vote on a motion of censure of the Commission. If such a motion is carried, the members of the Commission shall resign as a body and the High Representative of the Union for Foreign Affairs and Security Policy shall resign from the duties that he carries out in the Commission.

Article 18

1   The European Council, acting by a qualified majority, with the agreement of the President of the Commission, shall appoint the High Representative of the Union for Foreign Affairs and Security Policy. The European Council may end his term of office by the same procedure.

2   The High Representative shall conduct the Union's common foreign and security policy. He shall contribute by his proposals to the development of that policy, which he shall carry out as mandated by the Council. The same shall apply to the common security and defence policy.

3   The High Representative shall preside over the Foreign Affairs Council.

4   The High Representative shall be one of the Vice-Presidents of the Commission. He shall ensure the consistency of the Union's external action. He shall be responsible within the Commission for responsibilities incumbent on it in external relations and

for coordinating other aspects of the Union's external action. In exercising these responsibilities within the Commission, and only for these responsibilities, the High Representative shall be bound by Commission procedures to the extent that this is consistent with paragraphs 2 and 3.

Article 19

1   The Court of Justice of the European Union shall include the Court of Justice, the General Court and specialised courts. It shall ensure that in the interpretation and application of the Treaties the law is observed.

   Member States shall provide remedies sufficient to ensure effective legal protection in the fields covered by Union law.

2   The Court of Justice shall consist of one judge from each Member State. It shall be assisted by Advocates-General.

   The General Court shall include at least one judge per Member State.

   The Judges and the Advocates-General of the Court of Justice and the Judges of the General Court shall be chosen from persons whose independence is beyond doubt and who satisfy the conditions set out in Articles 253 and 254 of the Treaty on the Functioning of the European Union. They shall be appointed by common accord of the governments of the Member States for six years. Retiring Judges and Advocates-General may be reappointed.

3   The Court of Justice of the European Union shall, in accordance with the Treaties:

   a)   rule on actions brought by a Member State, an institution or a natural or legal person;
   b)   give preliminary rulings, at the request of courts or tribunals of the Member States, on the interpretation of Union law or the validity of acts adopted by the institutions;
   c)   rule in other cases provided for in the Treaties.

European Union law

NV Algemene Transport – en Expeditie Onderneming van Gend & Loos v Netherlands Inland Revenue Administration, Judgment of 5 February 1963, Court of Justice of the European Union

Case 26–62, [1963] EU:C:1963:1.

The objective of the EEC Treaty, which is to establish a Common Market, the functioning of which is of direct concern to interested parties in the Community, implies that this Treaty is more than an agreement which merely creates mutual obligations between the contracting states. This view is confirmed by the preamble to the Treaty which refers not only to governments but to peoples. It is also confirmed more specifically by the establishment of institutions endowed with sovereign rights, the exercise of which affects Member States and also their citizens. Furthermore, it must be noted that the nationals of the states brought together in the Community are called upon to cooperate in the functioning of this Community through the intermediary of the European Parliament and the Economic and Social Committee.

In addition the task assigned to the Court of Justice under Article 177, the object of which is to secure uniform interpretation of the Treaty by national courts and tribunals, confirms that the states have acknowledged that Community law has an authority which can be invoked by their nationals before those courts and tribunals.

The conclusion to be drawn from this is that the Community constitutes a new legal order of international law for the benefit of which the states have limited their sovereign rights, albeit within limited fields, and the subjects of which comprise not only Member States but also their nationals. Independently of the legislation of Member States, Community law therefore not only imposes obligations on individuals but is also intended to confer upon them rights which become part of their legal heritage. These rights arise not only where they are expressly granted by the Treaty, but also by reason of obligations which the Treaty imposes in a clearly defined way upon individuals as well as upon the Member States and upon the institutions of the Community.

European Union law

Flaminio Costa v ENEL, The Judgment of 15 July 1964, Court of Justice of the European Union
Case 6–64, [1964] EU:C:1964:66.

By contrast with ordinary international treaties, the EEC Treaty has created its own legal system which, on the entry into force of the Treaty, became an integral part of the legal systems of the Member States and which their courts are bound to apply.

By creating a Community of unlimited duration, having its own institutions, its own personality, its own legal capacity and capacity of representation on the international plane and, more particularly, real powers stemming from a limitation of sovereignty or a transfer of powers from the States to the Com munity, the Member States have limited their sovereign rights, albeit within limited fields, and have thus created a body of law which binds both their nationals and themselves.

The integration into the laws of each Member State of provisions which derive from the Community, and more generally the terms and the spirit of the Treaty, make it impossible for the States, as a corollary, to accord precedence to a unilateral and subsequent measure over a legal system accepted by them on a basis of reciprocity. Such a measure cannot therefore be inconsistent with that legal system. The executive force of Community law cannot vary from one State to another in deference to subsequent domestic laws, without jeopardizing the attainment of the objectives of the Treaty set out in Article 5 (2) and giving rise to the discrimination prohibited by Article 7.

The obligations undertaken under the Treaty establishing the Community would not be unconditional, but merely contingent, if they could be called in question by subsequent legislative acts of the signatories. Wherever the Treaty grants the States the right to act unilaterally, it does this by clear and precise provisions (for example Articles 15, 93 (3), 223, 224 and 225). Applications, by Member States for authority to derogate from the Treaty are subject to a special authorization procedure (for example Articles 8 (4), 17 (4), 25, 26, 73, the third subparagraph of Article 93 (2), and 226) which would lose their purpose if the Member States could renounce their obligations by means of an ordinary law.

The precedence of Community law is confirmed by Article 189, whereby a regulation 'shall be binding' and 'directly applicable in all Member States'. This provision, which is subject to no reservation, would be quite meaningless if a State could unilaterally nullify its effects by means of a legislative measure which could prevail over Community law.

It follows from all these observations that the law stemming from the Treaty, an independent source of law, could not, because of its special and original nature, be overridden by domestic legal provisions, however framed, without being deprived of its character as Community law and without the legal basis of the Community itself being called into question.

The transfer by the States from their domestic legal system to the Community legal system of the rights and obligations arising under the Treaty carries with it a permanent limitation of their sovereign rights, against which a subsequent unilateral act incompatible with the concept of the Community cannot prevail. Consequently Article 177 is to be applied regardless of any domestic law, whenever questions relating to the interpretation of the Treaty arise.

NATO

The North Atlantic Treaty
of 4 April 1949
Entry into force: 24 August 1949

Article 1

The Parties undertake, as set forth in the Charter of the United Nations, to settle any international dispute in which they may be involved by peaceful means in such a manner that international peace and security and justice are not endangered, and to refrain in their international relations from the threat or use of force in any manner inconsistent with the purposes of the United Nations.

Article 2

The Parties will contribute toward the further development of peaceful and friendly international relations by strengthening their free institutions, by bringing about a better understanding of the principles upon which these institutions are founded, and by promoting conditions of stability and well-being. They will seek to eliminate conflict in their international economic policies and will encourage economic collaboration between any or all of them.

Article 3

In order more effectively to achieve the objectives of this Treaty, the Parties, separately and jointly, by means of continuous and effective self-help and mutual aid, will maintain and develop their individual and collective capacity to resist armed attack.

Article 4

The Parties will consult together whenever, in the opinion of any of them, the territorial integrity, political independence or security of any of the Parties is threatened.

Article 5

The Parties agree that an armed attack against one or more of them in Europe or North America shall be considered an attack against them all and consequently they agree that, if such an armed attack occurs, each of them, in exercise of the right of individual or collective self-defence recognised by Article 51 of the Charter of the United Nations, will assist the Party or Parties so attacked by taking forthwith, individually and in concert with the other Parties, such action as it deems necessary, including the use of armed force, to restore and maintain the security of the North Atlantic area.

Any such armed attack and all measures taken as a result thereof shall immediately be reported to the Security Council. Such measures shall be terminated when the Security Council has taken the measures necessary to restore and maintain international peace and security.

Article 6[594]

For the purpose of Article 5, an armed attack on one or more of the Parties is deemed to include an armed attack:

- on the territory of any of the Parties in Europe or North America, on the Algerian Departments of France,[595] on the territory of or on the Islands under the jurisdiction of any of the Parties in the North Atlantic area north of the Tropic of Cancer;
- on the forces, vessels, or aircraft of any of the Parties, when in or over these territories or any other area in Europe in which occupation forces of any of the Parties were stationed on the date when the Treaty entered into force or the Mediterranean Sea or the North Atlantic area north of the Tropic of Cancer.

594 The definition of the territories to which Article 5 applies was modified through Article 2 of the Protocol to the North Atlantic Treaty on the accession of Greece and Turkey signed in 1951. 'For the purpose of Article 5, an armed attack on one or more of the Parties is deemed to include an armed attack: 1. on the territory of any of the Parties in Europe or North America, on the Algerian Departments of France, on the territory of Turkey or on the islands under the jurisdiction of any of the Parties in the North Atlantic area north of the Tropic of Cancer; 2. on the forces, vessels, or aircraft of any of the Parties, when in or over these territories or any other area in Europe in which occupation forces of any of the Parties were stationed on the date when the Treaty entered into force or the Mediterranean Sea or the North Atlantic area north of the Tropic of Cancer.'

595 In 1963, the North Atlantic Council stated that insofar as the former Algerian Departments of France were concerned, the relevant clauses of this Treaty had become inapplicable as from 3 July 1962.

Article 7

This Treaty does not affect, and shall not be interpreted as affecting in any way the rights and obligations under the Charter of the Parties which are members of the United Nations, or the primary responsibility of the Security Council for the maintenance of international peace and security.

Article 8

Each Party declares that none of the international engagements now in force between it and any other of the Parties or any third State is in conflict with the provisions of this Treaty, and undertakes not to enter into any international engagement in conflict with this Treaty.

Article 9

The Parties hereby establish a Council, on which each of them shall be represented, to consider matters concerning the implementation of this Treaty. The Council shall be so organised as to be able to meet promptly at any time. The Council shall set up such subsidiary bodies as may be necessary; in particular it shall establish immediately a defence committee which shall recommend measures for the implementation of Articles 3 and 5.

Article 10

The Parties may, by unanimous agreement, invite any other European State in a position to further the principles of this Treaty and to contribute to the security of the North Atlantic area to accede to this Treaty. Any State so invited may become a Party to the Treaty by depositing its instrument of accession with the Government of the United States of America. The Government of the United States of America will inform each of the Parties of the deposit of each such instrument of accession.

Article 11

This Treaty shall be ratified and its provisions carried out by the Parties in accordance with their respective constitutional processes. The instruments of ratification shall be deposited as soon as possible with the Government of the United States of America, which will notify all the other signatories of each deposit. The Treaty shall enter into force between the States which have ratified it as soon as the ratifications of the majority of the signatories, including the ratifications of Belgium, Canada, France, Luxembourg, the Netherlands, the United Kingdom and the United States, have been deposited and shall come into effect with respect to other States on the date of the deposit of their ratifications.

Article 12

After the Treaty has been in force for ten years, or at any time thereafter, the Parties shall, if any of them so requests, consult together for the purpose of reviewing the Treaty, having regard for the factors then affecting peace and security in the North Atlantic area, including the development of universal as well as regional arrangements under the Charter of the United Nations for the maintenance of international peace and security.

Article 13

After the Treaty has been in force for twenty years, any Party may cease to be a Party one year after its notice of denunciation has been given to the Government of the United States of America, which will inform the Governments of the other Parties of the deposit of each notice of denunciation.

Article 14

This Treaty, of which the English and French texts are equally authentic, shall be deposited in the archives of the Government of the United States of America. Duly certified copies will be transmitted by that Government to the Governments of other signatories.

Organisation of American States

Charter of the Organisation of American States of 30 April 1948
Entry into force: 13 December 1951[596]

Part One

Chapter I

NATURE AND PURPOSES

Article 1

The American States establish by this Charter the international organization that they have developed to achieve an order of peace and justice, to promote their solidarity, to strengthen their collaboration, and to defend their sovereignty, their territorial integrity, and their independence. Within the United Nations, the Organization of American States is a regional agency.

---

596 As amended by the Protocol of Amendment to the Charter of the Organisation of American States 'Protocol of Buenos Aires', signed on 27 February 1967, at the Third Special Inter-American Conference, by the Protocol of Amendment to the Charter of the Organisation of American States 'Protocol of Cartagena de Indias', approved on 5 December 1985, at the Fourteenth Special Session of the General Assembly, by the Protocol of Amendment to the Charter of the Organisation of American States 'Protocol of Washington', approved on 14 December 1992, at the Sixteenth Special Session of the General Assembly, and by the Protocol of Amendment to the Charter of the Organisation of American States 'Protocol of Managua', adopted on 10 June 1993, at the Nineteenth Special Session of the General Assembly.

The Organization of American States has no powers other than those expressly conferred upon it by this Charter, none of whose provisions authorizes it to intervene in matters that are within the internal jurisdiction of the Member States.

Chapter III Members

Article 4

All American States that ratify the present Charter are Members of the Organization.

Article 5

Any new political entity that arises from the union of several Member States and that, as such, ratifies the present Charter, shall become a Member of the Organization. The entry of the new political entity into the Organization shall result in the loss of membership of each one of the States which constitute it.

Article 6

Any other independent American State that desires to become a Member of the Organization should so indicate by means of a note addressed to the Secretary General, in which it declares that it is willing to sign and ratify the Charter of the Organization and to accept all the obligations inherent in membership, especially those relating to collective security expressly set forth in Articles 28 and 29 of the Charter.

Article 7

The General Assembly, upon the recommendation of the Permanent Council of the Organization, shall determine whether it is appropriate that the Secretary General be authorized to permit the applicant State to sign the Charter and to accept the deposit of the corresponding instrument of ratification. Both the recommendation of the Permanent Council and the decision of the General Assembly shall require the affirmative vote of two thirds of the Member States.

Article 8

Membership in the Organization shall be confined to independent States of the Hemisphere that were Members of the United Nations as of December 10, 1985, and the non autonomous territories mentioned in document OEA/Ser. P, AG/doc.1939/85, of November 5, 1985, when they become independent.

Article 9

A Member of the Organization whose democratically constituted government has been overthrown by force may be suspended from the exercise of the right to participate in the sessions of the General Assembly, the Meeting of Consultation, the Councils of the Organization and the Specialized Conferences as well as in the commissions, working groups and any other bodies established.

a) The power to suspend shall be exercised only when such diplomatic initiatives undertaken by the Organization for the purpose of promoting the restoration of representative democracy in the affected Member State have been unsuccessful;

b) The decision to suspend shall be adopted at a special session of the General Assembly by an affirmative vote of two-thirds of the Member States;

c) The suspension shall take effect immediately following its approval by the General Assembly;

d) The suspension notwithstanding, the Organization shall endeavor to undertake additional diplomatic initiatives to contribute to the re-establishment of representative democracy in the affected Member State;

e) The Member which has been subject to suspension shall continue to fulfill its obligations to the Organization;

f) The General Assembly may lift the suspension by a decision adopted with the approval of two-thirds of the Member States;

g) The powers referred to in this article shall be exercised in accordance with this Charter.

Chapter IV

FUNDAMENTAL RIGHTS AND DUTIES OF STATES

Article 10

States are juridically equal, enjoy equal rights and equal capacity to exercise these rights, and have equal duties. The rights of each State depend not upon its power to ensure the exercise thereof, but upon the mere fact of its existence as a person under international law.

Article 11

Every American State has the duty to respect the rights enjoyed by every other State in accordance with international law.

Article 12

The fundamental rights of States may not be impaired in any manner whatsoever.

Article 13

The political existence of the State is independent of recognition by other States. Even before being recognized, the State has the right to defend its integrity and independence, to provide for its preservation and prosperity, and consequently to organize itself as it sees fit, to legislate concerning its interests, to administer its services, and to determine the jurisdiction and competence of its courts. The exercise of these rights is limited only by the exercise of the rights of other States in accordance with international law.

Article 14

Recognition implies that the State granting it accepts the personality of the new State, with all the rights and duties that international law prescribes for the two States.

Article 15

The right of each State to protect itself and to live its own life does not authorize it to commit unjust acts against another State.

Article 16

The jurisdiction of States within the limits of their national territory is exercised equally over all the inhabitants, whether nationals or aliens.

Article 17

Each State has the right to develop its cultural, political, and economic life freely and naturally. In this free development, the State shall respect the rights of the individual and the principles of universal morality.

Article 18

Respect for and the faithful observance of treaties constitute standards for the development of peaceful relations among States. International treaties and agreements should be public.

Article 19

No State or group of States has the right to intervene, directly or indirectly, for any reason whatever, in the internal or external affairs of any other State. The foregoing principle prohibits not only armed force but also any other form of interference or attempted threat against the personality of the State or against its political, economic, and cultural elements.

Article 20

No State may use or encourage the use of coercive measures of an economic or political character in order to force the sovereign will of another State and obtain from it advantages of any kind.

Article 21

The territory of a State is inviolable; it may not be the object, even temporarily, of military occupation or of other measures of force taken by another State, directly or indirectly, on any grounds whatever. No territorial acquisitions or special advantages obtained either by force or by other means of coercion shall be recognized.

Article 22

The American States bind themselves in their international relations not to have recourse to the use of force, except in the case of selfdefense in accordance with existing treaties or in fulfillment thereof.

Article 23

Measures adopted for the maintenance of peace and security in accordance with existing treaties do not constitute a violation of the principles set forth in Articles 19 and 21.

The international protection of human rights

DOI: 10.4324/9781003213772-8

TO THE BASICS OF THE CONCEPT

<blockquote>
universal and eternal
inalienable
indivisible
natural law theory
value-based core
</blockquote>

From the roots to the modern concept

The roots of the human rights concept can be discovered deep in the past centuries, mostly in the philosophy of the ancient times and the world religions and, in sum, in the whole of what can be broadly termed as the cultural legacy of the humankind. However, the modern concept of human rights as we know it was formed only after these rights came to be considered as (1) **universal and eternal**, (2) **inalienable**, and (3) **indivisible** (interrelated and interdependent). Meanwhile, the primary intellectual forces to advance the human rights concept were the **natural law theory** thinkers.

The three pillars of human rights

Thus, the human rights concept is founded on respect for the dignity and worth of each individual and the following three pillars:

1   Human rights are eternal and universal, meaning that they shall be applied equally and without discrimination to all persons in time and space. However, they are not static but are a subject to redevelopment and redetermination, even though the core of those norms is predefined.

2   Human rights are inalienable, meaning that:

   a)   an individual as a human being obtains these rights from birth (they are either given by God or derive from human nature);

   b)   they are not granted by a state, a government, or any other entity or person; and

   c)   no one can have his or her human rights taken away other than in certain specific circumstances and only regarding those rights which do not possess the absolute character.

3   Human rights are an interrelated and interdependent complex of rights and therefore are indivisible, which means that human rights should be respected in their totality and human rights norms cannot be applied selectively. Consequently, all human rights shall be regarded to be of equal importance and equally essential for the respect of the dignity and worth of every individual.

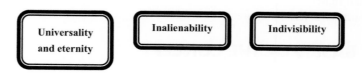

FIGURE 8.1 The pillars of the human rights concept

The dimension – individual-state

Human rights are realised at the individual-to-state level (of interrelationship). Hence, they are the rights of human beings (individual or collective) and the obligations of the states.

Human rights as a value-based core of international law

Nowadays, the international human rights concept is challenging the very essence of international law as an 'interstate' law which is based on the doctrines of state sovereignty and state jurisdiction. Nevertheless, international law in principle still remains an interstate law, but considering the challenge posed by the human rights concept, it might be subject to redevelopment.

Numerous authors, as well as the decisions of some international tribunals, emphasise the rethinking model of international law, in which human rights generate the **value-based core** of international law. Such a value-based core (of international law) cannot disappear or be destroyed by the states through multilateral agreements or customary norms.[597] From

---

597 As the International Criminal Tribunal for the former Yugoslavia stated: 'Fourthly, the impetuous development and propagation in the international community of human rights doctrines, particularly after the adoption of the Universal Declaration of Human Rights in 1948, has brought about significant changes in international law, notably in the approach to problems besetting the world community. A State-sovereignty-oriented approach has been gradually supplanted by a human-being-oriented approach. Gradually the maxim of Roman law *hominum causa omne jus constitutum est* (all law is created for the benefit of human beings) has gained a firm foothold in the international community as well.' *Prosecutor v Dusko Tadić* a/k/a 'DULE', Decision on the Defence Motion for Interlocutory Appeal on Jurisdiction of 2 October 1995, International Criminal Tribunal for the Former Yugoslavia.

the theoretical point of view, this rethinking model may be considered as some kind of a recognition of the natural law view on the natural rights, which shall have a higher standing than human-made law and exist as a set of principles governing all human beings in time and space.

HUMAN RIGHTS MILESTONES

universal regime of human rights
UN Commission on Human Rights
Universal Declaration of Human Rights
international refugee law
principle of non-refoulement
refugee
asylum-seeker
migrant
United Nations High Commissioner for Refugees
racial discrimination
Committee on the Elimination of Racial Discrimination
Human Rights Committee
Committee on Economic, Social, and Cultural Rights
Committee on the Elimination of Discrimination against Women
torture
Committee against Torture
Committee on the Rights of the Child
Committee on the Protection of the Rights of All Migrant Workers and Members of their Families
Committee on the Rights of Persons with Disabilities
Office of the High Commissioner for Human Rights
UN Human Rights Council
regional human rights regimes
International Bill of Human Rights

Introductory remark

The modern complex perception of human rights is the result of the collision of historical forces, milestone documents, and the ensuing political and legal developments leading humankind to a progressive vision of (international) human rights.[598]

---

598 In this regard, it is notable: Code of Hammurabi – Babylonian code of law (eighteenth century BC), teachings of Confucius (sixth–fifth century BC), Old Testament (thirteenth–first century BC), New Testament (first century AD), the Koran (seventh century), Magna Carta – the 'great charter' of liberties signed by John I of England (1215), the English Bill of Rights (1689), and so on.

The illustration of the modern concept of human rights

The substantial official documents which enshrined the modern essence of the human rights concept were:

- American Declaration of Independence (1776), which expressed a central statement on the human rights as follows: 'We hold these truths to be self-evident, that all men are created equal, that they are endowed by their Creator with certain unalienable Rights, that among these are Life, Liberty and the pursuit of Happiness.'
- French Declaration of Human and Civic Rights (1789), which listed 'the natural, unalienable and sacred rights of man', and, among other things, pronounced that

> [l]iberty consists in being able to do anything that does not harm others: thus, the exercise of the natural rights of every man has no bounds other than those that ensure to the other members of society the enjoyment of these same rights. These bounds may be determined only by Law.

The universal regime of human rights

After the UN Charter entered into force, the Charter era regarding international law began, which, among other things, stimulated development of international human rights law and respectively, an increase in popularity of the term 'human rights' itself. The UN Charter affirmed the fundamental UN mission of being a promoter of 'respect for human rights and for fundamental freedoms for all without distinction as to race, sex, language, or religion'.[599]

On the whole, the Charter stipulated the gradual establishment and development of the **universal regime of human rights**, which is composed of many material and implementing components. (The term 'universal' concerning the global regime of human rights in this book is used in the sense that the human rights instruments and mechanisms discussed in this chapter are introduced at the global level for universal application, despite the fact that not all of them are [universally] recognised by all subjects of international law). The first part is reflected in particular global treaties, general customary international law, and general principles of law, as well as subsidiary means or soft law examples concerning the human rights content. The second represents the global institutions (mechanisms) which are entitled to implement their mandate in the field of the human rights. An exceptional contribution to the formation of human rights has been performed by the **UN Commission on Human Rights**, which was established in 1946.

The Universal Declaration of Human Rights

On 10 December 1948, the **Universal Declaration of Human Rights** was adopted (Human Rights Day is observed every year on 10 December), in which '[m]ember States have pledged themselves to achieve, in co-operation with the United Nations . . . a common standard . . . for all peoples and all nations'. It was the first time in history that human rights and fundamental freedoms were outlined in such detail in a universal document. At the same time, even though the Universal Declaration was adopted as a legally non-binding

599 Article 1 (3) of the Charter.

document, it is generally regarded to be the foundation (mainly in the form of customary law) for universal, regional, and national human rights law.

The Universal Declaration is constructed on the pillars of freedom[600] and equality[601] and recognises fundamental rights, which are the inherent rights of every human being including, among others, the right to life, liberty, and security of person;[602] the right to recognition everywhere as a person before the law[603] and equality before the law;[604] the right to an adequate standard of living;[605] and the right to freedom of opinion and expression.[606]

The global treaties

The Universal Declaration has also inspired a rich body of legally binding international human rights treaties:

- Convention Relating to the Status of Refugees of 1951, which initially covered only those persons who became refugees as a result of events occurring before 1 January 1951. Nevertheless, the 1967 Protocol Relating to the Status of Refugees removed the time limits and has been applied to refugees 'without any geographic limitation'. These two legal instruments of **international refugee law** are central to the universal refugee protection system. These documents established the principle that refugees should not be forcibly returned to a territory where their lives or freedom would be threatened (the **principle of non-refoulement**). However, who is a **refugee**? According to the Convention, a refugee is a person who has a well-founded fear of being persecuted if returned to his or her country of origin or habitual residence and is unable or unwilling to return there due to severe threats posed to his or her life, physical integrity, or freedom. This well-founded fear must relate to one or more of the five grounds set out in the Convention – race, religion, nationality, membership of a particular social group, or political opinion.[607]

  At the same time, there is a need to distinguish the notion of the refugee from the terms '**asylum-seeker**' and '**migrant**'. Asylum-seeker is a general designation for someone who is seeking and has applied for a refugee status, but not every asylum-seeker will finally be recognised as a refugee. As for the migrant, he or she is a person who chooses to move not because of a direct threat to life or freedom, but in order to find work, receive education, reunite with the family, or for some other personal reasons.

  Unlike in cases of other Conventions reviewed subsequently, the Convention Relating to the Status of Refugees did not entail the establishment of the new special body which would monitor the implementation of the Convention since the United

---

600 Article 1 of the Universal Declaration of Human Rights.
601 Article 2 of the Universal Declaration of Human Rights.
602 Article 3 of the Universal Declaration of Human Rights.
603 Article 6 of the Universal Declaration of Human Rights.
604 Article 7 of the Universal Declaration of Human Rights.
605 Article 25 of the Universal Declaration of Human Rights.
606 Article 19 of the Universal Declaration of Human Rights.
607 Article 1 A(2) of the Convention Relating to the Status of Refugees.

Nations General Assembly had already established the Office of the **United Nations High Commissioner for Refugees** (UNHCR) in 1950, which was mandated with the protection and support of refugees.

- International Convention on the Elimination of All Forms of Racial Discrimination of 1965, which defined the term '**racial discrimination**' as 'any distinction, exclusion, restriction or preference based on race, colour, descent, national or ethnic origin with the purpose or effect of nullifying or impairing the recognition, enjoyment or exercise, on an equal footing, of human rights in any field of public life, including political, economic, social or cultural life.'[608] Therefore, it is notable that this definition envisions a much more extensive range of grounds than "race" on which discrimination may take place.

    The Committee on the Elimination of Racial Discrimination was also established by the Convention to ensure that state parties to the convention fulfil their obligations.

- International Covenant on Civil and Political Rights of 1966, which (together with the second Covenant on Economic, Social, and Cultural Rights) is widely regarded as having developed the provisions defined in the Universal Declaration. Many of the provisions in the Covenant address the relationship between the individual and the state. The civil and political rights provided in the Covenant include, inter alia, the right to self-determination of peoples;[609] the right to life;[610] freedom of movement within the territory of a state, including freedom to choose a place of residence and the right to leave the country;[611] freedom of thought, conscience, religion,[612] expression,[613] peaceful assembly,[614] and association;[615] freedom from torture or cruel, inhuman, or degrading treatment or punishment;[616] freedom from slavery or forced or compulsory labour;[617] freedom from arbitrary arrest or detention;[618] the right to a fair and prompt trial;[619] and the right to privacy.[620] As regards the right to life, according to the Covenant:

> In countries which have not abolished the death penalty, sentence of death may be imposed only for the most serious crimes in accordance with the law in force at the time of the commission of the crime and not contrary to the provisions of the present Covenant and to the Convention on the Prevention and Punishment of the Crime of Genocide. This penalty can only be carried out pursuant to a final judgement rendered by a competent court.

608 Article 1 of the International Convention on the Elimination of All Forms of Racial Discrimination.
609 Article 1 of the International Covenant on Civil and Political Rights.
610 Article 6 of the International Covenant on Civil and Political Rights.
611 Article 11 of the International Covenant on Civil and Political Rights.
612 Article 18 of the International Covenant on Civil and Political Rights.
613 Article 19 of the International Covenant on Civil and Political Rights.
614 Article 21 of the International Covenant on Civil and Political Rights.
615 Article 22 of the International Covenant on Civil and Political Rights.
616 Article 7 of the International Covenant on Civil and Political Rights.
617 Article 8 of the International Covenant on Civil and Political Rights.
618 Article 9 of the International Covenant on Civil and Political Rights.
619 Articles 9, 14 of the International Covenant on Civil and Political Rights.
620 Article 17 of the International Covenant on Civil and Political Rights.

Under the Covenant, the **Human Rights Committee**, which is responsible for overseeing the implementation of the Covenant, was established.
- International Covenant on Economic, Social, and Cultural Rights of 1966, which contained some of the most significant international legal provisions concerning economic, social, and cultural rights, encompassing, inter alia, the right to work[621] in just and favourable conditions;[622] social security, including social insurance;[623] an adequate standard of living, including clothing, food, and housing;[624] the highest attainable standards of physical and mental health;[625] education;[626] take part in cultural life; and the right to enjoy the benefits of scientific progress and its applications.[627]

  Monitoring the fulfilment of the Covenant by states parties was the responsibility of the UN Economic and Social Council, which delegated this responsibility to a committee of independent experts established for this purpose – the **Committee on Economic, Social, and Cultural Rights**.
- Convention on the Elimination of All Forms of Discrimination against Women of 1979, which identified a number of specific areas where discrimination against women had been horrific, specifically concerning participation in public life, marriage, family life, and sexual exploitation. Under the Convention: '[T]he term "discrimination against women" shall mean any distinction, exclusion or restriction made on the basis of sex which has the effect or purpose of impairing or nullifying the recognition, enjoyment or exercise by women, irrespective of their marital status, on a basis of equality of men and women, of human rights and fundamental freedoms in the political, economic, social, cultural, civil or any other field.'[628]

  In addition, the Convention established the **Committee on the Elimination of Discrimination against Women** to oversee the implementation of its provisions.[629]
- Convention against Torture and other Cruel, Inhuman, or Degrading Treatment or Punishment of 1984, which defined '**torture**' as 'any act by which severe pain or suffering, whether physical or mental, is intentionally inflicted on a person for such purposes as obtaining from him or a third person information or a confession, punishing him for an act he or a third person has committed or is suspected of having committed, or intimidating or coercing him or a third person, or for any reason based on discrimination of any kind, when such pain or suffering is inflicted by or at the instigation of or with the consent or acquiescence of a public official or other person

---

621 Article 6 of the International Covenant on Economic, Social and Cultural Rights.
622 Article 7 of the International Covenant on Economic, Social and Cultural Rights.
623 Article 9 of the International Covenant on Economic, Social and Cultural Rights.
624 Article 11 of the International Covenant on Economic, Social and Cultural Rights.
625 Article 12 of the International Covenant on Economic, Social and Cultural Rights.
626 Article 13 of the International Covenant on Economic, Social and Cultural Rights.
627 Article 15 of the International Covenant on Economic, Social and Cultural Rights.
628 Article 1 of the Convention on the Elimination of All Forms of Discrimination against Women.
629 Article 17 of the Convention on the Elimination of All Forms of Discrimination against Women.

acting in an official capacity. it does not include pain or suffering arising only from, inherent in or incidental to lawful sanctions.'[630]

For the implementation of the Convention, a monitoring body – the **Committee against Torture** – was established.

- The Convention on the Rights of the Child of 1989, which defined the term 'child' as 'every human being below the age of eighteen years'[631] and embodied four general principles for guiding the implementation of the rights of the child:

    - Non-Discrimination – 'States parties shall respect and ensure the rights set forth in the present convention to each child within their jurisdiction without discrimination of any kind, irrespective of the child's parents or legal guardian, race, colour, sex, language, religion, political or other opinion, national, ethnic or social origin, poverty, disability, birth or other status.'[632]
    - Best interests of the child – 'In all actions concerning children whether undertaken by public or private social welfare institution, courts of law, administrative authorities or legislative bodies, the best interest of the child shall be a primary consideration.'[633]
    - The right to life, survival, and development.[634]
    - The views of the child – 'States parties shall assure to the child who is capable of forming his or her own views the rights to express those views freely in all matters affecting the child, the view of the child being given due weight in accordance with the age and maturity of the child.'[635]

    According to the Convention, the **Committee on the Rights of the Child** was established to monitor the implementation of the Convention.[636]

- International Convention on the Protection of the Rights of all Migrant Workers and Members of Their Families of 1990, which entitled the protected persons to enjoy their human rights throughout the migration process. For instance, the right of migrant workers and members of their families to leave any state, including their state of origin;[637] the right to life;[638] protection from torture or cruel, inhuman, or degrading treatment or punishment;[639] arbitrary deprivation of property, whether owned individually or in association with others;[640] and so on.

---

630 Article 1 of the Convention against Torture and other Cruel, Inhuman, or Degrading Treatment or Punishment.

631 Article 1 of the Convention on the Rights of the Child.

632 Paragraph 1 of Article 2 of the Convention on the Rights of the Child.

633 Paragraph 1 of Article 3 of the Convention on the Rights of the Child.

634 Article 6 of the Convention on the Rights of the Child.

635 Paragraph 1 of Article 12 of the Convention on the Rights of the Child.

636 Article 43 of the Convention on the Rights of the Child.

637 Article 8 of the International Convention on the Protection of the Rights of all Migrant Workers and Members of Their Families.

638 Article 9 of the International Convention on the Protection of the Rights of all Migrant Workers and Members of Their Families.

639 Article 10 of the International Convention on the Protection of the Rights of all Migrant Workers and Members of Their Families.

640 Article 15 of the International Convention on the Protection of the Rights of all Migrant Workers and Members of Their Families.

According to the Convention, the **Committee on the Protection of the Rights of All Migrant Workers and Members of Their Families** was instituted as the body of independent experts which monitors implementation of the Convention.[641]

- Convention on the Rights of Persons with Disabilities of 2006, which prohibited all discrimination on the basis of disability and guaranteed to persons with disabilities equal and effective legal protection against discrimination on all grounds,[642] especially stressed the significance of protection of women and children with disabilities,[643] targeted raising awareness throughout society,[644] prescribed the states to implement measures to enable persons with disabilities to live independently and participate fully in all aspects of life,[645] and so forth.

Under the Convention, the **Committee on the Rights of Persons with Disabilities**, which is the body of independent experts monitoring the implementation of the Convention by the parties, was established.[646]

There were many other outcomes within the UN framework regarding the human rights. For example: The Declaration on the Right to Development (1986), the Declaration on the Elimination of Violence against Women (1993), the World Conference on Human Rights (1993), establishment of the **Office of the High Commissioner for Human Rights** (1993), the Millennium Declaration (2000), establishment of the **UN Human Rights Council** (2006), the UN Declaration on the Rights of Indigenous Peoples (2007), the Resolution on Treaty Body Strengthening (2014), and so on.

In 2002 the Rome Statute entered into force, and the International Criminal Court (ICC) was established, which is the first permanent court with a world-wide reach mandated to investigate, charge, and try those accused of crime of genocide, crimes against humanity, war crimes, and the crime of aggression.

Regional human rights regimes

On the other hand, **regional human rights regimes** were established in Europe, the Americas, and Africa. These systems are harmonised with the universal human rights framework; however, their specific nature varies in every regime. In addition, the transatlantic model of human rights was built based on the regional pattern of the 1975 Final Act of Helsinki.

The interplay between the distinct areas of international law

At the same time, it is notable that the development of international human rights law was accompanied by the gradual development of other fields of international law, which are more or less interlinked with human rights.

641 Article 72 of the International Convention on the Protection of the Rights of all Migrant Workers and Members of Their Families.
642 Article 5 of the Convention on the Rights of Persons with Disabilities.
643 Articles 6, 7 of the Convention on the Rights of Persons with Disabilities.
644 Article 8 of the Convention on the Rights of Persons with Disabilities.
645 Article 9 of the Convention on the Rights of Persons with Disabilities.
646 Article 34 of the Convention on the Rights of Persons with Disabilities.

In this respect, it is necessary to specify international humanitarian law and international criminal law. Regarding the interrelationship between these two areas of international law and human rights law, it must first be emphasised that without the modern concept of human rights, neither international humanitarian law nor international criminal law would have a robust value-based foundation. On the other hand, although they have specific subjects/fields of operation, they overlap in some specific areas. For example, when distinguishing international human rights law from international humanitarian law, one can stress that the first sets standards for state conduct in guaranteeing the rights and freedoms of individuals, and the second provides standards for the protection of certain persons and objects during an armed conflict and the manner in which hostilities are to be conducted. However, human rights must be protected during hostilities as well; at the same time, there are some specific limits in this context which will be examined in the chapter on international humanitarian law. Hence, the aforementioned fields of international law are deeply interdependent.

International Bill of Human Rights

Finally, in international law scholarship, the term **International Bill of Human Rights** finds widespread usage. It refers to a collection of three international documents – (1) the Universal Declaration of Human Rights, (2) the International Covenant on Civil and Political Rights, and (3) the International Covenant on Economic, Social, and Cultural Rights (together with the Optional Protocols to the Covenants, such as the First Optional Protocol to the International Covenant on Civil and Political Rights of 1966, establishing an individual complaint mechanism for the International Covenant; the Second Optional Protocol to the International Covenant on Civil and Political Rights, aiming at the abolition of the death penalty of 1989; and the Optional Protocol to the International Covenant on Economic, Social, and Cultural Rights of 2008, creating an individual complaint mechanism for the International Covenant similar to those of the First Optional Protocol to the International Covenant on Civil and Political Rights).

By such a designation, the authors emphasise the remarkable role of these documents in the history of human rights law.

THREE GENERATIONS OF HUMAN RIGHTS

> three generations of human rights
> liberty, equality, and fraternity
> civil-political rights
> socio-economic rights
> collective-developmental rights
> fourth generation of human rights
> ideological approaches to human rights

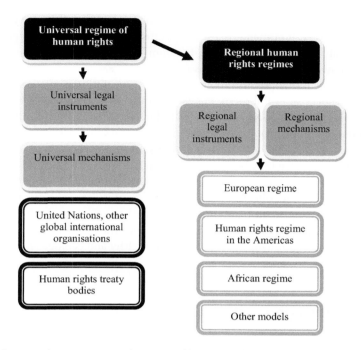

FIGURE 8.2 The complex international system of human rights

Three generations of human rights

In the international law scholarship, identification of particular human rights generations has become a conventional trait.

The prominent model of such a division was promoted by Karel Vasak, who furthered the concept of **three generations of human rights**.[647] The three categories align with the three tenets of the French Revolution – **liberty, equality, and fraternity** (solidarity); respectively, there can be three types of human rights identified – **civil-political**, **socio-economic**, and **collective-developmental**.

Under this model:

• Civil-political human rights are largely regarded as 'negative' rights, which require the state to abstain from violating them (demanding inaction).[648] Civil-political

647 'The first generation concerns "negative" rights, in the sense that their respect requires that the state do nothing to interfere with individual liberties, and correspond roughly to the civil and political rights. The second generation, on the other hand, requires positive action by the state to be implemented, as is the case with most social, economic and cultural rights. The international community is now embarking upon a third generation of human rights which may be called "rights of solidarity".' Karel Vasak, 'A Thirty-Year Struggle: the Sustained Efforts to give Force of law to the Universal Declaration of Human Rights' (1977) 30(11) *The UNESCO Courier* 29.

648 Of course, in order to protect civil-political human rights, the states have certain positive obligations as well, and in general, they must maintain the order enabling the exercise of these rights by the

human rights include the norms maintaining physical and civil security (for instance, no torture, slavery, inhumane treatment, arbitrary arrest) and norms for maintaining civil-political liberties (for example, freedom of thought, conscience, and religion; freedom of assembly and voluntary association).

- Socio-economic human rights rather impose positive duties on the states (demanding action) to respect and fulfil them. They cover the norms maintaining social rights (for instance, the rights to social security, including social insurance; health; and education), economic rights (for example, the rights to work, to form and join trade unions without restriction), and cultural needs (for example, the right to take part in cultural life and enjoy the benefits of scientific progress).
- Collective-developmental human rights are rights of individuals, but they affect and correspond with their collective interests. They include, inter alia, the right to self-determination of peoples and certain rights related to ethnic and religious minorities and indigenous peoples (for example, the right to the enjoyment of their own cultures, languages, and religions), 'the right to a healthy and ecologically balanced environment',[649] and so forth.

Rights of future generations

Nowadays some authors observe the outline for the **fourth generation of human rights** as rights belonging to future generations, which are rights that cannot appertain to an individual or be directed towards social groups only, but rather affect humanity as a whole. The fourth generation of human rights include the so-called 'rights related to genetic engineering' (with the central idea that human beings should not be genetically influenced in any way), rights deriving from exploration and exploitation of cosmic space, and so on.

A different point of view

Another group of writers introduce a distinct vision on a particular groups of human rights. They point out the '**ideological approaches to human rights**' which were prevalent during the Cold War era. Namely:

- The Western worldview, which generally tended to emphasise the fundamental civil and political rights of individuals with a focus on the human-to-state dimension;
- The Eastern (Socialist) worldview, which accentuated socio-economic human rights with a focus on the state-to-state dimension; and
- The Southern worldview, which highlighted the focus mainly on the collective-developmental human rights dimension.

---

individuals in the territories under their jurisdiction.

649 Karel Vasak identified the following rights among the third generation of human rights: '[T]he right to development, the right to a healthy and ecologically balanced environment, the right to peace, and the right to ownership of the common heritage of mankind.' (n 647) 29.

THE IMPLEMENTATION OF THE UNIVERSAL REGIME OF HUMAN RIGHTS

> human rights special mechanisms
> Committee of 24
> Special Committee against Apartheid
> Commission on Human Rights
> UN internal human rights bodies
> human rights treaty bodies

A complex framework of the implementation of the universal regime of human rights

The implementation model of the universal regime of human rights is a comprehensive framework which incorporates the institutions (mechanisms) primarily created to carry out other main purposes but also cover the human rights field, as well as those bodies designated for the protection of human rights. (The latter bodies are usually called **human rights special mechanisms**.)

Principal organs of the United Nations

Under the institutions established for other paramount purposes, firstly, the principal organs of the United Nations must be outlined.

For instance, the UN General Assembly is entitled under Article 13 of the UN Charter to initiate studies and, among other things, make recommendations regarding human rights. Additionally, with regard to human rights, the active role of General Assembly's Third Committee (Social, Humanitarian, and Cultural Committee) deserves close attention. At the same time, there were other subsidiary organs established by General Assembly, which assisted the Assembly concerning human rights issues, such as the **Committee of 24** (discussed earlier), the **Special Committee against Apartheid** created under the UN General Assembly Resolution of 1962,[650] and so on.

The other principal body of the UN which is directly related to human rights matters is the Economic and Social Council, which, under Article 62 of the UN Charter, has the power:

- to 'make recommendations for the purpose of promoting respect for, and observance of, human rights and fundamental freedoms for all';
- to draft conventions and call international conferences on human rights matters; and
- to hear annually the reports of a wide range of bodies and institutions regarding, among other things, the human rights.

In addition, initially, the former **Commission on Human Rights** (1946–2006) was established as a subsidiary organ of the Economic and Social Council.

---

650 A/RES/1761(XVII) of 6 November 1962.

United Nations agencies and partner institutions

On the other hand, many United Nations agencies and partner institutions are also involved in the promotion and protection of human rights and interact with the leading human rights bodies: for example, the International Labour Organisation, the World Health Organisation, the United Nations Educational, Scientific, and Cultural Organisation (UNESCO), and so forth.

The particular human rights bodies

As noted earlier, the universal regime of human rights is also built up with the bodies dedicated specifically to dealing with human rights matters. These bodies fall into two categories:

1   UN internal human rights bodies; and
2   Human rights treaty bodies, which are deeply interlinked with the UN internal bodies and the overall system of the UN. Nevertheless, they occupy a unique and autonomous place within the universal human rights protection framework.

The United Nations internal human rights bodies

> Charter-based bodies
> Human Rights Council
> Special Procedures
> Country Mandates
> Thematic Mandates
> Office of the High Commissioner for Human Rights
> High Commissioner for Human Rights

The UN Charter–based bodies

The United Nations human rights specific bodies category is basically constructed through the so-called **Charter-based bodies**:

- The **Human Rights Council** (which was created via the Resolution of the General Assembly of 2006[651] as a subsidiary organ of the Assembly in place of the Commission on Human Rights, which was a subsidiary organ of the Economic and Social Council).
- **Special Procedures**.

651 A/RES/60/251 of 15 March 2006 (Human Rights Council).

The Human Rights Council

The Human Rights Council meets in Geneva for ten weeks a year and is composed of 47 elected United Nations member states, which serve for an initial period of three years and cannot be elected for more than two consecutive terms. Under the Resolution of the General Assembly mentioned earlier, the Human Rights Council is a forum 'for promoting universal respect for the protection of all human rights and fundamental freedoms for all, without distinction of any kind and in a fair and equal manner.'[652]

The functions of the Council

The Council:

- addresses violations of human rights in relation to particular countries or thematic issues;
- adopts a position and makes recommendations;
- establishes international standards in the field of human rights (for example, the guidelines);
- develops instruments which are legally binding (e.g. the protocol providing for a complaints procedure for the Convention on the Rights of the Child);
- promotes human rights through dialogue by reinforcing capacity building and provision of technical assistance;
- promotes human rights education and learning; and
- makes recommendations to the General Assembly concerning the promotion and protection of human rights and supports further development of international law in the field of human rights.

Decisions of the Council

The Council adopts resolutions which are an expression of soft law. However, the resolutions made by the Council primarily have indirect and long-term repercussions and allow the international community's attention to be drawn to particular topics or country-specific situations. Some two-thirds of its resolutions are adopted by consensus, i.e. without a vote. On the whole, it is apparent that the Council represents a vital platform for attaining a compromise solution in various fields of human rights.

The unique character of the Council

The Council differs from the human rights treaty bodies in several ways:

- It is universal in the sense that it monitors human rights situation in all members of the United Nations.
- It is general in the sense that it protects all human rights.

652 ibid.

Special Procedures

Special Procedures is the general title given to the mechanisms initially established by the Commission on Human Rights and assumed by the Human Rights Council to address either specific country situations or thematic issues in all parts of the world. At the same time, the Special Procedures arise either in the form of an individual (a special rapporteur or independent expert) or a working group composed of independent experts. The Human Rights Council appoints these individuals, as well as the independent experts of the working group. In addition, Special Procedures' mandates, as a rule, address human rights situations in specific countries or territories, known as **Country Mandates**, or human rights issues of particular concern worldwide, known as **Thematic Mandates**.

Office of the High Commissioner for Human Rights

In the universal regime of human rights, the United Nations **Office of the High Commissioner for Human Rights**, which was established in 1993 by the UN General Assembly, plays a critical role.[653] According to this Resolution, the **High Commissioner for Human Rights** serves as 'the United Nations official with principal responsibility for United Nations human rights activities under the direction and authority of the Secretary-General' and is appointed by the Secretary-General of the UN and approved by the General Assembly, with due regard to geographical rotation, with a fixed term of four years and the possibility of one additional fixed term of four years.

The Office, in turn, represents a part of the United Nations Secretariat and works to offer the best expertise and support to the different human rights monitoring mechanisms at the human rights universal regime level, including the treaty bodies established to monitor states parties' compliance with the core international human rights treaties and the Special Procedures of the Human Rights Council.

Human rights treaty bodies

> four monitoring functions
> reports from the states parties
> inter-state complaints
> individual complaints
> general comments
> quasi-judicial body
> follow-up procedure

653 A/RES/48/141 of 20 December 1993 (High Commissioner for the promotion and protection of all human rights).

The human rights treaty bodies

There are ten human rights treaty bodies that monitor implementation of the core international human rights treaties:

- the Human Rights Committee;
- the Committee on Economic, Social, and Cultural Rights;
- the Committee on the Elimination of Racial Discrimination;
- the Committee on the Elimination of Discrimination against Women;
- the Committee against Torture;
- the Subcommittee on Prevention of Torture;
- the Committee on the Rights of the Child;
- the Committee on Migrant Workers;
- the Committee on the Rights of Persons with Disabilities; and
- the Committee on Enforced Disappearances.

These Committees are created by the particular treaties and operate in similar manner.

The Human Rights Committee

For instance, as a typical example, the Human Rights Committee was established under the International Covenant on Civil and Political Rights. There are 18 members on the committee, who are nationals of states parties to the Covenant. Members of the Committee, like the members of the other treaty bodies, are usually called 'experts'. Under the Covenant, Committee members shall be 'persons of high moral character and recognized competence in the field of human rights', with 'consideration given to the usefulness of the participation of some persons having legal experience'.[654] According to the Covenant, the Committee 'may not include more than one national of the same State'. In turn, 'consideration should be given to equitable geographical distribution of membership and to the representation of the different forms of civilization and of the principal legal systems'.[655] The state parties nominate members and then elect them by secret ballot to four-year terms during the meetings of the states parties.

The work of the Committee is supported by the UN Secretariat, especially by the Office of the High Commissioner for Human Rights. The Committee meets in regular sessions three times a year (as a rule, in Geneva and New York at United Nations Headquarters) and, according to the Rules of procedure of the Human Rights Committee, 'decisions of the Committee shall be made by a majority of the members present'.[656] However, during the very first session held by the Committee, 'members of the Committee generally expressed the view that its method of work normally should allow for attempts to reach decisions by consensus before voting'.[657]

654 Article 28 of the International Covenant on Civil and Political Rights.
655 Article 31 of the International Covenant on Civil and Political Rights.
656 Rule 51 of Rules of procedure of the Human Rights Committee.
657 Footnote to Rule 51.

Four monitoring functions

All treaty-based bodies are entitled to monitor the implementation of a respective treaty. To fulfil this function, they have special tools at their disposal, most of which are similar; however, they may also differ from one Committee to another. Generally, these tools are known as the '**four monitoring functions**'. These four functions are:

- receiving and examining **reports from the states parties**;
- elaboration of the **comments** designed to assist state parties to give effect to the provisions of the Covenant;
- receiving and examining **inter-state complaints** when a certain state party is not abiding by the obligations assumed under the Covenant; and
- receiving and considering **individual complaints** made by individuals who claim violations of their rights by the state party under the Covenant.

For example, state parties are obliged to submit regular reports to the Human Rights Committee on how the rights are being implemented. All states must initially report a year after acceding to the Covenant and then upon request of the Committee (usually every four years). The Committee examines all reports and addresses them with recommendations in the form of 'concluding observations'. At the same time, the Covenant provides specific provisions to the Committee to consider inter-state complaints.[658]

Moreover, the **First Optional Protocol to the International Covenant on Civil and Political Rights**[659] gives the Committee special competence regarding individual complaints 'to receive and consider communications from individuals subject to its jurisdiction who claim to be victims of a violation by that State Party of any of the rights set forth in the Covenant.'[660] Under this competence, the committee targets those individuals who claim that any of their rights included in the Covenant have been violated, and they have exhausted all available domestic remedies. According to the Protocol: 'Committee shall consider inadmissible any communication under the present Protocol which is anonymous, or which it considers to be an abuse of the right of submission of such communications or to be incompatible with the provisions of the Covenant.'[661] When implementing its mandate, the Committee shall bring any communications submitted to it under the Protocol to the attention of the state party; in turn, '[w]ithin six months, the receiving State shall submit to the Committee written explanations or statements clarifying the matter and the remedy, if any, that may have been taken by that State'.[662] As an outcome of the procedure, the Committee shall hold closed meetings when examining communications under the Protocol and finally, shall forward its views to the state party concerned

---

658 Article 41 of the International Covenant on Civil and Political Rights.

659 The First Optional Protocol was adopted and opened for signature, ratification, and accession by General Assembly Resolution A/RES/2200(XXI) of 16 December 1966 and entered into force on 23 March 1976.

660 Article 1 of the First Optional Protocol to the International Covenant on Civil and Political Rights.

661 Article 3 of the First Optional Protocol to the International Covenant on Civil and Political Rights.

662 Paragraph 2 of Article 4 of the First Optional Protocol to the International Covenant on Civil and Political Rights.

and to the individual. The Committee shall also include in its annual report a summary of its activities under the Protocol.[663]

Another principal function of the Committee is the interpretation of the Covenant and clarification of the scope and meaning of its Articles through the development and adoption of the so-called **general comments**, which are a very useful guide to the normative substance of international human rights obligations.[664]

Nevertheless, the Committee is not a court with the power to enact binding decisions. In turn, the competence of the Human Rights Committee is quasi-judicial. Therefore, the Committee itself is a **quasi-judicial body** and, among other things, represents the location for the individual's direct claims at the global level, although with limited legal mechanisms in its hands. Under such mechanisms, the so-called **follow-up procedure** and techniques shall be considered: for example, (1) the appointment of a Special Rapporteur to follow up cases; and (2) various forms of publicity, including separate sections in annual reports and the issuing of annual press communiqués.

REGIONAL PROTECTION OF HUMAN RIGHTS

> regional human rights legal instruments
> regional human rights mechanisms
> ASEAN Intergovernmental Commission on Human Rights
> ASEAN Commission for the Promotion and Protection of the Rights of Women and Children

Regional human rights legal instruments and mechanisms

Regional human rights regimes are composed of:

- **Regional human rights legal instruments** – regional treaties, customary norms, general principles of law, soft law, and so on – which assist in localising universal human rights norms and standards, reflecting the particular human rights concerns and developments in the region.
- **Regional human rights mechanisms** – e.g. institutions, special procedures, and judiciary structures – which subsequently help implement these instruments in practice.

The role of the regional human rights regimes

The existence of an effective regional human rights regime is of fundamental importance to monitor, promote, and protect human rights, since it:

---

663 Articles 5, 6 of the First Optional Protocol to the International Covenant on Civil and Political Rights.

664 It must be noted various general comments of the Committee; for instance, regarding Article 6 of the Covenant (the right to life) the conclusion: The 'production, testing, possession and deployment and use of nuclear weapons should be prohibited and recognised as crimes against humanity.'

- assists national governments with the implementation of their universal as well as regional human rights obligations;
- helps national governments better address regional human rights concerns and developments;
- provides individuals in the region with more accessible mechanisms for the protection of their human rights, once national remedies have been exhausted;
- reflects local contexts and specific human rights concerns; and
- provides regional input into the further development of universal human rights standards and the improvement of universal human rights legal instruments and institutional mechanisms.

The interdependence of the regional human rights regimes

Nowadays, the three most well-established regional human rights regimes exist in Africa, the Americas, and Europe. Despite the distinctions conditioned by the regional contexts, the three regimes display patterns of cross-influence, which are due to the spillover of the developments in each of them, and thus, they share the common features which, among other things, include the following:

- auxiliary to the national system of human rights protection;
- co-operation with universal human rights mechanisms;
- normative instruments which are not lower than the universal human rights standards;
- institutional building composed of diverse bodies with specific mandates, which serves as the structure for implementation of regional human rights concerns and developments; and
- institutional set-up with the mechanisms for effective interaction with the civil societies and respectively, with numerous representatives from a wide variety of non-governmental organisations engaged in the promotion of human rights at the regional level.

At the same time, regional human rights regimes in Europe, the Americas, and nowadays also in Africa maintain the well-established trend which contributed to similar movements in other regions as well. For instance, in Asia, ASEAN has made substantial progress in recent decades towards the establishment of regional human rights instruments and mechanisms for Southeast Asia. Specifically, ASEAN's members established such documents as the ASEAN Human Rights Declaration (AHRD), the Phnom Penh Statement on the Adoption of the ASEAN Human Rights Declaration, the Kuala Lumpur Declaration on ASEAN 2025: Forging Ahead Together, the Ha Noi Declaration on the Enhancement of Welfare and Development of ASEAN Women and Children, the Bali Declaration on the Enhancement of the Role and Participation of Persons with Disabilities in the ASEAN Community, and so on, and such mechanisms as the **ASEAN Intergovernmental Commission on Human Rights** in 2009 and the **ASEAN Commission for the Promotion and Protection of the Rights of Women and Children** in 2010 (which are an integral part of ASEAN's organisational structure; however, so far, they have limited powers compared to human rights mechanisms in Europe, the Americas, and Africa).

European human rights regime

Convention for the Protection of Human Rights and Fundamental Freedoms
European Social Charter
European Court of Human Rights
inter-state applications
individual applications
European Committee of Social Rights
reporting procedure
collective complaints procedure
Charter of Fundamental Rights of the European Union
human dimension of the OSCE's security concept
human dimension mechanism

A combined European regime of human rights

The edifice of the comprehensive European human rights regime is constructed by the Council of Europe, the European Union and Organisation for Security and Co-operation in Europe. (The OSCE mandate is not limited to European countries, i.e. it is not solely a European organisation; however, it is a structure which mostly targets security and co-operation in Europe.) Each of these intergovernmental organisations has its own regional human rights legal instruments and mechanisms.

The Council of Europe

However, the Council of Europe and the 1950 **Convention for the Protection of Human Rights and Fundamental Freedoms** (entered into force in 1953), which in common language is often referred to as the European Convention on Human Rights,[665] are respectively the international organisation and the international treaty on which the European human rights system was initially erected. At the same time, several additional Protocols have been added to the European Convention's substantive and procedural provisions. In 1961, a Council of Europe treaty was concluded – the **European Social Charter**, which became effective in 1965 and was revised in 1996 and which deals with economic and social rights.

Although these are the primary Council of Europe human rights conventions, within its framework, numerous other conventions on human rights were also adopted, which cover a wide range of areas, including migrant workers, national minorities, children and gender equality, and prohibition of torture.

665 The official text of the European Convention on Human Rights is available at <www.echr.coe.int/Documents/Convention_ENG.pdf> accessed 16 March 2021. This book refers to the version as amended by Protocols Nos. 11 and 14 and supplemented by Protocols Nos. 1, 4, 6, 7, 12, 13, and 16, and amended and supplemented by Protocol No. 15.

The European Convention on Human Rights

The European Convention on the Human Rights is one of the most significant codified treatments of civil and political rights in the world and the first legally binding international treaty codifying human rights, which has preconditioned the relevant developments at the global as well as the regional level.

The European Convention on Human Rights guarantees the classic human rights and freedoms, including the right to life;[666] the right not to be subject to torture or to inhuman or degrading treatment or punishment;[667] the prohibition of slavery and forced labour;[668] the right to liberty and security of person;[669] the right to a fair trial;[670] the right to respect for private and family life, home, and correspondence;[671] freedom of thought, conscience, and religion;[672] and freedom of expression.[673]

The European Social Charter

In 1996, the European Social Charter was revised. Hence, the revised Charter of 1996 comprises in one document all rights guaranteed by the Charter of 1961 and its additional Protocol of 1988 and adds new rights and amendments adopted by the parties. The Charter protects economic and social rights. For example, the right to work,[674] the right to just conditions of work,[675] the right to safe and healthy working conditions,[676] the right of children and young persons to protection,[677] the right of employed women to protection of maternity,[678] the right to protection of health,[679] the right to social security,[680] and so on.

666 Paragraph 1 of Article 2: 'Everyone's right to life shall be protected by law. No one shall be deprived of his life intentionally save in the execution of a sentence of a court following his conviction of a crime for which this penalty is provided by law.'
667 Article 3 of the European Convention on Human Rights.
668 Article 4 of the European Convention on Human Rights.
669 Article 5 of the European Convention on Human Rights.
670 Article 6 of the European Convention on Human Rights.
671 Article 8 of the European Convention on Human Rights.
672 Article 9 of the European Convention on Human Rights.
673 Article 10 of the European Convention on Human Rights.
674 Article 1 of the Revised European Social Charter of 1996.
675 Article 2 of the Revised European Social Charter of 1996.
676 Article 3 of the Revised European Social Charter of 1996.
677 Article 7 of the Revised European Social Charter of 1996.
678 Article 8 of the Revised European Social Charter of 1996.
679 Article 11 of the Revised European Social Charter of 1996.
680 Article 12 of the Revised European Social Charter of 1996.

Mechanisms of the European Convention on Human Rights

The mechanisms for the implementation of human rights standards and rules under the European Convention on Human Rights is one of the most efficient human rights systems in the world.

Regarding the enforcement mechanism, Protocol No. 11 (of 1994, entered into force in 1998) and Protocol No. 14 (of 2004, entered into force in 2010) to the European Convention on Human Rights shall be outlined.

The first Protocol revised the Articles of Convention in order to rationalise the control machinery. Thus, under the same protocol, the single full-time **European Court of Human Rights** was consolidated, replacing the previous mechanism composed of the European Commission on Human Rights and the European Court of Human Rights. The new machinery oversees the implementation of the European Convention on Human Rights through state and individual complaint systems. It also accentuated the role of the Committee of Ministers (of the Council of Europe) to focus on the supervision of the Court judgments to be executed.

Protocol No. 14, in its turn, for the more efficient operation of the European Court of Human Rights, targeted implementation of such changes as the introduction of the new admissibility criterion (which encourages the Court to declare inadmissible applications that do not demonstrate 'significant disadvantage' suffered by applicants), the introduction of the 'single-judge formation' to declare applications inadmissible,[681] and so on. In addition, according to the Protocol, the Committee of Ministers was empowered, if it decides by a two-thirds majority of votes, to bring proceedings before the Court where a state refuses to comply with a judgment. At the same time, the Committee of Ministers has a new competence, which allows it to request an interpretation of a judgment from the Court. This new competence was introduced to assist the Committee of Ministers in its task of supervising the execution of judgments, particularly by adjusting the measures necessary to comply with a judgment.

The European Court of Human Rights

The European Court of Human Rights is a judicial body set up in 1959, located in Strasbourg and composed of 'a number of judges equal to that of the High Contracting Parties' (currently, 47 states parties).[682]

The judges in the Court:

*   'shall be of high moral character and must either possess the qualifications required for appointment to high judicial office or be jurisconsults of recognised competence';[683]

---

681 Articles 7 and 12 of Protocol No. 14 to the Convention for the Protection of Human Rights and Fundamental Freedoms, amending the control system of the Convention.

682 Article 20 of the European Convention on Human Rights.

683 Article 21 of the European Convention on Human Rights.

- 'sit on the Court in their individual capacity';[684] and
- are 'elected by the Parliamentary Assembly with respect to each High Contracting Party by a majority of votes cast from a list of three candidates nominated by the High Contracting Party'[685] for a single period of nine years and 'terms of office of judges shall expire when they reach the age of 70'.[686]

Inter-state and individual applications

The jurisdiction of the Court extends to all matters concerning the interpretation and application of the European Convention on Human Rights and the Protocols thereto. Any contracting state ('**inter-state applications**') or person, non-governmental organisation, or group of individuals ('**individual applications**') claiming to be a victim of a violation of the Convention may lodge an application directly with the Court alleging a breach by a state party of one of the rights under the Convention.

The admissibility criteria of the individual applications

The European Convention on Human Rights prescribes a multifaceted system of admissibility criteria concerning individual applications. Notably, the Court may take up the matter when:

1   all domestic remedies have been exhausted;
2   the application is submitted within a period of six months from the date on which the final decision was taken; (This time limit will be reduced to four months in accordance with Protocol No. 15 to the Convention.)
3   the application is not anonymous;
4   the application is not 'substantially the same as the matter which has already been examined by the Court' or has not 'already been submitted to another procedure of international investigation or settlement';
5   the application:

   a)   is not incompatible with the provisions of the Convention or the Protocols thereto;
   b)   is not manifestly ill-founded; and
   c)   does not abuse the right to lodge an individual application; and

---

684 Article 21 of the European Convention on Human Rights.
685 'When selecting their three candidates, states should ensure that their national procedure is fair and transparent, for example by issuing public and open calls for candidates. All candidates must have appropriate legal qualifications and experience and must have an active knowledge of either English or French – the languages in which Court judgments are drafted – and at least a passive knowledge of the other language.' See the website of the Parliamentary Assembly of the Council of Europe (PACE).
686 Paragraph 2 of Article 23 of the Convention was deleted by Protocol No. 15 to the Convention, however, for example, in relation to judges in office, the previous rule on the expiry of their term of office when they reach the age of 70 continues to apply.

6   the applicant has 'suffered a significant disadvantage, unless respect for human rights
     as defined in the Convention and the Protocols thereto requires an examination of the
     application on the merits.'[687]

Adversarial and public procedure

The procedure before the Court is adversarial and, in principle, public. Memorials and
other documents filed with the Court's Registry by the parties are as a rule publicly available. At the same time, the hearings, although rare, are public unless, in exceptional cases,
the Court decides to proceed in a closed format.

Composition of the Court

The Court itself is divided into sections in which Chambers are formed.

Depending on the significance of the case, the Court's composition varies from one
case to another. 'To consider cases brought before it, the Court shall sit in a single-judge
formation, in committees of three judges, in Chambers of seven judges and in a Grand
Chamber of seventeen judges. The Court's Chambers shall set up committees for a fixed
period of time'.[688] Respectively, the cases are heard in one of the four main formations:

1   A single judge may declare inadmissible or strike out of the Court's list of cases an
     individual application 'where such a decision can be taken without further examina-
     tion.' This decision is final.[689]
2   A Committee may rule by a unanimous vote (a) on the admissibility or strike an indi-
     vidual application out of its list of cases 'where such decision can be taken without
     further examination' and (b) on the merits of individual application cases that are
     already covered by the well-established case law of the Court. These decisions and
     judgments are final as well.[690]
3   Individual applications and inter-state cases may be assigned to a Chamber which
     rules by a majority vote on the admissibility and merits of the case.[691] The decision on
     admissibility may be taken separately. At the same time, as regards the judgments of
     a Chamber, they become final:

     a)   when the parties declare that they will not request that the case be referred to the
          Grand Chamber or if the panel of the Grand Chamber rejects the request; or
     b)   three months after the date of the judgment, if reference of the case to the Grand
          Chamber has not been requested.
4   The Grand Chamber hears cases referred to it by the Chamber in case of the 'relin-
     quishment of jurisdiction' to the Grand Chamber or in exceptional cases, by any party

687 Paragraph 3 of Article 35 of the European Convention on Human Rights.
688 Paragraph 1 of Article 26 of the European Convention on Human Rights.
689 Article 27 of the European Convention on Human Rights.
690 Article 28 of the European Convention on Human Rights.
691 Article 29 of the European Convention on Human Rights.

to the case within a period of three months from the date of the judgment of the Chamber:

a) when a case concerns a serious question affecting the interpretation of the Convention or the Protocols thereto; or

b) in the event of a 'relinquishment of jurisdiction', also, if the resolution of a question before the Chamber might have a result inconsistent with a judgment delivered previously by the Court; or

c) in case of request of the parties, in addition, if the case raises 'a serious issue of general importance.'

5   The judgments of the Grand Chamber are final. The Grand Chamber, in addition, considers requests for advisory opinions on legal questions arising from the interpretation of the European Convention and its Protocols upon the request of the Committee of Ministers.

Final judgments

Final judgments are legally binding for state parties, and their execution will be supervised by the Committee of Ministers of the Council of Europe.

The new developments

The recent Protocols, which amended the European Convention on Human Rights, include Protocol No. 15 and Protocol No. 16 to the Convention. Both of them were 'opened for signature' in 2013. Protocol No. 16 came into force in 2018 but only with regard to the states which have signed and ratified it. Protocol No. 15 entered into force on 1 August 2021, as all states parties to the European Convention on Human Rights have ratified it.[692]

Protocol No. 15 articulates the principle of subsidiarity and the doctrine of the margin of appreciation:

> Affirming that the High Contracting Parties, in accordance with the principle of subsidiarity, have the primary responsibility to secure the rights and freedoms defined in this Convention and the Protocols thereto, and that in doing so they enjoy a margin of appreciation, subject to the supervisory jurisdiction of the European Court of Human Rights established by this Convention.[693]

Protocol No.15 also decreases from six to four months the time limit to submit an application to the Court following the date of a final domestic decision (which apply only after

---

692 The information on the status of Protocol No. 15 is available on the official website of the Council of Europe <www.coe.int/en/web/conventions/full-list/-/conventions/treaty/213/signatures?p_auth=s79IWQml> accessed 7 June 2021.

693 Article 1 of Protocol No. 15 amending the Convention for the Protection of Human Rights and Fundamental Freedoms.

a period of six months following the entry into force of the Protocol), as well as gives greater effect to the maxim *de minimis non curat praetor* (the law does not concern itself with trifles), as deletes one limiting provision in relation to the admissibility criterion of 'significant disadvantage' (Article 5 of the Protocol: 'In Article 35, paragraph 3, sub-paragraph b of the Convention, the words "and provided that no case may be rejected on this ground which has not been duly considered by a domestic tribunal" shall be deleted.'). Protocol No. 16, in its turn, introduces the right of the state parties' highest courts and tribunals to 'request the Court to give advisory opinions on questions of principle relating to the interpretation or application of the rights and freedoms defined in the Convention or the protocols thereto.'[694]

The European Committee of Social Rights

For supervision and enforcement of the European Social Charter provisions according to the Charter (of 1961),[695] initially, the Committee of Independent Experts was established. It is now called the **European Committee of Social Rights** and consists of 15 independent, impartial members (experts) who are elected by the Council of Europe's Committee of Ministers for a period of six years, renewable once.

The procedures of the Committee

The European Committee of Social Rights provides for the monitoring of reporting procedure and system of collective complaints:

- **Reporting procedure** – national reports have to be drawn up by the contracting parties. In the framework of the reporting system, states parties regularly submit a report on the legislative and practical implementation of the Charter. The European Committee of Social Rights adopts conclusions which are published every year.
- **Collective complaints procedure** – only certain social partners (e.g. the European Trade Union Confederation, Business Europe and the International Organisation of Employers) and other predefined organisations are entitled to lodge collective complaints concerning the Charter; individuals are not entitled to do so. This procedure was introduced by the Additional Protocol to the European Social Charter Providing for a System of Collective Complaints of 1995. 'The Committee of Independent Experts shall draw up a report in which it shall describe the steps taken by it to examine the complaint and present its conclusions as to whether or not the Contracting Party concerned has ensured the satisfactory application of the provision of the Charter referred to in the complaint.'[696] These reports shall be transmitted to the Committee of Ministers, as well as to the organisation which lodged the complaint and to the

---

694 Article 1 of Protocol No. 16 to the Convention for the Protection of Human Rights and Fundamental Freedoms.
695 Article 25 of the European Social Charter (of 1961).
696 Article 8 of the Additional Protocol.

contracting parties of the Charter. Under the Collective Complaints procedure, the Committee adopts two types of decisions – decisions on admissibility and decisions on the merits contained in the report.[697]

Committee's conclusions and decisions

Like the conclusions adopted by the European Committee of Social Rights within the reporting system, the decisions (contained in the reports) adopted in the framework of the Collective Complaints procedure are also of a declaratory nature. Nevertheless, the follow-up of the Committee's conclusions and decisions is ensured by the Committee of Ministers of the Council of Europe, which intervenes at the last stage of the enforcement system.

For instance, within the Collective Complaints procedure based on the report of the European Committee of Social Rights, 'the Committee of Ministers shall adopt a resolution by a majority of those voting.' In turn, the contracting party concerned 'shall provide information on the measures it has taken to give effect to the Committee of Ministers' recommendation.'[698]

The other institutions established on the European Council's framework

In addition, various specialised organs have been established to develop the European Council's work, as well as for the implementation of certain conventions in specific areas. Some of them bring together or are supported by all the member states, such as, for instance, the Commissioner for Human Rights (which is an independent institution within the Council of Europe, mandated to promote the awareness of and respect for human rights in Council of Europe member states) and the European Commission against Racism and Intolerance (which is a human rights body composed of independent experts monitoring problems of racism, xenophobia, anti-Semitism, intolerance, and discrimination on grounds such as 'race', national/ethnic origin, colour, citizenship, religion, and language [racial discrimination]; it prepares the reports and adopts the recommendations to the member states).

At the same time, on the European Council's framework and based on the partial agreements, other organs were also constructed.

* The European Committee for the Prevention of Torture and Inhuman or Degrading Treatment or Punishment – was established by the European Convention for the Prevention of Torture and Inhuman or Degrading Treatment or Punishment of 1987

697 'The Committee's decision on the merits of the complaint contained in the report provided for in Article 8 of the Protocol shall be accompanied by reasons and be signed by the President, the Rapporteur and the Executive Secretary. Any separate opinions shall be appended to the Committee's decision.' Rule 35 (1) of the Rules of Procedure of the European Committee of Social Rights adopted in 2004 and revised in 2005, 2009, 2011, 2013, 2014.

698 Articles 9 and 10 of the Additional Protocol.

and consists of 'independent and impartial experts' elected by the Committee of Ministers of the Council of Europe (one member is elected in respect of each state party).

- The Advisory Committee under the Framework Convention for the Protection of National Minorities – is the independent expert committee responsible for 'evaluating the adequacy of the measures taken by the Parties to give effect to the principles' set out in the Framework Convention for the Protection of National Minorities of 1995[699] and advising the Committee of Ministers of the Council of Europe. The Advisory Committee is composed of 18 independent experts elected for four years by the Committee of Ministers.[700]

- The Group of Experts on Action against Trafficking Human Beings (GRETA) – is instituted for monitoring the implementation of the Council of Europe Convention on Action against Trafficking in Human Beings of 2005 and is composed of independent and impartial experts 'taking into account a gender and geographical balance, as well as a multidisciplinary expertise', who are elected by the Committee of the Parties ('the representatives on the Committee of Ministers of the Council of Europe of the member States Parties to the Convention and representatives of the Parties to the Convention, which are not members of the Council of Europe')[701] for a term of office of four years, renewable once.

The European Union

The second pillar of the European human rights regime is the European Union. On its pattern are built the instruments and mechanisms which target the development and strengthening of the basic rules and institutions provided by the European Council framework.

The instruments of the European Union

In 2000, to further strengthen the human rights regime in the region, the European Union adopted the **Charter of Fundamental Rights of the European Union,**[702] which became a binding bill of rights for the EU, as well as the member countries:

---

699 Article 26 (1) of the Framework Convention for the Protection of National Minorities.

700 'The Advisory Committee is composed of up to 18 members elected by the Committee of Ministers from candidates proposed by States Parties. Not all countries can have one of their nominees serve on the Committee, so those candidates who are not elected are placed on a reserve list of additional members. On the basis of a rotation system, the composition of the Advisory Committee will change over time.' United Nations Office of the High Commissioner for Human Rights, 'The Council of Europe's Framework Convention for the Protection of National Minorities', Pamphlet No. 8 of the UN Guide for Minorities <www.ohchr.org/Documents/Publications/GuideMinorities8en.pdf> accessed 16 March 2021.

701 Article 37 (1) of the Council of Europe Convention on Action against Trafficking in Human Beings.

702 On 1 December 2009, with the entry into force of the Treaty of Lisbon, the Charter became legally binding on the EU institutions and national governments, just like the EU founding treaties themselves.

The provisions of this Charter are addressed to the institutions, bodies, offices and agencies of the Union with due regard for the principle of subsidiarity and to the Member States only when they are implementing Union law. They shall, therefore, respect the rights, observe the principles and promote the application thereof in accordance with their respective powers and respecting the limits of the powers of the Union as conferred on it in the Treaties.[703]

On the whole, the Charter is the most advanced human rights document in Europe, and in addition to traditional civil and political rights, it also includes economic, social, and cultural rights. Hence, the Charter covers some supplementary areas not covered by the European Convention on Human Rights, although, as stated in the Charter, any rights (in the Charter) that correspond with those articulated in the Convention should have the same meaning and scope in order to avoid discrepancies between the two documents.

At the same time, there is a need to emphasise the Charter's structure, which closely follows scientific developments in the field of human rights and reflects fundamental rights in six areas: dignity, freedoms, equality, solidarity, citizens' rights, and justice.

In each of the areas, the respective rights and freedoms are considered. For example, under category of dignity are expressed prescriptions on the respect for the human dignity, right to life, right to the integrity of the person,[704] and so forth; the category of freedoms includes the right to liberty and security, protection of personal data, freedom of the arts and sciences, right to asylum,[705] and so on; the category of equality includes equality before the law, equality between men and women, the rights of the elderly,[706] and so forth; the category of solidarity includes the right of collective bargaining and action, environmental protection, consumer protection,[707] and so forth; the category of citizens' rights includes the right to vote and to stand as a candidate, the right of access to documents, the right to petition,[708] and so forth; the category of justice includes the right to an effective remedy and to a fair trial, the presumption of innocence and right of defence, principles of legality and proportionality of criminal offences and penalties,[709] and so on.

The mechanisms of the European Union

As regards the mechanisms, all Union institutions are involved in the protection of human rights according to their respective powers and competencies. At the same time, there are special bodies with respect to human rights. For instance, the European Parliament established the Committee of Civil Liberties, Justice, and Home Affairs and the Subcommittee (of the Committee on Foreign Affairs) on Human Rights; the European Fundamental Rights Agency was established in 2007 as an independent body of the EU; the Treaty of

703 Paragraph 1 of Article 51 of the Charter of Fundamental Rights of the European Union.
704 Articles 1, 2, 3 of the Charter of Fundamental Rights of the European Union.
705 Articles 6, 8, 13, 18 of the Charter of Fundamental Rights of the European Union.
706 Articles 20, 23, 25 of the Charter of Fundamental Rights of the European Union.
707 Articles 28, 37, 38 of the Charter of Fundamental Rights of the European Union.
708 Articles 39, 40, 42, 44 of the Charter of Fundamental Rights of the European Union.
709 Articles 47, 48, 49 of the Charter of Fundamental Rights of the European Union.

Maastricht introduced an independent and impartial body – the European Ombudsmen – to investigate cases of maladministration by the Union institutions (and the first Ombudsman was elected by Parliament in 1995).

Nevertheless, the EU countries have their own systems for protecting fundamental rights through national constitutions and courts. The Charter does not replace them. Therefore, in the first place, it is up to the national institutions to ensure respect for the fundamental rights.

The Organisation for Security and Co-operation in Europe

Finally, the third pillar of the European human rights regime raised on the shoulders of the transatlantic Organisation for Security and Co-operation in Europe, which initially was considered as a process of the gathering to eliminate the threat of World War III in the Cold War era. Hence, in this framework, human rights protection was conceived as a necessary measure for peacebuilding, since the latter was the primary purpose for this transatlantic co-operation institution. Moreover, the inclusion of the principle of 'respect for human rights and fundamental freedoms' on the list of the Principles Guiding Relations between Participating States shall be regarded as key to the comprehensive security concept.

The human dimension of the OSCE's security concept

Beginning with the Helsinki Final Act of 1975, the existing 56 participating states of the OSCE and the Holy See (as participant subject as well) have adopted a large number of politically binding commitments relating to what has become known as the **human dimension of the OSCE's security concept**. In this regard, various documents were signed or otherwise adopted by various high-level CSCE (Conference on Security and Co-operation in Europe)/OSCE forums. While these documents do not have the character of legally binding treaties under international law, they represent political commitments, adopted by consensus and binding on each participating state.

Human dimension mechanism

In addition to these regular meetings, the OSCE has also created the so-called **human dimension mechanism** – the Vienna Mechanism as established in the Vienna Concluding Document of 1989 and the Moscow Mechanism as agreed upon at the meeting of the Conference on the Human Dimension of the CSCE in Moscow (1991). The Vienna Mechanism allows a participating subject through a set of procedures to raise questions relating to the human dimension in another OSCE participating subject. The Moscow Mechanism provides for the supplementary possibility to establish *ad hoc* missions of independent experts to assist in the resolution of the specific problems related to the human dimension.

Hence, strengthening and promoting the protection of human rights across the OSCE region is at the heart of its framework.

Office for Democratic Institutions and Human Rights and other institutions

The OSCE Office for Democratic Institutions and Human Rights (ODIHR) provides participating subjects with advice and assistance and supports individuals and civil societies with respect to human rights. As a specialised institution, ODIHR covers a broad spectrum of issues. In order to structure its human dimension activities, it conducts regular meetings and consolidates OSCE human dimension commitments and follow-up recommendations.

The OSCE High Commissioner on National Minorities is tasked to identify ethnic tensions that might endanger peace, stability, or friendly relations between OSCE participants. Therefore, the High Commissioner engages in preventative diplomacy at the earliest stage of tensions. Based on the defined mandate, the High Commissioner seeks to promote dialogue, confidence building, and co-operation.

The OSCE Representative on Freedom of the Media assists OSCE participants in furthering free, independent, and pluralistic media as one of the essential elements of a functioning pluralistic democracy. The Representative observes media developments in all participating states and promotes compliance with relevant OSCE principles and commitments.

Final assessment

On the whole, although some overlaps between the human rights regional systems examined here do exist, each of the pillars has a unique role to play in a combined European regime of human rights. At the same time, generally, the OSCE system remains more politically oriented (and is not limited to the European countries), while the Council of Europe and EU systems are primarily juridically focused.

Human rights regime in the Americas

American Declaration on the Rights and Duties of Man
American Convention on Human Rights
Inter-American Commission on Human Rights
Inter-American Court of Human Rights
Statute of the Inter-American Commission on Human Rights
petitions
other communications
Statute of the Inter-American Court of Human Rights

The Organisation of American States as a regional pole

In the Americas, the regional human rights arrangements have been developed within the intergovernmental organisation known as the Organisation of American States (OAS). Therefore, the Organisation of American States is the principal regional pole (including

North, South, and Central America) responsible for the overall development and oversight of regional human rights standards and mechanisms throughout the Western hemisphere.

Human rights instruments and mechanisms of the inter-American regime

The primary human rights legal instruments of the inter-American regime are (1) the 1948 **American Declaration on the Rights and Duties of Man** – the first general international human rights instrument which included enumerated particular human rights and duties (enacted as a legally non-binding Declaration, which predated the Universal Declaration of Human Rights by more than seven months) – adopted by the International Conference of American States, Bogota, Colombia, and (2) the **American Convention on Human Rights** (also known as the **Pact of San Jose**) adopted at the Inter-American Specialised Conference on Human Rights, San Jose, Costa Rica, in 1969 and entered into force in 1978.

The main mechanisms of the inter-American regime include the **Inter-American Commission on Human Rights** and the **Inter-American Court of Human Rights**.

American Declaration of the Rights and Duties of Man

The American Declaration of the Rights and Duties of Man, while being initially adopted as a legally non-binding instrument, is now considered a source of international obligations for OAS member states as a set of customary norms. The Declaration possesses a specified structure laying out not just the human rights of individuals but also their corresponding duties to society.

According to the Declaration, the fundamental rights include the right to life, liberty and personal security; equality before law; religious freedom and worship; freedom of investigation, opinion, expression, and dissemination; protection of honour, personal reputation, and private and family life; a family and protection thereof; residence and movement; leisure time and the use thereof;[710] and so on.

According to the Declaration, the 'rights of man are limited by the rights of others, by the security of all, and by the just demands of the general welfare and the advancement of democracy.'[711]

Consequently, the Declaration entails the following duties: general duty to a society ('It is the duty of the individual so to conduct himself in relation to others that each and every one may fully form and develop his personality'),[712] duties towards children and parents, a duty to receive instruction,[713] a duty to vote ('It is the duty of every person to vote in the popular elections of the country of which he is a national, when he is legally capable

---

710 Articles I, II, III, IV, V, VI, VIII, XV of the American Declaration of the Rights and Duties of Man.
711 Article XXVIII of the American Declaration of the Rights and Duties of Man.
712 Article XXIX of the American Declaration of the Rights and Duties of Man.
713 Articles XXX, XXXI of the American Declaration of the Rights and Duties of Man.

of doing so'),[714] a duty to obey the law, a duty to pay taxes, a duty to refrain from political activities in a foreign country,[715] and so on.

American Convention on Human Rights

Over time, however, states determined that the regional human rights regime in the Americas needed to be strengthened, and an American Convention on Human Rights was prepared as an international treaty. The Convention by itself represents a very progressive document for that era, codifying many rules in the human rights area and institutionalising the human rights mechanisms.

Initially, the Convention was focused on civil and political rights and freedoms, such as the rights to juridical personality ('Every person has the right to recognition as a person before the law'), life, humane treatment ('Every person has the right to have his physical, mental, and moral integrity respected'), personal liberty, a name, nationality, equal protection, freedoms of conscience and religion, thought and expression, association,[716] and so forth.

Over time, protocols to the Convention, which were made available for ratification, were also developed. Namely, the Additional Protocol to the American Convention on Human Rights in the Area of Economic, Social and Cultural Rights, adopted in 1988 (which was intended to provide a balance to the Convention's focus on civil and political rights), and the Protocol to the American Convention on Human Rights to Abolish the Death Penalty, adopted in 1990.

On the other hand, the relationship between the duties and rights in the Convention is conceived in terms of personal responsibilities to a family, a community, and humanity.

Inter-American Commission on Human Rights

The Inter-American Commission on Human Rights 'was formally established in 1960 when the Permanent Council of the [OAS] approved its Statute.'[717] The current **Statute of the Inter-American Commission on Human Rights** under which it works was adopted in 1979. The Commission is based in Washington, DC, and is an organ of the OAS, created to encourage compliance by American states with their commitments in the field of human rights. In its work, the Commission uses the American Convention on Human Rights and, in addition, the American Declaration on the Rights and Duties of Man.

The Commission is composed of seven members, 'who shall be persons of high moral character and recognized competence in the field of human rights',[718] elected in a personal capacity by the secret ballot of the General Assembly of the OAS from a list of candidates

---

714 Article XXXII of the American Declaration of the Rights and Duties of Man.
715 Articles XXXIII, Article XXXVI, Article XXXVIII of the American Declaration of the Rights and Duties of Man.
716 Articles 3, 4, 5, 7, 18, 20, 24, 12, 13, 16 of the American Convention on Human Rights.
717 See the official website of the Organisation of American States <www.oas.org/en/about/commission_human_rights.asp> accessed 16 March 2021.
718 Paragraph 1 of Article 2 of the Statute of the Inter-American Commission on Human Rights.

proposed by the governments of the member states for a term of four years and may be re-elected only once.

Based on the Charter of the Organisation of American States, the Commission has general powers with respect to all member states of the OAS: namely 'to promote the observance and protection of human rights and to serve as a consultative organ of the Organization in these matters.'[719] The general powers include raising awareness of human rights among the peoples of the Americas; making recommendations to the governments of the states on the adoption of progressive measures in favour of human rights in the framework of their legislation (including constitutional provisions) and international commitments, as well as appropriate measures to further the observance of those rights; requesting that the governments of the states provide reports on measures they adopt in matters of human rights; and so on.

Nevertheless, the principal source of the Commission's mandate is the American Convention on Human Rights. Therefore, with regard to those states which are the parties to the Convention, the Commission has the powers:

- to act on the **petitions** and **other communications**;
- to appear before the Inter-American Court of Human Rights;
- to request the Court to take provisional measures;
- 'to consult the Court on the interpretation of the American Convention on Human Rights or of other treaties concerning the protection of human rights in the American states;' and
- 'to submit additional draft protocols to the American Convention on Human Rights to the General Assembly, in order to progressively include other rights and freedoms under the system of protection of the Convention, and . . . to submit to the General Assembly, through the Secretary General, proposed amendments to the American Convention on Human Rights.'[720]

Petitions and other communications

The mandate of the Commission regarding petitions and other communications is especially remarkable.

- Petitions – under the American Convention on Human Rights, any person, group of persons, or non-governmental entity legally recognised in one or more member states of the OAS may lodge petitions with the Commission containing denunciations or complaints of violation of the Convention by a state party.[721]
- Other communications – according to the Convention, any state party may, when it deposits its instrument of ratification of or adherence to the Convention or at any later time, declare that it recognises the competence of the Commission to receive

719 Article 106 of the Charter of the Organisation of American States.
720 Article 19 of the Statute of the Inter-American Commission on Human Rights.
721 Article 44 of the American Convention on Human Rights.

and examine communications in which a state party alleges that another state party has committed a violation of a human right set forth in the Convention.[722]

The Convention also determined the admissibility criteria for the petitions and other communications:

a   that the remedies under domestic law have been pursued and exhausted in accordance with generally recognized principles of international law;
b   that the petition or communication is lodged within a period of six months from the date on which the party alleging violation of his rights was notified of the final judgment;
c   that the subject of the petition or communication is not pending in another international proceeding for settlement; and
d   that, in the case of Article 44 [concerning the petitions], the petition contains the name, nationality, profession, domicile, and signature of the person or persons or of the legal representative of the entity lodging the petition.[723]

Nevertheless, the Commission may not apply all these requirements to some cases – for instance, if, on the domestic level, there has been an unwarranted delay in rendering a final judgment.[724]

If the Commission considers the petition or communication admissible, first of all, it aims to reach a friendly settlement of the matter. However, when an amicable settlement cannot be reached, the Commission shall draw up a report setting forth the facts and stating its conclusions, which shall be transmitted to the states concerned. (These states do not have the liberty to publish a report.) At the same time, the Convention enumerates the measures targeting settlement of the matter in any of the forms, inter alia:

- to issue 'pertinent recommendations and . . . prescribe a period within which the state is to take the measures that are incumbent upon it to remedy the situation examined';
- to publish the report of the Commission in certain cases;
- to submit the case to the Inter-American Court of Human Rights; and
- to request (in cases of extreme urgency) that the Inter-American Court of Human Rights order the adoption of 'provisional measures' to prevent irreparable harm to persons, even when the case has not yet been submitted to the Court.

Inter-American Court on Human Rights

The other crucial organ of the regional human rights regime is the Inter-American Court on Human Rights, which was established after the entry into force of the Convention and is based in San Jose.

722 Article 45 of the American Convention on Human Rights.
723 Article 46 (1) of the American Convention on Human Rights.
724 Article 46 (2) of the American Convention on Human Rights.

The Court consists of seven judges, nationals of the member states of the OAS, elected in an individual capacity for a term of six years (they may be re-elected only once) in a secret ballot by an absolute majority of votes of the parties to the Convention, in the General Assembly of the Organisation, from a panel of candidates proposed by those states.

The Court elects from among its members the President and the Vice President, who serve for two years; they may be re-elected. The President shall direct the work of the Court, represent it, regulate the disposition of matters brought before the Court, and preside over its sessions. The Vice President takes the place of the President in the latter's temporary absence or if the office of President becomes vacant. The Secretariat of the Court functions under the direct authority of the Secretary, who is appointed by the Court.

Jurisdiction

According to the **Statute of the Inter-American Court of Human Rights**, the Court is 'an autonomous judicial institution whose purpose is the application and interpretation of the American Convention on Human Rights'; hence, it exercises the 'adjudicatory and advisory jurisdiction'.[725]

Under the adjudicatory cases, '[o]nly the States Parties and the Commission shall have the right to submit a case to the Court'.[726] Under the advisory jurisdiction, the Court issues opinions 'regarding the interpretation of [the] Convention or of other treaties concerning the protection of human rights in the American states'[727] which are brought before it by certain OAS bodies or the member states. In its advisory role in interpreting the Convention, the Court is available to all states of the OAS,[728] although, in adjudicating cases, the Court has jurisdiction only when the particular state involved has accepted the Court's binding jurisdiction.

Thus, unlike the European human rights system, individuals from the OAS member states are not permitted to take cases directly to the Court.

---

725 Articles 1 and 2 of the Statute of the Inter-American Court of Human Rights.

726 Article 61 of the American Convention on Human Rights.

727 Article 64 (1) of the American Convention on Human Rights.

728 As the Inter-American Court of Human Rights stated in its Advisory Opinion *'Other Treaties' Subject to the Consultative Jurisdiction of the Court (Art. 64 American Convention on Human Rights)* requested by Peru (Advisory Opinion OC-1/82 of September 24, 1982): 'Article 64 of the Convention confers on this Court an advisory jurisdiction that is more extensive than that enjoyed by any international tribunal in existence today. All the organs of the OAS listed in Chapter X of the Charter of the Organization and every OAS Member State, whether a party to the Convention or not, are empowered to seek advisory opinions. The Court's advisory jurisdiction is not limited only to the Convention, but extends to other treaties concerning the protection of human rights in the American States. In principle, no part or aspect of these instruments is excluded from the scope of its advisory jurisdiction. Finally, all OAS Member States have the right to request advisory opinions on the compatibility of any of their domestic laws with the aforementioned international instruments.' All Court cases are available at the official website of the Court <www.corteidh.or.cr/index.cfm?lang=en> accessed 16 March 2021. In this book, materials from the website are used, taking into account the disclaimer and applicable legal rules.

Decision-making process

The quorum for deliberations by the Court is five judges. Decisions of the Court are being taken by a majority vote of the judges present. In the event of a tie, the President shall cast the deciding vote.[729]

The hearings of the Court are public, along with the decisions, judgments, and opinions, although deliberations remain secret unless the Court decides otherwise.

The judgment of the Court is final and is not subject to appeal.

The positive impact of the American Convention on Human Rights in the region

On the whole, the American Convention on Human Rights strengthened the regional human rights regime by making the Commission more effective, creating a Court, and, on the whole, changing the legal nature of the instruments and mechanisms upon which the system is based.

While many countries have ratified the Convention,[730] only a few of them have accepted the special competence (developed by the Convention) of the Inter-American Commission on Human Rights, as well as the Inter-American Court on Human Rights, and most of them provided such recognition only with the reservations (for example, by referring to the 'condition of reciprocity').[731]

The instruments prescribing the specific areas of human rights

Over time, other legal instruments have been adopted in the Inter-American region to better protect specific areas of human rights concerns. These are the Inter-American Convention to Prevent and Punish Torture of 1985; the Inter-American Convention on Forced Disappearance of Persons of 1994; the Inter-American Convention on the Prevention, Punishment, and Eradication of Violence against Women of 1994; the Inter-American Convention on the Elimination of All Forms of Discrimination Against Persons with Disabilities of 1999; and so on.

---

729 Article 23 of the Statute of the Inter-American Court of Human Rights.

730 However, for example, Canada did not sign the Convention, and, while the United States signed the Convention on 1 June 1977, it has not yet ratified it.

731 'In the instrument of ratification dated August 14, 1984, and deposited with the General Secretariat of the OAS on September 5, 1984, the Government of Argentina recognizes the competence of the Inter-American Commission on Human Rights and on the jurisdiction of the Inter-American Court of Human Rights. This recognition is for an indeterminate period and *on condition of reciprocity* on all cases related to the interpretation or application of the Convention cited, with the partial reservation and bearing in mind the interpretative statements contained in the instrument of ratification.' All reservations and 'interpretative declarations' are available at <www.oas.org/en/iachr/mandate/Basics/conventionrat.asp> accessed 16 March 2021.

African human rights regime

African Charter on Human and Peoples' Rights
African Commission on Human and Peoples' Rights
African Court on Human and Peoples' Rights
Court of Justice of the African Union
report of states
communication from states
other communications
African Court of Justice and Human Rights
African Court of Justice and Human and Peoples' Rights

The African Union as a regional pole, the primary regional human rights instrument and mechanisms

The African regional human rights regime has been established within the regional inter-governmental organisation – the African Union. The primary regional human rights legal instrument in Africa is the 1981 **African Charter on Human and Peoples' Rights**, and the main mechanisms are the **African Commission on Human and Peoples' Rights** and the **African Court on Human and Peoples' Rights**, which is in the process of merging with the **Court of Justice of the African Union**.

African Charter on Human and Peoples' Rights

The African Charter on Human and Peoples' Rights, also known as the Banjul Charter, was adopted in 1981, is one of the youngest of the operational regional instruments, and enumerates the traditional list of civil and political rights and freedoms of individuals, as well as certain economic, social, and cultural rights.

Nevertheless, the main distinguishing feature of the Charter is already noted in the title and consists of addressing by the Charter the peoples' rights. This target is rooted in the African context since the main international political concerns for African peoples remain the elimination of all forms of colonialism and racial discrimination.

For example, the Charter determines that 'All peoples shall be equal; they shall enjoy the same respect and shall have the same rights. Nothing shall justify the domination of a people by another'[732] and prescribes that all peoples shall have the right to existence and self-determination, which in terms of the Charter means that they shall freely determine their political status and shall pursue their economic and social development according to the policy they have freely chosen.[733] At the same time, 'colonised or oppressed peoples shall have the right to free themselves from the bonds of domination by resorting to any means recognised by the international community', and moreover, these 'peoples

732 Article 19 of the African Charter on Human and Peoples' Rights.
733 Article 20 of the African Charter on Human and Peoples' Rights.

shall have the right to the assistance of the States parties to the present Charter in their liberation struggle against foreign domination, be it political, economic or cultural'. Simultaneously, the Charter defines the duty of the states to ensure the exercise of the right to development of peoples, underlines the right of peoples to national and international peace and security, the right of peoples to a general satisfactory environment favourable to their development,[734] and so on.

African Commission on Human and People's Rights

On the other hand, the Charter led to the creation of the African Commission on Human and People's Rights. The role of the Commission is to

- promote and protect human and people's rights on the African continent, and, inter alia, to
  - collect documents and undertake studies and researches on the problems in the field of human and peoples' rights; and
  - formulate and lay down principles and rules aimed at solving legal problems relating to human and peoples' rights; and
- interpret the Banjul Charter as requested by the states, AU institutions, or an African Organisation recognised by the AU.

The Commission is made up of 11 independent experts elected for six years in a secret ballot by the AU Assembly of Heads of State and Government from a list of persons nominated by the states parties to the Charter. The Commission members usually meet twice a year. In turn, the Commission elects its Chairman and Vice Chairman for a two-year period. Seven members form the quorum. It is notable that the members of the Commission enjoy certain diplomatic privileges and immunities.

The Commission's Secretariat is located in Banjul, Gambia.

The operational mechanisms of the Commission

The Commission is equipped with the following operational mechanisms:

- **Report of states** – on the legislative or other measures taken to give effect to the rights and freedoms recognised and guaranteed by the Charter. In terms of reporting, countries are required to submit a report in every two years.
- **Communication from states** – every state party to the Charter may draw, by written communication, the attention of the targeted state to a given matter. This communication shall also be addressed to the Secretary General of the AU and the Chairman of the Commission. Within three months of the receipt of the communication, the state to which the communication is addressed shall give the enquiring state a written

---

734 Articles 22, 23, 24 of the African Charter on Human and Peoples' Rights.

explanation or statement elucidating the matter. If the issue is not settled within three months, either state has the right to submit the matter to the Commission through the Chairman and notify the other states involved. The Commission prepares a report stating the facts and its findings, sends the report to the states concerned, and communicates to the Assembly of Heads of State and Government.

- **Other communications** – which shall be considered by the Commission if a simple majority of its members so decide. The Charter determines the admissibility criteria for such other communications. Individuals and NGOs in Africa and beyond have lodged this kind of complaints with the Commission over the years. 'When it appears after deliberations of the Commission that one or more communications apparently relate to special cases which reveal the existence of a series of serious or massive violations of human and peoples' rights, the Commission shall draw the attention of the Assembly of Heads of State and Government to these special cases.'[735]

The Commission may create subsidiary mechanisms (Special Mechanisms) such as special rapporteurs (for example, the Special Rapporteur on Freedom of Expression and Access to Information and the Special Rapporteur on Refugees, Asylum Seekers, Internally Displaced Persons, and Migrant in Africa were established), committees (e.g. the Committee for the Prevention of Torture in Africa, the Committee on the Protection of the Rights of People Living With HIV (PLHIV) and Those at Risk, Vulnerable to and Affected by HIV, and so forth), and working groups (e.g. the Working Group on Rights of Older Persons and People with Disabilities, the Working Group on Economic, Social, and Cultural Rights, and so forth).[736]

Nevertheless, it is especially notable that the mandate of the Commission is quasi-judicial in nature since its final recommendations are not legally binding.

African Court on Human and Peoples' Rights

Therefore, to ensure the protection of human and peoples' rights in Africa and reinforce the functions of the African Commission on Human and Peoples' Rights, the African Court on Human and Peoples' Rights was established under Article 1 of the Protocol to the African Charter on Human and Peoples' Rights on the Establishment of an African Court on Human and Peoples' Rights of 1998. (The Protocol came into force in 2004.) Under the Protocol, 'The jurisdiction of the Court shall extend to all cases and disputes submitted to it concerning the interpretation and application of the Charter, this Protocol and any other relevant Human Rights instrument ratified by the States concerned.'[737]

Generally, the Court has two types of jurisdiction – contentious and advisory.

---

735 Paragraph 1 of Article 58 of the African Charter on Human and Peoples' Rights.

736 The list of such Special Mechanisms, which were established over time, is available on the official website of the African Commission on Human and Peoples' Rights <www.achpr.org/specialmechanisms> accessed 16 March 2021.

737 Paragraph 1 of Article 3 of the Protocol to the African Charter on Human and Peoples' Rights on the Establishment of an African Court on Human and Peoples' Rights.

The Court is composed of 11 judges, nationals of member states of the African Union. The Court officially started its operations in Addis Ababa, Ethiopia, in 2006; in 2007, it moved to its current location in Arusha, the United Republic of Tanzania.

The Court may receive cases from the African Commission of Human and Peoples' Rights, states parties to the Protocol, or African intergovernmental organisations. At the same time, the non-governmental organisations with observer status in the African Commission and individuals can also file cases directly to the Court as long as the state against which they are complaining has deposited the appropriate declaration recognising the jurisdiction of the Court to accept cases from individuals and NGOs.[738]

The merging of two courts

In 2004, the African states decided to merge the two courts – the Court of Justice of the African Union and the African Court on Human and Peoples' Rights.[739] The first Court was initially intended to be the principal judicial organ of the African Union with the authority to rule on disputes regarding the interpretation of the AU treaties; nevertheless, the Court never came onto existence.

Regarding the merger of the courts, two protocols (respectively in 2008 and 2014) were adopted. The Protocol of 2008 (Protocol on the Statute of the African Court of Justice and Human Rights) aimed at the establishment of a single court called the **African Court of Justice and Human Rights** to avoid duplication of functions and waste of resources.

The second Protocol of 2014 (Protocol on Amendments to the Protocol on the Statute of the African Court of Justice and Human Rights) targeted modification of the Court to equip it with a tripartite mandate. Under this Protocol, the Court would have a General Affairs Section, a Human Rights Section, and an International Criminal Law Section. This contribution focuses on its newest mandate – international crimes. In addition, the Protocol changed the name of the Court to the **African Court of Justice and Human and Peoples' Rights**.[740]

The Protocol of 2014 is widely regarded as a new wave of attempt to modify international criminal law[741] since, in addition to the recognised list of international crimes (such

---

738 'As of December 2020, only six (6) of the thirty-one (31) State Parties to the Protocol have deposited the declaration recognizing the competence of the Court to receive cases directly from NGOs and individuals. The six States are: Burkina Faso, The Gambia, Ghana, Mali, Malawi and Tunisia. . . . Rwanda withdrew its declaration in 2017; Tanzania in 2019; Côte d'Ivoire and Benin in 2020.' <www.african-court.org/wpafc/welcome-to-the-african-court/> accessed 16 March 2021.

739 'FURTHER DECIDES that the African Court on Human and Peoples' Rights and the Court of Justice should be integrated into one Court'. Decision on the Seats of the African Union, AU Doc. Assembly/AU/Dec. 45 (III) of 2004, Paragraph 4.

740 Article 8 of the Protocol on Amendments to the Protocol on the Statute of the African Court of Justice and Human Rights.

741 'The Protocol and the Statute annexed to it provide for the establishment of a regional court in Africa to be known as the "African Court of Justice and Human and Peoples' Rights" (African Court). This Court will, among others, exercise criminal jurisdiction over a wide range of international crimes involving individual criminal responsibility and corporate criminal liability over legal persons (with

as genocide, crimes against humanity, war crimes, and the crime of aggression), it also enumerates other offences as well (covered by the international criminal jurisdiction of the Court): namely, the crime of unconstitutional change of a government; piracy; terrorism; mercenaryism; corruption; money laundering; trafficking in persons; trafficking in drugs; trafficking in hazardous wastes; and illicit exploitation of natural resources.

However, this new wave is considered to be mostly politically motivated, including, aiming at duplication of the International Criminal Court's jurisdiction. Besides, as of now, these Protocols which aimed to merge the two courts have still not entered into force.

The instruments prescribing the specific areas of human rights

Other legal instruments have also been adopted in the African region to help better protect specific human rights areas. These are, among others, the African Charter on the Rights and Welfare of the Child of 1990, the Protocol to the African Charter on Human and Peoples' Rights on the Rights of Women in Africa of 2003, and the African Charter on Democracy, Elections, and Governance of 2011.

CASES AND MATERIALS (*SELECTED PARTS*)

Development of the international human rights law

Declaration of Human and Civic Rights
Approved by the National Assembly of France on 26 August 1789.[742]

The representatives of the French People, formed into a National Assembly, considering ignorance, forgetfulness or contempt of the rights of man to be the only causes of public misfortunes and the corruption of Governments, have resolved to set forth, in a solemn Declaration, the natural, unalienable and sacred rights of man, to the end that this Declaration, constantly present to all members of the body politic, may remind them unceasingly of their rights and their duties; to the end that the acts of the legislative power and those of the executive power, since they may be continually compared with the aim of every political institution, may thereby be the more respected; to the end that the demands of the citizens, founded henceforth on simple and incontestable principles, may always be directed toward the maintenance of the Constitution and the happiness of all. In consequence whereof, the National Assembly recognises and declares, in the presence and under the auspices of the Supreme Being, the following Rights of Man and of the Citizen.

Article 1. Men are born and remain free and equal in rights. Social distinctions may be based only on considerations of the common good.

---

the exception of States), which goes beyond any other international court or hybrid tribunal.' Manisuli Ssenyonjo and Saidat Nakitto, 'The African Court of Justice and Human and Peoples' Rights "International Criminal Law Section": Promoting Impunity for African Union Heads of State and Senior State Officials?' (2016) 16(1) *International Criminal Law Review* 71.

742 Available at the official website of the French Constitutional Council <www.conseil-constitutionnel.fr/sites/default/files/as/root/bank_mm/anglais/cst2.pdf> accessed 16 March 2021.

Article 2. The aim of every political association is the preservation of the natural and imprescriptible rights of Man. These rights are Liberty, Property, Safety and Resistance to Oppression.

Article 3. The principle of any Sovereignty lies primarily in the Nation. No corporate body, no individual may exercise any authority that does not expressly emanate from it.

Article 4. Liberty consists in being able to do anything that does not harm others: thus, the exercise of the natural rights of every man has no bounds other than those that ensure to the other members of society the enjoyment of these same rights. These bounds may be determined only by Law.

Article 5. The Law has the right to forbid only those actions that are injurious to society. Nothing that is not forbidden by Law may be hindered, and no one may be compelled to do what the Law does not ordain.

Article 6. The Law is the expression of the general will. All citizens have the right to take part, personally or through their representatives, in its making. It must be the same for all, whether it protects or punishes. All citizens, being equal in its eyes, shall be equally eligible to all high offices, public positions and employments, according to their ability, and without other distinction than that of their virtues and talents.

Article 7. No man may be accused, arrested or detained except in the cases determined by the Law, and following the procedure that it has prescribed. Those who solicit, expedite, carry out, or cause to be carried out arbitrary orders must be punished; but any citizen summoned or apprehended by virtue of the Law, must give instant obedience; resistance makes him guilty.

Article 8. The Law must prescribe only the punishments that are strictly and evidently necessary; and no one may be punished except by virtue of a Law drawn up and promulgated before the offense is committed, and legally applied.

Article 9. As every man is presumed innocent until he has been declared guilty, if it should be considered necessary to arrest him, any undue harshness that is not required to secure his person must be severely curbed by Law.

Article 10. No one may be disturbed on account of his opinions, even religious ones, as long as the manifestation of such opinions does not interfere with the established Law and Order.

Article 11. The free communication of ideas and of opinions is one of the most precious rights of man. Any citizen may therefore speak, write and publish freely, except what is tantamount to the abuse of this liberty in the cases determined by Law.

Article 12. To guarantee the Rights of Man and of the Citizen a public force is necessary; this force is therefore established for the benefit of all, and not for the particular use of those to whom it is entrusted.

Article 13. For the maintenance of the public force, and for administrative expenses, a general tax is indispensable; it must be equally distributed among all citizens, in proportion to their ability to pay.

Article 14. All citizens have the right to ascertain, by themselves, or through their representatives, the need for a public tax, to consent to it freely, to watch over its use, and to determine its proportion, basis, collection and duration.

Article 15. Society has the right to ask a public official for an accounting of his administration.

Article 16. Any society in which no provision is made for guaranteeing rights or for the separation of powers, has no Constitution.

Article 17. Since the right to Property is inviolable and sacred, no one may be deprived thereof, unless public necessity, legally ascertained, obviously requires it, and just and prior indemnity has been paid.

Development of international human rights law

The Universal Declaration of Human Rights
Adopted by A/RES/217(III) D, 10 December 1948

Article 1

All human beings are born free and equal in dignity and rights. They are endowed with reason and conscience and should act towards one another in a spirit of brotherhood.

Article 2

Everyone is entitled to all the rights and freedoms set forth in this Declaration, without distinction of any kind, such as race, colour, sex, language, religion, political or other opinion, national or social origin, property, birth or other status. Furthermore, no distinction shall be made on the basis of the political, jurisdictional or international status of the country or territory to which a person belongs, whether it be independent, trust, non-self-governing or under any other limitation of sovereignty.

Article 3

Everyone has the right to life, liberty and security of person.

Article 4

No one shall be held in slavery or servitude; slavery and the slave trade shall be prohibited in all their forms.

Article 5

No one shall be subjected to torture or to cruel, inhuman or degrading treatment or punishment.

Article 6

Everyone has the right to recognition everywhere as a person before the law.

Article 7

All are equal before the law and are entitled without any discrimination to equal protection of the law. All are entitled to equal protection against any discrimination in violation of this Declaration and against any incitement to such discrimination.

Article 8

Everyone has the right to an effective remedy by the competent national tribunals for acts violating the fundamental rights granted him by the constitution or by law.

Article 9

No one shall be subjected to arbitrary arrest, detention or exile.

Article 10

Everyone is entitled in full equality to a fair and public hearing by an independent and impartial tribunal, in the determination of his rights and obligations and of any criminal charge against him.

Article 11

(1) Everyone charged with a penal offence has the right to be presumed innocent until proved guilty according to law in a public trial at which he has had all the guarantees necessary for his defence.

(2) No one shall be held guilty of any penal offence on account of any act or omission which did not constitute a penal offence, under national or international law, at the time when it was committed. Nor shall a heavier penalty be imposed than the one that was applicable at the time the penal offence was committed.

Article 12

No one shall be subjected to arbitrary interference with his privacy, family, home or correspondence, nor to attacks upon his honour and reputation. Everyone has the right to the protection of the law against such interference or attacks.

Article 13

(1) Everyone has the right to freedom of movement and residence within the borders of each state.

(2) Everyone has the right to leave any country, including his own, and to return to his country.

Article 14

(1) Everyone has the right to seek and to enjoy in other countries asylum from persecution.

(2) This right may not be invoked in the case of prosecutions genuinely arising from non-political crimes or from acts contrary to the purposes and principles of the United Nations.

Article 15

(1) Everyone has the right to a nationality.

(2) No one shall be arbitrarily deprived of his nationality nor denied the right to change his nationality.

Article 16

(1) Men and women of full age, without any limitation due to race, nationality or religion, have the right to marry and to found a family. They are entitled to equal rights as to marriage, during marriage and at its dissolution.
(2) Marriage shall be entered into only with the free and full consent of the intending spouses.
(3) The family is the natural and fundamental group unit of society and is entitled to protection by society and the State.

Article 17

(1) Everyone has the right to own property alone as well as in association with others.
(2) No one shall be arbitrarily deprived of his property.

Article 18

Everyone has the right to freedom of thought, conscience and religion; this right includes freedom to change his religion or belief, and freedom, either alone or in community with others and in public or private, to manifest his religion or belief in teaching, practice, worship and observance.

Article 19

Everyone has the right to freedom of opinion and expression; this right includes freedom to hold opinions without interference and to seek, receive and impart information and ideas through any media and regardless of frontiers.

Article 20

(1) Everyone has the right to freedom of peaceful assembly and association.
(2) No one may be compelled to belong to an association.

Article 21

(1) Everyone has the right to take part in the government of his country, directly or through freely chosen representatives.
(2) Everyone has the right to equal access to public service in his country.
(3) The will of the people shall be the basis of the authority of government; this will shall be expressed in periodic and genuine elections which shall be by universal and equal suffrage and shall be held by secret vote or by equivalent free voting procedures.

Article 22

Everyone, as a member of society, has the right to social security and is entitled to realization, through national effort and international co-operation and in accordance with the organization and resources of each State, of the economic, social and cultural rights indispensable for his dignity and the free development of his personality.

Article 23

(1) Everyone has the right to work, to free choice of employment, to just and favourable conditions of work and to protection against unemployment.
(2) Everyone, without any discrimination, has the right to equal pay for equal work.
(3) Everyone who works has the right to just and favourable remuneration ensuring for himself and his family an existence worthy of human dignity, and supplemented, if necessary, by other means of social protection.
(4) Everyone has the right to form and to join trade unions for the protection of his interests.

Article 24

Everyone has the right to rest and leisure, including reasonable limitation of working hours and periodic holidays with pay.

Article 25

(1) Everyone has the right to a standard of living adequate for the health and well-being of himself and of his family, including food, clothing, housing and medical care and necessary social services, and the right to security in the event of unemployment, sickness, disability, widowhood, old age or other lack of livelihood in circumstances beyond his control.
(2) Motherhood and childhood are entitled to special care and assistance. All children, whether born in or out of wedlock, shall enjoy the same social protection.

Article 26

(1) Everyone has the right to education. Education shall be free, at least in the elementary and fundamental stages. Elementary education shall be compulsory. Technical and professional education shall be made generally available and higher education shall be equally accessible to all on the basis of merit.
(2) Education shall be directed to the full development of the human personality and to the strengthening of respect for human rights and fundamental freedoms. It shall promote understanding, tolerance and friendship among all nations, racial or religious groups, and shall further the activities of the United Nations for the maintenance of peace.
(3) Parents have a prior right to choose the kind of education that shall be given to their children.

Article 27

(1) Everyone has the right freely to participate in the cultural life of the community, to enjoy the arts and to share in scientific advancement and its benefits.
(2) Everyone has the right to the protection of the moral and material interests resulting from any scientific, literary or artistic production of which he is the author.

Article 28

Everyone is entitled to a social and international order in which the rights and freedoms set forth in this Declaration can be fully realized.

Article 29

(1) Everyone has duties to the community in which alone the free and full development of his personality is possible.

(2) In the exercise of his rights and freedoms, everyone shall be subject only to such limitations as are determined by law solely for the purpose of securing due recognition and respect for the rights and freedoms of others and of meeting the just requirements of morality, public order and the general welfare in a democratic society.

(3) These rights and freedoms may in no case be exercised contrary to the purposes and principles of the United Nations.

Article 30

Nothing in this Declaration may be interpreted as implying for any State, group or person any right to engage in any activity or to perform any act aimed at the destruction of any of the rights and freedoms set forth herein.

Racial Discrimination

International Convention on the Elimination of All Forms of Racial Discrimination
Adopted and opened for signature and ratification by General Assembly resolution A/ RES/2106 (XX) of 21 December 1965
Entry into force: 4 January 1969

Part I

Article 1

1 In this Convention, the term "racial discrimination" shall mean any distinction, exclusion, restriction or preference based on race, colour, descent, or national or ethnic origin which has the purpose or effect of nullifying or impairing the recognition, enjoyment or exercise, on an equal footing, of human rights and fundamental freedoms in the political, economic, social, cultural or any other field of public life.

2 This Convention shall not apply to distinctions, exclusions, restrictions or preferences made by a State Party to this Convention between citizens and non-citizens.

3 Nothing in this Convention may be interpreted as affecting in any way the legal provisions of States Parties concerning nationality, citizenship or naturalization, provided that such provisions do not discriminate against any particular nationality.

4 Special measures taken for the sole purpose of securing adequate advancement of certain racial or ethnic groups or individuals requiring such protection as may be necessary in order to ensure such groups or individuals equal enjoyment or exercise of human rights and fundamental freedoms shall not be deemed racial discrimination, provided, however, that such measures do not, as a consequence, lead to the maintenance of separate rights for different racial groups and that they shall not be continued after the objectives for which they were taken have been achieved.

Article 2

1 States Parties condemn racial discrimination and undertake to pursue by all appropriate means and without delay a policy of eliminating racial discrimination in all its forms and promoting understanding among all races, and, to this end:

(a) Each State Party undertakes to engage in no act or practice of racial discrimination against persons, groups of persons or institutions and to ensure that all public authorities and public institutions, national and local, shall act in conformity with this obligation;

(b) Each State Party undertakes not to sponsor, defend or support racial discrimination by any persons or organizations;

(c) Each State Party shall take effective measures to review governmental, national and local policies, and to amend, rescind or nullify any laws and regulations which have the effect of creating or perpetuating racial discrimination wherever it exists;

(d) Each State Party shall prohibit and bring to an end, by all appropriate means, including legislation as required by circumstances, racial discrimination by any persons, group or organization;

(e) Each State Party undertakes to encourage, where appropriate, integrationist multiracial organizations and movements and other means of eliminating barriers between races, and to discourage anything which tends to strengthen racial division.

2 States Parties shall, when the circumstances so warrant, take, in the social, economic, cultural and other fields, special and concrete measures to ensure the adequate development and protection of certain racial groups or individuals belonging to them, for the purpose of guaranteeing them the full and equal enjoyment of human rights and fundamental freedoms. These measures shall in no case entail as a consequence the maintenance of unequal or separate rights for different racial groups after the objectives for which they were taken have been achieved.

Article 3

States Parties particularly condemn racial segregation and apartheid and undertake to prevent, prohibit and eradicate all practices of this nature in territories under their jurisdiction.

Article 5

In compliance with the fundamental obligations laid down in article 2 of this Convention, States Parties undertake to prohibit and to eliminate racial discrimination in all its forms and to guarantee the right of everyone, without distinction as to race, colour, or national or ethnic origin, to equality before the law, notably in the enjoyment of the following rights:

(a) The right to equal treatment before the tribunals and all other organs administering justice;

(b) The right to security of person and protection by the State against violence or bodily harm, whether inflicted by government officials or by any individual group or institution;

(c) Political rights, in particular the right to participate in elections – to vote and to stand for election – on the basis of universal and equal suffrage, to take part in the Government as well as in the conduct of public affairs at any level and to have equal access to public service;

(d) Other civil rights, in particular:

   (i) The right to freedom of movement and residence within the border of the State;
   (ii) The right to leave any country, including one's own, and to return to one's country;
   (iii) The right to nationality;
   (iv) The right to marriage and choice of spouse;
   (v) The right to own property alone as well as in association with others;
   (vi) The right to inherit;
   (vii) The right to freedom of thought, conscience and religion;
   (viii) The right to freedom of opinion and expression;
   (ix) The right to freedom of peaceful assembly and association;

(e) Economic, social and cultural rights, in particular:

   (i) The rights to work, to free choice of employment, to just and favourable conditions of work, to protection against unemployment, to equal pay for equal work, to just and favourable remuneration;
   (ii) The right to form and join trade unions;
   (iii) The right to housing;
   (iv) The right to public health, medical care, social security and social services;
   (v) The right to education and training;
   (vi) The right to equal participation in cultural activities;

(f) The right of access to any place or service intended for use by the general public, such as transport hotels, restaurants, cafes, theatres and parks.

Part II

Article 8

1   There shall be established a Committee on the Elimination of Racial Discrimination (hereinafter referred to as the Committee) consisting of eighteen experts of high moral standing and acknowledged impartiality elected by States Parties from among their nationals, who shall serve in their personal capacity, consideration being given to equitable geographical distribution and to the representation of the different forms of civilization as well as of the principal legal systems.

2   The members of the Committee shall be elected by secret ballot from a list of persons nominated by the States Parties. Each State Party may nominate one person from among its own nationals.

3   The initial election shall be held six months after the date of the entry into force of this Convention. At least three months before the date of each election the Secretary-General of the United Nations shall address a letter to the States Parties inviting them to submit their nominations within two months. The Secretary-General shall prepare a list in alphabetical order

of all persons thus nominated, indicating the States Parties which have nominated them, and shall submit it to the States Parties.

4   Elections of the members of the Committee shall be held at a meeting of States Parties convened by the Secretary-General at United Nations Headquarters. At that meeting, for which two-thirds of the States Parties shall constitute a quorum, the persons elected to the Committee shall be nominees who obtain the largest number of votes and an absolute majority of the votes of the representatives of States Parties present and voting.

5   (a) The members of the Committee shall be elected for a term of four years. However, the terms of nine of the members elected at the first election shall expire at the end of two years; immediately after the first election the names of these nine members shall be chosen by lot by the Chairman of the Committee;

(b) For the filling of casual vacancies, the State Party whose expert has ceased to function as a member of the Committee shall appoint another expert from among its nationals, subject to the approval of the Committee.

6   States Parties shall be responsible for the expenses of the members of the Committee while they are in performance of Committee duties.

Article 9

1   States Parties undertake to submit to the Secretary-General of the United Nations, for consideration by the Committee, a report on the legislative, judicial, administrative or other measures which they have adopted and which give effect to the provisions of this Convention:

(a) within one year after the entry into force of the Convention for the State concerned; and

(b) thereafter every two years and whenever the Committee so requests. The Committee may request further information from the States Parties.

2   The Committee shall report annually, through the Secretary-General, to the General Assembly of the United Nations on its activities and may make suggestions and general recommendations based on the examination of the reports and information received from the States Parties. Such suggestions and general recommendations shall be reported to the General Assembly together with comments, if any, from States Parties.

Article 10

1   The Committee shall adopt its own rules of procedure.
2   The Committee shall elect its officers for a term of two years.
3   The secretariat of the Committee shall be provided by the Secretary-General of the United Nations.
4   The meetings of the Committee shall normally be held at United Nations Headquarters.

Article 11

1   If a State Party considers that another State Party is not giving effect to the provisions of this Convention, it may bring the matter to the attention of the Committee. The Committee shall then transmit the communication to the State Party concerned. Within three months, the

receiving State shall submit to the Committee written explanations or statements clarifying the matter and the remedy, if any, that may have been taken by that State.

2   If the matter is not adjusted to the satisfaction of both parties, either by bilateral negotiations or by any other procedure open to them, within six months after the receipt by the receiving State of the initial communication, either State shall have the right to refer the matter again to the Committee by notifying the Committee and also the other State.

3   The Committee shall deal with a matter referred to it in accordance with paragraph 2 of this article after it has ascertained that all available domestic remedies have been invoked and exhausted in the case, in conformity with the generally recognized principles of international law. This shall not be the rule where the application of the remedies is unreasonably prolonged.

4   In any matter referred to it, the Committee may call upon the States Parties concerned to supply any other relevant information.

5   When any matter arising out of this article is being considered by the Committee, the States Parties concerned shall be entitled to send a representative to take part in the proceedings of the Committee, without voting rights, while the matter is under consideration.

Article 12

1   (a) After the Committee has obtained and collated all the information it deems necessary, the Chairman shall appoint an ad hoc Conciliation Commission (hereinafter referred to as the Commission) comprising five persons who may or may not be members of the Committee. The members of the Commission shall be appointed with the unanimous consent of the parties to the dispute, and its good offices shall be made available to the States concerned with a view to an amicable solution of the matter on the basis of respect for this Convention;
(b) If the States parties to the dispute fail to reach agreement within three months on all or part of the composition of the Commission, the members of the Commission not agreed upon by the States parties to the dispute shall be elected by secret ballot by a two-thirds majority vote of the Committee from among its own members.

2   The members of the Commission shall serve in their personal capacity. They shall not be nationals of the States parties to the dispute or of a State not Party to this Convention.

3   The Commission shall elect its own Chairman and adopt its own rules of procedure.

4   The meetings of the Commission shall normally be held at United Nations Headquarters or at any other convenient place as determined by the Commission.

5   The secretariat provided in accordance with article 10, paragraph 3, of this Convention shall also service the Commission whenever a dispute among States Parties brings the Commission into being.

6   The States parties to the dispute shall share equally all the expenses of the members of the Commission in accordance with estimates to be provided by the Secretary-General of the United Nations.

7   The Secretary-General shall be empowered to pay the expenses of the members of the Commission, if necessary, before reimbursement by the States parties to the dispute in accordance with paragraph 6 of this article.

8   The information obtained and collated by the Committee shall be made available to the Commission, and the Commission may call upon the States concerned to supply any other relevant information.

Article 13

1   When the Commission has fully considered the matter, it shall prepare and submit to the Chairman of the Committee a report embodying its findings on all questions of fact relevant to the issue between the parties and containing such recommendations as it may think proper for the amicable solution of the dispute.

2   The Chairman of the Committee shall communicate the report of the Commission to each of the States parties to the dispute. These States shall, within three months, inform the Chairman of the Committee whether or not they accept the recommendations contained in the report of the Commission.

3   After the period provided for in paragraph 2 of this article, the Chairman of the Committee shall communicate the report of the Commission and the declarations of the States Parties concerned to the other States Parties to this Convention.

Article 14

1   A State Party may at any time declare that it recognizes the competence of the Committee to receive and consider communications from individuals or groups of individuals within its jurisdiction claiming to be victims of a violation by that State Party of any of the rights set forth in this Convention. No communication shall be received by the Committee if it concerns a State Party which has not made such a declaration.

2   Any State Party which makes a declaration as provided for in paragraph I of this article may establish or indicate a body within its national legal order which shall be competent to receive and consider petitions from individuals and groups of individuals within its jurisdiction who claim to be victims of a violation of any of the rights set forth in this Convention and who have exhausted other available local remedies.

3   A declaration made in accordance with paragraph 1 of this article and the name of any body established or indicated in accordance with paragraph 2 of this article shall be deposited by the State Party concerned with the Secretary-General of the United Nations, who shall transmit copies thereof to the other States Parties. A declaration may be withdrawn at any time by notification to the Secretary-General, but such a withdrawal shall not affect communications pending before the Committee.

4   A register of petitions shall be kept by the body established or indicated in accordance with paragraph 2 of this article, and certified copies of the register shall be filed annually through appropriate channels with the Secretary-General on the understanding that the contents shall not be publicly disclosed.

5   In the event of failure to obtain satisfaction from the body established or indicated in accordance with paragraph 2 of this article, the petitioner shall have the right to communicate the matter to the Committee within six months.

6   (a) The Committee shall confidentially bring any communication referred to it to the attention of the State Party alleged to be violating any provision of this Convention, but the identity of the individual or groups of individuals concerned shall not be revealed without his or their express consent. The Committee shall not receive anonymous communications;
(b) Within three months, the receiving State shall submit to the Committee written explanations or statements clarifying the matter and the remedy, if any, that may have been taken by that State.

7   (a) The Committee shall consider communications in the light of all information made available to it by the State Party concerned and by the petitioner. The Committee shall not consider any communication from a petitioner unless it has ascertained that the petitioner has exhausted all available domestic remedies. However, this shall not be the rule where the application of the remedies is unreasonably prolonged;
(b) The Committee shall forward its suggestions and recommendations, if any, to the State Party concerned and to the petitioner.

8   The Committee shall include in its annual report a summary of such communications and, where appropriate, a summary of the explanations and statements of the States Parties concerned and of its own suggestions and recommendations.

9   The Committee shall be competent to exercise the functions provided for in this article only when at least ten States Parties to this Convention are bound by declarations in accordance with paragraph I of this article.

Article 15

1   Pending the achievement of the objectives of the Declaration on the Granting of Independence to Colonial Countries and Peoples, contained in General Assembly resolution 1514 (XV) of 14 December 1960, the provisions of this Convention shall in no way limit the right of petition granted to these peoples by other international instruments or by the United Nations and its specialized agencies.

2   (a) The Committee established under article 8, paragraph 1, of this Convention shall receive copies of the petitions from, and submit expressions of opinion and recommendations on these petitions to, the bodies of the United Nations which deal with matters directly related to the principles and objectives of this Convention in their consideration of petitions from the inhabitants of Trust and Non-Self-Governing Territories and all other territories to which General Assembly resolution 1514 (XV) applies, relating to matters covered by this Convention which are before these bodies;
(b) The Committee shall receive from the competent bodies of the United Nations copies of the reports concerning the legislative, judicial, administrative or other measures directly related to the principles and objectives of this Convention applied by the administering Powers within the Territories mentioned in subparagraph (a) of this paragraph, and shall express opinions and make recommendations to these bodies.

3   The Committee shall include in its report to the General Assembly a summary of the petitions and reports it has received from United Nations bodies, and the expressions of opinion and recommendations of the Committee relating to the said petitions and reports.

4   The Committee shall request from the Secretary-General of the United Nations all information relevant to the objectives of this Convention and available to him regarding the Territories mentioned in paragraph 2 (a) of this article.

Article 16

The provisions of this Convention concerning the settlement of disputes or complaints shall be applied without prejudice to other procedures for settling disputes or complaints in the field of discrimination laid down in the constituent instruments of, or conventions adopted by, the United Nations and its specialized agencies, and shall not prevent the States Parties from having recourse to other procedures for settling a dispute in accordance with general or special international agreements in force between them.

Civil and political rights
Human Rights Committee

International Covenant on Civil and Political Rights
Adopted and opened for signature, ratification and accession by General Assembly resolution A/RES/2200A (XXI) of 16 December 1966
Entry into force: 23 March 1976

Part I

Article 1

1   All peoples have the right of self-determination. By virtue of that right they freely determine their political status and freely pursue their economic, social and cultural development.
2   All peoples may, for their own ends, freely dispose of their natural wealth and resources without prejudice to any obligations arising out of international economic co-operation, based upon the principle of mutual benefit, and international law. In no case may a people be deprived of its own means of subsistence.
3   The States Parties to the present Covenant, including those having responsibility for the administration of Non-Self-Governing and Trust Territories, shall promote the realization of the right of self-determination, and shall respect that right, in conformity with the provisions of the Charter of the United Nations.

Part II

Article 2

1   Each State Party to the present Covenant undertakes to respect and to ensure to all individuals within its territory and subject to its jurisdiction the rights recognized in the present Covenant, without distinction of any kind, such as race, colour, sex, language, religion, political or other opinion, national or social origin, property, birth or other status.
2   Where not already provided for by existing legislative or other measures, each State Party to the present Covenant undertakes to take the necessary steps, in accordance with its constitutional processes and with the provisions of the present Covenant, to adopt such laws or other measures as may be necessary to give effect to the rights recognized in the present Covenant.
3   Each State Party to the present Covenant undertakes:

(a)   To ensure that any person whose rights or freedoms as herein recognized are violated shall have an effective remedy, notwithstanding that the violation has been committed by persons acting in an official capacity;
(b)   To ensure that any person claiming such a remedy shall have his right thereto determined by competent judicial, administrative or legislative authorities, or by any other competent authority provided for by the legal system of the State, and to develop the possibilities of judicial remedy;
(c)   To ensure that the competent authorities shall enforce such remedies when granted.

Article 3

The States Parties to the present Covenant undertake to ensure the equal right of men and women to the enjoyment of all civil and political rights set forth in the present Covenant.

Part IV

Article 28

1   There shall be established a Human Rights Committee (hereafter referred to in the present Covenant as the Committee). It shall consist of eighteen members and shall carry out the functions hereinafter provided.
2   The Committee shall be composed of nationals of the States Parties to the present Covenant who shall be persons of high moral character and recognized competence in the field of human rights, consideration being given to the usefulness of the participation of some persons having legal experience.
3   The members of the Committee shall be elected and shall serve in their personal capacity.

Article 29

1   The members of the Committee shall be elected by secret ballot from a list of persons possessing the qualifications prescribed in article 28 and nominated for the purpose by the States Parties to the present Covenant.
2   Each State Party to the present Covenant may nominate not more than two persons. These persons shall be nationals of the nominating State.
3   A person shall be eligible for renomination.

Article 30

1   The initial election shall be held no later than six months after the date of the entry into force of the present Covenant.
2   At least four months before the date of each election to the Committee, other than an election to fill a vacancy declared in accordance with article 34, the Secretary-General of the United Nations shall address a written invitation to the States Parties to the present Covenant to submit their nominations for membership of the Committee within three months.
3   The Secretary-General of the United Nations shall prepare a list in alphabetical order of all the persons thus nominated, with an indication of the States Parties which have nominated them, and shall submit it to the States Parties to the present Covenant no later than one month before the date of each election.
4   Elections of the members of the Committee shall be held at a meeting of the States Parties to the present Covenant convened by the Secretary-General of the United Nations at the Headquarters of the United Nations. At that meeting, for which two thirds of the States Parties to the present Covenant shall constitute a quorum, the persons elected to the Committee shall be those nominees who obtain the largest number of votes and an absolute majority of the votes of the representatives of States Parties present and voting.

Article 31

1 The Committee may not include more than one national of the same State.
2 In the election of the Committee, consideration shall be given to equitable geographical distribution of membership and to the representation of the different forms of civilization and of the principal legal systems.

Article 32

1 The members of the Committee shall be elected for a term of four years. They shall be eligible for re-election if renominated. However, the terms of nine of the members elected at the first election shall expire at the end of two years; immediately after the first election, the names of these nine members shall be chosen by lot by the Chairman of the meeting referred to in article 30, paragraph 4.
2 Elections at the expiry of office shall be held in accordance with the preceding articles of this part of the present Covenant.

Article 33

1 If, in the unanimous opinion of the other members, a member of the Committee has ceased to carry out his functions for any cause other than absence of a temporary character, the Chairman of the Committee shall notify the Secretary-General of the United Nations, who shall then declare the seat of that member to be vacant.
2 In the event of the death or the resignation of a member of the Committee, the Chairman shall immediately notify the Secretary-General of the United Nations, who shall declare the seat vacant from the date of death or the date on which the resignation takes effect.

Article 34

1 When a vacancy is declared in accordance with article 33 and if the term of office of the member to be replaced does not expire within six months of the declaration of the vacancy, the Secretary-General of the United Nations shall notify each of the States Parties to the present Covenant, which may within two months submit nominations in accordance with article 29 for the purpose of filling the vacancy.
2 The Secretary-General of the United Nations shall prepare a list in alphabetical order of the persons thus nominated and shall submit it to the States Parties to the present Covenant. The election to fill the vacancy shall then take place in accordance with the relevant provisions of this part of the present Covenant.
3 A member of the Committee elected to fill a vacancy declared in accordance with article 33 shall hold office for the remainder of the term of the member who vacated the seat on the Committee under the provisions of that article.

Article 35

The members of the Committee shall, with the approval of the General Assembly of the United Nations, receive emoluments from United Nations resources on such terms and conditions as the General Assembly may decide, having regard to the importance of the Committee's responsibilities.

Article 36

The Secretary-General of the United Nations shall provide the necessary staff and facilities for the effective performance of the functions of the Committee under the present Covenant.

Article 37

1   The Secretary-General of the United Nations shall convene the initial meeting of the Committee at the Headquarters of the United Nations.
2   After its initial meeting, the Committee shall meet at such times as shall be provided in its rules of procedure.
3   The Committee shall normally meet at the Headquarters of the United Nations or at the United Nations Office at Geneva.

Article 38

Every member of the Committee shall, before taking up his duties, make a solemn declaration in open committee that he will perform his functions impartially and conscientiously.

Article 39

1   The Committee shall elect its officers for a term of two years. They may be re-elected.
2   The Committee shall establish its own rules of procedure, but these rules shall provide, inter alia, that:

    (a)   Twelve members shall constitute a quorum;
    (b)   Decisions of the Committee shall be made by a majority vote of the members present.

Article 40

1   The States Parties to the present Covenant undertake to submit reports on the measures they have adopted which give effect to the rights recognized herein and on the progress made in the enjoyment of those rights:

    (a)   Within one year of the entry into force of the present Covenant for the States Parties concerned;
    (b)   Thereafter whenever the Committee so requests.

2   All reports shall be submitted to the Secretary-General of the United Nations, who shall transmit them to the Committee for consideration. Reports shall indicate the factors and difficulties, if any, affecting the implementation of the present Covenant.
3   The Secretary-General of the United Nations may, after consultation with the Committee, transmit to the specialized agencies concerned copies of such parts of the reports as may fall within their field of competence.
4   The Committee shall study the reports submitted by the States Parties to the present Covenant. It shall transmit its reports, and such general comments as it may consider appropriate, to the States Parties. The Committee may also transmit to the Economic and Social Council these comments along with the copies of the reports it has received from States Parties to the present Covenant.

5   The States Parties to the present Covenant may submit to the Committee observations on any comments that may be made in accordance with paragraph 4 of this article.

Article 41

1   A State Party to the present Covenant may at any time declare under this article that it recognizes the competence of the Committee to receive and consider communications to the effect that a State Party claims that another State Party is not fulfilling its obligations under the present Covenant. Communications under this article may be received and considered only if submitted by a State Party which has made a declaration recognizing in regard to itself the competence of the Committee. No communication shall be received by the Committee if it concerns a State Party which has not made such a declaration. Communications received under this article shall be dealt with in accordance with the following procedure:

(a) If a State Party to the present Covenant considers that another State Party is not giving effect to the provisions of the present Covenant, it may, by written communication, bring the matter to the attention of that State Party. Within three months after the receipt of the communication the receiving State shall afford the State which sent the communication an explanation, or any other statement in writing clarifying the matter which should include, to the extent possible and pertinent, reference to domestic procedures and remedies taken, pending, or available in the matter;

(b) If the matter is not adjusted to the satisfaction of both States Parties concerned within six months after the receipt by the receiving State of the initial communication, either State shall have the right to refer the matter to the Committee, by notice given to the Committee and to the other State;

(c) The Committee shall deal with a matter referred to it only after it has ascertained that all available domestic remedies have been invoked and exhausted in the matter, in conformity with the generally recognized principles of international law. This shall not be the rule where the application of the remedies is unreasonably prolonged;

(d) The Committee shall hold closed meetings when examining communications under this article;

(e) Subject to the provisions of subparagraph (c), the Committee shall make available its good offices to the States Parties concerned with a view to a friendly solution of the matter on the basis of respect for human rights and fundamental freedoms as recognized in the present Covenant;

(f) In any matter referred to it, the Committee may call upon the States Parties concerned, referred to in subparagraph (b), to supply any relevant information;

(g) The States Parties concerned, referred to in subparagraph (b), shall have the right to be represented when the matter is being considered in the Committee and to make submissions orally and/or in writing;

(h) The Committee shall, within twelve months after the date of receipt of notice under subparagraph (b), submit a report:

(i)   If a solution within the terms of subparagraph (e) is reached, the Committee shall confine its report to a brief statement of the facts and of the solution reached;

      (ii) If a solution within the terms of subparagraph (e) is not reached, the Committee shall confine its report to a brief statement of the facts; the written submissions and record of the oral submissions made by the States Parties concerned shall be attached to the report. In every matter, the report shall be communicated to the States Parties concerned.

2   The provisions of this article shall come into force when ten States Parties to the present Covenant have made declarations under paragraph I of this article. Such declarations shall be deposited by the States Parties with the Secretary-General of the United Nations, who shall transmit copies thereof to the other States Parties. A declaration may be withdrawn at any time by notification to the Secretary-General. Such a withdrawal shall not prejudice the consideration of any matter which is the subject of a communication already transmitted under this article; no further communication by any State Party shall be received after the notification of withdrawal of the declaration has been received by the Secretary-General, unless the State Party concerned has made a new declaration.

Article 42

1   (a) If a matter referred to the Committee in accordance with article 41 is not resolved to the satisfaction of the States Parties concerned, the Committee may, with the prior consent of the States Parties concerned, appoint an ad hoc Conciliation Commission (hereinafter referred to as the Commission). The good offices of the Commission shall be made available to the States Parties concerned with a view to an amicable solution of the matter on the basis of respect for the present Covenant;
(b) The Commission shall consist of five persons acceptable to the States Parties concerned. If the States Parties concerned fail to reach agreement within three months on all or part of the composition of the Commission, the members of the Commission concerning whom no agreement has been reached shall be elected by secret ballot by a two-thirds majority vote of the Committee from among its members.

2   The members of the Commission shall serve in their personal capacity. They shall not be nationals of the States Parties concerned, or of a State not Party to the present Covenant, or of a State Party which has not made a declaration under article 41.

3   The Commission shall elect its own Chairman and adopt its own rules of procedure.

4   The meetings of the Commission shall normally be held at the Headquarters of the United Nations or at the United Nations Office at Geneva. However, they may be held at such other convenient places as the Commission may determine in consultation with the Secretary-General of the United Nations and the States Parties concerned.

5   The secretariat provided in accordance with article 36 shall also service the commissions appointed under this article.

6   The information received and collated by the Committee shall be made available to the Commission and the Commission may call upon the States Parties concerned to supply any other relevant information.

7   When the Commission has fully considered the matter, but in any event not later than twelve months after having been seized of the matter, it shall submit to the Chairman of the Committee a report for communication to the States Parties concerned:

      (a) If the Commission is unable to complete its consideration of the matter within twelve months, it shall confine its report to a brief statement of the status of its consideration of the matter;

(b)   If an amicable solution to the matter on the basis of respect for human rights as recognized in the present Covenant is reached, the Commission shall confine its report to a brief statement of the facts and of the solution reached;

(c)   If a solution within the terms of subparagraph (b) is not reached, the Commission's report shall embody its findings on all questions of fact relevant to the issues between the States Parties concerned, and its views on the possibilities of an amicable solution of the matter. This report shall also contain the written submissions and a record of the oral submissions made by the States Parties concerned;

(d)   If the Commission's report is submitted under subparagraph (c), the States Parties concerned shall, within three months of the receipt of the report, notify the Chairman of the Committee whether or not they accept the contents of the report of the Commission.

8   The provisions of this article are without prejudice to the responsibilities of the Committee under article 41.

9   The States Parties concerned shall share equally all the expenses of the members of the Commission in accordance with estimates to be provided by the Secretary-General of the United Nations.

10   The Secretary-General of the United Nations shall be empowered to pay the expenses of the members of the Commission, if necessary, before reimbursement by the States Parties concerned, in accordance with paragraph 9 of this article.

Article 43

The members of the Committee, and of the ad hoc conciliation commissions which may be appointed under article 42, shall be entitled to the facilities, privileges and immunities of experts on mission for the United Nations as laid down in the relevant sections of the Convention on the Privileges and Immunities of the United Nations.

Article 44

The provisions for the implementation of the present Covenant shall apply without prejudice to the procedures prescribed in the field of human rights by or under the constituent instruments and the conventions of the United Nations and of the specialized agencies and shall not prevent the States Parties to the present Covenant from having recourse to other procedures for settling a dispute in accordance with general or special international agreements in force between them.

Article 45

The Committee shall submit to the General Assembly of the United Nations, through the Economic and Social Council, an annual report on its activities.

European Court of Human Rights
Convention for the Protection of Human Rights and Fundamental Freedoms
(European Convention on Human Rights) of 4 November 1950 as amended by Protocols
Nos. 11 and 14. Entry into force: 3 September 1953

Section II – European Court of Human Rights

Article 19 – Establishment of the Court

To ensure the observance of the engagements undertaken by the High Contracting Parties in the Convention and the Protocols thereto, there shall be set up a European Court of Human Rights, hereinafter referred to as "the Court". It shall function on a permanent basis.

Article 20 – Number of judges

The Court shall consist of a number of judges equal to that of the High Contracting Parties.

Article 21 – Criteria for office

1   The judges shall be of high moral character and must either possess the qualifications required for appointment to high judicial office or be jurisconsults of recognised competence.
2   The judges shall sit on the Court in their individual capacity.
3   During their term of office the judges shall not engage in any activity which is incompatible with their independence, impartiality or with the demands of a full-time office; all questions arising from the application of this paragraph shall be decided by the Court.

Article 22 – Election of judges

The judges shall be elected by the Parliamentary Assembly with respect to each High Contracting Party by a majority of votes cast from a list of three candidates nominated by the High Contracting Party.

Article 23 – Terms of office and dismissal

1   The judges shall be elected for a period of nine years. They may not be re-elected.
2   The terms of office of judges shall expire when they reach the age of 70.
3   The judges shall hold office until replaced. They shall, however, continue to deal with such cases as they already have under consideration.
4   No judge may be dismissed from office unless the other judges decide by a majority of two-thirds that that judge has ceased to fulfil the required conditions.

Article 24 – Registry and rapporteurs

1   The Court shall have a registry, the functions and organisation of which shall be laid down in the rules of the Court.
2   When sitting in a single-judge formation, the Court shall be assisted by rapporteurs who shall function under the authority of the President of the Court. They shall form part of the Court's registry.

Article 25 – Plenary Court

The plenary Court shall

a)   elect its President and one or two Vice-Presidents for a period of three years; they may be re-elected;

b)   set up Chambers, constituted for a fixed period of time;

c)   elect the Presidents of the Chambers of the Court; they may be re-elected;

d)   adopt the rules of the Court;

e)   elect the Registrar and one or more Deputy Registrars;

f)   make any request under Article 26, paragraph 2.

Article 26 – Single-judge formation, committees, Chambers and Grand Chamber

1   To consider cases brought before it, the Court shall sit in a single-judge formation, in committees of three judges, in Chambers of seven judges and in a Grand Chamber of seventeen judges. The Court's Chambers shall set up committees for a fixed period of time.

2   At the request of the plenary Court, the Committee of Ministers may, by a unanimous decision and for a fixed period, reduce to five the number of judges of the Chambers.

3   When sitting as a single judge, a judge shall not examine any application against the High Contracting Party in respect of which that judge has been elected.

4   There shall sit as an ex officio member of the Chamber and the Grand Chamber the judge elected in respect of the High Contracting Party concerned. If there is none or if that judge is unable to sit, a person chosen by the President of the Court from a list submitted in advance by that Party shall sit in the capacity of judge.

5   The Grand Chamber shall also include the President of the Court, the Vice-Presidents, the Presidents of the Chambers and other judges chosen in accordance with the rules of the Court. When a case is referred to the Grand Chamber under Article 43, no judge from the Chamber which rendered the judgment shall sit in the Grand Chamber, with the exception of the President of the Chamber and the judge who sat in respect of the High Contracting Party concerned.

Article 27 – Competence of single judges

1   A single judge may declare inadmissible or strike out of the Court's list of cases an application submitted under Article 34, where such a decision can be taken without further examination.

2   The decision shall be final.

3   If the single judge does not declare an application inadmissible or strike it out, that judge shall forward it to a committee or to a Chamber for further examination.

Article 28 – Competence of committees

1   In respect of an application submitted under Article 34, a committee may, by a unanimous vote,

a)   declare it inadmissible or strike it out of its list of cases, where such decision can be taken without further examination; or

b)   declare it admissible and render at the same time a judgment on the merits, if the underlying question in the case, concerning the interpretation or the application of the Convention or the Protocols thereto, is already the subject of well-established case-law of the Court.

2   Decisions and judgments under paragraph 1 shall be final.

3   If the judge elected in respect of the High Contracting Party concerned is not a member of the committee, the committee may at any stage of the proceedings invite that judge to take the place of one of the members of the committee, having regard to all relevant factors, including whether that Party has contested the application of the procedure under paragraph 1.b.

Article 29 – Decisions by Chambers on admissibility and merits

1   If no decision is taken under Article 27 or 28, or no judgment rendered under Article 28, a Chamber shall decide on the admissibility and merits of individual applications submitted under Article 34. The decision on admissibility may be taken separately.
2   A Chamber shall decide on the admissibility and merits of inter-State applications submitted under Article 33. The decision on admissibility shall be taken separately unless the Court, in exceptional cases, decides otherwise.

Article 30 – Relinquishment of jurisdiction to the Grand Chamber

Where a case pending before a Chamber raises a serious question affecting the interpretation of the Convention or the protocols thereto, or where the resolution of a question before the Chamber might have a result inconsistent with a judgment previously delivered by the Court, the Chamber may, at any time before it has rendered its judgment, relinquish jurisdiction in favour of the Grand Chamber, unless one of the parties to the case objects.

Article 31 – Powers of the Grand Chamber

The Grand Chamber shall:

a)   determine applications submitted either under Article 33 or Article 34 when a Chamber has relinquished jurisdiction under Article 30 or when the case has been referred to it under Article 43;
b)   decide on issues referred to the Court by the Committee of Ministers in accordance with Article 46, paragraph 4; and
c)   consider requests for advisory opinions submitted under Article 47.

Article 32 – Jurisdiction of the Court

1   The jurisdiction of the Court shall extend to all matters concerning the interpretation and application of the Convention and the protocols thereto which are referred to it as provided in Articles 33, 34, 46 and 47.
2   In the event of dispute as to whether the Court has jurisdiction, the Court shall decide.

Article 33 – Inter-State cases

Any High Contracting Party may refer to the Court any alleged breach of the provisions of the Convention and the protocols thereto by another High Contracting Party.

Article 34 – Individual applications

The Court may receive applications from any person, non-governmental organisation or group of individuals claiming to be the victim of a violation by one of the High Contracting Parties of the rights set forth in the Convention or the protocols thereto. The High Contracting Parties undertake not to hinder in any way the effective exercise of this right.

Article 35 – Admissibility criteria

1   The Court may only deal with the matter after all domestic remedies have been exhausted, according to the generally recognised rules of international law, and within a period of six months from the date on which the final decision was taken.

2   The Court shall not deal with any application submitted under Article 34 that

   a)   is anonymous; or
   b)   is substantially the same as a matter that has already been examined by the Court or has already been submitted to another procedure of international investigation or settlement and contains no relevant new information.

3   The Court shall declare inadmissible any individual application submitted under Article 34 if it considers that:

   a)   the application is incompatible with the provisions of the Convention or the Protocols thereto, manifestly ill-founded, or an abuse of the right of individual application; or
   b)   the applicant has not suffered a significant disadvantage, unless respect for human rights as defined in the Convention and the Protocols thereto requires an examination of the application on the merits and provided that no case may be rejected on this ground which has not been duly considered by a domestic tribunal.

4   The Court shall reject any application which it considers inadmissible under this Article. It may do so at any stage of the proceedings.

Article 36 – Third party intervention

1   In all cases before a Chamber or the Grand Chamber, a High Contracting Party one of whose nationals is an applicant shall have the right to submit written comments and to take part in hearings.

2   The President of the Court may, in the interest of the proper administration of justice, invite any High Contracting Party which is not a party to the proceedings or any person concerned who is not the applicant to submit written comments or take part in hearings.

3   In all cases before a Chamber or the Grand Chamber, the Council of Europe Commissioner for Human Rights may submit written comments and take part in hearings.

Article 37 – Striking out applications

1   The Court may at any stage of the proceedings decide to strike an application out of its list of cases where the circumstances lead to the conclusion that:

   a)   the applicant does not intend to pursue his application; or

b) the matter has been resolved; or
c) for any other reason established by the Court, it is no longer justified to continue the examination of the application.

However, the Court shall continue the examination of the application if respect for human rights as defined in the Convention and the protocols thereto so requires.

2   The Court may decide to restore an application to its list of cases if it considers that the circumstances justify such a course.

Article 38 – Examination of the case

The Court shall examine the case together with the representatives of the parties and, if need be, undertake an investigation, for the effective conduct of which the High Contracting Parties concerned shall furnish all necessary facilities.

Article 39 – Friendly settlements

1   At any stage of the proceedings, the Court may place itself at the disposal of the parties concerned with a view to securing a friendly settlement of the matter on the basis of respect for human rights as defined in the Convention and the Protocols thereto.
2   Proceedings conducted under paragraph 1 shall be confidential.
3   If a friendly settlement is effected, the Court shall strike the case out of its list by means of a decision which shall be confined to a brief statement of the facts and of the solution reached.
4   This decision shall be transmitted to the Committee of Ministers, which shall supervise the execution of the terms of the friendly settlement as set out in the decision.

Article 40 – Public hearings and access to documents

1   Hearings shall be in public unless the Court in exceptional circumstances decides otherwise.
2   Documents deposited with the Registrar shall be accessible to the public unless the President of the Court decides otherwise.

Article 41 – Just satisfaction

If the Court finds that there has been a violation of the Convention or the protocols thereto, and if the internal law of the High Contracting Party concerned allows only partial reparation to be made, the Court shall, if necessary, afford just satisfaction to the injured party.

Article 42 – Judgments of Chambers

Judgments of Chambers shall become final in accordance with the provisions of Article 44, paragraph 2.

Article 43 – Referral to the Grand Chamber

1   Within a period of three months from the date of the judgment of the Chamber, any party to the case may, in exceptional cases, request that the case be referred to the Grand Chamber.

2   A panel of five judges of the Grand Chamber shall accept the request if the case raises a serious question affecting the interpretation or application of the Convention or the protocols thereto, or a serious issue of general importance.
3   If the panel accepts the request, the Grand Chamber shall decide the case by means of a judgment.

Article 44 – Final judgments

1   The judgment of the Grand Chamber shall be final.
2   The judgment of a Chamber shall become final:

   a)   when the parties declare that they will not request that the case be referred to the Grand Chamber; or
   b)   three months after the date of the judgment, if reference of the case to the Grand Chamber has not been requested; or
   c)   when the panel of the Grand Chamber rejects the request to refer under Article 43.

3   The final judgment shall be published.

Article 45 – Reasons for judgments and decisions

1   Reasons shall be given for judgments as well as for decisions declaring applications admissible or inadmissible.
2   If a judgment does not represent, in whole or in part, the unanimous opinion of the judges, any judge shall be entitled to deliver a separate opinion.

Article 46 – Binding force and execution of judgments

1   The High Contracting Parties undertake to abide by the final judgment of the Court in any case to which they are parties.
2   The final judgment of the Court shall be transmitted to the Committee of Ministers, which shall supervise its execution.
3   If the Committee of Ministers considers that the supervision of the execution of a final judgment is hindered by a problem of interpretation of the judgment, it may refer the matter to the Court for a ruling on the question of interpretation. A referral decision shall require a majority vote of two thirds of the representatives entitled to sit on the Committee.
4   If the Committee of Ministers considers that a High Contracting Party refuses to abide by a final judgment in a case to which it is a party, it may, after serving formal notice on that Party and by decision adopted by a majority vote of two thirds of the representatives entitled to sit on the Committee, refer to the Court the question whether that Party has failed to fulfil its obligation under paragraph 1.
5   If the Court finds a violation of paragraph 1, it shall refer the case to the Committee of Ministers for consideration of the measures to be taken. If the Court finds no violation of paragraph 1, it shall refer the case to the Committee of Ministers, which shall close its examination of the case.

Article 47 – Advisory opinions

1   The Court may, at the request of the Committee of Ministers, give advisory opinions on legal questions concerning the interpretation of the Convention and the protocols thereto.
2   Such opinions shall not deal with any question relating to the content or scope of the rights or freedoms defined in Section I of the Convention and the protocols thereto, or with any other question which the Court or the Committee of Ministers might have to consider in consequence of any such proceedings as could be instituted in accordance with the Convention.
3   Decisions of the Committee of Ministers to request an advisory opinion of the Court shall require a majority vote of the representatives entitled to sit on the Committee.

Article 48 – Advisory jurisdiction of the Court

The Court shall decide whether a request for an advisory opinion submitted by the Committee of Ministers is within its competence as defined in Article 47.

Article 49 – Reasons for advisory opinions

1   Reasons shall be given for advisory opinions of the Court.
2   If the advisory opinion does not represent, in whole or in part, the unanimous opinion of the judges, any judge shall be entitled to deliver a separate opinion.
3   Advisory opinions of the Court shall be communicated to the Committee of Ministers.

Article 50 – Expenditure on the Court

The expenditure on the Court shall be borne by the Council of Europe.

Article 51 – Privileges and immunities of judges

The judges shall be entitled, during the exercise of their functions, to the privileges and immunities provided for in Article 40 of the Statute of the Council of Europe and in the agreements made thereunder.

CHAPTER 9

Responsibility in international law

DOI: 10.4324/9781003213772-9

THE GENERAL CONCEPT OF RESPONSIBILITY

> existence of an international legal norm
> existence of a breach of an international obligation
> act or omission
> injury
> force majeure
> legal consequences of an internationally wrongful act or omission
> full reparation
> injured subject
> serious breach of an obligation arising under a peremptory norm
> international community as a whole
> absolute liability

Introductory remark

All general rules and principles defined in this section and introduced initially in terms of state responsibility now exist as applicable rules for other subjects of international law as well.

The subjects of the international responsibility system

The subjects of the international responsibility system are the subjects of international law. Every subject's responsibility shall be measured within the limits of its subjectivity. Since states possess universal subjectivity under international law, accordingly, their responsibility may not be limited. The other subject's responsibility is derived from their limited international subjectivity.

The essential preconditions of responsibility in international law

The essential preconditions of responsibility in international law are:

1   the **existence of an international legal norm** and derived obligation;

2   the **existence of a breach of an international obligation**;
3   the existence of an **act or omission** imputable to the subject responsible; and
4   the **injury** which resulted from this act or omission.

The existence of an international legal norm establishing an obligation

The existence of the legal norms is the first and crucial precondition for international responsibility. There should be an international legal norm in any form of the sources of international law which provides the subject or subjects with the specific obligation.

The existence of a breach of an international obligation

The subject, through its act or omission, violates the specific obligation derived from the particular norm of law. That is, when an act or omission by a subject is in breach of the requirements set forth by its own obligation(s), the act or omission is wrongful.

There are two different categories of breach of an international obligation:

- A breach not having a continuing character, which occurs at the moment when the act or omission is performed, even if its effects continue later on; and
- A breach having a continuing character, which extends over the entire period of time during which the act or omission continues and remains out of conformity with the obligation.

Force majeure

At the same time, not every formal violation of an international norm turns on the engine of the international responsibility system. For instance, generally, the wrongfulness of an act or omission is precluded if the act is due to **force majeure**: that is, the occurrence of an irresistible force or an unforeseen event, beyond the control of the subject, making it materially impossible in such circumstances to perform that very obligation.

Attribution of conduct to a subject

The wrongful act or omission of a subject of international law happens when an act or omission is committed by a representative person (either a physical person or entity) which can be imputable to a responsible subject (attribution of conduct to a subject).

The conduct of a person or entity shall be considered an act of a subject if the person or entity exercise the elements of the representative authority or if they are in fact acting on the instructions of, or under the direction or control of, that subject in carrying out the conduct.

In addition, the conduct shall be considered an act or omission of that subject if the subject acknowledges and adopts the conduct as its own.

Injury

The nature of an injury can either be determined in broad terms or conceived more narrowly as a material loss or damage. Based on the first understanding, every violation of an obligation may affect the injury – be it material, political, or moral. Under international law, injury includes any damage, whether material, political, or moral, caused by the internationally wrongful act.

Legal consequences of an internationally wrongful act or omission

The international responsibility system provides **legal consequences of an internationally wrongful act or omission**.

Under the legal consequences of an internationally wrongful act are the following obligations of the subject responsible for the internationally wrongful act:

- to cease that act (if it is continuing);
- to offer appropriate assurances and guarantees of non-repetition (if circumstances so require); and
- to make full reparation for the injury caused by the internationally wrongful act. Injury includes any damage, whether material, political, or moral.

The legal consequences of an internationally wrongful act under international responsibility do not affect the continued general duty of the responsible subject to perform the obligation breached.

If the internationally wrongful act constitutes a **serious breach of an obligation arising under a peremptory norm** of general international law by a subject of international law, the breach may result in further legal consequences for those responsible, as well as the injured and other subjects. Notably, the subjects in such cases shall co-operate to put an end to the wrongful act, not recognise a situation as lawful which stems out of the breach, and not assist the subject which bears the responsibility for wrongdoing to enjoy the benefits of maintaining the situation it is responsible for creating.

The key to the international legal responsibility engine

The key to the international legal responsibility engine is mostly in the hands of the **injured subject**, who can switch on the engine to achieve the result in terms of legal consequences. This injured subject can initiate the process and select the forms of response to the wrongful act or omission. Where the same internationally wrongful act injures several subjects, each injured subject may separately invoke the responsibility of the subject which has committed the internationally wrongful act.

Nevertheless, in those cases when the **international community as a whole** is regarded as the addressee of a particular wrongful act or omission, the key to the international legal responsibility moves to the international community despite the position of the particularly affected (injured) subject/subjects: for example, in the fields of international peace and security, international criminal law, and so on.

Absolute liability

In international law, there exists a principle of **absolute liability** in the fields where risk is qualitatively higher (e.g. nuclear technologies, space programs, and so forth), and there is a high probability that an injury will occur which is not induced by the breach of any legal obligation but is caused by the conduct of that subject. In these cases, the subject of international law nevertheless finds itself placed in the international responsibility system and is liable for reparation regardless of any fault on its part.[743]

As described in the *Explanatory Texts* issued by the International Atomic Energy Agency (concerning the nuclear liability regime):

> There is a long established tradition of legislative action or judicial interpretation that a presumption of liability for hazards created arises when a person engages in a dangerous activity. Owing to the special dangers involved in the activities within the scope of the Conventions and the difficulty of establishing negligence in particular cases, this presumption has been adopted for nuclear liability. Strict liability is therefore the rule; liability results from the risk, irrespective of fault.[744]

STATE RESPONSIBILITY

Draft Articles on Responsibility of States for Internationally Wrongful Acts
content of the international responsibility
circumstances precluding wrongfulness
implementation of the international responsibility

Introductory remark

Generally, the rights accorded to states imply responsibilities.

---

743 For example, under Paragraph 1 of Article IV of the Vienna Convention on Civil Liability for Nuclear Damage of 21 May 1963: 'The liability of the operator for nuclear damage under this Convention shall be absolute.' Accordingly, '[u]nder this principle, which greatly facilitates the bringing of claims on behalf of the victims of a nuclear incident, the operator of the nuclear installation is liable for compensation regardless of any fault on his part; the claimant is only required to prove the relationship of cause and effect between the nuclear incident and the damage for which compensation is sought, and the operator cannot escape liability by proving diligence on his part (Articles II and IV).' *The 1997 Vienna Convention on Civil Liability for Nuclear Damage and the 1997 Convention on Supplementary Compensation for Nuclear Damage: Explanatory Texts*, IAEA International Law Series No. 3 (International Atomic Energy Agency 2007) 9.

744 ibid 1.

Draft Articles on Responsibility of States for Internationally Wrongful Acts

As mentioned earlier, in 2001 the International Law Commission adopted **Draft Articles on Responsibility of States for Internationally Wrongful Acts** at its 53rd session and submitted this document to the General Assembly as a part of the Commission's report covering the work of that session.[745]

The Draft Articles as a general legal framework for the state responsibility system

This document amasses all rules and principles discussed in the previous section in order to establish the general framework for the state responsibility system. At the same time, it provides the interstate system with norms on the:

- **content of the international responsibility** of a state;
- **circumstances precluding wrongfulness**; and
- **implementation of the international responsibility** of a state.

Attribution of conduct to a state

> attributable to the state
> governmental authority
> elements of the governmental authority
> under the direction or control of the state

Preliminary remark

States are liable for breaches of their obligations if the breach is **attributable to the state** itself.

State organs

Every state is liable for breaches committed by its organs exercising **governmental authority**. (The term 'organ' in this context includes any person or entity having such a status in accordance with the national law of a state.) That is, 'whether the organ exercises legislative, executive, judicial or any other functions, whatever position it holds in the

---

745 As stated earlier (n 155), the text of the Draft Articles was annexed to the UN General Assembly Resolution A/RES/56/83 of 12 December 2001 (Annex – Responsibility of States for internationally wrongful acts).

organization of the State, and whatever its character as an organ of the central Government or of a territorial unit of the State.'[746]

Persons or entities exercising the elements of the governmental authority

If a person or entity is not an organ of the state but the domestic law of that state allows that person or entity to exercise **elements of the governmental authority**, an act or omission by that person or entity may also be considered an act of the state in particular instances.

This rule concerns the persons or entities which are empowered by the national legislation of a state to exercise functions of a public character that are usually exercised by state organs, if the conduct of the person or entity relates to the exercise of the governmental authority concerned.

Excess of authority or contravention of instructions

Moreover, the conduct of an organ, as well as an entity or person empowered to exercise elements of governmental authority, may be considered an act of the state if the organ, entity, or person acts in that capacity, even if it exceeds its authority or contravenes instructions.[747]

Other cases

In addition, conduct is attributable to a state if it is performed by person or entity acting **under the direction or control of the state**.

And finally, the state may, in any case, acknowledge conduct as its own, even if it was not committed by state organs or the persons or entities mentioned in this subsection.

Circumstances precluding wrongfulness

consent of counter state
self-defence
countermeasures
limits set for the countermeasures
force majeure
distress
necessity

746 Article 4 (1) of the Draft Articles on Responsibility of States for Internationally Wrongful Acts.
747 Article 7 of the Draft Articles on Responsibility of States for Internationally Wrongful Acts.

Introductory remark

There are certain circumstances which preclude wrongfulness, even if the subject, through its act or omission, formally violates a specific obligation derived from a particular norm of international law.

Consent of counter state

Consent by a state to the commission of a given act by another state (**consent of counter state**) precludes the wrongfulness of that act in relation to that state.

Self-defence

The wrongfulness of an act is precluded if it represents a lawful measure of **self-defence** under the Charter of the United Nations.

Countermeasures in respect of an internationally wrongful act

The wrongfulness of an act is precluded if and to the extent that an injured state retaliates with the countermeasures taken against a state which is responsible for an internationally wrongful act (**countermeasures in respect of an internationally wrongful act**) and only if they are taken under the **limits set for the countermeasures**.

Force majeure

Regarding **force majeure**, there are certain limits defined under international law. Namely, the wrongfulness of an act of a state which is not in conformity with an international obligation is not precluded if (1) 'the situation of force majeure is due, either alone or in combination with other factors, to the conduct of the state invoking it' or (2) the state 'has [previously] assumed the risk of that situation occurring'.[748]

Distress

Generally, the wrongfulness of an act is precluded 'if the author of the act in question has no other reasonable way, in a situation of distress, of saving the author's life or the lives of other persons entrusted to the author's care.'[749] In turn, there are certain limits to invoking the grounds of **distress** by a state in international law. For example, it cannot be invoked if 'the situation of distress is due, either alone or in combination with other factors, to the conduct of the State invoking it.'

---

748 Article 23 of the Draft Articles on Responsibility of States for Internationally Wrongful Acts.
749 Article 24 of the Draft Articles on Responsibility of States for Internationally Wrongful Acts.

Necessity

The grounds of **necessity** as a circumstance precluding the wrongfulness of an act may be invoked if:

- it 'is the only way for the State to safeguard an essential interest against a grave and imminent peril';
- it 'does not seriously impair an essential interest of the State or States towards which the obligation exists, or of the international community as a whole'; and
- the state invoking this ground has not contributed to the situation of necessity.[750]

Content of the international responsibility of a state

deterrence function

reparation

forms of material responsibility

satisfaction

form of moral responsibility

enforcement

forms of political responsibility

injury in static

injury in dynamic

Chorzów Factory case

restitution

compensation

legal restitution

substitution

sanctions

reprisals

countermeasures

retorsions

pacific reprisals

belligerent reprisals

Naulila dispute

The horizontal arrangement model

The nature of the international responsibility of a state is stipulated due to the specifics of interstate relations and the horizontal arrangement model of the interstate system, which in

750 Article 25 of the Draft Articles on Responsibility of States for Internationally Wrongful Acts.

this regard means that international responsibility can be organised only through the horizontal arrangement model. The horizontal model is a basis for any rights, either of the injured state (states) or the representatives speaking on behalf of the international community as a whole.

Purposes of international responsibility

There are three primary purposes which the international responsibility system aims to fulfil. At the same time, each of them involves a **deterrence function** restraining a state from breach of the international legal obligation:

1   Reparation – which takes the **forms of material responsibility**;
2   Satisfaction – which takes the **form of moral responsibility**; and
3   Enforcement – which takes the **forms of political responsibility**.

Reparation

Reparation targets the material injury caused by an internationally wrongful act committed by a state. It may be invoked if the internationally wrongful act results in material loss or damage.

The twofold nature of material injury

Material injury may be considered in two terms – either as static damage (**injury in static**) or as any financially assessable damage, including loss of profits insofar as it is established (**injury in dynamic**).

In this context, the **Chorzów Factory** case (*Germany v Poland*) should be outlined. This was a case heard before the Permanent Court of International Justice. Under its Judgment, the Court articulated several essential principles in the field of the international responsibility of states.[751]

For example, on the principle of international responsibility, 'the Court observes that it is a principle of international law, and even a general conception of law, that any breach of an engagement involves an obligation to make reparation'. About the content of the reparation:

> The essential principle contained in the actual notion of an illegal act – a principle which seems to be established by international practice and in particular by the decisions of arbitral tribunals – is that reparation must, as far as possible, wipe-out all the consequences of the illegal act and re-establish the situation which would, in, all probability, have existed if that act had not been committed.

On the nature of restitution and compensation:

> Restitution in kind, or, if this is not possible, payment of a sum corresponding to the value which a restitution in kind would bear; the award, if need be, of damages for loss sustained which would not be covered by restitution in kind or payment in place of it – such are the principles which should serve to determine the amount of compensation due for an act contrary to international law.

751 *Chorzów Factory (Germany v Poland)*, Judgment No.13 of 13 September 1928, PCIJ Ser A – No. 17.

Moreover, concerning an injury, there is an obvious conclusion in the Dissenting Opinion by M. Ehrlich that the loss shall be calculated on the grounds of a corresponding interest which, in its turn, depends on what kind of an interest was held by the injured subject before the wrongful act was committed.[752]

Therefore, generally, the injury:

* may not include loss of profits – for example in case of the destruction of a house which was only owned by the person and where there is no additional corresponding interest (injury in static); and
* may also include loss of profits – for example in case of the destruction of a house which was owned by the person and, at the same time, an additional corresponding interest in favour of that person existed (for example, if the house was rented or leased) (injury in dynamic).

Meanwhile, the forms of material responsibility are:

* **restitution**; and
* **compensation**.

Restitution

Restitution is the re-establishment of the situation (legal right) which existed before the wrongful act was committed. It is the initial form of material responsibility; it shall be invoked by the injured state at first. The object of material restitution can be the restoration of the damaged property, the return of illegally seized or illegally detained property, and so on.

In litigation and arbitration practice, the term '**legal restitution**' is also often used. This type of restitution requires or involves a change in the legal situation, which is delivered by the changes in the national legislation or international obligations (towards third parties) of the responsible state, resulting in the modifications of its legal relations with the injured state. Cases of this type include recall, cancellation or amendment of a legislative provision or international obligation, and cancellation or revision of an administrative or judicial measure(s) taken against a person or a property, if such conduct was adopted in violation of an international legal obligation before the injured state.

In some cases, both material and legal restitution can be applied, provided there is at hand a material loss which was conditioned by the changes in the national legislation or international obligations (towards third parties) mentioned earlier. At the same time, such changes may stipulate not only material injury. Hence, in principle, 'legal restitution' cannot be limited within the bounds of the material responsibility system.

---

752 'The loss caused to any given person can only be *quantum ejus interest*. If two persons have different rights over a piece of land, one being the owner, and the other being owner of land in favour of which a servitude over the land has been established, the reparation due to each of these persons will be represented by the value of his right, excluding the value of the rights of the other person. . . . On the other hand, the reparation of the loss caused, for instance, by the destruction of a house – whether the person concerned be owner, tenant, or owner of a property in favour of which a servitude exists – would only cover the value of the rights of the particular person, excluding the rights of every other person.' *Chorzów Factory (Germany v Poland)*, Judgment No.13 of 13 September 1928, PCIJ Ser A – No. 17, Dissenting Opinion by M. Ehrlich.

Compensation

Compensation is the secondary form of reparation. The state responsible for an internationally wrongful act is obliged to compensate for the damage caused by such an act when such damage is not redressed by restitution: namely, when restitution is:

1   not materially possible; or
2   not sufficient and appropriate (e.g. loss of profits).

Consequently, in the first case, compensation is the only possible form of material responsibility, while in the second case, it may be applied as an additional form in combination with restitution.

The function of compensation is to address the actual losses incurred as a result of the internationally wrongful act. In other words, it is purely compensating a victim of a wrongful act.

Meanwhile, compensation typically consists of a monetary payment, but it may be carried out in any other means approved by the parties. Simultaneously, it may be provided in the form of **substitution**, as with the replacement of illegally destroyed or damaged property (buildings, vehicles, other property).

Satisfaction

Satisfaction is a form which aims to alleviate the moral injury (to honour and dignity of the injured state) caused by the internationally wrongful act.

The ILC acknowledged the priority of a particular type in favour of the forms of the material responsibility by developing the following rule: 'The State responsible for an internationally wrongful act is under an obligation to give satisfaction for the injury caused by that act insofar as it cannot be made good by restitution or compensation.'[753] At the same time, as articulated by the ILC in the Commentary to the relevant Article:

> Material and moral damage resulting from an internationally wrongful act will normally be financially assessable and hence covered by the remedy of compensation. Satisfaction, on the other hand, is the remedy for those injuries, not financially assessable, which amount to an affront to the State.

Examples of relevant internationally wrongful acts, among other things,

> include situations of insults to the symbols of the State, such as the national flag, violations of sovereignty or territorial integrity, attacks on ships or aircraft, ill-treatment of or deliberate attacks on heads of State or Government or diplomatic or consular representatives or other protected persons and violations of the premises of embassies or consulates or of the residences of members of the mission.[754]

Satisfaction may take the form of an acknowledgement of the breach, an expression of regret which may be given verbally or in writing by an appropriate official, assurances

753 Article 37 (1) of the Draft Articles on Responsibility of States for Internationally Wrongful Acts.
754 This list was demonstrated by the ILC in the Commentary to Article 37 of the Draft Articles on Responsibility of States for Internationally Wrongful Acts.

or guarantees of non-repetition, disciplinary or penal action against the individuals whose conduct caused the internationally wrongful act, honouring the flag of the injured state or performance of its anthem in an appropriate solemn atmosphere, an award of symbolic damages for non-pecuniary injury, and so on.

At the same time, satisfaction is not intended to be punitive in character. Thus, there are two limitations on the obligation to give satisfaction:

- the proportionality of satisfaction to the injury incurred; and
- the requirement that the satisfaction not be humiliating to the honour and dignity of a responsible state.

Political responsibility

The modes of political responsibility are also not intended as the forms of mere punishment for a wrongful conduct, but as the instruments for (1) achieving compliance with the obligations of the responsible state or (2) the enforcement of the reparation.

Such modes are named as forms of political responsibility while the responsible state violates the political rules of the interstate system, which conditions the political injury of another state or the international community as a whole. The most common forms of political responsibility are (1) **sanctions**, (2) **reprisals**, (3) **countermeasures**, and (4) **retorsions**. They are all counter-acts directed against the conduct of the responsible state; however, at the same time, the forms of political responsibility are significantly different from each other.

Sanctions

1 refers to the multilateral measures;
2 is implemented without violation of international law, primarily by the states or the international organisations, on the basis of authorisation obtained from the United Nations; and
3 is triggered by the wrongful conduct of the responsible state.

Reprisal

1 is a unilateral response;
2 is generally illegal; and
3 is stipulated by the wrongful conduct of the responsible state.

Retorsion

1 is a unilateral response;
2 does not violate international law; and
3 is usually taken in response to the unfriendly conduct of the responsible state.

Under Draft Articles on Responsibility of States for Internationally Wrongful Acts, the political responsibility is interlinked with the concept of countermeasures. The latter nowadays denotes non-forcible measures, which were formerly regarded as the **pacific reprisals** in peacetime: i.e. countermeasures to a large extent replaced the concept of reprisals in contemporary international law, and the term 'reprisals' now only depicts forcible measures.

Sanctions

Sanctions are enforcement measures applied to the responsible state. There appears to be a commonly shared understanding that the term refers to multilateral measures which are adopted by states or other subjects of international law after obtaining the appropriate authorisation from the United Nations or by the UN itself.

For instance, the basis for UN sanctions derives from Chapter VII of the UN Charter. Article 41 covers enforcement measures not involving the use of armed force. (The list is not exhaustive.)

> The Security Council may decide what measures not involving the use of armed force are to be employed to give effect to its decisions, and it may call upon the Members of the United Nations to apply such measures. These may include complete or partial interruption of economic relations and of rail, sea, air, postal, telegraphic, radio, and other means of communication, and the severance of diplomatic relations.

The amount or type of sanctions depends on the severity of the offence committed and the damage done. For example, according to Article 42:

> Should the Security Council consider that measures provided for in Article 41 would be inadequate or have proved to be inadequate, it may take such action by air, sea, or land forces as may be necessary to maintain or restore international peace and security. Such action may include demonstrations, blockade, and other operations by air, sea, or land forces of Members of the United Nations.

Finally, it is notable that sanctions as a form of enforcement must be applied only in the case of a wilful and significant violation of international law. The application of such sanctions in other cases cannot be considered legitimate.

Countermeasures

The ILC described countermeasures in the following way: 'In certain circumstances, the commission by one State of an internationally wrongful act may justify another State injured by that act in taking non-forcible countermeasures in order to procure its cessation and to achieve reparation for the injury.'[755] However, there are certain 'legal limits' to such countermeasures.

First of all, the countermeasures 'must be commensurate with the injury suffered, taking into account the gravity of the internationally wrongful act and the rights in question'.[756] (The countermeasures must be proportionate.)

---

755 Paragraph (1) of the Commentary to Article 22 of the Draft Articles on Responsibility of States for Internationally Wrongful Acts.
756 Article 51 of the Draft Articles on Responsibility of States for Internationally Wrongful Acts.

In addition, the countermeasures:

- shall be directed at the responsible state and not at third parties;
- shall be limited 'to procuring cessation of and reparation for the internationally wrongful act and not by way of punishment';[757]
- shall be terminated as soon as the responsible state has complied with its obligations;
- shall be taken in such a way as to permit the resumption of performance of the obligations in question, since the countermeasures should be taken on a temporary basis;
- may not be taken if the dispute is pending before a court or tribunal; and
- shall not affect the 'fundamental substantive obligations'. The Draft Articles on Responsibility of States for Internationally Wrongful Acts enumerates the following obligations: (a) the obligation to refrain from the threat or use of force, (b) obligations for the protection of fundamental human rights, (c) obligations of humanitarian character prohibiting reprisals, and (d) other obligations under the peremptory norms of general international law.[758]

Reprisal

Reprisal refer to an act which, according to contemporary international law, is mostly illegal *per se* and which is adopted by one state in retaliation for an earlier illegal act committed by another state.

The ILC applied the term 'reprisal' in order to designate the measures taken in time of the international armed conflict:

> [T]raditionally the term 'reprisals' was used to cover otherwise unlawful action, including forcible action, taken by way of self-help in response to a breach. More recently, the term 'reprisals' has been limited to action taken in time of international armed conflict; i.e. it has been taken as equivalent to **belligerent reprisals**.[759]

However, the legitimate application of belligerent reprisals is also extremely limited by international humanitarian law and is subject to stringent conditions since they usually breach the rights of non-combatants and other protected persons, as well as damaging objects which are under the protection of international humanitarian law. (The limits of belligerent reprisals will be examined in detail in the chapter on international humanitarian law.)

The most cited case concerning the law of reprisals which existed before the UN Charter era is the **Naulila** dispute *(Portugal v Germany)*. After considering the case, the

---

757 Paragraph (6) of the Commentary to the Chapter II Countermeasures of the Draft Articles on Responsibility of States for Internationally Wrongful Acts.

758 In the commentary to Article 50 of the Draft Articles on Responsibility of States for Internationally Wrongful Acts, the ILC emphasised that: 'The reference to "other" obligations under peremptory norms makes it clear that subparagraph (d) does not qualify the preceding subparagraphs, some of which also encompass norms of a peremptory character.'

759 Paragraph (3) of the Commentary to the Chapter II Countermeasures of the Draft Articles on Responsibility of States for Internationally Wrongful Acts.

international tribunal developed the following preconditions for lawful reprisals to be carried out:

- There must be a previous violation of international law by the responsible state.
- An unsatisfied demand for reparation or compliance with the obligations of the responsible state must precede the reprisal.
- There must be proportionality between the wrongful conduct and the reprisal.[760]

These rules shall be applied even today in order to claim in rare cases the legitimacy of a belligerent reprisal,[761] taking into consideration the prohibition on the use of force formulated in the UN Charter. At the same time, at present, there is a clear tendency to outlaw belligerent reprisals at all.

Retorsion

Retorsion is a counter-action of one state, directed against the unfriendly and injurious conduct of another state which, in turn, may not necessarily be an internationally wrongful act. It is in conformity with international law; however, it certainly is an unfriendly act towards another state. Generally, the retorsion aims at presenting discontent in a form that is detrimental to another state, albeit without crossing the bounds of legality.

The following acts can be termed as acts of retorsion: Recalling an ambassador from a state that has committed an unfriendly act; expulsion from the country of an equal number of diplomats of a state which earlier expelled from its territory the diplomats of the state in question; various economic and travel restrictions (which do not violate existing international law norms), including prohibition of entry into the country or the cancellation of visits by delegations; and so on.

Implementation of the international responsibility of a state

> giving notice of its claim
> offer appropriate assurances and guarantees of non-repetition
> forms of material, moral, or political responsibility
> individually or in combination with other forms of responsibility

---

760 *Naulila* dispute *(Portugal v Germany)*, Award of 31 July 1928, Reports of International Arbitral Awards, Volume II 1011–1033 <https://legal.un.org/riaa/states/portugal.shtml> accessed 17 March 2021.

761 Some authors also assume that there is a need to apply the prerequisites of legitimate countermeasures to belligerent reprisals.

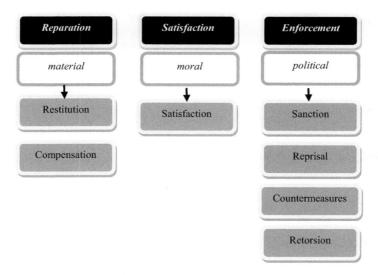

FIGURE 9.1 The purposes and forms of state responsibility

The key to the state responsibility engine

As noted earlier, the mechanism of international responsibility generally starts with an appeal made by an injured subject or subjects or the international community as a whole. Thus, being an injured state, every state becomes entitled by **giving notice of its claim** to a responsible state to invoke the responsibility of a responsible state, if the obligation breached is owed to:

1 that state individually; or
2 a group of states including that state, or the international community as a whole; and
3 at the same time, the breach of the obligation either (a) particularly affects that state or (b) 'is of such a character as radically to change the position of all the other States to which the obligation is owed with respect to the further performance of the obligation.'[762]

Where several states are responsible for the same internationally wrongful act, the responsibility of each state may be invoked by the injured state.

In addition, when the obligation breached is owed to a group of states or to the international community as a whole, in the first case, any state member of that group or, in the second case, every state shall be considered an injured state and, consequently, be entitled to invoke the responsibility of a respective state.

However, the responsibility cannot be invoked if the injured state has validly waived the claim or 'is to be considered as having, by reason of its conduct, validly acquiesced in the lapse of the claim.'[763]

762 Articles 42 and 43 of the Draft Articles on Responsibility of States for Internationally Wrongful Acts.
763 Article 47 of the Draft Articles on Responsibility of States for Internationally Wrongful Acts.

Legal consequences

Any state entitled to invoke international responsibility may claim to have ceased that act (if it was continuing); to **offer appropriate assurances and guarantees of non-repetition** (if circumstances so require); or to take the **forms of material, moral, or political responsibility** corresponding with the injury suffered (**individually or in combination with other forms of responsibility**).

RESPONSIBILITY OF INTERNATIONAL ORGANISATIONS

Draft Articles on the Responsibility of International Organisations
international organisation
organisation established by a treaty or other instrument governed by international law
possessing its own international legal personality

Preliminary remark

To date, there are numerous international intergovernmental organisations in the world. The functioning of such a number of subjects of international law inevitably poses the question of how the international community should react if such actors commit a breach of an international obligation.

Draft Articles on the Responsibility of International Organisations

At present, the only attempt to codify the liability provisions concerning international organisations is the **Draft Articles on the Responsibility of International Organisations** of 2011 adopted by the International Law Commission, which, like the Draft Articles on Responsibility of States for Internationally Wrongful Acts, does not yet have the status of a legally binding international treaty.[764]

---

764 Since the adoption of the Draft Articles on Responsibility of States for Internationally Wrongful Acts, the UN General Assembly has addressed the issue several times. In more recent times, the Resolution A/RES/74/180 of 18 December 2019 on Responsibility of States for Internationally Wrongful Acts was adopted without a vote; the General Assembly '[a]cknowledged that a growing number of decisions of international courts, tribunals and other bodies refer to the articles' and requested 'the Secretary-General to update the compilation of decisions of international courts, tribunals and other bodies referring to the articles and to invite Governments to submit information on their practice in this regard, and also requests the Secretary-General to submit such material well in advance of its seventy-seventh session;' As regards the Draft Articles on the Responsibility of International Organisations, in its Resolution A/RES/66/100 of 9 December 2011, the General Assembly took note of the Articles on the Responsibility of International Organizations presented by the International Law Commission,

The notion of an international organisation

Under the Draft Articles on the Responsibility of International Organisations, **international organisation** means an **organisation** 'established by a treaty or other instrument governed by international law and possessing its own international legal personality'. International organisations may include as members the states, as well as other entities.[765]

Similar approaches

Generally, the Draft Articles are built on the same structure as ILC's Draft Articles on Responsibility of States for Internationally Wrongful Acts. Moreover, there are many similar approaches, starting with the general rule that every internationally wrongful act of an international organisation entails the international responsibility of that organisation, continuing with the rules on attribution of conduct to an international organisation, circumstances precluding wrongfulness, legal consequences of an internationally wrongful act or omission, implementation of the international responsibility, countermeasures, and so forth.

Attribution of conduct to an international organisation

For example, with regard to the attribution of conduct to an international organisation, it is determined that

> The conduct of an organ or agent of an international organization in the performance of functions of that organ or agent shall be considered an act of that organization under international law, whatever position the organ or agent holds in respect of the organization.[766]

INDIVIDUAL CRIMINAL RESPONSIBILITY IN INTERNATIONAL LAW

direct addressees of the international responsibility system
serious violation
international crimes
international criminal law
violation of a criminal norm derived from international law

---

the text of which was annexed to the Resolution. More recently, the General Assembly requested 'the Secretary-General to update the compilation of decisions of international courts, tribunals and other bodies referring to the articles and to invite Governments and international organizations to submit information on their practice in this regard, as well as written comments on any future action regarding the articles, and also requests the Secretary-General to submit this material well in advance of its seventy-fifth session' (A/RES/ 72/122 of 7 December 2017).

765 Article 2 of the Draft Articles on the Responsibility of International Organisations.

766 Paragraph 1 of Article 6 of the Draft Articles on the Responsibility of International Organisations.

> offensive to the international community as a whole
> criminal liability
> *actus reus*
> *mens rea*
> physical component
> mental component

Individual as a direct addressee of international responsibility

Even though individuals are not regarded as subjects of international law, they can be considered **direct addressees of the international responsibility system** if a **serious violation** of the most fundamental rules of conduct emerges at the interstate level. These very dangerous breaches of fundamental international legal norms undertaken by individuals are called **international crimes**. Hence, international crimes may be committed only by a natural person and not by the entities.[767]

International criminal law

The twentieth century was the bloodiest and most violent in the human history; however, it also reflects extensive efforts to use international treaties and other international law norms to restrain ever more terrible crimes against peace and humanity and establish standards of war. Thus, a particular field of international law – **international criminal law** – was developed.

The characteristics of international crime

Hence, international crime represents a grave violation of international law by individuals. An act can be assessed as an international crime when the following five conditions are met:

1   There is a **violation of a criminal norm derived from international law**.
2   This violation is treated as being **offensive to the international community as a whole**.
3   International law itself establishes **criminal liability** for the act committed.
4   The criminal norms (both material and processual norms) of international law may be prosecuted and tried by the international criminal institutions (tribunals or court).[768]
5   The criminal norms (both material and processual norms) of international law shall be binding on the vast majority of states.

767 'Crimes against international law are committed by men, not by abstract entities, and only by punishing individuals who commit such crimes can the provisions of international law be enforced', reads the judgment of the Nuremberg International Military Tribunal.
768 Since, for example, the International Criminal Court is considered complementary to national criminal systems, which means that international crimes can and shall be tried in domestic courts.

Thus, only a few of the gravest violations of international law may be committed by natural persons, which accumulate the characteristics noted earlier and are, therefore, determined to be international crimes.

Actus reus and *mens rea*[769]

Under international law, establishment of criminal culpability requires certain prerequisites. For example, the Trial Chamber of the International Criminal Tribunal for the former Yugoslavia confirmed in one of its judgments that:

> It is apparent that it is a general principle of law that the establishment of criminal culpability requires an analysis of two aspects. The first of these may be termed the *actus reus* – the physical act necessary for the offence. . . . The second aspect of the analysis of any homicide offence relates to the necessary mental element, or *mens rea*.[770]

Hence, to place an act under international criminal responsibility, it is necessary that a **physical component** (physical act) and a **mental component** (intent component), which is the knowledge that one's action or omission would cause a crime to be committed, are both present.

From the *ad hoc* tribunals to the permanent international criminal court

> military tribunals
> Nuremberg International Military Tribunal
> Tokyo International Military Tribunal
> crimes against peace
> war crimes
> crimes against humanity
> *ad hoc* Tribunals
> criminal tribunals of international character
> International Criminal Tribunal for the former Yugoslavia
> ICTY
> International Criminal Tribunal for Rwanda
> ICTR

769 *Actus reus* – '"Guilty act." The physical conduct element of a criminal offense. Most crimes have both a conduct component (*actus reus*) and a mental or intent component (*mens rea*).' *Guide to Latin in International Law* (n 71) 14.

770 *Prosecutor v Zejnil Delalic, Zdravko Mucic also known as 'Pavo', Hazim Delic, Esad Landzo also known as 'Zenga'* (IT-96–21-T) Judgment of 16 November 1998.

The first effort

The first treaty that provided for the enforcement of individual criminal responsibility at the international level was the Treaty of Peace with Germany (Treaty of Versailles) of 1919. The treaty recognised 'the right of the Allied and Associated Powers to bring before military tribunals persons accused of having committed acts in violation of the laws and customs of war'.[771] Under this Treaty, the persons guilty of criminal acts against the nationals of one or more of the Allied and Associated Powers should had been brought before the **military tribunals** of an affected power or the mixed tribunals of the powers concerned.

At the same time, basing its claims on the Treaty, the Allied and Associated Powers attempted to arraign the former German Emperor Kaiser Wilhelm II 'for a supreme offense against international morality and the sanctity of treaties'.[772] According to the Treaty, the establishment of a special tribunal was also intended. This was reserved as an institute composed of five judges, with the right to appoint one judge per each of the following countries: the United States of America, Great Britain, France, Italy, and Japan.

However, Wilhelm II went into exile in the neutral Netherlands. The Netherlands refused to extradite him based on international law provisions of that time.[773]

On the other hand, attempts to bring to justice the persons accused of having committed acts in violation of the laws and customs of war fared a little better from 1921 through 1925. However, only a minor number of cases were finalised, and even these trials were not conducted by the international tribunal. (For example, German individuals were tried in the German court [the so-called Leipzig War Crimes Trials].)[774] In the end, only a handful of individuals were tried.

Origination of the international criminal responsibility

The genesis of individual criminal responsibility under international law came at the end of World War II when it became apparent to the international community that there ought to be real punishment for 'the major war criminals' with respect to the violation of the most fundamental international law norms concerning war. On this premise, the **Nuremberg** and **Tokyo International Military Tribunals** were established.

---

771 Article 228 of the Treaty of Versailles.

772 Article 227 of the Treaty of Versailles.

773 Article 227 of the Treaty of Versailles thus remained a dead letter.

774 'In the period from 10 January 1921 to 3 July 1922, the German Supreme Court (Reichsgericht) in Leipzig conducted 12 trials involving 17 accused Germans on charges relating to allegations of criminal conduct by German citizens during the First World War ("Leipzig War Crimes Trials")'. Matthias Neuner, 'When Justice Is Left to the Losers: The Leipzig War Crimes Trials' in Morten Bergsmo, CHEAH Wui Ling, and YI Ping (eds), *Historical Origins of International Criminal Law: Volume 1* (FICHL Publication Series No. 20, Torkel Opsahl Academic EPublisher 2014) 333.

Nuremberg Tribunal

Under the London Agreement of 1945, which was concluded by the Government of the United States of America, the Provisional Government of the French Republic, the Government of the United Kingdom of Great Britain and Northern Ireland, and the Government of the Union of Soviet Socialist Republics for the prosecution and punishment of the major war criminals of the European Axis, the International Military Tribunal (the so-called Nuremberg Tribunal) was created.

According to the Charter of the International Military Tribunal, which consisted of four members and alternates (each of the signatories appointed one member and one alternate), the Tribunal had jurisdiction over the following acts (named as the crimes) stipulating the individual responsibility:

(a) *Crimes against peace*: namely, planning, preparation, initiation or waging of a war of aggression, or a war in violation of international treaties, agreements or assurances, or participation in a Common Plan or Conspiracy for the accomplishment of any of the foregoing;
(b) *War crimes*: namely, violations of the laws or customs of war. Such violations shall include, but not be limited to, murder, ill-treatment or deportation to slave labour or for any other purpose of civilian population of or in occupied territory, murder or ill-treatment of prisoners of war or persons on the seas, killing of hostages, plunder of public or private property, wanton destruction of cities, towns, or villages, or devastation not justified by military necessity;
(c) *Crimes against humanity*: namely, murder, extermination, enslavement, deportation, and other inhumane acts committed against any civilian population, before or during the war, or persecutions on political, racial, or religious grounds in execution of or in connection with any crime within the jurisdiction of the Tribunal, whether or not in violation of domestic law of the country where perpetrated.[775]

With this famous provision, the Charter of the International Military Tribunal laid the foundation of the traditional tripartition of international crimes – **crimes against peace**, **war crimes**, and **crimes against humanity**. In 1946, the International Military Tribunal handed down its verdicts in the trials of 22 Nazi leaders – 12 of them were sentenced to death by hanging.

Tokyo Tribunal

The second international tribunal was established as the International Military Tribunal for the Far East (the so-called Tokyo Tribunal) in 1946. Under the Charter of the International Military Tribunal for the Far East, the Tribunal was instituted 'by the Supreme

---

775 Article 6 of the Charter of the International Military Tribunal. The Charter is available at United Nations – Treaty Series, 1951, No. 251 <http://bit.ly/2Issmjf> accessed 16 March 2021.

Commander for the Allied Powers[776] from the names submitted by the Signatories to the Instrument of Surrender.'[777]

The Tribunal had the power to try and punish Far Eastern war criminals who, as individuals or as members of organisations, were charged with offences.

The Tokyo Tribunal Charter generally followed the model set by the Nuremberg Trials; it repeated the Nuremberg Tribunal Charter's attitude regarding the tripartition of international crimes. Class A charges, alleging crimes against peace, were to be brought against Japan's top leaders who had planned and directed the war while Class B and C charges – charges of conventional war crimes and crimes against humanity, respectively – could had been levelled at the Japanese of any rank. The crimes themselves were defined similarly, but with some changes. For example, war crimes were determined more broadly as violations of the laws or customs of war.

Development of international criminal law during the Cold War

From this historical point, the evolution of individual criminal responsibility gained momentum. Nevertheless, overshadowed by the Cold War, it would take more than 40 years until *ad hoc* international criminal tribunals would be set up once again.

However, at the same time, in the Cold War era, the international criminal law (material) norms were developed in many diverse directions – for instance, the Convention on the Prevention and the Punishment of the Crime of Genocide of 1948, the International Convention on the Suppression and the Punishment of the Crime of Apartheid of 1973, and so on.

Post–Cold War *ad hoc* Tribunals

The next crucial step in the process of developing rules on the direct enforcement of individual criminal responsibility under international law was taken only after the end of the Cold War era, with the setting up of the two *ad hoc* **Tribunals** as the bodies instituted by the UN Security Council for the prosecution of crimes committed in the former Yugoslavia and in Rwanda.

Simultaneously, other developments at the interstate level led to the establishment of several hybrid international tribunals, the so-called **criminal tribunals of international character**. They differ from the full-fledged international criminal tribunals due to a hybrid composition (uniting the 'international judges' and the 'national judges') and their subject-matter jurisdiction, which does not include any international crimes but only the crimes prescribed under the criminal legislation of a state concerned.

Such criminal tribunals of international character are usually established either as the products of treaty negotiations between a state in question and the UN (the Special Court

---

776 Douglas Macarthur – General of the Army, United States Army Supreme Commander for the Allied Powers.

777 Article 2 of the Charter of the International Military Tribunal for the Far East.

for Sierra Leone, the Extraordinary Chambers in the Courts of Cambodia, and the Special Tribunal for Lebanon) or as a feature of the UN transitional authority (the East Timor Special Panels).

For example, the Special Tribunal for Lebanon was established by Security Council Resolution[778] and the 'Agreement between the United Nations and the Lebanese Republic on the establishment of a Special Tribunal for Lebanon', which was annexed to the Resolution. According to the Agreement: 'There is hereby established a Special Tribunal for Lebanon to prosecute persons responsible for the attack of 14 February 2005 resulting in the death of former Lebanese Prime Minister Rafiq Hariri and in the death or injury of other persons'. The Tribunal was composed of the Lebanese and international judges appointed by the Secretary-General (after consultations with the Lebanese side) accordingly from a list presented by the Lebanese government and 'upon nominations forwarded by States at the invitation of the Secretary-General, as well as by competent persons'. Under the Statute of the Special Tribunal for Lebanon, the Lebanese criminal legislation as applicable criminal law was defined.[779]

International Criminal Tribunal for the former Yugoslavia

In the post–Cold War environment, it appeared that international crimes had returned to Europe in the form of mass deportations, concentration camps, ethnic cleansing, and mass killings. As a response to this dramatic comeback of the past, the United Nations Security Council established the **International Criminal Tribunal for the former Yugoslavia (ICTY)**.[780] Its mandate lasted from 1993 to 2017. The tribunal was located in The Hague, Netherlands.

The Tribunal was a United Nations body that, according to its Statute, had 'the power to prosecute persons responsible for serious violations of international humanitarian law committed in the territory of the former Yugoslavia since 1991.'

The Tribunal's permanent judges and *ad litem* judges were elected by the General Assembly of the United Nations from a list submitted by the Security Council for a term of four years, after which they were eligible for re-election. The *ad litem* judges were appointed on a temporary basis to serve in the Trial Chambers.

Under the Statute, the ICTY had the authority to prosecute and try individuals:

- committing or ordering to be committed grave breaches of the Geneva Conventions of 1949;
- violating the laws or customs of war;

---

778 S/RES/1757 of 30 May 2007.
779 '[T]he Lebanese Criminal Code relating to the prosecution and punishment of acts of terrorism, crimes and offences against life and personal integrity, illicit associations and failure to report crimes and offences, including the rules regarding the material elements of a crime, criminal participation and conspiracy; and (b) Articles 6 and 7 of the Lebanese law of 11 January 1958 on "Increasing the penalties for sedition, civil war and interfaith struggle".' Article 2 of the Statute of the Special Tribunal for Lebanon.
780 S/RES/827 of 25 May 1993.

- committing genocide; or
- committing crimes against humanity (murder; extermination; enslavement; deportation; imprisonment; torture; rape; persecutions on political, racial, and religious grounds; or other inhumane acts).

The maximum sentence the Tribunal could impose on a convicted person was life imprisonment.

International Criminal Tribunal for Rwanda

The other information on serious violations of international humanitarian law and the horrifying facts of genocide of colossal proportion came from Rwanda. The neutral commentators pointed out over a million deaths, overwhelmingly Tutsi; moderate Hutu, Twa, and other individuals also perished in less than three months.[781]

The Security Council of the United Nations could not ignore almost a million dead in Rwanda. Consequently, the Security Council instituted the **International Criminal Tribunal for Rwanda (ICTR)** as a United Nations body

> for the Prosecution of Persons Responsible for Genocide and Other Serious Violations of International Humanitarian Law Committed in the Territory of Rwanda and Rwandan citizens responsible for genocide and other such violations committed in the territory of the neighbouring States, between 1 January 1994 and 31 December 1994.[782]

The Tribunal was held in Arusha, Tanzania, and its Appeals Chamber in The Hague, Netherlands.[783] The mandate of Tribunal lasted from 1995 to 2015.

The General Assembly elected the judges of the International Tribunal for Rwanda from a list submitted to it by the Security Council.

According to its Statute, the Tribunal had the power to prosecute persons:

- committing genocide;
- committing crimes against humanity; or
- 'committing or ordering to be committed serious violations of Article 3 common to the Geneva Conventions of 12 August 1949 for the Protection of War Victims, and of Additional Protocol II thereto of 8 June 1977.'[784]

---

781 See <www.un.org/en/preventgenocide/rwanda/> accessed 17 March 2021.
782 S/RES/955 of 8 November 1994.
783 Under Article 12 of the Statute of the Tribunal: '2. The members of the Appeals Chamber of the International Tribunal for the Prosecution of Persons Responsible for Serious Violations of International Humanitarian Law Committed in the Territory of the Former Yugoslavia since 1991 ... shall also serve as the members of the Appeals Chamber of the International Tribunal for Rwanda.'
784 Article 4 of the Statute of the International Tribunal for Rwanda.

It is especially remarkable that for the first time in history, an international tribunal – the International Tribunal for Rwanda – delivered verdicts against persons directly responsible for committing the act of genocide.[785]

International Criminal Court

International Criminal Court
ICC
Rome Statute of the International Criminal Court
Assembly of States Parties
Presidency
Judicial Divisions
Office of the Prosecutor
Registry
Trust Fund for Victims

The standing international criminal court

It took a lot of time and effort from humankind to achieve the standing international criminal court, but ultimately, that attempt led to the Rome Statute System. The Diplomatic Conference on the Establishment of an **International Criminal Court (ICC)** was held in 1998 (Rome, Italy). A final statute – the **Rome Statute of the International Criminal Court** (also called the ICC Statute or Rome Statute) – was adopted at the Diplomatic Conference, which was attended by delegations from more than 100 states, intergovernmental organisations, and hundreds of non-governmental organisations.[786] The Statute entered into force on 1 July 2002, with the deposit of the 60th instrument of ratification.

Under the Rome Statute the ICC was established as 'a permanent institution and shall have the power to exercise its jurisdiction over persons for the most serious crimes of international concern'.[787]

It should specifically be mentioned that the ICC is intended to complement and not to replace national criminal systems. International crimes can and shall be tried in domestic courts. The preamble to the Rome Statute states that the ICC will 'complement the jurisdictions of national criminal courts', and that 'it is the duty of every State to exercise its

---

785 'The ICTR is the first ever international tribunal to deliver verdicts in relation to genocide, and the first to interpret the definition of genocide set forth in the 1948 Geneva Convention. It also is the first international tribunal to define rape in international criminal law and to recognise rape as a means of perpetrating genocide. . . . The ICTR in Brief' <http://unictr.unmict.org/en/tribunal> accessed 17 March 2021.

786 Only seven states voted against the statute: the United States, China, Israel, Qatar, Libya, Iraq, and Yemen.

787 Article 1 of the Rome Statute.

criminal jurisdiction over those responsible for international crimes.' Moreover, the ICC prosecutes cases only when a certain state is unwilling or unable to prosecute offenders in particular cases.

Jurisdiction of the International Criminal Court

The Rome Statute grants the ICC jurisdiction over four main types of crime:

- the crime of genocide;
- crimes against humanity;
- war crimes; and
- the crime of aggression.[788]

The ICC may exercise jurisdiction:

in a situation where genocide, crimes against humanity, or war crimes:

- were committed on or after 1 July 2002; and
- were committed by a national of a state party; or
- were committed in the territory of a state party; or
- were committed in a state that had accepted the jurisdiction of the ICC concerning a particular case; or
- were referred to the ICC Prosecutor by the United Nations Security Council through a resolution adopted under Chapter VII of the UN charter.

After initialisation of the jurisdiction of the Court over the crime of aggression as of 17 July 2018, cases of aggression could be referred to the Court:

- by the UN Security Council, enforcing Chapter VII of the United Nations Charter, 'irrespective as to whether it involves States Parties or non-States Parties' of the Rome Statute;[789] or

---

788 The definition of crime of aggression was adopted through amending the Rome Statute at the Review Conference of the Statute in Kampala, Uganda, in 2010. In 2017 the Assembly of states parties adopted by consensus Resolution ICC-ASP/16/Res.5 (of 14 December 2017) on the activation of the jurisdiction of the Court over the crime of aggression as of 17 July 2018. At the same time, according to the Resolution, 'the amendments to the Statute regarding the crime of aggression adopted at the Kampala Review Conference enter into force for those States Parties which have accepted the amendments one year after the deposit of their instruments of ratification or acceptance and that in the case of a State referral or *proprio motu* investigation the Court shall not exercise its jurisdiction regarding a crime of aggression when committed by a national or on the territory of a State Party that has not ratified or accepted these amendments'. <https://asp.icc-cpi.int/en_menus/asp/resolutions/sessions/Pages/2017-16th-session.aspx> accessed 17 March 2021.

789 'Jurisdiction', official website of the ICC <www.icc-cpi.int/about/how-the-court-works/Pages/default.aspx#legalProcess> accessed 17 March 2021. In this book, materials from the website are used, taking into account the disclaimer and applicable legal rules.

- even in the absence of a UN Security Council referral of an act of aggression, by the Prosecutor initiating an investigation *proprio motu*[790] i.e. on his or her initiative (after acquiring the authorisation from the Pre-Trial Chamber) or upon the request of a state party. In such cases, the investigation can be conducted only concerning the situations committed on the territory of states parties or by states parties' nationals. Moreover, the term 'states parties' includes only the states which specifically accept the Court's jurisdiction over the crime of aggression. At the same time, the competence of the Prosecutor to investigate a request from a state party (state referral) concerning the crime of aggression is limited since additional preconditions should also be met.[791]

The Court as an autonomous institution

The Court is an independent judicial institution; thus, it is not a United Nations body.

At the same time, the ICC does not have its own enforcement structure; instead, it relies on co-operation with countries and international organisations worldwide for making arrests, transferring arrested persons to the ICC detention centre in The Hague, freezing suspects' assets, enforcing sentences, and so forth.

The organisational structure of the Rome Statute system

As regards the organisational structure, the Rome Statute established three separate bodies:

- the **Assembly of States Parties** – which elects the judges and the Prosecutor and approves the ICC's budget;
- the International Criminal Court itself – which is composed of four organs: The **Presidency** (the President and First and Second Vice Presidents), the **Judicial Divisions** (18 judges in three divisions – Pre-Trial, Trial, and Appeals), the **Office of the Prosecutor** (including the Prosecutor and Deputy Prosecutor), and the **Registry**; and
- the **Trust Fund for Victims** – which was established by the Assembly of States Parties 'for the benefit of victims of crimes within the jurisdiction of the Court, and of the families of

---

790 'Proprio (suo) motu . . . "From its own motion."' *Guide to Latin in International Law* (n 71) 233.

791 According to Article 15 *bis* of the Rome Statute, '6. Where the Prosecutor concludes that there is a reasonable basis to proceed with an investigation in respect of a crime of aggression, he or she shall first ascertain whether the Security Council has made a determination of an act of aggression committed by the State concerned. The Prosecutor shall notify the Secretary-General of the United Nations of the situation before the Court, including any relevant information and documents. 7. Where the Security Council has made such a determination, the Prosecutor may proceed with the investigation in respect of a crime of aggression. 8. Where no such determination is made within six months after the date of notification, the Prosecutor may proceed with the investigation in respect of a crime of aggression, provided that the Pre-Trial Division has authorized the commencement of the investigation in respect of a crime of aggression in accordance with the procedure contained in article 15, and the Security Council has not decided otherwise in accordance with article 16 [Deferral of investigation or prosecution].'

such victims'.[792] In order to accumulate the necessary resources for the maintenance of the reparations for the victims of the Rome Statute crimes and their families and to support implementation of the Court-ordered reparations, the Fund asks individuals, legal persons, and governments to consider making voluntary contributions. In addition, the 'Court may order money and other property collected through fines or forfeiture to be transferred, by order of the Court, to the Trust Fund',[793] which are imposed on perpetrators.

The constraining challenge to the effective functioning of the Court

Although the Rome Statute now has more than 100 states parties, three of the five permanent members of the UN Security Council are not among them – namely, the USA, Russia, and China – as well as many other states. Consequently, this fact appears as a significant obstacle to the effective operation of the Court.

At the same time, there are other challenges concerning the successful functioning of the Court. For instance, the efficiency of the system of reparations for the victims of crimes and their families is questionable. Although the institution of the Trust Fund for Victims was important to assist and support the victims, in fact, fundraising for the trust fund is largely dependent on voluntary contributions.

International crimes

> crime of genocide
> crimes against humanity
> war crimes
> crime of aggression
> Convention on the Prevention and Punishment of the Crime of Genocide
> *Prosecutor v Jean-Paul Akayesu* case
> apartheid
> International Convention on the Suppression and Punishment of the Crime of Apartheid
> ethnic cleansing
> statute of limitations

Development of international criminal law

The meaning of international crimes has been specified over time in a range of international treaties and customary international norms, beginning with the Hague Conventions adopted in 1899 and 1907, which established rules for military conduct during wartime.

792 Article 79 (1) of the Rome Statute.
793 Article 79 (2) of the Rome Statute.

The concept which was reflected in these international agreements and customary norms extended criminal responsibility not just to the direct perpetrators of a certain crime, but also to those who commanded, planned, or allowed the crimes to take place. At the end of World War II, the development of international criminal law helped produce the tripartition of international crimes into crimes against peace, war crimes, and crimes against humanity.

More recent developments in the field led to the conventional list of international crimes – the **crime of genocide**, **crimes against humanity**, **war crimes**, and the **crime of aggression**, which are at present determined by the Rome Statute.

Genocide

Genocide[794] was codified as an independent crime in the 1948 **Convention on the Prevention and Punishment of the Crime of Genocide** (the Genocide Convention). An impressive majority of countries have ratified the Convention; however, from a legal point of view, nowadays all states are bound by the principle that genocide is a crime prohibited under international law. Moreover, the prohibition of genocide is generally recognised as a peremptory norm of contemporary international law, and therefore, no derogation from it is allowed.

According to the Genocide Convention, 'genocide, whether committed in time of peace or in time of war, is a crime under international law', and the crime of genocide includes two main elements:[795]

- A physical element – which includes the following five acts, enumerated exhaustively:

  (a) Killing members of the group;
  (b) Causing serious bodily or mental harm to the members of the group;
  (c) Deliberately inflicting on the group conditions of life calculated to bring about its physical destruction in whole or in part;
  (d) Imposing measures intended to prevent births within the group;
  (e) Forcibly transferring children of the group to another group.[796]

- A mental element – the 'intent to destroy, in whole or in part, a national, ethnical, racial or religious group, as such'.

  - To constitute genocide, there must be a proven 'specific intent' on the part of the perpetrator which clearly seeks to physically destroy a national, ethnical, racial, or religious group. (In some instances, the case law has associated intent with the existence of a state or organisational plan or policy).
  - The target of destruction must be the group as such and not its members as individuals.
  - The targeted groups are determined exhaustively; they should be national, ethnical, racial, or religious groups.

---

794 The word 'genocide' consists of the Greek prefix *genos*, meaning race or tribe, and the Latin suffix *cide*, meaning killing.

795 Articles 1 and 2 of the Genocide Convention.

796 Article 6 of the Rome Statute.

- The intention to destroy means the intention of physical destruction and not, for instance, attacks upon the cultural or sociological characteristics of a group in order to remove its separate identity.

- Genocide can also be committed against only a part of the group, as long as that part is identifiable and 'substantial'.

The third element of the genocide – a contextual component should be outlined, which stipulates that the 'conduct took place in the context of a manifest pattern of similar conduct directed against that group or was conduct that could itself effect such destruction.'[797]

Crimes against humanity

It was only after World War II that crimes against humanity were prosecuted for the first time at the Nuremberg and Tokyo Tribunals. Nowadays, the Rome Statute is the treaty that reflects the contemporary consensus among the international community on the definition of crimes against humanity. Unlike war crimes, crimes against humanity (according to the Rome Statute) do not always need to be linked with an armed conflict since, even though it is rare, they may also take place in times of peace.

Under the Rome Statute, crimes against humanity 'means any of the following acts when committed as part of a widespread or systematic attack directed against any civilian population, with knowledge of the attack.'[798] Consequently, crimes against humanity consist of three main components:

- A physical component – the commission of any of the following acts:

  (a) murder;
  (b) extermination;
  (c) enslavement;
  (d) deportation or forcible transfer of population;
  (e) imprisonment;
  (f) torture;
  (g) grave forms of sexual violence;
  (h) persecution;
  (i) enforced disappearance of persons;
  (j) the crime of apartheid; or
  (k) '[o]ther inhumane acts of a similar character intentionally causing great suffering, or serious injury to body or to mental or physical health.'[799]

- A contextual component – which excludes random, accidental, or isolated acts of violence. Firstly, the contextual component means that:

---

797 *Elements of Crimes* (International Criminal Court 2011, Printed by PrintPartners Ipskamp, Enschede) 2.

798 Article 7(1) of the Rome Statute.

799 Article 7(1) (k) of the Rome Statute

- crimes against humanity must be committed 'in furtherance of a State or organizational policy to commit such attack'.[800]

Also, this component prescribes that the commission of the acts mentioned earlier may involve:

- large-scale violence in relation to the number of victims; or
- its extension over a broad geographic area (widespread); or
- a methodical type of violence (systematic).

- A mental component – the perpetrator must act with the knowledge of the attack against the civilian population and 'that the conduct was part of or intended the conduct to be part of a widespread or systematic attack against a civilian population. . . . However, the last element should not be interpreted as requiring proof that the perpetrator had knowledge of all characteristics of the attack or the precise details of the plan or policy of the State or organization. In the case of an emerging widespread or systematic attack against a civilian population, the intent clause of the last element indicates that this mental element is satisfied if the perpetrator intended to further such an attack.'[801]
- In addition, as determined in the ***Prosecutor v Jean-Paul Akayesu*** case of the International Tribunal for Rwanda: 'An attack may also be non violent in nature, like imposing a system of apartheid, which is declared a crime against humanity in Article 1 of the Apartheid Convention of 1973, or exerting pressure on the population to act in a particular manner, may come under the purview of an attack, if orchestrated on a massive scale or in a systematic manner.'[802]

It is necessary to distinguish crimes against humanity from genocide in order to interpret notions accurately and contribute to their better performance. In contrast with the crime of genocide, crimes against humanity do not target a specific group, and, therefore, there is no need to prove a 'specific intent.' Intent to commit any of the acts mentioned earlier is sufficient for considering an act 'as part of a widespread or systematic attack directed against any civilian population'.

1 Hence, crimes against humanity and the crime of genocide have different *mens rea* (mental or intent components).
2 Consequently, the objectives of these two concepts are rather different since one (in the case of crimes against humanity) aims at the protection of an individual while the other (in the case of genocide) aims at the protection of a group of individuals.
3 At the same time, although a crime against humanity can only be committed against civilians, the crime of genocide may be committed against a targeted group which, by definition, may include combatants as well as civilians.

---

800 Article 7(2) (a) of the Rome Statute.
801 *Elements of Crimes* (n 797) 5.
802 *Prosecutor v Jean-Paul Akayesu* (ICTR-96–4-T) Judgment of 2 September 1998. All ICTR cases are available at the Legacy website of the International Criminal Tribunal for Rwanda < https://unictr. irmct.org/en/cases>. In this book, materials from the website are used, taking into account the disclaimer and applicable legal rules.

Apartheid

One of the brutal forms of crimes against humanity is **apartheid** – the systematic persecution of one racial group by another. The infamous historic lesson is attributed to the South African apartheid government.

Apartheid was recognised as a crime against humanity under the **International Convention on the Suppression and Punishment of the Crime of Apartheid**. According to the Convention, the crime of apartheid

> shall include similar policies and practices of racial segregation and discrimination as practised in southern Africa, shall apply to the . . . inhuman acts committed for the purpose of establishing and maintaining domination by one racial group[803] of persons over any other racial group of persons and systematically oppressing them.[804]

War crimes

The concept of war crimes undoubtedly developed at the end of the nineteenth century and the beginning of the twentieth century, when international humanitarian law, also known as the law of armed conflict, was codified for the first time.

War crimes are those violations of the international humanitarian treaty or customary law 'when committed as part of a plan or policy or as part of a large-scale commission of such crimes.'[805]

Under Article 8 of the Rome Statute, war crimes are categorised as follows:

- grave breaches of the 1949 Geneva Conventions, related to international armed conflict;
- other serious violations of the laws and customs applicable in international armed conflict;
- serious violations of Article 3 common to the four 1949 Geneva Conventions, related to armed conflict not of an international character; and
- other serious violations of the laws and customs applicable in armed conflict not of an international character.

At the same time, war crimes could be divided into:

---

803 'Racial group' in this context will include any group of people who are defined by reference to their race, colour, nationality (including citizenship), or ethnic or national origin; according to the United Nations Convention on the Elimination of All Forms of Racial Discrimination of 1965, the term 'racial discrimination' means 'any distinction, exclusion, restriction or preference based on *race, colour, descent, or national or ethnic origin* which has the purpose or effect of nullifying or impairing the recognition, enjoyment or exercise, on an equal footing, of human rights and fundamental freedoms in the political, economic, social, cultural or any other field of public life.'

804 Article II of the International Convention on the Suppression and Punishment of the Crime of Apartheid.

805 Article 82 of the Rome Statute.

- war crimes against persons requiring particular protection;
- war crimes against those providing humanitarian assistance and peacekeeping operations;
- war crimes against property and other rights;
- prohibited methods of warfare; and
- prohibited means of warfare.

War crimes contain three main components:

- A physical component – the commission of any of the following acts:

  (a) wilful killing;
  (b) torture or inhuman treatment, including biological experiments;
  (c) wilfully causing great suffering or serious injury to body or health;
  (d) extensive destruction and appropriation of property, not justified by military necessity and carried out unlawfully and wantonly;
  (e) compelling a prisoner of war or other protected person to serve in the forces of a hostile power;
  (f) wilfully depriving a prisoner of war or other protected person of the right to a fair and regular trial;
  (g) unlawful deportation or transfer or unlawful confinement; or
  (h) taking of hostages.[806]

- A contextual component – which means that the conduct took place in the context of and was associated with an international/non-international armed conflict and, as defined under the Rome Statute, when it is committed as part of a plan or policy or as part of a large-scale commission of such crimes; and
- A mental component – the perpetrator must have direct intent and knowledge concerning the committed act and the contextual component.

On the whole, war crimes:

1 take place in the context of an armed conflict, either international or non-international, in contrast to the crime of genocide and crimes against humanity;

---

806 From 2 to 7 December 2019, the Assembly of 122 states parties to the Rome Statute of the International Criminal Court (ASP) met in The Hague for its 18th session. Switzerland proposed to amend Article 8 (War crimes) of the Rome Statute to make the intentional starvation of civilians in a non-international armed conflict a war crime. As proclaimed on the official website of the Swiss government, 'Following a Swiss initiative, the International Criminal Court (ICC) will from now on be able to prosecute the intentional starvation of civilians in civil wars as a war crime. The ICC Assembly of States Parties took a unanimous decision to this effect earlier today. . . . Swiss initiative: intentional starvation of civilians in civil wars is now a war crime.' <http://bit.ly/38sFXmv> accessed 17 March 2021.

2 refer to serious breaches of international humanitarian law committed against either civilians or enemy combatants. In contrast, the crime of genocide and crimes against humanity are principally directed against civilian populations; and
3 can usually be perpetrated by members of an army of any rank. In contrast, the crime of genocide and crimes against humanity are commonly perpetrated by high-ranking governmental or military officials. However, in principle, civilians can also commit war crimes, as well as the crime of genocide and crimes against humanity.[807]

Crime of aggression

The concept of crimes against peace was framed at the end of World War II due to the foundational documents and judgments of the Nuremberg and Tokyo Tribunals. The embodiment of these crimes was termed 'crimes of aggression.' On the other hand, an act of aggression itself was comprehensively defined by the UN General Assembly Resolution 3314 (XXIX) of 1974 (Definition of Aggression).

At the Rome Conference, which adopted the Rome Statute, the crime of aggression was included as one of the crimes within the jurisdiction of the Court. However, participants in the Rome Conference could not agree on the definition of the crime, nor could they manage to agree on the conditions under which the Court would exercise jurisdiction on the issue. Only at the 2010 Review Conference did the states parties managed to agree by consensus to adopt a resolution accepting the amendments to the Statute, adding the definition of the crime and the conditions for the exercise of jurisdiction by the Court over this crime.

Under modern redaction of Article 8 *bis* of the Rome Statute,

> crime of aggression means the planning, preparation, initiation or execution, by a person in a position effectively to exercise control over or to direct the political or military action of a State, of an act of aggression which, by its character, gravity and scale, constitutes a manifest violation of the Charter of the United Nations.

At the same time, referring to UN General Assembly Resolution 3314 (XXIX) annexing the Definition of Aggression, an '"act of aggression" means the use of armed force by a State against the sovereignty, territorial integrity or political independence of another State, or in any other manner inconsistent with the Charter of the United Nations.'

---

807 'In principle, individuals may be indicted (and held criminally responsible if found guilty) regardless of their exact role in the commission of the crime as long as their contribution to the crime meets the above jurisdictional requirement of gravity and that it falls within one of the forms of criminal participation provided for in the statutes. The only relevant consideration to assign individual criminal responsibility is whether the accused, private individual, or state official, took part in one of the crimes covered by the statute, in one of the forms provided for in Articles 6(1) and 6(3) of the statute of the Rwanda tribunal or Articles 7(1) and 7(3) of the statute of the Yugoslav tribunal.' Guénaël Mettraux, 'The Person of the Perpetrator: Who Can Commit an International Crime?' in Guénaël Mettraux (ed), *International Crimes and the Ad Hoc Tribunals* (2010) Oxford Scholarship Online <http://bit.ly/2TccDvf> accessed 17 March 2021.

In sum, the crime of aggression can be committed only by high-ranking representatives of the state authority who are 'in a position to effectively exercise control over or to direct the political or military action' of a state.

In order to better distinguish the crime of aggression from other international crimes, we have to underline one additional element that it is the only crime under international law which at the same time requires a specific internationally wrongful act by a state – an act of aggression – to be committed.

Ethnic cleansing

Meanwhile, at the present moment, **ethnic cleansing** deserves particular attention since it has become widespread in the post–Cold War era: for example, with documented cases of ethnic cleansing taking place in the territory of Georgia, the former Yugoslavia, and so forth.

However, up until now, ethnic cleansing has not been recognised as an independent crime under international law. Furthermore, there is no precise definition of this concept.

Nevertheless, the United Nations Commission of Experts, which was established by the Secretary-General according to the request of the Security Council in order to look into violations of international humanitarian law committed in the territory of the former Yugoslavia,[808] defined ethnic cleansing in its interim report as 'rendering an area ethnically homogeneous by using force or intimidation to remove persons of given groups from the area.'[809] In the final report, the Commission stated that the '"ethnic cleansing" is a purposeful policy designed by one ethnic or religious group to remove by violent and terror-inspiring means the civilian population of another ethnic or religious group from certain geographic areas'[810] On the whole, the Commission concluded that the practices of ethnic cleaning could 'constitute crimes against humanity and can be assimilated to specific war crimes. Furthermore, such acts could also fall within the meaning of the Genocide Convention.'[811]

808 Under its Resolution S/RES/780 of 14 September 1992, the UN Security Council requested 'the Secretary-General to establish, as a matter of urgency, an impartial Commission of Experts to examine and analyse the information submitted pursuant to resolution 771 (1992) and the present resolution, together with such further information as the Commission of Experts may obtain through its own investigations or efforts, of other persons or bodies pursuant to resolution 771 (1992), with a view to providing the Secretary-General with its conclusions on the evidence of grave breaches of the Geneva Conventions and other violations of international humanitarian law committed in the territory of the former Yugoslavia'.

809 Interim Report of the United Nations Commission of Experts Established Pursuant to Security Council Resolution 780 (1992), annexed to the Letter Dated 9 February 1993 from the Secretary-General to the President of the Security Council, S/25274 <https://undocs.org/S/25274> accessed 17 March 2021.

810 Final Report of the Commission of Experts Established Pursuant to Security Council Resolution 780 (1992), annexed to the Letter Dated 24 May 1994 from the Secretary-General to the President of the Security Council, S/1994/674, Paragraph 130, <https://undocs.org/S/1994/674> accessed 17 March 2021.

811 ibid Paragraph 129.

No statute of limitations

Finally, it is especially notable that there is no **statute of limitations** on international crimes. For instance, under the Convention on the Non-Applicability of Statutory Limitations to War Crimes and Crimes Against Humanity of 1968, it is prescribed that 'statutory or other limitations shall not apply to the prosecution and punishment of the crimes . . . and that, where they exist, such limitations shall be abolished.'[812]

CASES AND MATERIALS (*SELECTED PARTS*)

Responsibility of States
Responsibility of States for Internationally Wrongful Acts. The UN General Assembly Resolution A/RES/56/83
of 12 December 2001

PART ONE THE INTERNATIONALLY WRONGFUL ACT OF A STATE

Chapter I General principles

Article 1 Responsibility of a State for its internationally wrongful acts

Every internationally wrongful act of a State entails the international responsibility of that State.

Article 2 Elements of an internationally wrongful act of a State

There is an internationally wrongful act of a State when conduct consisting of an action or omission:

(a) is att ributable to the State under international law; and
(b) constitutes a breach of an international obligation of the State.

CHAPTER II ATTRIBUTION OF CONDUCT TO A STATE

Article 4 Conduct of organs of a State

1   The conduct of any State organ shall be considered an act of that State under international law, whether the organ exercises legislative, executive, judicial or any other functions, whatever position it holds in the organization of the State, and whatever its character as an organ of the central Government or of a territorial unit of the State.
2   An organ includes any person or entity which has that status in accordance with the internal law of the State.

---

812 Article IV of the Convention on the Non-Applicability of Statutory Limitations to War Crimes and Crimes Against Humanity.

CHAPTER III BREACH OF AN INTERNATIONAL OBLIGATION

Article 12 *Existence of a breach of an international obligation*

There is a breach of an international obligation by a State when an act of that State is not in conformity with what is required of it by that obligation, regardless of its origin or character.

Article 13 *International obligation in force for a State*

An act of a State does not constitute a breach of an international obligation unless the State is bound by the obligation in question at the time the act occurs.

Article 14 *Extension in time of the breach of an international obligation*

1   The breach of an international obligation by an act of a State not having a continuing character occurs at the moment when the act is performed, even if its effects continue.
2   The breach of an international obligation by an act of a State having a continuing character extends over the entire period during which the act continues and remains not in conformity with the international obligation.
3   The breach of an international obligation requiring a State to prevent a given event occurs when the event occurs and extends over the entire period during which the event continues and remains not in conformity with that obligation.

Article 15 *Breach consisting of a composite act*

1   The breach of an international obligation by a State through a series of actions or omissions defined in aggregate as wrongful occurs when the action or omission occurs which, taken with the other actions or omissions, is sufficient to constitute the wrongful act.
2   In such a case, the breach extends over the entire period starting with the first of the actions or omissions of the series and lasts for as long as these actions or omissions are repeated and remain not in conformity with the international obligation.

CHAPTER V CIRCUMSTANCES PRECLUDING WRONGFULNESS

Article 20 *Consent*

Valid consent by a State to the commission of a given act by another State precludes the wrongfulness of that act in relation to the former State to the extent that the act remains within the limits of that consent.

Article 21 *Self-defence*

The wrongfulness of an act of a State is precluded if the act constitutes a lawful measure of self-defence taken in conformity with the Charter of the United Nations.

Article 22 Countermeasures in respect of an internationally wrongful act

The wrongfulness of an act of a State not in conformity with an international obligation towards another State is precluded if and to the extent that the act constitutes a countermeasure taken against the latter State in accordance with chapter II of part three.

Article 23 Force majeure

1   The wrongfulness of an act of a State not in conformity with an international obligation of that State is precluded if the act is due to force majeure, that is the occurrence of an irresistible force or of an unforeseen event, beyond the control of the State, making it materially impossible in the circumstances to perform the obligation.
2   Paragraph 1 does not apply if:

   (a)   the situation of force majeure is due, either alone or in combination with other factors, to the conduct of the State invoking it; or
   (b)   the State has assumed the risk of that situation occurring.

Article 24 Distress

1   The wrongfulness of an act of a State not in conformity with an international obligation of that State is precluded if the author of the act in question has no other reasonable way, in a situation of distress, of saving the author's life or the lives of other persons entrusted to the author's care.
2   Paragraph 1 does not apply if:

   (a)   the situation of distress is due, either alone or in combination with other factors, to the conduct of the State invoking it; or
   (b)   the act in question is likely to create a comparable or greater peril.

Article 25 Necessity

1   Necessity may not be invoked by a State as a ground for precluding the wrongfulness of an act not in conformity with an international obligation of that State unless the act:

   (a)   is the only way for the State to safeguard an essential interest against a grave and imminent peril; and
   (b)   does not seriously impair an essential interest of the State or States towards which the obligation exists, or of the international community as a whole.
2   In any case, necessity may not be invoked by a State as a ground for precluding wrongfulness if:

   (a)   the international obligation in question excludes the possibility of invoking necessity; or
   (b)   the State has contributed to the situation of necessity.

PART TWO CONTENT OF THE INTERNATIONAL RESPONSIBILITY OF A STATE

CHAPTER I GENERAL PRINCIPLES

Article 29 Continued duty of performance

The legal consequences of an internationally wrongful act under this part do not affect the continued duty of the responsible State to perform the obligation breached.

Article 30 Cessation and non-repetition

The State responsible for the internationally wrongful act is under an obligation:

(a) to cease that act, if it is continuing;
(b) to offer appropriate assurances and guarantees of non-repetition, if circumstances so require.

Article 31 Reparation

1   The responsible State is under an obligation to make full reparation for the injury caused by the internationally wrongful act.
2   Injury includes any damage, whether material or moral, caused by the internationally wrongful act of a State.

Article 32 Irrelevance of internal law

The responsible State may not rely on the provisions of its internal law as justification for failure to comply with its obligations under this part.

Article 33 Scope of international obligations set out in this part

1   The obligations of the responsible State set out in this part may be owed to another State, to several States, or to the international community as a whole, depending in particular on the character and content of the international obligation and on the circumstances of the breach.
2   This part is without prejudice to any right, arising from the international responsibility of a State, which may accrue directly to any person or entity other than a State.

CHAPTER II REPARATION FOR INJURY

Article 34 Forms of reparation

Full reparation for the injury caused by the internationally wrongful act shall take the form of restitution, compensation and satisfaction, either singly or in combination, in accordance with the provisions of this chapter.

Article 35 Restitution

A State responsible for an internationally wrongful act is under an obligation to make restitution, that is, to re-establish the situation which existed before the wrongful act was committed, provided and to the extent that restitution:

(*a*) is not materially impossible;

(*b*) does not involve a burden out of all proportion to the benefit deriving from restitution instead of compensation.

Article 36 Compensation

1 The State responsible for an internationally wrongful act is under an obligation to compensate for the damage caused thereby, insofar as such damage is not made good by restitution.

2 The compensation shall cover any financially assessable damage including loss of profits insofar as it is established.

Article 37 Satisfaction

1 The State responsible for an internationally wrongful act is under an obligation to give satisfaction for the injury caused by that act insofar as it cannot be made good by restitution or compensation.

2 Satisfaction may consist in an acknowledgement of the breach, an expression of regret, a formal apology or another appropriate modality.

3 Satisfaction shall not be out of proportion to the injury and may not take a form humiliating to the responsible State.

Article 38 Interest

1 Interest on any principal sum due under this chapter shall be payable when necessary in order to ensure full reparation. The interest rate and mode of calculation shall be set so as to achieve that result.

2 Interest runs from the date when the principal sum should have been paid until the date the obligation to pay is fulfilled.

Article 39 Contribution to the injury

In the determination of reparation, account shall be taken of the contribution to the injury by wilful or negligent action or omission of the injured State or any person or entity in relation to whom reparation is sought.

CHAPTER III SERIOUS BREACHES OF OBLIGATIONS UNDER PEREMPTORY NORMS OF GENERAL INTERNATIONAL LAW

Article 40 Application of this chapter

1 This chapter applies to the international responsibility which is entailed by a serious breach by a State of an obligation arising under a peremptory norm of general international law.

2   A breach of such an obligation is serious if it involves a gross or systematic failure by the responsible State to fulfil the obligation.

Article 41 Particular consequences of a serious breach of an obligation under this chapter

1   States shall cooperate to bring to an end through lawful means any serious breach within the meaning of article 40.
2   No State shall recognize as lawful a situation created by a serious breach within the meaning of article 40, nor render aid or assistance in maintaining that situation.
3   This article is without prejudice to the other consequences referred to in this part and to such further consequences that a breach to which this chapter applies may entail under international law.

Reparation

Chorzów Factory (Germany v Poland), Judgment No.13 of 13 September 1928, Permanent Court of International Justice
PCIJ Ser A – No.17.

Three fundamental questions arise:

(1) The existence of the obligation to make reparation.
(2) The existence of the damage which must serve as a basis for the calculation of the amount of the indemnity.
(3) The extent of this damage.

As regards the first point, the Court observes that it is a principle of international law, and even a general conception of law, that any breach of an engagement involves an obligation to make reparation. In Judgment No. 8, when deciding on the jurisdiction derived by it from Article 23 of the Geneva Convention, the Court has already said that reparation is the indispensable complement of a failure to apply a convention, and there is no necessity for this to be stated in the convention itself. The existence of the principle establishing the obligation to make reparation, as an element of positive international law, has moreover never been disputed in the course of the proceedings in the various cases concerning the Chorzów factory.

The obligation to make reparation being in principle recognized, it remains to be ascertained whether a breach of an international engagement has in fact taken place in the case under consideration. Now this point is *res judicata* . . .

[I]t should first be observed that, in estimating the damage caused by an unlawful act, only the value of property, rights and interests which have been affected and the owner of which is the person on whose behalf compensation is claimed, or the damage done to whom is to serve as a means of gauging the reparation claimed, must be taken into account. This principle, which is accepted in the jurisprudence of arbitral tribunals, has the effect, on the one hand, of excluding from the damage to be estimated, injury resulting for third parties from the unlawful act and, on the other hand, of not excluding from the damage the amount of debts and other obligations for which the injured party is responsible.

Nuremberg Tribunal

Charter of the International Military Tribunal

Annex to the Agreement for the Prosecution and Punishment of the Major War Criminals of the European Axis ('London Agreement') of 8 August 1945
Entry into force: 8 August 1945

I. CONSTITUTION OF THE INTERNATIONAL MILITARY TRIBUNAL

Article 1

In pursuance of the Agreement signed on 8 August 1945, by the Government of the United Kingdom of Great Britain and Northern Ireland, the Government of the United States of America, the Provisional Government of the French Republic and the Government of the Union of Soviet Socialist Republics, there shall be established an International Military Tribunal (hereinafter called "the Tribunal") for the just and prompt trial and punishment of the major war criminals of the European Axis.

Article 2

The Tribunal shall consist of four members, each with an alternate. One member and one alternate shall be appointed by each of the Signatories. The alternates shall, so far as they are able, be present at all sessions of the Tribunal. In case of illness of any member of the Tribunal or his incapacity for some other reason to fulfil his functions, his alternate shall take his place.

Article 4

(a) The presence of all four members of the Tribunal or the alternate for any absent member shall be necessary to constitute the quorum.
(b) The members of the Tribunal shall, before any trial begins, agree among themselves upon the selection from their number of a President, and the President shall hold office during that trial, or as may otherwise be agreed by a vote of not less than three members. The principle of rotation of presidency for successive trials is agreed. If, however, a session of the Tribunal takes place on the territory of one of the four Signatories, the representative of that Signatory on the Tribunal shall preside.
(c) Save as aforesaid the Tribunal shall take decisions by a majority vote and in case the votes are evenly divided, the vote of the President shall be decisive; provided always that convictions and sentences shall only be imposed by affirmative votes of at least three members of the Tribunal.

II. JURISDICTION AND GENERAL PRINCIPLES

Article 6

The Tribunal established by the Agreement referred to in Article 1 hereof for the trial and punishment of the major war criminals of the European Axis countries shall have the power to try and punish persons who, acting in the interests of the European Axis countries, whether as individuals or as members of organizations, committed any of the following crimes.

The following acts, or any of them, are crimes coming within the jurisdiction of the Tribunal for which there shall be individual responsibility:

a) Crimes against peace: namely, planning, preparation, initiation or waging of a war of aggression, or a war in violation of international treaties, agreements or assurances, or participation in a common plan or conspiracy for the accomplishment of any of the foregoing;

b) War crimes: namely, violations of the laws or customs of war. Such violations shall include, but not be limited to, murder, ill-treatment or deportation to Wave labour or for any other purpose of civilian population of or in occupied territory, murder or ill-treatment of prisoners of war or persons on the seas, killing of hostages, plunder of public or private property, wanton destruction of cities, towns or villages, or devastation not justified by military necessity;

c) Crimes against humanity: namely, murder, extermination, enslavement, deportation, and other inhumane acts committed against any civilian population, before or during the war, or persecutions on political, racial or religious grounds in execution of or in connection with any crime within the jurisdiction of the Tribunal, whether or not in violation of the domestic law of the country where perpetrated.

Leaders, organizers, instigators and accomplices participating in the formulation or execution of a common plan or conspiracy to commit any of the foregoing crimes are responsible for all acts performed by any persons in execution of such plan.

Article 7

The official position of defendants, whether as Heads of State or responsible officials in Government Departments, shall not be considered as freeing them from responsibility or mitigating punishment.

Article 8

The fact that the Defendant acted pursuant to order of his Government or of a superior shall not free him from responsibility, but may be considered in mitigation of punishment if the Tribunal determines that justice so requires.

Article 9

At the trial of any individual member of any group or organization the Tribunal may declare (in connection with any act of which the individual may be convicted) that the group or organization of which the individual was a member was a criminal organization.

After receipt of the Indictment the Tribunal shall give such notice as it thinks fit that the prosecution intends to ask the Tribunal to make such declaration and any member of the organization will be entitled to apply to the Tribunal for leave to be heard by the Tribunal upon the question of the criminal character of the organization. The Tribunal shall have power to allow or reject the application. If the application is allowed, the Tribunal may direct in what manner the applicants shall be represented and heard.

III. COMMITTEE FOR THE INVESTIGATION AND PROSECUTION OF MAJOR WAR CRIMINALS

Article 14

Each Signatory shall appoint a Chief Prosecutor for the investigation of the charges against and the prosecution of major war criminals.

The Chief Prosecutors shall act as a committee for the following purposes:

a) to agree upon a plan of the individual work of each of the Chief Prosecutors and his staff,
b) to settle the final designation of major war criminals to be tried by the Tribunal,
c) to approve the Indictment and the documents to be submitted therewith,
d) to lodge the Indictment and the accompanying documents with the Tribunal,
e) to draw up and recommend to the Tribunal for its approval draft rules of procedure, contemplated by Article 13 of this Charter. The Tribunal shall have power to accept, with or without amendments, or to reject, the rules so recommended.

The Committee shall act in all the above matters by a majority vote and shall appoint a Chairman as may be convenient and in accordance with the principle of rotation: provided that if there is an equal division of vote concerning the designation of a Defendant to be tried by the Tribunal, or the crimes with which he shall be charged, that proposal will be adopted which was made by the party which proposed that the particular Defendant be tried, or the particular charges be preferred against him.

Article 15

The Chief Prosecutors shall individually, and acting in collaboration with one another, also undertake the following duties:

a) investigation, collection and production before or at the Trial of all necessary evidence,
b) the preparation of the Indictment for approval by the Committee in accordance with paragraph (c) of Article 14 hereof,
c) the preliminary examination of all necessary witnesses and of the Defendants,
d) to act as prosecutor at the Trial,
e) to appoint representatives to carry out such duties as may be assigned to them,
f) to undertake such other matters as may appear necessary to them for the purposes of the preparation for and conduct of the Trial.

It is understood that no witness or Defendant detained by any Signatory shall be taken out of the possession of that Signatory without its assent.

IV. FAIR TRIAL FOR DEFENDANTS

Article 16

In order to ensure fair trial for the Defendants, the following procedure shall be followed:

a) The Indictment shall include full particulars specifying in detail the charges against the Defendants. A copy of the Indictment and of all the documents lodged with the Indictment, translated

into a language which he understands, shall be furnished to the Defendant at a reasonable time before the Trial.
b)   During any preliminary examination or trial of a Defendant he shall have the right to give any explanation relevant to the charges made against him.
c)   A preliminary examination of a Defendant and his Trial shall be conducted in, or translated into, a language which the Defendant understands.
d)   A Defendant shall have the right to conduct his own defence before the Tribunal or to have the assistance of Counsel.
e)   A Defendant shall have the right through himself or through his Counsel to present evidence at the Trial in support of his defence, and to cross-examine any witness called by the Prosecution.

V. POWERS OF THE TRIBUNAL AND CONDUCT OF THE TRIAL

Article 17

The Tribunal shall have the power:

a)   to summon witnesses to the Trial and to require their attendance and testimony and to put questions to them,
b)   to interrogate any Defendant,
c)   to require the production of documents and other evidentiary material,
d)   to administer oaths to witnesses,
e)   to appoint officers for the carrying out of any task designated by the Tribunal including the power to have evidence taken on commission.

Article 18

The Tribunal shall:

a)   confine the Trial strictly to an expeditious hearing of the issues raised by the charges,
b)   take strict measures to prevent any action which will cause unreasonable delay, and rule out irrelevant issues and statements of any kind whatsoever,
c)   deal summarily with any contumacy, imposing appropriate punishment, including exclusion of any Defendant or his Counsel from some or all further proceedings, but without prejudice to the determination of the charges.

Article 24

The proceedings at the Trial shall take the following course:

a)   The Indictment shall be read in court.
b)   The Tribunal shall ask each Defendant whether he pleads "guilty" or "not guilty."
c)   The Prosecution shall make an opening statement.
d)   The Tribunal shall ask the Prosecution and the Defence what evidence (if any) they wish to submit to the Tribunal, and the Tribunal shall rule upon the admissibility of any such evidence.
e)   The witnesses for the Prosecution shall be examined and after that the witnesses for the Defence. Thereafter such rebutting evidence as may be held by the Tribunal to be admissible

shall be called by either the Prosecution or the Defence.

f)   The Tribunal may put any question to any witness and to any Defendant, at any time.

g)   The Prosecution and the Defence shall interrogate and may cross-examine any witnesses and any Defendant who gives testimony.

h)   Defence shall address the court.

i)   The Prosecution shall address the court.

j)   Each Defendant may make a statement to the Tribunal.

k)   The Tribunal shall deliver judgment and pronounce sentence.

Article 25

All official documents shall be produced, and all court proceedings conducted, in English, French and Russian, and in the language of the Defendant. So much of the record and of the proceedings may also be translated into the language of any country in which the Tribunal is sitting, as the Tribunal considers desirable in the interests of justice and public opinion.

VI. JUDGMENT AND SENTENCE

Article 26

The judgment of the Tribunal as to the guilt or the innocence of any Defendant shall give the reasons on which it is based, and shall be final and not subject to review.

Article 27

The Tribunal shall have the right to impose upon a Defendant, on conviction, death or such other punishment as shall be determined by it to be just.

Article 28

In addition to any punishment imposed by it, the Tribunal shall have the right to deprive the convicted person of any stolen property and order its delivery to the Control Council for Germany.

International Criminal Court

Rome Statute of the International Criminal Court

of 17 July 1998
Entry into force: 1 July 2002

PART 1. ESTABLISHMENT OF THE COURT

Article 1 The Court

An International Criminal Court ("the Court") is hereby established. It shall be a permanent institution and shall have the power to exercise its jurisdiction over persons for the most serious crimes of international concern, as referred to in this Statute, and shall be complementary to national criminal jurisdictions. The jurisdiction and functioning of the Court shall be governed by the provisions of this Statute.

PART 2. JURISDICTION, ADMISSIBILITY AND APPLICABLE LAW

Article 5 Crimes within the jurisdiction of the Court

The jurisdiction of the Court shall be limited to the most serious crimes of concern to the international community as a whole. The Court has jurisdiction in accordance with this Statute with respect to the following crimes:

(a) The crime of genocide;
(b) Crimes against humanity;
(c) War crimes;
(d) The crime of aggression.

Article 6 Genocide

For the purpose of this Statute, "genocide" means any of the following acts committed with intent to destroy, in whole or in part, a national, ethnical, racial or religious group, as such:

(a) Killing members of the group;
(b) Causing serious bodily or mental harm to members of the group;
(c) Deliberately inflicting on the group conditions of life calculated to bring about its physical destruction in whole or in part;
(d) Imposing measures intended to prevent births within the group;
(e) Forcibly transferring children of the group to another group.

Article 7 Crimes against humanity

1 For the purpose of this Statute, "crime against humanity" means any of the following acts when committed as part of a widespread or systematic attack directed against any civilian population, with knowledge of the attack:

   (a) Murder;
   (b) Extermination;
   (c) Enslavement;
   (d) Deportation or forcible transfer of population;
   (e) Imprisonment or other severe deprivation of physical liberty in violation of fundamental rules of international law;
   (f) Torture;
   (g) Rape, sexual slavery, enforced prostitution, forced pregnancy, enforced sterilization, or any other form of sexual violence of comparable gravity;
   (h) Persecution against any identifiable group or collectivity on political, racial, national, ethnic, cultural, religious, gender as defined in paragraph 3, or other grounds that are universally recognized as impermissible under international law, in connection with any act referred to in this paragraph or any crime within the jurisdiction of the Court;

    (i)   Enforced disappearance of persons;

    (j)   The crime of apartheid;

    (k)   Other inhumane acts of a similar character intentionally causing great suffering, or serious injury to body or to mental or physical health.

2   For the purpose of paragraph 1:

    (a)   "Attack directed against any civilian population" means a course of conduct involving the multiple commission of acts referred to in paragraph 1 against any civilian population, pursuant to or in furtherance of a State or organizational policy to commit such attack;

    (b)   "Extermination" includes the intentional infliction of conditions of life, inter alia the deprivation of access to food and medicine, calculated to bring about the destruction of part of a population;

    (c)   "Enslavement" means the exercise of any or all of the powers attaching to the right of ownership over a person and includes the exercise of such power in the course of trafficking in persons, in particular women and children;

    (d)   "Deportation or forcible transfer of population" means forced displacement of the persons concerned by expulsion or other coercive acts from the area in which they are lawfully present, without grounds permitted under international law;

    (e)   "Torture" means the intentional infliction of severe pain or suffering, whether physical or mental, upon a person in the custody or under the control of the accused; except that torture shall not include pain or suffering arising only from, inherent in or incidental to, lawful sanctions;

    (f)   "Forced pregnancy" means the unlawful confinement of a woman forcibly made pregnant, with the intent of affecting the ethnic composition of any population or carrying out other grave violations of international law. This definition shall not in any way be interpreted as affecting national laws relating to pregnancy;

    (g)   "Persecution" means the intentional and severe deprivation of fundamental rights contrary to international law by reason of the identity of the group or collectivity;

    (h)   "The crime of apartheid" means inhumane acts of a character similar to those referred to in paragraph 1, committed in the context of an institutionalized regime of systematic oppression and domination by one racial group over any other racial group or groups and committed with the intention of maintaining that regime;

    (i)   "Enforced disappearance of persons" means the arrest, detention or abduction of persons by, or with the authorization, support or acquiescence of, a State or a political organization, followed by a refusal to acknowledge that deprivation of freedom or to give information on the fate or whereabouts of those persons, with the intention of removing them from the protection of the law for a prolonged period of time.

3   For the purpose of this Statute, it is understood that the term "gender" refers to the two sexes, male and female, within the context of society. The term "gender" does not indicate any meaning different from the above

Article 8 War crimes

1   The Court shall have jurisdiction in respect of war crimes in particular when committed as part of a plan or policy or as part of a large-scale commission of such crimes.

2   For the purpose of this Statute, "war crimes" means:

(a)   Grave breaches of the Geneva Conventions of 12 August 1949, namely, any of the following acts against persons or property protected under the provisions of the relevant Geneva Convention:

(i)   Wilful killing;

(ii)   Torture or inhuman treatment, including biological experiments;

(iii)   Wilfully causing great suffering, or serious injury to body or health;

(iv)   Extensive destruction and appropriation of property, not justified by military necessity and carried out unlawfully and wantonly;

(v)   Compelling a prisoner of war or other protected person to serve in the forces of a hostile Power;

(vi)   Wilfully depriving a prisoner of war or other protected person of the rights of fair and regular trial;

(vii)   Unlawful deportation or transfer or unlawful confinement;

(viii)   Taking of hostages.

(b)   Other serious violations of the laws and customs applicable in international armed conflict, within the established framework of international law, namely, any of the following acts:

(i)   Intentionally directing attacks against the civilian population as such or against individual civilians not taking direct part in hostilities;

(ii)   Intentionally directing attacks against civilian objects, that is, objects which are not military objectives;

(iii)   Intentionally directing attacks against personnel, installations, material, units or vehicles involved in a humanitarian assistance or peacekeeping mission in accordance with the Charter of the United Nations, as long as they are entitled to the protection given to civilians or civilian objects under the international law of armed conflict;

(iv)   Intentionally launching an attack in the knowledge that such attack will cause incidental loss of life or injury to civilians or damage to civilian objects or widespread, long-term and severe damage to the natural environment which would be clearly excessive in relation to the concrete and direct overall military advantage anticipated;

(v)   Attacking or bombarding, by whatever means, towns, villages, dwellings or buildings which are undefended and which are not military objectives;

(vi)   Killing or wounding a combatant who, having laid down his arms or having no longer means of defence, has surrendered at discretion;

(vii)   Making improper use of a flag of truce, of the flag or of the military insignia and uniform of the enemy or of the United Nations, as well as of the distinctive emblems of the Geneva Conventions, resulting in death or serious personal injury;

(viii)   The transfer, directly or indirectly, by the Occupying Power of parts of its own civilian population into the territory it occupies, or the deportation or transfer of all or parts of the population of the occupied territory within or outside this territory;

(ix)   Intentionally directing attacks against buildings dedicated to religion, education, art, science or charitable purposes, historic monuments, hospitals and places where the sick and wounded are collected, provided they are not military objectives;

(x) Subjecting persons who are in the power of an adverse party to physical mutilation or to medical or scientific experiments of any kind which are neither justified by the medical, dental or hospital treatment of the person concerned nor carried out in his or her interest, and which cause death to or seriously endanger the health of such person or persons;

(xi) Killing or wounding treacherously individuals belonging to the hostile nation or army;

(xii) Declaring that no quarter will be given;

(xiii) Destroying or seizing the enemy's property unless such destruction or seizure be imperatively demanded by the necessities of war;

(xiv) Declaring abolished, suspended or inadmissible in a court of law the rights and actions of the nationals of the hostile party;

(xv) Compelling the nationals of the hostile party to take part in the operations of war directed against their own country, even if they were in the belligerent's service before the commencement of the war;

(xvi) Pillaging a town or place, even when taken by assault;

(xvii) Employing poison or poisoned weapons;

(xviii) Employing asphyxiating, poisonous or other gases, and all analogous liquids, materials or devices;

(xix) Employing bullets which expand or flatten easily in the human body, such as bullets with a hard envelope which does not entirely cover the core or is pierced with incisions;

(xx) Employing weapons, projectiles and material and methods of warfare which are of a nature to cause superfluous injury or unnecessary suffering or which are inherently indiscriminate in violation of the international law of armed conflict, provided that such weapons, projectiles and material and methods of warfare are the subject of a comprehensive prohibition and are included in an annex to this Statute, by an amendment in accordance with the relevant provisions set forth in articles 121 and 123;

(xxi) Committing outrages upon personal dignity, in particular humiliating and degrading treatment;

(xxii) Committing rape, sexual slavery, enforced prostitution, forced pregnancy, as defined in article 7, paragraph 2 (f), enforced sterilization, or any other form of sexual violence also constituting a grave breach of the Geneva Conventions;

(xxiii) Utilizing the presence of a civilian or other protected person to render certain points, areas or military forces immune from military operations;

(xxiv) Intentionally directing attacks against buildings, material, medical units and transport, and personnel using the distinctive emblems of the Geneva Conventions in conformity with international law;

(xxv) Intentionally using starvation of civilians as a method of warfare by depriving them of objects indispensable to their survival, including wilfully impeding relief supplies as provided for under the Geneva Conventions;

(xxvi) Conscripting or enlisting children under the age of fifteen years into the national armed forces or using them to participate actively in hostilities.

(c) In the case of an armed conflict not of an international character, serious violations of article 3 common to the four Geneva Conventions of 12 August 1949, namely, any of the following acts committed against persons taking no active part in the hostilities, including members of armed forces who have laid down their arms and those placed hors de combat by sickness, wounds, detention or any other cause:

(i) Violence to life and person, in particular murder of all kinds, mutilation, cruel treatment and torture;

(ii) Committing outrages upon personal dignity, in particular humiliating and degrading treatment;

(iii) Taking of hostages;

(iv) The passing of sentences and the carrying out of executions without previous judgement pronounced by a regularly constituted court, affording all judicial guarantees which are generally recognized as indispensable.

(d) Paragraph 2 (c) applies to armed conflicts not of an international character and thus does not apply to situations of internal disturbances and tensions, such as riots, isolated and sporadic acts of violence or other acts of a similar nature.

(e) Other serious violations of the laws and customs applicable in armed conflicts not of an international character, within the established framework of international law, namely, any of the following acts:

(i) Intentionally directing attacks against the civilian population as such or against individual civilians not taking direct part in hostilities;

(ii) Intentionally directing attacks against buildings, material, medical units and transport, and personnel using the distinctive emblems of the Geneva Conventions in conformity with international law;

(iii) Intentionally directing attacks against personnel, installations, material, units or vehicles involved in a humanitarian assistance or peacekeeping mission in accordance with the Charter of the United Nations, as long as they are entitled to the protection given to civilians or civilian objects under the international law of armed conflict;

(iv) Intentionally directing attacks against buildings dedicated to religion, education, art, science or charitable purposes, historic monuments, hospitals and places where the sick and wounded are collected, provided they are not military objectives;

(v) Pillaging a town or place, even when taken by assault;

(vi) Committing rape, sexual slavery, enforced prostitution, forced pregnancy, as defined in article 7, paragraph 2 (f), enforced sterilization, and any other form of sexual violence also constituting a serious violation of article 3 common to the four Geneva Conventions;

(vii) Conscripting or enlisting children under the age of fifteen years into armed forces or groups or using them to participate actively in hostilities;

(viii) Ordering the displacement of the civilian population for reasons related to the conflict, unless the security of the civilians involved or imperative military reasons so demand;

(ix) Killing or wounding treacherously a combatant adversary;

(x) Declaring that no quarter will be given;

(xi) Subjecting persons who are in the power of another party to the conflict to physical mutilation or to medical or scientific experiments of any kind which are neither justified by the medical, dental or hospital treatment of the person concerned nor carried out in his or her interest, and which cause death to or seriously endanger the health of such person or persons;

(xii) Destroying or seizing the property of an adversary unless such destruction or seizure be imperatively demanded by the necessities of the conflict;

(xiii) Employing poison or poisoned weapons;

(xiv) Employing asphyxiating, poisonous or other gases, and all analogous liquids, materials or devices;

(xv) Employing bullets which expand or flatten easily in the human body, such as bullets with a hard envelope which does not entirely cover the core or is pierced with incisions.

(f) Paragraph 2 (e) applies to armed conflicts not of an international character and thus does not apply to situations of internal disturbances and tensions, such as riots, isolated and sporadic acts of violence or other acts of a similar nature. It applies to armed conflicts that take place in the territory of a State when there is protracted armed conflict between governmental authorities and organized armed groups or between such groups.

3   Nothing in paragraph 2 (c) and (e) shall affect the responsibility of a Government to maintain or re-establish law and order in the State or to defend the unity and territorial integrity of the State, by all legitimate means.

Article 8 bis Crime of aggression

1   For the purpose of this Statute, "crime of aggression" means the planning, preparation, initiation or execution, by a person in a position effectively to exercise control over or to direct the political or military action of a State, of an act of aggression which, by its character, gravity and scale, constitutes a manifest violation of the Charter of the United Nations.

2   For the purpose of paragraph 1, "act of aggression" means the use of armed force by a State against the sovereignty, territorial integrity or political independence of another State, or in any other manner inconsistent with the Charter of the United Nations. Any of the following acts, regardless of a declaration of war, shall, in accordance with United Nations General Assembly resolution 3314 (XXIX) of 14 December 1974, qualify as an act of aggression:

(a) The invasion or attack by the armed forces of a State of the territory of another State, or any military occupation, however temporary, resulting from such invasion or attack, or any annexation by the use of force of the territory of another State or part thereof;

(b) Bombardment by the armed forces of a State against the territory of another State or the use of any weapons by a State against the territory of another State;

(c) The blockade of the ports or coasts of a State by the armed forces of another State;

(d) An attack by the armed forces of a State on the land, sea or air forces, or marine and air fleets of another State;

(e) The use of armed forces of one State which are within the territory of another State with the agreement of the receiving State, in contravention of the conditions provided for in the agreement or any extension of their presence in such territory beyond the termination of the agreement;

(f)   The action of a State in allowing its territory, which it has placed at the disposal of another State, to be used by that other State for perpetrating an act of aggression against a third State;

(g)   The sending by or on behalf of a State of armed bands, groups, irregulars or mercenaries, which carry out acts of armed force against another State of such gravity as to amount to the acts listed above, or its substantial involvement therein.

Article 9 Elements of Crimes

1   Elements of Crimes shall assist the Court in the interpretation and application of articles 6, 7, 8 and 8 bis. They shall be adopted by a two-thirds majority of the members of the Assembly of States Parties.

2   Amendments to the Elements of Crimes may be proposed by:

(a)   Any State Party;
(b)   The judges acting by an absolute majority;
(c)   The Prosecutor.

Such amendments shall be adopted by a two-thirds majority of the members of the Assembly of States Parties.

3   The Elements of Crimes and amendments thereto shall be consistent with this Statute.

Elements of Crimes

Elements of Crimes, International Criminal Court
(International Criminal Court 2011, Printed by PrintPartners Ipskamp, Enschede) 1.

'1   . . . The provisions of the Statute, including article 21 and the general principles set out in Part 3, are applicable to the Elements of Crimes.

2   As stated in article 30, unless otherwise provided, a person shall be criminally responsible and liable for punishment for a crime within the jurisdiction of the Court only if the material elements are committed with intent and knowledge. Where no reference is made in the Elements of Crimes to a mental element for any particular conduct, consequence or circumstance listed, it is understood that the relevant mental element, i.e. intent, knowledge or both, set out in article 30 applies. Exceptions to the article 30 standard, based on the Statute, including applicable law under its relevant provisions, are indicated below.

3   Existence of intent and knowledge can be inferred from relevant facts and circumstances.

4   With respect to mental elements associated with elements involving value judgement, such as those using the terms "inhumane" or "severe", it is not necessary that the perpetrator personally completed a particular value judgement, unless otherwise indicated.

5   Grounds for excluding criminal responsibility or the absence thereof are generally not specified in the elements of crimes listed under each crime.

6   The requirement of "unlawfulness" found in the Statute or in other parts of international law, in particular international humanitarian law, is generally not specified in the elements of crimes.

7   The elements of crimes are generally structured in accordance with the following principles:

(a)   As the elements of crimes focus on the conduct, consequences and circumstances associated with each crime, they are generally listed in that order;

(b) When required, a particular mental element is listed after the affected conduct, consequence or circumstance;

(c) Contextual circumstances are listed last.'

No statutory limitation

Convention on the Non-Applicability of Statutory Limitations to War Crimes and Crimes
Against Humanity
Adopted and opened for signature, ratification and accession by General Assembly resolu-
tion A/RES/2391 (XXIII) of 26 November 1968
Entry into force: 11 November 1970

Article I

No statutory limitation shall apply to the following crimes, irrespective of the date of their commission: (a) War crimes as they are defined in the Charter of the International Military Tribunal,
Nürnberg, of 8 August 1945 and confirmed by resolutions 3 (I) of 13 February 1946 and 95
(I) of 11 December 1946 of the General Assembly of the United Nations, particularly the "grave
breaches" enumerated in the Geneva Conventions of 12 August 1949 for the protection of war
victims; (b) Crimes against humanity whether committed in time of war or in time of peace as they
are defined in the Charter of the International Military Tribunal, Nürnberg, of 8 August 1945
and confirmed by resolutions 3 (I) of 13 February 1946 and 95 (I) of 11 December 1946 of the
General Assembly of the United Nations, eviction by armed attack or occupation and inhuman
acts resulting from the policy of apartheid, and the crime of genocide as defined in the 1948
Convention on the Prevention and Punishment of the Crime of Genocide, even if such acts do not
constitute a violation of the domestic law of the country in which they were committed.

Article II

If any of the crimes mentioned in article I is committed, the provisions of this Convention shall
apply to representatives of the State authority and private individuals who, as principals or accomplices, participate in or who directly incite others to the commission of any of those crimes, or who
conspire to commit them, irrespective of the degree of completion, and to representatives of the
State authority who tolerate their commission.

Article III

The States Parties to the present Convention undertake to adopt all necessary domestic measures,
legislative or otherwise, with a view to making possible the extradition, in accordance with international law, of the persons referred to in article II of this Convention.

Article IV

The States Parties to the present Convention undertake to adopt, in accordance with their respective constitutional processes, any legislative or other measures necessary to ensure that statutory
or other limitations shall not apply to the prosecution and punishment of the crimes referred to in
articles I and II of this Convention and that, where they exist, such limitations shall be abolished.

Jurisdiction

DOI: 10.4324/9781003213772-10

THE DIMENSIONS OF JURISDICTION

> concept of jurisdiction
> concept of state immunity
> state territory
> citizens
> territoriality and nationality principles
> sovereign rights
> functional jurisdiction

Interdependence between jurisdiction, state sovereignty, and immunity

In international law, the **concept of jurisdiction** is closely related to the doctrine of sovereignty. From state sovereignty also derives the **concept of state immunity**. On the other hand, both these concepts (jurisdiction and state immunity) are rooted in the general principle of law – one sovereign power cannot exercise jurisdiction over another sovereign power (Lat. – *par in parem non habet imperium*).

The broader sense of jurisdiction in international law

In international law, the term 'jurisdiction' is employed in a much broader sense than it is used in national law (and in private international law) and encompasses any exercise of regulatory power by a state. At the same time, the popular domestic sense of jurisdiction, which specifically links it with the powers of the courts, is also practised under international law concerning the power of international courts and tribunals.

Two dimensions of jurisdiction

Contemporary states enjoy jurisdiction over places and persons, which are the two distinct dimensions of jurisdiction. Therefore, the **state territory** and **citizens** comprise the two essential elements of the states' jurisdictional concerns. However, although the **territoriality and nationality principles** primarily and predominantly determine jurisdiction, it is not inevitably and exclusively so.

Territory

Initially, the concept of the jurisdiction of states was considered a legal monopoly over a certain area of the earth's solid surface (*terra firma*).[813]

---

813 '*Terra firma* . . . "Solid land." (1) Solid ground. (2) Land of the kind that forms territory subject to state sovereignty.' *Guide to Latin in International Law* (n 71) 276.

However, over time, additional places have attracted the attention of states. From the late Middle Ages, European states disputed the issue of whether the oceans and seas would be owned by a few or shared by the many. The beginning of the age of the aeroplane specified the need for involving the airspace above the state territories in the jurisdictional frame. Simultaneously, the Antarctic and Arctic areas attracted international interest in the post–Second World War period. Finally, the first satellite launched into the space created another jurisdictional area in outer space.

Nevertheless, the states' jurisdictional attention, of course, is focused mostly on the state territory, which itself represents a complex legal notion.

Functional jurisdiction of states

However, nowadays, state territories do not constitute the only places in which the states' jurisdictions apply. Modern international law also considers other places to which the states hold (functional) **sovereign rights**, and such territories, therefore, fall under the **functional jurisdiction** of states.

'Functional jurisdiction' is primarily used in the law of the sea, where it refers to coastal states' limited jurisdiction over the activities in the maritime zones (the contiguous zone, the exclusive economic zone, the continental shelf) and, to a limited extent, to any state's jurisdiction over certain activities on the high seas.[814] However, the term can be also applied to other cases as well: for example, in relation to the leased territory where a lessee state can exercise jurisdiction without having full sovereignty over that territory.

On the whole, functional jurisdiction means that there are the limits established by international law for the application of such jurisdiction. The scope of limits is defined by the permissive rules of international law authorising the application of the sovereign rights to those territories.

Natural and legal persons

States are concerned with more than the physical spaces of the world. There is also the jurisdictional focus over natural and legal persons. With regard to natural persons, the states in this context mostly consider their citizens, but at the same time, the states also apply their rules to legal persons, foreign businesspeople, tourists, and others who are located in the state's territory.

The comprehensive picture of jurisdictional concerns

Finally, the jurisdictional concerns of a state are not restricted by the principles of territoriality and nationality. They are comprehensive and, in some instances, overlap with the jurisdictional lines of the other subjects. Meanwhile, in the cross-cutting areas, there appear to be additional grounds to make jurisdictional claims.

814 See the chapter of this book 'The law of the sea.'

THE NOTION OF JURISDICTION

> legislative jurisdiction
> executive jurisdiction
> judicial jurisdiction

The three types of jurisdiction

Jurisdiction refers to the power of a state to affect persons, property, and circumstances. It may be exercised through legislative, executive, or judicial actions. Therefore, jurisdiction implies the authority to prescribe rules of law, to enforce the prescribed rules of law, and to consider legal cases.

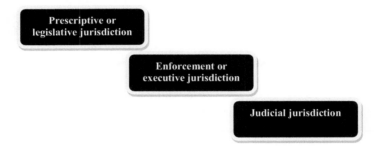

FIGURE 10.1 Three types of jurisdiction

Legislative jurisdiction

Prescriptive or **legislative jurisdiction** refers to the power of a state to make its laws applicable to persons, property, and circumstances since a state has the supremacy to make binding legislation within its territory. This supremacy is entrusted to certain organs and officials, which, in turn, are titled according to the national legal norms of a state.

Although legislation is primarily enforceable within state territory, it may extend beyond its borders in certain circumstances.[815]

Executive jurisdiction

Executive jurisdiction is the capacity of a state to enforce its legislation within its territory. As a rule, states have no authority to carry out their executive jurisdiction in foreign

---

815 For example, concerning the particular cases covered by the conflict of laws. Some aspects of international private law, including choice of law clauses in agreements between natural persons, companies, corporations, and other legal entities, that specify which laws the parties, court, or tribunal should apply to each aspect of the agreement will be examined later in this chapter.

territory since no state has the authority to interfere in the territorial sovereignty of another state. Therefore, a state cannot enforce its laws in foreign territory without the consent of the concerned state.

Judicial jurisdiction

Judicial jurisdiction is the power of a state to create courts, assign their jurisdiction, and lay down the procedures to be followed. At the same time, judicial jurisdiction refers to the capacity of the courts of a state to try legal cases.

LOTUS PRINCIPLE

> foundational principle of the jurisdiction of states
> Lotus principle
> *Lotus* case
> jurisdiction is certainly territorial
> wide measure of discretion, which is only limited in certain cases
> by prohibitive rules
> everything which is not forbidden is allowed
> everything which is not allowed is forbidden

The *Case of the S.S. 'Lotus'*

The Permanent Court of International Justice determined the **foundational principle of the jurisdiction of states** (the so-called **Lotus principle**) through Judgment No. 9 of 1927 on the ***Lotus* case** *(France v Turkey)*.[816]

Jurisdiction as limited within the territory of a state

The main target of the Lotus principle is to maintain the sovereignty of every state.

Consequently, on the one hand, a state cannot exercise its jurisdiction outside its territory unless international law permits it to do so in specific cases.

---

816 The *Lotus* case was the result of a collision which happened on the high seas between a French vessel – the *Lotus* – and a Turkish vessel – the *Boz-Kourt*. The victims were Turkish nationals, and the alleged offender was French. The survivors were transported to Turkey aboard the *Lotus*. Subsequently, in Turkey, the officer on watch on the *Lotus*, a French national, was charged with manslaughter and was sentenced. The primary legal question before the Court was the following: Did Turkey break the rules of international law by exercising jurisdiction over a crime committed by a French national on the high seas, i.e. outside the territory of Turkey?

In the *Lotus* case, the Court underlined that:

> Now the first and foremost restriction imposed by international law upon a State is that – failing the existence of a permissive rule to the contrary – it may not exercise its power in any form in the territory of another State. In this sense **jurisdiction is certainly territorial**; it cannot be exercised by a State outside its territory except by virtue of a permissive rule derived from international custom or from a convention.[817]

A considerable measure of discretion within its territory

On the other hand, within its territory, a state may exercise its jurisdiction with respect to any case, even if there is no specific rule of international law determining the exact scope of jurisdiction inside its borders. In these instances, the states have a considerable measure of discretion, which may only be limited by the restrictive rules of international law. The Court held that:

> It does not, however, follow that international law prohibits a State from exercising jurisdiction in its own territory, in respect of any case which relates to acts which have taken place abroad, and in which it cannot rely on some permissive rule of international law. . . . Far from laying down a general prohibition to the effect that States may not extend the application of their laws and the jurisdiction of their courts to persons, property and acts outside their territory, [international law] leaves them in this respect a **wide measure of discretion, which is only limited in certain cases by prohibitive rules**; as regards other cases, every State remains free to adopt the principles which it regards as best and most suitable.
>
> This discretion left to States by international law explains the great variety of rules which they have been able to adopt without objections or complaints on the part of other States. . . . In these circumstances, all that can be required of a State is that it should not overstep the limits which international law places upon its jurisdiction; within these limits, its title to exercise jurisdiction rests in its sovereignty.[818]

Two maxims

Since the adoption of this decision by the Permanent Court of International Justice, in the international law scholarship, the expression 'Lotus principle' became a widespread term denoting:

- the original freedom of states to act within their territory according to the maxim **'everything which is not forbidden is allowed'**; and, at the same time,
- the respective restrictions on states acting outside their territory – in particular, in the territory of another state. So, in this case, the states are subjected to the maxim **'everything which is not allowed is forbidden'**.

817 *Case of the S.S. 'Lotus' (France v Turkey)*, Judgment No. 9 of 7 September 1927.
818 ibid.

Territorial jurisdiction as a base

Although some findings of the Court regarding criminal jurisdiction, concurrent jurisdiction, and so forth were challenged by time and the new norms of international law, this foundational principle of jurisdiction remains a crucial frame for the contemporary concept of jurisdiction.

THE PRINCIPLES OF JURISDICTION

Preliminary remarks

As noted before, concerning the jurisdiction of states, there are three types of jurisdiction usually outlined.

Principally, states are considered as having prescriptive and judicial jurisdiction based on either the principle of territoriality, which reflects the crucial interdependence between the state territory and statehood in international law, or the nationality principle, which indicates the strong legal linkage between the nationals and the statehood.

Enforcement jurisdiction, in turn, is almost exclusively territorial. For instance, the law enforcement agencies of a state may only operate within its territory if there is no authorisation from another state or a clearly articulated permissive rule under international law.

Territoriality principle

> sovereignty
> jurisdiction
> territorial sovereignty
> territorial jurisdiction
> independence
> ownership and possession of a territory
> sovereign rights
> affect persons, property, and circumstances

Sovereignty, territorial sovereignty, jurisdiction, and territorial jurisdiction

The concepts of **sovereignty** and **jurisdiction** as well as the corresponding terms **territorial sovereignty** and **territorial jurisdiction** are sometimes confusing. Some even use these concepts interchangeably. However, there is a distinction to be made between these terms.

The term 'sovereignty' was examined earlier in this book in detail. It (1) signifies the supreme authority of a state over its territory, and (2) designates the ability to pursue domestic and foreign policy objectives independently. Hence, the main sense of sovereignty is **independence**.

The notion of territorial sovereignty (1) stems from the **ownership and possession of a territory** and (2) denotes entitlement of a state to exercise domestic and foreign policy and the jurisdiction over its territory independently.

In relation to the territories outside the state territory, a more accurate term is **sovereign rights** since this term reflects a limited or functional application of the sovereignty of a state beyond its borders.

On the other hand, jurisdiction (1) applies to both the state territory and the other matters as well (including non-territorial jurisdictional concerns). At the same time, the main focus of the jurisdiction is (2) to **affect persons, property, and circumstances**.

The territorial jurisdiction as a form of jurisdiction, in turn, signifies the competence to affect persons, property, and circumstances within the territory which is under the territorial sovereignty of a given state; i.e. the territorial jurisdiction is limited in relation to the state territory.

Coverage of territorial jurisdiction

Territorial jurisdiction covers:

- everybody living within the territory under the sovereignty of a given state (citizens, aliens);
- all things within the territory under the sovereignty of a given state (movable and immovable property); and
- every circumstance within the territory under the sovereignty of a given state.

Limits of territorial jurisdiction

At the same time, in executing its territorial jurisdiction, a state should refrain from harming the rights of the other states and their citizens. Therefore, among other things, a state:

- should give no permission for its territory to be used for activities which will cause the violation of the rights of the other states and their citizens; and
- cannot use its territory in a way that pollutes another state's territory.

The territoriality principle in particular fields of law

The territoriality principle dominates jurisdictional concerns in specific legal matters. For instance, in criminal law, as a rule, all crimes committed within the territory of a state may be taken up only by the national courts of that state, and the accused, if convicted of the wrongdoing, can be sentenced.

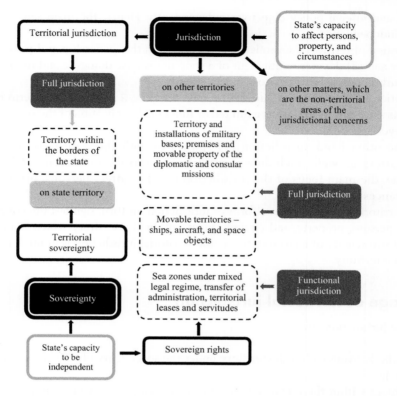

FIGURE 10.2 Sovereignty, territorial sovereignty, jurisdiction, and territorial jurisdiction

Nationality principle

nationality
passive personality
prevention of statelessness
presumption of nationality
Convention relating to the Status of Stateless Persons
Convention on the Reduction of Statelessness
citizenship
member of a state
ethnicity
jus soli
jus sanguinis
naturalisation
Convention on the Nationality of Married Women
dual nationality
flag state
movable territory

Jurisdiction over persons

Even though the primary source of jurisdiction under international law is usually considered to be territorial, there is also an active role held by the rules which are focused on persons, the primary reason being mostly related to the question of **nationality**.

Passive personality

Moreover, in some instances, the connecting factor of nationality operates as a basis for jurisdiction through the doctrine of **passive personality**. Passive personality refers to the state's authority to protect its nationals abroad, even outside its territory. Such an entitlement has commonly been controversial but has been increasingly accepted by a number of states – for instance, in the context of acts of terrorism which target a state by targeting its nationals.

Nationality

Nationality is an interrelationship between a person and a state, which affords the state jurisdiction over the person and grants the person the protection of the state.

International law generally does not regulate the granting of nationality by a state, and this question is regarded as a matter of domestic jurisdiction. However, sometimes particular rules on nationality are also governed by public international law.

Nationality as a right

Under contemporary international law, nationality is regarded as an inalienable right of every human being. For example, the International Covenant on Civil and Political Rights (1966) provides: 'Every child has the right to acquire a nationality.'[819] The United Nations Universal Declaration of Human Rights (1948) states that 'everyone has the right to a nationality' and that 'no one shall be arbitrarily deprived of his nationality'.

The same approach is taken up in many international documents and treaties targeting **prevention of statelessness**; for instance, under the Resolution adopted by the UN General Assembly in 2000 (Nationality of natural persons in relation to the succession of States),[820] which prescribes the prevention of statelessness and **presumption of nationality**. Meanwhile, the 1954 **Convention relating to the Status of Stateless Persons** and the 1961 **Convention on the Reduction of Statelessness** are the key international conventions addressing statelessness.

Different meanings of nationality

Nevertheless, the term 'nationality' in international practice and documents may be understood differently:

- Sometimes it is used interchangeably with the term '**citizenship.**'

---

819 Paragraph 3 of Article 24 of the International Covenant on Civil and Political Rights.
820 A/RES/55/153 of 12 December 2000.

- However, in specific cases, nationality is considered formally different in meaning from the formal understanding of the term 'citizenship.' The latter, in this context, is regarded as a stronger legal bond between a natural person and a country. In turn, the term 'nationality' can include both citizens and non-citizens, as well as natural persons and legal entities. Historically, the concept of citizenship is rooted in the rethinking of a natural person's role as an essential **member of a state**. The most traditional distinguishing feature of citizenship is that citizens have the right to participate in the political life of a state, such as by voting or standing as a candidate in elections.
- Nationality is sometimes used simply as an alternative word for **ethnicity** or national origin. For example, in the Soviet Union, (ethnic) nationality was recorded in the official identity documents.

Jus soli *and* jus sanguinis

Through national legislative provisions, the state sets the criteria for determining who shall be its nationals. By one rule of law, a person who is born within a state's territory and is a subject to its jurisdiction acquires that state's nationality simply due to the fact of birth in that territory (*jus soli*). By another rule, one has a nationality as an inheritance from one or both of one's parents (*jus sanguinis*). States vary in the use of the two principles. For example, continental European countries such as France, Germany, and Switzerland generally have used *jus sanguinis*; in turn, the common law countries have tended to adopt the *jus soli* rule. However, in some instances, the states have combined these principles and have used both of them.

Naturalisation

The other form of acquisition of nationality is **naturalisation**. The naturalisation process commonly involves a minimum legal residency requirement, knowledge of the language or culture of a titular nation, a promise to obey and uphold that country's laws, and so on.

Nevertheless, the requirements vary considerably from country to country. Marriage represents besides, one of the usual conditions for naturalisation. For instance, the **Convention on the Nationality of Married Women** of 1957 prescribes that an alien wife may acquire, at her request, the nationality of her husband through specially privileged naturalisation procedures.[821]

Dual nationality

Especially remarkable is the legal institute of the **dual nationality** (also called multiple nationality, multiple citizenship, or dual citizenship), which means that a person is concurrently regarded as a citizen of more than one state when these states permit dual citizenship.

---

821 Article 3 of the Convention on the Nationality of Married Women.

Movable territories and jurisdiction

Finally, the term 'nationality' also covers specific cases regarding ships, aircraft, and space objects. They also have 'nationality' under international law. For instance, a merchant ship has the nationality of its **flag state**. The flag state determines the conditions for the registration and granting of the right to fly its flag.

However, the nationality of ships, aircraft, and space objects is to some degree interlinked with the territoriality principle as well since, as is noted earlier in the section of this book dealing with the state, ships, aircraft, and space objects are sometimes assimilated to a state territory as a '**movable territory.**'

Extraterritorial jurisdiction

> *Banković and Others v Belgium and Others*
> effects within its territory
> active personality principle
> passive personality principle
> protective principle
> principle of universal jurisdiction
> jurisdictional rule of reason
> balancing test between the jurisdictional concerns
> MARPOL regime

The meaning of extraterritorial jurisdiction

Extraterritorial jurisdiction refers to the ability of a state to exercise its authority over persons and circumstances, regardless the principle of territoriality.

The following 'recognised instances of the extra-territorial exercise of jurisdiction by a State' are enumerated in the well-known Grand Chamber Decision of the European Court of Human Rights (the case – *Banković and Others v Belgium and Others*):

* Acts of the authorities of the states 'which produced effects or were performed outside their own territory';
* The 'activities of . . . diplomatic or consular agents abroad and on board craft and vessels registered in, or flying the flag of, that State';
* When 'through the consent, invitation or acquiescence of the Government of [the] territory, [another state] exercises all or some of the public powers normally to be exercised by that Government'.[822]

---

822 *Banković and Others v Belgium and Others* [GC] (dec.), no. 52207/99, ECHR 2001- XII § 69, § 71, § 73. All cases of the ECHR are available at <https://hudoc.echr.coe.int>.

Some other primary grounds for extraterritorial jurisdiction

The extension of jurisdiction commonly may occur abroad, when a state assumes jurisdiction on the basis that the behaviour of a party is producing **effects within its territory**. At the same time, extraterritorial jurisdiction may be claimed on the grounds of such principles as the nationality/**active personality principle** (conduct performed by the state's nationals), the **passive personality principle** (conduct having the state's nationals as its victims), the **protective principle** (conduct directed against a state's 'vital interests'), or the **principle of universal jurisdiction** (conduct recognised by the interstate system to be of 'universal concern'). These principles were reviewed earlier in this book, and further discussion will also be provided later.

Jurisdictional rule of reason

As regards the effects within the territory of a claimant state, the states usually refer to a '**jurisdictional rule of reason**', which means that the effect within the territory shall be substantial, and the exercise of jurisdiction should be reasonable (undergoing a **balancing test between the jurisdictional concerns**).

This mode of extraterritorial jurisdiction appears in such fields as anti-corruption, securities law, antitrust, environmental regulation, and so on.

For example, the USA, due to various cases, has extended its jurisdiction, particularly in the context of economic issues. Nevertheless, this approach has drawn sharp criticism from the states, as well as the international organisations.[823]

Environmental regulations

For instance, regarding environmental regulations, there are a small number of environmental regimes that permit and simultaneously require the use of direct extraterritorial jurisdiction over persons and conduct abroad.

The **MARPOL regime** on maritime pollution is definitely the best-known example. As prescribed under the International Convention for the Prevention of Pollution from Ships of 1973:

> Any violation of the requirements of the present Convention within the jurisdiction of any Party to the Convention shall be prohibited and sanctions shall be established therefor under the law of that Party. Whenever such a violation occurs, that Party shall either:
>
> **(a)** Cause proceedings to be taken in accordance with its law; or

---

823 For example, the European Community stressed in a letter to the Congressional Committee considering changes in the US export control legislation in 1984 that: 'US claims to jurisdiction over European subsidiaries of US companies and over goods and technology of US origin located outside the US are contrary to the principles of international law and can only lead to clashes of both a political and legal nature. These subsidiaries, goods and technology must be subject to the laws of the country where they are located.'

(b) Furnish to the Administration of the ship such information and evidence as may be in its possession that a violation has occurred.[824]

Criminal jurisdiction

subjective territorial principle
objective territorial principle
Lotus case
protective principle
principle of universal jurisdiction
Draft Code of Crimes against the Peace and Security of Mankind
international crimes
piracy
slavery
torture
taking of hostages
terrorism
hijacking
drug trafficking
corruption
crime of international nature
quasi-universal jurisdiction
Convention against Torture and Other Cruel, Inhuman or Degrading Treatment or Punishment

A central principle of criminal jurisdiction

As noted before, a fundamental principle of criminal jurisdiction is the territoriality principle. However, the territoriality principle in this context encompasses not only crimes committed entirely in the territory of a single state but also crimes which were only partially committed within the territory of that state.

Crimes occurring on the territories of more than one state

As regards the latter case, there are two approaches:

- **Subjective territorial principle**: A state would have the jurisdiction to investigate and try a crime initiated (started) on its territory but later completed abroad.

---

824 Paragraph 2 of Article 4 of the International Convention for the Prevention of Pollution from Ships.

- **Objective territorial principle**: A state would have the jurisdiction to investigate and try criminal offences regardless of where the acts actually initiated if they were completed on or produced harmful consequences for the territory of the state in question.

Thus, these approaches lead to cross-state territorial jurisdiction since the jurisdiction to prosecute the offender may be claimed by the state where the crime was initiated or the state where the crime was completed, as well as the state where the injury actually took place.

The territory in which a substantial or a more significant part of the crime was committed

Therefore, in this regard, it is crucial to define in which jurisdiction the substantial or a more significant part of the crime was committed.

Besides affirming the two fundamental maxims of jurisdiction examined earlier, the **Lotus** case *(France v Turkey)* played an additional, essential role at that very historical moment, in solving the existing challenges of cross-state territorial jurisdiction concerning criminal jurisdiction. The Court held that a state would have territorial jurisdiction, even if the crime was committed outside its territory, if a constitutive element of the crime was committed in that state ('an act – of negligence or imprudence – having its origin on board the Lotus, whilst its effects made themselves felt on board the Boz-Kourt'). Nevertheless, the value of the judgment regarding criminal jurisdiction on the high seas has been diminished by the new norms of international law. For example, the Geneva Convention on the High Seas (1958) reads:

> [I]n the event of collusion or of any other incident of navigation concerning a ship on the high seas . . . no penal or disciplinary proceedings may be instituted against master of the ship or any other person in the service of ship . . . except before the judicial or administrative authorities either of the flag state or of the state of which such person is a national.[825]

This provision was repeated in the United Nations Convention on the Law of the Sea of 1982.[826]

Nationality/active personality principle and criminal jurisdiction

As regards the second ground of jurisdiction – the nationality principle (also referred to as the active personality principle), traditionally, certain continental European countries with civil law legal system claim criminal jurisdiction over crimes committed by their

---

825 Article 11 of the Geneva Convention on the High Seas.

826 Article 97 (Penal jurisdiction in matters of collision or any other incident of navigation) of the United Nations Convention on the Law of the Sea.

nationals abroad. The common law states, in turn, tend to consider exercising jurisdiction over their nationals abroad only in severe cases.[827]

Protective principle and principle of universal jurisdiction

Sometimes, for the extension of criminal jurisdictional lines mostly constituted by the territoriality principle, the states use the other legal principles as well. In this respect, the **protective principle** and the **principle of universal jurisdiction** should be outlined.

The meaning of the protective principle

The protective principle refers to the power of a state to prosecute an alien for acts committed abroad that are directed against the existence, peace, and order of that state. As a rule, this principle is related to the 'vital interests of states' and is commonly practised because of insufficient national laws or enforcement mechanisms in other states.

The sense of universal jurisdiction

As regards the principle of universal jurisdiction, under international law, there are specific offences which provide the ground for criminal jurisdiction for every state, allowing them the right to prosecute and punish those crimes based on general customary international law 'irrespective of where or by whom those crimes were committed.'[828]

Thus, universal jurisdiction is an essential tool of international justice, empowering every state to prosecute and punish persons for crimes committed outside their territories which are not specifically linked to a state by the nationality of the suspect or the victims or by harm particularly inflicted upon the national interests of that state.

Universal jurisdiction stipulates the obligation – *aut dedere aut prosequi* (either to deliver or to prosecute),[829] which is reflected in the ILC **Draft Code of Crimes against the Peace and Security of Mankind** of 1996 with the following wording:

> Without prejudice to the jurisdiction of an international criminal court, the State Party in the territory of which an individual alleged to have committed a crime . . . shall extradite or prosecute that individual.[830]

---

827 'The nationality principle is more usually asserted by civil law, as opposed to common law, countries, although the latter do rely on the principle to claim jurisdiction over certain extraterritorial offences.' *Parry & Grant Encyclopaedic Dictionary of International Law* (n 165) 406.

828 Article 8 of the Draft Code of Crimes against the Peace and Security of Mankind.

829 *Aut dedere aut prosequi* . . .

"Either to deliver or to prosecute." An alternative phrase for *Aut dedere aut iudicare*. E.g., "There are . . . certain indications that a universal criminal jurisdiction for certain international crimes is clearly not regarded as unlawful. The duty to prosecute under those treaties which contain the aut dedere aut prosequi provisions opens the door to a jurisdiction based on the heinous nature of the crime rather than on links of territoriality or nationality." *Arrest Warrant of 11 April 2000* (Congo v. Belg.).

Guide to Latin in International Law (n 71) 42

830 Article 9 of the Draft Code of Crimes against the Peace and Security of Mankind.

International crimes as a field of application of universal jurisdiction

International crimes are undoubtedly covered by virtue of the principle of universal jurisdiction, because the crimes involved are regarded as being offensive to the international community as a whole.

In this respect, the crimes under consideration are usually the crimes of **piracy, slavery,** or **torture**, as well as genocide, crimes against humanity, and war crimes. The International Law Commission in its Draft Code of Crimes against the Peace and Security of Mankind in this context enumerated the following crimes: the crime of aggression, crime of genocide, crimes against humanity, crimes against UN and associated personnel, and war crimes.[831]

The suitable Commentary of the ILC stressed that 'the national courts of States parties would be entitled to exercise the broadest possible jurisdiction . . . under the principle of universal jurisdiction.'[832]

Crimes of international nature and quasi-universal jurisdiction

In addition, the principle of universal jurisdiction has been embodied in a specific form in the multilateral treaties dealing with **taking of hostages, terrorism, hijacking, drug trafficking, corruption,** and so forth, which are generally denoted as **crimes of international nature,** which itself covers (1) crimes determined under international law, (2) the avoidance of which requires international co-operation, (3) but the prosecution and trying of which are domains of national laws and institutions.

Because, in these cases, the universal jurisdiction is not based on general customary international law and, therefore, binds only the parties to a treaty, it is called **quasi-universal jurisdiction.** Hence, the jurisdiction is termed quasi-universal when it has substantially the same purpose as universal jurisdiction but is authorised only between the parties to a particular treaty (and with regard to only certain proceedings). Its primary purpose is to ensure that there will be no place to hide for the alleged offenders in those states which are the parties to a respective treaty.

The transformation of quasi-universal jurisdiction into universal jurisdiction

However, in certain cases, quasi-universal jurisdiction can be transformed into universal jurisdiction if either (1) a treaty entailing quasi-universal jurisdiction attains universal (or almost universal) recognition, or (2) its rules stipulate the creation of the norm of general customary international law, enabling all states to exercise universal jurisdiction.

---

831 Articles 16, 17, 18, 19, 20 of the Draft Code of Crimes against the Peace and Security of Mankind.
832 Commentary to Article 9.

A good example of such a modification is the **Convention against Torture and Other Cruel, Inhuman or Degrading Treatment or Punishment** of 1984. The Convention obliged every party:

1   to criminalise 'all acts of torture' as the 'offences under its criminal law' and to 'make these offences punishable by appropriate penalties which take into account their grave nature';[833]
2   to exercise its jurisdiction either based on the territoriality principle ('When the offences are committed in any territory under its jurisdiction or on board a ship or aircraft registered in that State'), active personality principle ('When the alleged offender is a national of that State'), or passive personality principle ('When the victim is a national of that State if that State considers it appropriate'); and
3   to exercise 'likewise' a (quasi) universal jurisdiction (to 'take such measures as may be necessary to establish its jurisdiction over such offences in cases where the alleged offender is present in any territory under its jurisdiction and it does not extradite him . . . to any of the States').[834]

For example, at the regional level, the Inter-American Convention to Prevent and Punish Torture of 1985 was adopted to prevent torture and other similar activities and prescribed that '[e]very State Party shall also take the necessary measures to establish its jurisdiction over the crime described in this Convention when the alleged criminal is within the area under its jurisdiction and it is not appropriate to extradite him'.[835]

In addition, torture is currently included in the definition of war crimes (whether committed in an international or non-international armed conflict) and crimes against humanity (when it is 'committed as part of a widespread or systematic attack directed against any civilian population, with knowledge of the attack'). Hence, within the meanings of those crimes, torture is subject to universal jurisdiction.

As regards, 'all [other] acts of torture', as described by the aforementioned Conventions, initially, the jurisdictional rules mentioned here were applicable only between the parties to the Convention against Torture and Other Cruel, Inhuman or Degrading Treatment or Punishment or the Inter-American Convention to Prevent and Punish Torture. The almost-universal recognition of those norms (concerning some non-party states in the status of general customary international law) currently seems to be the basis for identifying torture to be within the universal jurisdiction of every country.[836]

---

833 Article 4 of the Convention against Torture and Other Cruel, Inhuman or Degrading Treatment or Punishment.

834 Article 5 of the Convention against Torture and Other Cruel, Inhuman or Degrading Treatment or Punishment.

835 Article 12 of the Inter-American Convention to Prevent and Punish Torture.

836 See, for example, 'Universal Jurisdiction: The duty of states to enact and implement legislation', Chapter Nine, 'Torture: The legal basis for universal jurisdiction' (31 August 2001, Index number: IOR 53/012/2001) <www.amnesty.org/en/documents/ior53/012/2001/en/?OpenDocument> accessed 17 March 2021.

FIGURE 10.3 International crime and crime of international nature

Civil jurisdiction

conflict of laws
private international law
foreign element
Hague Conference on Private International Law
Statute of the Hague Conference on Private International Law
party autonomy
choice of law
forum selection clause
Hague Choice of Court Convention
Convention on the Recognition and Enforcement of Foreign Arbitral Awards
Principles on Choice of Law in International Commercial Contracts
international contracts
exclusive choice of court agreements
overriding mandatory rules
public policy
forum state
choice of law agreement

A limited number of the general international law rules on civil jurisdiction

Aside from the rules of diplomatic and consular law which, in some instances, concern jurisdictional aspects in civil matters, there are at present no rules of general international law specifically governing the jurisdiction of states in civil matters. However, at the bilateral, regional, and multilateral levels, international law norms sometimes prescribe the particular international obligations between the parties on this subject.

The nature of private international law

Therefore, state jurisdiction in civil matters is mostly prescribed by the norms of another legal framework – namely, **conflict of laws** or **private international law**, which:

* concerns relations across different legal jurisdictions between natural persons and legal entities; and
* consists of conflict of laws norms of national laws with regard to the **foreign element** (persons and things) and the international law bilateral, regional, and multilateral treaty and customary norms on the civil matters. Consequently, private international law embodies a complex composition of the norms of two legal systems – national and international – while it is mainly part of national law. However, to some degree it, also constitutes part of international law as well.

The Hague Conference on Private International Law

Although the rules of private international law are mostly national in their source, the efforts towards the international harmonisation of private international law through treaties, spearheaded by the **Hague Conference on Private International Law**[837] (the intergovernmental organisation for cross-border co-operation in civil and commercial matters) should be regarded as a reflection of a deeper connection between public and private international law.

Under the **Statute of the Hague Conference on Private International Law**, the members of the Conference may be both the states[838] and the 'Regional Economic Integration Organisations'.[839]

---

837 The First to Sixth Diplomatic Sessions of the Hague Conference on Private International Law held in 1893, 1894, 1900, 1904, 1925, and 1928 respectively. They stipulated the conclusion of several multilateral treaties, which unified the rules of private international law in the areas of marriage, divorce, guardianship, civil procedure, and deprivation of civil rights. 'The Seventh Session in 1951 marked the beginning of a new era with the preparation of a Statute which made the Conference a permanent intergovernmental organisation. The Statute entered into force on 15 July 1955.' <www.hcch.net/en/about/more-about-hcch> accessed 17 March 2021. As of 17 March 2021, the Hague Conference has 88 Members: 87 states and the European Union.

838 According to Article 2 of the Statute: 'The admission of new Member States shall be decided upon by the Governments of the participating States, upon the proposal of one or more of them, by a majority of the votes cast, within a period of six months from the date on which that proposal is submitted to the Governments.'

839 Under Article 3(1): 'The Member States of the Conference may, at a meeting concerning general affairs and policy where the majority of Member States is present, by a majority of the votes cast, decide to admit also as a Member any Regional Economic Integration Organisation which has submitted an application

A wide range of grounds for civil jurisdictional concerns

In the context of jurisdiction, the rules of private international law accept a wide range of grounds for national courts to exercise jurisdiction over private law disputes and thus readily accept the possibility that more than one court may have jurisdiction based on territorial or personal connections with the parties or the subject matter of their dispute.

Party autonomy

On the whole, the questions of jurisdiction are implemented in private international law through the principle of **party autonomy**, which commonly refers to the power of parties to a contract to choose the law that governs that contract (**choice of law**). However, party autonomy may also include the right of the parties to choose an adjudicatory forum (court or arbitral tribunal) to determine the rights and obligations arising from their legal relationships (by the so-called **forum selection clause**).

The principle of party autonomy is almost universally recognised and has traditionally functioned in the context of commercial contractual relations; however, sometimes it is also applied beyond this context (for example, in family law).

The international acknowledgement of party autonomy in the context of civil jurisdiction has been confirmed by the **Hague Choice of Court Convention** (Convention on Choice of Court Agreements) of 2005, prepared by the Hague Conference on Private International Law, the 1958 New York **Convention on the Recognition and Enforcement of Foreign Arbitral Awards** ('Contracting States' of which are a vast majority of states), and the **Principles on Choice of Law in International Commercial Contracts**, which was approved in 2015 in the format of Hague Conference on Private International Law and embodies 'a model law that states are encouraged to enact'.

International contracts and international cases

The principle of party autonomy may be applied only in relation to **international contracts**. Under the Principles on Choice of Law in International Commercial Contracts, a contract is international unless each party has its establishment in the same state, and the relationship of the parties and all other relevant elements, regardless of the chosen law, are connected only with that state.

The Hague Choice of Court Convention provides a similar approach but with reference to the term 'international cases', stating that the Convention shall apply in international cases to **exclusive choice of court agreements** concluded in civil or commercial matters. At the same time, according to the Convention,

> a case is international unless the parties are resident in the same Contracting State and the relationship of the parties and all other elements relevant to the dispute, regardless of the location of the chosen court, are connected only with that State.[840]

---

for membership to the Secretary General. References to Members under this Statute shall include such Member Organisations, except as otherwise expressly provided. The admission shall become effective upon the acceptance of the Statute by the Regional Economic Integration Organisation concerned.'

840 Article 1 of the Convention on Choice of Court Agreements.

Restrictions of the principle of party autonomy

However, the principle of party autonomy does not provide that autonomy is unlimited even concerning the international cases. The states implement various restrictions (1) regarding particular matters and (2) based on certain grounds. These restrictions, on the other hand, must be precisely and exhaustively formulated under the national law of a state without placing substantial limitation on the party autonomy.

Particular matters

The particular matters, where the principle of party autonomy is not commonly applicable, include, among other things, the capacity of natural and legal persons, insolvency, anti-trust (competition) matters, and tort or delict claims for damage to tangible property that do not arise from a contractual relationship.

Overriding mandatory rules and public policy (*ordre public*)

Under the internationally acknowledged approach, the power of the parties to a contract to choose the law is usually limited if their choice contradicts the **overriding mandatory rules** or **public policy** (*ordre public*) of the **forum state** (the state where the proceedings are carried out). Hence, these categories are treated as a necessary counter-balance to the principle of party autonomy. The categories – the overriding mandatory rules and the public policy – are closely interlinked since both meanings exist primarily to protect the national interests and policies of the forum state; nevertheless, they differ from each other:

1   An overriding mandatory rule is a specific, positive rule of the *lex fori*,[841] from which the parties cannot derogate by the terms of their contract or otherwise. Consequently, these rules are the imperative provisions of national law, and respect for them is regarded to be crucial by the forum country for safeguarding its own vital interests (and the interests of private persons). On the other hand, by referring to the public policy, the adjudicatory forum (court or arbitral tribunal) shall consider only fundamental notions of public policy and the basic legal principles of national law.[842]
2   The overriding mandatory rules are concerned with the positive application of the laws of a country which reflect the public interests of the forum state. On the other hand, the reservation of the public policy protects particular fundamental interests

---

841   'LEX FORI [L. *lex* + *forum, fori* / market-place, public square, courthouse, court] The law of the court or forum; the law of the jurisdiction in which an action is commenced or is pending. The lex fori will control all procedural and substantive matters required for decision except in those instances in which some principle of conflicts resolution requires the court to look at the law of another jurisdiction.' Emanuel (n 90) 217.

842   For example, Article 5 (Public order) of the Law of Georgia on Private International Law of 1998: 'The rules of a foreign law shall not be applied in Georgia, if it contradicts the basic legal principles of Georgia.'

which are contrary to the chosen law and represents a negative response by the adjudicatory forum to the consequences of otherwise applicable law.

Consequently, party autonomy shall not prevent a court from applying overriding mandatory provisions of the law of the forum state, which apply irrespective of the law chosen by the parties. The same approach is introduced with respect to the public policy of a concerned country when the application of the chosen law is blocked because its application in a particular case is manifestly incompatible with the fundamental notions and principles.

The overriding mandatory rules may be, for example, the imperative rules that are adopted to protect customers and employees (the so-called 'protection of weaker parties').

One example of inconsistency with the public policy is a case relating to a wagering contract when such an activity is prohibited in the forum state and is considered to be against the fundamental public policy of that state. This may lead to the refusal to apply the rules upholding the enforceability of the contract under the law chosen by the parties.

The international obligations of the forum state shall also be regarded as possible references to public policy. For instance, if the court ascertains that the parties to the contract intended to avoid the sanctions imposed by a United Nations Security Council resolution, it may refuse by invoking the ground of a public policy to enforce a contract, valid under the law chosen by the parties.

Lastly, as opposed to the courts, arbitral tribunals have a different relation to overriding mandatory rules and public policy reservations as, in the first instance, they must follow their mandate and the choice of law undertaken by the parties. Nevertheless, an arbitral tribunal may apply or take into account the provisions or policies of the law of the forum state, contrary to the parties' choice, if it concludes that it is under a legal obligation or is otherwise entitled to do so. For this decision, arbitral tribunals usually pay attention to the institutional rules applicable to the arbitration in a forum state and the potentially controlling influence of the forum state's court system.

Choice of law

According to the common law and the EU rules, generally, there is no requirement for a connection between the parties or their dispute and the institute or law they have chosen. However, some countries have more restrictive approach to matters related to the choice of law.

Similarly, under the Principles on Choice of Law in International Commercial Contracts, which is a model law reflecting the best practises of the states, '[n]o connection is required between the law chosen and the parties or their transaction'.

Besides, in this document, the general provisions governing the choice of law are formulated. According to these provisions, among other things, (1) the parties may either choose the applicable law in their main contract or make a separate agreement on the choice of law (**choice of law agreement**); (2) the parties may choose both – the law applicable to the entire contract or to only the part of it – and may also select different laws applicable to different parts of the contract; and (3) the choice may be made or modified at any time.

Lastly, according to the Principles on Choice of Law in International Commercial Contracts, the law chosen by the parties governs all aspects of the contract between the parties, including interpretation; rights and obligations arising from the contract; performance and the consequences of non-performance, including the assessment of damages; the various ways of extinguishing obligations; prescription and limitation periods; validity and the consequences of invalidity of the contract; burden of proof and legal presumptions; and pre-contractual obligations.

Forum selection clauses

The Principles on Choice of Law in International Commercial Contracts distinguishes choice of law agreements from 'forum selection clauses', 'choice of court clauses', 'arbitration clauses'; all of which are synonyms for the parties' agreement on the forum that shall decide their dispute. However, in practice, dispute resolution clauses are often combined with choice of law provisions. Nevertheless, it is a fact that they have different aims and foci. Therefore, in order to eliminate the contradictions, the parties should separately proclaim their will on both matters.

The Hague Choice of Court Convention specifies that an exclusive choice of court agreement must be concluded or documented either in writing or by any other means of communication which renders information accessible so as to be usable for subsequent reference. In addition, according to the Convention, if an exclusive choice of court agreement forms the part of a contract, it should be regarded as an independent agreement. Hence, the 'validity of the exclusive choice of court agreement cannot be contested solely on the ground that the contract is not valid.'[843]

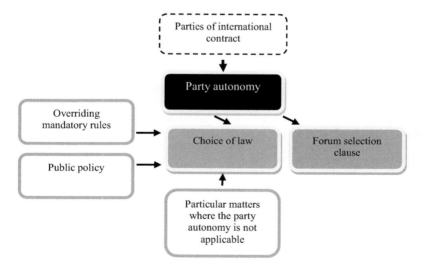

FIGURE 10.4 The principle of party autonomy

---

843 Article 3 of the Convention on Choice of Court Agreements.

The New York Convention on the Recognition and Enforcement of Foreign Arbitral Awards is similarly founded on the principle of party autonomy, providing that the parties are free to grant exclusive jurisdiction over their private disputes to the arbitrators appointed for each case and permanent arbitral bodies. Under the Convention, each contracting state shall recognise an agreement in writing and arbitral awards as binding and enforce them.[844]

According to the provisions of the Convention, the 'term "agreement in writing" shall include an arbitral clause in a contract or an arbitration agreement, signed by the parties or contained in an exchange of letters or telegrams.'[845]

RECOGNITION AND ENFORCEMENT OF FOREIGN JUDGMENTS, ARBITRAL AWARDS, AND CROSS-BORDER CRIMINAL JUSTICE CO-OPERATION

foreign judgments
comity
judgment creditor
judgment debtor
foreign arbitral awards
Statute of the Hague Conference on Private International Law
law enforcement co-operation
INTERPOL
extradition
Model Treaty on Extradition
principle of speciality
dual-criminality principle
death penalty

The legal grounds for the recognition and enforcement of foreign judgments

Foreign judgments may be recognised and enforced within the multilateral regimes established by international treaties or through bilateral international agreements between the countries.

In the absence of a valid international treaty, foreign judgments may be recognised and enforced either unilaterally or based on the principles of **comity**, hence, mutual deference between courts in different countries.

---

844 Paragraph 1 of Article II and Article III of the New York Convention on the Recognition and Enforcement of Foreign Arbitral Awards.

845 Paragraph 2 of Article II of the New York Convention on the Recognition and Enforcement of Foreign Arbitral Awards.

At the same time, in this context, the term 'foreign judgment' usually includes any judgment given by a court or tribunal of a state, 'whatever the judgment may be called'.[846]

Enforcement of foreign judgments after recognition

Before a judgment can be enforced, usually, it must first be recognised since a judgment of a foreign court cannot operate outside its own territorially circumscribed jurisdiction without the medium of the relevant courts. The recognition and enforcement of a judgment is as a rule claimed by the so-called **judgment creditor** against the **judgment debtor**.

The preconditions of the recognition and enforcement of the foreign judgments vary across multilateral regimes, as well as in the legal practice of states – i.e. the states have distinct approaches concerning the grounds of rejection as well as recognition or enforcement of foreign judgments; however, in most cases, recognition (and enforcement)[847] of foreign judgments may be denied on the following grounds:

- If the foreign judgment contradicts the multilateral regime or bilateral international norms on recognition and enforcement of foreign judgments which are valid for the country addressed;
- If the foreign judgment is not final and conclusive;[848]
- If a previous final and conclusive judgment of the court in the country addressed conflicts with the judgment, the recognition or enforcement of which is claimed by the judgment creditor;[849]
- If a foreign court did not possess jurisdiction over the parties;[850]

---

846 For instance, according to Article 2 of the Regulation (EU) No 1215/2012 of the European Parliament and of the Council of 12 December 2012 on jurisdiction and the recognition and enforcement of judgments in civil and commercial matters (recast) – the so-called Brussels I Regulation (recast), '(a) "judgment" means any judgment given by a court or tribunal of a Member State, whatever the judgment may be called, including a decree, order, decision or writ of execution, as well as a decision on the determination of costs or expenses by an officer of the court.'

847 The enforcement procedure usually corresponds to the grounds of the refusal of recognition. See Article 46 of the Convention on Jurisdiction and the Recognition and Enforcement of Judgments in Civil and Commercial matters (the so-called Lugano Convention) of 2007.

848 For example, in the UK '[a] judgment that is subject to appeal can still be final and conclusive for these purposes. However, recognition and enforcement of foreign judgments under the common law regime is discretionary and the court may stay any relevant proceedings if the judgment is subject to appeal in the state of origin.' Anna Pertoldi and Gary Horlock, 'Conditions for Recognition and Enforcement of Foreign Judgments in the United Kingdom' (24 January 2019) <http://bit.ly/2Q8QHhY> accessed 17 March 2021.

849 In certain circumstances, the relevant judgment of the foreign competent court involving the same cause of action and the same parties, which can be recognised in the country addressed, may also be examined.

850 According to the approach of some countries, it is not sufficient for the foreign court to have jurisdiction according to its own legislation; a foreign judgment is only enforceable if the foreign court had jurisdiction according to the domestic principles of the private international law of the country

- If a judgment was acquired by fraud;
- If a judgment contradicts the public policy of the country addressed; or
- If the recognition of a foreign judgment would result in the contravention of the overriding mandatory rules (including the principles of justice) of the country addressed.[851]

Multilateral regimes for the recognition and enforcement of foreign judgments

There are several multilateral regimes regarding recognition and enforcement of foreign judgments. For example:

- The EU internal regime under the legislative acts on jurisdiction and the recognition and enforcement of judgments in civil and commercial matters;[852]
- Convention of 2007 on Jurisdiction and the Recognition and Enforcement of Judgments in Civil and Commercial matters (the so-called new Lugano Convention) between EU member states and certain European countries that are not the EU members;[853] and
- The multilateral regimes under the Hague Conference on Private International Law, which, among other things, includes:

  - Convention of 1971 on the Recognition and Enforcement of Foreign Judgments in Civil and Commercial Matters;[854]

---

addressed. For example, under the 'common law regime', '[a] foreign judgment is only enforceable if the foreign court had jurisdiction according to English principles of private international law.' Louise Freeman and Shivani Sanghi, 'England & Wells: Enforcement of Foreign Judgements and Regulations 2020' (8 April 2020) <https://iclg.com/practice-areas/enforcement-of-foreign-judgments-laws-and-regulations/england-and-wales> accessed 17 March 2021.

851 For example, under the USA Securing the Protection of our Enduring and Established Constitutional Heritage Act, 'a domestic court shall not recognize or enforce a foreign judgment for defamation unless the domestic court determines that – (A) the defamation law applied in the foreign court's adjudication provided at least as much protection for freedom of speech and press in that case as would be provided by the first amendment to the Constitution of the United States and by the constitution and law of the State in which the domestic court is located', *SPEECH Act* H.R.2765–111th Congress (2009–2010) Public Law No: 111–223 (08/10/2010) §4102. 'Recognition of Foreign Defamation Judgments' <http://bit.ly/35Gmv3E> accessed 17 March 2021.

852 For example, Regulation (EU) No 1215/2012 of the European Parliament and of the Council of 12 December 2012 on jurisdiction and the recognition and enforcement of judgments in civil and commercial matters (recast).

853 'Known as the new Lugano Convention, it replaces the Lugano Convention of 1988. . . . The convention, signed by the European Community, along with Denmark, Iceland, Norway and Switzerland, was to come into force once it is ratified by the signatories. Denmark was a separate contracting party to this convention, because it had opted out of the then Brussels I regulation (Council Regulation (EC) No 44/2001) – subsequently replaced by Regulation (EU) No 1215/2012 on court jurisdiction and the recognition and enforcement of judgments in civil and commercial matters.' 'Strengthening Cooperation with Switzerland, Norway and Iceland: The Lugano Convention' (31 July 2018) <http://bit.ly/3cHW5U0> accessed 17 March 2021.

854 Contracting Parties of the Convention are only: Albania, Cyprus, Kuwait, Netherlands and Portugal <http://bit.ly/2EDiUre> accessed 17 March 2021.

- Convention of 1996 on Jurisdiction, Applicable Law, Recognition, Enforcement and Co-operation in Respect of Parental Responsibility and Measures for the Protection of Children; and
- Hague Choice of Court Convention of 2005.

Foreign arbitral awards

In the field of the **foreign arbitral awards**, the fundamental framework is prescribed by the New York Convention on the Recognition and Enforcement of Foreign Arbitral Awards of 1958.[855] Under the Convention, the term 'arbitral awards' shall include not only awards made by arbitrators appointed for each case but also those made by permanent arbitral bodies to which the parties have submitted.

According to the New York Convention, recognition and enforcement of the award may be refused at the request of the party against whom it is invoked only if that party delivers to the competent authority, where the recognition and enforcement is sought, proof that: 'The party against whom the award is invoked was not given proper notice of the appointment of the arbitrator or of the arbitration proceedings or was otherwise unable to present his case'; the 'composition of the arbitral authority or the arbitral procedure was not in accordance with the agreement of the parties, or, failing such agreement, was not in accordance with the law of the country where the arbitration took place'; or the 'award has not yet become binding on the parties, or has been set aside or suspended by a competent authority of the country in which, or under the law of which, that award was made'.[856]

Law enforcement co-operation

As regards **law enforcement co-operation**, in the majority of jurisdictions, it is possible to rely on two channels of cross-border law enforcement co-operation:

- International co-operation involving operational police assistance before any judicial proceedings are in place. In these instances, the necessary arrangements can usually be made between the relevant police agencies without reference to mutual legal assistance legal norms.
- International co-operation based upon formal 'letters of request' made after judicial proceedings have been commenced or when an official investigation is underway.

INTERPOL

The essential role in this regard is performed by intergovernmental co-operation through the combined framework of **INTERPOL**, which is the world's largest international police organisation, with more than 190 member countries.

---

855 Together with the Geneva Protocol on Arbitration Clauses of 1923 and the Geneva Convention on the Execution of Foreign Arbitral Awards of 1927, which ceased to have effect between the contracting states of the New York Convention (Article VII of the New York Convention).

856 Article V of the New York Convention.

INTERPOL provides the tools and services necessary to facilitate exchanges between the member states. In order to affect these channels of communication, INTERPOL offers to the member states four 'core services':

1 Secure Global Police Communications Services;
2 Operational Data Services and Databases for Police;
3 Operational Police Support Services; and
4 Training and Development.

On the whole, effective communication between the INTERPOL member countries not only facilitates but also dramatically enhances the chances for a successful collaborative effort of law enforcement and other local, regional, and international organisations in fighting crimes on a worldwide scale.

Extradition

Bilateral treaties, national laws of several states, and the judicial decisions of national courts led to the development of certain principles regarding **extradition**, which are deemed general rules of international law. Though there are numerous provisions regulating extradition, each case has to be considered individually and according to the applicable provisions.

In 1990, the General Assembly of the United Nations approved a **Model Treaty on Extradition** containing many of these principles. According to the Model Treaty,

> extraditable offences are offences that are punishable under the laws of both Parties by imprisonment or other deprivation of liberty for a maximum period of at least [one/two] year(s), or by a more severe penalty. Where the request for extradition relates to a person who is wanted for the enforcement of a sentence of imprisonment or other deprivation of liberty imposed for such an offence, extradition shall be granted only if a period of at least [four/six] months of such sentence remains to be served.[857]

At the same time, the Model Treaty prescribes, among other things, the following mandatory grounds for refusal:

• If the state which received the request for extradition regards the offence committed as an offence of a political nature. However, in recent years, certain limitations were placed on offences of a political nature, and international terrorism, anarchistic offences, and international crimes may not be considered offences of a political nature.
• If the state which received a request has solid grounds to consider that the request for extradition is intended to prosecute or punish a person 'on account of that person's race, religion, nationality, ethnic, origin, political opinions, sex, or status'.

857 Article 1 of the Model Treaty on Extradition.

- 'If the offence for which extradition is requested is an offence under military law, which is not also an offence under ordinary criminal law'.
- 'If the person whose extradition is requested has, under the law of either Party, become immune from prosecution or punishment for any reason, including lapse of time or amnesty'.
- 'If the person whose extradition is requested has been or would be subjected in the requesting State to torture or cruel, inhuman or degrading treatment or punishment or if that person has not received or would not receive the minimum guarantees in criminal proceedings, as contained in the International Covenant on Civil and Political Rights, article 14'.[858]

In addition, under the Model Treaty are enumerated, inter alia, the following optional grounds to refuse a request for extradition:

- 'If the person whose extradition is requested is a national of the requested State'. At the same time, when extradition is refused on this ground, the requested state shall, if the other state so requests, submit the case to its competent authorities to take appropriate action against this person.
- 'If the competent authorities of the requested State have decided either not to institute or to terminate proceedings against the person for the offence in respect of which extradition is requested'.[859]

In sum, according to the internationally acknowledged approach of extradition:

1   The states do not extradite criminals in the absence of a treaty or national legislation which empowers them to do so. International extradition agreements are usually bilateral treaties.
2   The existing system of extradition already incorporates checks to safeguard individual rights, such as the political offence exception and the **principle of speciality**, which prescribes that the extradited individual will only stand trial for the offence specified in the extradition.
3   According to the **dual-criminality principle**, a person may be extradited only when his or her actions constitute an offence in both the requesting and the requested states.
4   A lot of states refuse extradition when the offender is likely to be subjected to the **death penalty** and make extradition conditional upon an assurance that the death penalty, if imposed, will be commuted to a sentence of imprisonment.
5   A large number of states, as a rule, do not allow the extradition of their nationals to another state.
6   But not all civil and human rights concerns are as efficiently upheld during the process of extradition; conflicts in specific cases have revolved around the use of torture in criminal proceedings, harsh interrogation methods, questionable trial (the standard of the justice in the requesting state) and incarceration, and inhuman or degrading treatment and punishment.

---

858 Article 3 of the Model Treaty on Extradition.
859 Article 4 of the Model Treaty on Extradition.

IMMUNITY FROM JURISDICTION

> sovereign immunity
> immunity from jurisdiction
> restrictive approach to foreign sovereign immunity
> public acts
> private acts
> Convention on Jurisdictional Immunities of States and Their Property
> European Convention on State Immunity
> counterclaim

State immunity as immunity from jurisdiction

Generally, state immunity derives from the principle of the sovereign equality of states, which itself is a central pillar of the international legal order.

State immunity or **sovereign immunity** is a principle of international law, by virtue of which one sovereign state cannot be sued before the power (legislative, executive, or judicial) of another sovereign state without its consent. State immunity is also referred to as '**immunity from jurisdiction**'.

Hence, sovereign immunity protects a state and its property from the jurisdiction of the legislative, executive, and judicial powers of another state. It covers administrative, civil, and criminal proceedings, as well as enforcement measures.

The limitations of state immunity

However, state immunity is not absolute. It obtains some limitations in international practice.

For instance, the United States and some Western European and other countries have adopted a **restrictive approach to foreign sovereign immunity**. The restrictive approach of state immunity means that foreign states are immune from jurisdiction relating to their **public acts** (*acta jure imperii*); however, they have no immunity from jurisdiction for their **private acts** (*acta jure gestionis*), including commercial activities.

Convention on Jurisdictional Immunities of States and Their Property

The United Nations **Convention on Jurisdictional Immunities of States and Their Property** of 2004 (not yet in force) encompasses a narrow understanding (immunity from judicial power) of state immunity:[860]

---

860 However, it is also reserved that 'The present Convention is without prejudice to the privileges and immunities enjoyed by a State under international law.'

A State enjoys immunity, in respect of itself and its property, from the jurisdiction of the courts of another State subject to the provisions of the present Convention.[861]

The Convention contains the rules and proceedings in which state immunity cannot be invoked: for example, commercial transactions; contracts of employment; personal injuries and damage to property; ownership, possession, and use of property; and so forth. In case of commercial transactions:

> If a State engages in a commercial transaction with a foreign natural or juridical person and, by virtue of the applicable rules of private international law, differences relating to the commercial transaction fall within the jurisdiction of a court of another State, the State cannot invoke immunity from that jurisdiction in a proceeding arising out of that commercial transaction.[862]

However, this rule does not apply to commercial transactions between states.[863]

European Convention on State Immunity

Similar approaches can be discovered in the **European Convention on State Immunity** of 1972,[864] which also prescribed the rules with regard to the scope of the immunity of one state from the jurisdiction of the courts of another state, including the restrictions from the immunity rule.

First of all, under the Convention, the principle was defined stipulating that a state cannot claim immunity from the jurisdiction of a court of another state if it has previously agreed to the jurisdiction of that court either by international treaty, 'an express term contained in a contract in writing', or 'an express consent given after a dispute between the parties has arisen'.

Secondly, the consent of a state to the jurisdiction of the court of another state may be assumed, if it 'institutes or intervenes in proceedings before a court' of that other state. Consequently, such a state has no right to claim immunity with respect to any **counterclaim** within the 'instituted' or 'intervened' proceedings.

In addition, the Convention also determined particular fields in which a state cannot claim the immunity. For instance, 'if the proceedings relate to a contract of employment between the State and an individual where the work has to be performed on the territory

---

861 Article 5 of the Convention on Jurisdictional Immunities of States and Their Property.

862 Paragraph 1 of Article 10 of the Convention on Jurisdictional Immunities of States and Their Property.

863 Paragraph 2(a) of Article 10 of the Convention on Jurisdictional Immunities of States and Their Property.

864 The Convention entered into force in 1976, according to Article 38: 'The Convention shall enter into force three months after the date of the deposit of the third instrument of ratification or acceptance.' Nevertheless, as of the time this book was written, it had only eight member states. See <www.coe.int/en/web/conventions/full-list/-/conventions/treaty/074> accessed 17 March 2021.

of the State of the forum'[865] (Nevertheless, this rule has exceptions, for example, it is not applicable in case of a contract concluded between states or 'the individual is a national of the employing State at the time when the proceedings are brought'.);[866]

> if [the State] participates with one or more private persons in a company, association or other legal entity having its seat, registered office or principal place of business on the territory of the State of the forum, and the proceedings concern the relationship, in matters arising out of that participation, between the State on the one hand and the entity or any other participant on the other hand. (However, this rule is not applicable 'if it is otherwise agreed in writing.')[867]

Privileges and immunities of state representatives

The concepts of state sovereignty, sovereign rights, and state immunity concern 'the privileges and immunities enjoyed by a State under international law in relation to the exercise of the functions' of (1) its diplomatic missions, consular posts, special missions, missions to international organisations or delegations to organs of international organisations or international conferences; and (2) persons connected with them; (3) privileges and immunities accorded under international law to the heads of states and governments or minister for foreign affairs *ratione personae*[868] (because of the nature or position of the relevant person);[869] and so forth.

There are different approaches to the relationship between immunity *ratione materiae*[870] (persons enjoying immunity) and immunity of the State (*stricto sensu*).[871] As was rightly assumed by the Special Rapporteur of the ILC Concepción Escobar Hernández in the Fourth Report on the Immunity of State Officials from Foreign Criminal Jurisdiction: 'It should be borne in mind that the immunity of State officials from jurisdiction has traditionally been viewed as a form of State immunity and has been conflated with that concept.'[872] Some authors, however, argue 'that the immunity of State officials from

---

865 Article 5 of the European Convention on State Immunity.

866 Paragraph 2 (a) of Article 4 and Paragraph 2 (a) of Article 5 of the European Convention on State Immunity.

867 Article 6 of the European Convention on State Immunity.

868 See Article 3 of the United Nations Convention on Jurisdictional Immunities of States and Their Property.

869 *Guide to Latin in International Law* (n 71) 247.

870 'Ratione materiae. ratēō'nā matā'rē-ī. rāšō'nē mutē'rē-ā. adv. "By reason of the matter." Because of the nature of the relevant subject matter. The immunity of a diplomat or head of state to most criminal and civil actions brought in the courts of the receiving state based on the official's acts on behalf of the sending state is immunity ratione materiae and outlives the official's tenure in office.' *Guide to Latin in International Law* (n 71) 247.

871 'Stricto sensu. strēk'tō sān'sū. strik'tō sen'sū. adj. or adv. "In the strict sense."' *Guide to Latin in International Law* (n 71) 269.

872 Concepción Escobar Hernández enumerated almost all relevant arguments: 'This conclusion is the outcome of various arguments, including the following: (i) the immunity from jurisdiction enjoyed

foreign criminal jurisdiction *ratione materiae* is individual in nature and distinct from the immunity of the State *stricto sensu*.'[873] Moreover, a few of them are convinced that the 'theory of representation – that would root the rule in the same principles that underlie the immunity of the state – is no longer accepted.'[874] Although the differences between the two forms of immunity may be outlined (for example, with regard to the immunity of state officials from foreign criminal jurisdiction),[875] nevertheless, it is clear that the 'indirect or ultimate beneficiary' of the immunity enjoyed by the state officials is the state concerned and 'that officials are given immunity from jurisdiction in the interest of the State and in order to safeguard values and principles that pertain solely and exclusively to the State.'[876]

CASES AND MATERIALS (*SELECTED PARTS*)

Lotus principle

Case of the S.S. 'Lotus' (France v Turkey), Judgment No.9 of 7 September 1927
PCIJ Ser A (1927) – No.10.

International law governs relations between independent States. The rules of law binding upon States therefore emanate from their own free will as expressed in conventions or by usages

---

by State officials is a consequence of the principle of the sovereign equality of States, as expressed by the phrase *par in parem non habet imperium*; (ii) immunity is recognized in order to protect State sovereignty and ensure that international relations can be carried on peacefully and sustainably; (iii) the immunity of State officials is not in fact immunity of the officials but immunity of the State, as demonstrated by the State's freedom of choice with regard to such immunity, including the freedom to lift or waive it; and (iv) bringing suit against a State official in a foreign court is an indirect way of bringing suit against the State when the latter cannot be prosecuted in the courts of a third State, meaning that the official's immunity from jurisdiction serves as a safeguard against frivolous challenges to State immunity, and is therefore equivalent to State immunity.' Paragraph 102 of the Fourth Report on the Immunity of State Officials from Foreign Criminal Jurisdiction, available at <https://undocs.org/A/CN.4/686> accessed 17 March 2021.

873 ibid, Paragraph 105.

874 Rosanne Van Alebeek, *The Immunity of States and Their Officials in International Criminal Law and International Human Rights Law* (Oxford University Press 2008) 160.

875 'This differentiation between the immunity of State officials from foreign criminal jurisdiction and the immunity of the State *stricto sensu* is still more evident in the case of immunity *ratione personae*, as an official who enjoys such immunity (a Head of State, Head of Government or Minister for Foreign Affairs) may do so even in respect of acts which are performed in a private capacity and which thus are not attributable to the State and do not engage its responsibility. In such cases, the immunity of these three officials from foreign criminal jurisdiction for a criminal act committed in a private capacity has no equivalent whatsoever in the realm of State immunity.' Paragraph 109 of the Fourth Report on the Immunity of State Officials from Foreign Criminal Jurisdiction.

876 ibid, Paragraph 103.

generally accepted as expressing principles of law and established in order to regulate the relations between these co-existing independent communities or with a view to the achievement of common aims. Restrictions upon the independence of States cannot therefore be presumed.

Now the first and foremost restriction imposed by international law upon a State is that – failing the existence of a permissive rule to the contrary – it may not exercise its power in any form in the territory of another State. In this sense jurisdiction is certainly territorial; it cannot be exercised by a State outside its territory except by virtue of a permissive rule derived from international custom or from a convention.

It does not, however, follow that international law prohibits a State from exercising jurisdiction in its own territory, in respect of any case which relates to acts which have taken place abroad, and in which it cannot rely on some permissive rule of international law. Such a view would only be tenable if international law contained a general prohibition to States to extend the application of their laws and the jurisdiction of their courts to persons, property and acts outside their territory, and if, as an exception to this general prohibition, it allowed States to do so in certain specific cases. But this is certainly not the case under international law as it stands at present. Far from laying down a general prohibition to the effect that States may not extend the application of their laws and the jurisdiction of their courts to persons, property and acts outside their territory, it leaves them in this respect a wide measure of discretion which is only limited in certain cases by prohibitive rules; as regards other cases, every State remains free to adopt the principles which it regards as best and most suitable.

This discretion left to States by international law explains the great variety of rules which they have been able to adopt without objections or complaints on the part of other States; it is in order to remedy the difficulties resulting from such variety that efforts have been made for many years past, both in Europe and America, to prepare conventions the effect of which would be precisely to limit the discretion at present left to States in this respect by international law, thus making good the existing lacunae in respect of jurisdiction or removing the conflicting jurisdictions arising from the diversity of the principles adopted by the various States.

In these circumstances, all that can be required of a State is that it should not overstep the limits which international law places upon its jurisdiction; within these limits, its title to exercise jurisdiction rests in its sovereignty. . . .

It is certainly true that-apart from certain special cases which are defined by international law-vessels on the high seas are subject to no authority except that of the State whose flag they fly. In virtue of the principle of the freedom of the seas, that is to say, the absence of any territorial sovereignty upon the high seas, no State may exercise any kind of jurisdiction over foreign vessels upon them. Thus, if a war vessel, happening to be at the spot where a collision occurs between a vessel flying its flag and a foreign vessel, were to send on board the latter an officer to make investigations or to take evidence, such an act would undoubtedly be contrary to international law.

But it by no means follows that a State can never in its own territory exercise jurisdiction over acts which have occurred on board a foreign ship on the high seas. A corollary of the principle of the freedom of the seas is that a ship on the high seas is assimilated to the territory of the State the flag of which it flies, for, just as in its own territory, that State exercises its authority upon it, and no other State may do so. All that can be said is that by virtue of the principle of the freedom of the seas, a ship is placed in the same position as national territory; but there is nothing to support the claim according to which the rights of the State under whose flag the vessel sails may go farther than the rights which it exercises within its territory properly so called. It follows that what occurs on board a vessel on the high seas must be regarded as if it occurred on the territory of the State whose flag the ship flies. If, therefore, a guilty act committed on the high seas produces its effects on a vessel flying another flag or in foreign territory, the same principles must be applied as if the territories of two different States were concerned, and the conclusion must therefore be drawn that there is no rule of international law prohibiting the State to which the ship on which the effects of the offence have taken place belongs, from regarding the offence as having been committed in its territory and prosecuting, accordingly, the delinquent.

Extraterritorial jurisdiction

Banković and Others v Belgium and Others [GC] (dec.), European Court of Human Rights Grand Chamber Decision as to the Admissibility of Application no. 52207/99, ECHR 2001- XII

(c) Extra-territorial acts recognised as constituting an exercise of jurisdiction

67. In keeping with the essentially territorial notion of jurisdiction, the Court has accepted only in exceptional cases that acts of the Contracting States performed, or producing effects, outside their territories can constitute an exercise of jurisdiction by them within the meaning of Article 1 of the Convention. . . .

69. In addition, . . . the Court accepted that the responsibility of Contracting Parties . . . could, in principle, be engaged because of acts of their authorities (judges) which produced effects or were performed outside their own territory . . .

70. Moreover, . . . the Court found that, bearing in mind the object and purpose of the Convention, the responsibility of a Contracting Party was capable of being engaged when as a consequence of military action (lawful or unlawful) it exercised effective control of an area outside its national territory. The obligation to secure, in such an area, the Convention rights and freedoms was found to derive from the fact of such control whether it was exercised directly, through the respondent State's armed forces, or through a subordinate local administration . . .

On the merits, the Court found that it was not necessary to determine whether Turkey actually exercised detailed control over the policies and actions of the authorities of the "Turkish Republic of Northern Cyprus" ("TRNC"). It was obvious from the large number of troops engaged in active duties in northern Cyprus that Turkey's army exercised "effective overall control over that part of the island". Such control, according to the relevant test and in the circumstances of the case, was found to entail the responsibility of Turkey for the policies and actions of the "TRNC". The Court concluded that those affected by such policies or actions therefore came within the "jurisdiction" of Turkey for the purposes of Article 1 of the Convention. Turkey's obligation to secure the rights and freedoms set out in the Convention was found therefore to extend to northern Cyprus.

In its subsequent Cyprus v. Turkey judgment . . ., the Court added that since Turkey had such "effective control", its responsibility could not be confined to the acts of its own agents therein but was engaged by the acts of the local administration which survived by virtue of Turkish support. Turkey's "jurisdiction" under Article 1 was therefore considered to extend to securing the entire range of substantive Convention rights in northern Cyprus.

71. In sum, the case-law of the Court demonstrates that its recognition of the exercise of extra-territorial jurisdiction by a Contracting State is exceptional: it has done so when the respondent State, through the effective control of the relevant territory and its inhabitants abroad as a consequence of military occupation or through the consent, invitation or acquiescence of the Government of that territory, exercises all or some of the public powers normally to be exercised by that Government. . . .

73. Additionally, the Court notes that other recognised instances of the extra-territorial exercise of jurisdiction by a State include cases involving the activities of its diplomatic or consular agents abroad and on board craft and vessels registered in, or flying the flag of, that State. In these specific situations, customary international law and treaty provisions have recognised the extra-territorial exercise of jurisdiction by the relevant State.

Ships on the high seas

United Nations Convention on the Law of the Sea
of 10 December 1982
Entry into force: 16 November 1994

Article 97

Penal jurisdiction in matters of collision or any other incident of navigation

1   In the event of a collision or any other incident of navigation concerning a ship on the high seas, involving the penal or disciplinary responsibility of the master or of any other person in the service of the ship, no penal or disciplinary proceedings may be instituted against such person except before the judicial or administrative authorities either of the flag State or of the State of which such person is a national.
2   In disciplinary matters, the State which has issued a master's certificate or a certificate of competence or licence shall alone be competent, after due legal process, to pronounce the withdrawal of such certificates, even if the holder is not a national of the State which issued them.
3   No arrest or detention of the ship, even as a measure of investigation, shall be ordered by any authorities other than those of the flag State.

Crimes against the peace and security of mankind

Draft Code of Crimes against the Peace and Security of Mankind of 1996 with Commentaries, International Law Commission

Adopted by the International Law Commission at its forty-eighth session, *Yearbook of the International Law Commission*, 1996, vol. II, Part Two.

Article 3. Punishment

An individual who is responsible for a crime against the peace and security of mankind shall be liable to punishment. The punishment shall be commensurate with the character and gravity of the crime.

Commentary

(5) In the case of a system of universal jurisdiction, it is each State declaring that it is competent that will determine the applicable penalty; the penalty may, for example, involve a maximum and a minimum, and may or may not admit extenuating or aggravating circumstances.

Article 8. Establishment of jurisdiction

Without prejudice to the jurisdiction of an international criminal court, each State Party shall take such measures as may be necessary to establish its jurisdiction over the crimes set out in articles 17, 18, 19 and 20, irrespective of where or by whom those crimes were committed. Jurisdiction over the crime set out in article 16 shall rest with an international criminal court. However, a State referred to in article 16 is not precluded from trying its nationals for the crime set out in that article.

Commentary

(5) The Commission considered that the effective implementation of the Code required a combined approach to jurisdiction based on the broadest jurisdiction of national courts together with the possible jurisdiction of an international criminal court. The article therefore establishes the principle of the concurrent jurisdiction of the national courts of all States parties to the Code based on the principle of universal jurisdiction and the jurisdiction of an international criminal court for the crimes set out in articles 17 to 20 of part two. . . .

(7) Jurisdiction over the crimes covered by the Code is determined in the first case by international law and in the second case by national law. As regards international law, any State party is entitled to exercise jurisdiction over an individual allegedly responsible for a crime under international law set out in articles 17 to 20 who is present in its territory under the principle of "universal jurisdiction" set forth in article 9. The phrase "irrespective of where or by whom those crimes were committed" is used in the first provision of the article to avoid any doubt as to the existence of universal jurisdiction for those crimes.

(8) As regards the crime of genocide, the Commission noted that the Convention on the Prevention and Punishment of the Crime of Genocide (art. VI) restricted national court jurisdiction for this crime to the State in whose territory the crime occurred. The provision extends national court jurisdiction over the crime of genocide set out in article 17 to every State party to the Code. The Commission considered that such an extension was fully justified in view of the character of the crime of genocide as a crime under international law for which universal jurisdiction existed as a matter of customary law for those States that were not parties to the Convention and therefore not subject to the restriction contained therein. . . .

(9) The provision is intended to give effect to the entitlement of States parties to exercise jurisdiction over the crimes set out in articles 17 to 20 under the principle of universal jurisdiction by ensuring that such jurisdiction is appropriately reflected in the national law of each State party. The phrase "shall take such measures as may be necessary" defines the relevant obligation of a State party in flexible terms to take account of the fact that constitutional and other national law requirements for the exercise of criminal jurisdiction vary from State to State. . . .

(10) In addition, the provision is intended to require a State party to enact any procedural or substantive measures that may be necessary to enable it to effectively exercise jurisdiction in a particular case with respect to an individual who is allegedly responsible for a crime set out in articles 17 to 20. . . .

(11) The recognition of the principle of the universal jurisdiction of the national courts of States parties to the Code for the crimes set out in articles 17 to 20 does not preclude the possibility of the jurisdiction of an international criminal court for those crimes, as indicated by the opening clause of the first provision which states that it is "without prejudice to the jurisdiction of an international criminal court". . . .

(12) The provision envisages the concurrent jurisdiction of an international criminal court in relation to the crimes set out in articles 17 to 20 to complement the national court jurisdiction envisaged for those crimes and thereby enhance the effective implementation of the Code in that respect. The priority to be given to national court jurisdiction or international court jurisdiction is not addressed in the article since this question would no doubt be addressed in the statute of the international criminal court. . . .

Article 9. Obligation to extradite or prosecute

Without prejudice to the jurisdiction of an international criminal court, the State Party in the territory of which an individual alleged to have committed a crime set out in article 17,18,19 or 20 is found shall extradite or prosecute that individual.

Commentary

(1) Article 8 of the Code envisages the establishment of two separate jurisdictional regimes for the crimes set out in articles 17 to 20 in the first instance and for the crime set out in article 16 in the second instance. In the first instance, the national courts of States parties would be entitled to exercise the broadest possible jurisdiction over genocide, crimes against humanity, crimes against United Nations and associated personnel and war crimes under the principle of universal jurisdiction. In addition, an international criminal court would be entitled to exercise concurrent jurisdiction over those crimes in accordance with its statute. . . .

(2) Article 9 establishes the general principle that any State in whose territory an individual alleged to have committed a crime set out in articles 17 to 20 of part two is bound to extradite or prosecute the alleged offender. The *aut dedere aut judicare* principle is reflected in several of the relevant conventions referred to in the commentary to the previous article. The fundamental purpose of this principle is to ensure that individuals who are responsible for particularly serious crimes are brought to justice by providing for the effective prosecution and punishment of such individuals by a competent jurisdiction.

(3) The obligation to prosecute or extradite is imposed on the custodial State in whose territory an alleged offender is present. The custodial State has an obligation to take action to ensure that such an individual is prosecuted either by the national authorities of that State or by another State which indicates that it is willing to prosecute the case by requesting extradition. . . .

(6) The custodial State has a choice between two alternative courses of action either of which is intended to result in the prosecution of the alleged offender. The custodial State may fulfil its obligation by granting a request for the extradition of an alleged offender made by any other State or by prosecuting that individual in its national courts. Article 9 does not give priority to either alternative course of action. The custodial State has discretion to decide whether to transfer the individual to another jurisdiction for trial in response to a request received for extradition or to try the alleged offender in its national courts.

Forum selection

Convention on Choice of Court Agreements
of 30 June 2005
Entry into force: 1 October 2015

Chapter I – Scope and definitions

Article 1 Scope

(1) This Convention shall apply in international cases to exclusive choice of court agreements concluded in civil or commercial matters.

(2) For the purposes of Chapter II, a case is international unless the parties are resident in the same Contracting State and the relationship of the parties and all other elements relevant to the dispute, regardless of the location of the chosen court, are connected only with that State.

(3) For the purposes of Chapter III, a case is international where recognition or enforcement of a foreign judgment is sought.

Article 2 Exclusions from scope

(1) This Convention shall not apply to exclusive choice of court agreements –

   a) to which a natural person acting primarily for personal, family or household purposes (a consumer) is a party;

   b) relating to contracts of employment, including collective agreements.

(2) This Convention shall not apply to the following matters –

   a) the status and legal capacity of natural persons;

   b) maintenance obligations;

   c) other family law matters, including matrimonial property regimes and other rights or obligations arising out of marriage or similar relationships;

   d) wills and succession;

   e) insolvency, composition and analogous matters;

   f) the carriage of passengers and goods;

   g) marine pollution, limitation of liability for maritime claims, general average, and emergency towage and salvage;

   h) anti-trust (competition) matters;

   i) liability for nuclear damage;

   j) claims for personal injury brought by or on behalf of natural persons;

   k) tort or delict claims for damage to tangible property that do not arise from a contractual relationship;

   l) rights in rem in immovable property, and tenancies of immovable property;

   m) the validity, nullity, or dissolution of legal persons, and the validity of decisions of their organs;

   n) the validity of intellectual property rights other than copyright and related rights;

   o) infringement of intellectual property rights other than copyright and related rights, except where infringement proceedings are brought for breach of a contract between the parties relating to such rights, or could have been brought for breach of that contract;

   p) the validity of entries in public registers.

(3) Notwithstanding paragraph 2, proceedings are not excluded from the scope of this Convention where a matter excluded under that paragraph arises merely as a preliminary question and not as an object of the proceedings. In particular, the mere fact that a matter excluded under paragraph 2 arises by way of defence does not exclude proceedings from

the Convention, if that matter is not an object of the proceedings.

(4) This Convention shall not apply to arbitration and related proceedings.

(5) Proceedings are not excluded from the scope of this Convention by the mere fact that a State, including a government, a governmental agency or any person acting for a State, is a party thereto.

(6) Nothing in this Convention shall affect privileges and immunities of States or of international organisations, in respect of themselves and of their property.

Article 3 Exclusive choice of court agreements

For the purposes of this Convention –

a) "exclusive choice of court agreement" means an agreement concluded by two or more parties that meets the requirements of paragraph c) and designates, for the purpose of deciding disputes which have arisen or may arise in connection with a particular legal relationship, the courts of one Contracting State or one or more specific courts of one Contracting State to the exclusion of the jurisdiction of any other courts;

b) a choice of court agreement which designates the courts of one Contracting State or one or more specific courts of one Contracting State shall be deemed to be exclusive unless the parties have expressly provided otherwise;

c) an exclusive choice of court agreement must be concluded or documented –

   i) in writing; or
   ii) by any other means of communication which renders information accessible so as to be usable for subsequent reference;

d) an exclusive choice of court agreement that forms part of a contract shall be treated as an agreement independent of the other terms of the contract. The validity of the exclusive choice of court agreement cannot be contested solely on the ground that the contract is not valid.

Chapter II – Jurisdiction

Article 5 Jurisdiction of the chosen court

(1) The court or courts of a Contracting State designated in an exclusive choice of court agreement shall have jurisdiction to decide a dispute to which the agreement applies, unless the agreement is null and void under the law of that State.

(2) A court that has jurisdiction under paragraph 1 shall not decline to exercise jurisdiction on the ground that the dispute should be decided in a court of another State.

(3) The preceding paragraphs shall not affect rules –

   a) on jurisdiction related to subject matter or to the value of the claim;
   b) on the internal allocation of jurisdiction among the courts of a Contracting State. However, where the chosen court has discretion as to whether to transfer a case, due consideration should be given to the choice of the parties.

Article 6 Obligations of a court not chosen

A court of a Contracting State other than that of the chosen court shall suspend or dismiss proceedings to which an exclusive choice of court agreement applies unless –

a) the agreement is null and void under the law of the State of the chosen court;
b) a party lacked the capacity to conclude the agreement under the law of the State of the court seised;
c) giving effect to the agreement would lead to a manifest injustice or would be manifestly contrary to the public policy of the State of the court seised;
d) for exceptional reasons beyond the control of the parties, the agreement cannot reasonably be performed; or
e) the chosen court has decided not to hear the case.

Article 7 Interim measures of protection

Interim measures of protection are not governed by this Convention. This Convention neither requires nor precludes the grant, refusal or termination of interim measures of protection by a court of a Contracting State and does not affect whether or not a party may request or a court should grant, refuse or terminate such measures.

Chapter III – Recognition and enforcement

Article 8 Recognition and enforcement

(1) A judgment given by a court of a Contracting State designated in an exclusive choice of court agreement shall be recognised and enforced in other Contracting States in accordance with this Chapter. Recognition or enforcement may be refused only on the grounds specified in this Convention.
(2) Without prejudice to such review as is necessary for the application of the provisions of this Chapter, there shall be no review of the merits of the judgment given by the court of origin. The court addressed shall be bound by the findings of fact on which the court of origin based its jurisdiction, unless the judgment was given by default.
(3) A judgment shall be recognised only if it has effect in the State of origin, and shall be enforced only if it is enforceable in the State of origin.
(4) Recognition or enforcement may be postponed or refused if the judgment is the subject of review in the State of origin or if the time limit for seeking ordinary review has not expired. A refusal does not prevent a subsequent application for recognition or enforcement of the judgment.
(5) This Article shall also apply to a judgment given by a court of a Contracting State pursuant to a transfer of the case from the chosen court in that Contracting State as permitted by Article 5, paragraph 3. However, where the chosen court had discretion as to whether to transfer the case to another court, recognition or enforcement of the judgment may be refused against a party who objected to the transfer in a timely manner in the State of origin.

Article 9 Refusal of recognition or enforcement

Recognition or enforcement may be refused if –

a) the agreement was null and void under the law of the State of the chosen court, unless the chosen court has determined that the agreement is valid;
b) a party lacked the capacity to conclude the agreement under the law of the requested State;

c) the document which instituted the proceedings or an equivalent document, including the essential elements of the claim,

   i) was not notified to the defendant in sufficient time and in such a way as to enable him to arrange for his defence, unless the defendant entered an appearance and presented his case without contesting notification in the court of origin, provided that the law of the State of origin permitted notification to be contested; or

   ii) was notified to the defendant in the requested State in a manner that is incompatible with fundamental principles of the requested State concerning service of documents;

d) the judgment was obtained by fraud in connection with a matter of procedure;

e) recognition or enforcement would be manifestly incompatible with the public policy of the requested State, including situations where the specific proceedings leading to the judgment were incompatible with fundamental principles of procedural fairness of that State;

f) the judgment is inconsistent with a judgment given in the requested State in a dispute between the same parties; or

g) the judgment is inconsistent with an earlier judgment given in another State between the same parties on the same cause of action, provided that the earlier judgment fulfils the conditions necessary for its recognition in the requested State.

Recognition and Enforcement of Foreign Arbitral Awards

Convention on the Recognition and Enforcement of Foreign Arbitral Awards
of 10 June 1958
Entry into force: 7 June 1959

Article I

1 This Convention shall apply to the recognition and enforcement of arbitral awards made in the territory of a State other than the State where the recognition and enforcement of such awards are sought, and arising out of differences between persons, whether physical or legal. It shall also apply to arbitral awards not considered as domestic awards in the State where their recognition and enforcement are sought.

2 The term "arbitral awards" shall include not only awards made by arbitrators appointed for each case but also those made by permanent arbitral bodies to which the parties have submitted.

Article II

1 Each Contracting State shall recognize an agreement in writing under which the parties undertake to submit to arbitration all or any differences which have arisen or which may arise between them in respect of a defined legal relationship, whether contractual or not, concerning a subject matter capable of settlement by arbitration.

2 The term "agreement in writing" shall include an arbitral clause in a contract or an arbitration agreement, signed by the parties or contained in an exchange of letters or telegrams.

3 The court of a Contracting State, when seized of an action in a matter in respect of which the parties have made an agreement within the meaning of this article, shall, at the request of one of the parties, refer the parties to arbitration, unless it finds that the said agreement is null and void, inoperative or incapable of being performed.

Article III

Each Contracting State shall recognize arbitral awards as binding and enforce them in accordance with the rules of procedure of the territory where the award is relied upon, under the conditions laid down in the following articles. There shall not be imposed substantially more onerous conditions or higher fees or charges on the recognition or enforcement of arbitral awards to which this Convention applies than are imposed on the recognition or enforcement of domestic arbitral awards.

Article IV

1   To obtain the recognition and enforcement mentioned in the preceding article, the party applying for recognition and enforcement shall, at the time of the application, supply:

   (a)   The duly authenticated original award or a duly certified copy thereof;
   (b)   The original agreement referred to in article II or a duly certified copy thereof.

2   If the said award or agreement is not made in an official language of the country in which the award is relied upon, the party applying for recognition and enforcement of the award shall produce a translation of these documents into such language. The translation shall be certified by an official or sworn translator or by a diplomatic or consular agent.

Article V

1   Recognition and enforcement of the award may be refused, at the request of the party against whom it is invoked, only if that party furnishes to the competent authority where the recognition and enforcement is sought, proof that:

   (a)   The parties to the agreement referred to in article II were, under the law applicable to them, under some incapacity, or the said agreement is not valid under the law to which the parties have subjected it or, failing any indication thereon, under the law of the country where the award was made; or
   (b)   The party against whom the award is invoked was not given proper notice of the appointment of the arbitrator or of the arbitration proceedings or was otherwise unable to present his case; or
   (c)   The award deals with a difference not contemplated by or not falling within the terms of the submission to arbitration, or it contains decisions on matters beyond the scope of the submission to arbitration, provided that, if the decisions on matters submitted to arbitration can be separated from those not so submitted, that part of the award which contains decisions on matters submitted to arbitration may be recognized and enforced; or
   (d)   The composition of the arbitral authority or the arbitral procedure was not in accordance with the agreement of the parties, or, failing such agreement, was not in accordance with the law of the country where the arbitration took place; or
   (e)   The award has not yet become binding on the parties, or has been set aside or suspended by a competent authority of the country in which, or under the law of which, that award was made.

2   Recognition and enforcement of an arbitral award may also be refused if the competent authority in the country where recognition and enforcement is sought finds that:

   (a)   The subject matter of the difference is not capable of settlement by arbitration under the law of that country; or

(b)   The recognition or enforcement of the award would be contrary to the public policy of that country.

Article VI

If an application for the setting aside or suspension of the award has been made to a competent authority referred to in article V (1) (e), the authority before which the award is sought to be relied upon may, if it considers it proper, adjourn the decision on the enforcement of the award and may also, on the application of the party claiming enforcement of the award, order the other party to give suitable security.

Extradition

Model Treaty on Extradition
The UN General Assembly Resolution A/RES/45/116 of 14 December 1990, subsequently amended by the General Assembly Resolution A/RES/52/88 of 12 December 1997

Article 1 Obligation to extradite

Each Party agrees to extradite to the other, upon request and subject to the provisions of the present Treaty, any person who is wanted in the requesting State for prosecution for an extraditable offence or for the imposition or enforcement of a sentence in respect of such an offence.

Article 2 Extraditable offences

1   For the purposes of the present Treaty, extraditable offences are offences that are punishable under the laws of both Parties by imprisonment or other deprivation of liberty for a maximum period of at least [one/two] year(s), or by a more severe penalty. Where the request for extradition relates to a person who is wanted for the enforcement of a sentence of imprisonment or other deprivation of liberty imposed for such an offence, extradition shall be granted only if a period of at least [four/six] months of such sentence remains to be served.

2   In determining whether an offence is an offence punishable under the laws of both Parties, it shall not matter whether:

(a)   The laws of the Parties place the acts or omissions constituting the offence within the same category of offence or denominate the offence by the same terminology;

(b)   Under the laws of the Parties the constituent elements of the offence differ, it being understood that the totality of the acts or omissions as presented by the requesting State shall be taken into account.

3   Where extradition of a person is sought for an offence against a law relating to taxation, customs duties, exchange control or other revenue matters, extradition may not be refused on the ground that the law of the requested State does not impose the same kind of tax or duty or does not contain a tax, customs duty or exchange regulation of the same kind as the law of the requesting State.

4   If the request for extradition includes several separate offences each of which is punishable under the laws of both Parties, but some of which do not fulfil the other conditions set out in

paragraph 1 of the present article, the requested Party may grant extradition for the latter offences provided that the person is to be extradited for at least one extraditable offence.

Article 3 Mandatory grounds for refusal

Extradition shall not be granted in any of the following circumstances:

(a) If the offence for which extradition is requested is regarded by the requested State as an offence of a political nature. Reference to an offence of a political nature shall not include any offence in respect of which the Parties have assumed an obligation, pursuant to any multilateral convention, to take prosecutorial action where they do not extradite, or any other offence that the Parties have agreed is not an offence of a political character for the purposes of extradition;

(b) If the requested State has substantial grounds for believing that the request for extradition has been made for the purpose of prosecuting or punishing a person on account of that person's race, religion, nationality, ethnic, origin, political opinions, sex or status, or that that person's position may be prejudiced for any of those reasons;

(c) If the offence for which extradition is requested is an offence under military law, which is not also an offence under ordinary criminal law;

(d) If there has been a final judgment rendered against the person in the requested State in respect of the offence for which the person's extradition is requested;

(e) If the person whose extradition is requested has, under the law of either Party, become immune from prosecution or punishment for any reason, including lapse of time or amnesty;

(f) If the person whose extradition is requested has been or would be subjected in the requesting State to torture or cruel, inhuman or degrading treatment or punishment or if that person has not received or would not receive the minimum guarantees in criminal proceedings, as contained in the International Covenant on

Civil and Political Rights, article 14;

(g) If the judgment of the requesting State has been rendered in absentia, the convicted person has not had sufficient notice of the trial or the opportunity to arrange for his or her defence and he has not had or will not have the opportunity to have the case retried in his or her presence.

Article 4 Optional grounds for refusal

Extradition may be refused in any of the following circumstances:

(a) If the person whose extradition is requested is a national of the requested State. Where extradition is refused on this ground, the requested State shall, if the other State so requests, submit the case to its competent authorities with a view to taking appropriate action against the person in respect of the offence for which extradition had been requested;

(b) If the competent authorities of the requested State have decided either not to institute or to terminate proceedings against the person for the offence in respect of which extradition is requested;

(c) If a prosecution in respect of the offence for which extradition is requested is pending in the requested State against the person whose extradition is requested;

(d) If the offence for which extradition is requested carries the death penalty under the law of the requesting State, unless that State gives such assurance as the requested State considers sufficient that the death penalty will not be imposed or, if imposed, will not be carried out. Where extradition is refused on this ground, the requested State shall, if the other State so requests, submit the case to its competent authorities with a view to taking appropriate action against the person for the offence for which extradition had been requested;

(e) If the offence for which extradition is requested has been committed outside the territory of either Party and the law of the requested State does not provide for jurisdiction over such an offence committed outside its territory in comparable circumstances;

(f) If the offence for which extradition is requested is regarded under the law of the requested State as having been committed in whole or in part within that State. Where extradition is refused on this ground, the requested State shall, if the other State so requests, submit the case to its competent authorities with a view to taking appropriate action against the person for the offence for which extradition had been requested;

(g) If the person whose extradition is requested has been sentenced or would be liable to be tried or sentenced in the requesting State by an extraordinary or ad hoc court or tribunal;

(h) If the requested State, while also taking into account the nature of the offence and the interests of the requesting State, considers that, in the circumstances of the case, the extradition of that person would be incompatible with humanitarian considerations in view of age, health or other personal circumstances of that person.

Article 5 Channels of communication and required documents

1 A request for extradition shall be made in writing. The request, supporting documents and subsequent communications shall be transmitted through the diplomatic channel, directly between the ministries of justice or any other authorities designated by the Parties.

2 A request for extradition shall be accompanied by the following:

(a) In all cases,

(i) As accurate a description as possible of the person sought, together with any other information that may help to establish that person's identity, nationality and location;

(ii) The text of the relevant provision of the law creating the offence or, where necessary, a statement of the law relevant to the offence and a statement of the penalty that can be imposed for the offence;

(b) If the person is accused of an offence, by a warrant issued by a court or other competent judicial authority for the arrest of the person or a certified copy of that warrant, a statement of the offence for which extradition is requested and a description of the acts or omissions constituting the alleged offence, including an indication of the time and place of its commission;

(c) If the person has been convicted of an offence, by a statement of the offence for which extradition is requested and a description of the acts or omissions constituting the offence and by the original or certified copy of the judgment or any other document setting out the conviction and the sentence imposed, the fact that the sentence is enforceable, and the extent to which the sentence remains to be served;

(d) If the person has been convicted of an offence in his or her absence, in addition to the documents set out in paragraph 2 (c) of the present article, by a statement as to the legal means available to the person to prepare his or her defence or to have the case retried in his or her presence;

(e) If the person has been convicted of an offence but no sentence has been imposed, by a statement of the offence for which extradition is requested and a description of the acts or omissions constituting the offence and by a document setting out the conviction and a statement affirming that there is an intention to impose a sentence.

3   The documents submitted in support of a request for extradition shall be accompanied by a translation into the language of the requested State or in another language acceptable to that State.

Article 9 Provisional arrest

1   In case of urgency the requesting State may apply for the provisional arrest of the person sought pending the presentation of the request for extradition. The application shall be transmitted by means of the facilities of the International Criminal Police Organization, by post or telegraph or by any other means affording a record in writing.

2   The application shall contain a description of the person sought, a statement that extradition is to be requested, a statement of the existence of one of the documents mentioned in paragraph 2 of article 5 of the present Treaty, authorizing the apprehension of the person, a statement of the punishment that can be or has been imposed for the offence, including the time left to be served and a concise statement of the facts of the case, and a statement of the location, where known, of the person.

3   The requested State shall decide on the application in accordance with its law and communicate its decision to the requesting State without delay.

4   The person arrested upon such an application shall be set at liberty upon the expiration of [40] days from the date of arrest if a request for extradition, supported by the relevant documents specified in paragraph 2 of article 5 of the present Treaty, has not been received. The present paragraph does not preclude the possibility of conditional release of the person prior to the expiration of the [40] days.

5   The release of the person pursuant to paragraph 4 of the present article shall not prevent rearrest and institution of proceedings with a view to extraditing the person sought if the request and supporting documents are subsequently received.

State immunity

Convention on Jurisdictional Immunities of States and Their Property
of 2 December 2004
Not yet in force

PART II
GENERAL PRINCIPLES

Article 5 State immunity

A State enjoys immunity, in respect of itself and its property, from the jurisdiction of the courts of another State subject to the provisions of the present Convention.

Article 6 Modalities for giving effect to State immunity

1   A State shall give effect to State immunity under article 5 by refraining from exercising jurisdiction in a proceeding before its courts against another State and to that end shall ensure that its courts determine on their own initiative that the immunity of that other State under article 5 is respected.

2   A proceeding before a court of a State shall be considered to have been instituted against another State if that other State:

(a)   is named as a party to that proceeding; or

(b)   is not named as a party to the proceeding but the proceeding in effect seeks to affect the property, rights, interests or activities of that other State.

Article 7 Express consent to exercise of jurisdiction

1   A State cannot invoke immunity from jurisdiction in a proceeding before a court of another State with regard to a matter or case if it has expressly consented to the exercise of jurisdiction by the court with regard to the matter or case:

(a)   by international agreement;

(b)   in a written contract; or

(c)   by a declaration before the court or by a written communication in a specific proceeding.

2   Agreement by a State for the application of the law of another State shall not be interpreted as consent to the exercise of jurisdiction by the courts of that other State.

Article 8 Effect of participation in a proceeding before a court

1   A State cannot invoke immunity from jurisdiction in a proceeding before a court of another State if it has:

(a)   itself instituted the proceeding; or

(b)   intervened in the proceeding or taken any other step relating to the merits. However, if the State satisfies the court that it could not have acquired knowledge of facts on which a claim to immunity can be based until after it took such a step, it can claim immunity based on those facts, provided it does so at the earliest possible moment.

2   A State shall not be considered to have consented to the exercise of jurisdiction by a court of another State if it intervenes in a proceeding or takes any other step for the sole purpose of:

(a)   invoking immunity; or

(b)   asserting a right or interest in property at issue in the proceeding.

3   The appearance of a representative of a State before a court of another State as a witness shall not be interpreted as consent by the former State to the exercise of jurisdiction by the court.

4   Failure on the part of a State to enter an appearance in a proceeding before a court of another State shall not be interpreted as consent by the former State to the exercise of jurisdiction by the court.

PART III
PROCEEDINGS IN WHICH STATE IMMUNITY
CANNOT BE INVOKED

Article 10 *Commercial transactions*

1   If a State engages in a commercial transaction with a foreign natural or juridical person and, by virtue of the applicable rules of private international law, differences relating to the commercial transaction fall within the jurisdiction of a court of another State, the State cannot invoke immunity from that jurisdiction in a proceeding arising out of that commercial transaction.

2   Paragraph 1 does not apply:

(*a*)   in the case of a commercial transaction between States; or

(*b*)   if the parties to the commercial transaction have expressly agreed otherwise.

3   Where a State enterprise or other entity established by a State which has an independent legal personality and is capable of:

(*a*)   suing or being sued; and

(*b*)   acquiring, owning or possessing and disposing of property, including property which that State has authorized it to operate or manage, is involved in a proceeding which relates to a commercial transaction in which that entity is engaged, the immunity from jurisdiction enjoyed by that State shall not be affected.

Article 11 *Contracts of employment*

1   Unless otherwise agreed between the States concerned, a State cannot invoke immunity from jurisdiction before a court of another State which is otherwise competent in a proceeding which relates to a contract of employment between the State and an individual for work performed or to be performed, in whole or in part, in the territory of that other State.

2   Paragraph 1 does not apply if:

(*a*)   the employee has been recruited to perform particular functions in the exercise of governmental authority;

(*b*)   the employee is:

(*i*)   a diplomatic agent, as defined in the Vienna Convention on Diplomatic Relations of 1961;

(*ii*)   a consular officer, as defined in the Vienna Convention on Consular Relations of 1963;

(*iii*) a member of the diplomatic staff of a permanent mission to an international organization or of a special mission, or is recruited to represent a State at an international conference; or

(*iv*)   any other person enjoying diplomatic immunity;

(*c*)   the subject-matter of the proceeding is the recruitment, renewal of employment or reinstatement of an individual;

(*d*)   the subject-matter of the proceeding is the dismissal or termination of employment of an individual and, as determined by the head of State, the head of Government or the

Minister for Foreign Affairs of the employer State, such a proceeding would interfere with the security interests of that State;

(e) the employee is a national of the employer State at the time when the proceeding is instituted, unless this person has the permanent residence in the State of the forum; or

(f) the employer State and the employee have otherwise agreed in writing, subject to any considerations of public policy conferring on the courts of the State of the forum exclusive jurisdiction by reason of the subject-matter of the proceeding.

Article 12 Personal injuries and damage to property

Unless otherwise agreed between the States concerned, a State cannot invoke immunity from jurisdiction before a court of another State which is otherwise competent in a proceeding which relates to pecuniary compensation for death or injury to the person, or damage to or loss of tangible property, caused by an act or omission which is alleged to be attributable to the State, if the act or omission occurred in whole or in part in the territory of that other State and if the author of the act or omission was present in that territory at the time of the act or omission.

Article 13 Ownership, possession and use of property

Unless otherwise agreed between the States concerned, a State cannot invoke immunity from jurisdiction before a court of another State which is otherwise competent in a proceeding which relates to the determination of:

(a) any right or interest of the State in, or its possession or use of, or any obligation of the State arising out of its interest in, or its possession or use of, immovable property situated in the State of the forum;

(b) any right or interest of the State in movable or immovable property arising by way of succession, gift or bona vacantia; or

(c) any right or interest of the State in the administration of property, such as trust property, the estate of a bankrupt or the property of a company in the event of its winding up.

Article 14 Intellectual and industrial property

Unless otherwise agreed between the States concerned, a State cannot invoke immunity from jurisdiction before a court of another State which is otherwise competent in a proceeding which relates to:

(a) the determination of any right of the State in a patent, industrial design, trade name or business name, trademark, copyright or any other form of intellectual or industrial property which enjoys a measure of legal protection, even if provisional, in the State of the forum; or

(b) an alleged infringement by the State, in the territory of the State of the forum, of a right of the nature mentioned in subparagraph (a) which belongs to a third person and is protected in the State of the forum.

Article 15 Participation in companies or other collective bodies

1   A State cannot invoke immunity from jurisdiction before a court of another State which is otherwise competent in a proceeding which relates to its participation in a company or other collective body, whether incorporated or unincorporated, being a proceeding concerning the relationship between the State and the body or the other participants therein, provided that the body:

(a) has participants other than States or international organizations; and
(b) is incorporated or constituted under the law of the State of the forum or has its seat or principal place of business in that State.

2   A State can, however, invoke immunity from jurisdiction in such a proceeding if the States concerned have so agreed or if the parties to the dispute have so provided by an agreement in writing or if the instrument establishing or regulating the body in question contains provisions to that effect.

Article 16 Ships owned or operated by a State

1   Unless otherwise agreed between the States concerned, a State which owns or operates a ship cannot invoke immunity from jurisdiction before a court of another State which is otherwise competent in a proceeding which relates to the operation of that ship if, at the time the cause of action arose, the ship was used for other than government non-commercial purposes.

2   Paragraph 1 does not apply to warships, or naval auxiliaries, nor does it apply to other vessels owned or operated by a State and used, for the time being, only on government non-commercial service.

3   Unless otherwise agreed between the States concerned, a State cannot invoke immunity from jurisdiction before a court of another State which is otherwise competent in a proceeding which relates to the carriage of cargo on board a ship owned or operated by that State if, at the time the cause of action arose, the ship was used for other than government non-commercial purposes.

4   Paragraph 3 does not apply to any cargo carried on board the ships referred to in paragraph 2, nor does it apply to any cargo owned by a State and used or intended for use exclusively for government non-commercial purposes.

5   States may plead all measures of defence, prescription and limitation of liability which are available to private ships and cargoes and their owners.

6   If in a proceeding there arises a question relating to the government and non-commercial character of a ship owned or operated by a State or cargo owned by a State, a certificate signed by a diplomatic representative or other competent authority of that State and communicated to the court shall serve as evidence of the character of that ship or cargo.

Article 17 Effect of an arbitration agreement

If a State enters into an agreement in writing with a foreign natural or juridical person to submit to arbitration differences relating to a commercial transaction, that State cannot invoke immunity from jurisdiction before a court of another State which is otherwise competent in a proceeding which relates to:

(a) the validity, interpretation or application of the arbitration agreement;
(b) the arbitration procedure; or
(c) the confirmation or the setting aside of the award, unless the arbitration agreement otherwise provides.

CHAPTER 11

Diplomatic and consular law

DOI: 10.4324/9781003213772-11

DISTINCTION BETWEEN DIPLOMATIC AND CONSULAR RELATIONS

> diplomatic law
> subject-to-subject political relations
> consular law
> relationship between individuals of sending and receiving states
> high-level diplomatic relations
> administrative functions, protection, co-operation, and friendship on an individual level
> general representative role
> in matters within their competence
> consular district

Diplomats and consuls

Diplomats[877] and consuls[878] perform useful functions in the host subjects (in case of diplomats, both in the states and in some other subjects of international law) for the benefit of the sending subject and issues of mutual interest. They provide a permanent presence and temporary missions in the receiving subjects and pursue friendly relations between the sending and the receiving subjects.

The leading criterion for the distinction

Generally, **diplomatic law**, which is the area of international law that prescribes permanent and temporary diplomatic relations, is concerned with **subject** (of international law)–to–**subject** (of international law) **political relations**, whereas **consular law** primarily encourages the **relationship between individuals of sending and receiving states**.[879]

---

877 The term 'diplomat' derives from the Latin 'diploma' (letter of recommendation or authority) and from the Greek δίπλωμα (folded double). Rev. Walter W. Skeat, *An Etymological Dictionary of the English Language* (Oxford at the Clarendon Press, impression of 1963) 171.

878 'CONSUL, a (Roman) chief magistrate. L.) . . . – L. consul, a consul. Etym. doubtful, but allied to the verb consulere, to consult, deliberate.' ibid 131.

879 Some functions aimed at protecting the persons in the territory under the jurisdiction of another subject of international law, which are similar to consular functions, may also be performed by other subjects of international law. However, strictly speaking, the general concept of consular law applies only to states.

Different functions

Embassies and ambassadors establish **high-level diplomatic relations**, whereas consulates and consuls deal with **administrative functions** (such as issuing visas and passports), **protection** (assisting their nationals in distress), **co-operation**, and **friendship on an individual level**.

Different scopes of representation

On the whole, diplomatic agents have a **general representative role** since they represent their senders in all matters and relations in the receiving subject to which they are accredited. Consuls, on the other hand, also represent their senders in the receiving state, but only **in matters within their competence**.

Therefore, the diplomatic mission to a receiving subject is accomplished by one permanent representation covering the receiving subject entirely, while the consulates operate in the particular region(s) of a receiving state (**consular districts**) as specified under the bilateral agreement between the states.

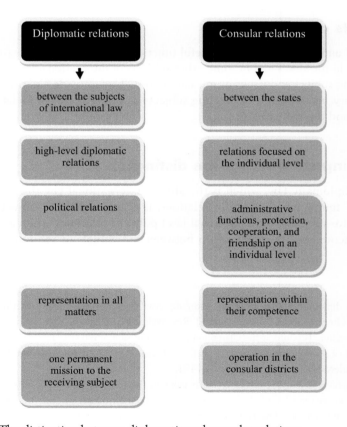

Diplomatic relations	Consular relations
between the subjects of international law	between the states
high-level diplomatic relations	relations focused on the individual level
political relations	administrative functions, protection, cooperation, and friendship on an individual level
representation in all matters	representation within their competence
one permanent mission to the receiving subject	operation in the consular districts

FIGURE 11.1 The distinction between diplomatic and consular relations

DIPLOMATIC RELATIONS AND DIPLOMATIC MISSION

> state-to-state diplomatic relations
> permanent diplomatic missions
> apostolic nunciatures
> temporary diplomatic missions
> special missions
> Convention on Special Missions
> Congress of Vienna
> Vienna Convention on Diplomatic Relations
> sending state
> receiving state

The meaning of diplomatic relations

Many forms of the foreign relations fall within the scope of the term 'diplomatic relations.'

- In the broad sense, diplomatic relations include a wide range of foreign relations involving internal bodies and officials of the subjects of international law (mostly the employees of the agencies of foreign affairs), as well as foreign temporary and permanent missions.
- In a narrow sense, the term 'diplomatic relations' concerns foreign missions, i.e. the group of people from the sending subject of international law who officially represent that subject in the receiving subject.
- In the strict conceptual sense, diplomatic law is concerned with **state-to-state diplomatic relations**; however, diplomatic relations (in the broad sense) may be exercised by some other subjects of international law as well.

The permanent and temporary diplomatic missions

There are many types of diplomatic relations and missions at the international level. Some of them obtain a permanent character (the **permanent diplomatic missions**) – for example, the permanent missions of the states and the Holy See (the **apostolic nunciatures**).

According to the conventional position, the emergence of permanent diplomatic missions as a distinct form from temporary diplomatic missions dates back to the seventeenth century, following the 1648 Treaty of Westphalia.

In the majority of cases, diplomatic relations emerge in the form of **temporary diplomatic missions**: for example, the **special missions** of states, which are defined under the **Convention on Special Missions** of 1969 as 'temporary mission[s], representing the State, which [are] sent by one State to another State with the consent of the latter for the purpose of dealing with it on specific questions or of performing in relation to it a specific task'.

It should be noted that special missions are the oldest form of diplomatic relations and have been utilised as a kind of *ad hoc* form of diplomacy for hundreds of years.

Development of diplomatic law

The legal norms regulating the various aspects of diplomatic relations are the result of centuries of the interstate practice of relations. They were developed mostly by the forms of customary international norms and bilateral treaties. In the early nineteenth century, some common understandings on the rules of the diplomatic relations were reached at the **Congress of Vienna** of 1815 in the aftermath of the Napoleonic wars.

The new and the most extensive codification of diplomatic law was achieved in 1961 with the conclusion of the **Vienna Convention on Diplomatic Relations**.

While the Vienna Convention on Diplomatic Relations is one of the most important treaties in the field of diplomacy, it only regulates a limited part mostly of the state-to-state diplomatic relations and, therefore, is not a comprehensive document regulating all questions arising in the area of diplomatic relations, even concerning the field of state-to-state diplomacy.

Common terms used in state-to-state diplomatic relations

To denote the states which engage in the state-to-state diplomatic relations, the following two terms are usually applied: the **sending state** and the **receiving state**.

The term 'diplomatic mission' is generic, designating all forms of either permanent or temporary missions.

Most permanent diplomatic missions are called embassies; however, in certain cases, some have unique titles; for instance, the diplomatic mission of one Commonwealth state,[880] to another is generally called a high commission and their ambassadors are called the high commissioners. When a country withdraws from the Commonwealth, their permanent representative structures also change their names to embassies.

The origination of diplomatic relations between states

The establishment of diplomatic relations and either permanent or temporary diplomatic missions take place by mutual consent, which, as a rule, is performed by the conclusion of the corresponding international treaty.

At the same time, this consent represents the *de jure* recognition of a state (or its government). On the other hand, the *de jure* recognition itself, which is provided in the form of a separate declaration or other document, is usually soon followed by the establishment of diplomatic relations.

---

880 'The Commonwealth is a voluntary association of 54 independent and equal countries. . . . The Commonwealth's roots go back to the British Empire. But today any country can join the modern Commonwealth. The last country to join the Commonwealth was Rwanda in 2009.' <https://thecommonwealth.org/about-us> accessed 17 March 2021.

Functions of a diplomatic mission of a state

> represent
> protect
> negotiate
> inform and report
> promote friendly relations

The functions of a diplomatic mission enumerated in the Vienna Convention

The functions of a diplomatic mission, as stated in the Vienna Convention on Diplomatic Relations, consist of, among other things:

(a) representing the sending State in the receiving State;
(b) protecting in the receiving State the interests of the sending State and of its nationals, within the limits permitted by international law;
(c) negotiating with the Government of the receiving State;
(d) ascertaining by all lawful means conditions and developments in the receiving State, and reporting thereon to the Government of the sending State;
(e) promoting friendly relations between the sending State and the receiving State, and developing their economic, cultural and scientific relations.

Cardinal functions of a diplomatic mission

Consequently, the primary functions are:

* to **represent** (a sending state);
* to **protect** (the interests of a sending state and its nationals);
* to **negotiate** (with the government of a receiving state);
* to **inform and report** (by all lawful means); and
* to **promote friendly relations** (between sending and receiving states).

The fulfilment of the consular functions by diplomatic missions

This list does not provide an exhaustive set of the functions fulfilled by diplomatic missions. For example, in addition to the listed functions, a diplomatic mission can perform consular functions as well. Moreover, nowadays, performing consular functions is an essential role for the most diplomatic missions, as is undoubtedly recognised by both the Vienna Convention on Diplomatic Relations and the Vienna Convention on Consular Relations of 1963.[881] The latter provides that, although consular functions are to be exercised by the consular posts, they may also be exercised by the diplomatic missions. In such a case, the diplomatic mission does so in accordance with the Vienna Convention on Consular Relations, but it also retains all its diplomatic privileges and immunities.

However, when a member of a diplomatic mission performs consular functions, that member should generally deal with the local authorities, police, judiciary, and so forth, instead of the central government. To avoid misunderstandings as to the nature of the duties being performed in such cases, it is desirable that a member of the diplomatic mission receive a consular appointment in addition to the diplomatic post, and the receiving state should be notified of both appointments.

Members of a diplomatic mission of a state

members of a mission
head of a mission
members of the staff of a mission
members of diplomatic staff
diplomatic rank
members of administrative and technical staff
members of service staff
Ambassador
Minister
Counsellor
First Secretary
Second Secretary
Third Secretary
Attaché
Assistant Attaché
diplomatic classes
Charges d'affaires
Ambassador-in-Residence
Ambassador-at-Large
diplomatic corps
diplomatic service
Dean of the Diplomatic Corps

881 Article 3 of the Vienna Convention on Diplomatic Relations and Article 2 of the Vienna Convention on Consular Relations.

Composition of the members of a diplomatic mission

Under the Vienna Convention on Diplomatic Relations, the **members of a mission** are the **head of a mission,** who is a person charged by the sending state with the duty of acting in that capacity, and the **members of the staff of a mission**.

In turn, the members of the staff of a mission are:

1   members of **diplomatic staff**, who possess a **diplomatic rank;**
2   members of **administrative and technical staff**, who are employed in the administrative and technical service of a mission (translators, referents, and so on); and
3   members of **service staff**, who are employed to perform domestic services for the mission (drivers, cleaners, gardeners, cooks, and so on).

Location and size of a mission

A permanent mission to a state, as a rule, is located in the capital of the receiving state. At the same time, a sending state without the prior express consent of a receiving state may not establish offices forming part of a mission in areas other than those in which the mission itself is established.

As for the size of a diplomatic mission, in the absence of a specific agreement, the receiving state may require that the size of a mission be kept within the limits it considers reasonable with regard to the specific local conditions and the needs of the particular mission in the receiving state.

Members of diplomatic staff should be nationals of the sending state; however, although it is uncommon, they may also be the nationals of the receiving state if the latter agrees to it. As for the rest of the staff of the mission, many of them may be nationals of the receiving state. The reasons for such a choice may be related to convenience, lower costs, and so on.

Diplomatic ranks

Diplomatic ranks designate the career and protocol status of personnel holding diplomatic positions in line with international customs and reflect their professional competence and suitability to perform foreign service.

The internal legislation of each state regulates the granting of the diplomatic ranks and the list of the ranks. Consequently, there are differences from country to country in this regard. As a result, the diplomatic ranks 'can be confusing and unfamiliar.'[882]

The order of diplomatic ranks

Taking into account that there are certain states which follow their traditional diplomatic ranks system with a clear individuality and that it is challenging to locate such systems in any general model, nevertheless, the existing differences in the system of diplomatic ranks

---

882 *Protocol for the Modern Diplomat* (Foreign Service Institute, US Department of State, July 2013) 10 <http://bit.ly/3bswrRE> accessed 17 March 2021.

can still be integrated under a single structure. Hence, to make such a generalisation, the individual precedence *inter se* of diplomats in formal or diplomatic functions from highest to lowest can be demonstrated as follows:

- **Ambassador** (rank);
- **Minister** (rank);
- **Counsellor** (rank);
- **First Secretary** (rank);
- **Second Secretary** (rank);
- **Third Secretary** (rank);
- **Attaché** (rank).[883]

Some diplomatic ranks enumerated here may not be available in smaller missions.

In some countries, particular ranks may be added, or some ranks listed here may be more divided.[884] For example, there can be two ranks for a Minister and a Counsellor,[885] several ranks for a Secretary,[886] and so on. In several countries, some diplomatic ranks include the words 'extraordinary' and 'plenipotentiary.' For instance, the rank of Ambassador is often

883 For instance, under Article 13 of Law of the People's Republic of China on Diplomatic Personnel Stationed Abroad: 'Basic relations between diplomatic posts and diplomatic ranks are as follows: (1) Ambassador Extraordinary and Plenipotentiary: rank of Ambassador; (2) Representative or Vice-Representative: rank of Ambassador, Minister or Counselor; (3) Minister and Minister-Counselor: rank of Minister; (4) Counselor: rank of Counselor; (5) First Secretary: rank of First Secretary; (6) Second Secretary: rank of Second Secretary; (7) Third Secretary: rank of Third Secretary; and (8) Attaché: rank of Attaché.' Available at <www.npc.gov.cn/zgrdw/englishnpc/Law/2011-02/16/content_1620759.htm> accessed 17 March 2021. According to the official website of the Ministry of Foreign and European Affairs of the Slovak Republic, there are in the Slovak Republic the following diplomatic ranks: I. Lower diplomatic ranks – (1) Attaché (Attaché) ('This diplomatic rank is also sometimes conferred or breveted to non-diplomatic staff temporarily assigned to serve at diplomatic missions in order to carry out economic management tasks, or to other administrative or technical staff in so-called risk countries.') and (2) Third Secretary (*Troisième Secrétaire*); II. Mid-level diplomatic ranks – (3) Second Secretary (*Deuxième Secrétaire*) and (4) First Secretary (*Premier Secrétaire*); III. Higher diplomatic ranks – (5) Counsellor (*Conseiller*), (6) Minister Counsellor (*Ministre Conseiller*) and (7) Ambassador (*Ambassadeur*). <https://bit.ly/36fJm7v> accessed 17 March 2021.
884 'The following list ranks many of the positions (from the top down) one may find in a U.S. embassy. Not all positions exist in every embassy. Ambassador Extraordinary and Plenipotentiary[;] Ministers Plenipotentiary[;] Ministers[;] Chargé d'Affaires ad hoc or pro tempore[;] Chargé d'Affaires ad interim[;] Minister-Counselors[;] Counselors (or Senior Secretaries in the absence of Counselors) [;] Army, Naval and Air Attachés[;] Civilian Attaches not in the Foreign Service[;] First Secretaries[;] Second Secretaries[;] Assistant Army, Naval and Air Attachés[;] Civilian Assistant Attaches not in the Foreign Service[;] Third Secretaries and Assistant Attachés.' *Protocol for the Modern Diplomat* (n 882) 10.
885 For example, Minister First Class, Minister Second Class, Counsellor First Class, and Counsellor Second Class in Kazakhstan, the Russian Federation, and Uzbekistan.
886 For example, First Secretary of the First Class, First Secretary of the Second Class, Second Secretary of the First Class, and Second Secretary of the Second Class in Kazakhstan, the Russian Federation, and Uzbekistan.

formulated as 'Ambassador Extraordinary and Plenipotentiary'; there can also be 'Minister Plenipotentiary.'

Attaché sometimes denotes a rank of the persons who do not fit strictly into the standard diplomatic ranking, often because they are not (or were not traditionally) members of the sending country's diplomatic service or foreign ministry and were therefore only 'attached' to the diplomatic mission. However, 'Attaché' clearly denotes a diplomatic rank in some European countries, as well as in China, Russia, and so on, where Attaché is the lowest diplomatic rank for a career diplomat. The post titled 'Attaché' is also sometimes conferred on or breveted to the staff assigned to serve at diplomatic missions in order to carry out some specific types of work (mostly military, naval, air, commercial, cultural, press, and information). Sometimes, such service and specialist attaches are also placed in the diplomatic ranking system.[887] In some states, the rank of **Assistant Attaché** is added to the list as the lowest diplomatic rank.

The head of mission

Meanwhile, the Convention on Diplomatic Relations divides the heads of diplomatic missions into three **diplomatic classes**, namely:

- Ambassadors and High Commissioners (in Commonwealth missions to other Commonwealth countries) accredited to Heads of States. This class also includes Nuncios of the Holy See, which, as examined earlier, is a *sui generis* subject of international law.
- Envoys[888] and Ministers (Ministers as the heads of the mission and not within the meaning of the second diplomatic rank mentioned earlier)[889] accredited to Heads of States. This class also includes Internuncios of the Holy See.
- **Charges d'affaires**[890] accredited to Ministers for Foreign Affairs.

Under the Convention, if the post of the head of a mission is vacant, or if the head of a mission is incapable performing the functions, a chargé d'affaires ad interim[891] shall act provisionally as the head of the mission.

887 For example, in the US diplomatic service.
888 'Envoy . . . Nowadays used to refer to any senior diplomat. Earlier it had a specific hierarchical connotation, being used to designate diplomatic agents of less than the highest rank.' 'Glossary of Diplomatic Terms' <www.ediplomat.com/nd/glossary.htm> accessed 17 March 2021.
889 'Minister, Minister-Counselor . . . a minister has traditionally been a chief of diplomatic mission who headed a legation rather than an embassy. As so few legations are left, the title is now borrowed more and more to designate the second-ranking officer of a large embassy. It has, therefore, come increasingly to mean the senior counselor under the ambassador. To avoid confusion with the old connotation, the United States and a number of governments designate these senior deputy chiefs of mission by the hyphenated title "minister-counselor".' ibid.
890 'Chargé d'Affaires, a.i. . . . Formerly, a chargé d'affaires was the title of a chief of mission, inferior in rank to an ambassador or a minister. Today with the a.i. (ad interim) added, it designates the senior officer taking charge for the interval when a chief of mission is absent from his post.' ibid.
891 'AD INTERIM [L. *ad* + *interim* / meanwhile, in the meantime] In the meantime; for a limited time; temporary. *Ad interim* alimony is temporary support pending the outcome of the proceeding. [Ad]

The name of the charge d'affaires ad interim shall be notified, either by the head of the mission or, in case he is unable to do so, by the Ministry for Foreign Affairs of the sending State to the Ministry for Foreign Affairs of the receiving State or such other ministry as may be agreed.[892]

The class to which the head of mission is assigned is a matter of agreement between the concerned states. Except precedence and etiquette, there is no differentiation between heads of missions due to the class assigned to them. However, the heads of missions are to take precedence 'in their respective classes in the order of the date and time of taking up their functions.'[893] In many countries with Roman Catholicism as the dominant religion, the precedence of the representative of the Holy See is accepted.

Some countries recognise a difference between an **Ambassador-in-Residence**, whose competence is commonly limited to a particular country, and an **Ambassador-at-Large**, who is entrusted with special duties (specific foreign policy issues) and is not appointed to a particular country.[894] Some subjects of international law also assign Special Representatives or Special Envoys for particular fields (usually with the diplomatic rank of Ambassador).[895]

Diplomatic corps

One of the most apparent fields in which precedence is expressed is the **diplomatic corps** or corps diplomatique, which is the collective body of foreign diplomats accredited to a particular state (or, in some instances, to another subject of international law). At the same time, the term 'diplomatic corps' is sometimes confused with the collective body of diplomats from a particular country, the proper term for which is '**diplomatic service**'.

The diplomatic corps may refer to a collective of the accredited heads of missions (ambassadors, high commissioners, and others). In many countries, the heads of major international organisations are also considered members of the diplomatic corps.

---

interim copyright is a copyright for a limited time, shorter than for a conventional copyright.' Emanuel (n 90) 12.

892 Article 19 (1) of the Vienna Convention on Diplomatic Relations.

893 Article 16 (1) of the Vienna Convention on Diplomatic Relations.

894 For example, as noted on the official website of the US Department of State: 'John Cotton Richmond serves as the United States Ambassador-at-Large to Monitor and Combat Trafficking in Persons and leads the Department's Office to Monitor and Combat Trafficking in Persons. In October 2018, the Senate unanimously confirmed him and President Trump appointed him to lead the United States' global engagement to combat human trafficking and support the coordination of anti-trafficking efforts across the U.S. government.' <https://2017-2021.state.gov/biographies/john-cotton-richmond/index.html> accessed 17 March 2021.

895 In the US, '[t]he President and the Secretary of State appoint special representatives, envoys, advisers, and coordinators for top-level foreign policy issues.' <https://2009-2017.state.gov/s/index.htm> accessed 17 March 2021. For example, James F. Jeffrey served as the Special Representative for Syria Engagement and Special Envoy to the Global Coalition to Defeat ISIS; his term ended in November 2020. The official website of the US Embassy in Syria <https://sy.usembassy.gov/on-the-departure-of-ambassador-james-f-jeffrey/> accessed 17 March 2021.

The diplomatic corps usually assembles to attend state functions like coronations, inaugurations, national days, visits by foreign leaders, and so forth, depending on local customs. The diplomatic corps has a senior member – a **Dean of the Diplomatic Corps** (Doyen of the Corps Diplomatique) – who is usually the longest-serving ambassador to a country and the corps' spokesman on formal occasions. At the same time, in many countries where Roman Catholicism is the dominant religion, the Apostolic Nuncio (also referred to as the Papal Nuncio) is *ex officio* dean of the diplomatic corps.[896]

Appointment of the heads and members of the diplomatic staff of missions of a state

> principle of reciprocity
> *agrément*
> letter of credence
> credentials
> ceremonial reception

The principle of reciprocity

Under the Vienna Convention on Diplomatic Relations, the appointment of members of the diplomatic staff is founded on the **principle of reciprocity**. Both the sending and receiving states participate in the appointment process.

The participation of the sending and receiving states in the appointment of the members of staff

Of course, every candidate may be selected and assigned by the sending state and, generally, the sending state may freely appoint the members of the staff of the mission, according to the Vienna Convention on Diplomatic Relations.[897]

However, at the same time, the appointment is subject to the agreement of the receiving state, which has the right to refuse it:

- in case of accreditation of a head of mission;
- if a member of the diplomatic staff of the mission is appointed from among persons having the nationality of the receiving state or third state;

---

896 'In determining the appointment of the Dean or Doyen, the seniority of a head of mission is based on the length of time that he has continuously held his appointment at that post. In certain countries (especially in Latin America) the Apostolic Nuncio is always Dean'. R. G. Feltham, *Diplomatic Handbook* (7th edn, Longman 1998) 14.

897 Article 7 of the Vienna Convention on Diplomatic Relations.

- if a diplomatic agent is declared *persona non grata*;
- in the absence of a specific agreement as to the size of the mission.

Therefore, in practice, the sending states, as a rule, notify the receiving states of the appointment of diplomatic agents.

Agrément and the letter of credence

The principle of reciprocity is clearly expressed in the case of the head of the mission.

The sending state shall notify the receiving state of the name of the person proposed to be appointed as head of a mission. When the receiving state gives its consent to the proposed person through sending the ***agrément***, then the sending state can continue with the formal appointment procedure and accredit a candidate.

Accreditation is done by furnishing the head of the mission with certain official papers known as '**letter of credence**' or **credentials**. The credentials of the head of a mission are presented to the head of the receiving state in a **ceremonial reception**.

Diplomatic privileges and immunities

diplomatic immunity
diplomatic privileges
premises of the mission
means of transport
archives and documents of the mission
official correspondence of the mission
diplomatic bag
property placed in the premises of the mission
inviolability
furnishings of the premises of the mission
bank accounts of a diplomatic mission
private servants of members of the mission
diplomatic courier
United States Diplomatic and Consular Staff in Tehran case

Difference between diplomatic immunity and diplomatic privileges

In essence, **diplomatic immunity** puts some persons and things outside the scope of the legislative, executive, and judicial system of the receiving state.

Diplomatic privileges refer more to benefits, as opposed to the protections allowed by immunity. One such privilege is the immunity itself. Other types of privileges afforded to diplomatic staff include special handling at a port of entry and expedited baggage service, as well as reduced rates for certain goods and services.

Persons and things as the holders of diplomatic immunity and diplomatic privileges

Diplomatic privileges and immunities fall into two different categories:

1 Privileges and immunities accorded to the things of the diplomatic mission; and
2 Privileges and immunities of persons.

Things

The following are considered things of a diplomatic mission:

- **Premises of the mission;**
- **Means of transport;**
- **Archives and documents of the mission;**
- **Official correspondence of the mission;**
- **Diplomatic bag;**
- Other **property placed in the premises of the mission.**

According to contemporary international law, the **inviolability** rule as an expression of diplomatic immunity applies to the properties mentioned here.

Under the Vienna Convention on Diplomatic Relations, 'the "premises of the mission" are the buildings or parts of buildings and the land ancillary thereto, irrespective of ownership, used for the purposes of the mission including the residence of the head of the mission.'[898]

Under the Convention, the premises of the mission shall be inviolable, which first of all means that agents of the receiving state may not enter them, except with the consent of the head of the mission. On the other hand, the receiving state 'is under a special duty to take all appropriate steps to protect the premises of the mission against any intrusion or damage and to prevent any disturbance of the peace of the mission or impairment of its dignity.'[899]

At the same time, the Convention, in addition to the premises of the mission, also protects the **furnishings of premises of the mission**, other property thereon, and the means of transport of the mission, which shall be immune from search, requisition, attachment, or execution.[900] This does not amount to complete inviolability in every case. For instance, the transport of a mission may be towed away if it is causing a serious obstruction[901] or creating a public hazard.

---

898 Article 1 (i) of the Vienna Convention on Diplomatic Relations.
899 Article 22 (1) and 22 (2) of the Vienna Convention on Diplomatic Relations.
900 Article 22 (3) of the Vienna Convention on Diplomatic Relations.
901 'Towing away a vehicle which is causing serious traffic obstruction is by contrast carried out not primarily to penalize the driver but in order to keep the highway clear, and since it does not fall squarely within the forms of interference specifically prohibited by Article 22.3 the view has been taken in

Meanwhile, although the Convention leaves the question of whether the **bank accounts of a diplomatic mission** also enjoy immunity, nowadays, the established practice of the various countries is that the bank accounts of a diplomatic mission at least hold immunity from search, requisition, attachment, or execution.[902]

According to the Convention, the archives and documents of the mission shall be under the highest protection. 'They shall be inviolable at any time and wherever they may be.' The term 'documents' today would also include documents held via electronic means (computer hard and floppy disks, CD-ROMs, memory sticks, and so on). Inviolability should be determined extensively and shall apply to the documents wherever they may be. At the same time, inviolability lasts indefinitely. Closure of the mission, severance of diplomatic relations, or an armed conflict is not grounds to violate the immunity.

In addition, the official correspondence of the mission shall be inviolable. According to the Convention, the same rule has been applied to the diplomatic bag. In this context, official correspondence means all correspondence relating to the mission and its functions. On the other hand, the packages constituting the diplomatic bag must bear visible external marks of their character and may contain only diplomatic documents or articles intended for official use. Since secure electronic communications (secure fax, email, and so forth) were developed and have become widely used for diplomatic communications, the diplomatic bag is still used for sending lengthy classified documents and sensitive items of equipment, but of course, it is nowadays used less frequently.

The premises of the mission enjoy certain diplomatic privileges. For example, they are exempt from all national, regional, or municipal dues and taxes, other than the payments for specific services rendered (for example, the utilities actually supplied).

Privileges and immunities – personal

As regards the privileges and immunities of persons, the Convention has a differentiated approach:

1   Members of the diplomatic staff who are not nationals or permanent residents of the receiving state enjoy almost complete immunity from the jurisdiction of the receiving state, with certain exceptions outlined later.
2   Members of the diplomatic staff who are nationals or permanent residents of the receiving state enjoy immunity only from jurisdiction and inviolability concerning the official acts performed in the exercise of their functions. Meanwhile, additional privileges and immunities may be granted by the receiving state or bilateral agreement.

---

most congested capitals that it is permissible in relation to diplomatic vehicles.' Eileen Denza, *Diplomatic Law: Commentary on the Vienna Convention on Diplomatic Relations* (4th edn, Oxford University Press 2016) 133.

902 'In most jurisdictions where the possibility arises, superior courts have concluded that embassy bank accounts maintained to cover a mission's costs and running expenses are not subject to enforcement. The leading case, *Philippine Embassy Bank Account*, was decided by the German Federal Constitutional Court in 1977. The court concluded [that] . . . [c]laims against a general current bank account of the embassy of a foreign State which exists in the State of the forum and the purpose of which is to cover the embassy's costs and expenses are not subject to forced execution by the State of the forum.' ibid 129.

3   Members of the family of a diplomatic agent forming part of his or her household, if they are not nationals of the receiving state, likewise enjoy the same privileges and immunities.

4   Members of the administrative and technical staff, if they are not nationals or permanent residents of the receiving state, also enjoy privileges and immunities but to a lesser degree than the diplomatic agents. Their immunity from the civil and administrative jurisdiction of the receiving state does not extend to acts performed outside the course of their duties. The same privileges and immunities are applied to the members of the families of the administrative and technical staff if they are not nationals or permanent residents of the receiving state.[903]

5   Members of the service staff of the mission who are not nationals or permanent residents of the receiving state enjoy immunity only with respect to acts performed in the course of their duties and exemption from dues and taxes on the emoluments they receive because of their employment.

6   **Private servants of members of the mission** shall, if they are not nationals or permanent residents of the receiving state, be exempt from dues and taxes on the emoluments they receive because of their employment.

7   Other members of the staff of the mission and private servants who are not nationals or permanent residents of the receiving state enjoy privileges and immunities only to the extent admitted by the receiving state.

8   The **diplomatic courier**, who shall be provided with an official document indicating his or her status and the number of packages constituting the diplomatic bag, shall be protected by the receiving state in the performance of his or her duties. The courier enjoys personal inviolability and shall not be liable to any form of arrest or detention.

The moment when the application of privileges and immunities begins

An entitled person enjoys the privileges and immunities from the moment of entering the territory of the receiving state on proceeding to take up the post or, if he or she is already in its territory, from the moment when the Ministry for Foreign Affairs, or any other government agency of the receiving state as may be agreed, is notified of the appointment. An entitled person also enjoys such privileges and immunities when travelling via or is in the territory of a third state on proceeding to take up or to return to his or her post or when returning to his or her own country.

---

903 Article 37 (2) of the Vienna Convention on Diplomatic Relations: 'Members of the administrative and technical staff of the mission, together with members of their families forming part of their respective households, shall, if they are not nationals of or permanently resident in the receiving State, enjoy the privileges and immunities specified in Articles 29 to 35, except that the immunity from civil and administrative jurisdiction of the receiving State specified in paragraph 1 of Article 31 shall not extend to acts performed outside the course of their duties. They shall also enjoy the privileges specified in Article 36, paragraph 1, in respect of articles imported at the time of first installation.'

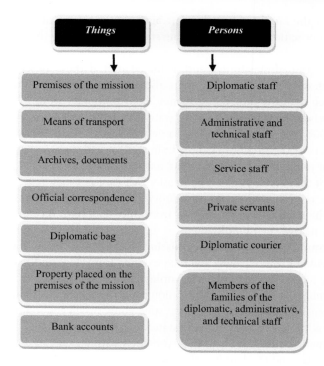

FIGURE 11.2 The holders of diplomatic privileges and immunities

Privileges and immunities of diplomatic agents

The central privileges and immunities granted to a diplomatic agent are:

- Complete immunity from the criminal jurisdiction of the receiving state.
- Immunity from the civil and administrative jurisdiction of the receiving state, except in case of:
  - a real action relating to private immovable property situated in the territory of the receiving state, unless he/she holds it on behalf of the sending state for the purposes of the mission;
  - an action relating to a succession in which the diplomatic agent is involved as executor, administrator, heir, or legatee as a private person and not on behalf of the sending state; or
  - an action relating to any professional or commercial activity exercised by the diplomatic agent in the receiving state outside his or her official functions.
- The inviolability of his or her person.
- Exemption from giving evidence as a witness.
- Exemption from all dues and taxes, personal or real, national, regional, or municipal, except, among others:

- dues and taxes on private immovable property situated in the territory of the receiving state, unless he/she holds it on behalf of the sending state for the purposes of the mission;
- estate, succession, or inheritance duties levied by the receiving state;
- dues and taxes on private income having its source in the receiving state and capital taxes on investments made in commercial undertakings in the receiving state; and
- charges levied for specific services rendered.

- Freedom of communication with a sending state for official purposes.
- The right to move freely on the territory of the receiving state.
- Inviolability of his or her private residence.
- Inviolability of his or her papers, correspondence, and property.

However, the immunity from jurisdiction granted to a diplomatic agent is immunity from the jurisdiction of the receiving state and not from legal liability. Diplomatic agents are not immune from the jurisdiction of the sending state. Moreover, they can be sued in the receiving state after a reasonable time elapses from the end of the mission.

The sending state may waive the immunity of a diplomatic agent from jurisdiction of the receiving state. The waiver must be express. However, a general waiver of immunity from jurisdiction does not imply a waiver of immunity with respect to the execution of the judgment; in such a case, a separate waiver is required. Immunity may also be waived by the diplomatic agent by submitting voluntarily to the jurisdiction of the court of the receiving state.

United States Diplomatic and Consular Staff in Tehran case

Generally, all rules on diplomatic privileges and immunities are duly recognised and performed by the subjects of international law. Nevertheless, in exceptional cases, violations still occur. One of the gravest breaches of the norms of diplomatic (and consular) privileges and immunities took place in Iran in 1979, when in the beginning, the Iranian authorities failed to protect the US Embassy in Tehran and the Consulates at Tabriz and Shiraz from rallying students ('militants'); however, subsequently, they themselves were involved in seizing the premises and in the illegal 'seizure and detention as hostages' of the US diplomatic and consular officers (as well as other individuals) for 444 days.

The case was brought before the International Court of Justice, which responded in the **United States Diplomatic and Consular Staff in Tehran** case *(United States of America v Iran)* by articulating that

> the principle of the inviolability of the persons of diplomatic agents and the premises of diplomatic missions is one of the very foundations of this long-established regime, to the evolution of which the traditions of Islam made a substantial contribution. . . . Even in the case of armed conflict or in the case of a breach in diplomatic

relations those provisions require that both the inviolability of the members of a diplomatic mission and of the premises, property and archives of the mission must be respected by the receiving State.[904]

Termination of a diplomatic mission or of the functions of a diplomatic agent of a state

> breaking of diplomatic relations
> functions of the mission have come to an end
> recall of the diplomatic agent
> functions of the diplomatic agent have come to an end
> *persona non grata*
> resignation of the diplomatic agent
> death of the diplomatic agent

Various means of and reasons for termination

A diplomatic mission or the functions of a diplomatic agent may be terminated permanently or temporarily by various means and for various reasons. Some are defined in the Vienna Convention on Diplomatic Relations, and others are established by state practice.

An illustrative list of the means and reasons

Among these means and reasons are:

1   Termination of the diplomatic mission by:

   a)   the **breaking of diplomatic relations** between the sending and receiving states because of war or due to any other reason; and
   b)   the notification by the sending state to the receiving state that the **functions of the mission have come to an end**;

2   Termination of the functions of a diplomatic agent by:

   a)   the **recall of the diplomatic agent** by his or her sending state upon its initiative or at the request of the receiving state;
   b)   the notification of the sending state to the receiving state that the **functions of the diplomatic agent have come to an end**;
   c)   the notification by the receiving state that the diplomatic agent is a *persona non grata*;
   d)   the **resignation of the diplomatic agent**; or
   e)   the **death of the diplomatic agent**.

904 *United States Diplomatic and Consular Staff in Tehran (United States of America v Iran)* Judgment of 24 May 1980, ICJ Reports 1980, 3.

The procedure of *persona non grata*

A unique role in this regard is performed by the procedure of *persona non grata*, which is a vital tool in the hands of the receiving state. According to the Vienna Convention on Diplomatic Relations, a receiving state may

> at any time and without having to explain its decision, notify the sending State that the head of the mission or any member of the diplomatic staff of the mission is *persona non grata* or that any other member of the staff of the mission is not acceptable. In such a case, the sending State shall, as appropriate, either recall the person concerned or terminate his functions with the mission. A person may be declared *non grata* or not acceptable before arriving in the territory of the receiving State.[905]

However, this procedure is rarely used because it leads to the complication of interstate relations and the counter response from the sending state regarding the diplomatic agents of the receiving state. In practice, it is done if the diplomatic agent commits a crime or seeks to obtain information through illegal methods (espionage, other actions against the security of the receiving state) or sometimes even for sending a political message. When a serious offence has been committed, the sending state may have the choice of waiving the person's immunity or withdrawing them from the receiving state.

DIPLOMATIC LAW AND INTERNATIONAL ORGANISATIONS

Convention on the Privileges and Immunities of the United Nations
juridical personality
immunity from every form of legal process
representatives of members to the principal and subsidiary organs
officials of the UN
constituent treaty
Headquarters agreement
host state

Preliminary remarks

As long as, in parallel with the main subjects of international law, there are also other subjects of international law, they all enter into foreign relations as separate subjects. The questions which should be posed here are as follows: Can the foreign relations in which these subjects are involved be elevated to the status of diplomatic relations? And hence, should the rules and approaches of diplomatic law be applied to them?

905 Article 9 (1) of the Vienna Convention on Diplomatic Relations.

There is no doubt that particular foreign actions undertaken by certain *sui generis* subjects of international law (for instance, the Holy See, the diplomatic relations of which is covered by express provisions of the Vienna Convention on Diplomatic Relations; the Sovereign Order of Malta) are acknowledged to be an integral part of the network of diplomatic relations. However, concerning other non-state subjects, the positions vary.

Moreover, as mentioned earlier, for many experts, in the strict sense, diplomatic relations concern only state-to-state foreign relations. Therefore, to designate foreign representations, officials involved in the foreign service, as well as the privileges and immunities of such non-state actors, more neutral terms, such as missions; international staff; international officials; and international privileges and immunities without using the terms 'diplomatic', 'diplomat', 'embassy', and so on are often formally utilised. Nevertheless, with regard to international organisations, as well as some other subjects of international law, in practice, the latter wordings were not so rarely used. Furthermore, some references to the terms 'diplomat' or 'diplomatic' or the application of concepts and rules similar to diplomatic law can be found in international treaties which address the representations of states to international organisations and vice versa.

Diplomatic law as such is related to the concepts of state sovereignty and immunity. Since both concepts were implemented, for example, with regard to the Holy See, the theoretical foundation for covering that case by diplomatic law was obtained. However, the question is whether one can apply, in terms of an analogy, these concepts (sovereignty and immunity) to other cases, such as international organisations or some other subjects of international law, as well.

United Nations Organisation

The **Convention on the Privileges and Immunities of the United Nations** of 1946 was one of the first conventions which was adopted and widely recognised immediately after the establishment of the UN.

Firstly, it defined that the United Nations possesses **juridical personality** by having the capacity (1) to contract, (2) to acquire and dispose of immovable and movable property, and (3) to institute legal proceedings.[906]

Secondly, the Convention recognised that the UN itself, 'its property and assets wherever located and by whomsoever held, shall enjoy **immunity from every form of legal process** except insofar as in any particular case it has expressly waived its immunity' and that its premises are 'immune from search, requisition, confiscation, expropriation and any other form of interference, whether by executive, administrative, judicial or legislative action.' The inviolability rule also covers the archives, funds, gold, and currency of any kind of the United Nations.[907]

Thirdly, the Convention afforded to the UN privileges similar to those of the diplomatic missions: for example, by proclaiming that the assets, income and, other property of the UN shall be 'exempt from all direct taxes' and 'from customs duties and prohibitions and restrictions on imports and exports in respect of articles imported or exported by the

906 Article I of the Convention on the Privileges and Immunities of the United Nations.
907 Article II of the Convention on the Privileges and Immunities of the United Nations.

United Nations for its official use'. Moreover, under the Convention, the UN enjoys, in the territory of each member,

> for its official communications treatment not less favourable than that accorded by the Government of that Member to any other Government including its diplomatic mission in the matter of priorities, rates and taxes on mails, cables, telegrams, radiograms, telephotos, telephone and other communications; and press rates for information to the press and radio. No censorship shall be applied to the official correspondence and other official communications of the United Nations.[908]

Fourthly, in order to safeguard the independent exercise of their functions in connection with the United Nations, the Convention provided the **representatives of members to the principal and subsidiary organs** of the United Nations and to conferences convened by the UN with 'immunity from personal arrest or detention and from seizure of their personal baggage, and, in respect of words spoken or written and all acts done by them in their capacity as representatives, immunity from legal process of every kind'. The Convention specifically enumerated other immunities and privileges of such officials and finally declared that it would also include

> such other privileges, immunities and facilities not inconsistent with the foregoing as diplomatic envoys enjoy, except that they shall have no right to claim exemption from customs duties on goods imported (otherwise than as part of their personal baggage) or from excise duties or sales taxes.[909]

However, according to the Convention, the member countries have a duty to waive the immunity of their representatives if 'in the opinion of the Member the immunity would impede the course of justice'.

Fifthly, the Convention furnished some categories of '**officials of the UN**' specified by the Secretary-General with certain immunities and privileges, which include immunity from legal process in respect of words spoken or written and all acts performed by them in their official capacity, exemption from taxation on the salaries and emoluments paid to them by the United Nations, immunity from immigration restrictions and alien registration (this rule was also applied to 'their spouses and relatives dependent on them'), and so forth. Generally, the immunities and privileges of the officials of the UN aim to safeguard the independent exercise of their functions and are more limited than those of diplomatic agents as well as the members of the administrative and technical staffs of the diplomatic mission if they are not nationals or permanent residents of the receiving state. However, at the same time, the Convention provided the UN Secretary-General and all Assistant Secretaries-General 'in respect of themselves, their spouses and minor children, the privileges and immunities, exemptions and facilities accorded to diplomatic envoys, in accordance with international law.'[910] The Secretary-General has a duty to waive the

---

908 Article III of the Convention on the Privileges and Immunities of the United Nations.
909 Article IV of the Convention on the Privileges and Immunities of the United Nations.
910 Article V of the Convention on the Privileges and Immunities of the United Nations.

immunity of the UN officials when 'in his opinion, the immunity would impede the course of justice.' With regard to the Secretary-General, only the UN Security Council can waive immunity.

On the whole, under the Convention, state sovereignty and immunity concepts were in a particular way also extended to the UN. Hence, it afforded the United Nations, its premises, its assets, representatives of members, and officials with immunities and privileges which were very similar to diplomatic ones. However, some specifics can also be outlined. For example, regarding persons, those immunities and privileges were substantially limited for officials of the UN (except the UN Secretary-General and the Assistant Secretaries-General) and significantly equated to those of diplomatic agents in the case of the representatives of members to the principal and subsidiary organs of the United Nations and to conferences convened by the UN.

Other international organisations

Generally, any international organisation derives its immunity from the **constituent treaty** establishing the organisation, the **Headquarters agreement** made between that organisation and respective **host state**, and the norms of international law. On particular occasions, in the absence of a specific international norm, the scopes of immunity may also be defined by the national legislation of the host state.[911] Therefore, the rules on immunities and privileges concerning the international organisations were usually specified case by case, according to the legal sources enumerated here, and mostly by the bilateral agreements between the organisation and the state concerned.

Vienna Convention on the Representation of States in their Relations with International Organisations of a Universal Character

In 1975, the Vienna Convention on the Representation of States in their Relations with International Organisations of a Universal Character was adopted.

However, as long no more than 30 states delivered their consent to be bound by the Convention, it did not attain a universal character. The main reason for the cold attitude towards the Convention from the states was the choice of the ILC to award high immunities and privileges with regard to the representation of states in their relations with international organisations of a universal character, making them substantially similar to diplomatic ones and, therefore, sometimes even moving away from the cautious approach of the Convention on the Privileges and Immunities of the United Nations.

---

911 For example, the UK International Organisations Act 2005 ('An Act to make provision about privileges, immunities and facilities in connection with certain international organisations') <www.legislation.gov.uk/ukpga/2005/20/introduction/enacted> accessed 17 March 2021.

In sum, the Convention mostly followed the architecture of the Vienna Convention on Diplomatic Relations and adapted the terms and approaches of the latter to the representation of states in their relations with international organisations – for instance, by dividing their staffs into 'the members of the diplomatic staff, the administrative and technical staff, and the service staff of the mission, the delegation, or the observer delegation'.

The Convention obliged the host state (which was defined as a state in whose territory either the organisation has its seat or an office or where a meeting of an organ or a conference is held), as well as the organisation concerned with guaranteeing the immunities and privileges afforded by the Convention, including the absolute inviolability of premises, archives, and documents; the immunity from search, requisition, attachment, or execution of the 'premises of the mission, their furnishings and other property thereon and the means of transport';[912] the complete immunity from the criminal jurisdiction of the host state concerning the head of the mission, the members of the diplomatic staff, 'members of the administrative and technical staff of the mission, together with members of their families forming part of their respective households who are not nationals of or permanently resident in the host state';[913] and rules similar to diplomatic law concerning civil and administrative jurisdiction, freedom of movement and communication, and so forth.

The equating approach

Although the transfer of rules of diplomatic law to the representation of states in their relations with international organisations in such high proportions, as introduced by the Vienna Convention on the Representation of States in their Relations with International Organisations of a Universal Character, and making it universal in character did not receive sufficient formal recognition from the states, in fact, for example, the permanent missions of members and permanent observers or representatives of non-members to the international organisation are very reminiscent of the permanent diplomatic missions of states to the receiving states. They all consist of officials having diplomatic ranks and functions. The Host States award the permanent missions immunities and privileges very similar to those of the diplomatic missions, despite the fact that a member of a mission to an international organisation is a representative of his or her state in that organisation and not in the host state.

On the other hand, the same equating approach was implemented to a greater degree in practice with regard to the representatives of international organisations in states as well.

---

912 Article 23 of the Vienna Convention on the Representation of States in their Relations with International Organisations of a Universal Character.

913 Articles 30 and 36 of the Vienna Convention on the Representation of States in their Relations with International Organisations of a Universal Character.

CONSULAR RELATIONS AND CONSULAR POSTS

> Vienna Convention on Consular Relations
> consulate-general
> consulate
> vice-consulate
> consular agency
> seat of the consular post
> classification of the consular post
> career consular officers
> honorary consular officers

The general multilateral international treaty concerning consular relations

The 1963 **Vienna Convention on Consular Relations** is the almost universally recognised international treaty governing consular relations.

Formation and severance of consular relations

Under the Convention, consular relations between states may be established by mutual consent. The consent given to the establishment of diplomatic relations between the two states implies, unless otherwise stated, consent to the establishment of consular relations. However, the severance of diplomatic relations shall not *ipso facto* involve the severance of consular relations.[914]

Consular post

The **consular post** is one of the most ancient in international relations, and its institution is much older than that of the diplomatic mission.

The consular post means any **consulate-general**, **consulate**, **vice-consulate**, or **consular agency**.

The establishment of consular relations should not be confused with the establishment of a consular post in the territory of the receiving state, which is subject to the individual consent of the receiving state. The **seat of the consular post**; its **classification**; the consular district; and the subsequent changes in the seat of the consular post, its classification, or the consular district shall be provided by the sending state and approved by the receiving state.[915]

A consular post operates in a consular district, which is the area assigned to a consular post in order to exercise its consular functions.

914 Article 2 of the Vienna Convention on Consular Relations.
915 Article 4 of the Vienna Convention on Consular Relations.

The number of consular posts

There can be more than one consular post of a sending state in a receiving state. The number of consular posts depends on the consular needs of the sending state. For example, a sending state with a significant number of its citizens in the receiving state may have a higher number of consulates in that state than the latter has in the territory of the sending state. However, when countries have similar interests in protecting individual interests in each other's territory, or they are neighbouring countries, the rule of parity will usually apply.

Career and honorary consular officers

There are two categories of consular officers – **career consular officers** and **honorary consular officers**. The latter means any citizen or permanent resident of a receiving state, including the head of a foreign consular post, entrusted in that capacity with the exercise of consular functions without being employed in the career consular service of a sending state and often without receiving the remuneration and emoluments of such a job.

Honorary consular officers are usually selected from persons who have significant business or cultural connections with the recipient country. However, they possess limited privileges and immunities, since they are citizens or permanent residents of the receiving state. Honorary consular officers, unlike career consular officers, carry on for personal profit any professional or commercial activity in the receiving state.

Consular functions

> protection
> administrative functions
> co-operation
> friendship

Difference between diplomatic and consular functions

The consular post is different from the diplomatic mission concerning the functions it performs. While the diplomatic mission is mostly concerned with the political relations between the two states, the consular post exercises a variety of administrative, protective, economic, and cultural functions on an individual level.

An illustrative list of consular functions

According to the Vienna Convention on Consular Relations,[916] the functions of consular posts are:

---

916 Article 5 of the Vienna Convention on Consular Relations.

1 Protection

- Protecting the interests of the sending state and its nationals (both natural and legal persons) in the receiving state;
- '[S]ubject to the practices and procedures obtaining in the receiving State, representing or arranging appropriate representation for nationals of the sending State before the tribunals and other authorities of the receiving State, for the purpose of obtaining, in accordance with the laws and regulations of the receiving State, provisional measures for the preservation of the rights and interests of these nationals, where, because of absence or any other reason, such nationals are unable at the proper time to assume the defence of their rights and interests;' and
- Safeguarding, in accordance with the laws and regulations of the receiving state, the interests of minors and other persons lacking full capacity who are nationals of the sending state.

2 Administrative functions

- Helping and assisting nationals of the sending state;
- Issuing passports and travel documents to the nationals of the sending state;
- Giving visas to persons wishing to travel to the sending state;
- Acting as a notary and civil registrar and in capacities of a similar kind and performing certain functions of an administrative nature;
- Safeguarding the interests of nationals of the sending state 'in cases of succession *mortis causa* in the territory of the receiving state';
- Transmitting judicial and extra-judicial documents or executing letters to the receiving state;
- Exercising supervision and inspection powers over vessels and aircraft having the nationality of the sending state and over the crews of these vessels and aircraft; and
- Extending assistance to vessels and aircraft having the nationality of the sending state and to their crews, 'taking statements regarding the voyage of a vessel, examining and stamping the ship's papers, and, without prejudice to the powers of the authorities of the receiving State, conducting investigations into any incidents which occurred during the voyage, and settling disputes of any kind between the master, the officers and the seamen in so far as this may be authorized by the laws and regulations of the sending State'.

3 Co-operation

- Furthering the commercial, economic, cultural, and scientific relations between the sending state and the receiving state; and
- Reporting to the sending state on the conditions and developments of the commercial, economic, cultural, and scientific life of the receiving state, as well as providing such information to interested persons.

4 Friendship

- Promoting friendly relations between the sending state and the receiving state and their nationals, both individuals and bodies corporate.

In addition, the consular post can perform other functions entrusted to it by the sending state provided that:

- such functions are not prohibited by the laws and regulations of the receiving state; or
- there is no objection by the receiving state; or
- such functions are envisaged by the international treaties between the states concerned.

The performance of diplomatic acts by a consular officer

In a state where the sending state has no diplomatic mission and is not represented by the diplomatic mission of a third state, the consular officer may, with the consent of the receiving state and without affecting the consular status, be authorised to perform diplomatic acts/duties. The performance of such acts by a consular officer shall not confer upon the officer any right to claim diplomatic privileges and immunities.[917]

Members of a consular post

members of the consular post
consular officers
consular employees
members of the service staff
consuls-general
consuls
vice-consuls
consular agents
members of the consular staff
members of the private staff

The size of the consular staff

As to the size of the consular staff, the sending state needs an express agreement from the receiving state; otherwise, the receiving state may require that the size of the staff be kept within the limits it considers reasonable and normal, having regard for the circumstances and conditions in the consular district and for the needs of the particular consular post.[918]

---

917 Article 17 (1) of the Vienna Convention on Consular Relations.
918 Article 20 of the Vienna Convention on Consular Relations.

Composition of the consular post

Under the Vienna Convention on Consular Relations, **members of the consular post** consist of the **consular officers**, **consular employees**, and **members of the service staff**.

According to the Convention:

- A consular officer is any person, including the head of a consular post, entrusted in that capacity to exercise consular functions. Consular officers, in principle, have the nationality of the sending state and may not be appointed from among persons having the nationality of the receiving state except with the express consent of that state, which may be withdrawn at any time.[919]
- The head of a consular post is the person with the duty to act in that capacity. The heads of a consular post are divided into four classes:

  - **Consuls-general;**
  - **Consuls;**
  - **Vice-consuls**; and
  - **Consular agents.**

  The class to which the head of a consular post is assigned is a matter of agreement between the concerned states. At the same time, the parties can agree to assign classes to other consular officers as well.[920]
- A consular employee is any person employed to provide administrative or technical services for a consular post.
- A member of the service staff is any person employed in the domestic service of a consular post.
- **Members of the consular staff** are the consular officers other than the head of a consular post, consular employees, and members of the service staff.
- **Members of the private staff** are persons who are employed exclusively in the private service of a member of the consular post.

Appointment of heads of consular posts and other consular officers

consular commission
notification of appointment
exequatur
precedence rules under consular law

---

919 Article 22 of the Vienna Convention on Consular Relations.

920 '2. Paragraph 1 of this Article in no way restricts the right of any of the Contracting Parties to fix the designation of consular officers other than the heads of consular posts.' Article 9 of the Vienna Convention on Consular Relations.

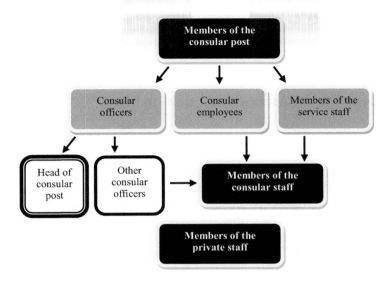

FIGURE 11.3 The composition of the consular post

The heads of the consular posts

The heads of the consular posts are appointed and admitted to exercise consular functions by the sending state.

In the process of appointment, they are provided by the sending state with a **consular commission** or similar instrument, intended for each appointment, certifying their capacity and showing the full name, the category and class, the consular district, and the seat of the consular post. This document shall be transmitted through the diplomatic or another appropriate channel to the sending state. However, if the receiving state agrees, the sending state may, instead of a commission or similar instrument, send to the receiving state only a **notification of appointment** containing the aforementioned particulars.[921]

Exequatur

An *exequatur* is an official written recognition and authorisation of a consular officer. If the receiving state has no objection to the appointment, the *exequatur* is issued.

An *exequatur*, as a rule, is issued concerning the head of a consular post, and usually, the head of a consular post does not take his or her post until receiving an *exequatur*.

The receiving state has the right either to issue an *exequatur* or to refuse to issue it without obligation to provide an explanation.

Other consular officers

As regards the other consular officers, generally, the sending state may freely appoint them. The full name, category, and class of all consular officers, other than the head of a consular

921 Article 11 of the Vienna Convention on Consular Relations.

post, shall be notified by the sending state to the receiving state in a reasonable timeframe for the receiving state. In some instances, if required by the laws and internal regulations of the sending state or the receiving state, the sending state may request, and the receiving state may grant, an *exequatur* to a consular officer other than the head of a consular post.[922]

The precedence rules under consular law

There exist the following **precedence rules under consular law**:

1 Heads of consular posts have precedence over consular officers not having that status.
2 The heads of consular posts rank in each class according to the date of the *exequatur* granted.
3 If the head of a consular post is admitted to exercise their functions before the *exequatur* is obtained, precedence is determined according to the date of the provisional admission.
4 'Acting heads of posts shall rank after all heads of consular posts and, as between themselves, they shall rank according to the dates on which they assumed their functions as acting heads of posts'.[923]
5 The order of precedence as between two or more heads of consular posts who received the *exequatur* or provisional admission on the same date is specified according to the dates on which their commissions or similar instruments or the notifications were presented to the receiving state.
6 Honorary consular officers who are heads of consular posts rank in each class after career heads of consular posts.[924]

Notice of the order of precedence as between the consular officers of a consular post and any change thereof shall be provided by the diplomatic mission or the head of the consular post to the authority designated by the receiving state.[925]

Consular privileges and immunities

consular premises
means of transport
consular archives and documents
official correspondence of the consular post
consular bags and messages in code or cypher
other property of the consular post
consular courier

922 Article 19 of the Vienna Convention on Consular Relations.
923 Article 16 (4) of the Vienna Convention on Consular Relations
924 Paragraphs 3 and 5 of Article 16 of the Vienna Convention on Consular Relations.
925 Article 21 of the Vienna Convention on Consular Relations.

The moment of the origination of the consular privileges and immunities

> Every member of the consular post shall enjoy the privileges and immunities . . . from the moment he enters the territory of the receiving State on proceeding to take up his post or, if already in its territory, from the moment when he enters on his duties with the consular post.[926]

The scope of consular privileges and immunities

Generally, there are fewer consular privileges and immunities than are provided to certain persons and things under diplomatic law, and on the whole, they are primarily limited to the acts performed in the exercise of consular functions.

Nevertheless, in recent decades, there has been an observable tendency of approximation between the approaches in these two areas. At the same time, the receiving states consider the limitations on consular privileges and immunities very carefully.

According to consular law, there is a similar list of privileges and immunities which, as in the case of diplomatic privileges and immunities, may also be divided between things and persons.

Things

Under the protected things of the consular post shall be considered:

- consular premises;
- means of transport;
- consular archives and documents;
- official correspondence of the consular post;
- consular bags and messages in code or cypher; and
- other property of the consular post.

According to the Vienna Convention on Consular Relations:

> '[C]onsular premises' means the buildings or parts of buildings and the land ancillary thereto, irrespective of ownership, used exclusively for the purposes of the consular post. . . .
>
> '[C]onsular archives' includes all the papers, documents, correspondence, books, films, tapes and registers of the consular post, together with the ciphers and codes, the card-indexes and any article of furniture intended for their protection or safe keeping.

Under the Convention, the receiving state shall, even in case of armed conflict, respect and protect the consular premises, together with the property of the consular post and the consular archives.[927]

926 Article 53 (1) of the Vienna Convention on Consular Relations.
927 Article 27 (1) (a) of the Vienna Convention on Consular Relations.

As for the immunities of the consular premises, the authorities of the receiving state shall not enter that part of the consular premises which is used exclusively for the work of the consular post, except with the consent of the head of the consular post, his or her designee, or the head of the diplomatic mission of the sending state. However, unlike in cases of diplomatic premises, the consent of the head of the consular post may be assumed as given in case of fire or other disaster requiring prompt protective action.[928]

In addition, the consular premises, their furnishings, the property of the consular post, and its means of transport in principle are immune from any form of requisition for purposes of national defence or public utility. However, if expropriation is necessary for such purposes, all possible steps shall be taken to avoid impeding the performance of consular functions, and prompt, adequate, and effective compensation shall be paid to the sending state.

According to the Convention, archives and documents of the post are under the highest protection, as with diplomatic archives and documents. 'The consular archives and documents shall be inviolable at all times and wherever they may be.'[929]

The official correspondence of the post is inviolable in much the same way. According to the Convention, the same rule has been applied to the consular bag, which shall be neither opened nor detained. Nevertheless, if competent authorities of the receiving state have serious reason to believe that the bag contains something other than the correspondence, documents, or articles, they may request that the bag be opened in their presence by an authorised representative of the sending state. In turn, if the authorities of the sending state refuse such a request, the bag shall be returned to its place of origin.

Regarding the privileges of the consular premises, they, together with

> the residence of the career head of consular post of which the sending State or any person acting on its behalf is the owner or lessee shall be exempt from all national, regional or municipal dues and taxes whatsoever, other than such as represent payment for specific services rendered.[930]

Another significant privilege under consular law is that the consular post may levy in the territory of the receiving state the fees and charges provided by the laws and regulations of the sending state for consular acts.

Persons

As regards the privileges and immunities of persons, the Vienna Convention on Consular Relations has a differentiated approach:

- Consular officers enjoy immunity from the criminal jurisdiction of the receiving state with certain exceptions. (1) A consular officer is immune from an arrest or detention pending trial, except in case of a grave crime and according to a decision by the

928 Article 31 (2) of the Vienna Convention on Consular Relations.
929 Article 33 of the Vienna Convention on Consular Relations.
930 Article 32 (1) of the Vienna Convention on Consular Relations.

competent judicial authority. (2) He or she is immune from imprisonment or any other restriction put on his or her personal freedom save in execution of a final judicial decision. If criminal proceedings are instituted against a consular officer, he or she must appear before the competent authority. The proceedings must be conducted in a manner that respects his or her official position and does not hamper the exercise of consular functions and with the minimum delay.

- Consular officers and consular employees are immune from the jurisdiction of the judicial or administrative authorities of the receiving state only with respect to acts performed in the exercise of consular functions.[931] However, they do not enjoy such immunity with respect to a civil action either 'arising out of a contract concluded by a consular officer or a consular employee in which he did not contract expressly or impliedly as an agent of the sending State' or 'by a third party for damage arising from an accident in the receiving State caused by a vehicle, vessel or aircraft.'[932]
- Members of a consular post may be called upon to attend as witnesses in the course of judicial or administrative proceedings. At the same time, if a consular officer declines to do so, no coercive measure or penalty may be applied to him or her. Nevertheless, members of the consular post are under no obligation to give evidence concerning matters connected with the exercise of their functions or to provide official correspondence and documents related to them. They are also entitled to decline to give evidence as an expert witness concerning the law of the sending state.[933]
- Consular officers, consular employees, and members of their families forming part of their households are exempted from all obligations under the laws and regulations of the receiving state with regard to: the registration of aliens; residence permits; social security provisions; all dues and taxes except in certain specified cases (for example, they should pay dues or taxes on private immovable property, private income, capital taxes relating to investments made in commercial or financial undertakings in the receiving state, and so on); and 'all personal services . . . all public service of any kind whatsoever, and . . . military obligations such as those connected with requisitioning, military contributions and billeting.'[934]
- Members of the consular post enjoy freedom of movement and travel in its territory, freedom of communication with the sending state for official purposes and, on the other hand, with the authorities of the receiving state.
- Consular officers are free to communicate with nationals of the sending state and have access to them, including the right to visit a national of the sending state who is in custody, detention, or prison, to converse and correspond with and provide legal representation for them. At the same time, nationals of the sending state have the same freedom concerning communication with and access to consular officers of the sending state. Moreover, the receiving state has the obligation to inform the consular post without delay if a national of that state is arrested, committed to prison or custody pending trial, or is detained in any other manner within its consular district.

---

931 Article 43 (1) of the Vienna Convention on Consular Relations.
932 Article 43 (2) of the Vienna Convention on Consular Relations.
933 Article 44 of the Vienna Convention on Consular Relations.
934 Article 52 of the Vienna Convention on Consular Relations.

- In the performance of his or her functions, a **consular courier** enjoys personal inviolability and shall not be liable to any form of arrest or detention.

Under the Convention, the privileges and immunities are not accorded to (1) consular employees, (2) members of the service staff, (3) members of their family and private staff, or (4) members of the family of a consular officer, if the persons listed here 'themselves carry on any private gainful occupation in the receiving State'.[935]

Summary of the distinction between the diplomatic and consular privileges and immunities

Comparing diplomatic and consular privileges and immunities, it is remarkable that diplomatic immunity and privileges are of a general character while, for consular posts, they are mostly focused on and limited to acts performed in the exercise of consular functions and, therefore, are primarily of the functional nature. At the same time, consular privileges and immunities are more restricted in their scope. For example:

- Whereas, under diplomatic law, the diplomatic premises are absolutely immune, in contrast, regarding the consular premises even without the express consent of the head of the consular post, consent may be assumed in case of fire or other disasters requiring prompt protective action.
- Whereas diplomatic agents have complete immunity from the criminal jurisdiction of the receiving state, consular officers:
  - 'shall not be liable to arrest or detention pending trial, except in the case of a grave crime and pursuant to a decision by the competent judicial authority'; and
  - are immune from imprisonment or any other restriction on their personal freedom save in execution of a final judicial decision.

Waiver

As in the case of the diplomatic privileges and immunities, under consular law, the sending state also may waive any privileges and immunities of a member of the consular post.

This waiver shall in all cases be express and shall be communicated to the receiving state in writing.

Honorary consular officers and consular posts

Finally, the specific regime of privileges and immunities relating to honorary consular officers and consular posts headed by such officers should also be outlined.

On the one hand, according to the Convention, certain privileges and immunities apply to consular posts headed by an honorary consular officer. For instance, freedom of movement and travel, freedom of communication with the sending state for official purposes

935 Article 57 (2) of the Vienna Convention on Consular Relations.

and with the authorities of the receiving state, freedom of communication and contact with nationals of the sending state, and so on.

However, some of them are narrower or were adjusted. For example, the consular archives and documents of a consular post headed by an honorary consular officer are inviolable at all times and wherever they may be, but only when they are kept separately from other papers and documents and, in particular, from the private correspondence of the head of the consular post of any person working with him or her and from the materials, books, and documents relating to their profession or trade.[936] Moreover, concerning immunity from the criminal jurisdiction of the receiving state, the only limitation is that criminal proceedings shall be conducted with due respect to an official post held by an honorary consular officer and shall be instituted with the minimum delay in time.

Termination of the consular functions

notification by the sending state to the receiving state
withdrawal of the *exequatur*
receiving state ceases to consider the person a member of the consular staff
persona non grata
not acceptable
resignation of the member of the consular post
death of the member of the consular post
breaking of consular relations

Various ways of and reasons for the termination of consular functions

Among these ways and reasons are the following:

- A **notification by the sending state to the receiving state** that the functions of the post or any of its members have come to an end.
- The **withdrawal of the *exequatur*** or when the **receiving state ceases to consider the person a member of the consular staff**. The receiving state may, at any time and without providing reasons for its decision, notify the sending state that a consular officer is ***persona non grata*** or that any other member of the consular staff is **not acceptable**. If the sending state refuses or fails within a reasonable time to carry out its obligations to recall the person concerned or terminate his or her functions, the receiving state may either withdraw the *exequatur* from the person concerned or cease to consider him or her a member of the consular staff.[937] On the other hand, a person appointed as a member of a consular post may be declared unacceptable by the receiving state

---

936 Article 61 of the Vienna Convention on Consular Relations.
937 Article 23 of the Vienna Convention on Consular Relations.

before arriving in its territory or, if already in the receiving state, before entering into his or her duties with the consular post. In such cases, the sending state shall withdraw the appointment.

- **Resignation of the member of the consular post.**
- **Death of the member of the consular post.**
- The **breaking of consular relations** between the sending and receiving states. For example, when the sending or receiving state becomes extinct.

CASES AND MATERIALS (*SELECTED PARTS*)

Diplomatic law

Vienna Convention on Diplomatic Relations
of 18 April 1961
Entry into force: 24 April 1964

Article 2

The establishment of diplomatic relations between States, and of permanent diplomatic missions, takes place by mutual consent.

Article 3

1   The functions of a diplomatic mission consist inter alia in:

   (a)   representing the sending State in the receiving State;
   (b)   protecting in the receiving State the interests of the sending State and of its nationals, within the limits permitted by international law;
   (c)   negotiating with the Government of the receiving State;
   (d)   ascertaining by all lawful means conditions and developments in the receiving State, and reporting thereon to the Government of the sending State;
   (e)   promoting friendly relations between the sending State and the receiving State, and developing their economic, cultural and scientific relations.

2   Nothing in the present Convention shall be construed as preventing the performance of consular functions by a diplomatic mission.

Article 4

1   The sending State must make certain that the agrément of the receiving State has been given for the person it proposes to accredit as head of the mission to that State.
2   The receiving State is not obliged to give reasons to the sending State for a refusal of agrément.

Article 5

1   The sending State may, after it has given due notification to the receiving States concerned, accredit a head of mission or assign any member of the diplomatic staff, as

the case may be, to more than one State, unless there is express objection by any of the receiving States.

2   If the sending State accredits a head of mission to one or more other States it may establish a diplomatic mission headed by a charge d'affaires ad interim in each State where the head of mission has not his permanent seat.

3   A head of mission or any member of the diplomatic staff of the mission may act as representative of the sending State to any international organization.

Article 6

Two or more States may accredit the same person as head of mission to another State, unless objection is offered by the receiving State.

Article 7

Subject to the provisions of Articles 5, 8, 9 and 11, the sending State may freely appoint the members of the staff of the mission. In the case of military, naval or air attaches, the receiving State may require their names to be submitted beforehand, for its approval.

Article 8

1   Members of the diplomatic staff of the mission should in principle be of the nationality of the sending State.

2   Members of the diplomatic staff of the mission may not be appointed from among persons having the nationality of the receiving State, except with the consent of that State which may be withdrawn at any time.

3   The receiving State may reserve the same right with regard to nationals of a third State who are not also nationals of the sending State.

Article 9

1   The receiving State may at any time and without having to explain its decision, notify the sending State that the head of the mission or any member of the diplomatic staff of the mission is persona non grata or that any other member of the staff of the mission is not acceptable. In any such case, the sending State shall, as appropriate, either recall the person concerned or terminate his functions with the mission. A person may be declared non grata or not acceptable before arriving in the territory of the receiving State.

2   If the sending State refuses or fails within a reasonable period to carry out its obligations under paragraph 1 of this Article, the receiving State may refuse to recognize the person concerned as a member of the mission.

Article 10

1   The Ministry for Foreign Affairs of the receiving State, or such other ministry as may be agreed, shall be notified of:

(a)   the appointment of members of the mission, their arrival and their final departure or the termination of their functions with the mission;

(b) the arrival and final departure of a person belonging to the family of a member of the mission and, where appropriate, the fact that a person becomes or ceases to be a member of the family of a member of the mission;

(c) the arrival and final departure of private servants in the employ of persons referred to in sub-paragraph (a) of this paragraph and, where appropriate, the fact that they are leaving the employ of such persons;

(d) the engagement and discharge of persons resident in the receiving State as members of the mission or private servants entitled to privileges and immunities.

2   Where possible, prior notification of arrival and final departure shall also be given.

Article 11

1   In the absence of specific agreement as to the size of the mission, the receiving State may require that the size of a mission be kept within limits considered by it to be reasonable and normal, having regard to circumstances and conditions in the receiving State and to the needs of the particular mission.

2   The receiving State may equally, within similar bounds and on a non-discriminatory basis, refuse to accept officials of a particular category.

Article 12

The sending State may not, without the prior express consent of the receiving State, establish offices forming part of the mission in localities other than those in which the mission itself is established.

Article 13

1   The head of the mission is considered as having taken up his functions in the receiving State either when he has presented his credentials or when he has notified his arrival and a true copy of his credentials has been presented to the Ministry for Foreign Affairs of the receiving State, or such other ministry as may be agreed, in accordance with the practice prevailing in the receiving State which shall be applied in a uniform manner.

2   The order of presentation of credentials or of a true copy thereof will be determined by the date and time of the arrival of the head of the mission.

Article 14

1   Heads of mission are divided into three classes, namely:

(a) that of ambassadors or nuncios accredited to Heads of State, and other heads of mission of equivalent rank;

(b) that of envoys, ministers and internuncios accredited to Heads of State;

(c) that of charges d'affaires accredited to Ministers for Foreign Affairs.

2   Except as concerns precedence and etiquette, there shall be no differentiation between heads of mission by reason of their class.

Article 15

The class to which the heads of their missions are to be assigned shall be agreed between States.

Article 16

1   Heads of mission shall take precedence in their respective classes in the order of the date and time of taking up their functions in accordance with Article 13.
2   Alterations in the credentials of a head of mission not involving any change of class shall not affect his precedence.
3   This article is without prejudice to any practice accepted by the receiving State regarding the precedence of the representative of the Holy See.

Article 17

The precedence of the members of the diplomatic staff of the mission shall be notified by the head of the mission to the Ministry for Foreign Affairs or such other ministry as may be agreed.

Article 18

The procedure to be observed in each State for the reception of heads of mission shall be uniform in respect of each class.

Article 19

1   If the post of head of the mission is vacant, or if the head of the mission is unable to perform his functions, a charge d'affaires ad interim shall act provisionally as head of the mission. The name of the charge d'affaires ad interim shall be notified, either by the head of the mission or, in case he is unable to do so, by the Ministry for Foreign Affairs of the sending State to the Ministry for Foreign Affairs of the receiving State or such other ministry as may be agreed.
2   In cases where no member of the diplomatic staff of the mission is present in the receiving State, a member of the administrative and technical staff may, with the consent of the receiving State, be designated by the sending State to be in charge of the current administrative affairs of the mission.

Article 20

The mission and its head shall have the right to use the flag and emblem of the sending State on the premises of the mission, including the residence of the head of the mission, and on his means of transport.

Article 21

1   The receiving State shall either facilitate the acquisition on its territory, in accordance with its laws, by the sending State of premises necessary for its mission or assist the latter in obtaining accommodation in some other way.
2   It shall also, where necessary, assist missions in obtaining suitable accommodation for their members.

Article 22

1   The premises of the mission shall be inviolable. The agents of the receiving State may not enter them, except with the consent of the head of the mission.

2   The receiving State is under a special duty to take all appropriate steps to protect the premises of the mission against any intrusion or damage and to prevent any disturbance of the peace of the mission or impairment of its dignity.

3   The premises of the mission, their furnishings and other property thereon and the means of transport of the mission shall be immune from search, requisition, attachment or execution.

Article 23

1   The sending State and the head of the mission shall be exempt from all national, regional or municipal dues and taxes in respect of the premises of the mission, whether owned or leased, other than such as represent payment for specific services rendered.

2   The exemption from taxation referred to in this Article shall not apply to such dues and taxes payable under the law of the receiving State by persons contracting with the sending State or the head of the mission.

Article 24

The archives and documents of the mission shall be inviolable at any time and wherever they may be.

Article 25

The receiving State shall accord full facilities for the performance of the functions of the mission.

Article 26

Subject to its laws and regulations concerning zones entry into which is prohibited or regulated for reasons of national security, the receiving State shall ensure to all members of the mission freedom of movement and travel in its territory.

Article 27

1   The receiving State shall permit and protect free communication on the part of the mission for all official purposes. In communicating with the Government and the other missions and consulates of the sending State, wherever situated, the mission may employ all appropriate means, including diplomatic couriers and messages in code or cipher. However, the mission may install and use a wireless transmitter only with the consent of the receiving State.

2   The official correspondence of the mission shall be inviolable. Official correspondence means all correspondence relating to the mission and its functions.

3   The diplomatic bag shall not be opened or detained.

4   The packages constituting the diplomatic bag must bear visible external marks of their character and may contain only diplomatic documents or articles intended for official use.

5   The diplomatic courier, who shall be provided with an official document indicating his status and the number of packages constituting the diplomatic bag, shall be protected by the receiving State in the performance of his functions. He shall enjoy personal inviolability and shall not be liable to any form of arrest or detention.

6   The sending State or the mission may designate diplomatic couriers ad hoc. In such cases the provisions of paragraph 5 of this Article shall also apply, except that the immunities therein mentioned shall cease to apply when such a courier has delivered to the consignee the diplomatic bag in his charge.

7   A diplomatic bag may be entrusted to the captain of a commercial aircraft scheduled to land at an authorized port of entry. He shall be provided with an official document indicating the number of packages constituting the bag but he shall not be considered to be a diplomatic courier. The mission may send one of its members to take possession of the diplomatic bag directly and freely from the captain of the aircraft.

Article 28

The fees and charges levied by the mission in the course of its official duties shall be exempt from all dues and taxes.

Article 29

The person of a diplomatic agent shall be inviolable. He shall not be liable to any form of arrest or detention. The receiving State shall treat him with due respect and shall take all appropriate steps to prevent any attack on his person, freedom or dignity.

Article 30

1   The private residence of a diplomatic agent shall enjoy the same inviolability and protection as the premises of the mission.

2   His papers, correspondence and, except as provided in paragraph 3 of Article 31, his property, shall likewise enjoy inviolability.

Article 31

1   A diplomatic agent shall enjoy immunity from the criminal jurisdiction of the receiving State. He shall also enjoy immunity from its civil and administrative jurisdiction, except in the case of:

(a)   a real action relating to private immovable property situated in the territory of the receiving State, unless he holds it on behalf of the sending State for the purposes of the mission;

(b)   an action relating to succession in which the diplomatic agent is involved as executor, administrator, heir or legatee as a private person and not on behalf of the sending State;

(c)   an action relating to any professional or commercial activity exercised by the diplomatic agent in the receiving State outside his official functions.

2   A diplomatic agent is not obliged to give evidence as a witness.

3   No measures of execution may be taken in respect of a diplomatic agent except in the cases coming under sub-paragraphs (a), (b) and (c) of paragraph 1 of this Article, and provided that the measures concerned can be taken without infringing the inviolability of his person or of his residence.

4   The immunity of a diplomatic agent from the jurisdiction of the receiving State does not exempt him from the jurisdiction of the sending State.

Article 32

1   The immunity from jurisdiction of diplomatic agents and of persons enjoying immunity under Article 37 may be waived by the sending State.

2   Waiver must always be express.

3   The initiation of proceedings by a diplomatic agent or by a person enjoying immunity from jurisdiction under Article 37 shall preclude him from invoking immunity from jurisdiction in respect of any counter-claim directly connected with the principal claim.

4   Waiver of immunity from jurisdiction in respect of civil or administrative proceedings shall not be held to imply waiver of immunity in respect of the execution of the judgment, for which a separate waiver shall be necessary.

Article 33

1   Subject to the provisions of paragraph 3 of this Article, a diplomatic agent shall with respect to services rendered for the sending State be exempt from social security provisions which may be in force in the receiving State.

2   The exemption provided for in paragraph 1 of this Article shall also apply to private servants who are in the sole employ of a diplomatic agent, on condition:

(a) that they are not nationals of or permanently resident in the receiving State; and

(b) that they are covered by the social security provisions which may be in force in the sending State or a third State.

3   A diplomatic agent who employs persons to whom the exemption provided for in paragraph 2 of this Article does not apply shall observe the obligations which the social security provisions of the receiving State impose upon employers.

4   The exemption provided for in paragraphs 1 and 2 of this Article shall not preclude voluntary participation in the social security system of the receiving State provided that such participation is permitted by that State.

5   The provisions of this Article shall not affect bilateral or multilateral agreements concerning social security concluded previously and shall not prevent the conclusion of such agreements in the future.

Article 34

A diplomatic agent shall be exempt from all dues and taxes, personal or real, national, regional or municipal, except:

(a) indirect taxes of a kind which are normally incorporated in the price of goods or services;

(b) dues and taxes on private immovable property situated in the territory of the receiving State, unless he holds it on behalf of the sending State for the purposes of the mission;

(c) estate, succession or inheritance duties levied by the receiving State, subject to the provisions of paragraph 4 of Article 39;

(d) dues and taxes on private income having its source in the receiving State and capital taxes on investments made in commercial undertakings in the receiving State;

(e) charges levied for specific services rendered;

(f) registration, court or record fees, mortgage dues and stamp duty, with respect to immovable property, subject to the provisions of Article 23.

Article 35

The receiving State shall exempt diplomatic agents from all personal services, from all public service of any kind whatsoever, and from military obligations such as those connected with requisitioning, military contributions and billeting.

Article 36

1   The receiving State shall, in accordance with such laws and regulations as it may adopt, permit entry of and grant exemption from all customs duties, taxes, and related charges other than charges for storage, cartage and similar services, on:

(a) articles for the official use of the mission;

(b) articles for the personal use of a diplomatic agent or members of his family forming part of his household, including articles intended for his establishment.

2   The personal baggage of a diplomatic agent shall be exempt from inspection, unless there are serious grounds for presuming that it contains articles not covered by the exemptions mentioned in paragraph 1 of this Article, or articles the import or export of which is prohibited by the law or controlled by the quarantine regulations of the receiving State. Such inspection shall be conducted only in the presence of the diplomatic agent or of his authorized representative.

Article 37

1   The members of the family of a diplomatic agent forming part of his household shall, if they are not nationals of the receiving State, enjoy the privileges and immunities specified in Articles 29 to 36.

2   Members of the administrative and technical staff of the mission, together with members of their families forming part of their respective households, shall, if they are not nationals of or permanently resident in the receiving State, enjoy the privileges and immunities specified in Articles 29 to 35, except that the immunity from civil and administrative jurisdiction of the receiving State specified in paragraph 1 of Article 31 shall not extend to acts performed outside the course of their duties. They shall also enjoy the privileges specified in Article 36, paragraph 1, in respect of articles imported at the time of first installation.

3   Members of the service staff of the mission who are not nationals of or permanently resident in the receiving State shall enjoy immunity in respect of acts performed in the course of their duties, exemption from dues and taxes on the emoluments they receive by reason of their employment and the exemption contained in Article 33.

4   Private servants of members of the mission shall, if they are not nationals of or permanently resident in the receiving State, be exempt from dues and taxes on the emoluments they receive by reason of their employment. In other respects, they may enjoy privileges and immunities only to the extent admitted by the receiving State. However, the receiving State must exercise its jurisdiction over those persons in such a manner as not to interfere unduly with the performance of the functions of the mission.

Article 38

1   Except insofar as additional privileges and immunities may be granted by the receiving State, a diplomatic agent who is a national of or permanently resident in that State shall enjoy only immunity from jurisdiction, and inviolability, in respect of official acts performed in the exercise of his functions.

2   Other members of the staff of the mission and private servants who are nationals of or permanently resident in the receiving State shall enjoy privileges and immunities only to the extent admitted by the receiving State. However, the receiving State must exercise its jurisdiction over those persons in such a manner as not to interfere unduly with the performance of the functions of the mission.

Article 39

1   Every person entitled to privileges and immunities shall enjoy them from the moment he enters the territory of the receiving State on proceeding to take up his post or, if already in its territory, from the moment when his appointment is notified to the Ministry for Foreign Affairs or such other ministry as may be agreed.

2   When the functions of a person enjoying privileges and immunities have come to an end, such privileges and immunities shall normally cease at the moment when he leaves the country, or on expiry of a reasonable period in which to do so, but shall subsist until that time, even in case of armed conflict. However, with respect to acts performed by such a person in the exercise of his functions as a member of the mission, immunity shall continue to subsist.

3   In case of the death of a member of the mission, the members of his family shall continue to enjoy the privileges and immunities to which they are entitled until the expiry of a reasonable period in which to leave the country.

4   In the event of the death of a member of the mission not a national of or permanently resident in the receiving State or a member of his family forming part of his household, the receiving State shall permit the withdrawal of the movable property of the deceased, with the exception of any property acquired in the country the export of which was prohibited at the time of his death. Estate, succession and inheritance duties shall not be levied on movable property the presence of which in the receiving State was due solely to the presence there of the deceased as a member of the mission or as a member of the family of a member of the mission.

Article 40

1   If a diplomatic agent passes through or is in the territory of a third State, which has granted him a passport visa if such visa was necessary, while proceeding to take up or to return to his post, or when returning to his own country, the third State shall accord him inviolability and such other immunities as may be required to ensure his transit or return. The same shall apply in the case of any members of his family enjoying privileges or immunities who are

accompanying the diplomatic agent, or travelling separately to join him or to return to their country.

2   In circumstances similar to those specified in paragraph 1 of this Article, third States shall not hinder the passage of members of the administrative and technical or service staff of a mission, and of members of their families, through their territories.

3   Third States shall accord to official correspondence and other official communications in transit, including messages in code or cipher, the same freedom and protection as is accorded by the receiving State. They shall accord to diplomatic couriers, who have been granted a passport visa if such visa was necessary, and diplomatic bags in transit the same inviolability and protection as the receiving State is bound to accord.

4   The obligations of third States under paragraphs 1, 2 and 3 of this Article shall also apply to the persons mentioned respectively in those paragraphs, and to official communications and diplomatic bags, whose presence in the territory of the third State is due to force majeure.

Article 41

1   Without prejudice to their privileges and immunities, it is the duty of all persons enjoying such privileges and immunities to respect the laws and regulations of the receiving State. They also have a duty not to interfere in the internal affairs of that State.

2   All official business with the receiving State entrusted to the mission by the sending State shall be conducted with or through the Ministry for Foreign Affairs of the receiving State or such other ministry as may be agreed.

3   The premises of the mission must not be used in any manner incompatible with the functions of the mission as laid down in the present Convention or by other rules of general international law or by any special agreements in force between the sending and the receiving State.

Article 42

A diplomatic agent shall not in the receiving State practise for personal profit any professional or commercial activity.

Article 43

The function of a diplomatic agent comes to an end, inter alia:

(a)   on notification by the sending State to the receiving State that the function of the diplomatic agent has come to an end;

(b)   on notification by the receiving State to the sending State that, in accordance with paragraph 2 of Article 9, it refuses to recognize the diplomatic agent as a member of the mission.

Article 44

The receiving State must, even in case of armed conflict, grant facilities in order to enable persons enjoying privileges and immunities, other than nationals of the receiving State, and members of the families of such persons irrespective of their nationality, to leave at the earliest possible moment. It must, in particular, in case of need, place at their disposal the necessary means of transport for themselves and their property.

Article 45

If diplomatic relations are broken off between two States, or if a mission is permanently or temporarily recalled:

(a) the receiving State must, even in case of armed conflict, respect and protect the premises of the mission, together with its property and archives;
(b) the sending State may entrust the custody of the premises of the mission, together with its property and archives, to a third State acceptable to the receiving State;
(c) the sending State may entrust the protection of its interests and those of its nationals to a third State acceptable to the receiving State.

Article 46

A sending State may with the prior consent of a receiving State, and at the request of a third State not represented in the receiving State, undertake the temporary protection of the interests of the third State and of its nationals.

Diplomatic and consular privileges and immunities

United States Diplomatic and Consular Staff in Tehran (United States of America v Iran),
    Judgment of 24 May 1980, International Court of Justice
ICJ Reports 1980, 3.

68. The Court is therefore led inevitably to conclude, in regard to the first phase of the events which has so far been considered, that on 4 November 1979 the Iranian authorities:

(a) were fully aware of their obligations under the conventions in force to take appropriate steps to protect the premises of the United States Embassy and its diplomatic and consular staff from any attack and from any infringement of their inviolability, and to ensure the security of such other persons as might be present on the said premises;
(b) were fully aware, as a result of the appeals for help made by the United States Embassy, of the urgent need for action on their part;
(c) had the means at their disposal to perform their obligations;
(d) completely failed to comply with these obligations.

Similarly, the Court is led to conclude that the Iranian authorities were equally aware of their obligations to protect the United States Consulates at Tabriz and Shiraz, and of the need for action on their part, and similarly failed to use the means which were at their disposal to comply with their obligations.

69. The second phase of the events which are the subject of the United States' claims comprises the whole series of facts which occurred following the completion of the occupation of the United States Embassy by the militants, and the seizure of the Consulates at Tabriz and Shiraz. The occupation having taken place and the diplomatic and consular personnel of the United States' mission having been taken hostage, the action required of the Iranian Government by the Vienna Conventions and by general international law was manifest. Its plain duty was at once to make every effort, and to take every appropriate step, to bring these flagrant infringements of the inviolability of the premises, archives and diplomatic and consular staff

of the United States Embassy to a speedy end, to restore the Consulates at Tabriz and Shiraz to United States control, and in general to re-establish the status quo and to offer reparation for the damage.

70. No such step was, however, taken by the Iranian authorities. At a press conference on 5 November the Foreign Minister, Mr. Yazdi, conceded that "according to international regulations the Iranian Government is dutybound to safeguard the life and property of foreign nationals". But he made no mention of Iran's obligation to safeguard the inviolability of foreign embassies and diplomats; and he ended by announcing that the action of the students "enjoys the endorsement and support of the government, because America herself is responsible for this incident". As to the Prime Minister, Mr. Bazargan, he does not appear to have made any statement on the matter before resigning his office on 5 November.

71. In any event expressions of approval of the take-over of the Embassy. and indeed also of the Consulates at Tabriz and Shiraz by militants came immediately from numerous Iranian authorities, including religious, judicial, executive, police and broadcasting authorities. Above all, the Ayatollah Khomeini himself made crystal clear the endorsement by the State both of the take-over of the Embassy and Consulates and of the detention of the Embassy staff as hostages. . . .

72. At any rate, thus fortified in their action, the militants at the Embassy at once went one step farther. On 6 November they proclaimed that the Embassy, which they too referred to as "the U.S. centre of plots and espionage", would remain under their occupation. and that they were watching "most closely" the members of the diplomatic staff taken hostage whom they called "U.S. mercenaries and spies". . . .

76. The Iranian authorities' decision to continue the subjection of the premises of the United States Embassy to occupation by militants and of the Embassy staff to detention as hostages, clearly gave rise to repeated and multiple breaches of the applicable provisions of the Vienna Conventions even more serious than those which arose from their failure to take any steps to prevent the attacks on the inviolability of these premises and staff. . . .

84. The Vienna Conventions of 1961 and 1963 contain express provisions to meet the case when members of an embassy staff, under the cover of diplomatic privileges and immunities, engage in such abuses of their functions as espionage or interference in the internal affairs of the receiving State. It is precisely with the possibility of such abuses in contemplation that Article 41, paragraph 1, of the Vienna Convention on Diplomatic Relations, and Article 55, paragraph 1, of the Vienna Convention on Consular Relations, provide

> "Without prejudice to their privileges and immunities, it is the duty of all persons enjoying such privileges and immunities to respect the laws and regulations of the receiving State. They also have a duty not to interfere in the internal affairs of that State."

Paragraph 3 of Article 41 of the 1961 Convention further States: "The premises of the mission must not be used in any manner incompatible with the functions of the missions . . .": an analogous provision, with respect to consular premises is to be found in Article 55, paragraph 2, of the 1963 Convention.

85. Thus, it is for the very purpose of providing a remedy for such possible abuses of diplomatic functions that Article 9 of the 1961 Convention on Diplomatic Relations stipulates:

> "1   The receiving State may at any time and without having to explain its decision, notify the sending State that the head of the mission or any member of the diplomatic staff of the mission

is persona non grata or that any other member of the staff of the mission is not acceptable. In any such case, the sending State shall, as appropriate, either recall the person concerned or terminate his functions with the mission. A person may be declared non grata or not acceptable before arriving in the territory of the receiving State.

2   If the sending State refuses or fails within a reasonable period to carry out its obligations under paragraph 1 of this Article, the receiving State may refuse to recognize the person concerned as a member of the mission."

The 1963 Convention contains, in Article 23, paragraphs 1 and 4, analogous provisions in respect of consular officers and consular staff. Paragraph 1 of Article 9 of the 1961 Convention, and paragraph 4 of Article 23 of the 1963 Convention, take account of the difficulty that may be experienced in practice of proving such abuses in every case or, indeed, of determining exactly when exercise of the diplomatic function, expressly recognized in Article 3 (1) (d) of the 1961 Convention, of "ascertaining by all lawful means conditions and developments in the receiving State" may be considered as involving such acts as "espionage" or "interference in internal affairs". The way in which Article 9, paragraph 1, takes account of any such difficulty is by providing expressly in its opening sentence that the receiving State may "at any time and without having to explain its decision" notify the sending State that any particular member of its diplomatic mission is "persona non grata" or "not acceptable" (and similarly Article 23, paragraph 4, of the 1963 Convention provides that "the receiving State is not obliged to give to the sending State reasons for its decision"). Beyond that remedy for dealing with abuses of the diplomatic function by individual members of a mission, a receiving State has in its hands a more radical remedy if abuses of their functions by members of a mission reach serious proportions. This is the power which every receiving State has, at its own discretion, to break off diplomatic relations with a sending State and to call for the immediate closure of the offending mission.

86. The rules of diplomatic law, in short, constitute a self-contained regime which, on the one hand, lays down the receiving State's obligations regarding the facilities, privileges and immunities to be accorded to diplomatic missions and, on the other, foresees their possible abuse by members of the mission and specifies the means at the disposal of the receiving State to counter any such abuse. These means are, by their nature, entirely efficacious, for unless the sending State recalls the member of the mission objected to forthwith, the prospect of the almost immediate loss of his privileges and immunities, because of the withdrawal by the receiving State of his recognition as a member of the mission, will in practice compel that person, in his own interest, to depart at once. But the principle of the inviolability of the persons of diplomatic agents and the premises of diplomatic missions is one of the very foundations of this long-established regime, to the evolution of which the traditions of Islam made a substantial contribution. The fundamental character of the principle of inviolability is, moreover, strongly underlined by the provisions of Articles 44 and 45 of the Convention of 1961 (cf. also Articles 26 and 27 of the Convention of 1963). Even in the case of armed conflict or in the case of a breach in diplomatic relations those provisions require that both the inviolability of the members of a diplomatic mission and of the premises, property and archives of the mission must be respected by the receiving State. Naturally, the observance of this principle does not mean – and this the Applicant Government expressly acknowledges – that a diplomatic agent caught in the act of committing an assault or other offence may not, on occasion, be briefly arrested by the police of the receiving State in order to prevent the commission of the particular crime. But such eventualities bear no relation at all to what occurred in the present case.

Vienna Convention on Consular Relations
of 24 April 1963
Entry into force: 19 March 1967

CHAPTER I. CONSULAR RELATIONS IN GENERAL

SECTION I. ESTABLISHMENT AND CONDUCT OF CONSULAR RELATIONS

Article 2 Establishment of consular relations

1   The establishment of consular relations between States takes place by mutual consent.
2   The consent given to the establishment of diplomatic relations between two States implies, unless otherwise stated, consent to the establishment of consular relations.
3   The severance of diplomatic relations shall not ipso facto involve the severance of consular relations.

Article 3 Exercise of consular functions

Consular functions are exercised by consular posts. They are also exercised by diplomatic missions in accordance with the provisions of the present Convention.

Article 4 Establishment of a consular post

1   A consular post may be established in the territory of the receiving State only with that State's consent.
2   The seat of the consular post, its classification and the consular district shall be established by the sending State and shall be subject to the approval of the receiving State.
3   Subsequent changes in the seat of the consular post, its classification or the consular district may be made by the sending State only with the consent of the receiving State.
4   The consent of the receiving State shall also be required if a consulate-general or a consulate desires to open a vice-consulate or a consular agency in a locality other than that in which it is itself established.
5   The prior express consent of the receiving State shall also be required for the opening of an office forming part of an existing consular post elsewhere than at the seat thereof.

Article 5 Consular functions

Consular functions consist in:

(a)   protecting in the receiving State the interests of the sending State and of its nationals, both individuals and bodies corporate, within the limits permitted by international law;
(b)   furthering the development of commercial, economic, cultural and scientific relations between the sending State and the receiving State and otherwise promoting friendly relations between them in accordance with the provisions of the present Convention;

(c) ascertaining by all lawful means conditions and developments in the commercial, economic, cultural and scientific life of the receiving State, reporting thereon to the Government of the sending State and giving information to persons interested;

(d) issuing passports and travel documents to nationals of the sending State, and visas or appropriate documents to persons wishing to travel to the sending State;

(e) helping and assisting nationals, both individuals and bodies corporate, of the sending State;

(f) acting as notary and civil registrar and in capacities of a similar kind, and performing certain functions of an administrative nature, provided that there is nothing contrary thereto in the laws and regulations of the receiving State;

(g) safeguarding the interests of nationals, both individuals and bodies corporate, of the sending States in cases of succession mortis causa in the territory of the receiving State, in accordance with the laws and regulations of the receiving State;

(h) safeguarding, within the limits imposed by the laws and regulations of the receiving State, the interests of minors and other persons lacking full capacity who are nationals of the sending State, particularly where any guardianship or trusteeship is required with respect to such persons;

(i) subject to the practices and procedures obtaining in the receiving State, representing or arranging appropriate representation for nationals of the sending State before the tribunals and other authorities of the receiving State, for the purpose of obtaining, in accordance with the laws and regulations of the receiving State, provisional measures for the preservation of the rights and interests of these nationals, where, because of absence or any other reason, such nationals are unable at the proper time to assume the defence of their rights and interests;

(j) transmitting judicial and extrajudicial documents or executing letters rogatory or commissions to take evidence for the courts of the sending State in accordance with international agreements in force or, in the absence of such international agreements, in any other manner compatible with the laws and regulations of the receiving State;

(k) exercising rights of supervision and inspection provided for in the laws and regulations of the sending State in respect of vessels having the nationality of the sending State, and of aircraft registered in that State, and in respect of their crews;

(l) extending assistance to vessels and aircraft mentioned in subparagraph (k) of this article, and to their crews, taking statements regarding the voyage of a vessel, examining and stamping the ship's papers, and, without prejudice to the powers of the authorities of the receiving State, conducting investigations into any incidents which occurred during the voyage, and settling disputes of any kind between the master, the officers and the seamen insofar as this may be authorized by the laws and regulations of the sending State;

(m) performing any other functions entrusted to a consular post by the sending State which are not prohibited by the laws and regulations of the receiving State or to which no objection is taken by the receiving State or which are referred to in the international agreements in force between the sending State and the receiving State.

Article 9 Classes of heads of consular posts

1 Heads of consular posts are divided into four classes, namely

(a) consuls-general;

(b) consuls;

(c)   vice-consuls;

(d)   consular agents.

2   Paragraph 1 of this article in no way restricts the right of any of the Contracting Parties to fix the designation of consular officers other than the heads of consular posts.

Article 10 Appointment and admission of heads of consular posts

1   Heads of consular posts are appointed by the sending State and are admitted to the exercise of their functions by the receiving State.

2   Subject to the provisions of the present Convention, the formalities for the appointment and for the admission of the head of a consular post are determined by the laws, regulations and usages of the sending State and of the receiving State respectively.

Article 11 The consular commission or notification of appointment

1   The head of a consular post shall be provided by the sending State with a document, in the form of a commission or similar instrument, made out for each appointment, certifying his capacity and showing, as a general rule, his full name, his category and class, the consular district and the seat of the consular post.

2   The sending State shall transmit the commission or similar instrument through the diplomatic or other appropriate channel to the Government of the State in whose territory the head of a consular post is to exercise his functions.

3   If the receiving State agrees, the sending State may, instead of a commission or similar instrument, send to the receiving State a notification containing the particulars required by paragraph 1 of this article.

Article 12 The *exequatur*

1   The head of a consular post is admitted to the exercise of his functions by an authorization from the receiving State termed an *exequatur*, whatever the form of this authorization.

2   A State which refused to grant an *exequatur* is not obliged to give to the sending State reasons for such refusal.

3   Subject to the provisions of articles 13 and 15, the head of a consular post shall not enter upon his duties until he has received an *exequatur*.

Article 17 Performance of diplomatic acts by consular officers

1   In a State where the sending State has no diplomatic mission and is not represented by a diplomatic mission of a third State, a consular officer may, with the consent of the receiving State, and without affecting his consular status, be authorized to perform diplomatic acts. The performance of such acts by a consular officer shall not confer upon him any right to claim diplomatic privileges and immunities.

2   A consular officer may, after notification addressed to the receiving State, act as representative of the sending State to any intergovernmental organization. When so acting, he shall be entitled to enjoy any privileges and immunities accorded to such a representative

by customary international law or by international agreements; however, in respect of the performance by him of any consular function, he shall not be entitled to any greater immunity from jurisdiction than that to which a consular officer is entitled under the present Convention.

Article 19 Appointment of members of consular staff

1 Subject to the provisions of articles 20, 22 and 23, the sending State may freely appoint the members of the consular staff.
2 The full name, category and class of all consular officers, other than the head of a consular post, shall be notified by the sending State to the receiving State in sufficient time for the receiving State, if it so wishes, to exercise its rights under paragraph 3 of article 23.
3 The sending State may, if required by its laws and regulations, request the receiving State to grant an *exequatur* to a consular officer other than the head of a consular post.
4 The receiving State may, if required by its laws and regulations, grant an *exequatur* to a consular officer other than the head of a consular post.

Article 23 Persons declared "non grata"

1 The receiving State may at any time notify the sending State that a consular officer is persona non grata or that any other member of the consular staff is not acceptable. In that event, the sending State shall, as the case may be, either recall the person concerned or terminate his functions with the consular post.
2 If the sending State refuses or fails within a reasonable time to carry out its obligations under paragraph 1 of this article, the receiving State may, as the case may be, either withdraw the *exequatur* from the person concerned or cease to consider him as a member of the consular staff.
3 A person appointed as a member of a consular post may be declared unacceptable before arriving in the territory of the receiving State or, if already in the receiving State, before entering on his duties with the consular post. In any such case, the sending State shall withdraw his appointment.
4 In the cases mentioned in paragraphs 1 and 3 of this article, the receiving State is not obliged to give to the sending State reasons for its decision.

SECTION II. END OF CONSULAR FUNCTIONS

Article 25 Termination of the functions of a member of a consular post

The functions of a member of a consular post shall come to an end, inter alia:

(a) on notification by the sending State to the receiving State that his functions have come to an end;
(b) on withdrawal of the *exequatur*;
(c) on notification by the receiving State to the sending State that the receiving State has ceased to consider him as a member of the consular staff.

Article 27 Protection of consular premises and archives and of the interests of the sending State in exceptional circumstances

1 In the event of the severance of consular relations between two States:

   (a) the receiving State shall, even in case of armed conflict, respect and protect the consular premises, together with the property of the consular post and the consular archives;

   (b) the sending State may entrust the custody of the consular premises, together with the property contained therein and the consular archives, to a third State acceptable to the receiving State;

   (c) the sending State may entrust the protection of its interests and those of its nationals to a third State acceptable to the receiving State.

2 In the event of the temporary or permanent closure of a consular post, the provisions of sub-paragraph (a) of paragraph 1 of this article shall apply. In addition,

   (a) if the sending State, although not represented in the receiving State by a diplomatic mission, has another consular post in the territory of that State, that consular post may be entrusted with the custody of the premises of the consular post which has been closed, together with the property contained therein and the consular archives, and, with the consent of the receiving State, with the exercise of consular functions in the district of that consular post; or

   (b) if the sending State has no diplomatic mission and no other consular post in the receiving State, the provisions of subparagraphs (b) and (c) of paragraph 1 of this article shall apply.

CHAPTER II. FACILITIES, PRIVILEGES AND IMMUNITIES RELATING TO CONSULAR POSTS, CAREER CONSULAR OFFICERS AND OTHER MEMBERS OF A CONSULAR POST

SECTION I. FACILITIES, PRIVILEGES AND IMMUNITIES RELATING TO A CONSULAR POST

Article 28 Facilities for the work of the consular post

The receiving State shall accord full facilities for the performance of the functions of the consular post.

Article 31 Inviolability of the consular premises

1 Consular premises shall be inviolable to the extent provided in this article.

2 The authorities of the receiving State shall not enter that part of the consular premises which is used exclusively for the purpose of the work of the consular post except with the consent of the head of the consular post or of his designee or of the head of the diplomatic mission of the sending State. The consent of the head of the consular post may, however, be assumed in case of fire or other disaster requiring prompt protective action.

3 Subject to the provisions of paragraph 2 of this article, the receiving State is under a special duty to take all appropriate steps to protect the consular premises against any intrusion or damage and to prevent any disturbance of the peace of the consular post or impairment of its dignity.

4   The consular premises, their furnishings, the property of the consular post and its means of transport shall be immune from any form of requisition for purposes of national defence or public utility. If expropriation is necessary for such purposes, all possible steps shall be taken to avoid impeding the performance of consular functions, and prompt, adequate and effective compensation shall be paid to the sending State.

Article 32 Exemption from taxation of consular premises

1   Consular premises and the residence of the career head of consular post of which the sending State or any person acting on its behalf is the owner or lessee shall be exempt from all national, regional or municipal dues and taxes whatsoever, other than such as represent payment for specific services rendered.

2   The exemption from taxation referred to paragraph 1 of this article shall not apply to such dues and taxes if, under the law of the receiving State, they are payable by the person who contracted with the sending State or with the person acting on its behalf.

Article 33 Inviolability of the consular archives and documents

The consular archives and documents shall be inviolable at all times and wherever they may be.

Article 34 Freedom of movement

Subject to its laws and regulations concerning zones entry into which is prohibited or regulated for reasons of national security, the receiving State shall ensure freedom of movement and travel in its territory to all members of the consular post.

Article 35 Freedom of communication

1   The receiving State shall permit and protect freedom of communication on the part of the consular post for all official purposes. In communicating with the Government, the diplomatic missions and other consular posts, wherever situated, of the sending State, the consular post may employ all appropriate means, including diplomatic or consular couriers, diplomatic or consular bags and messages in code or cipher. However, the consular post may install and use a wireless transmitter only with the consent of the receiving State.

Article 36 Communication and contact with nationals of the sending State

1   With a view to facilitating the exercise of consular functions relating to nationals of the sending State:

   (a) consular officers shall be free to communicate with nationals of the sending State and to have access to them. Nationals of the sending State shall have the same freedom with respect to communication with and access to consular officers of the sending State;

   (b) if he so requests, the competent authorities of the receiving State shall, without delay, inform the consular post of the sending State if, within its consular district, a national of that State is arrested or committed to prison or to custody pending trial or is detained in any other manner. Any communication addressed to the consular post by the person arrested, in prison, custody or detention shall be forwarded by the said authorities without delay. The said authorities shall inform the person concerned without delay of his rights under this subparagraph;

(c) consular officers shall have the right to visit a national of the sending State who is in prison, custody or detention, to converse and correspond with him and to arrange for his legal representation. They shall also have the right to visit any national of the sending State who is in prison, custody or detention in their district in pursuance of a judgement. Nevertheless, consular officers shall refrain from taking action on behalf of a national who is in prison, custody or detention if he expressly opposes such action.

2 The rights referred to in paragraph 1 of this article shall be exercised in conformity with the laws and regulations of the receiving State, subject to the proviso, however, that the said laws and regulations must enable full effect to be given to the purposes for which the rights accorded under this article are intended.

SECTION II. FACILITIES, PRIVILEGES AND IMMUNITIES RELATING TO CAREER CONSULAR OFFICERS AND OTHER MEMBERS OF A CONSULAR POST

Article 40 Protection of consular officers

The receiving State shall treat consular officers with due respect and shall take all appropriate steps to prevent any attack on their person, freedom or dignity.

Article 41 Personal inviolability of consular officers

1 Consular officers shall not be liable to arrest or detention pending trial, except in the case of a grave crime and pursuant to a decision by the competent judicial authority.

2 Except in the case specified in paragraph 1 of this article, consular officers shall not be committed to prison or be liable to any other form of restriction on their personal freedom save in execution of a judicial decision of final effect.

3 If criminal proceedings are instituted against a consular officer, he must appear before the competent authorities. Nevertheless, the proceedings shall be conducted with the respect due to him by reason of his official position and, except in the case specified in paragraph 1 of this article, in a manner which will hamper the exercise of consular functions as little as possible. When, in the circumstances mentioned in paragraph 1 of this article, it has become necessary to detain a consular officer, the proceedings against him shall be instituted with the minimum of delay.

Article 42 Notification of arrest, detention or prosecution

In the event of the arrest or detention, pending trial, of a member of the consular staff, or of criminal proceedings being instituted against him, the receiving State shall promptly notify the head of the consular post. Should the latter be himself the object of any such measure, the receiving State shall notify the sending State through the diplomatic channel.

Article 43 Immunity from jurisdiction

1 Consular officers and consular employees shall not be amenable to the jurisdiction of the judicial or administrative authorities of the receiving State in respect of acts performed in the exercise of consular functions.
2 The provisions of paragraph 1 of this article shall not, however, apply in respect of a civil action either:

(a) arising out of a contract concluded by a consular officer or a consular employee in which he did not contract expressly or impliedly as an agent of the sending State; or
(b) by a third party for damage arising from an accident in the receiving State caused by a vehicle, vessel or aircraft.

Article 44 Liability to give evidence

1 Members of a consular post may be called upon to attend as witnesses in the course of judicial or administrative proceedings. A consular employee or a member of the service staff shall not, except in the cases mentioned in paragraph 3 of this article, decline to give evidence. If a consular officer should decline to do so, no coercive measure or penalty may be applied to him.
2 The authority requiring the evidence of a consular officer shall avoid interference with the performance of his functions. It may, when possible, take such evidence at his residence or at the consular post or accept a statement from him in writing.
3 Members of a consular post are under no obligation to give evidence concerning matters connected with the exercise of their functions or to produce official correspondence and documents relating thereto. They are also entitled to decline to give evidence as expert witnesses with regard to the law of the sending State.

Special missions

Convention on Special Missions
of 8 December 1969
Entry into force: 21 June 1985

Article 1 Use of terms

For the purposes of the present Convention:

(a) a "special mission" is a temporary mission, representing the State, which is sent by one State to another State with the consent of the latter for the purpose of dealing with it on specific questions or of performing in relation to it a specific task;

Article 2 Sending of a special mission

A State may send a special mission to another State with the consent of the latter, previously obtained through the diplomatic or another agreed or mutually acceptable channel.

Article 3 Functions of a special mission

The functions of a special mission shall be determined by the mutual consent of the sending and the receiving State.

Article 4 Sending of the same special mission to two or more States

A State which wishes to send the same special mission to two or more States shall so inform each receiving State when seeking the consent of that State.

Article 5 Sending of a joint special mission by two or more States

Two or more States which wish to send a joint special mission to another State shall so inform the receiving State when seeking the consent of that State.

Article 9 Composition of the special mission

1   A special mission shall consist of one or more representatives of the sending State from among whom the sending State may appoint a head. It may also include diplomatic staff, administrative and technical staff and service staff.
2   When members of a permanent diplomatic mission or of a consular post in the receiving State are included in a special mission, they shall retain their privileges and immunities as members of their permanent diplomatic mission or consular post in addition to the privileges and immunities accorded by the present Convention.

Article 10 Nationality of the members of the special mission

1   The representatives of the sending State in the special mission and the members of its diplomatic staff should in principle be of the nationality of the sending State.
2   Nationals of the receiving State may not be appointed to a special mission except with the consent of that State, which may be withdrawn at any time.
3   The receiving State may reserve the right provided for in paragraph 2 of this article with regard to nationals of a third State who are not also nationals of the sending State.

Article 12 Persons declared "non grata" or not acceptable

1   The receiving State may, at any time and without having to explain its decision, notify the sending State that any representative of the sending State in the special mission or any member of its diplomatic staff is persona non grata or that any other member of the staff of the mission is not acceptable. In any such case, the sending State shall, as appropriate, either recall the person concerned or terminate his functions with the mission. A person may be declared non grata or not acceptable before arriving in the territory of the receiving State.
2   If the sending State refuses, or fails within a reasonable period, to carry out its obligations under paragraph 1 of this article, the receiving State may refuse to recognize the person concerned as a member of the special mission.

Article 13 Commencement of the functions of a special mission

1 The functions of a special mission shall commence as soon as the mission enters into official contact with the Ministry of Foreign Affairs or with such other organ of the receiving State as may be agreed.
2 The commencement of the functions of a special mission shall not depend upon presentation of the mission by the permanent diplomatic mission of the sending State or upon the submission of letters of credence or full powers.

Article 20 End of the functions of a special mission

1 The functions of a special mission shall come to an end, inter alia, upon:

(a) the agreement of the States concerned;
(b) the completion of the task of the special mission;
(c) the expiry of the duration assigned for the special mission, unless it is expressly extended;
(d) notification by the sending State that it is terminating or recalling the special mission;
(e) notification by the receiving State that it considers the special mission terminated.

2 The severance of diplomatic or consular relations between the sending State and the receiving State shall not of itself have the effect of terminating special missions existing at the time of such severance.

Article 21 Status of the Head of State and persons of high rank

1 The Head of the sending State, when he leads a special mission, shall enjoy in the receiving State or in a third State the facilities, privileges and immunities accorded by international law to Heads of State on an official visit.
2 The Head of the Government, the Minister for Foreign Affairs and other persons of high rank, when they take part in a special mission of the sending State, shall enjoy in the receiving State or in a third State, in addition to what is granted by the present Convention, the facilities, privileges and immunities accorded by international law.

Article 22 General facilities

The receiving State shall accord to the special mission the facilities required for the performance of its functions, having regard to the nature and task of the special mission.

Article 23 Premises and accommodation

The receiving State shall assist the special mission, if it so requests, in procuring the necessary premises and obtaining suitable accommodation for its members.

Article 29 Personal inviolability

The persons of the representatives of the sending State in the special mission and of the members of its diplomatic staff shall be inviolable. They shall not be liable to any form of arrest or detention.

The receiving State shall treat them with due respect and shall take all appropriate steps to prevent any attack on their persons, freedom or dignity.

Article 30 Inviolability of the private accommodation

1   The private accommodation of the representatives of the sending State in the special mission and of the members of its diplomatic staff shall enjoy the same inviolability and protection as the premises of the special mission.
2   Their papers, their correspondence and, except as provided in paragraph 4 of article 31, their property shall likewise enjoy inviolability.

Article 31 Immunity from jurisdiction

1   The representatives of the sending State in the special mission and the members of its diplomatic staff shall enjoy immunity from the criminal jurisdiction of the receiving State.
2   They shall also enjoy immunity from the civil and administrative jurisdiction of the receiving State, except in the case of:

(a)   a real action relating to private immovable property situated in the territory of the receiving State, unless the person concerned holds it on behalf of the sending State for the purposes of the mission;
(b)   an action relating to succession in which the person concerned is involved as executor, administrator, heir or legatee as a private person and not on behalf of the sending State;
(c)   an action relating to any professional or commercial activity exercised by the person concerned in the receiving State outside his official functions;
(d)   an action for damages arising out of an accident caused by a vehicle used outside the official functions of the person concerned.

3   The representatives of the sending State in the special mission and the members of its diplomatic staff are not obliged to give evidence as witnesses.
4   No measures of execution may be taken in respect of a representative of the sending State in the special mission or a member of its diplomatic staff except in the cases coming under subparagraphs (a), (b), (c) and (d) of paragraph 2 of this article and provided that the measures concerned can be taken without infringing the inviolability of his person or his accommodation.
5   The immunity from jurisdiction of the representatives of the sending State in the special mission and of the members of its diplomatic staff does not exempt them from the jurisdiction of the sending State.

Article 41 Waiver of immunity

1   The sending State may waive the immunity from jurisdiction of its representatives in the special mission, of the members of its diplomatic staff, and of other persons enjoying immunity under articles 36 to 40.
2   Waiver must always be express.

3 The initiation of proceedings by any of the persons referred to in paragraph 1 of this article shall preclude him from invoking immunity from jurisdiction in respect of any counterclaim directly connected with the principal claim.

4 Waiver of immunity from jurisdiction in respect of civil or administrative proceedings shall not be held to imply waiver of immunity in respect of the execution of the judgment, for which a separate waiver shall be necessary.

Territory

DOI: 10.4324/9781003213772-12

TERRITORY UNDER INTERNATIONAL LAW

land territory and its subsoil
airspace
sea territory
outer space
moon and other celestial bodies
state territory
international territory
territories where the states retain functional sovereign rights
contiguous zone
exclusive economic zone
continental shelf
territories under the sovereignty or control of the subjects of international law
territories under international administration
maritime zones
province of mankind
common heritage of mankind

Territory as a paramount matter in the clash of states' interests

Since the avoidance of war and the maintenance of peace are the main concerns of international law, as a legal system, it aims to determine and adjust the fields where clashes between states' interests have a higher probability.

Traditionally, territory has been the source of conflicts between states. That is the primary reason the specific norms designed to regulate issues related to territory are considered the building blocks of international law.

Definition of territory

Generally, 'territory' in international law means any area of the earth and outer space which may be the source for either sovereignty or sovereign rights for particular subjects of international law or is ordered by the international regime.

At the same time, in defining a territory, international law divides the territories based on (1) geographical criterion or (2) legal criterion.

The geographical criterion

Based on the first characteristic, international law selects all possible and useful categories, such as:

- Earth's surface
  - **land territory** and its **subsoil**;
  - **airspace**; and
  - **sea territory**.
- **Outer space**
  - the **moon and other celestial bodies**.

The legal criterion

Based on the second measure, the following types of territory can be identified:

1 **State territory**, which is under the sovereignty of a certain state.
2 **International territory**, which is not under the sovereignty of states or other subjects of international law, such as outer space, the Antarctic, the high seas, and the deep seabed.
3 **Territories where the states retain the functional sovereign rights** or, in other words, the territories under a mixed legal regime, which mostly hold international status but where the functional sovereign rights of the states are preserved, such as the **contiguous zone**, the **exclusive economic zone**, and the **continental shelf**.
4 **Territories under the sovereignty or control of subjects of international law** other than states, such as the Vatican City under the sovereignty of the Holy See and the territories under the sovereignty or control of other subjects of international law.
5 **Territories under international administration**, such as the territories of the four Cambodian factions under the civil administrative functions of the United Nations and Bosnia and Herzegovina, according to the Dayton Agreement.

The sea territory or the so-called **maritime zones** are governed by the law of the sea and, like the land territory, may belong to any of the aforementioned types of territory.[938]

---

938 Under Article 1 of the United Nations Convention on the Law of the Sea: 'This Convention applies *mutatis mutandis* to the entities referred to in article 305, paragraph l(b), (c), (d), (e) and (f), which

Outer space is an international territory being regulated by the **province of mankind** and the **common heritage of mankind** (concerning the moon) principles, which will be examined in detail later in this book.

STATE TERRITORY

territorial sovereignty
principle of territorial sovereignty
principle of respect for territorial integrity
Declaration on Principles Guiding Relations between Participating States
obligation to protect the rights of other states within its territory
obligation to refrain from the acts which would do damage to the rights of
other states
no-harm principle
Trail Smelter case

Territory as an attribute of statehood

As noted in the section of this book dealing with the state, territory is the crucial criterion (attribute) of statehood. Therefore, statehood is traditionally inconceivable in the absence of a defined geographical base.[939]

---

become Parties to this Convention in accordance with the conditions relevant to each, and to that extent "States Parties" refers to those entities.' Hence, not just the states can enjoy the rights enshrined in the Convention. For instance, this Article of the Convention applies to the *territories which enjoy full internal self-government but have not attained full independence.*

939 'Traditionally' because, in the recent decades, several international processes have challenged the established approach claiming that a state without territory is unconceivable, mostly in relation to the so-called 'Islamic State', the effects of technological developments on statehood (the imagined 'blockchain-based state') and, more essentially, in regard to the island states, which may disappear as a result of climate change. As pointed out by Emma Allen: 'According to data published by the Inter-governmental Panel on Climate Change (IPCC), a number of small low-lying islands located in both the South Pacific and Indian Oceans stand to be submerged in the next fifty to one hundred years. This situation raises a number of important questions from an international law perspective, including whether the affected island communities – following the complete loss of their territorial basis – could cease to be states.' However, even concerning a more practical challenge – regarding the island states – the authors usually suggest the 'strategies of territory retention', which, with the assertion of Emma Allen, 'include the building of artificial islands, the appropriation of unclaimed land (*terra nullius*) and cooperation with third states.' However, 'whilst theoretically available, these strategies are unlikely to succeed due to legal restrictions and practical limitations.' Finally, she also considers the 'as yet largely uninvestigated option of pursuing remedial territory, i.e. territory transferred from responsible to injured states as redress for climate change induced deterritorialisation.' Emma Allen, 'Climate

Indeed, possession of a territory provides a state with an opportunity to perform acts and take on duties which would be impossible in the absence of such a possession.

Boundaries as an essential attribute of the state territory

As outlined earlier, there is no defined minimum territory which would serve as a prerequisite for statehood; however, a piece of land in the possession of a state is essential for the recognition of the establishment or continuation of the existence of a state. On the other hand, the territory must be definable with certain boundaries.[940]

Territorial sovereignty over state territory and sovereign rights over other territories

The system-forming principle which governs state territory is the **principle of territorial sovereignty**.

At the same time, many norms of international law have been developed to regulate the sovereign rights of the states over the land, sea, airspace. and outer space territories.

The principle of respect for territorial integrity

The other crucial principle with regard to state territory is the **principle of respect for territorial integrity**, which, as determined under the **Declaration on Principles Guiding Relations between Participating States**, means that the states

> will refrain from any action inconsistent with the purposes and principles of the Charter of the United Nations against the territorial integrity, political independence or the unity of any participating State, and in particular from any such action constituting a threat or use of force. The participating States will likewise refrain from making each other's territory the object of military occupation or other direct or indirect measures of force in contravention of international law, or the object of acquisition by means of such measures or the threat of them. No such occupation or acquisition will be recognized as legal.

The obligations of states stemming from the fact that they own the territory

In addition to the rights which generate from territorial sovereignty, there are, of course, the duties imposed upon a state as well. These duties involve the **obligation to protect the rights of other states within its territory** and the **obligation to refrain from the acts which would do damage to the rights of other states**.

Change and Disappearing Island States: Pursuing Remedial Territory' (2018) *Brill Open Law* <http://bit.ly/2vYLfHX> accessed 17 March 2021.

940 See the section of this book dealing with the state.

For example, as regards the so-called '**no harm**' **principle**, a state cannot use its own territory in a way which would lead to the pollution of the territory of another state. A significant crystallising factor concerning this principle was the landmark arbitral award in the ***Trail Smelter*** case *(United States of America v Canada)*. The dispute arose over the emission of sulphur fumes from a smelter located in Canada, which produced damage in the United States. The tribunal determined that

> under the principles of international law . . . no State has the right to use or permit the use of its territory in such a manner as to cause injury by fumes in or to the territory of another or the properties or persons therein, when the case is of serious consequence and the injury is established by clear and convincing evidence.[941]

STATE BOUNDARIES

> boundary
> imaginary line
> *uti possidetis*
> delimitation
> demarcation
> bilateral boundary commissions

The meaning and types of boundaries

A state exercises its territorial sovereignty within its **boundary**, which is an **imaginary line** that delineates the territory which belongs to a state from the territory of another subject of international law or from territory which is not under the sovereignty of states or other subjects of international law.

Boundaries are either topographical, having distinguishable natural features, such as mountains, rivers, or lakes, and reflecting the relief, or they are imaginary and artificial, such as, for instance, the lines of latitude and longitude.

Sovereignty within the boundaries

A state enjoys sovereignty within its boundaries, including:

- land territory (terrestrial territory) within its land borders;
- sea territory – the internal waters and territorial sea;
- subsoil beneath its land and sea territory; and
- airspace above its land and sea territory until the edge of the earth's atmosphere.

---

941 *Trail Smelter* case *(United States of America v Canada)*, Decision of 11 March 1941 of the Arbitral Tribunal, Reports of International Arbitral Awards, Volume III, 1905–1982.

The peaceful means for the adjustment of disputes concerning boundaries

In the interstate system, disputes over the precise location of the states' boundaries are widespread and are mainly settled by diplomatic negotiations. However, there are also other peaceful means available to settle disputes of this type, such as enquiry, mediation, conciliation, arbitration, and judicial settlement.

Uti possidetis

Of fundamental importance to the determination of boundaries in the twentieth century has been the principle of *uti possidetis*, which, as mentioned earlier, in the process of Decolonisation stresses respect for the frontiers existing during the colonial administration of those territories. However, nowadays, it is considered a principle of general international law which has been applied to recent cases as well.

Delimitation and demarcation

For the **delimitation** of the boundary, the states use either bilateral or multilateral formats, but more commonly, bilateral treaties are concluded to settle issues related to borders. Delimitation means the legal adjustment of a state boundary with a treaty, in which the boundary is graphically outlined, usually on a topographic map, and duly specified in a corresponding written description. The map and the description commonly become an integral part of the treaty (usually as its annex).

Meanwhile, the states also need more precise identification of the boundary. For that reason, the term **demarcation** is given consideration. Demarcation means the adoption of relatively permanent geographical elements, such as mountains, rivers, lakes, roads, and so on, to describe the exact borderline. This mechanism is usually implemented by **bilateral boundary commissions**.

THE ACQUISITION OF ADDITIONAL TERRITORY

> *terra nullius*
> original title
> derivative title
> effective administration
> principle of effectiveness

The importance of the determination of modes of the acquisition of additional territory

How does a state acquire sovereignty over more territory? It is the question which often arises in international relations. Therefore, the precise determination of the modes of the acquisition of a territory is a vital precondition for international peace.

The subjects of the acquisition of additional territory

The provisions of this section primarily concern the states. However, some modes of the acquisition of additional territory (for example, cession) may also be utilised by some other subjects of international law (taking into account the specifics of the subject concerned). Moreover, currently, some *sui generis* subjects hold sovereignty over a piece of land (for example, the Holy See), and there is no rule of international law restricting the acquisition of additional territory by such subjects.

Original and derivative titles

Generally, the title to a territory is acquired either by claiming land not previously owned by anyone (***terra nullius*** – a territory belonging to no one) or through the transfer of title from one subject to another. When the title is acquired according to the first method, it is called an **original title** while, in the second case, it is called a **derivative title**.

Modes of the original acquisition of territory are:

- occupation; and
- accretion (usually from a natural cause).

Derivative modes of acquisition include:

- self-determination (which may be a mode of acquisition of additional territory, if a people realise their right to external self-determination by free integration with an independent state in exceptional cases when such external self-determination is permitted by international law. This matter was examined earlier in this book);
- prescription;
- cession;
- boundary allocation decisions (taken by international organisations, international conferences, and, in rare cases, judicial bodies and other third parties); and
- annexation.

There is also the so-called confirming (crystallising) mechanism concerning the acquisition of a territory, which is called adjudication.

Effective administration

At the heart of several modes of acquisition of the title to a territory, there is the need for the claimant state to prove that it had exercised an **effective administration** of the functions of a state within that territory.

In short, the state claiming the title must establish that it has behaved like a state with respect to a territory it has a claim to. What actually is required for a state to satisfy this prerequisite will depend on the nature of the modes of the acquisition. Therefore, under international law, the **principle of effectiveness** is considered to be a guiding principle in territorial matters.

Occupation and accretion

occupation of the *terra nullius*
military occupation
effective control
law of belligerent occupation
Advisory Opinion on *Western Sahara*
act of the presence
intention to occupy
effective and continuous exercise of authority
Clipperton Island case
avulsion
presumption of effective occupation
artificial accretion

Two meanings of occupation

Firstly, it is notable that the term 'occupation' may be misleading since, in international practice, it has two primary meanings:

- **Occupation of the *terra nullius*** – the state peacefully and effectively exercises the functions of a state within a territory which does not belong to any other state; and
- Occupation of the territory of another state through the use of force without the consent of the domestic government, which, following the generally accepted approach, is called **military occupation** in this book as well.

Military occupation

The Hague Conventions of 1899 and 1907 included similar definitions of and approaches to military occupation. According to the Convention (II) with Respect to the Laws and Customs of War on Land (the Annex – Regulations Respecting the Laws and Customs of War on Land) of 1899: 'Territory is considered occupied when it is actually placed under the authority of the hostile army. The occupation applies only to the territory where such authority is established, and in a position to assert itself.' Under the Convention (IV) Respecting the Laws and Customs of War on Land (the Annex – Regulations Concerning the Laws and Customs of War on Land) of 1907: 'Territory is considered occupied when it is actually placed under the authority of the hostile army. The occupation extends only to the territory where such authority has been established and can be exercised.'

The Hague Conventions of 1899 and 1907, as well as the norms of international law that were developed after this period, make the occupying power responsible for the maintenance of public order and safety and the application of the relevant rules of international law on the occupied territory.

Even if there is no fighting, once territory comes under the **effective control** of the foreign armed forces, the so-called **law of belligerent occupation** (the body of norms of international law adjusting the relationship during or following an international armed conflict between an occupying power on the one hand, and a fully or partially occupied state and its inhabitants on the other) should be applied. The basic pattern of international legal obligations for the occupying state (and for the law of belligerent occupation) currently is established by the norms of international human rights law and international humanitarian law. Hence, the occupying power shall protect human rights and fundamental freedoms, as well as the principles and certain rules of international humanitarian law in the occupied territory.[942]

At the same time, the application of international legal norms concerning the military occupation does not in any way affect the sovereign rights in relation to the occupied territory since sovereignty is not transferred to the occupying power.

Occupation of the *terra nullius*

Only the occupation of the *terra nullius*, i.e. the first meaning, represents one of the modes for the acquisition of a territory. It assumes the establishment of the title to a territory not under the authority of any other state when:

- newly discovered, or
- abandoned by the state which was formerly in control of that territory.

In the meantime, the essential threshold question is what does *terra nullius* or newly discovered actually mean? The ICJ notable **Advisory Opinion on** *Western Sahara* of 1975 attempted to clarify that very question: 'According to the State practice of that period, territories inhabited by tribes or peoples having a social and political organization were not regarded as *terrae nullius*' (even if these tribes or peoples were nomadic, provided that they were socially and politically organised).[943] With this

---

942 For example, see the Decision of the Committee of Ministers of the Council of Europe of 2 May 2019 (CM/Del/Dec(2019)1345/2.1) concerning 'continuing military presence in the Georgian regions of Abkhazia and Tskhinvali region/South Ossetia' of the Russian Federation, in which is outlined the following: '[B]earing in mind that human rights and fundamental freedoms shall be protected by all relevant States Parties to the European Convention on Human Rights in the Georgian regions of Abkhazia and Tskhinvali region/South Ossetia, reiterated their call to the authorities exercising effective control: – to create conditions for the voluntary, safe and dignified return of all IDPs and refugees; – to cease any form of ethnic discrimination towards the residents of the Georgian regions, first and foremost, the ethnic discriminatory measures against the Georgian population of Gali and Akhalgori districts, including demands to register as foreign residents or to change the surnames in order to be granted access to full civil rights.'

943 'In the present instance, the information furnished to the Court shows that at the time of colonization Western Sahara was inhabited by peoples which, if nomadic, were socially and politically organized in tribes and under chiefs competent to represent them.' *Western Sahara*, Advisory Opinion of 16 October 1975.

formulation, the ICJ reflected the modification of the approach concerning the uninhabited territory since, for a long time, the territories inhabited by tribes, even those tribes having a social as well as political organisation, were regarded as uninhabited territory for this purpose.

At the same time, another disputable question which arises in this context concerns occupation and the meaning of 'abandoned by the state'. Under international law, the term 'abandoned by the state' suggests not only the failure to exercise authority over the territory on the part of the state which formally possessed the territory, but also an intention to abandon that territory.

Mandatory prerequisites of the occupation of the *terra nullius*

To occupy the land, one needs to take possession of it. For a title acquired through occupation to be final and valid, the following prerequisites must be fulfilled:

1   An **act of the presence** on the concerned territory imputable to a particular state.
2   An **intention** or will **to occupy** the territory.
3   An **effective and continuous exercise of authority** over the concerned territory.

1   The first prerequisite means that only a state can initiate the process of occupation. The activities by private persons without the direct link with a state shall not be regarded as acts of presence of a state.[944]
2   In the general case, the intention or the will to occupy the territory can be presumed from the simple fact that the state is exercising such an authority in the territory. However, when there is a dispute on this issue, the intention or the will may be inferred from all the facts and documents, including the official notifications to the other states.
3   The most critical and contradictory criterion is the effective exercise of authority, which first of all shall be understood as an actual exercise of authority by maintaining legislative, administrative, quasi-judicial, and judicial acts. In addition, the exercise of authority must be continuous and uninterrupted over a considerable period of time.[945]

944 In the *Sovereignty over Pulau Ligitan and Pulau Sipadan* case *(Indonesia/Malaysia)*, the International Court of Justice concluded that 'activities by private persons cannot be seen as effectivités if they do not take place on the basis of official regulations or under governmental authority'. Judgment of 17 December 2002, ICJ Reports 2002, 625.

945 In the *Sovereignty over Pulau Ligitan and Pulau Sipadan* case *(Indonesia/Malaysia)*, the International Court of Justice stated that 'the activities relied upon by Malaysia . . . are modest in number but that they are diverse in character and include legislative, administrative and quasi-judicial acts. They cover a considerable period of time and show a pattern revealing an intention to exercise State functions in

With respect to the effective and continuous exercise of authority, there are a number of arbitral and judiciary decisions. The most cited is the **Clipperton Island** case *(France v Mexico)*.[946] The award, rendered by the arbitrator, King Victor Emmanuel III of Italy, holds that

> the actual, and not the nominal, taking of possession is a necessary condition of occupation. This taking of possession consists in the act, or series of acts, by which the occupying state reduces to its possession the territory in question and takes steps to exercise exclusive authority there. Strictly speaking, and in ordinary cases, that only takes place when the state establishes in the territory itself an organization capable of making its laws respected.

However, if a territory 'was completely uninhabited' and in the absence of a competing claim, 'from the first moment when the occupying state makes its appearance there, at the absolute and undisputed disposition of that state, from that moment the taking of possession must be considered as accomplished, and the occupation is thereby completed.'[947]

So, there may be different standards for the effective and continuous exercise of authority with respect to various cases, depending on the concerned territory and the absence of a competing claim.[948]

The possibility of contemporary cases on the occupation of *terra nullius*

Today, however, almost the whole of the earth's surface is under the sovereignty of some state or other subject of international law, and occupation is obsolescent except:

- in relation to the proof of historical titles; and
- concerning newly appearing *terra nullius* as a result of

---

respect of the two islands in the context of the administration of a wider range of islands.' Judgment of 17 December 2002.

946 Mexico and France signed a Special Agreement in 1909 on submission of the dispute regarding the sovereignty over Clipperton Island to the binding international arbitration of King Victor Emanuel III of Italy. In 1931 King Victor Emanuel III issued his award and concluded that the Clipperton was a French possession.

947 *Clipperton Island* case *(France v Mexico)*, Award of 28 January 1931. Translated from *Revue Generale du Droit International Public*, 3d series, Volume 6 (1932) 129–132 <http://bit.ly/38RbxJx> accessed 17 March 2021.

948 The same approach was maintained by the International Court of Justice in its Advisory Opinion, delivered on 16 October 1975 concerning the *Western Sahara*: 'True, the Permanent Court recognized that in the case of claims to sovereignty over areas in thinly populated or unsettled countries, "very little in the way of actual exercise of sovereign rights" might be sufficient in the absence of a competing claim.'

- abandonment by the previous owner;
- the appearance of new territories as a result of such natural phenomena as, for example, volcanic activity, if the legal institute of accretion does not cover this case. In other words, if a newly formed peace of solid earth does not emerge within the territory (including the territorial waters) of any state, it cannot be considered a subject of natural accretion for the existing state territory.

The meaning of accretion

Accretion is the extension of sovereignty over new territory because of an increase in a state's land territory, primarily through natural causes.[949] Under international law, the term 'accretion', in addition to the gradual enlargement of state territory, also covers so-called **avulsion**, which commonly refers to an immediate and noticeable addition to a territory caused, for instance, by a sudden change in a water bed or the course of a stream.

Examples of accretion

Examples of accretion include the creation of islands in a river mouth; the drying up or change in course of a boundary river; an increase in riparian land by ocean action, causing land previously covered by water to become dry; or a more dramatic increase in a state's territory, such as the creation of new islands in existing territorial waters as a result of volcanic activity.

Enlargement of territories *ipso facto* by accretion

In practice, accretion is not a widespread mode since such changes occur very rarely, and even then, if new land is created within the territory of a state, it usually automatically forms a part of its territory without causing any reaction from other states. The basis of this approach appears to be a **presumption of effective occupation**. Thus, accretion as a mode of acquisition of a territory is largely interlinked with the mode of occupation of *terra nullius* discussed earlier.

Disputes between concerned parties

The particular case is drying or shifting of a boundary river, which sometimes leads to a dispute between the concerned parties.[950]

---

949 Accretion 'is a generic term for methods by which a State may acquire title to territory through the gradual operations of nature and requiring no formal acts of appropriation, e.g., alluvial deposits at the mouths of rivers, significant changes in the course of rivers'. *Parry & Grant Encyclopaedic Dictionary of International Law* (n 165) 5.

950 See the *Chamizal Case (US v Mexico)*, Award of 15 June 1911, Award by the International Boundary Commission (which consisted of three officials – a Mexican, an American, and a Canadian) in the Matter of the International Title to the Chamizal Tract of 15 June 1911, Reports of International

With regard to this case, international law provides that if such a change is slow and gradual, the boundary may be shifted, but if the change is excessive (momentous) – for example, when a stream suddenly abandons its bed and seeks a new bed – as a rule, the boundary line does not change. It remains at the same point of the original bed, even if water no longer flows through it (the so-called rule of avulsion).

Artificial accretion

Finally, accretion may also be the result of artificial forces (**artificial accretion**), such as, for example, the construction of jetties upland. However, if the utilisation of the artificial forces concerns the territory of a neighbouring state or states, there may be no accretion without their consent (for instance, concerning the boundary river).

Prescription

act of the presence
intention to prescribe
effective, peaceful, and continuous display of authority
publicly known
lack of objection
acquiescence
effective and continuous exercise of authority
Islands of Palmas case

The meaning of prescription

Prescription is a mode of establishing title for a territory which is subject to the formal authority of another state (not a territory belonging to no one).

Nowadays, this mode is considered mostly in relation to the proof of historical titles.

Mandatory prerequisites of prescription

For a title acquired through prescription to be valid, the following prerequisites must be fulfilled:

1 An **act of the presence** on the concerned territory imputable to a particular state.
2 An **intention** or the will **to prescribe** the territory.
3 An **effective, peaceful, and continuous display of authority** over the concerned territory for an extended period of time.

Arbitral Awards, Volume XI, 309–347. Available at <www.internationalwaterlaw.org/cases/Chamizal_Arbitration.pdf>.

4   A display of state authority that is **publicly known**.
5   A **lack of objection** (or **acquiescence**) by the former holder of the title.

The content of the first three prerequisites is similar to the occupation of *terra nullius*; however, some differences are also present. For instance, in this case, the **effective and continuous exercise of authority** should be expressly peaceful and of sufficient duration in time, which leads up to the critical date at which the dispute over the territorial sovereignty is considered to be decisive. Hence, the adequacy of the length of the period would be decided on a case-by-case basis. At the same time, the exercise of *de facto* authority must be publicly known. As the arbitrator Max Huber stressed in the award of the tribunal of arbitration of 1928 in the **Islands of Palmas** case *(United States of America v Netherlands)*:

> As to the conditions of acquisition of sovereignty by way of continuous and peaceful display of State authority (so-called prescription), some of which have been discussed in the United States Counter-Memorandum, the following must be said: The display has been open and public, that is to say that it was in conformity with usages as to exercise of sovereignty over colonial States. A clandestine exercise of State authority over an inhabited territory during a considerable length of time would seem to be impossible.[951]

Finally, the lack of objection (or acquiescence) by the former holder of the title is the crucial precondition for the title acquired through prescription to be valid. Although there is some debate as to what form this lack of objection or acquiescence should take, the consensus among international legal scholars is that the objection may consist of diplomatic protests, statements in the international organisations, the enactment of national legislation applying to the territory, or referral to a tribunal. These instruments and mechanisms overall should prove that there is not a lack of objection by the former holder of the title.

Cession, adjudication, and boundary allocation decisions

right to transfer its own territory
nemo dat non quod habet
Islands of Palmas case
benefit and burden principle
purchase
exchange
gift

---

951 *Islands of Palmas* case *(United States of America v Netherlands)*, Award of the tribunal of arbitration of 4 April 1928. All Permanent Court of Arbitration cases are available at the official website of the Court <https://pca-cpa.org/en/cases/>. In this book, materials from the website are used, according to applicable legal rules.

bilateral cession
Final Act of the Congress of Vienna
Treaty of Versailles
international peace conferences
Congress of Berlin
boundary allocation decisions
incorporation
arbitral tribunal
international court
quasi-judicial adjudication

The meaning of cession

Cession is the transfer of a territory from one sovereign to another with the consent of both parties. The situation is rather like the transfer of property in national law. In sum, in order for the cession of a territory to take place, the following two preconditions must be present:

- Direct will of the parties to cede a territory; and
- Agreement between the parties concerned, which is typically accomplished by international treaty.

The parties to the cession are (1) the ceding sovereign and (2) the acquiring sovereign. The object of cession is sovereignty over the territory, which belonged to the ceding subject before.

As articulated earlier, the predominant subjects of a cession are the states; nevertheless, the ceding and acquiring subjects may also be some other subjects of international law having sovereignty over a piece of territory.

The fundamental principles of cession

Fundamentally, cession rests on the **right to transfer its own territory**, which is an inherent attribute of the territorial sovereignty of a subject and, generally, of every territorial possession.

The second principle of cession, as in national law, is the Latin rule ***nemo dat non quod habet*** (no one gives what one does not have), which, with respect to international law, means that you can only cede that to which you have title. The principle was prominently affirmed by the Permanent Court of Arbitration in the **Islands of Palmas** case *(United States of America v Netherlands)*.[952]

---

952 'It is evident that Spain could not transfer more rights than she herself possessed.' *Islands of Palmas case (United States of America v Netherlands)*, Award of the tribunal of arbitration of 4 April 1928.

The third significant rule is that the cession shall be made with unambiguous language, which means that the cession may be considered final only with precise formulations, usually in a treaty concerning the cession of a territory.[953]

The parties to the cession should apply to the cession the principles and rules of succession, as well as the **benefit and burden principle** (a person who acquires an interest in or goes into an occupation of any land will automatically be subject to the burden of any subsisting land obligations). Therefore, a territory may be transferred only together with the obligations of the predecessor towards third parties, unless the ceding and acquiring subjects agree otherwise to distribute those obligations between themselves.

Since the cession of a territory occurs, as a rule, in the form of an international treaty, the modern norms relating to the formation and validity of treaties apply to it. For example, the incapacity of a party, vitiation of consent, and illegality of the object shall be considered grounds for invalidity.

Finally, since the sea territories, the subsoil, and airspace are 'inalienable appurtenances of the land', there is a traditional approach that they cannot be ceded without a piece of land.[954]

The categories of cession

Historically, there are two categories of cession – one which designates non-voluntary transfers and one which takes place as a result of a **purchase**, an **exchange**, a **gift**, or any other peaceful and voluntary manner.

In the UN Charter era, non-voluntary transfers of territories are prohibited. Hence, currently, cession is a method of peaceful transfer of a territory which, in practice, usually arises in rare cases, most of which concern marginal areas.

The forms of cession

The most common form of cession arises as a result of the bilateral transfer of a territory between the parties concerned (**bilateral cession**).

However, sometimes, cession may also be carried out via a multilateral treaty. For example, some transfers of territory which were enshrined in the General Treaty of the

---

953 As it is rightly articulated by the US District Court for the District of Hawaii in the *United States v Ushi Shiroma* case, 123 F. Supp. 145 (D. Haw. 1954), 'the Sovereignty over a territory may be transferred by an agreement of cession. See 1 Hackworth, Digest of International Law 421 (1940). Here neither in Article 3 nor in any other article of the Treaty of Peace does Japan cede Okinawa to the United States. In Article 2, Japan formally "renounces all right, title and claim" to certain specified territories, including Korea, Formosa and the Kurile Islands. However, there is no such renunciation as to territories named in Article 3.' Available at <www.jstor.org/stable/2194115?seq=1> accessed 17 March 2021.

954 Oppenheim (n 276) 377.

Final Act of the Congress of Vienna of 9 June 1815,[955] as well as certain Articles of the Treaty of Peace with Germany (**Treaty of Versailles**) of 1919[956] are notable examples of such cessions.

Nevertheless, not all territorial transfers which resulted from the **international peace conferences** or other multilateral treaties (albeit labelled as cessions) constitute a mode of cession. The particular non-voluntary transfers of the territories related to certain vulnerable countries based on the outcome documents of the peace conferences or other international agreements which were agreed by the great powers without the appropriate participation of those countries in the decision-making process and the signing of the outcome document or other international agreement, essentially may not be regarded as cessions. In such cases, the foundational preconditions of cession – direct will of the parties to cede a territory and agreement between the parties concerned – are absent. Examples of such cessions are the transfer of the south of Bessarabia from Rumania to Russia in exchange for part of Dobruja, as well as some other territories, following the **Congress of Berlin** of 1878[957] and 'the cession to Germany of the Sudeten German territory' from Czechoslovakia in 1938.[958] In this book, such cases are covered by the mode **boundary allocation decisions**, discussed later in this chapter.

---

955 For example. 'ART. V. His Majesty the Emperor of all the Russias, cedes to his Imperial and Royal Apostolic Majesty [the Emperor of Austria, King of Hungary and Bohemia] the districts which have been separated from Eastern Gallicia, in consequence of the Treaty of Vienna of 1809, from the circles of Zloozow, Brzezan, Tarnopole, and Zalesczyk, and the frontiers on this side shall be re-established, such as they were before the date of the said Treaty.'

956 Since certain provisions of the Treaty of Versailles – e.g. Articles 45 (regarding the Saar Basin) and 51 (concerning the Alsace-Lorraine) – which reflected the 'redistribution of Europe' (parts of the defeated Germany) by the victorious states entailed a substantial degree of violence, some authors (who recognised only voluntary transfers to be cession) regarded this method as distinct from cession – a separate mode of the acquisition of territory – via the decisions of the conferences of states.

957 The Treaty of Berlin (the Treaty between Austria-Hungary, France, Germany, Great Britain and Ireland, Italy, Russia, and the Ottoman Empire for the Settlement of Affairs in the East) was concluded in 1878 after the Russo-Turkish War (1877–1878) and the peace Treaty of San Stefano between Russia and the Ottoman Empire and following the Congress of Berlin (13 June–13 July 1878). Among other things, under the Treaty of Berlin, Romania achieved full independence. At the same time, some territorial issues were also determined. For instance, the cession of part of Bessarabia was prescribed in ARTICLE XLV. 'The Principality of Roumania restores to His Majesty the Emperor of Russia that portion of the Bessarabian territory detached from Russia by the Treaty of Paris of 1856'. On the other hand, the case of the Dobruja and other territories was defined in ARTICLE XLVI. 'The islands forming the Delta of the Danube, as well as the Isle of Serpents, the Sandjak of Toultcha, comprising the districts (eazas) of Kilia . . . are added to Roumania. The Principality receives in addition the territory situated to the south of the Dobroutcha.'

958 On 29 September 1938, the Munich Pact (also referred to as the Munich Betrayal) between Germany, Great Britain, France, and Italy (without the direct participation of Czechoslovakia) was concluded, resulting in the incorporation of Sudetenland directly into the Reich. The Pact itself used the following formulation: '[T]he cession to Germany of the Sudeten German territory'. See <https://avalon.law.yale.edu/imt/munich1.asp> accessed 16 March 2021. Five months later, Adolf Hitler summoned

Usually, the cession refers to the transfer of the portion of state territory but rarely may embrace the entire territory of ceding state. Ceding of the whole territory of a state amounts to the **incorporation** (the merger) and it results in the disappearance of the ceding state.

Examples of cession

Examples of cession in the nineteenth century include the purchase of Alaska by the United States from Russian Empire and the Louisiana Purchase by the United States from France (the purchase); Britain's cession of the island of Heligoland to Germany, mostly in exchange for Zanzibar, according to the so-called Heligoland-Zanzibar Treaty, which also regulated other territorial issues in Africa between the parties (the exchange); and the gift of Venice by Austria to France (the gift).[959]

Adjudication as a confirming mechanism of a title

In many situations, the title to a territory is in dispute. International adjudication is a method of international dispute settlement that involves the referral of a dispute, usually to an **arbitral tribunal** or an **international court**.

However, according to the traditional viewpoint, the common task of such tribunals and courts is to clarify the rights which the parties already have (not to establish new ones). Hence, the binding decisions of the arbitral or judicial bodies determining the title to a territory provide only a confirming mechanism (confirmation or declaration) of a title that has been in doubt.

The traditional approach, according to which the decisions of the courts and international tribunals were regarded 'as declaratory of existing rights and not as constitutive of new rights',[960] was challenged by several authors. Some of them argued that when an adjudicating

---

Czechoslovak President Emil Hácha to Berlin, where, after waiting for hours, during the early hours of 15 March 1939, Hácha was informed of the impending German invasion. Threatening a Luftwaffe attack on Prague, Hitler intimidated him into accepting the German occupation of the remaining Czech territory (the territory of Czechoslovakia at that time was significantly reduced as a result of processes in which almost all neighbours of Czechoslovakia were involved) and its conversion into a German protectorate. Hácha suffered a heart attack during the meeting and had to be kept awake by the medical staff, eventually gave in, and accepted the terms of surrender put forth by Hitler. On 16 March 1939, Adolf Hitler announced the establishment of the Protectorate of Bohemia and Moravia by a proclamation made from the Prague Castle.

959 'Austria, during war with Prussia and Italy in 1866, ceded Venice to France as a gift, and some weeks afterwards France on her part ceded Venice to Italy.' Oppenheim (n 276) 378.

960 Harry Post, 'Adjudication as a Mode of Acquisition of Territory? Some Observations on the Iraq-Kuwait Boundary Demarcation in Light of the Jurisprudence of the International Court of Justice'. Vaughan Lowe and Malgosia Fitzmaurice (eds), *Fifty Years of the International Court of Justice; Essays in Honour of Sir Robert Jennings* (digitally printed version, Cambridge University Press 2008) 239.

body was entitled to allocate a territory to a state which previously did not belong to it, the act of adjudication could be considered a separate mode of acquisition of the territory.[961]

Harry Post, who, under the label of adjudication, also united the '**quasi-judicial adjudication**' exercised by non-judicial bodies (namely, by the international organisations), enumerated the following 'traditional modes of acquiring dominion over property' (known in Roman law) – cession, conquest, occupation, accretion, prescription, and adjudication – and remarked that adjudication 'was the only one of these Roman law modes not adopted in international law.'[962] He finally concluded that 'within international law, indeed, such a way of acquiring territory is perfectly possible.'[963]

However, strictly speaking, such adjudicating authorities as tribunals and courts, as a rule, should deduce their findings based on the sources of international law or, in rare cases, on the principle of *ex aequo et bono*, but only if the parties specifically authorise such a foundation. Consequently, in principle, they can only apply or interpret the existing norms and have no power to establish new ones. Nor they can make a decision at sole will or based on political considerations. In exceptional cases, the parties may empower a judicial body with such unusual authority, but this would not be a common approach. To cover such exceptional cases of judicial adjudication in this book, this mode of acquisition of the territory is referred to as a boundary allocation decision.

Boundary allocation decisions

In most cases, boundary allocations are fulfilled by international (as a rule, bilateral) treaties with the direct participation of the countries concerned, and such an allocation should be regarded as a subtype of cession.

However, sometimes boundary allocation decisions are provided by the 'third parties', such as international organisations, international peace conferences, superpowers, international judicial bodies, or other third parties.[964]

---

961 Jan Hendrik Willem Verzijl, *International Law in Historical Perspective, State Territory* (Brill/Nijhoff 1970), Volume 3, 378. See also Robert Y. Jennings, *The Acquisition of Territory in International Law* (Manchester University Press 1963) 13.

962 Post (n 960) 237.

963 ibid 262.

964 One such decision was referred to in the ICJ Judgment of 16 March 2001 on the case *Maritime Delimitation and Territorial Questions between Qatar and Bahrain (Qatar v Bahrain)*: 'Qatar also advances in support of its position the 19 October 1981 arbitral award rendered by the Court of Arbitration in the *Dubai/Sharjah Border* case; in that award, which in Qatar's view was rendered under circumstances comparable to those of the present case, the Court of Arbitration concluded that boundary delimitation decisions taken by the British Government were not arbitral awards but rather *administrative decisions* of a binding character'. The Court favoured the position that the administrative decisions made by the British government were not arbitral awards but had a binding character since 'Bahrain and Qatar consented to the British Government settling their dispute over the Hawar Islands. The 1939 decision must therefore be regarded as a decision that was binding from the outset on both

Among such decisions, in this context, particular interest should be payed to the constitutive (not declaratory or interpretive) decisions of the third parties. The common characteristic in all such cases is the special competence of these parties to determine boundaries (usually concerning the disputed parts of the border), i.e. the authority not only to confirm but rather to establish title to a territory.

As the cases of such mandatory boundary allocation decisions are commonly regarded: the Council of the League of Nations' decisions on that matter, certain arbitral awards with a special competence to determine the border, and so forth.

Currently, the most significant institution with the power to make boundary allocation decisions is the United Nations; under Chapter VII of the Charter, the UN Security Council has the capacity to determine boundaries. The notable example of the implementation of this right was the case of the demarcation of the border between Iraq and Kuwait by the United Nations Iraq-Kuwait Boundary Demarcation Commission after the Gulf War in 1993.[965] The Security Council exercised its mandate, even though the representatives of Iraq declared their objections during the demarcation process.[966] Hence, the boundary allocation decisions were made largely based on the exclusive authority of the UN Security Council.

Annexation

> formal act
> incorporated territory
> threat or use of force
> lawful incorporation
> military occupation
> no legal validity
> null and void

The meaning of annexation

Annexation was a traditional means of acquisition of a territory for centuries. It is a **formal act** whereby a state declares a part or the full territory of another state as an **incorporated territory** under its sovereignty.

States and continued to be binding on those same States after 1971, when they ceased to be British protected States'. ICJ Reports 2001, 40.

965 See UN Security Council Resolutions: S/RES/687 of 3 April 1991, S/RES/689 of 9 April 1991, S/RES/773 of 21 August 1992. According to Resolution 687, the Security Council '[c]alls upon the Secretary-General to lend his assistance to make arrangements with Iraq and Kuwait to demarcate the boundary between Iraq and Kuwait.'

966 'On several occasions, in particular when the demarcation process of the Iraq-Kuwait international boundary was initiated, the government of Iraq has made clear that it believed that boundary issues could only be solved subject to agreement between the states concerned. In its view, this was not only so because such an agreement was the only real basis for guaranteeing the stability of boundaries, but also because international law so demands.' Post (n 960) 260.

Annexation is the result of the **threat or use of force**. This is a crucial element to determine annexation and distinguish it from the **lawful incorporation** of one or more states or parts of a territory into another state. Annexation may be exercised only by a state against another state.

Usually, annexation is the result of the use of military force and **military occupation**. However, it may also be exercised by the threat of the use of force.[967]

Mandatory prerequisites of annexation

The following prerequisites are necessary to determine annexation:

1 An act of the presence on the concerned territory imputable to a particular state.
2 A threat or use of force by a state against another state.
3 An effective and continuous display of authority over the concerned territory.
4 An intention or will to the annexation of the territory expressed through a formal act of the state acquiring the new territory.

The difference between annexation and military occupation

A vital element to distinguish annexation exercised as the result of the use of military force from military occupation is the fourth precondition of an annexation. There must be a precise proclamation of the incorporation of the territory under its sovereignty, which is usually fulfilled by the adoption of an internal formal act with respect to the territory concerned.

Contemporary prohibition of annexation

Meanwhile, at the present time, the threat or use of force is prohibited under international law. Therefore, only the title to a territory which was annexed with the threat or use of force before this prohibition was put into place can be considered valid.

The most notable modern example of annexation is Iraq's annexation of Kuwait in 1990. With respect to this annexation, the Security Council adopted Resolution 662 of 1990 declaring that 'annexation of Kuwait by Iraq under any form and whatever pretext has **no legal validity**, and is considered **null and void**'.[968] With this formulation, the Security Council reaffirmed the assessment of annexation by the use of force as a violation of the peremptory norm of general international law, disseminating the appropriate legal sanction, i.e. considering it to be null and void.

Nowadays, in particular cases, the interstate system faces a challenge from the individual states sometimes derogating from the *jus cogens* norm and annexing parts of other states by the use of force, as in the case of 'the illegal annexation of Crimea and Sevastopol' by

---

967 As in the case of the Baltic states (Estonia, Latvia, and Lithuania), which were annexed by the Soviet Union in 1940.
968 S/RES/662 of 9 August 1990.

the Russian Federation (as, for example, it is referred to in the European Council Decision 2014/386/CFSP of 23 June 2014 concerning restrictive measures in response to the illegal annexation of Crimea and Sevastopol, which was amended several times – most recently on 18 June 2020). However, these cases are still very rare exceptions and, most importantly, do not provide the legal basis for the acquisition of the territory.

MINOR RIGHTS OVER STATE TERRITORY

> functionally limited transfer of rights
> transfer of administration
> international lease
> international servitude
> international rivers
> international canals
> condominium

The functionally limited transfer of rights

The territorial supremacy of one state may be narrowed by the **functionally limited transfer of rights** to another state. However, the transfer of the particular right to another state, even in the case of the transfer of the administration of the territory, does not substitute the owner of the title to a territory.

Forms of the transfer of rights

There are several legal forms of this transfer:

- **Transfer of administration** of part of the territory of the state together with the complex of the rights related to its administration.
- **International lease** of part of the territory of the state together with the complex of rights related to the utilisation of the leased territory.
- **International servitude** of part or all of the territory of the state related to the exercise of a specific right or some particular rights.

Generally, these forms of transfer are regarded as the means by which states may exercise certain rights over territories without having sovereignty over them. At the same time, some scholars unite these forms of transfer under the label 'servitudes'. Hence, they do not separate the forms of the transfer of administration and international lease.

Different scopes of the transfer of rights

As mentioned earlier, the complex of rights transferred might concern a particular territory as a whole (as in the cases of the transfer of administration and international lease); however, sometimes it might be limited to a specific right or rights. In this book, the latter cases are regarded as servitudes, including the transfer of minor rights with regard to **international rivers** and **international canals**.

Condominium

Two states may formally agree to exercise sovereignty jointly over a certain territory or a border area. This is known as a **condominium**. Usually, condominium arrangements are designed to be temporary in nature.

Modern condominium proposals

In recent years, the condominium has been proposed as a solution to several boundary disputes, including Gibraltar (dispute between the UK and Spain), the West Bank and Gaza (dispute between Israel, the Palestinian Authority, and Jordan) and the Caspian Sea (dispute between the Caspian Sea countries).[969]

Transfer of administration

> territory as a whole
> indefinite or definite period of time
> Hay-Bunau-Varilla Treaty
> rights, power, and authority
> Panama Canal Treaty
> rights to manage, operate, and maintain

Definition of the transfer of administration

In case of a transfer of administration, one state gives the right to govern and administer a **territory as a whole**[970] and for an **indefinite or definite period of time** to another state with or without compensation.

Panama Canal Zone

The best-known example of the transfer of administration is the case of the Panama Canal Zone, which was constituted under the **Hay-Bunau-Varilla Treaty** (Convention between

---

969 Until 1998, the condominium was the arrangement proposed by Russia and supported by Iran to resolve the dispute among those two nations, as well as Kazakhstan, Turkmenistan, and Azerbaijan.

970 'A state may also, by treaty, be given the right to administer part of the territory of another state. For instance, the Treaty of Berlin 1878 gave the United Kingdom the right to administer the Turkish island of Cyprus (the subsequent British annexation of Cyprus in 1915 was recognized by Turkey in the Treaty of Lausanne 1923).' Malanczuk (n 72) 158.

the United States and the Republic of Panama for the Construction of a Ship Canal to Connect the Waters of the Atlantic and Pacific Oceans) of 1903 concluded between the United States and Panama. According to the Treaty: 'The Republic of Panama grants to the United States in perpetuity the use, occupation and control of a zone of land and land under water for the construction maintenance, operation, sanitation and protection of said Canal'.[971] In addition:

> The Republic of Panama grants to the United States of the **rights, power and authority** within the zone mentioned . . . and within the limits of all auxiliary lands and waters mentioned . . . which the United States would possess and exercise if it were the sovereign of the territory within which said lands and waters are located to the entire exclusion of the exercise by the Republic of Panama of any such sovereign rights, power or authority.[972]

In 1977, a new treaty (**Panama Canal Treaty**) was signed. According to this Treaty, on the one hand, some provisions of the previous status were reaffirmed, especially regarding the transfer of administration. As stated in the Treaty:

> The Republic of Panama, as territorial sovereign, grants to the United States of America the **rights to manage, operate, and maintain** the Panama Canal, its complementary works, installations, and equipment and to provide for the orderly transit of vessels through the Panama Canal.[973]

Upon the entry into the force of this Treaty, the United States government agencies known as the Panama Canal Company and the Canal Zone Government ceased to operate. At the same time, a new administrative body was created – a United States government agency called the Panama Canal Commission, which was supervised by a board composed of nine members, five of whom were nationals of the United States, and four of whom were the Panamanian nationals proposed by the Republic of Panama.

On the other hand, the Republic of Panama was regarded as being responsible for providing, in all areas comprising the former Canal Zone, services of a general jurisdictional nature, such as customs and immigration, postal services, courts, and licensing, in accordance with the Treaty and related agreements.

In general, this Treaty maintained the transitional status of the Canal and allowed the gradual transfer of control over the Canal Zone to Panama and the handover of full control of the Panama Canal on December 31, 1999, when, according to its provision, the Panama Canal Treaty was terminated.

With the full restoration of Panama's territorial sovereignty over the Panama Canal Zone, cases of the transfer of administration have become obsolete.

---

971 Article II of the Hay-Bunau-Varilla Treaty.
972 Article III of the Hay-Bunau-Varilla Treaty.
973 Article III (1) of the Panama Canal Treaty.

International lease

territory as a whole
right-of-use
definite period of time
competences
duration of the arrangement
compensation
sole jurisdiction
complete jurisdiction and control

The meaning of the lease of territories under international law

More frequently, state practice has led to the lease of territories. The lease under international law is a temporary transfer of a part of a **territory as a whole** with a **right-of-use** and, as a rule, for a **defined period of time**.

Primary conditions of lease treaties

In lease treaties, the parties usually determine:

- **Competences** to be transferred to the lessee state, which have substantial scope for variation.
- **Duration of the arrangement**, which may be a fixed term, a fixed term with automatic renewal, a term contingent on events, or an indefinite term with the provision of termination.
- **Compensation** to be paid to the lessor, which is not necessarily monetary. Sometimes the lessee state may not be required to make any payment to the lessor state.[974]

Lease as a mechanism of the transfer of functionally limited rights

Generally, through the lease, only functionally limited, particular rights are transferred to another state since sovereignty over the leased territory remains with the lessor, and the subject of lease is divorced from the jurisdiction for a certain period of time. Comparing the lease with the transfer of administration, the following distinctive features of a lease should be outlined:

---

974 For example, under the Convention Between the United Kingdom and China Respecting an Extension of Hong Kong Territory, the compensation to be paid to the lessor was not defined.

- The special focus in case of the lease of a territory should, by definition, be made on the usage of a territory.
- A lease may usually be concluded for a defined duration of the arrangement or of time.

However, considering the practical examples, the boundaries between these legal forms are mobile.[975]

Examples of international leases

Examples of leases include the international treaties with which China leased Kiautschou Bay to Germany (1898–1914) and Port Arthur to Russia in 1898. On the latter matter, the parties have concluded the Convention between Russia and China for Lease to Russia of Port Arthur, Talienwan, and the Adjacent Waters. According to the Convention, 'this lease is to be without prejudice to China's authority in that territory.'[976] Therefore, this formulation clearly expresses the main content of the lease treaty, which does not stipulate substitution of the authority over the leased territory.

Probably the best-known example of the lease of a territory in the interstate system is the Convention Between the United Kingdom and China Respecting an Extension of Hong Kong Territory of 1898. Simultaneously, in this case, the lessee was equipped with full jurisdiction with regard to the territory, and, in fact, the United Kingdom exercised the full administration. As stated in the Convention: 'Within the remainder of the newly leased territory Great Britain shall have **sole jurisdiction**.'

The other notable example is the lease of Guantanamo Bay, which the United States leased for use as a coaling station and naval base in 1903.[977] According to the Agreement Between the United States and Cuba for the Lease of Lands for Coaling and Naval Stations:

> While on the one hand the United States recognizes the continuance of the ultimate sovereignty of the Republic of Cuba over the above described areas of land and water, on the other hand the Republic of Cuba consents that during the period of the occupation by the United States of said areas under the terms of this agreement the United States shall exercise **complete jurisdiction and control** over and within said areas.[978]

International servitude

> **benefit of the servitude**
> **burden of the servitude**
> **positive (active) servitudes**
> **negative (passive) servitudes**

975 For example, see in detail the Hay-Bunau-Varilla Treaty.

976 Article II of the Convention.

977 Since 2002, the naval base has contained a military prison. Nowadays, it has a notorious reputation.

978 Article III of the Agreement Between the United States and Cuba for the Lease of Lands for Coaling and Naval Stations.

transit servitudes
boundary servitudes
economic servitudes
military servitudes
demilitarised or neutral zones
erga omnes obligations

Definition of international servitude

International servitude has been transferred from private law. Under international law, servitude represents a regime of restrictions applicable to part or the whole of the territory of one state in the interest of one or more other states. These restrictions find their legal foundation in an international treaty or a local custom.

Servitudes may be established for a state enjoying the **benefit of the servitude** or for a state on whom the **burden of the servitude** is imposed; accordingly, there are **positive (active)** and **negative (passive) servitudes**. In the first case, the beneficiary state is entitled to the individual rights concerning the territory; in the second case, the liable state has an obligation to refrain from certain actions. An example of a negative servitude is the demilitarisation of certain areas.

The continuity of servitudes

As an obligation under international law, servitudes exist irrespective of any change of a holder of the title to the territory concerned. In other words, the state which has replaced another in the responsibility for the international relations of the territory is bound by the previous obligations.

An example of the survival of a servitude despite the change of the landlord is the servitude to the benefit of the Swiss troops created by the Vienna Congress Final Act of 1815 in respect of the Chablais and Faucigny provinces, and the whole of the territory of Savoy to the North of Ugine, belonging at that moment to the King of Sardinia.[979] Since 1860, these areas had been under the jurisdiction of France; nevertheless, the Swiss retain their rights to these areas.

The parties of international servitude

International servitude is usually established among states. However, international law does not restrict other subjects of international law from participation in this process.

---

979 'Whenever, therefore, the neighbouring powers to Switzerland are in a stale of open or impending hostility, the troops of his Majesty the King of Sardinia which may be in those provinces, shall retire, and may for that purpose pass through the Vallais, if necessary. No other armed troops of any other power shall have the privilege of passing through or remaining in the said territories and provinces, excepting those which the Swiss Confederation shall think proper to place there'. Article XCII of the Final Act of the Congress of Vienna.

For example, in 2002, a Joint Statement was signed between the European Union and the Russian Federation, which constituted international servitude with regard to the legal regime for the citizens of the Russian Federation travelling from the Kaliningrad region to rest of the Russian Federation and from the main part of Russia to Kaliningrad, crossing the territory of Lithuania (Kaliningrad transit). In this international servitude, three subjects of international law – the European Union, the Russian Federation, and the Republic of Lithuania – participate.

The forms of international servitudes

With respect to the content of the servitudes, they fall into four groups:

1 **transit servitudes**;
2 **boundary servitudes**;
3 **economic servitudes**; and
4 **military servitudes**.

An example of transit servitude is the aforementioned servitude regarding the citizens of the Russian Federation; boundary servitudes include, for example, cases in which railway stations are located (partly) in a foreign territory;[980] economic servitudes give the beneficiary state the opportunity to use the defined territory in economic terms, but generally only to a limited extent in the fields of fishing, mining, navigation, the use of the port facilities, and the establishment of free ports or free zones in favour of other states;[981] and finally, military servitudes are mainly exercised for the establishment of **demilitarised or neutral zones** and the deployments or passage of foreign military troops.[982]

Servitudes for the benefit of all states or a large number of states

Servitudes may exist for the benefit of all states or a large number of states. Thus, some obligations which arise from the establishment of these international servitudes are considered *erga omnes* **obligations**. Such obligations, for instance, are established for the states which administer the Suez and the Panama Canals.

---

980 An example of this is Baden's Basel train station, which is located entirely in Swiss territory.

981 For instance, France was authorised by Article 65 of the Versailles Treaty of 1919 '[w]ithin a period of three weeks after the coming into force of the present Treaty, the port of Strasburg and the port of Kehl shall be constituted, for a period of seven years, a single unit from the point of view of exploitation. The administration of this single unit will be carried on by a manager named by the Central Rhine Commission to exercise certain rights over the port of Kehl.'

982 For example, the demilitarisation of the Aland Islands (Finland), established by a tripartite convention between Great Britain, France, and Russia and confirmed in the 1856 Treaty of Paris, which ended the Crimean War. The logic of the demilitarisation was that this small piece of territory would not be fortified and therefore would be less attractive militarily and less dangerous than it would otherwise be.

International canals and rivers

> international waterways
> freedom of passage
> Convention on the Law of the Non-navigational Uses of International Watercourses
> Convention of Constantinople
> Hay-Bunau-Varilla Treaty
> Treaty Concerning the Permanent Neutrality and Operation of the Panama Canal
> Convention Regarding the Regime of Navigation on the Danube
> Danube Commission
> Central Commission for the Navigation of the Rhine
> Mannheim Act

The characteristics of international canals and rivers

International canals and rivers form a vital part of **international waterways**. In order to apply international status to a particular canal or river, it must satisfy several characteristics:

1   A canal or a river should ultimately connect two areas of the high seas or enable ocean shipping to reach internal ports which otherwise would be land locked.
2   It should be of interest, if not to all, then at least to a significant number of states.
3   There should be in force the norms of international law with regard to a canal or a river typically, in the form of a multilateral treaty or a bilateral treaty for the benefit of the world community.

The principles governing international canals and rivers

The main target of international law arrangement on this matter traditionally was to guarantee **freedom of passage** to vessels through international waterways. However, in recent times, there have been other remarkable fields added, mostly aimed at the protection and sustainable use of the watercourses. In this respect, the **Convention on the Law of the Non-navigational Uses of International Watercourses** of 1997 has made a sizable impact. It stipulates the principle of equitable and reasonable utilisation and participation as the cornerstone of the Convention. It requires that a state sharing an international watercourse with other states utilise the watercourse in its territory in a manner that is equitable and reasonable vis-à-vis the other states sharing it. In addition, the Convention reflects the general principle of international law regarding the territory: that the states exercising the territorial sovereignty over its territory shall take all appropriate measures to prevent the causing of significant harm to other states.[983]

---

983 Article 7 of the Convention on the Law of the Non-navigational Uses of International Watercourses.

International canals

International canals are human-made waterways which link two geographically separate marine areas and pass through the territory of one or some states, which are regarded as the owners of the territorial sovereignty over the waterway. The canal is therefore considered as forming part of the national waters of the state (or states) concerned, which exercises its full sovereignty by issuing regulations, collecting taxes, and taking all self-defensive measures.

At the same time, the international canal is also an international maritime passageway connecting two free seas, and the holder shall comply with the obligations before the international community as they are disclosed in the international treaties.

Examples of such treaties include the **Convention of Constantinople** (Convention Respecting the Free Navigation of the Suez Maritime Canal) of 1888 for the Suez Canal[984] and the **Hay-Bunau-Varilla Treaty** of 1903 for the Panama Canal.[985]

The Convention of Constantinople decrees a very emphatic status of neutrality for the Suez Canal waterway and the highest degree of freedom of passage, stating that this canal

> shall always be free and open to vessels of commerce or of war, without distinction of flag . . . in time of war as in time of peace. . . . The Canal shall never be subjected to the exercise of the right of blockade.[986]

It is especially notable that freedom of passage means that a waterway is open to vessels founded on the non-discriminatory treatment in all matters connected with the usage of the waterway, but it does not mean that there may be no requirements for the vessels enjoying this freedom.[987]

In 1956, after the end of the British presence in the canal zone and the nationalisation of the assets of the canal company by the Egyptian government, Egypt reaffirmed its commitment to the provisions of the Convention of Constantinople, although, in fact, during the war of 1967, the Canal was closed for navigation until 1975, when it was reopened. After the conclusion of the Peace Treaty between Israel and Egypt in 1979, the provision of the Convention of Constantinople mentioned earlier was applied to Israel too.[988]

---

984 The Convention was signed between the United Kingdom, Germany, Austria-Hungary, Spain, France, Italy, the Netherlands, the Russian Empire, and the Ottoman Empire on 29 October 1888.

985 The other notable example is the Kiel Canal, the status of which as an international canal was originally defined by the Treaty of Versailles of 1919.

986 Article 1 of the Convention of Constantinople.

987 For instance, with respect to the Suez Canal, there exist the Rules of Navigation issued by the Suez Canal Authority. Article 1: '(1) Transit through the SC is open to vessels of all nations *subject to their complying with the conditions stated in the present Rules of Navigation.*' Article 12: '(1) Vessels may book for transiting the Canal. The booking notice shall reach the SCA Offices not later than four days prior to the transit date.' and so forth.

988 'Ships of Israel, and cargoes destined for or coming from Israel, shall enjoy the right of free passage through the Suez Canal and its approaches through the Gulf of Suez and the Mediterranean Sea on the basis of the Constantinople Convention of 1888, applying to all nations, Israeli nationals,

Concerning the Panama Canal, according to the Hay-Bunau-Varilla Treaty of 1903, the bilateral rule for the benefit of the world community was declared: 'The Canal, when constructed, and the entrances thereto shall be neutral in perpetuity, and shall be opened'.[989] In addition, the content of neutrality and freedom of passage was defined via reference to the following provision of the Hay-Pauncefote Treaty:

> The canal shall be free and open to the vessels of commerce and of war of all nations observing these Rules, on terms of entire equality, so that there shall be no discrimination against any such nation, or its citizens or subjects, in respect of the conditions or charges of traffic, or otherwise. Such conditions and charges of traffic shall be just and equitable.[990]

This status of the Panama Canal was reasserted under the 1977 **Treaty Concerning the Permanent Neutrality and Operation of the Panama Canal** (between the United States and Panama). In addition, the parties agreed to uphold the regime of neutrality over the Panama Canal, 'which shall be maintained in order that the Canal shall remain permanently neutral, notwithstanding the termination of any other treaties entered into by the two Contracting Parties.'[991]

International rivers

As for the rivers, in order to obtain international status, in addition to the characteristics listed earlier, a river must be shared by two or more states. The most remarkable example of an international river is the Danube, whose international status has been maintained by the **Convention Regarding the Regime of Navigation on the Danube** (Belgrade Convention) of 1948 and relevant bilateral treaties between the parties. Under the Convention, the '[n]avigation on the Danube shall be free and open for the nationals, vessels of commerce and goods of all States, on a footing of equality in regard to port and navigation charges and conditions for merchant shipping.'[992] This regime is effective regarding the navigable part of the Danube River between Ulm and the Black Sea through the Sulina arm, with the outlet to the sea through the Sulina channel. The right to free navigation does not apply to naval vessels.

Therefore, freedom of passage is regarded with respect to:

- nationals;
- vessels of commerce; and
- goods.

---

vessels and cargoes, as well as persons, vessels and cargoes destined for or coming from Israel, shall be accorded non-discriminatory treatment in all matters connected with usage of the canal.' Paragraph 1 of Article V of the Peace Treaty between Israel and Egypt.

989 Article XVIII of the Hay-Bunau-Varilla Treaty.

990 The Treaty was signed by the United States and the United Kingdom in 1901.

991 Article IV of the Treaty Concerning the Permanent Neutrality and Operation of the Panama Canal.

992 Articles 1 and 2 of the Convention Regarding the regime of navigation on the Danube.

The Convention established the **Danube Commission** as an international intergovernmental organisation whose main objectives are to provide and develop free navigation on the Danube for commercial vessels flying the flags of all states in accordance with the interests and sovereign rights of the member states of the Convention. Since 1954, the Commission has had its seat in Budapest. The Danube Commission in its work rests on the best practice of international river commissions, including the European Danube Commission, established under the Paris Peace Treaty of 1856.

The Danube Commission has a small organisational structure. It consists of one representative of each Danubian state; among its members, it elects a chairman, a vice-chairman and a secretary for a term of three years. The Commission takes decisions by a majority of the members present, unless otherwise expressly provided for in the Convention.

With respect to the utilisation and protection of the Danube, there are other international treaties concluded. Several other bodies in various fields of operation were also established. For example, in 1998, the International Commission for the Protection of the Danube River created under the Convention on Cooperation for the Protection and Sustainable Use of the River Danube (Convention for the Protection of the Danube) of 1994 became active.[993]

The other river which holds international status is the River Rhine.[994] The principle of freedom of navigation on major multinational rivers of Europe, including the Rhine, was laid down in the Final Act of the Congress of Vienna of 1815. In the same year, the **Central Commission for the Navigation of the Rhine** was formally constituted, which adopts the common regulations necessary for the safety of navigation on the Rhine. Up until now, it administers certain issues under its competence; for example, it has a decision-making authority with respect to appeals against court judgments involving navigation on the Rhine (exercised by the Central Commission's Chamber of Appeals).

The **Mannheim Act** of 1868 prescribed both the principle of free navigation on the Rhine and the possibility for member states of the Central Commission to adopt common regulations. According to the Mannheim Act, the

> navigation of the Rhine and its estuaries from Basel to the open sea either down or upstream is free to the vessels of all nations for the transport of merchandise and persons, provided that they conform to the provisions contained in this Convention and to the measures prescribed for the maintenance of general safety.[995]

993 The objectives of the Commission include to ensure sustainable water management, conservation, improvement, and rational use of surface waters and ground water; control pollution; and reduce inputs of nutrients and hazardous substances, as well as control floods and ice hazards.

994 Unlike the Rhine or the Danube River, which allow for co-operation between European states, such river as the Nile and the Euphrates lack co-operation between the riparian states, making agreement on the use of the river difficult to reach.

995 Article 1 of the Revised Convention for Rhine Navigation as set out in the text of 20 November 1963.

At the same time, the member states must refrain from imposing any toll, tax, duty, or charge based directly on the fact of navigation.[996]

POLAR REGIONS

> Antarctic
> Antarctica
> Arctic Ocean
> isolated politically
> global legal regime

Similarities and differences of the polar regions

The polar regions are often referred to together due to their parallel physical locations; algid temperatures; and, consequently, minimal accessibility.

However, geographically, they differ appreciably, since one polar region – the **Antarctic** – is located around the Earth's South Pole and comprises the continent of **Antarctica** and surrounding ice shelves, waters and the island territories, whereas the other is the **Arctic Ocean** surrounded by the land and ice masses.

Political interests

The Antarctic region is more **isolated politically** than the Arctic since the Arctic is very near to the territories belonging to the superpowers. The Arctic region ties together three geopolitical areas: Asia, Europe, and North America. Eight states located within these three areas are considered Arctic states. Perhaps that's why the legal status of the territory of the Arctic remained, to a greater degree and for a long time, a matter of diverging views and interests.

Distinct legal regimes

In terms of international law, the Antarctic has been under the protection of the binding **global legal regime** (the single international governance regime) since the mid–twentieth century. The Arctic, in contrast, has not yet received the same legal treatment. The

---

996 As noted on the official website of the Commission: 'Navigation is open to vessels of any nation, although there are certain limits resulting from Additional Protocol No. 2 of 1982. The limitations concern vessels registered in a country that is neither a Contracting State of the Convention nor a Member State of the European Union. For these States, although transit traffic is free, "exchange" traffic is subject to agreements with the States concerned and cabotage traffic on the Rhine is subject to the conditions laid down by the Central Commission.' <www.ccr-zkr.org/11020100-en.html> accessed 17 March 2021.

Antarctic is, in fact, internationalised, while considerable parts of the Arctic were claimed by certain states to be under the territorial sovereignty of those states.

Antarctic

> Antarctic Treaty system
> Antarctic Treaty
> Protocol on Environmental Protection to the Antarctic Treaty
> Convention for the Conservation of Antarctic Seals
> Convention of Antarctic Marine Living Resources
> for peaceful purposes only
> natural reserve, devoted to peace and science
> common heritage of mankind

The internationalised status of the Antarctic

The **Antarctic Treaty System** provides for the internationalised status of Antarctica and the surrounding ice shelves, waters, and island territories. At its core is the **Antarctic Treaty** of 1959, but it also includes the **Protocol on Environmental Protection to the Antarctic Treaty** (Madrid Protocol) of 1991, the **Convention for the Conservation of Antarctic Seals** of 1972, and the **Convention of Antarctic Marine Living Resources** of 1980.

Antarctic Treaty

The Antarctic Treaty was signed by the 12 countries which were active in and around Antarctica during the International Geophysical Year of 1957–1958, but since then, some other states have also acceded to it.

The Antarctic Treaty and the Antarctic Treaty system apply to the area south of 60° South Latitude, including all ice shelves, waters, and islands. According to the Antarctic Treaty:

> 'The provisions of the present Treaty shall apply to the area south of 60° South Latitude, including all ice shelves, but nothing in the present Treaty shall prejudice or in any way affect the rights, or the exercise of the rights, of any State under international law with regard to the high seas within that area.[997]

Hence, all provisions which are prescribed under the Treaty concerning Antarctica cover the surrounding ice shelves, waters, and island territories as well, which together with Antarctica, are usually referred to as 'the Antarctic Treaty area' or simply the Antarctic.

997 Article VI of the Antarctic Treaty.

The Antarctic Treaty declares Antarctica an internationalised territory, where no country shall claim sovereignty or attempt to establish the rights of sovereignty. Although the claims to sovereignty in Antarctica that existed at the moment of the conclusion of the Treaty were not affected by the Treaty, nevertheless, according to the Treaty:

> No acts or activities taking place while the present Treaty is in force shall constitute a basis for asserting, supporting or denying a claim to territorial sovereignty in Antarctica or create any rights of sovereignty in Antarctica. No new claim, or enlargement of an existing claim, to territorial sovereignty in Antarctica shall be asserted while the present Treaty is in force.[998]

Simultaneously, according to the Treaty,

> Antarctica shall be used **for peaceful purposes only**. There shall be prohibited, inter alia, any measures of a military nature, such as the establishment of military bases and fortifications, the carrying out of military maneuvers, as well as the testing of any types of weapons.[999]

With this formulation, the parties acknowledged one of the main targets of the Treaty – the use of this continent and its surrounding area for peaceful purposes only. Furthermore, any nuclear explosions in Antarctica and the disposal of radioactive waste material there are prohibited.

The Treaty guarantees freedom of scientific investigation in Antarctica and co-operation towards that end, which is regarded as a freedom for every existing state. The scientific observations and results from Antarctica shall be exchanged and made freely available. In order to promote the objectives and ensure the observance of the provisions of the Treaty, all areas of Antarctica, including all stations, installations, and equipment within those areas, are open at all times to inspection.

Antarctic as a natural reserve, devoted to peace and science

The Protocol on Environmental Protection to the Antarctic Treaty designates the Antarctic Treaty area as a '**natural reserve, devoted to peace and science**',[1000] whose protection is in the interest of humanity as a whole. Although this is a very similar concept to the **common heritage of mankind** principle, which was originally proclaimed solely with regard to the deep seabed beyond national jurisdiction and the resources contained therein, they differ considerably.

The focus of the concept applied to Antarctica (and to the entire Antarctic Treaty area) is that it is a natural reserve devoted to peace and science, which, inter alia, means that the activities in the Antarctic Treaty area shall be planned and conducted so as 'to limit adverse

---

998   Paragraph 2 of Article IV of the Antarctic Treaty.
999   Article I of the Antarctic Treaty.
1000   Article 2 of the Protocol on Environmental Protection to the Antarctic Treaty.

impacts on the Antarctic environment' and 'to accord priority to scientific research and to preserve the value of Antarctica as an area for the conduct of such research'. The Protocol on Environmental Protection to the Antarctic Treaty prescribes that the activities in the Antarctic Treaty area shall be planned and conducted so as to avoid, among other things,

- adverse effects on climate or weather patterns;
- significant adverse effects on air or water quality;
- significant changes in the atmospheric, terrestrial, glacial, or marine environments; and
- degradation of, or substantial risk to, areas of biological, scientific, historic, aesthetic, or wilderness significance.[1001]

Furthermore, the Protocol on Environmental Protection to the Antarctic Treaty prohibits all activities relating to Antarctic mineral resources, except for scientific research.[1002]

The common heritage of mankind approach

On the other hand, the aim of the common heritage of mankind approach is that certain global commons or elements which are considered to be beneficial to the humanity as a whole should not be exclusively exploited by individual states or their nationals.

Consequently, the common heritage of mankind approach stipulated the establishment of the international regimes (such as the International Seabed Authority and international rules concerning the deep seabed) in order to provide coordinated exploration and exploitation of the resources of such a type.

Arctic

> soft law mechanisms
> eight Arctic states
> Arctic indigenous peoples
> Declaration on the establishment of the Arctic Council
> high-level forum
> Agreement on Enhancing International Arctic Scientific Cooperation
> Agreement on Cooperation on Marine Oil Pollution Preparedness and Response in the Arctic
> Agreement on Cooperation on Aeronautical and Maritime Search and Rescue in the Arctic
> Arctic sector theory

1001   Article 3 of the Protocol on Environmental Protection to the Antarctic Treaty.
1002   Article 7 of the Protocol on Environmental Protection to the Antarctic Treaty.

Specific legal regime concerning the Arctic

In contrast to the legal regime of the Antarctic, the Arctic is not explicitly governed by multilateral treaty aiming for the creation of the single comprehensive international governance regime.

However, nowadays, several global treaties, such as the United Nations Convention on the Law of the Sea of 1982, the International Convention for the Prevention of Pollution from Ships of 1973 as modified by the Protocol of 1978 (MARPOL 73/78), the Polar Bear Treaty of 1973, and various other bilateral and multilateral agreements regulate particular aspects of activity in the Arctic.

Instead of a single international governance regime, the Arctic legal framework is widely regarded as a complex system of fragmented but, in recent decades, dynamically developing regional regulations. These regulations are complemented by **soft law mechanisms**, usually under the auspices of the Arctic Council, which is a forum with no real power to make binding law but which serves as an advisory body.

The Arctic Council

The Arctic Council consists of the **eight Arctic states**: Canada, the Kingdom of Denmark (including Greenland and the Faroe Islands), Finland, Iceland, Norway, Russia, Sweden, and the United States. Six international organisations representing **Arctic indigenous peoples** have permanent participant status.[1003]

According to the 1996 **Declaration on the establishment of the Arctic Council** (Ottawa Declaration), the Council was established as a **high-level forum**, which should 'normally meet on a biennial basis, with meetings of senior officials taking place more frequently, to provide for liaison and co-ordination', at the same time, hosting meetings of the Arctic Council, including maintaining the secretariat functions, is sequentially rotated among the Arctic States. The decisions of the Arctic Council are made by consensus of the Members.[1004]

In addition, nowadays, the Arctic Council is regarded as a forum to conduct negotiations on three modern agreements: the **Agreement on Enhancing International Arctic Scientific Cooperation** of 2017,[1005] the **Agreement on Cooperation on Marine Oil Pollution Preparedness and Response in the Arctic** of 2013, and the 2011 **Agreement on Cooperation on Aeronautical and Maritime Search and Rescue in the Arctic**.

1003   Aleut International Association (AIA), Arctic Athabaskan Council (AAC), Gwich'in Council International (GCI), Inuit Circumpolar Council (ICC), Russian Association of Indigenous Peoples of the North (RAIPON), and Saami Council (SC).

1004   Paragraphs 1, 4, 5, 6, 7 of the Ottawa Declaration.

1005   For example, this Agreement specifically stresses the role of the Arctic Council in Paragraph 1 of Article 12: 'The Parties shall meet no later than one year after the entry into force of this Agreement, as convened by the depositary, and from then on as decided by the Parties. The Parties may elect to convene such meetings in conjunction with meetings of the Arctic Council including inviting Arctic Council Permanent Participants and Arctic Council Observers to observe and provide information.'

Arctic sector theory

The absence of a consolidated approach to the territory of the Arctic for a long time incentivised different treatments regarding the boundaries of the territorial sovereignty of the concerned states. Early in the twentieth century, the **Arctic sector**[1006] **theory** made an appearance.[1007]

According to this theory, as formulated by Senator Pascal Poirier in the Senate, the upper house of Canada's bi-cameral Parliament, in 1907:

> In future partition of northern lands, a country whose possession today goes up to the Arctic regions, will have a right, or should have a right, or has a right to all the lands that are to be found in the waters between a line extending from its eastern extremity north, and another line extending from the western extremity north. All the lands between the two lines up to the north pole should belong and do belong to the country whose territory abuts up there.[1008]

Thus, this formulation is focused on the land territories (not the sea territories) within the denoted lines.

Nevertheless, no general conventions have been concluded acknowledging the Arctic sectors principle, nor is it commonly accepted in international practice. The Soviet Union is the only concerned state that, in 1926, formally incorporated it into its national law, referring, in a style similar to Senator Poirier's, to 'all lands and islands in the Arctic north of the coast of the Union of Soviet Socialist Republics up to the North Pole.'[1009] Others have either officially rejected it or, as in the case of Canada, despite the unconsolidated

---

1006 In geographical terms, 'a sector means a triangular slice of polar territory, with its apex at the pole, bounded by two meridians of longitude, and usually having a parallel of latitude or a territorial coast-line as its base. Arctic sectors converge at the North Pole whereas Antarctic sectors meet at the South Pole. However, in some cases a longitudinal line must deviate to circumvent foreign territory; both Greenland and Spitsbergen necessitate such deviations.' Elmer Plischke, 'Territorial Sovereignty in the Arctic' (1 January 1950) *Encyclopedia Arctica 11: Territorial Sovereignty and History*, Dartmouth College Library <https://collections.dartmouth.edu/arctica-beta/html/EA11-03.html> accessed 17 March 2021.

1007 This theory represents a specific application of the *contiguity theory*, which was rejected by the Arbitrator Max Huber in the *Island of Palmas* case *(Netherlands v USA)* (Award of the tribunal of arbitration of 4 April 1928, Reports of International Arbitral Awards, Volume II, 829–871), who stated, 'The title of contiguity, understood as a basis of territorial sovereignty, has no foundation in international law', but it is often used in the states' practice.

1008 'Poirier's resolution was abortive. His motion was neither seconded nor put to a vote. The draft resolution embodied in the motion was not accepted by the Senate, and never reached the floor of the House of Commons.' Ivan L. Head, Canadian Claims to Territorial Sovereignty in the Arctic Regions (1963) 9 *McGill Law Journal* 203.

1009 A Decree of the Presidium of the Central Executive Committee of the Union of Soviet Socialist Republics, dated 15 April 1926, and entitled 'Territorial Rights of the Soviet Union in the Arctic' reads: 'Are declared forming part of the territory of the Union of Soviet Socialist Republics all lands

individual statements on the part of some officials, the government has neither manifestly confirmed nor denied it.

Besides, there appears to be a problem with interpretation, even with respect to the Arctic sector theory. Notably, should the polar states acquire sovereignty over the seas, floating ice, and permanent ice within the limits of their sectors of attraction or not? If ice formations and the seas surrounding the Arctic lands were not included, then the polar sector adjacent to it would have to be considered an open sea, with all the consequences resulting from such an interpretation. On the other hand, the states that have rejected the Arctic sector theory constantly consider the Arctic a region to which the United Nations Convention on the Law of the Sea should be applied, including the principles and provisions on the high seas. Furthermore, even the Russian Federation, the successor of the Soviet Union with respect to the relevant boundary, legally abandoned the sectoral approach of 1926 due to the ratification of the United Nations Convention on the Law of the Sea in 1997.

CASES AND MATERIALS (*SELECTED PARTS*)

No-harm principle

Trail Smelter case *(United States of America v Canada)*, Decision of 11 March 1941 of the Arbitral Tribunal
Reports of International Arbitral Awards, Volume III, 1905–1982.

The Tribunal, therefore, finds that the above decisions, taken as a whole, constitute an adequate basis for its conclusions, namely, that, under the principles of international law, as well as of the law of the United States, no State has the right to use or permit the use of its territory in such a manner as to cause injury by fumes in or to the territory of another or the properties or persons therein, when the case is of serious consequence and the injury is established by clear and convincing evidence.

The decisions of the Supreme Court of the United States which are the basis of these conclusions are decisions in equity and a solution inspired by them, together with the regime hereinafter prescribed, will, in the opinion of the Tribunal, be "just to all parties concerned", as long, at least, as the present conditions in the Columbia River Valley continue to prevail.

Considering the circumstances of the case, the Tribunal holds that the Dominion of Canada is responsible in international law for the conduct of the Trail Smelter. Apart from the undertakings in the Convention, it is, therefore, the duty of the Government of the Dominion of Canada to see to it that this conduct should be in conformity with the obligation of the Dominion under international law as herein determined.

Terra nullius

Western Sahara, Advisory Opinion of 16 October 1975, International Court of Justice
ICJ Reports 1975, 12.

---

and islands already discovered, as well as those which are to be discovered in the future, which . . . lie in the Arctic north of the coast of the Union of Soviet Socialist Republics up to the North Pole.'

79. Turning to Question 1, the Court observes that the request specifically locates the question in the context of "the time of colonization by Spain", and it therefore seems clear that the words "Was Western Sahara . . . a territory belonging to no one (*terra nullius*)?" have to be interpreted by reference to the law in force at that period. The expression "*terra nullius*" was a legal term of art employed in connection with "occupation" as one of the accepted legal methods of acquiring sovereignty over territory. "Occupation" being legally an original means of peaceably acquiring sovereignty over territory otherwise than by cession or succession, it was a cardinal condition of a valid "occupation" that the territory should be *terra nullius* – a territory belonging to no-one – at the time of the act alleged to constitute the "occupation" (cf. Legal Status of Eastern Greenland, P.C.I.J., Series A/B, No. 53, pp. 44 f. and 63 f.). In the view of the Court, therefore, a determination that Western Sahara was a "*terra nullius*" at the time of colonization by Spain would be possible only if it were established that at that time the territory belonged to no-one in the sense that it was then open to acquisition through the legal process of "occupation".

80. Whatever differences of opinion there may have been among jurists, the State practice of the relevant period indicates that territories inhabited by tribes or peoples having a social and political organization were not regarded as *terrae nullius*. It shows that in the case of such territories the acquisition of sovereignty was not generally considered as effected unilaterally through "occupation" of *terra nullius* by original title but through agreements concluded with local rulers. On occasion, it is true, the word "occupation" was used in a non-technical sense denoting simply acquisition of sovereignty; but that did not signify that the acquisition of sovereignty through such agreements with authorities of the country was regarded as an "occupation" of a "*terra nullius*" in the proper sense of these terms. On the contrary, such agreements with local rulers, whether or not considered as an actual "cession" of the territory, were regarded as derivative roots of title, and not original titles obtained by occupation of *terrae nullius*.

81. In the present instance, the information furnished to the Court shows that at the time of colonization Western Sahara was inhabited by peoples which, if nomadic, were socially and politically organized in tribes and under chiefs competent to represent them. It also shows that, in colonizing Western Sahara, Spain did not proceed on the basis that it was establishing its sovereignty over *terrae nullius*. In its Royal Order of 26 December 1884, far from treating the case as one of occupation of *terra nullius*, Spain proclaimed that the King was taking the Rio de Oro under his protection on the basis of agreements which had been entered into with the chiefs of the local tribes: the Order referred expressly to "the documents which the independent tribes of this part of the coast" had "signed with the representative of the Sociedad Espanola de Africanistas", and announced that the King had confirmed "the deeds of adherence" to Spain. Likewise, in negotiating with France concerning the limits of Spanish territory to the north of the Rio de Oro, that is, in the Sakiet El Hamra area, Spain did not rely upon any claim to the acquisition of sovereignty over a *terra nullius*.

82. Before the Court, differing views were expressed concerning the nature and legal value of agreements between a State and local chiefs. But the Court is not asked by Question 1 to pronounce upon the legal character or the legality of the titles which led to Spain becoming the administering Power of Western Sahara. It is asked only to state whether Western Sahara (Rio de Oro and Sakiet El Hamra) at the time of colonization by Spain was "a territory belonging to no one (*terra nullius*)". As to this question, the Court is satisfied that, for the reasons which it has given, its answer must be in the negative. Accordingly, the Court does not find it necessary first to pronounce upon the correctness or otherwise of Morocco's view that the territory was not *terra nullius* at that time because the local tribes, so it maintains, were then subject to the sovereignty

of the Sultan of Morocco; nor upon Mauritania's corresponding proposition that the territory was not *terra nullius* because the local tribes, in its view, then formed part of the "Bilad Shinguitti" or Mauritanian entity. Any conclusions that the Court may reach with respect to either of these points of view cannot change the negative character of the answer which, for other reasons already set out, it has found that it must give to Question 1.

Effective exercise of state authority

Sovereignty over Pulau Ligitan and Pulau Sipadan case (*Indonesia/Malaysia*), Judgment of
   17 December 2002, International Court of Justice
   ICJ Reports 2002, 625.

137. Turning now to the *effectivités* relied on by Indonesia, the Court will begin by pointing out that none of them is of a legislative or regulatory character. Moreover, the Court cannot ignore the fact that Indonesian Act No. 4 of 8 February 1960, which draws Indonesia's archipelagic baselines, and its accompanying map do not mention or indicate Ligitan and Sipadan as relevant base points or turning points.

138. Indonesia cites in the first place a continuous presence of the Dutch and Indonesian navies in the waters around Ligitan and Sipadan. It relies in particular on the voyage of the Dutch destroyer *Lynx* in November 1921. This voyage was part of a joint action of the British and Dutch navies to combat piracy in the waters east of Borneo. According to the report by the commander of the *Lynx*, an armed sloop was despatched to Sipadan to gather information about pirate activities and a seaplane flew a reconnaissance flight through the island's airspace and subsequently flew over Ligitan. Indonesia concludes from this operation that the Netherlands considered the airspace, and thus also the islands, as Dutch territory.

139. In the opinion of the Court, it cannot be deduced either from the report of the commanding officer of the Lynx or from any other document presented by Indonesia in connection with Dutch or Indonesian naval surveillance and patrol activities that the naval authorities concerned considered Ligitan and Sipadan and the surrounding waters to be under the sovereignty of the Netherlands or Indonesia.

140. Finally, Indonesia States that the waters around Ligitan and Sipadan have traditionally been used by Indonesian fishermen. The Court observes, however, that activities by private persons cannot be seen as *effectivités* if they do not take place on the basis of official regulations or under governmental authority.

141. The Court concludes that the activities relied upon by Indonesia do not constitute acts *a titre de souverain* reflecting the intention and will to act in that capacity. . . .

148. The Court notes that the activities relied upon by Malaysia, both in its own name and as successor State of Great Britain, are modest in number but that they are diverse in character and include legislative, administrative and quasi-judicial acts. They cover a considerable period of time and show a pattern revealing an intention to exercise State functions in respect of the two islands in the context of the administration of a wider range of islands. The Court moreover cannot disregard the fact that at the time when these activities were carried out, neither Indonesia nor its predecessor, the Netherlands, ever expressed its disagreement or protest. In this regard, the Court notes that in 1962 and 1963 the Indonesian authorities did not even remind the authorities of the colony of North Borneo, or Malaysia after its independence, that the construction of the lighthouses at those times had taken place on territory which they considered Indonesian; even if they regarded these lighthouses as merely destined for safe navigation in

an area which was of particular importance for navigation in the waters off North Borneo, such behaviour is unusual.

149. Given the circumstances of the case, and in particular in view of the evidence furnished by the Parties, the Court concludes that Malaysia has title to Ligitan and Sipadan on the basis of the *effectivités* referred to above.

Continuous and peaceful display of state authority

Islands of Palmas case (*United States of America v Netherlands*), Award of the tribunal of arbitration of 4 April 1928
PCA, Award of the Tribunal, Arbitrator M. Huber.

As to the conditions of acquisition of sovereignty by way of continuous and peaceful display of State authority (so-called prescription) . . . the following must be said:

The display has been open and public, that is to say that it was in conformity with usages as to exercise of sovereignty over colonial States. A clandestine exercise of State authority over an inhabited territory during a considerable length of time would seem to be impossible. An obligation for the Netherlands to notify to other Powers the establishment of suzerainty over the Sangi States or of the display of sovereignty in these territories did not exist.

Such notification, like any other formal act, can only be the condition of legality as a consequence of an explicit rule of law. A rule of this kind adopted by the Powers in 1885 for the African continent does not apply *de plano* to other regions, and thus the contract with Taruna of 1885, or with Kandahar-Taruna of 1889, even if they were to be considered as the first assertions of sovereignty over Palmas (or Miangas) would not be subject to the rule of notification.

There can further be no doubt that the Netherlands exercised the State authority over the Sangi States as sovereign in their own right, not under a derived or precarious title.

Finally it is to be observed that the question whether the establishment of the Dutch on the Talautse Isles (Sangi) in 1677 was a violation of the Treaty of Münster and whether this circumstance might have prevented the acquisition of sovereignty even by means of prolonged exercise of State authority, need not be examined, since the Treaty of Utrecht recognized the state of things existing in 1714 and therefore the suzerain right of the Netherlands over Tabukan and Miangas.

Transfer of administration and free navigation

Hay-Bunau-Varilla Treaty
(Convention between the United States and the Republic of Panama for the Construction of a Ship Canal to Connect the Waters of the Atlantic and Pacific Oceans) of 1903
Entry into force: 26 February 1904

ARTICLE II

The Republic of Panama grants to the United States in perpetuity the use, occupation and control of a zone of land and land under water for the construction maintenance, operation, sanitation and protection of said Canal of the width of ten miles extending to the distance of five miles on each side of the center line of the route of the Canal to be constructed; the said zone beginning in the Caribbean Sea three marine miles from mean low water mark and extending to and across the Isthmus of Panama into the Pacific ocean to a distance of three marine miles from mean low water mark with the proviso that the cities of Panama and Colon and the harbors adjacent to said cities, which are included within the boundaries of the zone above described, shall not be included within this grant. The Republic of Panama further grants to the United States in perpetuity the use, occupation and control of any other lands and waters outside of the zone above described which may be necessary and convenient for the construction, maintenance, operation, sanitation and protection of the said Canal or of any auxiliary canals or other works necessary and convenient for the construction, maintenance, operation, sanitation and protection of the said enterprise.

The Republic of Panama further grants in like manner to the United States in perpetuity all islands within the limits of the zone above described and in addition thereto the group of small islands in the Bay of Panama, named, Perico, Naos. Culebra and Flamenco.

ARTICLE III

The Republic of Panama grants to the United States all the rights, power and authority within the zone mentioned and described in Article II of this agreement and within the limits of all auxiliary lands and waters mentioned and described in said Article II which the United States would possess and exercise if it were the sovereign of the territory within which said lands and waters are located to the entire exclusion of the exercise by the Republic of Panama of any such sovereign rights, power or authority.

ARTICLE IV

As rights subsidiary to the above grants the Republic of Panama grants in perpetuity to the United States the right to use the rivers, streams, lakes and other bodies of water within its limits for navigation, the supply of water or water-power or other purposes, so far as the use of said rivers, streams, lakes and bodies of water and the waters thereof may be necessary and convenient for the construction, maintenance, operation, sanitation and protection of the said Canal.

ARTICLE V

The Republic of Panama grants to the United States in perpetuity a monopoly for the construction, maintenance and operation of any system of communication by means of canal or railroad across its territory between the Caribbean Sea and the Pacific Ocean.

ARTICLE VI

The grants herein contained shall in no manner invalidate the titles or rights of private land holders or owners of private property in the said zone or in or to any of the lands or waters granted to the United States by the provisions of any Article of this treaty, nor shall they interfere with the rights of way over the public roads passing through the said zone or over any of the said lands or waters unless said rights of way or private rights shall conflict with rights herein granted to the

United States in which case. the rights of the United States shall be superior. All damages caused to the owners of private lands or private property of any kind by reason of the grants contained in this treaty or by reason of the operations of the United States, its agents or employees, or by reason of the construction, maintenance, operation, sanitation and protection of the said Canal or of the works of sanitation and protection herein provided for, shall be appraised and settled by a joint Commission appointed by the Governments of the United States and the Republic of Panama, whose decisions as to such damages shall be final and whose awards as to such damages shall be paid solely by the United States. No part of the work on said Canal or the Panama railroad or on any auxiliary works relating thereto and authorized by the terms of this treaty shall be prevented, delayed or impeded by or pending such proceedings to ascertain such damages. The appraisal of said private lands and private property and the assessment of damages to them shall be based upon their value before the date of this convention.

ARTICLE X

The Republic of Panama agrees that there shall not be imposed any taxes, national, munici-pal, departmental, or of any other class, upon the Canal, the railways and auxiliary works, tugs and other vessels employed in bye service of the Canal, store houses, work shops, offices, quarters for laborers, factories of all kinds, warehouses, wharves, machinery and other works, property, and effects appertaining to the Canal or railroad and auxiliary works, or their officers or employees, situated within the cities of Panama and Colon, and that there shall not be imposed contributions or charges of a personal character of any kind upon offi-cers, employees, laborers, and other individuals in the service of the Canal and railroad and auxiliary works.

ARTICLE XII

The Government of the Republic of Panama shall permit the immigration and free access to the lands and workshops of the Canal and its auxiliary works of all employees and workmen of Whatever nationality under contract to work upon or seeking employment upon or in any wise connected with the said Canal and its auxiliary works, with their respective families, and all such persons shall be free and exempt from the military service of the Republic of Panama.

ARTICLE XIII

The United States may import at any time into the said zone and auxiliary lands, free of custom duties, imposts, taxes, or other charges, and without any restrictions, any and all vessels, dredges, engines, cars, machinery, tools, explosives, materials, supplies, and other articles necessary and convenient in the construction, maintenance, operation, sanitation and protection of the Canal and auxiliary works, and all provisions, medicines, clothing, supplies and other things necessary and convenient for the officers, employees, workmen and laborers in the service and employ of the United States and for their families. If any such articles are disposed of for use outside of the zone and auxiliary lands granted to the United States and within the territory of the Republic, they shall be subject to the same import or other duties as like articles imported under the laws of the Republic of Panama.

ARTICLE XIV

As the price or compensation for the rights, powers and privileges granted in this convention by the Republic of Panama to the United States, the Government of the United States agrees to pay to the Republic of Panama the sum of ten million dollars ($10,000,000) in gold coin of the United States on the exchange of the ratification of this convention and also an annual payment during the life of this convention of two hundred and fifty thousand dollars ($250,000) in like gold coin, beginning nine years after the date aforesaid.

The provisions of this Article shall be in addition to all other benefits assured to the Republic of Panama under this convention.

But no delay or difference opinion under this Article or any other provisions of this treaty shall affect or interrupt the full operation and effect of this convention in all other respects.

ARTICLE XV

The joint commission referred to in Article VI shall be established as follows:

The President of the United States shall nominate two persons and the President of the Republic of Panama shall nominate two persons and they shall proceed to a decision; but in case of disagreement of the Commission (by reason of their being equally divided in conclusion) an umpire shall be appointed by tire two Governments who shall render the decision. In the event of the death, absence, or incapacity of a Commissioner or Umpire, or of his omitting, declining or ceasing to act, his place shall be filled by the appointment of another person in the manner above indicated. All decisions by a majority of the Commission or by the Umpire shall be final.

ARTICLE XVIII

The Canal, when constructed, and the entrances thereto shall be neutral in perpetuity, and shall be opened upon the terms provided for by Section I of Article three of, and in conformity with all the stipulations of, the treaty entered into by the Governments of the United States and Great Britain on November 18,1901.

ARTICLE XIX

The Government of the Republic of Panama shall have the right to transport over the Canal its vessels and its troops and munitions of war in such vessels at all times without paying charges of any kind. The exemption is to be extended to the auxiliary railway for the transportation of persons in the service of the Republic of Panama, or of the police force charged with the preservation of public order outside of said zone, as well as to their baggage, munitions of war and supplies.

ARTICLE XXI

The rights and privileges granted by the Republic of Panama to the United States in the preceding Articles are understood to be free of all anterior debts, liens, trusts, or liabilities, or concessions or privileges to other Governments, corporations, syndicates or individuals, and consequently, if there should arise any claims on account of the present concessions and privileges or otherwise, the claimants shall resort to the Government of the Republic of Panama and not to the United States for any indemnity or compromise which may be required.

ARTICLE XXII

The Republic of Panama renounces and grants to the United States the participation to which it might be entitled in the future earnings of the Canal under Article XV of the concessionary contract with Lucien N. B. Wyse now owned by the New Panama Canal Company and any and all other rights or claims of a pecuniary nature arising under or relating to said concession, or arising under or relating to the concessions to the Panama Railroad Company or any extension or modification thereof; and it likewise renounces, confirms and grants to the United States, now and hereafter, all the rights and property reserved in the said concessions which otherwise would belong to Panama at or before the expiration of the terms of ninety-nine years of the concessions granted to or held by the above mentioned party and companies, and all right, title and interest which it now has or many hereafter have, in and to the lands, canal, works, property and rights held by the said companies under said concessions or otherwise, and acquired or to be acquired by the United States from or through the New Panama Canal Company, including any property and rights which might or may in the future either by lapse of time, forfeiture or otherwise, revert to the Republic of Panama, under any contracts or concessions, with said Wyse, the Universal Panama Canal Company, the Panama Railroad Company and the New Panama Canal Company.

The aforesaid rights and property shall be and are free and released from any present or reversionary interest in or claims of Panama and the title of the United States thereto upon consummation of the contemplated purchase by the United States from the New Panama Canal (company, shall be absolute, so far as concerns the Republic of Panama, excepting always the rights of the Republic specifically secured under this treaty.

ARTICLE XXIII

If it should become necessary at any time to employ armed forces for the safety or protection of the Canal, or of the ships that make use of the same, or the railways and auxiliary works, the United States shall have the right, at all times and in its discretion, to use its police and its land and naval forces or to establish fortifications for these purposes.

ARTICLE XXIV

No change either in the Government or in the laws and treaties of the Republic of Panama shall, without the consent of the United States, affect any right of the United States under the present convention, or under any treaty stipulation between the two countries that now exists or may hereafter exist touching the subject matter of this convention.

If the Republic of Panama shall hereafter enter as a constituent into any other Government or into any union or confederation of states, so as to merge her sovereignty or independence in such Government, union or confederation, the rights of the United States under this convention shall not be in any respect lessened or impaired.

ARTICLE XXV

For the better performance of the engagements of this convention and to the end of the efficient protection of the Canal and the preservation of its neutrality, the Government of the Republic of Panama will sell or lease to the United States lands adequate and necessary for naval or coaling stations on the Pacific coast and on the western Caribbean coast of the Republic at certain points to be agreed upon with the President of the United States.

Convention Between the United Kingdom and China Respecting an Extension of Hong Kong
   Territory
of 1898
Ratification: Exchanged at London on 6 August 1898

WHEREAS it has for many years past been recognized that an extension of Hong Kong territory is necessary for the proper defence and protection of the Colony,

It has now been agreed between the Governments of Great Britain and China that the limits
of British territory shall be enlarged under lease to the extent indicated generally on the annexed
map. The exact boundaries shall be hereafter fixed when proper surveys have been made by officials appointed by the two Governments. The term of this lease shall be ninety-nine years.

It is at the same time agreed that within the city of Kowloon the Chinese officials now stationed
there shall continue to exercise jurisdiction except so far as may be inconsistent with the military
requirements for the defence of Hong Kong. Within the remainder of the newly leased territory
Great Britain shall have sole jurisdiction. Chinese officials and people shall be allowed as hereto-
fore to use the road from Kowloon to Hsinan.

It is further agreed that the existing landing-place near Kowloon city shall be reserved for the
convenience of Chinese men-of-war, merchant and passenger vessels, which may come and go
and lie there at their pleasure; and for the convenience of movement of the officials and people
within the city.

When hereafter China constructs a railway to the boundary of the Kowloon territory under
British control, arrangements shall be discussed.

It is further understood that there will be no expropriation or expulsion of the inhabitants of the
district included within the extension, and that if land is required for public offices, fortifications,
or the like official purposes, it shall be bought at a fair price.

If cases of extradition of criminals occur, they shall be dealt with in accordance with the existing
Treaties between Great Britain and China and the Hong Kong Regulations.

The area leased to Great Britain as shown on the annexed map, includes the waters of Mirs
Bay and Deep Bay, but it is agreed that Chinese vessels of war, whether neutral or otherwise, shall
retain the right to use those waters.

This Convention shall come into force on the first day of July, eighteen hundred and nine-
ty-eight, being the thirteenth day of the fifth moon of the twenty-fourth year of Kuang Hsü. It shall
be ratified by the Sovereigns of the two countries, and the ratifications shall be exchanged in
London as soon as possible.

Free navigation

Convention Respecting the Free Navigation of the Suez Maritime Canal
Signed: at Constantinople, 29 October 1888
Entry into force: According to ARTICLE XVII, the '[t]reaty shall be ratified, and the ratifications
   shall be exchanged at Constantinople, within the space of one month, or sooner, if possible.'

ARTICLE I

The Suez Maritime Canal shall always be free and of commerce or of war, without distinction of flag.

Consequently, the High Contracting Parties agree not in any way to interfere with the free use of the Canal, in time of war as in time of peace.

The Canal shall never be subjected to the exercise of the right of blockade.

ARTICLE IV

The Maritime Canal remaining open in time of war as a free passage, even to ships of war of belligerents, according to the terms of Article I of the present Treaty, the High Contracting Parties agree that no right of war, no act of hostility, nor any act having for its object to obstruct the free navigating of the Canal, shall be committed in the Canal and its ports, even though the Ottoman Empire should be one of the belligerent Powers.

Vessels of war of belligerents shall not re-victual or take in stores in the Canal and its ports of access, except in so far may be strictly necessary. The transit of the aforesaid vessels through the Canal shall be affected with the least possible delay, in accordance with the Regulations in force, and without any intermission than the resulting from the necessities of the service.

Their stay at Port Said and in the roadstead of Suez shall not exceed twenty-four hours, except in case if distress. In such case they shall be bound to leave as soon as possible. An interval of twenty-four hours shall always elapse between the sailing of a belligerent ship from one of the ports of access and the departure of a ship belonging to the hostile Power.

ARTICLE V

In time of war belligerent Powers shall not disembark nor embark within the Canal and its ports of access either troops, munitions, or materials of war. But in case of an accidental hindrance in the Canal, men may be embarked or disembarked at the ports of access by detachments not exceeding 1,000 men, with a corresponding amount of war material.

ARTICLE VI

Prizes shall be subjected, in all respects, to the same rules as the vessels of war of belligerents.

ARTICLE VII

The Powers shall not keep any vessel of war in the waters of the Canal (including lake Timsah and the Bitter Lakes).

Nevertheless, they may station vessel of war in the ports of access of Port Said and Suez, the number of which shall not exceed two for each power.

This right shall not be exercised by belligerents.

ARTICLE VIII

The agents in Egypt of the Signatory Powers of the present Treaty shall be charged to watch over its execution. In case of any event threatening the security or the free passage of the Canal, they shall meet on the summons of three of their number under the presidency of their Doyen, in order to proceed to the necessary verifications. They shall inform the Khedivial Government of the danger which they may have perceived, in order that that Government may take proper steps to insure the protection and the free use of the Canal. Under any circumstances, they shall meet once a year to take note of the due execution of the Treaty.

The last mentioned meetings shall take place under the presidency of a Special Commissioner nominated for that purpose by the Imperial Ottoman Government. A Commissioner of the Khedive may also take part in the meeting, and may preside over it in case of the absence of the Ottoman Commissioner.

They shall especially demand the suppression of any work or the dispersion of any assemblage on either bank of the Canal, the object or effect of which might be to interfere with the liberty and the entire security of the navigation.

Article XII

The High Contracting Parties, by application of the principle of equality as regards the free use of the Canal, a principle which forms one of the bases of the present Treaty, agree that none of them shall endeavour to obtain with respect to the Canal territorial or commercial advantages or privileges in any international arrangements which may be concluded. Moreover, the rights of Turkey as the territorial Power are reserved.

Article XV

The stipulations of the present Treaty shall not interfere with the sanitary measures in force in Egypt.

Free navigation

Treaty Concerning the Permanent Neutrality and Operation of the Panama Canal
Signed: 7 September 1977
Entry into force: According to Article VIII, 'six calendar months from the date of the exchange of the instruments of ratification.'

Article I

The Republic of Panama declares that the Canal, as an international transit waterway, shall be permanently neutral in accordance with the regime established in this Treaty. The same regime of neutrality shall apply to any other international waterway that may be built either partially or wholly in the territory of the Republic of Panama.

Article II

The Republic of Panama declares the neutrality of the Canal in order that both in time of peace and in time of war it shall remain secure and open to peaceful transit by the vessels of all nations on terms of entire equality, so that there will be no discrimination against any nation, or its citizens or subjects, concerning the conditions or charges of transit, or for any other reason, and so that the Canal, and therefore the Isthmus of Panama, shall not be the target of reprisals in any armed conflict between other nations of the world. The foregoing shall be subject to the following requirements:

(a) Payment of tolls and other charges for transit and ancillary services, provided they have been fixed in conformity with the provisions of Article III (c);

(b) Compliance with applicable rules and regulations, provided such rules and regulations are applied in conformity with the provisions of Article III;

(c) The requirement that transiting vessels commit no acts of hostility while in the Canal; and

(d) Such other conditions and restrictions as are established by this Treaty.

Article III

1 For purposes of the security, efficiency and proper maintenance of the Canal the following rules shall apply:

(a) The Canal shall be operated efficiently in accordance with conditions of transit through the Canal, and rules and regulations that shall be just, equitable and reasonable, and limited to those necessary for safe navigation and efficient, sanitary operation of the Canal;

(b) Ancillary services necessary for transit through the Canal shall be provided;

(c) Tolls and other charges for transit and ancillary services shall be just, reasonable, equitable and consistent with the principles of international law;

(d) As a pre-condition of transit, vessels may be required to establish clearly the financial responsibility and guarantees for payment of reasonable and adequate indemnification, consistent with international practice and standards, for damages resulting from acts or omissions of such vessels when passing through the Canal. In the case of vessels owned or operated by a State or for which it has acknowledged responsibility, a certification by that State that it shall observe its obligations under international law to pay for damages resulting from the act or omission of such vessels when passing through the Canal shall be deemed sufficient to establish such financial responsibility;

(e) Vessels of war and auxiliary vessels of all nations shall at all times be entitled to transit the Canal, irrespective of their internal operation, means of propulsion, origin, destination or armament, without being subjected, as a condition of transit, to inspection, search for surveillance. However, such vessels may be required to certify that they have complied with all applicable health, sanitation and quarantine regulations. In addition, such vessels shall be entitled to refuse to disclose their internal operation, origin, armament, cargo or destination. However, auxiliary vessels may be required to present written assurances, certified by an official at a high level of the government of the State requesting the exemption, that they are owned or operated by that government and in this case are being used only on government non-commercial service.

Article IV

The United States of America and the Republic of Panama agree to maintain the regime of neutrality established in this Treaty, which shall be maintained in order that the Canal shall remain permanently neutral, notwithstanding the termination of any other treaties entered into by the two Contracting Parties.

Article V

After the termination of the Panama Canal Treaty, only the Republic of Panama shall operate the Canal and maintain military forces, defense sites and military installations within its national territory.

Article VI

1   In recognition of the important contributions of the United States of America and of the Republic of Panama to the construction, operation, maintenance, and protection and defense of the Canal, vessels of war and auxiliary vessels of those nations shall, notwithstanding any other provisions of this Treaty, be entitled to transit the Canal irrespective of their internal operation, means of propulsion, origin, destination, armament or cargo carried. Such vessels of war and auxiliary vessels will be entitled to transit the Canal expeditiously.

2   The United States of America, so long as it has responsibility for the operation of the Canal, may continue to provide the Republic of Colombia toll-free transit through the Canal for its troops, vessels and materials of war. Thereafter, the Republic of Panama may provide the Republic of Colombia and the Republic of Costa Rica with the right of toll-free transit.

Article VII

1   The United States of America and the Republic of Panama shall jointly sponsor a resolution in the Organization of American States opening to accession by all nations of the world the Protocol to this Treaty whereby all the signatories will adhere to the objective of this Treaty, agreeing to respect the regime of neutrality set forth herein.

2   The Organization of American States shall act as the depositary for this Treaty and related instruments.

Article VIII

This Treaty shall be subject to ratification in accordance with the constitutional procedures of the two Parties. The instruments of ratification of this Treaty shall be exchanged at Panama at the same time as the instruments of ratification of the Panama Canal Treaty, signed this date, are exchanged. This Treaty shall enter into force, simultaneously with the Panama Canal Treaty, six calendar months from the date of the exchange of the instruments of ratification.

Free navigation

Protocol to the Treaty Concerning the Permanent Neutrality and Operation of the Panama Canal of 1977
Accession: open to accession by all states of the world at the OAS General Secretariat
Entry into force: For each state at the time of deposit of its instrument of accession[1010]

Article I

The Contracting Parties hereby acknowledge the regime of permanent neutrality for the Canal established in the Treaty Concerning the Permanent Neutrality and Operation or the Panama Canal and associate themselves with its objectives.

Article II

The Contracting Parties agree to observe and respect the regime of permanent neutrality of the Canal in time of war as in time of peace, and to ensure that vessels of their registry strictly observe the applicable rules.

1010   See <www.oas.org/juridico/english/Sigs/h-9.html> accessed 17 March 2021.

Article III

This Protocol shall be open to accession by all states of the world, and shall enter into force for each State at the time of deposit of its instrument of accession with the Secretary General of the Organisation of American States.

Free navigation
Danube Commission

Convention Regarding the Regime of Navigation on the Danube
of 1948
Entry into force: 11 May 1949 *Non-official version*[1011]

CHAPTER I
GENERAL PROVISIONS

Article 1

Navigation on the Danube shall be free and open for the nationals, vessels of commerce and goods of all States, on a footing of equality in regard to port and navigation charges and conditions for merchant shipping. The foregoing shall not apply to traffic between ports of the same State.

Article 2

The regime established by this Convention shall apply to the navigable part of the Danube River between Ulm and the Black Sea through the Sulina arm, with outlet to the sea through the Sulina channel.

Article 3

The Danubian States undertake to maintain their sections of the Danube in a navigable condition for river-going and, on the appropriate sections, for sea-going vessels, to carry out the works necessary for the maintenance and improvement of navigation conditions and not to obstruct or hinder navigation on the navigable channels of the Danube. The Danubian States shall consult the Danube Commission (art. 5) on matters referred to in this article.

The riparian States may, within their own jurisdiction, undertake works for the maintenance of navigation, the execution of which is necessitated by urgent and unforeseen circumstances. The States shall inform the Commission of the reasons which have necessitated the works, and shall furnish a summary description thereof.

Article 4

Should a Danubian State be unable itself to undertake works within its own territorial jurisdiction which are necessary for the maintenance of normal navigation it shall be bound to allow the Danube Commission (art. 5) to carry them out under conditions determined by the Commission,

---

1011 <www.danubecommission.org/dc/en/danube-commission/convention-regarding-the-regime-of-navigation-on-the-danube/> accessed 17 March 2021.

which may not entrust the execution of such works to another State unless the section in question of the waterway forms the frontier of such State. In the latter case, the Commission shall decide the conditions on which the works shall be carried out.

The Danubian States agree to afford the Commission or the State executing the said works all necessary assistance.

CHAPTER II
ADMINISTRATIVE PROVISIONS

Section I. The Danube Commission

Article 5

There shall be established a Danube Commission, hereinafter called "the Commission", to consist of one representative of each Danubian State.

Article 6

The Commission shall elect from among its members a chairman, a vice-chairman and a secretary for a term of three years.

Article 7

The Commission shall determine the times of its meetings and its own rules of procedure.

The first meeting of the Commission shall be held within six months after the entry into force of the present Convention.

Article 8

The jurisdiction of the Commission shall extend to the Danube as defined in article 2.

The functions of the Commission shall be:

(a) to supervise the implementation of the provisions of this Convention;
(b) to prepare a general plan of the principal works called for in the interests of navigation on the basis of proposals and projects presented by the Danubian States and the Special River Administrations (articles 20 and 21), and likewise to draw up a general budget in connection with such works;
(c) to execute the works in the cases provided for in article 4;
(d) to consult with, and make recommendations to the Danubian States in respect of the execution of the works referred to in paragraph (b) of this article, with due consideration for the technical and economic interests, plans and possibilities of the respective States;
(e) to consult with, and make recommendations to the Special River Administrations (articles 20 and 21), and to exchange information with them;
(f) to establish a uniform system of standards on the whole navigable portion of the Danube and to lay down the basic provisions governing navigation on the Danube, including those governing the pilot service, with due consideration for the specific conditions obtaining on particular sections;
(g) to unify the regulations governing river inspection;
(h) to co-ordinate the hydro-meteorological services on the Danube, and to publish a single hydrological bulletin and short-term and long-term hydrological forecasts for the Danube;

(i) to produce statistics on aspects of navigation on the Danube within the competence of the Commission;

(j) to publish reference works, sailing directions, navigational charts and atlases for purposes of navigation;

(k) to prepare and approve the budget of the Commission and to fix and levy the charges provided for in article 10.

Article 9

In order to carry out the tasks referred to in the foregoing article, the Commission shall have its own secretariat and the necessary office services, the staff of which shall be recruited from nationals of the Danubian States.

The organization of the secretariat and services shall be determined by the Commission itself.

Article 10

The Commission shall draw up its budget and approve it by a majority vote of all its members. The budget shall provide for the expenses for the maintenance of the Commission and its services, to be met by equal contributions from the Danubian States, payable annually.

In order to defray the cost of executing special works for the maintenance or improvement of navigability, the Commission may establish special charges.

Article 11

The Commission's decisions shall be taken by a majority of the members present, unless otherwise specifically provided for in this Convention (articles 10, 12 and 13).

Five members of the Commission shall constitute a quorum.

Article 12

The Commission's decisions on matters provided for in article 8, paragraphs (b), (c), (f) and (g) shall be taken by a majority vote of all members of the Commission but without outvoting the State of the territory on which the works are to be carried out.

Article 14

The Commission shall have the rights of a legal entity in accordance with the laws of the State in which the Commission has its seat.

Article 15

The official languages of the Commission shall be Russian and French.

Article 16

Members of the Commission and officers authorized by it shall enjoy diplomatic immunity. Its official buildings, archives and documents of all kinds shall be inviolable.

CHAPTER III
REGIME OF NAVIGATION

Section I. Navigation

Article 23

Navigation on the lower part of the Danube and in the Iron Gates section shall be carried out in accordance with the regulations on navigation established by the Administrations of the respective sections. Navigation on other parts of the Danube shall be carried out in accordance with the regulations established by the respective Danubian States through whose territory the Danube flows and, in those sections where the banks of the Danube belong to two different States, in accordance with the regulations established by agreement between such States.

In establishing regulations on navigation, the Danubian States and Administrations shall have regard to the basic provisions governing navigation on the Danube established by the Commission.

Antarctic

Antarctic Treaty
of 1959.
Entry into force: 23 June 1961

Article I

1   Antarctica shall be used for peaceful purposes only. There shall be prohibited, inter alia, any measures of a military nature, such as the establishment of military bases and fortifications, the carrying out of military maneuvers, as well as the testing of any types of weapons.
2   The present Treaty shall not prevent the use of military personnel or equipment for scientific research or for any other peaceful purpose.

Article II

Freedom of scientific investigation in Antarctica and co-operation towards that end, as applied during the International Geophysical Year, shall continue, subject to the provisions of the present Treaty.

Article III

1   In order to promote international co-operation in scientific investigation in Antarctica, as provided for in Article II of the present Treaty, the Contracting Parties agree that, to the greatest extent feasible and practicable:

a)   information regarding plans for scientific programs in Antarctica shall be exchanged to permit maximum economy and efficiency of operations;
b)   scientific personnel shall be exchanged in Antarctica between expeditions and stations;
c)   scientific observations and results from Antarctica shall be exchanged and made freely available.

2   In implementing this Article, every encouragement shall be given to the establishment of co-operative working relations with those Specialized Agencies of the United Nations and other international organizations having a scientific or technical interest in Antarctica.

Article IV

1 Nothing contained in the present Treaty shall be interpreted as:

    a) a renunciation by any Contracting Party of previously asserted rights of or claims to territorial sovereignty in Antarctica;

    b) a renunciation or diminution by any Contracting Party of any basis of claim to territorial sovereignty in Antarctica which it may have whether as a result of its activities or those of its nationals in Antarctica, or otherwise;

    c) prejudicing the position of any Contracting Party as regards its recognition or nonrecognition of any other State's right of or claim or basis of claim to territorial sovereignty in Antarctica.

2 No acts or activities taking place while the present Treaty is in force shall constitute a basis for asserting, supporting or denying a claim to territorial sovereignty in Antarctica or create any rights of sovereignty in Antarctica. No new claim, or enlargement of an existing claim, to territorial sovereignty in Antarctica shall be asserted while the present Treaty is in force.

Article V

1 Any nuclear explosions in Antarctica and the disposal there of radioactive waste material shall be prohibited.

2 In the event of the conclusion of international agreements concerning the use of nuclear energy, including nuclear explosions and the disposal of radioactive waste material, to which all the Contracting Parties whose representatives are entitled to participate in the meetings provided for under Article IX are parties, the rules established under such agreements shall apply in Antarctica.

Article VI

The provisions of the present Treaty shall apply to the area south of 60° South Latitude, including all ice shelves, but nothing in the present Treaty shall prejudice or in any way affect the rights, or the exercise of the rights, of any State under international law with regard to the high seas within that area.

Article VII

1 In order to promote the objectives and ensure the observance of the provisions of the present Treaty, each Contracting Party whose representatives are entitled to participate in the meetings referred to in Article IX of the Treaty shall have the right to designate observers to carry out any inspection provided for by the present Article. Observers shall be nationals of the Contracting Parties which designate them. The names of observers shall be communicated to every other Contracting Party having the right to designate observers, and like notice shall be given of the termination of their appointment.

2 Each observer designated in accordance with the provisions of paragraph 1 of this Article shall have complete freedom of access at any time to any or all areas of Antarctica.

3 All areas of Antarctica, including all stations, installations and equipment within those areas, and all ships and aircraft at points of discharging or embarking cargoes or personnel in

Antarctica, shall be open at all times to inspection by any observers designated in accordance with paragraph 1 of this article.

4   Aerial observation may be carried out at any time over any or all areas of Antarctica by any of the Contracting Parties having the right to designate observers.

5   Each Contracting Party shall, at the time when the present Treaty enters into force for it, inform the other Contracting Parties, and thereafter shall give them notice in advance, of

a)   all expeditions to and within Antarctica, on the part of its ships or nationals, and all expeditions to Antarctica organized in or proceeding from its territory;

b)   all stations in Antarctica occupied by its nationals; and

c)   any military personnel or equipment intended to be introduced by it into Antarctica subject to the conditions prescribed in paragraph 2 of Article I of the present Treaty.

Article VIII

1   In order to facilitate the exercise of their functions under the present Treaty, and without prejudice to the respective positions of the Contracting Parties relating to jurisdiction over all other persons in Antarctica, observers designated under paragraph 1 of Article VII and scientific personnel exchanged under subparagraph 1 (b) of Article III of the Treaty, and members of the staffs accompanying any such persons, shall be subject only to the jurisdiction of the Contracting Party of which they are nationals in respect of all acts or omissions occurring while they are in Antarctica for the purpose of exercising their functions.

2   Without prejudice to the provisions of paragraph 1 of this Article, and pending the adoption of measures in pursuance of subparagraph 1 (e) of Article IX, the Contracting Parties concerned in any case of dispute with regard to the exercise of jurisdiction in Antarctica shall immediately consult together with a view to reaching a mutually acceptable solution.

Arctic

Declaration on the establishment of the Arctic Council
(Ottawa Declaration) of 1996

The representatives of the Governments of Canada, Denmark, Finland, Iceland, Norway, the Russian Federation, Sweden and the United States of America (hereinafter referred as the Arctic States) meeting in Ottawa . . .

HEREBY DECLARE

1   The Arctic Council is established as a high level forum to:

a   provide a means for promoting cooperation, coordination and interaction among the Arctic States, with the involvement of the Arctic indigenous communities and other Arctic inhabitants on common arctic issues, in particular issues of sustainable development and environmental protection in the Arctic.

b   oversee and coordinate the programs established under the AEPS on the Arctic Monitoring and Assessment Program (AMAP); conservation of Arctic Flora and Fauna (CAFF); Protection of the Arctic Marine Environment (PAME); and Emergency Preparedness and Response (EPPR).

c   adopt terms of reference for and oversee and coordinate a sustainable development program.

d   disseminate information, encourage education and promote interest in Arctic-related issues.

2   Members of the Arctic Council are: Canada, Denmark, Finland, Iceland, Norway, the Russian Federation, Sweden and the United States of America (the Arctic States).

The Inuit Circumpolar Conference, the Saami Council and the Association of Indigenous Minorities in the Far north, Siberia, the Far East of the Russian Federation are Permanent Participants in the Arctic Council. Permanent participation is equally open to other Arctic organizations of indigenous peoples with majority Arctic indigenous constituency, representing:

a   a single indigenous people resident in more than one arctic State; or

b   more than one Arctic indigenous people resident in a single Arctic State.

The determination that such an organization has met this criterion is to be made by decision of the Council. The number of Permanent Participants should at any time be less than the number of members.

The category of Permanent Participation is created to provide for active participation and full consultation with the Arctic indigenous representatives within the Arctic Council.

3   Observer status in the Arctic Council is open to:

a   Non-arctic states;

b   inter-governmental and inter-parliamentary organizations, global and regional; and

c   non-governmental organizations

that the Council determines can contribute to its work.

4   The Council should normally meet on a biennial basis, with meetings of senior officials taking place more frequently, to provide for liaison and coordination. Each arctic State should designate a focal point on matters related to the Arctic Council.

5   Responsibility for hosting meetings of the Arctic Council, including provision of secretariat functions, should rotate sequentially among the Arctic States.

6   The Arctic Council, as its first order of business, should adopt rules of procedure for its meetings and those of its working groups.

7   Decisions of the Arctic Council are to be by consensus of the Members.

8   The Indigenous Peoples' secretariat established under AEPS is to continue under the framework of the Arctic Council.

9   The Arctic Council should regularly review the priorities and financing of its programs and associated structures.

THEREFORE, we the undersigned representatives of our respective Governments, recognizing the Arctic Council's political significance and intending to promote its results, have signed this declaration.

The law of the sea

DOI: 10.4324/9781003213772-13

THE COMPLEX APPROACH

inland waters
enclosed or semi-enclosed seas
mare liberum
De Jure Belli ac Pacis
mare clausum
internal waters
territorial sea
exclusive economic zone
contiguous zone
continental shelf
deep seabed
Area
archipelagic waters
United Nations Convention on the Law of the Sea
Third UN Conference on the Law of the Sea
constitution of the oceans
land-locked states

The scope of the application of the law of the sea

As a separate area (branch) of international law, the law of the sea regulates the activities of the subjects on the sea (the ocean). The 'sea' (the ocean), in terms of the international law of the sea, is a whole which unites all marine spaces naturally connected with each other on our planet. At the same time, the sea in this context includes the seabed and the subsoil, the adjacent waters, and the airspace above the sea.

As a result, waters not connected with the single marine space with at least a narrow outlet are generally beyond the scope of application of the international law of the sea.[1012]

Consequently, the **inland waters** (rivers, lakes, and other land-locked waters) of the states, even if such inland waters are shared by two or more states, fall within the scope of regulation of another field of international law – 'territory (in international law)' or 'international law of territory' (discussed earlier in this book).

1012 'Moreover, in order to freely and naturally communicate through the ocean, the water level must essentially be the same. Indeed, it appears to be unreasonable to argue that rules of the law of the sea are applicable to a distinct body of water at an altitude different from sea level, such as a lake located in a mountain several hundred or even thousand metres high. It must be concluded, therefore, that rivers and lakes are part of terrestrial territory and are not governed by the law of the sea.' Yoshifumi Tanaka, *The International Law of the Sea* (2nd edn, Cambridge University Press 2015), Scope of the oceans in the law of the sea.

On the other hand, the **enclosed or semi-enclosed seas** – 'a gulf, basin or sea surrounded by two or more states and connected to another sea or the ocean by a narrow outlet or consisting entirely or primarily of the territorial seas and exclusive economic zones of two or more coastal States'[1013] – are embraced by the universal framework of the law of the sea, although the states concerned usually establish regional norms of international law to regulate particular activities (relating to, inter alia, the management, conservation, exploration, and exploitation of the living resources) on such seas.[1014]

Mare liberum and mare clausum

Historically, there were two main and, at the same time, competing approaches concerning the legal status of the sea:

1   The first approach regarded the seas as a domain of the freedom of commerce and navigation. It is rooted in the Roman law and was called the **mare liberum** (free sea) doctrine. In 1609, Hugo Grotius wrote his *Mare Liberum*, in which he advocated the unrestricted right of all ships to use all waters. A more comprehensive formulation of his early ideas regarding the *mare liberum* was presented in his great work **De Jure Belli ac Pacis** (*On the Law of War and Peace*), which had a significant impact on the overall development of international law.
2   The second approach, in contrast, maintained state dominion over the seas. It considered the sea a subject of occupation and sovereignty in the same manner as any area of a land territory of the solid earth. This approach was called the **mare clausum** (closed sea) doctrine. An important book on this subject by the English jurist John Selden (1584–1654), *Mare Clausum*, appeared in 1635 to justify the English claims to the surrounding seas.

The modern international law of the sea is a very complex composition which incorporates ideas from both these two approaches, where *mare clausum* prevails over the internal waters and territorial sea and *mare liberum* obtains precedence gradually by moving from the coast towards the high seas.

Therefore, for legal purposes, the sea, which covers more than 70% of the surface of the globe, was divided into:

*   The domain of the *mare clausum*:

    *   **Internal waters**, which are under the full sovereignty of the coastal state; and
    *   **Territorial sea**, which is also under the sovereignty of the coastal state but includes one specific right of the *mare liberum*.

1013 Article 122 of the United Nations Convention on the Law of the Sea.
1014 For example, concerning the Black Sea, the passage through Turkish Straits – the Bosphorus, and Dardanelles is regulated by the Montreux Convention of 1936 (the Convention Regarding the Regime of the Straits), which, however, can be challenged to a significant degree when Turkey completes its new Canal Istanbul and if the states concerned do not come to an agreement on the extension of the current legal regime to the Canal.

- The domain of the *mare liberum*:

  - **Exclusive economic zone**, including **contiguous zone**, where only certain sovereign rights of a coastal state apply; and
  - High seas.

Modern international law also outlines other distinct zones where specific legal regimes apply. Two of them, which concern the seabed and subsoil – the **continental shelf** and **deep seabed** (also referred to as the **Area**) – are primarily in the domain of the *mare liberum* while in the **archipelagic waters**, introduced in relation to the so-called archipelagic states, the approach of *mare clausum* prevails.

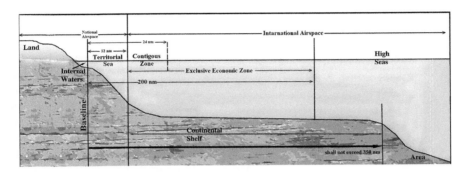

FIGURE 13.1 Maritime zones

United Nations Convention on the Law of the Sea

The 1982 **United Nations Convention on the Law of the Sea** is a global treaty that resulted from the **Third UN Conference on the Law of the Sea** (UNCLOS III), which took place between 1973 and 1982. This Convention is regarded to be the **constitution of the oceans** and represents a comprehensive agreement, which replaced among its parties (along with the states, the parties to the Convention may also be some other subjects of international law,[1015]

1015 According to Article 305 of the United Nations Convention on the Law of the Sea: '1. This Convention shall be open for signature by: (a) all States; (b) Namibia, represented by the United Nations Council for Namibia; (c) all self-governing associated States which have chosen that status in an act of self-determination supervised and approved by the United Nations in accordance with General Assembly resolution 1514 (XV) and which have competence over the matters governed by this Convention, including the competence to enter into treaties in respect of those matters; (d) all self-governing associated States which, in accordance with their respective instruments of association, have competence over the matters governed by this Convention, including the competence to enter into treaties in respect of those matters; (e) all territories which enjoy full internal self-government, recognized as such by the United Nations, but have not attained full independence in accordance with General Assembly resolution 1514 (XV) and which have competence over the matters governed by this Convention, including the competence to enter into treaties in respect of those matters; (f) international organizations, in accordance with Annex IX.'

and the term 'States Parties' *mutatis mutandis*[1016] refers to such subjects as well) the earlier treaties (the four 1958 Conventions)[1017] and the existing customary norms on that matter.

The United Nations Convention on the Law of the Sea is intended to govern the use of seas, and it is one of the most complete treaties in public international law, covering a wide range of topics regulating almost all aspects related to the law of the sea (e.g. delimitation of maritime boundaries; use of marine areas, including the airspace above and the seabed and subsoil below; marine environment protection; marine scientific research; right of access of **land-locked states** to and from the sea and freedom of transit; and so forth.

INTERNAL WATERS

baseline
normal baseline
straight baseline
baselines in special cases
closing line
Fisheries case
waters of the port
outermost permanent harbour works
Maritime Delimitation in the Black Sea case
distress
International Convention on Maritime Search and Rescue
merchant ships
flag state
good order of the coastal state
warships
government vessels used for non-commercial purposes

Definition of internal waters

Internal waters are commonly described with respect to the territorial sea as the waters inside the inner limit of the territorial sea. According to the formulation of the United Nations Convention on the Law of the Sea, 'waters on the landward side of the **baseline** of the territorial sea form part of the internal waters of the State.'[1018]

1016 A medieval Latin phrase 'denoting that a statement applies to matters or things other than those mentioned, with appropriate alterations or adjustments as to the particularities or details.' *Guide to Latin in International Law* (n 71) 189.

1017 Convention on the Territorial Sea and the Contiguous Zone, Convention on the Continental Shelf, Convention on Fishing and the Conservation of the Living Resources of the High Seas, Convention on the High Seas.

1018 Article 8 (1) of the United Nations Convention on the Law of the Sea.

Baselines

The Convention identifies the following methods of determining the baselines, which may be applied in combination:

- **Normal baseline** is a primary method. It is 'the low-water line along the coast as marked on large-scale charts officially recognized by the coastal State.'[1019] In the case of islands situated on atolls or having fringing reefs, the baseline is 'the seaward low-water line of the reef'.
- The **straight baseline** method is applied in highly complicated coastal configurations when the primary method of normal baseline can be replaced – namely, in 'localities where the coastline is deeply indented and cut into, or if there is a fringe of islands along the coast in its immediate vicinity' or where, because of the presence of a delta and other natural conditions, the coastline is highly unstable. However, the drawing of straight baselines:
  - should not depart to any appreciable extent from the general direction of the coast;
  - must sufficiently closely link the sea areas lying within the lines to the mainland of that state;
  - shall not be drawn to and from low-tide elevations unless lighthouses or similar installations, which are permanently above sea level, have been built on them or except in cases of general international recognition;
  - shall take into account the economic interests of the region concerned; and
  - generally, should not be realised 'in such a manner as to cut off the territorial sea of another State from the high seas or an exclusive economic zone.'[1020]

    It is noteworthy that in practice, application of the straight baselines became debatable stipulating conflict of interpretations.[1021]

- **Baselines in special cases**
  - Mouths of rivers – in cases when 'a river flows directly into the sea, the baseline shall be a straight line across the mouth of the river between points on the low-water line of its banks.'[1022]

1019 'The level of the low-water line relies on the tidal datum. Tidal datum has several definitions and the selection is left to the discretion of each State. Obviously the lower the low-water line selected, the further seaward the normal baseline will lie. However, the impact of a lower-tidal datum will be minimal, unless there is a significant tidal range.' Tanaka (n 1012) Normal baselines.

1020 Articles 5, 6, 7 of the United Nations Convention on the Law of the Sea.

1021 'Almost all East Asian coastal countries (i.e. Burma, Cambodia, China, Japan, North Korea, South Korea, Malaysia, the Philippines, Russian Federation, Taiwan, Thailand and Vietnam) have implemented a straight baseline system. In most cases, the use of straight baselines has been controversial'. Sam Bateman and Clive Schofield, 'State Practice Regarding Straight Baselines in East Asia: Legal, Technical and Political Issues in a Changing Environment' <https://bit.ly/2A6QQNX> accessed 20 December 2021.

1022 Article 9 of the United Nations Convention on the Law of the Sea.

- Bays – if the coasts of a bay belong to a single state and 'the distance between the low-water marks of the natural entrance points of a bay does not exceed 24 nautical miles,[1023] a **closing line** may be drawn between these two low-water marks, and the waters enclosed thereby shall be considered as internal waters.'[1024] On the other hand, when the distance between the low-water marks of the natural entrance points of a bay is more than 24 nautical miles, a straight baseline of 24 nautical miles shall be drawn within the bay. However, there is an exception to the '24 nautical miles rule' concerning so-called 'historic bays' which exceed the established limit but are traditionally regarded to be the internal waters of a given state. As articulated by the ICJ in the well-known [Anglo-Norwegian] *Fisheries* **case** *(United Kingdom v Norway)*, which highly influenced the development of certain rules concerning the baselines in the law of the sea: 'By "historic waters" are usually meant waters which are treated as internal waters but which would not have that character were it not for the existence of a historic title.'[1025]
- Ports – the **waters of the port** are regarded as internal waters according to the law of the sea. The waters of the port are waters within the straight lines drawn between the **outermost permanent harbour works**, which form an integral part of the harbour system (with the exclusion of the off-shore installations and artificial islands) and which, according to the United Nations Convention on the Law of the Sea, 'are regarded as forming part of the coast'.[1026] The permanent harbour works, as defined by the ICJ in the ***Maritime Delimitation in the Black Sea* case** *(Romania v Ukraine)*, include the 'installations which allow ships to be harboured, maintained or repaired and which permit or facilitate the embarkation and disembarkation of passengers and the loading or unloading of goods.'[1027]

Composition of internal waters

In sum, the internal waters consist of waters on the landward side of the baselines, including:

1 parts of the sea along the coast down to either the low-water mark or the straight baselines;
2 estuaries;
3 landward waters from the closing line of bays; and
4 waters of the ports.

A special case is the archipelagic states, which will be discussed later in this chapter.

1023 One nautical mile is slightly longer than a mile on land. 1 nautical mile is 1.1508 statute miles and 1.852 kilometers.
1024 Article 10 (4) of the United Nations Convention on the Law of the Sea.
1025 *Fisheries* case *(United Kingdom v Norway)*, Judgment of 18 December 1951, ICJ Reports 1951, 116.
1026 Article 11 of the United Nations Convention on the Law of the Sea.
1027 *Maritime Delimitation in the Black Sea (Romania v Ukraine)*, Judgment of 3 February 2009, ICJ Reports 2009, 61.

Sovereignty over internal waters

States have the same sovereignty over internal waters, including the airspace above and the seabed and subsoil below, as they do over a piece of land which is under their sovereignty. Accordingly, a coastal state has the right to prohibit the foreign ships from entering its internal waters, except for:

- Ships in **distress**. As defined by the 1979 **International Convention on Maritime Search and Rescue**, the 'distress phase' means a 'situation wherein there is a reasonable certainty that a vessel or a person is threatened by grave and imminent danger and requires immediate assistance.' The causes of a distress can be various: storms, faulty navigation, mutiny, the need for essential repairs, and so forth. According to the old general rule of international customary law, ships in distress always have the right to enter any port or place of refuge whatsoever, regardless of the cause of the distress. However, when the interests or rights of the coastal state or the risks to which it is exposed are higher than those of the ship, access may be refused.[1028] In addition, ships in distress hold some degree of immunity – for instance, concerning harbour duties and similar taxes.
- Certain cases when the determination of a straight baseline after the entry into force of the United Nations Convention on the Law of the Sea had the effect of enclosing certain areas as internal waters which were not previously considered as such. In those areas (internal waters), the right of innocent passage applies.

Jurisdiction over the ships

A particular question appears regarding the jurisdiction over the ships. In the internal waters, a coastal state may apply and enforce its laws in full against foreign **merchant ships**. The foreign merchant ships are subject to the coastal state's regulations on navigation and its sanitary, fiscal, technical, and customs controls.

At the same time, in some instances, the jurisdiction of the **flag state** may also be applied to a ship and its crew:

- Normally, the civil jurisdiction of the coastal state is not exercised concerning cases of a private nature between the members of the crew.
- As regards the criminal jurisdiction of the coastal state, it usually will not be applied if:
  - a case concerns solely the internal discipline on the ship;
  - non-members of the crew are not involved;
  - a crime committed by a member of the crew does not affect or is not likely to affect the peace, security, and **good order of the coastal state**;
  - intervention is not requested by the captain of the ship or a diplomatic agent or consular officer of the flag state; or
  - a case does not relate to matters to which, under international law, either universal or quasi-universal jurisdiction of the costal state should be applied (for example, in the case of pollution).

1028 This approach is called the *balancing interests theory*.

However, decisions on jurisdictional matters, as well as an assessment of the situation and conditions listed here, are normally made solely by the coastal state since it may apply and enforce its laws in full against foreign merchant ships in its internal waters.

On the other hand, foreign **warships** and other **government vessels used for non-commercial purposes** are exempt from the coastal state's jurisdiction due to the principle of sovereign immunity. Their crews are also immune from the jurisdiction of the coastal state (with respect to the acts exercised on board the ship).

However, if a warship does not comply with the laws and regulations of the coastal state, the coastal state has the right to request the warship leave its internal waters immediately.

At the same time, the flag state shall bear international responsibility for any loss or damage to the coastal state resulting from non-compliance by a warship or 'other government ship' operated for non-commercial purposes with the laws and regulations of the coastal state.[1029]

TERRITORIAL SEA

> territorial waters
> charts or lists of geographical coordinates
> innocent passage
> sea lanes and traffic separation schemes
> right for all categories of ships
> jurisdiction of the flag state

The meaning of the territorial sea

The sovereignty of a coastal state extends beyond its internal waters to an adjacent belt of sea called the territorial sea (also the **territorial waters**) and the airspace above the territorial sea, as well as its seabed and subsoil.

The breadth of the territorial sea may be established up to a limit not exceeding 12 nautical miles, measured from baselines which are the outer limits of the internal waters.[1030] Every coastal state has an obligation to establish the **charts or lists of geographical coordinates** of its territorial sea openly and transparently. In addition, it shall deposit a copy of each such chart or list with the Secretary-General of the United Nations.

1029   Article 31 of the United Nations Convention on the Law of the Sea.

1030   There are also some additional regulations under the United Nations Convention on the Law of the Sea with respect to the outer limits of the territorial sea. For example, pursuant to Article 12: 'Roadsteads which are normally used for the loading, unloading and anchoring of ships, and which would otherwise be situated wholly or partly outside the outer limit of the territorial sea, are included in the territorial sea.'

The right of innocent passage

However, in the territorial sea, on the main pattern of the *mare clausum*, the right of **innocent passage** of the ships of all states, whether coastal or land-locked, which is the first sign of the *mare liberum*, is engrafted. Innocent passage means navigation through the territorial sea on either (1) a lateral passage (i.e. 'traversing that sea without entering internal waters or calling at a roadstead or port facility outside internal waters') or (2) an inward/outward-bound passage (i.e. 'proceeding to or from internal waters or a call at such roadstead or port facility').[1031]

At the same time, the innocent passage must be continuous and expeditious, which does not mean that the ships cannot stop and anchor if such an action is 'incidental to ordinary navigation or [is] rendered necessary by force majeure or distress or for the purpose of rendering assistance to persons, ships, or aircraft in danger or distress.'

The ships enjoy the right of innocent passage so long as it is not prejudicial to the peace, good order, or security of the coastal state. The following activities are considered as prejudicial in this regard:

- the threat or use of force against the sovereignty, territorial integrity, or political independence of the coastal state;
- exercise or practice with weapons of any kind;
- acts of collecting information or disseminating propaganda aimed at affecting the defence or security of the coastal state;
- the launching, landing, or taking on the board of any aircraft or military device;
- the violation of the customs, fiscal, immigration, or sanitary laws and regulations of the coastal state;
- acts of wilful and serious pollution;
- fishing, research, or survey activities;
- acts aimed at interfering with any systems of communication or any other facilities or installations of the coastal state; and
- any other activity not having a direct bearing on passage.[1032]

For the safety of navigation, the coastal state may prescribe the **sea lanes and traffic separation schemes** for the regulation of the passage of ships. Nevertheless, the requirements imposed on foreign ships, in fact, should not result in denying or impairing the right of innocent passage or applying any other type of discriminatory measures.

Additionally, no charge may be levied upon foreign ships when the territorial sea is only used as the route of passage.[1033]

A coastal state is empowered to suspend temporarily the right of innocent passage in specified areas of its territorial sea if such suspension is essential for the protection of its security. At the same time, the suspension shall take effect only after it is duly published.[1034]

1031 Article 18 (1) of the United Nations Convention on the Law of the Sea.
1032 Article 19 (2) of the United Nations Convention on the Law of the Sea.
1033 Article 26 (1) of the United Nations Convention on the Law of the Sea.
1034 Article 25 (3) of the United Nations Convention on the Law of the Sea.

Finally, the right of the innocent passage concerns only the ships on the seas and does not extend to the freedom of overflight.

Innocent passage as a right of all categories of ships

According to the United Nations Convention on the Law of the Sea, the right of innocent passage was intended as a **right for all categories of ships** – merchant ships; government ships operated for commercial purposes; or warships and other government ships operated for non-commercial purposes, including submarines. There are many other provisions regarding warships and submarines as well. For instance, submarines and other underwater vehicles are required to navigate on the surface and display their flag. However, in practice, certain states have not applied the right of innocent passage in the proper form to warships, as they require prior authorisation for the passage.

The jurisdictional concerns in the territorial sea

When the ship navigates under the rule of innocent passage, it is considered a ship in the high seas (under the **jurisdiction of the flag state**).

Warships and other government ships operated for non-commercial purposes in the territorial sea are subject to the same rules on jurisdiction as in internal waters.

As for merchant ships and government ships operated for commercial purposes, in connection with any crime committed on board a ship during its passage, the criminal jurisdiction of the coastal state generally should not be exercised on board a foreign ship passing through the territorial sea. However, there also exist certain exemptions when the coastal state is entitled to intervene:

- If the consequences of the crime extend to the coastal state or the crime may disturb the peace of the country or the good order of the territorial sea.
- If the assistance of the local authorities has been requested by the master of the ship or by a diplomatic agent or consular officer of the flag state.
- If such measures are necessary for the suppression of illicit traffic in narcotic drugs or psychotropic substances.[1035]

Generally, during innocent passage, the coastal state may not take any steps on board a foreign ship to arrest any person or to conduct any investigation in connection with any crime committed before the ship entered the territorial sea, except in cases of (1) offences violating the specific norms of international law concerning the protection and preservation of the marine environment committed elsewhere, which entitle a coastal state to intervene, or (2) 'violations of laws and regulations adopted in accordance with Part V' (Part V. Exclusive Economic Zone).[1036]

As for civil jurisdiction, the coastal state should not stop or divert a foreign ship to exercise civil jurisdiction concerning a person on board the ship. Additionally, the 'coastal State

---

1035 Article 27 (1) of the United Nations Convention on the Law of the Sea.
1036 Article 27 (5) of the United Nations Convention on the Law of the Sea.

may not levy execution against or arrest the ship for the purpose of any civil proceedings, save only in respect of obligations or liabilities assumed or incurred by the ship itself in the course or for the purpose of its voyage through the waters of the coastal State.'[1037]

Finally, the coastal state has the general right to exercise criminal as well as civil jurisdiction authorised by its laws over a foreign ship passing through the territorial sea if the ship continues to sail after leaving the internal waters.[1038]

CONTIGUOUS ZONE

> initial part of the exclusive economic zone
> customs, fiscal, immigration, or sanitary laws
> Convention on the Territorial Sea and the Contiguous Zone

After the territorial sea comes the domain of the *mare liberum*. Nevertheless, in the maritime zones adjacent to the territorial sea, certain sovereign rights of the coastal state persist. In fact, the control rights the coastal state exercises in the sea zones contiguous to its territorial sea have been recognised for a long time.

Definition of the contiguous zone

The contiguous zone is a maritime zone which lies immediately beyond a coastal state's territorial sea and extends to a maximum of 24 nautical miles from the coastal state's baselines. It is the **initial part of the exclusive economic zone**. Therefore, the sovereign rights of a coastal state with regard to its exclusive economic zone apply in the contiguous zone accordingly.

Powers of coastal states in the contiguous zone

However, in the contiguous zone, the states have additional powers for the enforcement of **customs, fiscal, immigration, or sanitary laws**.

According to the United Nations Convention on the Law of the Sea, which in effect repeats the provisions of the 1958 **Convention on the Territorial Sea and the Contiguous Zone**:

> In a zone contiguous to its territorial sea, described as the contiguous zone, the coastal State may exercise the control necessary to:
>
> (a) prevent infringement of its customs, fiscal, immigration or sanitary laws and regulations within its territory or territorial sea;
> (b) punish infringement of the above laws and regulations committed within its territory or territorial sea.[1039]

1037 Article 28 (2) of the United Nations Convention on the Law of the Sea.
1038 Articles 27 (2) and 28 (3) of the United Nations Convention on the Law of the Sea.
1039 Article 33 (1) of the United Nations Convention on the Law of the Sea.

EXCLUSIVE ECONOMIC ZONE

> rights and jurisdiction of the coastal state
> rights and freedoms of other states
> freedom of navigation
> freedom of overflight
> freedom to lay submarine cables and pipelines
> sovereign rights to explore, exploit, conserve, and manage
> artificial islands, installations, and structures
> marine scientific research
> protection and preservation of the marine environment
> optimum utilisation of the living resources
> access to the surplus of the allowable catch

Specific legal regime of the exclusive economic zone

The exclusive economic zone is an area beyond and adjacent to the territorial sea and basically a domain of the *mare liberum*, where the **rights and jurisdiction of the coastal state** and the **rights and freedoms of other states** are complexly intertwined. The breadth of the exclusive economic zone must not extend beyond 200 nautical miles from the baselines from which the breadth of the territorial sea is measured.

Freedoms in the exclusive economic zone

As the exclusive economic zone is an area of the *mare liberum*, all states, whether coastal or land-locked, exercise **freedom of navigation**, **freedom of overflight**, and **freedom to lay submarine cables and pipelines**. The states (including the land-locked states) have the right to participate, on an equitable basis, in the exploitation of an appropriate part of the surplus of the living resources of the exclusive economic zones. Further discussion of this issue will be undertaken later in this book.

The sovereign rights of the coastal state in the exclusive economic zone

In the exclusive economic zone, the coastal state obtains:

- **sovereign rights to explore, exploit, conserve, and manage** the living or non-living natural resources

  - of the waters superjacent to the seabed; and
  - of the seabed and its subsoil.

- jurisdiction concerning

  - the establishment and use of **artificial islands, installations, and structures;**
  - **marine scientific research**; and
  - **protection and preservation of the marine environment**.

As is evident, the list of the rights of a coastal state in the exclusive economic zone generally also refers to the seabed and subsoil;[1040] however, these rights must be exercised in accordance with the rules of international law which govern the regime of the continental shelf. On the other hand, in the exclusive economic zone, the rights of a coastal state with regard to the natural resources do not command the same level of exclusivity as in the case of the continental shelf. The coastal state determines the allowable catch of the living resources, taking into account the **optimum utilisation of the living resources**, and when it does not have the capacity to harvest the entire allowable catch, it shall give other states **access to the surplus of the allowable catch** (including through the licensing of fishermen, fishing vessels, and equipment). At the same time, the nationals of other states fishing in the exclusive economic zone shall comply with the conservation measures and with the other terms and conditions as established by the laws and regulations of the coastal state.

On the other hand, in the exclusive economic zone, the coastal state has

> the exclusive right to construct and to authorize and regulate the construction, operation and use of: (a) artificial islands; (b) installations and structures . . . [and] (c) installations and structures which may interfere with the exercise of the rights of the coastal State in the zone.[1041]

Furthermore, the coastal state possesses exclusive jurisdiction over such artificial islands, installations, and structures, including jurisdiction with regard to customs, fiscal, health, safety, and immigration laws and regulations. In addition, it may establish reasonable **safety zones** around such artificial islands, installations, and structures aiming to take the appropriate measures to ensure the safety of both navigation and the artificial islands, installations, and structures. The breadth of the safety zones shall not exceed a distance of 500 metres around them.

CONTINENTAL SHELF

> seabed
> subsoil of the submarine areas

1040 '1. In the exclusive economic zone, the coastal State has: (a) sovereign rights for the purpose of exploring and exploiting, conserving and managing the natural resources, whether living or non-living, of the *waters superjacent to the seabed and of the seabed and its subsoil,* and with regard to other activities for the economic exploitation and exploration of the zone, such as the production of energy from the water, currents and winds'. Article 56 of the United Nations Convention on the Law of the Sea.
1041 Article 60 (1) of the United Nations Convention on the Law of the Sea.

> natural prolongation of its land territory
> outer edge of the continental margin
> exclusive sovereign rights to explore it and exploit its natural resources
> exclusive right to authorise and regulate drilling

Definition of the continental shelf

The continental shelf of a coastal state is the **seabed** and **subsoil of the submarine areas** that, according to the United Nations Convention on the Law of the Sea, extend beyond its territorial sea throughout the **natural prolongation of its land territory** to the **outer edge of the continental margin** (the so-called geological criterion) or to a distance of 200 nautical miles from the baselines from which the breadth of the territorial sea is measured (known as the distance criterion).

Besides, as clarified by the ICJ in the *Continental Shelf* case *(Libyan Arab Jamahiriya/ Malta)*:

> It is in the Court's view incontestable that . . . the institution of the exclusive economic zone, with its rule on entitlement by reason of distance, is shown by the practice of States to have become a part of customary law. . . . Although there can be a continental shelf where there is no exclusive economic zone, there cannot be an exclusive economic zone without a corresponding continental shelf.[1042]

Hence, the geological criterion can only be applied when the continental margin extends beyond 200 nautical miles. However, in such cases, the breadth of the continental shelf 'either shall not exceed 350 nautical miles from the baselines from which the breadth of the territorial sea is measured or shall not exceed 100 nautical miles from the 2,500 metre isobath, which is a line connecting the depth of 2,500 metres.'[1043]

Exclusive sovereign rights of coastal states

The coastal state has the **exclusive sovereign right to explore and exploit its natural resources** in its continental shelf. The exclusivity in this context means that 'if the coastal state does not explore the continental shelf or exploit its natural resources, no one may undertake these activities without the express consent of the coastal State.'[1044] In addition, the coastal state is armed with the **exclusive right to authorise and regulate drilling** on the continental shelf for all purposes.

The natural resources of continental shelf are the mineral and other non-living resources of the seabed and subsoil, together with the living organisms belonging to sedentary species.

1042 *Continental Shelf* case *(Libyan Arab Jamahiriya/Malta)*, Judgment of 3 June 1985.
1043 Article 76 (5) of the United Nations Convention on the Law of the Sea.
1044 Article 77 (2) of the United Nations Convention on the Law of the Sea.

Submarine cables and pipelines

Although all states have the right to lay submarine cables and pipelines on the continental shelf, the delineation of the course for the laying of such pipelines is subject to the consent of the coastal state.

STRAITS USED FOR INTERNATIONAL NAVIGATION

> *Corfu Channel* case
> innocent passage
> freedom of navigation and overflight
> transit passage
> continuous and expeditious transit
> sea lanes and traffic separation schemes
> freedom of passage

The legal status of the straits used for international navigation

By definition, a strait is a narrow area of sea that connects two larger areas of the sea.

As for the legal status with regard to the straits used for international navigation, the initial approach is reflected in the *Corfu Channel* case *(UK v Albania)*, in which the Court stated:

> It is, in the opinion of the Court, generally recognized and in accordance with inter-national custom that States in time of peace have a right to send their warships through straits used for international navigation between two parts of the high seas without the previous authorization of a coastal State.[1045]

Transit passage

In practice, the legal status of every strait did not result in a controversy between the strait states and other states; however, some additional disputes arose after the breadth of the territorial sea was expanded up to 12 nautical miles, and consequently, some international straits became part of the territorial sea of the strait states. In such cases, the strait states wanted to maintain the rule of **innocent passage**, which, as mentioned earlier, was applied to the territorial seas. However, the rule of innocent passage was not accepted by other states, which claimed the **freedom of navigation and overflight** (as in the high seas) to be applicable in those areas. Finally, under the United Nations Convention on the Law of the Sea, the rule of **transit passage** was adopted as a compromise formula.

1045 *Corfu Channel (UK v Albania)*, Judgment of 9 April 1949.

According to the Convention:

> Transit passage means the exercise . . . of the freedom of navigation and overflight solely for the purpose of **continuous and expeditious transit** of the strait between one part of the high seas or an exclusive economic zone and another part of the high seas or an exclusive economic zone. However, the requirement of continuous and expeditious transit does not preclude passage through the strait for the purpose of entering, leaving or returning from a State bordering the strait, subject to the conditions of entry to that State.[1046]

At the same time, the ships and aircraft which exercise the right of transit passage have to comply with the following specific obligations:

- Proceed without delay through or over the strait.
- Refrain from any threat or use of force against the sovereignty, territorial integrity, or political independence of the coastal states.
- Pursue the normal modes of continuous and expeditious transit unless rendered necessary by force majeure or by distress.
- Refrain from any research or survey activities without the prior authorisation of the states bordering straits.
- Comply with generally accepted international regulations provided for the safety of navigation and for the prevention, reduction, and control of pollution.
- Comply with the **sea lanes and traffic separation schemes** for navigation in straits established by the states bordering the strait in conformity with international law regulations.
- Be in conformity with the laws and regulations of the state bordering the strait relating to transit passage concerning (1) the safety of navigation; (2) the prevention, reduction, and control of pollution; (3) the prevention of fishing; (4) the loading or unloading of any commodity, currency, or person in contravention of the customs, fiscal, immigration, or sanitary laws and regulations of coastal state.

However, these 'laws and regulations shall not discriminate in form or in fact among foreign ships or in their application have the practical effect of denying, hampering or impairing the right of transit passage'.[1047]

In sum, foreign ships exercising the transit passage are more constrained than ships carrying out **freedom of passage** on the high seas. On the other hand, they enjoy more freedom than ships implementing the right of innocent passage in the territorial sea of a coastal state. This compromised regime of the transit passage, therefore, lies somewhere between them. The transit passage differs from the innocent passage model in the following ways:

1046 Article 38 (2) of the United Nations Convention on the Law of the Sea.
1047 Article 42 (2) of the United Nations Convention on the Law of the Sea.

- There is no right of innocent passage for aircraft, but transit passage provides the freedom of navigation and overflight (including to warships and military aircraft).
- Submarines enjoining the right of innocent passage must navigate on the surface and show their flags. However, there is no such rule concerning submarines in transit passage.
- The state bordering the strait may designate and prescribe the sea lanes and traffic separation schemes only after a 'competent international organisation' (which is the International Maritime Organisation in matters of navigational safety, safety of shipping traffic, and marine environmental protection)[1048] adopts it. On the other hand, there is no such requirement with regard to innocent passage.
- 'There shall be no suspension of transit passage.'[1049]
- The state bordering the strait may introduce fewer regulations with respect to transit passage, as in the case of innocent passage.

The categories of straits

Finally, according to the Convention, the straits fall into four different categories:

1 Straits governed by the long-standing special conventions.[1050]
2 Straits with central corridors of the high seas or the exclusive economic zone, i.e. straits wider than 24 nautical miles. The rule of innocent passage will apply to those parts of the strait which lie within the territorial sea limits. The freedoms of navigation and overflight of the high seas and the exclusive economic zones will apply in the middle section through the strait.
3 Straits where innocent passage should be applied, which, in turn, are of two categories:

   a) Straits formed by an island of a state bordering the strait and its mainland, where there exists seaward of the island an alternative route through the high seas or through an exclusive economic zone of similar convenience; and
   b) Straits connecting a part of the high seas or an exclusive economic zone and the territorial sea of a foreign state.

4 Straits where the regime of transit passage should be applied, such as the straits used for international navigation between one part of the high seas or an exclusive economic zone and another part of the high seas or an exclusive economic zone.

1048 See the official website of the IMO <www.imo.org/en/MediaCentre/SecretaryGeneral/Pages/itlos. aspx> accessed 18 March 2021.
1049 Article 44 of the United Nations Convention on the Law of the Sea.
1050 For example, the passage through Turkish Straits – the Bosphorus and Dardanelles is regulated by the Montreux Convention of 1936 (as mentioned earlier); the legal status of the Strait of Magellan is specifically prescribed by Article 5 of the Boundary Treaty of 1881 between Chile and Argentina: 'The Straits of Magellan shall be neutralized for ever, and free navigation assured to the flags of all nations. In order to assure this freedom and neutrality, no fortifications or military defences shall be constructed on the coasts that might be contrary to this purpose.'

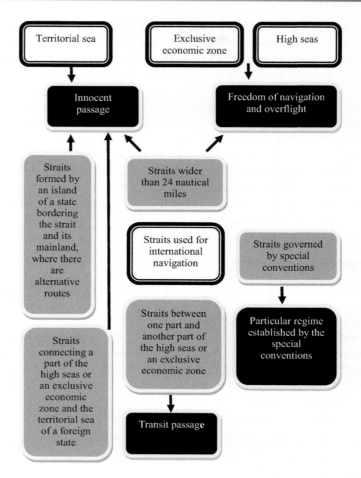

FIGURE 13.2 Passage regimes

ARCHIPELAGIC WATERS

archipelagic states
archipelago
archipelagic waters
archipelagic baselines
innocent passage
right of archipelagic sea lanes passage

Archipelagic states

The United Nations Convention on the Law of the Sea prescribed a particular legal regime for the **archipelagic states**, which are 'constituted wholly by one or more archipelagos and may include other islands as well'.[1051] An **archipelago** is defined as (1) a group of islands, including parts of islands, interconnecting waters, and other natural features (2) which are so closely interrelated that (3) such islands, waters, and other natural features form an intrinsic geographical, economic, and political entity (4) or which historically have been regarded as such.[1052]

Archipelagic states and the sea zones

In the case of the archipelagic states, in parallel with the ordinary maritime areas such as the internal waters, territorial sea, and so forth, a specific legal zone called the **archipelagic waters** was introduced, which was determined as the sea zone enclosed by the **archipelagic baselines**.

Archipelagic baselines

According to the Convention:

> An archipelagic State may draw straight archipelagic baselines joining the outermost points of the outermost islands and drying reefs of the archipelago provided that within such baselines are included the main islands and an area in which the ratio of the area of the water to the area of the land, including atolls, is between 1 to 1 and 9 to 1.[1053]

The length of such baselines shall typically not exceed 100 nautical miles, and only up to 3% of the total number of baselines may exceed that length, up to a maximum length of 125 nautical miles. Therefore, unlike straight baselines in ordinary cases, the maximum length of an archipelagic baseline is explicitly limited.

In addition, there were other rules developed concerning archipelagic baselines. For example, the baselines shall not be drawn in such a manner as to 'depart to any appreciable extent from the general configuration of the archipelago' or 'as to cut off from the high seas or the exclusive economic zone the territorial sea of another State'.[1054]

The peculiarity of the measurement of other sea zones

The introduction of a specific maritime area of archipelagic waters stipulated a need for the incorporation of this area into the general framework of the Convention. Hence, in the case of archipelagic states, the breadth of the territorial sea, the contiguous zone,

---

1051 As of the time this book was written, more than 20 states, parties to the Convention, have formally claimed archipelagic status. Among them are Antigua and Barbuda, the Bahamas, Cape Verde, Comoros, the Dominican Republic, Fiji, Grenada, Indonesia, and Jamaica.

1052 Article 46 (b) of the United Nations Convention on the Law of the Sea.

1053 Article 47 (1) of the United Nations Convention on the Law of the Sea.

1054 Article 47 of the United Nations Convention on the Law of the Sea.

the exclusive economic zone, and the continental shelf are measured from archipelagic baselines.

As regards internal waters, the archipelagic states are empowered to identify such a zone within its archipelagic waters by utilising 'closing lines for the delimitation of internal waters' concerning the mouths of rivers, bays, and ports. Consequently, the landward areas of those closing lines become internal waters of the archipelagic states.

The legal status of the archipelagic waters, the airspace over archipelagic waters, and their bed and subsoil

The concept of archipelagic waters is a complex combination of the concepts of the territorial sea and the straits used for international navigation.

Firstly, the full sovereignty of an archipelagic state extends to the waters enclosed by the archipelagic baselines and the airspace over the archipelagic waters, as well as their bed and subsoil.

Secondly, there is a difference from the internal waters and territorial sea regimes since an archipelagic state should respect existing agreements, submarine cables, traditional fishing rights, and other legitimate activities of certain states within the archipelagic waters.

Thirdly, ships of all states enjoy the right of **innocent passage** through archipelagic waters to the same extent as in the territorial sea, which accordingly does not include the right of overflight. An archipelagic state may also 'suspend temporarily in specified areas of its archipelagic waters the innocent passage of foreign ships if such suspension is essential for the protection of its security.'[1055]

In addition, the transit passage rule from the regime of the straits used for international navigation is also transmitted, which is called the **right of archipelagic sea lanes passage**.

The right of archipelagic sea lanes passage encompasses (1) the transit passage of either ships or aircraft (2) by passing through the sea lanes and air routes which are designated as such by the archipelagic state (3) for the continuous, expeditious, and unobstructed passage of foreign ships and aircraft (4) through or over its archipelagic waters and the adjacent territorial sea and (5) between one part of the high seas or an exclusive economic zone and another part of the high seas or exclusive economic zone.[1056]

As in the case of the transit passage, an archipelagic state should also specify the traffic separation schemes which, together with the sea lanes, are subject to adoption by the IMO. Moreover, if an archipelagic state does not designate sea lanes or air routes, the right of archipelagic sea lanes passage may be exercised on the routes normally used for international navigation.

Ships and aircraft during their passage, as well as the archipelagic states, have *mutatis mutandis* the same rights and obligations as in the case of the transit passage in the straits used for international navigation.

1055 Article 52 (2) of the United Nations Convention on the Law of the Sea.
1056 Article 53 of the United Nations Convention on the Law of the Sea.

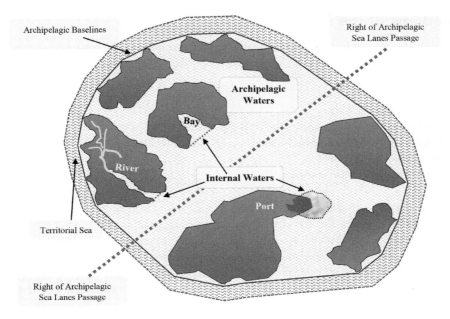

FIGURE 13.3 Delimitation of maritime zones – archipelagic state

HIGH SEAS

freedom of navigation
freedom of overflight
freedom to lay submarine cables and pipelines
freedom to construct artificial islands and other installations
freedom of fishing
freedom of scientific research
reasonable ground for suspecting
piracy
slave trade
unauthorised broadcasting
right of hot pursuit

Definition of the high seas

The high seas are those parts of the sea that do not belong to the internal waters, the territorial sea, the exclusive economic zone, or the archipelagic waters. This essentially means that the high seas start 200 nautical miles from the baselines.

Freedoms of the high seas

The high seas are open to all subjects of international law and are reserved for peaceful purposes. These subjects enjoy the freedoms of the high seas that include

1   **freedom of navigation;**
2   **freedom of overflight;**
3   **freedom to lay submarine cables and pipelines;**
4   **freedom to construct artificial islands and other installations;**
5   **freedom of fishing;** and
6   **freedom of scientific research.**[1057]

It is noteworthy that sometimes beneath the high seas is located the continental shelf of a coastal state when the breadth of the continental shelf exceeds 200 nautical miles from the baselines. Although, according to the Convention, generally, the 'rights of the coastal State over the continental shelf do not affect the legal status of the superjacent waters or of the air space above those waters' and 'the exercise of the rights of the coastal State over the continental shelf must not infringe or result in any unjustifiable interference with navigation and other rights and freedoms of other States', still, in such areas of the high seas, the freedom to lay submarine cables and pipelines, build artificial islands and do scientific research to some degree may concern the sovereign rights of the coastal state. For example, as regards the freedom to lay submarine cables and pipelines, although the coastal state generally may not impede the laying or maintenance of such cables or pipelines, at the same time, it has 'right to take reasonable measures for the exploration of the continental shelf, the exploitation of its natural resources and the prevention, reduction and control of pollution from pipelines'.[1058]

Consequently, without potential claims from the coastal states, the six freedoms listed here fully apply only to those parts of the high seas which are the superjacent waters of the Area.

Freedoms the states have related to the high seas do not amount to a license for their unrestricted exploitation. The freedoms allowed shall be exercised under the conditions as laid down by the United Nations Convention on the Law of the Sea (including the general obligations to protect and preserve the marine environment and, in certain cases, to conserve and manage living resources of the high seas), as well as in accordance with other norms of international law.

Every state, whether coastal or land-locked, has the right to sail ships and fly its flag on the high seas. These ships obtain the nationality of the state whose flag they are entitled to fly. In turn, the states establish the conditions for the granting of nationality, registration in its territory, and the right to fly its flag on ships. At the same time, the ships must sail under the flag of one state only and, therefore, are subject to its exclusive jurisdiction on the high seas. If a ship sails under the flags of two or more states, that ship may be regarded as a ship without nationality.

1057 Article 87 of the United Nations Convention on the Law of the Sea.
1058 Articles 78 and 79 (2) of the United Nations Convention on the Law of the Sea.

The ships on the high seas

The states should effectively exercise their jurisdiction and control in administrative, technical, and social matters over ships flying their flag; for example, they shall maintain a register of ships containing the names and particulars of ships flying its flag, assume jurisdiction under their internal law over each ship flying its flag, and so on.

On the high seas, warships, as well as ships owned or operated by a state and used only in government non-commercial service, have complete immunity from the jurisdiction of any state other than the flag state. As for other ships, according to the United Nations Convention on the Law of the Sea, a warship which encounters a foreign ship on the high seas is not justified in boarding it unless (1) there is an international treaty with the relevant state entitling it to exercise acts of interference, or (2) there is a **reasonable ground for suspecting** that the ship

- is engaged in **piracy**;[1059]
- is engaged in the **slave trade**;
- is engaged in **unauthorised broadcasting**;
- is without nationality;
- though flying a foreign flag or refusing to show its flag, is, in reality, of the same nationality as the warship.

Other exceptions from the immunity of the flag state

Nevertheless, this list of the exceptions from the general rule of the immunity on the high seas from the jurisdiction of any state other than the flag state is not exhaustive. States can specify other cases under new treaties or customary norms and, with the help of those legal instruments establish certain other types of limitations. For instance, the particular obligations in the field of the protection and preservation of the marine environment, including concerning the high seas, were enshrined in many legal instruments of international environmental law, which will be examined in detail later.

1059 Under Article 101 of the United Nations Convention on the Law of the Sea: 'Piracy consists of any of the following acts: (a) any illegal acts of violence or detention, or any act of depredation, committed for private ends by the crew or the passengers of a private ship or a private aircraft, and directed: (i) on the high seas, against another ship or aircraft, or against persons or property on board such ship or aircraft; (ii) against a ship, aircraft, persons or property in a place outside the jurisdiction of any State; (b) any act of voluntary participation in the operation of a ship or of an aircraft with knowledge of facts making it a pirate ship or aircraft; (c) any act of inciting or of intentionally facilitating an act described in subparagraph (a) or (b).'

The right of hot pursuit

International law recognises the **right of hot pursuit** of a foreign ship (or boat) with an aim to chase and arrest it, which may be undertaken when the competent authorities of the coastal state have good reason to believe that the ship has violated the laws and regulations of that state within the internal waters, the archipelagic waters, the territorial sea, or the contiguous zone of the pursuing state and may only be continued outside the territorial sea or the contiguous zone if the pursuit has not been interrupted.[1060]

At the same time, concerning a violation in the contiguous zone, the pursuit may only be undertaken if there has been a violation of the rights for the protection of which the zone was established. Moreover, the right of hot pursuit also applies *mutatis mutandis* to violations committed by foreign ships in the exclusive economic zone or on the continental shelf of the rights of the coastal state for the maintenance of which these legal zones were introduced.

The pursuit may only be initiated:

- by warships, military aircraft, or other ships or aircraft clearly marked and identifiable as being in government service; and
- after a visual or auditory signal to stop has been given at a distance which enables it to be seen or heard by the foreign ship.

The right of hot pursuit ceases as soon as:

- the ship pursued enters the territorial sea of another state; or
- the hot pursuit has been interrupted.

Under international law, the coastal state is justified in using force in a hot pursuit. However, the use of force is to be limited and only undertaken proportionately as much as necessary and as a measure of last resort.

THE DEEP SEABED

> **International Seabed Authority**
> **Area**
> **common heritage of mankind**

1060 The word 'interrupted' has not been defined clearly by the United Nations Convention on the Law of the Sea, but Article 111 states that the pursuit should be a continuous one as long it is not interrupted. Therefore, the hot pursuit can be continued by electronic means, that means other than visual watch can be employed to maintain contact with a pursued vessel, and observation is not limited to 'eyes on' surveillance. There can be a few reasons for interruptions: Some mechanical or technical failure in the pursuing vessel due to which it is compelled to discontinue the hot pursuit or any natural causes like darkness or bad climatic and weather conditions.

> beneficial to humanity as a whole
> parallel system of access to the Area
> Enterprise
> use of the Area exclusively for peaceful purposes

Discrepancy concerning the deep seabed

The adjustment of the deep seabed was one of the most controversial challenges of the United Nations Convention on the Law of the Sea, which stipulated different approaches to the subject from the developed and the developing countries.

Both the developed and the developing countries acknowledged the importance of the oceanic seabed and its recourses for the future generations but approached the matter from different perspectives and points of view. The developed countries had the necessary advanced technology and vast amounts of capital needed to exploit the resources of the seabed. The developing states, in turn, considered international co-operation and the establishment of appropriate international institutions as the only possibility for them to get their part of the pie. The Convention has not addressed all concerns accordingly. Consent concerning the deep seabed was reached only after the 1994 Agreement relating to the Implementation of Part XI of the United Nations Convention on the Law of the Sea.[1061] Thus, the Convention obtained a more universal recognition (including that it became effective for most developed countries), and the **International Seabed Authority** was established as an autonomous international organisation.

The Area

Under the Convention, 'the seabed and ocean floor and subsoil thereof' beyond the continental shelf (beyond the limits of the national functional jurisdiction) is termed the '**Area**' and declared to be the **common heritage of mankind**.[1062] In addition, under the Convention, the resources of the Area include the 'all solid, liquid or gaseous mineral resources *in situ* in the Area at or beneath the seabed, including polymetallic nodules.'

As noted earlier, the common heritage of mankind concept represents the approach that certain global commons or elements are considered **beneficial to humanity as a whole** and, therefore, should not be exploited exclusively by individual states or their nationals or by corporations or other entities. The International Seabed Authority, which organises and

---

1061 As stated in the UN General Assembly Resolution on Agreement relating to the implementation of Part XI of the United Nations Convention on the Law of the Sea of 10 December 1982: 'Prompted by the desire to achieve universal participation in the United Nations Convention on the Law of the Sea.' A/RES/48/263 of 17 August 1994.

1062 The concept actually finds its roots in the speech of Maltese Ambassador Arvid Pardo before the General Assembly of the United Nations, delivered at the United Nations General Assembly in November 1967, calling for the deep seabed to be placed beyond national jurisdiction and the resources contained therein to be declared the common heritage of mankind.

controls activities in the Area, is the body entitled to act on behalf of the humanity as a whole and, hence, to give concrete meaning to the concept of the common heritage of mankind. At the same time, the Convention permits individual exploitation of the resources in certain cases: 'No State or natural or juridical person shall claim, acquire or exercise rights with respect to the minerals recovered from the Area except in accordance with this Part. Otherwise, no such claim, acquisition or exercise of such rights shall be recognized.'[1063]

The parallel system of access to the Area

This formulation builds a bridge to the second general concept of the Convention with respect to the Area: the **parallel system of access to the Area**, which means that both states parties and the International Seabed Authority (or the **Enterprise**, to be specific, which initially was designed to be the Authority's mining arm, but partly as a result of the implementing agreement of 1994, it has not been established as an independent operational entity)[1064] would exploit the seabed side by side. A fundamental view of the arrangement of the parallel system is that activities in the Area shall be carried out in accordance with a formal written application for the approval of a plan of work for exploration, which should be considered and approved by the Council of the International Seabed Authority for 15 years.[1065] On this matter, the International Seabed Authority concludes the contracts for exploration with approved applicants.

The use of the Area exclusively for peaceful purposes

Finally, the vital governing principle of the activities in the Area is the **use of the Area exclusively for peaceful purposes** by all states, whether coastal or land-locked, and without discrimination.

1063 Article 137 (3) of the United Nations Convention on the Law of the Sea.
1064 On 25 July 2018, the International Seabed Authority adopted the Strategic Plan of the International Seabed Authority for the Period 2019–2023 (ISBA/24/A/CRP.3). According to the Strategic Plan, Direction 6.5. was specified as follows: 'Identify possible approaches to the independent operation of the Enterprise in a way that meets the objectives of the Convention and the 1994 Agreement while taking into account that the Enterprise lacks capital and is limited to operating through joint ventures.' At the same time, as noted on the official site of the International Seabed Authority: 'The Enterprise is the commercial arm of the Authority, empowered to conduct its own mining, initially through joint ventures with other entities. Until seabed mining becomes a commercial reality, the functions of the Enterprise are to be carried out by the Secretariat.' Recently, the 'Secretariat of the International Seabed Authority has received a proposal from Nautilus Minerals Inc. ('Nautilus'), a company incorporated in Canada, to enter into negotiations to form a joint venture with the Enterprise for the purpose of developing eight of the reserved area blocks in the Clarion Clipperton Zone (CCZ).' 'Nautilus Minerals Propose Joint Venture with the Enterprise' <www.isa.org.jm/news/nautilus-minerals-propose-joint-venture-enterprise> accessed 18 March 2021.
1065 In July 2015, the Council of the International Seabed Authority adopted a decision relating to the procedures and criteria for the extension of an approved plan of work for exploration according to section 1, Paragraph 9, of the annex to the Agreement relating to the Implementation of Part XI of the United Nations Convention on the Law of the Sea.

INTERNATIONAL INSTITUTIONS

> International Maritime Organisation
> International Seabed Authority
> international shipping
> Convention on the International Maritime Organisation
> Area
> regulations concerning the resources of the Area
> contracts for exploration

Preliminary remarks

Several international organisations are exercising their mandate in the field of the law of the sea. Among global intergovernmental organisations, the most notable institutions are the **International Maritime Organisation** and the **International Seabed Authority**.

International Maritime Organisation

The International Maritime Organisation (IMO) is a specialised agency of the United Nations. Its primary role is to develop and maintain a consistent regulatory framework for **international shipping** with a particular focus on the areas of safety, security, technical co-operation, and prevention of marine and atmospheric pollution by ships. Hence, it maintains a balance between protection of the environment and navigation rights.

In 1948, the international conference in Geneva adopted the **Convention on the International Maritime Organisation** formally establishing the IMO. (The original name was the Inter-Governmental Maritime Consultative Organisation or IMCO, but the name was changed in 1982 to IMO.) The IMO is based in London, England, and it has 174 member states and three associate members (Faroes; Hong Kong, China; and Macao, China).[1066]

The International Maritime Organisation serves as the repository for treaties related to maritime safety, marine pollution, liability and compensation, and other conventions which concern issues related to shipping. The key IMO Conventions are:

- The International Convention for the Safety of Life at Sea of 1974, which is generally regarded as the most important of all international treaties concerning the safety of merchant ships. Its main target is to specify minimum standards for the construction, equipment, and operation of ships, compatible with their safety.
- The International Convention for the Prevention of Pollution from Ships, 1973, as modified by the Protocol of 1978 relating thereto and by the Protocol of 1997 (MARPOL), which is the leading international treaty covering the prevention of pollution

---

1066 See the official website of the IMO <www.imo.org/en/About/Membership/Pages/MemberStates.aspx> accessed 18 March 2021.

of the marine environment by ships from operational or accidental causes. It covers the prevention of pollution by oil, noxious liquid substances, sewage, and garbage.

- The International Convention on Standards of Training, Certification, and Watch-keeping for Seafarers of 1978, which prescribes minimum standards relating to training, certification, and watchkeeping for seafarers. The states are obliged to meet or exceed these standards.

The internal structure of the International Maritime Organisation

- Assembly – consists of all the member states and is the highest governing body of the Organisation. It meets once every two years in regular sessions but may also assemble in extraordinary session. The Assembly is empowered to approve the work programme, vote on the budget, elect the Council for two-year terms, and approve the Secretary-General. In addition, it makes recommendations to the governments of the member states on maritime safety and pollution prevention.
- Council – consists of 40 members and is the executive organ of the IMO. It is responsible for the supervision (under the Assembly) of the IMO work, coordination of the activities of the organs of the Organisation, and the appointment of the Secretary-General. Between sessions of the Assembly, the Council maintains all the functions of the Assembly, except the function of making recommendations to governments on maritime safety and prevention of pollution.
- Committees:
  - Maritime Safety Committee – is the highest technical body of the IMO. It considers 'any matter within the scope of the Organization concerned with aids to navigation, construction and equipment of vessels, manning from a safety standpoint, rules for the prevention of collisions, handling of dangerous cargoes, maritime safety procedures and requirements, hydrographic information, log-books and navigational records, marine casualty investigations, salvage and rescue and any other matters directly affecting maritime safety.'[1067]
  - Marine Environment Protection Committee – considers any matter within the scope of the IMO related to the prevention and control of pollution from ships.
  - Sub-Committees – are established to assist and support the work of certain committees.
  - Legal Committee – is authorised to consider any legal matters within the scope of the IMO.
  - Technical Cooperation Committee – was created with the primary objective of implementing the technical co-operation projects for which the IMO acts as the executing or co-operating agency.

1067 Article 28 (a) of the Convention on the International Maritime Organisation.

- Facilitation Committee – deals with the elimination of redundant formalities and 'red tape' in international shipping by implementing relevant international legal instruments concerned with the facilitation of international maritime traffic.

• Secretariat – includes the Secretary-General and the international personnel. The Secretary-General is the chief administrative officer of the Organisation.

International Seabed Authority

The International Seabed Authority (ISA) is an autonomous international organisation established under the United Nations Convention on the Law of the Sea and the 1994 Agreement relating to the Implementation of Part XI of the United Nations Convention on the Law of the Sea. The Authority organises and oversees the activities in the **Area**, especially administering the resources of the Area. Its headquarters is based in Kingston, Jamaica. The Authority has almost 170 member states.

A primary target of the Authority is to regulate deep seabed exploration and exploitation by paying sufficient attention to the protection of the marine environment. Initially, one of its priorities was the establishment of the **regulations concerning the resources of the Area**. Thus, the Authority has issued the Regulations on Prospecting and Exploration for Polymetallic Nodules in the Area, the Regulations on Prospecting and Exploration for Polymetallic Sulphides in the Area and the Regulations on Prospecting and Exploration for Cobalt-Rich Crusts.

The internal structure of the International Seabed Authority

- Assembly – is composed of all ISA members and is the 'supreme organ' of the Authority, empowered to establish general policies and the rules, regulations, and procedures with regard to the exploration and exploitation of the Area. It sets the two-year budgets of the Authority. In addition, it elects the members of the Council and other bodies, as well as the Secretary-General. As a general rule, decision-making in the Assembly is by consensus. However, if consensus cannot be reached, the decisions are taken by a majority, or a two-thirds majority of members present and voting.[1068]
- Council – consists of 36 members and is the executive organ of the Authority. It establishes specific policies and supervises and coordinates implementation of the legal norms on exploration and exploitation of deep-sea minerals by states, corporations, and other entities. Under these norms, no such action may take place until contracts

---

1068 Paragraph 2 of Rule 61 of the Rules of Procedure of the Assembly of the International Seabed Authority states: 'If all efforts to reach a decision by consensus have been exhausted, decisions by voting in the Assembly on questions of procedure shall be taken by a majority of members present and voting, and decisions on questions of substance shall be taken by a two-thirds majority of members present and voting, as provided for in article 159, paragraph 8, of the Convention.'

have been signed between each interested person and the Authority. Hence, the Council draws up the terms of contracts, approves contract applications, supervises implementation of the contracts, and establishes environmental as well as other standards.

- Finance Committee – is elected by the Assembly and is responsible for overseeing the financing and financial management of the Authority.
- Legal and Technical Commission – is elected by the Council as an organ of the Council. Its main tasks are to review the applications for plans of work, supervise exploration and mining activities, assess the environmental impact of such activities, and provide advice to the International Seabed Authority's Assembly and Council on matters concerning the exploration and exploitation of non-living marine resources.
- Secretariat – is headed by the Secretary-General and is made up of four functional units: Office of the Secretary-General, Office of Environmental Management and Mineral Resources, Office of Legal Affairs, and Office for Administrative Services.

Contracts for exploration

To date, the International Seabed Authority has concluded 15-year **contracts for exploration** of polymetallic nodules, polymetallic sulphides, and cobalt-rich ferromanganese crusts in the Area with almost 30 contractors, allowing these contractors to explore specified parts of the deep oceans outside national jurisdiction.[1069]

SETTLEMENT OF INTERNATIONAL DISPUTES

peaceful means of dispute resolution
International Tribunal for the Law of the Sea
ITLOS
MOX Plant case
voluntary dispute settlement procedures
compulsory procedures for dispute settlement
International Court of Justice
arbitral tribunal
special arbitral tribunal
binding inquiry
Seabed Disputes Chamber
M/V Virginia G case

1069 For example, the International Seabed Authority and the China Minmetals Corporation have signed a 15-year exploration contract for polymetallic nodules. The exploration contract was signed in 2017 by the Secretary-General of the International Seabed Authority and the Chairman of China Minmetals Corporation. The allocated area covers a surface area of 72,745 km2 of the Clarion-Clipperton Fracture Zone in the Pacific Ocean. Available on the official website of the ISA <www.isa.org. jm/news/china-minmetals-corporation-signs-exploration-contract-international-seabed-authority> accessed 18 March 2021.

> voluntary conciliation
> compulsory conciliation
> Meeting of the States Parties
> contentious jurisdiction
> advisory jurisdiction

Complex approach to the settlement of disputes

The United Nations Convention on the Law of the Sea is widely regarded as a treaty which introduced in the area of the law of the sea a unique and comprehensive system for the settlement of disputes.

This system is made up of particular procedures immediately developed by the Convention and the **peaceful means of dispute resolution** embodied in the other sources of general, regional, or bilateral international law.

Peaceful means of dispute resolution

The peaceful means of dispute resolution, as examined earlier, are reflected in Article 33 of the UN Charter and include negotiation, enquiry, mediation, conciliation, arbitration, judicial settlement, resort to regional agencies or arrangements, and other peaceful means.

The Convention does not impair the right of any state 'to agree at any time to settle a dispute between them concerning the interpretation or application of this Convention by any peaceful means of their own choice.'[1070] As a result, the peaceful means chosen by the parties either by particular international treaties or *ad hoc* agreement concerning the existing dispute prevail over the dispute settlement procedures included in the United Nations Convention on the Law of the Sea.

At the same time, if the parties to the dispute agree through a general, regional, or bilateral agreement or otherwise that such dispute should be submitted to a procedure which entails a binding decision, that procedure shall apply instead of the procedures established by the Convention.

Moreover, if there is a particular mutual agreement between the parties obliging them

> to seek settlement of the dispute by a peaceful means of their own choice, the procedures provided for in [the Convention] apply only where no settlement has been reached by recourse to such means and the agreement between the parties does not exclude any further procedure.[1071]

In addition, the parties may agree on a time-limit for the 'peaceful means of their own choice'. In such a case, the procedures introduced by the Convention can be applied only upon the expiration of that time limit.

1070 Article 280 of the United Nations Convention on the Law of the Sea.
1071 Article 281 (1) of the United Nations Convention on the Law of the Sea.

The particular dispute settlement procedures of the Convention

In parallel, the Convention developed separate procedures which were integrated into the pattern of the peaceful means of dispute resolution established under other sources of general, regional, and bilateral international law and were prescribed in its following annexes: Annex V. Conciliation; Annex VI. Statute of the International Tribunal for the Law of the Sea; Annex VII. Arbitration; and Annex VIII. Special Arbitration.

Hence, the Convention offers to its members a wide range of voluntary and compulsory procedures (peaceful means) based on general, regional, and bilateral international law, as well as its own special mechanisms.

Obligations of the parties to a dispute

Firstly, the parties to the dispute are obliged to 'proceed expeditiously to an exchange of views regarding its settlement by negotiation or other peaceful means.'[1072] This provision means that views on the dispute settlement should be exchanged either at the preliminary stage or any further stages of the dispute resolution. However, as is articulated by the **International Tribunal for the Law of the Sea** (also referred to as the **ITLOS**), which was established under the Convention as a permanent judicial body, in the **MOX Plant case** *(Ireland v United Kingdom), Provisional Measures:* '[A] State Party is not obliged to continue with an exchange of views when it concludes that the possibilities of reaching agreement have been exhausted'.[1073]

Secondly, the Convention encourages the parties to the dispute to resolve disputes based on the **voluntary dispute settlement procedures** established by either the Convention or other bilateral or multilateral norms of international law, including by inviting the other party/parties to submit the dispute to conciliation in accordance with the procedure developed under Annex V to the Convention.

When no settlement can be reached by the voluntary dispute settlement procedures, the parties to the dispute should apply one of the **compulsory procedures for dispute settlement** if (as mentioned earlier) it is not precluded by a particular agreement between the parties.

Choice of the compulsory procedure

The parties to the Convention are free to choose, by means of a written declaration deposited with the Secretary-General of the United Nations, one or more of the following compulsory procedures (settlement means):

1072 Article 283 (1) of the United Nations Convention on the Law of the Sea.

1073 *MOX Plant case (Ireland v United Kingdom), Provisional Measures,* ITLOS, Case No. 10, Order of 3 December 2001, ITLOS Reports 2001 95. All cases considered by the ITLOS are available on the official website of the Tribunal <www.itlos.org/en/main/cases/list-of-cases/> accessed 18 March 2021. In this book, materials from the website are used, taking into account the disclaimer and applicable legal rules.

1   The International Tribunal for the Law of the Sea.
2   The **International Court of Justice**.
3   An **arbitral tribunal** (under Annex VII) which, in every case, consists of five members, unless the parties otherwise agree. The Secretary-General of the UN maintains the list of arbitrators. Every party to the Convention nominates four arbitrators, 'each of whom shall be a person experienced in maritime affairs and enjoying the highest reputation for fairness, competence and integrity.'[1074]
4   A **special arbitral tribunal** (under Annex VIII), constituted for one or more of the categories of disputes 'relating to (1) fisheries, (2) protection and preservation of the marine environment, (3) marine scientific research, or (4) navigation, including pollution from vessels and by dumping.'[1075] Unless the parties agree otherwise, the special arbitral tribunal shall consist of five members – experts in the particular fields listed earlier. As in the case of the arbitrators of an arbitral tribunal, there is no need for the special arbitrators to be lawyers. The lists of experts are maintained by the specialised institutions with competence in the fields enumerated earlier – for example, in the field of fisheries by the Food and Agriculture Organisation of the United Nations. A special arbitral tribunal is empowered to carry out an inquiry following the agreement between the parties to a dispute. Unless the parties agree otherwise, the finding of fact of the special arbitral tribunal is considered as conclusive between the parties. When 'all the parties to the dispute so request, the special arbitral tribunal may formulate recommendations which, without having the force of a decision, shall only constitute the basis for a review by the parties of the questions giving rise to the dispute.'[1076] In sum, the fact finding of the special arbitral tribunal is a remarkable example of the so-called **binding inquiry**.

Seabed Disputes Chamber

A declaration deposited with the Secretary-General of the UN (mentioned earlier) may not affect the obligations of a party to the Convention to accept the jurisdiction of the **Seabed Disputes Chamber** of the International Tribunal for the Law of the Sea, which, under the Convention, has the special competence to deal with disputes regarding activities in the Area between:

* the parties to the Convention, concerning the interpretation or application of the respective norms of the Convention;
* a party to the Convention and the International Seabed Authority, concerning some acts or omissions of the Authority or a party;
* the parties to a contract (the parties to the Convention, the Authority, the Enterprise, state enterprises, and natural or juridical persons); and
* the parties to any other disputes for which the jurisdiction of the Chamber is specifically foreseen in the Convention.[1077]

1074 Article 2 (1) of Annex VII. Arbitration.
1075 Article 1 of Annex VIII. Special Arbitration.
1076 Article 5 (3) of Annex VIII. Special Arbitration.
1077 Article 187 of the United Nations Convention on the Law of the Sea.

In addition, the Seabed Disputes Chamber is empowered to give advisory opinions at the request of the Assembly or the Council of the International Seabed Authority on legal questions arising within the scope of their activities.

The general assumption

Any party to a dispute which has not provided a declaration in force described earlier will be deemed to have accepted arbitration procedure under Annex VII to the Convention.

The arbitration procedure is also provided for such cases when the parties to the dispute have not chosen the identical procedure of the United Nations Convention on the Law of the Sea for the settlement of disputes, unless those parties otherwise agree.

The exhaustion of the local remedies

At the same time, the parties should submit a dispute to the compulsory procedures 'only after local remedies have been exhausted where this is required by international law.'[1078]

However, the scope of the exhaustion of the local remedies rule was sometimes disputed. In the *M/V Virginia G* case *(Panama/Guinea-Bissau)* the International Tribunal for the Law of the Sea articulated that

> It is a well-established principle of customary international law that the exhaustion of local remedies is a prerequisite for the exercise of diplomatic protection. . . . This principle is reflected in . . . the Draft Articles on Diplomatic Protection adopted by the International Law Commission in 2006, which provides that '[a] State may not present an inter-national claim in respect of an injury to a national . . . before the injured person has . . . exhausted all local remedies.'

At the same time, the Tribunal stressed the need to determine whether a direct injury to a state or an individual happened in particular case, and if both subjects are affected, which of the injuries is 'preponderant'. Finally, the Tribunal concluded that 'the exhaustion of local remedies rule does not apply where the claimant State is directly injured by the wrongful act of another State.'[1079]

Jurisdiction

The compulsory dispute settlement means enumerated here have jurisdiction over disputes concerning:

1078 Article 295 of the United Nations Convention on the Law of the Sea.
1079 *M/V Virginia G* case *(Panama/Guinea-Bissau)*, ITLOS, Case No. 19, Judgment of 14 April 2014, ITLOS Reports 2014 4.

- the interpretation or application of the Convention; and
- the interpretation or application of an international agreement related to the purposes of the Convention, which is submitted to a court or a tribunal listed earlier according to that agreement.[1080]

Consequently, a non-standard mechanism is enshrined in the Convention, since a party to another agreement may also use the dispute settlement procedures of the United Nations Convention on the Law of the Sea, even if it is not a party to the Convention.

The binding force of the decisions of the Court or tribunals

The decisions of the Court or a tribunal listed earlier which has sufficient jurisdiction over the case according to the Convention or the other sources of international law are binding. However, the binding force of such decisions applies only to the parties to the dispute and in relation to that specific dispute.

Sources

The decisions of the Court or a tribunal listed earlier should be based on the sources of international law, which are not incompatible with the United Nations Convention on the Law of the Sea, but they may also decide a case *ex aequo et bono* if the parties so agree. In addition, the Seabed Disputes Chamber acknowledges as the sources the rules, regulations, and procedures of the Authority and the terms of contracts concerning activities in the Area.

Conciliation

Firstly, the Convention includes two types of conciliation – **voluntary conciliation** and **compulsory conciliation**. Both are carried out by a commission composed of independent and impartial conciliators. The list of conciliators is maintained by the Secretary-General of the UN. Every party to the Convention is entitled to nominate four conciliators for inclusion in the list.

Unless the parties otherwise agree, the conciliation commission is composed of five members. Four of them are appointed by the parties to the dispute (preferably from the list of conciliators), and the fifth conciliator should be selected by the appointed conciliators (from the list of conciliators) within 30 days. The Secretary-General of the UN is also involved in the process and, upon the request of a relevant party, shall appoint the unassigned members of the commission (from the list of the conciliators) when a party or the conciliators did not select the conciliators within the defined term. In disputes involving more than two parties having separate interests, the parties shall apply these rules 'so far as possible'.[1081]

1080 Article 288 of the United Nations Convention on the Law of the Sea.
1081 Article 3 (h) of Annex V. Conciliation.

The commission reports within 12 months of its constitution. The report of the conciliation commission includes 'any agreements reached and, failing agreement, its conclusions on all questions of fact or law relevant to the matter in dispute and such recommendations as the commission may deem appropriate for an amicable settlement.'[1082] The report should be deposited with the Secretary-General of the UN and is immediately forwarded by the Secretary-General to the parties to the dispute.

The conciliation proceedings are terminated:

- when a settlement is reached;
- when the parties acknowledge or one party refuses the recommendations of the report; or
- when a period of three months from the date of transmission of the report to the parties expires.

All fees and expenses of the commission shall be borne by the parties to the dispute.

Voluntary conciliation

In cases of voluntary conciliation, there should be an agreement between the parties to take the dispute to conciliation, which can be initiated by a party through written notification (invitation) addressed to the other party or parties to the dispute. To proceed to the conciliation procedure, the party/parties concerned must accept the invitation.

Compulsory conciliation

As regards compulsory conciliation, the Convention introduced it concerning cases when the ordinary compulsory procedures listed earlier could not be applied (the so-called limitations to the compulsory procedures). For example, cases with regard to (a) marine scientific research in the Exclusive Economic Zone and on the continental shelf or (b) the living resources of the Exclusive Economic Zone. There can also be optional exceptions to the compulsory procedures since a party to the Convention has the right to declare in writing that it does not accept the compulsory procedures with respect to certain issues. For instance, with regard to the 'disputes concerning the interpretation or application of articles 15, 74 and 83 relating to sea boundary delimitations, or those involving historic bays or titles'.[1083]

Generally, in such cases, the Convention primarily offers the parties to the dispute the voluntary dispute settlement procedures. However, when no settlement is reached by these procedures, the compulsory conciliation mechanism is in the hands of the parties (for example, for disputes concerning the exercise of discretionary powers by the coastal state over fishing in its Exclusive Economic Zone). The procedure can be triggered by a party by written notification to the other party or parties to the dispute. In its turn, the other party or parties are 'obliged to submit to such proceedings'. However, as in the

---

1082 Article 7 (1) of Annex V. Conciliation.
1083 Article 298 (1) (a) (i) of the United Nations Convention on the Law of the Sea.

voluntary conciliation procedure, the report of the conciliation commission in cases of compulsory conciliation is not binding upon the disputing parties.

The International Tribunal for the Law of the Sea – organisational matters

One of the main achievements of the United Nations Convention on the Law of the Sea is the establishment of the International Tribunal for the Law of the Sea. The seat of the Tribunal is 'in the Free and Hanseatic City of Hamburg', Germany.

The Tribunal is 'a body of 21 independent members, elected from among persons enjoying the highest reputation for fairness and integrity and of recognized competence in the field of the law of the sea'. Additionally, they are selected from the principal legal systems of the world, and also taking into account the principle of equitable geographical distribution.[1084]

'No two members of the Tribunal may be nationals of the same State.'[1085] The members of the Tribunal are elected for nine years (and they may be re-elected) by a secret ballot at a **Meeting of the States Parties** to the Convention (convened by the Secretary-General of the UN) from the list of persons nominated by the states.

> Two thirds of the States Parties shall constitute a quorum at that meeting. The persons elected to the Tribunal shall be those nominees who obtain the largest number of votes and a two-thirds majority of the States Parties present and voting, provided that such majority includes a majority of the States Parties.[1086]

The President and the Vice-President of the Tribunal are elected for three years, and they may be re-elected.

The members of the Tribunal, when engaged in the business of the Tribunal, enjoy diplomatic privileges and immunities.

A very flexible system was established under the Convention, since the Tribunal allows consenting parties to choose chambers, which are composed of a few specialist judges. A judge of the Tribunal may participate in more than one chamber. Currently, there are the following Chambers established:

* Chamber of Summary Procedure – composed of five members and two alternates, it determines a case by 'summary procedure' if the parties so request or concerning the provisional measures when 'the Tribunal is not in session or a sufficient number of members is not available to constitute a quorum'.[1087]
* Chamber for Fisheries Disputes – consists of nine members empowered to deal with disputes concerning the conservation and management of marine living resources.

1084 Article 2 of Annex VI. Statute of the International Tribunal for the Law of the Sea.
1085 Article 3 (1) of Annex VI. Statute of the International Tribunal for the Law of the Sea.
1086 Article 4 (4) of Annex VI. Statute of the International Tribunal for the Law of the Sea.
1087 Article 25 (2) of Annex VI. Statute of the International Tribunal for the Law of the Sea.

- Chamber for Marine Environment Disputes – composed of nine members to consider disputes with regard to the protection and preservation of the marine environment.
- Chamber for Maritime Delimitation Disputes – consists of eleven members and deals with disputes on maritime delimitation.[1088]

At the request of the parties, the Tribunal shall form special chambers to deal with particular cases (according to Paragraph 2 of Article 15 of the Statute).

Disputes concerning activities in the Area are submitted to the Seabed Disputes Chamber of the Tribunal according to the Convention, which consists of 11 judges. A quorum of seven members is required to constitute the Chamber. In addition, any party to a dispute over which the Seabed Disputes Chamber has jurisdiction may request the Seabed Disputes Chamber to form an *ad hoc* chamber consisting of three members of the Seabed Disputes Chamber.

On the whole, the 'availability of chambers allows parties to choose a forum for either its efficiencies or its particular expertise. The members of these various chambers are selected by the Tribunal's judges, rather than by the States Parties.'[1089]

First of all, the 'Members of the Tribunal of the nationality of any of the parties to a dispute shall retain their right to participate as members of the Tribunal.'[1090] Secondly, if the Tribunal or a chamber does not include a judge with the same nationality as a party to the dispute, that party may choose a person to sit as a judge (judges *ad hoc*). At the same time, when there are 'several parties in the same interest', they are considered for this purpose as one party only. Judges *ad hoc* shall fulfil the requirements specified for the members of the Tribunal and 'shall participate in the decision on terms of complete equality with their colleagues.'[1091]

The International Tribunal for the Law of the Sea – jurisdiction and procedural matters

The jurisdiction of the Tribunal includes all disputes, all applications submitted to it in accordance with the Convention, and all matters specifically provided for in any other agreement 'related to the purposes of the Convention' and, additionally, confers jurisdiction on the Tribunal.[1092] Hence, the jurisdictional scope of the Tribunal is not limited to the parties to the Convention.[1093] Moreover, in certain cases, the Seabed

---

1088 See <www.itlos.org/en/main/the-tribunal/chambers/> accessed 18 March 2021.

1089 John E. Noyes, 'The International Tribunal for the Law of the Sea' (1999) 32(1) *Cornell International Law Journal* Article 3 128.

1090 Article 17 (1) of Annex VI. Statute of the International Tribunal for the Law of the Sea.

1091 Article 17 of Annex VI. Statute of the International Tribunal for the Law of the Sea.

1092 Article 21 of Annex VI. Statute of the International Tribunal for the Law of the Sea.

1093 'The Tribunal is open to States Parties to the Convention and, in certain cases, to entities other than States Parties (such as international organizations and natural or legal persons).' <www.itlos.org/en/main/the-tribunal/the-tribunal/> accessed 18 March 2021.

Disputes Chamber, in parallel with the states and other parties to the Convention or other international agreements, is also open to state enterprises and natural or juridical persons.

The Tribunal has **contentious jurisdiction** over the disputes, as well as **advisory jurisdiction** in particular cases. As emphasised earlier, the Seabed Disputes Chamber is empowered to give an advisory opinion within the scope of its competence. At the same time, the Tribunal may also give an advisory opinion on a legal question in particular cases if this is provided for by 'an international agreement related to the purposes of the Convention'.

Among the contentious cases of the Tribunal, the following types should be outlined:

- disputes concerning the interpretation or application of the Convention;
- disputes concerning the interpretation or application of other agreements; and
- particular disputes within the scope of the jurisdiction of the Seabed Disputes Chamber.

The Tribunal has the competence to determine provisional measures and prompt release of vessels and crews. (Unless the parties to the dispute agree otherwise, the jurisdiction of the Tribunal in such cases is mandatory.)[1094]

Generally, in the event of a dispute as to whether the Tribunal has jurisdiction, the issue shall be settled by the Tribunal.

'Disputes are submitted to the Tribunal, as the case may be, either by notification of a special agreement or by written application, addressed to the Registrar. In either case, the subject of the dispute and the parties shall be indicated.'[1095]

The hearings of the Tribunal are public unless the Tribunal decides otherwise or unless the parties demand that the hearing be closed. The Tribunal makes decisions based on the majority of votes of the members of the Tribunal present; in case of a tie, the President (or the member of the Tribunal who acts in President's place) has the deciding vote.

The decisions of the Tribunal are final. The President and the Registrar sign the judgment of the Tribunal. It shall be read in the open court.

CASES AND MATERIALS (*SELECTED PARTS*)

Sea zones

United Nations Convention on the Law of the Sea
of 1982
Entry into force: 16 November 1994

1094 Article 292 of the United Nations Convention on the Law of the Sea.
1095 Article 24 (1) of Annex VI. Statute of the International Tribunal for the Law of the Sea.

PART II
TERRITORIAL SEA AND CONTIGUOUS ZONE

SECTION 1. GENERAL PROVISIONS

Article 2 *Legal status of the territorial sea, of the air space over the territorial sea and of its bed and subsoil*

1   The sovereignty of a coastal State extends, beyond its land territory and internal waters and, in the case of an archipelagic State, its archipelagic waters, to an adjacent belt of sea, described as the territorial sea.
2   This sovereignty extends to the air space over the territorial sea as well as to its bed and subsoil.
3   The sovereignty over the territorial sea is exercised subject to this Convention and to other rules of international law.

SECTION 2. LIMITS OF THE TERRITORIAL SEA

Article 3 *Breadth of the territorial sea*

Every State has the right to establish the breadth of its territorial sea up to a limit not exceeding 12 nautical miles, measured from baselines determined in accordance with this Convention.

Article 4 *Outer limit of the territorial sea*

The outer limit of the territorial sea is the line every point of which is at a distance from the nearest point of the baseline equal to the breadth of the territorial sea.

Article 5 *Normal baseline*

Except where otherwise provided in this Convention, the normal baseline for measuring the breadth of the territorial sea is the low-water line along the coast as marked on large-scale charts officially recognized by the coastal State.

Article 6 *Reefs*

In the case of islands situated on atolls or of islands having fringing reefs, the baseline for measuring the breadth of the territorial sea is the seaward low-water line of the reef, as shown by the appropriate symbol on charts officially recognized by the coastal State.

Article 7 *Straight baselines*

1   In localities where the coastline is deeply indented and cut into, or if there is a fringe of islands along the coast in its immediate vicinity, the method of straight baselines joining appropriate points may be employed in drawing the baseline from which the breadth of the territorial sea is measured.

2   Where because of the presence of a delta and other natural conditions the coastline is highly unstable, the appropriate points may be selected along the furthest seaward extent of the low-water line and, notwithstanding subsequent regression of the low-water line, the straight baselines shall remain effective until changed by the coastal State in accordance with this Convention.

3   The drawing of straight baselines must not depart to any appreciable extent from the general direction of the coast, and the sea areas lying within the lines must be sufficiently closely linked to the land domain to be subject to the regime of internal waters.

4   Straight baselines shall not be drawn to and from low-tide elevations, unless lighthouses or similar installations which are permanently above sea level have been built on them or except in instances where the drawing of baselines to and from such elevations has received general international recognition.

5   Where the method of straight baselines is applicable under paragraph 1, account may be taken, in determining particular baselines, of economic interests peculiar to the region concerned, the reality and the importance of which are clearly evidenced by long usage.

6   The system of straight baselines may not be applied by a State in such a manner as to cut off the territorial sea of another State from the high seas or an exclusive economic zone.

Article 8 Internal waters

1   Except as provided in Part IV, waters on the landward side of the baseline of the territorial sea form part of the internal waters of the State.

2   Where the establishment of a straight baseline in accordance with the method set forth in article 7 has the effect of enclosing as internal waters areas which had not previously been considered as such, a right of innocent passage as provided in this Convention shall exist in those waters.

Article 9 Mouths of rivers

If a river flows directly into the sea, the baseline shall be a straight line across the mouth of the river between points on the low-water line of its banks.

Article 10 Bays

1   This article relates only to bays the coasts of which belong to a single State.

2   For the purposes of this Convention, a bay is a well-marked indentation whose penetration is in such proportion to the width of its mouth as to contain land-locked waters and constitute more than a mere curvature of the coast. An indentation shall not, however, be regarded as a bay unless its area is as large as, or larger than, that of the semi-circle whose diameter is a line drawn across the mouth of that indentation.

3   For the purpose of measurement, the area of an indentation is that lying between the low-water mark around the shore of the indentation and a line joining the low-water mark of its natural entrance points. Where, because of the presence of islands, an indentation has more than one mouth, the semi-circle shall be drawn on a line as long as the sum total of the lengths of the lines across the different mouths. Islands within an indentation shall be included as if they were part of the water area of the indentation.

4   If the distance between the low-water marks of the natural entrance points of a bay does not exceed 24 nautical miles, a closing line may be drawn between these two low-water marks, and the waters enclosed thereby shall be considered as internal waters.

5   Where the distance between the low-water marks of the natural entrance points of a bay exceeds 24 nautical miles, a straight baseline of 24 nautical miles shall be drawn within the bay in such a manner as to enclose the maximum area of water that is possible with a line of that length.

6   The foregoing provisions do not apply to so-called "historic" bays, or in any case where the system of straight baselines provided for in article 7 is applied.

Article 11 Ports

For the purpose of delimiting the territorial sea, the outermost permanent harbour works which form an integral part of the harbour system are regarded as forming part of the coast. Off-shore installations and artificial islands shall not be considered as permanent harbour works.

Article 12 Roadsteads

Roadsteads which are normally used for the loading, unloading and anchoring of ships, and which would otherwise be situated wholly or partly outside the outer limit of the territorial sea, are included in the territorial sea.

Article 13 Low-tide elevations

1   A low-tide elevation is a naturally formed area of land which is surrounded by and above water at low tide but submerged at high tide. Where a low-tide elevation is situated wholly or partly at a distance not exceeding the breadth of the territorial sea from the mainland or an island, the low-water line on that elevation may be used as the baseline for measuring the breadth of the territorial sea.

2   Where a low-tide elevation is wholly situated at a distance exceeding the breadth of the territorial sea from the mainland or an island, it has no territorial sea of its own.

Article 14 Combination of methods for determining baselines

The coastal State may determine baselines in turn by any of the methods provided for in the foregoing articles to suit different conditions.

Article 15 Delimitation of the territorial sea between States with opposite or adjacent coasts

Where the coasts of two States are opposite or adjacent to each other, neither of the two States is entitled, failing agreement between them to the contrary, to extend its territorial sea beyond the median line every point of which is equidistant from the nearest points on the baselines from which the breadth of the territorial seas of each of the two States is measured. The above provision does not apply, however, where it is necessary by reason of historic title or other special circumstances to delimit the territorial seas of the two States in a way which is at variance therewith.

Article 16 Charts and lists of geographical coordinates

1 The baselines for measuring the breadth of the territorial sea determined in accordance with articles 7, 9 and 10, or the limits derived therefrom, and the lines of delimitation drawn in accordance with articles 12 and 15 shall be shown on charts of a scale or scales adequate for ascertaining their position. Alternatively, a list of geographical coordinates of points, specifying the geodetic datum, may be substituted.
2 The coastal State shall give due publicity to such charts or lists of geographical coordinates and shall deposit a copy of each such chart or list with the Secretary-General of the United Nations.

SECTION 3. INNOCENT PASSAGE IN THE TERRITORIAL SEA

SUBSECTION A. RULES APPLICABLE TO ALL SHIPS

Article 17 Right of innocent passage

Subject to this Convention, ships of all States, whether coastal or land-locked, enjoy the right of innocent passage through the territorial sea.

Article 18 Meaning of passage

1 Passage means navigation through the territorial sea for the purpose of:

(a) traversing that sea without entering internal waters or calling at a roadstead or port facility outside internal waters; or
(b) proceeding to or from internal waters or a call at such roadstead or port facility.

2 Passage shall be continuous and expeditious. However, passage includes stopping and anchoring, but only in so far as the same are incidental to ordinary navigation or are rendered necessary by force majeure or distress or for the purpose of rendering assistance to persons, ships or aircraft in danger or distress.

Article 19 Meaning of innocent passage

1 Passage is innocent so long as it is not prejudicial to the peace, good order or security of the coastal State. Such passage shall take place in conformity with this Convention and with other rules of international law.
2 Passage of a foreign ship shall be considered to be prejudicial to the peace, good order or security of the coastal State if in the territorial sea it engages in any of the following activities:

(a) any threat or use of force against the sovereignty, territorial integrity or political independence of the coastal State, or in any other manner in violation of the principles of international law embodied in the Charter of the United Nations;
(b) any exercise or practice with weapons of any kind;

   (c)   any act aimed at collecting information to the prejudice of the defence or security of the coastal State;

   (d)   any act of propaganda aimed at affecting the defence or security of the coastal State;

   (e)   the launching, landing or taking on board of any aircraft;

   (f)   the launching, landing or taking on board of any military device;

   (g)   the loading or unloading of any commodity, currency or person contrary to the customs, fiscal, immigration or sanitary laws and regulations of the coastal State;

   (h)   any act of wilful and serious pollution contrary to this Convention;

   (i)   any fishing activities;

   (j)   the carrying out of research or survey activities;

   (k)   any act aimed at interfering with any systems of communication or any other facilities or installations of the coastal State;

   (l)   any other activity not having a direct bearing on passage.

Article 20 Submarines and other underwater vehicles

In the territorial sea, submarines and other underwater vehicles are required to navigate on the surface and to show their flag.

Article 24 Duties of the coastal State

1   The coastal State shall not hamper the innocent passage of foreign ships through the territorial sea except in accordance with this Convention. In particular, in the application of this Convention or of any laws or regulations adopted in conformity with this Convention, the coastal State shall not:

   (a)   impose requirements on foreign ships which have the practical effect of denying or impairing the right of innocent passage; or

   (b)   discriminate in form or in fact against the ships of any State or against ships carrying cargoes to, from or on behalf of any State.

2   The coastal State shall give appropriate publicity to any danger to navigation, of which it has knowledge, within its territorial sea.

Article 25 Rights of protection of the coastal State

1   The coastal State may take the necessary steps in its territorial sea to prevent passage which is not innocent.

2   In the case of ships proceeding to internal waters or a call at a port facility outside internal waters, the coastal State also has the right to take the necessary steps to prevent any breach of the conditions to which admission of those ships to internal waters or such a call is subject.

3   The coastal State may, without discrimination in form or in fact among foreign ships, suspend temporarily in specified areas of its territorial sea the innocent passage of foreign ships if such suspension is essential for the protection of its security, including weapons exercises. Such suspension shall take effect only after having been duly published.

SECTION 4. CONTIGUOUS ZONE

Article 33 Contiguous zone

1   In a zone contiguous to its territorial sea, described as the contiguous zone, the coastal State may exercise the control necessary to:

   (a) prevent infringement of its customs, fiscal, immigration or sanitary laws and regulations within its territory or territorial sea;
   (b) punish infringement of the above laws and regulations committed within its territory or territorial sea.

2   The contiguous zone may not extend beyond 24 nautical miles from the baselines from which the breadth of the territorial sea is measured.

PART V EXCLUSIVE ECONOMIC ZONE

Article 55 Specific legal regime of the exclusive economic zone

The exclusive economic zone is an area beyond and adjacent to the territorial sea, subject to the specific legal regime established in this Part, under which the rights and jurisdiction of the coastal State and the rights and freedoms of other States are governed by the relevant provisions of this Convention.

Article 56 Rights, jurisdiction and duties of the coastal State in the exclusive economic zone

1   In the exclusive economic zone, the coastal State has:

   (a) sovereign rights for the purpose of exploring and exploiting, conserving and managing the natural resources, whether living or non-living, of the waters superjacent to the seabed and of the seabed and its subsoil, and with regard to other activities for the economic exploitation and exploration of the zone, such as the production of energy from the water, currents and winds;
   (b) jurisdiction as provided for in the relevant provisions of this Convention with regard to:

   (i) the establishment and use of artificial islands, installations and structures;
   (ii) marine scientific research;
   (iii) the protection and preservation of the marine environment;

   (c) other rights and duties provided for in this Convention.

2   In exercising its rights and performing its duties under this Convention in the exclusive economic zone, the coastal State shall have due regard to the rights and duties of other States and shall act in a manner compatible with the provisions of this Convention.

3   The rights set out in this article with respect to the seabed and subsoil shall be exercised in accordance with Part VI.

Article 57 Breadth of the exclusive economic zone

The exclusive economic zone shall not extend beyond 200 nautical miles from the baselines from which the breadth of the territorial sea is measured.

Article 58 Rights and duties of other States in the exclusive economic zone

1   In the exclusive economic zone, all States, whether coastal or land-locked, enjoy, subject to the relevant provisions of this Convention, the freedoms referred to in article 87 of navigation and overflight and of the laying of submarine cables and pipelines, and other internationally lawful uses of the sea related to these freedoms, such as those associated with the operation of ships, aircraft and submarine cables and pipelines, and compatible with the other provisions of this Convention.

PART VI CONTINENTAL SHELF

Article 76 Definition of the continental shelf

1   The continental shelf of a coastal State comprises the seabed and subsoil of the submarine areas that extend beyond its territorial sea throughout the natural prolongation of its land territory to the outer edge of the continental margin, or to a distance of 200 nautical miles from the baselines from which the breadth of the territorial sea is measured where the outer edge of the continental margin does not extend up to that distance.

2   The continental shelf of a coastal State shall not extend beyond the limits provided for in paragraphs 4 to 6.

3   The continental margin comprises the submerged prolongation of the land mass of the coastal State, and consists of the seabed and subsoil of the shelf, the slope and the rise. It does not include the deep ocean floor with its oceanic ridges or the subsoil thereof.

4.   (a) For the purposes of this Convention, the coastal State shall establish the outer edge of the continental margin wherever the margin extends beyond 200 nautical miles from the baselines from which the breadth of the territorial sea is measured, by either:

   (i)   a line delineated in accordance with paragraph 7 by reference to the outermost fixed points at each of which the thickness of sedimentary rocks is at least 1 per cent of the shortest distance from such point to the foot of the continental slope; or

   (ii) a line delineated in accordance with paragraph 7 by reference to fixed points not more than 60 nautical miles from the foot of the continental slope.

   (b) In the absence of evidence to the contrary, the foot of the continental slope shall be determined as the point of maximum change in the gradient at its base.

5   The fixed points comprising the line of the outer limits of the continental shelf on the seabed, drawn in accordance with paragraph 4 (a)(i) and (ii), either shall not exceed 350 nautical miles from the baselines from which the breadth of the territorial sea is measured or shall not exceed 100 nautical miles from the 2,500 metre isobath, which is a line connecting the depth of 2,500 metres.

6   Notwithstanding the provisions of paragraph 5, on submarine ridges, the outer limit of the continental shelf shall not exceed 350 nautical miles from the baselines from which the breadth of the territorial sea is measured. This paragraph does not apply to submarine elevations that are natural components of the continental margin, such as its plateaux, rises, caps, banks and spurs.

7   The coastal State shall delineate the outer limits of its continental shelf, where that shelf extends beyond 200 nautical miles from the baselines from which the breadth of the territorial sea is measured, by straight lines not exceeding 60 nautical miles in length, connecting fixed points, defined by coordinates of latitude and longitude.

8   Information on the limits of the continental shelf beyond 200 nautical miles from the baselines from which the breadth of the territorial sea is measured shall be submitted by the coastal State to the Commission on the Limits of the Continental Shelf set up under Annex II on the basis of equitable geographical representation. The Commission shall make recommendations to coastal States on matters related to the establishment of the outer limits of their continental shelf. The limits of the shelf established by a coastal State on the basis of these recommendations shall be final and binding.

9   The coastal State shall deposit with the Secretary-General of the United Nations charts and relevant information, including geodetic data, permanently describing the outer limits of its continental shelf. The Secretary-General shall give due publicity thereto.

10 The provisions of this article are without prejudice to the question of delimitation of the continental shelf between States with opposite or adjacent coasts.

Article 77 Rights of the coastal State over the continental shelf

1   The coastal State exercises over the continental shelf sovereign rights for the purpose of exploring it and exploiting its natural resources.

2   The rights referred to in paragraph 1 are exclusive in the sense that if the coastal State does not explore the continental shelf or exploit its natural resources, no one may undertake these activities without the express consent of the coastal State.

3   The rights of the coastal State over the continental shelf do not depend on occupation, effective or notional, or on any express proclamation.

4   The natural resources referred to in this Part consist of the mineral and other non-living resources of the seabed and subsoil together with living organisms belonging to sedentary species, that is to say, organisms which, at the harvestable stage, either are immobile on or under the seabed or are unable to move except in constant physical contact with the seabed or the subsoil.

Article 78 Legal status of the superjacent waters and air space and the rights and freedoms of other States

1   The rights of the coastal State over the continental shelf do not affect the legal status of the superjacent waters or of the air space above those waters.

2   The exercise of the rights of the coastal State over the continental shelf must not infringe or result in any unjustifiable interference with navigation and other rights and freedoms of other States as provided for in this Convention.

PART VII HIGH SEAS

SECTION 1. GENERAL PROVISIONS

Article 87 Freedom of the high seas

1   The high seas are open to all States, whether coastal or land-locked. Freedom of the high seas is exercised under the conditions laid down by this Convention and by other rules of international law. It comprises, inter alia, both for coastal and land-locked States:
  (a) freedom of navigation;
  (b) freedom of overflight;
  (c) freedom to lay submarine cables and pipelines, subject to Part VI;
  (d) freedom to construct artificial islands and other installations permitted under international law, subject to Part VI;
  (e) freedom of fishing, subject to the conditions laid down in section 2;
  (f) freedom of scientific research, subject to Parts VI and XIII.

2   These freedoms shall be exercised by all States with due regard for the interests of other States in their exercise of the freedom of the high seas, and also with due regard for the rights under this Convention with respect to activities in the Area.

Article 88 Reservation of the high seas for peaceful purposes

The high seas shall be reserved for peaceful purposes.

Article 89 Invalidity of claims of sovereignty over the high seas

No State may validly purport to subject any part of the high seas to its sovereignty.

Article 90 Right of navigation

Every State, whether coastal or land-locked, has the right to sail ships flying its flag on the high seas.

Article 91 Nationality of ships

1   Every State shall fix the conditions for the grant of its nationality to ships, for the registration of ships in its territory, and for the right to fly its flag. Ships have the nationality of the State whose flag they are entitled to fly. There must exist a genuine link between the State and the ship.
2   Every State shall issue to ships to which it has granted the right to fly its flag documents to that effect.

Article 92 Status of ships

1   Ships shall sail under the flag of one State only and, save in exceptional cases expressly provided for in international treaties or in this Convention, shall be subject to its exclusive jurisdiction on the high seas. A ship may not change its flag during a voyage or while in a port of call, save in the case of a real transfer of ownership or change of registry.
2   A ship which sails under the flags of two or more States, using them according to convenience,

may not claim any of the nationalities in question with respect to any other State, and may be assimilated to a ship without nationality.

PART XI THE AREA

SECTION 2. PRINCIPLES GOVERNING THE AREA

Article 136 Common heritage of mankind

The Area and its resources are the common heritage of mankind.

Article 137 Legal status of the Area and its resources

1   No State shall claim or exercise sovereignty or sovereign rights over any part of the Area or its resources, nor shall any State or natural or juridical person appropriate any part thereof. No such claim or exercise of sovereignty or sovereign rights nor such appropriation shall be recognized.
2   All rights in the resources of the Area are vested in mankind as a whole, on whose behalf the Authority shall act. These resources are not subject to alienation. The minerals recovered from the Area, however, may only be alienated in accordance with this Part and the rules, regulations and procedures of the Authority.
3   No State or natural or juridical person shall claim, acquire or exercise rights with respect to the minerals recovered from the Area except in accordance with this Part. Otherwise, no such claim, acquisition or exercise of such rights shall be recognized.

Article 140 Benefit of mankind

1   Activities in the Area shall, as specifically provided for in this Part, be carried out for the benefit of mankind as a whole, irrespective of the geographical location of States, whether coastal or land-locked, and taking into particular consideration the interests and needs of developing States and of peoples who have not attained full independence or other self-governing status recognized by the United Nations in accordance with General Assembly resolution 1514 (XV) and other relevant General Assembly resolutions.
2   The Authority shall provide for the equitable sharing of financial and other economic benefits derived from activities in the Area through any appropriate mechanism, on a non-discriminatory basis, in accordance with article 160, paragraph 2(f)(i).

Article 141 Use of the Area exclusively for peaceful purposes

The Area shall be open to use exclusively for peaceful purposes by all States, whether coastal or land-locked, without discrimination and without prejudice to the other provisions of this Part.

Straits used for international navigation
Enclosed or semi-enclosed seas
Dardanelles and Bosphorus

Convention Regarding the Regime of the Straits
(Montreux Convention) of 1936
Entry into force: 9 November 1936

Article 1

The High Contracting Parties recognise and affirm the principle of freedom of transit and navigation by sea in the Straits.

The exercise of this freedom shall henceforth be regulated by the provisions of the present Convention.

SECTION I. MERCHANT VESSELS

Article 2

In time of peace, merchant vessels shall enjoy complete freedom of transit and navigation in the Straits, by day and by night, under any flag and with any kind of cargo, without any formalities, except as provided in Article 3 below. No taxes or charges other than those authorised by Annex I to the present Convention shall be levied by the Turkish authorities on these vessels when passing in transit without calling at a port in the Straits.

In order to facilitate the collection of these taxes or charges merchant vessels passing through the Straits shall communicate to the officials at the stations referred to in Article 3 their name, nationality, tonnage, destination and last port of call (provenance).

Pilotage and towage remain optional.

Article 3

All ships entering the Straits by the Aegean Sea or by the Black Sea shall stop at a sanitary station near the entrance to the Straits for the purposes of the sanitary control prescribed by Turkish law within the framework of international sanitary regulations. This control, in the case of ship possessing a clean bill of health or presenting a declaration of health testifying that they do not fall within the scope of the provisions of the second paragraph of the present Article, shall be carried out by day and by night with all possible speed, and the vessels in question shall not be required to make any other stop during their passage through the Straits.

Vessels which have on board cases of plague, cholera, yellow fever, exanthematic typhus or smallpox, or which have had such cases on board during the previous seven days, and vessels which have left an infected port within less than five times twenty-four hours shall stop at the sanitary stations indicated in the preceding paragraph in order to embark such sanitary guards as the Turkish authorities may direct. No fax or charge shall be levied in respect of these sanitary guards and they shall be disembarked at a sanitary station on departure from the Straits.

Article 4

In time of war, Turkey not being belligerent, merchant vessels, under any flag or with any kind of cargo, shall enjoy freedom of transit and navigation in the Straits subject to the provisions of Articles 2 and 3.

Pilotage and towage remain optional.

Article 5

In time of war, Turkey being belligerent, merchant vessels not belonging to a country at war with Turkey shall enjoy freedom of transit and navigation in the Straits on condition that they do not in any way assist the enemy.

Such vessels shall enter the Straits by day and their transit shall be effected by the route which shall in each case be indicated by the Turkish authorities.

Article 6

Should Turkey consider herself to be threatened with imminent danger of war, the provisions of Article 2 shall nevertheless continue to be applied except that vessels must enter the Straits by day and that their transit must be effected by the route which shall, in each case, be indicated by the Turkish authorities.

Pilotage may, in this case, be made obligatory, but no charge shall be levied.

Article 7

The term "merchant vessels" applies to all vessels which are not covered by Section II of the present Convention.

SECTION II. VESSELS OF WAR

Article 9

Naval auxiliary vessels specifically designed for the carriage of fuel, liquid or non-liquid, shall not be subject to the provisions of Article 13 regarding notification, nor shall they be counted for the purpose of calculating the tonnage which is subject to limitation under Articles 14 and 18, on condition that they shall pass through the Straits singly. They shall, however, continue to be on the same footing as vessels of war for the purpose of the remaining provisions governing transit.

The auxiliary vessels specified in the preceding paragraph shall only be entitled to benefit by the exceptional status therein contemplated if their armament does not include: for use against floating targets, more than two guns of a maximum calibre of 105 millimetres; for use against aerial targets, more than two guns of a maximum calibre of 75 millimetres.

Article 10

In time of peace, light surface vessels, minor war vessels and auxiliary vessels, whether belonging to Black Sea or non-Black Sea Powers, and whatever their flag, shall enjoy freedom of transit through the Straits without any taxes or charges whatever, provided that such transit is begun during daylight and subject to the conditions laid down in Article 13 and the Articles following thereafter.

Vessels of war other than those which fall within the categories specified in the preceding paragraph shall only enjoy a right of transit under the special conditions provided by Articles 11 and 12.

Article 11

Black Sea Powers may send through the Straits capital ships of a tonnage greater than that laid down in the first paragraph of Article 14, on condition that these vessels pass through the Straits singly, escorted by not more than two destroyers.

Article 12

Black Sea Powers shall have the right to send through the Straits, for the purpose of rejoining their base, submarines constructed or purchased outside the Black Sea, provided that adequate notice of the laying down or purchase of such submarines shall have been given to Turkey.

Submarines belonging to the said Powers shall also be entitled to pass through the Straits to be repaired in dockyards outside the Black Sea on condition that detailed information on the matter is given to Turkey.

In either case, the said submarines must travel by day and on the surface, and must pass through the Straits singly.

Article 13

The transit of vessels of war through the Straits shall be preceded by a notification given to the Turkish Government through the diplomatic channel. The normal period of notice shall be eight days; but it is desirable that in the case of non-Black Sea Powers this period should be increased to fifteen days. The notification shall specify the destination, name, type and number of the vessels, as also the date of entry for the outward passage and, if necessary, for the return journey. Any change of date shall be subject to three days' notice.

Entry into the Straits for the outward passage shall take place within a period of five days from the date given in the original notification. After the expiry of this period, a new notification shall be given under the same conditions as for the original notification.

When effecting transit, the commander of the naval force shall, without being under any obligation to stop, communicate to a signal station at the entrance to the Dardanelles or the Bosphorus the exact composition of the force under his orders.

Article 14

The maximum aggregate tonnage of all foreign naval forces which may be in course of transit through the Straits shall not exceed 15,000 tons, except in the cases provided for in Article 11 and in Annex III to the present Convention.

The forces specified in the preceding paragraph shall not, however, comprise more than nine vessels.

Vessels whether belonging to Black Sea or non-Black Sea Powers, paying visits to a port in the Straits, in accordance with the provisions of Article 17, shall not be included in this tonnage.

Neither shall vessels of war which have suffered damage during their passage through the Straits be included in this tonnage; such vessels, while undergoing repair, shall be subject to any special provisions relating to security laid down by Turkey.

Article 15

Vessels of war in transit through the Straits shall in no circumstances make use of any aircraft which they may be carrying.

Article 16

Vessels of war in transit through the Straits shall not, except in the event of damage or peril of the sea, remain therein longer than is necessary for them to effect the passage.

Article 17

Nothing in the provisions of the preceding Articles shall prevent a naval force of any tonnage or composition from paying a courtesy visit of limited duration to a port in the Straits, at the invitation of the Turkish Government. Any such force must leave the Straits by the same route as that by which it entered, unless it fulfils the conditions required for passage in transit through the Straits as laid down by Articles 10, 14 and 18.

Article 18

(1) The aggregate tonnage which non-Black Sea Powers may have in that sea in time of peace shall be limited as follows:

(a) Except as provided in paragraph *(b)* below, the aggregate tonnage of the said Powers shall not exceed 30,000 tons;

(b) If at any time the tonnage of the strongest fleet in the Black Sea shall exceed by at least 10,000 tons the tonnage of the strongest fleet in that sea at the date of the signature of the present Convention, the aggregate tonnage of 30,000 tons mentioned in paragraph *(a)* shall be increased by the same amount, up to a maximum of 45,000 tons. For this purpose, each Black Sea Power shall, in conformity with Annex IV to the present Convention, inform the Turkish Government, on the 1st January and the 1st July of each year, of the total tonnage of its fleet in the Black Sea; and the Turkish Government shall transmit this information to the other High Contracting Parties and to the Secretary-General of the League of Nations;

(c) The tonnage which any one non-Black Sea Power may have in the Black Sea shall be limited to two-thirds of the aggregate tonnage provided for in paragraphs *(a)* and *(b)* above;

(d) In the event, however, of one or more non-Black Sea Powers desiring to send naval forces into the Black Sea, for a humanitarian purpose, the said forces, which shall in no case exceed 8,000 tons altogether, shall be allowed to enter the Black Sea without having to give the notification provided for in Article 13 of the present Convention, provided an authorisation is obtained from the Turkish Government in the following circumstances: if the figure of the aggregate tonnage specified in paragraphs *(a)* and *(b)* above has not been reached and will not be exceeded by the despatch of the forces which it is desired to send, the Turkish Government shall grant the said authorisation within the shortest possible time after receiving the request which has been addressed to it; if the said figure has already been reached or if the despatch of the forces which it is desired to send will cause it to be exceeded, the Turkish Government will immediately inform the other Black Sea Powers of the request for authorisation, and if the said Powers make no objection within twenty-four hours of having received this information, the Turkish Government shall, within forty-eight hours at the latest, inform the interested Powers of the reply which it has decided to make to their request.

Any further entry into the Black Sea of naval forces of non-Black Sea Powers shall only be effected within the available limits of the aggregate tonnage provided for in paragraphs *(a)* and *(b)* above.

(2) Vessels of war belonging to non-Black Sea Powers shall not remain in the Black Sea more than twenty-one days, whatever be the object of their presence there.

Article 19

In time of war, Turkey not being belligerent, warships shall enjoy complete freedom of transit and navigation through the Straits under the same conditions as those laid down in Articles 10 to 18.

Vessels of war belonging to belligerent Powers shall not, however, pass through the Straits except in cases arising out of the application of Article 25 of the present Convention, and in cases of assistance rendered to a State victim of aggression in virtue of a treaty of mutual assistance binding Turkey, concluded within the framework of the Covenant of the League of Nations, and registered and published in accordance with the provisions of Article 18 of the Covenant.

In the exceptional cases provided for in the preceding paragraph, the limitations laid down in Articles 10 to 18 of the present Convention shall not be applicable.

Notwithstanding the prohibition of passage laid down in paragraph 2 above, vessels of war belonging to belligerent Powers, whether they are Black Sea Powers or not, which have become separated from their bases, may return thereto.

Vessels of war belonging to belligerent Powers shall not make any capture, exercise the right of visit and search, or carry out any hostile act in the Straits.

Article 20

In time of war, Turkey being belligerent, the provisions of Articles 10 to 18 shall not be applicable; the passage of warships shall be left entirely to the discretion of the Turkish Government.

Article 21

Should Turkey consider herself to be threatened with imminent danger of war she shall have the right to apply the provisions of Article 20 of the present Convention.

Vessels which have passed through the Straits before Turkey has made use of the powers conferred upon her by the preceding paragraph, and which thus find themselves separated from their bases, may return thereto. It is, however, understood that Turkey may deny this right to vessels of war belonging to the State whose attitude has given rise to the application of the present Article.

Should the Turkish Government make use of the powers conferred by the first paragraph of the present Article, a notification to that effect shall be addressed to the High Contracting Parties and to the Secretary-General of the League of Nations.

If the Council of the League of Nations decides by a majority of two-thirds that the measures thus taken by Turkey are not justified, and if such should also be the opinion of the majority of the High Contracting Parties signatories to the present Convention, the Turkish Government under-takes to discontinue the measures in question as also any measures which may have been taken under Article 6 of the present Convention.

Article 22

Vessels of war which have on board cases of plague, cholera, yellow fever, exanthematic typhus or smallpox or which have had such cases on board within the last seven days and vessels of war which have left an infected port within less than five times twenty-four hours must pass through the Straits in quarantine and apply by the means on board such prophylactic measures as are necessary in order to prevent any possibility of the Straits being infected.

Section III. Aircraft

Article 23

In order to assure the passage of civil aircraft between the Mediterranean and the Black Sea, the Turkish Government will indicate the air routes available for this purpose, outside the forbidden zones which may be established in the Straits. Civil aircraft may use these routes provided that they give the Turkish Government, as regards occasional flights, a notification of three days, and as regards flights on regular services, a general notification of the dates of passage.

The Turkish Government moreover undertake, notwithstanding any remilitarisation of the Straits, to furnish the necessary facilities for the safe passage of civil aircraft authorised under the air regulations in force in Turkey to fly across Turkish territory between Europe and Asia. The route which is to be followed in the Straits zone by aircraft which have obtained an authorisation shall be indicated from time to time.

Straits used for international navigation

Corfu Channel (UK v Albania), International Court of Justice, Judgment of 9 April 1949
ICJ Reports 1949, 4.

The Court will now consider the Albanian contention that the United Kingdom Government violated Albanian sovereignty by sending the warships through this Strait without the previous authorization of the Albanian Government.

It is, in the opinion of the Court, generally recognized and in accordance with international custom that States in time of peace have a right to send their warships through straits used for international navigation between two parts of the high seas without the previous authorization of a coastal State, provided that the passage is innocent. Unless otherwise prescribed in an international convention, there is no right for a coastal State to prohibit such passage through straits in time of peace.

The Albanian Government does not dispute that the North Corfu Channel is a strait in the geographical sense; but it denies that this Channel belongs to the class of international highways through which a right of passage exists, on the grounds that it is only of secondary importance and not even a necessary route between two parts of the high seas, and that it is used almost exclusively for local traffic to and from the ports of Corfu and Saranda.

It may be asked whether the test is to be found in the volume of traffic passing through the Strait or in its greater or lesser importance for international navigation. But in the opinion of the Court the decisive criterion is rather its geographical situation as connecting two parts of the high seas and the fact of its being used for international navigation. Nor can it be decisive that this Strait is not a necessary route between two parts of the high seas, but only an alternative passage between the Aegean and the Adriatic Seas. It has nevertheless been a useful route for international maritime traffic. In this respect, the Agent of the United Kingdom Government gave the Court the following information relating to the period from April 1st, 1936, to December 31st, 1937: "The following is the total number of ships putting in at the Port of Corfu after passing through or just before passing through the Channel. During the period of one year nine months, the total number of ships was 2,884. The flags of the ships are Greek, Italian, Roumanian, Yugoslav, French, Albanian and British. Clearly, very small vessels are included, as the entries for Albanian vessels are high, and of course one vessel may make several journeys, but 2,884 ships for a period of one year nine months is quite a large figure. These figures relate to vessels visited by the Customs at Corfu and so do not include the large number of vessels which went through the Strait without calling at Corfu at all." There were also regular sailings through the Strait by Greek vessels three times weekly, by a British ship fortnightly, and by two Yugoslav vessels weekly and by two others fortnightly. The Court is further informed that the British Navy has regularly used this Channel for eighty years or more, and that it has also been used by the navies of other States.

One fact of particular importance is that the North Corfu Channel constitutes a frontier between Albania and Greece, that a part of it is wholly within the territorial waters of these States, and that the Strait is of special importance to Greece by reason of the traffic to and from the port of Corfu.

Having regard to these various considerations, the Court has arrived at the conclusion that the North Corfu Channel should be considered as belonging to the class of international highways through which passage cannot be prohibited by a coastal State in time of peace.

On the other hand, it is a fact that the two coastal States did not maintain normal relations, that Greece had made territorial claims precisely with regard to a part of Albanian territory bordering on the Channel, that Greece had declared that she considered herself technically in a state of war with Albania, and that Albania, invoking the danger of Greek incursions, had considered it necessary to take certain measures of vigilance in this region. The Court is of opinion that Albania, in view of these exceptional circumstances, would have been justified in issuing regulations in respect of the passage of warships through the Strait, but not in prohibiting such passage or in subjecting it to the requirement of special authorization.

For these reasons the Court is unable to accept the Albanian contention that the Government of the United Kingdom has violated Albanian sovereignty by sending the warships through the Strait without having obtained the previous authorization of the Albanian Government.

Exchange of views regarding dispute settlement

MOX Plant case (*Ireland v United Kingdom*), Provisional Measures, ITLOS, Case No. 10,
    Order of 3 December 2001
ITLOS Reports 2001 95.
55. *Considering* that article 283 of the Convention reads as follows:

1   When a dispute arises between States Parties concerning the interpretation or application of this Convention, the parties to the dispute shall proceed expeditiously to an exchange of views regarding its settlement by negotiation or other peaceful means.
2   The parties shall also proceed expeditiously to an exchange of views where a procedure for the settlement of such a dispute has been terminated without a settlement or where a settlement has been reached and the circumstances require consultation regarding the manner of implementing the settlement;

56. *Considering* that the United Kingdom maintains that the correspondence between Ireland and the United Kingdom did not amount to an exchange of views on the dispute said to arise under the Convention;
57. *Considering* that the United Kingdom contends further that its request for an exchange of views under article 283 of the Convention was not accepted by Ireland;

58. *Considering* that Ireland contends that, in its letter written as early as 30 July 1999, it had drawn the attention of the United Kingdom to the dispute under the Convention and that further exchange of correspondence on the matter took place up to the submission of the dispute to the Annex VII arbitral tribunal;

59. *Considering* that Ireland contends further that it has submitted the dispute to the Annex VII arbitral tribunal only after the United Kingdom failed to indicate its willingness to consider the immediate suspension of the authorization of the MOX plant and a halt to related international transports;

60. *Considering* that, in the view of the Tribunal, a State Party is not obliged to continue with an exchange of views when it concludes that the possibilities of reaching agreement have been exhausted;

61. *Considering* that, in the view of the Tribunal, the provisions of the Convention invoked by Ireland appear to afford a basis on which the jurisdiction of the Annex VII arbitral tribunal might be founded;

62. *Considering* that, for the above reasons, the Tribunal finds that the Annex VII arbitral tribunal would *prima facie* have jurisdiction over the dispute;

Exhaustion of local remedies

M/V Virginia G case (*Panama/Guinea-Bissau*), ITLOS, Case No. 19, Judgment of 14 April 2014
ITLOS Reports 2014 4.

152. The next question the Tribunal has to examine is the nature of the claims made by Panama.

153. It is a well-established principle of customary international law that the exhaustion of local remedies is a prerequisite for the exercise of diplomatic protection. This principle is reflected in article 14, paragraph 1, of the Draft Articles on Diplomatic Protection adopted by the International Law Commission in 2006, which provides that "[a] State may not present an international claim in respect of an injury to a national . . . before the injured person has . . . exhausted all local remedies". It is also established in international law that the exhaustion of local remedies rule does not apply where the claimant State is directly injured by the wrongful act of another State.

154. The Tribunal thus has to consider whether the claims of Panama relate to a "direct" violation on the part of Guinea-Bissau of the rights of Panama. If the answer is in the affirmative, the rule that local remedies must be exhausted does not apply.

155. It should be recalled in this respect that the Tribunal in the M/V "SAIGA" (No. 2) Case, faced with a similar situation, proceeded to examine the nature of the rights which Saint Vincent and the Grenadines claimed had been violated by Guinea (see M/V "SAIGA" (No. 2) (Saint Vincent and Grenadines v. Guinea), Judgment, ITLOS Reports 1999, p. 10, at p. 45, para. 97). The Tribunal will follow the approach of the M/V "SAIGA" (No. 2) Case in the present case.

156. The rights which Panama claims have been violated by Guinea-Bissau are set out in its final submissions referred to in paragraph 54. The Tribunal notes that most provisions of the Convention referred to in the final submissions of Panama confer rights mainly on States. The Tribunal further notes that in some of the provisions referred to by Panama, however, rights appear to be conferred on a ship or persons involved. The term "ship" in those provisions can be understood to denote persons with an interest in that ship, such as an owner or operator of it.

157. When the claim contains elements of both injury to a State and injury to an individual, for the purpose of deciding the applicability of the exhaustion of local remedies rule, the Tribunal has to determine which element is preponderant. In the present case, the Tribunal is of the view that the principal rights that Panama alleges have been violated by Guinea-Bissau include the

right of Panama to enjoy freedom of navigation and other internationally lawful uses of the seas in the exclusive economic zone of the coastal State and its right that the laws and regulations of the coastal State are enforced in conformity with article 73 of the Convention. Those rights are rights that belong to Panama under the Convention, and the alleged violations of them thus amount to direct injury to Panama. Given the nature of the principal rights that Panama alleges have been violated by the wrongful acts of Guinea-Bissau, the Tribunal finds that the claim of Panama as a whole is brought on the basis of an injury to itself.

158. The Tribunal considers that the claim for damage to the persons and entities with an interest in the ship or its cargo arises from the alleged violations referred to in the preceding paragraph. Accordingly, the Tribunal concludes that the claims in respect of such damage are not subject to the rule of exhaustion of local remedies.

159. In light of the above conclusion, the Tribunal does not consider it necessary to address the arguments of the Parties on either the question of a jurisdictional link or the question whether local remedies were available and, if so, whether they were effective.

160. The Tribunal, therefore, rejects the objection of Guinea-Bissau, based on the non-exhaustion of local remedies, to the admissibility of the claims made by Panama in the interests of individuals or private entities.

International air and space law

DOI: 10.4324/9781003213772-14

DIFFERENT APPROACHES

air law
airspace law
space law
outer space law
aerospace law
international air law
international space law

Meaning of terms

The **air law** (also called **airspace law**) and the **space law** (also called **outer space law**) are distinct branches of law; however, they are sometimes treated as one, called **aerospace law**. Air law represents the body of public and private law, both national and international, which regulates aeronautical activities and other uses of airspace. The term '**international air law**', in its current usage, primarily refers to that part of international law that affects civil aviation, including international institutions concerned with civil aviation. Space law (or **international space law**), on the other hand, regulates the activities of states, international organisations, and private entities in outer space, including the use of satellites.

The different legal status of airspace and outer space

The essential difference between international air law and space law stems from the legal status of airspace and outer space. Whereas airspace, except in international territories and territories under a mixed legal regime, is under the sovereignty of subjacent states or other subjects of international law (for instance, the Holy See), international outer space law is based on the free exploitation and use of outer space and non-appropriation of outer space and celestial bodies.

WHERE AIRSPACE ENDS AND OUTER SPACE BEGINS

Chicago Convention on International Civil Aviation
point where airspace meets space
Karman line

Chicago Convention and the boundary of airspace

One of the fundamental international treaties determining the further development of international space law is the 1944 **Chicago Convention on International Civil Aviation**, which reaffirmed the approach regarding airspace as a subject of the territorial sovereignty of subjacent states. However, according to the Chicago Convention, the sovereignty of a state is understood to extend an unlimited distance into the airspace above its territory since there was no delimitation of the boundaries in this regard.

The appearance of a necessity of delimitation

However, the approach has been modified by the emergence of space law, which naturally caused a demand for the delimitation between airspace and outer space.

The issue – where does airspace end and outer space begin? – has been debated since the 1950s, particularly after the Soviet Union launched its first artificial earth satellite, Sputnik 1, in 1957.

The point where airspace meets space

However, so far, the question of boundaries between outer space and airspace has not yet found international agreement. Nevertheless, although the states have yet to legally introduce a demarcation line between airspace and outer space, their practice proves the existence of the international rule that national sovereignty shall extend over the airspace up to a specific limit, which ends at some altitude above the earth – at most, to the **point where airspace meets space**.

To define such a point, proposals have been suggested from a variety of scientific and technological standpoints, taking into account that the airspace as such is not readily susceptible to accurate measurement. Among these criteria are:

- the theoretical limits of air flight;[1096]
- the lowest altitude at which an artificial satellite can remain in orbit;[1097] and
- the theoretical line of 100 kilometres (the so-called **Karman line**),[1098] where aircraft aerodynamic controls become ineffective and which is recognised by the Fédération Aéronautique Internationale (World Air Sports Federation) and certain states.[1099]

1096 18 km – the upper limit of civil aviation traffic; 50 km – the upper limit of atmospheric buoyancy (balloons); 80 km – the threshold altitude that defines 'astronauts' in the US, and so forth.

1097 120 km – the re-entry threshold for space systems; 160 km – the lowest practical operating orbit for satellites, and so forth.

1098 The line is named after Theodore von Kármán (1881–1963), a Hungarian American engineer and physicist.

1099 One alternative modern theoretical approach suggests defining the 50–160 km region as 'near space', and treating it legally as open to peaceful use and innocent passage. Thus, there would be three zones: (1) the airspace zone, below 50 km, subject to the territorial sovereignty of the underlying state; 2) the near space zone; and 3) the outer space zone, subject to space law.

AIRSPACE

> International Convention for Regulation of Aerial Navigation
> Pan American Convention on Commercial Aviation
> Chicago Convention on International Civil Aviation

The emergence of the need to regulate activities in airspace

The development of science and technologies causing the origination of aviation, as well as the outbreak of the First World War in 1914, aroused the states' security concerns regarding the use of airspace, which, in turn, led to the emergence of the new rules of customary international law concerning airspace.

The leading customary rule

Since then, the principal international customary norm has been that aircraft of one state have the right to fly freely over the high seas, but flight over the territory or territorial sea of another state can only be permitted with the consent of the state concerned.

This rule was reflected in the Paris Convention of 1919 (**International Convention for Regulation of Aerial Navigation**) and the Havana Convention of 1928 (**Pan American Convention on Commercial Aviation**) and was reaffirmed by the 1944 **Chicago Convention on International Civil Aviation**, which superseded the first two.

The Chicago Convention provides that 'every State has complete and exclusive sovereignty over the airspace above its territory.' At the same time, the territory of a state consists of 'the land areas and territorial waters adjacent thereto under the sovereignty, suzerainty, protection or mandate of such State.'[1100]

Air services

> concept of bilateralism
> freedoms of the air
> International Air Services Transit Agreement
> technical freedoms of the air
> International Air Transport Agreement
> commercial freedoms of the air
> mutual advantage

1100 Articles 1 and 2 of the Chicago Convention on International Civil Aviation.

> civil aircraft
> nationality
> International Civil Aviation Organisation
> scheduled and non-scheduled air services
> Standards and Recommended Practices
> interception

Civil aviation as a field of application of the Chicago Convention

For a start, it is notable that the Chicago Convention on International Civil Aviation applies only to civil aircraft and not to state aircraft, which are used in military, customs, and police services.[1101] Such state aircraft, therefore, cannot enjoy the legal framework incorporated by the Chicago Convention.

The concept of bilateralism

On the other hand, the recognition of the exclusive sovereignty of a state over its airspace by the Chicago Convention has led to the **concept of bilateralism** in air services between states. Currently, international air traffic is primarily based on a complex web of bilateral treaties. The Chicago Convention and other multilateral international treaties, in turn, provide the general legal framework for such bilateral agreements. Between these multilateral treaties, a special place is occupied by two supplementary Agreements adopted during the Chicago Conference of 1944. These Agreements introduced the so-called **freedoms of the air**.

Freedoms of the air

The 1944 Chicago **International Air Services Transit Agreement** allowed aircraft of any contracting state with respect to scheduled international air services to fly over or to land for non-traffic purposes (for technical reasons) in the territory of any other party. These are known as the first (the freedom to overfly, also called as the transit freedom) and second (the freedom of technical stop) freedoms of the air or the **technical freedoms of the air**, which, according to this Agreement, are formulated as follows:

> Each contracting State grants to the other contracting States the following freedoms of the air in respect of scheduled international air services:
>
> 1   The privilege to fly across its territory without landing;
> 2   The privilege to land for non-traffic purposes.[1102]

1101 'a) This Convention shall be applicable only to civil aircraft, and shall not be applicable to state aircraft. b) Aircraft used in military, customs and police services shall be deemed to be state aircraft.' Article 3 of the Chicago Convention on International Civil Aviation.

1102 Section 1 of Article I of the International Air Services Transit Agreement.

The 1944 Chicago **International Air Transport Agreement** repeated these freedoms and, in relation to scheduled international air services, added the other three freedoms of the air, which collectively came to be known as the **commercial freedoms of the air**. Namely, the third freedom allows passengers, mail, and cargo from the home state to be set down in the state of arrival (the freedom to set down traffic); the fourth freedom allows passengers, mail, and cargo to be picked up for transport to the home state (the freedom to pick up traffic); and the fifth freedom allows passengers, mail, and cargo coming from or destined to a third state to be picked up or set down in the territory of the intermediate state (the freedom to carry traffic to or from third state).[1103]

The experts additionally describe the other four freedoms: (6) carry traffic via home state; (7) operate from second state to or from third state; (8) carry traffic between two points in a foreign state on a flight that has originated or will terminate in a home state; (9) operate only in a foreign state.[1104]

The genuine meaning of the freedoms of the air

However, these 'freedoms' are not actually rights. Firstly, they only apply to states parties to the agreements mentioned earlier. Secondly, air services have to be agreed on between the states concerned, usually in some form of bilateral agreement, since there is certainly no obligation according to the Chicago Convention for states to accept scheduled service into or over their territory.

In sum, exclusive sovereignty has led to the right of each state to conclude a bilateral agreement with another state on the basis of **mutual advantage**. The mutual advantage is based on the perceived and agreed advantage of each side.[1105]

Other essential principles of international air law

At the same time, the Chicago Convention laid down other fundamental principles of international air law as well. For example, it expressed the principle that aircraft have the **nationality** and remain subject to the laws of the state where they are registered (similarly

---

1103 '3.The privilege to put down passengers, mail and cargo taken on in the territory of the State whose nationality the aircraft possesses; 4. The privilege to take on passengers, mail and cargo destined for the territory of the State whose nationality the aircraft possesses; 5. The privilege to take on passengers, mail and cargo destined for the territory of any other contracting State and the privilege to put down passengers, mail and cargo coming from any such territory.' Section 1 of Article I of the International Air Transport Agreement.

1104 *See ICAO Manual on the Regulation of International Air Transport*, Doc 9626 (3rd edn, 2016) Chapter 4.1. The International Civil Aviation Organisation characterises these additional four freedoms as the 'so-called' freedoms since only the five freedoms listed earlier have been officially recognised as such by the international treaties. See the official website of the ICAO at <www.icao.int/Pages/freedomsAir.aspx> accessed 18 March 2021.

1105 National airlines generally participate in the intergovernmental agreements to obtain as much commercial advantage as possible.

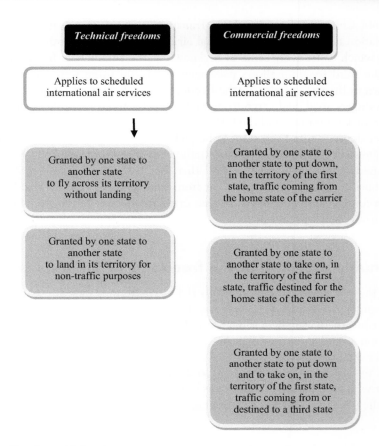

FIGURE 14.1 Freedoms of the air

to ships under the law of the sea). Each state's national law determines eligibility and criteria for aircraft registration. The registering states provide such aircraft with a certificate of airworthiness and issue certificates of competency and licenses for pilots and flight crew. Each state undertakes to supply any other state or the **International Civil Aviation Organisation** (ICAO), which was established by the Chicago Convention, the information concerning the registration and ownership of any particular aircraft registered in that state.

In addition, the Convention stressed the distinction between **scheduled and non scheduled air services**. Generally, as noted earlier, no scheduled international air service may be operated over or into the territory of a state, 'except with the special permission or other authorization' of that state.[1106]

On the other hand, as a practical consequence of the provisions of the Convention concerning the flights of the aircraft 'not engaged in scheduled international air services', the regulation of international non-scheduled traffic is usually governed by the national

---

1106 Article 6 of the Chicago Convention on International Civil Aviation.

laws of individual states, and only a few bilateral and multilateral treaties establish joint regulations.

The Annexes of the Chicago Convention provide the **Standards and Recommended Practices** (also referred to as the SARPs), which are regularly amended and published by the ICAO in the form of Annexes to the Chicago Convention. All member states are expected to incorporate the standards into their national law since their application 'is recognized as necessary'. As for the recommended practices, they are the practices which states are recommended to adopt since their application 'is recognized as desirable'.[1107]

Interception

Hence, as a rule, aircraft may only traverse the airspace of states with the agreement of these states. However, when such an agreement is not obtained and the aircraft crosses into the airspace of another state, such an act amounts to an illegal intrusion, which justifies **interception** by the state which has had its airspace violated by the aircraft; however, it does not justify (save in very exceptional cases) an actual attack on the aircraft.

Violation of national airspace by unauthorised foreign aircraft has led to many international incidents and disputes. These incidents have resulted in the need for a more detailed description of the limits of the right to interception. Ultimately, the Chicago Convention was supplemented with the new article,[1108] which specified the limits of interception, stating 'that every State must refrain from resorting to the use of weapons against civil aircraft in flight and that, in case of interception, the lives of persons on board and the safety of aircraft must not be endangered.' With this rule, the Convention restricted the **direct resort to the weapons** (without warning and giving the appropriate instructions) against intruding civil aircraft. Moreover, by entitling the states (1) to require the landing at some designated airport of a civil aircraft flying above its territory without authority or (2) to provide such aircraft with any other instructions to put an end to such violations, the Convention prescribed that the states may resort to any appropriate means which are consistent with the relevant rules of international law, including with the aforementioned restriction of the direct resort to the weapons.[1109] As was stressed by Oliver J. Lissitzyn:

> In its efforts to control the movements of intruding aircraft the territorial sovereign must not expose the aircraft and its occupants to unnecessary or unreasonably great danger – unreasonably great, that is, in relation to the reasonably apprehended

---

1107 As referred to by the ICAO itself.

1108 The most well-known incident is the destruction by a Soviet military aircraft of a Korean civil airliner, with heavy loss of life, in 1983, which contributed considerably to the adoption in 1984 by ICAO member states of an amendment to the Chicago Convention (Art. 3 *bis*) designed to prevent similar attacks on civil aircraft straying into foreign airspace without authorisation.

1109 Article 3 *bis* of the Chicago Convention on International Civil Aviation.

harmfulness of the intrusion. The application of this standard must of necessity be flexible and take into account a large variety of factors.[1110]

The Chicago Convention also provides the transparency obligation as a mechanism to limit the unrestricted use of interception since every state has an obligation to publish its regulations in force regarding interception.

Liability

> Warsaw Convention for the Unification of Certain Rules Relating to International Carriage by Air
>
> Warsaw system
>
> Montreal Convention for the Unification of Certain Rules for International Carriage by Air
>
> damage
>
> death or wounding of a passenger
>
> bodily injury
>
> accident
>
> fixed monetary limitation on the imposed liability
>
> two-tier liability system
>
> action for damages
>
> damage resulting from the death or injury

From the Warsaw Convention to the Montreal Convention

The **Warsaw Convention for the Unification of Certain Rules Relating to International Carriage by Air**, originating the so-called **Warsaw system**, was concluded in 1929. The primary goal of the Convention was to unify the private law rules that regulated aviation liability, thereby avoiding major conflicts of law. It established a fault-based liability system with a fixed monetary limitation on the imposed liability.

The original Convention was amended at various times.[1111] The co-existence of several amendments and numerous bilateral agreements created confusion among the states. In order to end the confusion, the **Montreal Convention for the Unification of Certain Rules for International Carriage by Air** of 1999 was adopted.

1110 Oliver J. Lissitzyn, 'The Treatment of Aerial Intruders in Recent Practice and International Law' (October 1953) 47(4) *The American Journal of International Law* 586.

1111 The original Convention was amended by the Hague Protocol of 1955, the Guadalajara Convention of 1961, the Montreal Agreement of 1966, the Guatemala City Protocol of 1971, Montreal Additional Protocol Nos. 1 to 3 and Montreal Protocol No. 4 of 1975.

The Warsaw system

As for the contribution made by the Warsaw Convention, it has harmonised air law with respect to:

- documents of carriage, such as passenger tickets, baggage checks, and air waybills;
- air carrier's liability; and
- jurisdictional concerns.

The liability rules of the Convention apply to the 'international carriage' of persons or property by aircraft. International carriage itself is defined as transportation between two states parties to the Convention or between two points in the same state where an agreed stopping point is in another state.

Under the Warsaw Convention, the carrier is liable for **damage** sustained (1) in the event of the **death or wounding of a passenger** or any other **bodily injury** (suffered by a passenger), (2) if the **accident** which caused the damage so sustained took place (3) on board the aircraft or (4) in the course of any of the operations of embarking or disembarking.[1112]

However, the legal meanings of the terms 'accident' and 'bodily injury' have drawn significant controversy.

In practice, under the first term is regarded an unexpected or unusual event that is external to the passenger and where there exists a causal connection between the cause of the damage and the operation of the aircraft. This definition, however, should be flexibly applied after the assessment of all circumstances.

As for the second term, a heated discussion was triggered on the question of whether or not 'bodily injury' extends to the cases when purely emotional distress and psychic injury is at hand but is not accompanied by a physical injury. Although there were different approaches to the question, many states did not recognise purely emotional distress and mental injury as launching the liability for damages.

The other purpose of the Warsaw Convention was to determine a **fixed monetary limitation on the imposed liability**, which was defined for each claim for injuries, checked baggage, and goods.[1113] Over time, the Warsaw Convention was amended several times; hence, the parties changed the fixed monetary limitations and increased their value.

Nevertheless, in some instances, according to the Convention, the carrier's liability could have been unlimited: for instance, if the claimant proved that the carrier had caused the damage by wilful misconduct or a passenger was not adequately informed about the

---

1112 Article 17 of the Warsaw Convention for the Unification of Certain Rules Relating to International Carriage by Air.

1113 '1. In the carriage of passengers the liability of the carrier for each passenger is limited to the sum of 125,000 francs. . . . Nevertheless, by special contract, the carrier and the passenger may agree to a higher limit of liability. 2. In the carriage of registered luggage and of goods, the liability of the carrier is limited to a sum of 250 francs per kilogram . . .' Article 22 of the Warsaw Convention for the Unification of Certain Rules Relating to International Carriage by Air.

existing (limitation) rules while the ticket was not delivered or was delivered in a non-proper state.

In the meanwhile, the Convention does not address the liability of the airport or aircraft manufacturers or liability for the damage done to persons and property on the surface of the earth.

Modernisation of the Warsaw system

The Montreal Convention of 1999 reaffirms some provisions of the Warsaw Convention (for example, the aforementioned definition of the damage which involves the liability of the carrier underwent only minor cosmetic changes), but, in sum, the convention introduced some modifications to modernise the Warsaw system and consolidate all related legal instruments.

It is also necessary to mention that the provisions on documentation have been changed to fit modern technological developments. With the new and a much simpler system for managing documentation, only one document that states the place of departure and destination and the applicability of the new Convention has to be delivered to a passenger. Furthermore, allowing 'any other means' which preserves the information noted here, the Convention has contributed to the development of the electronic ticket system.[1114]

However, the leading principal modification is considered a new **two-tier liability system**, with:

1 strict liability for death or bodily injury 'upon condition only that the accident which caused the death or injury took place on board the aircraft or in the course of any of the operations of embarking or disembarking' up to the fixed monetary limitation amount,[1115] and

2 a second tier of liability (above the fixed monetary limitation's amount) – the so-called presumptive liability in an unlimited amount – based on the presumed fault of the carrier, which the latter may avoid only by proving that:

    a) such damage was not due to the negligence or other wrongful act or omission of the carrier or its servants or agents; or

    b) a third person solely caused the damage.

In the event of second tier of liability, the burden of proof is on the carrier.

In any case, the carrier's liability may be discounted by the claimant's negligence or wrongful act. Under the Convention, 'punitive, exemplary or other non-compensatory

---

1114 'Today it is time to celebrate a great achievement: US$3 billion in cost savings; the making of history; the end of the paper ticket; and the convenience of ET everywhere and for everyone. Ladies and gentlemen, together we made 100 % e-ticketing a reality.' 'State of the Air Transport Industry delivered by Giovanni Bisignani at the 2008 IATA Annual General Meeting in Istanbul' (2 June 2008). <www.iata.org/en/pressroom/speeches/2008-06-02-01/> accessed 18 March 2021.

1115 Air carriers are strictly liable for proven damages (in case of death or injury of passengers) up to 128,821 special drawing rights (SDR) per passenger. The SDR is a mix of currency values established by the International Monetary Fund. The exchange rates are regularly published on the official website of the IMF. See 'SDRs per Currency unit and Currency units per SDR last five days', <www.imf.org/external/np/fin/data/rms_five.aspx> accessed 18 March 2021.

damages' are not recoverable. Also, no provision was made for recovery of purely emotional distress and mental injury.

The Montreal Convention changed and, in general, increased the maximum liability of carriers for cargo and baggage loss or damage, as well as in the case of damage caused by delay.

A particular rule of the Convention obliges the carrier to maintain adequate insurance to cover their liability. Finally, the Convention's liability limits shall be reviewed every five years and adjusted for inflation.

As for jurisdictional conflicts, according to the Montreal Convention, **action for damages** may be brought at the option of the plaintiff before the court:

- of the domicile of the carrier;
- of the carrier's principal place of business or where the carrier has a place of business through which the contract was made; or
- of the place of destination.

Concerning the **damage resulting from the death or injury** of a passenger, an action may be brought:

- before one of the courts mentioned earlier, or
- in the territory of a state party of the Convention in which the passenger has his or her principal and permanent residence if, at the same time, the carrier has some establishment there.[1116]

Aviation security

security
aircraft hijacking
Tokyo Convention on Offences and Certain Other Acts Committed on Board Aircraft
Hague Hijacking Convention
Montreal Sabotage Convention
Beijing Convention on the Suppression of Unlawful Acts Relating to International Civil Aviation
crime of international nature

1116 '[I]n the territory of a State Party of the Convention in which at the time of the accident the passenger has his or her principal and permanent residence and to or from which the carrier operates services for the carriage of passengers by air, either on its own aircraft, or on another carrier's aircraft pursuant to a commercial agreement, and in which that carrier conducts its business of carriage of passengers by air from premises leased or owned by the carrier itself or by another carrier with which it has a commercial agreement.' Paragraph 2 of Article 33 of the Montreal Convention for the Unification of Certain Rules for International Carriage by Air.

biological, chemical, and nuclear weapons
territorial jurisdiction
jurisdiction based on the nationality principle
quasi-universal jurisdiction
unmarked plastic explosives
aviation security audits
terrorism
extradition
Declaration on Measures to Eliminate International Terrorism

Aviation security as a concern of all states and other subjects of international law

Generally, aviation **security** is a combination of human and material resources to safeguard civil aviation against unlawful interference.[1117]

At the same time, in general, the changing nature of security threats has made traditional national security policies (including with regard to aviation security) largely useless. The new security environment is marked with new actors, targets, and victims and, in general, higher risk diffusion. In the new security environment, the security of aviation cannot be regarded nor can it be effectively dealt with at the level of an individual state.

Aircraft hijacking and other forms of offences

The history of **aircraft hijacking**, which is the act of illegally seizing an aircraft, is proof that this particular form of the security threat in aviation cannot be dealt with effectively by a particular state.

Moreover, although aircraft hijackings account for the most significant percentage of all attacks against civil aviation, there are other forms of offence as well, which include airport attacks, bombings, shootings on board civil aircraft, off-airport facility attacks, and so forth.

1117 In English, the terms 'security' and 'safety" are too often used interchangeably. However, numerous commentators argue that there is a need for a distinction between these terms. One of the most popular explanations suggests that 'security' refers to the overall system of measures established to reach the safety of particular addressees of the security. Hence, according to such interpretation, security is perceived to be the overarching umbrella protecting the safety of individuals, as well as entities and states. In the aviation field, aviation security is usually regarded as the set of measures and resources implemented to prevent unlawful interference with aircraft, their passengers, and members of crew. Aviation safety, in turn, 'relates to protection against all accidents, errors or unintentional defects in the design, construction, maintenance and operation of aircraft.' See <www.aeronewstv.com/en/lifestyle/in-your-opinion/3000-safety-and-security-whats-the-difference.html> accessed 18 March 2021. Also, a similar approach is reflected on the website of the ICAO <www.icao.int/Security/Pages/default.aspx> accessed 18 March 2021.

The terrorist attacks on 11 September 2001 in the USA were a clear illustration of the dangers and destruction which aircraft hijacking might result in when, for example, the hijacked aircraft itself is used as a missile.

Challenges of contemporary international air law

Therefore, contemporary international air law is concerned with:

1 offences and certain other acts committed on board of an aircraft;
2 suppression of the unlawful seizure of aircraft; and
3 suppression of unlawful acts against the safety of civil aviation.

International treaties on aviation security

Consequently, to address these concerns, the states have concluded:

* the **Tokyo Convention on Offences and Certain Other Acts Committed on Board Aircraft** of 1963;
* the Hague Convention for the Suppression of Unlawful Seizure of Aircraft (the so-called **Hague Hijacking Convention**) of 1970;
* the Montreal Convention for the Suppression of Unlawful Acts against the Safety of Civil Aviation (also referred to as the **Montreal Sabotage Convention**) of 1971; and
* the **Beijing Convention on the Suppression of Unlawful Acts Relating to International Civil Aviation** of 2010 that entered into force in 2018.

Offence

Firstly, it is notable that these Conventions do not apply to aircraft used in military, customs, or police services.

Secondly, according to the Tokyo Convention, it applies to '(a) offences against penal law; (b) acts which, whether or not they are offences, may or do jeopardize the safety of the aircraft or of persons or property therein or which jeopardize good order and discipline on board.'[1118]

Nevertheless, the Convention did not provide clear definitions for such crucial terms as 'offence' and 'jeopardizing acts'. Consequently, the offence was not made a **crime of international nature**, and even the definition of the offence was left to the prescriptive jurisdiction of the states. On the other hand, the term 'jeopardizing acts' stimulated broad interpretations. In sum, although the Tokyo Convention was a significant step forward in the development of international air law, it was not without significant legal weaknesses. For instance, as one of its key weaknesses is commonly regarded that it is applicable only to the unlawful acts committed on board of an aircraft.

1118 Paragraph 1 of Article 1 of the Tokyo Convention on Offences and Certain Other Acts Committed on Board Aircraft.

The Hague Convention also shared the same deficiency, since it excluded any offence committed by a person not on board the aircraft (such as saboteurs who remain on the ground; unlawful interference with air navigation facilities and services such as airports, radio communications, and so on). However, it certainly improved specific rules. For example, it explicitly determined the nature of the offences as follows:

> Any person who on board an aircraft in flight: (a) unlawfully, by force or threat thereof, or by any other form of intimidation, seizes, or exercises control of, that aircraft, or attempts to perform any such act, or (b) is an accomplice of a person who performs or attempts to perform any such act commits an offence.[1119]

Thus, the offence must be committed by any person 'on board an aircraft in flight', and the Hague Convention does not apply to any hijacking committed before the closing or after the opening of the aircraft doors. As a result, such acts were punishable only under the national law of the relevant state. At the same time, the application of the Convention was limited to flights of 'international character', and domestic flights were left out of the reach of the Convention.

Hence, the Tokyo Convention did not provide precise definitions of the offences, and the Hague Convention addressed only the offence of unlawful seizure of an aircraft during flights of 'international character'. However, the Montreal Convention introduced a new approach by providing a broader definition incorporating many acts, including unlawful interference with air navigation facilities and services such as airports and radio communications.[1120] According to the Convention, a person also commits an offence if he or she is an accomplice to an offender who commits or attempts to commit any of these offences.

Some new rules were introduced by the 1988 Protocol for the Suppression of Unlawful Acts of Violence at Airports Serving International Civil Aviation, supplementary to the Montreal Sabotage Convention, which specifically recognised the need to protect international airports.

The Beijing Convention modernises and consolidates the Montreal Convention and its supplementary Protocol. On the one hand, this Convention incorporates all relevant elements of offence's definition provided by the previous Conventions; on the other

---

1119 Article 1 of the Hague Convention for the Suppression of Unlawful Seizure of Aircraft.

1120 'Any person commits an offence if he unlawfully and internationally: (a) performs an act of violence against a person on board an aircraft in flight if that act is likely to endanger the safety of that aircraft; or (b) destroys an aircraft in service or causes damage to such an aircraft which renders it incapable of flight or which is likely to endanger its safety in flight; or (c) places or causes to be placed on an aircraft in service, by any means whatsoever, a device or substance which is likely to destroy that aircraft, or to cause damage to it which renders it incapable of flight, or to cause damage to it which is likely to endanger its safety in flight; or (d) destroys or damages air navigation facilities or interferes with their operation, if any such act is likely to endanger the safety of aircraft in flight; or (e) communicates information which he knows to be false, thereby endangering the safety of an aircraft in flight.' Paragraph 1 of Article 1 of the Montreal Convention for the Suppression of Unlawful Acts against the Safety of Civil Aviation.

hand, develops the definition, reflecting the contemporary challenges, namely, additionally criminalises:

- the act of using civil aircraft as a weapon to cause death, injury, or damage;
- the act of using civil aircraft to discharge **biological, chemical, and nuclear** (BCN) **weapons** or similar substances to cause death, injury, or damage or the act of using such substances to attack civil aircraft;
- the act of unlawful transport of biological, chemical, and nuclear weapons or particular related material; and
- a cyber-attack on air navigation facilities.

With this definition, the Convention consolidated and developed the offence against aviation security as a crime of an international nature.

In addition, under the Beijing Convention, a threat to commit an offence may be an offence itself, if the threat is credible. Furthermore, the Convention provides explicitly for the criminal liability of the directors and organisers of an offence, as well as the responsibility of those who knowingly assist an offender in evading investigation, prosecution, or punishment.[1121]

Jurisdiction

Another significant concern which, in this context, was regarded as a considerable challenge, is jurisdiction. All the Conventions mentioned here addressed this matter. However, the final legal treatment was implemented by the Beijing Convention, which required each contracting state to take necessary mandatory measures to establish the following:

Territorial jurisdiction

1 when the offence is committed in the territory of that state;
2 when the offence is committed against or on board an aircraft registered in that state;
3 when the aircraft on board which the offence is committed lands in its territory with the alleged offender still on board; or
4 when the offence is committed against or on board an aircraft leased without a crew to a lessee whose principal place of business or, if the lessee has no such place of business, whose permanent residence is in that state.

Jurisdiction based on the nationality principle

5 when the offence is committed by a national of that state;
6 when the offence is committed against a national of that state; or
7 when the offence is committed by a stateless person, whose habitual residence is in the territory of that state.

1121 Article 1 of the Beijing Convention on the Suppression of Unlawful Acts Relating to International Civil Aviation.

Quasi-universal jurisdiction

The Beijing Convention supplements the other precondition of jurisdiction and repeats the approach of the Hague and Montreal Conventions by stating that:

> Each State Party shall likewise take such measures as may be necessary to establish its jurisdiction over the offences . . . in the case where the alleged offender is present in its territory and it does not extradite that person.[1122]

This provision seems to reaffirm the principle of quasi-universal jurisdiction in international air law concerning the offences mentioned here since, in these cases, the principle is binding for only the treaty parties and is primarily binding with regard to an obligation to institute internal legal proceedings (prosecute or extradite).

Hence, the Beijing Convention empowers several states to exercise concurrent jurisdiction over the offences which may be a source of disputes between the states. However, commonly, the state which first apprehends the offender or the alleged offender exercises the primary jurisdiction.

The new challenges to aviation security

Over time, aviation security has faced new challenges which provided a new impetus for the international community to adopt new and improved instruments for dealing with them. Accordingly, the states reacted to the new developments by modernising and supplementing the global and regional norms. Among such global and regional norms, the following instruments should be outlined:

- The Montreal Convention on the Marking of Plastic Explosives for the Purpose of Detection of 1991, which requires each state party to prohibit and prevent manufacturing of **unmarked plastic explosives** in its territory.
- The 2010 Protocol Supplementary to the Convention for the Suppression of Unlawful Seizure of Aircraft expands the scope of the Hague Hijacking Convention to cover different forms of aircraft hijackings, including through advanced technological means. It also incorporates the provisions of the Beijing Convention relating to a threat or conspiracy to commit an offence.
- The instruments provided by the ICAO as the worldwide auditor of safety and security standards for international civil aviation, which, by performing its legislative function, is empowered to formulate and adopt the Standards and Recommended Practices (SARPs). For instance, the SARPs for international aviation security designated as Annex 17 of the Chicago Convention; the Aviation Security Plan of Action of 2002, a central element of which is regular, mandatory, systematic, and harmonised **aviation security audits** through evaluation security in place and to identify deficiencies. To this end, the ICAO launched the Universal Security Oversight Audit Programme.

1122 Paragraph 3 of Article 8 of the Beijing Convention on the Suppression of Unlawful Acts Relating to International Civil Aviation.

- The European Convention on the Suppression of Terrorism of 1977, which targeted depoliticising certain acts of **terrorism** or violence, including offences within the scope of the Hague Hijacking Convention and the Montreal Sabotage Conventions. According to the European Convention, for **extradition** between contracting states, none of these offences shall be regarded as political offences, as offences connected with a political offence, or as offences inspired by political motives. In addition, it entails the rules of quasi-universal jurisdiction concerning the cases in which the suspected offender is present in the territory of the given state, and it does not extradite him or her.

Terrorism

As for terrorism, which is a constant threat in the modern world, it is obvious that terrorist acts are not just directed against civil aviation. Nevertheless, civil aviation is the most vulnerable among potential targets.

Terrorism is usually considered to refer to acts of violence that predominately target civilians in the pursuit of political or ideological aims.

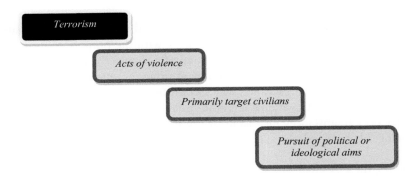

FIGURE 14.2 Definition of terrorism

Until now, the international community has not yet adopted an elaborate definition of terrorism. The existing declarations, statements, resolutions, and global or regional sectoral treaties relate to specific aspects of it, comprising core elements and certain acts only. The majority of these legal instruments were developed under the auspices of the United Nations or other international organisations at the global level. Under such sectoral instruments, the principal place is occupied by treaties:

- regarding civil aviation, reviewed earlier;
- concerning the protection of international staff;[1123]
- regarding the taking of hostages;[1124]

1123 1973 Convention on the Prevention and Punishment of Crimes against Internationally Protected Persons.

1124 1979 International Convention against the Taking of Hostages.

- regarding nuclear material and nuclear terrorism;[1125]
- relating to maritime navigation;[1126]
- regarding explosive materials;[1127]
- concerning the terrorist bombings;[1128] and
- regarding the financing of terrorism.[1129]

In 1994, the UN General Assembly's **Declaration on Measures to Eliminate International Terrorism** emphasised that: 'Acts, methods and practices of terrorism constitute a grave violation of the purposes and principles of the United Nations' and that the terrorism includes

> Criminal acts intended or calculated to provoke a state of terror in the general public, a group of persons or particular persons for political purposes are in any circumstance unjustifiable, whatever the considerations of a political, philosophical, ideological, racial, ethnic, religious or any other nature that may be invoked to justify them.[1130]

In 2004, the UN Security Council, in its Resolution 'Threats to international peace and security caused by terrorist acts', referred to

> criminal acts, including against civilians, committed with the intent to cause death or serious bodily injury, or taking of hostages, with the purpose to provoke a state of terror in the general public or in a group of persons or particular persons, intimidate a population or compel a government or an international organization to do or to abstain from doing any act, which constitute offences within the scope of and as defined in the international conventions and protocols relating to terrorism, are under no circumstances justifiable by considerations of a political, philosophical, ideological, racial, ethnic, religious or other similar nature.[1131]

Nowadays, the UN General Assembly is working towards the adoption of a Comprehensive Convention on International Terrorism. However, the negotiations currently are deadlocked because of differences over the definition of terrorism.[1132]

1125 1980 Convention on the Physical Protection of Nuclear Material, 2005 Amendments to the Convention on the Physical Protection of Nuclear Material, 2005 International Convention for the Suppression of Acts of Nuclear Terrorism.

1126 1988 Convention for the Suppression of Unlawful Acts against the Safety of Maritime Navigation, 1988 Protocol for the Suppression of Unlawful Acts against the Safety of Fixed Platforms Located on the Continental Shelf, and so forth.

1127 Montreal Convention on the Marking of Plastic Explosives for the Purpose of Detection of 1991.

1128 1997 International Convention for the Suppression of Terrorist Bombings.

1129 1999 International Convention for the Suppression of the Financing of Terrorism.

1130 A/RES/49/60 of 9 December 1994.

1131 S/RES/1566 of 8 October 2004.

1132 For instance, the debatable questions are: What distinguishes a terrorist organisation from a liberation movement? Do we exclude activities of national armed forces, even if they are perceived to commit acts of terrorism?

OUTER SPACE

Outer Space Treaty
Agreement on the Rescue of Astronauts
Convention on International Liability for Damage Caused by Space Objects
Convention on Registration of Objects Launched into Outer Space
Moon Agreement

International space law as the norms regulating space-related activities

International space law can generally be introduced as the field of international law regulating space-related activities. Ever since the launch of the first artificial satellite in 1957, space has been a concern of international law. Hence, the law of outer space has emerged, providing the legal regime to govern outer space and the activities therein.

The composition of international space law

International space law comprises a variety of international treaties, international customary rules, and the rules and regulations of international organisations, as well as examples of soft law, such as the United Nations General Assembly Resolutions. Beginning in 1957, the General Assembly of the United Nations adopted several Resolutions containing the foundational principles applicable to outer space.

However, the bulk of international space law consists of norms incorporated in the five multilateral treaties:

- the Treaty on Principles Governing the Activities of States in the Exploration and Use of Outer Space, including the Moon and Other Celestial Bodies of 1967 (the so-called **Outer Space Treaty**);
- the Agreement on the Rescue of Astronauts, the Return of Astronauts and the Return of Objects Launched into Outer Space of 1968 (also referred to as the **Agreement on the Rescue of Astronauts**);
- the **Convention on International Liability for Damage Caused by Space Objects** of 1972;
- the **Convention on Registration of Objects Launched into Outer Space** of 1975; and
- the Agreement Governing the Activities of States on the Moon and Other Celestial Bodies of 1979 (commonly called the **Moon Agreement**).

The principles of space law

province of mankind
natural reserve, devoted to peace and science

> common heritage of mankind
> astronauts as the envoys of mankind
> direct television broadcasting
> remote sensing

The Outer Space Treaty

The crucial international treaty prescribing the principles of space law is the Treaty on Principles Governing the Activities of States in the Exploration and Use of Outer Space, including the Moon and Other Celestial Bodies of 1967 (the Outer Space Treaty).

The Treaty utilises the internationally recognised approach of outer space as a **province of mankind**. The concept is very similar to the legal regimes adopted concerning the Antarctic as a **natural reserve devoted to peace and science** and to the deep seabed (Area) as a **common heritage of mankind**. However, these legal concepts retain the individual characteristics they possess and, therefore, are partially different from each other, as are their application fields – the Antarctic, the deep seabed, and outer space. In the meantime, the Moon Agreement acknowledges the common heritage of mankind principle concerning the moon and its natural resources. Furthermore, defining this concept, the Agreement specifically links it to the establishment of an 'international regime' and appropriate procedures 'to govern the exploitation of the natural resources of the Moon as such exploitation is about to become feasible.'[1133]

Province of mankind

According to the Outer Space Treaty, the province of mankind approach is formulated as follows:

> The exploration and use of outer space, including the Moon and other celestial bodies, shall be carried out for the benefit and in the interests of all countries, irrespective of their degree of economic or scientific development.[1134]

At the same time, the Treaty pronounced the other fundamental principles of space law, the majority of which were reflected before in the Declaration of Legal Principles Governing the Activities of States in the Exploration and Uses of Outer Space of 1962 (General Assembly Resolution XVIII).

1133 Paragraph 5 of Article 11 of the Moon Agreement.
1134 Article I of the Treaty on Principles Governing the Activities of States in the Exploration and Use of Outer Space, including the Moon and Other Celestial Bodies.

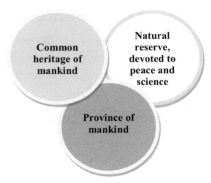

FIGURE 14.3 The concepts of the province of mankind, the natural reserve devoted to peace and science, and the common heritage of mankind

Non-appropriation of outer space by any one country

'Outer space, including the moon and other celestial bodies, is not subject to national appropriation by claim of sovereignty, by means of use or occupation, or by any other means.'[1135]

Outer space as the domain of international law

The activities of states in the exploration and use of outer space shall be carried out in accordance with international law in the interest of maintaining international peace and security and promoting international co-operation and understanding. Although particular rules of space law are also integrated into the domestic laws of the states, the main legal framework for space law is determined and prescribed by international law.

Freedom of access to and use of outer space

Outer space, including the moon and other celestial bodies, is free for exploration and use by all states without discrimination, and there is free access to all areas of celestial bodies. The freedom of access to and use of outer space should be exercised based on equality without discrimination of any kind.

Freedom of scientific investigation

There is the freedom of scientific investigation in outer space, including the moon and other celestial bodies, and states shall facilitate and encourage international co-operation in such an investigation.

1135 Article II of the Treaty on Principles Governing the Activities of States in the Exploration and Use of Outer Space, including the Moon and Other Celestial Bodies.

Prohibition of weapons of mass destruction

It is prohibited to place in orbit around the Earth any objects carrying nuclear weapons or any other kinds of weapons of mass destruction and to install such weapons on celestial bodies or station such weapons in outer space in any other manner.

Demilitarisation of the moon and other celestial bodies

The moon and other celestial bodies shall be used by all states exclusively for peaceful purposes. Establishment of military bases, installations, and fortifications; testing of any type of weapons; or conducting military exercises on celestial bodies is prohibited.

Liability for damage caused by space objects

The states bear the international responsibility for national activities in outer space, whether such activities are carried out by governmental agencies or by authorised non-governmental entities.

Jurisdiction of a state that registered an object

'A state . . . on whose registry an object launched into outer space is carried shall retain jurisdiction and control over such object, and over any personnel thereof, while in outer space or on a celestial body.'[1136]

Continuity of ownership

Ownership of objects launched into outer space, including objects landed or constructed on a celestial body, and of their component parts, is not affected by their presence in outer space or on a celestial body or by their return to the Earth. Such objects or component parts found beyond the limits of the State Party to the Treaty on whose registry they are carried shall be returned to that State Party, which shall, upon request, furnish identifying data prior to their return.[1137]

Astronauts as the envoys of mankind

There exists the duty to provide assistance to space vehicles and astronauts in distress or an emergency landing in the territory of another state or on the high seas and to return

---

1136 Article VIII of the Treaty on Principles Governing the Activities of States in the Exploration and Use of Outer Space, including the Moon and Other Celestial Bodies.
1137 ibid.

them safely and promptly to the state of registry of their space vehicle since the states have to regard **astronauts as the envoys of mankind** in outer space.

According to the Agreement on the Rescue of Astronauts, the Return of Astronauts and the Return of Objects Launched into Outer Space, each party which receives information or discovers that the personnel of a spacecraft have suffered an accident, are experiencing conditions of distress, or have made an emergency or unintended landing in territory under its jurisdiction, on the high seas, or in any other place not under the jurisdiction of any state should immediately either (1) notify the launching authority or promptly make a public announcement by all appropriate means of communication at its disposal or (2) notify the Secretary-General of the United Nations.[1138]

In turn, the astronauts of one state shall render all possible assistance to the astronauts of other states in outer space and on celestial bodies.

Co-operation and mutual assistance

States shall be guided by the principle of co-operation and mutual assistance and shall conduct all their activities in outer space with due regard for the corresponding interests of all other states.

Protection of the environment

The states have the duty to avoid harmful contamination and adverse changes in the environment. If a state has reason to believe that an activity or experiment planned in outer space by another state would cause potentially harmful interference with the activities of peaceful exploration and use of outer space, it may request consultation concerning that activity or experiment.

Duty to notify and registration of space activities

States are obliged to inform the Secretary-General of the United Nations as well as the public and the international scientific community of the nature, conduct, locations, and results of their activities in outer space. At the same time, the Secretary-General should be prepared to disseminate the information 'immediately and effectively.'

As for the registration duty, the Convention on Registration of Objects Launched into Outer Space states that when a space object is launched into earth orbit or beyond, the launching state shall register the space object through an entry into an appropriate registry which it shall maintain. When there are two or more launching states, they shall jointly determine which one of them shall register the object. There is also an obligation to provide the Secretary-General of the United Nations with the data from the register, such as the name of the launching state or states, an appropriate designator of the space

---

1138 Article 1 of the Agreement on the Rescue of Astronauts, the Return of Astronauts and the Return of Objects Launched into Outer Space.

object or its registration number, the date and territory or location of launch, basic orbital parameters, and so on.[1139]

Other principles of international space law

In addition, there are other principles of international space law as well, which were embodied in certain UN General Assembly Resolutions:

- The Principles Governing the Use by States of Artificial Earth Satellites for International Direct Television Broadcasting of 1982 (General Assembly Resolution 37/92) adapted these principles to the satellite broadcasting field. At the same time, it promoted in the area of international **direct television broadcasting** by satellite the balanced approach between the sovereign rights of states and the implementation of the right of everyone to seek, receive, and impart information and ideas.[1140] It also added several specific principles applicable to the use of satellites, such as the protection of copyright and neighbouring rights through appropriate agreements between the interested states or the competent legal entities acting under their jurisdiction.
- The Principles Relating to Remote Sensing of the Earth from Outer Space of 1986 (General Assembly Resolution 41/65), which defined the term '**remote sensing**' as 'the sensing of the Earth's surface from space by making use of the properties of electromagnetic waves emitted, reflected or diffracted by the sensed objects, for the purpose of improving natural resources management, land use and the protection of the environment.' The Resolution stated that remote sensing activities shall be carried out for the benefit and in the interests of all countries through co-operation between the states, including by making available technical assistance to other interested states on mutually agreed terms.
- The Principles Relevant to the Use of Nuclear Power Sources in Outer Space of 1992 (General Assembly resolution 47/68), which aimed to minimise the quantity of radioactive material in space and the risks involved with it. The use of nuclear power sources in outer space, therefore, was restricted to those space missions which cannot be operated by non-nuclear energy sources in a reasonable way.
- The Declaration on International Cooperation in the Exploration and Use of Outer Space for the Benefit and in the Interest of All States, Taking into Particular Account the Needs of Developing Countries of 1996 (General Assembly resolution 51/122), which reaffirmed the aforementioned legal principles governing the activities of states in the exploration and uses of outer space, with a particular focus on the needs of developing countries. Towards this end, it declared that international co-operation

---

1139 Article IV of the Convention on Registration of Objects Launched into Outer Space.

1140 'Activities should be carried out in a manner compatible with the sovereign rights of States, including the principle of non-intervention, as well as with the right of everyone to seek, receive and impart information and ideas as enshrined in the relevant United Nations instruments.' Paragraph A of the Principles Governing the Use by States of Artificial Earth Satellites for International Direct Television Broadcasting.

should aim, inter alia, at the following goals: (1) promoting the development of space science and technology and of its applications; (2) fostering the development of relevant and appropriate space capabilities in interested states; and (3) facilitating the exchange of expertise and technology among countries on a mutually acceptable basis.

Moon Agreement

> exclusively for peaceful purposes
> province of mankind
> common heritage of mankind
> international regime
> human-crewed and crewless stations

The moon and other celestial bodies

The so-called Moon Agreement implements these principles with regard to the moon. At the same time, according to this Agreement, the provisions relating to the moon also are applied to other celestial bodies within the solar system, except for the earth.

International law as a legal system governing all activities on the moon

Firstly, the Moon Agreement states that all activities on the moon, including its exploration and use, shall be carried out in compliance with international law and taking into account the Declaration on Principles of International Law concerning Friendly Relations and Co-operation among States in accordance with the Charter of the United Nations.[1141]

Peaceful purposes

Secondly, it provides that the moon should be used by all states **exclusively for peaceful purposes**. Thus, any threat or use of force or any other hostile act or threat of hostile act on the moon is prohibited. Among other things, states shall not place in orbit around or on another trajectory to or around the moon objects carrying nuclear weapons or any other kinds of weapons of mass destruction or place or use such weapons on the moon. They should not establish military bases, installations, or fortifications or test any type of weapons there. The use of military personnel is allowed only for scientific research or for any other peaceful purposes.

1141 Article 2 of the Agreement Governing the Activities of States on the Moon and Other Celestial Bodies.

Province of mankind and the common heritage of mankind

The Agreement introduces a very specific adaptation and combination of two concepts mentioned earlier – the **province of mankind** and the **common heritage of mankind**. The first is employed concerning the exploration and use of the moon for the benefit and in the interests of all countries, irrespective of their degree of economic or scientific development. The second is applied to the natural resources of the moon and prescribes the establishment of an **international regime** to govern the exploitation of the natural resources of the moon. The primary purposes of this international regime are:

- the orderly and safe development of the natural resources of the moon;
- the rational management of those resources;
- the expansion of opportunities in the use of those resources; and
- an equitable sharing by all states in the benefits derived from those resources.

According to the Agreement, neither the surface nor the subsurface of the moon, nor any part thereof or natural resources in place, shall become the property of any state, international intergovernmental or non-governmental organisation, national organisation or non-governmental entity, or any natural person.

Other principles of international space law

Additionally, the Moon Agreement includes the following other basic principles of international space law:

- The principle of co-operation and mutual assistance of states in all their activities concerning the exploration and use of the Moon.
- The duty to notify and register space activities, in which the UN Secretary-General occupies a crucial place.
- The freedom of scientific investigation: among other things, the right to collect on and remove from the Moon samples of its mineral and other substances.
- The duty to prevent the disruption of the existing balance of the environment of moon.
- The right to establish **human-crewed and crewless stations** on the moon under the jurisdiction of a concerned state. However, in establishing such stations, the states may use only that area which is required for the needs of the station and in such a manner that they do not impede the free access to all areas of the moon of personnel, vehicles, and equipment of other states.
- The duty to safeguard the life and health of persons on the moon, who shall be regarded and protected as astronauts.
- The international responsibility for national activities on the Moon.

International liability for damage caused by space objects

claim for compensation
Claims Commission
good faith
absolutely liable
exoneration from absolute liability
liability due to fault
joint and several liability

Responsibility of a subject who undertakes activities in outer space

As noted earlier, the states bear the international responsibility for national activities in outer space, whether such activities are carried out by governmental agencies or by authorised non-governmental entities. Meanwhile, when activities are carried out in outer space by an international organisation, responsibility is borne by both the international organisation and the states participating in such an organisation.

A state launching or procuring the launch of an object into outer space, including the moon and other celestial bodies, and the state from whose territory or facility an object is launched are internationally liable for damages caused to another state or its natural or juridical persons by such object or its component parts on the earth, in airspace, or in outer space, including the moon and other celestial bodies.

International liability

The process of international liability shall be initialised due to a **claim for compensation** by a claimant state that may be:

- a state which suffers damage or whose natural or juridical persons suffer damage;
- another state, with respect to damage sustained in its territory by any natural or juridical person if the state of nationality has not presented a claim; or
- another state, with respect to damage sustained by its permanent residents if neither the state of nationality nor the state in whose territory the damage was sustained has presented a claim or notified its intention of presenting a claim.

Under the Convention on International Liability for Damage Caused by Space Objects, this claim may be presented to a launching state not later than one year following the date of the occurrence of the damage or the identification of the launching state which is liable. If the claim is not settled through diplomatic negotiations within one year from the date on which the claimant state notifies the launching state that it has submitted the documentation of its claim, the parties concerned shall establish a **Claims Commission**, which, as a rule, should be composed of three members – one appointed by the claimant state, one appointed by the launching state, and the third member, the Chairman, to be chosen by both parties jointly. The decision of the Commission shall be final and binding if the parties have so agreed; otherwise, the Commission shall render a final and recommendatory award, which the parties shall consider in **good faith**. In addition, the Convention included other procedural provisions regarding the Commission.

Absolute liability and liability due to fault

Notably, the Convention introduces two forms of liability:

1   The launching states are '**absolutely liable**' for damage caused by their space objects on the surface of the earth or to aircraft in flight. However, **exoneration from absolute liability** shall be granted to the extent that a launching state establishes that the damage resulted either wholly or partially from gross negligence or from an act or omission done with intent to cause damage on the part of a claimant state or of natural or juridical persons it represents.
2   If the damage was caused elsewhere than on the surface of the earth to a space object of one state or to persons or property on board such a space object by a space object of another state, the latter shall be liable only if the damage is due to its fault (**liability due to fault**) or the fault of persons for whom it is responsible.[1142]

Joint and several liability

At the same time, the Convention entails the rules of **joint and several liability**, which first of all apply to two or more states that jointly launch a space object.

When damage is caused elsewhere than on the surface of the earth to a space object of one launching state or to persons or property on board such a space object by a space object of another launching state, and damage thereby is caused to a third state or its natural or juridical persons, the first two states are jointly and severally liable to the third state. At the same time:

*   If the damage was caused to the third state on the surface of the earth or to aircraft in flight, their liability to the third state shall be absolute.
*   If the damage was caused to a space object of the third state or to persons or property on board that space object elsewhere than on the surface of the earth, their liability to the third state shall be based on the fault of either of the first two states or on the fault of persons for whom either is responsible.[1143]

1142   Articles II and III of the Convention on International Liability for Damage Caused by Space Objects.
1143   Paragraph 1 of Article IV of the Convention on International Liability for Damage Caused by Space Objects.

As for the burden of compensation for the damage denoted here, it is apportioned between the first two states following the extent to which they were at fault or equally if the extent of the fault of each of these states cannot be determined.[1144]

Liability of international organisations

Finally, according to the Convention, these provisions also apply to any international intergovernmental organisation conducting space activities if the organisation declares its acceptance of the rights and obligations provided for in this Convention and if a majority of the states members of the organisation are parties to the Convention.

Jurisdiction

> particular module of space object
> International Space Station
> criminal jurisdiction
> nationality principle of jurisdiction
> protective principle

The registry holder state

A state on whose registry an object launched into outer space is carried retains jurisdiction and control over that object and over any personnel thereof in outer space or on a celestial body.

International Space Station

Sometimes the states that registered a **particular module of space object** exercise jurisdiction over that specific part of the object, as was provided with regard to the 'civil international Space Station' under the agreements of 1998 establishing the framework for co-operation among Europe, the United States, Russia, Canada, and Japan on the design, development, operation, and utilisation of the **International Space Station**.[1145] Moreover, the states are entitled to elaborate a specific regime of jurisdiction regarding particular programs, as was the case concerning the International Space Station when, with regard to

---

1144 Paragraph 2 of Article IV of the Convention on International Liability for Damage Caused by Space Objects

1145 According to Paragraph 2 of Article 5 of the Agreement among the Government of Canada, Governments of Member States of the European Space Agency, the Government of Japan, the Government of the Russian federation, and the Government of the United States of America Concerning Cooperation on the Civil International Space Station of 1998: 'each Partner shall retain jurisdiction and control over the elements it registers in accordance with paragraph 1 above and over personnel in or on the Space Station who are its nationals.'

criminal jurisdiction, the parties combined the **nationality principle of jurisdiction** with the **protective principle**.

According to the agreement, the engaged states may exercise criminal jurisdiction over personnel who are their nationals in or on any flight element. However, in a case involving the misconduct in orbit (1) affecting the life or safety of a national of another state or (2) causing damage to the flight element of another party, the state whose national is the alleged perpetrator shall, at the request of any affected state, consult with such state concerning their respective prosecutorial interests. Following such consultation, an affected party may exercise criminal jurisdiction over the alleged perpetrator, provided that within 90 days of the date of such consultation or within such other period as may be mutually agreed, the state whose national is the alleged perpetrator either:

- concurs in such exercise of criminal jurisdiction, or
- fails to provide assurances that it will submit the case to its competent authorities for the purpose of prosecution.[1146]

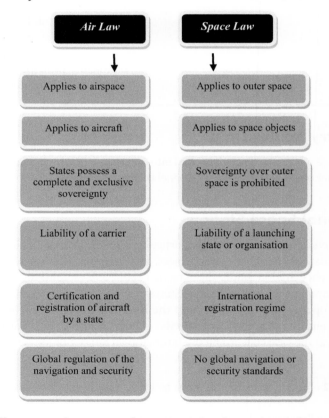

FIGURE 14.4 Differences in the regimes of international air law and space law

---

1146 Article 22 of the Agreement among the Government of Canada, Governments of Member States of the European Space Agency, the Government of Japan, the Government of the Russian federation, and the Government of the United States of America Concerning Cooperation on the Civil International Space Station.

INTERNATIONAL INSTITUTIONS

> International Civil Aviation Organisation
> International Telecommunication Union
> Committee on the Peaceful Uses of Outer Space
> right to communicate
> Register of Objects Launched into Outer Space

Preliminary remarks

The co-operation among states with respect to airspace and outer space led to the establishment of several international institutions. Among them, a unique place is occupied by the **International Civil Aviation Organisation, International Telecommunication Union** and, with regard to outer space, the **Committee on the Peaceful Uses of Outer Space**.

International Civil Aviation Organisation

International Civil Aviation Organisation (ICAO) is a specialised agency of the United Nations. Its central role is to guide the administration and governance of the Convention on International Civil Aviation (Chicago Convention) to reach a safe, efficient, secure, economically sustainable, and environmentally responsible civil aviation sector. Thus, by implementing these goals, ICAO has done much for the development of civil aviation, mainly defining a common legal framework for civil aviation.

As noted earlier, in 1944, the Chicago International Conference adopted the Convention on International Civil Aviation establishing the ICAO, which is headquartered in Montreal, Canada. The Organisation serves as the forum for co-operation in all fields of civil aviation among its 193 member states and several 'invited' organisations.

ICAO's aims and objectives, as stated in the Chicago Convention, are to determine or improve the principles and techniques of international civil air navigation and to foster the planning and development of international air transport.

To ensure the prompt development of the civil aviation sector, the ICAO sets Standards and Recommended Practices (SARPs), Procedures for Air Navigation (PANS), and policies for international civil aviation.

ICAO has established three strategic objectives:

- Safety – enhance civil aviation safety.
- Security – enhance civil aviation security.
- Environmental Protection and Sustainable Development of Air Transport – foster harmonized and economically viable development of international civil aviation that does not unduly harm the environment.

The composition of the International Civil Aviation Organisation

- Assembly – consists of all the member states. It meets once every three years in regular sessions but may also meet in an extraordinary meeting that may be held at any time upon the call of the Council or at the request of not less than one-fifth of the total number of contracting states addressed to the Secretary General. The Assembly is empowered to set the policy for the coming years, vote on the budget and determine the financial arrangements, consider proposals for the modification or amendment of the provisions of the Chicago Convention, elect the Council, and deal with any matter within the sphere of action of the Organisation not explicitly assigned to the Council.
- Council – consists of 36 members and is a permanent governing body responsible to the Assembly. Decisions by the Council require approval by a majority of its members. The Council submits annual reports to the Assembly, appoints and defines the duties of an Air Transport Committee (which shall be chosen from among the representatives of the members of the Council and assists it on economic matters), establishes an Air Navigation Commission, appoints a Secretary-General, adopts the international standards and recommended practices, and, for convenience, designates them as Annexes to the Chicago Convention.
- Air Navigation Commission – composed of 19 members appointed by the Council from among persons nominated by contracting states. These persons shall have suitable qualifications and experience in the science and practice of aeronautics. In addition, the Council appoints the President of the Air Navigation Commission. The Commission, as the technical body of the Organisation, recommends to the Council adoption and modifications of the Standards and Recommended Practices, establishes technical subcommissions, and advises the Council concerning the collection of all information which it considers necessary and useful for the advancement of air navigation.
- Secretariat – headed by the Secretary-General, a chief executive officer of the Organisation. The Secretariat consists of five bureaus:

  - Air Navigation Bureau;
  - Air Transport Bureau;
  - Technical Co-operation Bureau;
  - Legal Affairs and External Relations Bureau; and
  - Bureau of Administration and Services.

International Telecommunication Union

The International Telecommunication Union (ITU) is a specialised agency of the United Nations whose purpose is to coordinate telecommunication operations and services throughout the world. Founded in 1865 as the International Telegraph Union, the

ITU is the oldest existing global intergovernmental organisation. The International Telegraph (later Telecommunication) Convention, today the revised Constitution and Convention of the International Telecommunication Union of 1992,[1147] are the treaties that establish the legal basis for the Union and determine its purposes and structure.

The ITU headquarters are in Geneva, Switzerland. In addition to almost all countries of the world, ITU brings together more than 700 sector members and associates from the industry and international and regional organisations, as well as representatives from academia.

The ITU operates in three sectors:

- Radiocommunication – where a target is the optimal, fair, and rational use of the radio frequency (RF) spectrum. ITU allocates global radio spectrum.
- Telecommunication standardisation – which is crucial to ensure the seamless interconnection of networks and technologies. In this field, the ITU establishes the recommendations for standardising telecommunication devices and services worldwide. The ITU sets and publishes regulations and standards relevant to electronic communication and broadcasting technologies of all kind, including radio, television, satellite, telephone, and the internet.
- Telecommunication development – by maintaining this direction, the ITU assists countries in developing internal telecommunication operations.

Although the recommendations of the ITU are non-binding, most countries adhere to them in the interest of maintaining an effective international electronic communication environment.

Through its operation, the ITU protects and supports everyone's fundamental **right to communicate**.

The composition of the International Telecommunication Union

- Plenipotentiary Conference – is the supreme organ of the Union, composed of delegations representing member states, and convened every four years. It determines the general policies of the ITU, considers and adopts proposals for amendments to the Constitution and the Convention, considers the reports by the Council, provides any general directives dealing with the staffing of the Union, elects the member states which are to serve on the Council, and elects the Secretary-General, the Deputy Secretary-General, and the Directors of the Bureaux of the Sectors and the Radio Regulations Board.

1147 Subsequent plenipotentiary conferences have adopted only amending instruments to the 1992 documents.

- Council – acts on behalf of the Plenipotentiary Conference and in the interval between Plenipotentiary Conferences as the governing body of the Union. The member states of the Council are elected with due regard to the need for equitable distribution of the seats on the Council among all regions of the world. It takes all steps to facilitate the implementation by the member states of the provisions of the Constitution, the Convention, and the Administrative Regulations.
- World conferences on international telecommunication – may partially or, in exceptional cases, completely revise the International Telecommunication Regulations and may deal with any question of a worldwide character within its competence and related to its agenda.
- Radiocommunication sector, including world and regional radiocommunication conferences, radiocommunication assemblies, and the Radio Regulations Board.
- Telecommunication standardisation sector, including world telecommunication standardisation assemblies.
- Telecommunication development sector, including world and regional telecommunication development conferences.
- General Secretariat – directed by a Secretary-General, who is assisted by a Deputy Secretary-General. The Secretary-General acts as the legal representative of the Union and may act as a depositary.

Committee on the Peaceful Uses of Outer Space

The United Nation Committee on the Peaceful Uses of Outer Space (COPUOS) was instituted by the General Assembly in 1959 through its Resolution[1148] as a General Assembly's permanent Committee. Its primary focus is to review international co-operation in peaceful uses of outer space, study space-related activities which could be undertaken by the UN, promote space research programmes, and examine the nature of legal problems which may arise from the exploration of outer space.

Initially, the Committee had 18 members. Since then, it has grown to include 95 members. Thus, it is one of the largest Committees in the United Nations. In addition to states, other subjects of international law – such as the Holy See, the Sovereign Order of Malta and a number of international organisations – have observer status with COPUOS and its Subcommittees.

The United Nations Office for Outer Space Affairs serves as the Committee secretariat. In addition, it is responsible for implementing the Secretary-General's responsibilities under international space law and maintaining the United Nations **Register of Objects Launched into Outer Space**.

The Committee on the Peaceful Uses of Outer Space played the cardinal role in the creation of the five treaties and many principles of outer space. In sum, it represents a unique platform at the global level to monitor and discuss outer space matters. The Committee has two subsidiary bodies: the Scientific and Technical Subcommittee and the Legal Subcommittee.

1148 RES/1472(XIV) A of 12 December 1959.

CASES AND MATERIALS (*SELECTED PARTS*)

The freedoms of the Air

International Air Services Transit Agreement, Signed at Chicago, on 7 December 1944 (Transit Agreement)
Entry into force: 30 January 1945
Status: 133 Parties

Article I

Section 1

Each contracting State grants to the other contracting States the following freedoms of the air in respect of scheduled international air services:

1   The privilege to fly across its territory without landing;
2   The privilege to land for non-traffic purposes.

The privileges of this section shall not be applicable with respect to airports utilized for military purposes to the exclusion of any scheduled international air services. In areas of active hostilities or of military occupation, and in time of war along the supply routes leading to such areas, the exercise of such privileges shall be subject to the approval of the competent military authorities.

Section 2

The exercise of the foregoing privileges shall be in accordance with the provisions of the Interim Agreement on International Civil Aviation and, when it comes into force, with the provisions of the Convention on International Civil Aviation, both drawn up at Chicago on December 7, 1944.

Section 3

A contracting State granting to the airlines of another contracting State the privilege to stop for non-traffic purposes may require such airlines to offer reasonable commercial service at the points at which such stops are made.

Such requirement shall not involve any discrimination between airlines operating on the same route, shall take into account the capacity of the aircraft, and shall be exercised in such a manner as not to prejudice the normal operations of the international air services concerned or the rights and obligations of a contracting State.

Section 4

Each contracting State may, subject to the provisions of this Agreement,

1   Designate the route to be followed within its territory by any international air service and the airports which any such service may use;

2 Impose or permit to be imposed on any such service just and reasonable charges for the use of such airports and other facilities; these charges shall not be higher than would be paid for the use of such airports and facilities by its national aircraft engaged in similar international services: provided that, upon representation by an interested contracting State, the charges imposed for the use of airports and other facilities shall be subject to review by the Council of the International Civil Aviation Organization established under the above-mentioned Convention, which shall report and make recommendations thereon for the consideration of the State or States concerned.

Section 5

Each contracting State reserves the right to withhold or revoke a certificate or permit to an air transport enterprise of another State in any case where it is not satisfied that substantial ownership and effective control are vested in nationals of a contracting State, or in case of failure of such air transport enterprise to comply with the laws of the State over which it operates, or to perform its obligations under this Agreement.

Article II

Section 1

A contracting State which deems that action by another contracting State under this Agreement is causing injustice or hardship to it, may request the Council to examine the situation. The Council shall thereupon inquire into the matter, and shall call the States concerned into consultation. Should such consultation fail to resolve the difficulty, the Council may make appropriate findings and recommendations to the contracting States concerned. If thereafter a contracting State concerned shall in the opinion of the Council unreasonably fail to take suitable corrective action, the Council may recommend to the Assembly of the above-mentioned Organization that such contracting State be suspended from its rights and privileges under this Agreement until such action has been taken. The Assembly by a two-thirds vote may so suspend such contracting State for such period of time as it may deem proper or until the Council shall find that corrective action has been taken by such State.

Section 2

If any disagreement between two or more contracting States relating to the interpretation or application of this Agreement cannot be settled by negotiation, the provisions of Chapter XVIII of the above-mentioned Convention shall be applicable in the same manner as provided therein with reference to any disagreement relating to the interpretation or application of the above-mentioned Convention.

Article III

This Agreement shall remain in force as long as the abovementioned Convention; provided, however, that any contracting State, a party to the present Agreement, may denounce it on one year's notice given by it to the Government of the United States of America, which shall at once inform all other contracting States of such notice and withdrawal.

The freedoms of the Air

International Air Transport Agreement, Signed at Chicago, on 7 December, 1944 (Transport Agreement)
Entry into force: 8 February 1945
Status: 11 Parties

Article I

Section 1

Each contracting State grants to the other contracting States the following freedoms of the air in respect of scheduled international air services:

1   The privilege to fly across its territory without landing;
2   The privilege to land for non-traffic purposes;
3   The privilege to put down passengers, mail and cargo taken on in the territory of the State whose nationality the aircraft possesses;
4   The privilege to take on passengers, mail and cargo destined for the territory of the State whose nationality the aircraft possesses;
5   The privilege to take on passengers, mail and cargo destined for the territory of any other contracting State and the privilege to put down passengers, mail and cargo coming from any such territory.

With respect to the privileges specified under paragraphs 3, 4 and 5 of this section, the undertaking of each contracting State relates only to through services on a route constituting a reasonably direct line out from and back to the homeland of the State whose nationality the aircraft possesses.

The privileges of this section shall not be applicable with respect to airports utilized for military purposes to the exclusion of any scheduled international air services. In areas of active hostilities or of military occupation, and in time of war along the supply routes leading to such areas, the exercise of such privileges shall be subject to the approval of the competent military authorities.

Section 2

The exercise of the foregoing privileges shall be in accordance with the provisions of the Interim Agreement on International Civil Aviation and, when it comes into force, with the provisions of the Convention on International Civil Aviation, both drawn up at Chicago on December 7, 1944.

Section 3

A contracting State granting to the airlines of another contracting State the privilege to stop for nontraffic purposes may require such airlines to offer reasonable commercial service at the points at which such stops are made.

Such requirement shall not involve any discrimination between airlines operating on the same route, shall take into account the capacity of the aircraft, and shall be exercised in such a manner as not to prejudice the normal operations of the international air services concerned or the rights and obligations of any contracting State.

Section 4

Each contracting State shall have the right to refuse permission to the aircraft of other contracting States to take on in its territory passengers, mail and cargo carried for remuneration or hire and destined for another point within its territory. Each contracting State undertakes not to enter into any arrangements which specifically grant any such privilege on an exclusive basis to any other State or an airline of any other State, and not to obtain any such exclusive privilege from any other State.

Section 5

Each contracting State may, subject to the provisions of this Agreement,

1 Designate the route to be followed within its territory by any international air service and the airports which any such service may use;
2 Impose or permit to be imposed on any such service just and reasonable charges for the use of such airports and other facilities; these charges shall not be higher than would be paid for the use of such airports and facilities by its national aircraft engaged in similar international services: provided that, upon representation by an interested contracting State, the charges imposed for the use of airports and other facilities shall be subject to review by the Council of the International Civil Aviation Organization established under the above-mentioned Convention, which shall report and make recommendations thereon for the consideration of the State or States concerned.

Section 6

Each contracting State reserves the right to withhold or revoke a certificate or permit to an air transport enterprise of another State in any case where it is not satisfied that substantial ownership and effective control are vested in nationals of a contracting State, or in case of failure of such air transport enterprise to comply with the laws of the State over which it operates, or to perform its obligations under this Agreement.

Article II

Section 1

The contracting States accept this Agreement as abrogating all obligations and understandings between them which are inconsistent with its terms, and undertake not to enter into any such obligations and understandings. A contracting State which has undertaken any other obligations inconsistent with this Agreement shall take immediate steps to procure its release from the obligations. If an airline of any contracting State has entered into any such inconsistent obligations, the State of which it is a national shall use its best efforts to secure their termination forthwith and shall in any event cause them to be terminated as soon as such action can lawfully be taken after the coming into force of this Agreement.

Section 2

Subject to the provisions of the preceding section, any contracting State may make arrangements concerning international air services not inconsistent with this Agreement. Any such arrangement shall be forthwith registered with the Council, which shall make it public as soon as possible.

Article III

Each contracting State undertakes that in the establishment and operation of through services due consideration shall be given to the interests of the other contracting States so as not to interfere unduly with their regional services or to hamper the development of their through services.

Article V

This agreement shall remain in force as long as the abovementioned Convention; provided, however, that any contracting State, a party to the present Agreement, may denounce it on one year's notice given by it to the Government of the United States of America, which shall at once inform all other contracting States of such notice and withdrawal.

Air transport agreement

EU-US Air Transport Agreement
of 2007
The Agreement has provisionally applied since 30 March 2008
Entry into force: 29 June 2020
Note: Norway and Iceland acceded to the Agreement in 2011
Prior to the 2007 Agreement, air transport relations with the US were governed by bilateral
   agreements between EU countries and the US.

Article 3 Grant of rights

1   Each Party grants to the other Party the following rights for the conduct of international air transportation by the airlines of the other Party:

    (a)   the right to fly across its territory without landing;
    (b)   the right to make stops in its territory for non-traffic purposes;
    (c)   the right to perform international air transportation between points on the following routes:

        (i)   for airlines of the United States (hereinafter US airlines), from points behind the United States via the United States and intermediate points to any point or points in any Member State or States and beyond; and for all-cargo service, between any Member State and any point or points (including in any other Member States);
        (ii) for airlines of the European Community and its Member States (hereinafter Community airlines), from points behind the Member States via the Member

States and intermediate points to any point or points in the United States and beyond; for all-cargo service, between the United States and any point or points; and, for combination services, between any point or points in the United States and any point or points in any member of the European Common Aviation Area (hereinafter the ECAA) as of the date of signature of this Agreement; and

(d) the rights otherwise specified in this Agreement.

2 Each airline may on any or all flights and at its option:

(a) operate flights in either or both directions;

(b) combine different flight numbers within one aircraft operation;

(c) serve behind, intermediate, and beyond points and points in the territories of the Parties in any combination and in any order;

(d) omit stops at any point or points;

(e) transfer traffic from any of its aircraft to any of its other aircraft at any point;

(f) serve points behind any point in its territory with or without change of aircraft or flight number and hold out and advertise such services to the public as through services;

(g) make stopovers at any points whether within or outside the territory of either Party;

(h) carry transit traffic through the other Party's territory;

and

(i) combine traffic on the same aircraft regardless of where such traffic originates; without directional or geographic limitation and without loss of any right to carry traffic otherwise permissible under this Agreement.

3 The provisions of paragraph 1 of this Article shall apply subject to the requirements that:

(a) for US airlines, with the exception of all-cargo services, the transportation is part of a service that serves the United States, and

(b) for Community airlines, with the exception of (i) all-cargo services and (ii) combination services between the United States and any member of the ECAA as of the date of signature of this Agreement, the transportation is part of a service that serves a Member State.

4 Each Party shall allow each airline to determine the frequency and capacity of the international air transportation it offers based upon commercial considerations in the marketplace. Consistent with this right, neither Party shall unilaterally limit the volume of traffic, frequency or regularity of service, or the aircraft type or types operated by the airlines of the other Party, nor shall it require the filing of schedules, programs for charter flights, or operational plans by airlines of the other Party, except as may be required for customs, technical, operational, or environmental (consistent with Article 15) reasons under uniform conditions consistent with Article 15 of the Convention.

5 Any airline may perform international air transportation without any limitation as to change, at any point, in type or number of aircraft operated; provided that, (a) for US

airlines, with the exception of all-cargo services, the transportation is part of a service that serves the United States, and (b) for Community airlines, with the exception of (i) all-cargo services and (ii) combination services between the United States and a member of the ECAA as of the date of signature of this Agreement, the transportation is part of a service that serves a Member State.

6 Nothing in this Agreement shall be deemed to confer on:

   (a) US airlines the right to take on board, in the territory of any Member State, passengers, baggage, cargo, or mail carried for compensation and destined for another point in the territory of that Member State;

   (b) Community airlines the right to take on board, in the territory of the United States, passengers, baggage, cargo, or mail carried for compensation and destined for another point in the territory of the United States.

7 Community airlines' access to US Government procured transportation shall be governed by Annex 3.

Article 4 Authorisation

On receipt of applications from an airline of one Party, in the form and manner prescribed for operating authorisations and technical permissions, the other Party shall grant appropriate authorisations and permissions with minimum procedural delay, provided:

   (a) for a US airline, substantial ownership and effective control of that airline are vested in the United States, US nationals, or both, and the airline is licensed as a US airline and has its principal place of business in US territory;

   (b) for a Community airline, substantial ownership and effective control of that airline are vested in a Member State or States, nationals of such a State or States, or both, and the airline is licensed as a Community airline and has its principal place of business in the territory of the European Community;

   (c) the airline is qualified to meet the conditions prescribed under the laws and regulations normally applied to the operation of international air transportation by the Party considering the application or applications;
   and

   (d) the provisions set forth in Article 8 (Safety) and Article 9 (Security) are being maintained and administered.

Article 5 Revocation of authorisation

1 Either Party may revoke, suspend or limit the operating authorisations or technical permissions or otherwise suspend or limit the operations of an airline of the other Party where:

   (a) for a US airline, substantial ownership and effective control of that airline are not vested in the United States, US nationals, or both, or the airline is not licensed as a US airline or does not have its principal place of business in US territory;

   (b) for a Community airline, substantial ownership and effective control of that airline are not vested in a Member State or States, nationals of such a State or States, or both, or the airline is not licensed as a Community airline or does not have its principal place of business in the territory of the European Community; or

(c)   that airline has failed to comply with the laws and regulations referred to in Article 7 (Application of Laws) of this Agreement.

2   Unless immediate action is essential to prevent further noncompliance with subparagraph 1(c) of this Article, the rights established by this Article shall be exercised only after consultation with the other Party.

3   This Article does not limit the rights of either Party to withhold, revoke, limit or impose conditions on the operating authorisation or technical permission of an airline or airlines of the other Party in accordance with the provisions of Article 8 (Safety) or Article 9 (Security).

Article 6   Additional matters related to ownership, investment, and control

Notwithstanding any other provision in this Agreement, the Parties shall implement the provisions of Annex 4 in their decisions under their respective laws and regulations concerning ownership, investment and control.

Article 7   Application of laws

1   The laws and regulations of a Party relating to the admission to or departure from its territory of aircraft engaged in international air navigation, or to the operation and navigation of such aircraft while within its territory, shall be applied to the aircraft utilised by the airlines of the other Party, and shall be complied with by such aircraft upon entering or departing from or while within the territory of the first Party.

2   While entering, within, or leaving the territory of one Party, the laws and regulations applicable within that territory relating to the admission to or departure from its territory of passengers, crew or cargo on aircraft (including regulations relating to entry, clearance, immigration, passports, customs and quarantine or, in the case of mail, postal regulations) shall be complied with by, or on behalf of, such passengers, crew or cargo of the other Party's airlines.

Article 8   Safety

1   The responsible authorities of the Parties shall recognise as valid, for the purposes of operating the air transportation provided for in this Agreement, certificates of airworthiness, certificates of competency, and licences issued or validated by each other and still in force, provided that the requirements for such certificates or licences at least equal the minimum standards that may be established pursuant to the Convention. The responsible authorities may, however, refuse to recognise as valid for purposes of flight above their own territory, certificates of competency and licences granted to or validated for their own nationals by such other authorities.

2   The responsible authorities of a Party may request consultations with other responsible authorities concerning the safety standards maintained by those authorities relating

to aeronautical facilities, aircrews, aircraft, and operation of the airlines overseen by those authorities. Such consultations shall take place within 45 days of the request unless otherwise agreed. If following such consultations, the requesting responsible authorities find that those authorities do not effectively maintain and administer safety standards and requirements in these areas that at least equal the minimum standards that may be established pursuant to the Convention, the requesting responsible authorities shall notify those authorities of such findings and the steps considered necessary to conform with these minimum standards, and those authorities shall take appropriate corrective action. The requesting responsible authorities reserve the right to withhold, revoke or limit the operating authorisation or technical permission of an airline or airlines for which those authorities provide safety oversight in the event those authorities do not take such appropriate corrective action within a reasonable time and to take immediate action as to such airline or airlines if essential to prevent further non-compliance with the duty to maintain and administer the aforementioned standards and requirements resulting in an immediate threat to flight safety.

3   The European Commission shall simultaneously receive all requests and notifications under this Article.

4   Nothing in this Article shall prevent the responsible authorities of the Parties from conducting safety discussions, including those relating to the routine application of safety standards and requirements or to emergency situations that may arise from time to time.

Article 9   Security

1   In accordance with their rights and obligations under international law, the Parties reaffirm that their obligation to each other to protect the security of civil aviation against acts of unlawful interference forms an integral part of this Agreement. Without limiting the generality of their rights and obligations under international law, the Parties shall in particular act in conformity with the following agreements: the Convention on Offences and Certain Other Acts Committed on Board Aircraft, done at Tokyo, 14 September 1963, the Convention for the Suppression of Unlawful Seizure of Aircraft, done at The Hague, 16 December 1970, the Convention for the Suppression of Unlawful Acts against the Safety of Civil Aviation, done at Montreal, 23 September 1971, and the Protocol for the Suppression of Unlawful Acts of Violence at Airports Serving International Civil Aviation, done at Montreal, 24 February 1988.

2   The Parties shall provide upon request all necessary assistance to each other to address any threat to the security of civil aviation, including the prevention of acts of unlawful seizure of civil aircraft and other unlawful acts against the safety of such aircraft, of their passengers and crew, and of airports and air navigation facilities.

3   The Parties shall, in their mutual relations, act in conformity with the aviation security standards and appropriate recommended practices established by the International Civil Aviation Organisation and designated as Annexes to the Convention; they shall require that operators of aircraft of their registries, operators of aircraft who have their principal place of business or permanent residence in their territory, and the operators of airports in their territory act in conformity with such aviation security provisions.

4   Each Party shall ensure that effective measures are taken within its territory to protect aircraft and to inspect passengers, crew, and their baggage and carry-on items, as

well as cargo and aircraft stores, prior to and during boarding or loading; and that those measures are adjusted to meet increased threats to the security of civil aviation. Each Party agrees that the security provisions required by the other Party for departure from and while within the territory of that other Party must be observed. Each Party shall give positive consideration to any request from the other Party for special security measures to meet a particular threat.

5   With full regard and mutual respect for each other's sovereignty, a Party may adopt security measures for entry into its territory. Where possible, that Party shall take into account the security measures already applied by the other Party and any views that the other Party may offer. Each Party recognises, however, that nothing in this Article limits the ability of a Party to refuse entry into its territory of any flight or flights that it deems to present a threat to its security.

6   A Party may take emergency measures including amendments to meet a specific security threat. Such measures shall be notified immediately to the responsible authorities of the other Party.

7   The Parties underline the importance of working towards compatible practices and standards as a means of enhancing air transport security and minimising regulatory divergence. To this end, the Parties shall fully utilise and develop existing channels for the discussion of current and proposed security measures. The Parties expect that the discussions will address, among other issues, new security measures proposed or under consideration by the other Party, including the revision of security measures occasioned by a change in circumstances; measures proposed by one Party to meet the security requirements of the other Party; possibilities for the more expeditious adjustment of standards with respect to aviation security measures; and compatibility of the requirements of one Party with the legislative obligations of the other Party. Such discussions should serve to foster early notice and prior discussion of new security initiatives and requirements.

8   Without prejudice to the need to take immediate action in order to protect transportation security, the Parties affirm that when considering security measures, a Party shall evaluate possible adverse effects on international air transportation and, unless constrained by law, shall take such factors into account when it determines what measures are necessary and appropriate to address those security concerns.

9   When an incident or threat of an incident of unlawful seizure of aircraft or other unlawful acts against the safety of passengers, crew, aircraft, airports or air navigation facilities occurs, the Parties shall assist each other by facilitating communications and other appropriate measures intended to terminate rapidly and safely such incident or threat.

10   When a Party has reasonable grounds to believe that the other Party has departed from the aviation security provisions of this Article, the responsible authorities of that Party may request immediate consultations with the responsible authorities of the other Party. Failure to reach a satisfactory agreement within 15 days from the date of such request shall constitute grounds to withhold, revoke, limit, or impose conditions on the operating authorisation and technical permissions of an airline or airlines of that Party. When required by an emergency, a Party may take interim action prior to the expiry of 15 days.

11   Separate from airport assessments undertaken to determine conformity with the aviation security standards and practices referred to in paragraph 3 of this Article, a

Party may request the cooperation of the other Party in assessing whether particular security measures of that other Party meet the requirements of the requesting Party. The responsible authorities of the Parties shall coordinate in advance the airports to be assessed and the dates of assessment and establish a procedure to address the results of such assessments. Taking into account the results of the assessments, the requesting Party may decide that security measures of an equivalent standard are applied in the territory of the other Party in order that transfer passengers, transfer baggage, and/ or transfer cargo may be exempted from re-screening in the territory of the requesting Party. Such a decision shall be communicated to the other Party.

Terrorism

Threats to international peace and security caused by terrorist acts – S/RES/1566 of 8 October 2004

The Security Council . . .

1   Condemns in the strongest terms all acts of terrorism irrespective of their motivation, whenever and by whomsoever committed, as one of the most serious threats to peace and security;
2   Calls upon States to cooperate fully in the fight against terrorism, especially with those States where or against whose citizens terrorist acts are committed, in accordance with their obligations under international law, in order to find, deny safe haven and bring to justice, on the basis of the principle to extradite or prosecute, any person who supports, facilitates, participates or attempts to participate in the financing, planning, preparation or commission of terrorist acts or provides safe havens;
3   Recalls that criminal acts, including against civilians, committed with the intent to cause death or serious bodily injury, or taking of hostages, with the purpose to provoke a state of terror in the general public or in a group of persons or particular persons, intimidate a population or compel a government or an international organization to do or to abstain from doing any act, which constitute offences within the scope of and as defined in the international conventions and protocols relating to terrorism, are under no circumstances justifiable by considerations of a political, philosophical, ideological, racial, ethnic, religious or other similar nature, and calls upon all States to prevent such acts and, if not prevented, to ensure that such acts are punished by penalties consistent with their grave nature;
4   Calls upon all States to become party, as a matter of urgency, to the relevant international conventions and protocols whether or not they are a party to regional conventions on the matter;
5   Calls upon Member States to cooperate fully on an expedited basis in resolving all outstanding issues with a view to adopting by consensus the draft comprehensive convention on international terrorism and the draft international convention for the suppression of acts of nuclear terrorism;
6   Calls upon relevant international, regional and subregional organizations to strengthen international cooperation in the fight against terrorism and to intensify their interaction with the United Nations and, in particular, the CTC [United Nations Security Council

Counter-Terrorism Committee] with a view to facilitating full and timely implementation of resolution 1373 (2001);

7   Requests the CTC in consultation with relevant international, regional and subregional organizations and the United Nations bodies to develop a set of best practices to assist States in implementing the provisions of resolution 1373 (2001) related to the financing of terrorism;

8   Directs the CTC, as a matter of priority and, when appropriate, in close cooperation with relevant international, regional and subregional organizations to start visits to States, with the consent of the States concerned, in order to enhance the monitoring of the implementation of resolution 1373 (2001) and facilitate the provision of technical and other assistance for such implementation;

9   Decides to establish a working group consisting of all members of the Security Council to consider and submit recommendations to the Council on practical measures to be imposed upon individuals, groups or entities involved in or associated with terrorist activities, other than those designated by the Al-Qaida/Taliban Sanctions Committee, including more effective procedures considered to be appropriate for bringing them to justice through prosecution or extradition, freezing of their financial assets, preventing their movement through the territories of Member States, preventing supply to them of all types of arms and related material, and on the procedures for implementing these measures;

10   Requests further the working group, established under paragraph 9 to consider the possibility of establishing an international fund to compensate victims of terrorist acts and their families, which might be financed through voluntary contributions, which could consist in part of assets seized from terrorist organizations, their members and sponsors, and submit its recommendations to the Council;

11   Requests the Secretary-General to take, as a matter of urgency, appropriate steps to make the CTED [Counter-Terrorism Committee Executive Directorate] fully operational and to inform the Council by 15 November 2004;

12   Decides to remain actively seized of the matter.

Terrorism

Threats to international peace and security caused by terrorist acts: Preventing and combating the financing of terrorism – S/RES/2462
of 28 March 2019
The Security Council . . .

2. Emphasizes its decision in resolution 1373 that all Member States shall criminalize the wilful provision or collection, by any means, directly or indirectly, of funds by their nationals or in their territories with the intention that the funds should be used, or in the knowledge that they are to be used, in order to carry out terrorist acts; and its decision in resolution 2178 that all Member States shall establish serious criminal offenses regarding the travel, recruitment, and financing of foreign terrorist fighters;

3. Highlights that the obligation regarding the prohibition in paragraph 1 (d) of resolution 1373 applies to making funds, financial assets or economic resources or financial or other related services available, directly or indirectly, for the benefit of terrorist organizations or individual terrorists for any purpose, including but not limited to recruitment, training, or travel, even in the absence of a link to a specific terrorist act; . . .

7. Calls upon Member States to conduct financial investigations in terrorism related cases and to seek ways to address the challenges in obtaining evidence to secure terrorist financing convictions. . . .

10. Stresses the need for effective implementation of asset freezing mechanisms pursuant to resolution 1373 (2001), including considering third party requests from other States;

19. Calls upon Member States to intensify and accelerate the timely exchange of relevant operational information and financial intelligence regarding actions or movements, and patterns of movements, of terrorists or terrorist networks, including Foreign Terrorist Fighters (FTFs) and FTF returnees and relocators, in compliance with international law, including international human rights law, and domestic law, including by: (a) Ensuring that competent authorities can use financial intelligence shared by financial intelligence units, and relevant financial information obtained from the private sector, in compliance with international law, including international human rights law; (b) Enhancing the integration and use of financial intelligence in terrorism related cases, including through enhanced inter-agency coordination; (c) Using financial intelligence and financial footprints as a tool to detect networks of terrorists and their financiers; (d) Considering the establishment of a mechanism by which competent authorities can obtain relevant information, including but not limited to bank accounts, to facilitate the detection of terrorist assets, in compliance with international law, including international human rights law. . . .

24. Urges States, when designing and applying measures to counter the financing of terrorism, to take into account the potential effect of those measures on exclusively humanitarian activities, including medical activities, that are carried out by impartial humanitarian actors in a manner consistent with international humanitarian law. . . .

31. Encourages Member States to make the best use of INTERPOL policing capabilities, such as relevant databases and analytical files, in order to prevent and counter the financing of terrorism;

32. Encourages Member States as well as the United Nations, in particular the United Nations Office on Drugs and Crime (UNODC), to continue conducting research and collecting information to better understand the nature and scope of the links that may exist between terrorism, in particular the financing of terrorism, and transnational organized crime;

Outer space – principles

Treaty on Principles Governing the Activities of States in the Exploration and Use of Outer Space, including the Moon and Other Celestial Bodies of 1967
Entry into force: 10 October 1967

Article I

The exploration and use of outer space, including the Moon and other celestial bodies, shall be carried out for the benefit and in the interests of all countries, irrespective of their degree of economic or scientific development, and shall be the province of all mankind.

Outer space, including the Moon and other celestial bodies, shall be free for exploration and use by all States without discrimination of any kind, on a basis of equality and in accordance with international law, and there shall be free access to all areas of celestial bodies.

There shall be freedom of scientific investigation in outer space, including the Moon and other celestial bodies, and States shall facilitate and encourage international cooperation in such investigation.

Article II

Outer space, including the Moon and other celestial bodies, is not subject to national appropriation by claim of sovereignty, by means of use or occupation, or by any other means.

Article III

States Parties to the Treaty shall carry on activities in the exploration and use of outer space, including the Moon and other celestial bodies, in accordance with international law, including the Charter of the United Nations, in the interest of maintaining international peace and security and promoting international cooperation and understanding.

Article IV

States Parties to the Treaty undertake not to place in orbit around the Earth any objects carrying nuclear weapons or any other kinds of weapons of mass destruction, install such weapons on celestial bodies, or station such weapons in outer space in any other manner.

The Moon and other celestial bodies shall be used by all States Parties to the Treaty exclusively for peaceful purposes. The establishment of military bases, installations and fortifications, the testing of any type of weapons and the conduct of military manoeuvres on celestial bodies shall be forbidden. The use of military personnel for scientific research or for any other peaceful purposes shall not be prohibited. The use of any equipment or facility necessary for peaceful exploration of the Moon and other celestial bodies shall also not be prohibited.

Article V

States Parties to the Treaty shall regard astronauts as envoys of mankind in outer space and shall render to them all possible assistance in the event of accident, distress, or emergency landing on the territory of another State Party or on the high seas. When astronauts make such a landing, they shall be safely and promptly returned to the State of registry of their space vehicle.

In carrying on activities in outer space and on celestial bodies, the astronauts of one State Party shall render all possible assistance to the astronauts of other States Parties.

States Parties to the Treaty shall immediately inform the other States Parties to the Treaty or the Secretary-General of the United Nations of any phenomena they discover in outer space, including the Moon and other celestial bodies, which could constitute a danger to the life or health of astronauts.

Article VI

States Parties to the Treaty shall bear international responsibility for national activities in outer space, including the Moon and other celestial bodies, whether such activities are carried on by governmental agencies or by non-governmental entities, and for assuring that national activities are carried out in conformity with the provisions set forth in the present Treaty. The activities of non-governmental entities in outer space, including the Moon and other celestial bodies, shall require authorization and continuing supervision by the appropriate State Party to the Treaty.

When activities are carried on in outer space, including the Moon and other celestial bodies, by an international organization, responsibility for compliance with this Treaty shall be borne both by the international organization and by the States Parties to the Treaty participating in such organization.

Article VII

Each State Party to the Treaty that launches or procures the launching of an object into outer space, including the Moon and other celestial bodies, and each State Party from whose territory or facility an object is launched, is internationally liable for damage to another State Party to the Treaty or to its natural or juridical persons by such object or its component parts on the Earth, in air space or in outer space, including the Moon and other celestial bodies.

Article VIII

A State Party to the Treaty on whose registry an object launched into outer space is carried shall retain jurisdiction and control over such object, and over any personnel thereof, while in outer space or on a celestial body. Ownership of objects launched into outer space, including objects landed or constructed on a celestial body, and of their component parts, is not affected by their presence in outer space or on a celestial body or by their return to the Earth. Such objects or component parts found beyond the limits of the State Party to the Treaty on whose registry they are carried shall be returned to that State Party, which shall, upon request, furnish identifying data prior to their return.

Article IX

In the exploration and use of outer space, including the Moon and other celestial bodies, States Parties to the Treaty shall be guided by the principle of cooperation and mutual assistance and shall conduct all their activities in outer space, including the Moon and other celestial bodies, with due regard to the corresponding interests of all other States Parties to the Treaty. States Parties to the Treaty shall pursue studies of outer space, including the Moon and other celestial bodies, and conduct exploration of them so as to avoid their harmful contamination and also adverse changes in the environment of the Earth resulting from the introduction of extraterrestrial matter and, where necessary, shall adopt appropriate measures for this purpose. If a State Party to the Treaty has reason to believe that an activity or experiment planned by it or its nationals in outer space, including the Moon and other celestial bodies, would cause potentially harmful interference with activities of other States Parties in the peaceful exploration and use of outer space, including the Moon and other celestial bodies, it shall undertake appropriate international consultations before proceeding with any such activity or experiment. A State Party to the Treaty which has reason to believe that an activity or experiment planned by another State Party in outer space, including the Moon and other celestial bodies, would cause potentially harmful interference with activities in the peaceful exploration and use of outer space, including the Moon and other celestial bodies, may request consultation concerning the activity or experiment.

Article X

In order to promote international cooperation in the exploration and use of outer space, including the Moon and other celestial bodies, in conformity with the purposes of this Treaty, the States Parties to the Treaty shall consider on a basis of equality any requests by other States Parties to the Treaty to be afforded an opportunity to observe the flight of space objects launched by those States. The nature of such an opportunity for observation and the conditions under which it could be afforded shall be determined by agreement between the States concerned.

Article XI

In order to promote international cooperation in the peaceful exploration and use of outer space, States Parties to the Treaty conducting activities in outer space, including the Moon and other celestial bodies, agree to inform the Secretary-General of the United Nations as well as the public and the international scientific community, to the greatest extent feasible and practicable, of the nature, conduct, locations and results of such activities. On receiving the said information, the Secretary-General of the United Nations should be prepared to disseminate it immediately and effectively.

Article XII

All stations, installations, equipment and space vehicles on the Moon and other celestial bodies shall be open to representatives of other States Parties to the Treaty on a basis of reciprocity. Such representatives shall give reasonable advance notice of a projected visit, in order that appropriate consultations may be held and that maximum precautions may be taken to assure safety and to avoid interference with normal operations in the facility to be visited.

Outer space – liability

Convention on International Liability for Damage Caused by Space Objects
of 1972
Entry into force: 1 September 1972

Article I

For the purposes of this Convention:

(a) The term "damage" means loss of life, personal injury or other impairment of health; or loss of or damage to property of States or of persons, natural or juridical, or property of international intergovernmental organizations;

(b) The term "launching" includes attempted launching;

(c) The term "launching State" means:

(i) A State which launches or procures the launching of a space object;

(ii) A State from whose territory or facility a space object is launched;

(d) The term "space object" includes component parts of a space object as well as its launch vehicle and parts thereof.

Article II

A launching State shall be absolutely liable to pay compensation for damage caused by its space object on the surface of the Earth or to aircraft in flight.

Article III

In the event of damage being caused elsewhere than on the surface of the Earth to a space object of one launching State or to persons or property on board such a space object by a space object of another launching State, the latter shall be liable only if the damage is due to its fault or the fault of persons for whom it is responsible.

Article IV

1   In the event of damage being caused elsewhere than on the surface of the Earth to a space object of one launching State or to persons or property on board such a space object by a space object of another launching State, and of damage thereby being caused to a third State or to its natural or juridical persons, the first two States shall be jointly and severally liable to the third State, to the extent indicated by the following:

(a) If the damage has been caused to the third State on the surface of the Earth or to aircraft in flight, their liability to the third State shall be absolute;

(b) If the damage has been caused to a space object of the third State or to persons or property on board that space object elsewhere than on the surface of the Earth, their liability to the third State shall be based on the fault of either of the first two States or on the fault of persons for whom either is responsible.

2   In all cases of joint and several liability referred to in paragraph 1 of this article, the burden of compensation for the damage shall be apportioned between the first two States in accordance with the extent to which they were at fault; if the extent of the fault of each of these States cannot be established, the burden of compensation shall be apportioned equally between them. Such apportionment shall be without prejudice to the right of the third State to seek the entire compensation due under this Convention from any or all of the launching States which are jointly and severally liable.

Article V

1   Whenever two or more States jointly launch a space object, they shall be jointly and severally liable for any damage caused.

2   A launching State which has paid compensation for damage shall have the right to present a claim for indemnification to other participants in the joint launching. The participants in a joint launching may conclude agreements regarding the apportioning among themselves of the financial obligation in respect of which they are jointly and severally liable. Such agreements shall be without prejudice to the right of a State sustaining damage to seek the entire compensation due under this Convention from any or all of the launching States which are jointly and severally liable.

3   A State from whose territory or facility a space object is launched shall be regarded as a participant in a joint launching.

Article VI

1 Subject to the provisions of paragraph 2 of this article, exoneration from absolute liability shall be granted to the extent that a launching State establishes that the damage has resulted either wholly or partially from gross negligence or from an act or omission done with intent to cause damage on the part of a claimant State or of natural or juridical persons it represents.

2 No exoneration whatever shall be granted in cases where the damage has resulted from activities conducted by a launching State which are not in conformity with international law including, in particular, the Charter of the United Nations and the Treaty on Principles Governing the Activities of States in the Exploration and Use of Outer Space, including the Moon and Other Celestial Bodies.

Article VII

The provisions of this Convention shall not apply to damage caused by a space object of a launching State to:

(a) Nationals of that launching State;

(b) Foreign nationals during such time as they are participating in the operation of that space object from the time of its launching or at any stage thereafter until its descent, or during such time as they are in the immediate vicinity of a planned launching or recovery area as the result of an invitation by that launching State.

Article VIII

1 A State which suffers damage, or whose natural or juridical persons suffer damage, may present to a launching State a claim for compensation for such damage.

2 If the State of nationality has not presented a claim, another State may, in respect of damage sustained in its territory by any natural or juridical person, present a claim to a launching State.

3 If neither the State of nationality nor the State in whose territory the damage was sustained has presented a claim or notified its intention of presenting a claim, another State may, in respect of damage sustained by its permanent residents, present a claim to a launching State.

Article IX

A claim for compensation for damage shall be presented to a launching State through diplomatic channels. If a State does not maintain diplomatic relations with the launching State concerned, it may request another State to present its claim to that launching State or otherwise represent its interests under this Convention. It may also present its claim through the Secretary-General of the United Nations, provided the claimant State and the launching State are both Members of the United Nations.

Article X

1 A claim for compensation for damage may be presented to a launching State not later than one year following the date of the occurrence of the damage or the identification of the launching State which is liable.

2 If, however, a State does not know of the occurrence of the damage or has not been able to identify the launching State which is liable, it may present a claim within one year following the date on which it learned of the aforementioned facts; however, this period shall in no event exceed one year following the date on which the State could reasonably be expected to have learned of the facts through the exercise of due diligence.

3 The time limits specified in paragraphs 1 and 2 of this article shall apply even if the full extent of the damage may not be known. In this event, however, the claimant State shall be entitled to revise the claim and submit additional documentation after the expiration of such time limits until one year after the full extent of the damage is known.

Article XI

1 Presentation of a claim to a launching State for compensation for damage under this Convention shall not require the prior exhaustion of any local remedies which may be available to a claimant State or to natural or juridical persons it represents.

2 Nothing in this Convention shall prevent a State, or natural or juridical persons it might represent, from pursuing a claim in the courts or administrative tribunals or agencies of a launching State. A State shall not, however, be entitled to present a claim under this Convention in respect of the same damage for which a claim is being pursued in the courts or administrative tribunals or agencies of a launching State or under another international agreement which is binding on the States concerned.

Article XII

The compensation which the launching State shall be liable to pay for damage under this Convention shall be determined in accordance with international law and the principles of justice and equity, in order to provide such reparation in respect of the damage as will restore the person, natural or juridical, State or international organization on whose behalf the claim is presented to the condition which would have existed if the damage had not occurred.

Article XIII

Unless the claimant State and the State from which compensation is due under this Convention agree on another form of compensation, the compensation shall be paid in the currency of the claimant State or, if that State so requests, in the currency of the State from which compensation is due.

Article XIV

If no settlement of a claim is arrived at through diplomatic negotiations as provided for in article IX, within one year from the date on which the claimant State notifies the launching State that it has submitted the documentation of its claim, the parties concerned shall establish a Claims Commission at the request of either party.

Article XV

1　The Claims Commission shall be composed of three members: one appointed by the claimant State, one appointed by the launching State and the third member, the Chairman, to be chosen by both parties jointly. Each party shall make its appointment within two months of the request for the establishment of the Claims Commission.

2　If no agreement is reached on the choice of the Chairman within four months of the request for the establishment of the Commission, either party may request the Secretary-General of the United Nations to appoint the Chairman within a further period of two months.

Article XVI

1　If one of the parties does not make its appointment within the stipulated period, the Chairman shall, at the request of the other party, constitute a single-member Claims Commission.

2　Any vacancy which may arise in the Commission for whatever reason shall be filled by the same procedure adopted for the original appointment.

3　The Commission shall determine its own procedure.

4　The Commission shall determine the place or places where it shall sit and all other administrative matters.

5　Except in the case of decisions and awards by a single-member Commission, all decisions and awards of the Commission shall be by majority vote.

Article XVII

No increase in the membership of the Claims Commission shall take place by reason of two or more claimant States or launching States being joined in any one proceeding before the Commission. The claimant States so joined shall collectively appoint one member of the Commission in the same manner and subject to the same conditions as would be the case for a single claimant State. When two or more launching States are so joined, they shall collectively appoint one member of the Commission in the same way. If the claimant States or the launching States do not make the appointment within the stipulated period, the Chairman shall constitute a single-member Commission.

Article XVIII

The Claims Commission shall decide the merits of the claim for compensation and determine the amount of compensation payable, if any.

Article XIX

1 The Claims Commission shall act in accordance with the provisions of article XII.
2 The decision of the Commission shall be final and binding if the parties have so agreed; otherwise the Commission shall render a final and recommendatory award, which the parties shall consider in good faith. The Commission shall state the reasons for its decision or award.
3 The Commission shall give its decision or award as promptly as possible and no later than one year from the date of its establishment, unless an extension of this period is found necessary by the Commission.
4 The Commission shall make its decision or award public. It shall deliver a certified copy of its decision or award to each of the parties and to the Secretary-General of the United Nations.

Article XX

The expenses in regard to the Claims Commission shall be borne equally by the parties, unless otherwise decided by the Commission.

Article XXI

If the damage caused by a space object presents a large-scale danger to human life or seriously interferes with the living conditions of the population or the functioning of vital centres, the States Parties, and in particular the launching State, shall examine the possibility of rendering appropriate and rapid assistance to the State which has suffered the damage, when it so requests. However, nothing in this article shall affect the rights or obligations of the States Parties under this Convention.

Article XXII

1 In this Convention, with the exception of articles XXIV to XXVII, references to States shall be deemed to apply to any international intergovernmental organization which conducts space activities if the organization declares its acceptance of the rights and obligations provided for in this Convention and if a majority of the States members of the organization are States Parties to this Convention and to the Treaty on Principles Governing the Activities of States in the Exploration and Use of Outer Space, including the Moon and Other Celestial Bodies.
2 States members of any such organization which are States Parties to this Convention shall take all appropriate steps to ensure that the organization makes a declaration in accordance with the preceding paragraph.
3 If an international intergovernmental organization is liable for damage by virtue of the provisions of this Convention, that organization and those of its members which are States Parties to this Convention shall be jointly and severally liable; provided, however, that:

   (a) Any claim for compensation in respect of such damage shall be first presented to the organization;
   (b) Only where the organization has not paid, within a period of six months, any sum agreed or determined to be due as compensation for such damage, may the claimant

State invoke the liability of the members which are States Parties to this Convention for the payment of that sum.

4 Any claim, pursuant to the provisions of this Convention, for compensation in respect of damage caused to an organization which has made a declaration in accordance with paragraph 1 of this article shall be presented by a State member of the organization which is a State Party to this Convention.

International economic law

DOI: 10.4324/9781003213772-15

DEFINITION, SOURCES, AND SUBFIELDS OF INTERNATIONAL ECONOMIC LAW

international economic affairs
soft law
hard law
multilateral agreements
bilateral treaties
international finance law
international trade law
international investment law

The definition of international economic law

International economic law deals primarily with the regulation of **international economic affairs** between two or more states. Nonetheless international economic relations also engage other subjects of international law, as well as private natural and legal persons operating in cross-border economic transactions.

The legal rules for international economic relations are provided substantially by international private law and the national laws of states, which are, however, beyond the scope of this chapter. Thus, this chapter discusses predominantly only that part of the legal regulations which holds an intergovernmental nature and, therefore, is an essential component of international public law.

International economic law plays a significant role in maintaining the world economy and protecting long-term common interests. It serves as a legal tool to mitigate the contradictions between the political and economic goals of individual states, other subjects of international law, and the interests of the whole world economy.

Sources

International economic law deals with two kinds of legal instruments – **soft law** instruments and **hard law** instruments.

As regards soft law, numerous documents intended to establish particular arrangements in the international economic area operate in this field. Among them, a unique place belongs to the decisions of the internal bodies of international organisations, as these decisions, being remarkable expressions of soft law, possess a legally non-binding nature.

Concerning the instruments of hard law in this regard, customary international law and the general principles of law have developed only very general rules and principles in the area of international economic law. Hence, international economic relations between the subjects of international law are primarily regulated by international treaties. Among such treaties, **multilateral agreements** build a global or regional framework, and **bilateral treaties** establish the particular norms of economic interaction between the parties involved.

The subfields of international economic law

International economic law covers many areas of cross-border economic co-operation between the subjects of international law. However, its main objectives are the international financial system, international trade, and investment. Thus, under the umbrella of international economic law, such subfields as **international finance law**, **international trade law**, and **international investment law** have been developed.

Additionally, international economic law embraces such areas as economic development, the relationship between economic issues and environmental protection or human rights, the role of transnational enterprises, international commercial dispute resolution, and so one. Some of them are addressed in other chapters of this book. (For example, the modern concept of economic development without harming the environment is discussed in the next chapter – International environmental law.)

THE BRETTON WOODS SYSTEM

> Marshall Plan
> Bretton Woods system
> gold standard
> U.S. dollar standard
> liberal international economic order
> International Monetary Fund
> International Bank for Reconstruction and Development
> World Bank
> General Agreement on Tariffs and Trade
> stagflation
> Special Drawing Rights
> Jamaica Accords
> SDR standard
> global economic crisis

The post–Second World War period

The leading international political and economic challenge in the immediate aftermath of the Second World War was to rebuild Europe and, on the other hand, to create an international legal framework to help the global community achieve sustainable economic growth. A comprehensive plan for the recovery of Europe became known as the **Marshall Plan** (after General George C. Marshall).[1149] At the same time, in order to achieve these grand objectives, the following were considered to be the foundational tools:

1149 The Marshall Plan was a program sponsored by the United States, which was executed following the Second World War to support the European countries. It was announced by US Secretary of State George Marshall in 1947. The plan was authorised by Congress as the European Recovery Program.

- the free movement of goods and capital across borders;
- enabling states to exploit their natural resources to the maximum extent possible for their economic development;
- reduction of tariffs and other barriers to international trade;
- correcting the monetary disorders of earlier decades in the future and establishing international trade discipline; and
- minimisation of the possibility of economic conflicts between states.

The rise of the Bretton Woods system

However, the comprehension that the world or at least a large part of it was facing an economic collapse came before the Second World War was even over. Consequently, the allied (united) nations (Allied Powers) of World War II gathered at a conference in July 1944, which took place in Bretton Woods, New Hampshire (USA).

Before the **Bretton Woods system**, most countries followed the so-called **gold standard** or at least a special form of this standard (for instance, the so-called inter-war gold standard, also known as the gold exchange standard),[1150] which eventually meant that each state guaranteed the redemption of its currency for its value in gold, affirming by this the existence of a gold-based economy.

However, there were many reasons which led to the fall of the gold standard system. Among other things, the downfall of the system was the result of monetary disorders, hyperinflation of the currencies, the Great Depression of the 1930s, and so forth.

In 1944, the participants of the Bretton Woods conference opted to address the main economic challenges of that period by planting the seeds of the Bretton Woods system to promote international trade, global investments, and monetary discipline. The most important part of the international regulations developed in Bretton Woods concerned monetary rules. Under these regulations, each participant in the monetary system agreed to redeem its currency for US dollars (not gold), based on a fixed exchange rate to the US dollar, creating with this a **U.S. dollar standard**.[1151] The USA agreed to fix the convertibility of the US dollar into gold at the rate of US $35 per ounce.

However, the new system would not be successful without a coherent legal framework and institutionalised co-operation for the maintenance of the agreed international regulations.

As regards the basics of the established legal framework, the parties established the economic order for the free movement of goods and capital, the reduction of tariffs and

---

1150 The system of the *gold exchange standard* was the result of the decisions of the Genoa Conference of 1922 and was shaped by the outcome of the First World War. This model was a form of gold standard that conserved gold stocks; the gold remained in their vaults, and day-to-day transactions were conducted with representative paper notes. At the same time, citizens following this new gold exchange standard (gold bullion standard) would not receive gold coins freely in exchange for their notes, although *this was a significant version of the original gold standard.*

1151 The United States held three-fourths of the world's supply of gold. The Bretton Woods system allowed all countries to gradually transition from a gold standard to a U.S. dollar standard.

other barriers to international trade, and the maintenance of monetary and trade discipline, as well as other tools mentioned earlier.

As for the institutionalised safeguarding of the Bretton Woods system, the conference gave birth to three international structures of considerable importance for international economic order: the **International Monetary Fund** (IMF); the **International Bank for Reconstruction and Development** (IBRD), usually referred to as the **World Bank**, and the **General Agreement on Tariffs and Trade** (GATT).

The principal outcome documents of the Bretton Woods conference were the following agreements:

1   Articles of Agreement establishing the International Monetary Fund, adopted to promote stability of exchange rates and financial flows;
2   Articles of Agreement creating the International Bank for Reconstruction and Development, concluded to maintain the reconstruction agenda after the Second World War and to stimulate the economic development of all countries; and
3   Other means of international financial co-operation.

The fall of the Bretton Woods monetary system

There were numerous reasons for the collapse of the monetary part of the Bretton Woods system. Firstly, the system maintained a unique place for the United States, establishing this country as the dominant power in the world economy.

However, it was done with a great deal of criticism from many states, and such a position was painful for the American economy itself. Thus, over time, the Bretton Woods monetary system was shaken by the particular internal troubles of the system.

The main factors of the downfall of the Bretton Woods monetary system were related especially to the troubles of the dominant economic power, such as the depletion of the United States gold reserves and, in the early 1970s, the **stagflation** (as a combination of stagnant economic growth, high unemployment, and high inflation) of the United States economy.

There were several attempts to rescue the monetary system but without tangible results. One of the attempts to rescue the system was the introduction of an international currency issued by the IMF called **Special Drawing Rights** (SDR). This currency was intended to take the dollar's place as the international reserve currency. However, as its first issuance did not occur until 1969, it proved to be too late to correct the problems of the international monetary system. Finally, the states and involved international organisations introduced a system allowing currencies to float freely, bringing the Bretton Woods monetary system of fixed-but-adjustable rates to an unambiguous end.

The post–Bretton Woods monetary system

At the regular session of the IMF in Kingston, Jamaica, in 1976, the foundations of the multilateral system of payments were identified, and the **Jamaica Accords** as a set of international agreements were signed.

Under the Jamaica Accords, the function of gold as an exchange rate standard was finally abolished. Gold was turned into a regular commodity with a free price. At the same time, as a collective reserve currency, the **SDR standard** was reaffirmed. States were given the right to choose any exchange rate regime. Consequently, the states were free to either allow their currency to float freely or to peg it to another currency or basket of currencies. Moreover, they were allowed to adopt the currency of another country or participate in a monetary union as well.[1152]

At times, the global economy has faced several critical crises, such as the **global economic crisis** which started with the collapse of mortgage lending in the USA in 2007 and spread around the world in the next year. However, the numerous legal, political, and economic tools in the hands of the states and international institutions have more or less maintained the stability of the world economic system, which to date develops under the constant influence of globalisation. At the same time, among other things, the enormous leap of technologies led to new challenges for the stability of the world economy. For instance, the internet and blockchain technology are nowadays regarded as both challenges and possibilities for further development of the entire world economy.

INTERNATIONAL FINANCE LAW

> balance of payments
> negative or positive balance of payments
> Special Drawing Rights
> multilateral system of payments
> Articles of Agreement of the International Monetary Fund
> quota system
> voting power
> Articles of Agreement of the International Bank for Reconstruction and Development
> World Bank Group
> Group of 7
> Group of 20
> Group of 24

The fields of operation of international finance law

The areas of legal relations in international finance law are national, multinational, and regional legal regimes in the financial sphere; national currencies; international accounting units (reserve assets); conditions for convertibility of currencies; forms of international

---

1152 As a result, several countries pegged their rates to the US dollar, a number of countries to the French franc and other currencies; others to the SDR or to another basket of currencies. Some countries (for example, the USA) have established an independent navigation regime. Within the European countries, the mechanisms of the European Monetary System were developed.

payments; balance of payments; international currency markets; loans; debentures; and the list can be continued further.

Finances maintain international trade in goods and services, capital migration, and the labour markets. The national financial systems are linked via the exchange rate – that is, the price of the national currency expressed in the currency of another state, a basket of currencies, or international accounting units. At the same time, currency by itself became a commodity which could be traded in foreign exchange markets. To date, the global currency market is decentralised; stock exchanges, banks, transnational corporations, brokerage firms, and investment funds operate there.

The balance of payments

The **balance of payments** is the record of all economic transactions that systematically accumulates for a specific period (which usually can be a quarter or a year) the economic transactions of an economy with the rest of the world.

> A transaction itself is defined as an economic flow that reflects the creation, transformation, exchange, transfer, or extinction of economic value and involves changes in ownership of goods and/or financial assets, the provision of services, or the provision of labor and capital.[1153]

The **negative or positive balance of payments** in the interstate financial system indicates an imbalance in the transactions. A positive (surplus) balance specifies that the country accumulates the economy's claims on the rest of the world, and, therefore, it has investment potential. A negative (deficit) balance indicates an outflow of funds; the country becomes a debtor in relation to the outside world, the exchange rate of the national currency is deteriorating, and the state proceeds with the sale of reserves. As reserves, the state can accumulate, in particular, gold reserves, foreign currency, and **Special Drawing Rights** (SDR).

Special Drawing Rights

As noted earlier, Special Drawing Rights were initially introduced as a supplementary international reserve asset to the Bretton Woods fixed and adjusted exchange rate system. The establishment of floating exchange rate regimes changed its nature to a global reserve asset. At the same time, SDR serves as the unit of account for the several international organisations, including the IMF.

The SDR basket is revised, as a rule, every five years to ensure that the SDR mirrors the relative importance of the currencies in the international financial system. Nowadays, the value of the SDR is based on a basket of five currencies – the US dollar, the euro, the Chinese renminbi,[1154] the Japanese yen, and the British pound sterling.

1153 International Monetary Fund, *Balance of Payments Manual* (Washington, DC: International Monetary Fund 1993) 6.

1154 The Chinese renminbi (RMB) was included in the SDR basket in November 2015.

The IMF allocates SDRs to members participating in the SDR Department in proportion to their quotas. The SDRs are tradable between the members through the voluntary market.

When an IMF member state with a negative balance of payments consumes its foreign exchange reserve, it can use its SDRs and apply to the IMF for a loan. In this case, the IMF refers to another member state with a large foreign exchange reserve to allocate the necessary funds. The creditor country receives additional SDRs. The result of the actions of the borrowing system is expressed in maintaining the relative equilibrium of balances and exchange rate ratios.

The International Monetary Fund

Although the Bretton Woods monetary system has mostly given way to new arrangements, even today, international monetary law mainly exists under the shadow of this system since the institutional solutions introduced by the Bretton Woods system still represent the backbone of the current **multilateral system of payments**.

The founders considered the leading mission of the IMF to be the promotion of international monetary co-operation and exchange rate stability for the fostering of global economic growth and stability.

The members and status of the International Monetary Fund

To date, the IMF has almost 190 member states. It is an independent international organisation. At the same time, it is a Specialised Agency of the United Nations, and its relationship with the UN is regulated by a separate agreement between these two organisations. The IMF headquarters are based in Washington, DC (USA).

The purposes of the International Monetary Fund

Under the **Articles of Agreement of the International Monetary Fund**, the primary purposes of the organisation are:

- promotion of international monetary co-operation;
- facilitation of the expansion and balanced growth of international trade;
- maintenance of exchange stability;
- assistance in the establishment of a multilateral system of payments with respect to current transactions between members and in the elimination of foreign exchange restrictions which hamper the growth of world trade; and
- ensuring the availability of resources (with adequate safeguards) for members having balance of payments difficulties.[1155]

1155 Article I of the Articles of Agreement of the International Monetary Fund. This book refers to the version 'with the latest amendment adopted on December 15, 2010 (effective January 26, 2016)', available on the official website of the IMF <www.imf.org/external/pubs/ft/aa/index.htm> accessed 18 March 2021.

The quota system in the International Monetary Fund

The members of the IMF are represented through a **quota system** following their relative size in the world economy. The size of the quota of each state is calculated according to the standard formula, taking into account a number of economic factors. 'The current quota formula is a weighted average of GDP[1156] (weight of 50 percent), openness (30 percent), economic variability (15 percent), and international reserves (5 percent).' Quotas are denominated in Special Drawing Rights (SDRs), the international unit of account.[1157]

Over time, quotas are revised by the IMF's Board of Governors to adequately reflect the relative position of states in the world economy (normally, every five years).

The quota generally determines various aspects of a member's relations with the IMF. When joining the IMF, each state subscribes to a certain share of its capital. The member must pay its subscription in full: up to 25% in SDRs or foreign currencies acceptable to the IMF and the rest in the member's own currency.

The quotas also define the states' **voting power** in the internal bodies of the IMF. The votes of each member amount to the sum of its basic votes, which are equally distributed among all members, and quota-based votes.[1158] Finally, quotas affect the amount of financing a member can obtain from the IMF and the distribution of SDRs.

The internal structure of the International Monetary Fund

* Board of Governors – consists of all the member states and is the highest decision-making body of the Fund. Each state has the right to send two persons to the Board – one Governor and one Alternate (usually the Minister of Finance or the Head of the Central Bank), appointed in such a manner as that state may determine.

1156 Gross domestic product (GDP) represents the measure of the size of an economy. GDP can be calculated for a state, a region of a country, or several countries aggregated. The GDP is equal to the sum of all value added created in an economy. The 'value added' means the value of the goods and services that have been produced minus the value of the goods and services needed to produce them, the so-called intermediate consumption.

1157 'The largest member of the IMF is the United States, with a current quota (as of March 2017) of SDR82.99 billion (about US$118 billion), and the smallest member is Tuvalu, with a quota of SDR2.5 million (about US$3.5 million).' 'International Monetary Fund, Factsheet' <www.imf.org/~/media/Files/Factsheets/English/quotas.ashx> accessed 18 March 2021.

1158 'The quota largely determines a member's voting power in IMF decisions. Each IMF member's votes are comprised of basic votes plus one additional vote for each SDR100,000 of quota. The 2008 reforms fixed the number of basic votes at 5.502 percent of total votes. The current share of basic votes in total votes represents close to a tripling of their share prior to the implementation of the 2008 reforms.' ibid. The largest quota belongs to the United States (17.44%), which gives it a voting share of 16.51% of the total in the IMF internal system. See the official website of the IMF <www.imf.org/external/np/sec/memdir/members.aspx> accessed 18 March 2021.

The Board of Governors selects one of the Governors as a Chairman. Board meetings are held ordinarily once a year. At the same time, the meetings may be called whenever requested by 15 members or by members having one-quarter of the total voting power. A quorum for any meeting of the Board of Governors is a majority of the Governors having not less than two-thirds of the total voting power. The Board makes its decisions either by organising a meeting or remotely (via courier services, electronic mail, facsimile, or the internal secure online voting system) by a majority of the total voting power unless otherwise specified in the Articles of Agreement. For example, 'An eighty-five percent majority of the total voting power shall be required for any change in quotas.'[1159] Actually, the Board of Governors has delegated most of its powers to the Executive Board of the Fund; nevertheless, it reserves the right to approve quota increases, the Special Drawing Rights allocations, the admittance of new members, compulsory withdrawal of members, amendments to the Articles of Agreement of the International Monetary Fund, determination of the remuneration of the Executive Directors and their Alternates, and the salary and terms of the contract of service of the IMF's Managing Director.

- Ministerial Committees – composed of two ministerial committees, the International Monetary and Financial Committee and the Development Committee. The Committees serve as advisors to the Board of Governors.

  - The International Monetary and Financial Committee consists of 24 members drawn from the governors. It meets twice a year to discuss the general management of the international monetary system or any other matters of aggregate concern with respect to the global economy. The Committee issues a communiqué by consensus and without a formal vote.
  - The Development Committee is a joint committee advising the IMF (Board of Governors) and the World Bank regarding issues of economic development in developing countries. There are 25 members on the committee (commonly, ministers of finance or development), and it is primarily a forum for building intergovernmental consensus on crucial development-related issues.

- Executive Board – which is responsible for conducting the daily business of the Fund, as well as exercising the functions delegated by the Board of Governors. 'It is composed of 24 Directors, who are elected by member countries or by groups of countries, and the Managing Director, who serves as its Chairman.'[1160] Each Executive Director shall appoint an Alternate with full power to act on his or her behalf when he or she is not present. The Executive Board meets several times each week. It usually makes decisions via consensus, but sometimes formal votes are taken based on the sophisticated voting system described earlier.[1161]

1159 Section 2 (c) of Article III of the Articles of Agreement of the International Monetary Fund.
1160 See the official website of the IMF, 'IMF Executive Directors and Voting Power' <www.imf.org/external/np/sec/memdir/eds.aspx> accessed 18 March 2021.
1161 For instance, as of 4 May 2020, the Executive Director Domenico G. Fanizza (Alternate – Michael Massourakis) represented the votes (voting power) of Albania, Greece, Italy, Malta, Portugal, and

- Managing Director – holds the position of the chairman of the Executive Board and head of the staff. He or she is appointed by the Executive Board for a renewable term of five years and has a First Deputy Managing Director and three Deputy Managing Directors. The Executive Board may select a Managing Director by a majority of votes cast; however, until now, the Board has made such appointments by consensus. The Managing Director shall not be a Governor or an Executive Director. Although the Managing Director serves as the chairman of the Executive Board, he or she has no vote except a deciding vote in case of a tie. Besides, as the head of the staff, he or she is responsible for the organisation, appointment, and dismissal of the staff of the IMF.

The International Bank for Reconstruction and Development

The second international institution established at Bretton Woods was the International Bank for Reconstruction and Development (IBRD), also commonly called World Bank. The foundational agreement of the Bank is the **Articles of Agreement of the International Bank for Reconstruction and Development**, which became effective in 1945 and has been amended several times.

As is clearly visible from the title of this international organisation, two principal targets of the Bank were determined to be reconstruction and development. Therefore, from the very beginning, the Bank was intended as the largest development-oriented institution in the world, which would assist war-affected and developing countries by providing loans, necessary knowledge, and advice.

The World Bank Group

To address predefined objectives, over time, the International Bank for Reconstruction and Development has expanded to a closely associated group of five development organisations called the **World Bank Group**, including the World Bank; the International Finance Corporation, which accommodates the financial resources to private companies and financial institutions in less developed countries; the International Development Association, which targets the poorest countries by providing them with concessional financing; the International Centre for Settlement of Investment Disputes, which is an international arbitration institution established for international investment dispute resolution and conciliation; and the Multilateral Investment Guarantee Agency, which provides political risk insurance and credit enhancement guarantees.

Like the IMF, the International Bank for Reconstruction and Development, the International Development Association, and the International Finance Corporation are UN Specialised Agencies.

San Marino, which gave him a voting share of 4.13% of the total on the IMF Executive Board. 'IMF Executive Directors and Voting Power' ibid.

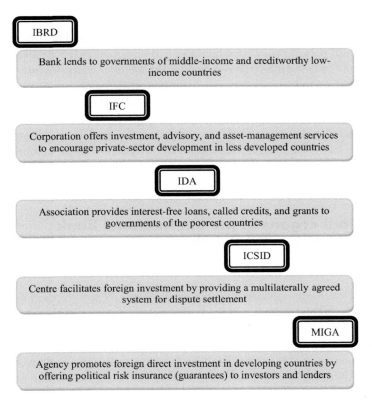

FIGURE 15.1 The five institutions of the World Bank Group

The members and status of the International Bank for Reconstruction and Development

At the heart of the World Bank Group's system is the International Bank for Reconstruction and Development, which currently has nearly 190 member states or shareholders. A prerequisite for membership in the IBRD is membership in the IMF.[1162] At the same time, like the International Monetary Fund, the International Bank for Reconstruction and Development is an independent international organisation with the status of a Specialised Agency of the United Nations. Its headquarters are in Washington, DC (USA).

The purposes of the International Bank for Reconstruction and Development

Under the Articles of Agreement of the International Bank for Reconstruction and Development, its primary objectives are:

1162 Article II of the Articles of Agreement of the International Bank for Reconstruction and Development. This book applies the version 'as amended effective June 27, 2012', available at <www.world-bank.org/en/about/articles-of-agreement/ibrd-articles-of-agreement> accessed 18 March 2021.

- Facilitation of the investment of capital for productive purposes, including the restoration of economies destroyed or disrupted by war and the encouragement of the development of productive facilities and resources in less developed countries.
- Promotion of private foreign investment in the member countries through guarantees or participation in loans and other investments made by private investors.
- Promotion of the long-range balanced growth of international trade and the maintenance of equilibrium in balances of payments, among other things, by assisting in raising productivity, the standard of living, and conditions of labour in member countries.
- Arrangement of 'the loans made or guaranteed by it in relation to international loans through other channels so that the more useful and urgent projects, large and small alike, will be dealt with first.'[1163]

The principal organs of the International Bank for Reconstruction and Development

The organisational structure of the IBRD is similar to that of the IMF:

- Board of Governors – consists of all the member states. The Governors serve as the ultimate policymakers of the World Bank. The governors of the IBRD are the ministers of finance or the ministers of development of the member countries. Typically, they meet once a year at the Annual Meetings of the Boards of Governors of the World Bank Group and the International Monetary Fund. Each state appoints two persons – one Governor and one Alternate. However, no Alternate may vote except in the absence of his or her principal. The Articles of Agreement of the International Bank for Reconstruction and Development determine the exclusive competences of the Board: the admission of new members and the conditions of their admission; the increase or decrease of the capital stock and the determination of the distribution of the net income of the Bank; permanent suspension of the bank operations and the distribution of its assets; suspension of membership; the final decision on the interpretation of the founding Articles of Agreement; and co-operation with other international organisations.

  A quorum for any meeting of the Board of Governors is a majority of the Governors, who have to cumulatively exercise not less than two-thirds of the total voting power. The voting system in the Board is identical to the IMF voting system, based on the voting power of member countries, which is equal to the sum of their basic votes and share votes.[1164] Governors and Alternates exercise their functions without compensation from the Bank, but the Bank pays them reasonable expenses incurred in attending meetings. At the same time, the Board of Governors determines the remuneration to be paid to the Executive Directors and the salary and terms of the contract of service of the President of the Bank.

1163 Article I of the Articles of Agreement of the International Bank for Reconstruction and Development.
1164 '(i) The basic votes of each member shall be the number of votes that results from the equal distribution among all members of 5.55 percent of the aggregate sum of the voting power of all the members, provided that there shall be no fractional basic votes. (ii) The share votes of each member shall be the number of votes that results from the allocation of one vote for each share of stock held.' Section 3 of Article V of the Articles of Agreement of the International Bank for Reconstruction and Development.

- Board of Directors – tasked with the day-to-day business of the Bank and the specific duties delegated by the Board of Governors. Currently, there are 25 Executive Directors on the board. Unlike the IMF, where the reform of the appointment/election system is implemented and all members of the Executive Board now are elected, the Bank, as of the time this book was written, retains the older system since the five largest shareholders appoint their respective Executive Directors, while elected Executive Directors represent other member countries. Each director is entitled to cast the number of votes allotted to the member state(s) appointing or electing him or her.

  The term 'World Bank Group Boards of Directors', on the other hand, refers to four separate Boards of Directors – namely the Boards of all institutions associated with the World Bank Group except the International Centre for Settlement of Investment Disputes. Each Board is responsible for the general operations of their respective organisation; the Corporate Secretariat assists them. At the same time, the IBRD Executive Directors serve *ex officio* as Directors for International Finance Corporation and International Development Association.[1165]

- President and staff – the Executive Directors select a President for a five-year term, who shall not be a Governor or an Executive Director or an Alternate for either. The President is the chairman of the Board of Directors but has no vote except a deciding vote in case of a tie. The President is simultaneously the chief of the staff of the Bank and conducts the ordinary business of the Bank and is responsible for the organisation, appointment, and dismissal of the officers and staff.

Concluding remarks

The IMF – the World Bank Group system – is, in fact, becoming the principal global financial and economic centre, which addresses not only issues related to the member states and groups of states but also issues which are of interest to the world community as a whole. Hence, this system is actually one of the cornerstones of the international economic security system in the community of states.

Informal groups of countries

Informal groups of countries occupy a special place in the field of international economic law. Informality in this context means that they represent mostly the political forums with minimal legal regulation and without a sophisticated structure. These groups, among other things, coordinate the common economic interests of the member states and are in close co-operation with the IMF and the World Bank. Among such groups, in the context of international finance law, are the **Group of 7**, the **Group of 20**, and the **Group of 24**.

1165 In the World Bank Group Boards of Directors, the voting power of each member country is based on the number of shares it holds. However, the shares are distributed differently in each organisation, resulting in the allocation of the different voting powers.

The Group of 7

Before 1975, there was a 'G5' of the five countries who had largest voting powers at the Fund and the Bank (France, Japan, the United Kingdom, the United States, and West Germany). In 1976, the 'Group of 7' (G7) was formed as an informal deliberation structure consisting of Canada, France, Italy, Japan, the United Kingdom, the United States, and West Germany.[1166]

So, under the umbrella of the G7, the major industrial countries started to hold annual economic summits (meetings at the level of head of state or government). IMF and IBRD bodies prepared special reports for G7 meetings. The decisions of the Group as informal advice are usually transferred for revision and execution to the internal organs of the Fund and the Bank. For example, in 1987–1988, the decisions of the Group of 7 on writing off part of the debts of the least developed countries were presented and approved.

The Group of 20

The 'Group of 20' (G20)[1167] is a group of major advanced and emerging market economies which was instituted in 1999 to strengthen policy coordination between its members and promote financial stability.

Initially, the G20 meetings of Finance Ministers and Central Bank Governors were held to discuss international financial and monetary policies and related economic issues.

The first G20 Leaders' Summit at the level of heads of state and government was held in 2008 to address the global financial crisis.

The IMF and IBRD are substantially engaged in the G20 deliberations. Moreover, the Managing Director of the IMF and the President of the World Bank, as a rule, participate in the G20 meetings on an *ex officio* basis. At the same time, the decisions of the countries at the G20 level are taken into consideration in the internal structure of the Fund and the Bank.

The Group of 24

The aforementioned forums brought together strong players in the global economy. However, at the same time, developing countries also needed to encourage their specific interests. To address this issue, in 1971, the 'Group of 77' (G77)[1168] established

---

1166 The Russian Federation joined the political forum from 1997, which the following year was renamed the G8. However, in 2014, Russia was suspended from the group following violations of the fundamental rules of international law in relation to Ukraine ('Russia's annexation of Crimea'). After that, the political forum's name reverted to G7.

1167 The G20 Members are Argentina, Australia, Brazil, Canada, China, France, Germany, India, Indonesia, Italy, Japan, the Republic of Korea, Mexico, Russia, Saudi Arabia, South Africa, Turkey, the United Kingdom, the United States, and the European Union.

1168 The Group of 77 (G77) was instituted in 1964 with the purpose of ensuring adequate representation of the interests of developing countries at the international level. Over time, it developed its permanent institutional structure, which led to the creation of 'Chapters of the Group of 77' with Liaison offices in Geneva (UNCTAD), Nairobi (UNEP), Paris (UNESCO), Rome (FAO/IFAD), Vienna (UNIDO), and the Group of 24 (G24) in Washington, DC (IMF and World Bank). The Group currently has 134 members. The G77 has a more multifaceted focus and is generally aimed at

the Intergovernmental Group of Twenty-Four on International Monetary Affairs and Development – commonly referred to as the 'Group of 24' or G24.

The member countries of the G24 primarily aimed to coordinate the joint efforts of the developing countries on international monetary and development issues and articulate and promote the interests of member countries within the Bretton Woods institutions, including in the Development Committee meetings of the IMF and World Bank.

The G24 is an independent co-operative format of member countries, though basically, the IMF provides secretariat services for the Group.

INTERNATIONAL TRADE LAW

reduction of tariffs and other barriers to international trade
General Agreement on Tariffs and Trade
GATT 1947
World Trade Organisation
GATT 1994
Uruguay Round agreements
Marrakesh Agreement Establishing the WTO
General Agreement on Trade in Services
Trade-Related Aspects of Intellectual Property Rights
Dispute Settlement Understanding
Trade Policy Review Mechanism
Plurilateral Trade Agreements
separate customs territory
principle of non-discrimination
most-favoured-nation treatment principle
national treatment principle
market access principle
schedule of concessions
principle of reciprocity
transparency obligation
exceptions
principle of the preferential treatment of developing countries
International Civil Aviation Organisation
International Maritime Organisation
World Tourism Organisation
United Nations Conference on Trade and Development
World Intellectual Property Rights Organisation
negative consensus
international commodity agreements
Organisation of Petroleum Exporting Countries

the entire United Nations system. It is usually regarded as the largest intergovernmental institution of developing countries in the United Nations.

The long road to the adoption of a multilateral system of international trade

International trade has long been one of the areas of the foreign affairs of states that influenced the development of co-operation in the interstate system and served as the engine to propel the economies of different countries and the global economy as well.

Initially, it developed mainly in a bilateral format; however, gradually, in the twentieth century, it took the form of multilateral agreements. The decisions made at Bretton Woods laid the foundation for the stabilisation of the international monetary and financial system, which, in turn, served as a pivot for the introduction of new regulations in international trade, targeting the development of the free movement of goods and capital across borders as a substantial basis for the development of the economies of different countries and the global economy as a whole. To this end, the initial objectives were the **reduction of tariffs and other barriers to international trade**, the maintenance of non-discriminatory international trade, and the minimisation of the trade conflicts between the states.

The establishment of the GATT 1947

In 1946, at the first session of the United Nations Economic and Social Council, the Resolution[1169] was adopted on the Calling of an International Conference on Trade and Employment, and based on the Resolution, the Preparatory Committee was created. The Preparatory Committee developed the Charter of the International Trade Organisation and the draft **General Agreement on Tariffs and Trade** (GATT). The GATT was signed in 1947 (therefore, it is known as the **GATT 1947**) and took effect on 1 January 1948 on a provisional basis. In 1948, the United Nations Conference on Trade and Employment was held in Havana, which adopted the Charter of the International Trade Organisation.

It was assumed that the GATT 1947 would operate under the umbrella of the International Trade Organisation. However, the Charter of the International Trade Organisation did not enter into force. So the GATT became the only multilateral legal instrument and institutional mechanism governing international trade from 1948 until the **World Trade Organisation** (WTO) was established in 1995.

The main focus of the GATT 1947

The primary focus of the GATT 1947 was the conduct of multilateral trade negotiations ('rounds') to reduce the level of customs taxation of goods and the elimination of non-tariff restrictions. Since its establishment, some general tariff negotiations rounds have taken place. The final Uruguay Round (1986–1994) led to the establishment of the World Trade Organisation. The GATT has endured a few amendments over the course of its operation.

1169 Resolution E/13(I) of 18 February 1946. All UN ECOSOC resolutions are available at the official website of the UN <https://research.un.org/en/docs/ecosoc/resolutions> accessed 18 March 2021.

The GATT 1947 as an organisational structure

The establishment of the GATT 1947 as a unique international organisational structure was gradual. Unlike other international organisations, the GATT system did not have such features as a single-constituent international treaty that would define its competence, scope, organisational structure, privileges, immunity, and so forth. For this reason, the GATT has often been qualified as a *de facto* international trade organisation.

However, at the same time, the GATT had an organisational structure. The supreme body of the GATT was the Session of the Contracting Parties, which was held once a year or as necessary and had a broad competence. Each participating state had one vote. Decisions were made by majority vote or by a qualified majority, although, in practice, most decisions were taken by consensus (i.e. in the absence of objection). Over time, a permanent operational governing body has been created – the Council of Representatives. The Secretariat provided technical support for the work of the GATT. The Secretariat was headed by the Director General, who was responsible for supervising the administrative functions. In addition, standing committees, subcommittees, and groups were created as subsidiary bodies.

From the GATT 1947 to the GATT 1994

The GATT 1947 was substituted in 1995. Nevertheless, the provisions of the GATT 1947 were incorporated into the **GATT 1994**. Generally, the GATT 1994 assembles the legal provisions from different sources. It consists of:

- the provisions of the GATT 1947;
- the legal instruments concluded under the GATT 1947;
- the Understandings reached during the Uruguay Round; and
- the Marrakesh Protocol of Tariff Concessions.

The provisions of the GATT 1947, currently incorporated into the GATT 1994, consist of the Articles, which are split up into four Parts.[1170]

Among the legal instruments concluded under the GATT 1947 are understood the protocols and certifications related to tariff concessions, protocols of accession, decisions on waivers granted under the GATT 1947, and other decisions of the contracting parties to the GATT 1947.

1170 Part I of the GATT contains Article I, which defines the most-favoured-nation treatment obligation, and Article II, which determines the obligations applicable to the Schedules of Concessions of each WTO Member. Part II enshrines the national treatment obligation; the non-tariff measures, such as unfair trade practices (dumping and export subsidies); quantitative restrictions; restrictions for balance-of-payments reasons; state-trading enterprises; government assistance to economic development; and emergency safeguard measures. Part III mainly concerns customs unions and free trade areas and the responsibility of the members for the acts of their regional and local governments. Part IV targets increasing trade opportunities for developing country members in various ways.

Under Understandings are considered the Understanding on the Balance-of-Payments Provisions of the General Agreement on Tariffs and Trade 1994; the Understanding in Respect of Waivers of Obligations under the GATT 1994; and the Understandings on the interpretation of the particular Articles of the GATT 1994, which aimed to either introduce further transparency obligation or refine terms or paragraphs of the relevant GATT articles.

Finally, the Marrakesh Protocol to the GATT 1994 is the legal instrument incorporating the Schedules of Concessions and Commitments on Goods into the GATT 1994, which were negotiated during the Uruguay Round.

Accordingly, the GATT 1947 is at the very heart of the GATT 1994 and the existing WTO system.[1171] Moreover, the principles of the GATT 1947 discussed here were included in the GATT 1994. Besides, although these principles initially were intended to apply to trade in goods, some of them have been integrated into other WTO agreements dealing with such areas as trade in services and trade in intellectual property products.

The foundation of the WTO

The World Trade Organisation was officially established in 1995 under the package of the **Uruguay Round agreements**, which represents a set of international treaties finalising the Uruguay Round signed in Marrakesh in 1994. First, it was composed of the **Marrakesh Agreement Establishing the WTO** (also referred to as the WTO Agreement). In addition, agreements on goods, services, and intellectual property; dispute settlement; trade policy review mechanism; and the plurilateral agreements were annexed. Namely, Annex 1 consisted of the GATT 1994 and other sectoral multilateral agreements on trade in goods, the **General Agreement on Trade in Services** (GATS), and the **Trade-Related Aspects of Intellectual Property Rights** (TRIPS); Annex 2 was the **Dispute Settlement Understanding**; Annex 3 was the **Trade Policy Review Mechanism**; and Annex 4 was the **Plurilateral Trade Agreements** (such as the Agreement on Trade in Civil Aircraft, the Agreement on Government Procurement). The agreements and associated legal instruments included in Annexes 1, 2, and 3 were referred to as 'Multilateral Trade Agreements' in the Marrakesh Agreement and were integral parts of this Agreement, binding on all members. The 'Plurilateral Trade Agreements' and associated legal instruments included in Annex 4 were also part of the Marrakesh Agreement but only for those members that have accepted them.

1171 'The "GATT 1994" is the basic set of trade rules, largely taken over from the GATT 1947, that in conjunction with the other agreements in Annex 1A to the WTO agreement now represents the goods-related obligations of WTO members. The GATT 1947 is no longer in effect. However, it is still necessary to read it. Its successor, the GATT 1994, is defined only by a brief agreement that, although entitled "General Agreement on Tariffs and Trade 1994", is little more than a series of references to other texts. Most of the provisions of the GATT 1947 are included by reference, along with many other legal instruments adopted by the GATT Contracting Parties and some new understandings and explanatory notes.' 'General Agreement on Tariffs and Trade', The WTO Agreements Series 2 <www.wto.org/english/res_e/booksp_e/agrmntseries2_gatt_e.pdf> accessed 18 March 2021.

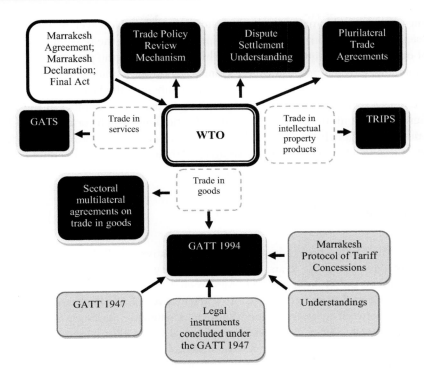

FIGURE 15.2 The legal basis of the WTO system

The creation of the WTO was a significant shift towards the comprehensive regulation of international trade under the watchful eye of the fully fledged international organisation. Currently, the WTO has over 160 members. Its headquarters is located in Geneva, Switzerland.

The principal functions of the WTO

The World Trade Organisation (WTO) ensures the implementation of two primary functions. First, it guides the development of the international rules mirrored by the Marrakesh Agreement, affecting both trade in goods and services and the protection of intellectual property. Second, it is a forum for administering the rules and settling the trade disputes.

Membership in the WTO system

Under the Marrakesh Agreement, any state or **separate customs territory** which has 'full autonomy in the conduct of its external commercial relations and of the other matters provided for in the Agreement and the Multilateral Trade Agreements may accede to the Agreement establishing the WTO.'[1172]

1172 Article XII of the Marrakesh Agreement Establishing the World Trade Organisation.

Hence, states are the main members of the organisation. However, by introducing the term 'separate customs territory', the Agreement also foresaw the possibility of the accession of other subjects of international law which would meet the preliminary (accession) conditions. Indeed, the European Union, Hong Kong (in the name of 'Hong Kong, China'), and Taiwan (referred to as 'Chinese Taipei') are members of the WTO.

A State or a separate customs territory aspiring to become a member of the WTO has to generally accept all the agreements and understandings which form the WTO. At the same time, even though the WTO allows waivers in particular cases, under exceptional circumstances, and for a limited period of time,[1173] their use is definitely limited compared to GATT 1947.

The internal structure of the WTO

* Ministerial Conference – composed of representatives of all the members and meets at least once every two years. It has the authority to make decisions on all matters under any of the Multilateral Trade Agreements.
* General Council – also composed of representatives of all the members. During the intervals between meetings of the Ministerial Conference, its functions are performed by the General Council. Additionally, the General Council carries out the tasks assigned to it by the Marrakesh Agreement. Simultaneously, it serves as the Dispute Settlement Body (appeals are also considered by the permanent seven-member Appellate Body established by the Dispute Settlement Body) and the Trade Policy Review Body. Both of them have separate chairmen and established rules of procedure for the fulfilment of those responsibilities. At the same time, the General Council delegates its responsibility to three other significant bodies accordingly – the Council for Trade in Goods, the Council for Trade in Services, and the Council for Trade-Related Aspects of Intellectual Property Rights – which oversee the functioning of the relevant trade agreements. At the same time, other bodies are also established by the Ministerial Conference and are responsible to the General Council, such as the Trade and Environment Committee, which is dedicated to finding a balance between trade and environment policies; the Committee on Trade and Development, which is concerned with issues relating to developing countries, especially to the 'least-developed' among them (through its Sub-Committee on Least-Developed countries); and the Committee on Balance of Payments, which is responsible for consultations between WTO members and countries which take trade-restrictive measures to cope with balance-of-payments difficulties. Finally, matters relating to the WTO's financing and budget are dealt with by a Committee on Budget.
* Secretariat and Director-General – responsible for the administrative functions. The Secretariat is headed by a Director-General appointed by the Ministerial Conference.

1173 '3. In exceptional circumstances, the Ministerial Conference may decide to waive an obligation imposed on a Member by this Agreement or any of the Multilateral Trade Agreements, provided that any such decision shall be taken by three fourths of the Members unless otherwise provided for in this paragraph.' Article IX of the Marrakesh Agreement Establishing the World Trade Organisation.

The Director-General, in turn, appoints the members of the staff of the Secretariat and determines their duties and conditions of service following the regulations adopted by the Ministerial Conference. The Marrakesh Agreement emphasises that the 'responsibilities of the Director-General and of the staff of the Secretariat shall be exclusively international in character. In the discharge of their duties, the Director-General and the staff of the Secretariat shall not seek or accept instructions from any government or any other authority external to the WTO.'[1174]

As in the case of the GATT 1947, the decision making in the General Council and the Ministerial Conference is based on consensus as much as possible. Only when a decision cannot be made by consensus is the matter decided by a majority of the votes cast or, in specified cases (such as decisions relating to the interpretation of the WTO Agreement and the Multilateral Trade Agreements), by a three-quarters majority. At the meetings of the Ministerial Conference and the General Council, each member has one vote. However, when the European Union exercises the right to vote, it has a number of votes equal to the number of its member states which are the members of the WTO (provided that the number of votes of the EU and their member states shall in no case exceed the number of the member states of the EU).

The multilateral agreements on trade in goods

The multilateral agreements on trade in goods comprise the GATT 1994 and other sectoral agreements, which deal with such matters as (1) agriculture, (2) sanitary and phytosanitary measures, (3) technical barriers to trade, (4) trade-related investment measures, (5) anti-dumping, (6) customs valuation, (7) pre-shipment inspection, (8) rules of origin, (9) import licensing, (10) subsidies and countervailing measures, (11) safeguards, and (12) trade facilitation.[1175] On the whole, the multilateral agreements on trade in goods aim to regulate the following four fields: market access, rules governing non-tariff measures, customs and trade administration, and trade protection measures.

The principles of the GATT 1994

The GATT 1994 is founded on the following principles:

- The **principle of non-discrimination** concerning the GATT members means that 'any advantage, favour, privilege or immunity granted by any contracting party to any product originating in or destined for any other country shall be accorded immediately and unconditionally to the like product originating in or destined for the territories of all other contracting parties.'[1176] The principle of non-discrimination does not

---

1174 Paragraph 4 of Article VI of the Marrakesh Agreement Establishing the World Trade Organisation.

1175 <www.wto.org/english/docs_e/legal_e/legal_e.htm> accessed 18 March 2021.

1176 Article I of the General Agreement on Tariffs and Trade (GATT 1947), as published on the official website of the World Trade Organisation <www.wto.org/english/docs_e/legal_e/gatt47_01_e.htm#fntext-1> accessed 18 March 2021. In this book, materials from the website are used, taking into account the disclaimer and applicable legal rules.

provide the obligation to treat all products alike; it allows individual treatment with regard to specific products and 'like products.' At the same time, it is difficult to find a universal formula to define the term 'like products.' Therefore, the like products are identified on a case-by-case basis, taking into account such determinants as the product's end use in a given market, consumer habits, and so forth. In general, the principle of non-discrimination in international trade aims to develop two standards – (1) the **most-favoured-nation treatment principle** and (2) the **national treatment principle**.

- The most-favoured-nation treatment principle requires the members of the GATT 1994 and, accordingly, of the WTO not to discriminate between products originating in or destined for different members. In other words, if a member grants someone a special favour (for instance, a lower customs duty rate for one of their products), it has to do the same for all other GATT 1994/WTO members.

  Hence, to be in conformity with the most-favoured-nation treatment obligation, the member shall undertake a measure with regard to (1) all members and (2) all like products (3) immediately and unconditionally. On the whole, the most-favoured-nation treatment principle targets equality of opportunity to import from or to export to all contracting parties.

  On the other hand, '[s]ome exceptions are allowed. For example, countries can set up a free trade agreement that applies only to goods traded within the group – discriminating against goods from outside. Or they can give developing countries special access to their markets. Or a country can raise barriers against products that are considered to be traded unfairly from specific countries.'[1177]

- The national treatment principle, on the other hand, requires GATT/WTO members to treat imported and locally produced goods equally once the imported products have entered the domestic market (the obligation to treat the products of another member no less favourably than their own national products). Notably, the principle aims to ensure that taxes or other internal regulations are not utilised to discriminate against foreign products and, accordingly, to protect local products. At the same time, 'charging customs duty on an import is not a violation of national treatment even if locally produced products are not charged an equivalent tax.'[1178]

- The **market access principle** is provided for the establishment of discipline regarding the barriers to market access. Generally, such barriers include tariffs or customs duties,[1179] which are imposed on goods when imported; quantitative restrictions (including quotas); other duties and financial charges; and other non-tariff measures, such as customs procedures, technical regulations, sanitary and phytosanitary measures, and anti-dumping and countervailing duties and fees. The GATT (for decades) has taken a differentiated approach to these barriers. For example, while quantitative restrictions (including import or export quotas, restrictive use of import or export licences, and so

---

1177 'Principles of the Trading System' <www.wto.org/english/thewto_e/whatis_e/tif_e/fact2_e.htm> accessed 18 March 2021.

1178 ibid.

1179 Customs duties are either specific (amount based on weight, volume, and so one) or *ad valorem* (amount based on value).

forth) are generally prohibited, tariffs and customs duties are allowed. However, concerning the later barrier, it requires members to negotiate the reduction of tariffs. Correspondingly, the eight successive 'rounds' of multilateral trade negotiations (between 1947 and 1994) have led to a decrease in tariffs.

- The **schedule of concessions** on goods binds the members to treat the products of other members no less favourably than it is provided in their respective schedules. The tariff concessions (also referred to as the bound rate) are included in the schedule of concessions for each member and are annexed to the GATT 1994. At the same time, the tariff negotiations were conducted on a bilateral basis; however, if a member agrees to any reduction in customs duties in its separate consultations with another member, it has to also benefit all other members as a result of the fulfilment of the non-discrimination principle.

- The **principle of reciprocity** is a basis for any trade negotiations. This principle ensures balanced outcomes to the negotiations, which notably means that each member is obliged to make equivalent tariff concessions.

- The **transparency obligation** is one of the cornerstones of the GATT 1994 system. The members are required to publish all trade and trade-related measures to ensure certainty, predictability, and accountability of the established measures in such a manner as to enable governments and traders to become acquainted with them. Furthermore, measures 'effecting an advance in a rate of duty or other charge on imports under an established and uniform practice, or imposing a new or more burdensome requirement, restriction or prohibition on imports, or on the transfer of payments therefor'[1180] may not be enforced before the official publication.

- **Exceptions** allow the members to derogate from the GATT 1994 disciplines to safeguard societal values in some particular conditions. Such exceptions, among other things, can be imposed:

  - based on the need for an emergency action regarding the import of specific products;
  - to safeguard public morale or to protect humans, animals, or plant life or health;
  - to protect national treasures of artistic, historic, or archaeological value;
  - for the necessity of the conservation of exhaustible natural resources;
  - to preserve the members' balance of payments; and
  - to protect national security.

Additionally, the members may vote to waive certain obligations of a member. Moreover, the GATT 1994 allows exceptions for the free-trade areas and customs unions, which results in permitting preferential treatment between members of such free-trade areas and customs unions.

Nonetheless, these exceptions have a limited scope of application. They cannot be used to derogate from the principles mentioned earlier and must satisfy the so-called 'necessity' test and 'requirement that such measures are not applied in a manner which would constitute a means of arbitrary or unjustifiable discrimination between countries where the same conditions prevail, or a disguised restriction on international trade.'[1181]

1180 Article X of the General Agreement on Tariffs and Trade (GATT 1947).
1181 Article XX of the General Agreement on Tariffs and Trade (GATT 1947).

- The **principle of the preferential treatment of developing countries** was developed in the 1950s. Finally, in 1965, Part IV on Trade and Development was added to the GATT 1947. The next step was the so-called 'enabling clause', intended to bene-fit developing countries, which limited the application of the most-favoured-nation treatment principle, as well as the principle of reciprocity, concerning developing countries. Currently, the GATT 1994 permits developing countries[1182] to take bal-ance-of-payments measures, to provide governmental assistance to promote an infant industry, to protect themselves from full reciprocity in trade negotiations among developed and developing country members, and to enter into regional or global arrangements among themselves for their mutual benefit.

The General Agreement on Trade in Services

The issue of international legal regulation of the services sector was included in the sub-ject of negotiations of the Uruguay Round. Initially, it was assumed that trade in services would be part of the GATT regime. However, finally, the entire area of services became the subject of a new, separate multilateral agreement – the General Agreement on Trade in Services (GATS).

In the interstate system, there are a large number of governmental and non-governmen-tal organisations that perform particular functions in the services sectors. Therefore, with respect to the international trade in services, the legal framework is rather complicated. For example, concerning their fields of operation, there are such Specialised Agencies of the United Nations engaged as the **International Civil Aviation Organisation** (ICAO) con-cerning civil aviation services, the **International Maritime Organisation** (IMO) regarding sea transportation services, the **World Tourism Organisation** (UNWTO) concerning the standards of the services in the tourism field, and the **United Nations Conference on Trade and Development** (UNCTAD), which is a permanent intergovernmental body established by the UN General Assembly and represents a part of the UN Secretariat aimed at facili-tating trade, investment, and development opportunities for developing countries.

The GATS by itself consists of a framework agreement, annexes relating to certain types of services, schedules of specific commitments, and the list of exemptions submitted by members.

According to the GATS, trade in services is defined as the supply of a service

> (a) from the territory of one Member into the territory of any other Member; (b) in the territory of one Member to the service consumer of any other Member; (c) by a service supplier of one Member, through commercial presence in the territory of any other Member; (d) by a service supplier of one Member, through presence of natural persons of a Member in the territory of any other Member.[1183]

1182 To date, the WTO system divides its membership into four groups: The developed country members, the developing country members (which are self-elected as such), the least developed country mem-bers (which are specified by the UN system), and the transitional economies (Central and Eastern European countries and the states which were established after the collapse of the Soviet Union).

1183 Article I of the General Agreement on Trade in Services.

Here, the term 'services' means any service in any sector except services supplied in the exercise of governmental authority.

In fact, the General Agreement on Trade in Services formalises the existence of a differentiated legal regime in the services sector. On the one hand, within the framework of the GATS regime, there are generally binding norms that apply to all types of services; however, on the other hand, the specific obligations of the individual members of the GATS for certain types of services agreed upon on a bilateral or group basis are allowed.

Generally, the GATS principles are very similar to the GATT 1994. For example, the GATS introduces such principles on trade in services as transparency on measures taken by a country that could affect trade in services; the national treatment principle, in accordance with which foreign service providers and the services themselves should use the same regime as national service providers and services; and the most-favoured-nation treatment principle, which stipulates that GATS members provide each other with the most-favoured-nation treatment in the services sector. At the same time, the GATS allows for specific treatment with regard to the particular types of services – for example, regarding the most-favoured-nation treatment principle, such as maritime transport services, telecommunications, and so forth. Furthermore, members can conclude a separate free trade agreement or enter into a customs union and liberalise trade in services between themselves without having to extend the agreement to the other GATS members, provided that such bilateral or regional arrangements have substantial sectoral coverage and should aim to reduce or avoid discrimination.

The Agreement on Trade-Related Aspects of Intellectual Property Rights

Under the Agreement on Trade-Related Aspects of Intellectual Property Rights (TRIPS), the members have recognised the applicability of the basic principles of GATT 1994 to trade-related aspects of intellectual property. Notably, it introduces the national treatment principle, the most-favoured-nation treatment principle, and the list can be continued further.

At the same time, the Agreement refers to the general international treaties that govern intellectual property rights, such as the Paris Convention for the Protection of Industrial Property of 1883; the Berne Convention for the Protection of Literary and Artistic Works of 1886; the Rome Convention for the Protection of Performers, Producers of Phonograms and Broadcasting Organisations of 1961; and the Washington Treaty on Intellectual Property in Respect of Integrated Circuits. Among other legal instruments, these international treaties are also administered by the **World Intellectual Property Rights Organisation** (WIPO), which is the Specialised Agency of the United Nations designed to promote intellectual property rights worldwide.

The categories of intellectual property rights covered by the Agreement on Trade-Related Aspects of Intellectual Property Rights include copyright and related rights, trademarks, geographical indications, industrial designs, patents, layout designs (topographies) of integrated circuits, and the protection of undisclosed information. The Agreement also deals with the enforcement of intellectual property rights by providing its members with the civil and administrative procedures and remedies, as well as the criminal procedures.

Dispute Settlement Understanding

Dispute settlement is the key pillar of the multilateral trading system introduced at the foundation of the WTO system. After adopting the comprehensive rules of the dispute settlement, over 600 disputes have been brought to the WTO and over 350 rulings have been issued.[1184] The General Council of the WTO convenes as the Dispute Settlement Body to deal with disputes between the WTO members (as 'a political institution'). The Dispute Settlement Body has the 'authority to establish panels, adopt panel and Appellate Body reports, maintain surveillance of implementation of rulings and recommendations, and authorize suspension of concessions and other obligations under the covered agreements.'[1185] Generally, the decisions of the Dispute Settlement Body are made by consensus; however, the **negative consensus** method is applied to issues of establishment of panels, adoption of reports of a panel or the Appellate Body, and compensation and the suspension of concessions. This means that the requested action is approved unless all participating members present at the Dispute Settlement Body meeting unanimously object.

The Dispute Settlement Understanding sets out in detail the stages and the timetable to be followed in resolving disputes. These stages are:

1   Consultations, good offices, conciliation, or mediation. The term of the 60 days is prescribed for this stage. The primary target of the WTO dispute settlement system is settling disputes first through consultations, good offices, conciliation, or mediation, and even when the case has progressed to other stages, the mechanisms of this stage are still always acceptable.
2   Set up of the panel and the appointment of the panellists, which usually continues for up to 45 days. If the first stage fails, the complaining member of the WTO can ask for a panel to be appointed. In the majority of cases, the panels are established at the second meeting of the Dispute Settlement Body since the parties other than the complaining party which requested the establishment of a panel are entitled to block the panel establishment but only once. At the same time, the panel members are 'selected with a view to ensuring the independence of the members, a sufficiently diverse background and a wide spectrum of experience.'[1186] Selection of the panellists is conducted by the WTO Secretariat. A panel consists of three individuals as agreed upon by the parties concerned. However, if the parties cannot agree on the composition of the panel within 20 days, the Director-General of the WTO appoints the panel members following the appropriate consultations.
3   Final panel report to parties, which normally lasts up to six months.
4   Final panel report to the WTO members, which usually lasts up to three weeks. Formally, the panel is assisting the Dispute Settlement Body in making rulings or recommendations. However, while the panel's report can only be rejected by negative consensus in the Dispute Settlement Body, its conclusions are difficult to refute.
5   The Dispute Settlement Body adopts its report (if there is no appeal) and issues its recommendations and rulings. This stage takes three weeks.

1184 Available on the official website of the WTO 'Dispute Settlement' <www.wto.org/english/tratop_e/dispu_e/dispu_e.htm> accessed 18 March 2021.
1185 Paragraph 1 of Article 2 of the Dispute Settlement Understanding.
1186 Paragraph 2 of Article 8 of the Dispute Settlement Understanding.

6   The appeals report, which commonly continues for 60 to 90 days. A standing Appellate Body is established to hear the appeals from panel cases. It is composed of seven persons, three of whom serve on any one case. Persons serving on the Appellate Body serve in rotation. The Dispute Settlement Body appoints the persons to serve on the Appellate Body for a four-year term; at the same time, each person may be reappointed once.
7   The Dispute Settlement Body adopts the appeals report, which needs up to 30 days.

If a case runs its full course to a first ruling without appeal, it should not normally take more than one year; if the case is appealed, the term is usually 15 months. Together with a panel report, a report of the Appellate Body becomes the official recommendations and rulings of the Dispute Settlement Body after adoption at the Dispute Settlement Body meeting.

As regards the implementation of these decisions, the Dispute Settlement Understanding comprises such tools as the resort to the original panel, the mandatory arbitration, and the countermeasures, such as compensation or suspension of concessions or other obligations against the party who fails to implement the recommendations and rulings.

For example, there is a general rule that the WTO member is given a reasonable period for the implementation of the recommendations and rulings, which may be decided by the mutual agreement of the disputing parties concerned or proposed by the member concerned and approved by the Dispute Settlement Body. Meanwhile, in the absence of such an agreement or decision, the parties may refer to binding arbitration. Such arbitration shall be carried out by agreement between the parties or by an arbitrator appointed by the Director-General. The arbitrator determines the 'reasonable period of time.' However, the reasonable period of time to implement a panel or Appellate Body recommendations should not exceed 15 months from the date of the adoption of a panel or Appellate Body report.[1187]

Trade Policy Review Mechanism

Annex 3 to the Marrakesh Agreement provides for the procedures concerning the Trade Policy Review Mechanism to conduct periodical reviews of the members' trade policies and practices by the Trade Policy Review Body. The WTO General Council convenes as the Trade Policy Review Body to accomplish trade policy reviews of the members and to study the regular reports of the Director-General on trade policy development. Hence, the Trade Policy Review Mechanism is the primary accountability, predictability, and transparency instrument of the WTO.[1188]

Plurilateral Trade Agreements

The plurilateral agreements of the WTO (such as the agreements on civil aircraft and government procurement) institute their management bodies, which are required to report to

---

1187 Paragraph 3 of Article 21 of the Dispute Settlement Understanding.
1188 The 4 biggest traders (as of October 2019, the European Union, the United States, China, and Japan) are considered once every three years. The next 16 most significant countries in terms of their share of world trade are reviewed every five years and the remaining members of the WTO approximately every seven years.

the General Council of the WTO. The basic principles of the GATT 1994 are also applied to the plurilateral agreements. For example, the Agreement on Government Procurement requires national treatment and non-discriminatory treatment in the area of government procurement (such as the purchase or lease of goods and services by governments) and calls for fair and transparent procurement procedures. It also includes complaint and dispute settlement procedures.

International commodity agreements

Currently, the predominant part of all commodity markets is placed within the legal framework of the package of the WTO agreements. At the same time, both within the WTO and outside this system, legal regimes have been created that regulate individual commodity markets.

International commodity agreements are inherently multilateral instrumentalities of intergovernmental control that target to secure stable prices and demand, assist in establishing predictable incomes for particular countries, and secure supplies for the consumer countries. All these goals are maintained through such arrangements as, for instance, export quotas or ensured access to markets. Over time, the particular states are engaged in commodity arrangements on wheat, sugar, olive oil, coffee, cocoa, dairy products, beef, natural rubber, jute, tropical wood, and so forth.

International commodity agreements contain conditions that may well be considered preferential quotas in terms of prices. However, actually, international commodity agreements are beyond the scope of the most-favoured-nation treatment principle. For example, regarding the export quota established by the commodity agreements, it is hard to apply the most-favoured-nation treatment mechanism since commodity agreements are often considered an integral part of the general preferential measures in favour of developing countries (principle of the preferential treatment of developing countries). Therefore, these agreements may be regarded as outside the scope of the most-favoured-nation treatment principle. In addition, sometimes the states refer to the GATT 1994 general exceptions – notably to the norm which provides that nothing in the GATT shall be construed to prevent the adoption or enforcement by any contracting party of measures 'undertaken in pursuance of obligations under any intergovernmental commodity agreement which conforms to criteria submitted to the Contracting Parties and not disapproved by them or which is itself so submitted and not so disapproved'.[1189]

Generally, international commodity agreements institute at least one organ, which is usually a council comprising representatives of all member countries overseeing the implementation of the agreement.

A particular case forms the so-called international commodity cartels, the members of which are only the producing countries of the concerned commodity.[1190] The most

---

1189 Article XX (h) of the General Agreement on Tariffs and Trade (GATT 1947).

1190 Typically, the definition of an international commodity agreement is limited to agreements involving both producers and consumers of the specific commodity, and international commodity cartels, by definition, do not satisfy this requirement.

well-known example of such a cartel is the **Organisation of Petroleum Exporting Countries (OPEC),**[1191] which is a permanent intergovernmental organisation of oil-exporting nations that coordinates and unifies the petroleum policies of its member countries, and thus, it has a sizable influence on the global oil supply and price formation.

INTERNATIONAL INVESTMENT LAW

capital-exporting countries
developed states
capital-importing countries
developing states
international investment national insurance schemes
bilateral investment treaties
investment dispute settlement mechanisms
international investment multilateral insurance schemes
International Centre for the Settlement of Investment Disputes
NAFTA
United States-Mexico-Canada Agreement
Energy Charter Treaty
dominant and effective nationality
Nottebohm case
Nottebohm principles
transnational corporations
direct investments
portfolio investments
Multilateral Investment Guarantee Agency
fair and equitable treatment
full protection and security
compensation in case of expropriation
appropriate compensation
prompt, adequate, and effective compensation
ICSID
UNCITRAL
UNCITRAL Arbitration Rules
UNCITRAL Model Law on International Commercial Arbitration

1191 The OPEC was founded by five countries: Islamic Republic of Iran, Iraq, Kuwait, Saudi Arabia, and Venezuela. These countries were later joined by Qatar (1961), Indonesia (1962), Libya (1962), the United Arab Emirates (1967), Algeria (1969), Nigeria (1971), Ecuador (1973), Gabon (1975), Angola (2007), Equatorial Guinea (2017), and Congo (2018). Indonesia suspended its membership in 2016. Qatar terminated its membership in 2019.

Capital-exporting and capital-importing countries

The strong international economic growth after the end of World War II soon led to an expansion of the export activities also expressed in the movement of the production and businesses of the nationals (natural and legal persons) from industrial nations to developing countries. There are many reasons for such activities, among them, significantly lower labour costs than in the industrialised countries. This economic activity was also in line with the interests of the developing countries, which, having obtained their political independence, could not satisfy their economic needs independently with their own means.

Nonetheless, private-sector companies were very reluctant to invest in these countries due to fears that the developing countries would expropriate foreign investment or otherwise hinder foreign capital and investors. For these reasons, the governments of capital-exporting countries have often begun to secure the political (non-commercial) risks of such transactions by bilateral international treaties, guarantees, or other mechanisms.

Thus, on the world economic map, there appeared two categories of countries – the **capital-exporting countries** or **developed states** and the **capital-importing countries** or **developing states**, both engaged in international investment transactions and interested in the maintenance of such activities, however, with differing interests and practical concerns.

The primary concern for the developed countries was the protection of investments of their nationals, including from the possibility of expropriation. However, the developing states were focused mainly on the promotion of their national interests by regaining sovereign control over crucial parts of their economies. To adjust these conflicting interests, the exporting and importing countries begun to develop **international investment national insurance schemes** at the national and international levels and the process of concluding **bilateral investment treaties**. On the other hand, they attempted to develop multilateral mechanisms to encourage free investment flows between the states and the security of investments. Over time, several multilateral mechanisms have been introduced to create a favourable investment climate under public international law, including **investment dispute settlement mechanisms** and **international investment multilateral insurance schemes**, although, as of now, the efforts to develop a general multilateral agreement on the promotion and protection of foreign investments at the global level have failed. However, there are still certain multilateral legal instruments which address foreign investment related issues.

- TRIMS (The WTO Agreement on Trade Related Investment Measures), GATS, and TRIPS partly cover investment matters.
- The Convention on the Settlement of Investment Disputes between States and Nationals of Other States, on the basis of which the **International Centre for the Settlement of Investment Disputes** (ICSID) was established, deals with investment disputes.
- Several regional economic arrangements contain particular investment rules. Notably:

  - Chapter Eleven (Investment) of the North American Free Trade Agreement (**NAFTA**), which came into force in 1994. The NAFTA eliminated most tariffs on trade among Mexico, Canada, and the United States. In 2018, the parties signed the new treaty – the **United States-Mexico-Canada Agreement** (USMCA), which replaced the NAFTA.[1192] However, it is basically an updated version of the original North American Free Trade Agreement and thus is often referred to as NAFTA 2.0. Chapter 14 of the USMCA provides the revised rules on the investment matter.

- Protocols on foreign investment (for instance, Protocol on Investment Cooperation and Facilitation of 2017) from states within and outside the Southern Common Market (MERCOSUR), which is a South American trade arrangement founded by Brazil, Argentina, Paraguay, and Uruguay in 1991.
- Comprehensive Investment Agreement of the Association of Southeast Asian Nations (ASEAN) of 2009.

- Multilateral sectoral treaties. For example, Part III (Investment Promotion and Protection) of the **Energy Charter Treaty** of 1994,[1193] which is a multilateral framework for energy co-operation establishing investment discipline in the sector.

Defining 'foreign investor'

The definitions of (foreign) **investor** and **investment** are among the critical elements determining the scope of application of rights and obligations under international investment law.

Foreign investors may be individuals, incorporated or unincorporated private or public enterprises, associated groups of individuals or enterprises, estates, trusts, or other organisations (including governments and government agencies) that invest in countries other than those in which the investors reside.

Thus, generally, there are two categories of investors – natural and legal persons.

Natural persons

In the cases of natural persons, international investment law, as a rule, refers to nationality, which is understood exclusively based on the national law of a state of claimed nationality. Some bilateral investment agreements also reflect alternative criteria, such as residency or domicile.

A particularly complicated situation arises by the occurrence of dual or multiple nationalities of the natural persons concerned. Customary international law links such situations with the understanding of **dominant and effective nationality**.

1192 According to the Preamble of the United States-Mexico-Canada Agreement, the parties resolved to 'REPLACE the 1994 North American Free Trade Agreement with a 21st Century, high standard new agreement to support mutually beneficial trade leading to freer, fairer markets, and to robust economic growth in the region'.

1193 'The Energy Charter Treaty was signed in December 1994 and entered into legal force in April 1998. Currently there are fifty-three Signatories and Contracting Parties to the Treaty. This includes both the European Union and Euratom.' The Energy Charter Treaty <www.energycharter.org/process/energy-charter-treaty-1994/energy-charter-treaty/> accessed 18 March 2021.

International law practice on questions of nationality has developed mainly in the context of diplomatic protection. In the ***Nottebohm* case** *(Liechtenstein v Guatemala)* the International Court of Justice articulated that even though a state may decide based on national legislation whether or not to grant nationality to a person, there must be a real connection between the state and the person – namely, that

> nationality is a legal bond having as its basis a social fact of attachment, a genuine connection of existence, interests and sentiments, together with the existence of reciprocal rights and duties. It may be said to constitute the juridical expression of the fact that the individual upon whom it is conferred, either directly by the law or as the result of an act of the authorities, is in fact more closely connected with the population of the State conferring nationality than with that of any other State.[1194]

So far, the **Nottebohm principles** are still applicable in cases of dual or multiple nationalities to address the question of which nationality is predominant in the event of a dispute.

For example, one of the most recent international treaties – the United States-Mexico-Canada Agreement – defined an investor as a party, a national, or an enterprise of a party, provided, however, that '(a) a natural person who is a dual citizen is deemed to be exclusively a national of the State of his or her dominant and effective citizenship'. At the same time, the USMCA reflects the rule that citizenship prevails over permanent residency when a concerned natural person is a citizen of a party and a permanent resident of another party.[1195]

Legal persons

The nationality of legal persons under international investment law is more complicated since legal persons often operate with a web of establishments in different countries – for example, as in the case of **transnational corporations**, which are the entities with substantial operations in many countries but controlled from their original home base.

Usually, in international practice, the test of incorporation or seat rather than control is used when determining the nationality of a juridical person, unless the test of control is provided for in the applicable international treaty.[1196]

1194 *Nottebohm (Liechtenstein v Guatemala)*, Judgment of 6 April 1955, ICJ Reports 1955, 4.

1195 Article 14.1 of the United States-Mexico-Canada Agreement. As of October 2019, available at https://ustr.gov/trade-agreements/free-trade-agreements/united-states-mexico-canada-agreement/agreement-between.

1196 The country of control is defined by taking into consideration ownership, which includes direct, indirect, and beneficial ownership. At the same time, for the determination of the country of control, preference will be given to the state of an owner exercising direct (rather than indirect) control. On the other hand, control means control in fact, including the ability to exercise substantial influence over the legal entity's management and operation and the selection of members of its board of directors or any other managing body.

To overcome the difficulties of the definition, in bilateral investment treaties, the parties as a rule specifically determine the objective criteria which make a legal person a national or investor of a party for the purposes of the agreements.[1197]

Defining 'international investment'

Numerous multilateral and bilateral investment treaties and trade agreements with investment sections include a broad definition of 'investment.' They commonly assign 'every kind of asset' followed by an illustrative but, at the same time, non-exhaustive list of included assets. At the same time, the new international investment agreements require that covered assets have the characteristics of an investment, including commitment of capital or other resources, an expectation of profit, or an assumption of risk.

For instance, according to the USMCA,

> investment means every asset that an investor owns or controls, directly or indirectly, that has the characteristics of an investment, including such characteristics as the commitment of capital or other resources, the expectation of gain or profit, or the assumption of risk. An investment may include: (a) An enterprise; (b) shares, stock and other forms of equity participation in an enterprise; (c) bonds, debentures, other debt instruments, and loans; (d) futures, options, and other derivatives; (e) turnkey, construction, management, production, concession, revenue-sharing, and other similar contracts; (f) intellectual property rights; (g) licenses, authorizations, permits, and similar rights conferred pursuant to a Party's law; and (h) other tangible or intangible, movable or immovable property, and related property rights, such as liens, mortgages, pledges, and leases.[1198]

International investment treaties also exclude some types of assets from their scope. For instance, the Pacific Agreement on Closer Economic Relations (PACER) Plus, which is a comprehensive free trade agreement (FTA) covering goods, services, and investment concluded in 2017 between Australia, New Zealand, and nine Pacific island countries, excludes

> (a) claims to payment resulting solely from the commercial sale of goods and services unless it is a loan that has the characteristics of an investment; (b) a bank letter of credit; or (c) the extension of credit in connection with a commercial transaction, such as trade financing.[1199]

1197 Notably, the bilateral investment treaties usually refer to (1) the place of constitution in accordance with the national law in force in the state; (2) the place of incorporation or where the registered office is; (3) the country of the seat or where the place of administration is; and (4) less frequently, the country of control. However, most of them use a combination of criteria to determine the nationality of legal persons.

1198 Article 14.1 of the United States-Mexico-Canada Agreement.

1199 Article 1 of Chapter 9 of the Pacific Agreement on Closer Economic Relations Plus. The Agreement is available at <https://dfat.gov.au/trade/agreements/not-yet-in-force/pacer/Pages/documents.aspx>

In addition, recent trade and investment agreements tend to demand that the investor have substantial business activities either in the territory of the host state, in the home state, or in other states. Sometimes, the requirement for substantial business activities is interlinked with the 'denial of benefits clause.' For example, the Pacific Agreement on Closer Economic Relations Plus provides for a procedure according to which a contracting party may deny the benefits of the investment chapter to the investor (1) if the investment is made by an enterprise that is owned or controlled by persons of a non-party or (2) 'where the covered investment is being made by an enterprise that is owned or controlled by persons of the denying Party' and provided that in both cases 'the enterprise has no substantive business operations in the territory of any other Party.'[1200]

Direct investments and portfolio investments

Traditionally, in international practice, foreign investments have been categorised as either **direct investments** or **portfolio investments**.

Direct investments include setting a substantial business interest in a foreign country, such as buying or establishing a manufacturing business or buying or constructing warehouses or buildings. Generally, investments in an enterprise giving the investor a significant degree of influence on the management of the enterprise are called direct investments.[1201] Usually, a direct investment enterprise is understood as an incorporated or unincorporated enterprise in which a direct investor owns a certain percentage (for instance, 10% or more) of the ordinary shares or the voting power (for an incorporated enterprise) or the equivalent (for an unincorporated enterprise). Hence, a direct investment tends to involve developing more of a long-term interest in the economy of a foreign country.

As a form of financial investment, so-called portfolio investments refer to the investment of money in a set (portfolio) of various securities with the expectation of earning a return, such as investment of money in stocks, bonds, or even shares of a company providing no significant degree of influence on the management of the enterprise (for example, so-called nonparticipating preferred shares). Such portfolio investments can be sold off promptly and, therefore, are regarded as short-term attempts to make money, rather than long-term investments in the economy of a foreign country.

Although traditionally, international investment law was primarily focused on the protection of a direct investment (including through the customary international law), over time, both investment forms reviewed here came to be considered essential concerns

---

accessed 18 March 2021. According to Article 14.1. of the USMCA, 'investment does not mean: (i) an order or judgment entered in a judicial or administrative action; (j) claims to money that arise solely from: (i) commercial contracts for the sale of goods or services by a natural person or enterprise in the territory of a Party to an enterprise in the territory of another Party, or (ii) the extension of credit in connection with a commercial contract referred to in subparagraph (j)(i)'.

1200 Article 18 of Chapter 9 of the Pacific Agreement on Closer Economic Relations Plus.

1201 'There can be no doubt that the transfer of physical property such as equipment or the physical property that is bought or constructed such as plantations or manufacturing plants constitute foreign direct investment.' Muthucumaraswamy Sornarajah, *The International Law on Foreign Investment* (3nd edn, Cambridge University Press 2010) 8.

for states. However, so far, portfolio investments generally are not protected to the same degree as foreign direct investments under international law unless specified in the definition of 'investment' in the bilateral and multilateral treaties.

Bilateral investment treaties

Bilateral investment treaties (BITs) are provided for the protection of foreign investments in the countries participating in the agreements. Starting in the 1950s, the European states began to conclude such international agreements. Gradually, other countries also followed best practices developed by the European nations; however, some of them had addressed foreign investment issues already by entering into the more general agreements called the Friendship, Commerce, and Navigation Treaties. During the past decades, the rapid increase of investment inflows into developing countries has been accompanied by a considerable proliferation of BITs concluded by developing countries, initially with developed countries and, more recently, also with other developing countries.

The states established the patterns of bilateral investment treaties either individually or in co-operation, as in the case of the model agreement elaborated by the Organisation for Economic Co-operation and Development.[1202] Such patterns or model agreements encourage the implementation of the common standards and typical provisions in bilateral investment treaties. Thus, several topics can be specified, which are usually addressed in the BITs. For example, the definition of 'investor' and 'investment', standards regarding the treatment of investments, protection against expropriation, dispute settlement provisions between the parties to the agreement or the host state and the foreign investor, and so forth.

The role of regional institutions in relation to BITs needs to be outlined as well. Notably, in this regard, a unique place is occupied by the European Union, which is the most advanced regional arrangement embracing all fields of international economic law by addressing monetary, trade, and investment matters at the regional and international levels. On the other hand, over the decades, the EU member states entered into close to half of all concluded bilateral investment treaties. However, after the entry into force in 2009 of the Treaty of Lisbon, which transferred the competence to conclude the agreements covering foreign direct investment from the member states to the Union, the EU appears as a party:

1   elaborating the standards of investment agreements;
2   engaging directly in negotiations with other states or regional organisations;
3   concluding bilateral treaties affecting foreign direct investment issues on behalf of the Union; and
4   authorising several individual EU member states to negotiate BITs.[1203]

1202 The Organisation for European Economic Cooperation was established in 1948 to run the US-financed Marshall Plan for the reconstruction of the continent ruined by World War II. In 1960, it was succeeded by the Organisation for Economic Co-operation and Development (OECD), which is an international organisation that works to build better policies.

1203 '(1) Following the entry into force of the Treaty of Lisbon, foreign direct investment is included in the list of matters falling under the common commercial policy. In accordance with Article 3(1) (e) of the Treaty on the Functioning of the European Union ('TFEU'), the European Union has

It is established that the EU member states should terminate all bilateral investment treaties (BITs) between themselves (intra-EU BITs), and, in the long run, BITs with third countries are to be substituted through the respective agreements concluded by the EU. However, the ultimate replacement of all the existing BITs of the member states by EU agreements will take time, and a large number of authorisations conferred to the member countries designate that they remain active in negotiating BITs with the non-member subjects.

As regards the EU side, there are three main types of EU trade agreements: (1) Customs Unions, which aim to eliminate customs duties in bilateral trade and establish a joint customs tariff for foreign importers; (2) Association Agreements, Stabilisation Agreements, (Deep and Comprehensive) Free Trade Agreements, and Economic Partnership Agreements, which sometimes remove, but usually at least reduce, customs tariffs in bilateral trade; and (3) Partnership and Cooperation Agreements, which establish a general framework for bilateral economic relations but do not concern customs tariffs.

One of the recent agreements relating to the investment matters is the EU-Singapore trade and investment agreements signed in 2018,[1204] which are usually referred to as a 'new generation' agreements, with an ambitious and comprehensive scope. The Investment Protection Agreement, which the EU and Singapore concluded in parallel to the EU-Singapore Free Trade Agreement, was intended to replace the existing bilateral investment treaties between Singapore and EU member states and to ensure a high level of investment protection. As a result, this treaty represents an example of the inclusion in an agreement of almost all the latest developments in the field of international investment law.

The international investment insurance schemes

The political (non-commercial) risk insurance industry includes two categories of providers and involves both export or trade credit and investment insurance:

- the public political risk insurance entities, consisting of the national and multilateral providers; and
- the private market's insurance entities.

The national political risk insurance providers include national export credit agencies and investment insurance entities. They aim at the cross-border trade and investments undertaken by their nationals.

---

exclusive competence with respect to the common commercial policy. Accordingly, only the Union may legislate and adopt legally binding acts within that area. The Member States are able to do so themselves only if so empowered by the Union, in accordance with Article 2(1) TFEU.' Regulation (EU) No 1219/2012 of the European Parliament and of the Council of 12 December 2012, available at <https://eur-lex.europa.eu/eli/reg/2012/1219/oj> accessed 18 March 2021.

1204 The Free Trade Agreement entered into force on 21 November 2019. The Investment Protection Agreement will enter into force after it has been ratified by all EU Member States; the agreements are available at <https://ec.europa.eu/trade/policy/countries-and-regions/countries/singapore/> accessed 18 March 2021.

The multilateral political risk insurance sector comprises such institutions as the African Trade Insurance Agency, the Asian Development Bank, the Inter-American Development Bank, the Arab Investment and Export Credit Guarantee Corporation, and the Islamic Corporation for the Insurance of Investment and Export Credit. The World Bank, the Asian Development Bank, and the Inter-American Development Bank also provide risk-mitigation instruments, such as partial risk guarantees. A notable role in this system belongs to the **Multilateral Investment Guarantee Agency** (MIGA), which will be given a thorough description later in this chapter.

The public political risk insurance entities' primarily focus is on expropriation, political violence (such as war, terrorism, and civil disturbance), currency inconvertibility and transfer restrictions, breach of contract/arbitration award default, non-honouring of sovereign financial obligations, and so forth.

The private political risk insurance market includes many syndicates and numerous private insurance companies. The private market offers protection from a wide variety of risks, either for political hazards alone or comprehensive non-payment situations. The private sector political risk insurance activities are similar to those of the public insurers, such as the coverage of investments in developing countries against expropriation, political violence, and other similar risks. On the other hand, the private political risk insurance entities also operate in the developing country non-payment insurance field, covering contract frustration and default by governments.

The Multilateral Investment Guarantee Agency (MIGA)

In 1985, the World Bank's Board of Governors began the process of establishing a new investment insurance affiliate by endorsing the Convention Establishing the Multilateral Investment Guarantee Agency, which defined its principal mission as

> to encourage the flow of investments for productive purposes among member countries, and in particular to developing member countries, thus supplementing the activities of the International Bank for Reconstruction and Development . . . the International Finance Corporation and other international development finance institutions.[1205]

Finally, in 1988, following the entry into force of the Convention, the MIGA was created as a legally separate and financially independent entity (with 'full juridical personality') and, at the same time, the newest member of the World Bank Group.

Membership in the MIGA is open to all members of the International Bank for Reconstruction and Development.

The structure of the MIGA

The structure of the Agency is similar to that of the other World Bank institutions. The MIGA has a three-tiered structure composed of (1) a Council of Governors, (2) a Board of Directors, and (3) a President and staff.

1205 Article 2 of the Convention Establishing the Multilateral Investment Guarantee Agency.

As noted earlier, the constituent parts of the World Bank Group in particular cases share certain officials, who sometimes undertake functions in the internal structure of interlinked organs *ex officio* as, for example, in the case of Executive Directors and Alternates of the Bank, who serve as Executive Directors and Alternates of the International Development Association and the International Finance Corporation. Concerning the MIGA, there is a particular approach developed, as separate elections are held for the Bank and MIGA Board of Directors.

In addition, according to the Convention, the President of the IBRD is an *ex officio* Chairman of the Board of Directors of the MIGA but has no vote except a deciding vote in case of a tie.[1206] Even though, under the Convention, the Agency could have its own President, the role of the President from the beginning was assigned to the President of the Bank. As of now, the functions of the chief executive officer of the Agency are performed by the Executive Vice President.

The operations of the MIGA

The Agency has a share capital and can issue guarantees in its own right, which are supplemented by guarantees issued for investments sponsored by the members; in the latter case, the Agency acts only as an administrator. The subscribed capital can be leveraged, allowing for guarantee coverage several times its size.

It is noteworthy that, according to the Convention, investments may be guaranteed by the 'operations' of the MIGA only if they are to be made in the territory of a developing member country.[1207] Under the MIGA's three-year strategy for the period FY18–20,[1208] the Agency serves as the World Bank Group's risk mitigator, providing investors with the level of comfort necessary to invest in developing countries through its political risk insurance and credit enhancement products. Its strategic priorities aim at the investments in International Development Association countries, projects in fragile and conflict-afflicted environments, and projects with positive climate change impact.

The Convention Establishing the Multilateral Investment Guarantee Agency covers the following categories of political (non-commercial) risk:

- Currency transfer – the currency transfer risk resulting from host government restrictions and delays in converting and transferring local currency earned by an investor into a freely usable currency or another currency acceptable to the holder of the guarantee.
- Expropriation and similar measures – the legislative or administrative action or omission of the host government, which deprives the holder of a guarantee of its ownership or control of or a substantial benefit from the investment. The protection from the means mentioned here does not include the non-discriminatory measures of general

---

1206 Paragraph (b) of Article 32 of the Convention Establishing the Multilateral Investment Guarantee Agency.

1207 Article 14 of the Convention Establishing the Multilateral Investment Guarantee Agency.

1208 MIGA's three-year strategy is available at <www.miga.org/report/strategy-business-outlook-fy18-20> accessed 18 March 2021.

application, which governments usually undertake for regulating economic activity under their jurisdictions.

- Breach of contract – the breach or repudiation of a contractual commitment by the host government in relation to an investor when the investor has no forum to pursue the contractual claim against the government, or recourse to such a forum is hampered by an unreasonable delay, or when, after obtaining a final decision in its favour, the investor is unable to enforce it.
- War and civil disturbance – military action or civil disturbance in any territory under the jurisdiction of the host country.
- Other cases – the Board of Directors of the MIGA may approve other specific non-commercial risks covered by the Convention; however, in no case can it be the risk of devaluation or depreciation of the currency.

At the same time, there is a general rule according to which losses resulting from (1) a host government action or omission to which the holder of the guarantee has agreed or for which the holder is responsible or (2) any event occurring before the conclusion of the contract of guarantee are not regarded as 'covered losses.'

Eligible investments and investors under the MIGA Convention

As regards eligible investments, according to the Convention, the MIGA's primary focus is direct investments; however, it may also include investments related to a specific investment or projects in which direct investment is present in some form. The main approach is that investments in which the investor demonstrates both the development benefits of and a long-term commitment to the project shall be covered. Nevertheless, the Board of Directors, by a special majority, may extend eligibility to any other medium- or long-term form of investment.

The Convention also defines the term 'eligible investors', which may be a natural person or a juridical person provided that

> (i) such natural person is a national of a member other than the host country; (ii) such juridical person is incorporated and has its principal place of business in a member or the majority of its capital is owned by a member or members or nationals thereof, provided that such member is not the host country in any of the above cases; and (iii) such juridical person, whether or not it is privately owned, operates on a commercial basis.

At the same time, the Convention addresses the dual or multiple nationality problem and determines a prevalence of the nationality of a member over the nationality of a non-member and the nationality of the host country over the nationality of any other member subject.[1209]

1209 Paragraphs (a) and (b) of Article 13 of the Convention Establishing the Multilateral Investment Guarantee Agency.

Investments' protection standards in international investment law

Bilateral investment treaties, as well as multilateral investment agreements, provide specific standards concerning the treatment of foreign investments.

At the heart of the protection model are located the principles comprising the WTO international trade system, such as the non-discrimination maxim, including the national treatment and most-favoured-nation treatment principles.

However, specific standards have also been developed which may be regarded as specific to international investment law, such as the guarantees of (1) **fair and equitable treatment**, (2) **full protection and security**, and (3) **compensation in case of expropriation**.

The standards of fair and equitable treatment and full protection and security are often reflected in recent international investment treaties. Generally, they, in combination, establish the so-called 'Minimum Standard of Treatment' obligation, which shall be followed as the basic rule of international investment law. A notable example of such a modern treaty is the United States-Mexico-Canada Agreement, according to which the parties 'shall accord to covered investments treatment in accordance with customary international law, including fair and equitable treatment and full protection and security.' At the same time, the '"fair and equitable treatment" includes the obligation not to deny justice in criminal, civil, or administrative adjudicatory proceedings in accordance with the principle of due process embodied in the principal legal systems of the world'. On the other hand, '"full protection and security" requires each Party to provide the level of police protection required under customary international law.'[1210]

To turn to a recent example, under breach of the obligation of fair and equitable treatment in the EU-Singapore Investment Protection Agreement, the following terms are outlined: '(a) denial of justice in criminal, civil and administrative proceedings; (b) a fundamental breach of due process; (c) manifestly arbitrary conduct; (d) harassment, coercion, abuse of power or similar bad faith conduct.'[1211]

Hence, fair and equitable treatment and full protection and security standards primarily refer to general international law and, particularly, to the customary international law rule on the minimum standard of treatment of aliens.

In addition, the fair and equitable treatment standard is an expression and itself part of the good faith general principle of law, which is also recognised in international law: '[T]he good faith principle established by international law, requires the Contracting Parties to provide to international investments treatment that does not affect the basic expectations that were taken into account by the foreign investor to make the investment.'[1212] So,

---

1210 Article 14.6 (Minimum Standard of Treatment) of the United States-Mexico-Canada Agreement.

1211 Paragraph 2 of Article 2.4 of the EU-Singapore Investment Protection Agreement.

1212 'The foreign investor expects the host State to act in a consistent manner, free from ambiguity and totally transparently in its relations with the foreign investor, so that it may know beforehand any and all rules and regulations that will govern its investments, as well as the goals of the relevant policies and administrative practices or directives, to be able to plan its investment and comply with such regulations. Any and all State actions conforming to such criteria should relate not only to the guidelines, directives or requirements issued, or the resolutions approved thereunder, but also to the

in practice, fair and equitable treatment is closely linked with the legitimate expectations of the foreign investor, which, among other things, may include the expectations that the host state's behaviour will be free from ambiguity and that the host state will act transparently and with a high degree of consistency.

On the other hand, the focus of the full protection and security standard is usually on protecting the investors and investments from physical violence. As stated in the EU-Singapore Investment Protection Agreement, '[f]or greater certainty, "full protection and security" only refers to a Party's obligation relating to physical security of covered investors and investments.'[1213]

Finally, it is established in the practice that both standards (fair and equitable treatment and full protection and security) have, to some extent, flexible meanings, which should be adjusted to the specific circumstances each case provides. However, regardless of circumstances, a country as a system must provide a minimum standard of investor treatment.

Expropriation

Generally, states have the right to permanent sovereignty over their natural wealth and resources. This right is explicitly founded in state sovereignty and was reaffirmed several times. However, as regards nationalisation, expropriation, or requisitioning, the states' ability to apply such measures for protecting these intrinsic rights is clearly limited and restricted by international law.

The UN General Assembly Resolution 'Permanent Sovereignty over Natural Resources' of 1962[1214] promoted the right of peoples and nations to permanent sovereignty over their natural wealth and resources and pronounced that this right should be exercised in the interest of their national development and of the well-being of the people of the state concerned. As regards investments, the Resolution applied to them the national legislation of the host state and the international agreements.

Moreover, the Resolution articulated that the

> profits derived must be shared in the proportions freely agreed upon, in each case, between the investors and the recipient State, due care being taken to ensure that there is no impairment, for any reason, of that State's sovereignty over its natural wealth and resources.

---

goals underlying such regulations. The foreign investor also expects the host State to act consistently, i.e. without arbitrarily revoking any preexisting decisions or permits issued by the State that were relied upon by the investor to assume its commitments as well as to plan and launch its commercial and business activities. The investor also expects the State to use the legal instruments that govern the actions of the investor or the investment in conformity with the function usually assigned to such instruments, and not to deprive the investor of its investment without the required compensation.' *Técnicas Medioambientales Tecmed, S.A. v United Mexican States*, Award ICSID Case No. ARB(AF)/00/ 2, 29 May 2003. In Dixon, McCorquodale, Williams (n 172) 517.

1213 Paragraph 5 of Article 2.4 of the EU-Singapore Investment Protection Agreement.

1214 A/RES/1803(XVII) of 14 December 1962.

At the same time, the Resolution also concerned the nationalisation and expropriation problem, and within the scope of its primary objective to protect the right of peoples and nations to permanent sovereignty over their natural wealth and resources, the Resolution reflected the shared vision that nationalisation, expropriation, and requisitioning should be founded on the grounds or reasons of public utility, security, or the national interest if they override purely individual or private interests. At the same time, it prescribed that, in such cases, **appropriate compensation** must be paid according to the rules of national and international law. In the event of controversy, the national jurisdiction of the state taking such measures shall be exhausted. It also referred to the possibility of the settlement of a dispute through arbitration or international adjudication if a relevant international agreement is in force.

Recent agreements mostly follow the trend of more detailed limitation and prescription of the grounds and scopes of nationalisation, expropriation, and requisitioning. They usually define that such measures are prohibited except when made:

1 in the public interest;
2 in accordance with due process of law;
3 on a non-discriminatory basis; and
4 against payment of compensation.

Nevertheless, the meaning and scope of 'compensation' have been the source of many disputes.

The USA follows the higher standard of **prompt, adequate, and effective compensation**,[1215] which is usually interpreted as 'the fair market value of the investment including expected profits'.[1216] At the same time, in interstate practice as well as in international adjudication, the term 'full compensation' is also widely applied, which 'is sometimes equated with the . . . prompt, adequate, and effective compensation'.[1217]

Such a high standard of compensation is included in certain global[1218] as well as regional international treaties – for example, in the United States-Mexico-Canada Agreement.

1215 'This is commonly referred to as the Hull doctrine named after the United States Sectary of State Cordell Hull. Hull accurately presented the then current position in international law in 1938 when he wrote his famous letter to the Mexican Government asking Mexico for "prompt, adequate and effective" compensation for the expropriated land of US nationals. . . . However, support for this position outside the US is sparse and even within the US, the courts are somewhat reluctant to apply this standard.' Kevin Smith, 'The Law of Compensation for Expropriated Companies and the Valuation Methods Used to Achieve that Compensation' (Law & Valuation, Professor Palmiter, Spring 2001) <https://users.wfu.edu/palmitar/Law&Valuation/Papers/2001/Smith.htm> accessed 18 March 2021.

1216 'The first alternative is prompt, adequate, and effective compensation: often interpreted as the fair market value of the investment including expected profits.' Mark A. Chinen, 'The Standard of Compensation for Takings' (2016) 25(2) *Minnesota Journal of International Law* 335 <https://digitalcommons.law.seattleu.edu/faculty/741> accessed 18 March 2021.

1217 ibid 338.

1218 For example, according to Article 31 (4) of the Vienna Convention on Consular Relations: 'The consular premises, their furnishings, the property of the consular post and its means of transport shall be immune from any form of requisition for purposes of national defence or public utility. If

In sum, according to this Agreement and certain other international treaties, there are requirements defined for the legitimate compensation; namely, that it shall:

- be paid without delay;
- be equivalent to the fair market value of the expropriated investment immediately before the expropriation took place (the so-called date of expropriation);
- not reflect any change in value occurring because the intended expropriation had become known earlier;
- include interest at a commercially reasonable rate, established on a market basis, taking into account the length of time from the time of expropriation until the time of payment; and
- be fully realisable and freely transferable.[1219]

The second standard of compensation is referred to as 'appropriate compensation', which was utilised by the UN in the Resolution mentioned earlier. However, in practice, appropriate compensation itself 'can range from full compensation to much less depending on the circumstances.'[1220]

To assess the scope of compensation, the central role is played by the so-called valuation methods. They usually utilise the following three techniques:

1 Book Value – 'is an assets method of valuation that is often referred to as net asset value. This valuation represents the net worth of the company (assets minus liabilities) as seen on the balance sheet.'[1221]
2 Going Concern Value – 'is based on the projected earnings or cash flow of a company. This method will also take into account the goodwill of the company which includes its brand names, reputation and customer loyalty.'[1222]

---

expropriation is necessary for such purposes, all possible steps shall be taken to avoid impeding the performance of consular functions, and prompt, adequate and effective compensation shall be paid to the sending State.'

1219 Paragraph 2 of Article 14.8 of the United States-Mexico-Canada Agreement: 'Compensation shall amount to the fair market value of the covered investment immediately before its expropriation or impending expropriation became public knowledge plus interest at a commercially reasonable rate, established on a market basis taking into account the length of time from the time of expropriation until the time of payment. Such compensation shall be effectively realisable, freely transferable in accordance with Article 2.7 (Transfer) and made without delay. Valuation criteria used to determine fair market value may include going concern value, asset value including the declared tax value of tangible property, and other criteria, as appropriate.' See also Paragraph 2 of Article 2.6 of the EU-Singapore Investment Protection Agreement: 'Compensation shall amount to the fair market value of the covered investment immediately before its expropriation or impending expropriation became public knowledge plus interest at a commercially reasonable rate, established on a market basis taking into account the length of time from the time of expropriation until the time of payment. Such compensation shall be effectively realisable, freely transferable in accordance with Article 2.7 (Transfer) and made without delay.'

1220 Chinen (n 1216).

1221 Kevin Smith (n 1215).

1222 ibid.

3   Discounted Cash Flow – 'is often considered the most appropriate. Because a company can be expected to grow at a constant or continuous rate, the value of an asset today can be assessed by taking the projected cash flows at a certain growth rate for the period of the investment and then discounting them back to a present value.'[1223]

The utilisation of a valuation method should be interlinked with the standards of the compensation since the application of the incorrect method of valuation can ultimately destroy the compensation standard.

Investment dispute settlement

The establishment of efficient mechanisms to address investment disputes is a crucial precondition for the facilitation of international trade and investment. Thus, bilateral and multilateral investment treaties articulate detailed rules concerning dispute settlement between the parties of the treaty (the states or other subjects of international law) and among the host subjects and foreign investors.

As a rule, such international agreements provide that a foreign investor may choose from the following possibilities:

1   Settlement in a court or administrative tribunals of a host state.
2   Arbitration by utilising the framework of the International Centre for Settlement of Investment Disputes (**ICSID**).
3   Arbitration through a sole arbitrator or *ad hoc* arbitration tribunal established under the Arbitration Rules of the United Nations Commission on International Trade Law (**UNCITRAL**).
4   Settlement under any applicable previously agreed dispute settlement procedure.

For example, the Energy Charter Treaty refers specifically to the mechanisms mentioned here, if a dispute cannot be settled amicably within a period of three months from the date on which either party to the dispute requested amicable settlement. However, it additionally enumerates 'an arbitral proceeding under the Arbitration Institute of the Stockholm Chamber of Commerce'.[1224]

Consent by a party to be bound by an international investment treaty, at the same time, means a general acceptance of compulsory international arbitration if the treaty includes provisions on dispute settlement through arbitration. On the other hand, the submission of a claim before the mechanism established by the international treaty concerned (for example, before an international arbitral tribunal) shall be considered as constituting the investor's consent to this mechanism.

1223 ibid.
1224 Article 26 of the Energy Charter Treaty.

UNCITRAL

The United Nations Commission on International Trade Law (UNCITRAL), created by UN General Assembly Resolution 2205 (XXI) of 1966,[1225] plays a vital role in developing 'the progressive harmonization and unification of the law of international trade' by preparing and encouraging the adoption and implementation of legal instruments in a number of critical areas of international economic law.

The members of the Commission are selected from the member states of the UN by the General Assembly. The selection process aims to have representation of different legal traditions and levels of economic development. In 2002, the number of members was expanded to 60 states. The Commission carries out its work at annual sessions, which are held alternately at United Nations Headquarters in New York and the Vienna International Centre.

To provide the member states and all participants in the commercial relations with a consolidated and comprehensive framework for commercial disputes, the Commission elaborated two essential legal instruments:

1   Arbitration Rules of the United Nations Commission on International Trade Law (**UNCITRAL Arbitration Rules**), originally adopted in 1976. However, the Arbitration Rules currently exist in three different versions: (a) the 1976 version; (b) the 2010 revised version; and (c) the 2013 version, which incorporates the UNCITRAL Rules on Transparency for Treaty-based Investor-State Arbitration.[1226] Hence, when referring to the UNCITRAL Arbitration Rules, it is advisable to specify which version of these rules the parties rely on.[1227]
2   **UNCITRAL Model Law on International Commercial Arbitration** of 1985, which was amended in 2006.

As follow-up actions, the UN General Assembly reacted with the respective Resolutions and recommended the member states to give due consideration to these legal documents. In its Resolution of 1985, the UN General Assembly enumerated three key legal instruments which 'significantly [contribute] to the establishment of a unified legal framework for the fair and efficient settlement of disputes arising in international commercial

---

1225 A/RES/2205(XXI) of 17 December 1966 – Establishment of the United Nations Commission on International Trade Law.

1226 Namely, a new Paragraph 4 of Article 1 was added to the text of the Arbitration Rules (as revised in 2010) to incorporate the Rules on Transparency.

1227 At the same time, it should be noted that Article 1 of the 2010 and 2013 UNCITRAL Arbitration Rules includes a provision intended to resolve conflicts in case of disagreement on this matter: '2. The parties to an arbitration agreement concluded after 15 August 2010 shall be presumed to have referred to the Rules in effect on the date of commencement of the arbitration, unless the parties have agreed to apply a particular version of the Rules. That presumption does not apply where the arbitration agreement has been concluded by accepting after 15 August 2010 an offer made before that date.'

relations'; among them, along with the Arbitration Rules and the Model Law, the UN General Assembly indicated the New York Convention on the Recognition and Enforcement of Foreign Arbitral Awards of 1958.[1228]

UNCITRAL Arbitration Rules

UNCITRAL Arbitration Rules consist of procedural rules upon which parties may agree for the conduct of arbitral proceedings 'in the context of international commercial relations'[1229] and are universally used in *ad hoc* arbitrations; however, sometimes they also provide the framework for administered or so-called institutional arbitrations, which embody a form of arbitration conducted with the support of and according to the rules of an arbitral institution.

It is noteworthy that the UNCITRAL Arbitration Rules are dispositive in nature, and parties to the contract may refer to them generally or in combination with particular rules agreed between them in the individual contract.

The 2013 UNCITRAL Arbitral Rules obtained a particular significance in the field of international investment law since they incorporated the so-called 'Rules on Transparency' aiming to ensure transparency in investor-state arbitration while, under previous versions of the UNCITRAL Arbitration Rules, disputes between investors and states were often not made public. In all other respects, the 2013 Arbitration Rules remain unchanged from the 2010 revised version.

The UNCITRAL Rules on Transparency in Treaty-based Investor-State Arbitration generally encourage openness – for example, by mandating the disclosure of the numerous types of documents submitted to or issued by the tribunal (the notice of arbitration, the response to the notice of arbitration, the statement of claim, the statement of defence, and any further written statements or written submissions by any disputing party, and so on).

Nevertheless, to balance the provisions on disclosure, the Rules on Transparency also specify that disclosure is subject to exceptions concerning transparency on:

- information which is confidential or protected (including information the disclosure of which would impede law enforcement);
- information the disclosure of which would compromise the essential security interests of a state; and
- information which, if made available to the public, would jeopardize the integrity of the arbitral process.

1228 A/RES/40/72 of 11 December 1985 – Model Law on International Commercial Arbitration of the United Nations Commission on International Trade Law.

1229 As specified in the UN General Assembly Resolution (A/RES/65/22 of 6 December 2010 – UNCITRAL Arbitration Rules as revised in 2010), 'the Arbitration Rules are recognized as a very successful text and are used in a wide variety of circumstances covering a broad range of disputes, including disputes between private commercial parties, investor-State disputes, State-to-State disputes and commercial disputes administered by arbitral institutions, in all parts of the world'.

Finally, according to the Rules on Transparency, the repository of published information is identified as 'the Secretary-General of the United Nations or an institution named by UNCITRAL'.[1230] However, currently, the functions of the Transparency Registry are undertaken by the UN Secretary-General, through the UNCITRAL secretariat.[1231]

As regards the general rules on arbitration reflected in both the 2010 and 2013 versions of the Arbitration Rules, at first, they included the 'model arbitration clause for contracts', which was formulated as follows:

> Any dispute, controversy or claim arising out of or relating to this contract, or the breach, termination or invalidity thereof, shall be settled by arbitration in accordance with the UNCITRAL Arbitration Rules.
>
> Note. Parties should consider adding: (a) The appointing authority shall be . . . [name of institution or person]; (b) The number of arbitrators shall be . . . [one or three]; (c) The place of arbitration shall be . . . [town and country]; (d) The language to be used in the arbitral proceedings shall be . . .[1232]

A particular provision of the Arbitral Rules concerns the issue of the composition of the arbitral tribunal; according to the 2010 and 2013 Arbitral Rules:

> If the parties have not previously agreed on the number of arbitrators, and if within 30 days after the receipt by the respondent of the notice of arbitration the parties have not agreed that there shall be only one arbitrator, three arbitrators shall be appointed.[1233]

The Arbitration Rules prescribe the appointment procedures in both cases (one arbitrator or three arbitrators) and the functions of the 'appointing authority' defined later with regard to a sole arbitrator as well as in cases of a panel of three arbitrators. For example, if under the contract, three arbitrators are to be appointed, each party shall appoint one arbitrator. The appointed two arbitrators choose the third arbitrator, who acts as the presiding arbitrator of the tribunal. However, if within 30 days, calculated from the moment an arbitrator is appointed by a party, the other party does not assign an arbitrator, or if within 30 days after the appointment of the second arbitrator, the two arbitrators cannot agree on the selection of the presiding arbitrator, the appointing authority enters into the procedure and assigns the corresponding arbitrators. At the same time, if the parties have agreed that the arbitral tribunal is to be composed of a number of arbitrators other than one or three, the appointment procedure of the arbitrators shall be determined in the contract concerned.

Under the 2010 and 2013 Arbitral Rules, the 'appointing authority' may be:

1230 Article 8 of the UNCITRAL Rules on Transparency in Treaty-based Investor-State Arbitration.
1231 Available at <www.uncitral.org/transparency-registry> accessed 18 March 2021.
1232 Annex to the UNCITRAL Arbitration Rules, as adopted in 2013.
1233 Paragraph 1 of Article 8 of the UNCITRAL Arbitration Rules, as adopted in 2013.

- the authority on which the parties have already agreed, either in the contract or otherwise; or
- the authority designated by the Secretary-General of the Permanent Court of Arbitration (PCA), if all parties have not decided on the choice of an appointing authority within 30 days after the parties have received a proposal, and at least one party requests the Secretary-General of the Permanent Court of Arbitration to designate the appointing authority.[1234]

The 2010 and 2013 Arbitral Rules explicitly define the conditions of disclosures by and challenges to arbitrators; their replacement provisions; detailed arbitration proceedings, including the rules on the statements of claim and defence, which should be communicated in writing; interim measures; evidence; the requirements of the hearing, which should be an open procedure unless it is determined otherwise by the tribunal in exceptional cases, and so forth. The periods determined by the arbitral tribunal for the communication of written statements (including the statement of claim and statement of defence) typically should not exceed 45 days.

As regards the awards, according to the 2010 and 2013 Arbitral Rules, in case there is more than one arbitrator, any award or other decision of the arbitral tribunal is made by a majority of the arbitrators. The arbitral tribunal may make separate awards on different issues at different times, which shall be made in writing and are final and binding on the parties. Thus, the parties should carry out all awards without delay.

The award of the arbitral tribunal usually is based on the law designated by the parties to be applicable to the substance of the dispute. However, if there is no such designation, the arbitral tribunal shall apply the law which it determines to be appropriate. The *ex aequo et bono* may be regarded as an additional source for the decisions – however, only if the parties have expressly authorised the arbitral tribunal to do so.

In case of the settlement of the dispute by the parties before an award is made, the arbitral tribunal shall either issue an order for the termination of the arbitral proceedings or record the settlement in the form of an arbitral award on the agreed terms.

The arbitral tribunal commonly fixes the costs of arbitration in the final award. However, sometimes the arbitral tribunal may define this issue in another decision 'if it deems appropriate'.

UNCITRAL Model Law on International Commercial Arbitration

The Model Law is designed to assist states in harmonising their legislation on the arbitral procedure. It defines the crucial terms, such as:

- 'arbitration', which under the Model Law means any arbitration whether administered by a permanent arbitral institution or not;
- 'arbitral tribunal', which means a sole arbitrator or a panel of arbitrators; and

---

1234 Paragraphs 1 and 2 of Article 6 of the UNCITRAL Arbitration Rules, as adopted in 2013.

- 'arbitration agreement', which may be concluded in the form of an arbitration clause in a contract or a separate agreement and which shall be formulated in writing.

The Model Law is designed to address almost all significant issues and challenges in arbitration proceedings, such as the principles in relation to arbitration, the composition of the arbitral tribunal, the jurisdiction of the arbitral tribunal, interim measures and preliminary orders, the conduct of arbitral proceedings, making awards and terminating proceedings, recourse against award (determining only limited and precise preconditions for the recourse), and so forth.

International Centre for Settlement of Investment Disputes

The International Centre for Settlement of Investment Disputes (ICSID) was created in 1966 as part of the World Bank Group, under the so-called ICSID Convention. The mission of the Centre was to provide facilities for (1) conciliation and (2) arbitration of investment disputes between contracting states and nationals of other contracting states.

The ICSID consists of the Administrative Council and the Secretariat. It also 'maintains' a Panel of Arbitrators and a Panel of Conciliators.

- The Administrative Council – is the governing body of the ICSID. It is composed of one Representative from each contracting state. An Alternate may act as a representative in case of the principal's absence from a meeting or inability to act in such a capacity. If a state does not designate a Representative or Alternate, the Governor and Alternate Governor of the International Bank for Reconstruction and Development for that state act in the capacity of its representatives on the Administrative Council. At the same time, the President of the Bank is an *ex officio* Chairman of the Administrative Council. A member of the Administrative Council has one vote. Generally, all matters before the Council shall be decided by a majority of the votes cast. The Administrative Council, among other things, adopts the administrative and financial regulations of the ICSID and the rules of procedure for conciliation and arbitration proceedings, determines the conditions of service of the Secretary-General and any Deputy Secretary-General, and adopts the annual budget of revenues and expenditures of the Centre.[1235]
- The Secretariat – consists of a Secretary-General, one or more Deputy Secretaries-General, and the staff. The Secretary-General and the Deputy Secretaries-General are elected by the Administrative Council by a two-thirds majority of its members upon the nomination of the Chairman for a term of service not exceeding six years. (They may be re-elected.) The Secretary-General is the 'legal representative and the principal officer of the Centre' and is responsible for its administration and the appointment of staff.[1236]

1235 Articles 4–7 of the Convention on the Settlement of Investment Disputes between States and Nationals of Other States.
1236 Articles 9–11 of the Convention on the Settlement of Investment Disputes between States and Nationals of Other States.

- The Panels – the Panel of Conciliators and the Panel of Arbitrators are composed of qualified persons who are designated for renewable periods of six years either by the contracting states (four persons to each Panel, who may but need not be their nationals) or by the Chairman, who may designate to each Panel ten persons of different nationalities, paying due regard to 'the principal legal systems of the world and of the main forms of economic activity'.[1237] A person may serve on both Panels.

The ICSID currently administers the majority of all international investment cases. The states worldwide have agreed on it as a forum for investor-state dispute settlement under many international investment treaties and numerous investment laws and contracts. The Centre provides for settlement of disputes by:

1   conciliation;
2   arbitration; and
3   fact finding.

Conciliation and arbitration under the ICSID framework

Strictly speaking, the ICSID does not itself consider a case. It embodies an institutional facility (a framework) which provides organisational support and numerous procedural rules for independent conciliation commissions and arbitral tribunals established to deal with each case.

In order to use this facility, a contracting state and an investor of another contracting state may submit a request for the particular proceeding (either for a conciliation or arbitration proceeding) to the Secretary-General of the ICSID, which will launch the process unless the dispute is manifestly outside the jurisdiction of the Centre.

At the same time, the ICSID has sets of rules that govern most proceedings under its framework: (1) the ICSID Convention, Regulations and Rules; and (2) the ICSID Additional Facility Rules. (3) The Centre may administer investment cases under other rules as well, such as the UNCITRAL Arbitral Rules and *ad hoc* rules for the investor-state and state-state cases.

Based on the ICSID Convention and the Regulations and Rules within the scope of the Convention, the 'jurisdiction of the Centre' extends

> to any legal dispute arising directly out of an investment, between a Contracting State (or any constituent subdivision or agency of a Contracting State designated to the Centre by that State) and a national of another Contracting State, which the parties to the dispute consent in writing to submit to the Centre. When the parties have given their consent, no party may withdraw its consent unilaterally.[1238]

1237 Paragraph 2 of Article 14 of the Convention on the Settlement of Investment Disputes between States and Nationals of Other States.
1238 Paragraph 1 of Article 25 of the Convention on the Settlement of Investment Disputes between States and Nationals of Other States.

Hence, both the foreign investor and the contracting state have to agree to submit a case to the Centre. As a rule, the consent of a state is reflected in the bilateral or multilateral investment agreements between subjects of international law. However, in particular cases, consent can be established in the national legislation of some states and contracts between a foreign investor and a state.

Under the Conciliation proceeding, the Commission targets the agreement between the parties. In such cases, it draws up a report recording that the parties have reached an agreement. If at any stage of the proceeding, the Commission considers that there is no likelihood the parties will reach the agreement, it closes the proceeding and draws up a report recording the failure of the parties to reach an agreement. The ICSID conciliation is a non-adversarial and specific dispute resolution process. Moreover, usually,

> neither party to a conciliation proceeding shall be entitled in any other proceeding, whether before arbitrators or in a court of law or otherwise, to invoke or rely on any views expressed or statements or admissions or offers of settlement made by the other party in the conciliation proceedings, or the report or any recommendations made by the Commission.[1239]

Arbitration under the ICSID Convention involves an effective enforcement mechanism. An award by an ICSID tribunal is final and binding on all parties to the proceeding, and all member states must recognise and enforce the award as if it were a final judgment of a court in that state.

Furthermore, arbitration awards are not subject to any appeal or any other remedy at the national level. However, they could be subject to an internal annulment procedure through an *ad hoc* committee of three persons appointed by the Chairman from the Panel of Arbitrators. The parties may request annulment of an award through an application in writing addressed to the Secretary-General, stating

> (a) that the Tribunal was not properly constituted; (b) the Tribunal has manifestly exceeded its powers; (c) that there was corruption on the part of a member of the Tribunal; (d) that there has been a serious departure from a fundamental rule of procedure; or (e) that the award has failed to state the reasons on which it is based.[1240]

ICSID Additional Facility Rules

Over time, the ICSID Additional Facility Rules instrument was introduced to expand the ICSID framework with regard to the issues which were not covered by the ICSID Convention.[1241] The ICSID Additional Facility Rules are administered by the Secretariat of the

---

1239 Article 35 of the Convention on the Settlement of Investment Disputes between States and Nationals of Other States.

1240 Paragraph 1 of Article 52 of the Convention on the Settlement of Investment Disputes between States and Nationals of Other States.

1241 The Rules Governing the Additional Facility for the Administration of Proceedings by the Secretariat of the International Centre for Settlement of Investment Disputes are available at <http://icsidfiles.worldbank.org/icsid/icsid/StaticFiles/facility/partA-article.htm#a0> accessed 18 March 2021.

Centre.[1242] Currently, the disputes between a state (or a constituent subdivision or agency of a state) and a national of another state are eligible for arbitration and conciliation under the Additional Facility Rules:

- in 'legal disputes arising directly out of an investment' if 'either the State party to the dispute or the State whose national is a party to the dispute is not a [ICSID] Contracting State'; or
- if a dispute does not directly arise out of an investment between the parties (provided that the underlying transaction is not an ordinary commercial transaction), at least one of which is an ICSID member state or a national of an ICSID member state.

At the same time, a special fact-finding mechanism was incorporated in the ICSID Additional Facility Rules.

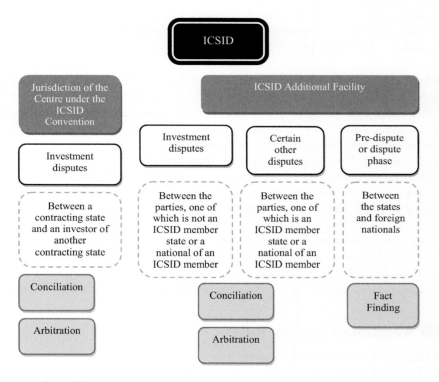

FIGURE 15.3 The ICSID institutional facility

1242 According to Article 6 of the Additional Facility Rules, 'Fact-finding, conciliation and arbitration proceedings under the Additional Facility shall be conducted in accordance with the respective Fact-finding (Additional Facility), Conciliation (Additional Facility) and Arbitration (Additional Facility) Rules set forth in Schedules A, B and C.'

Fact finding under the ICSID framework

Fact-Finding (Additional Facility) Rules allow any state or national of a state to request the establishment of a committee of inquire for examination and reporting on facts and circumstances either in the pre-dispute or dispute phase. Such request must be formulated in writing and sent to the Secretary-General of the ICSID. The request may be made jointly by the parties to the fact-finding proceeding.

Usually, the Committee consists of a sole commissioner or any uneven number of commissioners. Under the proceeding, the parties must present all the explanations and evidence, and the witnesses (if any) should be heard.

Finally, the President of the Committee shall declare the fact-finding proceeding closed, and the Committee shall draw up its Report adopted by a majority of all the commissioners. According to the Fact-Finding (Additional Facility) Rules, the 'parties shall be entirely free as to the effect to be given to the Report.'[1243]

CASES AND MATERIALS (*SELECTED PARTS*)

General obligations of members of the IMF

Articles of Agreement of the International Monetary Fund
Adopted at Bretton Woods in 1944. With the latest amendment adopted on 15 December 2010 (effective 26 January 2016)

Article VIII General obligations of members

Section 2. Avoidance of restrictions on current payments

(a) Subject to the provisions of Article VII, Section 3(b) and Article XIV, Section 2, no member shall, without the approval of the Fund, impose restrictions on the making of payments and transfers for current international transactions.
(b) Exchange contracts which involve the currency of any member and which are contrary to the exchange control regulations of that member maintained or imposed consistently with this Agreement shall be unenforceable in the territories of any member. In addition, members may, by mutual accord, cooperate in measures for the purpose of making the exchange control regulations of either member more effective, provided that such measures and regulations are consistent with this Agreement.

Section 3. Avoidance of discriminatory currency practices

No member shall engage in, or permit any of its fiscal agencies referred to in Article V, Section 1 to engage in, any discriminatory currency arrangements or multiple currency practices, whether within or outside margins under Article IV or prescribed by or under Schedule C, except as authorized under this Agreement or approved by the Fund. If such arrangements and practices are

---

1243 Article 16 of the Fact-Finding (Additional Facility) Rules.

engaged in at the date when this Agreement enters into force, the member concerned shall consult with the Fund as to their progressive removal unless they are maintained or imposed under Article XIV, Section 2, in which case the provisions of Section 3 of that Article shall apply.

Section 4. Convertibility of foreign-held balances

(a) Each member shall buy balances of its currency held by another member if the latter, in requesting the purchase, represents:

(i) that the balances to be bought have been recently acquired as a result of current transactions; or

(ii) that their conversion is needed for making payments for current transactions.

The buying member shall have the option to pay either in special drawing rights, subject to Article XIX, Section 4, or in the currency of the member making the request.

(b) The obligation in (a) above shall not apply when:

(i) the convertibility of the balances has been restricted consistently with Section 2 of this Article or Article VI, Section 3;

(ii) the balances have accumulated as a result of transactions effected before the removal by a member of restrictions maintained or imposed under Article XIV, Section 2;

(iii) the balances have been acquired contrary to the exchange regulations of the member which is asked to buy them;

(iv) the currency of the member requesting the purchase has been declared scarce under Article VII, Section 3(a); or

(v) the member requested to make the purchase is for any reason not entitled to buy currencies of other members from the Fund for its own currency.

Section 5. Furnishing of information

(a) The Fund may require members to furnish it with such information as it deems necessary for its activities, including, as the minimum necessary for the effective discharge of the Fund's duties, national data on the following matters:

(i) official holdings at home and abroad of (1) gold, (2) foreign exchange;

(ii) holdings at home and abroad by banking and financial agencies, other than official agencies, of (1) gold, (2) foreign exchange;

(iii) production of gold;

(iv) gold exports and imports according to countries of destination and origin;

(v) total exports and imports of merchandise, in terms of local currency values, according to countries of destination and origin;

(vi) international balance of payments, including (1) trade in goods and services, (2) gold transactions, (3) known capital transactions, and (4) other items;

(vii) international investment position, i.e. investments within the territories of the member owned abroad and investments abroad owned by persons in its territories so far as it is possible to furnish this information;

(viii) national income;

(ix) price indices, i.e. indices of commodity prices in wholesale and retail markets and of export and import prices;

(x) buying and selling rates for foreign currencies;

(xi) exchange controls, i.e. a comprehensive statement of exchange controls in effect at the time of assuming membership in the Fund and details of subsequent changes as they occur; and

(xii) where official clearing arrangements exist, details of amounts awaiting clearance in respect of commercial and financial transactions, and of the length of time during which such arrears have been outstanding.

(b) In requesting information the Fund shall take into consideration the varying ability of members to furnish the data requested. Members shall be under no obligation to furnish information in such detail that the affairs of individuals or corporations are disclosed. Members undertake, however, to furnish the desired information in as detailed and accurate a manner as is practicable and, so far as possible, to avoid mere estimates.

(c) The Fund may arrange to obtain further information by agreement with members. It shall act as a centre for the collection and exchange of information on monetary and financial problems, thus facilitating the preparation of studies designed to assist members in developing policies which further the purposes of the Fund.

Section 6. Consultation between members regarding existing international agreements

Where under this Agreement a member is authorized in the special or temporary circumstances specified in the Agreement to maintain or establish restrictions on exchange transactions, and there are other engagements between members entered into prior to this Agreement which conflict with the application of such restrictions, the parties to such engagements shall consult with one another with a view to making such mutually acceptable adjustments as may be necessary. The provisions of this Article shall be without prejudice to the operation of Article VII, Section 5.

Section 7. Obligation to collaborate regarding policies on reserve assets

Each member undertakes to collaborate with the Fund and with other members in order to ensure that the policies of the member with respect to reserve assets shall be consistent with the objectives of promoting better international surveillance of international liquidity and making the special drawing right the principal reserve asset in the international monetary system.

Loans and Guarantees of the IBRD

Articles of Agreement of the International Bank for Reconstruction and Development Adopted at Bretton Woods in 1944. As amended effective 27 June 2012

ARTICLE III General provisions relating to loans and guarantees

SECTION 1. *Use of resources*

(a) The resources and the facilities of the Bank shall be used exclusively for the benefit of members with equitable consideration to projects for development and projects for reconstruction alike.

(b) For the purpose of facilitating the restoration and reconstruction of the economy of members whose metropolitan territories have suffered great devastation from enemy occupation or hostilities, the Bank, in determining the conditions and terms of loans made to such members, shall pay special regard to lightening the financial burden and expediting the completion of such restoration and reconstruction.

Section 2. Dealings between members and the bank

Each member shall deal with the Bank only through its Treasury, central bank, stabilization fund or other similar fiscal agency, and the Bank shall deal with members only by or through the same agencies.

Section 3. Limitations on guarantees and borrowings of the bank

The total amount outstanding of guarantees, participations in loans and direct loans made by the Bank shall not be increased at any time, if by such increase the total would exceed one hundred percent of the unimpaired subscribed capital, reserves and surplus of the Bank.

Section 4. Conditions on which the bank may guarantee or make loans

The Bank may guarantee, participate in, or make loans to any member or any political sub-division thereof and any business, industrial, and agricultural enterprise in the territories of a member, subject to the following conditions:

  (i) When the member in whose territories the project is located is not itself the borrower, the member or the central bank or some comparable agency of the member which is acceptable to the Bank, fully guarantees the repayment of the principal and the payment of interest and other charges on the loan.
 (ii) The Bank is satisfied that in the prevailing market conditions the borrower would be unable otherwise to obtain the loan under conditions which in the opinion of the Bank are reasonable for the borrower.
(iii) A competent committee, as provided for in Article V, Section 7, has submitted a written report recommending the project after a careful study of the merits of the proposal.
 (iv) In the opinion of the Bank the rate of interest and other charges are reasonable and such rate, charges and the schedule for repayment of principal are appropriate to the project.
  (v) In making or guaranteeing a loan, the Bank shall pay due regard to the prospects that the borrower, and, if the borrower is not a member, that the guarantor, will be in position to meet its obligations under the loan; and the Bank shall act prudently in the interests both of the particular member in whose territories the project is located and of the members as a whole.
 (vi) In guaranteeing a loan made by other investors, the Bank receives suitable compensation for its risk.
(vii) Loans made or guaranteed by the Bank shall, except in special circumstances, be for the purpose of specific projects of reconstruction or development.

Section 5. Use of loans guaranteed, participated in or made by the bank

(a) The Bank shall impose no conditions that the proceeds of a loan shall be spent in the territories of any particular member or members.

(b) The Bank shall make arrangements to ensure that the proceeds of any loan are used only for the purposes for which the loan was granted, with due attention to considerations of economy and efficiency and without regard to political or other non-economic influences or considerations.

(c) In the case of loans made by the Bank, it shall open an account in the name of the borrower and the amount of the loan shall be credited to this account in the currency or currencies in which the loan is made. The borrower shall be permitted by the Bank to draw on this account only to meet expenses in connection with the project as they are actually incurred.

Section 6. Loans to the International Finance Corporation

(a) The Bank may make, participate in, or guarantee loans to the International Finance Corporation, an affiliate of the Bank, for use in its lending operations. The total amount outstanding of such loans, participations and guarantees shall not be increased if, at the time or as a result thereof, the aggregate amount of debt (including the guarantee of any debt) incurred by the said Corporation from any source and then outstanding shall exceed an amount equal to four times its unimpaired subscribed capital and surplus.

(b) The provisions of Article III, Sections 4 and 5 (c) and of Article IV, Section 3 shall not apply to loans, participations and guarantees authorized by this Section.

WTO

Marrakesh Agreement Establishing the World Trade Organisation
of 1994
Entry into force: 1 January 1995

Article II *Scope of the WTO*

1 The WTO shall provide the common institutional framework for the conduct of trade relations among its Members in matters related to the agreements and associated legal instruments included in the Annexes to this Agreement.

2 The agreements and associated legal instruments included in Annexes 1, 2 and 3 (hereinafter referred to as "Multilateral Trade Agreements") are integral parts of this Agreement, binding on all Members.

3 The agreements and associated legal instruments included in Annex 4 (hereinafter referred to as "Plurilateral Trade Agreements") are also part of this Agreement for those Members that have accepted them, and are binding on those Members. The Plurilateral Trade Agreements do not create either obligations or rights for Members that have not accepted them.

4 The General Agreement on Tariffs and Trade 1994 as specified in Annex 1A (hereinafter referred to as "GATT 1994") is legally distinct from the General Agreement on Tariffs and Trade, dated 30 October 1947, annexed to the Final Act Adopted at the Conclusion of the

Second Session of the Preparatory Committee of the United Nations Conference on Trade and Employment, as subsequently rectified, amended or modified (hereinafter referred to as "GATT 1947").

Article III *Functions of the WTO*

1 The WTO shall facilitate the implementation, administration and operation, and further the objectives, of this Agreement and of the Multilateral Trade Agreements, and shall also provide the framework for the implementation, administration and operation of the Plurilateral Trade Agreements.

2 The WTO shall provide the forum for negotiations among its Members concerning their multilateral trade relations in matters dealt with under the agreements in the Annexes to this Agreement. The WTO may also provide a forum for further negotiations among its Members concerning their multilateral trade relations, and a framework for the implementation of the results of such negotiations, as may be decided by the Ministerial Conference.

3 The WTO shall administer the Understanding on Rules and Procedures Governing the Settlement of Disputes (hereinafter referred to as the "Dispute Settlement Understanding" or "DSU") in Annex 2 to this Agreement.

4 The WTO shall administer the Trade Policy Review Mechanism (hereinafter referred to as the "TPRM") provided for in Annex 3 to this Agreement.

5 With a view to achieving greater coherence in global economic policy-making, the WTO shall cooperate, as appropriate, with the International Monetary Fund and with the International Bank for Reconstruction and Development and its affiliated agencies.

Article IV *Structure of the WTO*

1 There shall be a Ministerial Conference composed of representatives of all the Members, which shall meet at least once every two years. The Ministerial Conference shall carry out the functions of the WTO and take actions necessary to this effect. The Ministerial Conference shall have the authority to take decisions on all matters under any of the Multilateral Trade Agreements, if so requested by a Member, in accordance with the specific requirements for decision-making in this Agreement and in the relevant Multilateral Trade Agreement.

2 There shall be a General Council composed of representatives of all the Members, which shall meet as appropriate. In the intervals between meetings of the Ministerial Conference, its functions shall be conducted by the General Council. The General Council shall also carry out the functions assigned to it by this Agreement. The General Council shall establish its rules of procedure and approve the rules of procedure for the Committees provided for in paragraph 7.

3 The General Council shall convene as appropriate to discharge the responsibilities of the Dispute Settlement Body provided for in the Dispute Settlement Understanding. The Dispute Settlement Body may have its own chairman and shall establish such rules of procedure as it deems necessary for the fulfilment of those responsibilities.

4 The General Council shall convene as appropriate to discharge the responsibilities of the Trade Policy Review Body provided for in the TPRM. The Trade Policy Review Body may have its own chairman and shall establish such rules of procedure as it deems necessary for the fulfilment of those responsibilities.

5   There shall be a Council for Trade in Goods, a Council for Trade in Services and a Council for Trade-Related Aspects of Intellectual Property Rights (hereinafter referred to as the "Council for TRIPS"), which shall operate under the general guidance of the General Council. The Council for Trade in Goods shall oversee the functioning of the Multilateral Trade Agreements in Annex 1A. The Council for Trade in Services shall oversee the functioning of the General Agreement on Trade in Services (hereinafter referred to as "GATS"). The Council for TRIPS shall oversee the functioning of the Agreement on Trade-Related Aspects of Intellectual Property Rights (hereinafter referred to as the "Agreement on TRIPS"). These Councils shall carry out the functions assigned to them by their respective agreements and by the General Council. They shall establish their respective rules of procedure subject to the approval of the General Council. Membership in these Councils shall be open to representatives of all Members. These Councils shall meet as necessary to carry out their functions.

6   The Council for Trade in Goods, the Council for Trade in Services and the Council for TRIPS shall establish subsidiary bodies as required. These subsidiary bodies shall establish their respective rules of procedure subject to the approval of their respective Councils.

7   The Ministerial Conference shall establish a Committee on Trade and Development, a Committee on Balance-of-Payments Restrictions and a Committee on Budget, Finance and Administration, which shall carry out the functions assigned to them by this Agreement and by the Multilateral Trade Agreements, and any additional functions assigned to them by the General Council, and may establish such additional Committees with such functions as it may deem appropriate. As part of its functions, the Committee on Trade and Development shall periodically review the special provisions in the Multilateral Trade Agreements in favour of the least-developed country Members and report to the General Council for appropriate action. Membership in these Committees shall be open to representatives of all Members.

8   The bodies provided for under the Plurilateral Trade Agreements shall carry out the functions assigned to them under those Agreements and shall operate within the institutional framework of the WTO. These bodies shall keep the General Council informed of their activities on a regular basis.

Article VI *The Secretariat*

1   There shall be a Secretariat of the WTO (hereinafter referred to as "the Secretariat") headed by a Director-General.

2   The Ministerial Conference shall appoint the Director-General and adopt regulations setting out the powers, duties, conditions of service and term of office of the Director-General.

3   The Director-General shall appoint the members of the staff of the Secretariat and determine their duties and conditions of service in accordance with regulations adopted by the Ministerial Conference.

4   The responsibilities of the Director-General and of the staff of the Secretariat shall be exclusively international in character. In the discharge of their duties, the Director-General and the staff of the Secretariat shall not seek or accept instructions from any government or any other authority external to the WTO. They shall refrain from any action which might adversely reflect on their position as international officials. The Members of the WTO shall respect the international character of the responsibilities of the Director-General and of the staff of the Secretariat and shall not seek to influence them in the discharge of their duties.

Article VIII *Status of the WTO*

1   The WTO shall have legal personality, and shall be accorded by each of its Members such legal capacity as may be necessary for the exercise of its functions.

2   The WTO shall be accorded by each of its Members such privileges and immunities as are necessary for the exercise of its functions.

3   The officials of the WTO and the representatives of the Members shall similarly be accorded by each of its Members such privileges and immunities as are necessary for the independent exercise of their functions in connection with the WTO.

4   The privileges and immunities to be accorded by a Member to the WTO, its officials, and the representatives of its Members shall be similar to the privileges and immunities stipulated in the Convention on the Privileges and Immunities of the Specialized Agencies, approved by the General Assembly of the United Nations on 21 November 1947.

5   The WTO may conclude a headquarters agreement.

Article IX *Decision-making*

1   The WTO shall continue the practice of decision-making by consensus followed under GATT 1947(1). Except as otherwise provided, where a decision cannot be arrived at by consensus, the matter at issue shall be decided by voting. At meetings of the Ministerial Conference and the General Council, each Member of the WTO shall have one vote. Where the European Communities exercise their right to vote, they shall have a number of votes equal to the number of their member States which are Members of the WTO. Decisions of the Ministerial Conference and the General Council shall be taken by a majority of the votes cast, unless otherwise provided in this Agreement or in the relevant Multilateral Trade Agreement.

2   The Ministerial Conference and the General Council shall have the exclusive authority to adopt interpretations of this Agreement and of the Multilateral Trade Agreements. In the case of an interpretation of a Multilateral Trade Agreement in Annex 1, they shall exercise their authority on the basis of a recommendation by the Council overseeing the functioning of that Agreement. The decision to adopt an interpretation shall be taken by a three-fourths majority of the Members. This paragraph shall not be used in a manner that would undermine the amendment provisions in Article X.

3   In exceptional circumstances, the Ministerial Conference may decide to waive an obligation imposed on a Member by this Agreement or any of the Multilateral Trade Agreements, provided that any such decision shall be taken by three fourths of the Members unless otherwise provided for in this paragraph.

   (a)   A request for a waiver concerning this Agreement shall be submitted to the Ministerial Conference for consideration pursuant to the practice of decision-making by consensus. The Ministerial Conference shall establish a time-period, which shall not exceed 90 days, to consider the request. If consensus is not reached during the time-period, any decision to grant a waiver shall be taken by three fourths of the Members.

   (b)   A request for a waiver concerning the Multilateral Trade Agreements in Annexes 1A or 1B or 1C and their annexes shall be submitted initially to the Council for Trade in Goods, the Council for Trade in Services or the Council for TRIPS, respectively, for consideration during a time-period which shall not exceed 90 days. At the end of the time-period, the relevant Council shall submit a report to the Ministerial Conference.

4   A decision by the Ministerial Conference granting a waiver shall state the exceptional circum-
     stances justifying the decision, the terms and conditions governing the application of the waiver,
     and the date on which the waiver shall terminate. Any waiver granted for a period of more
     than one year shall be reviewed by the Ministerial Conference not later than one year after it
     is granted, and thereafter annually until the waiver terminates. In each review, the Ministerial
     Conference shall examine whether the exceptional circumstances justifying the waiver still exist
     and whether the terms and conditions attached to the waiver have been met. The Ministerial
     Conference, on the basis of the annual review, may extend, modify or terminate the waiver.
5   Decisions under a Plurilateral Trade Agreement, including any decisions on interpretations
     and waivers, shall be governed by the provisions of that Agreement.

Core principles of the GATT

'General Agreement on Tariffs and Trade', The WTO Agreements Series 2
<www.wto.org/english/res_e/booksp_e/agrmntseries2_gatt_e.pdf>

'Most-favoured nation

The MFN rule is basic to the whole edifice of the GATT. Stated in Article I of the GATT, it requires
that if one GATT (now WTO) signatory grants to another country "more favourable treatment"
(such as a reduction in the customs duty payable on imports of a particular product), it must immediately and unconditionally give the same treatment to imports from all signatories.

    In other words, all GATT/WTO members are entitled to receive the most favourable treatment given
by any member – or to put it the other way round, they are entitled not to be discriminated against.

    This MFN, or non-discrimination, obligation applies to customs duties and charges of any kind
connected with importing and exporting, as well as to internal taxes and charges, and to all the
rules by which such duties, taxes and charges are applied.

    The major, and continuing, exceptions to the MFN rule are Article XXIV . . . which allows mem-
bers of customs unions and free trade areas to give more favourable treatment to imports from one
another, and a 1979 decision which permits preferences for and among developing countries.

Tariff reductions and bindings

The second core principle is that the members undertake commitments in which they state the maximum level of import duty or other charge or restriction that they will apply to imports of specified
types of goods.

    These commitments, or "bindings" may result initially from bilateral negotiations, in which (for
instance) the government concerned has agreed to another country's request that it reduce the
import duty on certain products. However, the commitments are then recorded in national schedules which, through the provisions of Article II, become part of each country's obligations under
the GATT and, because of the operation of the MFN rule, apply to imports from any member.'

'National treatment

The rule of national treatment, in Article III of the GATT, is also of fundamental importance. It
complements the MFN rule. Whereas Article I, by requiring MFN treatment, puts the products

of all of a country's trading partners on equal terms with one another, the national treatment principle puts those products on equal terms also with the products of the importing country itself.

It says that, once imports have passed the national frontier (and in so doing have paid whatever import duty is imposed) they must be treated no worse than domestic products. Internal taxes or other charges on the imports must be no higher than on domestic products, and laws and regulations affecting their sale, purchase, transportation, distribution or use must be no less favourable than for goods of national origin.

Tariffs preferred

The national treatment principle means that protection of the domestic supplier of a product should be given only through action at the frontier.

A further set of GATT rules has the shared aim of restricting even frontier protection, as far as possible, to the single instrument of import duties. Quantitative restrictions on imports, and on exports, are in general banned, by Article XI, although a number of provisions in this and other articles state exceptions to this general rule. (Two such exceptions are affected by the Uruguay Round agreements on balance-of-payments measures and safeguards . . .)'

'Transparency

A further principle carried over to GATT 1994 is that of transparency. Multilateral review and transparency is a major element in the WTO itself (i.e. in the Agreement Establishing the WTO). It is retained also in general requirements imposed by GATT Article X for trade policies and regulations affecting trade in goods, and in more specific requirements built into many other Uruguay Round agreements.'

Nationality and the conflict of nationality laws

Nottebohm (Liechtenstein v Guatemala), Judgment of 6 April 1955, International Court of Justice ICJ Reports 1955, 4.

The character thus recognized on the international level as pertaining to nationality is in no way inconsistent with the fact that international law leaves it to each State to lay down the rules governing the grant of its own nationality. The reason for this is that the diversity of demographic conditions has thus far made it impossible for any general agreement to be reached on the rules relating to nationality, although the latter by its very nature affects international relations. It has been considered that the best way of making such rules accord with the varying demographic conditions in different countries is to leave the fixing of such rules to the competence of each State. On the other hand, a State cannot claim that the rules it has thus laid down are entitled to recognition by another State unless it has acted in conformity with this general aim of making the legal bond of nationality accord with the individual's genuine connection with the State which assumes the defence of its citizens by means of protection as against other States.

The requirement that such a concordance must exist is to be found in the studies carried on in the course of the last thirty years upon the initiative and under the auspices of the League of

Nations and the United Nations. It explains the provision which the Conference for the Codification of International Law, held at The Hague in 1930, inserted in Article I of the Convention relating to the Conflict of Nationality Laws, laying down that the law enacted by a State for the purpose of determining who are its nationals 'shall be recognized by other States in so far as it is consistent with . . . international custom, and the principles of law generally recognized with regard to nationality'. In the same spirit, Article 5 of the Convention refers to criteria of the individual's genuine connections for the purpose of resolving questions of dual nationality which arise in third States.

According to the practice of States, to arbitral and judicial decisions and to the opinions of writers, nationality is a legal bond having as its basis a social fact of attachment, a genuine connection of existence, interests and sentiments, together with the existence of reciprocal rights and duties. It may be said to constitute the juridical expression of the fact that the individual upon whom it is conferred, either directly by the law or as the result of an act of the authorities, is in fact more closely connected with the population of the State conferring nationality than with that of any other State. Conferred by a State, it only entitles that State to exercise protection vis-à-vis another State, if it constitutes a translation into juridical terms of the individual's connection with the State which has made him its national.

Diplomatic protection and protection by means of international judicial proceedings constitute measures for the defence of the rights of the State. As the Permanent Court of International Justice has said and has repeated, 'by taking up the case of one of its subjects and by resorting to diplomatic action or international judicial proceedings on his behalf, a State is in reality asserting its own rights – its right to ensure, in the person of its subjects, respect for the rules of international law'.

MIGA

Convention Establishing the Multilateral Investment Guarantee Agency
Submitted to the Board of Governors of the International Bank for Reconstruction and Development: 11 October 1985
Entry into force: 12 April 1988
Amended by the Council of Governors of MIGA effective 14 November 2010

Chapter III Operations

Article 11. Covered risks

(a) Subject to the provisions of Sections (b) and (c) below, the Agency may guarantee eligible investments against a loss resulting from one or more of the following types of risk:

(i) *Currency Transfer*

any introduction attributable to the host government of restrictions on the transfer outside the host country of its currency into a freely usable currency or another currency acceptable to the holder of the guarantee, including a failure of the host government to act within a reasonable period of time on an application by such holder for such transfer;

    (ii) *Expropriation and Similar Measures*

any legislative action or administrative action or omission attributable to the host government which has the effect of depriving the holder of a guarantee of his ownership or control of, or a substantial benefit from, his investment, with the exception of non-discriminatory measures of general application which governments normally take for the purpose of regulating economic activity in their territories;

    (iii) *Breach of Contract*

any repudiation or breach by the host government of a contract with the holder of a guarantee, when (a) the holder of a guarantee does not have recourse to a judicial or arbitral forum to determine the claim of repudiation or breach, or (b) a decision by such forum is not rendered within such reasonable period of time as shall be prescribed in the contracts of guarantee pursuant to the Agency's regulations, or (c) such a decision cannot be enforced; and

    (iv) *War and Civil Disturbance*

any military action or civil disturbance in any territory of the host country to which this Convention shall be applicable as provided in Article 66.

(b) In addition, the Board, by special majority, may approve the extension of coverage under this Article to specific non-commercial risks other than those referred to in Section (a) above, but in no case to the risk of devaluation or depreciation of currency.

(c) Losses resulting from the following shall not be covered:

    (i) any host government action or omission to which the holder of the guarantee has agreed or for which he has been responsible; and

    (ii) any host government action or omission or any other event occurring before the conclusion of the contract of guarantee.

Article 12. Eligible investments

(a) Eligible investments shall include equity interests, including medium- or long-term loans made or guaranteed by holders of equity in the enterprise concerned, and such forms of direct investment as may be determined by the Board.

(b) Loans other than those mentioned in Section (a) above are eligible for coverage

    (i) if they are made to finance or are otherwise related to a specific investment or project in which some other form of direct investment is present, whether or not guaranteed by the Agency and regardless of when such other investment was made, or

    (ii) as may be otherwise approved by the Board by special majority.

(c) The Board, by special majority, may extend eligibility to any other medium- or long-term form of investment.

(d) Guarantees shall generally be restricted to investments the implementation of which begins subsequent to the registration of the application for the guarantee by the Agency or receipt by the Agency of other satisfactory evidence of investor intent to obtain guarantees from the Agency. Such investments may include:

(i) a transfer of foreign exchange made to modernize, expand, or develop an existing investment, in which case both the original investment and the additional investment may be considered eligible for coverage;

(ii) the use of earnings from existing investments which could otherwise be transferred outside the host country;

(iii) the acquisition of an existing investment by a new eligible investor;

(iv) existing investments where an eligible investor is seeking to insure a pool of existing and new investments;

(v) existing investments owned by an eligible investor where there is an improvement or enhancement of the underlying project or the investor otherwise demonstrates medium- or long-term commitment to the project, and the Agency is satisfied that the project continues to have a high developmental impact in the host country; and

(vi) such other investments as may be approved by the Board by special majority.

(e) In guaranteeing an investment, the Agency shall satisfy itself as to:

(i) the economic soundness of the investment and its contribution to the development of the host country;

(ii) compliance of the investment with the host country's laws and regulations;

(iii) consistency of the investment with the declared development objectives and priorities of the host country; and

(iv) the investment conditions in the host country, including the availability of fair and equitable treatment and legal protection for the investment.

Article 13. Eligible investors

(a) Any natural person and any juridical person may be eligible to receive the Agency's guarantee provided that:

(i) such natural person is a national of a member other than the host country;

(ii) such juridical person is incorporated and has its principal place of business in a member or the majority of its capital is owned by a member or members or nationals thereof, provided that such member is not the host country in any of the above cases; and

(iii) such juridical person, whether or not it is privately owned, operates on a commercial basis.

(b) In case the investor has more than one nationality, for the purposes of Section (a) above the nationality of a member shall prevail over the nationality of a non-member, and the nationality of the host country shall prevail over the nationality of any other member.

(c) Upon the joint application of the investor and the host country, the Board, by special majority, may extend eligibility to a natural person who is a national of the host country or a juridical person which is incorporated in the host country or the majority of whose capital is owned by its nationals, provided that the assets invested are transferred from outside the host country.

Article 14. Eligible host countries

Investments shall be guaranteed under this Chapter only if they are to be made in the territory of a developing member country.

Article 15. Host country approval

The Agency shall not conclude any contract of guarantee before the host government has approved the issuance of the guarantee by the Agency against the risks designated for cover.

The Panel of Conciliators and the Panel of Arbitrators
The jurisdiction of the ICSID

Convention on the Settlement of Investment Disputes between States and Nationals of Other States of 1965
Entry into force: 14 October 1966

Section 4

The Panels

Article 12

The Panel of Conciliators and the Panel of Arbitrators shall each consist of qualified persons, designated as hereinafter provided, who are willing to serve thereon.

Article 13

(1) Each Contracting State may designate to each Panel four persons who may but need not be its nationals.
(2) The Chairman may designate ten persons to each Panel. The persons so designated to a Panel shall each have a different nationality.

Article 14

(1) Persons designated to serve on the Panels shall be persons of high moral character and recognized competence in the fields of law, commerce, industry or finance, who may be relied upon to exercise independent judgment. Competence in the field of law shall be of particular importance in the case of persons on the Panel of Arbitrators.
(2) The Chairman, in designating persons to serve on the Panels, shall in addition pay due regard to the importance of assuring representation on the Panels of the principal legal systems of the world and of the main forms of economic activity.

Article 15

(1) Panel members shall serve for renewable periods of six years.
(2) In case of death or resignation of a member of a Panel, the authority which designated the member shall have the right to designate another person to serve for the remainder of that member's term.
(3) Panel members shall continue in office until their successors have been designated.

Article 16

(1) A person may serve on both Panels.
(2) If a person shall have been designated to serve on the same Panel by more than one Contracting State, or by one or more Contracting States and the Chairman, he shall be deemed to have been designated by the authority which first designated him or, if one such authority is the State of which he is a national, by that State.
(3) All designations shall be notified to the Secretary-General and shall take effect from the date on which the notification is received.

Chapter II

Jurisdiction of the Centre

Article 25

(1) The jurisdiction of the Centre shall extend to any legal dispute arising directly out of an investment, between a Contracting State (or any constituent subdivision or agency of a Contracting State designated to the Centre by that State) and a national of another Contracting State, which the parties to the dispute consent in writing to submit to the Centre. When the parties have given their consent, no party may withdraw its consent unilaterally.
(2) "National of another Contracting State" means:

   (a) any natural person who had the nationality of a Contracting State other than the State party to the dispute on the date on which the parties consented to submit such dispute to conciliation or arbitration as well as on the date on which the request was registered pursuant to paragraph (3) of Article 28 or paragraph (3) of Article 36, but does not include any person who on either date also had the nationality of the Contracting State party to the dispute; and

   (b) any juridical person which had the nationality of a Contracting State other than the State party to the dispute on the date on which the parties consented to submit such dispute to conciliation or arbitration and any juridical person which had the nationality of the Contracting State party to the dispute on that date and which, because of foreign control, the parties have agreed should be treated as a national of another Contracting State for the purposes of this Convention.

(3) Consent by a constituent subdivision or agency of a Contracting State shall require the approval of that State unless that State notifies the Centre that no such approval is required.
(4) Any Contracting State may, at the time of ratification, acceptance or approval of this Convention or at any time thereafter, notify the Centre of the class or classes of disputes which it would or would not consider submitting to the jurisdiction of the Centre. The Secretary-General shall forthwith transmit such notification to all Contracting States. Such notification shall not constitute the consent required by paragraph (1).

Article 26

Consent of the parties to arbitration under this Convention shall, unless otherwise stated, be deemed consent to such arbitration to the exclusion of any other remedy. A Contracting State may require the exhaustion of local administrative or judicial remedies as a condition of its consent to arbitration under this Convention.

Article 27

(1) No Contracting State shall give diplomatic protection, or bring an international claim, in respect of a dispute which one of its nationals and another Contracting State shall have consented to submit or shall have submitted to arbitration under this Convention, unless such other Contracting State shall have failed to abide by and comply with the award rendered in such dispute.

(2) Diplomatic protection, for the purposes of paragraph (1), shall not include informal diplomatic exchanges for the sole purpose of facilitating a settlement of the dispute.

UNCITRAL Arbitration Rules
the constitution of the arbitral tribunal

United Nations Commission on International Trade Law Rules on Transparency in Treaty-based Investor-State Arbitration and Arbitration Rules
(as revised in 2010, with new article 1, paragraph 4, as adopted in 2013), adopted on 16 December 2013 with the Resolution A/RES/68/109 of the UN General Assembly

Section I. Introductory rules

Scope of application

Article 1

1 Where parties have agreed that disputes between them in respect of a defined legal relationship, whether contractual or not, shall be referred to arbitration under the UNCITRAL Arbitration Rules, then such disputes shall be settled in accordance with these Rules subject to such modification as the parties may agree.

2 The parties to an arbitration agreement concluded after 15 August 2010 shall be presumed to have referred to the Rules in effect on the date of commencement of the arbitration, unless the parties have agreed to apply a particular version of the Rules. That presumption does not apply where the arbitration agreement has been concluded by accepting after 15 August 2010 an offer made before that date.

3 These Rules shall govern the arbitration except that where any of these Rules is in conflict with a provision of the law applicable to the arbitration from which the parties cannot derogate, that provision shall prevail.

4 For investor-State arbitration initiated pursuant to a treaty providing for the protection of investments or investors, these Rules include the UNCITRAL Rules on Transparency in Treaty-based Investor-State Arbitration ("Rules on Transparency"), subject to article 1 of the Rules on Transparency.

Notice of arbitration

Article 3

1   The party or parties initiating recourse to arbitration (hereinafter called the "claimant") shall communicate to the other party or parties (hereinafter called the "respondent") a notice of arbitration.

2   Arbitral proceedings shall be deemed to commence on the date on which the notice of arbitration is received by the respondent.

3   The notice of arbitration shall include the following:

    (a)   A demand that the dispute be referred to arbitration;
    (b)   The names and contact details of the parties;
    (c)   Identification of the arbitration agreement that is invoked;
    (d)   Identification of any contract or other legal instrument out of or in relation to which the dispute arises or, in the absence of such contract or instrument, a brief description of the relevant relationship;
    (e)   A brief description of the claim and an indication of the amount involved, if any;
    (f)   The relief or remedy sought;
    (g)   A proposal as to the number of arbitrators, language and place of arbitration, if the parties have not previously agreed thereon.

4   The notice of arbitration may also include:

    (a)   A proposal for the designation of an appointing authority referred to in article 6, paragraph 1;
    (b)   A proposal for the appointment of a sole arbitrator referred to in article 8, paragraph 1;
    (c)   Notification of the appointment of an arbitrator referred to in article 9 or 10.

5   The constitution of the arbitral tribunal shall not be hindered by any controversy with respect to the sufficiency of the notice of arbitration, which shall be finally resolved by the arbitral tribunal.

Response to the notice of arbitration

Article 4

1   Within 30 days of the receipt of the notice of arbitration, the respondent shall communicate to the claimant a response to the notice of arbitration, which shall include:

    (a)   The name and contact details of each respondent;
    (b)   A response to the information set forth in the notice of arbitration, pursuant to article 3, paragraphs 3 (c) to (g).

2   The response to the notice of arbitration may also include:

    (a)   Any plea that an arbitral tribunal to be constituted under these Rules lacks jurisdiction;
    (b)   A proposal for the designation of an appointing authority referred to in article 6, paragraph 1;
    (c)   A proposal for the appointment of a sole arbitrator referred to in article 8, paragraph 1;

(d) Notification of the appointment of an arbitrator referred to in article 9 or 10;

(e) A brief description of counterclaims or claims for the purpose of a set-off, if any, including where relevant, an indication of the amounts involved, and the relief or remedy sought;

(f) A notice of arbitration in accordance with article 3 in case the respondent formulates a claim against a party to the arbitration agreement other than the claimant.

3   The constitution of the arbitral tribunal shall not be hindered by any controversy with respect to the respondent's failure to communicate a response to the notice of arbitration, or an incomplete or late response to the notice of arbitration, which shall be finally resolved by the arbitral tribunal.

Designating and appointing authorities

Article 6

1   Unless the parties have already agreed on the choice of an appointing authority, a party may at any time propose the name or names of one or more institutions or persons, including the Secretary-General of the Permanent Court of Arbitration at The Hague (hereinafter called the "PCA"), one of whom would serve as appointing authority.

2   If all parties have not agreed on the choice of an appointing authority within 30 days after a proposal made in accordance with paragraph 1 has been received by all other parties, any party may request the Secretary-General of the PCA to designate the appointing authority.

3   Where these Rules provide for a period of time within which a party must refer a matter to an appointing authority and no appointing authority has been agreed on or designated, the period is suspended from the date on which a party initiates the procedure for agreeing on or designating an appointing authority until the date of such agreement or designation.

4   Except as referred to in article 41, paragraph 4, if the appointing authority refuses to act, or if it fails to appoint an arbitrator within 30 days after it receives a party's request to do so, fails to act within any other period provided by these Rules, or fails to decide on a challenge to an arbitrator within a reasonable time after receiving a party's request to do so, any party may request the Secretary-General of the PCA to designate a substitute appointing authority.

5   In exercising their functions under these Rules, the appointing authority and the Secretary-General of the PCA may require from any party and the arbitrators the information they deem necessary and they shall give the parties and, where appropriate, the arbitrators, an opportunity to present their views in any manner they consider appropriate. All such communications to and from the appointing authority and the Secretary-General of the PCA shall also be provided by the sender to all other parties.

6   When the appointing authority is requested to appoint an arbitrator pursuant to articles 8, 9, 10 or 14, the party making the request shall send to the appointing authority copies of the notice of arbitration and, if it exists, any response to the notice of arbitration.

7   The appointing authority shall have regard to such considerations as are likely to secure the appointment of an independent and impartial arbitrator and shall take into account the advisability of appointing an arbitrator of a nationality other than the nationalities of the parties.

Section II. Composition of the arbitral tribunal

Number of arbitrators

Article 7

1 If the parties have not previously agreed on the number of arbitrators, and if within 30 days after the receipt by the respondent of the notice of arbitration the parties have not agreed that there shall be only one arbitrator, three arbitrators shall be appointed.

2 Notwithstanding paragraph 1, if no other parties have responded to a party's proposal to appoint a sole arbitrator within the time limit provided for in paragraph 1 and the party or parties concerned have failed to appoint a second arbitrator in accordance with article 9 or 10, the appointing authority may, at the request of a party, appoint a sole arbitrator pursuant to the procedure provided for in article 8, paragraph 2, if it determines that, in view of the circumstances of the case, this is more appropriate.

Appointment of arbitrators (articles 8 to 10)

Article 8

1 If the parties have agreed that a sole arbitrator is to be appointed and if within 30 days after receipt by all other parties of a proposal for the appointment of a sole arbitrator the parties have not reached agreement thereon, a sole arbitrator shall, at the request of a party, be appointed by the appointing authority.

2 The appointing authority shall appoint the sole arbitrator as promptly as possible. In making the appointment, the appointing authority shall use the following list-procedure, unless the parties agree that the list-procedure should not be used or unless the appointing authority determines in its discretion that the use of the list-procedure is not appropriate for the case:

(a) The appointing authority shall communicate to each of the parties an identical list containing at least three names;

(b) Within 15 days after the receipt of this list, each party may return the list to the appointing authority after having deleted the name or names to which it objects and numbered the remaining names on the list in the order of its preference;

(c) After the expiration of the above period of time the appointing authority shall appoint the sole arbitrator from among the names approved on the lists returned to it and in accordance with the order of preference indicated by the parties;

(d) If for any reason the appointment cannot be made according to this procedure, the appointing authority may exercise its discretion in appointing the sole arbitrator.

Article 9

1 If three arbitrators are to be appointed, each party shall appoint one arbitrator. The two arbitrators thus appointed shall choose the third arbitrator who will act as the presiding arbitrator of the arbitral tribunal.

2   If within 30 days after the receipt of a party's notification of the appointment of an arbitrator the other party has not notified the first party of the arbitrator it has appointed, the first party may request the appointing authority to appoint the second arbitrator.

3   If within 30 days after the appointment of the second arbitrator the two arbitrators have not agreed on the choice of the presiding arbitrator, the presiding arbitrator shall be appointed by the appointing authority in the same way as a sole arbitrator would be appointed under article 8.

Article 10

1   For the purposes of article 9, paragraph 1, where three arbitrators are to be appointed and there are multiple parties as claimant or as respondent, unless the parties have agreed to another method of appointment of arbitrators, the multiple parties jointly, whether as claimant or as respondent, shall appoint an arbitrator.

2   If the parties have agreed that the arbitral tribunal is to be composed of a number of arbitrators other than one or three, the arbitrators shall be appointed according to the method agreed upon by the parties.

3   In the event of any failure to constitute the arbitral tribunal under these Rules, the appointing authority shall, at the request of any party, constitute the arbitral tribunal and, in doing so, may revoke any appointment already made and appoint or reappoint each of the arbitrators and designate one of them as the presiding arbitrator.

Disclosures by and challenge of arbitrators (articles 11 to 13)

Article 11

When a person is approached in connection with his or her possible appointment as an arbitrator, he or she shall disclose any circumstances likely to give rise to justifiable doubts as to his or her impartiality or independence. An arbitrator, from the time of his or her appointment and throughout the arbitral proceedings, shall without delay disclose any such circumstances to the parties and the other arbitrators unless they have already been informed by him or her of these circumstances.

Article 12

1   Any arbitrator may be challenged if circumstances exist that give rise to justifiable doubts as to the arbitrator's impartiality or independence.

2   A party may challenge the arbitrator appointed by it only for reasons of which it becomes aware after the appointment has been made.

3   In the event that an arbitrator fails to act or in the event of the de jure or de facto impossibility of his or her performing his or her functions, the procedure in respect of the challenge of an arbitrator as provided in article 13 shall apply.

Article 13

1   A party that intends to challenge an arbitrator shall send notice of its challenge within 15 days after it has been notified of the appointment of the challenged arbitrator, or within 15 days after the circumstances mentioned in articles 11 and 12 became known to that party.

2   The notice of challenge shall be communicated to all other parties, to the arbitrator who is challenged and to the other arbitrators. The notice of challenge shall state the reasons for the challenge.

3   When an arbitrator has been challenged by a party, all parties may agree to the challenge. The arbitrator may also, after the challenge, withdraw from his or her office. In neither case does this imply acceptance of the validity of the grounds for the challenge.

4   If, within 15 days from the date of the notice of challenge, all parties do not agree to the challenge or the challenged arbitrator does not withdraw, the party making the challenge may elect to pursue it. In that case, within 30 days from the date of the notice of challenge, it shall seek a decision on the challenge by the appointing authority.

International environmental law

DOI: 10.4324/9781003213772-16

INTERNATIONAL ENVIRONMENTAL LAW AS A BRANCH OF INTERNATIONAL LAW

> global environmental problems
> Global Environment Outlook
> United Nations Environment Programme
> sustainable development
> international environmental law
> branch of international law
> area of international law

The emergence of global environmental problems

Global environmental problems, as one of the central challenges faced by the contemporary interstate system, emerged on the principal agenda of international politics several decades ago. In responding to the new challenge, states focused their attention and resources on addressing the newly emerging environmental concerns; however, awareness of the need for quick and decisive actions grew very slowly.

Over time, global environmental problems gradually moved up in importance on the agenda concerning the overall influence on the fundamental purpose of international law – the maintenance of peace. Hence, the transition from traditional problems to new challenges also informed the development of international law.

The global environmental problems of paramount importance

Among the main global environmental problems, the following challenges usually make the list of top priorities: '[a]cid rain, ozone depletion, climate change, loss of biodiversity, toxic and hazardous products and wastes, pollution of rivers and depletion of freshwater resources'.[1244]

The first United Nations **Global Environment Outlook** referred to land degradation, forest loss and degradation, biodiversity loss and fragmentation of habitat, pollution and scarcity of fresh water, atmospheric pollution, urban and industrial contamination, and so on. The Global Environment Outlook 6 (2019) identified the five key thematic areas: air, biodiversity, oceans and coasts, land and soil, and fresh water.[1245]

The United Nations Global Environment Outlooks were developed under the auspices of the **United Nations Environment Programme** (UNEP). The UNEP is a central global environmental body dealing with the global environmental agenda and the coherent implementation of environmental solutions within and outside the United Nations system (the Outlooks were elaborated by bringing together hundreds of scientists, peer reviewers, specialised institutions, and collaborating partners).

The regulation of environmental problems by international law

Environmental regulations were gradually incorporated into international law.

The first attempts to deal with the matter were primarily dictated by the economic interests at the forefront of environmental regulations, i.e. the maintenance of the interest of the states concerned (including the bilateral fisheries treaties, bilateral agreements between the adjacent states concerning shared resources, e.g. regarding the watershed) or were fragmented endeavours to limit the exploitation of certain natural resources (for example, the Convention on Nature Protection and Wild Life Preservation in the Western

---

1244 Philippe Sands, Jacqueline Peel, Adriana Fabra, and Ruth MacKenzie, *Principles of International Environmental Law* (3rd edn, Cambridge University Press 2012) 3.

1245 *Global Environment Outlook GEO-6: Healthy Planet, Healthy People*, Paul Ekins, Joyeeta Gupta, and Pierre Boileau (eds) (Cambridge University Press 2019).

Hemisphere of 1940 had as its main purpose 'to protect and reserve in their natural habitat representatives of all species and genera of their native flora and fauna, including migratory birds').[1246]

The second phase (from 1945 to 1972) was mostly aimed at expansion of the regulations limiting pollution and conserving the environment in particular fields (by developing the fragmented treatment of the matter) or certain geographical areas.

The last developments (from 1972 until now) reflect increased knowledge on the need to mobilise international forces to conserve biodiversity on a global scale, implement preventive and effective policies to protect the environment, and ensure **sustainable development** (development harmonised with environmental protection) in developing as well as other countries.

All these developments led to the establishment of a separate area of international law called **international environmental law**.

The areas (branches) of international law

The establishment of international environmental law contributed to the long-standing disputes about the structure of international law.

Generally, the international law scholars follow the tradition of presenting general courses in two main parts – the first part reflects the general issues, and the second reflects particular fields of international law. Such a division is mainstream in numerous textbooks on international law.

However, in selecting the particular fields, the authors did not follow a unified pattern, although some coincidences are still obvious. For example, they usually identify as separate areas of international law such bodies of norms as the law of international organisations, international human rights law, the law of foreign affairs (diplomatic and consular law), the international law of territory, the law of the sea, international air law, international space law, international economic law, international environmental law, international humanitarian law, and so forth. Some of them additionally enumerate as branches of international law such system-forming bodies of norms as the law of treaties and responsibility in international law.

Generally, to designate a separate field of international law, authors label them differently, but they usually apply the following terms – '**branch of international law**' or '**area of international law**'. The terms are used interchangeably.

However, what do these interchangeable terms mean? Specialists in international law agree that (as concerning many other matters) the structural units of international law differ from the component parts of the national legal systems. Specifically, they articulate that the areas of international law display a more limited autonomy than the branches of the national legal systems, i.e. international law branches have fewer separate methodological approaches, and they do not have autonomous processual systems (as compared to, for example, criminal law and civil law in the Romano-Germanic family countries).

1246 Preamble to the Convention on Nature Protection and Wild Life Preservation in the Western Hemisphere.

In order to designate a separate branch (area) of international law, the following requirements should be more or less identifiable:

1 Sufficient accumulation of special (branch-specific) legal sources, subsidiary means of international law, and soft law instruments.
2 Sufficient accumulation of branch-specific principles and substantial rules. The special norms should establish the rules of the game in the field of their focus, including the branch-specific principles of the field.

These two criteria are the most essential preconditions demonstrating the awareness and readiness of the actors of the interstate system to identify and separate a set of branch-specific concerns within the critical mission of international law, which, as mentioned many times in this book, consists of the avoidance of war and the institution of peace.

3 The global multilateral convention/conventions codifying the field. The establishment of such conventions, usually thanks to the International Law Commission, should prove the awareness and readiness of the actors of the interstate system to identify a separate special complex of international law norms.
4 The establishment of an intergovernmental institution in a field at the global level as a full-fledged subject of international law with a mandate which goes far beyond a role of 'facilitation forum' and fulfils the principal characteristics of an international governmental organisation (enumerated earlier in this book) and has sufficient competence in the field assigned to it under the foundational international treaty (at least a minimal ability to make binding decisions for the states and other subjects of international law).
5 The creation of a sectoral dispute settlement body or bodies.[1247]

The last two criteria confirm the next phase of the accumulation of interest in the regulation of the field. However, some authors consider these criteria preferable but not

---

1247 Soviet authors paid meaningful attention to the identification and enumeration of international law branches. The criteria for the designation of such branches are summarised by Panos Terz as follows: 'Zunächst sei die Bemerkung vorangestellt, dass fast ausschließlich Völkerrechtler der ehemaligen Sowjetunion sich der Zweigproblematik zugewandt haben, und dass es außerdem über die Zweitkriterien keine einheitlich Auffassung festgestellt werden kann. Werden die verschiedenen Meinungen kritisch und wertend zusammengefasst, so müssen die folgenden Kriterien vorliegen, damit von einem Völkerrechtszweig gesprochen werden kann: a) Ein bestimmter Bereich der internationalen Beziehungen, in concreto ein spezieller Gegenstand; b) Auf alle Fälle ein mit dem Gegenstand in enger Verbindung stehendes spezielles Ziel; c) Spezielle Rechtsnormen mit inhaltlich ebenso speziellen Rechten und Pflichten; d) Die Normengruppe stützt sich auf ein grundlegendes Völkerrechtsprinzip und widerspricht keinem der sieben grundlegenden Völkerrechtsprinzipien; e) Die Zweigmaterie, also der Gegenstand ist von der Mehrheit der Staaten als wichtig und als normierungsnotwendig betrachtet worden; f) Möglicherweise liegt ein besonderes Rechtserzeugungsverfahren vor, wie z. B. bei der Internationalen Seerechtskonvention von 1982.' Panos Terz, 'Die Völkerrechtstheorie, Versuch einer Grund-legung in den Hauptzügen' (2006) 11(2) *Papel Politico* 722.

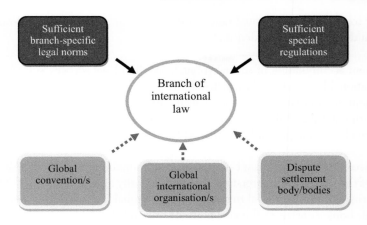

FIGURE 16.1 Defining the areas (branches) of international law

completely necessary. Moreover, if a scholar as a separate area of international law considers such system-forming complex of norms as, for example, the law of treaties, the fourth and fifth criteria, by definition, may not be applied to such fields. Lastly, as regards the third criterion, authors apply it flexibly and do not always regard it to be an absolute precondition for the identification of an autonomous area of international law.

International environmental law as a separate area of international law

In assessing the state of affairs with regard to international environmental law, researchers of international environmental law usually tend to assert that it is still 'a branch of international law',[1248] although 'at an early stage of practical development.'[1249] Some authors use the term 'area' and even though such authors regard the environmental field as a separate

---

1248 'International environmental law, as "a branch" of international law, has similarly as its purpose the maintenance of peace among states with regard to the management of global commons.' Elli Louka, *International Environmental Law: Fairness, Effectiveness, and World Order* (Cambridge University Press 2006) 67. 'It is a branch of public international law – a body of law created by states for states to govern problems that arise between states.' The University of Melbourne, Public International Law: International Environmental Law <http://unimelb.libguides.com/internationallaw/environmental> accessed 18 March 2021. 'Based on the increased awareness of the fragility of the environment and the dangers posed by the introduction of harmful substances and the overutilization of natural resources, and said by some to be based on an extensive interpretation of the award in the landmark *Trail Smelter Arbitration (1938, 1941) 3 R.I.A.A. 1905*, this branch of international law comprises international agreements, declarations, and regulations.' *Parry & Grant Encyclopaedic Dictionary of International Law* (n 165) 186.

1249 'It is quite clear that international environmental law remains, as a branch of general public international law, at an early stage of practical development, in spite of the large body of instruments and a

area of international law, nevertheless, they do not shy away from recognising the deficiencies of such treatment – namely that to designate it as a 'branch' or 'area', there are no:

1 global intergovernmental environmental organisation/organisations with a sufficient competence over environmental matters (as, for example, the ICAO in the field of the international air law);
2 sectoral dispute settlement body/bodies (as, for example, the WTO's Dispute Settlement Body in the field of international economic law);
3 global convention/conventions encompassing and codifying the entire area or at least a substantial part of the field (as the United Nations Convention on the Law of the Sea in the law of the sea); or
4 general legal obligation on subjects of international law 'to protect and preserve the environment *per se*.'[1250]

However, despite visible shortcomings in this regard, the existence of numerous conventions, customary norms, and soft law instruments in the field, as well as the subsidiary means of international law, including 'a burgeoning literature',[1251] may be considered a sufficient accumulation of special (sectoral) norms to regulate the field and establish sufficient substantial branch-specific obligations for the subjects of international law.

In addition, the functioning of the specialised intergovernmental formats at the interstate level, including the United Nations Environment Programme and other international bodies within or outside the UN system, as well as international conferences, contributed to the institution of the separate area of international law. Hence, international environmental law should be regarded as a branch of international law, albeit at an early stage of its development.

---

burgeoning literature. . . . [T]he subject of international environmental law has emerged as a discrete field of public international law'. *Principles of International Environmental Law* (n 1244) xxv, 3.

1250 'In this sense it is analogous to, say, international human rights law, the law of the sea, or international economic law. Institutionally it is less well-developed than these fields: there a no 'global environmental organization' with competence over environmental matter analogous to, say, the World Trade Organization, nor a dispute settlement body analogous to the WTO's Dispute Settlement Body or the Law of the Sea Convention's International Tribunal for the Law of the Sea. Moreover, notwithstanding significant growth in the body of general and particularized rules governing State conduct in respect of the environment, it remains the case that there is not yet any general customary or treaty law obligation on States to protect and preserve the environment *per se*. . . . Positive obligations, however, remain largely sectoral in focus, the most outstanding examples being the obligation in Article 192 of the 1982 Law of the Sea Convention to protect and preserve the marine environment and the obligation in Article 2 of the 1991 Protocol on Environmental Protection to the 1959 Antarctic Treaty comprehensively to protect the Antarctic environment and dependent and related ecosystems. But as for a general obligation to protect and preserve the environment wherever situated, one looks in vain.' Catherine Redgwell, '21. International Environmental Law' in Malcolm D. Evans (ed), *International Law* (1st edn, Oxford University Press 2003) 658.

1251 *Principles of International Environmental Law* (n 1244) xxv.

DEVELOPMENT OF INTERNATIONAL ENVIRONMENTAL LAW AND ITS SOURCES

United Nations Scientific Conference on the Conservation and Utilisation of Resources
United Nations Conference on the Human Environment
Stockholm Conference
International Union for Conservation of Nature and Natural Resources
sustainable development
United Nations Economic Commission for Europe
United Nations Conference on Environment and Development
Rio Conference
Agenda 21
international law of sustainable development
United Nations Commission on Sustainable Development
Rio Declaration on Environment and Development
sustainable use of natural resources
principle of fair and equitable use of natural resources
principle of common but differentiated responsibility
sustainable development principle
Rio United Nations Conference on Sustainable Development
United Nations High-level Political Forum on Sustainable Development
World Summits on Sustainable Development
green economy
Sustainable Development Goals
Rio Conventions
polluter-pays principle
ad hoc open-ended working group

The milestones of international environmental law

As mentioned earlier, there are two crucial milestones in the development of international environmental law.

The first milestone

The first is the establishments of the UN and the subsequent creation of a range of UN Specialised Agencies and other global international organisations, funds, and programmes, as well as regional institutions. Hence, 1945 was a critical moment in the development of both the fundamental principles of the new world order, which were enshrined in the UN Charter (i.e. in international law) and the specific areas of international law.

During this period, international organisations at the global and regional levels began to address environmental issues; however, at the same time, up until now, no United

Nations Specialised Agency or other sectoral full-fledged global international organisation has been established with an exclusive focus on environmental matters. The international institutions, such as the Food and Agriculture Organization (FAO); the United Nations Educational, Scientific and Cultural Organization (UNESCO); the International Maritime Organization (IMO;) and the General Agreement on Tariffs and Trade (GATT), only partially cover environmental issues within the broader scope of their competences.

The ideas on the reform of the UN Trusteeship Council (after the suspension of its work in 1994) to transfer its mandate to environmental issues yielded no results. For example, in 1997, the UN Secretary-General stated that:

> Member States appear to have decided to retain the Trusteeship Council. The Secretary-General proposes, therefore, that it be reconstituted as the forum through which Member States exercise their collective trusteeship for the integrity of the global environment and common areas such as the oceans, atmosphere and outer space.[1252]

However, the suggestion of the UN Secretary-General was not supported by a sufficient number of UN members.

Returning to the period before 1972, the UN itself applied soft law instruments to address environmental challenges, although environmental issues, as well as the competences in this regard, were not directly included in the Charter. Many UN General Assembly resolutions, as well as the activities of the UN Economic and Social Council, should also be remembered in this context.

Among other things, the UN General Assembly addressed such essential matters as the living resources of the sea, atmospheric nuclear tests and oil pollution, the use of nuclear energy, and the effects of nuclear radiation. The UN Specialised Agencies were also engaged in this process.

According to the ECOSOC Resolution of 1947,[1253] the **United Nations Scientific Conference on the Conservation and Utilisation of Resources** (the so-called UNCCUR) was convened in 1949, which was 'devoted solely to the exchange of ideas and experience on these matters among engineers, resource technicians, economists and other experts in related fields'. Under the Resolution, the ECOSOC recognised the 'importance of the world's natural resources' and 'the need for continuous development and widespread application of the techniques of resource conservation and utilization'.[1254] The Resolution

---

1252 Report of the Secretary-General 'Renewing the United Nations: A Programme for Reform', A/51/950 of 14 July 1997. Some states also maintained a similar position. For example, the government of Malta requested 'the inclusion of an item entitled "Review of the role of the Trusteeship Council"' in the agenda of the session of the General Assembly and declared that 'It is the belief of the Government of Malta that the role of the Trusteeship Council can be enhanced to that of trustee of the common heritage of humankind.' Letter dated 2 June 1995 from the Permanent Representative of Malta to the United Nations addressed to the Secretary-General, A/50/142 of 16 June 1995. See other developments on the official website of the UN <https://research.un.org/en/docs/tc/reform> accessed 18 March 2021.

1253 Resolution 32(IV) of 28 March 1947.

1254 ibid.

and the Conference ultimately resulted in the 1972 **United Nations Conference on the Human Environment** (also referred to as the **Stockholm Conference**), as well as other UN actions on environmental issues.

The activities of international organisations fed the conclusion of several treaties in the environmental field. Under the auspices of the UN, the Geneva Conventions on the Law of the Sea, which was partially related to environmental issues, was concluded in 1958. The Convention on Fishing and Conservation of the Living Resources of the High Seas introduced the rules on conservation, which in turn was defined as 'the aggregate of the measures rendering possible the optimum sustainable yield from those resources so as to secure a maximum supply to food and other marine products.'[1255] However, the primary purpose of the Convention was not to protect environment as such, but rather to guarantee the right of the nationals to engage in fishing on the high seas and to secure 'in the first place a supply of food for human consumption.'

The next essential field of the global effort was the ban on the testing of nuclear weapons. The states gradually prohibited the testing of nuclear weapons in nuclear-weapon-free zones (NWFZs) and, with the conclusion of the Treaty Banning Nuclear Weapon Tests in the Atmosphere, in Outer Space and Under Water of 1963, also in the atmosphere, in outer space, and under water.

In addition, in this period of time, steps were taken concerning (1) oil pollution, which ultimately resulted in the establishment of the MARPOL regime; (2) the regulation of whaling with the signing of the International Convention for the Regulation of Whaling in 1946; however, the regulation of whaling was a long-standing concern of the interstate system and had been addressed several times before (for example, in the International Agreement for the Regulation of Whaling [with Declaration] of 1937); (3) the wetlands, by concluding the Ramsar Convention on Wetlands of International Importance especially as Waterfowl Habitat of 1971, which is commonly regarded as the first international environmental treaty addressing the conservation of a particular type of ecosystem; and (4) specific territories, such as the Antarctic, which, under the Antarctic Treaty, was declared a natural reserve devoted to peace and science.

The regional developments also contributed to the creation of particular rules concerning the environment. For example, within the framework of the European Communities, special approaches and rules to protect the environment were adopted during the same period.

However, all these activities and even the international treaties were introduced 'in a piecemeal fashion'; lacked 'a coherent international environmental strategy'; and, as mentioned earlier, 'no international organisation had overall responsibility for co-ordinating international environmental policy and law, and few had a specific environmental mandate.'[1256]

The International Union for Conservation of Nature and Natural Resources

At the same time, there were some institutions established with the specific aim of facilitating the protection of the environment at the international level; however, these

---

1255 Article 2 of the Convention on Fishing and Conservation of the Living Resources of the High Seas.
1256 *Principles of International Environmental Law* (n 1244) 29.

environmental organisations did not enjoy the status of full-fledged international governmental organisations.

For example, in 1948, the International Union for the Protection of Nature (currently, the **International Union for Conservation of Nature and Natural Resources**) was created with the main task of examining the impact of human activities on nature through data analysis, field projects, advocacy, and education on environmental issues.

According to the Statutes: 'IUCN, International Union for Conservation of Nature and Natural Resources (also known as International Union for Conservation of Nature) is constituted in accordance with Article 60 of the Swiss Civil Code as an international association of governmental and non-governmental members.'[1257]

The Union has a vast and unique membership system, with over 1,300 members, including states and government agencies, political and/or economic integration organisations (Category A), international and national non-governmental organisations (Category B), indigenous peoples' organisations (Category C), and affiliates (Category D).[1258]

The IUCN World Conservation Congress assembles once in every four years. The IUCN Council is the principal governing body of the IUCN between sessions of the Congress. The IUCN Secretariat administers the issues according to its mandate. There are also IUCN Commissions, which connect over ten thousand experts.[1259] The headquarters of the Union is located in Gland, Switzerland.

The Stockholm Conference of 1972

The second milestone in the development of international environmental law was the United Nations Conference on the Human Environment, which was convened on 5 June 1972 in Stockholm, Sweden.

The Conference adopted such non-binding instruments as the Declaration of the United Nations Conference on the Human Environment (including 26 principles concerning the environment), the Action Plan for the Human Environment (containing 109 recommendations), and the Resolution on Institutional and Financial Arrangements (which led to the establishment of the United Nations Environment Programme in the same year), as well as several resolutions – the Resolution on World Environment Day (which recommended designating 5 June as World Environment Day), the Resolution on Nuclear Weapons Tests (which condemned nuclear weapons tests, especially those carried out in the atmosphere), and the Resolution Convening of a Second United Nations Conference on the Human Environment.

One of the main achievements of the Stockholm Conference was the reaffirmation of the obligation of the states not to harm the environment of other states as well as of the territories beyond their state borders. This obligation was enshrined in the 21st principle of the Declaration of the United Nations Conference on the Human Environment. According to this principle:

1257 Part I (Legal Status) of the Statutes of 5 October 1948, revised on 22 October 1996, and last amended on 27 September 2016.

1258 ibid, Part III (4).

1259 See the official website of the IUCN <www.iucn.org/about> accessed 18 March 2021.

States have, in accordance with the Charter of the United Nations and the principles of international law, the sovereign right to exploit their own resources pursuant to their own environmental policies, and the responsibility to ensure that activities within their jurisdiction or control do not cause damage to the environment of other States or of areas beyond the limits of national jurisdiction.

Although the Stockholm Conference only resulted in soft law instruments, they were nevertheless instrumental in the unification of approaches concerning environmental issues and consolidation of the focus on the protection of the environment, including by opening the door for the establishment of the programme at the level of the UN in order to achieve coordination and co-operation concerning the environment; therefore, the Stockholm Conference should be assessed as a very successful forum since it paved the way for a wide variety of further developments concerning international protection and co-operation on environment.

Nonetheless, the interstate system was still not prepared to incorporate into international law the uniform mandatory principles and codified norms encompassing the general positive obligations of the international actors in the field. Moreover, the fragmented treatment of the matter remained an essential pattern in the development of international environmental law; nevertheless, a solid foundation on which the new norms and regulations could be developed was laid.

The General Assembly resolutions after the Stockholm Conference

Among the direct follow-up actions of the Stockholm Conference, the UN General Assembly resolutions adopted following the Conference at the 27th session of the General Assembly should be outlined. The number of resolutions (more than ten) devoted to follow-up actions and environmental matters alone reflected increased attention by the world society to the outcomes of the Conference.

On the whole, the General Assembly demonstrated some kind of readiness, although perhaps weak, to link developmental issues with environmental matters, which, in a few decades, led to the development of a comprehensive approach to **sustainable development**. At that moment, however, the General Assembly only stressed that

environmental measures and programmes as may also constitute a necessary part of the process of accelerating the economic development of developing countries should receive special consideration in the formulation of programmes and priorities by the Governing Council of the United Nations Environment Programme.[1260]

The United Nations Environment Programme

The United Nations Environment Programme, headquartered in Nairobi, Kenya, was organised by the General Assembly Resolution on 'Institutional and financial arrangements

---

1260 A/RES/3002(XXVII) of 15 December 1972.

for international environmental co-operation',[1261] which mainly followed the recommendations of the Stockholm Conference's Resolution.

Under the General Assembly Resolution, the following organisational make-up was constituted:

- Governing Council (the designation of which was modified in 2013 and is currently called the United Nations Environment Assembly of the United Nations Environment Programme)[1262] – composed of 58 members elected by the General Assembly. The Council was mandated, among other things, to promote international co-operation in the field of the environment, to recommend policies towards this end, to provide general policy guidance for the environmental programmes of the United Nations system, to receive and review periodic reports of the Executive Director of the United Nations Environment Programme, and to review and approve annually the programme of utilisation of resources of the Environment Fund. It was also determined that the Governing Council must report annually to the General Assembly through the UN Economic and Social Council.

  After upgrading the Governing Council, in the United Nations Environment Assembly of the United Nations Environment Programme (also called the universal parliament for the environment),[1263] a universal membership system of all 193 member states of the UN was established,[1264] however, without changing the Council's initial mandate.[1265]

- Environment Secretariat – serves 'as a focal point for environmental action and co-ordination within the United Nations system'.[1266] The Secretariat is headed by the Executive Director of the United Nations Environment Programme, who is elected by the General Assembly on the nomination of the UN Secretary-General for a four-year term.

- Environment Fund – a 'voluntary fund' which was established to accumulate additional resources from the member states to finance environmental initiatives. Generally, for the UNEP, the Fund is a 'core source of flexible funds, complemented by softly earmarked funding provided by some Member States.'[1267]

1261 A/RES/2997(XXVII) of 15 December 1972.
1262 A/RES/67/251 of 13 March 2013.
1263 *Invest in a Healthy Planet Invest in UN Environment* (UN Environment Programme 2019) 6.
1264 'According to the decision adopted at the first session of the Governing Council with universal membership (27th session), UNEA will meet biennially in Nairobi starting in 2014. UNEA is mandated to ensure the active participation of all relevant stakeholders in the governance of UNEP and to promote a strong science-policy interface.' United Nations Environment Assembly of the UNEP (UNEA), available at the official website of the UNEP <www.unenvironment.org/events/civil-society-events/united-nations-environment-assembly-unep-unea> accessed 18 March 2021.
1265 '1. Takes note of Governing Council decision 27/2 of 22 February 2013, by which the Governing Council invited the General Assembly to adopt a resolution to change its designation to the United Nations Environment Assembly of the United Nations Environment Programme, it being understood that this change of designation in no way changes, nor will change, the present mandate, aims and purposes of the United Nations Environment Programme or the role and functions of its governing body.' A/RES/67/251 of 13 March 2013.
1266 A/RES/2997(XXVII) of 15 December 1972.
1267 *Invest in a Healthy Planet Invest in UN Environment* (n 1263) 27.

Currently, the United Nations Environment Programme is managed by a Senior Management Team, which is chaired by the Executive Director. The UNEP has several divisions, regional, liaison and out-posted offices.[1268]

From Stockholm to the Rio Conference of 1992

The Stockholm Conference and its follow-up actions facilitated the preparation and adoption of many international treaties as well as new soft law rules regarding the environment, including:

- The 1972 London Convention on the Prevention of Marine Pollution by Dumping of Wastes and Other Matter (also referred to as the London Dumping Convention).
- The MARPOL 73/78, addressing pollution from ships.
- The 1972 UNESCO Convention Concerning the Protection of the World Cultural and Natural Heritage,
- The treaties concluded under the auspices of the United Nations Environment Programme, such as the several regional seas agreements encompassing environmental protection provisions, the 1979 Convention on the Conservation of Migratory Species of Wild Animals (also called the Bonn Convention), the 1985 Vienna Convention for the Protection of the Ozone Layer, and the 1987 Montreal Protocol on Substances that Deplete the Ozone Layer, which were the most efficient treaties since the ozone hole in Antarctica is slowly recovering.
- International treaties to which the International Union for Conservation of Nature and Natural Resources made substantial contributions, such as the 1973 Convention on International Trade in Endangered Species of Wild Fauna and Flora (also known as the Washington Convention).[1269]
- The 1980 Convention on the Conservation of Antarctic Marine Living Resources, which developed the original special regime of the Antarctic Treaty by adding its new ecosystem approach.
- The 1982 United Nations Convention on the Law of the Sea, which also covered environmental matters with its unified framework, including comprehensive institutional arrangements on environmental assessment, technology transfer, liability, and dispute settlement.

1268 The General Assembly Resolution A/RES/2997(XXVII) of 15 December 1972 on institutional and financial arrangements for international environmental co-operation also established the Environment Co-ordination Board 'to provide for the most efficient co-ordination of United Nations environmental programmes, an Environment Co-ordination Board, under the chairmanship of the Executive Director of the United Nations Environment Programme'; however, in 1977, it merged with the Administrative Committee on Co-ordination, A/RES/32/197 of 20 December 1977. See also 6/18 'Enhancing United Nations co-ordination of environmental activities' of the Environment Governing Council (8th meeting, 31 May 1991).

1269 About the contribution of the IUCN, see International Union for Conservation of Nature and Natural Resources, 'The Impact of IUCN Resolutions on International Conservation Efforts' (IUCN 2018) <https://portals.iucn.org/library/node/47226> accessed 18 March 2021.

Finally, several international agreements were made at the regional level, such as:

- The 1979 Council of Europe's Convention on the Conservation of European Wildlife and Natural Habitats (also called the Bern Convention).[1270]
- The treaties adopted within the framework of the **United Nations Economic Commission for Europe** (also referred to as the UNECE or ECE), which was established in 1947 by ECOSOC and is one of five regional commissions of the United Nations.[1271] Among such conventions should be outlined the 1979 Geneva Convention on Long-Range Transboundary Air Pollution;[1272] the 1991 Espoo Convention on Environmental Impact Assessment in a Transboundary Context, which is a significant procedural treaty on general matters; and the 1992 Convention on the Protection and Use of Transboundary Watercourses and International Lakes.

The Rio Conference of 1992

In 1989, the UN General Assembly convened by its Resolution the **United Nations Conference on Environment and Development** for June 1992 in Rio de Janeiro, Brazil, to 'elaborate strategies and measures to halt and reverse the effects of environmental degradation in the context of increased national and international efforts to promote sustainable and environmentally sound development in all countries'.[1273]

The **Rio Conference** (also referred to as the 1992 Earth Summit in Rio) resulted in the **Agenda 21**, which is a comprehensive plan of action. Among other essential developments in the field, the Agenda 21 articulated a need for the 'efficacy' of international environmental law and attempted to marry environmental protection with the development in the form of the sustainable development approach.[1274]

The Conference led to the establishment of the **international law of sustainable development** and the creation of the **United Nations Commission on Sustainable Development**. These developments stipulated the rethinking of both environmental concerns and the need for development in order to find the right balance between them and, at the

---

1270 The Convention on the Conservation of European Wildlife and Natural Habitats is applicable to the natural habitats in Europe and in some African countries.

1271 'UNECE's major aim is to promote pan-European economic integration. UNECE includes 56 member States in Europe, North America and Asia. However, all interested United Nations member States may participate in the work of UNECE. Over 70 international professional organizations and other non-governmental organizations take part in UNECE activities.' <www.unece.org/mission. html> accessed 18 March 2021.

1272 According to Article 1 of the Convention on Long-Range Transboundary Air Pollution of 13 November 1979: '"Long-range transboundary air pollution" means air pollution whose physical origin is situated wholly or in part within the area under the national jurisdiction of one State and which has adverse effects in the area under the jurisdiction of another State at such a distance that it is not generally possible to distinguish the contribution of individual emission sources or groups of sources.'

1273 A/RES/44/228 of 22 December 1989.

1274 Paragraph 39.2. of the Agenda 21.

same time, to elaborate a holistic and comprehensive approach to overcome environmental threats.

Sustainable development

The Rio Conference strengthened the importance of the concept of 'sustainable development', which posits that development should be achieved without depletion of environmental resources. Principle 3 of the **Rio Declaration on Environment and Development** defined the term 'sustainable development' as follows: 'The right to development must be fulfilled so as to equitably meet developmental and environmental needs of present and future generations.'

On the whole, the concept of sustainable development emerged in the process of the consolidation of three different and sometimes opposing points of view – environmental, economic, and social ('ecology, economy and equity').[1275] It implies the adoption of measures aimed at maintaining the stability of social (including cultural) systems, as well as ensuring the integrity of natural systems, among other things, through the **sustainable use of natural resources** (which included the adoption of specific standards governing the rate of utilisation of natural resources) and the application of environmentally friendly technologies.

Hence, the concept of sustainable development imposed some limitations on economic development in favour of protecting the natural as well as the social environment.

On the other hand, the concept of sustainable development also took into account the **principle of fair and equitable use of natural resources**, which meant not only the 'fair and equitable' distribution of the shared resources (shared fisheries stocks, shared freshwater resources, and so on) between the states (also known as 'equitable and reasonable sharing of resources'),[1276] but also 'intergenerational equity', which provided that environmental protection should be implemented for the benefit of future generations.

However, on the side of responsibility, the **principle of common but differentiated responsibility** was introduced, which referred to the responsibility of all states but, at the same time, articulated the special role of the developed countries by taking into account their contribution to the creation of environmental problems and their ability to prevent, reduce, and control the threats.

1275 'Sustainable development objectives have been widely defined along three dimensions: "economic, environmental and social" or "ecology, economy and equity".' United Nations (2014), *Prototype Global Sustainable Development Report* (New York: United Nations Department of Economic and Social Affairs, Division for Sustainable Development July 2014) <http://sustainabledevelopment. un.org/globalsdreport/> accessed 18 March 2021.

1276 As concluded by the ICJ in the *Gabčíkovo-Nagymaros Project (Hungary/Slovakia)*: 'The Court considers that Czechoslovakia, by unilaterally assuming control of a shared resource, and thereby depriving Hungary of its right to an equitable and reasonable share of the natural resources of the Danube – with the continuing effects of the diversion of these waters on the ecology of the riparian area of the Szigetköz – failed to respect the proportionality which is required by international law.' Judgment of 25 September 1997, ICJ Reports 1997, 7.

The development of all countries was considered a crucial tool to protect the environment.

This innovative concept also stipulated a more inclusive collaboration between the developed and developing states in pursuit of a shared agenda. The development agenda of the world was considered less as a struggle between the developed and developing countries; rather, the states were supposed to co-operate to accomplish sustainable development goals.

Developed countries continued to provide financial and other types of assistance to the developing countries, but only for those development projects which were not harmful to the environment.

Over time, the sustainable development concept stipulated the establishment of the **sustainable development principle** in international law, which is shared by different branches of international law (such as international economic law and international environmental law) as one of their central principles.[1277]

The General Assembly resolutions after the Rio Conference

In December 1992, the UN General Assembly carried out follow-up actions and endorsed the principal decisions of the Rio Conference. Notably, in its Resolution named 'Report of the United Nations Conference on Environment and Development' it was proclaimed that the General Assembly

> Endorses the Rio Declaration on Environment and Development, 2/ Agenda 21 3/ and the Non-legally Binding Authoritative Statement of Principles for a Global Consensus on the Management, Conservation and Sustainable Development of All Types of Forests 4/ as adopted by the United Nations Conference on Environment and Development on 14 June 1992.[1278]

The Rio Declaration on Environment and Development, which developed the principles initially enshrined in the Stockholm Declaration of the United Nations Conference on the Human Environment and merged them with the sustainable development concept, is of special importance.

1277 By defining the principle (or concept) of 'sustainable development' in the book *Principles of International Environmental Law*, the following is outlined: 'The term needs to be taken, in the context of its historic evolution, as reflecting a range of procedural and substantive commitments and obligations. These are primarily, but not exclusively, recognition of: the need to take into consideration the needs of present and future generations; the acceptance, on environmental protection grounds, of limits placed upon the use and exploitation of natural resources; the role of equitable principles in the allocation of rights and obligations; the need to integrate all aspects of environment and development; and the need to interpret and apply rules of international law in an integrated and systemic manner.' *Principles of International Environmental Law* (n 1244) 217.

1278 A/RES/47/190 of 22 December 1992.

Although these principles, as well as other outcome documents of the Conference and follow-up decisions of the General Assembly, had in principle a soft law status, nevertheless, they all – particularly the Rio Declaration on Environment and Development – established a general framework for the international environmental approach. In addition, some of the principles of the Declaration were incorporated into customary international law, as well as international treaties. Hence, at present, the Rio principles, which will be examined in detail later, should be regarded as the pattern on which further development of international environmental law – namely, a possible general convention codifying the entire field (like the 1982 United Nations Convention on the Law of the Sea) – may be based, if such a development were to be considered in the future by the subjects of international law as the next necessary step to respond to the existing challenges.

At the same time, the UN General Assembly also addressed the 'recommendations' of the Rio Conference concerning institutional matters by its Resolution on 'Institutional arrangements to follow up the United Nations Conference on Environment and Development'[1279] and established the United Nations Commission on Sustainable Development.

The United Nations Commission on Sustainable Development

The United Nations Commission on Sustainable Development (CSD) was created by the UN General Assembly, through the UN Economic and Social Council, as 'a high-level Commission on Sustainable Development as a functional commission of the Council'.[1280]

From its inception, the Commission on Sustainable Development promoted the incorporation of the principles of the Rio Declaration and the implementation of Agenda 21 and, generally, has greatly contributed to the sustainable development agenda within the UN framework as well as outside the UN. It was rather inclusive by involving in its format a wide range of official stakeholders and partners. Over time, the CSD focused on clusters of specific thematic and cross-sectoral matters, which were described in its multi-year programme of work (2003–2017). There were 53 members in the United Nations Commission on Sustainable Development.

However, at the **Rio United Nations Conference on Sustainable Development** of 2012 (also referred to as the Rio+20), the participants agreed to establish the **United Nations High-level Political Forum on Sustainable Development**, which subsequently replaced the Commission on Sustainable Development.

The World Summits on Sustainable Development of 2002 and 2012

The next important consolidating conferences were the **World Summits on Sustainable Development**, held in Johannesburg and Rio, in 2002 and 2012, respectively, as the 10-year and 20-year follow-ups to the 1992 United Nations Conference on Environment and Development.

1279 A/RES/47/191 of 22 December 1992.
1280 ibid.

The Johannesburg World Summit on Sustainable Development of 2002 was mostly focused on the eradication of poverty. Although it did not produce a new wave of even a fragmented codification of international environmental law or other essential developments concerning principles and general approaches, nevertheless, its outcome document – the Plan of Implementation of the World Summit on Sustainable Development – articulated more practical methods for the implementation and development of the programmes which were adopted before.

The Rio World Summit on Sustainable Development was intended as a conference for maintaining the renewed political commitment to sustainable development by reviewing the progress achieved in this regard and addressing new and emerging environmental challenges. Particular attention at the Conference was paid to the so-called **'green economy'**, as well as other challenges, such as the elaboration of a strategy for financing sustainable development; 'the need for urgent action to reverse land degradation'; the urgent needs in the fields of energy, food security, oceans, and cities; and so forth. The additional concern was to develop the institutional framework at the international level to address the challenges.

An essential outcome of the Rio+20 was a soft law document 'The Future We Want', which, as in previous cases, was endorsed by the UN General Assembly.[1281] 'The Future We Want' substantially reaffirmed previous action plans – the Agenda 21 and the Plan of Implementation of the World Summit on Sustainable Development. However, it also stipulated the novelties with regard to the comprehensive connection of the 'green economy' concept with the sustainable development approach and also concerning the international governance of the environmental field.

As regards the 'green economy', the participants of the Conference recognised the 'green economy in the context of sustainable development and poverty eradication as one of the important tools available for achieving sustainable development and that it could provide options for policymaking but should not be a rigid set of rules.' At the same time, the UN General Assembly Resolution 'The Future We Want' identified the main frame for 'green economy policies', which should be exercised without violating international law and with respect for each country's national sovereignty over their natural resources and the needs of developing countries. Such policies shall '[p]romote sustained and inclusive economic growth, foster innovation and provide opportunities, benefits and empowerment for all and respect of all human rights'.[1282]

Concerning the international governance of the field, the Resolution 'The Future We Want' strengthened the role of the United Nations Environment Programme as the 'leading global environmental authority',[1283] led to the involvement in the Programme of all UN member states (universal membership model), and stipulated the advance of its position at the global level as well as the better engagement of the United Nations Environment

---

1281 A/RES 66/288 of 27 July 2012.

1282 ibid.

1283 '88. We are committed to strengthening the role of the United Nations Environment Programme as the leading global environmental authority that sets the global environmental agenda, promotes the coherent implementation of the environmental dimension of sustainable development within the United Nations system and serves as an authoritative advocate for the global environment.' ibid.

Programme in the coordination processes in environmental matters within the UN. On the other hand, the Rio+20 fed the establishment of the United Nations High-level Political Forum on Sustainable Development.

Finally, the launching of a process to develop a set of **Sustainable Development Goals** should be regarded as one of the main innovations of the Rio+20.

The United Nations High-level Political Forum on Sustainable Development

The United Nations High-level Political Forum on Sustainable Development (HLPF) was designed according to the General Assembly follow-up Resolution 'Format and organizational aspects of the high-level political forum on sustainable development'.[1284]

Starting in 2013, the Forum meets annually under the auspices of the UN Economic and Social Council, including a three-day ministerial segment, and every four years at the level of Heads of State and Government under the auspices of the General Assembly. The United Nations High-level Political Forum on Sustainable Development adopts important political declarations; therefore, it is a central platform on sustainable development within the UN system and maintains the follow-up and review actions of the outcomes of the World Summits.

For instance, the recent meeting of the High-level Political Forum on Sustainable Development convened under the auspices of the General Assembly (the so-called SDG Summit) was held in New York in September 2019, and it adopted the Political Declaration 'Gearing up for a decade of action and delivery for sustainable development'.[1285]

As regards the High-level Political Forum on Sustainable Development under the auspices of the UN Economic and Social Council, in such a format, it inter alia carries out regular voluntary reviews from developed and developing countries as well as relevant UN entities and other stakeholders.[1286]

The United Nations Sustainable Development Summit of 2015

The United Nations Sustainable Development Summit of 2015 was held as a high-level plenary meeting of the General Assembly at United Nations Headquarters in New York from 25 to 27 September 2015, which coincided with the 70th anniversary of the UN. The main outcome of the Summit was the 2030 Agenda for Sustainable Development, which was adopted by the UN General Assembly Resolution 'Transforming our world: the 2030 Agenda for Sustainable Development'.[1287] The 2030 Agenda included the Sustainable

---

1284 A/RES/67/290 of 9 July 2013.

1285 See the UN official website <https://sustainabledevelopment.un.org/sdgsummit> accessed 18 March 2021.

1286 As noted on the United Nations Sustainable Development Goals website: '47 countries carried out voluntary national reviews (VNRs) of their implementation of the 2030 Agenda in the 2020 HLPF from Friday, 10 July to Thursday, 16 July 2020.' <https://sustainabledevelopment.un.org/hlpf/2020> accessed 18 March 2021.

1287 A/RES/70/1 of 25 September 2015.

Development Goals and targets – namely, the '17 Sustainable Development Goals with 169 associated targets which are integrated and indivisible', which will be discussed later in this book. Currently, the Division for Sustainable Development Goals in the United Nations Department of Economic and Social Affairs performs the secretariat functions concerning Sustainable Development Goals and 'provides analytical inputs for intergovernmental deliberations on sustainable development'.[1288]

The General Assembly assessed the adoption of this Resolution with great optimism, articulating that '[n]ever before have world leaders pledged common action and endeavour across such a broad and universal policy agenda.'[1289] Indeed, the 2030 Agenda is a comprehensive document which builds on the previous developments in environment and development fields, addresses new challenges, and creates the general political agenda in this regard.

On the whole, in 2015, the interstate system took a big step forward towards shaping international policy on the basis of multilateralism, since in that year, in parallel with the United Nations Sustainable Development Summit and other significant international conferences, several other major international documents on the environment as well as development-related regulations were adopted. The documents adopted in this period which stand out in importance are the following: the Sendai Framework for Disaster Risk Reduction 2015–2030,[1290] which is a roadmap for making our environment safer and more resilient to disasters, and the Addis Ababa Action Agenda on Financing for Development 'of the Third International Conference on Financing for Development, which is an integral part of the 2030 Agenda for Sustainable Development, supports and complements it, helps to contextualize its means of implementation targets with concrete policies and actions'.[1291] In the same year, the international community shifted from the protracted debate on effective policy on climate change and the efficiency of the 1997 Kyoto Protocol and adopted the 2015 Paris Agreement.

The post-Rio (1992) multilateral environmental agreements

All these developments led to the establishment of a complex system of international environmental treaties without creating a single codified convention. However, at the

---

1288 'Division for Sustainable Development Goals', available at the United Nations Sustainable Development Goals website <https://sustainabledevelopment.un.org/about> accessed 18 March 2021.

1289 A/RES/70/1 of 25 September 2015.

1290 As outlined in Margareta Wahlström's (United Nations Special Representative of the Secretary-General for Disaster Risk Reduction) foreword: 'The Sendai Framework for Disaster Risk Reduction 2015–2030 was adopted at the Third UN World Conference in Sendai, Japan, on March 18, 2015. It is the outcome of stakeholder consultations initiated in March 2012 and inter-governmental negotiations from July 2014 to March 2015, supported by the United Nations Office for Disaster Risk Reduction at the request of the UN General Assembly. The Sendai Framework is the successor instrument to the Hyogo Framework for Action (HFA) 2005–2015: Building the Resilience of Nations and Communities to Disasters.' The Sendai Framework recognises that Member States have the primary responsibility for preventing and reducing disaster risk. It is available at <https://bit.ly/2Wzq3BM> accessed 18 March 2021.

1291 A/RES/70/204 of 22 December 2015.

same time, the complex system of international environmental law displays the tendency towards developing more general conventions while, in parallel, it continues to treat the subject through a rather selective and fragmented expansion of the regulations concerning specific environmental questions.

The tendency towards generalisation became especially visible after the Rio Conference of 1992. Two conventions were opened for signature at the 1992 Earth Summit in Rio: (1) the 1992 United Nations Framework Convention on Climate Change (UNFCCC),[1292] which was still a sectoral type of a treaty since it primarily dealt with questions of climate and atmosphere but, at the same time, reflected the broader impacts of climate change on ecosystems, food production, and sustainable development; and (2) the 1992 Convention on Biological Diversity (CBD),[1293] which aimed at the conservation of biodiversity, sustainable utilisation of its components, and fair and equitable distribution of the use of genetic resources. Towards these ends, it introduced a novel approach to agriculture, forestry, fishery, land use, and nature conservation. The United Nations Convention to Combat Desertification in those Countries Experiencing Serious Drought and/or Desertification, Particularly in Africa (UNCCD) was adopted later in 1994;[1294] it aimed specifically to mitigate the effects of drought and to promote sustainable land management in the arid, semi-arid, and dry sub-humid areas (the so-called drylands), where the most vulnerable ecosystems are located. Usually, these three conventions are together referred to as the '**Rio Conventions**'.

Over time, multilateral environmental agreements were developed under the umbrella of the existing conventions. For example, the 1997 Kyoto Protocol and its successor, the 2015 Paris Agreement, which enhanced and extended the climate change response under the United Nations Framework Convention on Climate Change. The 2000 Cartagena Protocol on Biosafety to the Convention on Biological Diversity and the 2010 Nagoya Protocol on Access to Genetic Resources and the Fair and Equitable Sharing of Benefits Arising from their Utilization to the Convention on Biological Diversity, which particularised commitments under the Convention on Biological Diversity.

The types of the environmental agreements

On the whole, all environmental agreements concluded before or after the Rio Conference of 1992 may be categorised as treaties concerning:

1292 As noted on the official website of the UN: 'The Convention was opened for signature at the Conference and, by the end of the Conference, on 14 June 1992, it had been signed by 154 States and one regional economic integration organization. The Convention entered into force on 21 March 1994'. <https://legal.un.org/avl/ha/ccc/ccc.html> accessed 18 March 2021.

1293 'The Convention was opened for signature on 5 June 1992 at the United Nations Conference on Environment and Development. . . . It remained open for signature until 4 June 1993, by which time it had received 168 signatures. The Convention entered into force on 29 December 1993, which was 90 days after the 30th ratification'. <www.cbd.int/history/> accessed 18 March 2021.

1294 As noted on the official website of the UN: 'The Convention was open for signature at Paris by all States and regional economic integration organizations on 14 and 15 October 1994. Thereafter, it remained open for signature at the United Nations Headquarters in New York until 13 October 1995'. <https://bit.ly/2JpelTQ> accessed 20 December 2020. The Convention entered into force on 18 March 2021.

1   general procedural matters – such as the 1998 Aarhus Convention on Access to Information, Public Participation in Decision-making and Access to Justice in Environmental Matters, which was established within the framework of the United Nations Economic Commission for Europe;

2   atmosphere – for example, the 1992 United Nations Framework Convention on Climate Change, including the 1997 Kyoto Protocol and the 2015 Paris Agreement;

3   marine environment and marine living resources – such as the 1996 International Convention on Liability and Compensation for Damage in Connection with the Carriage of Hazardous and Noxious Substances by Sea; the 2000 Protocol on Preparedness, Response and Co-operation to Pollution Incidents by Hazardous and Noxious Substances; the 1996 Agreement on the Conservation of Cetaceans in the Black Sea, Mediterranean Sea and contiguous Atlantic area; and the 2001 Agreement on the Conservation of Albatrosses and Petrels;

4   nature conservation and terrestrial living resources – such as the 1992 Convention on Biological Diversity, the 1994 Convention to Combat Desertification, and the 1994 International Tropical Timber Agreement; or

5   certain hazardous substances – such as the 1989 Basel Convention on the Transboundary Movement of Hazardous Wastes and their Disposal, the 1998 Rotterdam Convention on the Prior Informed Consent Procedure for Certain Hazardous Chemicals and Pesticides in International Trade, the 2001 Stockholm Convention on Persistent Organic Pollutants, and the 2013 Minamata Convention on Mercury.

Additional categories include treaties dealing with (6) freshwater resources (for example, the aforementioned 1992 Convention on the Protection and Use of Transboundary Watercourses and International Lakes); (7) nuclear safety (such as the 1996 Comprehensive Test Ban Treaty); (8) noise pollution (the 1979 Convention concerning the Protection of Workers against Occupational Hazards in the Working Environment due to Air Pollution, Noise and Vibration); (9) industry and industrial accidents (for example, the 1992 Helsinki Convention on the Transboundary Effects of Industrial Accidents), and (10) special regimes concerning certain territories (such as the Antarctic Treaty system examined earlier, the 1991 Alpine Convention, and the 1992 Bucharest Convention on the Protection of the Black Sea Against Pollution).

Other sources of international environmental law

As described earlier, soft law instruments occupy a special and perhaps unique place in international environmental law. In environmental and sustainable development fields, such documents were usually adopted before the interstate system achieved the point of readiness to introduce international legal norms and corresponding international legal obligations.

On the other hand, in parallel with the rules enshrined in international treaties, customary law principles and norms sprang up from the state practice, which are either of a general nature, since they also cover some other fields of international law, or are sectoral (i.e. were established to directly regulate environmental matters).

Among applicable customary norms are commonly enumerated the so-called 'no-harm' principle examined earlier in this book, the principle of equitable utilisation of shared resources, the obligation to notify on potential transboundary harm, and so forth.

Moreover, the third source of international law – the general principles of law – also contributes to the complex body of norms of international environmental law. For example, the so-called '**polluter-pays principle**' applies in international environmental law. First of all, it should be stressed that there is no unanimity of assessment on whether the polluter-pays principle should be recognised as a general principle of law or a customary rule (principle). Nevertheless, whereas the principle can be found in most national legal systems, as well as in an increasing number of international conventions and soft law documents (for example, Principle 16 of the Rio Declaration), this provides a sufficient basis for understanding the polluter-pays principle as a general principle of law.

Towards a Global Pact for the Environment

In 2018, the UN General Assembly adopted the Resolution 'Towards a Global Pact for the Environment'.[1295] With this Resolution, the interstate system addressed the long-standing challenge of creating a single framework agreement encompassing the entirety of international environmental law.

On the one hand, the General Assembly, with its Resolution, requested the Secretary-General to submit 'a technical and evidence-based report that identifies and assesses possible gaps in international environmental law and environment-related instruments' and, on the other hand, established an **ad hoc open-ended working group**, which was open to participation by all states members of the UN and all members of the UN Specialised Agencies.

By the end of November 2019, UN Secretary-General António Guterres had prepared the report 'Gaps in international environmental law and environment-related instruments: towards a global pact for the environment'. In the Report, he enumerated the following deficiencies in international environmental law:

1   'there is no single overarching normative framework that sets out what might be characterized as the rules and principles of general application in international environmental law';
2   'international environmental law is piecemeal and reactive. It is characterized by fragmentation and a general lack of coherence and synergy among a large body of sectoral regulatory frameworks';
3   'the articulation between multilateral environmental agreements and environment-related instruments remains problematic owing to the lack of clarity';
4   'the structure of international environmental governance is characterized by institutional fragmentation';
5   'the implementation of international environmental law is challenging at both the national and international levels'.[1296]

1295 A/RES/72/277 of 10 May 2018.
1296 'Gaps in international environmental law and environment-related instruments: towards a global pact for the environment', Report of the Secretary-General of 30 November 2018.

The Secretary-General suggested that the effective implementation of international environmental law 'could be strengthened through such actions as the clarification and reinforcement of principles of international environmental law. This could be done through a comprehensive and unifying international instrument that gathers all the principles of environmental law.'[1297]

Under the UN General Assembly Resolution, the mandate of the ad hoc open-ended working group was to consider the report of the UN Secretary-General and, if necessary, to define 'the scope, parameters and feasibility of an international instrument, with a view to making recommendations'.[1298] The working group held the Organisational Session in New York, the United States, in 2018, and three Substantive Sessions in Nairobi, Kenya, in 2018 and 2019.[1299] On 30 August 2019, the UN General Assembly adopted a new Resolution, which welcomed the work of the ad hoc open-ended working group and its report (recommendations of the *ad hoc* open-ended working group) and endorsed all its recommendations.[1300] However, as of now, the Global Pact for the Environment is still in the process of development, and currently, it is difficult to assess whether this process will result in the conclusion of an all-encompassing global treaty.

DEFINING THE ENVIRONMENT AND THE PRINCIPLES OF INTERNATIONAL ENVIRONMENTAL LAW

> natural environment
> human-made environment
> human environment
> environment of a quality that permits a life of dignity and well-being
> environmental impact assessment
> for the benefit of present and future generations
> right to a healthy and productive life in harmony with nature
> heritage of wildlife
> human's habitat
> principle of renewability
> no-harm principle
> pollution of seas
> means of mass destruction
> good faith
> spirit of partnership
> principle of prevention
> precautionary principle

1297 ibid.

1298 A/RES/72/277 of 10 May 2018.

1299 In addition, a portal dedicated to the establishment of the Global Pact for the Environment, which 'aims at providing existing information and material on international environmental law in an easily accessible manner', was created and is maintained. <https://globalpact.informea.org/about> accessed 18 March 2021.

1300 A/RES/73/333 of 30 August 2019.

The challenge of determining 'the environment'

Generally, the term 'environment' may be understood to cover 'all those elements which in their complex inter-relationships form the framework, setting and living conditions for mankind, by their very existence or by virtue of their impact.'[1301]

However, finding a unified definition of 'the environment' in the international legal norms or soft law documents is a thorny issue. The uncertainty in this matter is mostly stipulated by the fact that, as mentioned earlier, there is no all-encompassing and coherent international treaty in the field. Hence, it seems preferable to determine what is meant by the term 'environment' case by case from the treaty or other hard or soft law examples concerned.[1302]

What is the environment?

Nevertheless, the doctrine is based on a shared approach, which stipulates that the broad definition of the term can be deduced by generalising the norms from several international treaties and other hard or soft low sources of international law. One of the most cited generalisations about the term 'environment' combines the following three topics:

1   **natural environment**;
2   **human-made environment** ('including the cultural heritage', 'indoor and working environment'); and
3   **human environment** ('including regulations on food content, products, safety issues, leisure, and economic health [consumer protection, eco-labelling, and so forth]').[1303]

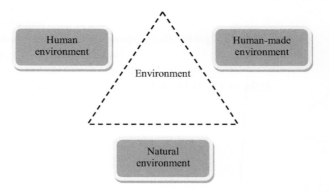

FIGURE 16.2 Defining 'environment'

1301 Draft Council resolution on the continuation and implementation of a European Community policy and Action Programme on the Environment (Submitted by the Commission to the Council on 24 March 1976) (1976) 19(C 115) *Official Journal of the European Communities* <https://bit.ly/2R6U1uE> accessed 18 March 2021.

1302 'In each case, what is meant by "the environment" must be gathered from the treaty concerned.' Anthony Aust, *Handbook of International Law* (2nd edn, Cambridge University Press 2010) 305.

1303 Marie-Louise Larsson, *The Law of Environmental Damage: Liability and Reparation* (the reference to John R. Salter, European Environmental Law, International Environmental Law and Policy Series (Kluwer Law International 1994) (Kluwer Law International, Norstedts Juridik AB 1999) 123.

Defining the environment in international treaties and soft law documents

Although international environmental documents usually evade introducing a general description of the term 'environment', nonetheless, sometimes a more or less general definition can still be discovered. For example, according to the 1993 Council of Europe Convention on Civil Liability for Damage Resulting from Activities Dangerous to the Environment, the definition of 'environment' includes:

- the 'natural resources both abiotic and biotic, such as air, water, soil, fauna and flora and the interaction between the same factors;'
- the 'property which forms part of the cultural heritage;' and
- 'the characteristic aspects of the landscape.'[1304]

Consequently, alongside the natural environment, this definition also covers protection of the cultural heritage, characteristic aspects of the landscape, and so on.

Sometimes international documents determine only the part of the term 'environment' which falls under their central scope and focus.

For instance, the 1972 Stockholm Declaration of the United Nations Conference on the Human Environment specified the notion of the 'natural resources of the earth', which include 'the air, water, land, flora and fauna and especially representative samples of natural ecosystems'. The natural environment was the primary focus of the Declaration and of the principles enshrined in that document. However, its particular provisions also addressed other aspects of the term 'environment', as in Principle 1, which declared that

> Man has the fundamental right to freedom, equality and adequate conditions of life, in an environment of a quality that permits a life of dignity and well-being, and he bears a solemn responsibility to protect and improve the environment for present and future generations. In this respect, policies promoting or perpetuating apartheid, racial segregation, discrimination, colonial and other forms of oppression and foreign domination stand condemned and must be eliminated.

Consequently, by articulating the fundamental right of a human to freedom, equality, and adequate conditions of life, the first principle of the Stockholm Declaration of the United Nations Conference on the Human Environment used a broad meaning of the term 'environment', which should permit 'life of dignity and well-being'; therefore, such an understanding may not be limited to the natural environment.

Comparing the Stockholm and Rio principles

Both documents – the Stockholm Declaration of the United Nations Conference on the Human Environment and the Rio Declaration on Environment and Development – were soft law instruments developing the fundamental principles of international environmental

---

1304 Article 2 of the Convention on Civil Liability for Damage Resulting from Activities Dangerous to the Environment.

law. Over time, these principles established a unified framework for environment and sustainable development matters. Nowadays, the principles which were reflected in these Declarations should be regarded as the source of the general legal obligations of the subjects of international law, at least in those portions that are enshrined in international treaties and in other sources of international law. On the other hand, after the adoption of the Declarations, these principles were further developed through hard and soft law instruments. Nevertheless, the main framework incorporated by the Declarations has not yet lost its significance.

Hence, both documents are crucial instruments. Therefore, the principles enshrined in these documents will be discussed here.

Meanwhile, the Declarations should be considered as supplementing each other; however, they do differ from each other to some degree.

The primary focus of the Stockholm Declaration was environmental protection. Thus, it introduced the definitions of the fundamental terms and main framework for the field. On the other hand, the Rio Declaration followed the developments in the area and shifted its main focus to the marriage of development and environment issues. Consequently, it provided the general definition, as well as the entire pattern, of sustainable development, on which all principles of international environmental law up until now were developed.

Of course, there were other novelties stemming from the Rio Declaration. For example, some new obligations were added to the co-operation and 'no-harm' principles; the need for introducing effective environmental norms at national and international levels was specified; and it also included a reference to **environmental impact assessment** as an essential national procedure for evaluating the likely impact of a proposed activity on the environment,[1305] declared support for the precautionary approach to the field, and so forth.

The Rio principles also addressed the promotion of the participation of particular groups of people to achieve their effective involvement in the process of sustainable development, including women, 'youth of the world', and indigenous peoples.

And finally, it connected the sustainable development concept with the central mission of international law to institute peace and, in particular, addressed the issue of protection of the environment in times of armed conflict.

Defining the purpose and the anthropocentric approach

By determining the central purpose of environmental protection, the Stockholm Declaration emphasised that the 'natural resources of the earth . . . must be safeguarded **for the benefit of present and future generations** through careful planning or management, as appropriate' (Principle 2).

The entire document is a manifestation and development of the fundamental right of all humans 'to freedom, equality and adequate conditions of life, in an environment of a quality that permits a life of dignity and well-being' (Principle 1).

1305 'Environmental impact assessment, as a national instrument, shall be undertaken for proposed activities that are likely to have a significant adverse impact on the environment and are subject to a decision of a competent national authority.' Principle 17 of the Rio Declaration.

The Rio Declaration also maintained the so-called 'anthropocentric approach' to environmental and developmental matters since, by addressing its main focus of 'sustainable development', it proclaimed that '[h]uman beings are at the centre of concerns for sustainable development' (Principle 1). Generally, in the Rio Declaration, the human's **right to a healthy and productive life in harmony with nature** is placed at the centre of its 'anthropocentric approach' (Principle 1).

The principle of protection of the heritage of wildlife and human's habitat

The norms in the field, producing the obligations for the main actors, aim 'to safeguard and wisely manage the **heritage of wildlife** and its habitat, which are now gravely imperilled by a combination of adverse factors', as articulated in Principle 4 of the Stockholm Declaration. Hence, protection of both the wildlife and **human's habitat** is the main concern of environmental regulations. The term 'human's habitat' should be interpreted in a broad sense, including not only the natural environment but also human-made and human environmental concerns.

The principle of renewability

To safeguard the heritage of wildlife and human's habitat, it is crucial to maintain the renewability of vital resources. Consequently, international environmental law is founded on the **principle of renewability**, which, according to the Stockholm Declaration, means that '[t]he capacity of the earth to produce vital renewable resources must be maintained and, wherever practicable, restored or improved' (Principle 3); '[t]he non-renewable resources of the earth must be employed in such a way as to guard against the danger of their future exhaustion' (Principle 5).

Sovereignty over natural resources and the 'no-harm' principle

As mentioned earlier, the Rio Declaration (Principle 2) reaffirmed Principle 21 of the Stockholm Declaration, enshrining the responsibility of the states not to cause damage to the environment of other states or to areas beyond national jurisdiction.

Thus, both documents:

1   refer to the UN Charter and the 'principles of international law' to articulate the sovereign right of the states to exploit their own resources according to their own policies;
2   entail a long-standing responsibility of states 'to ensure that activities within their jurisdiction or control do not cause damage to the environment of other States'; and
3   crystallise the principle of international environmental law according to which such responsibility of the states is not limited to state territories; rather, it also includes the 'areas beyond the limits of national jurisdiction' to which the 'no-harm' principle should be applied.

The **no-harm principle** includes certain substantial obligations. For example, the Stockholm Declaration enumerated the prohibition of '[t]he discharge of toxic substances or of other substances and the release of heat, in such quantities or concentrations as to exceed the capacity of the environment to render them harmless' (Principle 6); the **pollution of seas** 'by substances that are liable to create hazards to human health, to harm living resources and marine life, to damage amenities or to interfere with other legitimate uses of the sea' (Principle 7); and the protection from the **means of mass destruction** since '[m]an and his environment must be spared the effects of nuclear weapons and all other means of mass destruction' (Principle 26).

Obligation to co-operate

To 'conserve, protect and restore the health and integrity of the Earth's ecosystem', as well as to address other environmental problems, as reaffirmed by the Rio Declaration, the states have the obligation to co-operate 'in **good faith** and in a **spirit of partnership**' (Principles 7 and 27).

At the same time, the states should 'effectively co-operate' in order to prevent severe environmental degradation, i.e. any damage to the environment of other states or to areas beyond national jurisdiction.

The Stockholm Declaration additionally emphasised the 'efficient and dynamic' role of the international organisations in coordinating the activities of the actors for the better protection and improvement of the environment (Principle 24).

Engagement of all in the co-operation

The Rio Declaration specifically emphasised the need for the involvement of particular groups of people in solving environmental problems.

For example, the Declaration stated that '[w]omen have a vital role in environmental management and development.' On the other hand, it underlined the 'creativity, ideals and courage of the youth of the world . . . to forge a global partnership in order to achieve sustainable development and ensure a better future for all.' At the same time, it stressed the particular role of indigenous peoples, their communities, and other local communities in 'environmental management and development because of their knowledge and traditional practices'. Finally, the Declaration demanded that attention be paid to the environment and natural resources of peoples under oppression, domination, and occupation, who shall be protected by the parties concerned (Principles 20, 21, 22, and 23).

Access to information, the obligation to notify, and the principle of prevention

The Rio Declaration promoted an approach according to which the environmental issues are best handled with the participation of all concerned parties, including individuals. Therefore, it entailed the general duty of the states to 'facilitate and encourage public awareness and participation by making information widely available' and the obligation of the states to ensure at the national level the appropriate access of each individual 'to information concerning the environment that is held by public authorities, including information on hazardous materials and activities in their communities', as well as the opportunity to participate in decision-making processes and judicial and administrative proceedings (Principle 10).

At the international level, according to the Rio Declaration, the states have the obligation to immediately notify other states 'of any natural disasters or other emergencies that are likely to produce sudden harmful effects on the environment of those States'. At the same time, the states 'shall provide prior and timely notification and relevant information to potentially affected States . . . and shall consult with those States at an early stage and in good faith' (Principles 18 and 19).

Generally, international environmental law encourages the **principle of prevention**, according to which the states have a general duty to prevent, reduce, or limit activities that might cause or risk environmental damage.

Precautionary principle

The Rio Declaration also included the **precautionary principle**, which, according to the Declaration, should be widely applied by states according to their capabilities.

Under the Declaration, the principle is defined as follows: 'Where there are threats of serious or irreversible damage, lack of full scientific certainty shall not be used as a reason for postponing cost-effective measures to prevent environmental degradation' (Principle 15).

The development of the legal norms

To address all environmental and developmental issues, the subjects of international law should elevate the arrangements to the status of the legal norms at both the international and national levels. To this end, as determined by the Rio Declaration, the states must enact 'effective environmental legislation'. At the same time, the '[e]nvironmental standards, management objectives and priorities should reflect the environmental and developmental context to which they apply' (Principle 11).

The same approach in the formulation of the Stockholm Declaration reads as follows:

> International matters concerning the protection and improvement of the environment should be handled in a co-operative spirit by all countries, big and small, on an equal footing. Co-operation through multilateral or bilateral arrangements or other appropriate means is essential to effectively control, prevent, reduce and eliminate adverse environmental effects resulting from activities conducted in all spheres, in such a way that due account is taken of the sovereignty and interests of all States.
> (Principle 24)

Liability and compensation

The liability and compensation rules for the effective implementation of the responsibility system should be developed against the subjects of international law which violate the 'no-harm' principle as well as other relevant norms of international environmental law. Thus, the Stockholm Declaration articulated that the states 'shall co-operate to develop further the international law regarding liability and compensation for the victims of pollution and other environmental damage caused by activities within the jurisdiction or control of such States to areas beyond their jurisdiction' (Principle 22).

The Rio Declaration reaffirmed the same obligation of the states, but supplemented the duty to 'develop national law regarding liability and compensation for the victims of pollution and other environmental damage' (Principle 13).

The polluter-pays principle

The Rio Declaration reaffirmed the 'polluter-pays principle', which is examined earlier in this book. It urged the states to take into account 'the approach that the polluter should, in principle, bear the cost of pollution' (Principle 16).

Development as a tool for environmental protection and the principle of sustainable development

Although the principal focus of the Stockholm Declaration was not development, it attempted, nevertheless, to connect environmental protection with economic development with the following formulation: 'Nature conservation, including wildlife, must therefore receive importance in planning for economic development' (Principle 4).

On the other hand, the Declaration expressed the understanding that '[e]conomic and social development is essential for ensuring a favourable living and working environment for man and for creating conditions on earth that are necessary for the improvement of the quality of life' (Principle 8).

The Stockholm Declaration reaffirmed the strong awareness of humankind of addressing 'under-development', which can be overstepped only 'through the transfer of substantial quantities of financial and technological assistance as a supplement to the domestic effort of the developing countries and such timely assistance as may be required' (Principle 9).

Hence, sustainable development is unthinkable without environmental protection, as was clearly summarised in the Rio Declaration, which, as noted earlier, included a general definition of the term 'sustainable development' (Principle 3) and stated that 'to achieve sustainable development, environmental protection shall constitute an integral part of the development process and cannot be considered in isolation from it' (Principle 4).

However, protection of the environment, in turn, is impossible without (economic) development. Thus, there must be reciprocal movement in both directions in order to achieve the goal of sustainable development. Therefore, as declared in the Stockholm Declaration, 'the environmental policies of all States should enhance and not adversely affect the present or future development potential of developing countries, nor should they hamper the attainment of better living conditions for all' (Principle 11).

Hence, developing countries should be the focus of any environmental considerations. As noted in the Rio Declaration, '[t]he special situation and needs of developing countries, particularly the least developed and those most environmentally vulnerable, shall be given special priority' (Principle 6).

The principle of common but differentiated responsibility

The Rio Declaration acknowledged the principle of common but differentiated responsibility, taking into consideration the different contributions to global environmental degradation by the states and the special needs of developing countries.

The Declaration proclaimed that '[s]tates have common but differentiated responsibilities.'

With this formulation, firstly, the Declaration emphasised a common responsibility of states for the protection of the environment at the national, regional, and global levels.

However, secondly, the principle specifically requires a higher level of responsibility from the developed countries 'in view of the pressures their societies place on the global environment and of the technologies and financial resources they command' (Principle 7).

The principle of sustainable development and rational planning

The 'rational management of resources' was foreseen by the Stockholm Declaration to be a crucial factor in improving the environment. Therefore, the Declaration prescribed the implementation by the states of 'an integrated and co-ordinated approach to their development planning'. At the same time, rational planning was considered 'an essential tool for reconciling any conflict between the needs of development and the need to protect and improve the environment' (Principles 13 and 14).

Such rational planning should aim at enhancing environmental quality; therefore, it must be 'applied to human settlements and urbanization with a view to avoiding adverse effects on the environment and obtaining maximum social, economic and environmental benefits for all'. It should cover demographic policies, appropriate national institutions for enhancing environmental quality, science, and technology and must encourage education in environmental matters.

In the wording of the Rio Declaration, such rational planning should be incorporated to 'achieve sustainable development and a higher quality of life for all people'. Towards this end, the states 'should reduce and eliminate unsustainable patterns of production and consumption and promote appropriate demographic policies' and must co-operate 'by improving scientific understanding through exchanges of scientific and technological knowledge, and by enhancing the development, adaptation, diffusion and transfer of technologies, including new and innovative technologies' (Principles 8 and 9).

Peace and sustainable development

Principle 25 of the Rio Declaration prescribes that '[p]eace, development and environmental protection are interdependent and indivisible.'

With this formulation, the Declaration addressed the main mission of international law and proclaimed that without development and environmental protection, there may be no peace.

In addition, it emphasised the need for the peaceful resolution of all environmental disputes. Finally, it stated that the warfare is 'inherently destructive of sustainable development', but when such warfare occurs, states should 'respect international law providing protection for the environment in times of armed conflict' (Principles 24 and 26).

Development of the principles enshrined in the Declarations

Over time, the principles discussed here were embodied in the international treaties, as well as other hard and soft law sources and the subsidiary means of international law.

Of course, the new formulations sometimes modified the wordings which were introduced in the Declarations or even added specific meanings; however, the basic frame and substantial character of the principles generally remained unchanged.

For example, in the formulation of the 1992 (UNECE) Convention on the Protection and Use of Transboundary Watercourses and International Lakes, the precautionary principle is determined as follows:

> The precautionary principle by virtue of which action to avoid the potential transboundary impact of the release of hazardous substances shall not be postponed on the ground that scientific research has not fully proved a causal link between those substances, on the one hand, and the potential transboundary impact, on the other hand.[1306]

On the whole, whereas the existence of the principles of international environmental law is to date widely recognised, their legal status, the normative meaning, and the scope of applicability sometimes remain unsettled, especially when (1) a principle is not reflected in an international treaty, (2) the subject of international law is not a party to a treaty enshrining the principle, and (3) there is no consent on the status of a principle (for example, the acknowledgement of that principle as possessing a status of a general customary rule or a general principle of law).[1307]

SUSTAINABLE DEVELOPMENT GOALS AND TARGETS

Millennium Declaration
Millennium Development Goals
Sustainable Development Goals
associated targets
global indicator framework
COVID-19

1306 Article 2 (5) (a) of the UNECE Convention on the Protection and Use of Transboundary Watercourses and International Lakes of 17 March 1992.

1307 For instance, as regards the precautionary principle mentioned earlier, some subjects of international law argued that the principle had the status of a general customary rule or a general principle of law; 'in the *EC – Biotech case*, the WTO panel stated that the legal status of the precautionary principle was "unsettled", and since it did not need to take a position on whether or not the principle was a recognised principle of general or customary international law it would "refrain from expressing a view on th[e] issue".' *Principles of International Environmental Law* (n 1244) 226, 227.

Eight Millennium Development Goals

The **Millennium Declaration**[1308] and eight **Millennium Development Goals** (MDGs),[1309] which were adopted by the UN General Assembly in 2000, fixed 2015 as the year for measuring the progress achieved regarding sustainable development. Since the countries which adopted the MDGs generally recognised their success, as well as the need to adopt a new agenda after 2015, in 2012, at the UN Conference on Sustainable Development, they decided to start the process of developing a set of Sustainable Development Goals (SDGs).

Adopting the new sustainable development agenda

During the United Nations Sustainable Development Summit of 2015, the UN member states addressed some of the most pressing challenges faced by the world and approved the 'outcome document of the United Nations summit for the adoption of the post-2015 development agenda'. The new document, which was adopted by the UN General Assembly, as mentioned earlier, was titled 'Transforming our world: the 2030 Agenda for Sustainable Development'.

The document was intended to be 'a plan of action for people, planet, and prosperity' and was presented as an attempt to save humanity from poverty and heal the planet. As noted earlier, the 2030 Agenda for Sustainable Development included 17 **Sustainable Development Goals** with 169 **associated targets**.

Sustainable Development Goals

The Sustainable Development Goals are listed here in the form of subheadings as they are commonly referred to; the exact wording of the goals as defined in the Resolution[1310] is given in parentheses:

1 No poverty (End poverty in all its forms everywhere);
2 Zero hunger (End hunger, achieve food security and improved nutrition, and promote sustainable agriculture);
3 Good health and well-being (Ensure healthy lives and promote well-being for all at all ages);
4 Quality education (Ensure inclusive and equitable quality education and promote lifelong learning opportunities for all);
5 Gender equality (Achieve gender equality and empower all women and girls);

1308 A/RES/55/2 of 8 September 2000.
1309 Goal 1: Eradicate extreme poverty and hunger; Goal 2: Achieve universal primary education; Goal 3: Promote gender equality and empower women; Goal 4: Reduce child mortality; Goal 5: Improve maternal health; Goal 6: Combat HIV/AIDS, malaria, and other diseases; Goal 7: Ensure environmental sustainability; Goal 8: Develop a global partnership for development.
1310 A/RES/70/1 of 25 September 2015.

6 Clean water and sanitation (Ensure availability and sustainable management of water and sanitation for all);

7 Affordable and clean energy (Ensure access to affordable, reliable, sustainable, and modern energy for all);

8 Decent work and economic growth (Promote sustained, inclusive, and sustainable economic growth, full and productive employment, and decent work for all);

9 Industry, innovation, and infrastructure (Build resilient infrastructure, promote inclusive and sustainable industrialisation, and foster innovation);

10 Reducing inequality (Reduce inequality within and among countries);

11 Sustainable cities and communities (Make cities and human settlements inclusive, safe, resilient, and sustainable);

12 Responsible consumption and production (Ensure sustainable consumption and production patterns);

13 Climate action (Take urgent action to combat climate change and its impacts);

14 Life below water (Conserve and sustainably use the oceans, seas, and marine resources for sustainable development);

15 Life on land (Protect, restore, and promote sustainable use of terrestrial ecosystems, sustainably manage forests, combat desertification, and halt and reverse land degradation and halt biodiversity loss);

16 Peace, justice, and strong institutions (Promote peaceful and inclusive societies for sustainable development, provide access to justice for all, and build effective, accountable, and inclusive institutions at all levels);

17 Partnerships for the Goals (Strengthen the means of implementation and revitalise the Global Partnership for Sustainable Development).[1311]

The general meanings

The Sustainable Development Goals are comprehensive and ensure the balance of all three components of sustainable development – environmental, economic, and social.

As defined by the UN General Assembly Resolution, the Sustainable Development Goals and targets

> are integrated and indivisible, global in nature and universally applicable, taking into account different national realities, capacities and levels of development and respecting national policies and priorities. Targets are defined as aspirational and global, with each Government setting its own national targets guided by the global level of ambition but taking into account national circumstances. Each Government will also decide how these aspirational and global targets should be incorporated into national planning processes, policies and strategies. It is important to recognize

---

1311 The Goals in the shortened forms are formulated as they are listed on the United Nations Sustainable Development Goals website <www.un.org/sustainabledevelopment/> accessed 18 March 2021.

FIGURE 16.3 UN Sustainable Development Goals – SDGs[70]

the link between sustainable development and other relevant ongoing processes in the economic, social and environmental fields.[1312]

Implementation

To implement the Goals and targets, the three sectors – the environmental, economic, and social sectors in their broadest sense – should be unified under a single vision. Moreover, transdisciplinary research should be undertaken in order to support the holistic view of the aforementioned sectors.

The implementation of the SDGs started worldwide in 2016. The overall work to achieve the SDGs was supposed to be completed by 31 December 2030.

Countries should independently develop their own strategies, plans, and programs for sustainable development. The SDGs will play a guiding role in enabling countries to align their plans with their global commitments.

Achievement of the SDGs and the targets foreseen in the 2030 Agenda for Sustainable Development are monitored and tracked using the **global indicator framework**. An annual

1312 A/RES/70/1 of 25 September 2015.

1313 The SDG poster is included in this book with the permission of the DGC-sdgpermissions <sdgpermissions@un.org>. Its versions are available on the United Nations Sustainable Development Goals website <www.un.org/sustainabledevelopment/>. At the same time, the content of this publication has not been approved by the United Nations and does not reflect the views of the United Nations or its officials or Member States.

study of the results achieved and the follow-ups is usually organised under the format of the High-level Political Forum on Sustainable Development, based on the progress report on the SDGs prepared by the UN Secretary-General.

The global indicator framework for the Sustainable Development Goals and targets

To measure progress towards reaching the SDGs and targets, specific indicators were introduced according to the 'global indicator framework for the Sustainable Development Goals and targets of the 2030 Agenda for Sustainable Development',[1314] which was adopted by the UN General Assembly in 2017.[1315]

At the same time, the General Assembly requested

> the Secretary-General to continue to maintain the Sustainable Development Goals global indicator database to inform the yearly progress report on the Goals and to ensure transparency on the data, statistics and metadata presented on countries and used for the regional and global aggregates.

Currently, the Sustainable Development Goals global indicator database[1316] remains a substantial tool to observe the overall progress towards the goals and targets to be reached under SDGs. The tool also assists the Secretary-General in the preparation of the annual reports on the 'Progress towards the Sustainable Development Goals'.

Indivisibility of the SDGs

The SDGs concept demonstrates an all-encompassing approach to sustainable development and the separate Goals are to be considered indivisible and interdependent. Therefore, all Goals to some degree relate to environmental protection as well as to the economic and social components of sustainable development.

Nonetheless, some of them which largely concern 'traditional' environmental protection issues can be singled out.

COVID-19

In 2020, the United Nations Department of Economic and Social Affairs prepared the 'Sustainable Development Goals Report 2020', which identified certain 'devastating' initial impacts of **COVID-19** on the Goals and targets. The Report generally concluded that

---

1314 'The official indicator list . . . includes the global indicator framework as contained in A/RES/71/313, the refinements agreed by the Statistical Commission at its 49th session in March 2018 (E/CN.3/2018/2, Annex II) and 50th session in March 2019 (E/CN.3/2019/2, Annex II), and the changes from the 2020 Comprehensive Review (E/CN.3/2020/2, Annex II) and annual refinements (E/CN.3/2020/2, Annex III) from the 51st session in March 2020.' <https://unstats.un.org/sdgs/indicators/indicators-list/> accessed 18 March 2021.

1315 A/RES/71/313 of 6 July 2017.

1316 <https://unstats.un.org/sdgs/indicators/database/> accessed 18 March 2021.

'[b]efore the COVID-19 outbreak, progress had been uneven, and more focused attention was needed in most areas. The pandemic abruptly disrupted implementation towards many of the SDGs and, in some cases, turned back decades of progress.' The impact of COVID-19 on the SDGs has been further analysed by some other organisations, as well as individuals. Some interesting analytical material is displayed in 'Sustainable Development Report 2020. The Sustainable Development Goals and COVID-19', prepared by individual experts.[1317] In sum, the authors of the report assessed the short-term impact of COVID-19 on certain SDGs as 'highly negative' (for example, on SDG 1 – 'No poverty'), on some others as 'mixed or moderately negative' (for example, on SDG 6 – 'Clean water and sanitation') and, in relation to certain SDGs which will be partially represented later in this book as 'impact still unclear'.

Goal 13. Climate action

Resolution 'Transforming our world: the 2030 Agenda for Sustainable Development'[1318]

SDG 13 emphasises the need to take urgent action in order to combat climate change and its impacts. To this end, it enumerates such preconditions as the strengthening of 'resilience and adaptive capacity to climate-related hazards and natural disasters in all countries'; the prompt adoption of climate change measures into national policies; and improvement in education, 'awareness-raising and human and institutional capacity on climate change mitigation, adaptation, impact reduction and early warning'.

According to the Resolution, the determined targets include raising 'jointly $100 billion annually by 2020 from all sources to address the needs of developing countries in the context of meaningful mitigation actions and transparency on implementation and fully operationalize the Green Climate Fund through its capitalization as soon as possible', and to maintain the 'mechanisms for raising capacity for effective climate change–related planning and management in least developed countries and small island developing States, including focusing on women, youth and local and marginalized communities.'

The short-term impact of COVID-19 on Goal 13

The Sustainable Development Report 2020, first summarises that the impact is 'still unclear' but, at the same time, lists the following findings:

- Short-term reduction in global GHG emissions
- Pressure to reduce environmental safeguards
- Lack of clarity on environmental investments
- Slowdown in economic growth contributing to reduction in energy prices (e.g., oil), which might increase access to energy but reduce incentives for renewables.

1317 Jeffrey D. Sachs, Guido Schmidt-Traub, Christian Kroll, Guillaume Lafortune, Grayson Fuller, Finn Woelm, *The Sustainable Development Goals and COVID-19*, Sustainable Development Report 2020 (Cambridge: Cambridge University Press 2020).
1318 A/RES/70/1 of 25 September 2015.

Goal 14. Life below water

Resolution 'Transforming our world: the 2030 Agenda for Sustainable Development'

SDG 14 aims to 'conserve and sustainably use the oceans, seas and marine resources'. According to the Resolution, the following targets were identified:

- By 2025, prevent and significantly reduce marine pollution of all kinds;
- By 2020, sustainably manage and protect marine and coastal ecosystems to avoid significant adverse impacts;
- Minimize and address the impacts of ocean acidification;
- By 2020, effectively regulate harvesting and end overfishing;
- By 2020, conserve at least 10% of coastal and marine areas;
- By 2020, prohibit certain forms of fisheries subsidies which contribute to overcapacity and overfishing; and
- By 2030, increase the economic benefits to small island developing states and least developed countries from the sustainable use of marine resources.

To meet the targets, the states were obliged to increase scientific knowledge and co-operation (including concerning the marine technology), provide access for small-scale artisanal fishers to marine resources and markets, and enhance conservation and the sustainable use of the oceans and their resources through the effective implementation of the international obligations.

The short-term impact of COVID-19 on Goal 14

The Sustainable Development Report 2020 first articulates that the impact is 'still unclear' but, at the same time, enumerates the following conclusions:

- Short-term reduction in threats to marine biodiversity due to reduced global economic activity and consumption
- Pressure to reduce marine biodiversity and ecosystem safeguards.

Goal 15. Life on land

Resolution 'Transforming our world: the 2030 Agenda for Sustainable Development'

Goal 15 was introduced to stop land degradation and conserve terrestrial ecosystems. The main targets of SDG 15 were determined as follows:

- 'By 2020, ensure the conservation, restoration and sustainable use of terrestrial and inland freshwater ecosystems and their services, in particular forests, wetlands, mountains and drylands';

- By 2020, promote the implementation of sustainable management of all types of forests;
- By 2030, combat desertification, restore degraded land and soil;
- By 2030, ensure the conservation of mountain ecosystems;
- By 2020, protect and prevent the extinction of threatened species;
- Share the benefits arising from the utilisation of genetic resources;
- End poaching and trafficking of protected species of flora and fauna;
- By 2020, introduce measures to prevent the introduction and significantly reduce the impact of invasive alien species on land and water ecosystems and control or eradicate the priority species; and
- By 2020, integrate ecosystem and biodiversity values into national development processes.

Towards these ends, states were requested, in line with their international obligations, to significantly increase financial resources in order to finance sustainable forest management and to enhance global support for efforts to combat poaching and trafficking of protected species.

The short-term impact of COVID-19 on Goal 15

The Sustainable Development Report 2020 again concludes that the impact is 'still unclear' but, at the same time, enumerates the following deductions:

- Short-term reduction in threats to terrestrial and freshwater biodiversity due to reduced global economic activity and consumption
- Pressure to reduce terrestrial and freshwater biodiversity and ecosystem safeguards, including biodiversity and ecosystem regulations conventions (for instance, on deforestation).

INTERNATIONAL ENVIRONMENTAL GOVERNANCE AND DEFINING 'POLLUTION'

pollution
Conference of the Parties
Meeting of States Parties
secretariat
Commission on the Protection of the Black Sea Against Pollution
damage
liability
compensable damage
Trail Smelter case

Introductory remarks

Before the examination of some of the substantial fields of international environmental law, the system of institutions, which were introduced to oversee the implementation of the international obligations in the environmental area, should be briefly described. The term '**pollution**', as applied in certain international treaties, must also be determined since the essential parts of the international environmental norms address the effects of (environmental) pollution.

The institutional fragmentation of international environmental governance

As is rightly summarised by the UN Secretary-General in the Report 'Gaps in international environmental law and environment-related instruments: towards a global pact for the environment', the structure of international environmental governance is characterised by institutional fragmentation and 'a heterogeneous set of actors, revealing important coherence and coordination challenges'.[1319]

Hence, unlike some other branches of international law, the international environmental area does not have a unified global institutional architecture which could serve as a platform for the majority of related activities. Instead, each multilateral international agreement usually establishes its own institutional governance structure.

The variety of the bodies of the multilateral environmental agreements

As stated in the aforementioned Report of the UN Secretary-General:

> After the Stockholm Conference, international environmental law-making saw the proliferation of multilateral environmental agreements and the emergence of treaty-based bodies. According to the Environmental Law Information Service (ECOLEX), there are currently more than 500 multilateral environmental agreements, and it has been estimated that some 200 or so treaty-based institutions were established in the two decades after the Stockholm Conference.[1320]

The treaty-monitoring bodies of the multilateral environmental agreements

The plenary bodies of multilateral environmental agreements were typically called the '**Conference of the Parties**', '**Meeting of States Parties**', or some other similar combination of words. The plenary bodies are composed of representatives from each contracting party, who periodically meet.

1319 Report of the Secretary-General of 30 November 2018.
1320 ibid.

Such treaty-monitoring bodies are commonly designated to be the primary decision-making and supreme policy-making organs for multilateral treaties and are typically empowered to review compliance with and implementation of the treaties. Towards this end, they are given the power to establish subsidiary organs, share mandatory information and materials, adopt resolutions, and sometimes even modify the provisions of the original treaty.

The administrative and support functions

In addition, a **secretariat** is usually appointed to support the work of a treaty-monitoring body. Sometimes treaties share the same secretariat. The UN Environmental Programme provides secretariat support for many of the UN multilateral environmental agreements' treaty-monitoring bodies.

On specific occasions, the other internal UN bodies may also be authorised to act as secretariats or otherwise participate in the process of reviewing compliance with and implementation of a multilateral environmental agreement – for example, the United Nations Economic Commission for Europe in relation to the 1979 Geneva Convention on Long-Range Transboundary Air Pollution.[1321]

Specific cases

Some agreements dealing with particular topics or establishing a regime in certain regions created the specific bodies for their implementation. For example, under the framework of the 1992 Bucharest Convention on the Protection of the Black Sea against Pollution, the contracting parties instituted the **Commission on the Protection of the Black Sea Against Pollution** (known as the Black Sea Commission) as an intergovernmental implementing body of the Bucharest Convention, which is composed of the Commissioners, high officials from each of the six Black Sea countries. The Commission is assisted in its activities by a Permanent Secretariat headquartered in Istanbul, Turkey.[1322] At the same time, the Meetings of the Contracting Parties were established in order to review the implementation of the Bucharest Convention and the Protocols to the Convention based on the report of the Commission.[1323]

Defining 'pollution'

Most broad definitions of pollution stipulate that **damage** should take place before **liability** is assigned.

1321 Article 11 'The Executive Secretary of the Economic Commission for Europe shall carry out, for the Executive Body, the following secretariat functions: (a) To convene and prepare the meetings of the Executive Body; (b) To transmit to the Contracting Parties reports and other information received in accordance with the provisions of the present Convention; (c) To discharge the functions assigned by the Executive Body.'

1322 Article XVII of the Convention on the Protection of the Black Sea Against Pollution. Other relevant materials are available at <www.blacksea-commission.org/> accessed 18 March 2021.

1323 Article XIX of the Convention on the Protection of the Black Sea Against Pollution.

The broad definition of the term builds on two components: (1) the introduction by a human, directly or indirectly, of substances or energy (2) causing the damage (loss or harm) to a human, property, or the environment. The term '**compensable damage**' was also introduced, commonly determined in relation to the reparation and liability and exclusively covering the damage expressed in economic terms.

International treaties define the term 'pollution' within the confines of their own scope. For instance, according to the Geneva Convention on Long-Range Transboundary Air Pollution:

> 'Air Pollution' means the introduction by man, directly or indirectly, of substances or energy into the air resulting in deleterious effects of such a nature as to endanger human health, harm living resources and ecosystems and material property and impair or interfere with amenities and other legitimate uses of the environment, and 'air pollutants' shall be construed accordingly.[1324]

Liability

The first question which stems out in this regard is whether there can be a liability for the risk of damage or if actual damage must occur for liability to be assigned. According to the conventional approach, the risk of damage is generally not recognised as triggering liability in this context.

However, some definitions in specific treaties leave room for wider interpretations, as in the case of the United Nations Convention on the Law of the Sea, which includes the following provision: The '"pollution of the marine environment" means the introduction by man, directly or indirectly, of substances or energy into the marine environment, including estuaries, which results or is likely to result in . . . deleterious effects'.[1325]

A particular question is whether there must be a scale of damage so that a liability mechanism might be triggered.

In the ***Trail Smelter*** case *(United States of America v Canada)*, the arbitral tribunal articulated the need for the 'serious consequence' in order to establish international liability. The finding of the tribunal was founded on the principles of international law of that era.[1326]

The new norms of international law which were developed after that case was considered do not use the unified formulation to determine the damage (or loss, harm). The Conventions and other instruments utilise more or less comprehensive wordings when defining the term. For example, the definition in the Geneva Convention on Long-Range Transboundary Air Pollution, outlined earlier, refers to the 'deleterious effects of such a nature as to endanger human health, harm living resources and ecosystems and material property and impair or interfere with amenities and other legitimate uses of the environment'. Other treaties use a similar approach to identify the exact moment which triggers the liability. Hence, a certain threshold of damage should be determined case by case, based on the specific definitions in the treaty concerned.

1324 Article 1 (a) of the Geneva Convention on Long-Range Transboundary Air Pollution.

1325 Paragraph 1 (4) of Article 1 of the United Nations Convention on the Law of the Sea.

1326 *Trail Smelter* case *(United States of America v Canada)*, Decision of 11 March 1941 of the Arbitral Tribunal.

THE MAIN FIELDS OF SUBSTANTIVE INTERNATIONAL ENVIRONMENTAL LAW

Preliminary remarks

Among the main fields of substantive international environmental law, the following might be outlined:

- nature conservation and protection of the terrestrial and marine environment (including fresh water, international watercourses, and combat desertification);
- climate and atmosphere (including ozone depletion and climate change); and
- hazardous substances and activities (including the nuclear sector and other hazardous substances and activities sectors).

Certainly, other substantial fields of international environmental law might also be identified, such as noise pollution, industry and industrial accidents, and so forth; however, the fields which will be examined here traditionally represent the bulk of the problems for the interstate system.

Conservation of nature and protection of the terrestrial and marine environments

conservation
sustainable
preservation
ecosystem
natural heritage
cultural heritage
wetlands
waterfowl
Conference of the Contracting Parties
General Assembly of States Parties
United Nations Educational, Scientific and Cultural Organisation
endangered species
migratory species
biological diversity
in-situ conservation
ex-situ conservation
combat desertification
tropical timber
MARPOL 73/78

Conservation

Generally, **conservation** means the management and usage of the environment in a way that is **sustainable** (i.e. the environment and its components or the resources it provides shall not be exhausted or destroyed). Consequently, among other things, conservation ensures that natural resources will be used in a manner that meets the present-day needs without endangering the availability of the resources for future generations. The second method of the protection of the environment is **preservation**, which is much stricter than conservation since preservation of the environment is aimed at banning the use by humans of certain components of the environment in order to maintain them in their pristine form. In such cases, humans can have access to the protected environment but usually only for observation and inspiration.

The object of conservation can be the entire **ecosystem** in an area – i.e. a complex of the particular physical environment and the living organisms, such as animals, plants, or micro-organisms interacting as a system – or a particular segment of the ecosystem.[1327] For the purposes of this subsection, conservation also refers to the heritage systems (**natural heritage** and **cultural heritage**) which are located in the environment.

The conservation rules of international environmental law cover the terrestrial and marine ecosystems. They are usually focused on species and habitat protection, the maintenance of regional ecosystems (for instance, the Antarctic area), protection from the pollution (for example, in relation to marine pollution), and so forth.

Development of the fields of conservation

The treaties which aimed at protecting species and their habitats can be found at the earliest stage of the development of international environmental law; however, the primary motives behind those agreements were mostly economic rather than environmental (for example, the 1902 Paris Convention for the Protection of Birds Useful to Agriculture, which introduced the principle by which birds that are useful to agriculture, especially insectivores, were to enjoy absolute protection).[1328]

Over time, numerous bilateral, regional, and multilateral agreements were concluded which targeted these fields of conservation (for example, concerning seals, bears, vicuna, whales, and turtles).

1327 As defined by Article 2 of the Convention on Biological Diversity, '"Ecosystem" means a dynamic complex of plant, animal and micro-organism communities and their non-living environment interacting as a functional unit.'

1328 'Birds useful to agriculture, particularly the insect-eaters and namely those birds enumerated in the first Schedule attached to the present Convention (which Schedule the Parliaments of the several countries may enlarge by additions) shall be unconditionally protected by a prohibition forbidding them to be killed in any way whatsoever, as well as the destruction of their nests, eggs and broods.' Article 1 of the Convention for the Protection of Birds Useful to Agriculture.

Wetlands

The 1971 Ramsar Convention on Wetlands of International Importance especially as Waterfowl Habitat was intended to protect the **wetlands**, which were defined as the

> areas of marsh, fen, peatland or water, whether natural or artificial, permanent or temporary, with water that is static or flowing, fresh, brackish or salt, including areas of marine water the depth of which at low tide does not exceed six metres.[1329]

The second aim of the Convention was **waterfowl** – the birds ecologically dependent on wetlands.

The Convention established 'a List of Wetlands of International Importance', which included the 'suitable wetlands' within the territories of states. The states have the obligation to designate at least one wetland to be included in the List. The Convention declared the duty of the parties to 'formulate and implement their planning so as to promote the conservation of the wetlands included in the List, and as far as possible, the wise use of wetlands in their territory.' Over time, particularly after the integration of the sustainable development concept into international environmental law, the term 'wise use' was interpreted to mean 'sustainable use'. The states also have the general obligation to 'promote the conservation of wetlands and waterfowl by establishing nature reserves on wetlands, whether they are included in the list or not'.[1330]

The Convention created a treaty-monitoring body which was called the Conference on the Conservation of Wetlands and Waterfowl and is currently referred to as the **Conference of the Contracting Parties** (COP), which meets every three years. The Conferences have an 'advisory character' and are empowered to discuss the implementation of the Convention; to consider the additions to and changes in the List; to make general or specific recommendations to the contracting parties regarding the conservation, management, and 'wise use' of wetlands and their flora and fauna; and so forth. In addition, the International Union for the Conservation of Nature and Natural Resources was appointed as the 'continuing bureau' to, among other things, assist in the convening and organising of Conferences and to maintain the List of Wetlands of International Importance.[1331]

World heritage

The second principal international treaty dealing with conservation is the 1972 Convention Concerning the Protection of the World Cultural and Natural Heritage (also known

---

1329 Article 1 of the Ramsar Convention on Wetlands of International Importance especially as Waterfowl Habitat.

1330 Articles 3 and 4 of the Ramsar Convention on Wetlands of International Importance especially as Waterfowl Habitat.

1331 The Secretariat fulfils the day-to-day coordination functions. It is based at the headquarters of the International Union for the Conservation of Nature (IUCN) in Gland, Switzerland.

as the World Heritage Convention), which was adopted following the 1972 Stockholm Conference under the **United Nations Educational, Scientific and Cultural Organisation** (UNESCO) auspices. The UNESCO performs a unique role in fortifying the foundations of lasting peace and sustainable development by advancing co-operation in education, science, culture, communication, and information. Moreover, its programmes are regarded as essential contributions in the achievement of Sustainable Development Goals.

The World Heritage Convention determined as 'cultural heritage' the monuments, the groups of buildings, and the sites.[1332] The Convention also defined the term 'natural heritage', which includes the

> natural features consisting of physical and biological formations or groups of such formations, which are of outstanding universal value from the aesthetic or scientific point of view; geological and physiographical formations and precisely delineated areas which constitute the habitat of threatened species of animals and plants of outstanding universal value from the point of view of science or conservation; natural sites or precisely delineated natural areas of outstanding universal value from the point of view of science, conservation or natural beauty.[1333]

According to the Convention, states recognised 'the duty of ensuring the identification, protection, conservation, presentation and transmission to future generations of the cultural and natural heritage' and the obligation 'not to take any deliberate measures which might damage directly or indirectly the cultural and natural heritage'. Consequently, the

> international protection of the world cultural and natural heritage shall be understood to mean the establishment of a system of international co-operation and assistance designed to support States Parties to the Convention in their efforts to conserve and identify that heritage.[1334]

Hence, the primary duty to protect the heritage is on the states concerned and their authorities.

Heritage should be designated by a state, which provides to the World Heritage Committee an inventory of the property. The Committee has no independent listing authority. The heritage can be added to the World Heritage List of natural and cultural sites if it satisfies the inscription criteria.

The **General Assembly of States Parties** to the World Heritage Convention unites the representatives from all of the states' parties. It convenes every two years during the sessions of the General Conference of the UNESCO. Each country has one vote. The primary function of the Assembly is to elect the 21 members of the World Heritage Committee, which was established within the UNESCO.

The Committee is responsible for the implementation of the Convention and determines the use of the World Heritage Fund. It establishes and publishes, under the title

---

1332 Article 1 of the World Heritage Convention.
1333 Article 2 of the World Heritage Convention.
1334 Articles 4, 6 and 7 of the World Heritage Convention.

of the 'World Heritage List', a list of properties forming part of the cultural heritage and natural heritage.[1335] It also maintains, under the title of 'List of World Heritage in Danger', 'a list of the property appearing in the World Heritage List for the conservation of which major operations are necessary and for which assistance has been requested'.[1336] The World Heritage Committee submits reports on its activities at each of the ordinary sessions of the General Conference of the UNESCO.[1337] It is assisted by the Secretariat appointed by the Director-General of the UNESCO (from 1992 called the World Heritage Centre).

Finally, the Committee has limited but effective mechanisms in its hands, such as the deletion of a property from the List. On particular occasions, when a property is under 'serious and specific dangers', it can be placed on the List of World Heritage in Danger. However, when 'the Outstanding Universal Value of the property which justified its inscription on the World Heritage List is lost, the Committee considers deleting the property from the World Heritage List.'[1338]

Endangered species

The 1973 Convention on International Trade in **Endangered Species** of Wild Fauna and Flora (also known as the CITES) was concluded to regulate the trade – the 'export, re-export, import and introduction from the sea' – of some species through the licensing and/or permission systems existing at the national level. For the purposes of the Convention, the term species includes any species, subspecies, or geographically separate population thereof.[1339]

The scope of the regulation depends on the quality of the threat. The species are divided into three groups and listed in the Appendices to the Convention according to the degree of protection they need. Consequently, Appendix I includes all species facing the threat of extinction, which are or may be affected by trade and, therefore, are under 'strict regulation' by utilising export, re-export, import, and introduction from the sea permits. Appendix II covers such species 'which although not necessarily now threatened with extinction may become so' if trade is not regulated.[1340] The Convention applies a

1335 As of 18 March 2021, there were 1,121 properties on the World Heritage List, including 869 cultural, 213 natural, and 39 mixed properties. The list is available at <https://whc.unesco.org/en/list/stat> accessed 18 March 2021.

1336 Article 11 (4) of the World Heritage Convention.

1337 Article 29 (3) of the World Heritage Convention.

1338 Paragraph 9 of the Operational Guidelines for the Implementation of the World Heritage Convention, available at <https://whc.unesco.org/en/guidelines/> accessed 18 March 2021.

1339 'Over 38,700 species – including roughly 5,950 species of animals and 32,800 species of plants – are protected by CITES against over-exploitation through international trade. They are listed in the three CITES Appendices. The species are grouped in the Appendices according to how threatened they are by international trade. They include some whole groups, such as primates, cetaceans (whales, dolphins and porpoises), sea turtles, parrots, corals, cacti and orchids. But in some cases only a subspecies or geographically separate population of a species (for example the population of just one country) is listed.' 'The CITES Species' <www.cites.org/eng/disc/species.php> accessed 18 March 2021.

1340 Article II (2) of the Convention on International Trade in Endangered Species of Wild Fauna and Flora.

more relaxed set of regulations to such species.[1341] Appendix III refers to species which are protected in at least one country. In such cases, there is some variation in the requirements from a country to another; however, usually, export permits are required, and limited regulations are established concerning import and re-export.[1342]

The CITES introduced a general framework, but the primary instruments and mechanisms were implemented by the parties to the Convention at the national level. Specifically, each party designated one or more Management Authorities in charge of administering the licensing, permission, and certification system and Scientific Authorities to advise on the effects of trade on endangered species.

The Convention instituted the ordinary system of international governance in the field of the endangered species. The supreme decision-making body of the Convention is the Conference of the Parties (COP), consisting of all parties (the states and regional economic integration organisations, such as the EU) and holding the regular meetings at least once every two to three years. Each state has one vote, and the regional economic integration organisation has a number of votes equal to the number of their member states that are parties to the Convention, provided that such an organisation 'shall not exercise their right to vote if their Member States exercise theirs, and vice versa.' Such a rule usually applies to COPs comprising the economic integration organisations.

The COP is empowered to review the implementation of the Convention, consider and adopt amendments to Appendices I and II, receive the reports presented by the CITES Secretariat, and make recommendations for improving the effectiveness of the Convention. Upon entry into force of the Convention, the CITES Secretariat is administered by the United Nations Environment Programme and it is located in Geneva, Switzerland. Among other important functions performed by the Secretariat, it periodically publishes updated editions of Appendices I, II, and III.

The Conference of the Parties determined the so-called 'biological and trade criteria' to assist in the identification of species that should be included in Appendices I or II. Normally, states submit proposals based on those criteria, and the COP decides by a two-thirds majority of parties present and voting. In exceptional cases, it is also allowed to amend Appendices I and II by a 'postal procedure' between meetings of the COP. For this procedure, the communications between the parties should be organised by the Secretariat, but in practice, the postal procedure is rarely used.

Migratory species

The 1979 Convention on the Conservation of **Migratory Species** of Wild Animals (Bonn Convention) determined 'migratory species' to mean 'the entire population or any geographically separate part of the population of any species or lower taxon of wild animals,

---

1341 For example, as relates to import, 'the prior presentation of either an export permit or a re-export certificate' may be required, and usually, no import permit is needed.

1342 '3. The import of any specimen of a species included in Appendix III shall require, except in circumstances to which paragraph 4 of this Article applies, the prior presentation of a certificate of origin and, where the import is from a State which has included that species in Appendix III, an export permit.' Article V of the Convention on International Trade in Endangered Species of Wild Fauna and Flora.

a significant proportion of whose members cyclically and predictably cross one or more national jurisdictional boundaries'.[1343]

The Convention introduced two Appendices: Appendix I lists the migratory species which are endangered, and Appendix II encompasses the migratory species

> which have an unfavourable conservation status and which require international agreements for their conservation and management, as well as those which have a conservation status which would significantly benefit from the international co-operation that could be achieved by an international agreement.

The states should provide immediate protection for migratory species included in Appendix I and 'shall endeavour to conclude AGREEMENTS covering the conservation and management of migratory species included in Appendix II.'[1344]

As in the case of the Convention concerning Endangered Species, the Bonn Convention also established a Conference of the Parties (COP) as its decision-making organ, which usually meets once every three years and decides on the amendment of the Appendices, and the Secretariat, which is provided and administered by the United Nations Environment Programme and is located in Bonn, Germany. In addition, there is the Standing Committee, which is responsible for carrying out interim activities on behalf of the COP, and the Scientific Council, which makes the recommendations to the COP on such issues as conducting a research on migratory species, specific conservation and management measures, the inclusion of migratory species in the Appendices, and so forth.

Biological diversity

However, before the 1992 Rio Conference, international agreements usually addressed conservation issues in a piecemeal manner, perhaps with the exception of the World Heritage Convention and the treaties dealing with specific regional ecosystems. Only after the adoption of the 1992 United Nations Convention on **Biological Diversity** (CBD) was the holistic approach applied to the interaction of species, habitat, and ecosystems. The Convention acknowledged the cardinal importance of biodiversity and designated the conservation of biodiversity as a 'common concern of humankind'; however, it also took into account that the states have intrinsic sovereign rights over their own biological resources.

On the whole, the Convention has three central objectives: '[T]he conservation of biological diversity, the sustainable use of its components and the fair and equitable sharing of the benefits arising out of the utilization of genetic resources.'

It defines biological diversity broadly, including 'the variability among living organisms from all sources including, inter alia, terrestrial, marine and other aquatic ecosystems and the ecological complexes of which they are part; this includes diversity within species, between species and of ecosystems.'[1345] Under the auspice of the Convention, there were seven thematic programmes of work developed: Agricultural Biodiversity, Dry and

---

1343 Article I (1) (a) of the Convention on the Conservation of Migratory Species of Wild Animals.

1344 Articles IV (1) and II (3) of the Convention on the Conservation of Migratory Species of Wild Animals.

1345 Articles 1 and 2 of the United Nations Convention on Biological Diversity.

Sub-humid Land Biodiversity, Forest Biodiversity, Inland Waters Biodiversity, Island Biodiversity, Marine and Coastal Biodiversity, and Mountain Biodiversity.

The Convention also defined two types of conservation – **in-situ conservation** and **ex-situ conservation**. In-situ conservation is defined as 'the conservation of ecosystems and natural habitats and the maintenance and recovery of viable populations of species in their natural surroundings and, in the case of domesticated or cultivated species, in the surroundings where they have developed their distinctive properties.' Ex-situ conservation 'means the conservation of components of biological diversity outside their natural habitats.'[1346] The Convention formulated the obligations of the parties concerning both forms of the conservation, which the parties shall fulfil 'as far as possible and as appropriate.' For example, concerning in-situ conservation, they should '[d]evelop, where necessary, guidelines for the selection, establishment and management of protected areas or areas where special measures need to be taken to conserve biological diversity' and '[r]egulate or manage biological resources important for the conservation of biological diversity whether within or outside protected areas, with a view to ensuring their conservation and sustainable use'. The parties should apply ex-situ conservation 'predominantly for the purpose of complementing in-situ measures'. In such cases, they must adopt measures for the conservation of the components of biological diversity, preferably in the country of origin of such components; establish and maintain 'facilities for ex-situ conservation of and research on plants, animals and micro-organisms, preferably in the country of origin of genetic resources';[1347] and so on.

The Conference of the Parties is the governing body of the Convention, comprising all the member parties (the states and the regional economic integration organisations),[1348] which currently meets once every two years to oversee the implementation of the Convention. The CBD Secretariat, based in Montreal, Canada, operates under the United Nations Environment Programme. The Convention also established the Subsidiary Body for Scientific, Technical and Technological Advice; the Subsidiary Body on Implementation; and certain Working Groups to assist the COP in fulfilling its functions.

According to the Convention on Biological Diversity, the Conference of the Parties has the competence to adopt the protocols to the Convention. As a result, two protocols were developed: the 2000 Cartagena Protocol on Biosafety to the Convention on Biological Diversity (with the 2010 Nagoya-Kuala Lumpur Supplementary Protocol on Liability and Redress to the Cartagena Protocol on Biosafety), which governs the movements from one country to another of living modified organisms resulting from modern biotechnology, and the 2010 Nagoya Protocol on Access to Genetic Resources and the Fair and Equitable Sharing of Benefits Arising from their Utilization to the Convention on Biological Diversity, which addressed the third cardinal goal of the CBD and established an unambiguous legal framework for the implementation of the fair and equitable sharing of benefits arising out of the utilisation of genetic resources.

1346 Article 2 of the United Nations Convention on Biological Diversity.

1347 Articles 8 and 9 of the United Nations Convention on Biological Diversity

1348 In the status of the regional economic integration organisation, the party of the Convention is the European Union <www.cbd.int/information/parties.shtml> accessed 18 March 2021.

Currently, the adoption of the Post-2020 Biodiversity Framework is scheduled 'as a stepping stone towards the 2050 Vision of "Living in harmony with nature".'[1349]

Tropical timber

Sustainable forest management was a long-standing challenge before the interstate system. Many countries have constantly opposed the development of mandatory international standards in the field. Hence, the conclusion of an international legal agreement encompassing all problems in relation to the forest eventually was rescheduled. Nevertheless, some subjects of international law were able to adopt the International **Tropical Timber** Agreement in 1983 and its renewed versions in 1994 and 2006, but only with a limited scope – concerning tropical timber[1350] – and largely facilitating trade and not forest biodiversity *per se*. Consequently, this treaty can be regarded primarily as an international commodity agreement. Nevertheless, the International Tropical Timber Agreement and international intergovernmental organisation which operates under this Agreement, called the International Tropical Timber Organisation (ITTO), have contributed significantly to conservation, as well as to the promotion of the biodiversity of tropical forests.

During its existence, the International Tropical Timber Organisation has developed policy guidelines and norms to facilitate sustainable forest management and sustainable tropical timber industries and trade and generally assisted in developing the capacity of tropical forestry. ITTO members are the producing and consuming countries, which represent a substantial part of the global tropical timber trade and world's tropical forests.[1351]

The ITTO's governing body is the International Tropical Timber Council, comprising all members. It is assisted by the committees, which usually meet during the sessions of the Council. The decisions of the International Tropical Timber Council are made through a special voting procedure during which the producer members together hold 1,000 votes, and the consumer members together hold 1,000 votes. These votes are distributed between the members according to the International Tropical Timber Agreement.[1352] The Organisation has its own Executive Director and staff appointed by the Director and is located in Yokohama, Japan.

1349 Updates on the implementation of the process for developing the post-2020 global biodiversity framework are available at <www.cbd.int/conferences/post2020> accessed 18 March 2021.

1350 According to Article 2 (1) of the 2006 International Tropical Timber Agreement: '"Tropical timber" means tropical wood for industrial uses, which grows or is produced in the countries situated between the Tropic of Cancer and the Tropic of Capricorn. The term covers logs, sawn wood, veneer sheets and plywood'.

1351 As articulated on the official website of the Organisation, 'ITTO's membership represents about 90% of the global tropical timber trade and more than 80% of the world's tropical forests.' <www.itto.int/about_itto/> accessed 18 March 2021.

1352 Article 10 of the 2006 International Tropical Timber Agreement.

Desertification

The United Nations Convention to Combat **Desertification** in those Countries Experiencing Serious Drought and/or Desertification, Particularly in Africa (UNCCD) was adopted in 1994, following the Rio Conference. It applied a broad definition of the term 'desertification', which, according to the Convention, 'means land degradation in arid, semi-arid and dry sub-humid areas resulting from various factors, including climatic variations and human activities'. On the other hand, under the Convention, 'combating desertification' aims at the prevention and/or reduction of land degradation, rehabilitation of partly degraded land, and reclamation of decertified land.[1353]

To combat desertification and 'mitigate the effects of drought', the Convention requests from the parties the maintenance of 'a spirit of partnership' at all levels of government, local communities, non-governmental organisations, and landholders. The parties to the Convention are obliged to 'adopt an integrated approach addressing the physical, biological and socio-economic aspects of the processes of desertification and drought'. The call for an integrated approach in practice further included close interconnection and co-operation with other two 'Rio Conventions' – the Convention on Biological Diversity and the United Nations Framework Convention on Climate Change.

From the beginning, the UNCCD articulated the need for assistance (including financial assistance) to the developing countries and that the priority should be given to affected African countries 'in the light of the particular situation prevailing in that region'.[1354]

The Convention established a typical institutional framework to monitor the implementation process and fulfil the objectives outlined by the Convention. The Conference of the Parties was created as the supreme decision-making body, comprising the ratifying governments and regional economic integration organisations (the EU). The Bureau of the COP (the President and Vice-Presidents) organises the sessions. It is involved in the follow-up of the COP and the preparation of the next Conference and is elected at the beginning of the first meeting of each ordinary session.

The COP has the authority to amend the Convention and adopt new annexes, such as the regional implementation annexes.

The Permanent Secretariat was instituted in order to assist the COP and its subsidiary bodies. It is currently located in Bonn, Germany. The Secretariat is headed by the Executive Secretary, who is appointed by the United Nations Secretary-General as Under-Secretary-General and Executive Secretary of the UNCCD. Specific bodies, such as the Committee on Science and Technology and the Committee for the Review of the Implementation of the Convention, were created to assist the COP.

The parties to the Convention have developed the new UNCCD 2018–2030 Strategic Framework, which was elaborated under the auspice of the Convention and targets 'future that avoids, minimizes, and reverses desertification/land degradation and mitigates the effects of drought in affected areas at all levels'.[1355]

1353 Article 1 of the United Nations Convention to Combat Desertification in those Countries Experiencing Serious Drought and/or Desertification, Particularly in Africa.

1354 Articles 6 and 7 of the United Nations Convention to Combat Desertification in those Countries Experiencing Serious Drought and/or Desertification, Particularly in Africa.

1355 'About the Convention' <www.unccd.int/convention/about-convention> accessed 18 March 2021.

Protection of the marine environment

The 1982 United Nations Convention on the Law of the Sea is a central legal instrument codifying almost all necessary matters concerning the seas. Of course, it could not ignore one of the traditional concerns of the interstate system – the protection of the marine environment. Accordingly, in the Part titled 'Protection and Preservation of the Marine Environment', the Convention provided the general framework for the states' activities in that regard.

First of all, the Convention reflected the main principles of the field. It prescribed the central duty of the states to protect and preserve the marine environment, their 'sovereign right to exploit their natural resources pursuant to their environmental policies and in accordance with their duty to protect and preserve the marine environment', 'no-harm' obligation ('not to cause damage by pollution to other States and their environment') and 'polluter-pays principle.'[1356]

Secondly, the Convention covered all sources of pollution, such as the release of toxic, harmful, or noxious substances from land-based sources, from or through the atmosphere, or by dumping, and pollution from vessels, installations, and devices.

Thirdly, the Convention reaffirmed the obligations of the states to 'cooperate directly or through competent international organizations' to protect the marine environment, to notify all probably affected parties of even an imminent danger of being damaged by pollution, to advance scientific collaboration to protect the environment, to provide technical assistance to developing states, and so on.

Fourthly, the states were obliged to engage in the monitoring process; to observe, measure, evaluate, and analyse the risks and effects of pollution of the marine environment; to publish reports on that matter; to adopt laws and regulations to prevent, reduce, and control pollution of the marine environment; and so forth.

Lastly, the Convention enhanced the enforcement power of the coastal states with regard to pollution in order to protect the marine environment, including empowering the coastal states to 'establish particular requirements for the prevention, reduction and control of pollution of the marine environment as a condition for the entry of foreign vessels into their ports or internal waters' as well as in the territorial sea (however, without hampering the innocent passage of foreign vessels) and in their exclusive economic zones (provided that such rules are transparent and non-discriminatory in nature).

A particular case is the conservation and protection of marine living resources. Over time, the states concluded various bilateral and multilateral treaties for that reason.

Early agreements were mostly focused on the economic aspects of fisheries. Gradually, environmental protection bias was integrated into such treaties. On the whole, most fisheries treaties established a fixed quota (i.e. a total allowable catch), limited fishing methods, and introduced monitoring and reporting systems.

Some international regulations aimed at conservation of particular species, such as albatrosses and petrels (the 2001 Agreement on the Conservation of Albatrosses and Petrels) and cetaceans (the 1996 Agreement on the Conservation of Cetaceans of the Black Sea, Mediterranean Sea and contiguous Atlantic Area; the 1992 Agreement on the

---

1356 Articles 192, 193, 194, and 235 of the United Nations Convention on the Law of the Sea.

Conservation of Small Cetaceans of the Baltic, North East Atlantic, Irish and North Seas) and the conservation treaties of the Antarctic Treaty System.

In 2009, the Food and Agriculture Organisation (FAO) Conference approved the Agreement on Port State Measures to Prevent, Deter and Eliminate Illegal, Unreported and Unregulated Fishing, which is the binding international treaty specifically designed 'to prevent, deter and eliminate . . . [illegal, unreported, and unregulated fishing] through the implementation of effective port State measures, and thereby to ensure the long-term conservation and sustainable use of living marine resources and marine ecosystems' (Article 2). The Agreement applies to fishing vessels seeking entry into a port other than those of their own state.

Marine pollution

Before and after the adoption of the United Nations Convention on the Law of the Sea, certain international agreements were concluded at the global and regional levels dealing with such problems as dumping (for example, the 1972 London Convention on the Prevention of Marine Pollution by Dumping of Wastes and Other Matter) and marine pollution (for instance, the **MARPOL 73/78**).

Currently, concerning dumping, the 'prohibited unless permitted' approach is recognised. Particular attention should be paid to the MARPOL 73/78 regime, since it not only largely influenced developments with regard to its primary objective (pollution from ships) but also contributed to the crystallisation of many international approaches to marine regulation, as well as more general issues of international law (for example, as mentioned earlier, in relation to extraterritorial jurisdiction).

The International Convention for the Prevention of Pollution from Ships (MARPOL) is the main international treaty on the prevention of pollution of the oceans and seas by ships from operational or accidental causes. It was initially adopted in 1973, under the auspices of the International Maritime Organisation. The 1973 MARPOL Convention did not come into force until 1978, when the states concluded the 1978 MARPOL Protocol; the combined instrument entered into force in 1983. Over time, the MARPOL has been amended – for example, by the Protocol of 1997, which updated the provisions of the Convention and supplemented a new Annex VI.[1357]

MARPOL is divided into the following Annexes according to various categories of pollutants: the Regulations for the Prevention of Pollution by Oil (I), the Control of Pollution by Noxious Liquid Substances in Bulk (II), the Prevention of Pollution by Harmful Substances Carried by Sea in Packaged Form (III), the Prevention of Pollution by Sewage from Ships (IV), the Prevention of Pollution by Garbage from Ships (V), and the Prevention of Air Pollution from Ships (VI).

A principal regulative mechanism introduced by the MARPOL regime is the standardised International Oil Pollution Prevention Certificates (for 'any oil tanker of 150 gross tonnage and above and any other ship of 400 gross tonnage and above which is engaged in voyages to ports or offshore terminals'),[1358] the issuance of which is linked with the regular

---

1357 See the official website of the IMO <http://bit.ly/34xI6wO> accessed 18 March 2021.
1358 Regulation 5 of Annex I of MARPOL 73/78.

surveying and inspection of vessels by the officers appointed or authorised by the party concerned. Such Certificates should be accepted by the other parties to the Convention. In addition, tankers and other ships are required to carry an Oil Record Book detailing all operations involving oil. Any 'inspection is limited to verifying that there is on board a valid certificate, unless there are clear grounds for believing that the condition of the ship or its equipment does not correspond substantially with the particulars of that certificate.'[1359]

Fresh water

The 1992 Convention on the Protection and Use of Transboundary Watercourses and International Lakes (commonly referred to as the UNECE Water Convention) is one of the agreements which was adopted with the significant efforts and sponsorship of the United Nations Economic Commission for Europe. The parties to the Convention were the countries under the UNECE framework and the EU. However, in 2016 the 'Water Convention's global opening' was launched, which led to the accession to the Convention of other countries located outside the region. The Protocol on Water and Health (in co-operation with the WHO/Europe), which addressed the problems of water-related diseases, was also concluded.

According to the Convention, the term 'transboundary waters' refers to 'any surface or ground waters which mark, cross or are located on boundaries between two or more States', and 'transboundary impact' means 'any significant adverse effect on the environment resulting from a change in the conditions of transboundary waters caused by a human activity',[1360] which originated wholly or in part within an area under the jurisdiction of one party and influenced an area under the jurisdiction of another party.

The parties to the Convention were obliged: (1) to 'prevent, control and reduce pollution of waters causing or likely to cause transboundary impact;' (2) to 'ensure that transboundary waters are used with the aim of ecologically sound and rational water management, conservation of water resources and environmental protection' and to conserve and, where necessary, restore the ecosystems; and (3) to use transboundary waters 'in a reasonable and equitable way'. To implement their obligations, the parties were required to operate based on such principles as the precautionary principle, the 'polluter-pays' principle, and the utilisation of water recourses 'without compromising the ability of future generations to meet their own needs'.[1361]

As regards the institutional framework, the following organs were established: Meeting of the Parties – a main governing body comprising all parties; its Bureau (the Chairperson, Vice-Chairpersons, and other officers). which organises the Meeting; the Subsidiary Bodies to the Meeting of the Parties, such as the Working Group on Integrated Water Resources Management, the Working Group on Monitoring and Assessment, and other

---

1359 Article 5 (2) of the International Convention for the Prevention of Pollution from Ships.

1360 Article 1 of the Convention on the Protection and Use of Transboundary Watercourses and International Lakes.

1361 Article 2 of the Convention on the Protection and Use of Transboundary Watercourses and International Lakes.

bodies dealing with particular subject matters; and the Executive Secretary of the Economic Commission for Europe, carrying out the secretariat functions.[1362]

Climate and atmosphere

transboundary air pollution
ozone depletion
global warming
UNECE
Ozone Secretariat
non-compliance procedure

The principal concerns

In the twentieth century, three principal environmental concerns regarding climate and the atmosphere emerged – **transboundary air pollution, ozone depletion**, and **global warming**.

Although some doubt the very existence and extent of the problem, the awareness of humankind has gradually increased about these threats; thus, the interstate system reacted accordingly with the elaboration and adoption of the relevant international norms.

Transboundary air pollution

The 1979 Convention on Long-range Transboundary Air Pollution attempted to regulate transboundary air pollution in the **UNECE** (United Nations Economic Commission for Europe) region by utilising advanced scientific co-operation and focused negotiations in the policy-making field. Over time, eight protocols to the framework Convention were developed, addressing the need to cut the emissions of air pollutants and substantially enlarging the extent of the parties' commitment. Among them, a more recent document is the 1999 Protocol to Abate Acidification, Eutrophication and Ground-level Ozone.

The framework Convention by itself prescribes the obligation of states parties: To 'endeavour to limit and, as far as possible, gradually reduce and prevent air pollution including long-range transboundary air pollution'; to develop scientific collaboration and relevant policies and strategies; for the purposes of the Convention, to exchange information, including data on emissions; and, if it is necessary, to hold consultations at an early stage in case of a significant risk of long-range transboundary air pollution.[1363]

The parties to the Convention are the states of the UNECE region and the regional economic integration organisations (the EU).

1362 Article 19 of the Convention on the Protection and Use of Transboundary Watercourses and International Lakes.
1363 Articles 2–5 of the Convention on Long-range Transboundary Air Pollution.

Under the Convention, the Executive Body was established to assist in reviewing ongoing work and to plan for future activities in the field of transboundary air pollution. The Executive Body is composed of the representatives of the parties 'within the framework of the Senior Advisors to UNECE Governments on Environmental Problems' and meets at least annually in that capacity. Subsidiary bodies were also created, such as the Working Group on Effects, the Steering Body to EMEP (the European Monitoring and Evaluation Programme),[1364] and the Working Group on Strategies and Review, the Convention's Implementation Committee, which are accountable to the Executive Body. The Convention designated the Executive Secretary of UNECE to carry out secretariat functions, including convening and preparing for the meetings of the Executive Body.

On the whole, the Convention itself did not introduce a specific mechanism on liability if a country did not comply with its commitments. Therefore, 'the implementation mechanism is more supportive and persuasive in character', among other things, involving in the process the Convention's Implementation Committee, which is responsible for monitoring compliance with the various obligations of the parties.[1365] Nevertheless, the Convention and its implementation are commonly regarded as successful since, as summarised on the official website of the UNECE, the 'result of this collective effort has been remarkable: emissions of a series of harmful substances have been reduced by 40 to 80% since 1990 in Europe.'[1366]

Ozone depletion

The 1985 Vienna Convention for the Protection of the Ozone Layer was intended as the framework treaty to address ozone depletion and to minimalize the negative impact of certain human-made, ozone-depleting substances on the atmosphere[1367] since these chemicals were considered to be a major cause of ozone depletion.[1368] The ozone layer is an invisible shield which protects life on earth from harmful ultraviolet radiation from the sun.

1364 EMEP is a co-operative programme for monitoring and evaluating the long-range transmission of air pollutants in Europe by its Centers and Task Forces.

1365 'Some countries have not been able to comply with all commitments; some have problems with the reporting obligations, other have encountered problems in achieving the emission reductions they had signed up to.' *Clearing the Air: 25 Years of the Convention on Long-Range Transboundary Air Pollution*, Johan Sliggers and Willem Kakebeeke (eds) (UNECE 2004) 5.

1366 'The Convention and Its Achievements' <https://bit.ly/3aMeFaB> accessed 18 March 2021.

1367 In real life, a significant portion of such chemicals is made up of 'freon'. 'Freon [is] the proprietary name for any of a group of fluorocarbon or chlorofluorocarbon compounds that are clear, colourless liquids, chemically inert, and of low toxicity. They are useful as refrigerants, aerosol propellants, cleaning fluids, and solvents. These substances have been shown to be important in the chemical removal of ozone by chlorine-catalysed cycles in the polar region during winter and spring.' *Oxford Dictionary of Biochemistry and Molecular Biology*, R. Cammack (Managing ed) (2nd revised edn, Oxford University Press 2006) 256.

1368 As noted on the official website of the UNEP: 'In the mid-1970s, scientists realised that the ozone layer was threatened by the accumulation of gases containing halogens (chlorine and bromine) in the atmosphere. Then, in the mid-1980s, scientists discovered a "hole" in the ozone layer above Antarctica – the region of Earth's atmosphere with severe depletion.' <https://ozone.unep.org/ozone-and-you> accessed 18 March 2021.

The Vienna Convention defined the 'ozone layer' as the layer of atmospheric ozone above the planetary boundary layer and prescribed the general obligation of the parties to the Convention to take appropriate measures 'to protect human health and the environment against adverse effects resulting or likely to result from human activities which modify or are likely to modify the ozone layer.'[1369] According to the Convention, to implement the general obligation, the parties should co-operate through systematic observations, research, and information exchange, as well as adopting appropriate legislative or administrative measures and harmonising such measures.

The Vienna Convention is one of the most universally recognised treaties, since its parties are all UN member states, the EU, and some other subjects of international law (such as the Holy See).

The Vienna Convention established the typical institutional structure to implement its provisions. First of all, it constituted the Conference of the Parties, which meets once every three years, as well as the Bureau to assist the Conference in organisational matters. Secondly, the secretariat functions were assigned to the United Nations Environment Programme. Currently, the **Ozone Secretariat** of the UNEP provides administrative functions in relation to the Convention. One of the main outcomes of the Vienna Convention was the institution of the scientific forum of governmental atmospheric experts called the Meeting of Ozone Research Managers to overview ozone depletion and the state of affairs concerning the climate change and produce reports for the Conference of Parties.

However, the Vienna Convention did not include detailed provisions on the elimination or reduction of particular ozone-depleting substances; it only provided a platform of development of the field. As a result, this framework nourished the 1987 Montreal Protocol on Substances that Deplete the Ozone Layer, which is commonly regarded as a landmark agreement, resulting in the substantial phase-down of the particular chemicals depleting the ozone layer.[1370] It was adjusted and amended several times in order to effectively phase out both the production and consumption of ozone-depleting substances.[1371]

The Montreal Protocol established the Meeting of the Parties as its governing body, which meets every year to take decisions on all matters related to the Protocol. At the same time, the Ozone Secretariat (UNEP) provides administrative support to the Protocol.

Non-compliance

The Montreal Protocol introduced a new procedure for its implementation, which is called the '**non-compliance procedure**'. This procedure was effectively applied in the field of air pollution and was also used by the Kyoto Protocol, which will be examined later.

1369 Article 2 of the Vienna Convention for the Protection of the Ozone Layer.

1370 Article 2A: CFCs; Article 2B: Halons; Article 2C: Other fully halogenated CFCs; Article 2D: Carbon tetrachloride; Article 2E: 1,1,1-trichloroethane (methyl chloroform); etc.

1371 'The most recent amendment, the Kigali Amendment, called for the phase-down of hydrofluorocarbons (HFCs) in 2016. These HFCs were used as replacements for a batch of ozone-depleting substances eliminated by the original Montreal Protocol.' 'The Montreal Protocol on Substances that Deplete the Ozone Layer' <https://ozone.unep.org/treaties/montreal-protocol?q=treaties/montreal-protocol> accessed 18 March 2021.

The non-compliance procedure is based on the carrot-and-stick approach since it involves both incentives (for example, the benefits of the Multilateral Fund), as well as sanctions (for example, issuing cautions), and mostly, it is oriented on so-called 'soft enforcement.'

To embody the non-compliance procedure, the Meeting of the Parties approved appropriate Decisions.[1372] The triggering mechanisms for the non-compliance procedure may be a written submission of a party to the Ozone Secretariat or the Secretariat itself when 'during the course of preparing its report, becomes aware of possible non-compliance by any Party with its obligations under the Protocol'. The procedure involves the Implementation Committee elected by the Meeting of the Parties, which is empowered to 'identify the facts and possible causes relating to individual cases of non-compliance referred to the Committee, as best it can, and make appropriate recommendations to the Meeting of the Parties.' The Meeting of the Parties may issue an interim call and/or recommendation.[1373] In sum, the following measures might be taken by the Meeting of the Parties regarding non-compliance with the Protocol:

> A. Appropriate assistance, including assistance for the collection and reporting of data, technical assistance, technology transfer and financial assistance, information transfer and training. B. Issuing cautions. C. Suspension, in accordance with the applicable rules of international law concerning the suspension of the operation of a treaty, of specific rights and privileges under the Protocol, whether or not subject to time limits, including those concerned with industrial rationalization, production, consumption, trade, transfer of technology, financial mechanism and institutional arrangements.[1374]

Climate change

The third 'Rio Convention' – the 1992 United Nations Framework Convention on Climate Change (UNFCCC) is a landmark treaty which aimed to stabilize 'greenhouse gas concentrations in the atmosphere at a level that would prevent dangerous anthropogenic interference with the climate system.' It prescribed that 'such a level should be achieved within a time-frame sufficient to allow ecosystems to adapt naturally to climate change, to ensure that food production is not threatened, and to enable economic development to proceed in a sustainable manner.' At the same time, the Convention defined the greenhouse gases as 'those gaseous constituents of the atmosphere, both natural and anthropogenic, that absorb and re-emit infrared radiation.'[1375]

The members of the Convention include all the UN member states and other subjects of international law (for example, in the status of the regional economic integration

---

1372 Decision I/8, Decision II/5, Decision III/2, and so forth. Ozone Secretariat, UNEP *Handbook for the Montreal Protocol on Substances That Deplete the Ozone Layer* (14th edn, Ozone Secretariat, UNEP 2020) 430–436.

1373 ibid 798–800.

1374 ibid 800.

1375 Articles 1 and 2 of the United Nations Framework Convention on Climate Change.

organisation, the party is the EU). The Convention is based on the principles of international environmental law, such as the protection of the climate system for the benefit of present and future generations of humankind, the principles of equity and common but differentiated responsibility, the precautionary principle, the principle of co-operation, and so forth. At the same time, the Convention paid special attention to the need to support the developing countries for actions on climate change, including financially. On the other hand, it enumerated a detailed list of the general 'Commitments': for example, the commitment to

> [d]evelop, periodically update, publish and make available to the Conference of the Parties . . . national inventories of anthropogenic emissions by sources and removals by sinks of all greenhouse gases not controlled by the Montreal Protocol, using comparable methodologies to be agreed upon by the Conference of the Parties.[1376]

However, there were particular commitments determined which were exclusively reserved for the developed countries due to their expected leading role in advancing the longer-term trend to reverse the effects of the climate change and the fact that the developed countries were the major source of the greenhouse gas emissions.

The Convention established the Conference of the Parties 'as the supreme body of this Convention', with the authority to periodically examine the obligations of the parties and the institutional arrangements under the Convention and, generally, to monitor the implementation process, making the appropriate recommendations on any issue necessary for the implementation of the Convention. The UNFCCC secretariat is the United Nations entity located in Bonn, Germany.

On the whole, the Convention itself arranged no binding limits on greenhouse gas emissions for the states. Instead, it provided a framework agreement for negotiating particular international treaties, which may set binding limits on greenhouse gases. As a result, it is a parent treaty of the 1997 Kyoto Protocol and the 2015 Paris Agreement.

The Kyoto Protocol was the first agreement with legally binding obligations for limits and reductions concerning climate change.[1377] The period of applicability was set for the years 2008 to 2012 ('first quantified emission limitation and reduction commitment period') and 2013 to 2020, the binding targets of which stipulated debates between the states. Moreover, some signing countries either have not ratified the Kyoto Protocol (USA), have withdrawn from the Protocol (Canada), or have chosen not to taken on the new targets determined for the second commitment period (Japan, Russia).

On the other hand, the 2015 Paris Agreement received a more universal acknowledgement despite the inconsistent position of certain states.[1378] The central aim of the Paris

---

1376 Article 4 (1) (a) of the United Nations Framework Convention on Climate Change.

1377 The Kyoto Protocol applies to the following greenhouse gases: Carbon dioxide (CO_2), methane (CH_4), nitrous oxide (N_2O), hydrofluorocarbons (HFCs), perfluorocarbons (PFCs), and sulphur hexafluoride (SF_6). Annex A to the Protocol.

1378 First, on 4 November 2019, the government of the United States of America notified the UN Secretary-General of its decision to withdraw from the Agreement, which took effect on 4 November 2020. However, the new President of the United States of America, Joseph R. Biden Jr., reaccepted

Agreement was to hold 'the increase in the global average temperature to well below 2°C above pre-industrial levels' and to pursue 'efforts to limit the temperature increase to 1.5°C above pre-industrial levels'.[1379] Under the Agreement, each party must define, plan, and regularly report on the contribution that it undertakes to mitigate global warming.

Hazardous substances and activities

> hazardous substances
> hazardous activities
> waste
> environmentally sound management
> Draft Articles on Prevention of Transboundary Harm from Hazardous Activities
> ultrahazardous activity
> absolute liability
> Prior Informed Consent procedure
> non-compliance procedure

A typical piecemeal approach

As in the other areas of environmental protection, with regard to **hazardous substances** and **hazardous activities**, as well as **waste**, there is currently no single institutional structure which would generally oversee the production and movement of such substances or control the hazardous or dangerous activities carried out by the states and other actors of the interstate system.

The subjects of international law, on the one hand, adopted only the broad policy guidelines concerning hazardous substances and activities, and, on the other hand, attempted to deal with the matter in a piecemeal manner by concluding specific agreements in distinct fields.

The soft law instruments

The broad policy guidelines are specified in the soft law instruments examined earlier, such as the documents enshrining the Stockholm and Rio Principles and, more recently, the Sustainable Development Goals.

Principle 6 of the 1972 Stockholm Declaration prescribed that

> The discharge of toxic substances or of other substances and the release of heat, in such quantities or concentrations as to exceed the capacity of the environment to

---

the 'Agreement and every article and clause thereof on behalf of the United States of America'. Consequently, a new instrument of acceptance of the Agreement by the US was deposited with the UN Secretary-General on 20 January 2021. <https://bit.ly/3dGAon1> accessed 18 March 2021.

1379 Article 2 (1) (a) of the Paris Agreement.

render them harmless, must be halted in order to ensure that serious or irreversible damage is not inflicted upon ecosystems.

Principle 14 of the Rio Declaration specified that the '[s]tates should effectively cooperate to discourage or prevent the relocation and transfer to other States of any activities and substances that cause severe environmental degradation or are found to be harmful to human health.' Sustainable Development Goal 12 ('Ensure sustainable consumption and production patterns'), which was defined in the UN General Assembly Resolution 'Transforming our world: the 2030 Agenda for Sustainable Development', also partly covered the issue of hazardous substances and activities, as well as waste, by demanding 'sustainable consumption and production patterns.' Moreover, among the associated targets for Goal 12 is specified (by 2020) to

> achieve the **environmentally sound management** of chemicals and all wastes throughout their life cycle, in accordance with agreed international frameworks, and significantly reduce their release to air, water and soil in order to minimize their adverse impacts on human health and the environment.

Definition of 'hazardous substances and activities'

In 2001, the International Law Commission adopted the **Draft Articles on Prevention of Transboundary Harm from Hazardous Activities**, which, as stressed in the 'General commentary' of the ILC, dealt 'with the concept of prevention in the context of authorization and regulation of hazardous activities which pose a significant risk of transboundary harm'. In 2005, the ILC endorsed the subsequent document, which was titled the Draft Principles on the Allocation of Loss in the Case of Transboundary Harm Arising Out of Hazardous Activities.[1380]

According to the Draft Articles, as hazardous are defined the activities, which are not prohibited by international law, however, 'involve a risk of causing significant transboundary harm through their physical consequences'. In the same manner, the Draft Principles also referred to activities not prohibited by international law but which involve 'a risk of causing significant harm'. Thus, both documents utilise the formulation 'significant harm' to determine the meaning of the term 'hazardous activities.'[1381] At the same time, the ILC claimed in its Commentaries to the Draft Articles, that with the definition mentioned earlier,

---

1380 The General Assembly adopted some Resolutions concerning the ILC work on the topic. For example, by Resolution A/RES/62/68 of 7 December 2007, the General Assembly welcomed the adoption by the ILC of the respective Draft Articles, Draft Principles, and Commentaries on the subjects. It commended the 'articles on prevention of transboundary harm from hazardous activities, presented by the Commission, the text of which is annexed to the present resolution, to the attention of Governments, without prejudice to any future action, as recommended by the Commission regarding the articles'.

1381 '(4) The term "significant" is not without ambiguity and a determination has to be made in each specific case. It involves more factual considerations than legal determination. It is to be understood that "significant" is something more than "detectable" but need not be at the level of "serious" or "substantial". The harm must lead to a real detrimental effect on matters such as, for example, human

any hazardous and by inference any **ultrahazardous activity** which involves a risk of significant transboundary harm is covered. An ultrahazardous activity is perceived to be an activity with a danger that is rarely expected to materialize but might assume, on that rare occasion, grave (more than significant, serious or substantial) proportions.

On the other hand, there is no definition of 'hazardous substances' in these documents. Generally, hazardous substances can be outlined by their inherent characteristics, such as their toxicity, flammability, explosiveness, and oxidisation. However, since international environmental law concerning this matter is also based on a piecemeal approach, for the exact identification of the substances (which are regulated and limited by international law), the specific international treaties, which regulate specific substances and activities case by case, should be examined. Some of the most significant global treaties regulating the nuclear sector and the other hazardous substances and activities sector will be discussed next.

Nuclear sector

It is established that nuclear energy activities are ultrahazardous in nature. Therefore, the interstate system periodically aimed to regulate such activities in order to minimise the negative effects of nuclear energy on the environment and human well-being.

At first, the central concern of the subjects of international law was the liability matter, which was addressed at the global level by the 1963 Vienna Convention on Civil Liability for Nuclear Damage, which introduced the so-called **absolute liability** system of the operator for nuclear damage (examined earlier in this book). As a result, an 'operator of the nuclear installation is liable for compensation regardless of any fault on his part', and 'the claimant is only required to prove the relationship of cause and effect between the nuclear incident and the damage for which compensation is sought.'

1986 was a landmark year for the nuclear sector. The accident at the Chernobyl nuclear power plant in the Soviet Union caused serious damage to a very large region around Chernobyl. As a consequence, the subjects of international law under the leadership of the International Atomic Energy Agency (IAEA) adopted two significant international treaties in the same year:

- The Convention on Early Notification of a Nuclear Accident created the notification system for nuclear accidents 'from which a release of radioactive material occurs or is likely to occur and which has resulted or may result in an international transboundary release that could be of radiological safety significance for another State.' The Convention obliged the states to report the accident's time, location, nature, and other data necessary to assess the situation. Notification shall be made to affected states directly or through the International Atomic Energy Agency and to the IAEA itself.[1382]

---

health, industry, property, environment or agriculture in other States. Such detrimental effects must be susceptible of being measured by factual and objective standards.' ILC Commentary to Article 2 (Use of terms).

1382 Articles 1 and 2 of the Convention on Early Notification of a Nuclear Accident.

- The Convention on Assistance in the Case of a Nuclear Accident or Radiological Emergency, under which the parties agreed to co-operate in the case of a nuclear accident and provide the appropriate assistance to the affected states with their available experts, equipment, and materials.

More recently, under the auspices of the IAEA, two other important treaties were also adopted:

- The Convention on Nuclear Safety of 1994 aimed to achieve higher levels of safety through the enhancement of national measures and international co-operation, including regular meetings of the contracting parties, and by submitting reports on the implementation of their obligations for 'peer review' at meetings. The IAEA provides the secretariat functions for the meetings of the contracting parties.
- The Joint Convention on the Safety of Spent Fuel Management and on the Safety of Radioactive Waste Management of 1997 regulates the issue of spent fuel and radioactive waste management safety at a global level. In order to implement its objectives, the Joint Convention prescribed the fundamental safety principles and established a similar 'peer review' mechanism to that of the Convention on Nuclear Safety.

Other hazardous substances and activities

Another challenge for the interstate system was the environmentally sound management of hazardous chemicals. To address this challenge, four international treaties were adopted at the global level, to which the parties may be the states as well as the so-called integration organisations ('regional economic integration organisation' or 'political and/or economic integration organisation') and which established a similar institutional framework, including the Conferences of the Parties as the governing bodies for each Convention, as well as the Secretariats under the auspices of the UNEP. These Conventions are:

- The 1989 Basel Convention on the Transboundary Movement of Hazardous Wastes and their Disposal, which aimed to protect human health and the environment from the adverse effects of hazardous waste. The Convention's scope of application includes a wide range of waste, which was determined to be 'hazardous waste' based on its origin and/or composition and its characteristics, as well as 'other waste', such as household waste and incinerator ash.

   The Convention obligated the parties to follow the fundamental principles of environmentally sound waste management. Some prohibitions were also introduced – namely, that the hazardous waste cannot be exported to Antarctica, to a state which is not a party to the Convention or to any other international treaty permitting such a transboundary movement, or to a party that has explicitly banned the import of hazardous waste. The Convention established a prior informed consent system, which requires that, before an export may take place, the exporting state shall notify the authorities of the states of import and transit, and the export may only proceed if and when all the states involved in the transportation give their written consent.

In the case of the illegal transboundary movement of hazardous waste or when even a permitted movement 'cannot be completed in accordance with the terms of the contract', the Convention attributed the responsibility to the states of export, as well as imposing a duty to take back hazardous waste 'by the exporter or the generator' or, if necessary, by the state of export itself into the state of export or, if impracticable, to otherwise ensure the disposal of the waste in an environmentally sound manner.[1383]

- The 1998 Rotterdam Convention on the Prior Informed Consent Procedure for Certain Hazardous Chemicals and Pesticides in International Trade (revised in 2017). The objective of the Convention was 'to promote shared responsibility and cooperative efforts among Parties in the international trade of certain hazardous chemicals in order to protect human health and the environment from potential harm and to contribute to their environmentally sound use, by facilitating information exchange about their characteristics, by providing for a national decision-making process on their import and export and by disseminating these decisions to Parties.'

The Convention defined 'chemical' as 'a substance whether by itself or in a mixture or preparation and whether manufactured or obtained from nature, but does not include any living organism. It consists of the following categories: pesticide (including severely hazardous pesticide formulations) and industrial'.[1384]

Under the Convention was created a subsidiary body of the Conference of the Parties – the Chemical Review Committee, which, among other things, was empowered to recommend listing a chemical in Annex III ('Chemicals Subject to the Prior Informed Consent Procedure').

The Convention introduced the '**Prior Informed Consent procedure**'. It covered chemicals which were 'banned or severely restricted' for health or environmental reasons by the parties to the Convention and which have been notified by the parties for inclusion in the Prior Informed Consent (PIC) procedure. To maintain the PIC procedure, there was envisioned the inclusion of the chemicals in Annex III and delivering a 'decision guidance document' containing information concerning the chemical and the regulatory decisions to ban or severely restrict the chemical. According to the Convention, '[w]hen a decision to list a chemical in Annex III has been taken and the related decision guidance document has been approved by the Conference of the Parties, the Secretariat shall forthwith communicate this information to all Parties.' On the other hand, the parties had to implement appropriate legislative or administrative measures to ensure timely decisions concerning the import of chemicals listed in Annex III. At the same time, a nine-month period was provided for the parties to prepare an answer regarding future imports of the chemical. The answer could entail either a final decision (to allow the import of a chemical, prohibit the import, or to allow the import with specified conditions) or an interim response, which also should be circulated between the parties.

1383 Articles 8 and 9 of the Basel Convention on the Transboundary Movement of Hazardous Wastes and their Disposal.

1384 Articles 1 and 2 of the Rotterdam Convention on the Prior Informed Consent Procedure for Certain Hazardous Chemicals and Pesticides in International Trade.

- The 2001 Stockholm Convention on Persistent Organic Pollutants (revised in 2017). According to the Convention, the parties were obliged to 'prohibit and/or take the legal and administrative measures necessary to eliminate' the production, use, import, and export of the chemicals listed in Annex A; restrict the production and use of the chemicals listed in Annex B; and reduce or eliminate releases from unintentionally produced chemicals which are listed in Annex C.[1385] 'Exposure to Persistent Organic Pollutants (POPs) can lead to serious health effects including certain cancers, birth defects, dysfunctional immune and reproductive systems, greater susceptibility to disease and damages to the central and peripheral nervous systems.'[1386]

  At the same time, the Secretariat maintains the Register 'for the purpose of identifying the Parties that have specific exemptions listed in Annex A or Annex B'. The Persistent Organic Pollutants Review Committee (composed of experts in chemical assessment or management, who are appointed by the Conference of the Parties) was created to examine proposals for the listing of chemicals in Annexes A, B, and C. The final decision on the listing belongs to the Conference of the Parties by 'taking due account of the recommendations of the Committee, including any scientific uncertainty, shall decide, in a precautionary manner, whether to list the chemical, and specify its related control measures, in Annexes A, B and/or C.'[1387]

  In addition, to effectively implement its provisions, the Convention utilises some typical mechanisms developed in the substantive international environmental law fields – for example, the **non-compliance procedure**, regular reviews undertaken by the COP, and so forth.

- The 2013 Minamata Convention on Mercury aimed 'to protect the human health and the environment from anthropogenic emissions and releases of mercury and mercury compounds.'[1388]

  As articulated by UN Secretary-General António Guterres: 'In 1956, two sisters, aged two and five, were diagnosed in Minamata Bay, Japan, with the crippling, untreatable and stigmatizing effects of mercury poisoning. In the decades that followed, their story would be retold many times, becoming synonymous with the tens of thousands of adults, children and unborn infants to suffer from what is now known as Minamata disease.'[1389]

  In sum, the Convention addressed the entire life cycle of mercury, including the regulation of mercury-added products (Annex A), the manufacturing processes in which mercury or mercury compounds are used (Annex B), artisanal and small-scale gold mining (Annex C), the list of point sources of emissions of mercury and mercury compounds to the atmosphere (Annex D), the export and import of mercury, its safe storage and its disposal as waste, and so forth.

1385 Articles 3 and 5 of the Stockholm Convention on Persistent Organic Pollutants.
1386 <http://chm.pops.int/TheConvention/Overview/tabid/3351/Default.aspx> accessed 18 March 2021.
1387 Article 8 (9) of the Stockholm Convention on Persistent Organic Pollutants.
1388 Article 1 of the Minamata Convention on Mercury.
1389 *Minamata Convention on Mercury: Text and Annexes* (UNEP September 2019) Foreword by the Secretary-General of the United Nations António Guterres.

To 'promote implementation of, and review compliance with, all provisions of [the] Convention', the Implementation and Compliance Committee was established as a subsidiary body of the Conference of the Parties. The Committee consists of '15 members, nominated by parties and elected by the Conference of the Parties, with due consideration to equitable geographical representation based on the five regions of the United Nations'.[1390]

The Convention also introduced several obligations on the parties, such as the development and implementation of strategies and programmes to identify and protect populations at risk and promoting the development and implementation of science-based educational and preventive programmes, as well as appropriate health-care services; providing information exchange between the parties; promoting public information, awareness, and education; regularly reporting to the Conference of the Parties, through the Secretariat, on the measures taken to implement the provisions of the Convention; and so on.

CASES AND MATERIALS (*SELECTED PARTS*)

Stockholm principles

Declaration of the United Nations Conference on the Human Environment
(Stockholm 5–16 June 1972)

II

Principles

States the common conviction that:

Principle 1

Man has the fundamental right to freedom, equality and adequate conditions of life, in an environment of a quality that permits a life of dignity and well-being, and he bears a solemn responsibility to protect and improve the environment for present and future generations. In this respect, policies promoting or perpetuating apartheid, racial segregation, discrimination, colonial and other forms of oppression and foreign domination stand condemned and must be eliminated.

Principle 2

The natural resources of the earth, including the air, water, land, flora and fauna and especially representative samples of natural ecosystems, must be safeguarded for the benefit of present and future generations through careful planning or management, as appropriate.

Principle 3

The capacity of the earth to produce vital renewable resources must be maintained and, wherever practicable, restored or improved.

1390 Article 15 of the Minamata Convention on Mercury.

Principle 4

Man has a special responsibility to safeguard and wisely manage the heritage of wildlife and its habitat, which are now gravely imperilled by a combination of adverse factors. Nature conservation, including wildlife, must therefore receive importance in planning for economic development.

Principle 5

The non-renewable resources of the earth must be employed in such a way as to guard against the danger of their future exhaustion and to ensure that benefits from such employment are shared by all mankind.

Principle 6

The discharge of toxic substances or of other substances and the release of heat, in such quantities or concentrations as to exceed the capacity of the environment to render them harmless, must be halted in order to ensure that serious or irreversible damage is not inflicted upon ecosystems. The just struggle of the peoples of all countries against pollution should be supported.

Principle 7

States shall take all possible steps to prevent pollution of the seas by substances that are liable to create hazards to human health, to harm living resources and marine life, to damage amenities or to interfere with other legitimate uses of the sea.

Principle 8

Economic and social development is essential for ensuring a favourable living and working environment for man and for creating conditions on earth that are necessary for the improvement of the quality of life.

Principle 9

Environmental deficiencies generated by the conditions of under-development and natural disasters pose grave problems and can best be remedied by accelerated development through the transfer of substantial quantities of financial and technological assistance as a supplement to the domestic effort of the developing countries and such timely assistance as may be required.

Principle 10

For the developing countries, stability of prices and adequate earnings for primary commodities and raw materials are essential to environmental management since economic factors as well as ecological processes must be taken into account.

Principle 11

The environmental policies of all States should enhance and not adversely affect the present or future development potential of developing countries, nor should they hamper the attainment of better living conditions for all, and appropriate steps should be taken by States and international organizations with a view to reaching agreement on meeting the possible national and international economic consequences resulting from the application of environmental measures.

Principle 12

Resources should be made available to preserve and improve the environment, taking into account the circumstances and particular requirements of developing countries and any costs which may emanate from their incorporating environmental safeguards into their development planning and the need for making available to them, upon their request, additional international technical and financial assistance for this purpose.

Principle 13

In order to achieve a more rational management of resources and thus to improve the environment, States should adopt an integrated and co-ordinated approach to their development planning so as to ensure that development is compatible with the need to protect and improve environment for the benefit of their population.

Principle 14

Rational planning constitutes an essential tool for reconciling any conflict between the needs of development and the need to protect and improve the environment.

Principle 15

Planning must be applied to human settlements and urbanization with a view to avoiding adverse effects on the environment and obtaining maximum social, economic and environmental benefits for all. In this respect, projects which are designed for colonialist and racist domination must be abandoned.

Principle 16

Demographic policies which are without prejudice to basic human rights and which are deemed appropriate by Governments concerned should be applied in those regions where the rate of population growth or excessive population concentrations are likely to have adverse effects on the environment of the human environment and impede development.

Principle 17

Appropriate national institutions must be entrusted with the task of planning, managing or controlling the environmental resources of States with a view to enhancing environmental quality.

Principle 18

Science and technology, as part of their contribution to economic and social development, must be applied to the identification, avoidance and control of environmental risks and the solution of environmental problems and for the common good of mankind.

Principle 19

Education in environmental matters, for the younger generation as well as adults, giving due consideration to the underprivileged, is essential in order to broaden the basis for an enlightened opinion and responsible conduct by individuals, enterprises and communities in protecting and improving the environment in its full human dimension. It is also essential that mass media of communications avoid contributing to the deterioration of the environment, but, on the contrary, disseminate information of an educational nature on the need to protect and improve the environment in order to enable man to develop in every respect.

Principle 20

Scientific research and development in the context of environmental problems, both national and multinational, must be promoted in all countries, especially the developing countries. In this connexion, the free flow of up-to-date scientific information and transfer of experience must be supported and assisted, to facilitate the solution of environmental problems; environmental technologies should be made available to developing countries on terms which would encourage their wide dissemination without constituting an economic burden on the developing countries.

Principle 21

States have, in accordance with the Charter of the United Nations and the principles of international law, the sovereign right to exploit their own resources pursuant to their own environmental policies, and the responsibility to ensure that activities within their jurisdiction or control do not cause damage to the environment of other States or of areas beyond the limits of national jurisdiction.

Principle 22

States shall co-operate to develop further the international law regarding liability and compensation for the victims of pollution and other environmental damage caused by activities within the jurisdiction or control of such States to areas beyond their jurisdiction.

Principle 23

Without prejudice to such criteria as may be agreed upon by the international community, or to standards which will have to be determined nationally, it will be essential in all cases to consider the systems of values prevailing in each country, and the extent of the applicability of standards which are valid for the most advanced countries but which may be inappropriate and of unwarranted social cost for the developing countries.

Principle 24

International matters concerning the protection and improvement of the environment should be handled in a co-operative spirit by all countries, big and small, on an equal footing. Co-operation through multilateral or bilateral arrangements or other appropriate means is essential to effectively control, prevent, reduce and eliminate adverse environmental effects resulting from activities conducted in all spheres, in such a way that due account is taken of the sovereignty and interests of all States.

Principle 25

States shall ensure that international organizations play a co-ordinated, efficient and dynamic role for the protection and improvement of the environment.

Principle 26

Man and his environment must be spared the effects of nuclear weapons and all other means of mass destruction. States must strive to reach prompt agreement, in the relevant international organs, on the elimination and complete destruction of such weapons.

Rio principles

Report of the United Nations Conference on Environment and Development (Rio de Janeiro, 3–14 June 1992)

Annex I

RIO DECLARATION ON ENVIRONMENT AND DEVELOPMENT

The United Nations Conference on Environment and Development, . . . Proclaims that:

Principle 1

Human beings are at the centre of concerns for sustainable development. They are entitled to a healthy and productive life in harmony with nature.

Principle 2

States have, in accordance with the Charter of the United Nations and the principles of international law, the sovereign right to exploit their own resources pursuant to their own environmental and developmental policies, and the responsibility to ensure that activities within their jurisdiction or control do not cause damage to the environment of other States or of areas beyond the limits of national jurisdiction.

Principle 3

The right to development must be fulfilled so as to equitably meet developmental and environmental needs of present and future generations.

Principle 4

In order to achieve sustainable development, environmental protection shall constitute an integral part of the development process and cannot be considered in isolation from it.

Principle 5

All States and all people shall cooperate in the essential task of eradicating poverty as an indispensable requirement for sustainable development, in order to decrease the disparities in standards of living and better meet the needs of the majority of the people of the world.

Principle 6

The special situation and needs of developing countries, particularly the least developed and those most environmentally vulnerable, shall be given special priority. International actions in the field of environment and development should also address the interests and needs of all countries.

Principle 7

States shall cooperate in a spirit of global partnership to conserve, protect and restore the health and integrity of the Earth's ecosystem. In view of the different contributions to global environmental degradation, States have common but differentiated responsibilities. The developed countries acknowledge the responsibility that they bear in the international pursuit of sustainable development in view of the pressures their societies place on the global environment and of the technologies and financial resources they command.

Principle 8

To achieve sustainable development and a higher quality of life for all people, States should reduce and eliminate unsustainable patterns of production and consumption and promote appropriate demographic policies.

Principle 9

States should cooperate to strengthen endogenous capacity-building for sustainable development by improving scientific understanding through exchanges of scientific and technological knowledge, and by enhancing the development, adaptation, diffusion and transfer of technologies, including new and innovative technologies.

Principle 10

Environmental issues are best handled with the participation of all concerned citizens, at the relevant level. At the national level, each individual shall have appropriate access to information concerning the environment that is held by public authorities, including information on hazardous materials and activities in their communities, and the opportunity to participate in decision-making processes. States shall facilitate and encourage public awareness and participation by making information widely available. Effective access to judicial and administrative proceedings, including redress and remedy, shall be provided.

Principle 11

States shall enact effective environmental legislation. Environmental standards, management objectives and priorities should reflect the environmental and developmental context to which they apply. Standards applied by some countries may be inappropriate and of unwarranted economic and social cost to other countries, in particular developing countries.

Principle 12

States should cooperate to promote a supportive and open international economic system that would lead to economic growth and sustainable development in all countries, to better address the problems of environmental degradation. Trade policy measures for environmental purposes should not constitute a means of arbitrary or unjustifiable discrimination or a disguised restriction on international trade. Unilateral actions to deal with environmental challenges outside the jurisdiction of the importing country should be avoided. Environmental measures addressing transboundary or global environmental problems should, as far as possible, be based on an international consensus.

Principle 13

States shall develop national law regarding liability and compensation for the victims of pollution and other environmental damage. States shall also cooperate in an expeditious and more determined manner to develop further international law regarding liability and compensation for adverse effects of environmental damage caused by activities within their jurisdiction or control to areas beyond their jurisdiction.

Principle 14

States should effectively cooperate to discourage or prevent the relocation and transfer to other States of any activities and substances that cause severe environmental degradation or are found to be harmful to human health.

Principle 15

In order to protect the environment, the precautionary approach shall be widely applied by States according to their capabilities. Where there are threats of serious or irreversible damage, lack of full scientific certainty shall not be used as a reason for postponing cost-effective measures to prevent environmental degradation.

Principle 16

National authorities should endeavour to promote the internalization of environmental costs and the use of economic instruments, taking into account the approach that the polluter should, in principle, bear the cost of pollution, with due regard to the public interest and without distorting international trade and investment.

Principle 17

Environmental impact assessment, as a national instrument, shall be undertaken for proposed activities that are likely to have a significant adverse impact on the environment and are subject to a decision of a competent national authority.

Principle 18

States shall immediately notify other States of any natural disasters or other emergencies that are likely to produce sudden harmful effects on the environment of those States. Every effort shall be made by the international community to help States so afflicted.

Principle 19

States shall provide prior and timely notification and relevant information to potentially affected States on activities that may have a significant adverse transboundary environmental effect and shall consult with those States at an early stage and in good faith.

Principle 20

Women have a vital role in environmental management and development. Their full participation is therefore essential to achieve sustainable development.

Principle 21

The creativity, ideals and courage of the youth of the world should be mobilized to forge a global partnership in order to achieve sustainable development and ensure a better future for all.

Principle 22

Indigenous people and their communities and other local communities have a vital role in environmental management and development because of their knowledge and traditional practices. States should recognize and duly support their identity, culture and interests and enable their effective participation in the achievement of sustainable development.

Principle 23

The environment and natural resources of people under oppression, domination and occupation shall be protected.

Principle 24

Warfare is inherently destructive of sustainable development. States shall therefore respect international law providing protection for the environment in times of armed conflict and cooperate in its further development, as necessary.

Principle 25

Peace, development and environmental protection are interdependent and indivisible.

Principle 26

States shall resolve all their environmental disputes peacefully and by appropriate means in accordance with the Charter of the United Nations.

Principle 27

States and people shall cooperate in good faith and in a spirit of partnership in the fulfilment of the principles embodied in this Declaration and in the further development of international law in the field of sustainable development.

UNEP

Institutional and financial arrangements for international environmental cooperation, the UN General Assembly Resolution A/RES/2997(XXVII) of 15 December 1972

The General Assembly . . .

I
GOVERNING COUNCIL OF THE UNITED NATIONS ENVIRONMENT PROGRAMME

1   Decides to establish a Governing Council of the United Nations Environment Programme, composed of fifty-eight members elected by the General Assembly for three-year terms on the following basis:

(a)   Sixteen seats for African States;
(b)   Thirteen seats for Asian States;
(c)   Six seats for Eastern European States;
(d)   Ten seats for Latin American States;
(e)   Thirteen seats for Western European and other States;

2   Decides that the Governing Council shall have the following main functions and responsibilities:

(a)   To promote international co-operation in the field of the environment and to recommend, as appropriate, policies to this end;
(b)   To provide general policy guidance for the direction and co-ordination of environmental programmes within the United Nations system;
(c)   To receive and review the periodic reports of the Executive Director of the United Nations Environment Programme, referred to in section II, paragraph 2, below, on the implementation of environmental programmes within the United Nations system;
(d)   To keep under review the world environmental situation in order to ensure that emerging environmental problems of wide international significance receive appropriate and adequate consideration by Governments;
(e)   To promote the contribution of the relevant international scientific and other professional communities to the acquisition, assessment and exchange of environmental knowledge and information and, as appropriate, to the technical aspects of the formulation and implementation of environmental programmes within the United Nations system;
(f)   To maintain under continuing review the impact of national and international environmental policies and measures on developing countries, as well as the problem of additional costs that may be incurred by developing countries in the implementation of environmental programmes and projects, and to ensure that such programmes and projects shall be compatible with the development plans and priorities of those countries;

(g) To review and approve annually the programme of utilization of resources of the Environment Fund referred to in section III below;

3 Decides that the Governing Council shall report annually to the General Assembly through the Economic and Social Council, which will transmit to the Assembly such comments on the report as it may deem necessary, particularly with regard to questions of co-ordination and to the relationship of environmental policies and programmes within the United Nations system to overall economic and social policies and priorities;

II
ENVIRONMENT SECRETARIAT

1 Decides that a small secretariat shall be established in the United Nations to serve as a focal point for environmental action and co-ordination within the United Nations system in such a way as to ensure a high degree of effective management;

2 Decides that the environment secretariat shall be headed by the Executive Director of the United Nations Environment Programme, who shall be elected by the General Assembly on the nomination of the Secretary-General for a term of four years and who shall be entrusted, *inter alia*, with the following responsibilities:

(a) To provide substantive support to the Governing Council of the United Nations Environment Programme;

(b) To co-ordinate, under the guidance of the Governing Council, environmental programmes within the United Nations system, to keep their implementation under review and to assess their effectiveness;

(c) To advise, as appropriate and under the guidance of the Governing Council, intergovernmental bodies of the United Nations system on the formulation and implementation of environmental programmes;

(d) To secure the effective co-operation of, and contribution from, the relevant scientific and other professional communities in all parts of the world;

(e) To provide, at the request of all parties concerned, advisory services for the promotion of international co-operation in the field of the environment;

(f) To submit to the Governing Council, on his own initiative or upon request, proposals embodying medium-range and long-range planning for United Nations programmes in the field of the environment;

(g) To bring to the attention of the Governing Council any matter which he deems to require consideration by it;

(h) To administer, under the authority and policy guidance of the Governing Council, the Environment Fund referred to in section III below;

(i) To report on environmental matters to the Governing Council;

(j) To perform such other functions as may be entrusted to him by the Governing Council;

3 Decides that the costs of servicing the Governing Council and providing the small secretariat referred to in paragraph 1 above shall be borne by the regular budget of the United Nations and that operational programme costs, programme support and administrative costs of the Environment Fund established under section III below shall be borne by the Fund;

III
ENVIRONMENT FUND

1   Decides that, in order to provide for additional financing for environmental programmes, a voluntary fund shall be established, with effect from 1 January 1973, in accordance with existing United Nations financial procedures;

2   Decides that, in order to enable the Governing Council of the United Nations Environment Programme to fulfil its policy-guidance role for the direction and co-ordination of environmental activities, the Environment Fund shall finance wholly or partly the costs of the new environmental initiatives undertaken within the United Nations system – which will include the initiatives envisaged in the Action Plan for the Human Environment adopted by the United Nations Conference on the Human Environment with particular attention to integrated projects, and such other environmental activities as may be decided upon by the Governing Council – and that the Governing Council shall review these initiatives with a view to taking appropriate decisions as to their continued financing;

3   Decides that the Environment Fund shall be used for financing such programmes of general interest as regional and global monitoring, assessment and data-collecting systems, including, as appropriate, costs for national counterparts; the improvement of environmental quality management; environmental research; information exchange and dissemination; public education and training; assistance for national, regional and global environmental institutions; the promotion of environmental research and studies for the development of industrial and other technologies best suited to a policy of economic growth compatible with adequate environmental safeguards; and such other programmes as the Governing Council may decide upon, and that in the implementation of such programmes due account should be taken of the special needs of the developing countries;

4   Decides that, in order to ensure that the development priorities of developing countries shall not be adversely affected, adequate measures shall be taken to provide additional financial resources on terms compatible with the economic situation of the recipient developing country, and that, to this end, the Executive Director, in co-operation with competent organizations, shall keep this problem under continuing review;

5   Decides that the Environment Fund, in pursuance of the objectives stated in paragraphs 2 and 3 above, shall be directed to the need for effective co-ordination in the implementation of international environmental programmes of the organizations in the United Nations system and other international organizations;

6   Decides that, in the implementation of programmes to be financed by the Environment Fund, organizations outside the United Nations system, particularly those in the countries and regions concerned, shall also be utilized as appropriate, in accordance with the procedures established by the Governing Council, and that such organizations are invited to support the United Nations environmental programmes by complementary initiatives and contributions;

7   Decides that the Governing Council shall formulate such general procedures as are necessary to govern the operations of the Environment Fund;

IV
ENVIRONMENT CO-ORDINATION BOARD

1   Decides that, in order to provide for the most efficient co-ordination of United Nations environmental programmes, an Environment Co-ordination Board, under the chairmanship of the

Executive Director of the United Nations Environment Programme, shall be established under the auspices and within the framework of the Administrative Committee on Co-ordination;

2   Further decides that the Environment Co-ordination Board shall meet periodically for the purpose of ensuring co-operation and co-ordination among all bodies concerned in the implementation of environmental programmes and that it shall report annually to the Governing Council of the United Nations Environment Programme . . .

UNEP

Change of the designation of the Governing Council of the United Nations Environment Programme, the UN General Assembly Resolution A/RES/67/251 of 13 March 2013

The General Assembly . . .

1   Takes note of Governing Council decision 27/2 of 22 February 2013, by which the Governing Council invited the General Assembly to adopt a resolution to change its designation to the United Nations Environment Assembly of the United Nations Environment Programme, it being understood that this change of designation in no way changes, nor will change, the present mandate, aims and purposes of the United Nations Environment Programme or the role and functions of its governing body;

2   Decides to change the designation of the Governing Council of the United Nations Environment Programme to the United Nations Environment Assembly of the United Nations Environment Programme.

Sustainable Development Goals and targets

Transforming our world: the 2030 Agenda for Sustainable Development, the UN General Assembly Resolution A/RES/70/1 of 25 September 2015

Preamble

This Agenda is a plan of action for people, planet and prosperity. It also seeks to strengthen universal peace in larger freedom. We recognize that eradicating poverty in all its forms and dimensions, including extreme poverty, is the greatest global challenge and an indispensable requirement for sustainable development.

All countries and all stakeholders, acting in collaborative partnership, will implement this plan. We are resolved to free the human race from the tyranny of poverty and want and to heal and secure our planet. We are determined to take the bold and transformative steps which are urgently needed to shift the world on to a sustainable and resilient path. As we embark on this collective journey, we pledge that no one will be left behind.

The 17 Sustainable Development Goals and 169 targets which we are announcing today demonstrate the scale and ambition of this new universal Agenda.

They seek to build on the Millennium Development Goals and complete what they did not achieve. They seek to realize the human rights of all and to achieve gender equality and the empowerment of all women and girls. They are integrated and indivisible and balance the three dimensions of sustainable development: the economic, social and environmental.

The Goals and targets will stimulate action over the next 15 years in areas of critical importance for humanity and the planet.

Our shared principles and commitments

10. The new Agenda is guided by the purposes and principles of the Charter of the United Nations, including full respect for international law. It is grounded in the Universal Declaration of Human Rights, international human rights treaties, the Millennium Declaration and the 2005 World Summit Outcome. It is informed by other instruments such as the Declaration on the Right to Development.

11. We reaffirm the outcomes of all major United Nations conferences and summits which have laid a solid foundation for sustainable development and have helped to shape the new Agenda. These include the Rio Declaration on Environment and Development, the World Summit on Sustainable Development, the World Summit for Social Development, the Programme of Action of the International Conference on Population and Development, the Beijing Platform for Action and the United Nations Conference on Sustainable Development. We also reaffirm the follow-up to these conferences, including the outcomes of the Fourth United Nations Conference on the Least Developed Countries, the third International Conference on Small Island Developing States, the second United Nations Conference on Landlocked Developing Countries and the Third United Nations World Conference on Disaster Risk Reduction.

12. We reaffirm all the principles of the Rio Declaration on Environment and Development, including, inter alia, the principle of common but differentiated responsibilities, as set out in principle 7 thereof.

13. The challenges and commitments identified at these major conferences and summits are interrelated and call for integrated solutions. To address them effectively, a new approach is needed. Sustainable development recognizes that eradicating poverty in all its forms and dimensions, combating inequality within and among countries, preserving the planet, creating sustained, inclusive and sustainable economic growth and fostering social inclusion are linked to each other and are interdependent.

A call for action to change our world

49. Seventy years ago, an earlier generation of world leaders came together to create the United Nations. From the ashes of war and division they fashioned this Organization and the values of peace, dialogue and international cooperation which underpin it. The supreme embodiment of those values is the Charter of the United Nations.

50. Today we are also taking a decision of great historic significance. We resolve to build a better future for all people, including the millions who have been denied the chance to lead decent, dignified and rewarding lives and to achieve their full human potential. We can be the first generation to succeed in ending poverty; just as we may be the last to have a chance of saving the planet. The world will be a better place in 2030 if we succeed in our objectives.

51. What we are announcing today – an Agenda for global action for the next 15 years – is a charter for people and planet in the twenty-first century. Children and young women and men are critical agents of change and will find in the new Goals a platform to channel their infinite capacities for activism into the creation of a better world.

52. "We the peoples" are the celebrated opening words of the Charter of the United Nations. It is "we the peoples" who are embarking today on the road to 2030. Our journey will involve

Governments as well as parliaments, the United Nations system and other international institutions, local authorities, indigenous peoples, civil society, business and the private sector, the scientific and academic community – and all people. Millions have already engaged with, and will own, this Agenda. It is an Agenda of the people, by the people and for the people – and this, we believe, will ensure its success.

53. The future of humanity and of our planet lies in our hands. It lies also in the hands of today's younger generation who will pass the torch to future generations. We have mapped the road to sustainable development; it will be for all of us to ensure that the journey is successful and its gains irreversible.

Sustainable Development Goals and targets

54. Following an inclusive process of intergovernmental negotiations, and based on the proposal of the Open Working Group on Sustainable Development Goals, which includes a chapeau contextualizing the latter, set out below are the Goals and targets which we have agreed.

55. The Sustainable Development Goals and targets are integrated and indivisible, global in nature and universally applicable, taking into account different national realities, capacities and levels of development and respecting national policies and priorities. Targets are defined as aspirational and global, with each Government setting its own national targets guided by the global level of ambition but taking into account national circumstances. Each Government will also decide how these aspirational and global targets should be incorporated into national planning processes, policies and strategies. It is important to recognize the link between sustainable development and other relevant ongoing processes in the economic, social and environmental fields.

56. In deciding upon these Goals and targets, we recognize that each country faces specific challenges to achieve sustainable development, and we underscore the special challenges facing the most vulnerable countries and, in particular, African countries, least developed countries, landlocked developing countries and small island developing States, as well as the specific challenges facing the middle-income countries. Countries in situations of conflict also need special attention.

57. We recognize that baseline data for several of the targets remains unavailable, and we call for increased support for strengthening data collection and capacity-building in Member States, to develop national and global baselines where they do not yet exist. We commit to addressing this gap in data collection so as to better inform the measurement of progress, in particular for those targets below which do not have clear numerical targets.

58. We encourage ongoing efforts by States in other forums to address key issues which pose potential challenges to the implementation of our Agenda, and we respect the independent mandates of those processes. We intend that the Agenda and its implementation would support, and be without prejudice to, those other processes and the decisions taken therein.

59. We recognize that there are different approaches, visions, models and tools available to each country, in accordance with its national circumstances and priorities, to achieve sustainable development; and we reaffirm that planet Earth and its ecosystems are our common home and that "Mother Earth" is a common expression in a number of countries and regions.

The rethinking of the role of the UN Trusteeship Council

Renewing the United Nations: A Programme for Reform, Report of the Secretary-General of 14 July 1997, A/51/950.

PART ONE: OVERVIEW

I. INTRODUCTION

1   The United Nations is a noble experiment in human cooperation. In a world that remains divided by many and diverse interests and attributes, the United Nations strives to articulate an inclusive vision: community among nations, common humanity among peoples, the singularity of our only one Earth. Indeed, the historic mission of the United Nations is not merely to act upon, but also to expand the elements of common ground that exist among nations – across space to touch and improve more lives and over time to convey to future generations the material and cultural heritage that we hold in trust for them. The Charter of the United Nations, drafted with the searing experience of history's two most destructive wars fresh in mind, embraced each of these aspirations and provided institutional instruments for their pursuit.

2   Fifty-two years after the signing of the Charter, the world can celebrate numerous progressive changes in which the United Nations has played a significant part. The United Nations role in decolonization began almost instantly and remains one of its grandest achievements. The Universal Declaration of Human Rights soon celebrates its own fiftieth anniversary. United Nations peacekeepers have helped to stabilize regional disputes and its humanitarian missions have alleviated suffering throughout the world. The challenges faced by developing countries have been at the forefront of United Nations economic activities.

3   The smooth flow of international transactions is made possible by rules of the road devised by the United Nations and its agencies. The world's people are healthier and lead longer and more productive lives thanks to the eradication of diseases, the improvement of nutritional standards, the promotion of agricultural development, the campaigns for literacy and the advocacy of the rights of women and children in which United Nations organizations have featured prominently. And the United Nations has no peer among international organizations in identifying novel issues on the policy horizon and devising plans of action for dealing with them, including the environment, social development questions and such uncivil elements in global civil society as drug-trafficking, transnational criminal networks and terrorism.

4   At the same time, there remains a sizeable gap between aspiration and accomplishment. Despite the unprecedented prosperity that technological advances and the globalization of production and finance have brought to many countries, neither Governments, nor the United Nations, nor the private sector have found the key to eradicating the persistent poverty that grips the majority of humankind. Indeed, imbalances in the world economy today pose serious challenges to future international stability: imbalances in the distribution of wealth, between the forces driving economic integration and political fragmentation, between humanity's impact on, and the capacities of, planetary life-support systems.

C. The road ahead

•   A new concept of trusteeship

84. Although the United Nations was established primarily to serve Member States, it also expresses the highest aspirations of men, women and children around the world. Indeed, the Charter begins by declaring the determination of "We the peoples of the United Nations" to

achieve a peaceful and just world order. Relations between the United Nations and agencies of civil society are growing in salience in every major sector of the United Nations agenda. The global commons are the policy domain in which this intermingling of sectors and institutions is most advanced.

85. Member States appear to have decided to retain the Trusteeship Council. The Secretary-General proposes, therefore, that it be reconstituted as the forum through which Member States exercise their collective trusteeship for the integrity of the global environment and common areas such as the oceans, atmosphere and outer space. At the same time, it should serve to link the United Nations and civil society in addressing these areas of global concern, which require the active contribution of public, private and voluntary sectors.

Towards a global pact for the environment

Gaps in international environmental law and environment-related instruments: towards a global pact for the environment, Report of the Secretary-General of 30 November 2018, A/73/419.

VII. Conclusions

100. The above review and analysis of the state of international environmental law and environment-related instruments reveals gaps and deficiencies at multiple levels. There are significant gaps and deficiencies with respect to the applicable principles of environmental law; the normative and institutional content of the sectoral regulatory regimes, as well as their articulation with environment-related regimes; the governance structure of international environmental law; and the effective implementation of, compliance with and enforcement of international environmental law.

101. Environmental principles inform the way in which environmental treaties can be interpreted, and may fill gaps between the rules laid out in treaties. Such principles include the duty of States to prevent significant environmental harm beyond their national boundaries, exercise precaution in making decisions which may harm the environment, provide reparation for environmental harm, provide public access to information and decision-making involving potentially significant environmental harm and cooperate in environmental protection. Some of the principles have been incorporated into the issue-specific contexts of many multilateral environmental agreements. In addition, several international courts and tribunals have confirmed the existence of rules of customary international law relating to environmental protection, in particular the obligation to prevent environmental harm beyond national jurisdiction, the performance of due diligence, the duty to conduct an environmental impact assessment and the obligation of reparation for environmental damage.

102. There are important deficiencies with respect to principles of international environmental law, in particular with respect to their content and legal status. There are instances where there is no clarity as to the nature and content of a principle, or no judicial consensus as to its applicability, or no recognition in binding legal instruments, or all of the above. The degree of legal uncertainty surrounding many of these principles has a direct and indirect impact on the predictability and implementation of sectoral environmental regimes. Some principles, such as access to information, participation in decision-making and access to justice, have only regional application. Others, such as a right to a clean and healthy environment and the principles of non-regression and progression, have only recently, and only in a limited number of legal instruments, been recognized

and have not yet been fully developed. Although the principles of sustainable development and common but differentiated responsibilities and respective capabilities are inherently dynamic and flexible enough to allow international law to grow and respond to new challenges, their general application is hardly evident. There is a need to further clarify the principles of environmental law, without prejudice to the legal developments already achieved in the issue-specific contexts of various multilateral environmental agreements. A comprehensive and unifying international instrument that gathers all the principles of environmental law could provide for better harmonization, predictability and certainty.

103. International environmental law is characterized by fragmentation and a general lack of coherence and synergy among a large body of sectoral regulatory frameworks. This fragmentation is inevitable given the piecemeal, incremental and reactive nature of international environmental law-making. However, deliberate efforts will be required to harness the interlinkages and synergies inherent in specific areas such as biodiversity, atmosphere or chemicals and wastes. The governance structure of international environmental law corresponds to its fragmentation. A multiplicity of institutions have responsibilities and mandates with respect to the environment, including institutions of the United Nations system, treaty -based bodies established by multilateral environmental agreements and specialized agencies, as well as regional institutions. This institutional fragmentation requires better coordination at both the law-making and implementation levels in order to ensure policy coherence, mutual supportiveness and synergies in implementation. There is, however, an important coordination deficit within the United Nations system, between United Nations system institutions and multilateral environmental agreements, among multilateral environmental agreements and between multilateral environmental agreements and other environment-related instruments. Strengthened coordination and coherence could enhance the effectiveness of international environmental law.

104. There are important gaps and deficiencies in specific sectoral regulatory regimes. In general, the sectoral approach has also meant that some issues remain without specific, legally binding regulation, including regulations on the conservation and sustainable use of forests, the pollution of marine areas by land-based plastic waste, the protection of soil, human rights and climate change, biodiversity, nanomaterials and some geo-engineering activities. Some of these issues can, subject to political will, find a home in existing multilateral environmental agreements. With regard to the climate change regime, an important challenge is the articulation between multiple treaties that have different memberships and contain different, sometimes overlapping, obligations. There may be a need for the harmonization of various aspects of the treaties, such as reporting, in order to pre-empt potential tensions among them. In treaties that deal with the protection of the atmosphere, such as ozone and mercury regimes, challenges relate to implementation, monitoring, reporting and verification. On the other hand, air pollution has largely been framed as a regional issue, notwithstanding the growing evidence of its global effects. Regional approaches leave significant gaps in coverage in terms of countries and of pollutants or pollution sources. Some regional approaches show weak implementation and poor compliance with existing rules. A global approach to air pollution through a global air pollution treaty or the linking of regional treaties might be desirable.

105. The biodiversity cluster of treaties is also characterized by issues of ineffective implementation; ineffectual processes relating to monitoring, reporting, review and verification; and the absence of or inadequate procedures and mechanisms to promote and enforce compliance. The growing focus on the concept of ecosystem-services, which attaches economic value to biodiversity, could help better integrate and mainstream biodiversity into other policy and law-making arenas. Several more narrowly focused regional and subregional instruments exist, but there is

scope for further developments that would allow for the adjustment of rules pertaining to specific transboundary ecological areas or species. More attention needs to be given to direct and indirect drivers of biodiversity loss, as well as to cooperation and coherence with other areas of international law that govern those drivers, such as trade, food security, climate change and marine use.

106. Freshwater resources are regulated through a patchwork of global, regional and basin agreements which often utilize ambiguous terms, leading to uncertainty and a lack of uniformity as to how they are applied. Environmental principles could fill the resulting normative and institutional gaps in these instruments, and may serve to harmonize their application.

107. With regard to the marine environment, while the United Nations Convention on the Law of the Sea provides a comprehensive set of rules for the protection and preservation of the marine environment, different complementary instruments apply to various activities depending upon the subject matter and the geographical location concerned. This sectoral approach creates challenges to the implementation of integrated approaches. Compliance mechanisms are not common and disparities remain in terms of assessing implementation. No specific instruments comprehensively address the modern challenges of marine debris, plastics and microplastics. While the Convention provides a unifying legal framework to address fragmentation, its potential role in that regard has not yet been fully realized.

108. There are significant gaps in the regulatory regimes of hazardous substances, wastes and activities. With regard to hazardous substances, these gaps lie in the absence of global rules that address accident prevention, preparedness and response, as well as binding rules regarding classification, labelling, packaging and transport. International rules governing hazardous wastes do not impose quantitative restrictions on the generation of such wastes within specific time frames. The absence of an operative global liability and compensation regime with respect to the transboundary movements of hazardous wastes is a major gap in the international legal framework. Finally, in the area of hazardous activities, international regulation has focused mainly on nuclear activities. However, there are critical deficiencies with respect to legally binding global rules, principles and standards relating to the design, siting and safety of nuclear power plants.

109. The articulation between multilateral environmental agreements and environment-related instruments remains problematic owing to the lack of clarity, content-wise and status-wise, of many environmental principles. There is a need for greater mutual supportiveness of rules concerning trade and environment. Environmental concerns addressed in investment treaties have not generally evolved to include issues such as climate change and biodiversity. Intellectual property instruments have not interacted harmoniously with agricultural concerns, the rights of indigenous and local communities or access to genetic resources and benefit- sharing. Regional courts are left to integrate environmental considerations and human rights on a case-by-case basis.

110. International courts and tribunals often stress the lack of international consensus concerning environmental principles. Non-specialized courts and tribunals have faced obstacles related to assessing environmental data, situations where environmental harm has not yet occurred and applying general rules to environmental damage. Compliance regimes are largely inadequate and need to be strengthened to promote the effective implementation of multilateral environmental agreements. Outside the realm of oil pollution and nuclear damage, liability and redress regimes are either non-existent or consist of adopted instruments that have not entered into force. Implementation gaps also remain with respect to the enforcement of rights and obligations regarding the high seas and shared natural resources.

111. The implementation of international environmental law remains problematic at both the national and international levels. National implementation is constrained in many countries by a

lack of appropriate national legislation, financial resources, environmentally sound technologies and institutional capacities. National implementation could be improved through the mainstreaming of environmental considerations into other sectors and the enhanced participation of non-State actors in decision-making and implementation.

112. At the international level, implementation is also constrained by the lack of clarity of many environmental principles. Nevertheless, implementation at this level could be strengthened through more effective reporting, review and verification processes, as well as robust compliance and enforcement procedures and mechanisms. The role of non-State actors in international environmental law-making, implementation monitoring and compliance procedures needs to be enhanced in most sectoral regulatory regimes.

113. Building upon the creative approaches that States have thus far adopted to protect the environment, it is essential that States and the United Nations work together to address gaps in international environmental law. We must collectively seize the opportunity to use international environmental law in new and dynamic ways to provide a strong and effective governance regime with a view to better safeguarding the environment for future generations.

CHAPTER 17

International humanitarian law

DOI: 10.4324/9781003213772-17

FROM THE LAW OF WAR TO INTERNATIONAL HUMANITARIAN LAW

> *jus ad bellum*
> *jus contra bellum*
> *jus in bello*
> international humanitarian law
> law of war
> methods and means of warfare
> law of the Hague
> Hague Conventions of 1899 and 1907
> armed conflict
> protection and assistance of those affected by the hostilities
> Geneva Conventions of 1949
> law of the Geneva
> Additional Protocol I
> Additional Protocol II
> Additional Protocol III

Two dimensions of looking at war

There are two main dimensions in which international law navigates the phenomenon of war:

1   The legal limitations on starting a fight; and
2   How you fight (i.e. the methods and means of fighting a war).

Jus ad bellum

The first dimension refers to all modern principles and rules:

1   prohibiting the threat or the use of force against the territorial integrity or political independence of any state or in any other manner inconsistent with the Charter of the United Nations;
2   as well as defining, in exceptional cases, the legitimate reasons a state (sometimes also other subjects of international law – such as a people) may use force that would not contradict international law.

This area of international law is called ***jus ad bellum***.[1391] However, today, *jus ad bellum* has substantially changed to ***jus contra bellum*** (which combines two meanings – the law against war and the law/right in response to war) since:

1391 'jus âd be´lum. n. "Law/right relating to war."' *Guide to Latin in International Law* (n 71) 150.

1   its essential part consists of norms prohibiting the threat or the use of force (forming the body of norms against war), and
2   even the exceptions to the general prohibition concerning the threat or the use of force were legalised to be allowed as a counter-reaction in cases of individual and collective self-defence, as well as under UN Security Council enforcement measures and sometimes in order to enforce peoples' right to self-determination.

Nevertheless, in this book, the traditional approach to the terms is followed and, in this case, the term '*jus ad bellum*' is retained.

Jus in bello

In contrast, ***jus in bello***[1392] does not regulate legitimate reasons for the use of force – in other words, under which conditions a subject has the legal right to use force. *Jus in bello* is the set of principles and norms that come into effect once a war has started with the aim of putting a limit on conduct during warfare in order to place it under certain restrictions. This area (branch) of international law is called **international humanitarian law**, which is a set of principles and rules which, for humanitarian reasons, targets limiting the effects of armed conflict. Nevertheless, a party violating *jus ad bellum* would still have to comply with specific rules during a war (i.e. with the international humanitarian law).

Development of international humanitarian law

The origins of international humanitarian law can be traced back to at least the nineteenth century; however, some of its principles and practices are much older. Initially, international humanitarian law was referred to as the **law of war** since the outbreak of the war certainly triggered its operation, and the regulations under its framework were primarily concerned with the rules of war and limitations or prohibitions on some specific **methods and means of warfare**. These rules are also called the **law of the Hague**, a term that derives its name from the conventions concluded in The Hague, primarily the **Hague Conventions of 1899 and 1907**.[1393]

After the tragedy of two world wars and the certain impact of the Kellogg-Briand Pact of 1928, which renounced war as an instrument for solving international controversies, as well as due to the influence of other developments the term 'war' in international documents was to a great degree replaced by the term '**armed conflict**',[1394] which was considered a more neutral

---

1392 'jus in be'lō. n. "Law in war."' *Guide to Latin in International Law* (n 71) 155.
1393 As noted earlier, the Hague Conventions are a number of international treaties and declarations reached at two international peace conferences at the Hague in 1899 and 1907.
1394 In rare cases, the term 'war' is still used in some valid international norms. For example, Article 2 of the Geneva Convention for the Amelioration of the Condition of the Wounded and Sick in Armed Forces in the Field (the First Geneva Convention) of 12 August 1949 prescribes: 'In addition to the provisions which shall be implemented in peacetime, the present Convention shall apply to all cases of declared war or of any other armed conflict which may arise between two or more of the High Contracting Parties, even if the state of war is not recognized by one of them. The Convention shall

notion. At the same time, concerning *jus in bello*, there was a change in focus, and the states shifted to the **protection and assistance of those affected by the hostilities** since the protection of persons and objects has been envisaged as a more practical, necessary, and enforceable direction.

The famous work by Henri Dunant and the Red Cross Movement influenced the change in focus concerning *jus in bello*; however, the most comprehensive expression of this shift can be found in the four **Geneva Conventions of 1949**. The first Geneva Convention for the Amelioration of the Condition of the Wounded and Sick in Armed Forces in the Field[1395] protects wounded and sick soldiers on land; the second Convention for the Amelioration of the Condition of Wounded, Sick and Shipwrecked Members of Armed Forces at Sea[1396] safeguards wounded, sick, and shipwrecked military personnel at sea; the third Convention relative to the Treatment of Prisoners of War[1397] applies to prisoners of war; and the fourth Convention relative to the Protection of Civilian Persons in Time of War[1398] concerns protection of civilians, including in occupied territories. This direction of international humanitarian law was named after the city where the respective Conventions were adopted – the **law of the Geneva**.

Additional Protocols to the 1949 Geneva Conventions

With the adoption of the Additional Protocols to the 1949 Geneva Conventions that codify and develop rules on the conduct of hostilities, the dichotomy between the terms 'law of Geneva' and 'law of the Hague' largely lost its relevance. These are the 1977 Protocol Additional to the Geneva Conventions of 12 August 1949, and relating to the Protection of Victims of International Armed Conflicts (**Additional Protocol I**); the 1977 Protocol Additional to the Geneva Conventions of 12 August 1949, and relating to the Protection of Victims of Non-International Armed Conflicts (**Additional Protocol II**); and the Protocol Additional to the Geneva Conventions of 12 August 1949, and relating to the Adoption of an Additional Distinctive Emblem (**Additional Protocol III**) of 2005.

Prevalence of the term 'international humanitarian law'

In the meantime, this branch of international law itself almost entirely modified its own name to become international humanitarian law, and such a name is considered to more adequately reflect the principal purpose of contemporary legal regulation – the humanitarian content of

---

also apply to all cases of partial or total occupation of the territory of a High Contracting Party, even if the said occupation meets with no armed resistance.'

1395 'This Convention represents the fourth updated version of the Geneva Convention on the wounded and sick following those adopted in 1864, 1906 and 1929.' 'The Geneva Conventions of 1949 and their Additional Protocols' <https://bit.ly/2XOprKf> accessed 18 March 2021.

1396 'This Convention replaced Hague Convention of 1907 for the Adaptation to Maritime Warfare of the Principles of the Geneva Convention.' ibid.

1397 'This Convention replaced the Prisoners of War Convention of 1929.' ibid.

1398 'The Geneva Conventions, which were adopted before 1949, were concerned with combatants only, not with civilians. The events of World War II showed the disastrous consequences of the absence of a convention for the protection of civilians in wartime. The Convention adopted in 1949 takes account of the experiences of World War II.' ibid.

the protection of the victims of armed conflict. On the other hand, this change conformed to the general tendency in contemporary international law to abandon the term 'war.'

Two primary areas of international humanitarian law

Thus, modern international humanitarian law covers two key areas:

- regulation of the methods and means of warfare; and
- protection of and assistance to those affected by the hostilities.

General customary international law and the general principles of law as the substantial sources of international humanitarian law

Finally, it is notable that numerous rules of international humanitarian law obtained their legal force through customary international norms since numerous rules enshrined in treaty law have received widespread acceptance and have had a far-reaching effect on interstate practice. They, therefore, act in the force of general customary international law. In addition, the general principles of law also have an important imprint on international humanitarian law as a source of some key legal norms (for example, the prohibition of torture).

THE BASICS OF INTERNATIONAL HUMANITARIAN LAW

International Committee of the Red Cross
Declaration of Saint Petersburg
combatants
non-combatants
civilians
Hague Regulations
partisans
unlawful combatants
saboteurs
mercenaries
spies
prisoners of war
combatants' privileges
protection from direct attack
civilian persons
principle of distinction
Advisory Opinion on *Legality of the Threat or Use of Nuclear Weapons*
methods of warfare
means of warfare

The new vision concerning warfare

The attempts to introduce some minor standards and laws of war are as old as war itself. However, not until the second half of the nineteenth century did international developments eventually bring a new vision (shared between the main actors of the interstate system) concerning the need to regulate and put limits on the conduct of warfare, in this way also planting the seeds of modern international humanitarian law.

All this was due to a combination of factors, including the progressive change of humanity in moral values and scientific progress. (These factors were also intertwined.) Due to scientific progress, humanity invented arms that had the capacity to threaten large masses of people or even engender the extinction of every form of life on the earth. Personal contributions were also an important factor – for example, the impressive deeds of famous persons such as Henry Dunant and other contributors to the International Committee for Relief to the Wounded (from 1876, **International Committee of the Red Cross**); Francis Lieber, who designed his valuable document 'The Lieber Code' attempting to gather the laws and customs of war; and so on.

Two central postulates of the new vision

In 1868, the **Declaration of Saint Petersburg** (Declaration Renouncing the Use, in Time of War, of Explosive Projectiles Under 400 Grammes Weight) was adopted; this was the first formal international treaty prohibiting the use of certain weapons during war. However, at the same time, this Declaration pronounced that the progress of civilization should alleviate as much as possible the calamities of war and introduced a new vision of warfare, notably:

1 that the parties to a war are the states and not the peoples of the fighting states; and
2 '[t]hat the only legitimate object which States should endeavour to accomplish during war is to weaken the military forces of the enemy'.

These two central postulates of the new approach triggered a turnaround in thought. First of all, war, as a phenomenon, was no longer regarded as a conflict between the peoples of the fighting states. From that time on, only states and state mechanisms were to be considered as belligerents. Secondly, the legitimate object of war was not the destruction of the opposing side, but only the weakening of the enemy military forces that would allow effective self-defence.

The first postulate and the terms 'combatants', 'non-combatants', and 'civilians'

Hence, for the implementation of the first postulate, it was crucial to determine who should be considered the representatives of states during a war. In due course, it stipulated the logical distinction between the militaries and all peaceful inhabitants of a country.

Consequently, new terms were introduced – 'combatants', 'non-combatants', and 'civilians' – as well as the principle of international humanitarian law that the targets of war would only be the combatants. Hence, parties to a conflict are obliged to conduct military operations exclusively against military objectives.

Combatants

Combatants are all members of the armed forces of a party to a conflict, with the exception of medical and religious personnel (combat medics and military chaplains), who are regarded as non-combatants.[1399] The states' practice established this rule as a norm of customary international law in international armed conflicts. It goes back to the **Hague Regulations** (Convention IV Respecting the Laws and Customs of War on Land and its annex, Regulations Concerning the Laws and Customs of War on Land of 1907).

According to the Hague Regulations, the term 'combatant' was applied not only to the members of the armed forces, but also to the militia and the volunteer corps fulfilling the following conditions:

1. To be commanded by a person responsible for his subordinates;
2. To have a fixed distinctive emblem recognizable at a distance;
3. To carry arms openly; and
4. To conduct their operations in accordance with the laws and customs of war.[1400]

At the same time, under the Hague Regulations, the inhabitants of a territory which has not been occupied shall also be regarded as combatants who, upon enemy attack, take up arms spontaneously to resist the invading troops without prior organisation and mobilisation, if they carry arms openly and respect the laws and customs of war.

The Additional Protocol I of 1977 to the Geneva Conventions reaffirmed these requirements and designated as combatants persons who:

- have the right to participate directly in hostilities;
- are members of the armed forces of a party to a conflict (other than medical personnel and chaplains);
- are organised under a command responsible to that party for the conduct of its subordinates, even if that party is represented by a government or an authority not recognised by an adversary;
- are obliged to distinguish themselves from the civilian population; and
- shall retain his or her status as a combatant if he or she openly carries arms
  - during each military engagement, and
  - when he or she is visible to the adversary while he or she is engaged in a military deployment preceding the launching of an attack in which he or she is to participate.[1401]

1399 Article 3 of the Convention IV Respecting the Laws and Customs of War on Land and its annex: Regulations concerning the Laws and Customs of War on Land of 1907: 'The armed forces of the belligerent parties may consist of combatants and non-combatants.'

1400 Article 1 of the Annex to the Convention: Regulations Respecting the Laws and Customs of War on Land, Section I: On Belligerents, Chapter I: The Qualifications of Belligerents – Regulations.

1401 Paragraph 2 of Article 43 and Paragraph 3 of Article 44 of the Protocol Additional to the Geneva Conventions of 12 August 1949, and relating to the Protection of Victims of International Armed Conflicts.

Partisans

Although in practice the conditions listed here are rarely interpreted strictly, nevertheless, they are essential in determining the status of a combatant. For instance, **partisans** are regarded as combatants if they are under a command responsible for their conduct, have insignia distinguishing them from the civilian population, carry their arms openly, and respect the rules of international humanitarian law.

Saboteurs, mercenaries, and spies

On the other hand, **saboteurs**, **mercenaries**, and **spies** do not qualify as combatants because they do not always follow the laws and customs of war or usually do not wear a uniform or carry arms openly. Accordingly, they fall under the category of **unlawful combatants**. An unlawful combatant may be detained or prosecuted under the domestic law of the detaining state for unlawful acts of war.

Mercenary

According to the Additional Protocol I, a mercenary shall not be a combatant or a prisoner of war. At the same time, under the definition in Protocol I, a mercenary is any person who:

- is specially recruited to fight in an armed conflict and directly participates in the hostilities;
- is motivated essentially by the desire for private gain and, in fact, is promised, by or on behalf of a party to the conflict, material compensation which is substantially higher than that promised or paid to combatants of similar ranks and functions in the armed forces of that party; and
- is neither a national of a party to the conflict nor a resident of a territory controlled by a party to the conflict, is not a member of the armed forces of a party to the conflict, and was not sent by a state which is not a party to the conflict on official duty as a member of its armed forces.[1402]

Combatants' privileges

In turn, combatants may fight in legitimate acts of war, for which they may not be subjected to criminal prosecution. At the same time, combatants who are captured have the right to the status and guarantees accorded to **prisoners of war**, and their detention should not be a form of punishment, but shall only target prevention of their further participation in the conflict. These special rights are called the **combatants' privileges**.

1402 Article 47 of the Protocol Additional to the Geneva Conventions of 12 August 1949, and relating to the Protection of Victims of International Armed Conflicts.

Non-combatants

As for non-combatants (for example, combat medics and military chaplains), they are members of the armed forces but do not have any combat mission (i.e. do not directly participate in the hostilities).

Certain states additionally recognise as non-combatants judges, government officials, blue-collar workers,[1403] and so on.

The non-combatant members of the armed forces are not to be confused, however, with civilians accompanying the armed forces who are not the members of the armed forces.

The protection of non-combatants

Since the target of war should only be military objectives, non-combatants enjoy **protection from direct attack** and from any form of direct harm. According to the Hague Regulations, in case of capture by the enemy, non-combatants also have the right to be treated as prisoners of war.

Civilian persons and objects

On the other hand, international humanitarian law also assigns the specific legal protection regime to **civilian persons** and objects, which, by definition, shall be immune from direct attack.

The distinction between civilians and combatants

The **principle of distinction** prescribes the distinction between civilians and combatants and between civilian objects and military objects. In its **Advisory Opinion on Legality of the Threat or Use of Nuclear Weapons** of 1996, the International Court of Justice stated that the principle of distinction is one of the 'cardinal principles' of international humanitarian law and one of the 'intransgressible principles of international customary law'.[1404]

1403 For example, the military manuals of Germany.

1404 'It is undoubtedly because a great many rules of humanitarian law applicable in armed conflict are so fundamental to the respect of the human person and "elementary considerations of humanity" as the Court put it in its Judgment of 9 April 1949 in the *Corfu Channel* case . . . that the Hague and Geneva Conventions have enjoyed a broad accession. Further these fundamental rules are to be observed by all States whether or not they have ratified the conventions that contain them, because they constitute intransgressible principles of international customary law.' *Legality of the Threat or Use of Nuclear Weapons*, Advisory Opinion, 8 July 1996.

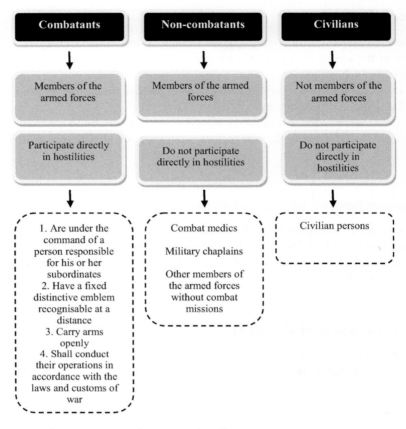

FIGURE 17.1 Combatants, non-combatants, and civilians

The second postulate of the new approach

Concerning the legitimate object of war, which is the weakening of the enemy military forces, the Declaration of Saint Petersburg articulated that it is sufficient to disable the greatest possible number of combatants and if this object would not be exceeded 'by the employment of arms which uselessly aggravate the sufferings of disabled men, or render their death inevitable'. This fundamental rule led to the necessity of:

- the regulation of the **methods of warfare**; and
- the prohibition or limitation of the **means of warfare**, i.e. the weapons, 'which uselessly aggravate the sufferings of disabled men, or render their death inevitable' since the employment of such arms at the time of the Declaration of Saint Petersburg was already considered to be 'contrary to the laws of humanity.'

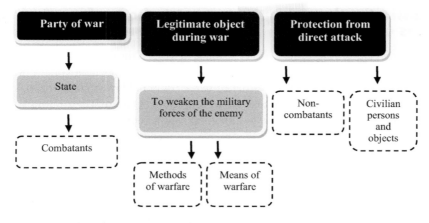

FIGURE 17.2 Basics of modern international humanitarian law

THE METHODS AND MEANS OF WARFARE

perfidy
improper use of distinctive emblems and signs
inhumane treatment
hors de combat
indiscriminate attacks
quarter
reprisals
belligerent reprisals
starvation
damage to the natural environment
damage to works and installations containing dangerous forces
exploding projectiles weighing less than 400 grams
bullets which expand or flatten easily in the human body
dumdum bullets
poison or poisoned weapons
asphyxiating, poisonous, or other gases
bacteriological methods of warfare
Biological Weapons Convention
Chemical Weapons Convention
conventional weapons
weapons that are not detectable in the human body by X-rays
incendiary weapons
blinding laser weapons
landmines, booby-traps, and other devices
anti-personnel landmines
cluster munitions
new weapons

The distinction between the terms 'methods of warfare' and 'means of warfare'

As noted earlier, the only legitimate object of war is to weaken the military forces of the enemy and disable the greatest possible number of combatants. To this end, international humanitarian law norms prohibit or otherwise restrict certain kinds of military strategy or behaviour and certain types of weapons or provide regulations concerning their use. These norms are usually referred to as the methods and means of warfare, where the term 'methods' describes the ways of conducting hostilities, and the term 'means' relates to all types of weapons.

The 'basic rules' of warfare

In order to result in the practical effect of the fundamental principles and postulates described earlier, international humanitarian law first determines that the right to choose methods and means of warfare is not unlimited. Secondly, it prohibits employing methods and means of warfare which cause superfluous injury or unnecessary suffering. Finally, it restrains methods and means of warfare which are intended, or may be expected, to cause widespread, long-term, and severe damage to the natural environment. These regulations are collectively known as the 'basic rules' of warfare.

The prohibited methods of warfare

Concerning the prohibited methods of warfare, international humanitarian law introduces numerous particular restrictions, which include the following prohibitions (this list is not exhaustive):

- **Perfidy** – Killing, injuring, or capturing an adversary by resorting to perfidy is prohibited. According to Additional Protocol I, perfidy is defined as the feigning of an intent to negotiate under a flag of truce or of a surrender; the feigning of an incapacitation by wounds or sickness; the feigning of being a civilian or non-combatant; and the feigning of having a protected status by the use of signs, emblems, or uniforms of the United Nations or other international organisations or of neutral or other states not parties to the conflict.[1405]
- **Improper use of distinctive emblems and signs** – Emblems and signs shall be used only for the reasons they were designed (to signify certain units, personnel, vehicles, and material). This includes the distinctive emblems of the red cross, red crescent, or red crystal or other emblems, signs, or signals, as well as the flags or military emblems, insignia, or uniforms of neutral or other states not parties to the conflict.
- **Inhumane treatment** of persons who are not directly participating or have ceased to take part in hostile actions, such as violence to the life, health, and physical or mental well-being of persons; collective punishments; taking of hostages; acts of terrorism; outrages upon personal dignity, in particular humiliating and degrading treatment, rape,

---

1405 Article 37 of the Protocol Additional to the Geneva Conventions of 12 August 1949, and relating to the Protection of Victims of International Armed Conflicts.

enforced prostitution, and any form of indecent assault; slavery and the slave trade in all their forms; pillage; and threats to commit any of the foregoing acts are prohibited.

- Attacks on persons **hors de combat** or parachuting from an aircraft in distress are prohibited. According to Additional Protocol I, a person is *hors de combat* if he or she is in the power of an adverse party, clearly expresses an intention to surrender, has been rendered unconscious or is otherwise incapacitated by wounds or sickness, or is incapable of defending him- or herself, provided that, in any of these cases, he or she abstains from any hostile act and does not attempt to escape.[1406] As for a person who has parachuted from an aircraft in distress, he or she shall be allowed to surrender before being made the object of attack, unless it is apparent that he or she is engaging in a hostile act.
- **Indiscriminate attacks** – i.e. attacks on military objectives, civilians, or civilian objects without distinction – are prohibited. For example, (1) attacks not directed against a specific military objective or (2) the employment of methods or means of combat which cannot be directed against a specific military objective.
- **Quarter** – The prohibition on declaring that no quarter will be given is a long-standing rule of customary international law. Thus, it is prohibited to order that there shall be no survivors, to threaten an adversary therewith, or to conduct hostilities on this basis.
- **Reprisals** (also referred to as the **belligerent reprisals**) – Any action which *per se* is illegal but only in exceptional cases is regarded to be lawful under international law when used as an enforcement measure in response to unlawful acts of an adversary. Reprisals are prohibited against non-military objectives and the persons or objects protected by international humanitarian law. In addition, even concerning military objectives, as referred to earlier in this book, belligerent reprisals are permitted if they are:
  - taken in reaction to a prior serious violation of international humanitarian law, only for the purpose of inducing the adversary to comply with the law and must cease as soon as the adversary complies with the law;
  - taken after the unsatisfied demand for the compliance with the norms of international humanitarian law;
  - carried out as a measure of last resort;
  - proportionate to the violation they aim to stop; and
  - taken at the highest level of government.
- **Starvation** – It is prohibited to attack, destroy, remove, or render useless, for that purpose, objects indispensable to the survival of the civilian population, such as foodstuffs, agricultural areas for the production of foodstuffs, crops, livestock, drinking water installations and supplies, and irrigation works.[1407]
- **Damage to the natural environment** or **to works and installations containing dangerous forces** – It is prohibited to use methods or means of warfare which are intended

---

1406 Article 41 of the Protocol Additional to the Geneva Conventions of 12 August 1949, and relating to the Protection of Victims of International Armed Conflicts.

1407 Article 14 of the Protocol Additional to the Geneva Conventions of 12 August 1949, and relating to the Protection of Victims of International Armed Conflicts.

or may be expected to cause widespread, long-term, and severe damage to the natural environment or attacks against dams, dykes, or nuclear electrical-generating stations if such attack may cause the release of dangerous forces and consequent severe losses among the civilian population.

The general principles guiding the prohibition of means of warfare

As regards means of warfare, the process of limitation of particular weapons is governed by three general principles of international humanitarian law, which are:

1   Means which would render the death of adverse persons inevitable are prohibited.
2   Means which would uselessly aggravate the sufferings of adverse persons are prohibited.
3   Means that have indiscriminate effects, hitting military and civilian objectives alike, are prohibited.

Prohibited means of warfare

At first, international treaties prohibited:

- 'the employment by . . . military or naval troops of any projectile of a weight below 400 grammes, which is either explosive or charged with fulminating or inflammable substances' – **exploding projectiles weighing less than 400 grams** (Declaration of Saint Petersburg of 1868);
- 'the use of **bullets which expand or flatten easily in the human body**, such as bullets with a hard envelope which does not entirely cover the core or is pierced with incisions' – this was introduced mostly with a view to banning British-made '**dumdum**' **bullets** (Hague Declaration Concerning Expanding Bullets of 1899);
- 'to employ **poison or poisoned weapons**' (Hague Regulations of 1907); and
- 'the use in war of **asphyxiating, poisonous, or other gases**, and of all analogous liquids, materials or devices' and of **bacteriological methods of warfare** (Geneva Protocol of 1925).

The Geneva Protocol of 1925 was updated by the **Biological Weapons Convention** of 1972 (Convention on the Prohibition of the Development, Production and Stockpiling of Bacteriological [Biological] and Toxin Weapons and on their Destruction) and the **Chemical Weapons Convention** of 1993 (Convention on the Prohibition of the Development, Production, Stockpiling and Use of Chemical Weapons and on their Destruction). These conventions strengthened the Geneva Protocol of 1925 by spreading prohibitions on the development, production, acquisition, stockpiling, retention, and transfer of biological and chemical weapons and requiring their destruction.

A number of **conventional weapons** are regulated in the 1980 Convention on Prohibitions or Restrictions on the Use of Certain Conventional Weapons which may be deemed to be Excessively Injurious or to have Indiscriminate Effects, which prescribes the elimination of effects of the explosive remnants of war (Protocol V (2003) to the Convention) and prohibits the use of:

- Any weapon, the primary effect of which is to injure by fragments that are **not detectable in the human body by X-rays.**
- **Incendiary weapons**, which are primarily designed to set fire to objects or to cause burn injury to persons through the action of flame, heat, or combination thereof (Protocol III (1980) to the Convention), inter alia:
  - to make the civilian population as such, individual civilians, or civilian objects the object of attack;
  - to make any military objective located within a concentration of civilians the object of attack by air-delivered incendiary weapons;
  - to make any military objective located within a concentration of civilians the object of an attack employing incendiary weapons other than air-delivered incendiary weapons, except when such military objective is clearly separated from the concentration of civilians;
  - to make forests or other kinds of plant cover the object of attack by incendiary weapons except when such natural elements are used to cover, conceal, or camouflage combatants or other military objectives or are themselves military objectives.
- **Blinding laser weapons** specifically designed, as their sole combat function or as one of their combat functions, to cause permanent blindness to unenhanced vision – that is, to the naked eye or to the eye with corrective eyesight devices (Protocol IV (1995) to the Convention).
- **Landmines, booby-traps, and other devices** (Protocol II as amended in 1996 covered 'the use on land of the mines, booby-traps and other devices'; however, it did not apply to 'the use of the anti-ship mines at sea or in inland waterways')[1408] if:
  - they are of a nature to cause unnecessary suffering or superfluous injury;
  - they are designed to explode when detected by mine-detection equipment;[1409] or
  - they are directed against civilians or civilian objects, i.e. are used indiscriminately.

In addition, under Protocol II, '[e]ffective advance warning shall be given of any emplacement of mines, booby-traps and other devices which may affect the civilian population, unless circumstances do not permit.'[1410] At the same time, Protocol III also prescribed other

---

1408 Article 1 of the Protocol on Prohibitions or Restrictions on the Use of Mines, Booby-Traps and Other Devices as amended on 3 May 1996 (Protocol II, as amended on 3 May 1996).

1409 'It is prohibited to use mines, booby-traps or other devices which employ a mechanism or device specifically designed to detonate the munition by the presence of commonly available mine detectors as a result of their magnetic or other non-contact influence during normal use in detection operations.' Article 3 (5) of the Protocol on Prohibitions or Restrictions on the Use of Mines, Booby-Traps and Other Devices as amended on 3 May 1996.

1410 Article 3 (11) of the Protocol on Prohibitions or Restrictions on the Use of Mines, Booby-Traps and Other Devices as amended on 3 May 1996.

preconditions when the prohibition of the use of such weapons shall be applied. For example, the use of anti-personnel mines are prohibited if they are not detectable.[1411]

The next significant step was the final ban of **anti-personnel landmines** under the 1997 Convention on the Prohibition of the Use, Stockpiling, Production and Transfer of Anti-Personnel Mines and on their Destruction, which aimed to eliminate anti-personnel landmines (AP mines) around the world.[1412] In other words, it is prohibited to use, develop, produce, or otherwise acquire, stockpile, retain, or transfer to anyone (directly or indirectly) anti-personnel mines, as well as to assist, encourage, or induce, in any way, anyone to engage in any activity prohibited to a party under the Convention.[1413]

In 2008, the majority of UN member states adopted the Convention on Cluster Munitions. According to the Convention, each state undertakes never, under any circumstances, to:

- use **cluster munitions**;
- develop, produce, otherwise acquire, stockpile, retain, or transfer to anyone, directly or indirectly, cluster munitions; or
- assist, encourage, or induce anyone to engage in any activity prohibited under the Convention.

Thus, the international community progressively prohibits or limits the weapons contradicting the principles of international humanitarian law, but the scientific and technical development of humanity leads to inventing **new weapons**. In order to respond to this challenge, Additional Protocol I of 1977 established explicitly the rule that, in the study, development, acquisition, or adoption of a new weapon, means, or method of warfare, a state is under an obligation to determine whether its employment would, in some or all circumstances, be prohibited by this Protocol or by any other applicable rule of international law.[1414]

A separate issue is **nuclear weapons**, which, despite their destructive power and threat to the whole of humankind, still occupy a special place in the interstate security system. Hence, with respect to nuclear weapons within the framework of international law, a particular and sophisticated approach was developed.

NUCLEAR WEAPONS

atomic bombs
thermonuclear bombs
threat or use of nuclear weapons

1411 Article 4 of the Protocol on Prohibitions or Restrictions on the Use of Mines, Booby-Traps and Other Devices as amended on 3 May 1996.

1412 However, as of the time this book was written, such superpowers as China, Russia, and the United States have not ratified the treaty.

1413 Article 1 of the Convention on the Prohibition of the Use, Stockpiling, Production and Transfer of Anti-Personnel Mines and on their Destruction.

1414 Article 36 of the Protocol Additional to the Geneva Conventions of 12 August 1949, and relating to the Protection of Victims of International Armed Conflicts.

Treaty on the Prohibition of Nuclear Weapons
self-defence
policy of deterrence
Advisory Opinion on *Legality of the Threat or Use of Nuclear Weapons*
good faith
protection of the environment
nuclear proliferation
nuclear-weapons-free zones
nuclear testing
nuclear disarmament
control over nuclear forces
Treaty on the Non-Proliferation of Nuclear Weapons
International Atomic Energy Agency

The current state of affairs

Although nuclear weapons (**atomic bombs** and **thermonuclear** [hydrogen] **bombs**)[1415] have the potential to threaten not only the whole of humanity but also the very possibility of life on earth, the interstate system has not yet been able to attain the universal consent reflected in international law on the general prohibition of the **threat or use of nuclear weapons**.

The campaign to abolish nuclear weapons

Nevertheless, the issue of a nuclear weapons ban has long been on the international agenda. In this process, the UN organs are involved (for example, the first resolution was adopted by the UN General Assembly in 1946), as well as numerous states, international organisations, and interested groups. Finally, the campaign to abolish nuclear weapons resulted in the **Treaty on the Prohibition of Nuclear Weapons** (also referred to as the Nuclear Weapon Ban Treaty) in 2017. The aim of the Treaty was to establish the first legally binding comprehensive international agreement to ban nuclear weapons. It contains prohibitions against the development, testing, production, stockpiling, stationing, otherwise acquiring, transferring, using, and threat of using nuclear weapons, as well as against assistance and encouragement of prohibited activities.

Although on 22 January 2021, the Treaty entered into force, the nuclear-weapon states did not sign the Treaty, and, furthermore, for instance, the United States, the United

---

1415 Nuclear weapons are explosive devices whose destructive force generates from either nuclear fission chain reactions (by splitting the nucleus of an atom) or combined nuclear fission and fusion reactions. The former devices are usually called atomic bombs, while those that start with the same fission reaction that powers atomic bombs but produce most of their energy in nuclear fusion reactions are termed thermonuclear (hydrogen) bombs.

Kingdom, and France issued a joint statement asserting that they did not intend to sign, ratify, or ever become the party to this agreement.

The arguments against the universal prohibition of nuclear weapons

Many countries are against the universal prohibition of nuclear weapons. Basically, their arguments are as follows:

1   Nuclear weapons are a mechanism to exercise the inherent right of every state to **self-defence**.
2   Nuclear weapons have been considered a vital tool for the policy of deterrence ever since the Cold War, and they serve as one of the most decisive obstacles to the unleashing of a world war by effectively eliminating the possibility of victory or making the gains of victory in the nuclear war extremely marginal for everyone.[1416]

Moreover, the strategic documents of some nuclear-weapon states certainly leave room for wider interpretations regarding use of the nuclear weapons. For example, one such recent document is the Decree of the President of the Russian Federation 'On the Fundamentals of State Policy of the Russian Federation in the Field of Nuclear Deterrence'. According to the Decree, the Russian Federation reserves the right to use nuclear weapons in response to the use of nuclear weapons and other weapons of mass destruction against it and/or its allies, as well as in the case of aggression against the Russian Federation using conventional weapons when the very existence of the state is threatened.[1417]

The Nuclear Weapons Advisory Opinion

In relation to the issue of the present state of international law with regard to the prohibition of the threat or use of nuclear weapons, the International Court of Justice was directed by the UN General Assembly to deliver its advisory opinion on the following question: 'Is the threat or use of nuclear weapons in any circumstance permitted under international law?'

In 1996, the International Court of Justice provided the **Advisory Opinion on *Legality of the Threat or Use of Nuclear Weapons*** . To address the request, the Court stressed that it cannot lose sight of the fundamental right of every state to survival and the right

---

1416 In the discipline of International Relations, many authors share these assumptions, such as the supporters of the deterrence theory and the nuclear peace theory. Proponents of nuclear peace argue that controlled nuclear proliferation may be beneficial for inducing stability. The prominent founder of neorealist theory in the International Relations, Kenneth Waltz, argued that 'the gradual spread of nuclear weapons is better than no spread and better than rapid spread'. Kenneth Waltz, 'The Spread of Nuclear Weapons: More May Better', Adelphi Papers, Number 171 (London: International Institute for Strategic Studies 1981).

1417 Paragraph 17 of the Decree of the President of the Russian Federation of 2 June 2020 No. 355 on the Fundamentals of State Policy of the Russian Federation in the Field of Nuclear Deterrence.

to resort to self-defence under Article 51 of the UN Charter when its survival is at stake. Accordingly, it concluded: 'A threat or use of force by means of nuclear weapons that is contrary to Article 2, paragraph 4, of the United Nations Charter and that fails to meet all the requirements of Article 51, is unlawful'. At the same time, ICJ emphasised that it could not ignore the practice referred to as the policy of deterrence, to which an appreciable section of the international community had adhered to for many years.

On the other hand, the ICJ acknowledged that the methods and means of warfare which would preclude any distinction between the civilian and military targets or would result in unnecessary suffering of combatants are prohibited by international humanitarian law. Because of the 'unique characteristics of nuclear weapons . . . the use of such weapons in fact seems scarcely reconcilable with respect for such requirements.' Thus, the threat or use of such weapons 'would generally be contrary to the rules of international law applicable in armed conflict.' However, the Court abandoned to resolve precisely when (in which cases) the threat or use of nuclear weapons would be lawful or unlawful in an exceptional circumstance of self-defence, in which the very survival of a state would be at stake.

In addition, the ICJ studied the nuclear disarmament matter and, in this context, reaffirmed the obligation of the states to pursue in **good faith** and bring to conclusion the 'negotiations leading to nuclear disarmament in all its aspects under strict and effective international control.'

Finally, the ICJ concluded that:

> There is in neither customary nor conventional international law any comprehensive and universal prohibition of the threat or use of nuclear weapons as such.

The Nuclear Weapons Advisory Opinion has led to contradictory assessments among scholars as well as representatives of international organisations. A particularly critical assessment came from the International Committee of the Red Cross – specifically that the ICRC found it difficult to envisage how any use of nuclear weapons could be compatible with the rules of international humanitarian law.

An additional issue of interest in this regard was the norms of international law related to the **protection of the environment**, as well as the principle of international humanitarian law restricting the employment of methods or means of warfare which are intended or may be expected to cause widespread, long-term, and severe damage to the natural environment. However, the ICJ envisaged that the obligations stemming from the environmental treaties were neither intended to be 'obligations of total restraint during military conflict' nor to 'deprive a State of the exercise of its right of self-defence under international law because of its obligations to protect the environment'. Rather, the ICJ introspected respect for the environmental rules as 'one of the elements that go to assessing whether an action is in conformity with the principles of necessity and proportionality'.

The practical matters concerning nuclear weapons

Despite the unsuccessful universal prohibition of nuclear weapons under international law, the subjects of international law are fully aware of the relevance of legal limitations that might be put on nuclear weapons. To this end, more practical matters were identified to which the global agreement of states was obtainable. Hence, over the years, a number of multilateral treaties have been established with the aim of:

- preventing **nuclear proliferation,**
  - including the establishment of **nuclear-weapons-free zones** as an additional component of the non-proliferation regime;
- regulating **nuclear testing;**
- promoting progress in the **nuclear disarmament;** or
- preventing nuclear war.

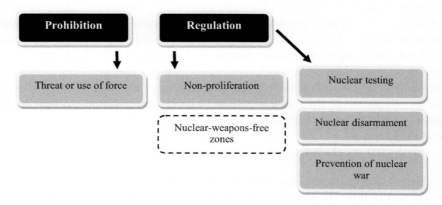

FIGURE 17.3 Challenges concerning nuclear weapons

Non-proliferation

The **Treaty on the Non-Proliferation of Nuclear Weapons** of 1968 is a landmark, universally agreed legal instrument. The structure of the treaty is based on three central pillars:

1   Non-proliferation. The nuclear-weapon states pledge not to transfer nuclear weapons or other nuclear explosive devices to any recipient or in any way assist, encourage, or induce any non-nuclear-weapon state to manufacture or acquire nuclear weapons. On their part, non-nuclear-weapon states take up the obligation not to acquire or exercise control over nuclear weapons or other nuclear explosive devices and not to seek or receive assistance to make such weapons or devices.[1418]
2   Peaceful use of nuclear energy. The Treaty acknowledges the right of all Parties to develop research, production, and use of nuclear energy for peaceful purposes without discrimination, but only in conformity with their nonproliferation obligations.[1419]
3   Disarmament. According to the Treaty, all parties undertake to pursue good-faith negotiations 'on effective measures relating to cessation of the nuclear arms race at

1418 Articles I, II of the Treaty on the Non-Proliferation of Nuclear Weapons.
1419 Article IV of the Treaty on the Non-Proliferation of Nuclear Weapons.

an early date and to nuclear disarmament, and on a treaty on general and complete disarmament under strict and effective international control.'[1420]

At the current moment, only nine states possess nuclear weapons. These states are the five permanent members of the UN Security Council, which are recognised nuclear-weapon states under the Treaty on the Non-Proliferation of Nuclear Weapons, as well as the Democratic People's Republic of Korea, India, Israel, and Pakistan, which are not parties to the Treaty and, therefore, are not recognised in such status under the Treaty.

International Atomic Energy Agency

According to the Treaty, the so-called safeguards system under the auspices of the **International Atomic Energy Agency** was introduced. Created in 1957, the Agency is an autonomous international organisation within the United Nations system,[1421] with its headquarters in Vienna, Austria.

The **International Atomic Energy Agency's safeguards system** (also referred to as the IAEA Safeguards) was developed for the exclusive purpose of verification of the fulfilment of states' obligations. The legal framework for the safeguards system consists of, among other things:

- the International Atomic Energy Agency's Statute;
- the States' obligations under the Treaty on the Non-Proliferation of Nuclear Weapons;
- the safeguards agreements:
  - the comprehensive safeguards agreements with non-nuclear-weapon states parties to the Treaty on the Non-Proliferation of Nuclear Weapons;
  - voluntary safeguards agreements with the nuclear-weapon states parties to the Treaty;
  - item-specific safeguards agreements with non-Treaty states; and
- the treaties establishing nuclear-weapon-free zones.

Nuclear-weapons-free zones

Nuclear-weapons-free zones are significant complementary mechanisms for the non-proliferation regime and the peaceful use of nuclear energy. The Treaty on the Non-Proliferation of Nuclear Weapons itself contributed to the creation of such zones by maintaining the right of any group of states to conclude regional treaties in order to assure the total

1420 ibid.
1421 According to Article 1 of the Agreement Governing the Relationship between the United Nations and the International Atomic Energy Agency (IAEA) of 1957: 'The United Nations recognizes the International Atomic Energy Agency . . . as the agency, under the aegis of the United Nations as specified in this Agreement. . . . The United Nations recognizes that the Agency, by virtue of its inter-governmental character and international responsibilities, will function under its Statute as an autonomous international organization in the working relationship with the United Nations established by this Agreement'.

absence of nuclear weapons in their respective territories. So far, five regional treaties constituting nuclear-weapons-free zones have been concluded:

- the Treaty for the Prohibition of Nuclear Weapons in Latin America and the Caribbean (Treaty of Tlatelolco) of 1967;[1422]
- the South Pacific Nuclear Free Zone Treaty (Treaty of Rarotonga) of 1985;
- the Southeast Asian Nuclear-Weapon-Free Zone Treaty (Bangkok Treaty) of 1995;
- the African Nuclear Weapon Free Zone Treaty (Pelindaba Treaty) of 1996; and
- the Central Asian Nuclear-Weapon-Free Zone Treaty (Semipalatinsk Treaty) of 2006.

Mongolia's self-declared nuclear-weapon-free status has been recognised internationally through the adoption of UN General Assembly resolution on Mongolia's international security and nuclear-weapon-free status.

In addition, nuclear-weapons-free areas (zones) are:

- the Antarctic – under the Antarctic Treaty;
- outer space, including the moon and other celestial bodies – according to the Outer Space Treaty and the Moon Agreement; and
- the seabed, the ocean floor, and the subsoil thereof – under the Seabed Arms Control Treaty – Treaty on the Prohibition of the Emplacement of Nuclear Weapons and Other Weapons of Mass Destruction on the Sea-Bed and the Ocean Floor and in the Subsoil Thereof, which bans the emplacement of nuclear weapons or 'any other types of weapons of mass destruction' on the ocean floor beyond 12 nautical miles from the baseline from which the breadth of the territorial sea is measured.

Testing

As for the testing of nuclear weapons, this activity is prohibited in the nuclear-weapons-free zones according to the treaties mentioned here. Furthermore, there are other international treaties which also pursue the similar aim of banning the testing of the nuclear weapons in certain areas. For instance, the Treaty Banning Nuclear Weapon Tests in the Atmosphere, in Outer Space, and Under Water of 1963, also known as the Partial Test Ban Treaty.

The Treaty was signed between the United States of America, the United Kingdom of Great Britain and Northern Ireland, and the Union of Soviet Socialist Republics and prohibited any nuclear weapon test explosion

(a) in the atmosphere; beyond its limits, including outer space; or under water, including territorial waters or high seas; or (b) in any other environment if such explosion causes radioactive debris to be present outside the territorial limits of the State under whose jurisdiction or control such explosion is conducted.

1422 Under Article 1 of the Treaty, the contracting parties undertake the obligation to prohibit and prevent in their respective territories the 'testing, use, manufacture, production, or acquisition by any means whatsoever of any nuclear weapons' and 'receipt, storage, installation, deployment, and any form of possession of any nuclear weapons, directly or indirectly'.

The parties also proclaimed their aspiration to further the negotiations to achieve 'the permanent banning of all nuclear test explosions, including all such explosions underground'.[1423]

The next effort to achieve a permanent ban on all nuclear test explosions was the Comprehensive Nuclear-Test-Ban Treaty, which was signed in 1996 but has not yet entered into force (as of the time this book was written).

At the present time, the majority of the states as well as scholars claim that a ban on the testing of the nuclear weapons in the atmosphere, in outer space, and underwater has crystallised into general international law and is gradually being recognised by the nuclear-weapon states.[1424]

The same is not the case, however, concerning the underground testing of nuclear weapons.[1425]

Disarmament

As noted earlier, the Treaty on the Non-Proliferation of Nuclear Weapons is the key legal instrument concerning the pursuit in good faith and the conclusion of negotiations on nuclear disarmament.

A number of bilateral and multilateral agreements seek to reduce or fully eliminate certain categories of nuclear weapons:

*   The agreements between the United States of America and the Soviet Union. (In this matter, its principal successor is the Russian Federation.) For example, the

---

1423   Article I of the Treaty Banning Nuclear Weapon Tests in the Atmosphere, in Outer Space and Under Water.

1424   For example, France also declared the cessation of atmospheric nuclear tests. As noted on the website of the ICJ: 'On 9 May 1973, Australia and New Zealand each instituted proceedings against France concerning tests of nuclear weapons which France proposed to carry out in the atmosphere in the South Pacific region. . . . By two Orders of 22 June 1973, the Court, at the request of Australia and New Zealand, indicated provisional measures to the effect, *inter alia*, that pending judgment France should avoid nuclear tests causing radioactive fall-out on Australian or New Zealand territory. By two Judgments delivered on 20 December 1974, the Court found that the Applications of Australia and New Zealand no longer had any object and that it was therefore not called upon to give any decision thereon. In so doing the Court based itself on the conclusion that the objective of Australia and New Zealand had been achieved inasmuch as France, in various public statements, had announced its intention of carrying out no further atmospheric nuclear tests on the completion of the 1974 series.' <www.icj-cij.org/en/case/58> accessed 18 March 2021.

1425   'Unlike atmospheric testing, recent state practice regarding underground testing is not uniform. Certainly, since the CTBT was opened for signature in 1996, none of the NPT nuclear weapon states has conducted underground nuclear weapons tests. The three states that have tested since 1996 – India, Pakistan, and DPR Korea – faced international criticism and sanctions, and India and Pakistan have since declared moratoria. . . . Even if there was a general rule of customary international law prohibiting underground testing, India and Pakistan, and possibly DPR Korea, would doubtless argue that they have been persistent objectors to the applicability of any such rule to them.' Don MacKay, 'The Testing of Nuclear Weapons under International Law' in G. Nystuen, S. Casey-Maslen, and A. Bersagel (eds), *Nuclear Weapons under International Law* (Cambridge University Press 2014) 317, 318.

1987 Intermediate-Range Nuclear Forces Treaty required the United States and the Soviet Union to eliminate and permanently forswear all of their nuclear and conventional ground-launched ballistic and cruise missiles with ranges of 500 to 5,500 kilometres.[1426]

- Various other arrangements:

  - regarding nuclear exports and nuclear-related exports (Nuclear Suppliers Group);
  - limiting the proliferation of missiles and missile technology (Missile Technology Control Regime); and
  - the Hague Code of Conduct against Ballistic Missile Proliferation of 2002.

Prevention of nuclear war

The other crucial matter regarding the regulation of nuclear weapons is the prevention of nuclear war by co-operation between the nuclear-weapon states. A prominent example of such legal arrangement is represented by the 1971 Agreement on Measures to Reduce the Risk of Outbreak of Nuclear War Between the United States of America and the Union of Soviet Socialist Republics. Under this Agreement, each party undertook the obligation to maintain and improve its existing organisational and technical arrangements to guard against the accidental or unauthorised use of nuclear weapons under its control; to notify each other immediately in the event of an accidental, unauthorised, or any other unexplained incident involving a possible detonation of a nuclear weapon; and so on.

The same parties concluded the 1973 Agreement between the United States of America and the Union of Soviet Socialist Republics on the Prevention of Nuclear War, which reaffirmed the obligation of the parties to enter immediately into urgent consultations with each other and make every effort to avert the risk of a nuclear conflict. Similar international treaties were signed between other nuclear-weapon states too. For example, the French-Soviet Agreement of 1976 and the Soviet-United Kingdom Agreement of 1977 on the prevention of accidental or unauthorised use of nuclear weapons.

INTERNATIONAL AND NON-INTERNATIONAL ARMED CONFLICTS

> **Common Article 3**
> **minimum standards of humanity**
> **Additional Protocol II**

1426 'On Dec. 4, 2018, Secretary of State Mike Pompeo announced that the United States found Russia in "material breach" of the treaty and would suspend its treaty obligations in 60 days if Russia did not return to compliance in that time. On Feb. 2, the Trump administration declared a suspension of U.S. obligations under the INF Treaty and formally announced its intention to withdraw from the treaty in six months. Shortly thereafter, Russian President Vladimir Putin also announced that Russia will be officially suspending its treaty obligations as well. On Aug. 2, 2019, the United States formally withdrew from the INF Treaty.' See <www.armscontrol.org/factsheets/INFtreaty> accessed 18 March 2021.

> *Prosecutor v Dusko Tadić* case
> protracted armed violence
> organised armed groups
> non-discrimination precept
> absence of the combatant's status
> guarantees of persons whose liberty has been restricted

Inclusion of the regulations on non-international armed conflicts in international law

Initially, non-international armed conflicts were beyond the scope of the law of armed conflict. However, gradually, the states have acknowledged that there are some situations which cannot be left outside international law regulation since they are of concern to the international community as a whole.

The first significant step in this direction was the adoption of the four 1949 Geneva Conventions, which included **common Article 3** reflecting the **minimum standards of humanity** concerning non-international armed conflicts. In order to further develop those standards, the 1977 Protocol Additional to the Geneva Conventions of 12 August 1949, and relating to the Protection of Victims of Non-International Armed Conflicts (**Additional Protocol II**) was adopted.

The distinction between international and non-international armed conflict

An armed conflict between two or more states is considered an international conflict.

On the other hand, a non-international armed conflict is the prevalent form of the vast majority of armed conflicts in the world of today. These conflicts take place within the boundaries of a state and comprise an armed conflict between a state and an armed group or among armed groups which are outside the authority of a state. At the same time, non-international armed conflicts can be internationalised, for example, when a foreign state gets involved in the conflict on the side of the rebels.

Definition of a non-international armed conflict

Common Article 3 does not provide a definition of a non-international armed conflict. It merely refers to 'the case of armed conflict not of an international character occurring in the territory of one of the High Contracting Parties'. Nevertheless, the case law – for instance, the decision of the International Criminal Tribunal for the Former Yugoslavia in the *Prosecutor v Dusko Tadić* case – formulated the elements of a non-international armed conflict as follows: (1) **Protracted armed violence**

(2) between governmental authorities and **organised armed groups** or between such groups within a state.[1427]

Thus, there are the two key elements of a non-international armed conflict – protracted armed violence and the involvement of an organised armed group or groups. Meanwhile, in order to conclude that there is 'protracted armed violence', it is necessary to identify such characteristics as the intensity and duration of the confrontations, the type of weapons and other military equipment used, the number of persons and type of forces participating in the fighting, the extent of physical and material destruction, the involvement of international organisations, and so on. As for the 'organised armed groups', inter alia, the following factors would be indicative of the level of organisation of an armed group: The existence of a command structure and disciplinary rules and mechanisms; the existence of headquarters; the ability to plan, coordinate, and carry out military operations; the ability to negotiate and conclude agreements such as cease-fires or peace accords; and so on.

This definition does not include situations of internal disturbances and tensions such as riots, isolated and sporadic acts of violence, or other acts of a similar nature.

Additional Protocol II provides a more rigorous definition of a non-international armed conflict than Common Article 3. Hence, Additional Protocol II has a more limited scope of application. Whereas Common Article 3 refers generally to 'armed conflict not of an international character', Additional Protocol II applies only to armed conflict taking place:

- in the territory of a contracting state; and
- between the armed forces of a state, dissident armed forces, and/or other organised armed groups, which (1) under responsible command (2) exercise control over a part of their territory as to enable them (3) to carry out sustained and concerted military operations and (4) to implement the Protocol II.

The legal significance of the distinction

Although the contemporary trend stipulates amalgamation/integration between the substantial standards for the protection of human beings in an armed conflict,[1428] the distinction between international and non-international armed conflicts has not yet lost its legal significance since international humanitarian law still applies different rules to these

1427 *Prosecutor v Dusko Tadić* a/k/a 'DULE', Decision on the Defence Motion for Interlocutory Appeal on Jurisdiction of 2 October 1995, International Criminal Tribunal for the Former Yugoslavia.

1428 'It follows that in the area of armed conflict the distinction between interstate wars and civil wars is losing its value as far as human beings are concerned. Why protect civilians from belligerent violence, or ban rape, torture or the wanton destruction of hospitals, churches, museums or private property, as well as proscribe weapons causing unnecessary suffering when two sovereign States are engaged in war, and yet refrain from enacting the same bans or providing the same protection when armed violence has erupted "only" within the territory of a sovereign State? If international law, while of course duly safeguarding the legitimate interests of States, must gradually turn to the protection of human beings, it is only natural that the aforementioned dichotomy should gradually lose its weight.' *Prosecutor v Dusko Tadić* a/k/a 'DULE', Decision on the Defence Motion for Interlocutory Appeal on Jurisdiction of 2 October 1995, International Criminal Tribunal for the Former Yugoslavia, Paragraph 97.

conflicts. Thus, classifying the types of armed conflict is instrumental in order to correctly apply the rules and regulations to different cases of conflict.[1429]

The minimum standards of humanity concerning non-international conflicts

Common Article 3 of the four Geneva Conventions maintains the minimum standards of humanity with regard to non-international conflicts. It lists the following prohibited acts: The violence to life and person, in particular murder of all kinds, mutilation, cruel treatment, and torture; taking of hostages; outrages upon personal dignity, in particular, humiliating and degrading treatment; and the passing of sentences and the carrying out of executions without previous judgment pronounced by a regularly constituted court affording all the judicial guarantees, which are recognised as indispensable by civilised peoples.

Common Article 3 prescribes that the wounded and sick shall be collected and cared for. It also maintains the special status of the International Committee of the Red Cross, which may have an ability to offer its services to the parties to the conflict.

At the same time, the important point in this regard is to understand that the norms with respect to non-international armed conflicts essentially do not protect persons and objects based on their status or belonging to a certain category; rather, individuals as well as objects enjoy protection against the acts, which are prohibited. Only in some cases can the protected categories of individuals or objects in connection with non-international armed conflicts which are protected in a similar manner as persons and objects during international armed conflicts be identified – for instance, medical and religious personnel, cultural objects, and so on.

The protection against prohibited acts in times of non-international armed conflict should be performed without discrimination. Under Common Article 3, the **non-discrimination precept** is formulated as follows:

> Persons taking no active part in the hostilities, including members of armed forces who have laid down their arms and those placed *hors de combat* by sickness, wounds, detention, or any other cause, shall in all circumstances be treated humanely, without any adverse distinction founded on race, colour, religion or faith, sex, birth or wealth, or any other similar criteria.

Finally, it is essential to note that the application of the provisions of international humanitarian law to non-international armed conflicts does not affect the legal (international) status of the parties to the conflict, which should be considered under other norms

---

1429 In addition, there are subcategories of armed conflicts that have different applicable rules. For example, within international armed conflicts, there are more extensive rules that apply to situations of military occupation, which itself is not determined in the 1949 Geneva Conventions. However, Article 42 of the Annex to the 1907 Hague Convention IV includes the following definition: 'Territory is considered occupied *when it is actually placed under the authority of the hostile army*. The occupation extends only to the territory where such authority has been established and can be exercised.'

of general international law. Additional Protocol II develops this general approach reproduced in Common Article 3 with regard to its scope, which is purely humanitarian. Its regulations do not affect the sovereignty of a state or the responsibility of the government to maintain or re-establish law and order in the state or defend the national unity and territorial integrity of the state with the use of all legitimate means and methods at its disposal.

The applicable rules concerning non-international armed conflicts

The main distinction between the concepts and norms applicable to international and non-international armed conflicts is that in the case of non-international armed conflicts, the focus is on finding a balance between the humanitarian issues and the maintenance or re-establishment of law and order within a state. Indeed, the significant accent concerning non-international armed conflicts appears as the non-intervention rule maintaining the national unity and territorial integrity of a state.

As for the particular elements of the distinction, the following aspects, among others, may be outlined:

- The first feature of the law of non-international armed conflict is the **absence of the combatant's status**. National legislation usually regards rebellion as a crime; the legitimate armed forces of a state fight a rebellion under the domestic legislation, but the rebellious forces do not have the right to take up arms under national law. Meanwhile, the right to participate in hostilities is an essential feature (privilege) of the status of a combatant. The members of a dissident force who directly participate in hostilities in a non-international armed conflict cannot also possess the other privileges combatants are allowed. For instance, they may be prosecuted for all hostile acts, including violations of national legislation. Nevertheless, there are certain rules to safeguard such persons. For example, no sentence shall be passed or penalties executed for criminal offences related to the conflict except when a conviction is pronounced by an independent and impartial court. Persons under the age of 18 years at the time of the offence, pregnant women, and mothers of young children must not be punished with the death penalty.
- Persons captured during a non-international armed conflict are not entitled to prisoner of war status since such a status does not exist in the law of non-international armed conflict. Nevertheless, they shall be treated according to the minimum standards of humanity, and according to Additional Protocol II, the captives, whether they are interned or detained, should be given the **guarantees of persons whose liberty has been restricted**.[1430]
- As noted earlier, in extreme cases, parties to an international armed conflict may resort to **reprisals**, subject to stringent conditions when not expressly prohibited under international humanitarian law. However, parties to non-international armed conflicts do not have the right to resort to belligerent reprisals.

1430 Article 5 of the Protocol Additional to the Geneva Conventions of 12 August 1949, and relating to the Protection of Victims of Non-International Armed Conflicts.

Other sources of international law concerning non-international armed conflicts

Finally, several international treaties also partially address non-international armed conflicts. For instance:

- Article 19 of the 1954 Hague Convention for the Protection of Cultural Property in the Event of Armed Conflict, which prescribes that each party to the conflict shall be bound to apply, as a minimum, the provisions of the Convention concerning the requirements to respect the cultural property.[1431]

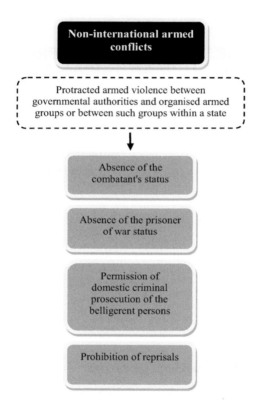

FIGURE 17.4 The approach of international law to non-international armed conflicts

1431 Article 19. Conflicts not of an international character '1. In the event of an armed conflict not of an international character occurring within the territory of one of the High Contracting Parties, each party to the conflict shall be bound to apply, as, a minimum, the provisions of the present Convention which relate to respect for cultural property. 2. The parties to the conflict shall endeavour to bring into force, by means of special agreements, all or part of the other provisions of the present Convention. 3. The United Nations Educational, Scientific and Cultural Organization may offer its services to the parties to the conflict. 4. The application of the preceding provisions shall not affect the legal status of the parties to the conflict.'

- Several international treaties which aim to prohibit or restrict certain means of warfare.
- The Rome Statute of the International Criminal Court, which empowers the Court (within the scope of its jurisdiction, examined earlier) to address the violations of international humanitarian law whether committed in international armed conflicts or in 'armed conflict not of an international character.'

In addition, some rules of customary international law are undoubtedly applicable to non-international armed conflicts. For example, rules such as the prohibition of attacks against civilians and civilian objects, the protection of religious objects and cultural property, and so on.

PERSONS AND OBJECTS UNDER THE PROTECTION OF INTERNATIONAL HUMANITARIAN LAW

> protected persons
> wounded and sick on land
> wounded, sick, and shipwrecked at sea
> prisoners of war and other detainees
> civilians and civilian objects
> fundamental guarantees
> Customary International Humanitarian Law Database
> journalists
> parlementaires
> red cross, red crescent, or red crystal
> Red Cross and Red Crescent Movement
> third Protocol emblem

Protected and safeguarded persons

The term '**protected persons**' refers to persons who possess the specific protection during an armed conflict afforded by the 1949 Geneva Conventions, their 1977 Additional Protocols, and customary international humanitarian law.

Formally, international humanitarian law uses the term 'protected persons' only in the context of international armed conflicts.

This term is not used precisely as a reference to internal armed conflicts since, as mentioned earlier, in that case, persons are primarily entitled to protection essentially not based on their status or membership in a particular group (such as the prisoners of war in an international armed conflict); rather, they are safeguarded against the acts, which are prohibited. However, one can still identify certain persons in times of non-international armed conflict to whom protection shall be applied based on their belonging to a certain category – for example, medical and religious personnel. As prescribed by Additional Protocol II, '[m]edical and religious personnel shall be respected and protected and shall be granted all available help for the performance of their duties.'[1432]

Objects under protection

At the same time, objects under the protection of international humanitarian law in cases of international or non-international armed conflicts should also be identified.

Four primary categories of protected persons and objects

Generally, there are four main categories of protected persons and objects affected by the hostilities during an international armed conflict, which accordingly are addressed by the four Geneva Conventions:

1   wounded and sick on land;
2   wounded, sick, and shipwrecked at sea;
3   prisoners of war and other detainees; and
4   civilians and civilian objects.

A more detailed list of protected persons and objects in times of international conflict is outlined next.

Combatants and non-combatants

1   The wounded and sick in armed forces on land – protected by the entire First Geneva Convention and by Additional Protocol I.
2   The wounded, sick, and shipwrecked members of armed forces at sea – protected by the entire Second Geneva Convention and by Additional Protocol I.
3   Medical and religious personnel attached to armed forces and other non-combatants – protected by the First and Second Geneva Conventions.
4   Prisoners of war – protected by the entire Third Geneva Convention and by Additional Protocol I.

Civilians and civilian objects which find themselves in the hands of a party to the conflict of which they are not nationals

5   Wounded and sick civilians, including pregnant women, maternity cases, newborn infants, and infirm persons – protected by the Fourth Geneva Convention and by Additional Protocol I.

1432 Article 9 (1) of the Protocol Additional to the Geneva Conventions of 12 August 1949, and relating to the Protection of Victims of Non-International Armed Conflicts.

6 Personnel of civil defence organisations – protected by Additional Protocol I.

7 Medical and religious civilian personnel – protected by the Fourth Geneva Convention and by Additional Protocol I.

8 Civilian population participating in relief actions – protected by Additional Protocol I.

9 Stateless persons – always protected civilians.

10 Nationals of a neutral state who find themselves in the territory of a belligerent state – 'shall not be regarded as protected persons while the State of which they are nationals has normal diplomatic representation in the State in whose hands they are.'[1433] Such nationals of a neutral state remain under diplomatic protection unless they commit hostile acts against a belligerent. If there are no such diplomatic relations, neutral persons are entitled to be treated as protected persons under the Fourth Geneva Convention.

11 Other civilians and civilian objects, including civilians detained, interned, or otherwise deprived of liberty; women; children; elderly, disabled, and infirm persons; foreigners; and refugees – protected by the Fourth Geneva Convention and by Additional Protocol I.

Civilians protected by their own national law or other branches of international law

International humanitarian law excludes some civilians from the category of protected persons because, presumably, their state of nationality can protect them through the ordinary mechanism of its national law or by normal diplomatic means.

Hence, civilians who are under the control of their own national authority are not regarded as protected persons in terms of international humanitarian law. Nationals of a co-belligerent (allied) state on the territory under the control of an allied state are also not subject to the protection of international humanitarian law if their state of nationality has normal diplomatic representation in the state concerned.

The categories of persons and objects under protection during non-international armed conflicts

In times of non-international armed conflict, the following categories may be selected:

1 Persons who do not directly participate or ceased to participate in hostilities. According to Article 4 ('Fundamental guarantees') of the Additional Protocol II, these persons shall benefit from the minimum **fundamental guarantees**, such as 'respect for their person, honour and convictions and religious practices'. Generally, they should be treated 'humanely.' Because of their greater vulnerability, the law of non-international armed conflict explicitly takes into account the treatment of children. It states that children must be provided with the care and aid they require: An education, including religious and moral education and the possibility to reunite with families who were temporarily separated. Children who are younger than 15 years old shall

---

1433 Article 4 of the Geneva Convention relative to the Protection of Civilian Persons in Time of War.

neither be recruited into the armed forces or groups nor allowed to take part in hostilities.[1434]

2   Objects, such as:

   a)   objects indispensable to the survival of the civilian population while starvation of civilians as a method of combat is prohibited;

   b)   works and installations containing dangerous forces, namely dams, dykes, and nuclear electrical generating stations. They 'shall not be made the object of attack, even where these objects are military objectives, if such attack may cause the release of dangerous forces and consequent severe losses among the civilian population';[1435]

   c)   cultural objects since 'it is prohibited to commit any acts of hostility directed against historic monuments, works of art or places of worship which constitute the cultural or spiritual heritage of peoples, and to use them in support of the military effort.'[1436]

3   Persons who have been deprived of liberty 'for reasons related to the armed conflict, whether they are interned or detained'. Among other things, these persons shall, to the same extent as the local civilian population, 'be provided with food and drinking water and be afforded safeguards as regards health and hygiene and protection against the rigours of the climate and the dangers of the armed conflict.'[1437]

4   The wounded, sick, and shipwrecked. '[A]ll possible measures shall be taken, without delay, to search for and collect the wounded, sick. and shipwrecked; to protect them against pillage and ill-treatment; to ensure their adequate care; and to search for the dead, prevent their being despoiled, and decently dispose of them.'[1438]

5   Medical and religious personnel, medical units, and transports. They shall not be compelled to carry out tasks which are not compatible with their humanitarian mission. Medical personnel in the cases of both international and non-international armed conflicts comprise military and civilian medical personnel assigned by a party to the conflict exclusively for medical purposes, the administration of medical units, or the operation or administration of medical transports, including medical personnel of national red cross and red crescent societies and 'other national voluntary aid societies duly recognized and authorized by a Party to the conflict . . . medical personnel of medical units or medical transports'.[1439]

1434 Article 4 of the Protocol Additional to the Geneva Conventions of 12 August 1949, and relating to the Protection of Victims of Non-International Armed Conflicts.

1435 Article 15 of the Protocol Additional to the Geneva Conventions of 12 August 1949, and relating to the Protection of Victims of Non-International Armed Conflicts.

1436 Article 16 of the Protocol Additional to the Geneva Conventions of 12 August 1949, and relating to the Protection of Victims of Non-International Armed Conflicts.

1437 Article 5 of the Protocol Additional to the Geneva Conventions of 12 August 1949, and relating to the Protection of Victims of Non-International Armed Conflicts.

1438 Article 8 of the Protocol Additional to the Geneva Conventions of 12 August 1949, and relating to the Protection of Victims of Non-International Armed Conflicts.

1439 Article 8 (c) of the Protocol Additional to the Geneva Conventions of 12 August 1949, and relating to the Protection of Victims of International Armed Conflicts.

Journalists

In 2005, the International Committee of the Red Cross conducted the Study on the Rules of Customary International Humanitarian Law.[1440] Currently, on the official website of the Committee is published the updated version of the Study, called the **Customary International Humanitarian Law Database**,[1441] which lists **journalists** among the persons who enjoy protection. Journalists shall be protected in situations of international and non-international armed conflicts.

Reproducing the development of norms of Additional Protocol I, which considers journalists to be civilians and grants them appropriate protection, the Additional Protocol II, which 'does not contain any specific provision on civilian journalists, [but] their immunity against attack is based on the prohibition on attacking civilians unless and for such time as they take a direct part in hostilities', the following 'Rule 34' is formulated in the Customary International Humanitarian Law Database: 'Civilian journalists engaged in professional missions in areas of armed conflict must be respected and protected as long as they are not taking a direct part in hostilities.'[1442] This 'respect' relates to the professional activities of journalists. Thus, the parties should refrain from any harassment and intimidation of journalists.

Meanwhile, according to the Database, civilian journalists are not to be confused with war correspondents, who are journalists accompanying the armed forces of a state without actually being members thereof. Consequently, they are not combatants and may not be made the object of attack. Nonetheless, according to the Third Geneva Convention, war correspondents are entitled to prisoner of war status when captured during a conflict.

Persons who use a distinctive emblem

Several categories of persons and objects displaying distinctive emblems in a manner foreseen by international humanitarian law are also under protection. Attacks directed against such persons or objects wearing those distinctive emblems are prohibited.

For instance, the white flag, as the flag of truce reserved for persons authorised to negotiate directly with the adversary, has the right to inviolability according to the Fourth 1907 Hague Convention on the laws and customs of war (hence, **parlementaires** authorised by military authorities to enter into direct parleys with the enemy are particularly protected by international humanitarian law); a **red cross, red crescent, or red crystal** on a white background[1443] protects the representatives and equipment of the International **Red Cross**

1440 The Study originally was published by the Cambridge University Press – Jean-Marie Henckaerts and Louise Doswald-Beck, *Customary International Humanitarian Law*, 2 volumes (Volume I. Rules, Volume II. Practice) (Cambridge University Press 2005).

1441 <https://ihl-databases.icrc.org/customary-ihl/eng/docs/v1_rul_rule34> accessed 18 March 2021.

1442 ibid.

1443 Initially, there was an emblem (with respect to Iran) – a red lion and sun – but in 1980, the government of the Islamic Republic of Iran renounced its right to use this emblem as an official emblem of the International Association of the Red Cross and declared that it would use the red crescent.

FIGURE 17.5 The third Protocol emblem

and **Red Crescent Movement**, as well as medical and religious personnel, medical units, and medical transports.[1444]

The Regulations on the use of the Emblem of the Red Cross or the Red Crescent by the National Societies adopted by the Red Cross and Red Crescent International Conference in 1965 and revised by the Council of Delegates in 1991 enumerated two types of permissible application of the emblem – protective and indicative. 'The protective use of the emblem is meant to mark medical and religious personnel and equipment which must be respected and protected in armed conflicts. . . . The indicative use of the emblem serves to show that persons or objects are linked to the [Red Cross and Red Crescent] Movement.'[1445]

1444 For example, according to Article 8 (l) of the Protocol Additional to the Geneva Conventions of 12 August 1949, and relating to the Protection of Victims of International Armed Conflicts, '"distinctive emblem" means the distinctive emblem of the red cross, red crescent or red lion and sun on a white ground when used for the protection of medical units and transports, or medical and religious personnel, equipment or supplies'.

1445 'There is only one emblem, but it can be used for two different purposes: the first use of the emblem is as a visible sign of the protection conferred by international humanitarian law on certain persons and objects, in particular those belonging to or made available to the Army Medical Service and medical staff from National Red Cross and Red Crescent Societies and from civil defence organizations (Articles 38 and 44, First Convention; Article 8 [c] of Protocol I). The second use of the emblem indicates only that persons or objects displaying it are linked to the Movement.' Article 1 of the Regulations on the use of the Emblem of the Red Cross or the Red Crescent by the National Societies, available at <www.icrc.org/en/doc/resources/documents/article/other/57jmbg.htm> accessed 18 March 2021.

Since 2005, the relevant persons (for instance, the members of the International Red Cross and Red Crescent Movement), units, and transports may use the red crystal as well, which, in Additional Protocol III to the Geneva Conventions, is referred to as the '**third Protocol emblem**'. The red crystal is a neutral symbol and does not have any national, religious, or cultural undertones. Thus, it is available for use by those national societies which do not wish to use any of the existing emblems. This additional distinctive emblem is 'composed of a red frame in the shape of a square on edge on a white ground'.[1446] The conditions for the use of and respect for this emblem are identical to the distinctive emblems of the red cross or red crescent maintained by the four Geneva Conventions and the 1977 Additional Protocols.

Fundamental guarantees

In contrast to international human rights law, international humanitarian law does not ordinarily include universal rights which should be applied to all individuals. Alternatively, it primarily introduces a system of categorisation of persons and grants different levels of protection to each category. A specific (preferential) legal regime for such groups is designated because of their engagement in an armed conflict or natural vulnerability.

Therefore, in order to limit the risk of leaving individuals without protection due to non-inclusion in any of the previously listed categories, international humanitarian law, together with international human rights law, establishes minimum fundamental guarantees that apply in times of armed conflict to everyone without discerning their status.

Such fundamental guarantees include:

- The inherent right to life, the prohibition of the torture or cruel, inhuman or degrading treatment or punishment, and so on, prescribed by international human rights law.
- Common Article 3 of the four Geneva Conventions, which maintains the minimum standards of humanity.
- The fundamental guarantees in times of international armed conflict, since Additional Protocol I relaxed the strict approach of the Geneva Conventions concerning the categorisation of protected persons and objects and applied the provisions ensuring a minimal level of protection to all victims of an armed conflict 'who are in the power of a Party to the conflict and who do not benefit from more favourable treatment under the Conventions or under this Protocol'.[1447]

1446 Article 2 (2) of the Protocol Additional to the Geneva Conventions of 12 August 1949, and relating to the Adoption of an Additional Distinctive Emblem.

1447 Article 75 of the Protocol Additional to the Geneva Conventions of 12 August 1949, and relating to the Protection of Victims of International Armed Conflicts.

- The fundamental guarantees in times of non-international armed conflict established for persons who do not or no longer participate in the hostilities, listed in Additional Protocol II.
- Other related norms of international humanitarian law.

Hence, during an armed conflict, the two areas of international law ensure sufficient protection of individuals by complex normative interplay since, as articulated by the International Court of Justice in its **Advisory Opinion** on *Legality of the Threat or Use of Nuclear Weapons* ,

> the protection of the International Covenant [on] Civil and Political Rights does not cease in times of war, except by operation of Article 4 of the Covenant whereby certain provisions may be derogated from in a time of national emergency. Respect for the right to life is not, however, such a provision. In principle, the right not arbitrarily to be deprived of one's life applies also in hostilities. The test of what is an arbitrary deprivation of life, however, then falls to be determined by the applicable *lex specialis*, namely, the law applicable in armed conflict which is designed to regulate the conduct of hostilities.[1448]

Thus, in a state of 'public emergency which threatens the life of the nation', the states may restrict some human rights, provided that such a limitation is strictly required by the exigencies of the situation,[1449] but the rules which form the body of the fundamental guarantees for humans may not be eliminated.

These fundamental guarantees should be safeguarded in both international and non-international armed conflicts. In the first case, both international humanitarian law and, within certain limits, international human rights law also apply. However, since 'it is the majority view that international human rights law only binds governments and not armed opposition groups',[1450] during a non-international conflict, international humanitarian law operates only as a binding source concerning the regulation of the conduct of hostilities for such groups.

1448 *Legality of the Threat or Use of Nuclear Weapons*, Advisory Opinion of 8 July 1996.

1449 According to Article 4 (1) of the International Covenant on Civil and Political Rights: 'In time of public emergency which threatens the life of the nation and the existence of which is officially proclaimed, the States Parties to the present Covenant may take measures derogating from their obligations under the present Covenant to the extent strictly required by the exigencies of the situation, provided that such measures are not inconsistent with their other obligations under international law and do not involve discrimination solely on the ground of race, colour, sex, language, religion or social origin.'

1450 'Introduction to Fundamental Guarantees' <https://ihl-databases.icrc.org/customary-ihl/eng/docs/v1_rul_intofugu#Fn_D6C0BE62_00001> accessed 18 March 2021.

Continued applicability of other areas of international law during an armed conflict

In sum, in relation to armed conflicts (as in the many other fields which are addressed by international law), certain areas (branches) of international law form a complex legal pattern which is primarily composed of international humanitarian law, together with international human rights law, but is partly covered by other areas of international law as well.

For example, when the question relates to the legal limitations on starting a fight, *jus ad bellum* establishes the binding rules; in case of the status of the parties to the conflict, the fundamental principles and rules are provided by the area of international law which is usually called the 'subjects of international law' and which combines the rules on the creation, the continuation of the existence, and the extinction of the subjects of international law, and this list can be continued further.

Each area of international law is designed to regulate a particular field, and within its mission, it shall be regarded as *lex specialis*. As a result, in each case, there emerges a comprehensive interplay of several areas of international law and their respective norms, including with regard to an armed conflict. As mentioned earlier, international humanitarian law is *lex specialis* 'designed to regulate the conduct of hostilities.' Hence, within this scope, the other rules of international law, including the norms of human rights law, may operate only if they do not contradict the specific regulations of international humanitarian law.

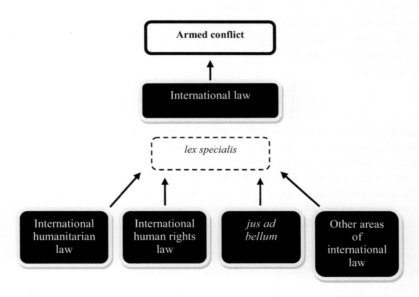

FIGURE 17.6 The complex framework of international law concerning armed conflicts

CASES AND MATERIALS (*SELECTED PARTS*)

The character of international humanitarian law

Legality of the Threat or Use of Nuclear Weapons, Advisory Opinion, 8 July 1996, International Court of Justice
ICJ Reports 1996, 226.

78. The cardinal principles contained in the texts constituting the fabric of humanitarian law are the following. The first is aimed at the protection of the civilian population and civilian objects and establishes the distinction between combatants and non-combatants; States must never make civilians the object of attack and must consequently never use weapons that are incapable of distinguishing between civilian and military targets. According to the second principle, it is prohibited to cause unnecessary suffering to combatants: it is accordingly prohibited to use weapons causing them such harm or uselessly aggravating their suffering. In application of that second principle, States do not have unlimited freedom of choice of means in the weapons they use.

The Court would likewise refer, in relation to these principles, to the Martens Clause, which was first included in the Hague Convention II with Respect to the Laws and Customs of War on Land of 1899 and which has proved to be an effective means of addressing the rapid evolution of military technology. A modern version of that clause is to be found in Article 1, paragraph 2, of Additional Protocol 1 of 1977, which reads as follows:

"In cases not covered by this Protocol or by other international agreements, civilians and combatants remain under the protection and authority of the principles of international law derived from established custom, from the principles of humanity and from the dictates of public conscience."

In conformity with the aforementioned principles, humanitarian law, at a very early stage, prohibited certain types of weapons either because of their indiscriminate effect on combatants and civilians or because of the unnecessary suffering caused to combatants, that is to Say, a harm greater than that unavoidable to achieve legitimate military objectives. If an envisaged use of weapons would not meet the requirements of humanitarian law, a threat to engage in such use would also be contrary to that law.

79. It is undoubtedly because a great many rules of humanitarian law applicable in armed conflict are so fundamental to the respect of the human person and "elementary considerations of humanity" as the Court put it in its Judgment of 9 April 1949 in the *Corfu Channel* case . . . that the Hague and Geneva Conventions have enjoyed a broad accession. Further these fundamental rules are to be observed by all States whether or not they have ratified the conventions that contain them, because they constitute intransgressible principles of international customary law.

80. The Nuremberg International Military Tribunal had already found in 1945 that the humanitarian rules included in the Regulations annexed to the Hague Convention IV of 1907 "were recognized by all civilized nations and were regarded as being declaratory of the laws and customs of war". . . .

81. The Report of the Secretary-General pursuant to paragraph 2 of Security Council resolution 808 (1993), with which he introduced the Statute of the International Tribunal for the Prosecution of Persons Responsible for Serious Violations of International Humanitarian Law Committed in

the Territory of the Former Yugoslavia since 1991, and which was unanimously approved by the Security Council (resolution 827 (1993)), stated:

> In the view of the Secretary-General, the application of the principle *nullum crimen sine lege* requires that the international tribunal should apply rules of international humanitarian law which are beyond any doubt part of customary law. . . .
>
> The part of conventional international humanitarian law which has beyond doubt become part of international customary law is the law applicable in armed conflict as embodied in: the Geneva Conventions of 12 August 1949 for the Protection of War Victims; the Hague Convention (IV) Respecting the Laws and Customs of War on Land and the Regulations annexed thereto of 18 October 1907; the Convention on the Prevention and Punishment of the Crime of Genocide of 9 December 1948; and the Charter of the International Military Tribunal of 8 August 1945.

82. The extensive codification of humanitarian law and the extent of the accession to the resultant treaties, as well as the fact that the denunciation clauses that existed in the codification instruments have never been used, have provided the international community with a corpus of treaty rules the great majority of which had already become customary and which reflected the most universally recognized humanitarian principles. These rules indicate the normal conduct and behaviour expected of States.

83. It has been maintained in these proceedings that these principles and rules of humanitarian law are part of *jus cogens* as defined in Article 53 of the Vienna Convention on the Law of Treaties of 23 May 1969.

Laws and Customs of War on Land

Convention Respecting the Laws and Customs of War on Land
(Hague IV) of 18 October 1907
Entry into force: 26 January 1910

Article 1

The Contracting Powers shall issue instructions to their armed land forces which shall be in conformity with the Regulations respecting the laws and customs of war on land, annexed to the present Convention.

Article 2

The provisions contained in the Regulations referred to in Article 1, as well as in the present Convention, do not apply except between Contracting Powers, and then only if all the belligerents are parties to the Convention.

Article 3

A belligerent party which violates the provisions of the said Regulations shall, if the case demands, be liable to pay compensation It shall be responsible for all acts committed by persons forming part of its armed forces.

Article 4

The present Convention, duly ratified, shall as between the Contracting Powers, be substituted for the Convention of 29 July 1899, respecting the laws and customs of war on land.

The Convention of 1899 remains in force as between the Powers which signed it, and which do not also ratify the present Convention.

Annex to the convention

Regulations respecting the laws and customs of war on land

SECTION I ON BELLIGERENTS

Chapter I The qualifications of belligerents

Article 1

The laws, rights, and duties of war apply not only to armies, but also to militia and volunteer corps fulfilling the following conditions:

1   To be commanded by a person responsible for his subordinates;
2   To have a fixed distinctive emblem recognizable at a distance;
3   To carry arms openly; and
4   To conduct their operations in accordance with the laws and customs of war.
5   In countries where militia or volunteer corps constitute the army, or form part of it, they are included under the denomination "army."

Article 2

The inhabitants of a territory which has not been occupied, who, on the approach of the enemy, spontaneously take up arms to resist the invading troops without having had time to organize themselves in accordance with Article 1, shall be regarded as belligerents if they carry arms openly and if they respect the laws and customs of war.

Article 3

The armed forces of the belligerent parties may consist of combatants and non-combatants. In the case of capture by the enemy, both have a right to be treated as prisoners of war.

The Geneva Conventions

Geneva Convention for the Amelioration of the Condition of the Wounded and Sick in Armed Forces in the Field
(the First Geneva Convention) of 12 August 1949

Entry into force: Six months after the deposit of at least two instruments of ratification (21 October 1950). Thereafter, it comes into force for each contracting party six months after it ratifies.

Article 2

In addition to the provisions which shall be implemented in peacetime, the present Convention shall apply to all cases of declared war or of any other armed conflict which may arise between two or more of the High Contracting Parties, even if the state of war is not recognized by one of them.

The Convention shall also apply to all cases of partial or total occupation of the territory of a High Contracting Party, even if the said occupation meets with no armed resistance.

Although one of the Powers in conflict may not be a party to the present Convention, the Powers who are parties thereto shall remain bound by it in their mutual relations. They shall furthermore be bound by the Convention in relation to the said Power, if the latter accepts and applies the provisions thereof.

Article 3

In the case of armed conflict not of an international character occurring in the territory of one of the High Contracting Parties, each Party to the conflict shall be bound to apply, as a minimum, the following provisions:

1) Persons taking no active part in the hostilities, including members of armed forces who have laid down their arms and those placed *hors de combat* by sickness, wounds, detention, or any other cause, shall in all circumstances be treated humanely, without any adverse distinction founded on race, colour, religion or faith, sex, birth or wealth, or any other similar criteria.

    To this end, the following acts are and shall remain prohibited at any time and in any place whatsoever with respect to the above-mentioned persons:

    a) violence to life and person, in particular murder of all kinds, mutilation, cruel treatment and torture;
    b) taking of hostages;
    c) outrages upon personal dignity, in particular humiliating and degrading treatment;
    d) the passing of sentences and the carrying out of executions without previous judgment pronounced by a regularly constituted court, affording all the judicial guarantees which are recognized as indispensable by civilized peoples.

2) The wounded and sick shall be collected and cared for.

    An impartial humanitarian body, such as the International Committee of the Red Cross, may offer its services to the Parties to the conflict.

    The Parties to the conflict should further endeavour to bring into force, by means of special agreements, all or part of the other provisions of the present Convention.

    The application of the preceding provisions shall not affect the legal status of the Parties to the conflict.

Article 4

Neutral Powers shall apply by analogy the provisions of the present Convention to the wounded and sick, and to members of the medical personnel and to chaplains of the armed forces of the Parties to the conflict, received or interned in their territory, as well as to dead persons found.

Article 5

For the protected persons who have fallen into the hands of the enemy, the present Convention shall apply until their final repatriation.

Article 6

In addition to the agreements expressly provided for in Articles 10, 15, 23, 28, 31, 36, 37 and 52, the High Contracting Parties may conclude other special agreements for all matters concerning which they may deem it suitable to make separate provision. No special agreement shall adversely affect the situation of the wounded and sick, of members of the medical personnel or of chaplains, as defined by the present Convention, nor restrict the rights which it confers upon them.

Wounded and sick, as well as medical personnel and chaplains, shall continue to have the benefit of such agreements as long as the Convention is applicable to them, except where express provisions to the contrary are contained in the aforesaid or in subsequent agreements, or where more favourable measures have been taken with regard to them by one or other of the Parties to the conflict.

Article 7

Wounded and sick, as well as members of the medical personnel and chaplains, may in no circumstances renounce in part or in entirety the rights secured to them by the present Convention, and by the special agreements referred to in the foregoing Article, if such there be.

Article 8

The present Convention shall be applied with the co-operation and under the scrutiny of the Protecting Powers whose duty it is to safeguard the interests of the Parties to the conflict. For this purpose, the Protecting Powers may appoint, apart from their diplomatic or consular staff, delegates from amongst their own nationals or the nationals of other neutral Powers. The said delegates shall be subject to the approval of the Power with which they are to carry out their duties.

The Parties to the conflict shall facilitate, to the greatest extent possible, the task of the representatives or delegates of the Protecting Powers.

The representatives or delegates of the Protecting Powers shall not in any case exceed their mission under the present Convention. They shall, in particular, take account of the imperative necessities of security of the State wherein they carry out their duties. Their activities shall only be restricted, as an exceptional and temporary measure, when this is rendered necessary by imperative military necessities.

Article 9

The provisions of the present Convention constitute no obstacle to the humanitarian activities which the International Committee of the Red Cross or any other impartial humanitarian organization may, subject to the consent of the Parties to the conflict concerned, undertake for the protection of wounded and sick, medical personnel and chaplains, and for their relief.

Article 10

The High Contracting Parties may at any time agree to entrust to an organization which offers all guarantees of impartiality and efficacy the duties incumbent on the Protecting Powers by virtue of the present Convention.

When wounded and sick, or medical personnel and chaplains do not benefit or cease to benefit, no matter for what reason, by the activities of a Protecting Power or of an organization provided for in the first paragraph above, the Detaining Power shall request a neutral State, or such an organization, to undertake the functions performed under the present Convention by a Protecting Power designated by the Parties to a conflict.

If protection cannot be arranged accordingly, the Detaining Power shall request or shall accept, subject to the provisions of this Article, the offer of the services of a humanitarian organization, such as the International Committee of the Red Cross, to assume the humanitarian functions performed by Protecting Powers under the present Convention.

Any neutral Power, or any organization invited by the Power concerned or offering itself for these purposes, shall be required to act with a sense of responsibility towards the Party to the conflict on which persons protected by the present Convention depend, and shall be required to furnish sufficient assurances that it is in a position to undertake the appropriate functions and to discharge them impartially.

No derogation from the preceding provisions shall be made by special agreements between Powers one of which is restricted, even temporarily, in its freedom to negotiate with the other Power or its allies by reason of military events, more particularly where the whole, or a substantial part, of the territory of the said Power is occupied.

Whenever in the present Convention mention is made of a Protecting Power, such mention also applies to substitute organizations in the sense of the present Article.

Article 11

In cases where they deem it advisable in the interest of protected persons, particularly in cases of disagreement between the Parties to the conflict as to the application or interpretation of the provisions of the present Convention, the Protecting Powers shall lend their good offices with a view to settling the disagreement.

For this purpose, each of the Protecting Powers may, either at the invitation of one Party or on its own initiative, propose to the Parties to the conflict a meeting of their representatives, in particular of the authorities responsible for the wounded and sick, members of medical personnel and chaplains, possibly on neutral territory suitably chosen. The Parties to the conflict shall be bound to give effect to the proposals made to them for this purpose. The Protecting Powers may, if necessary, propose for approval by the Parties to the conflict a person belonging to a neutral Power or delegated by the International Committee of the Red Cross, who shall be invited to take part in such a meeting.

Non-International Armed Conflicts

Protocol Additional to the Geneva Conventions of 12 August 1949, and relating to the
   Protection of Victims of Non-International Armed Conflicts
(Protocol II) of 8 June 1977
Entry into force: 7 December 1978

SCOPE OF THIS PROTOCOL

Article 1 – Material field of application

1   This Protocol, which develops and supplements Article 3 common to the Geneva Conventions of 12 August 1949 without modifying its existing conditions of applications, shall apply to all armed conflicts which are not covered by Article 1 of the Protocol Additional to the Geneva Conventions of 12 August 1949, and relating to the Protection of Victims of International Armed Conflicts (Protocol I) and which take place in the territory of a High Contracting Party between its armed forces and dissident armed forces or other organized armed groups which, under responsible command, exercise such control over a part of its territory as to enable them to carry out sustained and concerted military operations and to implement this Protocol.

2   This Protocol shall not apply to situations of internal disturbances and tensions, such as riots, isolated and sporadic acts of violence and other acts of a similar nature, as not being armed conflicts.

Article 2 – Personal field of application

1   This Protocol shall be applied without any adverse distinction founded on race, colour, sex, language, religion or belief, political or other opinion, national or social origin, wealth, birth or other status, or on any other similar criteria (hereinafter referred to as "adverse distinction") to all persons affected by an armed conflict as defined in Article 1.

2   At the end of the armed conflict, all the persons who have been deprived of their liberty or whose liberty has been restricted for reasons related to such conflict, as well as those deprived of their liberty or whose liberty is restricted after the conflict for the same reasons, shall enjoy the protection of Articles 5 and 6 until the end of such deprivation or restriction of liberty.

Article 3 – Non-intervention

1   Nothing in this Protocol shall be invoked for the purpose of affecting the sovereignty of a State or the responsibility of the government, by all legitimate means, to maintain or re-establish law and order in the State or to defend the national unity and territorial integrity of the State.

2   Nothing in this Protocol shall be invoked as a justification for intervening, directly or indirectly, for any reason whatever, in the armed conflict or in the internal or external affairs of the High Contracting Party in the territory of which that conflict occurs.

PART II
HUMANE TREATMENT

Article 4 – Fundamental guarantees

1   All persons who do not take a direct part or who have ceased to take part in hostilities, whether or not their liberty has been restricted, are entitled to respect for their person, honour and convictions and religious practices. They shall in all circumstances be treated

humanely, without any adverse distinction. It is prohibited to order that there shall be no survivors.

2   Without prejudice to the generality of the foregoing, the following acts against the persons referred to in paragraph 1 are and shall remain prohibited at any time and in any place whatsoever:

   a)   violence to the life, health and physical or mental well-being of persons, in particular murder as well as cruel treatment such as torture, mutilation or any form of corporal punishment;
   b)   collective punishments;
   c)   taking of hostages;
   d)   acts of terrorism;
   e)   outrages upon personal dignity, in particular humiliating and degrading treatment, rape, enforced prostitution and any form of indecent assault;
   f)   slavery and the slave trade in all their forms;
   g)   pillage;
   h)   threats to commit any of the foregoing acts.

3   Children shall be provided with the care and aid they require, and in particular:

   a)   they shall receive an education, including religious and moral education, in keeping with the wishes of their parents, or in the absence of parents, of those responsible for their care;
   b)   all appropriate steps shall be taken to facilitate the reunion of families temporarily separated;
   c)   children who have not attained the age of fifteen years shall neither be recruited in the armed forces or groups nor allowed to take part in hostilities;
   d)   the special protection provided by this Article to children who have not attained the age of fifteen years shall remain applicable to them if they take a direct part in hostilities despite the provisions of subparagraph c) and are captured;
   e)   measures shall be taken, if necessary, and whenever possible with the consent of their parents or persons who by law or custom are primarily responsible for their care, to remove children temporarily from the area in which hostilities are taking place to a safer area within the country and ensure that they are accompanied by persons responsible for their safety and well-being.

Article 5 – Persons whose liberty has been restricted

1   In addition to the provisions of Article 4, the following provisions shall be respected as a minimum with regard to persons deprived of their liberty for reasons related to the armed conflict, whether they are interned or detained:

   a)   the wounded and the sick shall be treated in accordance with Article 7;
   b)   the persons referred to in this paragraph shall, to the same extent as the local civilian population, be provided with food and drinking water and be afforded safeguards as regards health and hygiene and protection against the rigours of the climate and the dangers of the armed conflict;
   c)   they shall be allowed to receive individual or collective relief;
   d)   they shall be allowed to practise their religion and, if requested and appropriate, to receive spiritual assistance from persons, such as chaplains, performing religious functions;

e) they shall, if made to work, have the benefit of working conditions and safeguards similar to those enjoyed by the local civilian population.

2 Those who are responsible for the internment or detention of the persons referred to in paragraph 1 shall also, within the limits of their capabilities, respect the following provisions relating to such persons:

a) except when men and women of a family are accommodated together, women shall be held in quarters separated from those of men and shall be under the immediate supervision of women;

b) they shall be allowed to send and receive letters and cards, the number of which may be limited by competent authority if it deems necessary;

c) places of internment and detention shall not be located close to the combat zone. The persons referred to in paragraph 1 shall be evacuated when the places where they are interned or detained become particularly exposed to danger arising out of the armed conflict, if their evacuation can be carried out under adequate conditions of safety;

d) they shall have the benefit of medical examinations;

e) their physical or mental health and integrity shall not be endangered by any unjustified act or omission. Accordingly, it is prohibited to subject the persons described in this Article to any medical procedure which is not indicated by the state of health of the person concerned, and which is not consistent with the generally accepted medical standards applied to free persons under similar medical circumstances.

3 Persons who are not covered by paragraph 1 but whose liberty has been restricted in any way whatsoever for reasons related to the armed conflict shall be treated humanely in accordance with Article 4 and with paragraphs 1 a), c) and d), and 2 b) of this Article.

4 If it is decided to release persons deprived of their liberty, necessary measures to ensure their safety shall be taken by those so deciding.

Article 6 – Penal prosecutions

1 This Article applies to the prosecution and punishment of criminal offences related to the armed conflict.

2 No sentence shall be passed and no penalty shall be executed on a person found guilty of an offence except pursuant to a conviction pronounced by a court offering the essential guarantees of independence and impartiality. In particular:

a) the procedure shall provide for an accused to be informed without delay of the particulars of the offence alleged against him and shall afford the accused before and during his trial all necessary rights and means of defence;

b) no one shall be convicted of an offence except on the basis of individual penal responsibility;

c) no one shall be held guilty of any criminal offence on account of any act or omission which did not constitute a criminal offence, under the law, at the time when it was committed; nor shall a heavier penalty be imposed than that which was applicable at the time when the criminal offence was committed; if, after the commission of the offence, provision is made by law for the imposition of a lighter penalty, the offender shall benefit thereby;

d) anyone charged with an offence is presumed innocent until proved guilty according to law;

e) anyone charged with an offence shall have the right to be tried in his presence;

f) no one shall be compelled to testify against himself or to confess guilt.

3 A convicted person shall be advised on conviction of his judicial and other remedies and of the time-limits within which they may be exercised.

4 The death penalty shall not be pronounced on persons who were under the age of eighteen years at the time of the offence and shall not be carried out on pregnant women or mothers of young children.

5 At the end of hostilities, the authorities in power shall endeavour to grant the broadest possible amnesty to persons who have participated in the armed conflict, or those deprived of their liberty for reasons related to the armed conflict, whether they are interned or detained.

Non-International Armed Conflicts
Maxim – all law is created for the benefit of human beings
Development of international law

Prosecutor v Dusko Tadić a/k/a 'DULE', Decision on the Defence Motion for Interlocutory Appeal on Jurisdiction of 2 October 1995, International Criminal Tribunal for the Former Yugoslavia

Tadić (IT-94–1)

(iii) Customary Rules of International Humanitarian Law Governing Internal Armed Conflicts

a General

96. Whenever armed violence erupted in the international community, in traditional international law the legal response was based on a stark dichotomy: belligerency or insurgency. The former category applied to armed conflicts between sovereign States (unless there was recognition of belligerency in a civil war), while the latter applied to armed violence breaking out in the territory of a sovereign State. Correspondingly, international law treated the two classes of conflict in a markedly different way: interstate wars were regulated by a whole body of international legal rules, governing both the conduct of hostilities and the protection of persons not participating (or no longer participating) in armed violence (civilians, the wounded, the sick, shipwrecked, prisoners of war). By contrast, there were very few international rules governing civil commotion, for States preferred to regard internal strife as rebellion, mutiny and treason coming within the purview of national criminal law and, by the same token, to exclude any possible intrusion by other States into their own domestic jurisdiction. This dichotomy was clearly sovereignty-oriented and reflected the traditional configuration of the international community, based on the coexistence of sovereign States more inclined to look after their own interests than community concerns or humanitarian demands.

97. Since the 1930s, however, the aforementioned distinction has gradually become more and more blurred, and international legal rules have increasingly emerged or have been agreed upon to regulate internal armed conflict. There exist various reasons for this development. First, civil wars have become more frequent, not only because technological progress

has made it easier for groups of individuals to have access to weaponry but also on account of increasing tension, whether ideological, inter-ethnic or economic; as a consequence the international community can no longer turn a blind eye to the legal regime of such wars. Secondly, internal armed conflicts have become more and more cruel and protracted, involving the whole population of the State where they occur: the all-out resort to armed violence has taken on such a magnitude that the difference with international wars has increasingly dwindled (suffice to think of the Spanish civil war, in 1936–39, of the civil war in the Congo, in 1960–1968, the Biafran conflict in Nigeria, 1967–70, the civil strife in Nicaragua, in 1981–1990 or El Salvador, 1980–1993). Thirdly, the large-scale nature of civil strife, coupled with the increasing interdependence of States in the world community, has made it more and more difficult for third States to remain aloof: the economic, political and ideological interests of third States have brought about direct or indirect involvement of third States in this category of conflict, thereby requiring that international law take greater account of their legal regime in order to prevent, as much as possible, adverse spill-over effects. Fourthly, the impetuous development and propagation in the international community of human rights doctrines, particularly after the adoption of the Universal Declaration of Human Rights in 1948, has brought about significant changes in international law, notably in the approach to problems besetting the world community. A State-sovereignty-oriented approach has been gradually supplanted by a human-being-oriented approach. Gradually the maxim of Roman law *hominum causa omne jus constitutum est* (all law is created for the benefit of human beings) has gained a firm foothold in the international community as well. It follows that in the area of armed conflict the distinction between interstate wars and civil wars is losing its value as far as human beings are concerned. Why protect civilians from belligerent violence, or ban rape, torture or the wanton destruction of hospitals, churches, museums or private property, as well as proscribe weapons causing unnecessary suffering when two sovereign States are engaged in war, and yet refrain from enacting the same bans or providing the same protection when armed violence has erupted "only" within the territory of a sovereign State? If international law, while of course duly safeguarding the legitimate interests of States, must gradually turn to the protection of human beings, it is only natural that the aforementioned dichotomy should gradually lose its weight.

98. The emergence of international rules governing internal strife has occurred at two different levels: at the level of customary law and at that of treaty law. Two bodies of rules have thus crystallised, which are by no means conflicting or inconsistent, but instead mutually support and supplement each other. Indeed, the interplay between these two sets of rules is such that some treaty rules have gradually become part of customary law. This holds true for common Article 3 of the 1949 Geneva Conventions, as was authoritatively held by the International Court of Justice (Nicaragua Case, at para. 218), but also applies to Article 19 of the Hague Convention for the Protection of Cultural Property in the Event of Armed Conflict of 14 May 1954, and, as we shall show below (para. 117), to the core of Additional Protocol II of 1977.

99. Before pointing to some principles and rules of customary law that have emerged in the international community for the purpose of regulating civil strife, a word of caution on the law-making process in the law of armed conflict is necessary. When attempting to ascertain State practice with a view to establishing the existence of a customary rule or a general principle, it is difficult, if not impossible, to pinpoint the actual behaviour of the troops in the field for the purpose of establishing whether they in fact comply with, or disregard, certain standards of behaviour.

This examination is rendered extremely difficult by the fact that not only is access to the theatre of military operations normally refused to independent observers (often even to the ICRC) but information on the actual conduct of hostilities is withheld by the parties to the conflict; what is worse, often recourse is had to misinformation with a view to misleading the enemy as well as public opinion and foreign Governments. In appraising the formation of customary rules or general principles one should therefore be aware that, on account of the inherent nature of this subject-matter, reliance must primarily be placed on such elements as official pronouncements of States, military manuals and judicial decisions.

Nuclear Weapons

Treaty on the Non-Proliferation of Nuclear Weapons
of 1968
Entry into force: 5 March 1970

In 1995, the Review and Extension Conference of the Parties to the Treaty on the Non-Proliferation of Nuclear Weapons decided that the Treaty should continue in force indefinitely.

Article I

Each nuclear-weapon State Party to the Treaty undertakes not to transfer to any recipient whatsoever nuclear weapons or other nuclear explosive devices or control over such weapons or explosive devices directly, or indirectly; and not in any way to assist, encourage, or induce any non-nuclear-weapon State to manufacture or otherwise acquire nuclear weapons or other nuclear explosive devices, or control over such weapons or explosive devices.

Article II

Each non-nuclear-weapon State Party to the Treaty undertakes not to receive the transfer from any transferor whatsoever of nuclear weapons or other nuclear explosive devices or of control over such weapons or explosive devices directly, or indirectly; not to manufacture or otherwise acquire nuclear weapons or other nuclear explosive devices; and not to seek or receive any assistance in the manufacture of nuclear weapons or other nuclear explosive devices.

Article III

1   Each non-nuclear-weapon State Party to the Treaty undertakes to accept safeguards, as set forth in an agreement to be negotiated and concluded with the International Atomic Energy Agency in accordance with the Statute of the International Atomic Energy Agency and the Agency's safeguards system, for the exclusive purpose of verification of the fulfilment of its obligations assumed under this Treaty with a view to preventing diversion of nuclear energy from peaceful uses to nuclear weapons or other nuclear explosive devices. Procedures for the safeguards required by this Article shall be followed with respect to source or special fissionable material whether it is being produced, processed or used in any principal nuclear facility or is outside any such facility. The safeguards required by this Article shall

be applied on all source or special fissionable material in all peaceful nuclear activities within the territory of such State, under its jurisdiction, or carried out under its control anywhere.

2   Each State Party to the Treaty undertakes not to provide: (a) source or special fissionable material, or (b) equipment or material especially designed or prepared for the processing, use or production of special fissionable material, to any non-nuclear-weapon State for peaceful purposes, unless the source or special fissionable material shall be subject to the safeguards required by this Article.

3   The safeguards required by this Article shall be implemented in a manner designed to comply with Article IV of this Treaty, and to avoid hampering the economic or technological development of the Parties or international co-operation in the field of peaceful nuclear activities, including the international exchange of nuclear material and equipment for the processing, use or production of nuclear material for peaceful purposes in accordance with the provisions of this Article and the principle of safeguarding set forth in the Preamble of the Treaty.

4   Non-nuclear-weapon States Party to the Treaty shall conclude agreements with the International Atomic Energy Agency to meet the requirements of this Article either individually or together with other States in accordance with the Statute of the International Atomic Energy Agency. Negotiation of such agreements shall commence within 180 days from the original entry into force of this Treaty. For States depositing their instruments of ratification or accession after the 180-day period, negotiation of such agreements shall commence not later than the date of such deposit. Such agreements shall enter into force not later than eighteen months after the date of initiation of negotiations.

Article IV

1   Nothing in this Treaty shall be interpreted as affecting the inalienable right of all the Parties to the Treaty to develop research, production and use of nuclear energy for peaceful purposes without discrimination and in conformity with Articles I and II of this Treaty.

2   All the Parties to the Treaty undertake to facilitate, and have the right to participate in, the fullest possible exchange of equipment, materials and scientific and technological information for the peaceful uses of nuclear energy. Parties to the Treaty in a position to do so shall also co-operate in contributing alone or together with other States or international organizations to the further development of the applications of nuclear energy for peaceful purposes, especially in the territories of non-nuclear-weapon States Party to the Treaty, with due consideration for the needs of the developing areas of the world.

Article V

Each Party to the Treaty undertakes to take appropriate measures to ensure that, in accordance with this Treaty, under appropriate international observation and through appropriate international procedures, potential benefits from any peaceful applications of nuclear explosions will be made available to non-nuclear-weapon States Party to the Treaty on a non-discriminatory basis and that the charge to such Parties for the explosive devices used will be as low as possible and exclude any charge for research and development. Non-nuclear-weapon States Party to the Treaty shall be able to obtain such benefits, pursuant to a special international agreement or agreements, through an appropriate international body with adequate representation of non-nuclear-weapon States. Negotiations on this subject shall commence as soon as possible after the Treaty enters into force. Non-nuclear-weapon States Party to the Treaty so desiring may also obtain such benefits pursuant to bilateral agreements.

Article VI

Each of the Parties to the Treaty undertakes to pursue negotiations in good faith on effective measures relating to cessation of the nuclear arms race at an early date and to nuclear disarmament, and on a treaty on general and complete disarmament under strict and effective international control.

Article VII

Nothing in this Treaty affects the right of any group of States to conclude regional treaties in order to assure the total absence of nuclear weapons in their respective territories.

Nuclear Deterrence

Kenneth Waltz, 'The Spread of Nuclear Weapons: More May Better'
Adelphi Papers, Number 171 (London: International Institute for Strategic Studies 1981).

'Conclusion

The conclusion is in two parts. After saying what follows for American policy from my analysis, I briefly state the main reasons for believing that the slow spread of nuclear weapons will promote peace and reinforce international stability.

Implications for American policy

I have argued that the gradual spread of nuclear weapons is better than no spread and better than rapid spread. We do not face a set of happy choices. We may prefer that countries have conventional weapons only, do not run arms races, and do not fight. Yet the alternative to nuclear weapons for some countries may be ruinous arms races with high risk of their becoming engaged in debilitating conventional wars.

Countries have to care for their security with or without the help of others. If a country feels highly insecure and believes that nuclear weapons will make it more secure, America's policy of opposing the spread of nuclear weapons will not easily determine theirs'. 'The strongest means by which the United States can persuade a country to forgo nuclear weapons is a guarantee of its security, especially if the guarantee is made credible by the presence of American troops. But how many commitments do we want to make and how many countries do we want to garrison? We are wisely reluctant to give guarantees, but we then should not expect to decide how other countries are to provide for their security. As a neighbour of China, India no doubt feels more secure, and can behave more reasonably, with a nuclear weapons capability than without it. The thought applies as well to Pakistan as India's neighbour. We damage our relations with such countries by badgering them about nuclear weapons while being unwilling to guarantee their security. Under such circumstances they, not we, should decide what their national interests require.'

'Neither the gradual spread of nuclear weapons nor American and Russian acquiescence in this has opened the nuclear floodgates. Nations attend to their security in ways they think best. The fact that so many more countries can make nuclear weapons than do make them says more about the hesitation of countries to enter the nuclear military business than about the effectiveness of American policy. We can sensibly suit our policy to individual cases. Sometimes bringing pressure against a country moving towards nuclear-weapons capability and sometimes quietly acquiescing. No one policy is right for all countries. We should ask what our interests in regional peace and stability require in particular instances. We should also ask what the interests of other countries require before putting pressure on them. Some countries are likely to suffer more in cost and pain if they remain conventional states than if they become nuclear ones. The measured and selective spread of nuclear weapons does not run against our interests and can increase the security of some states at a price they can afford to pay.

It is not likely that nuclear weapons will spread with a speed that exceeds the ability of their new owners to adjust to them. The spread of nuclear weapons is something that we have worried too much about and tried too hard to stop.'

'The nuclear future

What will a world populated by a larger number of nuclear states look like? I have drawn a picture of such a world that accords with experience throughout the nuclear age. Those who dread a world with more nuclear states do little more than assert that more is worse and claim without substantiation that new nuclear states will be less responsible and less capable of self-control than the old ones have been. They express fears that many felt when they imagined how a nuclear China would behave. Such fears have proved un-rounded as nuclear weapons have slowly spread. I have found many reasons for believing that with more nuclear states the world will have a promising future.'

The principle of distinction between civilians and combatants

Jean-Marie Henckaerts and Louise Doswald-Beck, with contributions by Carolin Alvermann, Knut Dörmann and Baptiste Rolle, *Customary International Humanitarian Law*

Volume I. Rules (Cambridge University Press, reprinted with corrections 2009) 3–8.

'**Rule 1**. The parties to the conflict must at all times distinguish between civilians and combatants. Attacks may only be directed against combatants. Attacks must not be directed against civilians. . . .'

Summary

State practice establishes this rule as a norm of customary international law applicable in both international and non-international armed conflicts. The three components of this rule are interrelated and the practice pertaining to each of them reinforces the validity of the others. The term "combatant" in this rule is used in its generic meaning, indicating persons who do not enjoy the protection against attack accorded to civilians, but does not imply a right to combatant status or prisoner-of-war status. . . . This rule has to be read in conjunction with the prohibition to attack persons recognised to be *hors de combat* . . . and with the rule that civilians are protected against attack unless and for such time as they take a direct part in hostilities'.

'International armed conflicts

The principle of distinction between civilians and combatants was first set forth in the St. Petersburg Declaration, which states that "the only legitimate object which States should endeavour to accomplish during war is to weaken the military forces of the enemy". The Hague Regulations do not as such specify that a distinction must be made between civilians and combatants, but Article 25, which prohibits "the attack or bombardment, by whatever means, of towns, villages, dwellings, or buildings which are undefended", is based on this principle. The principle of distinction is now codified in Articles 48, 51(2) and 52(2) of Additional Protocol I, to which no reservations have been made. According to Additional Protocol I, "attacks" means "acts of violence against the adversary, whether in offence or in defence".

At the Diplomatic Conference leading to the adoption of the Additional Protocols, Mexico stated that Articles 51 and 52 of Additional Protocol I were so essential that they "cannot be the subject of any reservations whatsoever since these would be inconsistent with the aim and purpose of Protocol I and undermine its basis". Also at the Diplomatic Conference, the United Kingdom stated that Article 51(2) was a "valuable reaffirmation" of an existing rule of customary international law.

The prohibition on directing attacks against civilians is also laid down in Protocol II, Amended Protocol II and Protocol III to the Convention on Certain Conventional Weapons and in the Ottawa Convention banning anti-personnel landmines. In addition, under the Statute of the International Criminal Court, "intentionally directing attacks against the civilian population as such or against individual civilians not taking direct part in hostilities" constitutes a war crime in international armed conflicts.'

'Non-international armed conflicts

Article 13(2) of Additional Protocol II prohibits making the civilian population as such, as well as individual civilians, the object of attack. The prohibition on directing attacks against civilians is also contained in Amended Protocol II to the Convention on Certain Conventional Weapons. It is also set forth in Protocol III to the Convention on Certain Conventional Weapons, which has been made applicable in non-international armed conflicts pursuant to an amendment of Article 1 of the Convention adopted by consensus in 2001. The Ottawa Convention banning anti-personnel landmines states that the Convention is based, *inter alia*, on "the principle that a distinction must be made between civilians and combatants".

Under the Statute of the International Criminal Court, "intentionally directing attacks against the civilian population as such or against individual civilians not taking direct part in hostilities" constitutes a war crime in non-international armed conflicts. In addition, this rule is included in other instruments pertaining also to non-international armed conflicts.'

'Alleged violations of this rule have generally been condemned by States, irrespective of whether the conflict was international or non-international. Similarly, the UN Security Council has condemned or called for an end to alleged attacks against civilians in the context of numerous conflicts, both international and non-international, including in Afghanistan, Angola, Azerbaijan, Burundi, Georgia, Lebanon, Liberia, Rwanda, Sierra Leone, Somalia, Tajikistan, the former Yugoslavia and the territories occupied by Israel.'

'The jurisprudence of the International Court of Justice in the *Nuclear Weapons case*, of the International Criminal Tribunal for the Former Yugoslavia, in particular in the *Tadić case*, *Martić case* and *Kupreškić case*, and of the Inter-American Commission on Human Rights in the case relative to the events at La Tablada in Argentina provides further evidence that the obligation to make a distinction between civilians and combatants is customary in both international and non-international armed conflicts.

The ICRC has called on parties to both international and non-international armed conflicts to respect the distinction between combatants and civilians.'

Index